REFERENCE

VICTORIAN AMERICA 1876 to 1913

Crandall Shifflett

Richard Balkin
General Editor

Facts On File, Inc.

AN INFOBASE HOLDINGS COMPANY

For

Kirsten and Zachary with love

Victorian America, 1876 to 1913

Copyright © 1996 by Crandall Shifflett

Facts On File, Inc.
11 Penn Plaza
New York NY 10001

Library of Congress Cataloging-in-Publication Data
Shifflett, Crandall A.
    Victorian America, 1876 to 1913 / Crandall Shifflett.
        p.   cm.—(Almanacs of American life)
    Includes bibliographical references and index.
    ISBN 0-8160-2531-2 (alk. paper)
    1. United States—Social life and customs—1865–1918.   2. United States—History—1865–1921.   3. United States—Social life and customs—1865–1918—Statistics.   4. United States—History—1865–1921—Statistics.   I. Title.   II. Series.
E168.S55   1996
973.8—dc20   95-13553

Facts On File books are available at special discounts when purchased in bulk quantities for businesses, associations, institutions, or sales promotions. Please call our Special Sales Department in New York at 212/976-8800 or 800/322-8755.

Text and jacket design by F. C. Pusterla
Maps on pages 18, 38, 47, 73, 251, and 338 by Dale Williams

This book is printed on acid-free paper.

Printed in United States of America

BB VC 10 9 8 7 6 5 4 3 2 1

CONTENTS

LIST OF MAPS

PREFACE

The chapters in this book illustrate diverse aspects of life in America between the years 1876 and 1913: the rise of vaudeville and the nickelodeon, the state of the states and large cities, social services of neighborhood saloons, what Americans earned and how they budgeted it, the careers of prominent citizens, popular sports and leading athletes, celebrations of American culture at three World's Fairs, farm and factory production, and much more. The diversity of subject matter in the chapters that follow encourages a view of historical culture as a kind of mosaic, based on the idea that we can learn as much about an age and its people by looking at the material conditions of everyday life as we can by discerning an overarching historical theme.

Readers are invited to explore these pages for new ideas and evidence and fresh insights into the overlapping and sometimes contradictory boundaries of culture, economy, and politics. Make your own picture, rearrange the pieces, explore the contradictions; you will not only use this book effectively, but you will also gain an appreciation for the stunning diversity that was life in Victorian America.

A word about translating prices, wages, and costs of living during the Victorian Age into current dollars. Consumer Price Indexes (CPI) are maintained by the United States Bureau of Labor Statistics, and they exist for each year since 1800. The conversions can be made through a few simple operations using the CPI to translate the cost of living of any earlier year into contemporary dollars. For example, in 1900 the CPI value for all commodities was 25; in 1990 the CPI was 391.4. Consequently, the cost of living in 1900, *on average,* would be 15.7 times greater in 1990 (391.4 divided by 25). In other words, a wage worker who made $400 a year in 1900 would have made roughly $6,200 in 1990 dollars.

NOTE ON PHOTOS

Many of the illustrations and photographs used in this book are old, historical images. The quality of the prints is not always up to modern standards, as in many cases the originals are from glass negatives or the originals are damaged. The content of the illustrations, however, made their inclusion important despite problems in reproduction.

CHAPTER 1 Climate, Natural History, and Historical Geography

Climate

Daily weather observations of some continuity began in the eighteenth century at Charleston, South Carolina, and Cambridge, Massachusetts. Not until the 1850s, however, did the Smithsonian Institution develop a nationwide system of standardized observations, supplementing records that had previously been made by the U.S.

Army. The Smithsonian Institution began to make systematic observations and continued active work for more than 20 years. The data, including tables of rain and snow in the United States, were collected and published in *Smithsonian Contributions to Knowledge.*

In 1870, the Congress of the United States acted on a recommendation of Smithsonian Secretary Joseph Henry and U.S. Commisioner of Agriculture Issac Newton to establish a more extensive weather service for the benefit of agriculture. In 1874 the Smithsonian relinquished its meterological work and transferred its observers to the U.S. Army Signal Service. The geographical distribution of stations was unbalanced, however (most of them were in the East), and the distances between them great, so it soon became evident that a more systematic arrangement was needed.

In 1890, Congress established the Weather Bureau within the Department of Agriculture, and the legislation transferred all meteorological work to it. The act went into effect April 1, 1891, and provided for the "taking of such meteorological observations as may be necessary to establish and record climatic conditions in the United States." Congress undoubtedly did not realize the immense task involved. Thousands of stations were necessary, and funding was inadequate to finance such a large project.

Under these conditions, the bureau inaugurated an extensive network of cooperative observation stations that developed into one of the most extraordinary systems anywhere. Thousands of unpaid volunteer observers, in all parts of the country, to whom the Weather Bureau furnished thermometers, thermometer shelters, and rain gauges made daily recordings year after year. These 5,000 observers provided much of the weather data for the United States since 1891.

TABLE 1.1 ANNUAL PRECIPITATION IN SELECTED UNITED STATES CITIES

City	1876	1890	1913
Abilene	a	28.2	27.5
Albany	37.8	44.5	26.1
Charleston, S.C.	77.7	47.4	41.1
Chicago	36.2	32.4	26.9
Denver	19.9	9.2	18.2
Jacksonville	37.6	47.1	38.3
Nashville	a	59.4	40.3
New Haven	53.6	48.5	46.3
New Orleans	66.6	41.8	63.0
New York	40.2	43.3	55.6
Portland, Oreg.	54.4	40.0	36.0
St. Louis	48.0	37.3	38.3
St. Paul/Minneapolis	23.4	23.2	23.8
Salt Lake City	21.1	10.2	16.5
San Francisco	23.3	25.2	18.9
Spokane	a	16.4	16.6

^anot available
Source: B. R. Mitchell, *International Historical Statistics, the Americas and Australasia* (1983), 3–8, Table A1. Given in millimeters and converted to inches here.

TABLE 1.2 DATE OF LAST KILLING FROST IN SPRING AND FIRST IN FALL, WITH LENGTH OF GROWING SEASON, SELECTED PLACES

Place	Last	First	Days	Last	First	Days
	1899			1913		
Albany, N.Y.	Apr. 11	Oct. 3	175	Apr. 21	Sep. 15	147
Atlanta, Ga.	Apr. 10	Nov. 3	207	Mar. 28	Oct. 21	207
Boston, Mass.	Apr. 6	Oct. 3	180	Apr. 10	Nov. 1	205
Chicago, Ill.	Apr. 2	Sep. 30	181	Apr. 27	Oct. 20	196
Denver, Colo.	May 4	Oct. 16	165	Apr. 25	Oct. 16	174
Helena, Mo.	May 16	Oct. 10	147	May 1	Sep. 25	147
Hutchinson, Kans.	Apr. 4	Nov. 2	212	Apr. 12	Oct. 18	189
Jackson, Tenn.	Apr. 2	Nov. 4	216	Mar. 28	Oct. 21	207
Lansing, Mich.	Apr. 15	Sep. 13	151	May 11	Oct. 13	155
Lexington, Ky.	Apr. 9	Sep. 30	174	Mar. 29	Oct. 20	205
Milford, Del.	Apr. 10	Oct. 2	175	May 12	Oct. 22	163
Minneapolis, Minn.	Apr. 8	Sep. 30	175	Apr. 27	Sep. 22	148
Orono, Maine	May 17	Sep. 16	122	May 18	Sep. 15	120
Phoenix, Ariz.	Mar. 11	Dec. 11	275	Mar. 1	Dec. 5	279
Richmond, Va.	Mar. 28	Nov. 13	230	Mar. 29	Oct. 22	207
Sacramento, Calif.	Feb. 5	Dec. 18	316	Mar. 25	Dec. 4	254
San Antonio, Tex.	Mar. 4	Dec. 4	275	Mar. 27	Dec. 26	274
Uniontown, Pa.	Apr. 11	Oct. 1	173	May 12	Oct. 22	163
Vicksburg, Miss.	Mar. 7	Nov. 3	241	Mar. 16	Oct. 30	228
Walla Walla, Wash.	Apr. 23	Dec. 2	223	Apr. 2	Dec. 3	245

Source: Climate and Man: Yearbook of Agriculture 1941 (1941), 761–1170.

TABLE 1.3 AVERAGE TEMPERATURE IN JANUARY AND JULY FOR SELECTED CITIES (IN CENTIGRADE)

Year	Abilene Jan.	Abilene Jul.	Charleston, S.C. Jan.	Charleston, S.C. Jul.	Chicago Jan.	Chicago Jul.	Denver Jan.	Denver Jul.	Nashville Jan.	Nashville Jul.	New Haven Jan.	New Haven Jul.
1876	...	...	12.6	28.6	1.1	24.3	−2.2	24.2	8.4	27.6	0.9	25.2
1877	...	...	10.0	28.4	−5.1	24.1	−4.2	23.6	2.5	27.7	−2.7	23.2
1878	...	...	9.4	28.1	0.1	25.1	−3.1	23.7	3.7	28.7	−0.4	24.1
1879	...	...	9.4	28.2	−5.4	25.7	−4.4	23.9	2.8	28.9	−3.1	23.1
1880	...	...	14.2	28.3	5.0	23.7	2.1	21.8	11.3	25.8	3.1	23.2
1881	...	...	7.8	28.3	−6.4	24.0	−3.4	24.8	1.3	28.6	−5.9	21.5
1882	...	...	12.4	27.2	−1.6	21.6	−1.4	22.3	5.9	24.3	−2.9	22.1
1883	...	...	10.4	28.3	−8.2	22.9	−2.1	22.5	3.5	25.2	−4.6	21.8
1884	...	...	7.7	27.6	−6.6	21.9	−0.4	24.2	−1.1	26.1	−4.9	20.0
1885	...	...	10.0	27.4	−7.1	23.9	−1.7	22.0	0.6	26.2	−2.9	22.4
1886	1.6	29.2	6.0	26.7	−5.4	23.2	−6.3	24.0	−1.7	25.4	−3.7	21.3
1887	6.5	29.1	7.6	27.7	−7.1	25.3	−0.5	21.3	3.2	27.5	−3.8	23.7
1888	3.8	27.9	10.5	26.2	−8.3	23.1	−2.7	23.6	2.5	26.3	−6.4	20.1
1889	6.1	25.5	10.7	26.9	0.4	21.9	−2.9	22.3	4.3	25.44	1.2	20.8
1890	9.7	28.1	14.9	26.0	0.6	23.1	−2.4	23.9	9.3	26.4	1.9	20.4
1891	5.4	27.8	10.1	25.9	0.1	20.2	−3.9	20.6	4.6	23.6	−0.7	19.4
1892	4.6	27.9	8.6	26.2	−5.9	22.8	−3.6	22.3	0.4	24.8	−2.8	21.7
1893	7.3	30.0	6.1	27.7	−10.1	24.0	3.2	23.1	0.3	26.9	−6.6	21.3
1894	7.1	27.6	11.3	25.4	−1.4	23.8	−0.6	22.1	5.9	24.5	−0.8	22.5
1895	5.1	26.2	9.2	26.9	−6.9	22.0	−2.3	19.8	1.3	24.6	−2.9	20.0
1896	7.1	28.1	8.8	27.4	−1.7	23.1	2.7	22.3	4.1	25.9	−3.9	22.0
1897	4.2	28.7	8.3	27.0	−4.6	24.2	−3.3	21.1	1.9	26.1	−2.3	22.0
1898	8.0	27.2	12.5	26.9	−0.8	23.8	−1.8	22.6	7.1	25.8	−1.4	21.9
1899	5.6	27.3	9.7	26.6	−3.9	23.1	−1.2	21.4	3.4	26.2	−2.4	21.6
1900	8.3	26.8	9.7	27.7	−0.8	22.8	2.1	21.9	4.2	26.2	−1.1	22.6
1901	9.3	29.1	9.7	26.8	−2.3	26.0	1.0	24.9	4.3	28.3	−2.2	23.2
1902	6.3	26.2	8.2	27.7	−2.7	23.2	−1.9	21.3	2.9	26.8	−2.8	20.7
1903	7.2	27.7	8.9	26.7	−3.4	23.1	1.3	23.2	3.5	26.2	−1.6	21.9
1904	6.2	27.4	7.1	26.2	−6.9	22.4	−0.8	20.6	2.3	24.4	−6.2	21.4
1905	3.4	26.7	7.4	26.8	−6.7	21.6	−1.7	20.7	−1.1	25.1	−4.1	22.4
1906	8.3	25.7	10.5	26.0	0.4	21.8	2.3	20.2	6.0	24.4	1.7	21.8
1907	11.4	26.9	13.4	27.4	−2.2	22.8	−0.4	22.2	9.2	27.3	−2.0	22.0
1908	8.4	25.8	9.4	26.9	−1.8	23.3	0.8	21.1	3.5	25.5	−0.9	23.3
1909	9.2	29.2	11.8	26.2	−1.7	22.2	1.7	22.9	5.8	25.1	−0.7	21.3
1910	8.5	30.1	9.2	26.6	−3.4	24.3	−0.5	23.7	3.9	25.3	−0.8	23.1
1911	10.6	28.1	11.4	26.4	−1.4	24.3	3.2	21.0	6.6	24.5	0.1	23.4
1912	4.4	29.5	7.4	26.4	−11.1	22.6	0.2	20.8	0.0	25.2	−6.6	22.4
1913	6.6	28.9	14.4	27.6	−1.4	23.7	−1.2	22.1	7.3	27.2	3.4	22.7

Temperatures have not changed very much since the eighteenth century. Twentieth-century temperatures have been slightly warmer, but by less than 1°F. Oscillations around unchanging averages characterized the period from 1400 to 1900. Opinions differ among twentieth-century scientists as to whether the slightly warmer temperatures after 1900 are due to solar radiation, volcanic activity, greenhouse gases that warm the earth, or shifts in currents in the tropical Pacific Ocean (El Niño) that warm the globe.

Natural Disasters

Nature, in the form of violent weather (tornadoes, hurricanes, floods, blizzards) and earthquakes produced some major catastrophes in the late nineteenth and early twentieth centuries. Most notable were the southern tornado outbreak in 1884; the Johnstown flood of 1889; the Galveston, Texas, hurricane in 1900; two major earthquakes—the Charleston, South Carolina, quake of 1886 and the San Francisco quake of 1906—and a few severe blizzards.

Not only were these events catastrophic in terms of loss of life and property damage, but in some cases they also changed the course of history. The Galveston flood, for example, led to the firing of city officials and the inauguration of a commission form of city government to replace the strong-mayor type. Other cities copied

Year	New Orleans Jan.	Jul.	Portland, Oreg. Jan.	Jul.	St. Louis Jan.	Jul.	St. Paul/Minneapolis Jan.	Jul.	San Francisco Jan.	Jul.	Spokane Jan.	Jul.
1876	15.9	28.7	3.9	19.3	5.2	26.6	−8.7	23.9	9.2	14.5	. . .	. . .
1877	12.1	28.8	5.7	19.5	−0.4	26.0	−12.5	23.5	12.2	15.2	. . .	. . .
1878	10.4	28.8	5.5	18.6	2.1	27.9	−5.5	23.6	11.4	14.1	. . .	. . .
1879	11.6	27.7	3.6	18.6	−2.1	27.7	−9.0	23.5	8.9	14.1	. . .	. . .
1880	17.2	27.8	4.4	18.2	7.6	25.2	−3.4	22.1	8.2	14.1	. . .	. . .
1881	10.0	28.8	4.0	17.7	−5.8	27.5	−13.7	22.9	11.7	14.6	−5.6	19.0
1882	17.1	27.2	4.1	18.6	0.0	23.5	−7.3	19.6	9.0	14.4	−5.2	21.0
1883	13.7	28.7	3.1	19.5	−4.9	24.8	−17.3	21.6	7.7	14.6	−4.6	22.1
1884	8.3	29.0	3.7	17.6	−3.5	25.4	−13.6	21.1	9.7	15.3	−4.3	19.1
1885	11.0	28.6	2.4	20.1	−3.4	27.2	−15.4	22.9	10.0	15.6	−5.7	22.2
1886	7.7	27.4	2.3	19.8	−4.1	27.2	−15.7	23.0	10.2	14.8	−5.4	22.8
1887	10.4	28.0	6.0	19.1	−0.9	29.0	−17.4	23.8	11.0	12.9	−0.3	21.4
1888	13.6	28.7	−1.8	19.4	−4.3	26.4	−18.4	22.9	7.9	15.6	−9.2	19.8
1889	11.9	28.1	2.8	21.0	1.4	25.3	−6.4	21.9	10.0	14.2	−4.6	21.9
1890	18.4	27.6	−0.4	18.3	3.9	26.4	−12.2	22.3	7.7	14.7	−8.1	19.9
1891	11.8	27.3	5.9	20.1	2.4	23.7	−5.9	18.7	11.0	14.5	1.4	21.0
1892	9.6	26.7	4.1	17.8	−3.5	24.9	−12.1	21.9	10.7	13.8	−3.4	18.6
1893	10.1	28.4	0.9	17.7	−4.1	26.7	−15.9	23.1	8.3	12.9	−4.8	19.3
1894	14.4	26.2	4.4	19.2	1.8	26.1	−12.0	24.4	8.5	12.8	−3.3	20.8
1895	11.2	27.7	2.1	18.3	−3.3	24.6	−14.3	21.2	9.0	13.9	−3.1	19.4
1896	11.2	28.2	5.7	20.8	1.6	26.0	−9.0	21.7	11.0	14.5	−0.9	22.6
1897	10.6	28.7	3.5	17.8	−0.9	26.9	−12.6	23.3	9.0	13.8	−1.9	18.2
1898	14.8	27.4	3.6	18.8	2.8	25.6	−5.1	22.8	7.9	12.7	−3.6	20.5
1899	11.8	28.1	4.5	19.0	0.2	25.9	−10.1	22.8	11.4	12.6	−2.8	20.8
1900	11.2	27.3	6.4	18.9	2.9	25.9	−5.9	22.0	10.2	13.8	1.9	20.6
1901	13.1	28.1	3.9	16.8	2.8	30.7	−8.7	25.7	9.7	12.4	−1.3	19.5
1902	11.9	28.3	3.3	17.8	0.1	26.7	−7.4	22.0	7.9	14.4	−2.6	18.0
1903	11.1	27.7	5.7	17.7	0.8	27.0	−9.3	21.0	8.6	13.3	−0.2	18.3
1904	10.8	27.1	5.3	19.1	−2.4	24.3	−13.4	20.4	10.1	13.2	0.1	20.7
1905	9.8	27.6	4.4	19.9	−4.4	24.0	−13.7	21.3	10.5	14.6	−0.9	21.4
1906	12.2	28.0	5.8	22.1	2.6	24.6	−6.8	21.4	10.7	13.5	−0.9	24.1
1907	17.3	28.4	0.8	19.6	2.2	25.9	−13.5	21.6	8.2	13.7	−7.6	20.3
1908	11.9	27.3	5.4	20.6	1.0	25.3	−6.8	22.4	10.2	13.3	−1.1	21.8
1909	14.7	28.4	0.2	17.4	0.3	24.9	−9.7	21.7	10.6	13.6	−6.0	18.6
1910	12.9	27.3	2.8	19.2	0.2	24.8	−9.7	23.6	7.8	12.8	−2.3	21.7
1911	16.1	26.8	3.3	20.5	1.8	26.2	−11.6	21.6	10.3	12.8	−1.0	21.2
1912	10.1	27.7	4.9	19.3	−6.6	25.9	−18.8	21.5	10.8	13.7	−3.2	18.9
1913	15.5	27.6	3.2	19.6	1.4	27.0	−10.0	21.2	8.3	15.2	−4.5	19.6

Source: B. R. Mitchell, *International Historical Statistics, the Americas and Australasia* (1943), 28–30, Table A2.

the Galveston model. The San Francisco earthquake took that city in new directions. Upon the ruins of a corrupt city government that had built its power with protection money from gambling dens, brothels, and other illicit activities, a new San Francisco emerged. Mayor Eugene E. Schmitz, who had ordered execution squads to kill looters during the earthquake, and his partner in crime Abe Reuf were both convicted of extortion. In 1915, just nine years after the quake, the city had been rebuilt and hosted the Panama-Pacific International Exposition in honor of the opening of the Panama Canal. No traces of the earthquake and fire were visible anywhere.

Tornadoes

The Great Southern Tornado Outbreak in 1884 The great tornado outbreak of February 1884 stood out for the number of individual tornadoes, the geographic extent of severe turbulence, and the number of fatalities. Not until 1974 did another series of tornadoes produce destruction on the same scale.

On February 19, 1884, the states of Virginia, North Carolina, South Carolina, Georgia, Alabama, Mississippi, Tennessee, and Kentucky experienced the most terrible devastation by wind ever experienced in this country up to that time. Between 10 A.M. and midnight, 60 tornadoes touched down in a eight-state area. Rough estimates placed property damages between $3 million and $4 million. About 800 people died; 2,500 were injured. From 10,000 to 15,000 were left homeless as 10,000 buildings were destroyed. The victims were mostly black farmhands and their families living mainly on tenant farms and small plantations. Countless numbers of cattle, horses, hogs, and other domestic animals were killed as well.

TABLE 1.4 DEADLIEST TORNADOES OF THE UNITED STATES

Date	Place	Deaths	Property Losses[a]
Jun. 17, 1882	Grinnell, Iowa	100	$1.1 million
Feb. 19, 1884	Va., N.C., S.C., Ga., Ala. Miss., Tenn., Ky.	800	$3–4 million
Mar. 27, 1890	Louisville, Ky.	106	$3.5 million
Jul. 6, 1893	Pomeroy, Iowa	89	$213,000
May 15, 1896	Sherman, Tex.	78	$165,000
May 27, 1896	St. Louis, Mo.	306	$12.9 million
Jun. 12, 1899	New Richmond, Wis.	100	No estimate
May 18, 1902	Goliad, Tex.	114	$50,000
Jun. 1, 1903	Gainesville, Ga.	98	$1 million
May 10, 1905	Snyder, Okla.	87	$270,000
Apr. 24, 1908	Ala.	210	$733,000
Apr. 24, 1908	Miss.	100	$880,000
Mar. 8, 1909	Ark.	64	$660,000
Mar. 23, 1913	Omaha, Nebr.	94	$3.5 million

[a]Prices *on average* for all items in 1900 were 15.66 times higher than 1990, meaning that a $1-million loss in 1900 is equivalent to $15.7 million in 1990 dollars.
Sources: John L. Baldwin, *Climates of the States* (1974 reprint), 38; Snowden D. Flora, *Tornadoes of the United States* (1954), 191–94; David M. Ludlum, *The American Weather Book* (1982), 110–12.

TABLE 1.5 DEADLIEST HURRICANES IN THE UNITED STATES

Year	Place	Number of Victims
1893	South Carolina	1,000–2,000
1893	Louisiana	2,000
1900	Galveston, Tex.	6,000–7,000

Source: Ludlum, *The American Weather Book,* 206.

Floods

The Johnstown Flood of 1889 Johnstown, a manufacturing city of about 30,000 residents, is situated in a narrow river valley on the main line of the Pennsylvania Railroad, a third of the distance from Altoona to Pittsburgh. Estimates vary as to the exact amount of rainfall that fell on May 31, 1889, somewhere between 6 and 10 inches, maybe higher in the surrounding mountains.

TABLE 1.6 DEADLIEST FLOODS IN THE UNITED STATES

Date	Location	Deaths	Property Losses
May 1889	Conemaugh River, South Fork Creek of Little Conemaugh River, Johnstown, Pa.	2,200	$3 million
May–Jun. 1903	Lower Missouri & Upper Mississippi rivers, Kansas	100	$40 million
Jun. 1903	Willow Creek, Oreg.	236	$100 million
Mar. 1913	Ohio River & tributaries	467	$147 million
Dec. 1913	Rivers in Texas	177	$9 million

Sources: Baldwin, *Climates of the United States,* 44; Ludlum, *American Weather Book,* 80, 129.

TABLE 1.7 NOTABLE BLIZZARDS

A blizzard is a storm combining high winds, low temperatures, a great amount of snow, and poor visibility.

Date	Place	Event
Jan. 6–13, 1886	Iowa, Nebr., Kans., Okla.	Called "Great Blizzard" in Kans. Struck with no advance warning. Wind averaged 40 mph, drifted snow, and reduced visibility to 15 ft. Temperatures near 0°F. 20 deaths reported in Iowa, and 50–100 in Kans. An estimated 80% of cattle in Kans. perished; heavy livestock losses reported in other states.
Jan. 11–13, 1888	Wyo., Mont., N. Dak., S. Dak., Minn., Nebr., Kans., Okla., Tex.	Reported as most disastrous blizzard ever known in Mont., the Dakotas, and Minn. Combination of gale winds, blowing snow, and extremely rapid drop in temperatures made storm very dangerous. Thousands of cattle perished, and loss of human life was great.
Mar. 11–14, 1888	Eastern Seaboard	Unseasonably late heavy snowstorm under blizzard conditions from Chesapeake Bay area to Maine. Complete disruption of normal activity in Washington, D.C., Philadelphia, New York City, and Boston. Wind averaged 20–25 mph for 4 days. Peak winds passed 70 mph and blew 4-ft snowfall into drifts up to 20 ft high. Snowfall averaged 40 in. or more over southeast N.Y. and southern New England, with 50 in. at Middletown, Conn., a record storm total for the state. In New York City alone, 200 deaths, uncounted injuries, and damage near $20 million. Total deaths above 400; maritime losses above a half million dollars; railroad and business losses totaled several million dollars.
Feb. 11–14, 1899	Middle and North Atlantic States	Great eastern blizzard. Snowfall from 15 to over 40 in. from Va. to southern New England. Near Atlantic City and Philadelphia, snowfall 44 in.; Washington, D.C., 20.5 in. (with all-time record snow depth of 34.2 in.; New York City, 24 in. Drifts to 15 ft. high. Intense below-zero cold: −30°F at Woodstock, Vt.; −17°F at River Vale, N.J.; and −15°F at Washington, D.C. (lowest ever recorded). Wind speeds 40 mph to more than 70 mph.

Source: Baldwin, *Climates of the United States,* 29.

On Friday morning, May 31, the steady rain sent the Conemaugh River over its banks and into the factories, stores, and homes of local residents in the narrow valley above Johnstown. When the local water gauge washed away, the river stood at 20 feet above low water. Already a record flood, it would have been only of local historic importance were it not for the occurrences at South Fork

Creek of the Little Conemaugh River, about 15 miles upstream from Johnstown. There, an earthen dam, built in 1852 to supply water for the Pennsylvania Railroad, had been restored by wealthy fishermen in 1879 to create a fishing camp and lake. The lake measured 2 miles long and 1.5 miles wide, a considerable body of water.

About 3 P.M. on Friday afternoon, overtopping of the dam, which had been going on for three hours, weakened the earthen structure and in minutes a 300-foot-wide break sent a wall of water into the valley and Johnstown's main business district. Deaths from the flood have been estimated to be as high as 5,000, with as much as $3 million in property damage.

Earthquakes

Two major earthquakes struck the United States during the period 1876 to 1913. On August 31, 1886, an earthquake struck Charleston, South Carolina, killing 100 citizens. Shocks were felt as far north as New York and as far south as Mobile, Alabama. Charleston, however, was the center of the quake. Dozens of buildings, many of them historic landmarks, toppled. Most of the people who died in the quake were killed by falling buildings.

At 5:13 A.M. on April 18, 1906, an earthquake along the 600-mile-long San Andreas Fault hit San Francisco, Santa Rosa, and San Jose, California. The quake measured 8.3 on the Richter scale and lasted approximately 75 seconds. The first jolt was 40 seconds long, followed by a 10-second calm, and then a second tremor lasting 25

The San Francisco earthquake of April 18, 1906, virtually destroyed the old city and required its rebuilding. (Courtesy Prints and Photographs Division, Library of Congress)

During the earthquake of August 31, 1886—the only earthquake known to have caused extensive damage to an eastern city—citizens of Charleston, South Carolina, encamp in the city park. (Courtesy National Archives)

seconds. Between 500 and 700 people lost their lives and many more were injured. Thousands of cheaply constructed buildings in landfill areas of the city were demolished, great land fissures opened and closed, and most of San Francisco's gas and water mains ruptured.

Residents reported seeing the quake approach in the form of undulating streets that looked like waves on the ocean. Fires broke out shortly afterward, and an inferno of fire raged for three days, consuming 3,000 acres, or 4.7 square miles, including 520 city blocks, and 28,188 buildings, half of which were homes. Damages were estimated at $500 million; insurance companies, some of which were bankrupted by the disaster, paid about 70% of the claims.

Will Irvin, a San Francisco native and writer, wrote after the disaster:

> The Old San Francisco is dead . . . those who have known that peculiar city by the Golden Gate, who have caught the flavor of the Arabian Nights, feel that it can never be the same. It is as though a pretty, frivolous woman had passed through a great tragedy. She survives, but she is sobered and different. If it rises out of the ashes it must be a modern city much like other cities and without its old atmosphere.

Environmental Change

In the late Victorian period, the emergence of a national policy to conserve natural resources was a notable though limited departure from earlier practices of deforestation and reckless destruction of wildlife.

The National Forest Reserve, today's National Forest System, dates from 1891, when Congress authorized President Harrison to withhold forests in the public domain from private use. By the turn of the twentieth century, presidents had reserved 46 million acres, making them off-limits to loggers without government permission.

Enforcement was lax until President Theodore Roosevelt, prodded by Chief Forester Gifford Pinchot, began to prosecute cattle "raiders" and timber "pirates" who abused public forests and grasslands. Between 1901 and 1905, Roosevelt added 125 million acres to the public domain and reserved 68 million acres of coal deposits, almost 5 million acres of phosphate beds, a number of oil fields, and 2,565 sites suitable for the construction of dams to generate hydroelectric power.

Trapping and hunting was on the decline as a way to make a living, but some still pursued it, as shown in this picture of trappers and hunters in the Four Peak country on Brown's Basin, Salt River Project, Arizona Territory, January 1908. Two Crab Tree boys are shown with their father, their dogs, and the burros they used to hunt. Their cabin is located on Long Creek at the entrance of Hell's Hip Pocket in Brown's Basin. (Photo by Lubkin, courtesy National Archives)

Roosevelt's conservation policy of managing forests to assure an adequate supply of lumber into the future appealed to large lumber interests that had made huge capital investments. But his policy angered westerners, especially cattle ranchers, clear-cut loggers, and private power companies who banded together to force an amendment to the Forest Reserve Act of 1905 limiting the president's power to enlarge the national domain in six western states.

During the presidency of William Howard Taft (1909–1913), a dispute erupted between Secretary of the Interior Richard A. Ballinger and Chief Forester Pinchot. Ballinger released to private developers a number of hydroelectric sites that President Roosevelt had reserved. Pinchot appealed to Taft, Roosevelt's hand-picked successor, and gained his grudging support. The differences between the two men continued, however, until Taft fired Pinchot.

In the area of wildlife, another small and belated step was taken. For years, hunters had slaughtered large and small animals in such great numbers that entire species were being driven to extinction. The buffalo was the most visible, but by no means the only, example of how quickly a species could be destroyed. With the building of a transcontinental railroad in the 1860s, companies hired professional hunters to kill buffalo for meat to feed the railroad workers and to destroy buffalo because, they argued, stampeding herds were a danger to the trains. Perhaps the buffalo could have survived this slaughter, but an even more devastating blow came in 1872 when a Pennsylvania tannery discovered a commercially profitable process for preserving buffalo hides. Within two years, the buffalo were nearly exterminated.

Not until January 1902 did Congress pass a resolution instructing the secretary of the interior and the secretary of agriculture to inves-

tigate the condition of the buffalo in the United States and to recommend a plan to prevent its extinction. As a result, before the close of the Fifty-seventh Congress, Interior Secretary Ethan A. Hitchcock presented the following figures (excerpted) on the number of buffalo and a plan for their future protection, with these remarks:

In my judgment steps should be taken by the United States for the preservation from extinction of the buffalo or American bi-

TABLE 1.8 STATISTICS ON AMERICAN BUFFALO, 1902

Running Wild, Purebloods		In Captivity		Total Buffalo
Colorado	50	(Mont. with 366 and N.H. with 110 head had the largest number of purebloods with scattered numbers among 26 other states).		
Wyoming (Yellowstone Park)	22			
		Purebloods	Hybrids	
United States	72	896	175	1,143
Canada	600	44	25	669
Europe	. . .	114	14	128
Total	672	1,054	214	1,940

Source: *The American Almanac, Yearbook, Cyclopedia and Atlas*, 537.

In 1876 a Pennsylvania tannery developed a commercial process for turning buffalo hide into finished leather. Within three years, the herds of buffalo—once estimated to be 12 million head—on the Great Plains were reduced to less than a thousand head, deep in the Canadian woods. In this picture of Rath and Wright's buffalo-hide yard, Dodge City, Kansas, in 1878, about 40,000 buffalo hides are ready for shipment, probably to a commercial tannery. (Courtesy National Archives)

son, and with that end in view I have submitted to Congress an estimate of $30,000 for the purchase of buffalo and the corraling of them in the Yellowstone National Park. With these animals in a national reservation, under Government supervision, it is believed that a herd of pure-blooded American bison may be domesticated, which will increase in numbers, and the herds now running wild in the Park may be also benefited by the introduction therein of new blood.

With wild herds once estimated at 12 million now numbering only 672 head, few could contest the danger of the buffalo's extinction or the necessity of this desperate effort to save the remaining herds.

Hitchcock's report was referred to the Committee on Agriculture and Forestry and was later sent to Congress with the recommendation for similar resolutions to protect the grizzly bear, beaver, elk, moose, mountain sheep and goat, and in prophetic words, "other contemporaneous animals that will soon become as extinct as the mammoth if something is not done to check their destruction."

The National Forest Reserve Act, the actions of Victorian-era presidents and Secretary Hitchcock, and the resolution of the Ballinger-Pinchot dispute in favor of national planning to promote effi-

cient development of the forest reserves marked a new beginning in attitudes toward the environment. Pinchot's policy of management emerged as a pragmatic response to garner support from various groups at odds with one another, such as the preservationists and the lumber interests. Years would pass before the nation began to embrace conservation, and then mostly as a necessity rather than an ideal. Still these early steps set important precedents, establishing as a principle federal responsibility to protect the nation's scarce natural resources in order to ensure the welfare of future generations.

Historical Geography

Migration and Settlement

Migration and resettlement characterized Victorian America, a nation on the move. Homesteaders took up lands on the frontier in massive numbers, Indian lands and reservations were overrun and claimed, and public lands were gobbled up by land speculators and business interests.

The persecution of Latter-Day Saints, or Mormons, in the eastern United States led to a great migration organized by Brigham Young. Eventually, this group settled near the Great Salt Lake in Utah. Here, Mormon immigrants are seen on the westward trek, c. 1879. Within a few years, 10,000 people lived in the Salt Lake basin. (Photo by C. W. Carter, courtesy National Archives)

TABLE 1.9   UNITED STATES PUBLIC LANDS

State	Acres		
	1878	1893	1913
Ala.	32,462,080	32,462,115	77,600
Alaska	369,529,600	369,529,600	367,963,823
Ariz.	72,906,304	72,906,240	39,525,195
Ark.	33,406,720	33,410,063	467,489
Calif.	100,992,640	100,992,640	20,853,637
Colo.	66,880,000	66,880,000	19,353,231
Dakota[a]	96,595,840	. . .	. . .
Fla.	37,931,520	37,931,520	358,417
Idaho	55,228,160	55,228,160	17,915,622
Ill.	35,462,400	35,405,093	. . .
Ind.	21,637,760	21,637,760	. . .
Iowa	35,228,800	35,228,800	. . .
Kans.	51,769,976	51,770,240	92,568
La.	26,461,440	28,731,090	78,014
Mich.	36,128,640	36,128,640	89,057
Minn.	53,459,840	53,459,840	1,286,394
Miss.	30,179,840	30,179,840	41,660
Mo.	41,824,000	41,836,931	713
Mont.	92,016,640	92,016,640	21,542,853
Nebr.	48,636,800	47,468,800	405,469
Nev.	71,737,741	71,737,600	55,138,593
N. Mex.	77,568,640	77,568,640	31,298,621
N. Dak.	. . .	4,561,600	1,156,120
Ohio	25,576,960	25,581,976	. . .
Okla.	. . .	18,234,080	. . .
Oreg.	60,975,360	60,975,360	41,636
S. Dak.	50,643,200	3,805,432	. . .
Utah	54,065,075	54,064,640	33,837,596
Wash.	44,796,160	44,796,160	1,750,208
Wis.	34,511,360	34,511,360	9,880
Wyo.	62,645,120	62,645,120	32,255,679
Indian Territory	44,154,240	25,840,640[b]	. . .
Totals	1,865,412,856	1,727,526,620	645,540,075

[a] Dakota Territory included North and South Dakota until they became separate states simultaneously on November 2, 1889.
[b] The figures given for Indian Territory, the area set aside in the 1830s for the "Five Civilized Tribes," include the area of the Cherokee Outlet, roughly 6,265,600 acres. The area gradually receded due to the opening of these lands to white settlement.
Sources: An American Almanac for 1878 (1878), 236; The World Almanac (1893), 120; The World Almanac and Encyclopedia 1914 (1913), 152.

TABLE 1.10   STATES ADMITTED TO THE UNION DURING THE VICTORIAN AGE

Number	State	Admitted
38	Colo.	Aug. 1, 1876
39	N. Dak.	Nov. 2, 1889
40	S. Dak.	Nov. 2, 1889
41	Mont.	Nov. 8, 1889
42	Wash.	Nov. 11, 1889
43	Idaho	Jul. 3, 1890
44	Wyo.	Jul. 10, 1890
45	Utah	Jan. 4, 1896
46	Okla.	Nov. 16, 1907
47	N. Mex.	Jan. 6, 1912
48	Ariz.	Feb. 14, 1912

The age of prospecting in the West predated the Victorian Age; the great Colorado gold rush came in 1859. In 1889, William Henry Jackson, the great explorer-photographer, photographed "Mustang Jack," a Colorado prospector who still dreamed of finding gold and getting rich. (Photo by William Henry Jackson, courtesy Colorado Historical Society)

Hopes for quick fortunes propelled some migrants, such as those of the Klondike gold rush of 1897, the rapid settlement of Oregon's Christmas Valley in 1902, and the California real-estate boom between 1900 and 1915. The "push" factor was more important for other groups. In the first large-scale movement of blacks from the rural South, for example, 6,000 freedmen known as the Exodusters left the lower Mississippi for Kansas in 1879.

Though the 1870 census counted roughly the same number of men as of women nationwide, their distribution by region was uneven. The West was shy of women; the East short of men. On the western frontier, men outnumbered women 3 to 1. In Mormon Utah, which had attracted entire families, and New Mexico, where Spanish-speaking residents had settled earlier, the gender ratio was more even. In New England, where textile factories provided jobs, women outnumbered men, and in the Southeast, where so many men had died in the Civil War, women formed the majority.

Perhaps nowhere was the heady exuberance of settlement more excessive than in the Oklahoma Indian Territory. On April 22, 1889, a gun sounded at noon, a flag dropped, a bugle blared, and 10,000 anxious settlers raced to claim a part of America's final frontier. Many laid claim to Indian lands and refused to give them up. Within hours settlers had created the town of Guthrie, Oklahoma, and by sunset had claimed the homesteads and town lots of the surrounding cities of Kingfisher, Stillwater, Oklahoma City, El Reno, and Norman.

Climate, Natural History, and Historical Geography   9

As the Oklahoma Territory opened to settlement, "boomers" waited for the firing of a gun to signal the moment they could stake their claims. In this picture, the first train and wagons are shown leaving the line north of Orlembo (Orlando), Fort Perry (Oklahoma Territory), September 16, 1893. (Courtesy National Archives)

The town of Guthrie, Oklahoma, looking west from Division Street on Oklahoma Avenue, is shown here in April 1893, just a short time after its founding by those eager to take advantage of settlers and drifters. (From the records of the Secretary of the Interior, courtesy National Archives)

Eleven new states west of the Mississippi River entered the Union during the period from 1876 to 1913. The nation's supply of free land held by federal and state governments dwindled as settlers took advantage of the Homestead Act (1862) and sales of public lands. In 1881, about 180,000 homesteaders occupied 21 million acres of land. By 1902, however, only about 32,000 still held homestead status on just over 4 million acres of land. The rest possessed their plots outright or had lost those plots to land speculators.

The Homestead Act   The Homestead Act, passed by the Congress in 1862 in the midst of the Civil War, was scarcely noticed by most Americans. Before the war, the opening up of new territories became occasions for debates on slavery, which endangered the Union. Fears of disunity effectively barred the federal government from liberalizing its land policies to dispose of western lands. With the war in progress, land policy was no longer a dangerous sectional debate. Rather, it was now an opportunity for the dominant Republican Party to pass legislation that would make westerners loyal Republicans.

The Homestead Act proposed that every head of a family who was a citizen or proposed to become a citizen could receive 160 acres of public land. After six months on the land, homesteaders could buy it at $1.25 per acre. Alternatively, they could live on it for five years, and it would be theirs free of cost. As a great number of homesteaders took possession of the land formerly leased to them, the amount of land in the public domain was reduced by about two-thirds between 1878 and 1913.

The supply of free land diminished also because of lavish grants to railroad companies to finance the building of a national railroad network. Timber companies and other industries gained control over additional acres. Also, the Morrill Act of 1862 granted each loyal state 30,000 acres per member of Congress to be used by the states to finance agricultural and mechanical colleges, leading to the subsequent founding of 69 land-grant colleges.

The Exodusters The Exodusters were black sodbusters who settled on homesteads in Kansas. After Reconstruction was ended,

At first, Kansas welcomed the emigrants, but soon the state launched a campaign to discourage Singleton's work. While propagandists were publicizing a roseate view among potential white emigrants, they began to tell southern blacks about the hardships and risks of farming on the Great Plains, for fear that the state would become a black refuge.

The Oscar Bredeson family, shown here with their children and other relatives on their farm in Clay County, Minnesota, c. 1905, were homesteaders from Norway who settled in northwestern Minnesota. Thousands of other Norwegians and Swedes, mostly Lutherans, settled the states of Minnesota, the Dakotas, Iowa, Illinois, and Wisconsin. Their stories of hope and hardship are evoked in the moving novels of Vilhelm Moberg and O. E. Rölvaag. (Author's possession)

Free land lured black farmers westward just as it did whites. The African-American migration, however, was organized into a group called the Exodusters for the protection and assistance of those who sought free land in the West. This poster in 1877 announces that blacks in Lexington, Kentucky, have organized themselves into a colony in order to unite with other black settlers in Kansas and to settle on vacant lands there. (Courtesy Kansas State Historical Society)

Benjamin "Pap" Singleton, a black carpenter from Nashville dubbed the "Moses of the colored exodus," concluded that, just like whites, blacks could do better for themselves by moving west. Singleton traveled throughout the South to urge blacks to migrate to Kansas; his message struck a responsive chord in some communities.

By the end of 1878, more than 7,000 Exodusters took out homesteads in Kansas. In 1879, another 20,000 arrived, founding communities such as Nicodemus, which continues to preserve its African-American pioneer heritage.

The Turner Thesis and the End of the Frontier In 1893 at the Chicago Exposition, Frederick Jackson Turner, a 32-year-old University of Wisconsin history professor, addressed professional historians and declared the closing of the American frontier. For Turner the passing of the age of westward expansion was a momentous event because the frontier had defined the American character.

Known in countless textbooks as the "Turner thesis," the idea that the national culture was more a product of mobility and environment and less a derivation from European cultural origins came to be widely known. Equally well known is the "safety-valve" theory, spawned by Turner's followers but spurned by his critics, that the closing of the frontier also meant the loss of an alternative for discontented urban laborers in the East.

From homesteaders on the Plains, sodbusters in Kansas, Mormons trekking to a homeland, or claim jumpers in Oklahoma, whether by covered wagon or automobile, Americans of the Victorian Age were a people on the move. As time went on, that movement changed direction. As Turner later noted, of the 1,000 counties in the United

Settlers, such as the Hancock family from Benson, Minnesota, often made multiple moves on the frontier. In this picture, a little girl in the Hancock family is shown feeding chickens against the background of the house, buckboard wagon, and ridge of a plateau in Sun River, Montana. (Photo by Lubkin, June 23, 1910, courtesy National Archives)

Lacking wood and other materials to build homes, settlers used the earth itself, as illustrated by this sod home in western Kansas in the 1890s. (Courtesy Western History Collections, University of Oklahoma Library)

The Victorian Era bridged the Age of Settlement and the Age of Modern America—illustrated in this scene as a covered wagon with jackrabbit mules encounters an automobile on the trail near Big Springs, Nebraska, in 1912. (Photo by A. L. Westgard, courtesy National Archives)

States that decreased in population between 1910 and 1920, almost all were rural, and the 2,000 that increased in population were urban and industrial.

Later historians found a turnover of almost 78% in the five small towns of Grant County, Wisconsin, from 1880 to 1895; another study noted that twenty farmers flocked to the city for every laborer who took up farming. As early as the 1870s, in sections of New England, the Middle Atlantic states, and parts of the Midwest, an urban way of life began to take root.

Thus as one frontier closed, another was opening.

CHAPTER 2 Native American Life

Overview, 1876 to 1913

Federal policy toward Native Americans during the Victorian Age had two purposes. First, between 1867 and 1887, segregation was the goal, and during these two decades the greatest number of reservations were created. Indians were separated from whites, just as they had been with the earlier removal policy. The difference was that instead of one large Indian country like the Oklahoma Territory, lands were carved up piecemeal, with tribes restricted to specific reservation boundaries.

The confinement of Indians to reservations had been tested in the West, when in the 1850s the California gold rush and the westward movement brought whites onto Indian lands and created conflict. Whites viewed the reservation as a solution, and also saw it as a place where Indians might be taught white customs. Nomadic hunting tribes, such as many of the Plains Indians groups, who had their areas substantially reduced, had great difficulty adapting to an alien farming lifestyle—especially when given land ill-suited to farming.

Moving additional tribes onto existing reservations to detribalize them and to make more land available for white settlement, the federal government broke the back of distinct Indian cultures.

The second phase of federal Indian policy began in 1887. Assimilation was America's "final solution." It was not an entirely new policy since missionaries and educators had been practicing it since colonial times in efforts to Christianize and "civilize" Indians, but it became national policy in 1887 through the Dawes Severalty Act (also known as the General Allotment Act). Under this Act, Indian reservations were broken into 160-acre plots allotted to the heads of Indian families to be held in trust for 25 years, whereupon the Indians were to be granted citizenship. Officially, the rationale was self-sufficiency of Indian peoples but on terms dictated by whites—that is, the substitution of white customs, traditions, and technologies for the Indian heritage. Indians objected to the Dawes Act for many reasons. Some tribes challenged it legally. Many were upset

In present-day Arizona and New Mexico, the Pima, Zuni, and Hopi Indians farmed the desert for centuries before white settlement. Their pueblos were communal houses or groups of apartments that formed a quasi-urban culture. Pictured here are the terraced houses at Walpi, Hopi Pueblo, Walpi, Arizona, 1879. (Photo by John K. Hillers, courtesy National Archives)

The assimilation of Native Americans into mainstream culture was the goal of American policymakers in Victorian America. Promising youths were selected to study agriculture at Hampton Institute in Virginia. Photographs were taken of the first class of Indians at Hampton in 1878. In this "before" picture, back row, left to right: Laughing Face, an Arikara; White Breast, a Mandan; Carries Flying, a Blackfoot Sioux; Man Who Looks Around, a Mandan; and Sioux Boy (Ka-ru-nack), an Arikara. Second row, left to right: Sharphorn, tribe unknown; Walking Cloud, a Hunkpapa Lakota (Sitting Bull's tribe); One Who Hoots When He Walks, a Hunkpapa Lakota; White Wolf, an Arikara. Front seated: Long Arm, a Gros Ventre. (Courtesy Smithsonian Institution, National Museum of Natural History, National Anthropological Archives)

that it obliterated their identities as families in tribal nations. Many also objected to it because any tribal land "left over" after the allotment was sold, often to whites or land developers. During the entire allotment period, Indians lost nearly two-thirds of the land that they had in 1887—millions of acres.

Education was an essential part of the process of assimilation. In 1878, the first class of Indians graduated from Hampton Institute, founded in 1868 by General Samuel Chapman Armstrong, an agent of the Freedmen's Bureau. From 1878 until 1912 federal funding supported a program for Native American students, who continued to attend Hampton until 1923. In 1888, according to the commissioner of Indian affairs, Indians numbered 243,299. Of this number, 19,816 could read; 25,255 could use English in conversation; 58,590 wore "citizen's dress" entirely, and 32,507 wore citizen's dress in part. In 1913, there were 111 boarding schools for Indians and 223 day schools; churches and religious societies ran an additional 57

mission schools; many areas had no schools at all. The government reported that year that expenditures for Indian schools totaled $4,015,720, or $12.15 per capita compared to $5.43 per capita spent for all schools in 1913.[a]

In the 1890s, Congress and the courts attempted to squeeze the breath out of Indian resistance to the Dawes Act. In 1898, when the Cherokee and the Choctaw of the Indian Territory refused allotment and took their case to the federal court, Congress passed the Curtis Act, dissolving their tribal governments. Resistance took other forms (see section on the Ghost Dance), but Indians were gradually forced under the law to become "allotted," subject to state civil and criminal jurisdiction.

Thus, the Victorian Age ended with Indians facing a federal policy of acculturation under duress, detribalization, and Americanization, accompanied by a galling promise of future citizenship.

In this "after" picture of the first class, 1878 (subjects unidentified), the Indians have been stripped of their traditional clothes and long hair and transformed into the white view of "model Americans." (Courtesy Smithsonian Institution, National Museum of Natural History, National Anthropological Archives)

Chronology of Native American History in Victorian America, 1865–1913

The various conflicts during the twenty-five years between the end of the Civil War and the Wounded Knee Massacre in 1890, although scattered across the West, represented the final stage of the armed struggle between Native Americans and whites. The pace of change was accelerating. The transcontinental railroad was completed in 1869, bringing thousands of settlers and fortune-seekers across Indian hunting and tribal lands. The army now had thousands of battle-tested troops and experienced officers, such as Generals William Tecumseh Sherman and Philip Sheridan, plus an arsenal of technologically advanced weapons to turn upon the Plains Indians. The United States could now open a large-scale coordinated drive against its foes, using a network of frontier forts as bases from which to conquer resisting tribes and confine them to reservations.

These activities provoked open warfare that lasted until the 1890s. The Indian peoples most involved at this stage were Lakota, Cheyenne, Arapaho, Comanche, Kiowa, and Apache. Other tribes also played a part: Nez Percé, Ute, Bannock, Paiute, and Modoc. The Indian leaders from this period are among the most famous: Red Cloud, Sitting Bull, Crazy Horse, Black Kettle, Little Raven, Quanah Parker, Satanta, Geronimo, Chief Joseph, Ouray, and Captain Jack. From this post–Civil War period come many of the familiar legends and themes of the Old West.

aBased upon an Indian population of 330,603 in 1913. Total per-capita expenditures are based upon an estimated total population of 96,094,000 and expenditures for all schools of $521,546,000 in 1913. See *Historical Statistics of the United States, Colonial Times to 1957* (1961), 209; B. R. Mitchell, ed., *International Historical Statistics* (1983), 50, whose figures for the U.S. population were interpolated to get the 1913 population estimate; *The World Almanac and Encyclopedia 1914* (1913), 521.

According to some estimates, the United States organized more than a dozen military campaigns and conducted a thousand armed engagements with the Indians. By the end of this epic struggle, the great herds of buffalo, a distinct geographical frontier line, and the aboriginal way of life had all perished.

Hostilities began in the Civil War years with the Sand Creek Massacre of Black Kettle's Cheyenne, which may be seen as the beginning of this final struggle because the tragedy galvanized Indian determination and resistance. A summary of the main campaigns follows:

(1) the war for the Bozeman Trail in Wyoming and Montana (1866–68), involving mostly the Teton Lakota under Red Cloud and their allies the Northern Cheyenne and Northern Arapaho; (2) the Snake War in Oregon and Idaho (1866–68), involving the Yahuskin and Walpapi bands of Northern Paiute; (3) Hancock's campaign on the central plains (1867), primarily against the Southern Cheyenne, Southern Arapaho, and Lakota allies; (4) Sheridan's campaign on the southern and central plains (sometimes called the Southern Plains War, 1868–69) against Cheyenne, Arapaho, Lakota, Comanche, and Kiowa; (5) the Modoc War in California (1872–73), involving the Modoc under Captain Jack; (6) the Red River War on the southern plains (1874–75), involving the Comanche, Kiowa, and Southern Cheyenne under Quanah Parker; (7) the Sioux War for the Black Hills in South Dakota, Montana, and Wyoming (1876–77), involving the Lakota, Cheyenne, and Arapaho under Sitting Bull and Crazy Horse, with the famous Battle of Little Bighorn; (8) the flight of the Nez Percé in the Northwest under Chief Joseph (1877); (9) the Bannock War in Idaho and Oregon (1878), involving the Bannock, Northern Paiute, and Cayuse; (10) the flight of the Northern Cheyenne through the central plains (1878), involving the Northern Cheyenne under Dull Knife; (11) the Sheepeater War in Idaho (1879), involving the Sheepeaters; (12) the Ute War (1879) in Colorado, involving the Ute; (13) the ongoing Apache Wars in the Southwest, including Crook's Tonto Basin Campaign against Apache and Yavapai (1872–73), Victorio's Resistance (1877–80), and Geronimo's Resistance (1881–86).

In a sense, this list of wars represents an oversimplification. The term *war* suggests an equality between forces that did not exist and a discrete period of time—with a beginning and an end—when the reality was that the conflict was permanent. From the Indian perspective, the wars for the West are best seen as a single protracted struggle that did not start and stop with particular campaigns but became a way of life that stretched over nearly a third of a century between Sand Creek and Wounded Knee. The battle was waged not only against armies but against squatters who usurped the land, hunters who destroyed the Indians' livelihood by wiping out the buffalo, and previously unknown diseases spread by whites that decimated whole tribes. In the 1890s the Indian population reached its nadir at less than 250,000. The following chronology gives the major developments during the Victorian period:

1876–77 Sioux War for the Black Hills, including the Battle of Little Bighorn in 1876.
1877 Flight of the Nez Percé under Chief Joseph.
1877–80 Apache resistance in the Southwest under Victorio.
1878 Bannock War in Idaho and Oregon.
1878–79 Flight of the Northern Cheyenne under Dull Knife on the plains.
1879 Sheepeater War in Idaho; Ute War in Colorado.
1879 The Carlisle Indian School in Pennsylvania began under Richard Pratt to assimilate Indians into white culture. The Bureau of American Ethnology, a branch of the Smithsonian, was founded for anthropological studies.

1881 Sitting Bull surrendered to officials at Fort Buford, North Dakota.

1881–86 Apache resistance under Geronimo, who surrendered in 1886.

1885 Last great herd of buffalo exterminated.

1887 Congress passed the Dawes Act to divide the reservations into 160-acre parcels and distribute the land to family heads; Indians lost millions of acres.

1890 Ghost Dance movement led by Wovoka gained a large following among Western Indians, leading to an hysterical reaction of the U.S. troops: they killed 150 Lakota Indians at Wounded Knee, mistakenly believing that they were en route to a Ghost Dance.

1890–1910 Indian population reached its lowest level of 250,000.

1898 The Curtis Act dissolved tribal governments and required Indians to submit to allotment.

1901 A Snake uprising in Oklahoma Territory in which the Creek Indians resisted allotment.

1902 The secretary of the interior leased to companies the first oil and gas rights on Indian lands in Oklahoma.

1906 The federal government seized 50,000 acres of wilderness sacred to the Taos Pueblo Indians of New Mexico and made it a national park.

1909 Just before leaving office, President Theodore Roosevelt transferred 2.5 million acres of timbered Indian reservation lands to national forests.

1910 The federal government prohibited the Sun Dance among Plains Indians, giving self-torture as the reason.

1912 Jim Thorpe from the Carlisle School won the Olympic pentathlon and decathlon. (In 1913, the Olympic committee stripped him of the medals because he had played one season of semiprofessional baseball; in 1983 the medals were reinstated.)

1913 The federal government issues a "buffalo-head" nickel with the composite portrait of three Indian chiefs—a Cheyenne, a Seneca, and a Lakota—on one side, and a buffalo on the reverse side.

TABLE 2.1 REPORTED BIRTHS, DEATHS, AND RATES, INDIANS ON RESERVATIONS, EXCLUDING FIVE CIVILIZED TRIBES, 1875–1900 (RATES PER 1,000 POPULATION)

Year	Indian Population	Births		Deaths	
		Number	Rate	Number	Rate
1875	252,900	1,985	7.8	1,601	6.3
1880	196,940	3,430	17.4	2,020	10.3
1890	176,534	4,908	27.8	5,208	29.5
1895	182,370	3,502[a]	19.2	2,974[b]	16.3
1900	185,790	4,196[a]	22.6	3,698[b]	19.9

[a]"The Five Civilized Tribes," as they were known, included the Creek, Choctaw, Cherokee, Chikasaw, and Seminole.
[b]Only partially reported.
Source: Paul Stewart, *Nationals Within a Nation* (1987), 102. These rates compare with U.S. death rates per 1,000 population in 1900 of 17.0 for whites and 25.0 for blacks. National rates of birth are unavailable until 1909, when they were 29.2 for whites and in 1917 for blacks when 32.9 births were recorded per 1,000 population. See B. R. Mitchell, *International Statistics* (1983), 113.

TABLE 2.2 INDIAN POPULATION, 1913

The annual reports of the various Indian superintendents showed as of Jun. 30, 1913, that the Indian population was 330,603,[a] distributed among the states as follows:

State	Number
Ala.	909
Ariz.	41,505
Ark.	460
Calif.	16,513
Colo.	870
Conn.	152
Del.	5
D.C.	68
Fla.	600
Ga.	95
Idaho	3,841
Ill.	188
Ind.	279
Nebr.	3,890
Nev.	7,756
N.H.	34
N.J.	168
N. Mex.	21,725
N.Y.	6,029
N.C.	7,945
N. Dak.	8,538
Ohio	127
Okla.	117,274
Oreg.	6,414
R.I.	284
Iowa	365
Kans.	1,345
Ky.	234
La.	780
Maine	892
Md.	55
Mass.	688
Mich.	7,512
Minn.	11,338
Miss.	1,253
Mo.	313
Mont.	11,331
S.C.	331
S. Dak.	20,555
Tenn.	216
Tex.	702
Utah	3,231
Vt.	26
Va.	539
Wash.	11,547
W. Va.	36
Wis.	9,930
Wyo.	1,715
U.S. Total	330,603

[a]Prior to 1890, U.S. census enumeration was limited to Native Americans living in the general population. Indians in Indian Territory and or Indian reservations, the bulk of the Native-American population was excluded. In 1910, a special effort was made to enumerate all persons with any perceptible amount of Indian ancestry. This probably resulted in the enumeration of a considerable number of persons who had been counted as white in previous censuses; it is likely that this is the most accurate count. No special effort was made in 1920, the the returns showed a much smaller number of Native Americans than in 1910. In 1930, another special effort was made, resulting in a more accurate count.
Source: The World Almanac and Encyclopedia 1914 (1913), 521.

American Indian Reservations, 1890

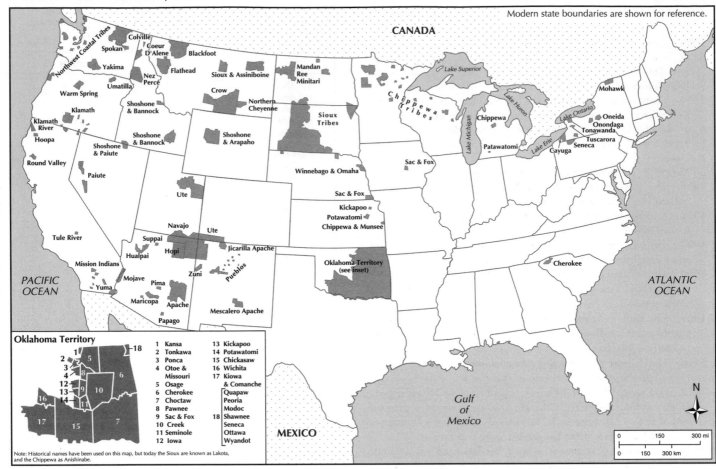

Modern state boundaries are shown for reference.

Oklahoma Territory

Note: Historical names have been used on this map, but today the Sioux are known as Lakota, and the Chippewa as Anishinabe.

1 Kansa	13 Kickapoo	
2 Tonkawa	14 Potawatomi	
3 Ponca	15 Chickasaw	
4 Otoe & Missouri	16 Wichita	
5 Osage	17 Kiowa & Comanche	
6 Cherokee		Quapaw
7 Choctaw		Peoria
8 Pawnee		Modoc
9 Sac & Fox	18	Shawnee
10 Creek		Seneca
11 Seminole		Ottawa
12 Iowa		Wyandot

This map shows Indian reservations in the United States as they were in the year 1890. By this time, most eastern tribes had been pushed west of their traditional homelands or had lost their land altogether. (Map by Dale Williams)

Buffalo Soldiers

Between 1866 and 1900, black men were included for the first time in the regular army. The post–Civil War army was largely engaged in Indian wars and was comprised of lower-class urban workers, European immigrants, and blacks. "Buffalo Soldiers" was the name usually given to members of the regular army sent to the Western territories to fight in the Indian wars. Black soldiers made up approximately one-tenth of the army, but in some western states they could constitute as much as one-half of the available military force.

In 1866, Congress passed a bill to reorganize the army. The reorganization included the establishment of four black units: the 9th and 10th Cavalry and the 24th and 25th Infantry. These were black units commanded by white officers; noncommissioned officers were black. White and black soldiers did serve concurrently at the same posts.

Racism played a role in virtually every facet of the Buffalo Soldiers' lives. Black soldiers were stationed at relatively remote and desolate locations because they were not welcome in the more populous eastern areas. They generally received inferior equipment, food, and other supplies and were obviously discriminated against in recruitment and promotion to officer status. Local newspapers often attacked them, and their abilities were constantly under scrutiny. Day-to-day life was boring and tedious; alcohol abuse was common. In all the Indian wars combined, a total of 18 black Buffalo Soldiers

received the Congressional Medal of Honor for heroism.

In one of the strangest ironies of American history, colonizers who had forced blacks against their will to come to America now called upon former slaves as soldiers to subdue a nation of people who had birthrights to the land.

Ghost Dance

In 1888, Wovoka, a Paiute Indian from Nevada, drew upon the mystic teachings of his father and his own vision during an eclipse to begin to spread a message that came to be called the Ghost Dance Religion. According to the vision, the Earth would soon perish and be replaced with a new land in its pure, aboriginal state, which would be inhabited by Indians who would be free from suffering forever. But this new paradise had to be earned by Indian cleansing, harmonious relations among themselves, and a shunning of the ways of whites, especially the use of alcohol, the "destroyer." Wovoka demanded the saying of prayers, meditations, and incantations, a ritual embodied in a dance during which one might "die" and catch a glimpse of the paradise of lush prairie grass, herds of buffalo, and Indian ancestors.

The Ghost Dance Religion spread to the conquered, impoverished, and forlorn tribes on reservations of the Far West, the Southwest, and the Plains. The message was especially popular with the

African-American soldiers were first used on a large scale during the Civil War when 180,000 served in the Union Army. After the war, Congress, for the first time, authorized black troops to serve in the regular peacetime army. Besides infantry, it created two cavalry regiments—the 9th and 10th—that became known as the Buffalo Soldiers. Like other black regiments, the 9th and 10th had white officers. The Buffalo Soldiers served in the West to police the Native American populations. This is a picture of Company "B," 25th Infantry, Captain Bentzoni commanding, Fort Randall, Dakota Territory, 1882. (Courtesy National Archives)

This picture shows the encampment on River Brulé near Pine Ridge, South Dakota, of 4,000 Lakota surrounded by 3,500 armed troopers just after the massacre of Wounded Knee. The village was established in January 1891 in defiance of the U.S. Army. Shortly afterward, these Lakota, who had made one final desperate effort to resist, were forced onto reservations. (Photo by John C. H. Grabill, courtesy National Archives)

Lakota (Sioux) who took to the new religion after one of their own shamans, Kicking Bear, learned of it in Nevada and began to dance the Ghost Dance.

Kicking Bear and Short Bull, both shamans of the Miniconjou Teton, put their own spin on the gospel. They choose to disregard Wovoka's antiviolence and emphasize the elimination of whites. They talked of special Ghost Dance shirts that were able to stop the white man's bullets.

As the Ghost Dance Religion spread and took on a more ominous tone of insurgency, the U.S. military became alarmed. In November 1890, the Ghost Dance was banned on Lakota reservations. When the practice continued, officials called in troops and prepared for one final Indian campaign, one that ended in the Wounded Knee Massacre.

Wounded Knee

The Wounded Knee Massacre resulted from U.S. Army's reaction to the Ghost Dance Religion that caught fire on Indian reservations in South Dakota. In November 1890, officials became overanxious and banned the Ghost Dance on Lakota reservations, but the rites continued. General Nelson Miles commanded the Division of the Missouri and set up his headquarters at Rapid City, South Dakota. The presence of troops only made matters worse. General Miles's troops stalked alleged followers of the religion, including Sitting Bull of the Hunkpapa, who was arrested to prevent him from joining in a dance at the Pine Ridge, South Dakota, reservation. While in custody, he was slain along with six of his warriors.

Miles also ordered the arrest of Big Foot, a Miniconjou leader living on the Cheyenne River in South Dakota, who had previously supported the Ghost Dance. But at this point Big Foot, who wanted to avoid any trouble, was leading his people not to the Ghost Dance, but to what he believed would be safety at Pine Ridge. The Seventh Cavalry, under Major S. M. Whitside, was sent to intercept Big Foot and his people, catching them at a point within 30 miles of Pine Ridge. The Indians put up no resistance; Big Foot was so ill with pneumonia that he rode in a wagon.

Whitside's soldiers instructed the Indians to encamp for the night on Wounded Knee Creek. Colonel James Forsyth arrived to take command and immediately ordered guards to place four Hotchkiss cannons in positions around the encampment. The soldiers numbered about 500; the Indians, 350, all but 120 of them women and children.

The next morning, December 29, 1890, the soldiers entered the Indian camp to collect all firearms. An Indian medicine man, Yellow Bird, advocated resistance with the claim that the Ghost Dance shirts would protect them. Big Foot, more cautious and believing that resistance would be suicidal, counseled cooperation. Then one of the soldiers attempted harshly to disarm Black Coyote, who was deaf, and the rifle discharged. Suddenly, the air was filled with gunfire. At first, soldiers fired at almost point blank range; then, as the Indians began to run for cover, the Hotchkiss artillery opened up on them—men, women, and children alike. When the firing stopped, 150 Indians lay dead and 50 were wounded. Army casualties were twenty-five killed and thirty-nine wounded. Forsyth was later exonerated from charges of killing innocent victims.

After Wounded Knee, the Ghost Dance declined. Wounded Knee marks the end of the Indian wars in many ways. It also became a symbol of the wrongs done to American Indians.

CHAPTER 3 Chronology of Important Events, 1876 to 1913

The period's politics began with a constitutional crisis on the anniversary of the nation's birth when the presidential election of 1876 produced no clear winner. At the end of the period, reform dominated the political agenda.

Issues such as prohibition, women's suffrage, business monopoly, labor conditions, farm foreclosures, crime and poverty in America's cities, unemployment and social unrest, and contamination of food spawned political and social movements—sometimes political parties—to deal with the problems.

Intervention in foreign affairs quickened noticeably during the Victorian period as America emerged as a world power. The Spanish-American War and intervention in the internal affairs of nations such as Nicaragua, Cuba, the Philippines, Mexico, Colombia, Panama, and China all underscored America's increasing involvement in world politics.

Minorities experienced some of the worst treatment in American history. Indians were forced onto reservations and virtually forgotten. African Americans were segregated by law in the South and by custom in the North. In the South, they were lynched with impunity, and the Supreme Court validated the doctrine of "separate but equal." Working women battled unequal pay, exclusion from positions of authority, and—except for teachers—confinement to low-paying factory and domestic-service occupations. Asian Americans, eastern Europeans, Jews, Italians, and Roman Catholics struggled against ethnic and religious intolerance. Immigration laws were enacted to exclude the Chinese and restrict other foreigners, especially nonwestern Europeans.

The economy grew at a dizzying pace, and corporate gigantism and monopoly characterized the evolution of business organization. Captains of industry amassed great fortunes, which they displayed in

Lynching, defined as "murder by mob action," predated the Victorian Age, having first become widespread in the territories of the West during the 1850s. During the Victorian Age, however, it moved south and increasingly became a weapon of white oppression against blacks. Between 1882 and 1903, the number of lynchings peaked at 3,337. Of this number 2,585 were in the South, and 1,985 were blacks, including 40 black women. Although the evidence belies the claim, the major pretext for lynching was to control black sexual assaults upon white women. This picture shows lynching to be a public spectacle as hundreds gather to watch the lynching of an unknown victim in Texas in 1893. (Courtesy Prints and Photographs Division, Library of Congress)

"conspicuous consumption." Laissez-faire economics gave way to a measure of government regulation as the nation struggled to control the power of corporations, the trusts, and financial chaos.

Confronting giant corporations and trusts, workers in the 1880s increased efforts to organize national unions. Labor conditions, including child labor (children as young as nine worked ten to fourteen hours a day), produced 14,800 strikes involving 4 million workers between 1881 and 1894. Employers fought these "muscle trusts" with injunctions, lockouts, blacklists, and armed assault. Unemployment and a devastating economic depression in the early 1890s caused mass unrest and hardship in the dense slum neighborhoods of American cities.

Inventions and technological breakthroughs also highlighted the era. The railroad led the postwar industrial revolution, but by 1913 Henry Ford had developed the automotive assembly line to produce the Model T, and the Wright Brothers had pioneered powered flight. Besides the automobile and airplane, the telephone, telegraph, typewriter, motion pictures, linotype machine, diesel engine, light bulb, X-ray and the cheap mass-produced camera, for use by amateurs were just a few of the many inventions and innovations that made an impact upon American life and culture.

Mass-circulation newspapers and magazines and three World's Fairs educated Americans about themselves and communicated to the world what the nation saw as its national heritage. Sports entertained increasing numbers. Baseball grew in importance, basketball was invented, football spread in colleges, and cycling increased with the invention of the safety bicycle. Women increasingly participated in athletics, and changes in dress made cycling a women's leisure activity for the first time.

The Centennial Exposition of 1876

In 1876, America celebrated its 100 years of independence with a Centennial Exposition, a "monster celebration," in Philadelphia. After the years of Civil War, Reconstruction, and scandal in the Grant administration, Americans were ready for a diversion. It emphasized the themes of unity, strength, and prosperity—goals more than accomplishments.

Physically, the Centennial Exposition was an imposing array of 167 buildings and 30,000 exhibits covering 236 acres in Fairmount Park. The Main Exhibition Building housed scientific and manufactured products, measured 1,800 feet in length and 464 feet in width, the largest building in the world at that time. Four buildings formed the core of the exhibition: Machinery Hall, Agricultural Hall, Horticultural Hall, and Memorial Hall. Unlike the other buildings whose name identified their purpose, Memorial Hall housed international displays of painting, sculpture, engraving, photography, and crafts. The U.S. Government Building included exhibits illustrating the work of federal agencies, such as an exhibit of military hardware and a working post office. A Women's Building highlighted "the results of woman's labors." Seventeen of thirty-nine participating states had exhibit buildings emphasizing their particular achievements.

Very expensive for the average citizen, railroad fare even after reductions meant that round-trip travel to the fair from Chicago cost (in 1990 dollars) about $422, from New Orleans $832, from Denver $1,303, and from San Francisco $2,495 (compared to today's average round-trip air fares of $181, $244, $366, and $386 from Chicago, New Orleans, Denver, and San Francisco, respectively, to Philadelphia). On May 10, 200,000 people came through the turnstiles to witness President Grant, the emperor of Brazil, and a group of military officers, politicians, and other official dignitaries officially open the Exposition. Ten million visitors came during its six-month run.

The fair mirrored late nineteenth-century hopes, assumptions, and fears. A heated debate over whether the fair should be open on Sundays preceded the opening. The directors bowed to pressure to "keep the Sabbath holy," and the gates remained closed. On the other hand, beer and liquor sales were allowed on the grounds, despite their prohibition at most county and state fairs, circuses, and other places of family entertainment. As for the items on display, most reflected the prevailing middle-class optimism about the industrial and mechanical transformation of everyday life in Victorian America.

Everywhere they turned, visitors saw depictions of day-to-day life: long rows of farm products and machinery, two buildings devoted exclusively to kindergarten training, a newspaper printing plant, demonstrations of the manufacture of everything from bricks to indoor plumbing, operating exhibits of typewriters and pneumatic tubes, a narrow-gauge railroad that transported fairgoers from place to place, botanical exhibits, Alexander Graham Bell personally demonstrating his telephone, Thomas Edison explaining his new automatic telegraph—all representative of the era's aspirations and optimistic faith in technology.

At Machinery Hall, the vision of the future reached its apogee. Here on prominent display was the mighty Corliss engine: two cylinders 40 inches in diameter with a stroke of 10 feet, a flywheel 30 feet in diameter, weighing 56 tons and spinning at 360 revolutions per minute, with 40 miles of belting, 23 miles of shafting—an engine powerful enough to run hundreds of other machines on display. According to one visitor, the Corliss was "Prometheus unbound"— but not for long. In 1910, after serving as the power source for the Pullman passenger-car plant in Chicago, "Prometheus" was dismantled and sold for scrap iron at eight dollars a ton.

Probably more revealing, for today's readers, were the exhibits that weren't there. African Americans had no exhibit of their own. Only two black artists, Edmonia Lewis and Edward Banister, had their paintings on display. African Americans received no acknowledgment in the Woman's Building. Frederick Douglass, the most prominent black in the United States, sat on the dignitaries' platform during the opening ceremonies, but he was not asked to speak. When African Americans were represented, they appeared in stereotypical form, as in the concession known variously as "The South" and the "Southern Restaurant," where guidebooks informed the public that "a band of old-time plantation 'darkies' . . . sing their quaint melodies and strum the banjo before visitors in every clime." On the grounds, blacks could be seen working as entertainers, waiters, hotel clerks, messengers, and janitors. Despite Philadelphia's large African-American population, no blacks were employed on construction jobs for the fairgrounds and its buildings.

In the United States Government Building was a spectacular display of Native American culture, a conglomeration of pottery, tools, weapons, wigwams, costumes, and wax figures, organized by the Smithsonian Institution. The display looked more like the results of an archaeological dig than an exhibit of a living people with multiple cultures. In fact, it portrayed Indians as the antithesis of civilization and progress. Visitors commented upon the wax figures that resembled "hideous demon[s]," and "red gentlemen, with . . . small, cruel, black eyes, . . . coarse, unkempt locks, . . . and large animal mouth."

Other minorities experienced similar treatment. Displays and exhibits from countries such as Japan, China, and the European empires of Africa drew little attention and much of that unfavorable. Wherever they went on the fairgrounds, visitors heard frequent expressions of xenophobic prejudice. Whether Asian, Turk, Slav, Egyptian, or Spaniard, foreign-looking people were "followed by large crowds of idle boys, and men, who hooted and shouted at them as if they had been animals of a strange species."

Most telling was the countercultural "Centennial City" that sprang up outside the gates of the Exposition. Like the slums and tenement districts of most American cities, Centennial City was actually a shantytown of hastily constructed structures of tin, wood, and canvas. Along a mile-long strip stood cheap food stalls, small hotels, beer stands, ice-cream parlors, peanut vendors, pie sellers, sausage makers, lemonade stands, balloon salesmen, and small circuslike sideshows, all for those unable to afford the fifty-cent admission fee to the exposition itself.

Centennial City was a striking contradiction to the exposition's optimistic assumptions about progress, prosperity, and the future. Both inside and outside the gates, the many incongruities and contradictions of American life, which the exposition was designed to disguise, were exposed. Side by side, visitors saw squalor and well-being, poverty and prosperity, national pride and ethnic and racial prejudice, celebrations of Indian life and depictions of Native Americans as savages, hunger and plenty, crime and high culture, all evidence, for those who chose to see, that America's promise did not include everyone.

The Columbian Exposition of 1893

Chicago launched its first World's Fair in 1893. The Columbian Exposition contrasted sharply with the Philadelphia fair.

Physically, the Chicago fairgrounds comprised a planned, urban environment. The White City, as it was called, was designed in the architecture of beaux-arts neoclassicism. Around a formal court with a central administrative building were clusters of buildings housing what Americans considered basic to their urban economy: Railroads, Machinery, Manufactures, and Agriculture. Two buildings, Mining and Electricity, signaled the importance of the extractive industries as a new source of power. Additional buildings included Louis Sullivan's Transportation Building, the Women's and adjoining Children's Buildings, and two large structures of state: the Illinois Building and the United States Building. Unlike the Philadelphia fair where the recreational activities were confined to the fringe of the fairground, the Midway Plaisance, a mile-long recreational corridor, was a part of the fair.

Exhibits displayed trends in domestic life, albeit mostly with a middle-class, consumerist emphasis. For example, the growing competition between gas and electricity as a source of home heating and lighting could be seen by visiting three model kitchens. In the Manufacturers and Liberal Arts Building, visitors viewed miles of displays of period room furniture, tableware, and textiles.

Visitors could glimpse the everyday life of laboring families in a special New York exhibit of a Workingman's Model Home. Katherine Davis, a Rochester social reformer, oversaw the design and furnishing of the residence. Her model family included a young engaged couple—a laborer who earned $500 per year and his fiancée, a domestic servant who earned $156 a year plus board. Their house was a two-story wood-frame dwelling designed to cost a maximum of $1,000, with a front parlor, a kitchen, and a bath with a tub and water closet. A range and wood stoves provided heat. Davis projected that the hypothetical couple would amass $400 in a two-year engagement, $100 of which would be retained as savings and $300 used to furnish their mortgaged dwelling. Lists of what household items cost and prices of clothing and other objects were posted throughout the model home. An eight-year-old boy, a five-year-old girl, and an infant represented the typical family. In addition, Davis researched feeding this family, according to Chicago market prices, and calculated the nutritional content of her purchases. During the fair, Davis prepared daily meals during a month of the fair and served them to a police officer and a widow and her three children.

Except for the New York exhibit, the overwhelming focus of the fair centered upon middle-class material culture. In the Electricity Building, another model home displayed the future household: electric stove, hot plates, washing machine, carpet sweepers, electric doorbell, fire alarms, and attractive lighting fixtures. The 54-acre Manufacturers and Liberal Arts Building, "the largest department store the world had ever seen," presented a "cornucopia of material culture" in the form of Morris chairs, zip lockers for shoes, garden furniture, baby carriages, and rural telephones. As the Corliss engine had impressed previous fairgoers, the Westinghouse Company's huge dynamos were, for Henry Adams and others, symbolic of a new force capable of transforming American life. Instead of the telephone and automatic telegraph that fascinated Philadelphia visitors, now phonographs and the Kinetoscope offered new visions of future communications.

The Chicago Exposition also highlighted the growth of American associational life, especially professional organizations. A separate World's Congress Auxiliary of 14,000 members organized 139 national conferences that attracted more than 700,000 participants. The most popular were those on education (with such speakers as G. Stanley Hall and John Dewey), labor (including addresses by Samuel Gompers and Henry George), and women (featuring Julia Ward Howe and Frances Willard). A World Parliament of Religions lasted more than two weeks and decried creeping materialism.

Chicago's Midway Plaisance, or the Midway as it came to be known (a new term thereafter applied to pleasure strips in the midst of county fairs, tent chautauquas, or trolley parks), achieved a kind of official status, unlike the fringe counterculture of Philadelphia. The polyglot Midway celebrated American diversity in foods, Turkish bazaars, Hawaiian volcanoes, and Hagenbeck's circus animals. Sideshow freaks, hootchy-kootchy dancers, strongmen, and magicians baffled and entertained visitors. George Ferris's wheel, a 264-foot "bicycle wheel in the sky," dominated the landscape. It had thirty-six cars, each capable of holding sixty people, and when fully loaded rotated 2,160 people in the air.

Various cultures received treatment in depictions, often stereotypical, on the Midway. Some, like the Javanese, were curiosities or were trophies, like the Lakota (Sioux). The exhibits were located, according to one visitor, on a "sliding scale of humanity." The Teutonic and Celtic cultures, depicted by two German and two Irish enclaves, had exhibits nearest the White City. The Midway's middle displayed the Arab and Asian worlds. Then, continued the visitor, "we descend to the savage races, the African of Dahomey and the North American Indian," located on the remotest part of the Midway. Blacks made several attempts to get Congress to put exhibits in both the fair's main structures and the state pavilions, but to no avail. The only black display presented the Hampton Institute's educational program. As was the case in Philadelphia, despite Chicago's large black population, discrimination barred them from the fair's construction crews and clerical staffs.

The Columbian Exposition introduced the first commemorative postage stamps and coins, and a new holiday and ceremony were added to American culture. Francis J. Bellamy, editor of *Youth's Companion,* proposed a plan for the fair's dedication of Columbus Day, October 12, 1892, which the nation's children might celebrate concurrently with a Pledge of Allegiance to the United States. Bellamy drafted the pledge, which the federal Bureau of Education circulated to teachers nationwide, launching an American ritual that has been repeated daily in the nation's classrooms.

More in keeping with the spirit of consumerism, other items introduced at the fair were Cream of Wheat, Aunt Jemima Pancake Mix, Postum, Juicy Fruit Gum, Shredded Wheat, and Pabst Blue Ribbon, the exposition's award-winning beer.

The Chicago Exposition closed on October 29, 1893, not in the heady atmosphere of prosperity, a theme the fair had stressed, but in the midst of the nation's worst economic depression. Wall Street stocks plunged on May 5 with the market all but collapsing on June 27. Six hundred banks closed their doors, business firms failed by the thousands, and seventy-four railroads went into receivership. In Washington, D.C., Coxey's Army of the unemployed marched on the city, demanding relief, but instead its members were arrested for walking on the Capitol grass. Fittingly, on January 8, 1894, fire destroyed nearly all the exposition's buildings. Without any federal controls on monetary and fiscal policy, the ups and downs of the business cycle continued to cause periods of boom and bust.

March 2, 1876 Impeachment proceedings against Secretary of War William W. Belknap for malfeasance in office were recommended by a House committee.

May 17, 1876 The Prohibition Party, during its second annual convention, nominated Green Clay Smith of Kentucky for president and Gideon T. Stewart of Ohio for vice president.

May 18, 1876 The Greenback Party, at its first convention, nominated Peter Cooper of New York for president and Samuel F. Perry of Ohio for vice president.

June 14–16, 1876 The Republican convention nominated Rutherford B. Hayes of Ohio for president and William A. Wheeler of New York for vice president.

June 25, 1876 At the battle of Little Bighorn in Montana, Gen. George A. Custer and all 265 men of the 7th Cavalry were killed by Lakota Indians led by Crazy Horse and Gall.

June 27–29, 1876 The Democratic convention nominated Samuel J. Tilden of New York for president and Thomas A. Hendricks of Indiana for vice president.

July 25, 1876 Free and unlimited coinage of silver was proposed by Rep. Richard P. Bland of Missouri.

August 1, 1876 Colorado was admitted as the thirty-eighth state.

November 7, 1876 The presidential election gave Samuel J. Tilden, the Democratic candidate, a popular vote plurality of 250,000, but Republicans contested returns in Florida, Louisiana, South Carolina, and Oregon. Dispute had to be settled by special commission made up of five members of each house of Congress and five members from the Supreme Court; in Congressional elections the Republicans lost seats in the Senate but maintained a 38–36 majority; in the House the Democrats held a 153–140 majority.

November 23, 1876 William Marcy "Boss" Tweed was captured in Spain and handed over to New York authorities to begin to serve his prison sentence.

December 5, 1876 New York City's worst theater fire occurred at the Brooklyn Theater, killing 289 people in an audience of 1,200.

December 12, 1876 A prohibition amendment to the constitution was introduced for the first time by Rep. Henry W. Blair of New Hampshire.

December 29, 1876 A railroad accident killed eighty-four when the Pacific Express plunged into a gorge in Ashtabula, Ohio.

January 2, 1877 "Carpetbag" government ended in Florida when George F. Drew, Democrat, was inaugurated governor.

March 5, 1877 Rutherford B. Hayes was inaugurated nineteenth president of the United States.

April 10, 1877 "Carpetbag" government ended in South Carolina when federal troops left Columbia.

June–October, 1877 Chief Joseph and the Nez Percé Indians fought federal troops before surrendering.

June 14, 1877 Flag Day was first observed to mark the adoption of the stars-and-stripes design by the Continental Congress. (It is not a legal holiday and is observed only by presidential proclamation.)

June 15, 1877 Henry O. Flipper became the first African American to graduate from U.S. Military Academy at West Point.

July 17, 1877 A crippling national railway strike spread across the nation when the Baltimore and Ohio workers went on strike.

August 29, 1877 Brigham Young died at 76.

November 23, 1877 The United States and Canada agreed on reciprocal fishing rights along the Canadian–U.S. border in Washington, and Canada received $5.5 million for its greater concessions.

December 6, 1877 Thomas A. Edison completed his phonograph.

January 28, 1878 The first commercial telephone exchange opened in New Haven, Connecticut, with eight lines and twenty-one phones.

February 22, 1878 The Greenback–Labor Party was formed, fusing elements of labor and farm parties.

June 11, 1878 The District of Columbia was given a government of three commissioners; residents would have no direct voice in either local or national government.

August 1, 1878 The American Bar Association was formed at Saratoga, New York, with James O. Broadhead as first president.

October 15, 1878 The first electric-light company, Edison Electric Light Company, opened in New York.

December 17, 1878 Greenbacks, issued in 1862 to finance the Civil War, achieved full value (meaning a dollar was worth a dollar) on Wall Street for the first time.

January 1, 1879 Trading in paper money for coins was resumed for the first time since 1861. (It has been maintained ever since.)

February 15, 1879 Women attorneys gained the right to argue cases before the U.S. Supreme Court.

May 8, 1879 George B. Selden of Rochester, New York, filed the first patent application for the gasoline engine, but the patent was not issued until November 5, 1895.

October 21, 1879 The first incandescent electric lamp was perfected by Thomas A. Edison in his Menlo Park, New Jersey, laboratories.

March 1, 1880 The U.S. Supreme Court declared that excluding African Americans from jury duty was unconstitutional under the provisions of the Fourteenth Amendment.

June 2–8, 1880 The Republican National Convention nominated James A. Garfield of Ohio for the presidency and Chester A. Arthur of New York as his running mate; Sen. Blanche Kelso Bruce of Mississippi was made temporary chairman of the Republican Party committee and became the first black to preside over a major party convention.

June 9, 1880 The Greenback-Labor National Convention nominated James B. Weaver of Iowa for president; he received 3.4% of the popular vote.

June 17, 1880 The Prohibition National Convention nominated Neal Dow of Maine for president; he received 10,305 votes, less than 1% of the popular vote.

June 22–24, 1880 The Democratic National Convention nominated Winfield S. Hancock of Pennsylvania for president.

November 2, 1880 James A. Garfield was elected president of the United States and Chester A. Arthur vice president; in congressional elections Republicans and Democrats achieved equal numbers in the Senate with thirty-seven seats each; in the House, the Republicans took a 147–135 majority.

November 17, 1880 The Chinese Exclusion Treaty was signed at

Peking (see Chapter 16), permitting the United States to regulate or limit but not exclude the immigration of Chinese laborers.

January 24, 1881 In *Springer v. United States,* the Supreme Court declared the federal income tax law of 1862 constitutional.

March 4, 1881 James A. Garfield was inaugurated twentieth president of the United States.

May 21, 1881 Clara Barton founded an American branch of the Red Cross.

July 2, 1881 President Garfield was shot in a Washington, D.C., railroad station by Charles J. Guiteau, a frustrated office seeker who believed his campaign efforts in Garfield's behalf entitled him to a government position; the act lead to the establishment of the civil service system (see January 16, 1883). Garfield lingered for eighty days before succumbing on September 19.

July 4, 1881 Tuskegee Institute opened, with Booker T. Washington as its first president.

September 20, 1881 Chester A. Arthur was inaugurated twenty-first president of the United States.

November 14, 1881 The trial of Charles J. Guiteau, President Garfield's assassin, began in Washington, D.C.; Guiteau was convicted on January 25, 1882, and was hanged in Washington on June 30, 1882.

March 16, 1882 The Geneva Convention of 1864, accepted by most European nations for the care of wounded war personnel, was ratified by the U.S. Senate.

March 22, 1882 The Edmunds Act, which forbade polygamy and was directed especially against the Mormons in Utah territory, was adopted by the U.S. Congress.

March 31, 1882 Congress voted a pension for widows of presidents.

April 3, 1882 Robert Ford shot and killed Jesse James.

April 28, 1882 The John F. Slater Fund for the education of emancipated blacks was established by a gift of $1 million from textile manufacturer John Fox Slater. This was the first major philanthropy in the field.

May 6, 1882 The Exclusion Act barred further Chinese emigration for ten years.

May 22, 1882 The United States recognized the independence of Korea.

August 2, 1882 An $18 million rivers and harbors bill was passed over President Arthur's veto.

August 3, 1882 The first federal emigration restriction law was passed; it restricted convicts, the insane, and those likely to become a public charge from entering the country.

November 7, 1882 In Congressional elections, the Democrats gained fifty seats to take a 197–118 majority; in the Senate, the Republicans gained one seat to take a 38–36 majority over the Democrats.

January 10, 1883 The worst hotel fire in U.S. history consumed the Newhall House in Milwaukee, Wisconsin, killing seventy-one persons.

January 16, 1883 The Pendleton Act established the civil service system.

March 3, 1883 Two measures were taken to reduce the U.S. Treasury surplus: U.S. postage was reduced to two cents per half ounce; the rebuilding of the U.S. Navy began with an appropriation from Congress.

May 9, 1883 The *New York World* newspaper was purchased by Joseph Pulitzer from Jay Gould.

May 24, 1883 The first telephone service between Chicago and New York City began. The Brooklyn Bridge, a 1,595-foot suspension bridge spanning the East River that had been begun in 1869, opened.

September 21, 1883 The first direct telegraph service to Brazil was established.

October 15, 1883 The Supreme Court vitiated the Civil Rights Act of 1875 to allow for segregation in public accommodations.

November 18, 1883 A system of standard time was adopted by the United States and Canada in order to set uniform time schedules and eliminate problems caused by a variety of local times.

February 19, 1884 A series of tornadoes killed 700 people in the southern states. From 10:00 A.M. until 12:00 P.M., sixty tornadoes occurred in parts of Virginia, North Carolina, South Carolina, Georgia, Alabama, Mississippi, Tennessee, and Kentucky. Rough estimates of damage placed the losses between $3 million and $4 million; the loss of life at 800; and the number of wounded at 2,500.

May 12, 1884 Mississippi Industrial Institute and College, the first state-supported women's college, was chartered; the Knights of Labor designated Labor Day to be celebrated annually on the first Monday in September.

May 14, 1884 The Anti-Monopoly Party was founded in Chicago and nominated Benjamin F. Butler of Massachusetts for the presidency.

May 28, 1884 The Greenback Party nominated Benjamin F. Butler for the presidency and Alanson M. West of Mississippi for the vice presidency.

June 3–6, 1884 The Republican National Convention nominated James G. Blaine of Maine for the presidency and Gen. John A. Logan of Illinois for the vice presidency.

June 6, 1884 The Mugwumps, reform-oriented independent Republicans, bolted the national convention upon Blaine's nomination, believing he would not support civil service reform.

July 8–11, 1884 The Democratic National Convention nominated Grover Cleveland of New York for the presidency and Thomas A. Hendricks of Indiana for the vice presidency.

July 23, 1884 The Prohibition National Convention nominated John P. St. John of Kansas for the presidency and William Daniel of Maryland for the vice presidency.

August 5, 1884 The cornerstone of the pedestal of the Statue of Liberty was laid.

October 6, 1884 The Naval War College was established at Newport, Rhode Island, with Commodore Stephen Bleecker Luce as its first president.

November 4, 1884 Grover Cleveland was elected president.

February 21, 1885 The Washington Monument was dedicated, having taken four-and-a-half years to build.

February 25, 1885 An act of Congress prohibited the fencing of public lands in the West.

March 4, 1885 Grover Cleveland was inaugurated twenty-second president of the United States.

July 1, 1885 Postal rates were lowered, creating a budget deficit in the Post Office Department.

July 23, 1885 Ulysses S. Grant died at 63 and was buried on Riverside Drive in New York City overlooking the Hudson River.

November 25, 1885 Vice President Thomas Hendricks died at 66 and was buried in Indianapolis; no provision for replacement of vice presidents was made until 1967.

January 19, 1886 A Presidential Succession Act was passed, replacing the statute of 1792: in the event of removal, disability, resignation, or death both of the president and vice president, the heads of the executive departments, in order of the creation of their departments, should succeed to the office of the president. This law remained in effect until 1947.

May 4, 1886 At Haymarket Square in Chicago, a bomb was thrown at a labor rally, killing seven police officers and wounding sixty others.

May 10, 1886 In two rulings, the Supreme Court introduced ambiguity into the meaning of the Fourteenth Amendment. In the case of *Yick Wo v. Hopkins,* the court defined an alien as a person in the eyes of the law, declaring that city ordinances against Chinese laundries violated the Fourteenth Amendment; in *Santa Clara County v. Southern Pacific Railroad Co.,* the court also held corporations to be legal persons under the Fourteenth Amendment and encouraged the substantive interpretation of the due process clause as a defense of corporate property rights.

June 2, 1886 President Cleveland married Frances Folsom at the White House in Washington, D.C.

June 19, 1886 Eight were convicted in the Haymarket incident, despite the lack of evidence proving any of them to be the bomb thrower. Seven were sentenced to death: four were hanged on November 11; one committed suicide in jail; and two had their sentences commuted to life imprisonment.

June 30, 1886 The Division of Forestry, established in 1881 in the Department of Agriculture, was recognized by Congress, and Dr. Bernhard E. Fernow, a professional forester, was named head.

September 4, 1886 Geronimo, the Apache raider along the Mexican border, surrendered, and all the Chiricahua Apaches were resettled in Florida as war prisoners.

September 14, 1886 The national convention of the Anti-Saloon Republicans met in Chicago.

October 12, 1886 A flood on the Texas Gulf coast killed 250.

October 28, 1886 The Statue of Liberty was dedicated.

November 2, 1886 In congressional elections, the Republicans lost four seats in the Senate but maintained a 39–37 majority; the Democrats lost fourteen seats but kept a 169–152 majority in the House of Representatives.

November 18, 1886 Former President Chester A. Arthur died at fifty-six and was buried in Albany, New York.

December 8, 1886 The American Federation of Labor (AFL) was organized in Columbus, Ohio. It was made up of twenty-five labor groups representing 150,000 members. Samuel Gompers, president of the Cigarmakers Union, was the AFL's first president.

January 20, 1887 Pearl Harbor, on the island of Oahu, Hawaii, was leased by the United States as a naval station.

February 3, 1887 The Electoral Count Act made each state responsible for its own election returns, which Congress was bound to accept, except in cases of irregularity.

February 8, 1887 The Dawes Severalty Act (General Allotment Act) attempted to replace the Indian reservation system by making individual Indians farmers of plots of land.

March 2, 1887 President Grover Cleveland signed the Hatch Act, which established agricultural experiment stations at all land-grant colleges and authorized annual appropriations to each state that began a station.

March 3, 1887 The American Protective Association, a secret anti-Catholic society dedicated to raising the fears concerning increasing Catholic influence in schools and public institutions, was founded in Clinton, Iowa.

August 10, 1887 A train wreck at Chadsworth, Illinois, killed 100 people.

February 19, 1888 A cyclone nearly destroyed Mt. Vernon, Illinois, killing thirty-five.

February 22, 1888 The Industrial Reform Party nominated Albert E. Redstone of California for president and John Colvin of Kansas for vice president.

March 12, 1888 A 36-hour blizzard, dropping 40 inches of snow, struck New York City, killing 400 and producing $20 million in property damage; New York City was virtually shut off from the world, and messages to Boston had to be relayed via England.

May 16, 1888 The Union Labor Party convention nominated Alson J. Streeter of Illinois for president and Charles E. Cunningham of Arkansas for vice president; they received 1.3% of the popular vote.

May 17, 1888 The United Labor Party convention nominated Robert H. Cowdrey of Illinois for president and William H. T. Wakefield of Kansas for vice president.

May 31, 1888 The Prohibition Party convention nominated Clifton B. Fisk of New Jersey for president and John A. Brooks of Missouri for vice president.

June 1888 Electrocution replaced hanging as the method of execution in New York State.

June 5, 1888 The Democratic convention nominated Pres. Grover Cleveland for a second term; Allen G. Thurman was nominated for vice president.

June 25, 1888 The Republicans nominated Benjamin Harrison of Indiana for president and Levi P. Morton of New York for vice president.

July 27, 1888 The first electric automobile, built by the Fred W. Kimball Company of Boston, was demonstrated.

July 29, 1888 A yellow-fever epidemic broke out in Jacksonville, Florida, and lasted until Dec 7; 4,500 cases of yellow fever were reported, and 400 died.

November 6, 1888 Benjamin Harrison was elected president of the United States; in congressional elections, the Republicans kept their 39–37 majority in the Senate and gained fourteen seats in the House to take a 166–159 majority.

December 24–26, 1888 In two separate incidents, steamboat fires on the Mississippi killed twenty-five when the *Kate Adams* burned on Christmas Eve, and thirty persons two nights later when the *John H. Hanna* burned.

February 11, 1889 The Department of Agriculture received cabinet status, with Norman J. Colman as its first secretary.

March 4, 1889 Benjamin Harrison was inaugurated as twenty-third president.

April 22, 1889 A pistol shot at noon started the Oklahoma land rush, opening up to settlement 1.9 million acres of land bought from the Creek and Seminole tribes in central Oklahoma.

May 31, 1889 The disastrous Johnstown, Pennsylvania, flood killed 2,295 people when the Conemaugh River dam broke, destroying four valley towns and putting Johnstown under 30 feet of water.

June 10, 1889 All Confederate veterans were united under the United Confederate Veterans organization, with John B. Gordon, governor of Georgia, as first general.

November 2, 1889 North and South Dakota were admitted to the Union as the thirty-ninth and fortieth states.

November 8, 1889 Montana was admitted as the forty-first state.

November 11, 1889 Washington was admitted as the forty-second state.

December 6, 1889 Jefferson Davis, former president of the Confederacy, died at 71 in New Orleans where he was buried; his remains were transferred to Richmond, Virginia, in 1893.

January 25, 1890 Nellie Bly (Elizabeth Cochrane Seaman), a *New York World* reporter, returned to New York City, having bested the record of Jules Verne's fictional hero Phineas Fogg who allegedly circled the globe in 80 days; Bly accomplished the journey in 72 days, 6 hours, 10 minutes, 58 seconds.

February 4, 1890 The Senate ratified the Samoan Treaty with Germany and Great Britain, placing Samoa under a tripartite protectorate.

February 10, 1890   Approximately 11 million acres of Lakota Indian territory were opened for general settlement.

February 24, 1890   The World's Columbian Exposition of 1893 to commemorate the 400th anniversary of the discovery of America was designated to be held in Chicago.

April 14, 1890   The Pan-American Union was created.

May 2, 1890   The Oklahoma Territory, the last territory in the contiguous United States, was created; it redefined Indian territory and created an area for settlers.

May 24, 1890   George Francis Train broke Nellie Bly's around-the-world record with a new time of 67 days, 13 hours, 3 minutes, and 3 seconds.

July 2, 1890   Congress passed the Sherman Antitrust Act, named for Sen. John Sherman of Ohio, to regulate trusts.

July 3, 1890   Wyoming was admitted as the forty-fourth state; it had the first state constitution to give women the vote.

July 8, 1890   The *Wall Street Journal* began publication; bare-knuckle boxing ended when John L. Sullivan knocked out Jake Kilrain in the seventy-fifth round.

July 13, 1890   A tornado drowned 100 people at Lake Pepin, Minnesota.

July 14, 1890   Congress passed the Sherman Silver Act, which required the federal government to purchase 4.5 million ounces of silver per month and issue paper notes against it.

October 1, 1890   Congress passed the McKinley Tariff Act, which raised import tariffs to the highest level ever in the United States; the Weather Bureau was created in the Department of Agriculture.

October 6, 1890   The Mormon Church discontinued the practice of sanctioning polygamy, though the practice continues among some Mormons to this day.

November 1, 1890   Mississippi was the first state to restrict the black suffrage with the device of a literacy clause, which required voters to be able to read and to understand a section of the constitution.

November 4, 1890   In congressional elections, the Republicans gained eight seats in the Senate to lead the Democrats 47–39; in the House, the Democrats gained a 235–88 majority in a landslide.

December 15, 1890   Sitting Bull, chief of the Teton Lakota Indians, was killed in a skirmish with U.S. soldiers in South Dakota.

December 29, 1890   In the Wounded Knee Massacre, 200–300 Lakota men, women, and children were killed by the Hotchkiss machine guns of the 7th Cavalry, Custer's old regiment.

March 3, 1891   The U.S. Circuit Courts of Appeal were created by an act of Congress.

March 4, 1891   Congress passed the International Copyright Act, which prohibited American publishers from pirating foreign works.

March 14, 1891   Eleven Sicilian immigrants who had been indicted for murder of an Irish chief of police in New Orleans were lynched, creating an international crisis.

May 5, 1891   Carnegie Hall at Seventh Avenue and 57th Street in New York City opened with an all-Tchaikovsky program conducted by the composer himself.

May 19, 1891   The People's or Populist Party was created in Cincinnati, Ohio, to voice the grievances of farmers in the throes of an economic depression.

September 22, 1891   Nine hundred thousand acres of Indian land in Oklahoma were opened for settlement.

October 16, 1891   A mob in Valparaiso, Chile, killed two sailors and wounded several others from the USS *Baltimore,* nearly setting off a war before Chile paid $75,000 to the injured and heirs of the dead.

January 1, 1892   Ellis Island, in New York Harbor, became the new entry point for immigrants.

February 29, 1892   The U.S. prohibition on hunting fur seals in the Bering Sea was submitted to international arbitration.

April 12, 1892   A $25,000 indemnity was paid to the heirs of the Sicilians lynched in New Orleans in 1891.

May 5, 1892   Chinese immigration restrictions were extended and tightened.

May 27, 1892   A cyclone killed thirty-one in Kansas.

June 7–11, 1892   The Republican convention nominated President Benjamin Harrison for president and Whitelaw Reid of New York for vice president.

June 21–23, 1892   The Democratic convention nominated Grover Cleveland of New York for president and Adlai Ewing Stevenson of Illinois for vice president.

June 29–July 1, 1892   The Prohibition National Convention nominated John Bidwell of California for president and James B. Cranfill of Texas for vice president.

July 4–5, 1892   The People's Party convention nominated James B. Weaver for president and James G. Field of Virginia for vice president.

August 4, 1892   In Fall River, Massachusetts, a famous trial began: Andrew J. Borden and his second wife, Abby, were axed to death in their home, allegedly by the Borden's 32-year-old unmarried daughter, Lisbeth A. Borden. Borden was acquitted, and the case was never solved, although it produced a famous jingle:

> Lizzie Borden took an ax,
> Gave her mother 40 whacks
> When she saw what she had done,
> She gave her father 41.

August 27, 1892   The New York Metropolitan Opera House was nearly destroyed by fire.

August 28, 1892   The Socialist Labor Party nominated Simon Wing of Massachusetts for president and Charles H. Matchett of New York for vice president.

October 20–23, 1892   The world's Columbian Exposition unofficially opened in Chicago; "After the Ball Is Over," composed by Charles K. Harris, became a tremendous hit during the exposition.

October 15, 1892   The Crow Indian reservation, covering 1.8 million acres in Montana, was opened to settlement by presidential proclamation.

October 28, 1892   A fire in Milwaukee burned more than 26 acres and caused $5 million in property damages.

November 8, 1892   Grover Cleveland was elected president and Adlai E. Stevenson vice president; in congressional elections, the Democrats gained five seats in the Senate for a 44–38 majority; in the House, the Democrats lost seats but retained a 218–127 majority.

December 2, 1892   Jay Gould, a railroad magnate, died at fifty-six, leaving an estate of $72 million.

December 27, 1892   On St. John's Day in New York City, the cornerstone was laid for the Protestant Episcopal Cathedral of St. John the Divine; the building is still not completed.

January 17, 1893   Former President Rutherford B. Hayes died at age seventy and was buried in Fremont, Ohio; a revolution in Hawaii deposed Queen Liliuokalani; a provisional government was headed by Sanford B. Dole under the protection of 300 U.S. Marines.

February 1, 1893   The provisional government of Hawaii was recognized by the United States, and the islands were declared an American protectorate.

February 15, 1893 A Hawaiian annexation treaty was withdrawn from Senate consideration by Pres. Grover Cleveland, who had begun to have doubts about U.S. actions in Hawaii.

March 1, 1893 The Diplomatic Appropriation Act was passed, creating the rank of ambassador and stipulating that U.S. ministers hold a rank equivalent to that of the ministers from the countries to which they are assigned.

March 4, 1893 Grover Cleveland was inaugurated twenty-fourth president of the United States, the only president to serve two nonconsecutive terms; Adlai E. Stevenson became vice president.

March 10, 1893 A fire in Boston killed several persons and destroyed $5 million in property.

March 26, 1893 The illegal immigration of Chinese was highlighted by the discovery of sixty-seven illegal immigrants entering Portland, Oregon, from Vancouver, Canada.

April 13, 1893 The Hawaiian protectorate was ended, and Commissioner James H. Blount ordered U.S. Marines to return to their ship.

May 15, 1893 The U.S. Supreme Court declared the Geary Chinese Exclusion Act of 1892 unconstitutional.

August 13, 1893 A fire in Minneapolis left 1,500 homeless and $2 million in property damages.

August 24, 1893 A cyclone in Savannah, Georgia, and Charleston, South Carolina, killed 1,000.

September 16, 1893 The Cherokee strip between Kansas and Oklahoma was opened for settlement.

September 17, 1893 A yellow-fever epidemic struck Brunswick, Georgia.

October 2, 1893 A cyclone killed 2,000 along Louisiana's Gulf coast.

November 7, 1893 Women's suffrage was adopted in Colorado.

December 24, 1893 Henry Ford assembled his first successful gasoline engine.

January 17, 1894 The U.S. Treasury issued $50 million in bonds to shore up the gold reserve and a similar amount on November 13.

January 30, 1894 The New York State Senate opened an investigation into corruption in the New York City Police Department.

January 30, 1894 Brazilian revolutionaries fired on the U.S. flag in Rio de Janeiro.

February 13, 1894 A mine cave-in at the Gaylord mine in Plymouth, Pennsylvania, killed thirteen miners.

March 17, 1893 A Chinese Exclusion Treaty was signed by which China agreed to exclude Chinese laborers from the United States.

March 25, 1894 Coxey's Army, a band of unemployed workers led by Jacob S. Coxey of Ohio, began a march from Massilon, Ohio, to Washington, D.C., to draw attention to the plight of the unemployed and to demand government action.

March 30, 1894 The Bland Bill, which would authorize coinage of silver bullion, was vetoed by Pres. Cleveland.

April 5, 1894 A riot of striking miners at Connellsville, Pennsylvania, killed eleven miners.

April 20, 1894 A strike by 136,000 coal miners for higher wages began at Columbus, Ohio.

April 24, 1894 A mine disaster at Franklin, Washington, killed thirty-seven miners.

May 11, 1894 The acrimonious Pullman strike began at the Pullman Palace Car Company in south Chicago after the company cut wages sharply without lowering rents in company-owned housing or prices in company-owned stores.

June 21, 1894 The Democratic Free Silver convention was held in Omaha, Nebraska, and it called for the free coinage on a silver-to-gold ratio of 16 to 1.

June 26, 1894 A general railway strike led by Eugene Debs's American Railway Union (ARU) in sympathy for the Pullman workers spread across the nation.

July 2, 1894 A U.S. federal court in Illinois issued an injunction against the ARU for interfering with the mails, marking the first use of the court injunction against labor.

July 3, 1894 President Cleveland ordered federal troops to Chicago to enforce the injunction against ARU.

July 6, 1894 Violence in the railway strike killed two men and injured several more when U.S. deputy marshals fired on strikers at Kensington near Chicago.

July 10, 1894 Eugene V. Debs was cited and jailed for contempt for failing to obey the injunction.

August 1, 1894 A fire in Chicago caused $3 million in property losses.

August 3, 1894 The Pullman strike was broken, and organized labor suffered a crushing blow with the loss of the ARU.

August 8, 1894 The Hawaiian Republic was officially recognized by the U.S. government.

August 27, 1894 The first graduated income tax, which was part of the Wilson–Gorman tariff bill, was passed by Congress without Pres. Cleveland's signature. In 1895, it was declared unconstitutional by the U.S. Supreme Court.

September 1, 1894 A fire, swept along by a cyclone, killed 500 in Hinckley, Minnesota, and eighteen neighboring towns.

September 4, 1894 A garment workers' strike protesting sweatshop conditions and the piecework system was begun in New York City by 12,000 tailors.

November 6, 1894 In congressional elections, the Republicans regained control of both houses of Congress, taking a 43–39 majority in the Senate and a 244–105 majority in the House.

December 14, 1894 Capt. Timothy J. Creeden of the New York City Police Department admitted paying $15,000 for his captaincy, providing evidence of corruption in the department; Eugene V. Debs was found guilty of contempt of court and sentenced to six months in jail; he was defended by Clarence Darrow, who achieved national prominence as Debs's counsel.

December 29, 1894 A fire at Silver Lake, Oregon, killed forty.

February 8, 1895 A federal gold purchase of $62 million was made by the Treasury Department from the banking houses of J. P. Morgan and Company and August Belmont and Company; due to hoarding, gold reserves had fallen to $41 million.

February 24, 1895 The revolt of Cuba against Spain broke out, caused in part by United States-induced depression in the sugar industry.

March 18, 1895 The emigration of U.S. blacks to Liberia, which had begun in 1822 with the establishment of Monrovia by free black settlers, continued with the departure of 200 blacks from Savannah, Georgia.

May 27, 1895 The Supreme Court ruled that a federal injunction could be used to prevent interference with interstate commerce.

June 11, 1895 The first U.S. patent for a gasoline-driven automobile by a U.S. inventor was issued to Charles E. Duryea.

September 27, 1895 A so-called Irish National Convention was held in Chicago and called for force to achieve separation of Ireland from British control.

November 5, 1895 The constitution of Utah provided for women's suffrage.

November 5, 1895 The Selden patent was issued to George B. Selden for his gasoline-driven automobile; alleged infringements brought a celebrated lawsuit against Henry Ford and others, but legal judgments allowed that changes in the construction of the gasoline engine meant that engines could be produced without violation of the Selden engine patent.

November 6, 1895 A boiler explosion in the headquarters of the *Evening Journal* of Detroit, Michigan, killed forty persons.

January 4, 1896 Utah was admitted as a state.

February 28, 1896 A congressional resolution granted belligerent rights to the Cuban revolutionaries, and the president was urged to use his good offices to obtain peace.

April 23, 1896 The first moving pictures on a public screen in America were shown at Koster and Bial's Music Hall in New York City.

May 18, 1896 The Jim Crow railroad-car law of Louisiana was declared constitutional by the Supreme Court in *Plessy v. Ferguson.*

May 27, 1896 A tornado killed 400 in St. Louis, Missouri.

May 27–28, 1896 The Prohibition National Convention nominated Joshua Levering of Maryland for president and Hale Johnson of Illinois for vice president.

June 4, 1896 At 2:00 A.M. the first Ford automobile rolled off Henry Ford's assembly line in Detroit, Michigan.

June 18, 1896 The Republican National Convention nominated William McKinley of Ohio for president and Garret A. Hobart of New Jersey for vice president.

July 4–9 The Socialist Labor National Convention nominated Charles H. Matchett of New York for president and Matthew Maguire of New Jersey for vice president.

July 7, 1896 The sentence "You shall not crucify mankind upon a cross of gold" elevated William Jennings Bryan's candidacy at the Democratic National Convention where Bryan uttered the words in his stirring speech, advocating silver, free coinage at 16 to 1.

July 11, 1896 The Democratic National Convention nominated William Jennings Bryan of Nebraska for president and Arthur Sewal of Maine for vice president.

July 22–24, 1896 The National Silver Republican Convention nominated William Jennings Bryan for president and Arthur Sewal for vice president.

July 25, 1896 The People's Party National Convention nominated William Jennings Bryan for president and Thomas E. Watson of Georgia as vice president.

August 12, 1896 Gold was discovered on the Klondike River in the Yukon Territory of northwest Canada, launching another great gold rush in 1897–98.

September 2–3, 1896 The National Democratic Party (Sound Money Democrats) nominated John M. Palmer of Illinois for the presidency and Simon P. Buckner of Kentucky for vice president.

October 1, 1896 Rural free delivery was inaugurated.

November 3, 1896 William McKinley was elected president of the United States and Garret A. Hobart vice president.

January 12, 1897 The National Monetary Conference at Indianapolis, Indiana, endorsed the gold standard.

February 2, 1897 Fire destroyed the Pennsylvania State Capitol at Harrisburg.

February 17, 1897 The National Congress of Mothers, forerunner of the Parent-Teachers Association, was organized in Washington, D.C.

March 2, 1897 An immigration bill that required a literacy test was vetoed by Pres. Cleveland as a "radical departure from national policy."

March 4, 1897 William McKinley was inaugurated twenty-fifth president of the United States.

May 5, 1897 The size of New York City was expanded to 326 square miles with a population of 3.4 million.

May 24, 1897 Congress appropriated $50,000 for relief of Americans in Cuba.

July 2, 1897 A coal miners' strike in Pennsylvania, Ohio, and West Virginia idled 75,000 men and produced violent incidents at Hazelton and Latimer, Pennsylvania, before miners won an eight-hour day, semimonthly pay, abolition of company stores, and biennial conferences.

July 14, 1897 The first shipment of Klondike gold, worth $750,000, reached the United States.

January 25, 1898 The U.S. battleship *Maine* docked at Havana, Cuba, to protect U.S. property and Americans' lives.

February 9, 1898 The famous de Lôme letter from the Spanish minister to the United States, Enrique de Lôme, was stolen by Cuban revolutionists and published in William Randolph Hearst's *Journal;* it depicted Pres. McKinley as feebleminded and lacking integrity.

February 15, 1898 The battleship *Maine* exploded in Havana harbor, killing 258 crew members; "Remember the Maine" became the U.S. war cry against Spanish tyranny, despite uncertainty over both the cause and the people responsible for the explosion.

April 5, 1898 U.S. consuls in Cuba were recalled by Pres. McKinley.

April 19, 1898 Congress authorized the use of armed force to end the civil war in Cuba.

April 22, 1898 A blockade of Cuban ports was ordered by Pres. McKinley; the Volunteer Army Act was passed in Congress to authorize the 1st Volunteer Cavalry, or "Rough Riders," under command of Col. Leonard Wood and Lt. Col. Theodore Roosevelt.

April 23, 1898 President William McKinley called for 125,000 volunteers to fight in the Cuban war.

April 24, 1898 The Spanish-American War officially began when Spain declared war on the United States.

April 25, 1898 Congress passed a declaration of war.

May 1, 1898 At the Battle of Manila in the Philippines, one of the most stunning defeats in the history of naval warfare occurred when the six-ship Asiatic squadron of Commodore George Dewey surprised and destroyed a larger but outgunned and unprepared Spanish fleet.

May 25, 1898 A call for 75,000 more volunteers to fight in Cuba was issued.

May 28, 1898 The U.S. Supreme Court declared that a child born of Chinese parents in the United States was a citizen and could not be deported under the Chinese Exclusion Act.

June 10, 1898 The War Revenue Act authorized the government to issue bonds up to $400 million and to tax liquor, tobacco, flour, and other items to pay for the war.

June 11, 1898 About 600 U.S. Marines landed at Guantanamo, Cuba.

June 15, 1898 The annexation of Hawaii was approved in a joint congressional resolution and signed by the president on July 7.

June 21, 1898 Guam, a Spanish possession, surrendered.

June 24, 1898 At the Battle of Las Guasimas in Cuba, U.S. troops won the first major land battle of the war with Spain.

July 1–2, 1898 El Caney and San Juan Heights, Spanish outposts to Santiago de Cuba, were taken with stiff resistance and heavy casualties on both sides; the Rough Riders participated in the attack.

July 3, 1898 The Spanish fleet at Cuba was destroyed by U.S. ships; 323 Spaniards were dead and 151 wounded; the United States lost one man.

July 17, 1898 Santiago de Cuba was surrendered along with 24,000 Spanish troops by General José Toral to U.S. General

William R. Sharter.

July 25, 1898 U.S. troops invaded Puerto Rico under Maj. Gen. Nelson D. Miles.

July 28, 1898 Ponce, Puerto Rico's second largest city, surrendered.

August 1, 1898 From disease, 4,200 U.S. personnel in Cuba are sick, mostly from yellow fever and typhoid; fewer than 400 U.S. troops were killed in battle or died of wounds in Cuba.

August 12, 1898 Hostilities ceased when Spain promised to give Cuba its independence, cede Puerto Rico and Guam to the United States, and negotiate the status of the Philippines.

November 8, 1898 In congressional elections, the Republicans took a 53–26 lead in the Senate and held a 185–163 lead in the House.

November 8, 1898 Theodore Roosevelt was elected governor of New York on the Republican ticket.

December 10, 1898 The treaty ending the Spanish-American War was signed in Paris.

February 4, 1899 Philippine nationalists under Emilio Aguinaldo fired on American forces at Manila, beginning a rebellion against U.S. rule that was to last until 1901.

February 10, 1899 The peace treaty with Spain was signed by President McKinley.

February 14, 1899 Congress authorized voting machines if individual states desired them.

April 27, 1899 A tornado killed forty and injured 100 in northern Missouri.

April 28, 1899 A Filipino peace commission proposed terms of armistice to the Americans, but the terms were rejected.

April 29, 1899 At Wardner, Idaho, on April 24, miners demanded $3.50 per day and the closed shop; employers refused to grant the closed shop, and strike violence erupted: on April 29, miners blew up mining property estimated at $250,000.

June 12, 1899 A tornado swept across Minnesota and Wisconsin, killing 250 persons at New Richmond, Wisconsin.

November 24, 1899 U.S. control of central Luzon in the Philippines was established; the president of the Filipino Congress, the Filipino secretary of state, and the Filipino treasurer were captured.

December 2, 1899 The Samoan Partition Treaty divided the Samoan Islands between the United States and Germany, and the United States received Tutila and its harbor at Pago Pago.

March 5, 1900 The Hall of Fame was founded in New York City to commemorate great Americans.

March 6–9, 1900 The Social Democratic Party nominated Eugene V. Debs of Indiana for president and Job Harriman of California for vice president.

March 14, 1900 Congress established the gold standard, ending the free-silver controversy.

April 30, 1900 The territory of Hawaii was established by an act of Congress.

April 30, 1900 At 3:52 A.M., railroad engineer John Luther "Casey" Jones died at the throttle of the Cannonball express from Memphis to Canton, Mississippi, as it slammed into the rear of a stopped train.

May 1, 1900 A mine explosion at Scofield, Utah, killed more than 200 persons.

May 10, 1900 The Populists nominated William Jennings Bryan of Nebraska for president and Charles A. Town of Minnesota for vice president; middle-of-the-road Populists nominated Wharton Barker of Pennsylvania and Ignatius Donnelly of Minnesota for president and vice president, respectively.

June 2–8, 1900 The Socialist Labor Party nominated Joseph P. Maloney of Massachusetts for president and Valentine Remmel of Pennsylvania for vice president.

June 19–21 The Republicans nominated William McKinley for reelection and Theodore Roosevelt for vice president.

June 21, 1900 Amnesty was granted to Filipino insurgents due to a proclamation of Gen. Arthur MacArthur, military governor of the Philippines.

June 27–28, 1900 The Prohibition Party nominated John G. Wooley of Illinois for president and Henry B. Metcalf of Rhode Island for vice president; the Democrats nominated William Jennings Bryan for president and Adlai E. Stevenson of Illinois for vice president.

September 8, 1900 A hurricane in Galveston, Texas, killed 6,000 persons as 120-mph winds drove Gulf waters over the land.

September 18, 1900 The first direct primary in the United States was tried in Hennepin County, Minnesota.

November 6, 1900 William McKinley was elected president of the United States and Theodore Roosevelt vice president; in congressional elections, the Republicans took a 55–31 majority in the Senate.

December 29, 1900 Congress announced that negotiations for the purchase of the Virgin Islands were complete and only awaited congressional appropriation.

January 10, 1901 The first great oil strike in Texas was made near Beaumont by Anthony F. Lucas. The first New York City public library system was made possible by a grant of $5.2 million from Andrew Carnegie.

February 2, 1901 The U.S. Army Dental Corps and the Army Nurse Corps were organized.

March 2, 1901 The Platt Amendment offered by Sen. Orville H. Platt of Connecticut was adopted by Congress and called for changes in the Cuban constitution in return for withdrawal of U.S. troops; it established a protectorate over Cuba that lasted until 1934.

March 23, 1901 Emilio Aguinaldo, nationalist leader of the Philippines, was captured in Luzon by a U.S. patrol.

April 19, 1901 The rebellion in the Philippines was ended; it had been the most unpopular war ever fought up to that time, largely because many in the United States felt the Philippines should have been given their independence.

May 3, 1901 A fire in Jacksonville, Florida, destroyed 1,700 buildings, cost $11 million in damages, and left 10,000 homeless.

May 27, 1901 A Supreme Court decision on the Insular Cases, involving the status of Puerto Rico and the Philippines, stated that territories acquired as a result of the Spanish-American war were neither foreign countries nor part of the United States.

September 6, 1901 President William McKinley, on a visit to the Pan-American Exposition in Buffalo, New York, was shot twice in the abdomen by a young anarchist, Leon Czolgosz, who carried a concealed pistol in a handkerchief.

September 14, 1901 President McKinley died and was succeeded by a young vice president, Theodore Roosevelt, age forty-three, former reform-minded governor of New York.

October 16, 1901 Booker T. Washington dined with President Theodore Roosevelt in the White House, causing an uproar, especially in the South.

November 18, 1901 The Hay-Pauncefote Treaty was signed, whereby the British consented to U.S. control of an isthmus connecting the Atlantic and Pacific Oceans.

January 24, 1902 A treaty with Denmark to purchase the Virgin Islands (Danish West Indies) was signed.

March 6, 1902 A permanent office of the Bureau of the Census was created.

April 29, 1902 The Chinese Exclusion Act was extended to prohibit the emigration of labor from the Philippines.

May 20, 1902 Cuban independence was granted, and the U.S. flag was replaced by the Cuban flag on government buildings.

June 28, 1902 The Isthmian Canal Act was passed by Congress, authorizing the financing and building of a canal across the Isthmus of Panama or Nicaragua.

July 1, 1902 The Philippine Government Act was passed in Congress; it declared the Philippine Islands to be an unorganized territory and all inhabitants territorial citizens.

September 3, 1902 President Roosevelt escaped serious injury in a train wreck near Pittsfield, Massachusetts.

November 4, 1902 In congressional elections, the Republicans kept their majority in the Senate, 57–33, and in the House, 208–178.

January 22, 1903 The Hay-Herran Treaty was signed with Colombia, giving the United States a 99-year lease and sovereignty over the Panama Canal Zone.

February 14, 1903 The Department of Commerce and Labor became the ninth cabinet office (divided in 1913).

February 19, 1903 The Elkins Act, named for Sen. Stephen B. Elkins, Republican of West Virginia, was passed making it illegal for railroads to give rebates on their advertised freight rates.

February 23, 1903 In the case *Champion v. Ames,* the Supreme Court ruled that Congress had the right to prohibit lottery tickets from being sent through the mails from one state to another.

May 1, 1903 New Hampshire licensed liquor sales, ending forty-eight years of total prohibition.

May 31, 1903 A flood of the Kansas, Missouri, and Des Moines rivers killed 200, left 8,000 homeless, and caused $4 million in property losses.

July 4, 1903 The first Pacific communications cable was opened.

November 3, 1903 A revolt in Panama against Colombian rule occurred one day after Pres. Roosevelt dispatched U.S. troops to prevent Colombian forces from stopping the rebellion.

November 6, 1903 The United States recognized the Republic of Panama.

November 18, 1903 The Hay-Bunau-Varilla Treaty gave the United States control of a 10-mile-wide canal zone in Panama in return for $10 million in gold and a yearly fee of $250,000.

December 17, 1903 The Wright brothers made the first powered flight in a heavier-than-air machine.

December 30, 1903 A fire at the Iroquois Theater in Chicago killed 588; public outcry led to new theater codes throughout the United States.

January 4, 1904 In a ruling on the status of territorial citizens, the Supreme Court declared that residents of Puerto Rico were not aliens and could not be refused admission to the United States, but the Court did not count them as U.S. citizens either.

February 7–8, 1904 A fire in Baltimore, Maryland, destroyed 2,600 buildings in an eighty-block area of the business district; it burned for thirty hours, making it the largest fire since the great Chicago fire of 1871.

February 29, 1904 The Panama Canal Commission was appointed by Pres. Roosevelt to oversee construction of the waterway.

May 5, 1904 The Socialist National Convention nominated Eugene V. Debs for president and Benjamin Hanford of New York for vice president.

March 11, 1904 Workers on the Morton Street Tunnel, working

west from New York City and east from New Jersey, linked beneath the Hudson River.

June 16, 1904 A fire on the steamship *General Slocum* in New York Harbor killed 900.

June 21–23, 1904 The Republicans nominated Pres. Roosevelt for election and Charles W. Fairbanks of Indiana for vice president.

June 29–30, 1904 The Prohibition Party nominated Dr. Silas C. Swallow of Pennsylvania for president and George W. Carroll of Texas for vice president.

July 2–8, 1904 The Socialist Labor Party nominated Charles H. Corregan of New York for president and William W. Cox of Illinois for vice president.

July 4–5, 1904 The People's Party (Populists) nominated Thomas E. Watson of Georgia for president and Thomas H. Tibbles of Nebraska for vice president.

July 6–9, 1904 The Democrats nominated Alton B. Parker of New York for president and Henry G. Davis of West Virginia for vice president.

September 9, 1904 Mounted police were used for the first time in New York City.

September 28, 1904 A woman was arrested for smoking a cigarette in public on New York's Fifth Avenue.

October 27, 1904 The first section of the New York subway system opened.

November 8, 1904 Theodore Roosevelt was reelected president of the United States; in congressional elections, the Republicans, who carried Missouri for the first time since the Civil War, maintained a 57–33 majority in the Senate and picked up forty-three seats in the House for a 250–136 majority.

February 20, 1905 A mine disaster in Virginia City, Alabama, southwest of Birmingham, killed 116 miners.

February 20, 1905 State compulsory vaccination laws were ruled constitutional by the U.S. Supreme Court.

March 4, 1905 Roosevelt was inaugurated as president and Charles W. Fairbanks as vice president.

April 17, 1905 The Supreme Court ruled unconstitutional state laws limiting working hours.

April 1905 Former president Grover Cleveland wrote against women's suffrage in the *Ladies' Home Journal* stating that "sensible and responsible women do not want to vote."

May 11, 1905 A tornado hit Snyder, Oklahoma, killing 100.

June 11, 1905 The Pennsylvania Railroad inaugurated eighteen-hour train service between New York and Chicago, and the New York Central followed shortly thereafter; within a week, both experienced train wrecks, costing nineteen lives.

June 27, 1905 The Industrial Workers of the World (Wobblies) were formed in Chicago as a reaction to the more conservative American Federation of Labor.

July 22, 1905 A severe yellow-fever epidemic struck New Orleans and lasted into October; it was finally brought under control by a federal antimosquito campaign after causing 400 deaths out of 3,000 cases.

November 8, 1905 Electric lamps were placed in a railroad train for the first time on the Chicago & North Western's Overland Limited, which ran from Chicago to California.

March 1, 1906 Woodrow Wilson, speaking before the North Carolina Association, said nothing had spread socialism in the country more than the automobile.

March 17, 1906 Roosevelt used the term *muckraker,* taken from a passage of John Bunyan's *Pilgrim's Progress,* in an address to the Gridiron Club in Washington, D.C.; the term was widely used to describe journalists who helped stimulate reform by uncovering some abuse.

April 18, 1906 A devastating earthquake struck San Francisco; it leveled 490 blocks, destroyed 25,000 buildings, caused 452 deaths, made 225,000 homeless, and produced damages of $350 million.

June 25, 1906 The killing of Stanford White, a prominent architect, by his wife's lover, Harry K. Thaw, became the most talked-about murder of the first decade of the twentieth century.

June 29, 1906 The Hepburn Act, called the Railroad Rate Act, gave the federal government authority to set rail rates for interstate shipment.

June 30, 1906 The Pure Food and Drug Act was passed along with a Meat Inspection Act on the same day.

August 23, 1906 Race riots in Atlanta, Georgia, left twenty-one dead, including eighteen blacks.

September 29, 1906 The Platt Amendment, authorizing U.S. intervention in Cuba, was invoked to allow the United States to take military control and make William Howard Taft provisional governor.

November 6, 1906 Charles Evans Hughes, made popular by his exposure of scandals in the life insurance business, was elected governor of New York.

November 9, 1906 The first foreign trip by a U.S. president was taken by Roosevelt to the Isthmus of Panama.

December 5, 1906 Rev. Algernon Sidney Crapsey, rector of St. Andrew's Protestant Episcopal Church in Rochester, New York, was tried and convicted for heresy (denial of Christ's divinity) and expelled from the ministry.

December 12, 1906 Oscar S. Straus of New York City, the first Jew to receive a cabinet appointment, was named secretary of commerce and labor by Pres. Roosevelt.

January 26, 1907 A law prohibiting corporate campaign contributions was passed by Congress.

February 12, 1907 The steamer *Larchmont* was swamped in Long Island Sound, causing 131 deaths.

February 20, 1907 The Immigration Act of 1907 was signed by Pres. Roosevelt; it included a provision to restrict the entry of Japanese laborers.

February 26, 1907 A General Appropriations Act increased the salaries of cabinet members, the speaker of the house, and the vice president to $12,000 and raised the salaries of senators and representatives to $7,500.

March 14, 1907 The Inland Waterways Commission was created to study forest preservation and commercial waterways.

March 21, 1907 U.S. Marines landed in Honduras to protect U.S. interests during a period of political disturbances.

July 20, 1907 A train wreck near Salem, Michigan, killed thirty and injured seventy.

July 28, 1907 A fire at Coney Island, New York, destroyed $1.5 million in property.

September 17, 1907 Oklahoma adopted a new constitution, which included prohibition.

October 21, 1907 Financial panic seized business and credit centers after a run on the Knickerbocker Trust Company in New York City; the bank was forced to close; the government called on J. P. Morgan for help; Morgan coaxed his fellow bankers into line and they borrowed $100 million in gold from Europe to restore confidence and end the panic.

November 16, 1907 Oklahoma was the forty-sixth state admitted to the Union.

December 6, 1907 A coal-mine explosion in Monongah, West Virginia, killed 361 miners in one of the worst explosions in U.S. coal-mining history.

December 19, 1907 A coal-mine explosion in Jacobs Creek, Pennsylvania, killed 239 persons.

February 3, 1908 In the so-called Danbury Hatters case, the U.S. Supreme Court decided that labor unions were also subject to antitrust laws.

February 18, 1908 A restriction on Japanese immigration was achieved when the Japanese government agreed not to issue any more passports to Japanese laborers.

March 4, 1908 A fire at the Collinwood School in Cleveland, Ohio, killed 176.

March 28, 1908 An explosion and cave-in at the Union Pacific Coal Company's mines at Hanna, Wyoming, entombed sixty miners.

April 2–3, 1908 The People's Party (Populist) nominated Thomas E. Watson of Georgia for president and Samuel W. Williams of Indiana for vice president.

April 12, 1908 A fire in Chelsea, Massachusetts, left 10,000 homeless and destroyed $10 million worth of property.

May 10–17, 1908 The Socialist Party nominated Eugene Debs of Indiana for president and Benjamin Hanford of New York for vice president.

May 13–15, 1908 A conservation conference held at the White House brought together the governors of forty-four states and territories to discuss natural resources.

May 28, 1908 A child-labor law for the District of Columbia was passed by Congress.

June 8, 1908 Pres. Roosevelt named a National Commission for the Conservation of Natural Resources with fifty-seven members, headed by Gifford Pinchot.

June 16–20, 1908 The Republicans nominated William Howard Taft of Ohio for president and James S. Sherman of New York for vice president.

June 24, 1908 Grover Cleveland, twenty-second and twenty-fourth president of the U.S., died at 71 and was buried at Princeton, New Jersey.

July 4, 1908 The Socialist Labor Party nominated Martin R. Preston of Nevada, then serving a jail sentence for murder in the Nevada penitentiary, for president and Donald L. Munro of Virginia for vice president. Forced to choose another presidential candidate, the party chose Augustus Gilhaus of New York.

July 7–10, 1908 The Democrats nominated William Jennings Bryan of Nebraska for president and John W. Kern of Indiana for vice president.

July 15–16, 1908 The Prohibition Party nominated Eugene W. Chafin of Illinois for president and Aaron S. Watkins of Ohio for vice president.

July 27, 1908 The Independence Party nominated Thomas L. Hisgen of Massachusetts for president and John Temple Graves of Georgia for vice president.

November 3, 1908 William Howard Taft was elected president of the United States and John S. Sherman vice president; in congressional elections, the Republicans held a 61–32 majority in the Senate and a 219–172 majority in the House.

November 28, 1908 An explosion and cave-in at the Marianna Mine in Monongahela, Pennsylvania, killed more than 100 miners.

January 28, 1909 The second military occupation of Cuba ended.

February 21, 1909 The Great White Fleet, an armada of sixteen battleships dispatched by Pres. Roosevelt in 1907, returned to Hampton Roads, Virginia.

March 4, 1909 William Howard Taft was inaugurated twenty-seventh president of the United States.

March 30, 1909 The Queensborough Bridge opened to traffic in New York City.

April 6, 1909 Robert Edwin Peary became the first person to reach the North Pole, accompanied by Matt Henson, an African American, and four Inuit.

May 22, 1909 Pres. Taft opened 700,000 acres of federal land to settlement in the states of Washington, Montana, and Idaho.

July 12, 1909 A resolution for the sixteenth (income tax) Amendment passed the Senate and went to the states for ratification.

September 1, 1909 Dr. Frederick Cook of Brooklyn, New York, claimed that he reached the North Pole about a year earlier, sparking a bitter debate before Congress; the scientific community recognized Peary's claim.

August 5, 1909 Pres. Taft signed the Payne-Aldrich Tariff Bill.

November 13, 1909 An explosion at the St. Paul mine, Cherry, Illinois, killed 259 miners.

November 18, 1909 Two U.S. warships were ordered to Nicaragua after a report that 500 revolutionaries, including two Americans, had been executed by Nicaraguan dictator Jose Santos Zelaya; Zelaya was forced to resign on December 16.

December 31, 1909 The Manhattan Bridge opened in New York City.

January 19, 1910 The Southern Health Conference was formed in Atlanta, Georgia, to combat hookworm, a scourge that afflicted perhaps 40% of southerners, most of them white.

January 24, 1910 Judge Kennesaw Mountain Landis launched an investigation into the beef trust in Chicago.

March 17, 1910 A bill passed to have the House Committee on Rules elected by the House instead of appointed by the Speaker, reducing the power of the Speaker Joseph G. Cannon, Republican of Illinois.

March 19, 1910 Corruption in Pittsburgh city government was disclosed by the confession of former councilman John F. Klein, implicating sixty municipal officers.

April 17, 1910 Mark Twain died.

April 25, 1910 Charles Evans Hughes, governor of New York, was appointed to the U.S. Supreme Court by President Taft.

May 18, 1910 Despite warnings of an apocalypse, rumors of catastrophe, suicides, and farmers and miners refusing to work, Halley's comet passed without incident.

May 26, 1910 The Immigration Act of 1907 was amended to forbid entrance to criminals, paupers, anarchists, and persons carrying disease.

June 20, 1910 A bill to allow New Mexico and Arizona to write state constitutions and form state governments was passed by the Senate.

June 25, 1910 The Mann Act, otherwise knows as the "white-slave traffic act," was passed by Congress to prohibit interstate or international transportation of women for "immoral purposes."

July 30, 1910 The Christian Endeavor Society began a campaign for movie censorship to ban motion pictures that showed nonrelatives kissing.

August 31, 1910 In a famous "New Nationalism" speech, Theodore Roosevelt stated his square-deal policy at Oswatomie, Kansas: graduated income tax, control of trusts, labor protection, conservation, and an adequate army and navy—all hallmarks of his presidency.

November 8, 1910 In congressional elections, the Democrats gained control of Congress for the first time since 1894: in the Senate the Republicans held a 51–41 majority; in the House, the Democrats held a 228–162 majority.

November 8, 1910 Washington State adopted women's suffrage.

January 21, 1911 The National Progressive Republican League was formed in Washington, D.C., by Sen. Robert M. La Follette of Wisconsin to enact progressive legislation and promote popular government.

March 7, 1911 Due to continued fighting in the Mexican revolution, the United States sent 20,000 troops to the Mexican border.

March 25, 1911 A horrendous industrial disaster occurred when the Triangle Shirtwaist Company, a New York City sweatshop, caught fire, trapping 850 employees in the building; 146 persons were killed, mostly women.

May 1, 1911 The Supreme Court ruled that forest reserves were to be under the control of the federal government, not the states.

May 15, 1911 The Supreme Court declared the Standard Oil Company of New Jersey, which controlled 85% of the oil business, to be a monopoly and in violation of the Sherman Antitrust Act of 1890.

May 29, 1911 The Supreme Court declared the American Tobacco Company dissolved on the grounds that it was a monopoly; however, under the new principle of "rule of reason," the Court orders it reorganized rather than dissolved.

August 22, 1911 Statehood for Arizona was vetoed by President Taft because he felt that the feature of the state constitution allowing for the recall of judges to be a threat to the judiciary; after removing this provision, Arizona was admitted.

October 16, 1911 The National Conference of Progressive Republicans was held in Chicago, and Sen. Robert La Follette was elected president.

December 18, 1911 Pres. Taft notified Russia that the 1832 treaty with Russia would be abrogated because of Russia's unwillingness to recognize U.S. passports carried by Jews, clergymen of certain denominations, and others; it was abrogated December 21.

December 23, 1911 Theodore Roosevelt wrote a letter to William B. Howland announcing his decision to seek the Republican presidential nomination.

January 6, 1912 New Mexico was admitted as the forty-seventh state of the Union.

January 22, 1912 U.S. troops began occupation of Tientsin to protect American interests in the Chinese revolution.

February 14, 1912 Arizona was admitted as the forty-eighth state of the Union.

April 15, 1912 The British liner *Titanic* sank on its maiden voyage after collision with an iceberg; more than 1,500 died; a later investigation found inadequate lifeboat numbers and safety procedures.

May 17, 1912 The Socialists nominated Eugene V. Debs for president and Emil Seidel of Wisconsin for vice president.

June 5, 1912 U.S. Marines landed in Cuba to protect American interests.

June 18–22, 1912 The Republicans nominated William Howard Taft for a second term; the progressive element nominated Theodore Roosevelt and James S. Sherman for president and vice president, respectively.

June 25–July 2, 1912 The Democrats nominated Woodrow Wilson of New Jersey for president and Hiram Johnson of California for vice president on a party platform calling for women's suffrage, direct primaries, and other progressive measures.

August 5, 1912 The Progressive (Bull Moose) Party nominated Theodore Roosevelt for president and Hiram Johnson of California for vice president.

August 24, 1912 The parcel-post system was authorized to begin on January 1, 1913.

October 14, 1912 Theodore Roosevelt was shot from a distance of 6 feet by John Schrank of New York; the incident took place in a Milwaukee hotel; the bullet struck a bulky manuscript and entered Roosevelt's chest; despite the wound, Roosevelt insisted on giving the speech before he was taken to a hospital.

November 5, 1912 Woodrow Wilson was elected president of the United States in a landslide; in congressional elections, the Democrats took a 51–44 majority in the Senate and a 291–127 majority in the House.

February 14, 1913 Pres. Taft vetoed an immigration bill with a literacy-test provision.

February 24, 1913 The Mann Act was ruled constitutional by the U.S. Supreme Court.

February 25, 1913 Congress adopted the Sixteenth Amendment to the Constitution, permitting the levying of an income tax on individuals and businesses.

March 1, 1913 Over Pres. Taft's veto, the Webb-Kenyon Interstate Liquor Act was passed, stating that no liquor could be shipped into states with prohibition; the bill was the first nationwide victory for the Anti-Saloon league.

March 4, 1913 Woodrow Wilson was inaugurated twenty-eighth president of the United States.

March 4, 1913 The Department of Commerce and Labor was split into two departments, each with cabinet status.

March 21–26, 1913 The Dayton flood in the Miami River valley of Ohio, killed 400 people; damages were estimated at $100 million.

April 8, 1913 Pres. Wilson's tariff-revision message was the first address to Congress by a president since John Adams in 1800.

May 2, 1913 Wilson officially recognized the Republic of China.

May 19, 1913 The Webb Alien Land-Holding Bill was signed by Gov. Hiram W. Johnson of California, despite objections by Pres. Wilson and Japan; the bill excluded Japanese from ownership of land in California.

May 31, 1913 The Seventeenth Amendment to the U.S. Constitution went into effect, providing for the election of U.S. senators by popular vote.

November 7, 1913 Wilson requested Mexican president Huerta's resignation, and Wilson later announced material support for Huerta's opponents.

December 10, 1913 The Nobel Peace Prize was awarded to Elihu Root in recognition of his work as president of the Carnegie Endowment for International Peace and as United States secretary of war.

December 23, 1913 The Owen-Glass Act became law, establishing the Federal Reserve System, the nation's first centralized control over currency and credit.

CHAPTER 4 The Economy

Agriculture

Agriculture is one of the great success stories of Victorian America; tremendous expansion of the area of arable land allowed the nation to feed a burgeoning population and created the surplus necessary to fuel the expansion of the industrial sector. Between 1870 and 1900, more than 431 million acres of virgin soil came under the plow, more than in all the country's prior history (408 million). Output was equally impressive. By 1900, American farmers had increased the production of staple crops—corn, cotton, and wheat—by 150%.

Commercial farming on a grand scale characterized certain areas of the nation. California mechanized its production of row crops, orchard products, and grapes, a pattern that also characterized the sugar-beet industry of Colorado, wheat farming in Oregon, and hop growing in Washington. Nothing symbolized the trend toward cultivation of immense acreages, mechanization, and crop specialization more than the "bonanza farms" of the Red River Valley of the North, especially in the Dakotas. Large-scale commercial, overcapitalized, and highly mechanized farming portended the future in American agriculture.

But while the American economy feasted on the agricultural surplus, many farmers more often saw famine. Beginning with the depression of 1873 and continuing until 1900—except for a brief interlude during 1885–1890—farm commodity prices slid steadily downward. Tenant farmers and sharecroppers were the hardest hit, but poverty and foreclosure of farms was not a stranger even on the rich soils of the newly settled West. Natural calamities—drought, soil erosion, plagues of grasshoppers, floods, and boll weevils—exacerbated the price collapse. Consequently, tenancy (a condition of renting rather than owning the land that is worked), increased from one-quarter of the farms in the nation in 1880 to more than one-third by the century's end. Throughout the country, farmers lost their farms, particularly during the 1893–1897 depression years.

The family farm, although already under the strain of market forces and threatened with extinction, was a common feature of rural America in the Victorian Age. Here, we see the yard of a family farm in Germantown, Pennsylvania, 1900–06. (Courtesy Prints and Photographs Division, Library of Congress)

TABLE 4.1 FARMS, NUMBER AND TOTAL ACREAGE BY STATE, 1880, 1910

	1880		1910	
	Number (000s)	Acreage (000s)	Number (000s)	Acreage (000s)
Ala.	136	18,855	263	20,732
Alaska	Unavailable			
Ariz.	1	136	9	1,246
Ark.	94	12,062	215	17,416
Calif.	36	16,594	88	27,931
Colo.	5	1,127	46	13,532
Conn.	31	2,476	27	2,185
Dakota	17	3,801	a	
Del.	9	1,090	11	1,038
D.C.	0	18	0	6
Fla.	23	3,297	50	5,253
Ga.	139	26,128	292	26,953
Hawaii	Unavailable			
Idaho	2	328	31	5,283
Ill.	256	32,402	252	32,522
Ind.	194	20,656	215	21,299
Iowa	185	25,055	217	33,930
Kans.	139	21,454	178	43,384
Ky.	166	21,942	259	22,189
La.	48	8,274	121	10,439
Maine	64	6,553	60	6,296
Md.	41	5,185	49	5,057
Mass.	38	3,359	37	2,875
Mich.	154	13,869	207	18,940
Minn.	92	13,043	156	27,675
Miss.	102	15,883	274	18,557
Mo.	216	28,178	277	34,591
Mont.	2	406	26	13,545
Nebr.	63	9,945	130	38,622
Nev.	1	531	3	2,714
N.H.	32	3,721	27	3,249
N.J.	34	2,930	33	2,573
N. Mex.	5	631	36	11,270
N.Y.	241	23,781	216	22,030
N.C.	157	22,640	254	22,439
N. Dak.	a	. . .	74	28,426
Ohio	247	24,529	272	24,105
Okla.	Unavailable	0	190	28,859
Oreg.	16	4,429	46	11,865
Pa.	213	20,060	219	18,586
R.I.	6	515	5	443
S.C.	94	13,535	176	13,512
S. Dak.	a	a	78	26,016
Tenn.	166	20,667	246	20,041
Tex.	174	36,303	418	112,435
Utah	9	656	22	3,397
Vt.	36	4,883	33	4,663
Va.	119	19,911	184	19,495
Wash.	7	1,409	56	11,712
W. Va.	63	10,255	97	10,026
Wis.	134	15,353	177	21,060
Wyo.	1	124	11	8,543
U.S.	4,008	538,979	6,363	878,955

a North and South Dakota were part of Dakota Territory in 1880.
Sources: The World Almanac and Encyclopedia 1921 (1921), 288; *The American Almanac for 1885* (1885), 373. Figures are in thousands of farms and acres.

TABLE 4.2 FARMS BY RACE AND TENURE OF OPERATOR, 1880, 1910

The U.S. Census was interested in counting farm opeators, not owners. Under the census definition, a farm operator was a person in charge of a farm, either performing the labor him- or herself or directly supervising it. Thus, in the table below, the number of farms indicates the number of farm operators, not the number of farm owners. Each farm was classified according to the tenure of the operator. *Full owners* meant that the operator or spouse or heirs held the title to all the land they operated. *Part owners* owned some and rented some; *managers* operated farms for others for wages or salaries; *tenants,* including sharecroppers, operated rented land only. Classification of farm operators by race and cross-classification by race and tenure were first made in 1900.

The rise in farm tenancy, especially in the South, is the most striking trend in agriculture that is revealed in this table. A pattern of dividing large plantations into multiple tenant farms characterized postbellum southern agriculture. Tenantry, though the increase was significant, rose less dramatically in the North, where full owners in 1910 composed 53% of all operators, compared to 43% in the South.

	Number of Farms	
	1880	1910
United States	4,009	6,362
Full owner		3,355
Part owner	2,984	594
Manager		58
Tenant	1,025	2,355
White		5,441
Full owner		3,159
Part owner	. . .	548
Manager		57
Tenant		1,677
Nonwhite		921
Full owner		196
Part owner	. . .	45
Manager		2
Tenant		678
South	1,531	3,098
Full owner		1,329
Part owner	977	215
Manager		16
Tenant	554	1,537
White		2,207
Full owner		1,154
Part owner	. . .	172
Manager		15
Tenant		866
Nonwhite		890
Full owner		175
Part owner	. . .	43
Manager		1
Tenant		670

Source: Historical Statistics of the United States: Colonial Times to 1957 (1961), 278.

The power and status of farmers eroded too, leading to farm protest organizations. The 1870 census for the first time found that farmers numbered less than one-half of the gainfully employed population. By 1920, the figure had dropped to 27%. Farmers organized to deal with the problems of depressed commodity prices, lack of credit, bank foreclosures, high interest rates and taxes, and unfair railroad practices. The farm-protest movement culminated in the

Some agricultural enterprises relied almost exclusively on hand labor, as shown by these apple workers in the Shenandoah Valley of Virginia, 1910. (Courtesy Prints and Photographs Division, Library of Congress)

formation of the People's Party. In 1892 the Populists, as they were called, put up candidates for president and vice president in the national election. Despite capturing 8.5% of the popular vote, the most successful third-party effort in American history, the Populists proved unable to build on their support and fused with the major political parties in subsequent elections. The trends toward mechanization, large farms, and highly capitalized farming continued.

TABLE 4.3 LEADING PRODUCERS OF CEREAL CROPS AND U.S. PRODUCTION, 1913 (MILLIONS OF BUSHELS)

Corn, oats, and wheat are the principal cereal crops in the United States. The following production figures are from a report of the Bureau of Statistics of the Department of Agriculture. They give the leading five states in the production of each crop for 1913.

Oats		Corn		Wheat	
Iowa	168.3	Iowa	338.2	Kansas	87.0
Minn.	112.5	Ill.	284.9	N. Dak.	79.7
Ill.	102.4	Ind.	176.3	Minn.	68.0
Wis.	83.8	Tex.	169.9	Nebr.	61.7
Nebr.	60.3	Ohio	149.8	Wash.	52.2
Total U.S.	1,122.1	Total U.S.	2,373.0	Total U.S.	753.2

Source: The World Almanac and Encyclopedia 1914 (1913), 239.

Bonanza Farms

By 1900, the self-sufficient and diversified family farm was still a national ideal, but a disappearing reality. As early as the 1870s, the famous "bonanza" farms of the Red River Valley signaled the new trends in American agriculture. The "day of the bonanza" foretold a highly capitalized, specialized, and mechanized business enterprise on a large scale.

Eastern capitalists or western speculators hired professional managers to organize and oversee 40,000-acre farms. Newspapers and farm journals produced countless articles on bonanza wheat farms; farm-implement dealers touted the use of their equipment on extensive acreages. Oliver Dalrymple, a Philadelphia lawyer, became the best-known bonanza farmer with 34 million acres in the Red River Valley (one wheat field alone was as big as Manhattan). Dalrymple

Economic Activities and Natural Resources in the United States, 1900

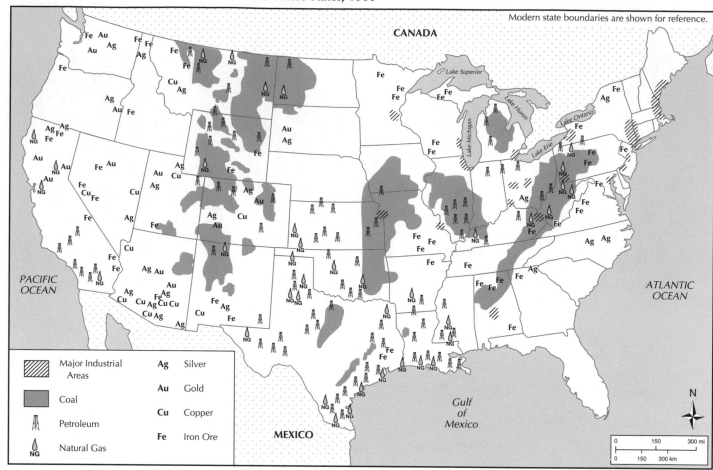

This map shows the locations of deposits of the following natural resources: iron ore, petroleum, natural gas, copper, silver, and gold. The major deposits of these resources in 1900 were: silver and gold in the West; copper in the Southwest and Great Lakes region; petroleum and natural gas in the southern Midwest; and iron ore in the Northeast. (Dale Williams)

divided his farms into 5,000-acre tracts, each with 250 farmhands and more than 400 horses and mules. Squads of threshers (with as many as forty horses) were pulled across wheat fields with military precision to glean the agricultural bounty.

Bonanza farming was highly organized. Echelons of managers, farmhands, and machines covered the landscape in regimentlike for-

mations. According to one observer, it was "the army system applied to agriculture . . . exact[ing] rich tribute from the land."

But bonanza farming could also be compared to the pace and precision of factory work. Wheat was threshed in the field in order to get the grain to market as quickly as possible. For instant communication, Dalrymple linked all his farms by telephone at a time when

TABLE 4.4 PRICES OF WHEAT, CORN, AND OATS PER BUSHEL, 1876–1913, U.S. AND CHICAGO MARKETS

The following is a history of farm prices for principal cereal crops in the United States. Note the collapse of commodity prices for all three crops between 1876 and 1900, when prices again began to rise. The depression of farm prices during these years produced severe trouble for thousands of farmers, especially those with mortgages to pay. Banks foreclosed, farmers brought more acreage under cultivation to make up for deflated prices and to cover their debts; their efforts led to overproduction and further price reductions. Many turned to farm labor organizations to protest their predicament and to advocate more and cheaper access to markets, regulation of corporate trusts, and government assistance for farm loans. Inflation of the currency (via free and unlimited coinage of silver) was the solution to farm problems that was most frequently advocated.

Wheat (Annual Range[a]), Corn and Oat[b] Prices						
Year	Month	Low	High	Avg.	Corn[b]	Oats[b]
1876	Jul.	$.83	$1.27	$1.05	$.36	$.35
1880	Aug.	$.87	$1.32	$1.10	$.39	$.35
1885	Mar.	$.73	$.92	$.83	$.32	$.28
1890	Feb.	$.74	$1.08	$.91	$.50	$.42
1900	Jan.	$.49	$.85	$.67	$.25	$.19
1900	Jan.	$.62	$.88	$.75	$.35	$.25
1905	Aug.	$.78	$1.24	$1.01	$.41	$.29
1910	Nov.	$.90	$1.28	$1.09	$.52	$.36
1913	Jul.–Aug.	$.84	$1.15	$1.00	$.70	$.39

[a] In the case of wheat, prices are Chicago market prices.
[b] In the case of corn and oats, prices are U.S. averages for the years as of Dec. 1.
Sources: The World Almanac and Encyclopedia 1914 (1914), 238; Historical Statistics of the United States, Colonial Times to 1957 (1961), 297.

TABLE 4.5 LEADING TOBACCO PRODUCERS, 1880, 1913

Historically, tobacco farming is associated with the southern United States where cash-crop farming grew out of plantation agriculture. But the following table of leading tobacco producers shows the states of Pennsylvania and Ohio in 1880 raising more tobacco than North Carolina, Virginia, or Tennessee. By 1913, except for Ohio, the leading producers were southern states.

1880		1913	
State	Lb. (Millions)	State	Lb. (Millions)
Ky.	171	Ky.	281
Va.	80	N.C.	168
Pa.	37	Va.	154
Ohio	45	Tenn.	65
Tenn.	41	Ohio	61

Source: American Almanac for 1885, 1885, 34; The World Almanac and Encyclopedia 1915, 1914, 255.

TABLE 4.6 LEADING COTTON PRODUCERS AND U.S. PRODUCTION, 1880, 1913

Cotton was king in the Old South. It remained important in the New South as the following table of leading producers indicates.

1880		1913	
	Bales (in thousands)		Bales (in thousands)
Miss.	956	Tex.	4,880
Ga.	814	Ga.	1,909
Tex.	804	Miss.	1,393
Ala.	700	S.C.	1,260
Ark.	608	Miss.	1,050
Total U.S.	5,737	Total U.S.	14,129

Source: American Almanac for 1885, 1885, 28; The World Almanac and Encyclopedia 1915, 1914, 234.

Cotton was less of a king in the postbellum South, but the vestiges of its reign remained, as in this scene of African-American farmhands picking cotton on a Mississippi plantation. Emancipation did not free blacks from white oppression; sharecropping was simply substituted for slavery. Under this system, croppers paid their landlords half the harvest (or more) from which the landowner deducted payments and usurious interest for loans of food, clothing, and other necessities. The labor system slowly changed, however, as blacks left the South for industrial jobs in the North. By 1935, tenant farmers in cotton involved more whites than blacks. (Courtesy State Historical Society of Wisconsin)

this new technology was yet to be used widely even in urban areas.

Bonanza farming was also practiced in California's central valley—the setting for Frank Norris's novel, *The Octopus* (1901)—and in parts of Nebraska and Kansas.

Besides being an indicator of agricultural trends, bonanza farming also stirred the imaginations of restless settlers who hoped to harvest

TABLE 4.7 LIVESTOCK ON FARMS IN UNITED STATES, 1876–1913, NUMBER (IN MILLIONS) AND AVERAGE VALUE

Livestock on farms grew in number and value during the period. The increases in the numbers of horses and mules are particularly significant because they were the "tractors" of nineteenth-century agriculture, providing the horsepower for the "plow that broke the plains." American agriculture is one of the most significant, and unsung, success stories of modern economic history. Farmers were able to feed a burgeoning population and create a surplus for industrial expansion.

Year	All Cattle Number	All Cattle Value	Hogs Number	Hogs Value	Stock Sheep Number	Stock Sheep Value	Horses Number	Horses Value	Mules Number	Mules Value
1876	36,140	$18.76	35,715	$5.97	37,477	$2.20	9,606	$56.48	1,608	$65.51
1885	52,463	$24.40	47,330	$5.06	49,620	$2.19	12,700	$72.94	2,102	$81.88
1895	49,510	$16.56	47,628	$5.09	41,827	$1.57	17,849	$35.57	2,708	$47.23
1905	66,111	$18.39	53,176	$5.89	40,410	$2.77	18,491	$69.73	3,586	$87.06
1913	56,592	$33.07	53,747	$9.89	40,544	$3.87	21,008	$110.58	4,683	$124.10

Source: Historical Statistics of the United States, Colonial Times to 1957, 1961, 289–290.

The mixture of men, women, and children, black and white farmhands, and perhaps members of different families in this scene of tobacco curing, Nash County, North Carolina, c. 1926, reveals the nature of tobacco culture in the South. Family labor, white supervision, and black dependency were familiar components of the southern tobacco economy. (Courtesy North Carolina Division of Archives and History)

Between 1860 and 1915, the manufacture of smoking tobacco and cigarettes continued to be southern-based industries. Older factory centers of Virginia and Kentucky were surpassed by the new centers in North Carolina, especially in places such as Durham, Winston-Salem, and Reidsville. Tobacco was marketed in urban centers, such as this tobacco market in Louisville, Kentury, 1906. (Courtesy Prints and Photographs Division, Library of Congress)

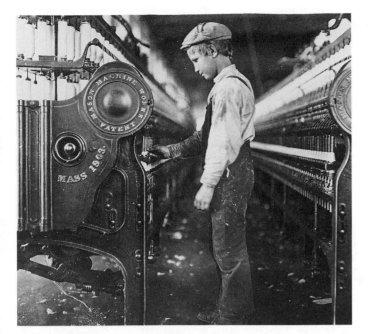

Before the Civil War, ginning of cotton was primarily done on plantations. The typical ginhouse was a two-story wooden building; the lower floor contained the running gear and the upper story the gin. After the Civil War, small plantation gins declined. They were replaced by an automated ginning system, such as the one shown here in this interior view of a cotton gin between 1900 and 1906, where the cotton moved automatically in one continuous process from the wagon to the gin stand until the bale was removed from the press. (Courtesy Prints and Photographs Division, Library of Congress)

TABLE 4.8   SHORN WOOL PRODUCTION AND PRICE, 1876–1913

Sheep farmers fared no better than other producers during this period, as the price of wool by 1895 dropped to nearly half the price of 1876 before again rising slowly but failing to recover completely.

Year	Production in lb (thousands)	Cents
1876	192,000	19.7
1880	232,500	23.1
1885	308,000	14.5
1890	276,000	17.1
1895	294,297	10.3
1900	259,973	13.7
1905	253,488	22.2
1910	305,834	21.7
1913	265,888	16.7

Source: Historical Statistics of the United States, Colonial Times to 1957, 1961, 294.

small bonanzas of their own as they migrated westward. Farm machine use among smaller farmers increased, encouraged by the example of bonanza farms. Between 1870 and 1920, the value of farm equipment rose from $271 million to $3.6 billion. Riding plows (with multiple plowheads); grain drills that planted, fertilized, and covered seed in one operation; and mammoth combines pulled by forty horses that could reap, thresh, and bag simultaneously typified farming on a grand scale. Grain elevators and giant silos sprouted on the landscape, landmarks of the new commercialized farming that

required finance capital on the scale of a large corporation. Commodity exchanges in distant cities became the farmer's markets. Together, capitalization, mechanization, and trading in commodities entangled local farmers in an international network of storing, shipping, and selling.

TABLE 4.9   LEADING HAY PRODUCERS AND U.S. PRODUCTION, 1880, 1913

Hay and dairy products, which are related because hay is a main forage crop for cattle, were expanding crops, especially in the older, settled states of New York and Pennsylvania. Dairy farming also became increasingly important in midwestern areas, such as Iowa, Wisconsin, and Ohio.

1880		1913	
States	Tons (thousands)	States	Tons (thousands)
N.Y.	5,240	N.Y.	5,358
Iowa	3,614	Iowa	4,440
Ill.	3,280	Pa.	4,146
Pa.	2,812	Ohio	3,848
Ohio	2,211	Wis.	3,848
Total U.S.	35,206	Total U.S.	64,116

Sources: American Almanac for 1885, 1885, 301; The World Almanac and Encyclopedia 1915, 1914, 253.

TABLE 4.10   DAIRY PRODUCTS PRODUCED, 1876, 1913

Year	Milk	Butter (thousands)	Cheese (thousands)
1876	a	677,424	214,334
1913	a	1,608,262	359,000

[a] None given for these years. In 1899, 62,486,000 pounds were produced; in 1909, 64,211,000 pounds.
Source: Historical Statistics of the United States, Colonial Times to 1957, 1961, 292–293.

TABLE 4.11   VALUE OF FARM PROPERTY IN UNITED STATES, 1880, 1910

The threefold increase in the value of farm property during this period included increases in land and buildings, but the most significant increase came in farm machinery and implements. The greater application of machinery allowed farming on a large scale, the most spectacular examples being the "bonanza" farms in the Midwest.

Property	1880 Dollars (thousands)	1910 Dollars (thousands)
All Farm Property	12,180,502	40,991,449
Land	10,197,097	28,476,674
Buildings	unavailable	6,325,452
Implements/Machinery	406,520	4,925,174

Source: The World Almanac and Encyclopedia 1921, 1921, 288.

In the late nineteenth century, cotton textiles that were concentrated in the Piedmont region of the Carolinas and Georgia emerged as the major industry of the South. As in New England, the family was employed by the mill as a unit, including children like this young mill worker in Lincolntown, North Carolina, 1908. (Photo by Lewis Hine, courtesy Prints and Photograph Division, Library of Congress)

TABLE 4.12   FARM MACHINERY, 1797–1915

Tractors were not developed as a power source until the first decade of the twentieth century. Throughout the Victorian Age, mechanical reapers, planters, cultivators, and harvesters were the major developments, along with the steel plow. Before 1915 and the coming of the tractor, draft animals pulled plows and machines through the fields. The following table gives patent dates for machinery. The major impact came years—sometimes decades later, depending on how rapidly the machinery could be adapted to regional conditions and on the financial ability of farmers to pay for the implements.

Date of Patent or Improvement	Type of Machinery
1797	Cast-iron plow
1830s	Steel plow, except for moldboards, braces, beams, and handles
1868	Soft-center steel, including moldboards
1856	Straddle-row, two-horse cultivator
1830s	Reaper
1875	Automatic self-binding reaper
1828; 1880	Combine; improved and used since
1851	Seed drill
1828; 1860	Corn-planter patent; cross-checking two-row planter
1825; 1875	Cotton planter; one mule improved planter

Source: Encyclopaedia Britannica (1960), 403–407.

TABLE 4.13   WORK-HOURS REQUIRED TO PRODUCE SPECIFIED AMOUNTS OF WHEAT, CORN, AND COTTON, 1880–1900

Mechanization of farming is best seen in the reduction of man-hours required to produce specific crops.

	1880	1900
Wheat		
Work-hours per acre	20	15
Yield per acre (bu)	13.2	13.9
Work-hours per 100 bushels	152	108
Corn		
Work-hours per acre	46	38
Yield per acre (bu)	25.6	25.9
Work-hours per 100 bushels	180	147
Cotton		
Work-hours per acre	119	112
Yield of lint per acre (lb)	179	191
Work-hours per bale[a]	318	280

[a] Yields are five-year averages, centered on year shown. For statistical purposes, a bale of cotton is 500 pounds gross weight or 480 pounds net weight of lint. Actual bale weights vary considerably.

Source: Historical Statistics of the United States, Colonial Times to 1957, 1961, 281.

Mechanization of American agriculture took place on a grand scale in areas of the Midwest and West. Here, something called bonanza farming emerged in the growth of certain crops. This picture of a bonanza farm in Oregon, c. 1890, shows people, animals, and machinery working together on an immense scale to harvest vast acreages of wheat in the plains. (Courtesy Washington State Historical Society)

TABLE 4.14   PER ACRE WORK-HOUR REQUIREMENTS IN WHEAT PRODUCTION

Date	Work-Hours 20 bu. per acre	Implements
1822	50–60	Walking plow, bundle of brush for harrow, hand broadcast of seed, sickle harvesting, flail threshing
1890	8–10	Gang plow, seeder, harrow, binder, reaper, harvester, thresher, wagons, and horses
1930	3–4	3-bottom gang plow, tractor, 10-ft tandem disk, harrow, 12-ft combine, and trucks.

Figures are from U.S. Department of Agriculture, *Yearbook,* 1941.
Source: Richard B. Morris, ed., *Encyclopedia of American History* (1965), 507.

Sharecropping

Sharecropping was a form of farm-lease contract that dominated agriculture in the South after the Civil War. In a cash-scarce region, the tenant farmer rented land from a landlord at an agreed-upon cash amount, payable at the end of the harvest season in the equivalent amount of corn, cotton, or tobacco. After the Civil War, many plantation masters hired former slaves under sharecropping contracts and divided their plantations into 40- to 50-acre plots, assigning one family to each plot.

TABLE 4.15   FARM WAGES, 1880–1913

Farm laborers in the North were more likely to be paid in cash while southern field workers more often worked under sharecropping arrangements where they received payments in the form of a part of the crop. The wage scales below, though helpful in understanding the general wage rate and trends for hired labor, are of limited value in determining how much farmworkers actually received. Individual case histories are necessary to account for time off for accidents and injuries, weather, economic conditions, and a variety of other forces.

Year	Per Month[a]		Per Day[b]		Index[c]
	With Board	Without Board	With Board	Without Board	
1880 or 1881	12.50	18.50	.65	.90	58
1884 or 1885	13.00	19.00	.70	.95	64
1889 or 1890	13.50	19.50	.70	.95	67
1895	12.50	18.50	.65	.85	60
1902	15.50	22.00	.85	1.10	75
1906	18.50	26.00	1.05	1.30	91
1910	21.00	28.00	1.05	1.35	96
1913	22.50	30.00	1.15	1.40	102

[a] Includes operators and family members doing farmwork without wages.
[b] Weighted averages as reported quarterly by crop reports.
[c] Composite farm-wage rates, 1910–1914 = 100.
Source: Historical Statistics of the United States, Colonial Times to 1957, 1961, 280–281.

By 1910, African Americans owned a quarter of a million farms in the Deep South, but for many others, the reality of life as a tenant farmer or field hand can be seen in this picture of mealtime in rural Virginia, 1899. (Courtesy Prints and Photographs Division, Library of Congress)

Sharecropping put severe limits upon a farmer's options. In addition to the land, the landlord furnished all the necessary equipment and supplies: tools, seed, fertilizer, farm animals, and usually housing. The sharecropper furnished labor. In return for using the land, equipment, and housing, the propertyless cropper turned over one-fourth to one-half his crop. The landlord often encumbered the remainder of the tenant's harvest with a "crop lien," which gave the landlord first claim. Then the landlord (or the merchant of the local country store) frequently advanced the cropper additional credit for food and clothing during the year, using the sharecropper's portion of the crop as collateral. Usurious interest rates, higher credit than cash prices at the country store, and sometimes outright cheating often led to debts that equaled or exceeded the cropper's income from the sale of the tenant's part of the crop.

Most sharecroppers shared a common way of life, a meager existence in which they saw little or no money and lived in one-room shacks in which they cooked, ate, and slept. According to one Georgia tenant, they were both astronomers and agronomists because they could study the stars through the roof and the soil through the holes in the floor. Personal possessions were scant, consisting of a bedstead, a table and a chair or two, a rickety cupboard that held a few dishes and pans, mattresses filled with corn shucks, a Bible, and maybe a few pictures cut from magazines or newspapers.

Despite their status as farmers, many sharecroppers had to purchase their food. Lease contracts often demanded the planting of a cash crop (corn, cotton, or tobacco). Tenants had to pay extra to rent pastureland for stock or space for vegetable gardens. Such practices meant that croppers relied heavily upon store-bought food, especially the region's three Ms: (corn)meal, molasses, and (hog)meat.

Tenant life also produced cycles of feast or famine, times of abundance, and periods of scarcity and habitual mobility. Because contracts lasted only one year (and tenants had no assurance of renewals), the lives of tenants meant constant movement and uncertainty. About one-third of all tenants moved each year. To make ends meet, many took two or three additional jobs. For example, the twelve black tenants on the Waverly Plantation in Mississippi in 1888, in addition to working their plots, also had part-time jobs at local sawmills, brickyards, and charcoal kilns.

Sharecropping was also detrimental to regional agriculture. High interest rates, the crop lien, and the cash-crop system produced overcropping and depleted the soil. The nature of the crop lien system often meant that "the merchant skinned the planter, the planter skinned the cropper, and the cropper skinned the land."

Consumers

Depressed farm prices hurt producers but benefited consumers. In certain areas of consumption—meat, potatoes, milk, and sugar—low prices were especially important because these commodities formed a fundamental part of the nation's diet. The following tables on the production, consumption, and prices of dairy products, potatoes, wool, sugarcane, and meat are some of the products important to consumers.

TABLE 4.16 APPARENT CIVILIAN PER CAPITA CONSUMPTION OF SELECTED FOODS, 1910, 1913, (IN POUNDS)

Year	Meat	Fruits	Potatoes (farm wt.)	Milk	Sugar, Cane and Beet
1910	146.4	137.9	198	759	75.4
1913	143.7	133.6	189	754	81.3

Source: Historical Statistics of the United States, Colonial Times to 1957, 1961, 186.

TABLE 4.17 WHITE POTATOES, ACREAGE, PRODUCTION, AND PRICE, 1876–1913

Year	Product, mils. lb	Price per 100 lb
1876	73,567	1.10
1880	99,095	.80
1885	118,286	.73
1890	102,065	1.26
1895	181,269	.44
1900	155,813	.72
1905	180,421	1.02
1910	205,231	.98
1913	199,468	1.14

Source: Historical Statistics of the United States Colonial, Colonial Times to 1957, 1961, 303.

TABLE 4.18 SUGAR PRODUCTION AND CONSUMPTION PER CAPITA, CANE AND BEET, 1880, 1884, 1913

Production		Consumption	
tons (thousands)		lb per capita	
1880	1913	1884	1913
3,670	18,180	53	85

Source: World Almanac and Encyclopedia 1915, 1914, 255.

Hogs, first introduced to America by early explorers, have remained a staple in the household economy, especially of rural folk in the southern United States, until the present day. The hardiness and ability of swine to forage for themselves make them choice livestock for anyone with a little land and a forested area in which to turn them loose. Typically, southerners choose cold weather for "hog-killing day" as shown in this picture of rural Virginia in 1899. The cold air preserves the pork for several weeks until the salt, rubbed into the fresh meat, cures it. Nearly every part of the hog was used: the fat as lard for cooking or oil for lamps; the meat for eating throughout the year; and the organs, intestines, feet, even the nose and ears were usually cooked on the day of the slaughter or ground into sausage. (Courtesy Prints and Photographs Division, Library of Congress)

TABLE 4.19 MEAT SLAUGHTERING, PRODUCTION, 1900, 1913

Year	Prod. Dressed Beef Weight mil. lb	Prod. Dressed Pork Weight mil. lb
1900	5,628	6,329
1913	6,182	6,979

Source: Historical Statistics of the United States, Colonial Times to 1957, 1961, 291.

Richard W. Sears saw the possibilities of the mail-order business. Beginning with watches and jewelry, he gradually expanded his offerings. In the early 1880s, he moved to Chicago, and with Alvah C. Roebuck, founded Sears, Roebuck and Company. Sears sold anything and everything. Six million catalogs of more than 500 pages each were distributed annually by the rural free delivery system, begun in 1893. By 1913, parcel post permitted the sending of packages through the U.S. mail, and mail order houses such as Sears and Montgomery Ward flourished as never before. While telephones and electricity did not reach most rural areas for decades, improved roads and mail-order catalogs knit farmers into mass society. A democracy of style led some Europeans to claim that it was impossible to tell a person's class from the clothing he/she wore. Shown here is the cover of the Sears catalog of 1902. (Author's possession)

The Mail-Order Catalog

Often called the "farmer's bibles," the mail-order catalogs of Sears, Roebuck and Company and Montgomery Ward brought the department store to the living rooms of thousands of isolated farm families. So accessible did it make consumer goods to rural folk that the story is told of the rural Idaho lad who, when asked by his Sunday-school teacher where the Ten Commandments came from, said, "From Sears, Roebuck, where else?" Gov. Eugene Talmadge of Georgia was once quoted as saying, "The poor dirt farmer ain't got but three friends on this earth: God Almighty; Sears, Roebuck; and Gene Talmadge."

In 1872, Montgomery Ward invaded rural communities with the help of the Grange movement and made his Chicago firm the official supply house of that rural organization. Richard Sears, a former Minnesota railway agent who got into mail-order retailing part-time selling watches, had launched his company in 1886. Within twenty years, Sears advertised itself as "the largest retail supply house in the world." Sears catalogs, soon over 500 pages, used four-color illustrations and other new techniques. More than 6 million catalogs were distributed annually in the 1900s.

Sears and Montgomery Ward sold anything and everything, prospering on the mutual faith between customers and distant distributors. A Kansas farmer wrote Sears in 1899: "Find enclosed one check; please send me wife Model #1242 on page 112 as soon as possible." A Montgomery Ward customer, anxious for embalming fluid for her dying husband, wrote: "When you send the stuff, please send instructions with it. Must I pour it down his throat just before he dies, or must I rub it on after he is dead? Please rush."

Many small-town businesses and country-store merchants fought the competition of the mail-order houses, which only seemed to provoke the Chicago giants into more innovative strategies. For example, when local businesses argued that mail-order firms sold merchandise of low quality or sent items that did not look like their catalog pictures, mail-order firms such as Sears and Wards mounted a national campaign to guarantee customer satisfaction or an immediate cash refund.

Several innovations of the U.S. post office—bulk mail rates, postal money orders, rural free delivery (RFD), and parcel post—fed the success of mail-order consumerism. Probably the most significant development was the nationwide RFD (rural free delivery) system of direct-to-the-home mail delivery that began in 1896. Postmaster General John A. Wanamaker endorsed the RFD system and farmers' organizations like the Grange championed it. Express companies, local stores, and the National Association of Grocers bitterly opposed RFD, and country storekeepers and small-town editors waged prolonged and vitriolic anticatalog campaigns. Some even offered a bounty of a dollar a catalog turned in to fuel a bonfire. Others found it easier to capitulate and make the catalogs available on their counters for customers to order from.

Of the 787 Wisconsin farm families sampled in 1920, 38% bought an annual average of about $60 worth of mail-order goods. Another survey of a Midwestern rural route found that every family received an average of seventeen mail-order parcels a year.

The effects of mail-order retailing were to wean rural people from a system of barter and extended credit and plunge them into a national market economy. For better or worse, installment buying came with the mail-order business. Rural patterns of socializing that had been encouraged by the local markets, and daily or weekly visits to the country stores were affected by mail-order consumerism.

Industry

During the Victorian Age, America witnessed a revolution in the size, power, and organization of business. A few numbers will illustrate the patterns. Between 1860 and 1920, the number of workers in the labor force who worked in manufacturing and transportation increased from about a quarter to more than one-half. Between 1880 and 1920, the gainfully employed rose from 17.4 to 41.6 million as approximately 21 million immigrants entered the United States during this forty-year period. Telegraph messages per year jumped from 9 million on 112,000 miles of wire in 1870 to 63 million messages on 933,000 miles of wire in 1900. The value of exports grew by twelve times between 1879 and 1920 as America became a world industrial power. By 1920, the United States was the world's largest producer of raw materials and food.

A more favorable climate for business growth and development could scarcely be imagined. Among the factors facilitating rapid expansion of the industrial sector were population growth, an expanding home market, the nation's great reservoirs of mineral and fossil fuels, the work of inventors, and the proindustry policies of both state and federal governments (such as land grants, protective tariffs, favorable tax rates, and the absence of state regulation of economic activities).

Manufacturers before the Civil War had concentrated upon producing textiles, clothing, and leather products or on processing agricultural and natural resources, such as hogs, lumber, or grain. Innovation in these industries continued, but it was heavy industry—steel, iron, petroleum, and machinery—that grew rapidly after the war. *Producer's goods* (goods intended for other producers rather than consumers) provided a new basis for economic growth. Farmers bought machinery for their farms; manufacturers wanted new equipment in their factories. The railroads linked the nation together, standardized time, spawned whole new industries, and provided a model of industrial organization.

Growth of the railroads, the first big business, is indicative of the modernizing and transforming force of industry in Victorian America. The railroads stimulated the demand for steel. In the 1870s, the introduction of the Bessemer and open-hearth processes of converting iron to hard steel lowered the demand for skilled workers. The steel industry expanded, production soared, and prices fell from $100 a ton in 1870 to $12 a ton by 1900. In turn, the production of steel generated demand for new goods and markets. Bridge building, coal mining, timbering, telegraph communications, and boilermaking were all stimulated by the railroads. In 1865, the typical railroad was only 100 miles long; in 1888, a medium-sized Boston railroad company had three times as many employees and received six times the income of the Massachusetts state government. The creation of a national railroad network required $10 billion in capital, which led to the growth of powerful investment banking houses such as Morgan & Company.

Unrestricted business growth and intense competition led to such

Farm Tenancy, 1900

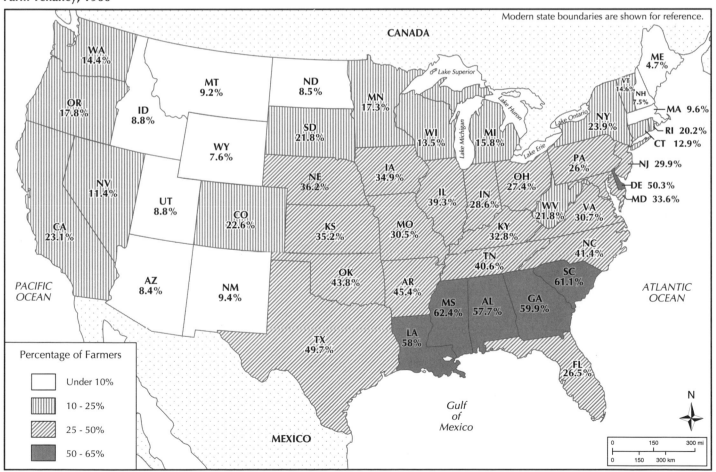

From the mid-1870s to the mid-1890s there was worldwide depression in farm prices. A symptom of this depression was the rise in farm tenancy. During the latter half of the nineteenth century, many farmers had bought their land on credit from speculators and railroads. In the depression, they found themselves unable to make payments and often lost their farms. In 1880 the government discovered that one-fourth of the nation's farmers were renting the land that they cultivated, and by 1900 one-third of all American farmers were tenants—cultivating land owned by someone else. (Dale Williams)

Mining copper was done with a form of shaft mining that required the miners to descend below ground as seen in this copper mine at the Calumet and Hecla Mine, Shaft #2, Calumet, Minnesota, c. 1906. (Courtesy Prints and Photograph Division, Library of Congress)

corrupt practices as price fixing, rebates to preferred customers, trusts and holding companies (consolidations of businesses to control the market), and even industrial violence to intimidate competitors. *Captains of industry,* or *robber barons* are terms writers have applied to the nation's new entrepreneurs, emphasizing either their business acumen or corrupt practices. Andrew Carnegie, John D. Rockefeller, J. Pierpont Morgan, Cornelius Vanderbilt, and others combined shrewdness with greed, accumulated fortunes—sometimes displaying their wealth in lavish homes and ostentatious lifestyles—and treated their workers like commodities to be bought and sold at the cheapest price.

As part of the trend toward bigness, centralization, and incorporation, middle management also grew rapidly. A host of white-collar clerks, engineers, timekeepers, accountants, and personnel managers became the new "invisible hands" of big business. Middle managers and their staffs changed the ways that factories and offices accomplished their work. Beginning with the railroads and spreading to oil, chemicals, rubber and other industries, American industry moved from entrepreneurial to managerial capitalism. Corporations divided their operations into bureaucratic departments of production, finance, shipping, receiving, purchasing, and marketing and applied the latest techniques to controlling costs, increasing production, and supervising the workforce. The managerial revolution changed fundamentally the way business did business and provided the model of corporate management for the twentieth century.

TABLE 4.20 PRINCIPAL RAILROADS (OPERATING EXPENSES MORE THAN $10 MILLION) OF THE UNITED STATES, 1901

Company	Miles	Operating Expenses	Net Earnings	Passengers Carried	Tons of Freight
Atchinson, Topeka & Santa Fe	7,810	$32.3	$22.2	a	a
Baltimore & Ohio	3,221	$31.0	$16.1	11.7	33.5
Boston & Maine	3,964	$21.5	$9.9	38.5	17.5
Canadian Pacific	8,647	$23.4	$15.0	4.8	8.8
Chicago & Northwestern	5,577	$25.9	$17.2	16.9	25.3
Chicago, Burlington & Quincy	8,284	$32.4	$18.0	a	a
Chicago, Milwaukee & St. Paul	6,747	$26.6	$15.9	8.3	18.0
Chicago, Rock Island & Pacific	3,910	$17.3	$12.0	8.2	8.2
Delaware, Lackawanna & Western	948	$40.0	$12.0	15.0	14.8
Erie	2,318	$27.3	$13.3	17.2	26.0
Grand Trunk of Canada	4,202	$16.5	$7.8	7.7	11.1
Great Northern	5,244	$15.8	$17.2	2.7	9.9
Illinois Central	4,266	$24.3	$16.2	17.9	17.7
Lehigh Valley	1,399	$20.1	$7.7	4.4	19.8
Missouri Pacific System	5,555	$21.2	$10.0	5.3	11.5
N.Y. Central & Hudson River	3,357	$42.5	$28.3	40.4	42.4
N.Y., New Haven, & Hartford	2,038	$28.0	$12.1	53.1	15.4
Northern Pacific	4,957	$16.6	$16.7	3.3	8.8
Pennsylvania	3,712	$19.7	$17.3	22.7	67.2
Reading Co.	1,455	$46.6	$15.5	. . .	. . .
Southern Pacific	9,017	$49.1	$28.1	27.4	17.7
Southern	6,729	$23.3	$11.0	7.7	15.0
Union Pacific	6,092	$23.7	$19.0	3.2	9.7
Wabash	2,367	$12.8	$5.1	4.9	8.4

a Not given
Source: *The American Almanac, Year Book, Cyclopedia and Atlas,* 1903, 509–510.

TABLE 4.21 MANUFACTURING OUTPUT IN METRIC TONS, 1876–1913

The nation's output of iron and steel allowed for the growth of heavy industry. Coal, especially in the form of coke, became the primary industrial fuel for the nation's factories, railroad boilers, and steamships. The opening of the coalfields in the southern Appalachian Mountains at the turn of the century provided a new and important source of coal, especially bituminous.

Year	Pig Iron (thousands)	Steel (thousands)	Coal	
			Anthra. (thousands)	Bitum. (thousands)
1876	1,899	542	28,868	20,677
1880	3,896	1,267	46,046	25,991
1890	9,350	4,346	100,972	42,156
1900	14,011	10,352	192,610	52,043
1910	27,742	26,514	378,397	76,644
1913	31,463	31,083	434,029	83,030

Source: B. R. Mitchell, *International Historical Statistics, the Americas and Australasia,* 1983, 399–400, 453–54, 457.

Iron ore mining was a different form of mining. Workers scraped off the topsoil, exposing the ore, which machines loaded onto railroad cars. In this photograph, workers and machines scrape the earth of its iron wealth at the Mesabi Range of northern Minnesota in 1903. The Mesabi Range was a major source of high grade iron ore in the United States. (Courtesy Prints and Photographs Division, Library of Congress)

TABLE 4.22 OUTPUT OF REFINED COPPER, LEAD, TIN, AND ZINC,[a] 1876, 1913

(thousands of metric tons)

Year	Copper	Lead	Zinc
1876	. . .	57	15
1913	796	486	395

[a] Production includes both primary and secondary sources.
Source: International Historical Statistics, 1983, 462, 464.

TABLE 4.23 MERCHANT VESSELS BUILT AND DOCUMENTED, BY MAJOR TYPE, 1876, 1913

(In Thousands of Tons, except Number of Vessels)

Year	No. of Vessels	Gross Tons	Steam & Motor	Sail	Canal Boats & Barges
1876	25,934	4,279	1,172	2,609	498
1913	27,070	7,887	[a]	1,508	1,406

[a] Steam and motor tonnage figures are not available, but most shipping would have been in coal and oil burning vessels. Also, not shown are small tonnages of trade in whale, cod, and mackerel fisheries.
Source: Historical Statistics of the United States, Colonial Times to 1957, 1961, 444–445.

TABLE 4.24 SHIPS OPERATING ON THE GREAT LAKES, 1868–1913

The number of vessels operating on the Great Lakes varied substantially during this period. Gas and steam vessels are lumped together; dates shown are for the year ending June 30. The application of steam power allows tonnages to increase as fewer vessels are able to carry more cargo.

Year	Sailships	Steamships	All Ships	Total Tons
1876	1,643	921	3,193	613,211
1877	1,604	923	3,191	610,160
1878	1,546	918	3,166	604,656
1879	1,473	896	3,087	597,376
1880	1,459	931	3,127	605,102
1881	1,417	988	3,207	663,383
1882	1,412	1,101	3,379	711,269
1883	1,373	1,149	3,403	723,911
1884	1,333	1,165	3,380	733,069
1885	1,322	1,175	3,379	749,948
1886	1,235	1,280	3,405	762,560
1887	1,286	1,225	3,144	683,721
1888	1,277	1,342	3,290	874,102
1889	1,285	1,455	3,412	972,271
1890	1,272	1,527	3,510	1,063,063

(continued)

TABLE 4.24 (continued)

Year	Sailships	Steamships	All Ships	Total Tons
1891	1,243	1,592	3,600	1,154,870
1892	1,226	1,631	3,657	1,183,582
1893	1,205	1,731	3,761	1,261,067
1894	1,139	1,731	3,341	1,227,400
1895	1,100	1,755	3,342	1,241,459
1896	1,044	1,792	3,333	1,324,067
1897	993	1,775	3,230	1,410,103
1898	960	1,764	3,256	1,437,500
1899	874	1,732	3,162	1,446,348
1900	832	1,739	3,167	1,565,587
1901	784	1,778	3,253	1,706,294
1902	726	1,795	3,172	1,816,511
1903	676	1,796	3,110	1,902,698
1904	623	1,820	3,075	2,019,208
1905	583	1,820	3,011	2,062,147
1906	519	1,844	3,052	2,234,432
1907	466	1,873	3,103	2,439,741
1908	429	1,942	3,172	2,729,169
1909	389	1,982	3,199	2,782,481
1910	362	2,107	3,273	2,895,102
1911	324	2,174	3,286	2,943,523
1912	303	2,269	3,367	2,949,924
1913	272	2,333	3,447	2,939,786

Source: Le Roy Barnett, Comp., *Shipping Literature of the Great Lakes: A Catalog of Company Publications, 1852–1990* (1992), 144.

TABLE 4.25   BULK CARGOES CARRIED ON THE GREAT LAKES, 1900–1913

Year	Iron	Coal	Grain	Stone
1900	18,570,315	8,907,663	5,591,208	Unknown
1901	20,157,522	9,819,615	4,667,820	Unknown
1902	27,039,169	9,196,039	4,893,812	Unknown
1903	23,649,550	13,351,291	5,732,468	Unknown
1904	21,226,591	12,370,023	4,186,824	Unknown
1905	33,476,904	14,401,199	6,112,859	Unknown
1906	37,513,589	17,273,718	6,863,068	Unknown
1907	41,290,709	21,486,927	7,010,937	Unknown
1908	25,427,094	19,288,098	6,024,493	Unknown
1909	41,683,599	18,617,396	6,651,245	Unknown
1910	42,618,758	26,478,068	5,803,514	Unknown
1911	32,130,411	25,700,104	6,959,465	Unknown
1912	47,435,771	24,673,210	9,372,252	Unknown
1913	49,070,478	33,362,379	11,697,160	Unknown

Source: Barnett, *Shipping Literature of the Great Lakes: A Catalog of Company Publications, 1852–1990,* 144.

Commercial Fishing

Yields of commercial United States and Alaskan fisheries continued to increase. Regionally, New England states led the nation, but the Chesapeake Bay area grew rapidly.

TABLE 4.26   YIELD AND VALUE OF UNITED STATES AND ALASKA FISHERIES, 1880, 1908

Year	Total		U.S.		Alaska	
	Yield	Value	Yield	Value	Yield	Value
1880	1,706	$39.1	1,598	$38.6	108	$ .5
1908	2,053	$62.7	1,829	$51.4	224	$11.3

Yield is given in millions of pounds. Value is given in millions of dollars.
Source: Historical Statistics of the United States, Colonial Times to 1957, 1961, 324.

Seaboard cities carried on a lively trade in fish. Pictured here is Boston's fisherman's wharf jammed with merchants and dock workers, c. 1890. (Courtesy National Archives)

Harvesting ice on lakes and ponds for commercial use became a big business. Consumption of manufactured ice quadrupled between 1899 and 1921 due to the proliferation of home iceboxes. The icebox enriched the American diet by putting a wide variety of foods—fresh fruit, vegetables, and meat—on the table, despite the season. Chains such as the Great Atlantic and Pacific Tea Company (A&P), with more than 1,000 stores by 1915, offered cash and carry groceries at lower prices. In this picture from 1903, a worker is sawing the ice into sections. (Courtesy Prints and Photographs Division, Library of Congress)

TABLE 4.27 LANDED CATCHES IN THE UNITED STATES BY REGIONS, 1880, 1908

Year	N. Eng.	Mid-Atl.	Chesap.	S. Atl.	Gulf	Pacif. C.	Lakes	Miss. R. & Tribs.
1880	726	412	250	43	24	73	65	. . .
1908	512	205	411	158	95	193	107	148

Catches given in millions of pounds.
Source: Historical Statistics of the United States, Colonial Times to 1957, 1961, 324.

Certain ethnic groups dominated specific occupations, as illustrated by these bearded Irish clamdiggers and a matronly companion on a wharf in Boston, 1882. (Courtesy National Archives)

Lumber Production

Deforestation continued in the United States with little significant change, despite the first efforts at conservation since the founding of the republic. Total lumber production more than doubled. Important changes occurred, however, in regional production of lumber. Re-ductions came in the mid-Atlantic and Lake regions; the South Atlantic, South, and West Coast regions showed great increases in lumber production. Softwoods, especially southern pine, showed the largest increases in cutting.

TABLE 4.28 LUMBER PRODUCTION BY REGION, 1879, 1913

Year	Total	N. Engl.	Mid-Atl.	Lake	Central	S. Atl.	South	R. Mtn.	W. Coast
1879	18,125	1,481	3,189	6,284	3,823	746	1,755	183	664
1913	38,387	1,672	1,425	3,866	3,953	3,983	14,329	1,266	7,892

Given in millions of board feet.
Source: Historical Statistics of the United States, Colonial Times to 1957, 1961, 313.

TABLE 4.29 ESTIMATES OF CROSSTIES USED AND ACRES OF FOREST CLEARED, 1870–1910

Year	Miles of Track	Ties Renewed Annually (millions)	Ties Used on New Construction (millions)	Total Ties Annually (millions)	Acres of Forest Cleared (thousands)
1870	60,000	21	18	39	195
1880	107,000	37	21	58	290
1890	200,000	70	19	89	445
1900	259,000	91		91	455
1910	357,000	124		124	620

Source: Michael Williams, *Americans and Their Forests* (1989), 352.

TABLE 4.30 ESTIMATED VALUE OF FOREST PRODUCTS, 1880

	Million Dollars	Percentage
Wood for domestic fuel	c. 307	43.9
Sawed logs	140	20.0
Unsawed timber (poles, spars, etc.)	c. 110	15.7
Wood for fencing	c. 100	14.3
Fuel, railroads	5	0.7
Fuel, steamships	2	0.3
Fuel, manufacturing	8	1.1
Charcoal	5	0.7
Naval stores	6	0.9
Railroad ties	10	1.4
All other	7	1.0
Total	700	100.0

Source: Williams, *Americans and Their Forests*, 194.

TABLE 4.31 AMOUNT OF FOREST CLEARING EACH DECADE, BY MAJOR REGION, 1850–1909

(in thousands of acres)

	1850–1859	1860–1869	1870–1879	1880–1889	1890–1899	1900–1909	Total
Northeast	1,417	619	1,339	62	80	228	3,745
Mid-Atlantic	4,283	2,811	4,278	295	646	87	12,400
Southeast	6,822	1,869	7,612	6,213	5,410	3,712	31,638
Northcentral	8,245	5,566	9,199	2,420	3,804	1,200	30,434
Southcentral	9,025	1,803	9,156	8,168	7,489	5,767	41,408
Lake	5,093	4,188	7,347	3,131	4,575	2,497	26,831
Southwest	3,018	1,422	7,796	7,148	8,020	7,832	35,236
Pacific	1,774	1,188	2,590	1,166	983	1,063	8,764
Total	39,677	19,466	49,317	28,603	31,007	22,386	190,456

Source: Williams, *Americans and Their Forests*, 361.

TABLE 4.32 LUMBER PRODUCTION BY SPECIFIC SPECIES, 1879, 1913

(millions of board feet)

Softwoods									
	Total	Softwoods	Douglas Fir	Southern Pine	Western Pine	Hemlock	Redwood	Eastern Pine	Other
1879	18,125	13,334	289	2,379	366	1,200	0	7,863	1,237
1913	38,387	30,303	5,556	14,839	1,768	2,320	510	2,229	3,080

Hardwoods						
	Total Hardwoods	Oak	Yellow Poplar	Sweet Gum	Maple	Cottonwood & Aspen	Other Hardwoods
1879	4,791	2,943	496	24	447	0	881
1913	8,084	3,212	620	773	901	209	2,370

Source: *Historical Statistics of the United States, Colonial Times to 1957*, 1961, 314.

TABLE 4.33 CHARCOAL PIG IRON PRODUCTION, BY STATE, 1866–1910 (TO NEAREST 1,000 TONS)

Year	Mass., Conn., N.Y., Maine	Pa.	Ohio	Md., Va.	Ky., Tenn., Ga.	Ala.	Mich.	Mo.	Wis.	Total
1866	. . .	58	88	. . .	. . .	. . .	35	. . .	. . .	181
1872	55	45	96	50	77	13	87	46	28	497
1880	64	43	69	47	45	38	154	16	43	519
1885	34	12	18	23	42	78	143	22	20	392
1890	47	18	26	24	64	110	259	34	95	677
1895	17	5	12	. . .	15	21	102	2	51	225
1900	24	4	9	7	29	65	176	38		352
1910	19	5	11	2	11	40	292	73		453

Source: Williams, *Americans and Their Forests,* 341.

TABLE 4.34 CHARCOAL IRON: BUSHELS OF WOOD USED PER TON PRODUCED, 1880–1900

Year	Bushels, Charcoal	Tons, Pig Iron	Bushels Per Ton
1888	53,910,000	480,000	112.31
1890	67,672,000	628,000	107.75
1900	31,422,000	385,000	81.61

Source: Williams, *Americans and Their Forests,* 343.

TABLE 4.35 PETROLEUM PRODUCTION IN UNITED STATES
(42-gallon barrels)

Year	Barrels (thousands)
1876	9,133
1880	26,286
1890	45,824
1900	63,621
1913	248,446

Source: The World Almanac and Encyclopedia 1921 (1920), 205.

In 1855, Benjamin Silliman discovered kerosene as one of the components into which crude oil could be broken. Four years later, Edwin Drake realized the commercial potential of cheap kerosene that, until mass production of the internal combustion engine, was used extensively for heating, lighting, or starting fires. Drake went to Titusville, Pennsylvania, and devised a drill and pump to extract crude oil in commercial quantities. The Pennsylvania oil rush that followed was as wild as the California gold rush of 1849. Because drilling for oil, like panning for gold, required only a small investment, thousands dreamed of instant riches and set up drilling operations in small fields. This is a picture of the Century Oil Company, Kern River District, California, 1898. (Courtesy National Archives)

Western needs for water to serve urban populations in arid areas grew in the early twentieth century. In this picture, a Class E9 Ingersoll drill is being used to dig a diversion channel, Minidoka Project, Idaho and Wyoming, July 30, 1905. (Courtesy National Archives)

Labor

The workforce in the extraction industries expanded fivefold. Large packing and canning industries processed foods and sold them as national brands. Sweatshops dominated the clothing and needle trades. Workers in mills and plants comprised two-thirds of the labor force by 1900, and by 1914 cars were rolling off assembly lines at Ford Motor Company. These are some of the trends in labor during the Victorian period. Mechanization, standardization, and automation of the workplace accelerated the pace of work, produced chronic health problems, and introduced labor to technological unemployment. Women often replaced men in the mechanized mills, and by 1900 they constituted a fifth of the workforce. Turbulent struggles between capital and labor raised fears of urban anarchy, leading to the erection of new armories to house a standing "national guard."

Meanwhile, the rise of a middle class and the professionalization of careers characterized changes in the upper echelons of American labor. The growing complexity and scale of American business produced new opportunities for clerks, bookkeepers, salespeople, typists, stenographers, telegraphers, messengers, and other low and midlevel workers. State agencies licensed and certified a variety of professionals who organized themselves into associations for the purpose of maintaining standards.

Distribution of the Workforce

Snapshots of the U.S. workforce in 1890 and 1914 show the economic transformation that the nation was undergoing during these years. The following excerpt from the U.S. Census of 1890 reveals that women outnumbered men in low-wage occupations such as teaching, domestic service (maids and laundresses), waiting tables, and dressmaking. Men predominated in the professions (medicine, engineering, and law), trade and transportation (banking, bookkeeping, draying, sales, and railroading), and the skilled trades and mechanical pursuits (carpentry, blacksmithing, tailoring, and mining). Still, however, America's 8 million farmworkers outnumbered jobholders in all other industries.

Labor Unions

In 1900, the average annual wage for manufacturing workers was $435, or $8.37 per week. But the higher wages for labor's "aristocracy"—locomotive engineers, machinists, master carpenters, printers, and other craftsworkers—inflated these statistics. Unskilled

TABLE 4.36   EMPLOYED IN OCCUPATIONS, 1880–1910

When occupations are grouped into categories of agriculture, extraction, manufacturing, construction, communication and finance, transportation, and communications and services, every occupational category can be seen to have grown between 1880 and 1910, except agriculture, which dropped from about one-half to just over one-third of the national work force.

Occupation	1880	Percent	1890	Percent	1900	Percent	1910	Percent
Agriculture, Forestry, and Fishing	8,705	50.1	10,170	42.8	10,920	37.6	11,590	31.6
Extractive Industries	310	1.8	480	2.0	760	2.6	1,050	2.9
Manufacturing	3,170	18.2	4,750	20.0	6,340	21.8	8,230	22.4
Construction	830	4.8	1,440	6.1	1,660	5.7	2,300	6.3
Commerce and Finance	1,220	7.0	1,990	8.4	2,760	9.5	3,890	10.6
Transportation and Communications	860	4.9	1,530	6.4	2,100	7.2	3,190	8.7
Services	2,100	12.1	3,210	13.5	4,160	14.3	5,880	16.0
Other	195	1.1	170	0.7	370	1.3	600	1.6
Total	17,390	100	23,740	100	29,070	100	36,730	100

Numbers given in thousands.
Source: International Historical Statistics, 154.

Henry Ford pioneered the use of the assembly line to build automobiles at his Ford Motor Company plant. With mass-production techniques, Ford managed to lower the price of a brand-new Model T (the "tin lizzie") to $260 in 1925 (about $2,000 in 1990 dollars). By 1927, he had sold 15 million tin lizzies, more than all the other automakers combined. Pictured here is one day's production—a thousand automobiles. (Courtesy Ford Motor Company)

workers received an average of ten cents per hour or about $5.50 per week ($286 per year). A young woman who worked a loom in a textile mill might earn as little as $2 per week. However, because the cost of food, clothing, and housing dropped, the real wages of many workers did rise during the Gilded Age.

In September 1882, the first Labor Day was celebrated with a parade up New York City's Fifth Avenue. One placard read: "EIGHT HOURS OF WORK, EIGHT HOURS OF REST, EIGHT HOURS FOR WHAT WE WILL." Most federal government workers had already won the eight-hour day, but many other workers, especially jewelers, masons, machinists, carpenters, iron puddlers (those who stirred liquid iron in furnaces during the steel-making process), bricklayers, and printers in the parade still worked ten- and twelve-hour days. By 1915, Labor Day had become a national holiday, signed into effect by President Grover Cleveland in 1894 to honor the contributions of working people to America. Labor unions used Labor Day, as they did May 1, to call strikes, to issue manifestoes, or to stage excursions, picnics, and athletic competitions. Labor Day also came to signal the end of summer vacations (for the middle class), the return to school, the closing of amusement parks, and the displaying of fall fashions.

In 1869 Uriah S. Stephens founded the Noble Order of the Knights of Labor, the first national labor union. It opened its ranks to all laborers, men and women, skilled and unskilled, white and black. In 1884, the Knights achieved popularity when they forced the powerful railroad magnate Jay Gould to roll back a wage cut. The next year, membership soared to 700,000. In 1886 the tragedy of the Haymarket incident in Chicago (police tried to break up a radical labor rally; a bomb was thrown, leading to the deaths of

seven policemen and the wounding of seventy people) quickly dampened public support for trade unionism. Despite having no role in the bombing, the Knights were held responsible for the violence by many, who alleged that its ranks were filled with foreign saboteurs and political schemers. By 1890, membership had declined to 100,000 and the Knights never recovered.

The American Federation of Labor

The American Federation of Labor (AFL) launched an American tradition of bread-and-butter unionism. Eschewing divisive and time-consuming ideologies of trade-union socialism and steering clear of anachronistic simple craft unionism, the AFL sprang to life in the antiradical atmosphere following the violence at Haymarket. From its inception, its leaders, including Adolph Strasser, president of the Cigarmakers' International, and Samuel Gompers, president of the AFL for forty-one years, avoided utopian political goals and focused upon plans to improve the conditions of the laboring masses.

The AFL traces its origins to a meeting of national unions in Pittsburgh in 1881. Later, it grew into an amalgamation of autonomous member unions of skilled workers only, all under the organizational umbrella of the larger federation that acted for the whole. The strike was the major weapon in the AFL's arsenal of industrial warfare. The fundamental principle to which the union dedicated itself was the right of collective bargaining by representatives of the workers' choice. It was to take fifty years before the courts gave legal protection to this principle. Meanwhile, the AFL brought a measure of equality to the bargaining process between executives of industrial corporations and workers. The impersonal corporation that the Supreme Court had declared a "person" faced a labor "person" who

Young women entered a variety of industrial occupations in the late nineteenth century, as illustrated by these women of the Paper Mills, Appleton, Wisconsin, 1880–1899. (Courtesy Prints and Photographs Division, Library of Congress)

was equally impersonal but less vulnerable than a single individual.

By 1900 the AFL claimed 500,000 members. It counted among its achievements the eight-hour day, the five- and six-day week, factory inspection, workmen's compensation, compulsory education, outlawing of the injunction, and other benefits. Bread-and-butter unionism brought an American solution to the problem of labor relations, attempting to meet labor's conflicting demands for equality, equity, and upward mobility.

Depression of 1893–1897

Victorian America experienced financial panics in 1873, 1884, and 1893, all of which led to depressions that lasted for several years. Business leaders disagreed over the causes. Some alleged overproduction; others underconsumption. Rapid economic growth, the need for credit, the absence of a centralized banking system to stabilize the supply of currency, and the inability or reluctance of the government to control monetary policy all contributed to financial panics. Silver and gold reserves fluctuated wildly, deepening the financial

crises and contributing to the cycles of boom and bust. The interdependence of world economies meant that economic troubles might begin in Europe and spread to the United States, as was the case in 1893.

The depression of 1893–1897 was the country's worst economic depression to date. On June 27, 1893, the Wall Street market virtually collapsed, companies plunged into bankruptcy, and the cycle of disaster spread. By the end of the year, 16,000 business and 500 banks had failed. Seventy-four railroads (including the Philadelphia & Reading, the North Pacific, the Erie, and the Sante Fe) went into receivership. Banks called in loans, the number of soup kitchens grew in the cities, and the unemployment rate reached 20% of the workforce. Jacob Coxey led a march of the unemployed on Washington, D.C., to demand federal relief for the unemployed. Meanwhile, Pres. Grover Cleveland declared that the government was not responsible, preferring instead to emphasize the "stupendous results of American enterprise" at the opening of the 1893 Chicago World's Fair.

TABLE 4.37   DISTRIBUTION OF THE WORKFORCE, 1890

Occupation	Male	Female
Agricultural Pursuits		
Dairymen, dairywomen	16,161	1,734
Farmowners, overseers	5,055,130	226,427
Hired hands (farm)	2,556,958	447,104
Lumbermen	65,838	28
Nurserymen, gardeners, florists	70,186	2,415
Wood choppers	33,665	32
Professional Service		
Actors	23,200	4,583
Architects, designers, draftsmen	17,134	327
Artists, art teachers	11,681	10,815
Clergymen	87,060	1,143
Dentists	17,161	337
Engineers, surveyors	43,115	124
Journalists	20,961	888
Lawyers	89,422	208
Musicians, music teachers	27,636	34,519
Literary, scientific persons	8,453	2,764
Officials (government)	77,715	4,875
Physicians, surgeons	100,248	4,557
Teachers, college professors	101,278	246,066
Domestic and Personal Service		
Barbers, hairdressers	82,157	2,825
Bartenders (hired)	55,660	146
Lodging-house keepers	11,756	32,593
Hotel keepers	38,800	5,276
Janitors, sextons	23,730	2,808
Launderers, laundresses	31,831	216,631
Nurses, midwives	6,190	41,396
Restaurant keepers	16,867	2,416
Saloon keepers	69,110	2,275
Servants, waiters	238,152	1,216,639
Watchmen, policemen, detectives	74,350	279
Trade and Transportation		
Bankers, brokers	35,458	510
Boatmen, sailors	76,823	51
Bookkeepers, accountants	131,602	27,772
Company executives	39,683	217
Draymen, hackmen, teamsters	368,265	234
Hostlers, stablemen (hired)	54,014	22
Hucksters, peddlers	56,824	2,259
Livery-stable owners	26,710	47
Messengers, office boys	48,446	2,909
Salesmen, saleswomen	205,943	58,451
Railroad employees	460,771	1,442
Stenographers, typewriters	12,148	21,270
Telegraph, telephone operators	43,740	8,474
Manufacturing and Mechanical Pursuits		
Bakers	57,910	2,287
Blacksmiths	209,521	60
Bookbinders	12,298	11,560
Brewers, maltsters	20,294	68
Broom, brush makers	8,949	1,166
Cabinet makers	35,891	24
Carpenters, joiners	618,044	198
Confectioners	17,577	5,674
Coopers	47,438	48
Dressmakers	836	292,668
Fishermen, oystermen	59,899	263
Harness, saddlemakers	42,647	833
Millers	52,747	94
Miners, quarrymen	386,872	376

Occupation	Male	Female
Paper hangers	12,315	54
Photographers	17,839	2,201
Tailors	123,516	64,509
Wheelwrights	12,855	1

Source: Eleventh Census of the United States (1890).

TABLE 4.38   U.S. WORKFORCE, 1914

By the end of the Victorian Age nearly one-third of the nation's workforce was concentrated in coal mining, lumber and timber, and textiles. Heavy industries (automakers, car builders, machinists, iron and steel, and structural iron) composed about 20% of the workforce. In 1914, when a special U.S. Census of manufactures was taken, the number at work in the chief occupations was as follows:

Industry	Number	Percent
Agricultural Implements	61,900	1
Automakers	151,054	2
Boots and Shoes	223,533	4
Boxes	92,903	1
Bakers	126,772	2
Brick and Tile	123,877	2
Canning	168,770	3
Car Builders	347,031	5
Clothing	373,057	6
Coal Mines	763,185	12
Confectionery	62,080	1
Cotton Textiles	389,980	6
Electrical	128,766	2
Flour	41,684	1
Machinists	384,214	6
Furniture	136,341	2
Gas (artificial)	47,572	1
Glass Works	86,461	1
Socks and Knit Goods	157,636	2
Iron and Steel	356,399	6
Leather	58,743	1
Liquors	78,177	1
Lumber and Timber	609,104	10
Metal Mines	158,115	3
Millinery	53,209	1
Paper and Pulp	89,916	1
Printing and Publishing	233,231	4
Quarries	87,936	1
Rubber Goods	58,246	1
Shipbuilding	49,582	1
Silk Goods	112,761	2
Meat Packing	108,440	2
Structural Iron	50,214	1
Tobacco	184,399	3
Wool Textiles	176,608	3
Total	6,331,896	100

Source: The World Almanac and Encyclopedia 1920 (1919), 136.

In 1910, Socialist writer John Spargo estimated that 1.8 million children under sixteen years of age were employed full time. Girls as young as twelve tended dangerous spinning machines in the textile mills. "Bobbin boys" of ten hauled boxes of heavy spindles from spinning to weaving rooms and back again. Children swept filings in machine shops. The anthracite coal mines of Pennsylvania employed boys as young as eight to separate slate rock from coal. It was a difficult labor carried out in filthy, frigid, wooden sheds in twelve-hour shifts that stole the youth of children and aged them prematurely. This is indicated in the faces of these breaker boys working in the Ewen Breaker in South Pittston, Pennsylvania, January 10, 1911. (Photo by Lewis Hine, courtesy National Archives)

TABLE 4.39   MINERS IN THE BITUMINOUS COAL INDUSTRY BY RACE, 1900–1920

In the late Victorian Period, the demand for labor in America's coal mines increased rapidly. Vast coal reserves were discovered in the Appalachian South where miners nearly doubled between 1900 and 1910. World War I kept the production of coal at high levels during this boom period, which would end quickly in the 1920s. Thereafter, the coal industry faced stiff competition from hydroelectric, oil, and natural gas as the nation's new sources of energy. Ironically, as the demand for miners increased, the proportion of African Americans in the industry declined, especially in the southern Appalachian states where they were in the greatest numbers. Increasingly, racial segregation and mechanization were forcing African Americans out of the industry.

State	1900			1910			1920		
	Total	Black	Percent Black	Total	Black	Percent Black	Total	Black	Percent Black
Southern Appalachian States									
Ala.	17,898	9,735	54.4	20,778	11,189	53.8	26,204	14,096	53.8
Ky.	9,299	2,206	23.7	18,310	3,888	21.2	44,269	7,407	16.7
Tenn.	10,890	3,092	28.4	11,094	1,609	14.5	12,226	913	7.5
Va.	7,369	2,651	35.9	7,291	1,719	23.6	12,418	2,450	19.8
W. Va.	20,797	4,620	22.2	54,884	11,237	20.5	87,728	17,799	20.3
Total	66,253	22,304	37.7	112,357	29,642	26.4	182,845	42,665	23.3
Northern States									
Ill.	38,184	1,368	3.6	58,738	1,512	2.6	82,305	2,194	2.7
Ind.	12,575	399	3.2	19,184	376	2.0	29,149	614	2.1
Iowa	11,078	1,065	9.6	13,990	1,600	11.4	12,809	1,103	8.6
Ohio	33,209	780	2.3	40,387	1,004	2.5	47,789	1,389	2.9
Pa.	180,474	1,616	.8	291,746	1,773	.6	297,345	2,930	.1
Total	275,520	5,228	1.9	424,045	6,265	1.5	469,397	8,230	1.8

Source: Ronald L. Lewis, *Black Coal Miners in America* (1987), 191.

Unlike the mining communities of the northern United States, which were situated in independent towns, most mining towns of the southern Appalachian Mountains were company towns. In these towns, the coal operators built the towns and owned everything in them. About 80% of West Virginia's coal towns, for example, were company towns. The company store, or commissary as the miners called it, was a central feature of the towns. They were places where miners bought groceries, supplies, and furniture and served a variety of social and economic needs. Depending upon the size of the company town, some stores might also serve as recreation centers, contain offices of the company, or provide such services as barbering, hairdressing, and billiard rooms. Pictured here is the Roda Company Store, Stonega Coke and Coal Company, Roda, Virginia. (Courtesy The Hagley Library)

TABLE 4.40   UNION MEMBERSHIP, 1900–1913

Figures on union membership are based on reports and statements made by unions in their official journals, reports, and convention proceedings; on correspondence with union officials; and on per-capita dues payments of national and international unions to overall federations. Different unions define membership differently. Some include and others exclude unemployed members, retired members, apprentices, members involved in work stoppages, and members in the armed forces.

The figures include Canadian members of unions with headquarters in the United States and some other members outside the continental United States.

Year	Total in Lab Force	Total Union Membership		AFL Number Affiliated Unions	Total Membership		Independent or Unaffiliated Membership
		BLS[a]	Wolman[a]	BLS	BLS	Wolman	Wolman
1900	28,376	791	868	82	548	625	243
1905	32,299	1,918	2,022	118	1,494	1,598	424
1910	36,709	2,116	2,140	120	1,562	1,587	554
1913	38,675	2,661	2,716	111	1,996	2,051	665

Numbers given in thousands.
Sources: [a]Bureau of Labor Statistics, records, and Leo Wolman, *Ebb and Flow in Trade Unionism,* National Bureau of Economic Research (New York, 1936), as reported in *Historical Statistics of the United States, Colonial Times to 1957,* 1961, 97; for estimated civilian labor force, see Erik W. Austin, *Political Facts of the United States Since 1789* (1986), Table 7.6.

TABLE 4.41 DURATION OF MAJOR DEPRESSIONS

Years	Months' Duration
1762–65	36
1768–69	12
1772–75	30
1784–88	**44**
1796–98	36
1802–03	24
1807–09	27
1815–21	**71**
1825–26	13
1833–34	9
1837–43	**72**
1857–58	18
1866–67	18
1873–78	**66**
1882–85	36
1890–91	9
1893–97	**48**
1907–08	12
1913–14	20
1920–21	18
1929–33	**42**
1937–38	10

Boldface type indicates the most major depressions.
Source: Richard B. Morris, ed., *Encyclopedia of American History* (1965), 536.

TABLE 4.42 UNEMPLOYMENT: NUMBERS AND PERCENTAGE OF WORKFORCE, 1891–1913

The harsh depression of the early 1890s is reflected in the high rates of unemployment of 1893–1894. Otherwise, finding work does not appear to have been difficult during the late Victorian Age. Except for 1908 when it rose again to 8% of the labor force, unemployment remained at what economists define as *nominal;* that is, about 4 to 6% of the labor force is typically but briefly unemployed in transition to other work.

Year	No. (thousands)	Percent
1891	1,265	5.4
1893	2,860	11.7
1894	4,612	18.4
1899	1,819	6.5
1906	574	1.7
1908	2,780	8
1913	1,671	4.3

Source: B. R. Mitchell, *International Historical Statistics* (1983), 161.

The Homestead Strike

On July 1, 1892, the contract between Andrew Carnegie's Homestead Steel Mill, just outside Pittsburgh, and the Amalgamated Association of Iron and Steel Workers expired. Plans had been laid by Carnegie and his manager Henry Clay Frick to use the occasion to rid the company of the union. Carnegie himself went home to Scotland, leaving Frick in charge. Frick first cut wages and then refused to negotiate, planning to secure the plant and bring in strikebreakers

Radical labor leaders sought to galvanize America's laboring class to action. Shown here are anarchists addressing a group of Wobblies, members of the International Workers of the World, in New York's Union Square, 1908. (Courtesy Prints and Photographs Division, Library of Congress)

TABLE 4.43 AVERAGE ANNUAL EARNINGS, SELECTED INDUSTRIES, 1890–1913

(in dollars)

Year	Mfg. Wages	RR[a] Wages	Street Railways	Telephone	Telegraph	Gas/ Electric	Bit.-Coal Mining	Clerks[b]	Farm Laborers	Federal Empls.	Postal Empls.	Public-School Teachers	Ministers
1890	439	560	557	...	...	687	406	848	233	...	878	256	794
1895	416	546	509	...	...	640	307	941	216	1,104	935	289	787
1900	435	548	604	...	...	620	438	1,011	247	1,033	925	328	731
1905	494	589	646	401	581	543	500	1,076	302	1,072	935	392	759
1910	558	677	681	417	649	622	558	1,156	336	1,108	1,049	492	802
1913	578	760	704	438	717	661	543	1,236	360	1,136	1,124	547	899

[a]Wage earners on steam railroads.
[b]Clerical workers are those in manufacturing and steam railroads.
Source: Historical Statistics of the United States, Colonial Times to 1957, 1961, 91–92. In terms of the 1910 and 1990 consumer price indices, 1910 wages *on average* were .072 percent (28 divided by 391.4) of those wages of 1990. The salaries of ministers in this table are lower than those of clergymen in Table 4.48, probably because the salaries of New England clergymen were generally higher than those of the southern United States.

to replace the workers. When the steelworkers struck as anticipated, Frick locked them out of the plant and called in a force of more than 300 armed Pinkerton detectives who were experienced in industrial warfare. In the early morning hours of July 5, the detectives were brought up the Monongahela River on two heavily armed barges specially outfitted with heavy wooden decking, partially reinforced metal plating, and boxlike enclosures to house them.

But the striking steelworkers had been alerted by union sentries who were posted along the river to report on any unusual activity. As the barges were towed closer to the plant, crowds along the riverbank swelled to nearly 10,000 men, women, and children—swearing, throwing objects at the barges, and hurling threats at those inside, who responded with sporadic gunfire. When the barges reached the riverbank beside the mill, strikers repulsed the armed

The Strike, an oil on canvas painting by Robert Koehler in 1886, represents the hostility and economic distance between employers and workers in the nineteenth century. (Courtesy Lee Baxandall, The Baxandall Company. Oshkosh, Wisconsin)

The depression of the 1890s threw thousands of people out of work, produced soup kitchens in the cities, and led to widespread economic distress. After the financial panic of 1893, hundreds of banks and thousands of businesses went into receivership. When the national government failed to act, Jacob Coxey, an Ohio businessman, organized and led a group of unemployed people from Massillon, Ohio, in March 1894, to Washington, D.C. In Washington, he was met with indifference and was arrested for stepping on the grass. (Courtesy Prints and Photographs Divsion, Library of Congress)

force on the landings, a final act of defiance. Frick appealed to the governor of Pennsylvania, who sent in 8,000 militiamen. Despite national sympathy for the steelworkers and Republican appeals to President Cleveland and to Andrew Carnegie to recognize the union, the Homestead mill reopened on July 15 with strikebreakers under guard.

TABLE 4.44 FAMILY SIZE, INCOME, AND EXPENDITURES, 1901, BY REGION OF THE UNITED STATES

Geographical Division	No. Families	Average Size	Average Income	Average Amounts Spent During the Year	
				For Food	For All
N. Atlantic	1,415	5.3	$835	$338	$778
S. Atlantic	219	5.3	$763	$299	$701
N. Central	721	5.5	$843	$322	$786
S. Central	122	5.7	$715	$293	$690
Western	90	4.7	$892	$309	$751

Source: The World Almanac and Encyclopedia 1921, 293. These averages, from the Annual Report of the Commissioner of Labor, are higher than those of Table 4.43 because they include all occupations.

TABLE 4.45 EXPENSES OF FAMILIES BY INCOME, 1902[a]

Expense	Under $450	$450– $600	$600– $750	$750– $1,200	More Than $1,200
Groceries	31	31	27	27	27
Rent	22	18	17	11	7
Meats, fish, and ice	17	16	17	17	16
Clothing	9	12	12	14	15
Fuel and light	8	7	7	5	5
Milk	5	4	4	4	3
Sickness/Funeral	2	3	2	3	4
Furniture/Household	2	2	2	3	2
Personal	1	2	3	4	7
Education	0	0.3	0.3	0.4	1
Newspapers/Periodicals	0.4	1	1	1	1
Relig./Charity	0.5	0.8	1	2	2
Societies/Unions	0.7	0.9	1	1	1
Insurance	1	2	2	2	3
Recreation	0	0.4	1	1	2
Getting to Work	0.4	0.2	0.5	0.5	1
Other	0	0.8	1	5	6

Numbers given are percentages of income.
[a] This table presents the result of the expenses of 104 "normal" families (father, mother, and immediate dependent relatives) whose income was based upon the labors of household members and was not increased by taking in boarders or lodgers. The Massachusetts Bureau of Labor made the compilation 1902, and the figures are representative of the town and cities in that commonwealth. In terms of 1990 dollars, prices were, *on average,* 15.1 times higher (based upon 26 and 391.4, the consumer price indices of 1902 and 1990 respectively in 1990).
Source: The American Almanac, Year Book, Cyclopedia and Atlas (1903), 356.

In the midst of the turmoil, a young anarchist, Alexander Berkman, burst into Frick's office, shot him twice in the abdomen, and stabbed him several times. Frick survived the attack and counterattacked in the courts, which indicted 185 men, forcing the union to raise more than $500,000 in bail money alone.

After nearly five months, it was all over. In the short run, the Homestead management had won. But in the long run, there were few winners. Carnegie's reputation had been tarnished beyond repair, Frick had been severely wounded, most of the workers lost their jobs to strikebreakers, and the defeat of the Amalgamated, the most important affiliate of the AFL, dealt organized labor a blow as devastating as Haymarket.

Nevertheless, the strike had familiarized a larger public with the conditions of labor and its need for an organized voice to give it protection and equality.

Garment Workers and the Triangle Fire

Thousands of young women worked in the garment district in New York City, most of them Jewish and Italian and between the ages of sixteen and twenty-five. Some lived with their families; others lived alone. All of them worked fifty-six-hour, six-day weeks for a wage of $6 per week. New York was the center of the American garment industry with 600 shirtwaist and dress factories that employed more than 30,000 workers. The operations had moved from tenement rooms to large loft buildings in lower Manhattan. These buildings were better than the dingy tenements, but were still overcrowded and had few safety features. Owners practiced "scientific" management techniques to increase profits: women had to rent their own sewing machines and pay for the electricity they used and were penalized for mistakes and talking too loudly. Male supervisors badgered them and sometimes asked for sexual favors.

On Saturday, March 25, 1910, a fire broke out at the ten-story

TABLE 4.46 COST OF LIVING IN THE UNITED STATES, 1872 AND 1902 [a]

Articles		Average Retail Price	
Groceries	Unit	1872	1902
Flour, wheat	Barrel	$12.75	$4.69
Corn Meal	Pound	$0.02	$0.03
Codfish, dry	Pound	$0.08	$0.10
Rice	Pound	$0.11	$0.08
Beans	Quart	$0.10	$0.10
Coffee, roasted	Pound	$0.43	$0.27
Sugar, granulated	Pound	$0.12	$0.05
Molasses, New Orleans	Gallon	$0.70	$0.49
Soap, common	Pound	$0.08	$0.05
Starch	Pound	$0.12	$0.08
Provisions			
Beef, Soup	Pound	$0.08	$0.07
Mutton, forequarter	Pound	$0.10	$0.11
Pork, fresh	Pound	$0.13	$0.14
Sausages	Pound	$0.13	$0.13
Lard	Pound	$0.15	$0.13
Butter	Pound	$0.39	$0.30
Cheese	Pound	$0.18	$0.16
Potatoes	Bushel	$1.02	$1.14
Milk	Quart	$0.08	$0.06
Eggs	Dozen	$0.30	$0.22
Fuel			
Coal	Ton	$9.25	$6.66
Wood, pine	Cord	$7.00	$6.79
Dry Goods			
Shirting 4-4 brown	Yard	$0.13	$0.07
Sheeting, 9-8 brown	Yard	$0.14	$0.13
Cotton flannel	Yard	$0.28	$0.11
Ticking	Yard	$0.24	$0.19
Prints	Yard	$0.12	$0.06
Boots			
Men's heavy	Pair	$3.94	$2.00
Rents			
Four-room tenements	Month	$14.75	$12.14
Six-room tenements	Month	$16.00	$19.30
Board			
Men	Week	$5.62	$3.91
Women	Week	$3.75	$3.34

[a] The comparisons of the cost of living were compiled in 1902 by the Massachusetts Bureau of Statistics of Labor. While restricted to the towns and cities in that state, they approximate those throughout New England and the middle and eastern states. The cost of transportation in the middle and western states would raise the price of a few articles produced in or imported into the East, but the average would be about the same because other articles could be bought more cheaply in the West. The South, however, cannot be classified in this table because living expenses were generally lower, and the average wage much less in that region.
Source: The American Almanac, Year Book, Cyclopedia and Atlas (1903), 355.

loft building of the Triangle Shirtwaist Company near Washington Square in New York. Within minutes, the top three floors were ablaze. Many exit doors were locked, elevators quit, and there were no fire escapes. Forty-six women jumped to their deaths, some holding hands, and more than 100 died in the flames.

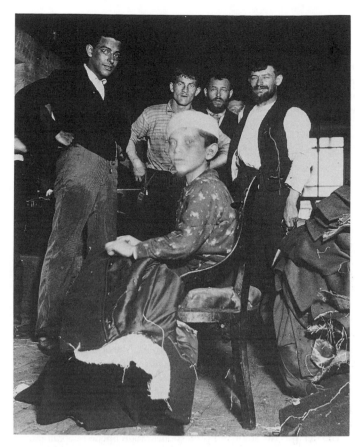

The sweatshops in the garment district of New York City were notorious for the exploitation of immigrant labor, especially children, as shown in this picture of a twelve-year-old boy at work pulling threads in a sweatshop, c. 1889. Whole families and their boarders sewed clothing in the cramped quarters of their own tenements. (Photo by Jacob Riis, courtesy, Prints and Photographs Division, Library of Congress)

In the aftershock, the state legislature appointed a commission to investigate working conditions in the state. Frances Perkins, who in 1933 became the first woman cabinet member, was one of the investigators. She led commissioners through dark lofts, dingy tenements, and unsafe factories all over the state to show them the conditions in which young women and children labored. The result was a raft of bills in the New York State Legislature that limited the work of women to fifty-four hours per week, abolished the labor of children under fourteen, and improved safety conditions in factories. Franklin Delano Roosevelt, who as president made Perkins his secretary of labor, was one of the legislators in Albany who helped pass the legislation.

Income and Cost of Living

In rough figures, in 1900 family size averaged about five members per family, average annual family income was around $800, and prices on average in 1990 were fifteen times those of 1900. Using these figures, a average family of five would have earned $12,000 in 1900, in terms of 1990 prices. It should be kept in mind, however, that in working-class families, women and children worked too to earn this average. Making a living on such a wage would have been even more difficult if the cost of living had been rising.

Fortunately, the cost of living fell during this period. Important items such as flour, which retailed at $12.75 a barrel in 1872, declined to $4.69 a barrel in 1902. Butter, milk, and eggs also declined, though less sharply. Meat prices stayed about the same. The costs of clothing and shoes also declined, as did rents. As a result of these deflationary trends, working families had a better chance of making ends meet.

Professionalization

After the Civil War, as the economy expanded, many new opportunities opened up for middle-class men. The growing complexity of the census categories reflected these changes. Whereas once the census taker had noted only the occupation of clerk, for example, the 1890 enumeration included bookkeepers, accountants, sales clerks, stenographers, "typewriters" (typists), telegraph operators, and a number of other specialized jobs open to the lower ranks of the white-collar world.

New careers required more education. Public schools in the United States increased from 160 in 1870 to 6,000 in 1900. By 1900, thirty-one states had passed compulsory-school-attendance laws.

Higher education experienced a similar growth. In the same period the number of students in colleges and universities doubled from 53,000 in 1870 to 101,000 by 1900.

Greater specialization and professionalization opened up still more occupations in various fields of education, medicine, law, and busi-

TABLE 4.47 PROFESSIONALS, OFFICE WORKERS, SKILLED, AND UNSKILLED WORKERS, 1900, 1910

Occupation	1900	1910	% Inc.
Professionals	1,234	1,758	42
Accountants & Auditors	23	39	70
Architects	11	16	45
Authors	3	4	33
Chemists	9	16	78
Clergymen	114	118	4
College[a]	7	16	129
Dentists	30	40	33
Editors & Reporters	32	36	13
Engineers	38	77	103
Lawyers & Judges	108	115	6
Nurses, Prof.	12	82	583
Physicians & Surgs.	131	152	16
Teachers	436	595	36
Veterinarians	8	12	50
Office Workers	3,881	6,204	60
Managerial[b]	1,697	2,462	45
Clerical & Kindred	877	1,987	127
Sales	1,307	1,755	34
Skilled Workers[c]	3,062	4,315	41
Unskilled Workers	8,387	11,630	39
Operatives & Kindred	3,720	5,441	46
Service Workers[d]	1,047	1,711	63
Laborers[e]	3,620	4,478	24

Numbers given in thousands.
[a] Presidents, professors, and instructors.
[b] Managers, officials, and proprietors, except farm.
[c] Craftsworkers, foremen, and kindred workers.
[d] Except private household.
[e] Except farm and mine.
Source: Historical Statistics of the United States, Colonial Times to 1957, 1961, 75.

TABLE 4.48 AVERAGE INCOME AND SAVINGS OF SALARIED MEN, 1910[a] (TRANSLATED INTO 1990 DOLLARS)

The savings of salaried men during the Victorian period seem quite remarkable. Bankers, brokers, and lawyers saved about one-third of their income; savings for the remainder of salaried men ranged between 18 and 22% of average income, except for clergymen (12%). Comparable figures are unavailable, but in 1989 the percentage of personal disposable income saved by workers at all levels was 4.6%.

Profession	Income in 1910 $	Income in 1990 $	Savings in 1910 $	Savings in 1990 $
Bankers & brokers	$7,726	108,009	$2,388	33,384
Lawyers	$4,169	58,283	$1,474	20,607
Physicians	$3,907	54,620	$717	10,024
Railroad officials	$3,441	48,105	$628	8,779
Supt. of mfg. cos.	$3,262	45,603	$729	10,191
Clergymen	$3,150	44,037	$369	5,159
Profs. & tutors	$2,878	40,234	$543	7,591

[a] The Massachusetts Labor Bureau in 1910 published statistics showing the average income and savings of various classes. The above figures approximate salaries and savings of professionals throughout New England and the middle and eastern states only. Translation into 1990 dollars was based upon the consumer price indices of 28 for 1910 and 391.4 for 1990, meaning that prices in 1990 on average were 13.98 (391.4 divided by 28) times higher than in 1910.
Source: The World Almanac and Encyclopedia 1913, 293; Historical Statistics of the United States, Colonial Times to 1970, 210–211; Statistical Abstract of the United States 1991 (1991), 438, 474.

ness. The rise of professional schools and government licensing meant that doctors and lawyers no longer "read up on" medical and legal cases by way of professional training. Rather, they were "certified" and licensed by the states through a process of education and testing. Not until 1893 did the word career take on its modern meaning. Professional organizations such as the American Medical Association and the American Bar Association were regulating and professionalizing membership. The number of law schools doubled, and eighty-six new medical schools were founded in the last quarter of the nineteenth century.

The need for lawyers, bankers, architects, and insurance agents to serve business and industry enlarged middle-class professional ranks. Between 1870 and 1900, the number of engineers, chemists, metallurgists, and architects grew substantially. Large companies required many more managerial positions. New careers in social service and government opened up, too, filled by professionals educated in the social sciences. Professional organizations also sprang up in the fields of history, sociology, economics, psychology, and political science, all during the last twenty years of the nineteenth century.

The Typewriter

Christopher L. Sholes invented the typewriter and first exhibited it at the 1876 Centennial Exposition. Prior to the introduction of the typewriter, everything had to be handwritten. Ironically, the typewriter eased the entry of women into the formerly all-male office; later, feminists made it a symbol of women's enslavement.

When first marketed, the typewriter was not associated with either sex. Women did not have to fight resentment (as did women in factories) over their operating a "man's machine." By the 1880s, however, marketing and office-management specialists had altered

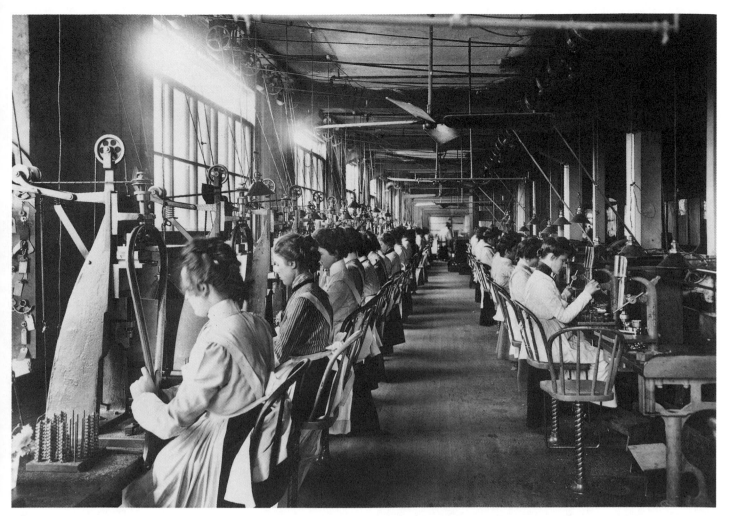

By 1900, women worked in larger and larger numbers. More than 5 million worked—one-fifth of all adult women. Among those employed, single women outnumbered married women by seven to one; yet more than one-third of married women worked due to the difficulty of supporting a family on one income. About 20% of the total labor force was female. Approximately 2 million were employed for subsistence wages or less in domestic service: cooking, cleaning, and tending the families of the rich. Women also worked in laborious and highly routinized factory jobs under male supervision where they were paid less than men such as these women in the lock-and-drill department, National Cash Register, Dayton, Ohio, c. 1902. (Courtesy Prints and Photograph Division, Library of Congress)

Trimming currency, 1907, was another example of women's work under male supervision. In 1900 about 30% of government clerks were women. (Courtesy National Archives)

the image, claiming that efficiency required the allegedly greater nimbleness of women's fingers. Hence, when Mark Twain bought his first machine, he had a "type girl" on hand to demonstrate it to him. In 1870, about 5% of all stenographers and typists were women; by 1930, the figure was about 92%.

Although some early typewriters resembled sewing machines (Remington) or had a semicircular keyboard (Hammond), by 1900 typical office models were black, with white lettering on black keys and a sturdy metal carriage.

Transportation

Railroads

Railroads transformed economic and social life in Victorian America. The "iron horse" symbolized the new unrestrained business climate of stock manipulations, monopolies, price conspiracies, and government subsidies. Railroading became the nation's largest industry, surpassing all others as a buyer of iron, steel, and coal. It stimu-

TABLE 4.49 RAILROAD PASSENGERS AND FREIGHT, 1876, 1913

Year	Passengers Carried Number (thousands)	Freight Carried Revenue Tons (thousands)
1876	136,121	691,344
1913	1,043,603	1,026,817

Source: Mitchell, *International Historical Statistics, The Americas and Australasia,* 669–670, 681–683.

TABLE 4.50 RAILROAD TRACK, 1876–1910

State	Miles		
	1876	1900	1910
Ala.	1,738	4,225	5,226
Alaska	0	0	0
Ariz.	0	1,511	2,097
Ark.	788	3,359	5,305
Calif.	1,919	5,751	7,771
Colo.	957	4,587	5,532
Conn.	918	1,023	1,000
Del.	285	346	334
D.C.[a]	0	21	35
Fla.	484	3,299	4,431
Ga.	2,306	5,651	7,056
Hawaii	0	0	0
Idaho	0	1,261	2,178
Ill.	7,285	11,002	11,878
Indian Territory	279	1,322	0[a]
Ind.	4,003	6,470	7,420
Iowa	3,939	9,185	9,754
Kans.	2,238	8,719	9,006
Ky.	1,475	3,059	3,526
La.	539	2,824	5,553
Maine	1,000	1,915	2,248
Md.[a]	1,107	1,376	1,426
Mass.	1,837	2,118	2,115
Mich.	3,395	8,195	9,021
Minn.	2,020	6,942	8,668
Miss.	1,044	2,919	4,506
Mo.	3,146	6,875	8,082
Mont.	0	3,010	4,207
Nebr.	1,150	5,684	6,067
Nev.	680	909	2,276
N.H.	940	1,239	1,245
N.J.	1,601	2,256	2,260
N. Mex.	0	1,752	3,032
N.Y.	5,525	8,121	8,429
N.C.	1,570	3,831	4,932
N. Dak.[a]	275	2,731	4,201
Ohio	4,687	8,807	9,134
Okla.	0	827	5,980
Oreg.	251	1,723	2,284
Pa.	5,983	10,330	11,290
R.I.	189	211	212
S.C.	1,353	2,817	3,441
S. Dak.[a]	0	2,849	3,947
Tenn.	1,645	3,136	3,815
Tex.	2,085	9,886	14,281
Utah	515	1,547	1,985
Vt.	810	1,012	1,100
Va.	1,649	3,779	4,534
Wash.	110	2,913	4,875
W. Va.	584	2,228	3,600
Wis.	2,707	6,530	7,475
Wyo.	459	1,228	1,644
U.S.	77,470	193,311	240,414

[a]The District of Columbia and Maryland are given together in 1876; the figure for North Dakota includes all the Dakota territory; most of the Indian Territory became the state of Oklahoma by 1913.
Source: Ainsworth R. Spofford, ed. *An American Almanac and Treasury of Facts, Statistical, Financial, and Political for the Year 1878,* 355; *The World Almanac and Encyclopedia 1921* (1921), 277.

Congestion of city streets may have been worse in the Victorian Age than it is today, especially during the transition stage of transportation. Shown here are horse-drawn wagons and carriages, an electric trolley car, and pedestrians congesting a cobblestone Philadelphia street in 1897. (Courtesy National Archives)

lated the growth of such industries as glass, lumber, and fabrics; created the telegraph system; standardized time and travel; nurtured the settlement of the West; lowered freight costs to previously unheard-of levels; and became the nation's largest employer (1.7 million workers in 1910). With unprecedented speed (by 1905 passenger trains sped between Chicago and New York in eighteen hours) and the ability to travel in all kinds of weather, the trains moved passengers and freight between cities and rural hamlets, breaking down provincialism and spreading mass culture.

Trains carried passengers across the country in the "era of the transcontinentals." In 1883, four railroads crossed the West, heading for the wheat fields of the Dakotas, Rocky Mountain mining towns, or California farmlands, hauling settlers and goods. They carried 289 million passengers; in 1913, more than a billion passengers traveled over the same routes.

TABLE 4.51 STREET RAILWAYS IN THE UNITED STATES MILES OF TRACK FOR CITIES OVER 100,000, IN 1900

Population based upon 1900 Census

City	Population	Miles
New York City	3,437,202	477
Chicago	1,698,575	1,187
Philadelphia	1,293,697	1,137
St. Louis	575,238	372
Boston	560,892	1,329
Baltimore	508,357	353
Cleveland	381,768	609
Buffalo	352,387	369
San Francisco	342,782	257
Cincinnati	325,902	460
Pittsburgh	321,616	379
New Orleans	287,104	192
Detroit	285,704	604
Milwaukee	285,315	158
Washington, D.C.	278,718	83
Newark	246,070 ⎫	255
Jersey City	206,433 ⎭	
Louisville	204,731	165
Minneapolis	202,718 ⎫	250
St. Paul	163,065 ⎭	
Providence	175,597	301
Indianapolis	169,164	217
Kansas City	163,752	179
Rochester, N.Y.	162,608	154
Denver	133,859	163
Toledo	131,822	269
Allegheny, Pa.	129,896	n.g.
Columbus, Ohio	125,560	282
Worcester, Mass.	118,421	69
Syracuse	108,374	99
New Haven	108,027	92
Paterson, N.J.	105,171	n.g.
Fall River, Mass.	104,863	n.g.
St. Joseph, Mo.	102,979	40
Omaha	102,555	135
Los Angeles	102,479	300
Memphis	102,320	70
Scranton	102,026	147

n.g. = none given
Sources: The American Almanac, Year Book, Cyclopedia and Atlas, 433, 516–521; The World Almanac and Encyclopedia 1902 (1901), 388.

TABLE 4.52 PASSENGER TRAFFIC ON RAILWAYS, 1882–1913

Year	Passengers Carried	Average Number of Passengers Per Mile of Railroad	Average Distance Traveled Per Passenger
1882	289	. . .	. . .
1892	561	3,375	23.59
1902	650*	3,098	29.63
1913	1,044	. . .	. . .

Numbers are given in millions of passengers.
Source: International Historical Statistics, 681, 683; The American Almanac, Year-Book, Cyclopedia, and Atlas, 511.
The fastest run from New York to Chicago, a distance of 964 miles, was made during this period by the New York Central and Harriman Railroad in nineteen hours, fifty-seven minutes, an average of 48.2 miles per hour with ten stops. *Ibid.,* 515.

TABLE 4.53 U.S. MOTOR-VEHICLE FACTORY SALES AND REGISTRATIONS, 1900–1915

Lack of mass-production techniques, affordable prices, and good roads limited the spread of motorized traffic until the end of the Victorian Age. In 1914, Ford Motor Company began to use assembly-line production, which explains the great increase in passenger cars from 1910 to 1915. In 1910, public roads totaled only about 2 million miles; most states had less than 10,000 miles in "improved roads" (packed dirt and gravel). In 1925, Henry Ford managed to set the price of a brand-new Model-T Ford, the "tin lizzie," at $260 (about $3,500 in 1990 prices), making it affordable to most workers.

Year	Factory Sales		Motor Vehicle Registrations[a]
	Passenger Cars	Trucks & Buses	
1900	4,192	. . .	8,000
1905	24,250	750	77,000
1910	181,000	6,000	468,500
1915	895,930	74,000	2,490,932

[a] Privately-owned vehicles only
Source: The Universal Almanac 1991 (1990), 276. Up through 1935, privately owned vehicles only; data exclude farm trucks registered at a nominal fee in certain states and restricted to use in the vicinity of owners' farms. Factory sales and vehicular registrations differ because registrations include vehicles registered in other years besides the sales year.

From Horsecars to the Elevateds: City Transportation, 1876–1913

The horsecar was introduced in American cities and its use expanded as steam railroads found it increasingly difficult to maintain the "nickel fare" for a thirty-minute commute.

In 1887 in Richmond, Virginia, electric streetcars were demonstrated and quickly adopted by most large cities within a year. They were cheaper to operate than horsecars because of the larger carrying capacity. The high capital investment spurred mergers of local horsecar companies and led to integration of services, lines, schedules, and the abolition of transfer charges. The increased range and speed of urban transit systems brought more passengers.

During the 1890s, electrified streetcar services expanded rapidly, and areas near the routes as far as six to eight miles from the urban center were now within a half hour of employment. An upswing in residential building, partially in response to extended transit service, stimulated further expansion of lines even after the building boom peaked, because companies felt development would continue into the countryside.

Central urban congestion, which threatened to nullify the advantages of speed, led to the development of the "el," trains that ran on trestle tracks elevated above street level, introduced in New York as early as 1878 and in Chicago in 1892. In Boston a combined subway and elevated system opened in 1897. Financial difficulties, partly the result of the costs of capital improvements and partly of inflation, led to a decline in revenue per passenger mile on the street railroads.

By the turn of the century, the street railway had become one of the most important and gigantic industries in the United States. Between 1890 and 1900, investment in trolley lines grew from $108 million to $1.5 billion; electric lines increased from 5,443 miles to

Despite the transcontinental railroad's completion in 1869, goods were still moved overland in many parts of the West. Not all areas were served by the railroad. In this picture, an ox train is seen transporting supplies in Arizona Territory in 1883. (Courtesy National Archives)

22,063 miles as mileage on the horsecar lines shrunk.

Residents who could afford the real estate and the commute continued to abandon the crowded inner cities for the quiet suburbs. Other services developed, too, such as the electric express service, postal cars, and even funeral cars to provide economical transportation to cemeteries. Lines were also extended to public parks and places of amusement. Excursion trains provided interurban transportation.

Communications

Mail: Distances and Time of Transit

In 1903, a letter sent from New York City reached Chicago, a rail distance of 964 miles, in twenty-five hours. San Francisco, a distance of 3,250 rail miles, could be reached in seventy-nine hours. A letter from New York to Washington, D.C., took six and one-half hours (228 miles). Wheeling, West Virginia (510 miles) could be reached in fourteen hours fifteen minutes; Topeka, Kansas (1,407 miles) in forty-eight hours.

Mail from New York City reached London and Paris in eight days; Berlin and Madrid were reached in nine days, but Rome got mail from New York City in thirteen days. More remote corners of the world took much longer to reach. A letter to Accra, in what is now Ghana, would not reach its addressee for twenty-nine days; Hong Kong took twenty-five days; Rio de Janeiro took twenty-three days; Mexico City, however, was just five days away. Odessa, Russia, was eleven days, Moscow ten days. Saigon took forty-four days via London and thirty-nine via San Francisco. Shanghai was forty-five days via London and twenty-five via San Francisco.

Time Zones

For the convenience of the railroads and business, a standard system of time was agreed upon in 1883. By this system, the United States was divided into four time zones extending from 65 degrees to 125 degrees west longitude. Each 15 degrees of longitude (7½ degrees, or 30 minutes, on each side of a meridian) beginning with the seventy-fifth meredian, constituted one zone. The time zones were named Eastern, Central, Mountain, and Pacific.

The Eastern Standard Time zone included all the territory between the Atlantic Ocean and an irregular line drawn from Buffalo to Charleston, South Carolina, the southernmost point of the zone. The Central zone included all the territory between the Eastern line and another irregular line from Bismarck, North Dakota, to the mouth of the Rio Grande. The Mountain zone included all territory from the Central line almost to the western borders of Idaho, Utah, and Arizona. The Pacific section included all territory from the Mountain section to the Pacific Ocean.

Time was uniform, or standard, throughout each zone, and, moving west, the time of each zone was an hour earlier than the preced-

Inevitably, narrow and crowded streets and the emergence of mass transit increased the dangers of city life, as shown in this cable-car accident, New York City, *Leslie's Weekly*, August 29, 1895. (Courtesy National Archives)

TABLE 4.54 POSTAL RATES FOR FIRST-CLASS LETTERS AND POSTAL CARDS, 1872, 1917

Year	Letters, Nonlocal	Postal Cards
1872	$.03 per ½ oz	$.01
1917	.03 per oz	.02

Source: Historical Statistics of the United States, Colonial Times to 1970, Part 2 (1975), 807.

TABLE 4.55 TELEGRAPH (WESTERN UNION), 1876, 1913

Rail and telegraph, the "Siamese twins of commerce," followed the route of the Pony Express. Telegraph companies won exclusive rights alongside the railroads and reciprocated by sending messages for the railroads. Use of domestic telegraph services increased until World War II when cheap telephone service caused telegrams to decline.

Year	Offices	Messages Handled
1876	7,072	18,730,000
1913	25,060	158,855,000

Source: Historical Atlas of the United States (1988), 217; The World Almanac and Encyclopedia 1913, 185.

ing zone. Times were based on Greenwich mean time, the time at Greenwich, England, located at 0 degrees longitude. Greenwich time is five hours later than New York, or Eastern Standard, time.

With some alterations in borders, and with the innovation of daylight saving time, this system is in use everywhere in the world today.

Traffic tickets are a century-old tradition. Pictured here is a traffic violator driving a 1900-vintage car being stopped by a policeman on a bicycle. (Courtesy National Archvies)

The Telephone and Telegraph

On May 27, 1844, Samuel F. B. Morse received the first telegraph message, on a Baltimore-to-Washington line. In a code of electric pulses—dots and dashes—that he had devised, the message read: "What hath God wrought?" Morse code and telegraphy spread rap-

TABLE 4.56 TELEPHONES AND CALLS: 1876, 1913

In the first decade after the arrival of the telephone, most phones were owned by doctors, lawyers, and businesspeople because monthly service cost more than one-half of the average worker's income. In 1894, when Alexander Graham Bell's patents expired, service was extended to rural areas. In 1907, the greatest concentrations of individually subscribed telephones were in Iowa, Nebraska, Washington, and California. In order to gain residential customers, telephone companies promoted practical uses, such as ordering groceries or calling the doctor. Only after World War I did the telephone industry recognize the profit potential of encouraging people to use the telephone to chat with friends and family.

Year	Number	Average Daily Local Calls	Calls/ 1,000 Popul.
1876	3,000	. . .	0.1
1913	9,543	39,895,000	97.2

Sources: Historical Atlas of the United States, 205; International Historical Statistics, 747; The World Almanac and Encyclopedia 1913, 185.

Workers at Ford Motor Company in 1913 worked on an assembly line 800 feet long. (Courtesy Ford Motor Company)

idly with the building of the railroads, allowing the railroads to keep schedules and spreading the technology across the country. By 1912, the day rate from New York City to California for every seven words in a message was one dollar; from New York City to Washington, D.C., the day rate was 25 cents per two words; from New York City to Dallas, Texas, the day rate was 75 cents for five words.

Rutherford B. Hayes put a telephone in the White House in 1878. By 1880, only four years after they had first heard of the invention, 50,000 Americans were using it. By 1890, 800,000 phones had been installed; in 1900, 1.5 million people in the smallest towns and rural areas knew about exchanges, party lines, and operators. As early as 1892, eastern and midwestern cities were connected to a long-distance network that soon reached the West Coast. Instantaneous communication was an invaluable asset to American business. In 1901, the average subscriber made about seven daily calls.

Trade and Finance

The Payne-Aldrich Tariff

In 1909, Pres. William Howard Taft called Congress into special session on the question of the tariff. The result was the Payne-Aldrich Act, which lowered duties to about 38% on imported manufactured goods (under the McKinley Tariff, duties had reached a peak of 49.5%).

Republican conservatives supported the tariff as protection for U.S. manufacturers and for the jobs of their factory workers, and to encourage capital investment. Some midwestern progressives disagreed, arguing that American business was strong enough to withstand fair competition. Farmers disliked the tariff because they were doubly affected. European nations, except Great Britain, retaliated against the previous tariff (Dingley Tariff) by imposing high duties on American agricultural products; high tariffs also drove up the prices of farm implements and machinery.

Taft hoped to placate both protectionists and free-traders in the Congress. The House of Representatives drafted a reasonable tariff-reduction schedule in the Payne bill, but in the Senate, Nelson Aldrich of Rhode Island, an ally of industrial capitalists, added 800 amendments to what became the Payne-Aldrich Act. Unlike Roosevelt, Taft lacked the political acumen to effect a reconciliation of the competing factions. Instead, he offered what he viewed as a compromise. In return for a reduced tariff, he proposed to make up the revenue loss with a mild corporate tax (2%) and a tax on personal incomes.

Imports and Exports

In 1876, exports of the United States consisted of food products, cotton, tobacco, and raw materials. By the close of the period, machinery, iron and steel, petroleum and petroleum products, coal, and motor vehicles had become a substantial part of the export trade.

Imports included products that were either difficult to produce in the United States or produced in insufficient quantity to satisfy national demand, such as coffee, tea, sugar, fruits, and nuts. Crude rubber imports rose with the increase in motor-vehicle production; the beginnings of petroleum imports in 1910 may also be attributed to the rise in demand for gasoline. The United States was also beginning to import more manufactured goods, including wool, iron and steel, cotton, and copper manufactures.

Throughout the Victorian Age, the United States enjoyed a favorable, and steadily improving, balance of trade; that is, the value of exports exceeded the value of all imports.

TABLE 4.57   MAJOR COMMODITY EXPORTS, 1876–1913

(millions of dollars)

Commodity	1876	1880	1890	1900	1910	1913
Coal	0	0	7	21	44	68
Cotton	193	212	251	242	450	547
Iron & Steel	0	0	3	39	60	124
Machinery	0	0	20	78	117	195
Meat	79	114	78	114	62	68
Motor Vehicles	0	0	0	0	11	33
Petro. & Prods	0	0	54	84	107	150
Leaf Tobacco	23	16	21	29	38	49
Wheat	93	226	102	141	95	142

Source: International Historical Statistics, The Americas and Australasia, 622, 628.

TABLE 4.58 MAJOR COMMODITY IMPORTS, 1876–1913

(millions of dollars)

Commodity	1876	1881	1890	1900	1910	1913
Coffee	57	57	78	52	69	119
Tea	20	21	12	11	14	17
Sugar	58	87	96	100	102	99
Crude Rubber	4.1	11	15	31	101	90
Raw Silk	5.4	11	23	45	65	82
Wool & Mohair	42.6	10	15	20	51	36
Wool Mfrs	. . .	31	57	16	24	16
Iron and Steel Mfrs	12.9	61	42	20	40	34
Tin (incl. ore value)	a	a	7	19	31	53
Cotton Mfrs	19.9	31	30	42	68	66
Copper & Mfrs	a	a	1	15	40	60
Hides and Skins	13.0	a	22	58	112	117
Fur & Mfrs	a	a	8	12	27	24
Fruits & Nuts	a	a	21	19	37	41
Forest Prods	a	a	13	15	40	48
Petrol & Prods	a	0	0	0	2	11

a Not available

Sources: Ainsworth R. Spofford, ed., An American Almanac and Treasury of Facts, Statistical, Finanical, and Political for the Year 1878 (1877), 214–15; An American Almanac for 1885, 318–19; Historical Statistics of the United States, Colonial Times to 1957, 548–549.

TABLE 4.59 VALUE OF IMPORTS AND EXPORTS, 1876–1913

(millions of U.S. dollars)

Year	Imports	Exports
1876	469	565
1880	680	850
1890	810	893
1900	885	1,451
1910	1,592	1,800
1913	1,854	2,538

Source: International Historical Statistics, the Americas and Australasia, 545.

The Money Question

After the Civil War, increased agricultural and industrial production caused a decline in prices. Farmers who were the deepest in debt suffered the most because they had to pay fixed interest and mortgage payments while the prices for their crops were falling. Seeing that the money supply was insufficient, which made their debts more onerous relative to commodity prices, farmers favored inflation, by means of the greater coinage of silver to increase the amount of money in circulation. Creditors wanted the opposite, a stable and tightly controlled money supply backed only by gold as a means of preserving the value of their investments. The money question divided Americans into debtors versus creditors, the agricultural South and West against the industrial Northeast, and rich against poor.

Prior to the 1870s, the government had coined both gold and silver dollars. A silver dollar weighed sixteen times more than a gold dollar, meaning that gold was officially worth sixteen times more than silver. Whenever gold discoveries increased the supply of this metal—as was the case in 1848, for example—its market value declined relative to silver's, and silver producers would sell their metal on the open market where they could get more than the official ratio that the government maintained. As a result, owners began to hoard silver dollars, and these coins disappeared from the market. In 1873, Congress officially stopped coining silver dollars, and European nations stopped buying them. Consequently, the U.S. government and its trading partners adopted the gold standard, meaning that their currencies were backed primarily by gold.

During the late 1870s, more silver mines opened in the American West and began to flood the market with silver. Gold was now worth more than sixteen times what silver was worth. It became more profitable to spend silver dollars. If the government had been buying silver, it would have been more profitable to sell silver to the government in return for gold. Debtors, who now favored expanding the money supply, joined with the silver producers to denounce the "crime of '73" and to agitate for resumption of coinage at the ratio of 16 to 1.

TABLE 4.60 OUTPUT OF GOLD AND SILVER, 1876–1913

(in metric tons)

Year	Gold	Silver
1876	60	933
1879	59	982
1884	46	1,174
1892	50	1,975
1900	119	1,793
1910	143	1,791
1913	134	2,214

Source: International Historical Statistics, 425–426, 437–438.

TABLE 4.61 CURRENCY IN CIRCULATION, 1876–1913

(millions of dollars)

Year	Currency	Notes
1876	807	672
1879	819	638
1884	1,244	817
1892	1,601	1,073
1900	2,081	1,302
1910	3,149	2,303
1913	3,419	2,529

Source: International Historical Statistics, 763–764.

The money question split Congress into silver and gold factions. The Bland-Allison Act of 1878 attempted to compromise on the issue by requiring the Treasury to buy $2 to $4 million worth of silver each month. In 1890, the Sherman Silver Purchase Act fixed the government's monthly purchase in weight (4.5 million ounces) rather than in dollars. Neither act pleased the interest groups. Nor did government purchases of silver expand the money supply because when the price of silver dropped, the government paid less for the same number of ounces, thereby putting less currency in circulation. In 1900, Pres. William McKinley signed the Gold Act, which required all paper money to be backed by gold and which lasted until 1933. The supply of currency was stabilized in 1913 with the passage of the Federal Reserve Act, establishing both the nation's first centralized banking system and government control over the currency by controlling credit.

The Federal Reserve System

In 1913, Pres. Woodrow Wilson signed into law a bill designed to bring order to the national banking system and to rein in the power of Wall Street. The Federal Reserve Act established twelve regional Federal Reserve Banks that did not deal directly with people but were bankers for other banks. The system was owned by private bankers, who were required to deposit 6% of their capital in it. In order to give the federal government control over the money supply, the president appointed the majority of the directors on the Federal Reserve Board, which sat in Washington.

The greatest power of the Federal Reserve System is the control over the discount rate, the rate of interest that banks charge to other banks that, in turn, lend money to private investors and buyers. In lowering the discount rate, the Federal Reserve can stimulate investment and economic expansion in slow times. By raising the discount, the Fed, as it is called, discourages investment and slows inflationary spending.

The Federal Reserve System did bring some order to the nation's banking system. It did not, however, tame the bankers, as progressives had hoped, because the Federal Reserve Board often included representatives of the private banks that the board was pledged to control.

TABLE 4.62   SAVINGS BANKS, DEPOSITS AND DEPOSITORS, AND COMMERCIAL DEPOSITS, 1876–1913

Year	Number of Banks	Number of Depositors	Savings Deposits	Commercial Deposits (millions)
1876	781	2,368,630	$941,350,255	$1,993
1880	921	2,335,582	$819,106,973	$2,222
1890	1,002	4,258,893	$1,524,844,506	$4,576
1900	1,759	6,107,083	$2,449,547,885	$4,345
1913	1,978	10,766,936	$4,727,403,950	$9,249

Sources: *International Historical Statistics*, 773, 783–784; *The World Almanac and Encyclopedia 1921*, 420.

TABLE 4.63   WHOLESALE AND CONSUMER PRICE INDICES, 1876–1913*

Year	Wholesale	Consumer
1876	110	108
1877	106	108
1878	91	98
1879	90	94
1880	100	98
1881	103	98
1882	108	98
1883	101	94
1884	93	91
1885	85	91
1886	82	91
1887	85	91
1888	86	91
1889	81	91
1890	82	91
1891	82	91
1892	76	91
1893	78	91
1894	70	88
1895	71	84
1896	68	84
1897	68	84
1898	71	84
1899	76	84
1900	82	84
1901	81	84
1902	86	88
1903	87	91
1904	87	91
1905	88	91
1906	90	91
1907	95	94
1908	92	91
1909	99	91
1910	103	94
1911	95	94
1912	101	98
1913	102	100

*Base period, wholesale: 1910–14 average (value 100). Base period, consumer: 1913 (value 100).
Source: *Historical Statistics of the United States, Colonial Times to 1970*, 210–211.

Income Tax

Congress passed the first income tax law July 1, 1862, to finance the Civil War. It taxed all annual incomes between $600 and $10,000 at the rate of 3%. Incomes of less than $600 were exempt; incomes of more than $10,000 were taxed at 5%. After the war, the income tax act was amended to tax incomes of more than a $1,000 at a flat 5%. It is estimated that only about 250,000 of a population of 40 million paid income tax under these provisions in 1868, and yet the returns of these persons provided an aggregate income of $800 million. Even though only a small number of the population wanted the income tax eliminated, Congress repealed the tax in 1871 on a narrow vote (the bill for repeal won by one vote in both houses of Congress).

During Woodrow Wilson's first administration, the need for an income tax increased when the Underwood Tariff was passed in 1913 to encourage imports by drastically reducing or eliminating tariff rates. To recover lost revenue due to the reductions by the tariff, the act levied a graduated income tax—an option made possible by the ratification earlier of the Sixteenth Amendment to the U.S. Constitution. Annual incomes of less than $4,000 (about $40,000 today) were nontaxable, exempting most factory and agricultural workers. Those individuals or corporations earning from $4,000 to $20,000 paid a 1% tax. The rate for higher incomes rose on a graduated scale to a maximum of 6% on earnings of more than $500,000 (about $6 million today).

CHAPTER 5 Population

Population Trends

During the Victorian Era, the population of the United States doubled. Natural increase and mass immigration fed the growth. At the beginning of the era, three-fourths of the population lived in rural areas; by 1913 nearly a half lived in cities. The African-American population was heavily concentrated in the eleven states of the former Confederacy; as a percentage of the total population, however, the black population declined.

The Victorian population was aging, the numbers over sixty-five years old increasing as a percentage of the total population. Males married in their mid-twenties, females in their early twenties. The number of marriages more than doubled, but the number of divorces grew fourfold. In 1913, overall life expectancy at birth was about fifty-three years, but women on average lived five years longer than men. These figures obscure a remarkable difference, however, in life expectancy by race. Nonwhites, on average, could expect to live only into their thirties.

Settled Areas, 1890

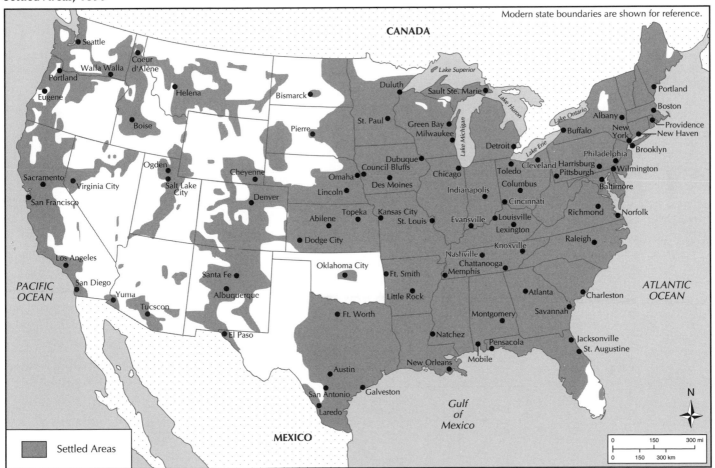

In this map showing the settled areas of the United States in 1890, only the territory in the West contained open land, and part of this area was occupied by Native Americans. As Frederick Jackson Turner observed, the once vast American frontier was no more. (Dale Williams)

TABLE 5.1 POPULATION OF THE UNITED STATES BY SEX AND RACE, 1880–1910

				Male			
					Other Races		
Year	All Races	White	Black	Total[a]	Native American	Japanese	Chinese
1880	25,518,820	22,130,900	3,253,115	134,805	33,985	134	100,686
1890	32,237,101	28,270,379	3,735,603	231,119	125,719	1,780	103,620
1900	38,816,448	34,210,735	4,386,547	228,166	119,484	23,341	85,341
1910	47,332,277	42,178,245	4,885,881	268,151	135,133	63,070	66,856

				Female			
					Other Races		
Year	All Races	White	Black	Total[a]	Native American	Japanese	Chinese
1880	24,636,963	21,272,070	3,327,678	37,215	32,422	14	4,779
1890	30,710,613	26,830,879	3,753,073	126,661	122,534	259	3,868
1900	37,178,127	32,607,461	4,447,447	123,219	117,712	985	4,522
1910	44,639,989	39,553,712	4,941,882	144,395	130,550	9,087	4,675

[a]Includes races now shown separately, of which Filipinos are most numerous. Filipino males: 1910—144; Filipino females: 1910—16.
Source: Erik W. Austin, *Political Facts of the United States Since 1789* (1986), Table 7.2.

TABLE 5.2 U.S. POPULATION, POPULATION DENSITY AND AREA OF RESIDENCE, 1880–1910

Year	Total Population	Percent Increase	Pop. Per Sq. Mi.[a]	Percent Urban	Percent Rural
1880	50,155,783	. . .	16.9	28.2	71.8
1890	62,947,714	25.5	21.2	35.1	64.9
1900	75,994,575	20.7	25.6	39.6	60.4
1910	91,972,266	21.0	31.0	45.6	54.4

[a]The areas and population of Alaska, Hawaii, and Puerto Rico in 1900 and of Indian Territory in 1880 are not considered in the calculations of density.
Source: The World Almanac and Encyclopedia 1920 (1919), 132.

TABLE 5.3 BLACK POPULATION OF THE UNITED STATES, 1880–1910

Year	Number (thousands)	Percent of Total Population
1880	6,581	13.1
1890	7,489	11.9
1900	8,834	11.6
1910	9,828	10.7

Source: The World Almanac and Encyclopedia 1914 (1913), 678.

TABLE 5.4 BLACK POPULATION, BY STATE, 1880–1910

(in thousands)

State	1880	1890	1900	1910
Ala.	600	678	827	908
Alaska	. . .	. . .	0	0
Ariz.	0	1	2	2
Ark.	211	309	367	443
Calif.	6	11	11	22
Colo.	2	6	9	11
Conn.	12	12	15	15
Del.	26	28	31	31
D.C.	60	76	87	94
Fla.	127	166	231	309
Ga.	725	859	1,035	1,177
Hawaii	. . .	. . .	0	1
Idaho	0	0	0	1
Ill.	46	57	85	109
Ind.	39	45	58	60
Iowa	10	11	13	15
Kans.	43	50	52	54
Ky.	271	268	285	262
La.	484	559	651	714
Maine	1	1	1	1
Md.	210	216	235	232
Mass.	19	22	32	38
Mich.	15	15	16	17
Minn.	2	4	5	7
Miss.	650	743	908	1,009
Mo.	145	150	161	157
Mont.	0	1	2	2
Nebr.	2	9	6	8
Nev.	0	0	0	1
N.H.	1	1	1	1
N.J.	39	48	70	90
N. Mex.	1	2	2	2
N.Y.	65	70	99	134
N.C.	531	561	624	698
N. Dak.	0	0	0	1
Ohio	80	87	97	111
Okla.	. . .	22	56	138
Oreg.	0	1	1	1
Pa.	86	108	157	194
R.I.	6	7	9	10
S.C.	604	689	782	836
S. Dak.	0	1	0	1
Tenn.	403	431	480	473
Tex.	393	488	621	690
Utah	0	1	1	1
Vt.	1	1	1	2
Va.	632	635	661	671
Wash.	0	2	3	6
W. Va.	26	33	43	64
Wis.	3	2	3	3
Wyo.	0	1	1	2

Source: Austin, Political Facts of the U.S. Since 1789, Table 7.3.

TABLE 5.5 AMERICANS OVER 65 YEARS OF AGE 1870–1920

Census Year	% Total Population 65 Years & Older	% Males 65 Years & Older	% Females 65 Years & Older
1870	2.99	2.97	3.02
1880	3.43	3.40	3.47
1890	3.87	3.86	3.88
1900	4.06	4.02	4.11
1910	4.30	4.18	4.43
1920	4.67	4.61	4.73

Source: Timothy J. Crimmins and Neil Larry Shumsky, American Life, American People (1988), 2:39.

TABLE 5.6 THE TEN MOST POPULOUS STATES AND THEIR POPULATIONS, 1880, 1910

Rank	State	1880	Rank	State	1910
1.	N.Y.	5,082,871	1.	N.Y.	9,113,279
2.	Pa.	4,282,891	2.	Pa.	7,665,111
3.	Ohio	3,198,062	3.	Ill.	5,638,591
4.	Ill.	3,077,871	4.	Ohio	4,767,121
5.	Mo.	2,168,380	5.	Tex.	3,896,542
6.	Ind.	1,978,301	6.	Mass.	3,366,416
7.	Mass.	1,783,085	7.	Mo.	3,293,335
8.	Ky.	1,648,690	8.	Mich.	2,810,173
9.	Mich.	1,636,937	9.	Ind.	2,700,876
10.	Iowa	1,624,615	10.	Ga.	2,609,121

Source: The World Almanac and Encyclopedia 1921 (1920), 446.

TABLE 5.7 MEDIAN AGE AT FIRST MARRIAGE, BY SEX, 1890–1910

Year	Male	Female
1890	26.1	22.0
1900	25.9	21.9
1910	25.1	21.6

Source: John W. Wright, ed., The Universal Almanac 1991 (1990), 196.

TABLE 5.8 MARRIAGES IN THE UNITED STATES 1887, 1896, 1906, 1916

Year	1887	1896	1906	1916
Number	483,069	483,069	853,290	1,040,778

Source: The World Almanac and Encyclopedia 1921, 463.

TABLE 5.9 DIVORCES IN THE UNITED STATES 1887, 1896, 1906, 1916

Year	1887	1896	1906	1916
Number	27,919	42,937	72,062	112,036

Source: The World Almanac and Encyclopedia 1921, 463.

TABLE 5.10 CHIEF CAUSES FOR DIVORCE IN THE UNITED STATES, 1916

Party to Which Granted	Unfaithful	Cruelty	Desertion
Husband	6,850	5,895	16,908
Wife	5,636	24,857	23,082

Source: The World Almanac and Encyclopedia 1921, 463.

TABLE 5.11 LIFE EXPECTANCY AT BIRTH BY RACE AND SEX, 1900–1913

In 1900, life expectancy at birth was about forty-seven years. Most parents did not live long enough to enjoy grandchildren. Only forty-one out of 100 people lived to age sixty-five. That's because in 1900 nearly one in four people died before the age of twenty (compared with one in fifty today). About half of twenty-year-olds lived to age sixty-five. Despite increases in life expectancy at birth, there has been only a one-year increase in life expectancy in older ages. At age eighty-five, life expectancy has grown by just over one year since 1900.

Year	Total			White			Nonwhite		
	Both Sexes	Male	Female	Both Sexes	Male	Female	Both Sexes	Male	Female
1900	47.3	46.3	48.3	47.6	46.6	48.7	33.0	32.5	33.5
1905	48.7	47.3	50.2	49.1	47.6	50.6	31.3	29.6	33.1
1910	50.0	48.4	51.8	50.3	48.6	52.0	35.6	33.8	37.5
1913	52.5	50.3	55.0	53.0	50.8	55.7	38.4	36.7	40.3
1990	75.6	72.1	79.0	76.2	72.7	79.6	71.4	67.7	75.0

Source: Historical Statistics of the United States, Colonial Times to 1957, 25. The first death statistics were collected in the federal Census of 1850, and incomplete reports were made in decennial censuses thereafter. The annual collection and publication of more complete mortality statistics, however, for areas having registration systems did not begin until 1900. These registration areas sent their data to the Bureau of the Census. The death registration area for 1900 consisted of ten states, the District of Columbia, and a number of cities located in nonregistration states. Gradually, the registration area was expanded until 1933, when it covered forty-eight states and the District of Columbia. Figures for 1990 are projections based on middle-mortality assumptions; for details see U.S. Bureau of the Census, Current Population Reports, series P-25, No. 1018. Figures are for blacks; nonwhite figures were unavailable. Statistical Abstract of the United States (1991), 73.

Disease and Death

Victorian America was a deadly place. Life expectancy improved if one lived to middle age, but infancy and childhood were risky periods. Rural Americans were likely to live longer than those in cities, whites outlived nonwhites, and women lived longer than men.

Infant mortality was high, especially in working-class families. In the coal fields of northeastern Pennsylvania, infant mortality was 33%, meaning that one in three infants died before reaching the first year. High rates of death among children, adolescents, and young adults also were prevalent. One demographic estimate claims that 35% to 40% of all American families would be disrupted by death before all the children had left home.

The leading killers were infectious diseases, which were especially deadly in population centers. Besides periodic outbreaks of cholera, yellow fever, and smallpox, diseases such as influenza, pneumonia, typhus, scarlet fever, measles, whooping cough, and especially tuberculosis took a large toll. Three energy-depleting diseases—malaria, hookworm, and pellagra—plagued the poor of the South. The lack of screens made southerners victims of malaria-bearing mosquitoes, the lack of shoes subjected them to hookworm, and diets of corn caused pellagra, a niacin-deficiency disease. In the urban industrial centers of the Northeast, diphtheria, a respiratory condition exacerbated by air pollution, was a problem.

Tuberculosis was the nation's greatest killer before 1915. The "white plague," also called consumption or TB, touched many lives. Doctors first tried to treat it with the so-called heroic therapies—purging, vomiting, sweating, diuresis, and bleeding. Nothing worked. After the Civil War, other therapies were tried. TB patients were often institutionalized in charity hospitals or sanitoriums. The TB industry in New Mexico helped populate and develop the state's economy as new hospitals, boardinghouses, and hotels proliferated with a steady stream of people seeking relief. Other states, such as Colorado and California, touted themselves as places to come for clean air and sunshine.

Tuberculosis also affected local life in a variety of ways. By 1915, most cities had passed ordinances requiring schoolteachers, nurses, and public-health officials to have regular examinations. New laws prohibited public spitting and the public drinking dipper, commonly found in railroad stations, schools, and offices. Glass-tank water coolers and the paper cup replaced them.

The middle class was subject to, or at least preoccupied with, two diseases: dyspepsia and neurasthenia. *Dyspepsia* was a term to describe the distress often associated with overeating: stomach cramps, heartburn, gas, and intestinal disorders. Middle-class men seemed most prone, if advertisements can be trusted, and they were treated with a myriad of diets, purgatives, suppositories, and tonics. Heavy multicourse meals often led to gastric distress. Rotundity ap-

TABLE 5.12 DEATHS PER 100,000 POPULATION IN NEW YORK, BOSTON, PHILADELPHIA, AND NEW ORLEANS (ANNUAL AVERAGES)

Cause	1864–1888	1899–1913
Tuberculosis	365	223
Stomach and intestinal disorders	299	196
Diphtheria	123	58
Typhoid and typhus	66	19
Smallpox	53	25

Source: Stephan Thernstrom, A History of the American People (1989), 467.

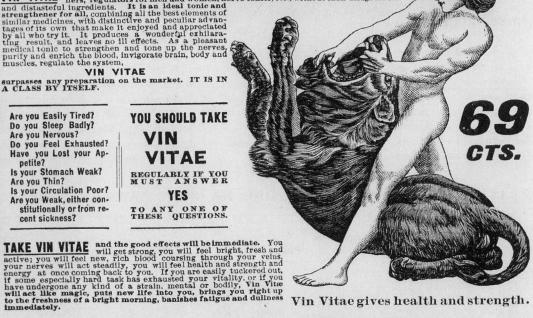
Nostrums and tonics, many containing generous shots of alcohol, to cure all ails were widely available through mail-order houses. In this picture of the 1902 Sears catalog, the "Wine of Life" promises to stimulate the tired and weak, renew the energy of the fatigued, and feed the brain and nerves. (Author's possession)

pears to have been a measure of status and achievement, the national model being Pres. William Howard Taft, who weighed more than 300 pounds.

Neurasthenia was first described by Dr. George Bard in 1881 in a medical treatise entitled *American Nervousness: Its Causes and Consequences*. Symptoms included sick headache, depression, insomnia, fidgetiness, palpitations, impotence, chills, morbid thoughts, and sundry other discomforts. It was treated with bromides, cannabis, opium, and sundry potions. Depending upon the severity or one's tolerance for alcohol or perhaps gullibility, patent medicines such as Baker's Stomach Bitters (about 43% alcohol) and Warner's Safe Tonic (about 36% alcohol) also brought relief. In retrospect, neurasthenia is probably best understood today as a blanket diagnosis for various stress disorders such as psychoneuroses, "a case of the nerves," anxieties associated with upwardly mobile professionals, or female menopausal and male "midlife crisis" syndromes.

Immigration, 1876–1913

One of the greatest mass movements of recorded history occurred during the nineteenth and early twentieth centuries as millions emigrated to the United States in search of economic betterment and political and religious freedom. Beginning in the 1830s, the annual numbers of newcomers swelled to 427,833 by 1854. This figure nearly doubled in 1882 when 788,992 arrived, a figure later eclipsed by the 1,285,349 who entered the United States in 1907, the peak year of the mass immigration experience.

But statistics tell only part of the story. During the Victorian Age, the sources of immigration shifted from the "old" immigrant areas, largely northern and western Europe. The "new" immigrants were Italians, Greeks, Slovaks, Poles, Russians, Austro-Hungarians, and smaller numbers of Asians (first the Chinese until they were excluded in 1882, then the Japanese, and the Filipinos) and Mexicans.

With the influx, a largely Protestant nation became much more diverse as many in this tidal wave of humanity were Greek Orthodox, Roman Catholic, Buddhist, or Jewish. The mixture of different tongues, religions, and ethnic heritages profoundly influenced American life, especially in the large urban centers where immigrants tended to concentrate, but also in the nation's heartland where Germans and Scandinavians clustered.

Whether homesteaders on the Plains or tenement dwellers on New York City's crowded Mulberry Street, mass immigration tested the fundamental premise of American nationality, *E pluribus unum*.

Not all stayed to witness the outcome; about a fourth to a third overall returned to their homelands. In some groups, the return migration reached 50%, as in the case of the Italians, Hungarians, and Slovaks who arrived between 1899 and 1924. About 12% of the Irish and 23% of the Scandinavians recrossed the Atlantic during this period. Mexicans and Canadians, who entered by America's side doors, often came with the intention of returning home.

Besides the diversity they brought to American culture, the most profound impact of the immigrants was on the political process. In most states, only a five-year wait was required before eligibility to vote. State and city governments with large numbers of immigrants

TABLE 5.13 IMMIGRANTS ARRIVING AT PORTS IN THE UNITED STATES, 1878–1902

Year	Boston & Charleston, Mass.	New York City	Philadelphia	Baltimore	San Francisco	All Other Ports	Total United States
1877	7,887	72,942	6,154	3,923	11,255	38,733	141,857
1882	58,186	502,171	36,284	41,739	32,668	116,933	788,992
1892	32,343	489,810	31,102	55,820	6,425	6,446	623,084
1902	39,465	493,262	17,175	39,679	5,271	53,891	648,743

Source: The American Almanac, Year Book, Cyclopedia, and Atlas (1903), 527.

TABLE 5.14 NUMBER OF IMMIGRANTS FROM SELECTED COUNTRIES ARRIVING IN THE UNITED STATES BY DECADE, 1871–1920

Years	Great Britain	Ireland	Scandinavia	Germany	Poland	U.S.S.R. and Baltic States	Italy	China	Japan	Canada and Newfoundland
1871–1880	548,043	436,871	243,016	691,813	12,970	39,284	55,759	123,201	149	383,640
1881–1890	807,357	655,482	656,494	1,452,970	51,876	213,282	307,309	61,711	2,270	393,304
1891–1900	271,538	388,416	371,512	505,152	96,720[a]	505,290	651,893	14,799[c]	25,942[c]	3,311[d]
1901–1910	525,950	399,065	505,324	341,498	n.a.	1,597,306	2,045,877	20,605	129,797	179,226
1911–1920	341,408	146,181	203,452	143,945	n.a.	921,957	1,109,524	21,278	83,837	742,185

Years	Mexico	Australia and New Zealand	Vietnam	Korea	Philippines	Other Asia	Africa	Cuba	Haiti and Dom. Rep.	Other W. Indies
1871–1880	5,162	9,886	n.a.	n.a.	n.a.	n.a.	n.a.	n.a.	n.a.	n.a.
1881–1890	1,913[b]	7,017	n.a.	n.a.	n.a.	n.a.	n.a.	n.a.	n.a.	n.a.
1891–1900	971[e]	2,740	n.a.	n.a.	n.a.	n.a.	n.a.	n.a.	n.a.	n.a.
1901–1910	49,642	11,975	n.a.	n.a.	n.a.	15,800	7,400	n.a.	n.a.	107,500
1911–1920	219,004	12,348	n.a.	n.a.	n.a.	8,100	8,400	n.a.	n.a.	123,400

[a] Data not available for the years 1899 to 1900.
[b] Data not available for the years 1886 to 1890.
[c] Data not available for 1892.
[d] Data not available for the years 1892 and 1893.
[e] Data not available for the years 1891 to 1893.
Source: Austin, Political Facts of the United States Since 1789, Table 7.5.

Ellis Island, New York, was the major entry port for New World immigrants after 1892. The U.S. Immigration Service set up the facility specifically for the processing of newcomers. It was laid out in long corridors where controlled lines flowed through examination rooms to be inspected by doctors, nurses, and officials. On some days, 15,000 passed through the turnstiles, and thousands more waited their turn to be examined. Six million immigrants passed through Ellis Island during the first decade of the twentieth century. Shown here are the many faces of fresh arrivals at Ellis Island, New York, in the 1910s. (Photo by Lewis Hine, courtesy Smithsonian Institution, National Museum of American History, Division of Costume)

TABLE 5.15 THE TOTAL IMMIGRATION RATE BY DECADE, 1871–1910

Period	Total Number (thousands)	Rate per 1000 U.S. Population
1871–1880	2,812	6.2
1881–1890	5,247	9.2
1891–1900	3,688	5.3
1901–1910	8,795	10.4

Source: The Universal Almanac 1991, 203.

TABLE 5.16 DECENNIAL IMMIGRATION TO THE UNITED STATES, 1880–1910

	1880–1889	1890–1899	1900–1909	1910–1919
Total in millions	5.2	3.7	8.2	6.3
Percent of Total From:				
Ireland	12.8	11.0	4.2	2.6
Germany[a]	27.5	15.7	4.0	2.7
United Kingdom	15.5	8.9	5.7	5.8
Scandinavia	12.7	10.5	5.9	3.8
Canada[b]	9.4	0.1	1.5	11.2
Russia	3.5	12.2	18.3	17.4
Austria-Hungary	6.0	14.5	24.4	18.2
Italy	5.1	16.3	23.5	19.4

[a]Continental European boundaries prior to the 1919 settlement.
[b]Canada includes Newfoundland; Canadian immigration was not recorded between 1886 and 1893.
Source: David Ward, Cities and Immigrants (1971), 53.

TABLE 5.17 REGIONAL DISTRIBUTION OF FOREIGN-BORN—PERCENTAGE OF TOTAL FOREIGN-BORN LIVING IN EACH REGION

Region	1870	1890	1910
New England	11.8	12.6	13.6
Middle Atlantic	34.1	30.0	36.1
East North Central	30.2	27.4	23.0
West North Central	12.2	17.0	12.1
South	7.2	5.6	5.4
Mountain	1.4	2.7	3.3
Pacific	3.1	4.6	6.5

Source: Ward, Cities and Immigrants, 67, 72, 74. For Ward's boundaries, see Fig. 2.3, 61.

TABLE 5.18 NATURALIZATION AND CITIZENSHIP, 1900

Year	Naturalized Foreigners	Foreign-Born of Voting Age
1890	2,545,753	4,348,459
1900	2,862,546	5,102,334

became heavily influenced by ethnic voters. Urban political machines rose to power on the strength of ethnic bloc voting; the presidential race of 1884 was said to have been decided on the swing of 10,000 Irish votes in New York.

Large numbers of immigrants entered the United States in the 1890s. By 1900, 316,793 had taken out "first papers," the initial step toward citizenship.

Any alien of "good intentions" and "moral character" who subscribed to the Constitution was entitled to declare his intentions. To do so, the aliens had to appear in District or Supreme Court of the United States or any of its territories, declare their intentions, and renounce forever allegiance to any foreign government. One Irishman is said to have immigrated in 1901 and declared his intentions within ten minutes of arrival in New York.

Aliens must have lived continuously for five years in the United States and within the state or territory of first declaration for at least one year. At least two years also had to lapse between the filing of the first declaration and the taking of the final oath of citizenship.

Soldiers who desired citizenship could do so provided they were at least twenty-one years old, honorably discharged, of good moral character, and had resided in a state for one year.

The citizenship of an American woman who married an alien remained unsettled. Some courts decided that a wife's political status followed that of her husband. So if she married a foreigner, she lost her citizenship and domicile. Other court decisions decided the opposite. Except for inheritance of property, it was generally held that an American woman was not entitled to the rights of citizenship if she married a foreigner.

Under the Constitution, citizenship and the right to vote are separate, and neither is dependent upon the other. Naturalization is a "federal gift," and the national government has the right to say who may or may not be naturalized. The right to vote, on the other hand, is a "state gift." Each state has a right to establish its own voting requirements. Consequently, nationwide variance in voting practices emerged. For example, in some states aliens who had been in the country just six months could vote if they had declared their intention to become citizens, while in others they might have to wait several years.

Housing

Housing during the Victorian Age underwent remarkable changes in design, building types, and methods of construction. Three new housing types emerged: the sod house on the western frontier, the bungalow in the rising suburbs, and the multiple-family apartment house in cities where real estate was expensive. The transportation revolution brought the streetcar suburb and made possible urban residential patterns of segregation by race and class. The size of the house and lot became symbols of status and affluence, or at least pretension.

Homesteading produced the sod house, a one-room dwelling made of the earth's sod containing a small window, a wooden door, and a dirt floor. By 1890, more than a million "soddies" could be found, mostly on the prairies of Kansas and Nebraska. Sod houses replaced dugouts, a temporary hole or cave dug into the side of a hill or ravine with sheets to partition rooms and a stove pipe through the earthen roof for cooking in the winter. Russian, German, and East European settlers brought their knowledge of sod-building techniques to the Plains.

A distinctive feature of housing during this period and one that has dominated American building since is the normative preference for the single detached home for both middle-class and working-class Americans. Between 1890 and 1930, approximately 60 to 80% of all urban housing starts were single-family residences. In most American cities in 1890 (seventeen of the twenty-eight largest), only 5% of the populations was housed in dwellings sheltering three or more families, the definition of a tenement.

In 1886 a worker's cottage, a one-story frame dwelling with a parlor, kitchen, and two bedrooms, could be built in Chicago for $600 (about $8,700 in 1990 prices). A two-story cottage with an indoor bath, fireplace, and three bedrooms cost about twice this amount. Workers' cottages might also be constructed by the householder from house plans or from prefabricated structures purchased from mail-order catalogs. Sears, Roebuck offered forty-four pages of house plans when first issued in 1908 and 146 pages by 1918. Other mail-order houses such as Montgomery Ward, Radford Company, and Aladin Homes in Bay City, Michigan, offered their own plan books. The plans and instructions arrived by mail; the materials by rail. Sears claimed its prefabricated houses could be built in 352 carpenter hours, compared to 583 hours for a conventional cottage.

The bungalow was a new house type that developed out of the housing shortage on the West Coast and spread eastward. By 1915, the bungalow dominated the mail-order business, and the "bungalow craze" lasted until the Great Depression.

The earliest apartment buildings, such as the Hotel Pelham built in Boston in 1855 and the 1869 Stuyvesant "French" Flats of New York City, appealed to young affluent families and bachelors. Elevators made this type of housing convenient and appealing. Large luxury hotels made their rooms into apartments and offered the amenities of hot water, bathrooms, kitchens, and the services of a domestic staff. Gradually, middle- and working-class families gravitated toward apartment living in larger and less-exclusive apartment houses. Units, without the servants and services of the apartment-hotels, ranged in size from an entire floor of a building to a single multipurpose room that included kitchen and sanitation facilities. The streetcar lines carved out corridors for apartment dwellers. Family flats or apartments had three and four rooms. They were built by real estate firms, insurance companies, and private developers; after 1911 Sears, Roebuck sold apartment houses.

Unique residential housing evolved with the peculiar circumstances and conditions of specific environments: in Boston, the "triple-decker," long, rectangular, multifamily buildings, housing one family on each of three floors; tenements like those on New York City's Lower East Side; company town housing like Homestead, near Pittsburgh or Pullman's town in Chicago; boardinghouses and flophouses; or the plain houses of black tenant farmers in the Mississippi Delta, two or three rooms built of rough pine boards with kitchen "lean-tos" and front porch "lean-ons."

New York's tenement district contained some of the worst housing in urban America. Immigrants arrived in the city in such great numbers that they overwhelmed the city's ability to provide for them; overnight, warehouses were turned into tenements. The poorest tenements had no piped water or baths. Shown here is a tenement dwelling of the Chinquanana family, 11 Hamilton Street, New York City, c. 1905. (Photo by Lewis Hine, courtesy Prints and Photographs Division, Library of Congress)

TABLE 5.19 DWELLING UNITS BEGUN IN NONFARM AREAS, BY TYPE OF HOUSING, 1900–1913

Year	Total	One-Family	Two-Family	Multifamily
1900	189	123	31	35
1905	507	336	64	107
1910	387	251	58	79
1913	421	263	72	85

Numbers given are in thousands.
Source: Historical Statistics of the United States, Colonial Times to 1957, 393.

TABLE 5.20 OCCUPIED DWELLINGS AND TENURE OF HOMES, 1890–1910

Year	Total Occup. Units	Number of Persons	Per Occupied Dwelling	% Owner Occupied	% Renter Occupied
1890	12,690,152	62,947,714	5	47.8	52.2
1900	15,963,965	75,994,575	4.8	46.7	52.3
1910	20,255,555	91,972,266	4.5	45.9	54.1

Source: Historical Statistics of the United States, Colonial Times to 1957, 395.

Tenements

In the 1880s and 1890s warehouses, factories, breweries, and residences in America were adapted as multiple family dwellings. New tenements grew up where previous buildings had been razed or where earlier structures had been dragged to the rear of lots as alley houses. Like *apartment building, tenement* was a term used to mean dwellings built to house three or more separate sets of tenants, living independently of one another under one roof and doing their cooking on the premises. Both were associated with dense urban living, but apartment buildings usually (after the 1890s) had private sanitary facilities, whereas tenements often had only communal plumbing.

Tenements came in a variety of shapes and sizes. Large family homes vacated by upwardly mobile families in center-of-the-city neighborhoods could be turned into tenements. Edith Abbott, author of *The Tenements of Chicago* (1936), found these kinds of tenements still expanding in 1910. *Light housekeeping rooms* meant furnished units, usually cheap efficiency apartments for poor workers who did their own cooking. The gas hot plate on a zinc-covered shelf in a bedroom corner became the trademark of widows or single working women who managed such units while living in one of them.

Investors in eastern cities built specially designed "tenement houses," typically three stories high with one family per floor, including the basement. Some had only one room per floor with enclosed stairways to upper floors. In Philadelphia, locals used terms such as *bandboxes* or *father-son-holy-ghost houses* to describe such dwellings. Laborers and newly arrived immigrants and their boarders inhabited these cramped quarters.

As one historian recently observed, the facile image of a tenement owner as an absentee landlord living in lordly style in the suburbs off the rents collected from tenement dwellers is a stereotype. While it is accurate to some extent—some great American fortunes were made or vastly increased by such developments—tenement owners often rose from the same ethnic group as the tenants, living close by and overseeing their property. Italians and Jews, for example, in late nineteenth-century Philadelphia found tenement real estate and proprietorship a convenient avenue of economic mobility.

Despite the preoccupation of contemporary reformers (and historians since), tenements never constituted more than a small fraction of the housing that was built. On New York City's Lower East Side, vast densely crowded slums and vile living conditions did exist, but only in a few other cities could similar tenement districts be found. Instead, multiple-family housing for the urban working class was characterized by all sorts of multiunit dwellings, made of brick, wood, or masonry, and usually three stories or less.

Slums

Slums are associated with late nineteenth-century American cities where swelling populations overwhelmed the capacity of urban governments to provide adequate housing, sanitation, water, electricity, fire protection, and public safety. Lewis Hine's photographs and Jacob Riis's book *How the Other Half Lives* (1890) exposed the hellish conditions in America's best known slum, New York City's Lower East Side. Riis estimated that 330,000 lived in one square mile of the slum or about 986 people per acre. On one tenement block in

No area of New York City was more representative of the city's ethnic diversity than Mulberry Street, shown here. (Courtesy Prints and Photographs Division, Library of Congress)

the Jewish section of the Lower East Side, 2,800 people lived on just over an acre.

Such crowding led to epidemic outbreaks of serious diseases such as smallpox, cholera, measles, typhus, scarlet fever, and diphtheria. Even less dangerous diseases such as chicken pox, mumps, whooping cough, croup, and influenza became killers in densely crowded areas. In 1889, when the national death rate was 17.2 per 1,000 (about 17 people in each 1,000 died annually), New York City's death rate was 25.2. In the slums it was 38; for children under five, 136 per 1,000. In one Chicago slum in 1900, the infant mortality rate was 200 (compared to today's national rate of 9 per 1,000).

Crowding was also the chief cause of poor sanitation. City governments provided for waste collection, but even honest administrations (which were not typical) could not keep up in densely populated areas. Horses compounded the problem, depositing tons of manure on city streets. When the beasts were no longer able to work, their owners removed their harnesses and turned them loose to die on the streets.

Water was often unavailable in the poorest tenements except in shared sinks in hallways. Heavy chemical treatment made it barely drinkable. Street wells and fire hydrants provided runoff water, often contaminated, for some. Children often used these for baths; adults frequented the public bathhouses where hot, clean water was available free or at low cost. (In New York, at least one remained in operation into the 1970s).

Slums bred vice and crime. With 14,000 homeless people on New York City's streets in 1890, many resorted to such crimes as sneak thievery (stealing unwatched property), pocket-picking, purse-snatching, and for the bolder, violent robbery. Strong-arm gangs preyed on New York's slum dwellers as early as the 1850s and defied the police (or paid them protection money), taking their names from their individual neighborhoods: the Five Points, Mulberry Bend, Hell's Kitchen, Poverty Gap, and Whyo gangs. During the 1880s, the homicide rate tripled in American cities, while it declined in German and British cities. By 1900, more sophisticated gangs moved into gambling, opium dens, and prostitution.

CHAPTER 6 Religion

Religion in Victorian America

Between 1870 and 1920, church membership and attendance increased steadily. At the end of the century, thousands of congregations erected church edifices in one of the greatest building booms in American religious history. According to H. C. Carroll, author of *The Religious Forces of the United States,* no nation in the world matched the variety of faiths present in 1900 America.

American Protestantism, led by the Methodists, Baptists, Presbyterians, and Disciples of Christ, constituted a semiofficial American religious establishment. Protestant clergy such as Walter Rauschenbusch, a Baptist minister in Hell's Kitchen, one of New York City's worst slums, and Washington Gladden, a Congregationalist minister highly critical of wealthy American industrialists, as well as nonclerical leaders, fashioned the "social gospel" as Protestantism's response to the massive urban problems of unemployment, poverty, crime, and neglect. In 1879 the Salvation Army, long active among the poor in East London's slums, opened corps and outposts in many American cities.

The Sunday-school movement, revivalism, and the camp meeting were the three most significant aspects of American Protestantism during the Victorian Age. Sunday schools became the means to convert the unchurched and "save the family." With the major push coming from the Baptists, Baraca (for men) and Philathea (for women) classes brought together several million members from thirty-two denominations each year into local and national conventions for teachers. The Sunday school at times seemed to overshadow the congregation and the Sunday-school superintendent could be as important as the local minister.

Revivalism made a spectacular reappearance in the form of William "Billy" Sunday and Dwight Moody. Sunday, from Ames, Iowa, a reformed hard-drinking, woman-chasing baseball star, an outfielder for the Chicago White Stockings (1883–1890), became a fiery evangelist after joining the Presbyterian Church. In Chicago, Sunday met Moody, founder of Moody Bible Institute and a well-known revivalist who preached what he called "old-fashioned gospel." Sunday learned from Moody and then struck out on his own in 1896 to "sell" religion with circus-style parades, marching bands, tent meetings, and large choirs. Millions of Americans were introduced to his "rapid-fire, wisecracking, emotional sermons and tirades in which he mixed slang and baseball terms with his hatred of rum, prostitution, card playing, and gambling."

Black Christians, who had separated themselves from white churches after the Civil War to form their own congregations, found the church a welcome haven in the hostile and segregated environment of the 1890s and thereafter. Institutionally, the black church became the most important agency for bringing social structure and leadership to black populations. By 1919, about 43% of black Americans were church members. But membership numbers understate the importance of the black church, which was, in the words of W. E. B. DuBois, a "social, intellectual, . . . economic [and] religious center of great power."

Roman Catholicism served another group of "outsiders," the immigrant populations. In 1880, Catholics already were the largest single religious group in the nation, with 6.3 million communicants; by 1920, this number had risen to 19.8 million, largely due to the immi-

TABLE 6.1 CHURCH DENOMINATIONS, MEMBERSHIP, AND EDIFICES, 1890–1916

Year	Denominations Reporting	Local Organizations	Members (thousands)	Church Edifices Number	Church Edifices Value (in thousands of dollars)
1890	145	165,151	21,699	142,487	$ 679,426
1906	186	212,230	35,068	192,795	$1,257,576
1916	200	227,487	41,927	203,432	$1,676,601

Source: Historical Statistics of the United States, Colonial Times to 1957 (1961), 228. The definition of a *member* depends upon the denomination. Due to variations, the figures do not furnish an adequate basis for measuring membership growth.

TABLE 6.2 MEMBERSHIP OF SELECTED RELIGIOUS BODIES, 1876, 1890, 1913

Year	Roman Catholic	Presbyterian	Methodist	Southern Baptist
1876	. . .	531	2,224	1,342
1890	. . .	761	3,442	1,236
1913	15,154	1,388	5,402	2,523

Numbers given in thousands.
Source: Historical Statistics of the United States, Colonial Times to 1957, 228–229.

TABLE 6.3 CHURCH CONGREGATIONS BY SELECTED DENOMINATIONS: 1890, 1906, 1916

Denomination	1890	1906	1916
Seventh-Day Adventist	995	1,889	2,011
Northern Baptist Conv	7,902	8,272	8,159
Southern Baptist Conv	16,238	21,104	23,627
National Baptist Conv	12,533	18,534	21,113
Churches of Christ	. . .	2,649	5,570
Congregational Churches	4,868	5,713	5,867
Disciples of Christ	7,246	8,293	8,408
Jewish congregations	533	1,769	1,901
Lutheran Synodical Conf	1,934	3,360	3,621
Methodist Episcopal	25,861	29,943	29,342
Methodist Episcopal South	15,017	17,831	19,220
African Methodist Episcopal	2,481	6,647	6,636
Presbyterian Church in USA	6,712	7,935	9,660
Protestant Episcopal Church	5,018	6,845	7,392
Roman Catholic Church	10,239	12,482	17,487
United Brethren in Christ	3,731	3,732	3,487
Totals	123,198	158,904	175,417

Source: Religious Bodies 1916, (1919), 25.

TABLE 6.4 MEMBERSHIP AND CHANGES IN PRINCIPAL DENOMINATIONS, 1906–1916

This table shows that for the denominations reporting more than a million members, there were few changes in rank with regard to members and numerical increase but significant changes in percent of increase. For example, the Roman Catholic Church ranked first in number of members and in numerical increase, but its rank was thirty-sixth in percent of increase due to a decrease in immigration and the emigration of Italians, Austrians, French, and others who returned to Europe because of World War I. The Russian Orthodox Church stands first in increase because of heavy gains through immigration. Other churches gained because of a more complete enumeration in 1916, such as the Churches of Christ, the Colored Methodist Episcopal Church, the African Methodist Episcopal Zion Church, the National Baptist Convention (African-American), and the Free Will Baptists.

| Denomination | Members 1916 | Increase Over 1906[a] | | Rank According To— | | |
| | | Number | Percent | Members in 1916 | Increase Over 1906 | |
					Number	Percent
Roman Catholic Church	15,721,815	1,511,060	10.6	1	1	36
Methodist Episcopal Church	3,717,785	731,631	24.5	2	2	21
Baptists—National Convention	2,938,579	676,972	29.9	3	4	15
Baptists—Southern Convention	2,708,870	699,399	34.8	4	3	11
Methodist Episcopal, South	2,114,479	475,999	29.1	5	5	16
Presbyterian Church in the United States of America	1,611,251	431,685	36.6	6	6	9
Baptists—Northern Convention	1,232,135	180,030	17.1	7	10	28
Disciples of Christ	1,226,028	243,327	24.8	8	7	20
Protestant Episcopal Church	1,092,821	205,879	23.2	9	8	23
Congregational Churches	791,274	90,794	13.0	10	15	34
Lutheran—Synodical Conference	777,701	117,031	17.7	11	12	26
African Methodist Episcopal	548,355	53,578	10.8	12	21	35
Lutheran—General Council	540,642	78,465	17.0	13	17	29
Latter Day Saints, Church of Jesus Christ	403,388	187,592	86.9	14	9	3
Lutheran—General Synod	370,715	100,494	37.2	15	13	8
Presbyterian Church in the United States	357,769	91,424	34.3	16	14	12
United Brethren in Christ	348,828	74,179	27.0	17	18	19
Reformed Church in the United States	344,374	51,720	17.7	18	22	27
German Evangelical Synod	339,853	46,716	15.9	19	23	32
Churches of Christ	317,937	158,279	99.1	20	11	2
African Methodist Episcopal Zion	257,169	72,627	39.4	21	20	6
Colored Methodist Episcopal	245,749	72,753	42.1	22	19	5
Methodist Protestant	186,908	8,364	4.7	23	38	38
United Norwegian Lutheran Church	176,084	−8,943	−4.8	24	42	41
Lutheran—Joint Synod of Ohio	164,968	41,560	33.7	25	24	13
United Presbyterian	160,726	30,384	23.3	26	25	22
Reformed Church in America	144,929	19,991	16.0	27	29	31
Lutheran—Synod of Iowa	130,793	20,539	18.6	28	28	25
Evangelical Association	120,756	15,858	15.1	29	33	33
Greek Orthodox (Hellenic)	119,871	29,120	32.1	30	26	14
Christian Church (Christian Convention)	118,737	8,620	7.8	31	37	37
Synod for Norwegian Lutheran Church	112,673	4,961	4.6	32	39	39
Church of the Brethren (Conservative)	105,102	28,555	37.3	33	27	7
Russian Orthodox Church	99,681	80,570	421.6	34	16	1
Friends (Orthodox)	92,379	1,218	1.3	35	40	40
United Evangelical	89,774	19,892	28.5	36	30	17
Unitarians	82,515	11,973	17.0	37	35	30
Primitive Baptists	80,311	−22,000	−21.5	38	43	43
Seventh-day Adventists	79,355	17,144	27.6	39	32	18
Cumberland Presbyterian	72,052	−123,718	−63.2	40	44	44
Latter Day Saints, Reorganized Church of Jesus Christ	58,941	18,090	44.3	41	31	4
Universalists	58,566	−5,592	−8.7	42	41	42
Lutheran—United Synod, South	56,656	8,909	18.7	43	36	24
Free Will Baptists	54,833	14,553	36.1	44	34	10

[a] A minus sign (−) denotes decrease.
Source: Religious Bodies 1916, 33.

TABLE 6.5 CHURCH EDIFICES BY SELECTED DENOMINATIONS: 1890, 1906, 1916

In 1916, five denominations accounted for about one-half of all church buildings: Methodist Episcopal Church, National Baptist Convention (African-American), the Southern Baptist Convention, the Methodist Episcopal Church and the Roman Catholic Church. The number of buildings was considerably smaller than the number of congregations. In 1916, nearly one congregation in ten had no building of its own but held its meetings in a hall, schoolhouse, rented building or elsewhere.

Denomination	1890	1906	1916
Seventh-Day Adventist	418	981	1,231
Northern Baptist Conv	7,066	8,244	8,105
Southern Baptist Conv	13,502	18,878	19,770
National Baptist Conv	11,987	17,913	20,146
Churches of Christ	. . .	1,974	4,342
Congregational Churches	4,736	5,792	5,744
Disciples of Christ	5,324	7,066	6,815
Jewish congregations	301	821	874
Lutheran Synodical Conf	1,531	2,899	3,301
Methodist Episcopal	22,844	28,345	28,406
Methodist Episcopal South	12,688	15,933	17,251
African Methodist Episcopal	4,124	6,538	6,302
Presbyterian Church in USA	6,660	8,185	9,068
Protestant Episcopal Church	5,018	6,922	6,726
Roman Catholic Church	8,784	11,881	15,120
United Brethren in Christ	2,837	3,410	3,244
Totals	109,710	147,688	158,361

Source: Religious Bodies 1916, 42–43.

TABLE 6.6 ANNUAL SALARIES OF MINISTERS BY SELECTED DENOMINATIONS: 1906, 1916

The following table gives salaries of ministers engaged in pastoral work only, i.e., those who gave their full time to the church work and who depend for their support upon the salary received. The 1906 averages were provided by the churches. In 1916, the ministers reported salaries themselves, and the average was derived from all those ministers who reported. The denominations reported here had five or more ministers reporting salaries.

Denomination	1906	1916
Seventh-Day Adventist	n.a.	823
Northern Baptist Conv	833	1,166
Southern Baptist Conv	367	1,072
National Baptist Conv	247	572
Congregational Churches	1,042	1,343
Disciples of Christ	587	1,251
Jewish congregations	1,222	1,655
Lutheran Synodical Conf	559	755
Methodist Episcopal	812	1,223
Methodist Episcopal South	714	1,037
African Methodist Episcopal	347	478
Presbyterian Church in USA	1,177	1,474
Protestant Episcopal Church	1,242	1,632
Roman Catholic Church	703	838
United Brethren in Christ	578	912
Average in U.S.	668	1,078

Source: Religious Bodies 1916, 72.

TABLE 6.7 OCCUPATIONS OF MINISTERS IN ADDITION TO PASTORAL WORK SPECIFIED DENOMINATIONS, 1916

Many ministers had to work in other occupations outside the church. The following table shows that 2,658 worked in distinctly rural labor, 526 worked in a business or trade, and 526 engaged in professional occupations.

Denomination	Total	Agents, Clerks, Salesmen, Etc.	Farmers	Laborers	Mechanics, Etc.	Owners, Managers, and Officials (Manufacturing, Trade, Etc.)	Professional Persons and Public Officials	Teachers, Principals, Professors, Etc.	All Other
Total	4,015	165	2,368	200	245	116	130	396	395
Baptists—Southern Convention	1,496	64	1,066	16	55	34	60	135	66
Church of the Brethren (Conservative)	709	22	462	13	26	25	16	34	111
Methodist Episcopal Church	245	20	98	2	19	11	15	44	36
Friends (Orthodox)	172	9	82	4	10	6	3	12	46
Methodist Protestant	163	6	96	4	10	5	4	17	21
Methodist Episcopal, South	59	5	21	3	4	2	7	17	. . .
Wesleyan Methodist	54	4	23	1	10	2	1	3	10
African Methodist Episcopal	743	23	326	127	65	22	14	90	76
African Methodist Episcopal Zion	191	1	89	23	26	6	5	25	16
Colored Methodist Episcopal	183	11	105	7	20	3	5	19	13

Source: Religious Bodies 1916, 71.

TABLE 6.8 MEMBERS BY SEX IN SELECTED DENOMINATIONS, 1906, 1916 (PERCENT)

Women constituted the largest percentage of church members in nearly every denomination. Race seemed to make no difference as the figures for the National Baptist Convention and the African Methodist Episcopal churches reflect similar patterns. Two striking exceptions stand out: in Jewish congregations, males denominated the membership; in Roman Catholic congregations, the percentages of men and women, unlike the national trend, were nearly equal.

Denomination	1906 Male	1906 Female	1916 Male	1916 Female
Seventh-Day Adventist	34.8	65.2	32.9	67.1
Northern Baptist Conv	36.5	63.5	37.8	62.2
Southern Baptist Conv	40.7	59.3	42.0	58.0
National Baptist Conv	37.3	62.7	38.5	61.5
Churches of Christ	41.5	58.5	41.8	58.2

Denomination	1906 Male	1906 Female	1916 Male	1916 Female
Congregational Churches	34.1	65.9	35.7	64.3
Disciples of Christ	39.7	60.3	40.6	59.4
Jewish congregations	n.a.	n.a.	60.7	39.3
Lutheran Synodical Conf	47.4	52.6	47.1	52.9
Methodist Episcopal	37.4	62.6	39.2	60.8
Methodist Episcopal South	40.5	59.5	40.6	59.4
African Methodist Episcopal	36.9	63.1	36.9	63.1
Presbyterian Church in USA	36.5	63.5	39.3	60.7
Protestant Episcopal Church	35.5	64.5	38.6	61.4
Roman Catholic Church	49.3	50.7	48.9	51.1
United Brethren in Christ	40.1	59.9	40.7	59.3
All Denominations	43.5	56.5	43.9	56.1

Source: Religious Bodies 1916, 40–41.

TABLE 6.9 RELIGIOUS STATISTICS BY SIZE OF CITIES: 1890, 1906, 1916

The number of church congregations per capita was greater in rural areas than in the principal cities. In 1916, there was one congregation to every 1,406 people; in rural areas the proportion was one to every 337 people. Despite having only 10.4% of the church organizations and buildings, city congregations had nearly 50% of the total value of church property and almost two-thirds (63.7%) of the total debt on church property.

Census Year and Item	Total for United States, Number or Amount	Principal Cities — Total Number or Amount	Per-cent	Cities of 300,000 and Over Number or Amount	Per-cent	Cities of 100,000 to 300,000 Number or Amount	Per-cent	Cities of 50,000 to 100,000 Number or Amount	Per-cent	Cities of 25,000 to 50,000 Number or Amount	Per-cent	Outside of Principal Cities Number or Amount	Per-cent
1916													
Number of cities in 1910	226	226	. . .	18	. . .	32	. . .	59	. . .	117	. . .	. . .	. . .
Population, 1916 (estimated)	102,017,312	33,334,907	32.7	17,535,610	17.2	6,098,864	6.0	5,013,690	4.9	4,686,743	4.6	68,682,405	67.3
Congregations	227,487	23,713	10.4	9,387	4.1	4,906	2.2	4,416	1.9	5,004	2.2	203,774	89.6
Members	41,926,854	15,291,245	36.5	7,686,860	18.3	2,751,017	6.6	2,495,401	6.0	2,357,967	5.6	26,635,609	63.5
Church edifices	203,432	21,237	10.4	8,022	3.9	4,468	2.2	4,081	2.0	4,666	2.3	182,195	89.6
Value of church property	$1,676,600,582	$824,216,547	49.2	$455,163,720	27.1	$132,128,314	7.9	$117,754,240	7.0	$119,170,273	7.1	$852,384,035	50.8
Debt of church property	$164,864,899	$104,939,733	63.7	$59,871,085	36.3	$17,203,445	10.4	$14,875,414	9.0	$12,989,789	7.9	$59,925,166	36.3
Value of parsonages	$218,846,096	$70,705,345	32.3	$33,561,881	15.3	$11,536,549	5.3	$12,107,585	5.5	$13,499,330	6.2	$148,140,751	67.7
Expenditures	$328,809,999	$134,054,781	40.8	$65,458,544	19.9	$24,095,290	7.3	$21,856,544	6.6	$22,644,403	6.9	$194,755,218	59.2
Sunday schools	194,759	22,251	11.4	8,186	4.2	4,820	2.5	4,293	2.2	4,952	2.5	172,508	88.6
Sunday school scholars	19,935,890	5,114,669	25.7	2,107,119	10.6	1,015,243	5.1	976,361	4.9	1,015,946	5.1	14,821,221	74.3
1906													
Number of cities in 1900	160	160	. . .	11	. . .	27	. . .	40	. . .	82	. . .	. . .	. . .
Population, 1906 (estimated)	85,837,372	23,632,153	27.5	11,519,172	13.4	5,319,883	6.2	3,322,515	3.9	3,470,583	4.0	62,205,219	72.5
Congregations	212,230	17,906	8.4	6,455	3.0	4,127	1.9	3,264	1.5	4,060	1.9	194,324	91.6
Members	ª35,068,058	ª11,478,706	32.7	ª5,503,800	15.7	ª2,556,182	7.3	ª1,687,073	4.8	ª1,731,651	4.9	ª23,589,352	67.3
Church edifices	192,795	16,517	8.6	5,770	3.0	3,903	2.0	3,075	1.6	3,769	2.0	176,278	91.4
Value of church property	$1,257,575,867	$612,833,315	48.7	$340,430,592	27.1	$110,357,931	8.8	$82,271,671	6.5	$79,773,121	6.3	$644,742,552	51.3
Debt on church property	$108,050,946	$70,262,228	65.0	$40,063,622	37.1	$14,052,537	13.0	$8,076,972	7.5	$8,069,097	7.5	$37,788,718	35.0
Value of parsonages	$143,495,853	$43,098,769	30.0	$20,497,480	14.3	$8,000,528	5.6	$6,583,350	4.6	$8,017,411	5.6	$100,397,084	70.0
Sunday schools	178,214	17,568	9.9	6,058	3.4	4,149	2.3	3,316	1.9	4,045	2.3	160,646	90.1
Sunday school scholars	14,685,997	3,603,872	24.5	1,511,809	10.3	802,078	5.5	610,933	4.2	679,052	4.6	11,082,125	75.5
1890													
Number of cities	124	124	. . .	7	. . .	21	. . .	30	. . .	66	. . .	. . .	. . .
Population	62,947,714	13,989,568	22.2	5,803,144	9.2	3,894,816	6.2	2,022,822	3.2	2,268,786	3.6	48,958,146	77.8
Congregations	165,151	10,241	6.2	3,117	1.9	2,840	1.7	1,859	1.1	2,425	1.5	154,910	93.8
Members	ª21,699,432	ª5,832,696	26.9	ª2,379,183	11.0	ª1,634,068	7.5	ª856,324	3.9	ª963,121	4.4	ª15,866,736	73.1
Church edifices	142,487	9,722	6.8	2,950	2.1	2,693	1.9	1,805	1.3	2,274	1.6	132,765	93.2
Value of church property	$679,426,489	$313,537,247	46.1	$146,916,242	21.6	$79,422,746	11.7	$42,693,776	6.3	$44,504,483	6.6	$365,889,242	53.9

ª Corrected figures.
Source: Religious Bodies 1916, 119.

TABLE 6.10 TOTAL MEMBERS IN AFRICAN-AMERICAN CONGREGATIONS BY STATES 1890, 1906, 1916

African-American members were concentrated in the southern United States. In 1916, the table shows about 79% of all black church members located in southern states.

State	African-American Congregations					
	1916		1906		1890	
	Number	Rank	Number	Rank	Number	Rank
Total[a]	4,602,805	. . .	[b]3,691,844	. . .	[c]2,676,549	. . .
Ga.	581,724	1	507,235	1	341,433	1
Ala.	475,140	2	397,243	2	297,161	3
S.C.	447,084	3	394,179	3	317,020	2
Miss.	403,881	4	359,001	4	224,404	6
Tex.	396,157	5	227,685	7	186,038	7
N.C.	359,380	6	283,717	6	290,755	4
Va.	328,230	7	307,463	5	238,617	5
Ark.	242,199	8	146,319	10	106,445	10
La.	209,843	9	187,500	8	108,872	9
Tenn.	196,022	10	172,972	9	131,015	8
Fla.	138,055	11	106,141	12	64,337	12
Ky.	137,211	12	117,373	11	92,768	11
Pa.	108,672	13	60,476	14	26,753	15
Md.	87,179	14	72,532	13	58,566	13
Mo.	75,792	15	50,165	15	42,452	14
Okla.	59,967	16	[d]29,153	20	[d]880	33
Ill.	49,633	17	32,058	18	15,635	19
Ohio	49,053	18	33,719	17	19,827	17
D.C.	48,377	19	47,119	16	22,965	16
N.Y.	43,921	20	30,857	19	17,216	18
N.J.	38,839	21	28,015	21	12,720	21
W. Va.	21,858	22	14,949	24	7,160	23
Kans.	21,842	23	17,273	23	9,750	22
Ind.	20,883	24	23,133	22	13,404	20
Del.	10,989	25	10,879	25	6,595	24
Mass.	8,610	26	9,402	26	3,638	27
Mich.	8,469	27	3,235	30	3,957	25
Calif.	6,906	28	4,564	27	3,720	26
Conn.	6,292	29	4,492	28	1,624	30
Iowa	5,313	30	4,108	29	2,643	28
Colo.	4,448	31	2,507	31	1,171	31
Minn.	2,629	32	1,453	33	958	32
R.I.	2,590	33	2,114	32	1,999	29
Nebr.	2,070	34	1,007	34	399	34
Wash.	1,204	35	614	35	66	39
Wis.	575	36	310	36	268	36
Ariz.	532	37	208	38	155	37
Mont.	310	38	135	40	32	42
Oreg.	291	39	160	39	291	35
N. Mex.	231	40	221	37	62	40
Wyo.	189	41	45	41	154	38
Utah	86	42	30	43	7	43
Idaho	50	43	. . .	. . .	. . .	. . .
N.H.	39	44	20	45	. . .	. . .
S. Dak.	18	45	38	42	. . .	. . .
Maine	17	46	25	44	45	41
Nev.	5	47	. . .	. . .	. . .	. . .

[a] North Dakota and Vermont had no African-American congregations in 1916, 1906, or 1890.
[b] Corrected figures.
[c] Corrected figures; also includes 2,562 members of the Roman Catholic African-American congregations, not distributed by states.
[d] Oklahoma and Indian Territory combined.
Source: Religious Bodies 1916, 139.

grants from eastern and southern Europe. American Catholicism fractured into a jigsaw pattern of national parishes—of Poles, Italians, Slovaks, and other nationalities.

In addition to providing houses of worship in various languages, the Catholic parishes became neighborhood community centers with schools, orphanages, homes for the elderly, newspapers, and even cemeteries. Lay organizations, such as sodalities, altar societies, literary groups, and temperance societies met the special needs of the parish community.

More than 2 million poor, working-class, east European and Russian Jewish immigrants arrived between 1880 and 1920. They organized synagogues and founded mutual-benefit societies to provide a range of services from funerals to recreation. They built Jewish hospitals, formed young-adult groups (YMHAs), and founded orphanages, settlement houses, and homes for the elderly. Jewish leaders also founded Hebrew and Talmud schools and established yeshivas or seminary schools to train rabbis. Jews also sustained a host of labor, Zionist, socialist, and other cultural institutions, including a large Yiddish press and theater.

CHAPTER 7 Government

Victorian Politics

The Victorian period began with a contested presidential election that had to be settled by Congress. Voter turnout remained heavy, at least in national election years.

Much of the political activity during these years was conducted in terms of values. The politics of moral purity raged in debates over activities to be allowed on Sundays. There was a proliferation of "blue laws," especially in the South, local statutes that regulated what could be bought and sold on Sundays. In areas with large immigrant populations, the language of instruction in education and the place of parochial schooling created conflict. Moral issues produced intense voter interest. Bread-and-butter issues or the economy seemed far less significant than whose values gained ascendancy in American politics.

In the North, much of the conflict arrayed the white, Protestant, Anglo-Saxon majority against a growing minority of immigrant Jews and Catholics of southern- and eastern-European descent. Entire elections hinged upon the ethnic vote in a few states. Local elections often became heated affairs over value-laden issues. Economic issues did surface, most notably with the rise of the People's (Populist) Party in 1892. But politics-as-usual during this age was the politics of morality, not of class.

In the South, the politics of race added additional fuel to the fires of moral argument. Newly enfranchised African Americans became the focus of political attention until the 1890s, when many southern states amended their constitutions to deny them the right to vote. Not until the Voting Rights Act of 1965 was the franchise extended again to black citizens in most of the South.

TABLE 7.1 AMERICAN PRESIDENTIAL CONVENTIONS, 1876–1912

Year	Party	City	Dates	Nominees	Number of Ballots
1876	Dem.	St. Louis	Jun. 27–29	Samuel J. Tilden, Thomas A. Hendricks	2
1876	Rep.	Cincinnati	Jun. 14–16	[a] Rutherford B. Hayes, William A. Wheeler	7
1880	Dem.	Cincinnati	Jun. 22–24	Winfield S. Hancock, Willliam H. English	2
1880	Rep.	Chicago	Jun. 2–8	[a] James A. Garfield, Chester A. Arthur	36
1884	Dem.	Chicago	Jul. 8–11	[a] Grover Cleveland, Thomas A. Hendricks	2
1884	Rep.	Chicago	Jun. 3–6	James G. Blaine, John A. Logan	4
1888	Dem.	St. Louis	Jun. 5–7	Grover Cleveland, Allen G. Thurman	1
1888	Rep.	Chicago	Jun. 19–25	[a] Benjamin Harrison, Levi P. Morton	8
1892	Dem.	Chicago	Jun. 21–23	[a] Grover Cleveland, Adlai E. Stevenson	1
1892	Rep.	Minneapolis	Jun. 7–10	Benjamin Harrison, Whitelaw Reid	1
1896	Dem.	Chicago	Jul. 7–11	William J. Bryan, Arthur Sewal	5
1896	Rep.	St. Louis	Jun. 16–18	[a] William McKinley, Garret A. Hobart	1
1900	Dem.	Kansas City	Jul. 4–6	William J. Bryan, Adlai E. Stevenson	1
1900	Rep.	Philadelphia	Jun. 5–6	[a] William McKinley, Theodore Roosevelt	1
1904	Dem.	St. Louis	Jul. 6–9	Alton S. Parker, Henry G. Davis	1
1904	Rep.	Chicago	Jun. 21–23	[a] Theodore Roosevelt, Charles W. Fairbanks	1
1908	Dem.	Denver	Jul. 7–10	William J. Bryan, John W. Kern	1
1908	Rep.	Chicago	Jun. 16–19	[a] William H. Taft, James S. Sherman	1
1912	Dem.	Baltimore	Jun. 25–Jul. 2	[a] Woodrow Wilson, Thomas R. Marshall	46
1912	Rep.	Chicago	Jun. 18–22	William H. Taft, James S. Sherman, Nicholas M. Butler[b]	1

[a] Elected president and vice-president
[b] The 1912 Republican Convention nominated James S. Sherman, who died on Oct. 30th. The Republican National Committee subsequently selected Nicholas M. Butler to receive the Republican electoral votes for vice-president.
Source: Erik W. Austin, *Political Facts of the United States Since 1789*, (1986), Table 3.10.

TABLE 7.2　NATIONAL VOTER TURNOUT, 1876–1912, (PERCENT)

Year	President	U.S. Representative	U.S. Senator[a]
1876	82.4	81.4	. . .
1878	. . .	64.6	. . .
1880	80.5	79.2	. . .
1882	. . .	65.3	. . .
1884	78.8	77.6	. . .
1886	. . .	63.8	. . .
1888	80.9	81.5	. . .
1890	. . .	64.8	. . .
1892	76.1	74.8	. . .
1894	. . .	67.4	. . .
1896	79.6	77.8	. . .
1898	. . .	60.0	. . .
1900	73.6	72.3	. . .
1902	. . .	55.5	. . .
1904	65.4	63.6	. . .
1906	. . .	52.0	. . .
1908	65.5	63.4	. . .
1910	. . .	51.3	. . .
1912	59.0	55.7	. . .

[a] As stipulated in Article 1, Section 3, of the Constitution, only one-third of the Senate is elected every two years. Consequently, turnout figures represent only those states electing senators. Elections usually result in only two-thirds of the states having a senatorial election in any election year. Before the adoption of the Twenty-Second Amendment (April 8, 1913), U.S. senators were selected by the state legislatures in most states, so turnout data are inappropriate.
Source: Austin, *Political Facts of the United States Since 1789,* Table 3.12.

TABLE 7.3　PRESIDENTS OF THE VICTORIAN AGE

No.	President	Birthdate	Birthplace	Year Married	Wife's Name	Religion
19	Hayes	Oct. 4, 1822	Delaware City, Ohio	1852	Lucy Ware Webb	Methodist
20	Garfield	Nov. 19, 1831	Cuyahoga Cty, Ohio	1858	Lucretia Rudolph	Disciples of Christ
21	Arthur	Oct. 5, 1830	Franklin Cty, Vt.	1859	Ellen Lewis Herndon	Episcopalian
22, 24	Cleveland	Mar. 18, 1837	Essex Cty, N.J.	1886	Frances Folsom	Presbyterian
23	Harrison	Aug. 20, 1833	Hamilton Cty, Ohio	1853	Caroline Lavinia Scott	Presbyterian
				1896	Mary Scott	
24	McKinley	Jan. 29, 1843	Trumbull Cty, Ohio	1871	Ida Saxton	Methodist
26	Roosevelt	Oct. 27, 1858	New York, N.Y.	1883	Alice Lee	Dutch
				1886	Edith Kermit Carow	Reformed
27	Taft	Sep. 15, 1857	Cincinnati, Ohio	1886	Helen Herron	Unitarian
28	Wilson	Dec. 28, 1856	Staunton, Va.	1885	Ellen Louise Axsen	Presbyterian

Source: The World Almanac and Encyclopedia 1914, (1913), 722.

Presidential Elections: Candidates, Votes, and Issues, 1876–1912

Presidential Election of 1876

The winner of the 1876 presidential election had to be decided by the House of Representatives. The election created a constitutional crisis when it ended in a stalemate with no clear winner. The significance of this election had far-reaching consequences for the nation.

Official returns reached Washington with two sets of ballots from each of three states, Florida, South Carolina, and Louisiana (one electoral vote in Oregon was also contested); Republicans and Dem-

ocrats each claimed that their candidate had won. Because the Constitution never planned for such an occurrence, a special commission was appointed to resolve the dispute, composed of eight Republicans and seven Democrats, including five members of each house of Congress and five members of the Supreme Court.

Voting 8 to 7 along strict party lines, the commission gave the Republican Hayes all three disputed states and the victory in the electoral college by one vote. The Democratic-controlled House had

TABLE 7.4 1876 ELECTION

Key Issues: Hayes, a three-term Ohio governor known for his impeccable integrity, ran against Tilden, the New York reform governor who had made a reputation cleaning up the notorious Tweed political machine. Both men held conservative economic views. Cooper and the Greenbacks wanted to expand the supply of currency. The election is unique in American political history, in having been thrown into the House of Representatives. The dealmaking preceding the House vote brought about the end of Reconstruction when Hayes took office.

Party	Candidate	Popular Vote	Percent	Electoral Vote
Republican	Rutherford B. Hayes (Ohio) and William A. Wheeler (N.Y.)	4,034,311	47.95	185
Democratic	Samuel J. Tilden (N.Y.) and Thomas A. Hendricks (Ind.)	4,288,546	50.97	184
ªGreenback	Peter Cooper (N.Y.)	75,973	0.90	. . .
Other		14,271	0.17	. . .
	Total votes 8,413,101			
	Tilden plurality 254,235			

ªThe Greenback Party platform called for an expansion of the money supply.
Source: Except for 1876, voter summaries are from Richard B. Morris, ed, *Encyclopedia of American History* (1982), 305–325; for 1876 and key issues, see John W. Wright, *The Universal Almanac* (1991), 75–80.

TABLE 7.5 1880 ELECTION

Key Issues: With the Civil War and Reconstruction behind, no major issues divided the major parties. The Democrats sought to shake its stigma as the party of secession and treason by nominating the Union General Hancock. Garfield grounded his campaign in a protectionist tariff. Republican strength in the Midwest and West and Democratic strength in the South resulted in a closely contested election and a plurality of less than 10,000 votes for Garfield out of more than 9 million votes cast. The Republicans regained control of the House for the first time since 1874. Four months into his term, Garfield was shot by a disappointed office seeker.

Party	Candidate	Popular Vote	Percent	Electoral Vote
Republican	James A. Garfield (Ohio) and Chester A. Arthur (N.Y.)	4,449,053	48.31	214
Democratic	Winfield S. Hancock (Pa.) and William H. English (Ind.)	4,442,035	48.23	155
Greenback	James B. Weaver (Iowa) and Benjamin J. Chambers (Tex.)	308,578	3.35	. . .
Other		10,305	0.11	. . .
	Total votes 9,209,971			
	Garfield plurality 7,018			

Source: Morris, ed., *Encyclopedia of American History (1982). The Universal Almanac (1991).*

TABLE 7.6 1884 ELECTION

Key Issues: The private lives and morals of the candidates took front-page headlines in a campaign notable for mudslinging. Blaine had previously denied before a congressional committee a charge of accepting bribes from a railroad company, and Republicans chided Cleveland for fathering a son out of wedlock. A popular campaign refrain of Democratic partisans was "Blaine! Blaine! James G. Blaine! Continental liar from the state of Maine!" The Republican faithful responded with: "Ma! Ma! Where's my Pa? Gone to the White House. Ha! Ha! Ha!" Still, Cleveland, known for his independence and integrity in public life, claimed the votes of many liberal Republicans and reformers unable to swallow Blaine. Cleveland carried all of the southern states as well as the key swing states of Indiana, New Jersey, Connecticut, and New York. He became the first Democrat elected president since the Civil War. During this colorful election, a Presbyterian minister making a campaign speech for Blaine in New York made the famous association of the Democratic Party with "Rum, Romanism, and Rebellion," insulting Irish Catholics and other critical voters in New York. Cleveland carried his home state of New York and its thirty-six electoral votes but by less than 1,200 votes. Some argue that the Irish vote gave Cleveland New York and the presidency. The Republicans gained eighteen seats in the House, but that body still remained under Democratic control (since 1882).

Party	Candidate	Popular Vote	Percent	Electoral Vote
Democratic	Grover Cleveland (N.Y.) and Thomas A. Hendricks (Ind.)	4,911,017	48.67	219
Republican	James G. Blaine (Maine) and John A. Logan (Ill.)	4,848,334	48.25	182
Greenback	Benjamin F. Butler (Mass.)	175,370	1.74	. . .
Prohibition	John P. St. John (Kans.)	150,369	1.49	. . .
Other		3,619	0.04	. . .
	Total votes 10,088,709			
	Cleveland plurality 62,683			

to approve the outcome, however, so the crisis was still not over. In a series of meetings, a group of prominent northern and southern politicians and businessmen came to an informal agreement that was satisfactory to the congressional leadership.

The Compromise of 1877 included various unwritten commitments, some of which were later disputed: northern support for investment in the South; a vague agreement by northern and southern conservatives to support a "lily-white" Republican Party in the South in the form of future federal appointments; and an end to Reconstruction. According to the bargain, the Democrats would accept the Republican Hayes as the winner in return for his withdrawal of all remaining northern troops from the South and a declaration that Reconstruction was officially over. Many southern Democrats readily supported the compromise because it meant the ouster of the Republicans in their states and the opportunity for them to check the political power of newly enfranchised blacks. Others, Democrats and Republicans, voted for the compromise because of a general lack of interest in the issues of the Civil War and Reconstruction and the desire to put political dissension behind them.

African Americans became casualties of this reconciliation, gradually losing at the hands of Democratic politicians what they had so recently gained from Republican reformers: the vote and the protection it gave them as a political constituency.

TABLE 7.7   1888 ELECTION

Key Issues: This was the first campaign in U.S. political history to be waged on the issue of the tariff. Cleveland hailed tariff reform as central to his administration, while the Republicans campaigned for a high tariff on imported goods and the promise of generous pensions to Civil War veterans. The Prohibition Party ran its first candidates for the presidency. Despite fears that tariff reform meant the end to protectionism, Cleveland managed to win the manufacturing states of New Jersey and Connecticut as well as most of the South. Despite winning the popular vote, Cleveland lost the election. On the eve of the election, the "Murchison letter," involving the British minister to the United States, Sackville-West, seemed to indicate British interference in America's internal affairs. Although the letter was a fraud, Sackville-West blundered in his handling of the affair, costing the Democrats many Irish-American votes. Harrison carried key protariff swing states, Indiana and New York, by slight margins to win the election in the electoral college.

Party	Candidate	Popular Vote	Percent	Electoral Vote
Republican	Benjamin Harrison (Ind.) and Levi P. Morton (N.Y.)	5,444,337	47.82	233
Democratic	Grover Cleveland (N.Y.) and Allen G. Thurman (Ohio)	5,540,050	48.66	168
Prohibition	Clinton B. Fisk (N.J.)	250,125	2.19	. . .
Union Labor	Alson J. Streeter (Ill.)	146,897	1.29	. . .
Other		2,808	0.02	. . .
	Total votes 11,384,217			
	Cleveland plurality 95,713			

TABLE 7.8   1892 ELECTION

Key Issues: Cleveland and Harrison again battled over the tariff, which the Republicans sharply increased in 1890. Neither man tapped into the growing agrarian and Populist discontent. Weaver got the Populist vote. Campaigning for free silver, he became the first third-party candidate to win electoral votes since the Civil War. Cleveland improved on his 1884 and 1888 showings to win the most decisive presidential victory in twenty years. He carried the swing states of New York, New Jersey, Connecticut, and Indiana as well as traditionally Republican strongholds of Illinois, California, and Wisconsin. Democrats secured control of both houses of Congress.

Party	Candidate	Popular Vote	Percent	Electoral Vote
Democratic	Grover Cleveland (N.Y.) and Adlai E. Stevenson (Ill.)	5,554,414	46.04	277
Republican	Benjamin Harrison (Ind.) and Whitelaw Reid (N.Y.)	5,190,802	43.02	145
Populist	James B. Weaver (Iowa) and James G. Field (Va.)	1,027,329	8.43	22
Prohibition	John Bidwell (Calif.)	271,058	2.25	. . .
Other		21,164	0.18	. . .
	Total votes 12,064,767			
	Cleveland plurality 363,612			

In resolving the crisis, an official end came to the process begun under Abraham Lincoln of reconstituting the Union. The resolution also allowed the Democratic Party to oust the Republicans from political control in three states, Florida, South Carolina, and Louisiana, and ultimately to destroy the political power and civil rights of blacks all over the "redeemed" South.

The Populists

After the Civil War, farm prices in the United States drifted steadily downward as farmers wrote one of the most extraordinary chapters in the history of American agriculture, bringing 431 million more acres of virgin land under cultivation between 1870 and 1900. Staple crop production of corn, wheat, and cotton increased 150%, but despite their success, farmers were not a people of plenty. Especially hard hit were farmers in debt because, as commodity prices fell, it became more difficult to meet mortgage payments or to get credit to expand production. In the southern states, a legacy of plantation agriculture, soil depletion, and the maldistribution of land combined with the scarcity of credit to produce the crop-lien system, sharecropping, and extensive poverty. Financial panic in 1873, a persistent drought in the Southeast in the late 1880s, and a deep depression between 1893 and 1896 led to foreclosures on family

TABLE 7.9   1896 ELECTION

Key Issues: The money question was the dominant issue of this election. The Democrats made a grab for the agrarian vote by nominating Bryan and adopted key elements of the Populist program, especially the call for free silver. Bryan delivered his eloquent "Cross of Gold" speech, closing with his challenge to the advocates of the gold standard: "You shall not press down upon the brow of labor this crown of thorns; you shall not crucify mankind upon a cross of gold." Progold Democrats nominated their own candidate, John M. Palmer (Illinois) for president and Simon B. Buckner (Kentucky) for vice president on a National Democratic Party ticket. McKinley led the protariff, progold Republicans, and Mark Hanna, the Cleveland industrialist named Republican Party manager, outspent the Democrats by almost 12 to 1. The Socialist Labor National Convention met in New York and nominated Charles H. Matchett (New York) for president and Matthew Maguire (New Jersey) for vice president. Bryan failed to garner the labor vote and carried no state north of Virginia or east of Missouri. Republican victories in key states broke Bryan's hold on the agricultural South and West. The Republicans retained control of both houses of Congress, which they had won in 1894.

Party	Candidate	Popular Vote	Percent	Electoral Vote
Republican	William McKinley (Ohio) and Garret A. Hobart (N.J.)	7,035,638	50.88	271
Democratic/ Populist	William J. Bryan (Nebr.) and Democ. Arthur Sewal (Maine)	6,467,946	46.78	176
National Democrat	John M. Palmer (Ill.)	131,529	0.95	. . .
Prohibition	Joshua L. Levering (Md.)	141,676	1.02	. . .
Socialist Labor National Convention	Charles Matchett	36,454	0.26	. . .
Other		13,969	0.41	. . .
	Total votes 13,827,212			
	McKinley plurality 567,692			

farms and stirred farmers and other laborers to political action. Farmers began to search for political solutions to their problems, first with the Patrons of Husbandry (Grangers) in the 1870s, more fraternal and social than political at first, and then the Northern and Southern Farmer's Alliances of the 1880s. In 1892, the Southern and Northern Alliances merged to form the People's Party, or the Populists, as they were called.

At their first exploratory gathering in Topeka, Kansas, in 1890, Mary Elizabeth Lease fired the assembled group with this exhortation: "What you farmers need to do is raise less corn and more hell!" Lease elaborated on her demands:

> We want money, land and transportation. We want the abolition of the national banks, and we want the power to make loans direct from the government. We want the accursed foreclosure system wiped out. . . . We will stand by our homes and stay by our firesides by force if necessary, and we will not pay our debts to the loanshark companies until the government pays its debts to us.

The Populists produced one of the most successful third-party efforts in American political history. In 1892, the Populists won the governorship and legislature of Kansas, took control of four midwestern states, held their own national convention, and nominated James Weaver for president. Despite having gained nearly 9% of the popular vote and twenty-two electoral votes in 1892, the Populists decided to abandon their third-party effort and united with the Democrats in 1896 behind William Jennings Bryan and a platform of free silver. Bryan lost, farm prices began to rise, and efforts to get urban-industrial labor's support failed, leading to the collapse of the Populists as an organized party. Yet many of their proposed reforms were later enacted by other political parties and accepted by American society as a whole.

TABLE 7.11   1904 ELECTION

Key Issues: Roosevelt seized the initiative from the Democrats on the issue of reform with his campaigns against "malefactors of great wealth." The Democrats veered to the right by nominating the lackluster Parker, a judge with close ties to Wall Street. Parker spurned Bryan Democrats by renouncing free silver. The Democratic platform assailed the trusts and called for supplementary powers for the Interstate Commerce Commission. The People's National Convention met at Springfield, Illinois, and nominated Thomas E. Watson for president and Thomas H. Tibbles (Nebraska) for vice president. Roosevelt won a landslide victory based largely on his own personality and popularity. The Democrats won only thirteen states, none outside the South. The Republicans retained control of both houses of Congress.

Party	Candidate	Popular Vote	Percent	Electoral Vote
Republican	Theodore Roosevelt (N.Y.) and Charles W. Fairbanks (Ind.)	7,628,834	56.41	336
Democratic	Alton B. Parker (N.Y.) and Henry G. Daws (W. Va.)	5,084,401	37.60	140
Socialist	Eugene V. Debs (Ind.)	402,460	2.98	. . .
Prohibition	Silas C. Swallow (Pa.)	259,257	1.92	. . .
Populist	Thomas E. Watson (Ga.)	114,753	0.85	. . .
Other		33,724	0.25	. . .
	Total votes 13,523,429			
	Roosevelt plurality 2,544,433			

TABLE 7.10   1900 ELECTION

Key Issues: The Democrats made imperialism the focus; Republicans stressed the "full dinner pail" as symbolic of the administration's success. Eugene V. Debs, a founder of the Socialist Party, ran for the first time as a candidate on the Socialist ticket (he also ran in 1904, 1908, 1912, and 1920). In a replay of the previous election, Bryan tried to unite the silver interests in the West and South with supporters of the gold standard in a coalition against imperialism, which the Democratic platform called the "paramount issue." But voters would not change horses in a time of prosperity, and McKinley won. Bryan carried only the solid South and four silver states in the West and was defeated in the silver states of Kansas, South Dakota, Utah, Wyoming, and his home state of Nebraska. Significant Republican majorities led both houses of Congress.

Party	Candidate	Popular Vote	Percent	Electoral Vote
Republican	William McKinley (Ohio) and Theodore Roosevelt (N.Y.)	7,219,530	51.82	292
Democratic	William J. Bryan (Nebr.) and Adlai E. Stevenson (Ill.)	6,358,071	45.64	155
Prohibition	John C. Woolley (Ill.)	209,166	1.50	. . .
Socialist	Eugene V. Debs (Ind.)	94,768	0.68	. . .
Other		50,232	0.36	. . .
	Total votes 13,931,767			
	McKinley plurality 861,459			

TABLE 7.12   1908 ELECTION

Key Issues: The enormously popular Roosevelt declined to run. Under his leadership, forest and mineral lands and water-power sites had come under federal protection for the first time. Taft, Roosevelt's secretary of war and handpicked successor, debated Bryan over who was better qualified to bring about Theodore Roosevelt's progressive program. Bryan abandoned silver and courted labor but ran a lackluster, losing campaign. Again Bryan carried the South. But the appeal of Roosevelt's reform programs helped the Republicans in the West, and Taft's background as a Yale graduate and federal jurist enabled him to carry the East as well. Republicans kept control of both houses of Congress.

Party	Candidate	Popular Vote	Percent	Electoral Vote
Republican	William H. Taft (Ohio) and James S. Sherman (N.Y.)	7,679,006	51.58	321
Democratic	William J. Bryan (Nebr.) and John W. Kern (Ind.)	6,409,106	43.05	162
Socialist	Eugene V. Debs (Ind.)	420,820	2.83	. . .
Prohibition	Eugene W. Chafin (Ill.)	252,683	1.70	. . .
Other		125,979	0.85	. . .
	Total votes 14,887,594			
	Taft plurality 1,269,900			

TABLE 7.13 1912 ELECTION

Key Issues: Taft's conservatism and political incompetence led Roosevelt to challenge him from within the party. Frustrated in his efforts to wrest the nomination from Taft, Roosevelt ran a third-party campaign. The election became a contest between Roosevelt and Wilson and their respective conceptions of progressivism. Roosevelt's New Nationalism stood for strong federal regulations to control the trusts and big businesses. Wilson's New Freedom sought instead to break them up and invigorate competition through energetic application of antitrust laws. The Progressives advocated a broad array of social reforms: tariff revision; stricter regulation of industrial combinations; direct election of U.S. senators; nationwide preferential primaries for presidential candidates; referendum, initiative, and recall; women's suffrage; prohibition of child labor; and minimum-wage standards for working women. Democrats emphasized the primacy of the states in such matters. Though he gained fewer votes than did Bryan in 1908, Wilson took advantage of the split in the Republican ranks to win a decisive plurality of the vote. He won convincing victories in traditional Democratic states but was able to win most traditionally Republican states, too. Roosevelt won only six states, including California, which he carried by fewer than 200 votes. Taft claimed Utah and Vermont. The Democrats also won control of both houses of Congress, their best overall showing since the Civil War.

Party	Candidate	Popular Vote	Percent	Electoral Vote
Democratic	Woodrow Wilson (N.J.) and Thomas Marshall (Ind.)	6,286,214	41.83	435
Progressive	Theodore Roosevelt (N.Y.) and Hiram Johnson (Calif.)	4,126,020	27.45	88
Republican	William H. Taft (Ohio) and James S. Sherman (N.Y.)	3,483,922	23.18	8
Socialist	Eugene V. Debs (Ind.)	897,011	5.97	. . .
Other		235,354	1.57	. . .
	Total votes 15,028,521			
	Wilson plurality 2,160,194			

TABLE 7.14 THE HAYES ADMINISTRATION

Title	Name	Years
President	Rutherford B. Hayes	1877–1881
Vice President	William A. Wheeler	1877–1881
Secretary of State	William B. Evarts	1877–1881
Secretary of Treasury	John Sherman	1877–1881
Secretary of War	George W. McCrary	1877–1879
	Alex Ramsey	1879–1881
Attorney General	Charles Devens	1877–1881
Postmaster General	David M. Key	1877–1880
	Horace Maynard	1880–1881
Secretary of Navy	Richard W. Thompson	1877–1880
	Nathan Goff, Jr.	1881
Secretary of Interior	Carl Schurz	1877–1881

Source: John W. Wright, ed., *The Universal Almanac* (1991), 88.

TABLE 7.15 THE GARFIELD ADMINISTRATION

Title	Name	Years
President	James A. Garfield	1881
Vice President	Chester A. Arthur	1881
Secretary of State	James G. Blaine	1881
Secretary of Treasury	William Windom	1881
Secretary of War	Robert T. Lincoln	1881
Attorney General	Wayne MacVeagh	1881
Postmaster General	Thomas L. James	1881
Secretary of Navy	William H. Hunt	1881
Secretary of Interior	Samuel J. Kirkwood	1881

Source: John W. Wright, ed., *The Universal Almanac* (1991), 88.

TABLE 7.16 THE ARTHUR ADMINISTRATION

Title	Name	Years
President	Chester A. Arthur	1881–1885
Vice President	None	
Secretary of State	F. T. Frelinghuysen	1881–1885
Secretary of Treasury	Charles J. Folger	1881–1884
	Walter Q. Gresham	1884
	Hugh McCulloch	1884–1885
Secretary of War	Robert T. Lincoln	1881–1885
Attorney General	Benjamin H. Brewster	1881–1885
Postmaster General	Timothy O. Howe	1881–1883
	Walter Q. Gresham	1883–1884
	Frank Hatton	1884–1885
Secretary of Navy	William H. Hunt	1881–1882
	William E. Chandler	1882–1885
Secretary of Interior	Samuel J. Kirkwood	1881–1882
	Henry M. Teller	1882–1885

Source: John W. Wright, ed., *The Universal Almanac* (1991), 88.

TABLE 7.17 THE CLEVELAND ADMINISTRATION

Title	Name	Years
President	Grover Cleveland	1885–1889
Vice President	Thomas A. Hendricks	1885–1889
Secretary of State	Thomas F. Bayard	1885–1889
Secretary of Treasury	Daniel Manning	1885–1887
	Charles S. Fairchild	1887–1889
Secretary of War	William C. Endicott	1885–1889
Attorney General	Augustus H. Garland	1885–1889
Postmaster General	William F. Vilas	1885–1888
	Don M. Dickinson	1888–1889
Secretary of Navy	William C. Whitney	1885–1889
Secretary of Interior	Lucius Q. C. Lamar	1885–1888
	William F. Vilas	1888–1889
Secretary of Agriculture	Norman J. Colman	1889

Source: John W. Wright, ed., *The Universal Almanac* (1991), 88.

TABLE 7.18 THE BENJAMIN HARRISON ADMINISTRATION

Title	Name	Years
President	Benjamin Harrison	1889–1893
Vice President	Levi P. Morton	1889–1893
Secretary of State	James G. Blaine	1889–1892
	John W. Foster	1892–1893
Secretary of Treasury	William Windom	1889–1891
	Charles Foster	1891–1893
Secretary of War	Redfield Proctor	1889–1891
	Stephen B. Elkins	1891–1893
Attorney General	William H. H. Miller	1889–1891
Postmaster General	John Wanamaker	1889–1893
Secretary of Navy	Benjamin F. Tracy	1889–1893
Secretary of Interior	John W. Noble	1889–1893
Secretary of Agriculture	Jeremiah M. Rusk	1889–1893

Source: John W. Wright, ed., *The Universal Almanac* (1991), 88.

TABLE 7.19 THE CLEVELAND ADMINISTRATION

Title	Name	Years
President	Grover Cleveland	1893–1897
Vice President	Adlai E. Stevenson	1893–1897
Secretary of State	Walter Q. Gresham	1893–1895
	Richard Olney	1895–1897
Secretary of Treasury	John G. Carlisle	1893–1897
Secretary of War	Daniel S. Lamont	1893–1897
Attorney General	Richard Olney	1893–1895
	James Harmon	1895–1897
Postmaster General	Wilson S. Bissell	1893–1895
	William L. Wilson	1895–1897
Secretary of Navy	Hilary A. Herbert	1893–1897
Secretary of Interior	Hoke Smith	1893–1896
	David R. Francis	1896–1897
Secretary of Agriculture	Julius S. Morton	1893–1897

Source: John W. Wright, ed., *The Universal Almanac* (1991), 88.

TABLE 7.20 THE MCKINLEY ADMINISTRATION

Title	Name	Years
President	William McKinley	1897–1901
Vice President	Garret A. Hobart	1897–1901
	Theodore Roosevelt	1901
Secretary of State	John Sherman	1897–1898
	William R. Day	1898
	John Hay	1898–1901
Secretary of Treasury	Lyman J. Gage	1897–1901
Secretary of War	Russell A. Alger	1897–1899
	Elihu Root	1899–1901
	Robert Bacon	1909
Attorney General	Joseph McKenna	1897–1898
	John W. Griggs	1898–1901
	Philander C. Knox	1901
Postmaster General	James A. Gary	1897–1898
	Charles E. Smith	1898–1901
Secretary of Navy	John D. Long	1897–1901
Secretary of Interior	Cornelius N. Bliss	1897–1899
	Ethan A. Hitchcock	1899–1901
Secretary of Agriculture	James Wilson	1897–1901

Source: John W. Wright, ed., *The Universal Almanac* (1991), 88.

TABLE 7.21 THE THEODORE ROOSEVELT ADMINISTRATION

Title	Name	Years
President	Theodore Roosevelt	1901–1909
Vice President	Charles Fairbanks	1905–1909
Secretary of State	John Hay	1901–1905
	Elihu Root	1905–1909
Secretary of Treasury	Lyman J. Gage	1901–1902
	Leslie M. Shaw	1902–1907
	George B. Cortelyou	1907–1909
Secretary of War	Elihu Root	1901–1904
	William H. Taft	1904–1908
	Luke E. Wright	1908–1909
Attorney General	Philander C. Knox	1901–1904
	William H. Moody	1904–1906
	Charles J. Bonaparte	1906–1909
Postmaster General	Charles E. Smith	1901–1902
	Henry C. Payne	1902–1904
	Robert J. Wynne	1904–1905
	George B. Cortelyou	1905–1907
	George von L. Meyer	1907–1909
Secretary of Navy	John D. Long	1901–1902
	William H. Moody	1902–1904
	Paul Morton	1904–1905
	Charles J. Bonaparte	1905–1906
	Victor H. Metcalf	1906–1908
	Truman H. Newberry	1908–1909
Secretary of Interior	Ethan A. Hitchcock	1901–1907
	James R. Garfield	1907–1909
Secretary of Agriculture	James Wilson	1901–1909
Secretary of Labor and Commerce	George B. Cortelyou	1903–1904
	Victor H. Metcalf	1904–1906
	Oscar S. Straus	1906–1909
	Charles Nagel	1909

Source: John W. Wright, ed., *The Universal Almanac* (1991), 88.

TABLE 7.22 THE TAFT ADMINISTRATION

Title	Name	Years
President	William H. Taft	1909–1913
Vice President	James S. Sherman	1909–1913
Secretary of State	Philander C. Knox	1909–1913
Secretary of Treasury	Franklin MacVeagh	1909–1913
Secretary of War	Jacob M. Dickinson	1909–1911
	Henry L. Stimson	1911–1913
Attorney General	George W. Wickersham	1909–1913
Postmaster General	Frank H. Hitchcock	1909–1913
Secretary of Navy	George von L. Meyer	1909–1913
Secretary of Interior	Richard A. Ballinger	1909–1911
	Walter L. Fisher	1911–1913
Secretary of Agriculture	James Wilson	1909–1913
Secretary of Labor and Commerce	Charles Nagel	1909–1913

Source: John W. Wright, ed., *The Universal Almanac* (1991), 89.

Biographies of Victorian Age Presidents

Rutherford B. Hayes, Nineteenth President (1877–1881)

Rutherford Birchard Hayes, the nineteenth president of the United States, was born on October 4, 1822, in Delaware, Ohio, where he was raised by his mother. After attending Harvard Law School, he established a successful law practice in Cincinnati in 1849. First as a Whig and then (after 1854) as a Republican, he served as city solicitor (1858–61) and governor of Ohio (1868–72), winning a third term in 1875. The following year the Republicans turned to Hayes as a scandal-free candidate and nominated him for president. He actually lost in the popular vote to Samuel Tilden, the Democrat, but Republicans in Congress disputed enough state vote totals to put "Rutherfraud" into office with the support of southern Democrats. Despite party factionalism and Democratic control of both houses of Congress, the Hayes administration put an end to military occupation of the South by withdrawing the last few remaining federal troops from South Carolina in 1877. Hayes also made progress toward civil service reform. He took conservative positions on issues of labor and finance, calling out federal troops to suppress the railroad strike of 1877 and vetoing the Bland-Allison silver coinage act (1878; enacted over his veto). After his presidency, Hayes worked quietly for charitable causes until his death on January 17, 1893.

James A. Garfield, Twentieth President (1881)

Called "the last log cabin president," James Abram Garfield was born near Orange, Ohio, on November 19, 1831. Like Rutherford B. Hayes, Garfield was raised by his mother. After he graduated from Williams College in 1856, he became president of Western Reserve Electric Institute (later Hiram College), 1857–61, was admitted to the bar, and elected to the Ohio Senate as a Republican (1859). During the Civil War, at age 30, he was the youngest general in the Union army. He distinguished himself at Shiloh, Middle Creek, Kentucky, and Chickamauga. Garfield left the army in 1864 to enter Congress, where he served until the Republicans nominated him for president in 1880, as a dark-horse compromise between Grant and James G. Blaine. Garfield defeated General Winfield Scott Hancock by less than one percent of the popular vote in a campaign stressing tariffs. Republicans, hungry for political patronage jobs, swarmed to Garfield, demanding appointments for their rival "Stalwart" (Grant supporters) and "Half-Breed" (opponents of Grant) factions. After only four months in office, Garfield was shot in a train station by Charles J. Guiteau, a disappointed Stalwart office-seeker. Garfield died 80 days later, on September 19, 1881, the second presidential assassination, ending the second-shortest presidency.

Chester A. Arthur, Twenty-first President (1881–1885)

The only president never elected to any political office (other than the vice presidency), Chester Alan Arthur, a preacher's son, was born in Fairfield, Vermont, on October 5, 1829. After graduation from Union College (1848), he was admitted to the New York State bar. He was an ardent abolitionist and a true machine politician, who worked for Republican candidates in New York and enjoyed several patronage jobs during the Civil War. President Ulysses S. Grant appointed him collector of the Port of New York in 1871, and in 1879 President Rutherford B. Hayes removed him in the name of reform. In 1880 "Half-Breed" Republicans nominated Arthur for vice president, and he became president after the death of Garfield. "The office of Vice President is a greater honor than I ever dreamed of attaining," he said. Arthur signed the Pendleton Act (1883), which laid the foundation for the present civil service system, used a treasury surplus to begin the rebuilding of the U.S. Navy, and vetoed a Chinese exclusion bill. Arthur ignored Republican calls for spoils and was consequently denied renomination in 1884. He lost a Senate race in New York and died two years later, on November 18, 1886. He was the last of three presidents who held office in the single year 1881.

Grover Cleveland, Twenty-second and Twenty-fourth President (1885–1889; 1893–1897)

The only president to serve two nonconsecutive terms, Stephen Grover Cleveland, a minister's son, was born in Caldwell, New Jersey, on March 18, 1837. He studied law in Buffalo and was admitted to the New York bar in 1859. He demonstrated little active interest in politics until Buffalo elected him mayor in 1881, and the next year Cleveland became governor. His fight against corruption in Tammany Hall, the New York City regular Democratic organization, made him the choice as Democratic reform candidate for president in 1884. During the election campaign, backers of James G. Blaine, the Republican candidate, accused Cleveland of fathering an illegitimate child. His open acknowledgment blunted the effect of the accusation and he won anyway—by 0.3 percent of the vote—but not before the Republicans came up with the popular campaign chant "Ma! Ma! Where's my Pa?/Gone to the White House/ Ha! Ha! Ha!" As the first Democratic president after the Civil War, Cleveland pushed for civil-service reform and lower tariffs. In the first White House wedding, he married Frances Folsom in 1886. During his first presidency, he took a conciliatory attitude toward the South. His vetoes of over two-thirds of the bills presented to him (mostly private pension bills) and a proposal to reduce the tariff (1887) led to his defeat by Harrison in 1888. Again elected in 1892, Cleveland underwent a secret operation to remove his cancerous upper jaw. His tight-money policies did nothing to help the depression after the Panic of 1893. By sending federal troops into Illinois to break up the Pullman strike (1894) and allowing Attorney General Olney to use a railroad attorney as special counsel to the government, he angered labor. As an anti-imperialist, he withdrew the U.S. treaty of annexation of Hawaii (1893), although he recognized the republic the following year. In 1896, he supported William McKinley, a Republican, for president. "I have tried so hard to do right," Cleveland said on his deathbed in Princeton, New Jersey, on June 24, 1908.

Benjamin Harrison, Twenty-third President (1889–1893)

Benjamin Harrison was born on August 20, 1833, at the North Bend, Ohio, farm of his grandfather William Henry Harrison, the ninth president. He graduated from Miami University (1852), was admitted to the Ohio bar (1853), and took up the law in Indianapolis before joining the Union army in 1862. Harrison finished the Civil War a brigadier general and returned to Indiana, where he became a prominent Republican. He was defeated for governor in 1876 but elected U.S. senator in 1881. In the Senate he opposed Cleveland's vetoes of pension bills and supported civil-service reform. A "colorless compromise candidate" for president, Harrison won the 1888 election despite receiving fewer popular votes than Grover Cleveland. During his administration, Harrison acquiesced to the "Billion Dollar Congress" of free-spending Republicans who escalated Civil War pensions, transportation subsidies, naval construction, and patronage. While he was president, the Congress also passed the McKinley Tariff Act, the Sherman Anti-Trust Act, and the Sherman Silver Purchase Act (all 1890); Secretary of State James G. Blaine's vigorous foreign policy was the mark of Harrison's administration, which oversaw the admission of six new states. Renominated in 1892, he was defeated by Cleveland, and resumed his law practice. He taught at Stanford University and became chief counsel for Venezeula in a boundary dispute with Britain before his death, on March 13, 1901. Harrison referred to the White House as "my jail."

William McKinley, Twenty-fifth President (1897–1901)

The last Civil War veteran to become president, William McKinley was born on January 29, 1843, in Niles, Ohio, the son of an iron founder. He studied at Allegheny College, but dropped out to become a post office clerk. When the Civil War began, he volunteered as a private, seeing action at South Mountain, Antietam, Winchester, and Cedar Creek before being mustered out as a 22-year-old major. McKinley studied law in Albany, New York, and was admitted to the Ohio bar in 1867. He was elected to Congress in 1876. In Congress he sponsored the unpopular McKinley Tariff Act (1890) and lost his reelection bid on this issue. In 1891 he was elected governor of Ohio, and reelected in 1893. Ohio millionaire Marcus Hanna, McKinley's political manager, who had engineered the two governor's terms for him, bankrolled McKinley's run for the presidency in 1896. Running on a sound-money (gold standard) and protective tariff platform, with the slogan a "full dinner pail," he defeated William Jennings Bryan, who ran on a free-silver platform. He won the election with the first popular majority since Grant's reelection in 1872. Strongly pro-business, McKinley raised the tariff to its highest level in U.S. history (Dingley Tariff, 1897), supported the Gold Standard Act (1900) and the annexation of Hawaii (July 7, 1898), and led the country into the Spanish-American War (1898). By acquiring the Philippines, Puerto Rico, and Guam as a result of the war with Spain, the United States became a world power. He went on to proclaim the "open-door" policy in China. He again defeated Bryan for president in 1900, by an even greater margin, again using "a full dinner pail" as his slogan. He was enjoying great popularity when anarchist Leon Czolgosz shot him in Buffalo, New York. McKinley died two weeks later on September 14, 1901.

Theodore Roosevelt, Twenty-sixth President (1901–1909)

Theodore Roosevelt was born in New York City on October 22, 1858, the only president born there. A small, sickly child plagued by asthma, Roosevelt overcame a pampered youth to live what he called the "strenuous life": he boxed, hiked, hunted, rode horses, and climbed the Matterhorn. For rich gentlemen of his day, politics was not considered a suitable vocation, but Roosevelt wanted "to be of the governing class." He graduated from Harvard (1880), read law briefly, and took up historical writing (*The Naval War of 1812,* 1882; *The Winning of the West,* 1889–96). After his mother and his first wife, Alice Lee, died in 1884, Roosevelt lived for a time on a ranch in the Dakotas. In 1886 he married Edith Kermit Carow, and they established a country home in Oyster Bay, New York. In 1886 he ran unsuccessfully for mayor of New York City, but achieved fame as a successful U.S. civil service commissioner (1889–95) and president of the board of police commissioners of New York City (1895–97). During the Spanish-American War, Roosevelt left a job at the Navy Department to lead the "Rough Riders" volunteer regiment in Cuba, achieving glory in the Battle of San Juan Hill. Elected governor of New York in 1898, his reform administration upset the Republican political machine, whose bosses arranged to have him nominated as McKinley's running mate in 1900. Roosevelt learned of McKinley's death while on a mountain-climbing expedition; he was elected in his own right in 1904. The youngest president at 42, "T.R." promised a Square Deal between capital and labor. He mounted well-known campaigns against monopolistic practices of big business and successfully arbitrated major strikes. In 1904 "Teddy"'s popularity soared when he humbled billionaire J. P. Morgan in the Northern Securities case. He gained a reputation as a "trust-buster," but distinguished between "good" and "bad" trusts. His most notable domestic achievements were progressive laws to regulate railroads, inspect food and drugs, and create more than 150 million acres of national parks and forests. No less active in foreign policy, Roosevelt promoted a corollary to the Monroe Doctrine that promised that the United States would intervene to prevent European involvement in Latin America. For helping to end the Russo-Japanese War, Roosevelt became the first American to win the Nobel Prize, but he regarded the Panama Canal as his greatest achievement. He kept his pledge not to seek a third term in 1908—but in 1912 he ran against his own chosen successor, William Howard Taft. He failed to win his party's nomination (while surviving an assassination attempt) but won more than four million votes as the Progressive, or Bull Moose, candidate, thereby denying Taft a second term. During World War I, Roosevelt bitterly denounced Woodrow Wilson's policy of neutrality. After the United States entered the war in 1917, Wilson denied Roosevelt's request to lead troops in France. Roosevelt's four sons fought there; Quentin, the youngest, was killed in action. In the midst of plans for another run at the White House, Roosevelt died suddenly of a cardiac embolism on January 6, 1919. "No President has ever enjoyed himself as much as I have enjoyed myself," he said.

William Howard Taft, Twenty-seventh President (1909–1913)

By far the largest president at more than 330 pounds, William Howard Taft was born in Cincinnati, Ohio, on Sept. 15, 1857. He graduated from Yale in 1878, Cincinnati Law College in 1880, and then began his practice in Cincinnati. He was assistant county prosecutor (1881–82, 1885–86), collector of internal revenue, first district of Ohio (1882–83), superior court judge (1887–90), and U.S. solicitor general under Harrison (1890–92). "I always had my plate right side up when offices were falling," Taft wrote. In 1900, President William McKinley appointed him president of the commission to govern the Philippines. President Theodore Roosevelt appointed him secretary of war in 1904. Taft traveled around the world as Roosevelt's emissary, becoming T.R.'s personal choice as Republican nominee in 1908. As president, Taft tried to carry on Roosevelt's policies, most notably a vigorous enforcement of antitrust laws (Standard Oil and American Tobacco trusts were dissolved during his term), but he divided the Republican party by alienating progressives from conservative "Stand-Patters" over tariff and conservation issues. Roosevelt became dissatisfied with Taft's leadership and challenged him unsuccessfully for the Republican nomination in 1912, then outpolled him as a third-party candidate in the election, giving Woodrow Wilson the victory. Taft, always more comfortable as a jurist, taught law at Yale until he was appointed chief justice of the United States (1921–30). On the Supreme Court, his labor decisions curtailed the Clayton Act, permitted injunctions in labor disputes, subjected labor unions to lawsuits, and invalidated Congressional legislation to impose a tax on the interstate products of child labor. Taft died on March 8, 1930. Never nostalgic about his stint in the White House, Taft once said, "I don't remember that I ever was President."

Woodrow Wilson, Twenty-eighth President (1913–1921)

Born on Dec. 28, 1856, in Staunton, Virginia, the son of a Presbyterian minister, Thomas Woodrow Wilson graduated from Princeton (1879), studied law at the University of Virginia (1880), and was admitted to the bar in 1881. He was the first southern president since Andrew Jackson. Probably dyslexic, Wilson had difficulty learning to read; yet he became the one of the best-educated presidents ever to hold the office. In 1885 he completed a notable doctoral thesis at Johns Hopkins entitled *Congressional Government*. He taught history at Bryn Mawr (1885–88) and Wesleyan (1888–90, and became professor of jurisprudence and political economics at Princeton (1890–1902). He was highly respected in his field and became a widely sought public lecturer. Wilson attracted the attention of New Jersey Democratic bosses after he was elected Princeton's president in (1902–10), and they persuaded him to run for governor. His term (1911–12) was marked by progressive stances in which he turned on the party bosses and sponsored antimachine reforms. In 1912 the Democrats nominated Wilson for president, and he won, with ex-president Theodore Roosevelt and President William Howard Taft splitting the Republican vote. His first administration was noted for such reforms as the Underwood Tariff, the Federal Reserve Act (1913), the Federal Trade Commission, and the Clayton Antitrust Act (1914). Restoring competition to the monopoly-plagued economy was the goal of Wilson's "New Freedom."

Presidential Assassinations

Two presidents were assassinated during the Victorian period: James A. Garfield and William McKinley. Both these assassinations had major policy implications, one in domestic and the other in foreign affairs.

On July 2, 1881, Garfield was shot in a Washington railway station by Charles Guiteau, a deranged lawyer frustrated because he had not received a federal job after working in Garfield's successful election campaign. Not seriously injured at first, the president lingered for seventy-nine days while doctors attempted to remove a bullet from his back. Finally succumbing to infection, he died on September 19.

Since the 1870s, the spoils system of filling federal appointments had been under attack. Reformers argued that dispensing jobs to the party faithful led to corruption and incompetence in office. Instead, they urged that appointments and promotions be based upon merit, rather than connections. Galvanized by Garfield's assassination at the hands of a discontented job seeker, Congress passed the Pendleton Civil Service Act late in 1882, and Pres. Chester Arthur signed it into law in 1883.

The act outlawed political contributions by officeholders and created the Civil Service Commission to supervise competitive examinations for government positions. Often considered one of the major political accomplishments of the period, the impact of civil-service reform was ambiguous. It did lay the foundation for a professional civil service, but it destroyed the means to finance party politics and increased candidates' dependence for campaign funds upon large special interests.

After just four months as president, James Garfield was assassinated. Charles Guiteau, a preacher and bill collector who had worked for the Republican Party but had not been rewarded with a government job, shot the president on July 2, 1881, in a Washington, D.C., train station. After lingering in great pain for eleven weeks, Garfield died on September 19. Shortly thereafter Congress passed legislation (Pendleton Act) that laid the basis for the present civil-service system of federal appointments. (Courtesy Prints and Photographs Division, Library of Congress)

TABLE 7.23 MAJORITY LEADERS OF THE UNITED STATES HOUSE OF REPRESENTATIVES, 1899–1915

Name	State	Party	Congresses	Years Served
Sereno E. Payne[a]	N.Y.	Republican	56th–61st	1899–1911
Oscar W. Underwood	Ala.	Democrat	62nd–63rd	1911–1915

[a]Sereno Payne was the first House member to be officially designated majority leader. Previously, the chairman of the Ways and Means Committee was looked upon as floor leader. Occasionally the speaker of the House had designated someone other than the Ways and Means chairman to serve as leader. The speaker selected the Majority Leader until 1911. After a "revolt" against Speaker Cannon in 1909–1910, House members took on the authority of selecting a leader through party caucuses or conferences.
Source: Austin, *Political Facts of the United States Since 1789,* Table 1.13.

TABLE 7.24 MAJORITY WHIPS OF THE UNITED STATES HOUSE OF REPRESENTATIVES, 1899–1915

Name	State	Party	Congresses	Years Served
James A. Tawney	Minn.	Republican	56th–58th	1899–1905
James E. Watson	Ind.	Republican	59th–60th	1905–1909
John W. Dwight	N.Y.	Republican	61st	1909–1911
. . .	. . .	. . .	62nd	1911–1913
Thomas M. Bell	Ga.	Democrat	63rd	1913–1915

Source: Austin, *Political Facts of the United States Since 1789,* Table 1.4.

TABLE 7.25 MINORITY LEADERS OF THE UNITED STATES HOUSE OF REPRESENTATIVES, 1899–1919[a]

Name	State	Party	Congresses	Years Served
James D. Richardson	Tenn.	Democrat	56th–57th	1899–1903
John Sharp Williams	Miss.	Democrat	58th–60th	1903–1909
Champ Clark	Mo.	Democrat	61st	1909–1911
James R. Mann	Ill.	Republican	62nd–65th	1911–1919

[a]Although first identifiable as early as 1883, the position of minority leader became officially recognized in 1899. After 1911, the selection was made by the party conferences or caucuses, with the choice usually being the candidate the minority party had nominated for the speakership of the House.
Source: Austin, *Political Facts of the United States Since 1789,* Table 1.15.

TABLE 7.26 MINORITY WHIPS OF THE UNITED STATES HOUSE OF REPRESENTATIVES, 1899–1915

Name	State	Party	Congresses	Years Served
Oscar W. Underwood	Ala.	Democrat	56th	1899–1901
James T. Lloyd	Mo.	Democrat	57th–60th	1901–1909
. . .	. . .	. . .	61st	1909–1911
John W. Dwight	N.Y.	Republican	62nd	1911–1913
Charles H. Burke	S. Dak.	Republican	63rd	1913–1915

Source: Austin, *Political Facts of the United States Since 1789,* Table 1.6.

Note: In tables below, d. = died, s. = seated, r. = resigned, t.a. = temporarily appointed.

TABLE 7.27 FORTY-FOURTH CONGRESS

Mar. 4, 1875 to Mar. 3, 1877

President of The Senate	President Pro Tempore of The Senate	Speakers of The House of Representatives
Henry Wilson	Thomas W. Ferry	Michael C. Kerr Samuel J. Randall

Alabama

Senators	Representatives
George E. Spencer (R) George T. Goldthwaite (D)	Taul Bradford (D) John Caldwell (D) William H. Forney (D) Jeremiah Haralson (R) Charles Hays (R) Goldsmith W. Hewitt (D) Burwell B. Lewis (D) Jeremiah N. Williams (D)

Arkansas

Senators	Representatives
Powell Clayton (R) Stephen W. Dorsey (R)	Lucien C. Gause (D) Thomas M. Gunter (D) William F. Slemons (D) William W. Wilshire (R)

California

Senators	Representatives
Aaron A. Sargent (R) Newton Booth (Anti-Monopolist)	John K. Luttrell (D) Horace F. Page (R) William A. Piper (D) Peter D. Wigginton (D)

Colorado

Senators	Representative
Jerome B. Chaffee (R) s. 1876 Henry M. Teller (R) s. 1876	James B. Belford (R) s. 1877

Connecticut

Senators	Representatives
Orris S. Ferry (R, D) d. Nov. 1875 James E. English (D) ta. 1875 William H. Barnum (D) s. 1876 William W. Eaton (D)	William H. Barnum (D) r. May 1876 George M. Landers (D) James Phelps (D) Henry H. Starkweather (R) d. Jan. 1876 John T. Wait (R) s. 1876 Levi Warner (D) s. 1876

Delaware

Senators	Representative
Thomas F. Bayard (D) Eli Saulsbury (D)	James Williams (D)

(continued)

TABLE 7.27 (continued)

Mar. 4, 1875 to Mar. 3, 1877

President of The Senate	President Pro Tempore of The Senate	Speakers of The House of Representatives
Henry Wilson	Thomas W. Ferry	Michael C. Kerr Samuel J. Randall

Florida

Senators	Representatives
Simon B. Conover (R) Charles W. Jones (D)	Jesse J. Finley (D) s. 1876 William J. Purman (R) Josiah T. Walls (R) r. Apr. 1876

Georgia

Senators	Representatives
Thomas M. Norwood (D) John B. Gordon (D)	James H. Blount (D) Milton A. Candler (D) Philip Cook (D) William H. Felton (D) Henry R. Harris (D) Julian Hartridge (D) Benjamin H. Hill (D) William E. Smith (D) Alexander H. Stephens (D)

Illinois

Senators	Representatives
John A. Logan (R) Richard J. Oglesby (R)	William B. Anderson (D) John C. Bagby (R) Horatio C. Burchard (R) Alexander Campbell Joseph G. Cannon (R) Bernard G. Caulfield (D) John R. Eden (D) Charles B. Farwell (R) r. May 1876 Greenbury L. Fort (R) Carter H. Harrison (D) William Hartzell (D) Thomas J. Henderson (R) Stephen A. Hurlbut (R) John V. Le Moyne (R) s. 1876 William R. Morrison (D) William A. J. Sparks (D) William M. Springer (D) Adlai E. Stevenson (D) Richard H. Whiting (R) Scott Wike (D)

Indiana

Senators	Representatives
Oliver H. P. T. Morton (R) Joseph E. McDonald (D)	John H. Baker (R) Nathan T. Carr (D) s. 1876 Thomas J. Cason (R) James L. Evans (R) Benoni S. Fuller (D) Andrew H. Hamilton (D) William S. Haymond (D) William S. Holman (D) Andrew Humphreys (D) s. 1876 Morton C. Hunter (R) Michael C. Kerr (D) d. Aug. 1876

Indiana

Senators	Representatives
	Franklin Landers (D) Jeptha D. New (D) Milton S. Robinson (R) James D. Williams (D) r. Dec. 1876

Iowa

Senators	Representatives
George G. Wright (R) William B. Allison (R)	Lucien L. Ainsworth (Anti-Monopolist) John A. Kasson (R) George W. McCrary (R) James W. McDill (R) S. Addison Oliver (R) Henry O. Pratt (R) Ezekiel S. Sampson (R) John Q. Tufts (R) James Wilson (R)

Kansas

Senators	Representatives
John J. Ingalls (R) James M. Harvey (R)	William R. Brown (R) John R. Goodin (D) William A. Phillips (R)

Kentucky

Senators	Representatives
John W. Stevenson (D) Thomas C. McCreery (D)	Joseph C. S. Blackburn (D) Andrew R. Boone (D) John Y. Brown (D) John B. Clarke (D) Milton J. Durham (D) Thomas L. Jones (D) J. Proctor Knott (D) Charles W. Milliken (D) Edward Y. Parsons (D) d. July 1876 Henry Watterson (D) s. 1876 John D. White (R)

Louisiana

Senators	Representatives
J. Rodman West (R) James B. Eustis (D) s. 1876	Chester B. Darrall (R) E. John Ellis (D) Randall L. Gibson (D) William M. Levy (D) Frank Morey (R) r. June 1876 Charles E. Nash (R) William B. Spencer (D) s. 1876 r. Jan. 1877

Maine

Senators	Representatives
Hannibal Hamlin (R) Lot M. Morrill (R) r. July 1876 James G. Blaine (R) s. 1876	James G. Blaine (R) r. July 1876 John H. Burleigh (R) Edwin Flye (R) s. 1876 William P. Frye (R) Eugene Hale (R) Harris M. Plaisted (R)

Maryland	
Senators	**Representatives**
George R. Dennis (D) William P. Whyte (D)	Eli J. Henkle (D) William J. O'Brien (D) Charles B. Roberts (D) Thomas Swann (D) Philip F. Thomas (D) William Walsh (D)

Massachusetts	
Senators	**Representatives**

George S. Boutwell (R)
Henry L. Dawes (R)
	Josiah G. Abbott (D)
	   s. 1876
	Nathaniel P. Banks (R)
	Chester W. Chapin (D)
	William W. Crapo (R)
	Rufus S. Frost (R)
	   r. July 1876
	Benjamin W. Harris (R)
	George F. Hoar (R)
	Henry L. Pierce (R)
	Julius H. Seelye (R)
	John K. Tarbox (D)
	Charles P. Thompson (D)
	William W. Warren (D)

Michigan	
Senators	**Representatives**
Thomas W. Ferry (R) Isaac P. Christiancy (R)	Nathan B. Bradley (R) Omar D. Conger (R) George H. Durand (D) Jay A. Hubbell (R) Allen Potter Henry Waldron (R) George Willard (R) Alpheus S. Williams (D) William B. Williams (R)

Minnesota	
Senators	**Representatives**
William Windom (R) Samuel J. R. McMillan (R)	Mark H. Dunnell (R) William S. King (R) Horace B. Strait (R)

Mississippi	
Senators	**Representatives**
James L. Alcorn (R) Blanche K. Bruce (R)	Charles E. Hooker (D) Lucius Q. C. Lamar (D) John R. Lynch (R) Hernando D. Money (D) Otho R. Singleton (D) G. Wiley Wells (R)

Missouri	
Senators	**Representatives**
Lewis V. Bogy (D) Francis M. Cockrell (D)	Richard P. Bland (D) Aylett H. Buckner (D) John B. Clark, Jr. (D) Rezin A. De Bolt (D) Benjamin J. Franklin (D) John M. Glover (D) Robert A. Hatcher (D) Edward C. Kehr (D) Charles H. Morgan (D) John F. Philips (D)

Missouri	
Senators	**Representatives**
	David Rea (D) William H. Stone (D) Erastus Wells (D)

Nebraska	
Senators	**Representative**
Phineas W. Hitchcock Algernon S. Paddock (R)	Lorenzo Crounse (R)

Nevada	
Senators	**Representative**
John P. Jones (R) William Sharon (R)	William Woodburn (R)

New Hampshire	
Senators	**Representatives**
Aaron H. Cragin (Amer) Bainbridge Wadleigh (R)	Samuel N. Bell (D) Henry W. Blair (R) Frank Jones (D)

New Jersey	
Senators	**Representatives**
Frederick T. Frelinghuysen (R) Theodore F. Randolph (D)	Samuel A. Dobbins (R) Augustus W. Cutler (D) Robert Hamilton (D) Augustus A. Hardenbergh (D) Miles Ross (D) Clement H. Sinnickson (R) Frederick H. Teese (D)

New York	
Senators	**Representatives**

Roscoe Conkling (R)
Francis Kernan (D)
	Charles H. Adams (R)
	George A. Bagley (R)
	John H. Bagley, Jr. (D)
	William H. Baker (R)
	Lyman K. Bass (R)
	George M. Beebe (D)
	Archibald M. Bliss (D)
	Simeon B. Chittenden (R)
	Samuel S. Cox (D)
	John M. Davy (R)
	Smith Ely, Jr. (D)
	   r. Dec. 1876
	David Dudley Field (D)
	   s. 1877
	Henry H. Hathorn (R)
	Abram S. Hewitt (D)
	George G. Hoskins (R)
	Elbridge G. Lapham (R)
	Elias W. Leavenworth (R)
	Scott Lord (D)
	Clinton D. MacDougall (R)
	Edwin R. Meade (D)
	Henry B. Metcalfe (D)
	Samuel F. Miller (R)
	Nelson I. Norton (R)
	N. Holmes Odell (D)
	Thomas C. Platt (R)
	John G. Schumaker (D)
	Martin I. Townsend (R)
	Charles C. B. Walker (D)
	Elijah Ward (D)
	William A. Wheeler (R)

(continued)

TABLE 7.27 (continued)

Mar. 4, 1875 to Mar. 3, 1877

President of The Senate	President Pro Tempore of The Senate	Speakers of The House of Representatives
Henry Wilson	Thomas W. Ferry	Michael C. Kerr Samuel J. Randall

| | | John O. Whitehouse (D)
Andrew Williams (R)
Benjamin A. Willis
Fernando Wood (D) |

North Carolina

Senators	Representatives
Matt W. Ransom (D) Augustus S. Merrimon (D)	Thomas S. Ashe (D) Joseph J. Davis (D) John A. Hyman (R) William M. Robbins (D) Alfred M. Scales (D) Robert B. Vance (D) Alfred M. Waddell (D) Jesse J. Yeates (D)

Ohio

Senators	Representatives
John Sherman (R) Allen G. Thurman (D)	Henry B. Banning (D) Jacob P. Cowan (D) Lorenzo Danford (R) Charles Foster (R) James Garfield (R) Frank H. Hurd (D) William Lawrence (R) John A. McMahon (D) James Monroe (R) Lawrence T. Neal (D) Henry B. Payne (D) Earley F. Poppleton (D) Americus V. Rice (D) John S. Savage (D) Milton Sayler (D) Milton I. Southard (D) John L. Vance (D) Nelson H. Van Vorhes (R) Ansel T. Walling (D) Laurin D. Woodworth (R)

Oregon

Senators	Representatives
James K. Kelly (D) John H. Mitchell (R)	George A. La Dow (D) d. May 1875 La Fayette Lane (D)

Pennsylvania

Senators	Representatives
Simon Cameron (R) William A. Wallace (D)	Hiester Clymer (D) Alexander G. Cochran (D) Francis D. Collins (D) Albert G. Egbert (D) Chapman Freeman (R) James H. Hopkins (D) George A. Jenks (D) William D. Kelley (R) Winthrop W. Ketchum (R) r. July 1876 Levi A. Mackey (D) Levi Maish (D) William Mutchler (D) Charles O'Neill (R)

Pennsylvania

Senators	Representatives
	John B. Packer (R) Joseph Powell (D) Samuel J. Randall (D) James B. Reilly (D) John Reilly (D) John Robbins (R) Sobieski Ross (R) James Sheakley (D) A. Herr Smith (R) William H. Stanton (D) s. 1876 William S. Stenger (D) Washington Townsend (R) Jacob Turney (D) John W. Wallace (R) Alan Wood, Jr. (R)

Rhode Island

Senators	Representatives
Henry B. Anthony (R) Ambrose E. Burnside (R)	Latimer W. Ballou (R) Benjamin T. Eames (R)

South Carolina

Senators	Representatives

Thomas J. Robertson (R)
John J. Patterson (R)
	Charles W. Buttz (R)
	  s. 1877
	Solomon L. Hoge (R)
	Edmund W. M. Mackey (R)
	  r. July 1876
	Joseph H. Rainey (R)
	Robert Smalls (R)
	Alexander S. Wallace (R)

Tennessee

Senators	Representatives

Henry Cooper (D)
Andrew Johnson (D)
  d. July 1875
David M. Key (D)
  ta. 1875
James E. Bailey (D)
  s. 1877
	John D. C. Atkins (D)
	John M. Bright (D)
	William P. Caldwell (D)
	George G. Dibrell (D)
	John F. House (D)
	William McFarland (D)
	Haywood Y. Riddle (D)
	  s. 1876
	Jacob M. Thornburgh (R)
	Washington C. Whitthorne (D)
	H. Casey Young (D)

Texas

Senators	Representatives
Morgan C. Hamilton (R) Samuel B. Maxey (D)	David B. Culberson (D) John Hancock (D) Roger Q. Mills (D) John H. Reagan (D) Gustave Schleicher (D) James W. Throckmorton (D)

Vermont

Senators	Representatives
George F. Edmunds (R) Justin S. Morrill (R)	Dudley C. Denison (R) George W. Hendee (R) Charles H. Joyce (R)

Virginia

Senators	Representatives
John W. Johnston (Con)	George C. Cabell (D)
Robert E. Withers (Con)	Beverly B. Douglas (Con)
	John Goode, Jr. (D)
	John T. Harris (D)
	Eppa Hunton (D)
	William H. H. Stowell (R)
	William Terry (Con)
	John R. Tucker (D)
	Gilbert C. Walker (Con)

West Virginia

Senators	Representatives
Henry G. Davis (D)	Charles J. Faulkner (D)
Allen T. Caperton (D)	Frank Hereford (D)
d. July 1876	r. Jan. 1877
Samuel Price	Benjamin Wilson (D)
ta. 1876	
Frank Hereford (D)	
s. 1877	

Wisconsin

Senators	Representatives
Timothy O. Howe (R)	Samuel D. Burchard (D)
Angus Cameron (R)	Lucien B. Caswell (R)
	George W. Cate
	Alanson M. Kimball (R)
	William P. Lynde (D)
	Henry S. Magoon (R)
	Jeremiah M. Rusk (R)
	Charles G. Williams (R)

Source: Notable Names in American History; A Tabulated Register. Third edition of *White's Conspectus of American Biography* (1973), 118–120.

TABLE 7.28 FORTY-FIFTH CONGRESS

Mar. 4, 1877 to Mar. 3, 1879

President of The Senate	President Pro Tempore of The Senate	Speaker of The House of Representatives
William A. Wheeler	Thomas W. Ferry	Samuel J. Randall

Alabama

Senators	Representatives
George E. Spencer (R)	William H. Forney (D)
John T. Morgan (D)	William W. Garth (D)
	Hilary A. Herbert (D)
	Goldsmith W. Hewitt (D)
	James T. Jones (D)
	Robert F. Ligon (D)
	Charles M. Shelley (D)
	Jeremiah N. Williams (D)

Arkansas

Senators	Representatives
Stephen W. Dorsey (R)	Jordan E. Cravens (D)
Augustus H. Garland (D)	Lucien C. Gause (D)
	Thomas M. Gunter (D)
	William F. Slemons (D)

President of The Senate	President Pro Tempore of The Senate	Speaker of The House of Representatives
William A. Wheeler	Thomas W. Ferry	Samuel J. Randall

California

Senators	Representatives
Aaron A. Sargent (R)	Horace Davis (R)
Newton Booth (Anti-Monopolist)	John K. Luttrell (D)
	Romualdo Pacheco (R)
	r. Feb. 1878
	Horace F. Page (R)
	Peter D. Wigginton (D)
	s. 1878

Colorado

Senators	Representatives
Jerome B. Chaffee (R)	James B. Belford (R)
Henry M. Teller (R)	r. Dec. 1877
	Thomas M. Patterson (D)

Connecticut

Senators	Representatives
William W. Eaton (D)	George M. Landers (D)
William H. Barnum (D)	James Phelps (D)
	John T. Wait (R)
	Levi Warner (D)

Delaware

Senators	Representative
Thomas F. Bayard (D)	James Williams (D)
Eli Saulsbury (D)	

Florida

Senators	Representatives
Simon B. Conover (R)	Horatio Bisbee, Jr. (R)
Charles W. Jones (D)	r. Feb. 1879
	Robert H. M. Davidson (D)
	Jesse J. Finley (D)
	s. 1879

Georgia

Senators	Representatives
John B. Gordon (D)	Hiram P. Bell (D)
Benjamin H. Hill (D)	James H. Blount (D)
	Milton A. Candler (D)
	Philip Cook (D)
	William H. Felton (D)
	William B. Fleming (D)
	s. 1879
	Henry R. Harris (D)
	Julian Hartridge (D)
	d. Jan. 1879
	William E. Smith (D)
	Alexander H. Stephens (D)

(continued)

TABLE 7.28 (continued)

Mar. 4, 1877 to Mar. 3, 1879

President of The Senate	President Pro Tempore of The Senate	Speaker of The House of Representatives
William A. Wheeler	Thomas W. Ferry	Samuel J. Randall

Illinois

Senators	Representatives
Richard J. Oglesby (R)	William Aldrich (R)
David Davis (R)	Thomas A. Boyd (R)
	Lorenzo Brentano (R)
	Horatio C. Burchard (R)
	Joseph G. Cannon (R)
	John R. Eden (D)
	Greenbury L. Fort (R)
	Carter H. Harrison (D)
	William Hartzell (D)
	Philip C. Hayes (R)
	Thomas J. Henderson (R)
	Robert M. Knapp (D)
	William Lathrop (D)
	Benjamin F. Marsh (R)
	William R. Morrison (D)
	William A. J. Sparks (D)
	William M. Springer (D)
	Thomas F. Tipton (R)
	Richard W. Townshend (D)

Indiana

Senators	Representatives
Oliver H. P. T. Morton (R)	John H. Baker (R)
d. 1877	George A. Bicknell (D)
Daniel W. Voorhees (D)	Thomas M. Browne (R)
Joseph E. McDonald (D)	William H. Calkins (R)
	Thomas R. Cobb (D)
	Benoni S. Fuller (D)
	James L. Evans (R)
	Andrew H. Hamilton (D)
	John Hanna (R)
	Morton C. Hunter (R)
	Milton S. Robinson (R)
	Leonidas Sexton (R)
	Michael D. White (R)

Iowa

Senators	Representatives
William B. Allison (R)	Theodore W. Burdick (R)
Samuel J. Kirkwood (R)	Rush Clark (R)
	Henry J. B. Cummings (R)
	Nathaniel C. Deering (R)
	S. Addison Oliver (R)
	Hiram Price (R)
	Ezekiel S. Sampson (R)
	William F. Sapp (R)
	Joseph C. Stone (R)

Kansas

Senators	Representatives
John J. Ingalls (R)	Dudley C. Haskell (R)
Preston B. Plumb (R)	William A. Phillips (R)
	Thomas Ryan (R)

Kentucky

Senators	Representatives
Thomas C. McCreery (D)	Joseph C. S. Blackburn (D)
James B. Beck (D)	Andrew R. Boone (D)
	John W. Caldwell (D)
	John G. Carlisle (D)
	John B. Clarke (D)
	Milton J. Durham (D)
	J. Proctor Knott (D)
	James A. McKenzie (D)
	Thomas Turner (D)
	Albert S. Willis (D)

Louisiana

Senators	Representatives
William P. Kellogg (R)	Joseph H. Acklen (D)
James B. Eustis (D)	s. 1878
	Chester B. Darrall (R)
	r. 1878
	Joseph B. Elam (D)
	E. John Ellis (D)
	Randall L. Gibson (D)
	John E. Leonard (R)
	d. 1878
	Edward W. Robertson (D)
	John S. Young (D)
	s. 1878

Maine

Senators	Representatives
Hannibal Hamlin (R)	William P. Frye (R)
James G. Blaine (R)	Eugene Hale (R)
	Stephen D. Lindsey (R)
	Llewellyn Powers (R)
	Thomas B. Reed (R)

Maryland

Senators	Representatives
George R. Dennis (D)	Eli J. Henkle (D)
William P. Whyte (D)	Daniel M. Henry (D)
	William Kimmel (D)
	Charles B. Roberts (D)
	Thomas Swann (D)
	William Walsh (D)

Massachusetts

Senators	Representatives
Henry L. Dawes (R)	Nathaniel P. Banks (R)
George F. Hoar (R)	Benjamin F. Butler (R)
	William Claflin (R)
	William W. Crapo (R)
	Benjamin Dean (D)
	s. 1878
	Walbridge A. Field (R)
	r. Mar. 1878
	Benjamin W. Harris (R)
	George B. Loring (R)
	Leopold Morse (D)
	Amasa Norcross (R)
	William W. Rice (R)
	George D. Robinson (R)

Michigan

Senators	Representatives

Thomas W. Ferry (R)
Isaac P. Christiancy (R)
  r. Feb. 1879
	Mark S. Brewer (R)
	Omar D. Conger (R)
	Charles C. Ellsworth (R)
	Jay A. Hubbell (R)
	Edwin W. Keightley (R)
	Jonas H. McGowan (R)
	John W. Stone (R)
	Alpheus S. Williams (D)
	  d. 1878
	Edwin Willits (R)

Minnesota

Senators	Representatives
William Windom (R) Samuel J. R. McMillan (R)	Mark H. Dunnell (R) Jacob H. Stewart (R) Horace B. Strait (R)

Mississippi

Senators	Representatives
Blanche K. Bruce (R) Lucius Q. C. Lamar (D)	James R. Chalmers (D) Charles E. Hooker (D) Vannoy H. Manning (D) Hernando D. Money (D) Henry L. Muldrow (D) Otho R. Singleton (D)

Missouri

Senators	Representatives

Lewis V. Bogy (D)
  d. Sep. 1877
David H. Armstrong (D)
  ta. 1877
James Shields (D)
  s. 1879
Francis M. Cockrell (D)
	Richard P. Bland (D)
	Aylett H. Buckner (D)
	John B. Clark, Jr. (D)
	Nathan Cole (R)
	Thomas T. Crittenden (D)
	Benjamin J. Franklin (D)
	John M. Glover (D)
	Robert A. Hatcher (D)
	Anthony Ittner (R)
	Lyne S. Metcalfe (R)
	Charles H. Morgan (D)
	Henry M. Pollard (R)
	David Rea (D)

Nebraska

Senators	Representatives

Algernon S. Paddock (R)
Alvin Saunders (R)
	Thomas J. Majors (R)
	  s. 1878
	Frank Welch (R)
	  d. 1878

Nevada

Senators	Representative
John P. Jones (R) William Sharon (R)	Thomas Wren (R)

New Hampshire

Senators	Representatives
Bainbridge Wadleigh (R) Edward H. Rollins (R)	Henry W. Blair (R) James F. Briggs (R) Frank Jones (D)

New Jersey

Senators	Representatives
Theodore F. Randolph (D) John R. McPherson (D)	Alvah A. Clark (D) Augustus W. Cutler (D) Augustus A. Hardenbergh (D) Thomas B. Peddie (R) John H. Pugh (R) Miles Ross (D) Clement H. Sinnickson (R)

New York

Senators	Representatives

Roscoe Conkling (R)
Francis Kernan (D)
	William J. Bacon (R)
	George A. Bagley (R)
	John H. Bailey (R)
	  s. 1878
	William H. Baker (R)
	George M. Beebe (D)
	Charles B. Benedict (D)
	Archibald M. Bliss (D)
	Solomon Bundy (R)
	John H. Camp (R)
	Simeon B. Chittenden (R)
	James W. Covert (D)
	Samuel S. Cox (D)
	Jeremiah W. Dwight (R)
	Anthony Eickhoff (D)
	E. Kirke Hart (D)
	Abram S. Hewitt (D)
	Frank Hiscock (R)
	John N. Hungerford (R)
	Amaziah B. James (R)
	John H. Ketcham (R)
	Elbridge G. Lapham (R)
	Daniel N. Lockwood (R)
	Anson G. McCook (R)
	Stephen L. Mayham (D)
	Nicholas Muller (D)
	George W. Patterson (R)
	Clarkson N. Potter (D)
	Terence J. Quinn (D)
	  d. Jun. 1878
	John H. Starin (R)
	Martin I. Townsend (R)
	William D. Veeder (D)
	Andrew Williams (R)
	Benjamin A. Willis (D)
	Fernando Wood (D)

North Carolina

Senators	Representatives
Matt W. Ransom (D) Augustus S. Merrimon (D)	Curtis H. Brogden (R) Joseph J. Davis (D) William M. Robbins (D) Alfred M. Scales (D) Walter L. Steele (D) Robert B. Vance (D) Alfred M. Waddell (D) Jesse J. Yeates (D)

(continued)

TABLE 7.28 (continued)

Mar. 4, 1877 to Mar. 3, 1879

President of The Senate	President Pro Tempore of The Senate	Speaker of The House of Representatives
William A. Wheeler	Thomas W. Ferry	Samuel J. Randall

Ohio

Senators	Representatives
Stanley Matthews (R) Allen G. Thurman (D)	Henry B. Banning (D) Jacob D. Cox (R) Lorenzo Danford (R) Henry L. Dickey (D) Thomas Ewing (D) Ebenezer B. Finley (D) Charles Foster (R) Mills Gardner (R) James A. Garfield (R) John S. Jones (R) J. Warren Keifer (R) William McKinley, Jr. (R) John A. McMahon (D) James Monroe (R) Henry S. Neal (R) Americus V. Rice (D) Milton Sayler (D) Milton I. Southard (D) Amos Townsend (R) Nelson H. Van Vorhes (R)

Oregon

Senators	Representative
John H. Mitchell (R) La Fayette Grover (D)	Richard Williams (R)

Pennsylvania

Senators	Representatives

Simon Cameron (R)
  r. Mar. 1877
J. Donald Cameron (R)
  s. 1877
William A. Wallace (D)
	Thomas M. Bayne (R)
	Samuel A. Bridges (D)
	Jacob M. Campbell (R)
	Hiester Clymer (D)
	Francis D. Collins (D)
	Russell Errett (R)
	I. Newton Evans (R)
	Chapman Freeman (R)
	Alfred C. Harmer (R)
	William D. Kelley (R)
	John W. Killinger (R)
	Levi A. Mackey (D)
	Levi Maish (D)
	John I. Mitchell (R)
	Charles O'Neill (R)
	Edward Overton, Jr. (R)
	Samuel J. Randall (D)
	James B. Reilly (D)
	William S. Shallenberger (R)
	A. Herr Smith (R)
	William S. Stenger (D)
	John M. Thompson (R)
	Jacob Turney (D)
	William Ward (R)
	Lewis F. Watson (R)
	Harry White (R)
	Hendrick B. Wright (D)

Rhode Island

Senators	Representatives
Henry B. Anthony (R) Ambrose E. Burnside (R)	Latimer W. Ballou (R) Benjamin T. Eames (R)

South Carolina

Senators	Representatives
John J. Patterson (R) Matthew C. Butler (D)	D. Wyatt Aiken (D) Richard H. Cain (D) John H. Evins (D) Joseph H. Rainey (R) Robert Smalls (R)

Tennessee

Senators	Representatives
James E. Bailey (D) Isham G. Harris (D)	John D. C. Atkins (D) John M. Bright (D) William P. Caldwell (D) George G. Dibrell (D) John F. House (D) James H. Randolph (R) Haywood Y. Riddle (D) Jacob M. Thornburgh (R) Washington C. Whitthorne (D) H. Casey Young (D)

Texas

Senators	Representatives
Samuel B. Maxey (D) Richard Coke (D)	David B. Culberson (D) De Witt C. Giddings (D) Roger Q. Mills (D) John H. Reagan (D) Gustave Schleicher (D) d. Jan. 1879 James W. Throckmorton (D)

Vermont

Senators	Representatives
George F. Edmunds (R) Justin S. Morrill (R)	Dudley C. Denison (R) George W. Hendee (R) Charles H. Joyce (R)

Virginia

Senators	Representatives

John W. Johnston (Con)
Robert E. Withers (Con)
	Richard Lee T. Beale (D)
	  s. 1879
	George C. Cabell (D)
	Beverly B. Douglas (D)
	  d. 1878
	John Goode, Jr. (Con)
	John T. Harris (D)
	Eppa Hunton (D)
	Joseph Jorgensen (R)
	Auburn L. Pridemore (D)
	John R. Tucker (D)
	Gilbert C. Walker (Con)

West Virginia

Senators	Representatives
Henry G. Davis (D) Frank Hereford (D)	John E. Kenna (D) Benjamin F. Martin (D) Benjamin Wilson (D)

Wisconsin	
Senators	**Representatives**
Timothy O. Howe (R) Angus Cameron (R)	Gabriel Bouck (D) Edward S. Bragg (D) Lucien B. Caswell (R) George C. Hazelton (R) Herman L. Humphrey (R) William P. Lynde (D) Thaddeus C. Pound (R) Charles G. Williams (R)

Source: Notable Names in American History; A Tabulated Register. Third edition of White's Conspectus of American Biography (1973), 120–22.

TABLE 7.29 FORTY-SIXTH CONGRESS

Mar. 4, 1879 to Mar. 3, 1881

President of The Senate	President Pro Tempore of The Senate	Speaker of The House of Representatives
William A. Wheeler	Allen G. Thurman	Samuel J. Randall

Alabama	
Senators	**Representatives**
John T. Morgan (D) George S. Houston (D) d. 1879 Luke Pryor (D) ta. 1880 James L. Pugh (D) s. 1880	Newton N. Clements s. 1880 William H. Forney (D) Hilary A. Herbert (D) Thomas H. Herndon (D) Burwell B. Lewis (D) r. Oct. 1880 William M. Lowe (D) William J. Samford Charles M. Shelley (D) Thomas Williams (D)

Arkansas	
Senators	**Representatives**
Augustus H. Garland (D) James D. Walker (D)	Jordan E. Cravens (D) Poindexter Dunn (D) Thomas M. Gunter (D) William F. Slemons (D)

California	
Senators	**Representatives**
Newton Booth (Anti-Monopolist) James T. Farley (R)	Campbell P. Berry (R) Horace Davis (R) Romualdo Pacheco (R) Horace F. Page (R)

Colorado	
Senators	**Representative**
Henry M. Teller (R) Nathaniel P. Hill (R)	James B. Belford (R)

Connecticut	
Senators	**Representatives**
William W. Eaton (D) Orville H. Platt (R)	Joseph R. Hawley (R) Frederick Miles (R) James Phelps (D) John T. Wait (R)

Delaware	
Senators	**Representative**
Thomas F. Bayard (D) Eli Saulsbury (D)	Edward L. Martin (D)

Florida	
Senators	**Representatives**
Charles W. Jones (D) Wilkinson Call (D)	Horatio Bisbee, Jr. (R) s. 1881 Robert H. M. Davidson (D) Noble A. Hull (D) r. Jan. 1881

Georgia	
Senators	**Representatives**
Benjamin H. Hill (D) John B. Gordon (D) r. May 1880 Joseph E. Brown (D) s. 1880	James H. Blount (D) Philip Cook (D) William H. Felton (D) Nathaniel J. Hammond (D) John C. Nicholls (D) Henry Persons (D) William E. Smith (D) Emory Speer (D) Alexander H. Stephens (D)

Illinois	
Senators	**Representatives**
David Davis (R) John A. Logan (R)	William Aldrich (R) Hiram Barber, Jr. (R) Thomas A. Boyd (R) Joseph G. Cannon (R) George R. Davis (R) Albert P. Forsythe (R) Greenbury L. Fort (R) Robert M. A. Hawk (R) Philip C. Hayes (R) Thomas J. Henderson (R) Benjamin F. Marsh (R) William R. Morrison (D) John C. Sherwin (R) James W. Singleton (D) William A. J. Sparks (D) William M. Springer (D) Adlai E. Stevenson (D) John R. Thomas (D) Richard W. Townshend (D)

Indiana	
Senators	**Representatives**
Joseph E. McDonald (D) Daniel W. Voorhees (D)	John H. Baker (R) George A. Bicknell (D) Thomas M. Browne (R) William H. Calkins (R) Thomas R. Cobb (D) Walpole G. Colerick (D) Calvin Cowgill (R) Gilbert De La Matyr (D) William Heilman (R) Abraham J. Hostetler (D) William R. Myers (D) Jeptha D. New (D) Godlove S. Orth (R)

(continued)

TABLE 7.29 (continued)

Mar. 4, 1879 to Mar. 3, 1881

President of The Senate	President Pro Tempore of The Senate	Speaker of The House of Representatives
William A. Wheeler	Allen G. Thurman	Samuel J. Randall

Iowa

Senators	Representatives
William B. Allison (R) Samuel J. Kirkwood (R)	Cyrus C. Carpenter (R) Rush Clark (R) d. Apr. 1879 Nathaniel C. Deering (R) Edward H. Gillette (Greenback) Moses A. McCoid (R) Hiram Price (R) William F. Sapp (R) William G. Thompson (R) Thomas Updegraff (R) James B. Weaver (Greenback)

Kansas

Senators	Representatives
John J. Ingalls (R) Preston B. Plumb (R)	John A. Anderson (R) Dudley C. Haskell (R) Thomas Ryan (R)

Kentucky

Senators	Representatives
James B. Beck (D) John S. Williams (D)	Joseph C. S. Blackburn (D) John W. Caldwell (D) John G. Carlisle (D) J. Proctor Knott (D) James A. McKenzie (D) Elijah C. Phister (D) Philip B. Thompson, Jr. (D) Oscar Turner (D) Thomas Turner (D) Albert S. Willis (D)

Louisiana

Senators	Representatives
William P. Kellogg (R) Benjamin F. Jonas (D)	Joseph H. Acklen (D) Joseph B. Elam (D) E. John Ellis (D) Randall L. Gibson (D) J. Floyd King (D) Edward W. Robertson (D)

Maine

Senators	Representatives
Hannibal Hamlin (R) James G. Blaine (R)	William P. Frye (R) George W. Ladd (Greenback, D) Stephen D. Lindsey (R) Thompson H. Murch (Greenback) Thomas B. Reed (R)

Maryland

Senators	Representatives
William P. Whyte (D) James B. Groome (D)	Eli J. Henkle (D) Daniel M. Henry (D) William Kimmel (D) Robert M. McLane (D) J. Fred C. Talbott (D) Milton G. Urner (R)

Massachusetts

Senators	Representatives
Henry L. Dawes (R) George F. Hoar (R)	Selwyn Z. Bowman (R) William Claflin (R) William W. Crapo (R) Walbridge A. Field (R) Benjamin W. Harris (R) George B. Loring (R) Leopold Morse (D) Amasa Norcross (R) William W. Rice (R) George D. Robinson (R) William A. Russell (R)

Michigan

Senators	Representatives

Thomas W. Ferry (R)
Zachariah Chandler (R)
   d. 1879
Henry P. Baldwin (R)
   s. 1879
	Mark S. Brewer (R)
	Julius C. Burrows (R)
	Omar D. Conger (R)
	   r. Mar. 1879
	Roswell G. Horr (R)
	Jay A. Hubbell (R)
	Jonas H. McGowan (R)
	John S. Newberry (R)
	John W. Stone (R)
	Edwin Willits (R)

Minnesota

Senators	Representatives
William Windom (R) Samuel J. R. McMillan (R)	Mark H. Dunnell (R) Henry Poehler (D) William D. Washburn (R)

Mississippi

Senators	Representatives
Blanche K. Bruce (R) Lucius Q. C. Lamar (D)	James R. Chalmers (D) Charles E. Hooker (D) Vannoy H. Manning (D) Hernando D. Money (D) Henry L. Muldrow (D) Otho R. Singleton (D)

Missouri

Senators	Representatives

Francis M. Cockrell (D)
George G. Vest (D)
	Richard P. Bland (D)
	Aylett H. Buckner (D)
	Martin L. Clardy (D)
	John B. Clark, Jr. (D)
	Lowndes H. Davis (D)
	Nicholas Ford (R)
	Richard G. Frost (D)
	William H. Hatch (D)
	Alfred M. Lay (D)
	   d. 1879
	John F. Philips (D)
	   s. 1880
	Gideon F. Rothwell (D)
	Samuel L. Sawyer (D)
	James R. Waddill (D)
	Erastus Wells (D)

Nebraska

Senators	Representative
Algernon S. Paddock (R) Alvin Saunders (R)	Edward K. Valentine (R)

Nevada	
Senators	**Representative**
John P. Jones (R)	Rollin M. Daggett (R)
William Sharon (R)	

New Hampshire	
Senators	**Representatives**
Edward H. Rollins (R)	James F. Briggs (R)
Charles H. Bell (R)	Evarts W. Farr (D)
ta. 1879	d. Nov. 1880
Henry W. Blair (R)	Joshua G. Hall (R)
s. 1879	Ossian Ray (R) s. 1881

New Jersey	
Senators	**Representatives**
Theodore F. Randolph (D)	John L. Blake (R)
John R. McPherson (D)	Lewis A. Brigham (R)
	Alvah A. Clark (D)
	George M. Robeson (R)
	Miles Ross (D)
	Hezekiah B. Smith (D)
	Charles H. Voorhis (R)

New York	
Senators	**Representatives**
Roscoe Conkling (R)	John M. Bailey (R)
Francis Kernan (D)	Archibald M. Bliss (D)
	John H. Camp (R)
	Simeon B. Chittenden (R)
	James W. Covert (D)
	Samuel S. Cox (D)
	Richard Crowley (R)
	Jeremiah W. Dwight (R)
	Edwin Einstein (R)
	John W. Ferdon (R)
	John Hammond (R)
	Frank Hiscock (R)
	Waldo Hutchins (D)
	Amaziah B. James (R)
	John H. Ketcham (R)
	Elbridge G. Lapham (R)
	William Lounsbery (D)
	Anson G. McCook (R)
	Joseph Mason (R)
	Warner Miller (R)
	Levi P. Morton (R)
	Nicholas Muller (D)
	James O'Brien (D)
	Daniel O'Reilly (D)
	Ray V. Pierce (R)
	r. 1880
	Cyrus D. Prescott (R)
	David P. Richardson (R)
	Jonathan Scovile (D)
	s. 1880
	John H. Starin (R)
	Henry Van Aernam (R)
	John Van Voorhis (R)
	David Wilber (R)
	Fernando Wood (D)
	d. Feb. 1881
	Walter A. Wood (R)

North Carolina	
Senators	**Representatives**
Matt W. Ransom (D)	Robert F. Armfield (D)
Zebulon B. Vance (D)	Joseph J. Davis (D)
	William H. Kitchin (D)
	Joseph J. Martin (R)
	r. Jan. 1881
	Daniel L. Russell (R)
	Alfred M. Scales (D)
	Walter L. Steele (D)
	Robert B. Vance (D)
	Jesse J. Yeates (D)
	s. 1881

Ohio	
Senators	**Representatives**
Allen G. Thurman (D)	Gibson Atherton (D)
George H. Pendleton (D)	Benjamin Butterworth (R)
	George L. Converse (D)
	Henry L. Dickey (D)
	Thomas Ewing (D)
	Ebenezer B. Finley (D)
	James A. Garfield (R)
	r. Nov. 1880
	George W. Geddes (D)
	William D. Hill (D)
	Frank H. Hurd (D)
	J. Warren Keifer (R)
	Benjamin Le Fevre (D)
	William McKinley, Jr. (R)
	John A. McMahon (D)
	James Monroe (R)
	Henry S. Neal (R)
	Ezra B. Taylor (R)
	s. 1880
	Amos Townsend (R)
	Jonathan T. Updegraff (R)
	Adoniram J. Warner (D)
	Thomas L. Young (R)

Oregon	
Senators	**Representative**
La Fayette Grover (D)	John Whiteaker (D)
James H. Slater (D)	

Pennsylvania	
Senators	**Representatives**
William A. Wallace (D)	Reuben K. Bachman (D)
J. Donald Cameron (R)	Thomas M. Bayne (R)
	Frank E. Beltzhoover (D)
	Henry H. Bingham (R)
	Hiester Clymer (D)
	Alexander H. Coffroth (D)
	Samuel B. Dick (R)
	Russell Errett (R)
	Horatio G. Fisher (R)
	William Godshalk (R)
	Alfred C. Harmer (R)
	William D. Kelley (R)
	John W. Killinger (R)
	Robert Klotz (D)
	John I. Mitchell (R)
	Charles O'Neill (R)
	James H. Osmer (R)
	Edward Overton, Jr. (R)
	Samuel J. Randall (D)
	John W. Ryon (D)
	William S. Shallenberger (R)
	A. Herr Smith (R)

(continued)

TABLE 7.29 (continued)

Mar. 4, 1879 to Mar. 3, 1881

President of The Senate	President Pro Tempore of The Senate	Speaker of The House of Representatives
William A. Wheeler	Allen G. Thurman	Samuel J. Randall

	William Ward (R) Harry White (R) Morgan R. Wise (D) Hendrick B. Wright (D) Seth H. Yocum (R)

Rhode Island

Senators	Representatives
Henry B. Anthony (R) Ambrose E. Burnside (R)	Nelson W. Aldrich (D) Latimer W. Ballou (R)

South Carolina

Senators	Representatives
Matthew C. Butler (D) Wade Hampton (D)	D. Wyatt Aiken (D) John H. Evins (D) Michael P. O'Connor (D) John S. Richardson (D) George D. Tillman (D)

Tennessee

Senators	Representatives
James E. Bailey (D) Isham G. Harris (D)	John D. C. Atkins (D) John M. Bright (D) George G. Dibrell (D) Leonidas C. Houk (R) John F. House (D) Benton McMillin (D) Charles B. Simonton (D) Robert L. Taylor (D) Washington C. Whitthorne (D) H. Casey Young (D)

Texas

Senators	Representatives
Samuel B. Maxey (D) Richard Coke (D)	David B. Culberson (D) George W. Jones (Greenback) Roger Q. Mills (D) John H. Reagan (D) Christopher C. Upson (D) Olin Wellborn (D)

Vermont

Senators	Representatives
George F. Edmunds (R) Justin S. Morrill (R)	Bradley Barlow (R) Charles H. Joyce (R) James M. Tyler (R)

Virginia

Senators	Representatives
John W. Jonston (C) Robert E. Withers (C)	Richard Lee T. Beale (D) George C. Cabell (D) John Goode, Jr. (D) John T. Harris (D) Eppa Hunton (D) Joseph E. Johnston (D) Joseph Jorgensen (R) James B. Richmond (D) John R. Tucker (D)

West Virginia

Senators	Representatives
Henry G. Davis (D) Frank Hereford (D)	John E. Kenna (D) Benjamin F. Martin (D) Benjamin Wilson (D)

Wisconsin

Senators	Representatives
Angus Cameron (R) Matthew H. Carpenter (R) d. Feb. 1881	Gabriel Bouck (D) Edward S. Bragg (D) Lucien B. Caswell (R) Peter V. Deuster (D) George C. Hazelton (R) Herman L. Humphrey (R) Thaddeus C. Pound (R) Charles G. Williams (R)

Source: Notable Names in American History; A Tabulated Register. Third edition of White's Conspectus of American Biography (1973), 122–24.

TABLE 7.30 FORTY-SEVENTH CONGRESS

Mar. 4, 1881 to Mar. 3, 1883

President of The Senate	Presidents Pro Tempore of The Senate	Speaker of The House of Representatives
Chester A. Arthur	Thomas F. Bayard David Davis George F. Edmunds	J. Warren Keifer

Alabama

Senators	Representatives
John T. Morgan (D) James L. Pugh (D)	William H. Forney (D) Hilary A. Herbert (D) Thomas H. Herndon (D) Goldsmith W. Hewitt (D) William M. Lowe (D) d. 1882 William C. Oates (D) Charles M. Shelley (D) Joseph Wheeler (D) Thomas Williams (D)

Arkansas

Senators	Representatives
Augustus H. Garland (D) James D. Walker (D)	Poindexter Dunn (D) Jordan E. Cravens (D) Thomas M. Gunter (D) James K. Jones (D)

California

Senators	Representatives
James T. Farley (R) John F. Miller (R)	Campbell P. Berry (R) Romualdo Pacheco (R) Horace F. Page (R) William S. Rosecrans (D)

Colorado

Senators	Representative
Henry M. Teller (R) r. Apr. 1882 George M. Chilcott (R) ta. 1882 Horace A. W. Tabor (R) s. 1883 Nathaniel P. Hill (R)	James B. Belford (R)

Connecticut	
Senators	**Representatives**
Orville H. Platt (R)	John R. Buck (R)
Joseph R. Hawley (R)	Frederick Miles (R)
	James Phelps (D)
	John T. Wait (R)

Delaware	
Senators	**Representative**
Thomas F. Bayard (D)	Edward L. Martin (D)
Eli Saulsbury (D)	

Florida	
Senators	**Representatives**
Charles W. Jones (D)	Horatio Bisbee, Jr. (R)
Wilkinson Call (D)	s. 1882
	Robert H. M. Davidson (D)
	Jesse J. Finley (D)
	r. Jun. 1882

Georgia	
Senators	**Representatives**
Benjamin H. Hill (D)	George R. Black (D)
d. 1882	James H. Blount (D)
M. Pope Barrow (D)	Hugh Buchanan (D)
s. 1882	Judson C. Clements (D)
Joseph E. Brown (D)	Philip Cook (D)
	Nathaniel J. Hammond (D)
	Seaborn Reese (D)
	s. 1882
	Emory Speer
	Alexander H. Stephens (D)
	r. Nov. 1882
	Henry G. Turner (D)

Illinois	
Senators	**Representatives**
David Davis (R)	William Aldrich (R)
John A. Logan (R)	Joseph G. Cannon (R)
	William Cullen (R)
	George R. Davis (R)
	Charles B. Farwell (R)
	Robert M. A. Hawk (R)
	d. June 1882
	Thomas J. Henderson (R)
	Robert R. Hitt (R)
	s. 1882
	John H. Lewis (R)
	Benjamin F. Marsh (R)
	William R. Morrison (D)
	Samuel W. Moulton (D)
	Lewis E. Payson (R)
	John C. Sherwin (R)
	James W. Singleton (D)
	Dietrich C. Smith (R)
	William A. J. Sparks (D)
	William M. Springer (D)
	John R. Thomas (R)
	Richard W. Townshend (D)

Indiana	
Senators	**Representatives**
Daniel W. Voorhees (D)	Thomas M. Browne (R)
Benjamin Harrison (R)	William H. Calkins (R)
	Thomas R. Cobb (D)
	Walpole G. Colerick (D)
	Mark L. DeMotte (R)
	Charles T. Doxey (R)
	s. 1883
	William Heilman (R)
	William S. Holman (D)
	Courtland C. Matson (D)
	Godlove S. Orth (R)
	d. Dec. 1882
	Stanton J. Peelle (R)
	Robert B. F. Pierce (R)
	George W. Steele (R)
	Strother M. Stockslager (D)

Iowa	
Senators	**Representatives**
William B. Allison (R)	Cyrus C. Carpenter (R)
Samuel J. Kirkwood (R)	Marsena E. Cutts (R)
r. Mar. 1881	Nathaniel C. Deering (R)
James W. McDill (R)	Sewall S. Farwell (R)
s. 1881	William P. Hepburn (R)
	John A. Kasson (R)
	Moses A. McCoid (R)
	William G. Thompson (R)
	Thomas Updegraff (R)

Kansas	
Senators	**Representatives**
John J. Ingalls (R)	John A. Anderson (R)
Preston B. Plumb (R)	Dudley C. Haskell (R)
	Thomas Ryan (R)

Kentucky	
Senators	**Representatives**
James B. Beck (D)	Joseph C. S. Blackburn (D)
John S. Williams (D)	John W. Caldwell (D)
	John G. Carlisle (D)
	J. Proctor Knott (D)
	James A. McKenzie (D)
	Elijah C. Phister (D)
	Philip B. Thompson, Jr. (D)
	Oscar Turner (D)
	JohnD. White (R)
	Albert S. Willis (D)

Louisiana	
Senators	**Representatives**
William P. Kellogg (R)	Newton C. Blanchard (D)
Benjamin F. Jonas (D)	Chester B. Darrall (R)
	E. John Ellis (D)
	Randall L. Gibson (D)
	J. Floyd King (D)
	Edward W. Robertson (D)

Maine	
Senators	**Representatives**
James G. Blaine (R)	Nelson Dingley, Jr. (R)
r. Mar. 1881	William P. Frye (R)
William P. Frye (R)	r. Mar. 1881
s. 1881	George W. Ladd (Greenback, D)
Eugene Hale (R)	Stephen D. Lindsey (R)
	Thompson H. Murch (Greenback)
	Thomas B. Reed (R)

(continued)

TABLE 7.30 (continued)

Mar. 4, 1881 to Mar. 3, 1883

President of The Senate	Presidents Pro Tempore of The Senate	Speaker of The House of Representatives
Chester A. Arthur	Thomas F. Bayard David Davis George F. Edmunds	J. Warren Keifer

Maryland

Senators	Representatives
James B. Groome (D) Arthur P. Gorman (D)	Andrew G. Chapman (D) George W. Covington (D) Fetter S. Hoblitzell (D) Robert M. McLane (D) J. Fred C. Talbott (D) Milton G. Urner (R)

Massachusetts

Senators	Representatives
Henry L. Dawes (R) George F. Hoar (R)	Selwyn Z. Bowman (R) John W. Candler (R) William W. Crapo (R) Banjamin W. Harris (R) Leopold Morse (D) Amasa Norcross (R) Ambrose A. Ranney (R) William W. Rice (R) George D. Robinson (R) William A. Russell (R) Eben F. Stone (R)

Michigan

Senators	Representatives
Thomas W. Ferry (R) Omar D. Conger (R)	Julius C. Burrows (R) Rosewell G. Horr (R) Jay A. Hubbell (R) Edward S. Lacey (R) Henry W. Lord (R) John T. Rich (R) Oliver L. Spaulding (R) George W. Webber (R) Edwin Willits (R)

Minnesota

Senators	Representatives

Samuel J. R. McMillan (R)
William Windom (R)
  r. Mar. 1881
Alonzo J. Edgerton (R)
  ta. 1881
	Mark H. Dunnell (R)
	Horace B. Strait (R)
	William D. Washburn (R)

Mississippi

Senators	Representatives

Lucius Q. C. Lamar (D)
James Z. George (D)
	James R. Chalmers (D)
	  r. Apr. 1882
	Charles E. Hooker (D)
	John R. Lynch (R)
	  s. 1882
	Vannoy H. Manning (D)
	Hernando D. Money (D)
	Henry L. Muldrow (D)
	Otho R. Singleton (D)

Missouri

Senators	Representatives

Francis M. Cockrell (D)
George G. Vest (D)
	Thomas Allen (D)
	  d. Apr. 1882
	Richard P. Bland (D)
	Aylett H. Buckner (D)
	Joseph H. Burrows (Greenback)
	Martin L. Clardy (D)
	John B. Clark, Jr. (D)
	Lowndes H. Davis (D)
	Nicholas Ford (R)
	Richard G. Frost (D)
	William H. Hatch (D)
	Ira S. Hazeltone (Greenback)
	James H. McLean (R)
	  s. 1882
	Theron M. Rice (Greenback)
	Robert T. Van Horn (R)

Nebraska

Senators	Representative
Alvin Saunders (R) Charles H. Van Wyck (R)	Edward K. Valentine (R)

Nevada

Senators	Representative
John P. Jones (R) James G. Fair (D)	George W. Cassidy (D)

New Hampshire

Senators	Representatives
Edward H. Rollins (R) Henry W. Blair (R)	James F. Briggs (R) Joshua G. Hall (R) Ossian Ray (R)

New Jersey

Senators	Representatives
John R. McPherson (D) William J. Sewell (R)	J. Hart Brewer (R) Augustus A. Hardenbergh (D) Henry S. Harris (D) John Hill (R) Phineas Jones (R) George M. Roseson (R) Miles Ross (D)

New York

Senators	Representatives
Elbridge G. Lapham (R) Warner Miller (R)	Lewis Beach (D) Perry Belmont (D) Archibald M. Bliss (D) John H. Camp (R) Thomas Cornell (R) Samuel S. Cox (D) Richard Crowley (R) P. Henry Dugro (D) Jeremiah W. Dwight (R) Roswell P. Flower (D) John Hammond (R) John Hardy (D) Abram S. Hewitt (D) Frank Hiscock (R) Waldo Hutchins (D) Ferris Jacobs (R) John Ketcham (R) Elbridge G. Lapham (R) r. 1881

New York	
Senators	**Representatives**
	Anson G. McCook (R)
	Joseph Mason (R)
	Warner Miller (R)
	r. Jul. 1881
	Levi P. Morton (R)
	r. Mar. 1881
	Michael N. Nolan (D)
	Abraham X. Parker (R)
	Cyrus D. Prescott (R)
	David P. Richardson (R)
	William E. Robinson (D)
	Jonathan Scoville (D)
	Charles R. Skinner (R)
	J. Hyatt Smith (R, D)
	Henry Van Aernam (R)
	John Van Voorhis (R)
	James W. Wadsworth (R)
	George West (R)
	Banjamin Wood (D)
	Walter A. Wood (R)

North Carolina	
Senators	**Representatives**
Matt W. Ransom (D)	Robert A. Armfield (D)
Zebulon B. Vance (D)	William R. Cox (D)
	Clement Dowd (D)
	Orlando Hubbs (R)
	Louis C. Latham (D)
	Alfred M. Scales (D)
	John W. Shackelford (D)
	d. 1883
	Robert B. Vance (D)

Ohio	
Senators	**Representatives**
George H. Pendleton (D)	Gibson Atherton (D)
John Sherman (R)	Benjamin Butterworth (R)
	George L. Converse (D)
	Rufus R. Dawes (R)
	George W. Geddes (D)
	J. Warren Keifer (R)
	John P. Leedom (D)
	Benjamin Le Fevre (D)
	Addison S. McClure (R)
	William McKinley, Jr. (R)
	Henry L. Morey (R)
	Henry S. Neal (R)
	John B. Rice (R)
	James M. Ritchie (R)
	James S. Robinson (R)
	Emanuel Shultz (R)
	Ezra B. Taylor (R)
	Joseph D. Taylor (R)
	s. 1883
	Amos Townsend (R)
	Jonathan T. Updegraff (R)
	d. Nov. 1882
	Thomas L. Young (R)

Oregon	
Senators	**Representative**
La Fayette Grover (D)	Melvin C. George (R)
James H. Slater (D)	

Pennsylvania	
Senators	**Representatives**
J. Donald Cameron (R)	Samuel F. Barr (R)
John I. Mitchell (R)	Thomas M. Bayne (R)
	Frank E. Beltzhoover (D)
	Henry H. Bingham (R)
	Charles N. Brumm (Greenback, R)
	Jacob M. Campbell (R)
	Andrew G. Curtin (D)
	Daniel Ermentrout (D)
	Russell Errett (R)
	Horatio G. Fisher (R)
	William Godshalk (R)
	Alfred C. Harmer (R)
	Cornelius C. Jadwin (R)
	William D. Kelley (R)
	Robert Klotz (D)
	Samuel H. Miller (R)
	James Mosgrove (Greenback, D)
	William Mutchler (D)
	Charles O'Neill (R)
	Samuel J. Randall (D)
	Joseph A. Scranton (R)
	William S. Shallenberger (R)
	A. Herr Smith (R)
	Robert J. C. Walker (R)
	William Ward (R)
	Lewis F. Watson (R)
	Morgan R. Wise (D)

Rhode Island	
Senators	**Representatives**
Henry B. Anthony (R)	Nelson W. Aldrich (R)
Ambrose E. Burnside (R)	r. Oct. 1881
d. Sep. 1881	Jonathan Chace (R)
Nelson W. Aldrich (R)	Henry J. Spooner (R)
s. 1881	

South Carolina	
Senators	**Representatives**
Matthew C. Butler (D)	D. Wyatt Aiken (D)
Wade Hampton (D)	Samuel Dibble (D)
	r. May 1882
	John H. Evins (D)
	Edmund W. M. Mackey (R)
	s. 1882
	Michael P. O'Connor (D)
	d. Apr. 1881
	John S. Richardson (D)
	Robert Smalls (R)
	s. 1882
	George D. Tillman (D)
	r. Jul. 1882

Tennessee	
Senators	**Representatives**
Isham G. Harris (D)	John D. C. Atkins (D)
Howell E. Jackson (D)	George G. Dibrell (D)
	Leonidas C. Houk (R)
	John F. House (D)
	Benton McMillin (D)
	William R. Moore (R)
	Augustus H. Pettibone (R)
	Charles B. Simonton (D)
	Richard Warner (D)
	Washington C. Whitthorne (D)

(continued)

TABLE 7.30   (continued)

Mar. 4, 1881 to Mar. 3, 1883

President of The Senate	Presidents Pro Tempore of The Senate	Speaker of The House of Representatives
Chester A. Arthur	Thomas F. Bayard David Davis George F. Edmunds	J. Warren Keifer

Texas

Senators	Representatives
Samuel B. Maxey (D) Richard Coke (D)	David B. Culberson (D) George W. Jones (Greenback) Roger Q. Mills (D) John H. Reagan (D) Christopher C. Upson (D) Olin Wellborn (D)

Vermont

Senators	Representatives
George F. Edmunds (R) Justin S. Morrill (R)	William W. Grout (R) Charles H. Joyce (R) James M. Tyler (R)

Virginia

Senators	Representatives
John W. Johnston (C) William Mahone (Readjuster)	John S. Barbour (D) George C. Cabell (D) John F. Dezendorf (R) Abram Fulkerson (Readjuster) George T. Garrison (D) Joseph Jorgensen (R) John Paul (Readjuster) John R. Tucker (D) George D. Wise (D)

West Virginia

Senators	Representatives
Henry G. Davis (D) Johnson N. Camden (D)	John B. Hoge (D) Benjamin Wilson (D)

Wisconsin

Senators	Representatives
Angus Cameron (R) Philetus Sawyer (R)	Edward S. Bragg (D) Lucien B. Caswell (R) Peter V. Deuster (D) Richard W. Guenther (R) George C. Hazelton (R) Herman L. Humphrey (R) Thaddeus C. Pound (R) Charles G. Williams (R)

Source: Notable Names in American History; A Tabulated Register. Third edition of White's Conspectus of American Biography (1973), 124–26.

TABLE 7.31   FORTY-EIGHTH CONGRESS

Mar. 4, 1883 to Mar. 3, 1885

President of The Senate	President Pro Tempore of The Senate	Speaker of The House of Representatives
None	George F. Edmunds	John G. Carlisle

Alabama

Senators	Representatives
John T. Morgan (D) James L. Pugh (D)	George H. Craig (R) s. 1885 William H. Forney (D) Hilary A. Herbert (D) Goldsmith W. Hewitt (D) James T. Jones (D) William C. Oates (D) Luke Pryor (D) Charles M. Shelley (D) r. Jan. 1885 Thomas Williams (D)

Arkansas

Senators	Representatives
Augustus H. Garland (D) James D. Walker (D)	Clifton R. Breckinridge (D) Poindexter Dunn (D) James K. Jones (D) r. Feb. 1885 Samuel W. Peel (D) John H. Rogers (D)

California

Senators	Representatives
James T. Farley (R) John F. Miller (R)	James H. Budd (D) John R. Glascock (D) Barclay Henley (D) William S. Rosecrans (D) Charles A. Sumner (D) Pleasant B. Tully (D)

Colorado

Senators	Representative
Nathaniel P. Hill (R) Thomas M. Bowen (R)	James B. Belford (R)

Connecticut

Senators	Representatives
Orville H. Platt (R) Joseph R. Hawley (R)	William W. Eaton (D) Charles L. Mitchell (D) Edward W. Seymour (D) John T. Wait (R)

Delaware

Senators	Representative
Thomas F. Bayard (D) Eli Saulsbury (D)	Charles B. Lore (D)

Florida

Senators	Representatives
Charles W. Jones (D) Wilkinson Call (D)	Horatio Bisbee, Jr. (R) Robert H. M. Davidson (D)

Georgia

Senators	Representatives
Joseph E. Brown (D) Alfred H. Colquitt (D)	James H. Blount (D) Hugh Buchanan (D) Allen D. Candler (D) Judson C. Clements (D) Charles F. Crisp (D) Nathaniel J. Hammond (D) Thomas Hardeman (D) John C. Nicholls (D) Seaborn Reese (D) Henry G. Turner (D)

Illinois

Senators	Representatives
John A. Logan (R) Shelby M. Cullom (R)	George E. Adams (R) Joseph G. Cannon (R) William Cullen (R) George R. Davis (R) Ransom W. Dunham (R) Reuben Ellwood (R) John F. Finerty (D) Thomas J. Henderson (R) Robert R. Hitt (R) William R. Morrison (D) Samuel W. Moulton (D) William H. Neece (D) Lewis E. Payson (R) James M. Riggs (D) Jonathan H. Rowell (R) Aaron Shaw (D) William M. Springer (D) John R. Thomas (R) Richard W. Townshend (D) Nicholas E. Worthington (D)

Indiana

Senators	Representatives

Daniel W. Voorhees (D)
Benjamin Harrison (R)
	Thomas M. Browne (R)
	William H. Calkins (R)
	   r. Oct. 1884
	Thomas R. Cobb (D)
	William E. English (D)
	   s. 1884
	William S. Holman (D)
	John J. Kleiner (D)
	John E. Lamb (D)
	Robert Lowry (D)
	Courtland C. Matson (D)
	Stanton J. Peelle (R)
	   r. May 1884
	Benjamin F. Shively (D)
	   s. 1884
	George W. Steele (R)
	Strother M. Stockslager (D)
	Thomas B. Ward (D)
	Thomas J. Wood (D)

Iowa

Senators	Representatives

William B. Allison (R)
James F. Wilson (R)
	John C. Cook (D)
	Benjamin T. Frederick (D)
	   s. 1885
	David B. Henderson (R)
	William P. Hepburn (R)
	Adoniram J. Holmes (R)
	John A. Kasson (R)
	   r. Jul. 1884
	Moses A. McCoid (R)
	Jeremiah H. Murphy (D)

Iowa

Senators	Representatives

	William H. M. Pusey (D)
	Hiram Y. Smith (R)
	   s. 1884
	Isaac S. Struble (R)
	Luman H. Weller (D)
	James Wilson (R)
	   r. Mar. 1885

Kansas

Senators	Representatives

John J. Ingalls (R)
Preston B. Plumb (R)
	John A. Anderson (R)
	Edward H. Funston (R)
	   s. 1884
	Lewis Hanback (R)
	Dudley C. Haskell (R)
	   d. Dec. 1883
	Edmund N. Morrill (R)
	Bishop W. Perkins (R)
	Samuel R. Peters (R)
	Thomas Ryan (R)

Kentucky

Senators	Representatives
James B. Beck (D) John S. Williams (D)	Joseph C. S. Blackburn (D) John G. Carlisle (D) James F. Clay (D) William W. Culbertson (R) John E. Halsell (D) Thomas A. Robertson (D) Philip B. Thompson, Jr. (D) Oscar Turner (D) John D. White (R) Albert S. Willis (D) Frank L. Wolford (D)

Louisiana

Senators	Representatives
Benjamin F. Jonas (D) Randall L. Gibson (D)	Newton C. Blanchard (D) E. John Ellis (D) Carleton Hunt (D) William P. Kellogg (R) J. Floyd King (D) Edward T. Lewis (D)

Maine

Senators	Representatives
Eugene Hale (R) William P. Frye (R)	Charles A. Boutelle (R) Nelson Dingley, Jr. (R) Seth L. Milliken (R) Thomas B. Reed (R)

Maryland

Senators	Representatives
James B. Groome (D) Arthur P. Gorman (D)	George W. Covington (D) John V. L. Findlay (D) Fetter S. Hoblitzell (D) Hart B. Holton (R) Louis E. McComas (R) J. Fred C. Talbott (D)

(continued)

TABLE 7.31 (continued)

Mar. 4, 1883 to Mar. 3, 1885

President of The Senate	President Pro Tempore of The Senate	Speaker of The House of Representatives
None	George F. Edmunds	John G. Carlisle

Massachusetts

Senators	Representatives
Henry L. Dawes (R)	Patrick A. Collins (D)
George F. Hoar (R)	Robert T. Davis (R)
	John D. Long (R)
	Henry B. Lovering (D)
	Theodore Lyman
	Leopold Morse (D)
	Ambrose A. Ranney (R)
	William W. Rice (R)
	George D. Robinson (R)
	r. Jan. 1884
	Francis W. Rockwell (R)
	s. Jan. 1884
	William A. Russell (R)
	Eben F. Stone (R)
	William Whiting (R)

Michigan

Senators	Representatives
Omar D. Conger (R)	Edward Breitung (R)
Thomas W. Palmer (R)	Ezra C. Carleton (D)
	Byron M. Cutcheon (R)
	Nathaniel B. Eldredge (D)
	Herschel H. Hatch (R)
	Roswell G. Horr (R)
	Julius Houseman (D)
	Edward S. Lacey (R)
	William C. Maybury (D)
	Edwin B. Winans (D)
	George L. Yaple (Un)

Minnesota

Senators	Representatives
Samuel J. R. McMillan (R)	Knute Nelson (R)
Dwight M. Sabin (R)	Horace B. Strait (R)
	James B. Wakefield (R)
	William D. Washburn (R)
	Milo White (R)

Mississippi

Senators	Representatives
Lucius Q. C. Lamar (D)	Ethelbert Barksdale (D)
James Z. George (D)	James R. Chalmers
	s. 1884
	Elza Jeffords (R)
	Hernando D. Money (D)
	Henry L. Muldrow (D)
	Otho R. Singleton (D)
	Henry S. Van Eaton (D)

Missouri

Senators	Representatives
Francis M. Cockrell (D)	Armstead M. Alexander (D)
George G. Vest (D)	Richard P. Bland (D)
	James O. Broadhead (D)
	Aylett H. Buckner (D)
	James N. Burnes (D)
	Martin L. Clardy (D)

Missouri

Senators	Representatives
	John Cosgrove (D)
	Lowndes H. Davis (D)
	Alexander M. Dockery (D)
	Robert W. Fyan (D)
	Alexander Graves (D)
	William H. Hatch (D)
	Charles H. Morgan (D)
	John J. O'Neill (D)

Nebraska

Senators	Representatives
Charles H. Van Wyck (R)	James Laird (R)
Charles F. Manderson (R)	Edward K. Valentine (R)
	Archibald J. Weaver (R)

Nevada

Senators	Representative
John P. Jones (R)	George W. Cassidy (D)
James G. Fair (D)	

New Hampshire

Senators	Representatives
Henry W. Blair (R)	Martin A. Haynes (R)
Austin F. Pike (R)	Ossian Ray (R)

New Jersey

Senators	Representatives
John R. McPherson (D)	J. Hart Brewer (D)
William J. Sewell (R)	Thomas M. Ferrell (D)
	William H. F. Fiedler (D)
	Benjamin F. Howey (R)
	John Kean (R)
	William McAdoo (D)
	William W. Phelps (R)

New York

Senators	Representatives
Warner Miller (R)	John J. Adams (D)
Elbridge G. Lapham (R)	John Arnot, Jr. (D)
	John H. Bagley, Jr. (D)
	Lewis Beach (D)
	Perry Belmont (D)
	Francis B. Brewer (R)
	Henry G. Burleigh (R)
	Felix Campbell (D)
	Samuel S. Cox (D)
	William Dorsheimer (D)
	Halbert S. Greenleaf (D)
	John Hardy (D)
	Abram S. Hewitt (D)
	Frank Hiscock (R)
	Waldo Hutchins (D)
	Darwin R. James (R)
	Frederick A. Johnson (R)
	John H. Ketcham (R)
	Stephen C. Millard (R)
	Nicholas Muller (R)
	Newton W. Nutting (R)
	Abraham X. Parker (R)
	Sereno E. Payne (R)
	Orlando B. Potter (D)
	George W. Ray (R)

New York	
Senators	**Representatives**
	William E. Robinson (D)
	William F. Rogers (D)
	Charles R. Skinner (R)
	Henry W. Slocum (D)
	John T. Spriggs (D)
	Robert S. Stevens (D)
	Thomas J. Van Alstyne (D)
	James W. Wadsworth (R)
	Edward Wemple (D)

North Carolina	
Senators	**Representatives**
Matt W. Ransom (D)	Risden T. Bennett (D)
Zebulon B. Vance (D)	William R. Cox (D)
	Clement Dowd (D)
	Wharton J. Green (D)
	James E. O'Hara (R)
	Walter F. Pool (R)
	d. Aug. 1883
	James W. Reid (D)
	s. 1885
	Alfred M. Scales (D)
	r. Dec. 1884
	Thomas G. Skinner (D)
	Tyre York (D)
	Robert B. Vance (D)

Ohio	
Senators	**Representatives**
George H. Pendleton (D)	James E. Campbell (D)
John Sherman (R)	s. 1884
	George L. Converse (D)
	John F. Follett (D)
	Martin A. Foran (D)
	George W. Geddes (D)
	Alphonso Hart (R)
	William D. Hill (D)
	Frank H. Hurd (D)
	Isaac M. Jordan (D)
	J. Warren Keifer (R)
	Benjamin Le Fevre (D)
	John W. McCormick (R)
	William McKinley, Jr. (R)
	r. May 1884
	Henry L. Morey (R)
	r. Jun. 1884
	Robert M. Murray (D)
	David R. Paige (D)
	James S. Robinson (R)
	r. Jan. 1885
	George E. Seney (D)
	Ezra B. Taylor (R)
	Joseph D. Taylor (R)
	Jonathan H. Wallace (D)
	s. 1884
	Adoniram J. Warner (D)
	Beriah Wilkins (D)

Oregon	
Senators	**Representative**
James H. Slater (D)	Melvin C. George (R)
Joseph N. Dolph (R)	

Pennsylvania	
Senators	**Representatives**
J. Donald Cameron (R)	Louis E. Atkinson (R)
John I. Mitchell (R)	Samuel F. Barr (R)
	Thomas M. Bayne (R)
	Henry H. Bingham (R)
	Charles E. Boyle (D)
	Samuel M. Brainerd (R)
	William W. Brown (R)
	Charles N. Brumm (Greenback)
	Jacob M. Campbell (R)
	Daniel W. Connolly (D)
	Andrew G. Curtin (D)
	William A. Duncan (D)
	d. Nov. 1884
	Mortimer F. Elliott (D)
	Daniel Ermentrout (D)
	I. Newton Evans (R)
	James B. Everhart (R)
	Alfred C. Harmer (R)
	James H. Hopkins (D)
	William D. Kelley (R)
	George V. Lawrence (R)
	Samuel H. Miller (R)
	William Mutchler (D)
	Charles O'Neill (R)
	John D. Patton (D)
	George A. Post (D)
	Samuel J. Randall (R)
	A. Herr Smith (R)
	John B. Storm (D)
	John A. Swope (D)
	s. 1885

Rhode Island	
Senators	**Representatives**
Henry B. Anthony (R)	Jonathan Chace (R)
d. Sep. 1884	r. Jan. 1885
William P. Sheffield (R)	Nathan F. Dixon (R)
ta. 1884	s. 1885
Jonathan Chace (R)	Henry J. Spooner (R)
s. 1885	
Nelson W. Aldrich (R)	

South Carolina	
Senators	**Representatives**
Matthew C. Butler (D)	D. Wyatt Aiken (D)
Wade Hampton (D)	John Bratton (D)
	s. 1884
	George W. Dargan (D)
	Samuel Dibble (D)
	John H. Evins (D)
	d. Oct. 1884
	John J. Hemphill (D)
	Edmund W. M. Mackey (R)
	d. Jan. 1884
	Robert Smalls (R)
	George D. Tillman (D)

Tennessee	
Senators	**Representatives**
Isham G. Harris (D)	John G. Ballentine (D)
Howell E. Jackson (D)	Andrew J. Caldwell (D)
	George G. Dibrell (D)
	Leonidas C. Houk (R)
	Benton McMillin (D)
	Augustus H. Pettibone (R)
	Rice A. Pierce (D)
	John M. Taylor (D)
	Richard Warner (D)
	H. Casey Young (D)

(continued)

TABLE 7.31 (continued)

Mar. 4, 1883 to Mar. 3, 1885

President of The Senate	President Pro Tempore of The Senate	Speaker of The House of Representatives
None	George F. Edmunds	John G. Carlisle

Texas

Senators	Representatives
Samuel B. Maxey (D) Richard Coke (D)	David B. Culberson (D) John Hancock (D) James H. Jones (D) Samuel W. T. Lanham (D) James F. Miller (D) Roger Q. Mills (D) Thomas P. Ochiltree John H. Reagan (D) Charles Stewart (D) James W. Throckmorton (D) Olin Wellborn (D)

Vermont

Senators	Representatives
George F. Edmunds (R) Justin S. Morrill (R)	Luke P. Poland (R) John W. Stewart (R)

Virginia

Senators	Representatives
William Mahone (Readjuster) Harrison H. Riddleberger (Readjuster)	John S. Barbour (D) Henry Bowen (Readjuster) George C. Cabell (D) George T. Garrison s. 1884 Benjamin S. Hooper (D) Harry Libbey (R) Robert M. Mayo (Readjuster) r. 1884 Charles T. O'Ferrall (D) s. 1884 John R. Tucker (D) George D. Wise (D)

West Virginia

Senators	Representatives
Johnson N. Camden (D) John E. Kenna (D)	Eustace Gibson (D) Nathan Goff (R) Charles P. Snyder (D) William L. Wilson (D)

Wisconsin

Senators	Representatives
Angus Cameron (R) Philetus Sawyer (R)	Peter V. Deuster (D) Richard W. Guenther (R) Burr W. Jones (D) William T. Price (R) Joseph Rankin (D) Isaac Stephenson (R) Daniel H. Sumner (D) John Winans (D) Gilbert M. Woodward (D)

Source: Notable Names in American History; A Tabulated Register. Third edition of White's Conspectus of American Biography (1973), 127–129.

TABLE 7.32 FORTY-NINTH CONGRESS

Mar. 4, 1885 to Mar. 3, 1887

President of The Senate	Presidents Pro Tempore of The Senate	Speaker of The House of Representatives
Thomas A. Hendricks	John Sherman John J. Ingalls	John G. Carlisle

Alabama

Senators	Representatives
John T. Morgan (D) James L. Pugh (D)	Alexander C. Davidson (D) William H. Forney (D) Hilary A. Herbert (D) James T. Jones (D) John M. Martin (D) William C. Oates (D) Thomas W. Sadler (D) Joseph Wheeler (D)

Arkansas

Senators	Representatives
Augustus H. Garland (D) r. Mar. 1885 James H. Berry (D) s. 1885 James K. Jones (D)	Clifton R. Breckinridge (D) Poindexter Dunn (D) Thomas C. McRae (D) Samuel W. Peel (D) John H. Rogers (D)

California

Senators	Representatives
John F. Miller (R) d. Mar. 1886 George Hearst (D) ta. 1886 Abram P. Williams (R) s. 1886 Leland Stanford (R)	Charles N. Felton (R) Barclay Henley (D) James A. Louttit (R) Joseph McKenna (R) Henry H. Markham (R) William W. Morrow (R)

Colorado

Senators	Representative
Thomas M. Bowen (R) Henry M. Teller (R)	George G. Symes (R)

Connecticut

Senators	Representatives
Orville H. Platt (R) Joseph R. Hawley (R)	John R. Buck (R) Charles L. Mitchell (D) Edward W. Seymour (D) John T. Wait (R)

Delaware

Senators	Representative
Thomas F. Bayard (D) r. Mar. 1885 George Gray (D) s. 1885 Eli Saulsbury (D)	Charles B. Lore (D)

Florida

Senators	Representatives
Charles W. Jones (D) Wilkinson Call (D)	Robert H. M. Davidson (D) Charles Dougherty (D)

Georgia	
Senators	**Representatives**
Joseph E. Brown (D)	George T. Barnes (D)
Alfred H. Colquitt (D)	James H. Blount (D)
	Allen D. Candler (D)
	Judson C. Clements (D)
	Charles F. Crisp (D)
	Nathaniel J. Hammond (D)
	Henry R. Harris (D)
	Thomas M. Norwood (D)
	Seaborn Reese (D)
	Henry G. Turner (D)

Illinois	
Senators	**Representatives**
John A. Logan (R)	George E. Adams (R)
d. Dec. 1886	Joseph G. Cannon (R)
Charles B. Farwell (R)	Ransom W. Dunham (R)
s. Jan. 1887	John R. Eden (D)
Shelby M. Cullom (R)	Reuben Ellwood (R)
	d. 1887
	Thomas J. Henderson (R)
	Robert R. Hitt (R)
	Albert J. Hopkins (R)
	Silas Z. Landes (D)
	Frank Lawler (D)
	William R. Morrison (D)
	William H. Neece (D)
	Lewis F. Payson (R)
	Ralph Plumb (R)
	James M. Riggs (D)
	Jonathan H. Rowell (R)
	William H. Springer (D)
	John R. Thomas (R)
	Richard W. Townshend (D)
	James H. Ward (D)
	Nicholas E. Worthington (D)

Indiana	
Senators	**Representatives**
Daniel W. Voorhees (D)	Thomas M. Browne (R)
Benjamin Harrison (R)	William D. Bynum (D)
	Thomas R. Cobb (D)
	George Ford (D)
	William S. Holman (D)
	Jonas G. Howard (D)
	James T. Johnston (R)
	John J. Kleiner (D)
	Robert Lowry (D)
	Courtland C. Matson (D)
	William D. Owen (R)
	George W. Steele (R)
	Thomas B. Ward (D)

Iowa	
Senators	**Representatives**
William B. Allison (R)	Edwin H. Conger (R)
James F. Wilson (R)	Benjamin T. Frederick (D)
	William E. Fuller (R)
	Benton J. Hall (D)
	David B. Henderson (R)
	William P. Hepburn (R)
	Adoniram J. Holmes (R)
	Joseph Lyman (R)
	Jeremiah H. Murphy (D)
	Isaac S. Struble (R)
	James B. Weaver (Greenback)

Kansas	
Senators	**Representatives**
John J. Ingalls (R)	John A. Anderson (R)
Preston B. Plumb (R)	Edward H. Funston (R)
	Lewis Hanback (R)
	Edmund N. Morrill (R)
	Bishop W. Perkins (R)
	Samuel R. Peters (R)
	Thomas Ryan (R)

Kentucky	
Senators	**Representatives**
James B. Beck (D)	William C. P. Breckinridge (D)
Joseph C. S. Blackburn (D)	John G. Carlisle (D)
	John E. Halsell (D)
	Polk Laffoon (D)
	James B. McCreary (D)
	Thomas A. Robertson (D)
	William J. Stone (D)
	William P. Taulbee (D)
	William H. Wadsworth (R)
	Albert S. Willis (D)
	Frank L. Wolford (D)

Louisiana	
Senators	**Representatives**
Randall L. Gibson (D)	Newton C. Blanchard (D)
James B. Eustis (D)	Edward J. Gay (D)
	Michael Hahn (R)
	d. Mar. 1886
	Alfred B. Irion (D)
	J. Floyd King (D)
	Louis St. Martin (D)
	Nathaniel D. Wallace (D)
	s. 1886

Maine	
Senators	**Representatives**
Eugene Hale (R)	Charles A. Boutelle (R)
William P. Frye (R)	Nelson Dingley, Jr. (R)
	Seth L. Miliken (R)
	Thomas B. Reed (R)

Maryland	
Senators	**Representatives**
Arthur P. Gorman (D)	William H. Cole (D)
Ephraim K. Wilson (D)	d. Jul. 1886
	Barnes Compton (D)
	John V. L. Dindlay (D)
	Charles H. Gibson (D)
	Louis E. McComas (R)
	Harry W. Rusk (D)
	s. 1886
	Frank T. Shaw (D)

(continued)

TABLE 7.32 (continued)

Mar. 4, 1885 to Mar. 3, 1887

President of The Senate	Presidents Pro Tempore of The Senate	Speaker of The House of Representatives
Thomas A. Hendricks	John Sherman John J. Ingalls	John G. Carlisle

Massachusetts

Senators	Representatives
Henry L. Dawes (R) George F. Hoar (R)	Charles H. Allen (R) Patrick A. Collins (D) Robert T. Davis (R) Frederick D. Ely (R) Edward D. Hayden (R) John D. Long (R) Henry B. Lovering (D) Ambrose A. Ranney (R) William W. Rice (R) Francis W. Rockwell (R) Eben F. Stone (R) William Whiting (R)

Michigan

Senators	Representatives
Omar D. Conger (R) Thomas W. Palmer (R)	Julius C. Burrows (R) Ezra C. Carleton (D) Charles C. Comstock (D) Byron M. Cutcheon (R) Nathaniel B. Eldredge (D) Spencer O. Fisher (D) William C. Maybury (D) Seth C. Moffatt (R) James O'Donnell (R) Timothy E. Tarsney (D) Edwin B. Winans (D)

Minnesota

Senators	Representatives
Samuel J. R. McMillan (R) Dwight M. Sabin (R)	John B. Gilfillan (R) Knute Nelson (R) Horace B. Strait (R) James B. Wakefield (R) Milo White (R)

Mississippi

Senators	Representatives

Lucius Q. C. Lamar (D)
  r. Mar. 1885
Edward C. Walthall (D)
  s. 1885
James Z. George (D)
	John M. Allen (D)
	Ethelbert Barksdale (D)
	Frederick G. Barry (D)
	Thomas C. Catchings (D)
	James B. Morgan (D)
	Otho R. Singleton (D)
	Henry S. Van Eaton (D)

Missouri

Senators	Representatives
Francis M. Cockrell (D) George G. Vest (D)	Richard P. Bland (D) James N. Burnes (D) Martin L. Clardy (D) William Dawson (D) Alexander M. Dockery (D) John M. Glover (D) John B. Hale (D) William H. Hatch (D)

Missouri

Senators	Representatives
	John T. Heard (D) John E. Hutton (D) John J. O'Neill (D) William J. Stone (D) William H. Wade (R) William Warner (R)

Nebraska

Senators	Representatives
Charles H. Van Wyck (R) Charles F. Manderson (R)	George W. E. Dorsey (R) James Laird (R) Archibald J. Weaver (R)

Nevada

Senators	Representative
John P. Jones (R) James G. Fair (D)	William Woodburn (R)

New Hampshire

Senators	Representatives

Austin F. Pike (R)
  d. Oct. 1886
Person C. Cheney (R)
  s. 1886
Henry W. Blair (R)
	Martin A. Haynes (R)
	Jacob H. Gallinger (R)

New Jersey

Senators	Representatives
John R. McPherson (D) William J. Sewell (R)	James Buchanan (R) Robert S. Green (D) r. Jan. 1887 George Hires (R) Herman Lehlbach (R) William McAdoo (D) William W. Phelps (R) James N. Pidcock (D)

New York

Senators	Representatives

Warner Miller (R)
William M. Evarts (R)
	John J. Adams (D)
	John Arnot, Jr. (D)
	  d. Nov. 1886
	Henry Bacon (D)
	  s. 1886
	Charles S. Baker (R)
	Lewis Beach (D)
	  d. Aug. 1886
	Perry Belmont (D)
	Archibald M. Bliss (D)
	Henry G. Burleigh (R)
	Felix Campbell (D)
	Timothy J. Campbell (D)
	Ira Davenport (R)
	Abraham Dowdney (D)
	  d. Dec. 1886
	John M. Farquhar (R)
	Abram S. Hewitt (D)
	  r. Dec. 1886
	Frank Hiscock (R)
	Darwin R. James (R)
	Frederick A. Johnson
	John H. Ketcham (R)

New York

Senators	Representatives
	James G. Lindsley (R)
	Peter P. Mahoney (D)
	Truman A. Merriman (D)
	Stephen C. Millard (R)
	Nicholas Muller (D)
	Abraham X. Parker (R)
	Sereno E. Payne (R)
	John S. Pindar (D)
	Joseph Pulitzer (D)
	r. Apr. 1886
	John G. Sawyer (R)
	Walter L. Sessions (R)
	William G. Stahlnecker (D)
	John T. Spriggs (D)
	John Swinburne (R)
	Egbert L. Viele (D)
	John B. Weber (R)
	George West (R)

North Carolina

Senators	Representatives
Matt W. Ransom (D)	Risden T. Bennett (D)
Zebulon B. Vance (D)	William H. H. Cowles (D)
	William R. Cox (D)
	Wharton J. Green (D)
	John S. Henderson (D)
	Thomas D. Johnston (D)
	James E. O'Hara (R)
	James W. Reid (D)
	r. Nov. 1886
	Thomas G. Skinner (D)

Ohio

Senators	Representatives
John Sherman (R)	Charles M. Anderson (D)
Henry B. Payne (D)	Charles E. Brown (R)
	Benjamin Butterworth (R)
	James E. Campbell (D)
	William C. Cooper (R)
	William W. Ellsberry (D)
	Martin A. Foran (D)
	George W. Geddes (D)
	Charles H. Grosvenor (R)
	William D. Hill (D)
	Benjamin Le Fevre (D)
	John Little (R)
	William McKinley, Jr. (R)
	Joseph H. Outhwaite (D)
	Jacob Romeis (R)
	George E. Seney (D)
	Ezra B. Taylor (R)
	Isaac H. Taylor (R)
	Albert C. Thompson (R)
	Adoniram J. Warner (D)
	Beriah Wilkins (D)

Oregon

Senators	Representative
Joseph N. Dolph (R)	Binger Hermann (R)
John H. Mitchell (R)	

Pennsylvania

Senators	Representatives
J. Donald Cameron (R)	Louis E. Atkinson (R)
John I. Mitchell (R)	Thomas M. Bayne (R)

Pennsylvania

Senators	Representatives
	Henry H. Bingham (R)
	Franklin Bound (R)
	Charles E. Boyle (D)
	William W. Brown (R)
	Charles N. Brumm (Greenback)
	Frank C. Bunnell (R)
	Jacob M. Campbell (R)
	Andrew G. Curtin (D)
	Daniel Ermentrout (D)
	I. Newton Evans (R)
	James B. Everhart (R)
	George W. Fleeger (R)
	Alfred C. Harmer (R)
	John A. Hiestand (R)
	Oscar L. Jackson (R)
	William D. Kelley (R)
	James S. Negley (R)
	Charles O'Neill (R)
	Edwin S. Osborne (R)
	Samuel J. Randall (D)
	William L. Scott (D)
	Joseph A. Scranton (R)
	William H. Sowden (D)
	John B. Storm (D)
	John A. Swope (D)
	Alexander C. White (R)

Rhode Island

Senators	Representatives
Nelson W. Aldrich (R)	Charles H. Page (D)
Jonathan Chace (R)	s. 1887
	William A. Pirce (R)
	r. Jan. 1887
	Henry J. Spooner (R)

South Carolina

Senators	Representatives
Matthew C. Butler (D)	D. Wyatt Aiken (D)
Wade Hampton (D)	George W. Dargan (D)
	Samuel Dibble (D)
	John J. Hemphill (D)
	William H. Perry (D)
	Robert Smalls (R)
	George D. Tillman (R)

Tennessee

Senators	Representatives
Isham G. Harris (D)	John G. Ballentine (D)
Howell E. Jackson (D)	Andrew J. Caldwell (D)
r. Apr. 1886	Presley T. Glass (D)
Washington C. Whitthorne (D)	Leonidas C. Houk (R)
s. 1886	Benton McMillin (D)
	John R. Neal (D)
	Augustus H. Pettibone (R)
	James D. Richardson (D)
	John M. Taylor (D)
	Zachary Taylor (R)

(continued)

TABLE 7.32   (continued)

Mar. 4, 1885 to Mar. 3, 1887

President of The Senate	Presidents Pro Tempore of The Senate	Speaker of The House of Representatives
Thomas A. Hendricks	John Sherman John J. Ingalls	John G. Carlisle

Texas

Senators	Representatives
Samuel B. Maxey (D) Richard Coke (D)	William H. Crain (D) David B. Culberson (D) James H. Jones (D) Samuel W. T. Lanham (D) James F. Miller (D) Roger Q. Mills (D) John H. Reagan (D) Joseph D. Sayers (D) Charles Stewart (D) James W. Throckmorton (D) Olin Wellborn (D)

Vermont

Senators	Representatives
George F. Edmunds (R) Justin S. Morrill (R)	William W. Grout (R) John W. Stewart (R)

Virginia

Senators	Representatives
William Mahone (Readjuster) Harrison H. Riddleberger (Readjuster)	John S. Barbour (D) James D. Brady (R) George C. Cabell (D) Thomas Croxton (D) John W. Daniel (D) Harry Libbey (R) Charles T. O'Ferrall (D) Connally F. Trigg (D) John R. Tucker (D) George D. Wise (D)

West Virginia

Senators	Representatives
Johnson N. Camden (D) John E. Kenna (D)	Eustace Gibson (D) Nathan Goff (R) Charles P. Snyder (D) William L. Wilson (D)

Wisconsin

Senators	Representatives

Philetus Sawyer (R)
John C. Spooner (R)
	Edward S. Bragg (D)
	Lucien B. Caswell (R)
	Richard W. Guenther (R)
	Thomas R. Hudd (D)
	  s. 1886
	Robert M. La Follette (R)
	Hugh H. Price (R)
	  s. 1887
	William T. Price (R)
	  d. Dec. 1886
	Joseph Rankin (D)
	  d. Jan. 1886
	Isaac Stephenson (R)
	Ormsby B. Thomas (R)
	Isaac W. Van Schaick (R)

Source: Notable Names in American History; A Tabulated Register. Third edition of White's Conspectus of American Biography (1973), 129–131.

TABLE 7.33   FIFTIETH CONGRESS

Mar. 4, 1887 to Mar. 3, 1889

President of The Senate	President Pro Tempore of The Senate	Speaker of The House of Representatives
Vacant	John J. Ingalls	John G. Carlisle

Alabama

Senators	Representatives
John T. Morgan (D) James L. Pugh (D)	John H. Bankhead (D) James E. Cobb Alexander C. Davidson (D) William H. Forney (D) Hilary A. Herbert (D) James T. Jones (D) William C. Oates (D) Joseph Wheeler (D)

Arkansas

Senators	Representatives
James K. Jones (D) James H. Berry (D)	Clifton R. Breckinridge (D) Poindexter Dunn (D) Thomas C. McRae (D) Samuel W. Peel (D) John H. Rogers (D)

California

Senators	Representatives
Leland Stanford (R) George Hearst (D)	Marion Biggs (D) Charles N. Felton (R) Joseph McKenna (R) William W. Morrow (R) Thomas L. Thompson (D) William Vandever (R)

Colorado

Senators	Representative
Thomas M. Bowen (R) Henry M. Teller (R)	George G. Symes (R)

Connecticut

Senators	Representatives
Orville H. Platt (R) Joseph R. Hawley (R)	Carlos French (D) Miles T. Granger (D) Charles A. Russell (R) Robert J. Vance (D)

Delaware

Senators	Representative
Eli Saulsbury (D) George Gray (D)	John B. Penington (D)

Florida

Senators	Representatives
Wilkinson Call (D) Samuel Pasco (D)	Robert H. M. Davidson (D) Charles Dougherty (D)

Georgia

Senators	Representatives
Joseph E. Brown (D)	George T. Barnes (D)
Alfred H. Colquitt (D)	James H. Blount (D)
	Allen D. Candler (D)
	Henry H. Carlton (D)
	Judson C. Clements (D)
	Charles F. Crisp (D)
	Thomas W. Grimes (D)
	Thomas M. Norwood (D)
	John D. Stewart (D)
	Henry G. Turner (D)

Illinois

Senators	Representatives
Shelby M. Cullom (R)	George E. Adams (R)
Charles B. Farwell (R)	George A. Anderson (D)
	Jehu Baker (R)
	Joseph G. Cannon (R)
	Ransom W. Dunham (R)
	William H. Gest (R)
	Thomas J. Henderson (R)
	Robert R. Hitt (R)
	Albert J. Hopkins (R)
	Silas Z. Landes (D)
	Edward Lane (D)
	Frank Lawler (D)
	William E. Mason (R)
	Lewis E. Payson (R)
	Ralph Plumb (R)
	Philip S. Post (R)
	Jonathan H. Rowell (R)
	William M. Springer (D)
	John R. Thomas (R)
	Richard W. Townshend (D)

Indiana

Senators	Representatives
Daniel W. Voorhees (D)	Thomas M. Browne (R)
David Turpie (D)	William D. Bynum (D)
	Joseph B. Cheadle (R)
	William S. Holman (D)
	Alvin P. Hovey (R)
	r. Jan. 1889
	Jonas G. Howard (D)
	James T. Johnston (R)
	Courtland C. Matson (D)
	John H. O'Neall (D)
	William D. Owen (R)
	Francis B. Posey (R)
	s. 1889
	Benjamin F. Shively (D)
	George W. Steele (R)
	James B. White

Iowa

Senators	Representatives
William B. Allison (R)	Albert R. Anderson (R)
James F. Wilson (R)	Edwin H. Conger (R)
	William E. Fuller (R)
	John H. Gear (R)
	Walter I. Hayes (D)
	David B. Henderson (R)
	Adoniram J. Holmes (R)
	Daniel Kerr (R)
	Joseph Lyman (R)
	Isaac S. Struble (R)
	James B. Weaver (D.G. Labor.)[a]

Kansas

Senators	Representatives
John J. Ingalls (R)	John A. Anderson (R)
Preston B. Plumb (R)	Edward H. Funston (R)
	Edmund N. Morrill (R)
	Bishop W. Perkins (R)
	Samuel R. Peters (R)
	Thomas Ryan (R)
	Erastus J. Turner (R)

Kentucky

Senators	Representatives
James B. Beck (D)	William C. P. Breckinridge (D)
Joseph C. S. Blackburn (D)	John G. Carlisle (D)
	Asher G. Caruth (D)
	Hugh F. Finley (R)
	W. Godfrey Hunter (R)
	Polk Laffoon (D)
	James B. McCreary (D)
	Alexander B. Montgomery (D)
	William J. Stone (D)
	William P. Taulbee (D)
	George M. Thomas (R)

Louisiana

Senators	Representatives
Randall L. Gibson (D)	Newton C. Blanchard (D)
James B. Eustis (D)	Edward J. Gay (D)
	Matthew D. Lagan (D)
	Cherubusco Newton (D)
	Samuel M. Robertson (D)
	Theodore S. Wilkinson (D)

Maine

Senators	Representatives
Eugene Hale (R)	Charles A. Boutelle (R)
William P. Frye (R)	Nelson Dingley, Jr. (R)
	Seth L. Milliken (R)
	Thomas B. Reed (R)

Maryland

Senators	Representatives
Arthur P. Gorman (D)	Barnes Compton (D)
Ephraim K. Wilson (D)	Charles H. Gibson (D)
	Louis E. McComas (R)
	Isidor Rayner (D)
	Harry W. Rusk (D)
	Frank T. Shaw (D)

Massachusetts

Senators	Representatives
Henry L. Dawes (R)	Charles H. Allen (R)
George F. Hoar (R)	Edward Burnett (D)
	William Cogswell (R)
	Patrick A. Collins (D)
	Robert T. Davis (R)
	Edward D. Hayden (R)
	Henry Cabot Lodge (R)
	John D. Long (R)
	Leopold Morse (D)
	Francis W. Rockwell (R)
	John E. Russell (D)
	William Whiting (R)

(continued)

TABLE 7.33 (continued)

Mar. 4, 1887 to Mar. 3, 1889

President of The Senate	President Pro Tempore of The Senate	Speaker of The House of Representatives
Vacant	John J. Ingalls	John G. Carlisle

Michigan

Senators	Representatives
Thomas W. Palmer (R)	Edward P. Allen (R)
Francis B. Stockbridge (R)	Mark S. Brewer (R)
	Julius C. Burrows (R)
	J. Logan Chipman (D)
	Byron M. Cutcheon (R)
	Spencer O. Fisher (D)
	Melbourne H. Ford (D)
	Seth C. Moffatt (R)
	d. Dec. 1887
	James O'Donnell (R)
	Henry W. Seymour (R)
	s. 1888
	Timothy E. Tarsney (D)
	Justin R. Whiting (Greenback, D)

Minnesota

Senators	Representatives
Dwight M. Sabin (R)	John Lind (R)
Cushman K. Davis (R)	John L. MacDonald (D)
	Knute Nelson (R)
	Edmund Rice (D)
	Thomas Wilson (D)

Mississippi

Senators	Representatives
James Z. George (D)	John M. Allen (D)
Edward C. Walthall (D)	Chapman L. Anderson (D)
	Frederick G. Barry (D)
	Thomas C. Catchings (D)
	Charles E. Hooker (D)
	James B. Morgan (D)
	Thomas R. Stockdale (D)

Missouri

Senators	Representatives
Francis M. Cockrell (D)	Richard P. Bland (D)
George G. Vest (D)	Charles F. Booher (D)
	s. 1889
	James N. Burnes (D)
	Martin L. Clardy (D)
	Alexander M. Dockery (D)
	John M. Glover (D)
	William H. Hatch (D)
	John T. Heard (D)
	John E. Hutton (D)
	Charles H. Mansur (D)
	John J. O'Neill (D)
	William J. Stone (D)
	William H. Wade (R)
	James P. Walker (D)
	William Warner (R)

Nebraska

Senators	Representatives
Charles F. Manderson (R)	George W. E. Dorsey (R)
Algernon S. Paddock (R)	James Laird (R)
	John A. McShane (D)

Nevada

Senators	Representative
John P. Jones (R)	William Woodburn (R)
William M. Stewart (R)	

New Hampshire

Senators	Representatives
Henry W. Blair (R)	Jacob H. Gallinger (R)
William E. Chandler (R)	Luther F. McKinney (D)

New Jersey

Senators	Representatives
John R. McPherson (D)	James Buchanan (R)
Rufus Blodgett (D)	George Hires (R)
	John Kean (R)
	Herman Lehlbach (R)
	William McAdoo (D)
	William W. Phelps (R)
	James N. Pidcock (D)

New York

Senators	Representatives
William M. Evarts (R)	Henry Bacon (D)
Frank Hiscock (R)	Charles S. Baker (R)
	James J. Belden (R)
	Perry Belmont (D)
	r. Dec. 1888
	Archibald M. Bliss (D)
	Lloyd S. Bryce (D)
	Felix Campbell (D)
	Timothy J. Campbell (D)
	W. Bourke Cockran (D)
	Samuel S. Cox (D)
	Amos J. Cummings (D)
	Ira Davenport (R)
	Milton De Lano (R)
	John M. Farquhar (R)
	Ashbel P. Fitch (R)
	Thomas S. Flood (R)
	Edward W. Greenman (D)
	Stephen T. Hopkins (R)
	John H. Ketcham (R)
	William G. Laidlaw (R)
	Peter P. Mahoney (D)
	Truman A. Merriman (D)
	John H. Moffitt (R)
	Newton W. Nutting (R)
	Abraham X. Parker (R)
	John G. Sawyer (R)
	James S. Sherman (R)
	Francis B. Spinola (D)
	William G. Stahlnecker (D)
	Charles Tracey (D)
	John B. Weber (R)
	George West (R)
	Stephen V. White (R)
	David Wilber (R)

North Carolina

Senators	Representatives
Matt W. Ransom (D)	John M. Brower (R)
Zebulon B. Vance (D)	William H. H. Cowles (D)
	John S. Henderson (D)
	Thomas D. Johnston (D)
	Louis C. Latham (D)
	Charles W. McClammy (D)
	John Nichols
	Alfred Rowland (D)
	Furnifold McL. Simmons (D)

Ohio

Senators	Representatives
John Sherman (R)	Melvin M. Boothman (R)
Henry B. Payne (D)	Charles E. Brown (R)
	Benjamin Butterworth (R)
	James E. Campbell (D)
	William C. Cooper (R)
	George W. Crouse (R)
	Martin A. Foran (D)
	Charles H. Grosvenor (R)
	Robert P. Kennedy (R)
	William McKinley, Jr. (R)
	Joseph H. Outhwaite (D)
	Jacob J. Pugsley (R)
	Jacob Romeis (R)
	George E. Seney (D)
	Ezra B. Taylor (R)
	Joseph D. Taylor (R)
	Albert C. Thompson (R)
	Charles P. Wickham (R)
	Beriah Wilkins (D)
	Elihu S. Williams (R)
	Samuel S. Yoder (D)

Oregon

Senators	Representative
Joseph N. Dolph (R)	Binger Hermann (R)
John H. Mitchell (R)	

Pennsylvania

Senators	Representatives
J. Donald Cameron (R)	Louis E. Atkinson (R)
Matthew S. Quay (R)	Thomas M. Bayne (R)
	Henry H. Bingham (R)
	Franklin Bound (R)
	Charles N. Brumm (Greenback)
	Charles R. Buckalew (D)
	Frank C. Bunnell (R)
	John Dalzell (R)
	Smedley Darlington (R)
	Daniel Ermentrout (D)
	Norman Hall (D)
	Alfred C. Harmer (R)
	John A. Hiestand (R)
	Oscar L. Jackson (R)
	William D. Kelley (R)
	John Lynch (D)
	Henry C. McCormick (R)
	Welty McCullogh (R)
	James T. Maffett (R)
	Levi Maish (D)
	Charles O'Neill (R)
	Edwin S. Osborne (R)
	John Patton (R)
	Samuel J. Randall (D)
	William L. Scott (D)
	Edward Scull (R)
	William H. Sowden (D)
	Robert M. Yardley (R)

Rhode Island

Senators	Representatives
Nelson W. Aldrich (R)	Warren O. Arnold (R)
Jonathan Chace (R)	Henry J. Spooner (R)

South Carolina

Senators	Representatives
Matthew C. Butler (D)	James S. Cothran (D)
Wade Hampton (D)	George W. Dargan (D)
	Samuel Dibble (D)
	William Elliott (D)
	John J. Hemphill (D)
	William H. Perry (D)
	George D. Tillman (D)

Tennessee

Senators	Representatives
Isham G. Harris (D)	Roderick R. Butler (R)
William B. Bate (D)	Benjamin A. Enloe (D)
	Presley T. Glass (D)
	Leonidas C. Houk (R)
	Benton McMillin (D)
	John R. Neal (D)
	James Phelan (D)
	James D. Richardson (D)
	Joseph E. Washington (D)
	Washington C. Whitthorne (D)

Texas

Senators	Representatives
Richard Coke (D)	Jo Abbott (D)
John H. Reagan (D)	William H. Crain (D)
	David B. Culberson (D)
	Silas Hare (D)
	Constantine B. Kilgore (D)
	Samuel W. T. Lanham (D)
	William H. Martin (D)
	Roger Q. Mills (D)
	Littleton W. Moore (D)
	Joseph D. Sayers (D)
	Charles Stewart (D)

Vermont

Senators	Representatives
George F. Edmunds (R)	William W. Grout (R)
Justin S. Morrill (R)	John W. Stewart (R)

Virginia

Senators	Representatives
Harrison H. Riddleberger (Readjuster)	George E. Bowden (R)
John W. Daniel (D)	Henry Bowen (R)
	John R. Brown (R)
	Thomas H. B. Browne (R)
	William E. Gaines (R)
	Samuel I. Hopkins (D)
	William H. F. Lee (D)
	Charles T. O'Ferrall (D)
	George D. Wise (D)
	Jacob Yost (R)

West Virginia

Senators	Representatives
John E. Kenna (D)	Charles E. Hogg (D)
Charles J. Faulkner (D)	Nathan Goff (R)
	Charles P. Snyder (D)
	William L. Wilson (D)

(continued)

TABLE 7.33 (continued)

Mar. 4, 1887 to Mar. 3, 1889

President of The Senate	President Pro Tempore of The Senate	Speaker of The House of Representatives
Vacant	John J. Ingalls	John G. Carlisle

Wisconsin

Senators	Representatives
Philetus Sawyer (R) John C. Spooner (R)	Lucien B. Caswell (R) Charles B. Clark (R) Richard W. Guenther (R) Nils P. Haugen (R) s. 1888 Thomas R. Hudd (D) Robert M. La Follette (R) Henry Smith (People's Party) Isaac Stephenson (R) Ormsby B. Thomas (R)

Source: Notable Names in American History; A Tabulated Register. Third edition of *White's Conspectus of American Biography* (1973), 131–134.
[a] Democratic-Greenback Laborite.

TABLE 7.34   FIFTY-FIRST CONGRESS

Mar. 4, 1889 to Mar. 3, 1891

President of The Senate	Presidents Pro Tempore of The Senate	Speaker of The House of Representatives
Levi P. Morton	John J. Ingalls Charles F. Manderson	Thomas B. Reed

Alabama

Senators	Representatives

John T. Morgan (D)
James L. Pugh (D)
	John H. Bankhead (D)
	Richard H. Clarke (R)
	James E. Cobb
	William H. Forney (D)
	Hilary A. Herbert (D)
	John V. McDuffie (R)
	  s. 1890
	William C. Oates (D)
	Louis W. Turpin (D)
	  r. Jun. 1890
	Joseph Wheeler (D)

Arkansas

Senators	Representatives

James K. Jones (D)
James H. Berry (D)
	Clifton R. Breckinridge (D)
	William H. Cate (D)
	  r. Mar. 1890
	Lewis P. Featherstone (Laborite)
	  s. 1890
	Thomas C. McRae (D)
	Samuel W. Peel (D)
	John H. Rogers (D)

California

Senators	Representatives

Leland Stanford (R)
George Hearst (D)
	Marion Biggs (D)
	Thomas J. Clunie (D)
	John J. De Haven (R)
	  r. Oct. 1890
	Thomas J. Geary (D)
	  s. 1890
	Joseph McKenna (R)
	William W. Morrow (R)
	William Vandever (R)

Colorado

Senators	Representative
Henry M. Teller (R) Edward O. Wolcott (R)	Hosea Townsend (R)

Connecticut

Senators	Representatives
Orville H. Platt (R) Joseph R. Hawley (R)	Frederick Miles (R) Charles A. Russell (R) William E. Simonds (R) Washington F. Willcox (D)

Delaware

Senators	Representative
George Gray (D) Anthony Higgins (R)	John B. Penington (D)

Florida

Senators	Representatives
Wilkinson Call (D) Samuel Pasco (D)	Robert Bullock (D) Robert H. M. Davidson (D)

Georgia

Senators	Representatives
Joseph E. Brown (D) Alfred H. Colquitt (D)	George T. Barnes (D) James H. Blount (D) Allen D. Candler (D) Henry H. Carlton (D) Judson C. Clements (D) Charles F. Crisp (D) Thomas W. Grimes (D) Rufus E. Lester (D) John D. Stewart (D) Henry G. Turner (D)

Idaho

Senators	Representative

George L. Shoup (R)
  s. 1890
William J. McConnell (R)
  s. 1891
	Willis Sweet (R)
	  s. 1890

Illinois

Senators	Representatives
Shelby M. Cullom (R) Charles B. Farwell (R)	George E. Adams (R) Joseph G. Cannon (R) George W. Fithian (D) William S. Forman (D) William H. Gest (R) Thomas J. Henderson (R) Charles A. Hill (R)

Illinois	
Senators	**Representatives**
	Robert H. Hitt (R)
	Albert J. Hopkins (R)
	Edward Lane (D)
	Frank Lawler (D)
	William E. Mason (R)
	Lewis E. Payson (R)
	Philip S. Post (R)
	Jonathan H. Rowell (R)
	George W. Smith (R)
	William M. Springer (D)
	Abner Taylor (R)
	Scott Wike (D)
	James R. Williams (R)

Indiana	
Senators	**Representatives**
Daniel W. Voorhees (D)	Elijah V. Brookshire (D)
David Turpie (D)	Jason B. Brown (D)
	Thomas M. Browne (R)
	William D. Bynum (D)
	Joseph B. Cheadle (R)
	George W. Cooper (D)
	William S. Holman (D)
	Charles A. O. McClellan (D)
	Augustus N. Martin (D)
	John H. O'Neall (D)
	William D. Owen (R)
	William F. Parrett (D)
	Benjamin F. Shively (D)

Iowa	
Senators	**Representatives**
William B. Allison (R)	Edwin H. Conger (R)
James F. Wilson (R)	r. Oct. 1890
	Jonathan P. Dolliver (R)
	James P. Flick (R)
	John H. Gear (R)
	Walter I. Hayes (D)
	Edward R. Hays (R)
	s. 1890
	David B. Henderson (R)
	Daniel Kerr (R)
	John F. Lacey (R)
	Joseph R. Reed (R)
	Isaac S. Struble (R)
	Joseph H. Sweney (R)

Kansas	
Senators	**Representatives**
John J. Ingalls (R)	John A. Anderson (R)
Preston B. Plumb (R)	Edward H. Funston (R)
	Harrison Kelley (R)
	Edmund N. Morrill (R)
	Samuel R. Peters (R)
	Bishop W. Perkins (R)
	Erastus J. Turner (R)

Kentucky	
Senators	**Representatives**
James B. Beck (D)	William C. P. Breckinridge (D)
d. May 1890	John G. Carlisle (D)
John G. Carlisle (D)	r. May 1890
s. 1890	Asher G. Caruth (D)
Joseph C. S. Blackburn (D)	William W. Dickerson (D)
	s. Jun. 1890

Kentucky	
Senators	**Representatives**
	William T. Ellis (D)
	Hugh F. Finley (R)
	Isaac H. Goodnight (D)
	James B. McCreary (D)
	Alexander B. Montgomery (D)
	Thomas H. Paynter (D)
	William J. Stone (D)
	John H. Wilson (R)

Louisiana	
Senators	**Representatives**
Randall L. Gibson (D)	Newton C. Blanchard (D)
James B. Eustis (D)	Charles J. Boatner (D)
	Hamilton D. Coleman (R)
	Andrew Price (D)
	Samuel M. Robertson (D)
	Theodore S. Wilkinson (D)

Maine	
Senators	**Representatives**
Eugene Hale (R)	Charles A. Boutelle (R)
William P. Frye (R)	Nelson Dingley, Jr. (R)
	Seth L. Milliken (R)
	Thomas B. Reed (R)

Maryland	
Senators	**Representatives**
Arthur P. Gorman (D)	Barnes Compton (D)
Ephraim K. Wilson (D)	r. Mar. 1890
d. Feb. 1890	Charles H. Gibson (D)
	Louis E. McComas (R)
	Sydney E. Mudd (R)
	s. 1890
	Harry W. Rusk (D)
	Henry Stockbridge (R)
	Herman Stump (D)

Massachusetts	
Senators	**Representatives**
Henry L. Dawes (R)	John F. Andrew (D)
George F. Hoar (R)	Nathaniel P. Banks (R)
	John W. Chandler (R)
	William Cogswell (R)
	Frederic T. Greenhalge (R)
	Henry Cabot Lodge (R)
	Elijah A. Morse (R)
	Joseph H. O'Neil (D)
	Charles S. Randall (R)
	Francis W. Rockwell (R)
	Joseph H. Walker (R)
	Rodney Wallace (R)

Michigan	
Senators	**Representatives**
Francis B. Stockbridge (R)	Edward P. Allen (R)
James McMillan (R)	Charles E. Belknap (R)
	Aaron T. Bliss (R)
	Mark S. Brewer (R)
	Julius C. Burrows (R)
	J. Logan Chipman (D)
	Byron M. Cutcheon (R)
	James O'Donnell (R)
	Samuel M. Stephenson (R)
	Frank W. Wheeler (R)
	Justin R. Whiting (D)

(continued)

TABLE 7.34 (continued)

Mar. 4, 1889 to Mar. 3, 1891

President of The Senate	Presidents Pro Tempore of The Senate	Speaker of The House of Representatives
Levi P. Morton	John J. Ingalls Charles F. Manderson	Thomas B. Reed

Minnesota

Senators	Representatives
Cushman K. Davis (R) William D. Washburn (R)	Solomon G. Comstock (R) Mark H. Dunnell (R) Darwin S. Hall (R) John Lind (R) Samuel P. Snider (R)

Mississippi

Senators	Representatives
James Z. George (D) Edward C. Walthall (D)	John M. Allen (D) Chapman L. Anderson (D) Thomas C. Catchings (D) Charles E. Hooker (D) Clarke Lewis (D) James B. Morgan (D) Thomas R. Stockdale (D)

Missouri

Senators	Representatives

Francis M. Cockrell (D)
George G. Vest (D)
	Richard P. Bland (D)
	Alexander M. Dockery (D)
	Nathan Frank (R)
	William H. Hatch (D)
	John T. Heard (D)
	William M. Kinsey (R)
	Charles H. Mansur (D)
	Frederick G. Niedringhaus (R)
	Richard H. Norton (D)
	William J. Stone (D)
	John C. Tarsney (D)
	William H. Wade (R)
	James P. Walker (D)
	   d. Jul. 1890
	Robert H. Whitelaw (D)
	   s. 1890
	Robert P. C. Wilson (D)

Montana

Senators	Representative

Thomas C. Power (R)
   s. 1890
Wilbur F. Sanders (R)
   s. 1890
	Thomas H. Carter (R)

Nebraska

Senators	Representatives
Charles F. Manderson (R) Algernon S. Paddock (R)	William J. Connell (R) George W. E. Dorsey (R) Gilbert L. Laws (R)

Nevada

Senators	Representative
John P. Jones (R) William M. Stewart (R)	Horace F. Bartine (R)

New Hampshire

Senators	Representatives
Henry W. Blair (R) William E. Chandler (R)	Alonzo Nute (R) Orren C. Moore (R)

New Jersey

Senators	Representatives
John R. McPherson (D) Rufus Blodgett (D)	Charles D. Beckwith (R) Christopher A. Bergen (R) James Buchanan (R) Samuel Fowler (D) Jacob A. Geissenhainer (D) Herman Lehlbach (R) William McAdoo (D)

New York

Senators	Representatives

William M. Evarts (R)
Frank Hiscock (R)
	Charles S. Baker (R)
	James J. Belden (R)
	Felix Campbell (D)
	John M. Clancy (D)
	James W. Covert (D)
	Amos J. Cummings (D)
	Milton De Lano (R)
	Edward J. Dunphy (D)
	John M. Farquhar (R)
	Ashbel P. Fitch (D)
	Thomas S. Flood (R)
	Roswell P. Flower (D)
	John H. Ketcham (R)
	Charles J. Knapp (R)
	William G. Laidlaw (R)
	Frederick Lansing (R)
	John H. McCarthy (D)
	   r. Jan 1891
	Thomas F. Magner (D)
	John H. Moffitt (R)
	Sereno E. Payne (R)
	John S. Pindar (D)
	   s. 1890
	John A. Quackenbush (R)
	John Quinn (D)
	John Raines (R)
	John Sanford (R)
	John G. Sawyer (R)
	James S. Sherman (R)
	Francis B. Spinola (D)
	William G. Stahlnecker (D)
	Moses D. Stivers (R)
	Charles Tracey (D)
	Charles H. Turner (D)
	William C. Wallace (R)
	David Wilber (R)
	   d. Apr. 1890
	John McC. Wiley (D)

North Carolina

Senators	Representatives
Matt W. Ransom (D) Zebulon B. Vance (D)	John M. Brower (R) Benjamin H. Bunn (D) Henry P. Cheatham (R) William H. H. Cowles (D) Hamilton G. Ewart (R) John S. Henderson (D) Charles W. McClammy (D) Alfred Rowland (D) Thomas G. Skinner (D)

North Dakota	
Senators	**Representative**
Lyman R. Casey (R) Gilbert A. Pierce (R)	Henry C. Hansbrough (R)

Ohio	
Senators	**Representatives**
John Sherman (R) Henry B. Payne (D)	Melvin M. Boothman (R) Thedore E. Burton (R) Benjamin Butterworth (R) John A. Caldwell (R) William C. Cooper (R) Charles H. Grosvenor (R) William E. Haynes (D) Robert P. Kennedy (R) William McKinley, Jr. (R) Henry L. Morey (R) Joseph H. Outhwaite (D) James W. Owens (D) Jacob J. Pugsley (R) George E. Seney (D) Martin L. Smyser (R) Ezra B. Taylor (R) Joseph D. Taylor (R) Albert C. Thompson (R) Charles P. Wickham (D) Elihu S. Williams (R) Samuel S. Yoder (D)

Oregon	
Senators	**Representative**
Joseph N. Dolph (R) John H. Mitchell (R)	Binger Hermann (R)

Pennsylvania	
Senators	**Representatives**

J. Donald Cameron (R)
Matthew S. Quay (R)
	Louis E. Atkinson (R)
	Thomas M. Bayne (R)
	Henry H. Bingham (R)
	Marriott Broslus (R)
	David B. Brunner (D)
	Charles R. Buckalew (D)
	Samuel A. Craig (R)
	William C. Culbertson (R)
	John Dalzell (R)
	Smedley Darlington (R)
	Alfred C. Harmer (R)
	William D. Kelley (R)
	  d. 1890
	James Kerr (D)
	Henry C. McCormick (R)
	Levi Maish (D)
	William Mutchler (D)
	Charles O'Neill (R)
	Edwin S. Osborne (R)
	Samuel J. Randall (D)
	  d. 1890
	Joseph W. Ray (R)
	James B. Reilly (D)
	John E. Reyburn (R)
	  s. 1890
	John W. Rife (R)
	Joseph A. Scranton (R)
	Edward Scull (R)
	Charles W. Stone (R)
	  s. 1890
	Charles C. Townsend (R)
	Richard Vaux (D)
	  s. 1890

Pennsylvania	
Senators	**Representatives**
	Lewis F. Watson (R) d. Aug. 1890 Myron B. Wright (R) Robert M. Yardley (R)

Rhode Island	
Senators	**Representatives**

Nelson W. Aldrich (R)
Jonathan Chace (R)
  r. Apr. 1889
Nathan F. Dixon (R)
  s. 1889
	Warren O. Arnold (R)
	Henry J. Spooner (R)

South Carolina	
Senators	**Representatives**

Matthew C. Butler (D)
Wade Hampton (D)
	James S. Cothran (D)
	George W. Dargan (D)
	Samuel Dibble (D)
	William Elliott (D)
	  r. Sep. 1890
	John J. Hemphill (D)
	Thomas E. Miller (R)
	  s. 1890
	William H. Perry (D)
	George D. Tillman (D)

South Dakota	
Senators	**Representatives**
Richard F. Pettigrew (R) Gideon C. Moody (R)	Oscar S. Gifford (R) John A. Pickler (R)

Tennessee	
Senators	**Representatives**
Isham G. Harris (D) William B. Bate (D)	Benjamin A. Enloe (D) H. Clay Evans (R) Leonidas C. Houk (R) Benton McMillin (D) James Phelan (D) d. Jan. 1891 Rice A. Pierce (D) James D. Richardson (D) Alfred A. Taylor (R) Joseph E. Washington (D) Washington C. Witthorne (D)

Texas	
Senators	**Representatives**
Richard Coke (D) John H. Reagan (D)	Jo Abbott (D) William H. Crain (D) David B. Culberson (D) Silas Hare (D) Constantine B. Kilgore (D) Samuel W. T. Lanham (D) William H. Martin (D) Roger Q. Mills (D) Littleton W. Moore (D) Joseph D. Sayers (D) Charles Stewart (D)

Vermont	
Senators	**Representatives**
George F. Edmunds (R) Justin S. Morrill (R)	William W. Grout (R) John W. Stewart (R)

(continued)

TABLE 7.34   (continued)

Mar. 4, 1889 to Mar. 3, 1891

President of The Senate	Presidents Pro Tempore of The Senate	Speaker of The House of Representatives
Levi P. Morton	John J. Ingalls Charles F. Manderson	Thomas B. Reed

Virginia

Senators	Representatives

John W. Daniel (D)
John S. Barbour (D)
	George E. Bowden (R)
	Thomas H. B. Browne (R)
	John A. Buchanan (D)
	Paul C. Edmunds (D)
	John M. Langston (R)
	  s. 1890
	William H. F. Lee (D)
	Posey G. Lester (D)
	Charles T. O'Ferrall (D)
	Henry St. George Tucker (D)
	Edward C. Venable (D)
	  r. Sep. 1890
	Edmund Waddill, Jr., (R)
	  s. 1890
	George D. Wise (R)
	  r. Apr. 1890

Washington

Senators	Representative
John B. Allen (R) Watson C. Squire (R)	John Wilson (R)

West Virginia

Senators	Representatives

John E. Kenna (D)
Charles J. Faulkner (D)
	John D. Alderson (D)
	George W. Atkinson (R)
	  s. 1890
	J. Monroe Jackson (D)
	  r. Feb. 1890
	John O. Pendleton (D)
	  r. Feb. 1890
	Charles B. Smith (R)
	  s. 1890
	William L. Wilson (D)

Wisconsin

Senators	Representatives
Philetus Sawyer (R) John C. Spooner (R)	Charles Barwig (D) George H. Brickner (D) Lucien B. Caswell (R) Charles B. Clark (R) Nils P. Haugen (R) Robert M. La Follette (R) Myron H. McCord (D) Ormsby B. Thomas (R) Isaac W. Van Schaick (R)

Wyoming

Senators	Representative

Joseph M. Carey (R)
  s. 1890
Francis E. Warren (R)
  s. 1890
	Clarence D. Clark (R)
	  s. 1890

Source: Notable Names in American History; A Tabulated Register. Third edition of White's Conspectus of American Biography (1973), 134–136.

TABLE 7.35   FIFTY-SECOND CONGRESS

Mar. 4, 1891 to Mar. 3, 1893

President of The Senate	President Pro Tempore of The Senate	Speaker of The House of Representatives
Levi P. Morton	Charles F. Manderson	Charles F. Crisp

Alabama

Senators	Representatives
John T. Morgan (D) James L. Pugh (D)	John H. Bankhead (D) Richard H. Clarke (R) James E. Cobb William H. Forney (D) Hilary A. Herbert (D) William C. Oates Louis W. Turpin (D) Joseph Wheeler (D)

Arkansas

Senators	Representatives
James K. Jones (D) James H. Berry (D)	Clifton R. Breckinridge (D) William H. Cate (D) Thomas C. McRae Samuel W. Peel (D) William L. Terry (D)

California

Senators	Representatives

Leland Stanford (R)
Charles N. Felton (R)
	William W. Bowers (R)
	Anthony Caminetti (D)
	John T. Cutting (R)
	Thomas J. Geary (D)
	Samuel G. Hilborn (R)
	  s. 1892
	Eugene F. Loud (R)
	Joseph McKenna (R)
	  r. Mar. 1892

Colorado

Senators	Representative
Henry M. Teller (R) Edward O. Wolcott (R)	Hosea Townsend (R)

Connecticut

Senators	Representatives
Orville H. Platt (R) Joseph R. Hawley (R)	Robert E. DeForest (D) Charles A. Russell (R) Lewis Sperry (D) Washington F. Willcox (D)

Delaware

Senators	Representative
George Gray (D) Anthony Higgins (R)	John W. Causey (D)

Florida

Senators	Representatives
Wilkinson Call (D) Samuel Pasco (D)	Robert Bullock (D) Stephen R. Mallory (D)

Georgia

Senators	Representatives
Alfred H. Colquitt (D) John B. Gordon (D)	James H. Blount (D) Charles F. Crisp (D) Robert W. Everett (D) Thomas G. Lawson (D) Rufus E. Lester (D) Leonidas F. Livingston (D) Charles L. Moses (D) Henry G. Turner (D) Thomas E. Watson (Pop) Thomas E. Winn (D)

Idaho

Senators	Representative
George L. Shoup (R) Fred T. Dubois (R)	Willis Sweet (R)

Illinois

Senators	Representatives
Shelby M. Cullom (R) John M. Palmer (D)	Samuel T. Busey (D) Benjamin T. Cable (D) Allan C. Durborow, Jr. (D) George W. Fithian (D) William S. Forman (D) Thomas J. Henderson (R) Robert R. Hitt (R) Albert J. Hopkins (R) Edward Lane (D) Lawrence E. McGann (D) Walter C. Newberry (D) Philip S. Post (R) Owen Scott (D) George W. Smith (R) Herman W. Snow (D) William M. Springer (D) Lewis Steward (D) Abner Taylor (R) Scott Wike (D) James R. Williams (D)

Indiana

Senators	Representatives
Daniel W. Voorhees (D) David Turpie (D)	John L. Bretz (D) Elijah V. Brookshire (D) Jason B. Brown (D) William D. Bynum (D) George W. Cooper (D) William S. Holman (D) Henry U. Johnson (R) Charles A. O. McClellan (D) Augustus N. Martin (D) William F. Parrett (D) David H. Patton (D) Benjamin F. Shively (D) Daniel W. Waugh (R)

Iowa

Senators	Representatives
William B. Allison (R) James F. Wilson (R)	Thomas Bowman (D) Walter H. Butler (D) Jonathan P. Dolliver (R) James P. Flick (R) John T. Hamilton (D) Walter I. Hayes (D) David B. Henderson (R) John A. T. Hull (R) George D. Perkins (R) John J. Seerley (D) Frederick E. White (D)

Kansas

Senators	Representatives
Preston B. Plumb (R) d. 1892 Bishop W. Perkins (R) s. 1892 William A. Peffer (Pop)	William Baker (People's Party) Case Broderick (R) Benjamin H. Clover (Farmer's Alliance) John Davis (People's Party) Edward H. Funston (R) John G. Otis (People's Party) Jeremiah Simpson (Pop)

Kentucky

Senators	Representatives
Joseph C. S. Blackburn (D) John G. Carlisle (D) r. Feb. 1893	William C. P. Breckinridge (D) Asher G. Caruth (D) William W. Dickerson (D) William T. Ellis (D) Isaac H. Goodnight (D) John W. Kendall (D) d. Mar. 1892 Joseph M. Kendall (D) s. 1892 James B. McCreary (D) Alexander B. Montgomery (D) Thomas H. Paynter (D) William J. Stone (D) John H. Wilson (R)

Louisiana

Senators	Representatives
Randall L. Gibson (D) d. Dec. 1892 Donelson Caffery, (D) s. 1893 Edward D. White (D)	Newton C. Blanchard (D) Charles J. Boatner (D) Matthew D. Lagan (D) Adolph Meyer (D) Andrew Price (D) Samuel M. Robertson (D)

Maine

Senators	Representatives
Eugene Hale (R) William P. Frye (R)	Charles A. Boutelle (R) Nelson Dingley, Jr. (R) Seth L. Milliken (R) Thomas B. Reed (R)

(continued)

TABLE 7.35   (continued)

Mar. 4, 1891 to Mar. 3, 1893

President of The Senate	President Pro Tempore of The Senate	Speaker of The House of Representatives
Levi P. Morton	Charles F. Manderson	Charles F. Crisp

Maryland

Senators	Representatives

Arthur P. Gorman (D)
Charles H. Gibson (D)
	John B. Brown (D)
	    s. 1892
	Barnes Compton (D)
	William M. McKaig (D)
	Henry Page (D)
	    r. Sep. 1892
	Isidor Rayner (D)
	Harry W. Rusk (D)
	Herman Stump (D)

Massachusetts

Senators	Representatives
Henry L. Dawes (R) George F. Hoar (R)	John F. Andrew (D) William Cogswell (R) Frederic S. Coolidge (D) John C. Crosby (D) Sherman Hoar (D) Henry Cabot Lodge (R) r. Mar. 1893 Elijah A. Morse (R) Joseph H. O'Neil (D) Charles S. Randall (R) Moses T. Stevens (D) Joseph H. Walker (R) George F. Williams (D)

Michigan

Senators	Representatives
Francis B. Stockbridge (R) James McMillan (R)	Charles E. Belknap (R) Julius C. Burrows (R) J. Logan Chipman (D) Melbourne H. Ford (D) d. Apr. 1891 James S. Gorman (D) James O'Donnell (R) Samuel M. Stephenson (R) Byron G. Stout (D) Thomas A. E. Weadock (D) Harrison H. Wheeler (R) Justin R. Whiting (Greenback, D) Henry M. Youmans (D)

Minnesota

Senators	Representatives
Cushman K. Davis (R) William D. Washburn (R)	James N. Castle (D) Osee M. Hall (D) Kittel Halvorson (Farmer's Alliance) William H. Harries (D) John Lind (R)

Mississippi

Senators	Representatives
James Z. George (D) Edward C. Walthall (D)	John M. Allen (D) Joseph H. Beeman (D) Thomas C. Catchings (D) Charles E. Hooker (D) John C. Kyle (D) Clarke Lewis (D) Thomas R. Stockdale (D)

Missouri

Senators	Representatives
Francis M. Cockrell (D) George G. Vest (D)	Marshall Arnold (D) Richard P. Bland (D) Samuel Byrns (D) Seth W. Cobb (D) David A. DeArmond (D) Alexander M. Dockery (D) Robert W. Fyan (D) William H. Hatch (D) John T. Heard (D) Charles H. Mansur (D) Richard H. Norton (D) John J. O'Neill (D) John C. Tarsney (D) Robert P. C. Wilson (D)

Montana

Senators	Representative
Thomas C. Power (R) Wilbur F. Sanders (R)	William W. Dixon (D)

Nebraska

Senators	Representatives
Charles F. Manderson (R) Algernon S. Paddock (R)	William Jennings Bryan (D) Omer M. Kem (Pop) William A. McKeighan (D)

Nevada

Senators	Representative
John P. Jones (R) William M. Stewart (R)	Horace F. Bartine (R)

New Hampshire

Senators	Representatives
William E. Chandler (R) Jacob H. Gallinger (R)	Warren F. Daniell (D) Luther F. McKinney (D)

New Jersey

Senators	Representatives
John R. McPherson (D) Rufus Blodgett (D)	Christopher A. Bergen (R) James Buchanan (R) Cornelius A. Cadmus (D) Thomas D. English (D) Samuel Fowler (D) Jacob A. Geissenhainer (D) Edward F. McDonald (D) d. Nov. 1892

New York	
Senators	**Representatives**

Frank Hiscock (R)
David B. Hill (D)
  s. 1892
	Henry Bacon (D)
	James J. Belden (R)
	Henry W. Bentley (D)
	Thomas L. Bunting (D)
	Timothy J. Campbell (D)
	Alfred C. Chapin (D)
	  r. Nov. 1892
	John M. Clancy (D)
	W. Bourke Cockran (D)
	William J. Coombs (D)
	James W. Covert (D)
	Isaac N. Cox (D)
	Amos J. Cummings (D)
	Newton M. Curtis (R)
	Edward J. Dunphy (D)
	John R. Fellows (D)
	Ashbel P. Fitch (D)
	Halbert S. Greenleaf (D)
	Warren B. Hooker (R)
	John H. Ketcham (R)
	Joseph J. Little (D)
	Daniel N. Lockwood (D)
	Thomas F. Magner (D)
	Sereno E. Payne (R)
	John A. Quackenbush (R)
	John Raines (R)
	George W. Ray (R)
	Hosea H. Rockwell (D)
	John Sanford (R)
	William G. Stahlnecker (D)
	Charles Tracey (D)
	George Van Horn (D)
	James W. Wadsworth (D)
	J. De Witt Warner (D)
	John M. Wever (R)

North Carolina	
Senators	**Representatives**
Matt W. Ransom (D) Zebulon B. Vance (D)	Sydenham B. Alexander (D) William A. B. Branch (D) Benjamin H. Bunn (D) Henry P. Cheatham (R) William H. H. Cowles (D) William T. Crawford (D) Benjamin F. Grady (D) John S. Henderson (D) Archibald H. A. Williams (D)

North Dakota	
Senators	**Representative**
Lyman R. Casey (R) Henry C. Hansbrough (R)	Martin N. Johnson (R)

Ohio	
Senators	**Representatives**
John Sherman (R) Calvin S. Brice (D)	John A. Caldwell (R) Robert E. Doan (R) Dennis D. Donovan (D) James Irvine Dungan (D) William H. Enochs (D) Martin K. Gantz (D) Darius D. Hare (D) Michael D. Harter (D) William E. Haynes (D) George W. Houk (D) Tom L. Johnson (D)

Ohio	
Senators	**Representatives**
	Fernando C. Layton (D) Lewis P. Ohliger (D) s. 1892 Joseph H. Outhwaite (D) James W. Owens (D) John M. Pattison (D) Albert J. Pearson (D) Bellamy Storer (R) Ezra B. Taylor (R) Joseph D. Taylor (R) Vincent A. Taylor (R) John G. Warwick (D)

Oregon	
Senators	**Representative**
Joseph N. Dolph (R) John H. Mitchell (R)	Binger Hermann (R)

Pennsylvania	
Senators	**Representatives**

J. Donald Cameron (R)
Matthew S. Quay (R)
	Lemuel Amerman (D)
	Louis E. Atkinson (R)
	Frank E. Beltzhoover (D)
	Henry H. Bingham (R)
	Marriott Brosius (R)
	David B. Brunner (D)
	Alexander K. Craig (D)
	  d. 1892
	John Dalzell (R)
	Eugene P. Gillespie (D)
	Matthew Griswold (R)
	Edwin Hallowell (D)
	Alfred C. Harmer (R)
	Albert C. Hopkins (R)
	George F. Huff (R)
	George F. Kribbs (D)
	William McAleer (D)
	William Mutchler (D)
	Charles O'Neill (R)
	James B. Reilly (D)
	John E. Reyburn (R)
	John W. Rife (R)
	John B. Robinson (R)
	Edward Scull (R)
	George W. Shonk (R)
	William A. Sipe (D)
	  s. 1892
	Andrew Stewart (R)
	  r. Feb. 1892
	Charles W. Stone (R)
	William A. Stone (R)
	Simon P. Wolverton (D)
	Myron B. Wright (R)

Rhode Island	
Senators	**Representatives**
Nelson W. Aldrich (R) Nathan F. Dixon (R)	Oscar Lapham (D) Charles H. Page (D)

(continued)

TABLE 7.35 (continued)

Mar. 4, 1891 to Mar. 3, 1893

President of The Senate	President Pro Tempore of The Senate	Speaker of The House of Representatives
Levi P. Morton	Charles F. Manderson	Charles F. Crisp

South Carolina

Senators	Representatives

Matthew C. Butler (D)
John L. M. Irby (D)
	William H. Brawley (D)
	William Elliott (D)
	John J. Hemphill (D)
	George Johnstone (D)
	John I. McLaurin (D)
	  s. 1892
	George W. Shell (D)
	Eli T. Stackhouse (D)
	  d. Jun. 1892
	George D. Tillman (D)

South Dakota

Senators	Representatives
Richard F. Pettigrew (R) James K. Kyle	John R. Gamble (R) d. Aug. 1891 John L. Jolley (R) John A. Pickler (R)

Tennessee

Senators	Representatives
Isham G. Harris (D) William B. Bate (D)	Nicholas N. Cox (D) Benjamin A. Enloe (D) John C. Houk (R) Benton McMillin (D) Josiah Patterson (D) Rice A. Pierce (D) James D. Richardson (D) Henry C. Snodgrass (D) Alfred A. Taylor (R) Joseph E. Washington (D)

Texas

Senators	Representatives

Richard Coke (D)
John H. Reagan (D)
  r. 1891
Horace Chilton (D)
  ta. 1891
Roger Q. Mills (D)
  s. 1892
	Jo Abbott (D)
	Edwin Le Roy Antony (D)
	  s. 1892
	Joseph W. Bailey (D)
	William H. Crain (D)
	David B. Culberson (D)
	Constantine B. Kilgore (D)
	Samuel W. T. Lanham (D)
	John B. Long (D)
	Roger Q. Mills (D)
	  r. Mar. 1892
	Littleton W. Moore (D)
	Joseph D. Sayers (D)
	Charles Stewart (D)

Vermont

Senators	Representatives

George F. Edmunds (R)
  r. Nov. 1891
Redfield Proctor (R)
  s. 1891
Justin S. Morrill (R)
	William W. Grout (R)
	H. Henry Powers (R)

Virginia

Senators	Representatives

John W. Daniel (D)
John S. Barbour (D)
  d. May 1892
Eppa Hunton (D)
  s. 1892
	John A. Buchanan (D)
	Paul C. Edmunds (D)
	James F. Epes (D)
	William A. Jones (D)
	John W. Lawson (D)
	Posey G. Lester (D)
	Elisha E. Meredith (D)
	Charles T. O'Ferrall (D)
	Henry St. George Tucker (D)
	George D. Wise (R)

Washington

Senators	Representative
John B. Allen (R) Watson C. Squire (R)	John L. Wilson (R)

West Virginia

Senators	Representatives

John E. Kenna (D)
  d. Jan. 1893
Johnson N. Camden (D)
  s. 1893
Charles J. Faulkner (D)
	John D. Alderson (D)
	James Capehart (D)
	John O. Pendleton (D)
	William L. Wilson (D)

Wisconsin

Senators	Representatives
Philetus Sawyer (R) William F. Vilas (D)	Clinton Babbitt (D) Charles Barwig (D) George H. Brickner (D) Allen R. Bushnell (D) Frank P. Coburn (D) Nils P. Haugen (R) Thomas Lynch (D) Lucas M. Miller (D) John L. Mitchell (D)

Wyoming

Senators	Representative
Joseph M. Carey (R) Francis E. Warren (R)	Clarence D. Clark (R)

Source: Notable Names in American History; A Tabulated Register. Third edition of *White's Conspectus of American Biography* (1973), 136–139.

TABLE 7.36   FIFTY-THIRD CONGRESS

Mar. 4, 1893 to Mar. 3, 1895

President of The Senate	Presidents Pro Tempore of The Senate	Speaker of The House of Representatives
Adlai E. Stevenson	Charles F. Manderson Isham G. Harris Matt W. Ransom	Charles F. Crisp

Alabama

Senators	Representatives

John T. Morgan (D)
James L. Pugh (D)
	John H. Bankhead (D)
	Richard H. Clarke (D)
	James E. Cobb
	William H. Denson (D)
	George P. Harrison (D)
	   s. 1894
	William C. Oates (D)
	   r. Nov. 1894
	Gaston A. Robbins (D)
	Jesse F. Stallings (D)
	Louis W. Turpin (D)
	Joseph Wheeler (D)

Arkansas

Senators	Representatives

James K. Jones (D)
James H. Berry (D)
	Clifton R. Breckinridge (D)
	   r. Aug. 1894
	Hugh A. Dinsmore (D)
	John S. Little (D)
	   s. 1894
	Philip D. McCulloch Jr. (D)
	Thomas C. McRae (D)
	Robert Neill (D)
	William L. Terry (D)

California

Senators	Representatives

Leland Stanford (R)
   d. 1893
George C. Perkins (R)
   s. 1893
Stephen M. White (D)
	William W. Bowers (R)
	Anthony Caminetti (D)
	Marion Cannon (People's Party)
	Warren B. English (D)
	Thomas J. Geary (D)
	Samuel G. Hilborn (R)
	   r. Apr. 1894
	Eugene F. Loud (R)
	James G. Maguire (D)

Colorado

Senators	Representatives
Henry M. Teller (R) Edward O. Wolcott (R)	John C. Bell (D) Lafayette Pence (D)

Connecticut

Senators	Representatives
Orville H. Platt (R) Joseph R. Hawley (R)	Robert E. DeForest (D) James P. Pigott (D) Charles A. Russell (R) Lewis Sperry (D)

Delaware

Senators	Representative
George Gray (D) Anthony Higgins (R)	John W. Causey (D)

Florida

Senators	Representatives
Wilkinson Call (D) Samuel Pasco (D)	Charles M. Cooper (D) Stephen R. Mallory (D)

Georgia

Senators	Representatives

Alfred H. Colquitt (D)
   d. Mar. 1894
Patrick Walsh (D)
   s. 1894
John B. Gordon (D)
	James C. C. Black (D)
	Thomas B. Cabaniss (D)
	Charles F. Crisp (D)
	Thomas G. Lawson (D)
	Rufus E. Lester (D)
	Leonidas F. Livingston (D)
	John W. Maddox (D)
	Charles L. Moses (D)
	Benjamin E. Russell (D)
	Farish C. Tate (D)
	Henry G. Turner (D)

Idaho

Senators	Representative
George L. Shoup (R) Fred T. Dubois (R)	Willis Sweet (R)

Illinois

Senators	Representatives

Shelby M. Cullom (R)
John M. Palmer (R)
	J. Frank Aldrich (R)
	John C. Black (D)
	   r. Jan. 1895
	Joseph G. Cannon (R)
	Robert A. Childs (R)
	Allan C. Durborow, Jr. (D)
	George W. Fithian (D)
	William S. Forman (D)
	Benjamin F. Funk (R)
	Julius Golozier (D)
	Thomas J. Henderson (R)
	Robert H. Hitt (R)
	Albert J. Hopkins (R)
	Andrew J. Hunter (D)
	Edward Lane (D)
	John J. McDannold (D)
	Lawrence E. McGann (D)
	Benjamin F. Marsh (R)
	Philip S. Post (R)
	   d. Jan. 1895
	George W. Smith (R)
	William M. Springer (D)
	Hamilton K. Wheeler (R)
	James R. Williams (R)

Indiana

Senators	Representatives
Daniel W. Voorhees (D) David Turpie (D)	John L. Bretz (D) Elijah V. Brookshire (D) Jason B. Brown (D) William D. Bynum (D) Charles G. Conn (D) George W. Cooper (D) Thomas Hammond (D) William S. Holman (D) Henry U. Johnson (R) William F. McNagny (D) Augustus N. Martin (D) Arthur H. Taylor (D) Daniel W. Waugh (R)

(continued)

TABLE 7.36 (continued)

Mar. 4, 1893 to Mar. 3, 1895

President of The Senate	Presidents Pro Tempore of The Senate	Speaker of The House of Representatives
Adlai E. Stevenson	Charles F. Manderson Isham G. Harris Matt W. Ransom	Charles F. Crisp

Iowa

Senators	Representatives
William B. Allison (R) James F. Wilson (R)	Robert G. Cousins (R) Jonathan P. Dolliver (R) John H. Gear (R) Alva L. Hager (R) Walter I. Hayes (D) David B. Henderson (R) William P. Hepburn (R) John A. T. Hull (R) John F. Lacey (R) George D. Perkins (R) Thomas Updegraff (R)

Kansas

Senators	Representatives

William A. Peffer (Pop)
John Martin (D)
	William Baker (People's Party)
	Case Broderick (R)
	Charles Curtis (R)
	John Davis (People's Party)
	Edward H. Funston
	   r. Aug. 1894
	William A. Harris (Pop)
	Thomas J. Hudson (Progressive)
	Horace L. Moore (D)
	   s. 1894
	Jeremiah Simpson (Progressive)

Kentucky

Senators	Representatives

Joseph C. S. Blackburn (D)
William Lindsay (D)
	Silas Adams (R)
	William M. Beckner (D)
	   s. 1894
	Albert S. Berry (D)
	William C. P. Breckinridge (D)
	Asher G. Caruth (D)
	William T. Ellis (D)
	Isaac H. Goodnight (D)
	Marcus C. Lisle (D)
	   d. Jul. 1894
	James B. McCreary (D)
	Alexander B. Montgomery (D)
	Thomas H. Paynter (D)
	   r. Jan. 1895
	William J. Stone (D)

Louisiana

Senators	Representatives

Edward D. White (D)
   r. Mar. 1894
Newton C. Blanchard (D)
   s. 1894
Donelson Caffery (D)
	Newton C. Blanchard (D)
	   r. Mar. 1894
	Charles J. Boatner (D)
	Robert C. Davey (D)
	Adolph Meyer (D)
	Henry W. Ogden (D)
	   s. 1894
	Andrew Price (D)
	Samuel M. Robertson (D)

Maine

Senators	Representatives
Eugene Hale (R) William P. Frye (R)	Charles A. Boutelle (R) Nelson Dingley, Jr. (R) Seth L. Milliken (R) Thomas B. Reed (R)

Maryland

Senators	Representatives

Arthur P. Gorman (D)
Charles H. Gibson (D)
	Robert F. Bratton (D)
	   d. May 1894
	Charles E. Coffin (R)
	   s. 1894
	Barnes Compton (D)
	   r. May 1894
	W. Laird Henry (D)
	   s. 1894
	William M. McKaig (D)
	Isidor Rayner (D)
	Harry W. Rusk (D)
	J. Fred C. Talbott (D)

Massachusetts

Senators	Representatives
George F. Hoar (R) Henry Cabot Lodge (R)	Lewis D. Apsley (R) William Cogswell (R) William F. Draper (R) William Everett (D) Frederick H. Gillett (R) Samuel W. McCall (R) Michael J. McEttrick (D) Elijah A. Morse (R) Joseph H. O'Neil (D) Charles S. Randall (R) Moses T. Stevens (D) Joseph H. Walker (R) Ashley B. Wright (R)

Michigan

Senators	Representatives

Francis B. Stockbridge (R)
   d. Apr. 1894
John Patton, Jr. (R)
   ta. 1894
Julius C. Burrows (R)
   s. 1895
James McMillan (R)
	David D. Aitken (R)
	John Avery (R)
	Julius C. Burrows (R)
	   r. 1895
	J. Logan Chipman (D)
	   d. Aug. 1893
	James S. Gorman (D)
	Levi T. Griffin (D)
	William S. Linton (R)
	John W. Moon (R)
	George F. Richardson (D)
	Samuel M. Stephenson (R)
	Henry F. Thomas (R)
	Thomas A. E. Weadock (D)
	Justin R. Whiting (Greenback)

Minnesota

Senators	Representatives
Cushman K. Davis (R) William D. Washburn (R)	Melvin R. Baldwin (D) Haldor E. Boen (People's Party) Loren Fletcher (R) Osee M. Hall (D) Andrew R. Kiefer (R) James T. McCleary (R) James A. Tawney (R)

Mississippi

Senators	Representatives
James Z. George (D)	John M. Allen (D)
Edward C. Walthall (D)	Thomas C. Catchings (D)
r. Jan. 1894	Charles E. Hooker (D)
Anselm J. McLaurin (D)	John C. Kyle (D)
s. 1894	Hernando D. Money (D)
	Thomas R. Stockdale (D)
	John Sharp Williams (D)

Missouri

Senators	Representatives
Francis M. Cockrell (D)	Marshall Arnold (D)
George G. Vest (D)	Richard Bartholdt (R)
	Richard P. Bland (D)
	Daniel D. Burnes (D)
	Champ Clark (D)
	Seth W. Cobb (D)
	David A. De Armond (D)
	Alexander M. Dockery (D)
	Robert W. Fyan (D)
	Uriel S. Hall (D)
	William H. Hatch (D)
	John T. Heard (D)
	Charles F. Joy (R)
	r. Apr. 1894
	Charles H. Morgan (D)
	John J. O'Neill (D)
	s. 1894
	John C. Tarsney (D)

Montana

Senators	Representative
Thomas C. Power (R)	Charles S. Hartman (R)
Lee Mantle (R)	

Nebraska

Senators	Representatives
Charles F. Manderson (R)	William Jennings Bryan (D)
William V. Allen (Pop)	Eugene J. Hainer (R)
	Omer M. Kem (Pop)
	William McKeighan
	George D. Meiklejohn (R)
	David H. Mercer (R)

Nevada

Senators	Representative
John P. Jones (R)	Francis G. Newlands (D)
William M. Stewart (R)	

New Hampshire

Senators	Representatives
William E. Chandler (R)	Henry M. Baker (R)
Jacob H. Gallinger (R)	Henry W. Blair (R)

New Jersey

Senators	Representatives
John R. McPherson (D)	Cornelius A. Cadmus (D)
James Smith, Jr. (D)	Johnston Cornish (D)
	John T. Dunn (D)
	Thomas D. English (D)
	George B. Fielder (D)
	John J. Gardner (D)
	Jacob A. Geissenhainer (D)
	Henry C. Loudenslager (R)

New York

Senators	Representatives
David B. Hill (D)	Franklin Bartlett (D)
Edward Murphy, Jr. (D)	James J. Belden (R)
	Timothy J. Campbell (D)
	Charles A. Chickering (R)
	John M. Clancy (D)
	W. Bourke Cockran (D)
	William J. Coombs (D)
	James W. Covert (D)
	Amos J. Cummings (D)
	r. Nov. 1893
	Newton M. Curtis (R)
	Charles Daniels (R)
	Edward J. Dunphy (D)
	John R. Fellows (D)
	r. Dec. 1893
	Ashbel P. Fitch (D)
	r. Dec. 1893
	Charles W. Gillet (R)
	John H. Graham (D)
	Charles D. Haines (D)
	Joseph C. Hendrix (D)
	Warren B. Hooker (R)
	Jacob Le Fever (R)
	Daniel N. Lockwood (D)
	Thomas F. Magner (D)
	Francis Marvin (R)
	Sereno E. Payne (R)
	Lemuel E. Quigg (R)
	s. 1894
	George W. Ray (R)
	William Ryan (D)
	Simon J. Schermerhorn (D)
	James S. Sherman (R)
	Daniel E. Sickles (D)
	Isidor Straus (D)
	s. 1894
	Charles Tracey (D)
	John Van Voorhis (R)
	James W. Wadsworth (R)
	J. De Witt Warner (D)
	John M. Wever (R)

North Carolina

Senators	Representatives
Matt W. Ransom (D)	Sydenham B. Alexander (D)
Zebulon B. Vance (D)	William H. Bower (D)
d. Apr. 1894	William A. B. Branch (D)
Thomas J. Jarvis (D)	Benjamin H. Bunn (D)
ta. 1894	William T. Crawford (D)
Jeter C. Pritchard (R)	Benjamin F. Grady (D)
s. 1895	John S. Henderson (D)
	Thomas Settle (R)
	Frederick A. Woodard (D)

North Dakota

Senators	Representative
Henry C. Hansbrough (R)	Martin N. Johnson (R)
William N. Roach (D)	

(continued)

TABLE 7.36 (continued)

Mar. 4, 1893 to Mar. 3, 1895

President of The Senate	Presidents Pro Tempore of The Senate	Speaker of The House of Representatives
Adlai E. Stevenson	Charles F. Manderson Isham G. Harris Matt W. Ransom	Charles F. Crisp

Ohio

Senators	Representatives

John Sherman (R)
Calvin S. Brice (D)
	Jacob H. Bromwell (R)
	  s. 1894
	Hezekiah S. Bundy (R)
	John A. Caldwell (R)
	  r. May 1894
	Dennis D. Dovovan (D)
	Charles H. Grosvenor (R)
	Darius D. Hare (D)
	Michael D. Harter (D)
	George W. Houk (D)
	  d. Feb. 1894
	George W. Hulick (R)
	George P. Ikirt (D)
	Tom L. Johnson (D)
	Fernando C. Layton (D)
	Stephen A. Northway (R)
	Joseph H. Outhwaite (D)
	Albert J. Pearson (D)
	James A. D. Richards (D)
	Byron F. Ritchie (D)
	Paul J. Sorg (D)
	  s. 1894
	Bellamy Storer (R)
	Luther M. Strong (R)
	Henry C. Van Voorhis (R)
	William J. White (R)
	George W. Wilson (R)

Oregon

Senators	Representatives
Joseph N. Dolph (R) John H. Mitchell (R)	William R. Ellis (R) Binger Hermann (R)

Pennsylvania

Senators	Representatives

J. Donald Cameron (R)
Matthew S. Quay (R)
	Robert Adams, Jr. (R)
	  s. 1894
	Frank E. Beltzhoover (D)
	Henry H. Bingham (R)
	Marriott Brosius (R)
	John Dalzell (R)
	Constantine J. Erdman (D)
	Galusha A. Grow (R)
	  s. 1894
	Alfred C. Harmer (R)
	Daniel B. Heiner (R)
	Josiah D. Hicks (R)
	William H. Hines (D)
	Albert C. Hopkins (R)
	Edwin J. Jorden (R)
	  s. 1895
	George F. Kribbs (D)
	William Lilly (R)
	  d. Dec. 1893
	William McAleer (D)
	Alexander McDowell (R)
	Thaddeus M. Mahon (R)

Pennsylvania

Senators	Representatives

	Howard Mutchler (D)
	Charles O'Neill (R)
	  d. Nov. 1893
	Thomas W. Phillips (R)
	James B. Reilly (D)
	John E. Reyburn (R)
	John B. Robinson (R)
	Joseph A. Scranton (R)
	Joseph C. Sibley (D)
	William A. Sipe (D)
	Charles W. Stone (R)
	William A. Stone (R)
	Irving P. Wanger (R)
	Simon P. Wolverton (D)
	Ephraim M. Woomer (R)
	Myron B. Wright (R)
	  d. Nov. 1894

Rhode Island

Senators	Representatives
Nelson W. Aldrich (R) Nathan F. Dixon (R)	Oscar Lapham (D) Charles H. Page (D)

South Carolina

Senators	Representatives

Matthew C. Butler (D)
John L. M. Irby (D)
	William H. Brawley (D)
	  r. Feb. 1894
	James F. Izlar (D)
	  s. 1894
	Asbury C. Latimer (D)
	John L. McLaurin (D)
	George W. Murray (R)
	George W. Shell (D)
	Thomas J. Strait (D)
	W. Jasper Talbert (D)

South Dakota

Senators	Representatives
Richard F. Pettigrew (R) James H. Kyle	William V. Lucas (R) John A. Pickler (R)

Tennessee

Senators	Representatives
Isham G. Harris (D) William B. Bate (D)	Nicholas N. Cox (D) Benjamin A. Enloe (D) John C. Houk (R) James C. McDearmon (D) Benton McMillin (D) Josiah Patterson (D) James Phelan (D) James D. Richardson (D) Henry C. Snodgrass (D) Alfred A. Taylor (R) Joseph E. Washington (D)

Texas	
Senators	Representatives
Richard Coke (D)	Jo Abbott (D)
Robert Q. Mills (D)	Joseph W. Bailey (D)
	Charles K. Bell (D)
	Jeremiah V. Cockrell (D)
	Samuel B. Cooper (D)
	William H. Crain (D)
	David B. Culberson (D)
	Walter Gresham (D)
	Joseph C. Hutcheson (D)
	Constantine B. Kilgore (D)
	Thomas M. Paschal (D)
	George C. Pendleton (D)
	Joseph D. Sayers (D)

Vermont	
Senators	Representatives
Justin S. Morrill (R)	William W. Grout (R)
Redfield Proctor (R)	H. Henry Powers (R)

Virginia	
Senators	Representatives
John W. Daniel (D)	Paul C. Edmunds (D)
Eppa Hunton (D)	James F. Epes (D)
	William A. Jones (D)
	James W. Marshall (D)
	Elisha E. Meredith (D)
	Charles T. O'Ferrall (D)
	r. Dec. 1893
	Claude A. Swanson (D)
	Henry St. George Tucker (D)
	Smith S. Turner (D)
	s. 1894
	D. Gardiner Tyler (D)
	George D. Wise (D)

Washington	
Senators	Representatives
Watson C. Squire (R)	William H. Doolittle (R)
John L. Wilson (R)	John L. Wilson (R)
s. 1895	r. Feb. 1895

West Virginia	
Senators	Representatives
Charles J. Faulkner (D)	John D. Alderson (D)
Johnson N. Camden (D)	James Capehart (D)
	John O. Pendleton (D)
	William L. Wilson (D)

Wisconsin	
Senators	Representatives
William F. Vilas (D)	Joseph W. Babcock (R)
John L. Mitchell (D)	Lyman E. Barnes (D)
	Charles Barwig (D)
	George H. Brickner (D)
	Henry Allen Cooper (R)
	Michael Griffin (R)
	s. 1894
	Nils P. Haugen (R)
	Thomas Lynch (D)
	George B. Shaw (R)
	d. Aug. 1894
	Peter J. Somers (D)
	Owen A. Wells (D)

Wyoming	
Senators	Representative
Joseph M. Carey (R)	Henry A. Coffeen (D)
Francis E. Warren (R)	
Clarence D. Clark (R)	
s. 1895	

Source: Notable Names in American History; A Tabulated Register. Third edition of White's Conspectus of American Biography (1973), 139–141.

TABLE 7.37   FIFTY-FOURTH CONGRESS

Mar. 4, 1895 to Mar. 3, 1897

President of The Senate	President Pro Tempore of The Senate	Speaker of The House of Representatives
Adlai E. Stevenson	William P. Frye	Thomas B. Reed

Alabama	
Senators	Representatives
John T. Morgan (D)	Truman H. Aldrich (R)
James L. Pugh (D)	s. 1896
	William F. Aldrich (R)
	s. 1896
	John H. Bankhead (D)
	Richard H. Clarke (D)
	James E. Cobb
	r. Apr. 1896
	Albert T. Goodwyn (D)
	s. 1896
	George P. Harrison (D)
	Milford W. Howard (Pop)
	Gatson A. Robbins (D)
	r. Mar. 1896
	Jesse F. Stallings (D)
	Oscar W. Underwood (D)
	r. 1896
	Joseph Wheeler (D)

Arkansas	
Senators	Representatives
James K. Jones (D)	Hugh A. Dinsmore (D)
James H. Berry (D)	John S. Little (D)
	Philip D. McCulloch Jr. (D)
	Thomas C. McRae (D)
	Robert Neill (D)
	William L. Terry (D)

California	
Senators	Representatives
Stephen M. White (D)	John A. Barham (R)
George C. Perkins (R)	William W. Bowers (R)
	Samuel G. Hillborn (R)
	Grove L. Johnson (R)
	Eugene F. Loud (R)
	James McLachlan (R)
	James G. Maguire (D)

Colorado	
Senators	Representatives
Henry M. Teller (R)	John C. Bell (D)
Edward O. Wolcott (R)	John F. Shafroth (R)

(continued)

TABLE 7.37 (continued)

Mar. 4, 1895 to Mar. 3, 1897

President of The Senate	President Pro Tempore of The Senate	Speaker of The House of Representatives
Adlai E. Stevenson	William P. Frye	Thomas B. Reed

Connecticut

Senators	Representatives
Orville H. Platt (R) Joseph R. Hawley (R)	E. Stevens Henry (R) Ebenezer J. Hill (R) Charles A. Russell (R) Nehemiah D. Sperry (R)

Delaware

Senators	Representative
George Gray (D) Richard R. Kennedy (D) s. 1897	Jonathan S. Willis (R)

Florida

Senators	Representatives
Wilkinson Call (D) Samuel Pasco (D)	Charles M. Cooper (D) Stephen M. Sparkman (D)

Georgia

Senators	Representatives
John B. Gordon (D) Augustus O. Bacon (D)	Charles L. Bartlett (D) James C. C. Black (D) Charles F. Crisp (D) d. Oct. 1896 Charles R. Crisp (D) s. 1896 Thomas G. Lawson (D) Rufus E. Lester (D) Leonidas F. Livingston (D) John W. Maddox (D) Charles L. Moses (D) Benjamin E. Russell (D) Farish C. Tate (D) Henry G. Turner (D)

Idaho

Senators	Representative
George L. Shoup (R) Fred T. Dubois (R)	Edgar Wilson (R)

Illinois

Senators	Representatives
Shelby M. Cullom (R) John McA. Palmer (D)	J. Frank Aldrich (R) Hugh R. Belknap (R) Orlando Burrell (R) Joseph G. Cannon (R) James A. Connolly (R) Edward D. Cooke (R) Finis E. Downing (R) r. Jun. 1896 George E. Foss (R) Joseph V. Graff (R) William F. L. Hadley (R) Robert R. Hitt (R) Albert J. Hopkins (R) William Lorimer (R)

Illinois

Senators	Representatives
	Lawrence E. McGann (D) r. Dec. 1895 Benjamin F. Marsh (R) Everett J. Murphy (R) George W. Prince (R) Walter Reeves (R) John I. Rinaker (R) s. 1896 George W. Smith (R) Vespasian Warner (R) George E. White (R) Benson Wood (R) Charles W. Woodman (R)

Indiana

Senators	Representatives
Daniel W. Voorhees (D) David Turpie (D)	George W. Faris (R) J. Frank Hanly (R) Alexander M. Hardy (R) Jethro A. Hatch (R) James A. Hemenway (R) Charles L. Henry (R) Henry U. Johnson (R) Jacob D. Leighty (R) Jesse Overstreet (R) Lemuel W. Royse (R) George W. Steele (R) Robert J. Tracewell (R) James E. Watson (R)

Iowa

Senators	Representatives
William B. Allison (R) James H. Gear (R)	Samuel M. Clark (R) Robert G. Cousins (R) George M. Curtis (R) Jonathan P. Dolliver (R) Alva L. Hager (R) David B. Henderson (R) William P. Hepburn (R) John A. T. Hull (R) John F. Lacey (R) George D. Perkins (R) Thomas Updegraff (R)

Kansas

Senators	Representatives
William A. Peffer (Pop) Lucien Baker (R)	William Baker (People's Party) Richard W. Blue (R) Case Broderick (R) William A. Calderhead (R) Charles Curtis (R) Snyder S. Kirkpatrick (R) Chester I. Long (R) Orrin L. Miller (R)

Kentucky

Senators	Representatives
Joseph C. S. Blackburn (D) William Lindsay (D)	Albert S. Berry (D) John D. Clardy (D) David G. Colson (R) Walter Evans (R) John K. Hendrick (D) Nathan T. Hopkins (R) s. 1897 W. Godfrey Hunter (R)

Kentucky	
Senators	**Representatives**
	Joseph M. Kendall (D)
	r. Feb. 1897
	John W. Lewis (R)
	James B. McCreary (D)
	William C. Owens (D)
	Samuel J. Pugh

Louisiana	
Senators	**Representatives**
Donelson Caffery (D)	Charles J. Boatner (D)
Newton C. Blanchard (D)	Charles F. Buck (D)
	Adolph Meyer (D)
	Henry W. Ogden (D)
	Andrew Price (D)
	Samuel M. Robertson (D)

Maine	
Senators	**Representatives**
Eugene Hale (R)	Charles A. Boutelle (R)
William P. Frye (R)	Nelson Dingley, Jr. (R)
	Seth L. Milliken (R)
	Thomas B. Reed (R)

Maryland	
Senators	**Representatives**
Arthur P. Gorman (D)	William B. Baker (R)
Charles H. Gibson (D)	Charles E. Coffin (R)
	John K. Cowen (D)
	Joshua W. Miles (D)
	Harry W. Rusk (D)
	George L. Wellington (R)

Massachusetts	
Senators	**Representatives**
George F. Hoar (R)	Lewis D. Apsley (R)
Henry Cabot Lodge (R)	Harrison H. Atwood (R)
	William E. Barrett (R)
	William F. Draper (R)
	John F. Fitzgerald (D)
	Frederick H. Gillett (R)
	William S. Knox (R)
	Samuel W. McCall (R)
	William H. Moody (R)
	Elijah A. Morse (R)
	John Simpkins (R)
	Joseph H. Walker (R)
	Ashley B. Wright (R)

Michigan	
Senators	**Representatives**
James McMillan (R)	David D. Aitken (R)
Julius C. Burrows (R)	John Avery (R)
	Roswell P. Bishop (R)
	John B. Corliss (R)
	Rousseau O. Crump (R)
	William S. Linton (D)
	Alfred Milnes (R)
	William Alden Smith (R)
	Horace G. Snover (R)
	George Spalding (R)
	Samuel M. Stephenson (R)
	Henry F. Thomas (R)

Minnesota	
Senators	**Representatives**
Cushman K. Davis (R)	Frank M. Eddy (R)
Knute Nelson (R)	Loren Fletcher (R)
	Joel P. Heatwole (R)
	Andrew R. Keifer (R)
	James T. McCleary (R)
	James A. Tawney (R)
	Charles A. Towne (R)

Mississippi	
Senators	**Representatives**
James Z. George (D)	John M. Allen (D)
Edward C. Walthall (D)	Thomas C. Catchings (D)
	Walter McK. Denny (D)
	John C. Kyle (D)
	Hernando D. Money (D)
	James G. Spencer (D)
	John Sharp Williams (D)

Missouri	
Senators	**Representatives**
Francis M. Cockrell (D)	Richard Bartholdt (R)
George G. Vest (D)	Charles G. Burton (R)
	Charles N. Clark (R)
	Seth W. Cobb (D)
	George C. Crowther (R)
	David A. De Armond (D)
	Alexander M. Dockery (D)
	Uriel S. Hall (D)
	Joel D. Hubbard (R)
	Charles F. Joy (R)
	Norman A. Mozley (R)
	John H. Raney (R)
	John C. Tarsney (D)
	r. Feb. 1896
	John P. Tracey (R)
	William M. Treloar (R)
	Robert T. Van Horn (R)
	s. 1896

Montana	
Senators	**Representative**
Lee Mantle (R)	Charles S. Hartman (R)
Thomas H. Carter (R)	

Nebraska	
Senators	**Representatives**
William V. Allen (Pop)	William E. Andrews (R)
John M. Thurston (R)	Eugene J. Hainer (R)
	Omer M. Kem (Pop)
	George D. Meiklejohn (R)
	David H. Mercer (R)
	Jesse B. Strode (R)

Nevada	
Senators	**Representative**
John P. Jones (R)	Francis G. Newlands (D)
William M. Stewart (R)	

New Hampshire	
Senators	**Representatives**
William E. Chandler (R)	Henry M. Baker (R)
Jacob H. Gallinger (R)	Cyrus A. Sulloway (R)

(continued)

TABLE 7.37 (continued)

Mar. 4, 1895 to Mar. 3, 1897

President of The Senate	President Pro Tempore of The Senate	Speaker of The House of Representatives
Adlai E. Stevenson	William P. Frye	Thomas B. Reed

New Jersey

Senators	Representatives
James Smith, Jr. (D)	Charles N. Fowler (R)
William J. Sewell (R)	John J. Gardner (D)
	Benjamin F. Howell (R)
	Henry C. Loudenslager (R)
	Thomas McEwan, Jr. (R)
	Richard W. Parker (R)
	Mahlon Pitney (R)
	James F. Stewart (R)

New York

Senators	Representatives
David B. Hill (D)	Franklin Bartlett (D)
Edward Murphy, Jr. (D)	Charles G. Bennett (R)
	Frank S. Black (R)
	r. Jan. 1897
	Henry C. Brewster (R)
	Charles A. Chickering (R)
	Amos J. Cummings (D)
	Newton M. Curtis (R)
	Charles Daniels (R)
	Benjamin L. Fairchild (R)
	Israel F. Fischer (R)
	Wallace T. Foote Jr. (R)
	Charles W. Gillet (R)
	Warren B. Hooker (R)
	James R. Howe (R)
	Dennis M. Hurley (R)
	Jacob Le Fever (R)
	Philip B. Low (R)
	George B. McClellan (D)
	Richard C. McCormick (R)
	Rowland B. Mahany (R)
	Henry Clay Miner (D)
	John M. Mitchell (R)
	s. Jun. 1896
	Benjamin B. Odell Jr. (R)
	Sereno E. Payne (R)
	Theodore L. Poole (R)
	Lemuel E. Quigg (R)
	George W. Ray (R)
	Richard C. Shannon (R)
	James S. Sherman (R)
	George N. Southwick (R)
	William Sulzer (D)
	James W. Wadsworth (R)
	James J. Walsh (D)
	r. Jun. 1896
	David F. Wilber (R)
	Francis H. Wilson (R)

North Carolina

Senators	Representatives
Jeter C. Pritchard (R)	Romulus Z. Linney (R)
Marion Butler (Pop)	James A. Lockhart (D)
	r. Jun. 1896
	Charles H. Martin (Pop)
	s. 1896
	Richard Pearson (R)
	Thomas Settle (R)

North Carolina

Senators	Representatives
	John G. Shaw (D)
	Alonzo C. Shuford (Pop)
	Harry Skinner (Pop)
	William F. Strowd (Pop)
	Frederick A. Woodard (D)

North Dakota

Senators	Representative
Henry C. Hansbroug (R)	Martin N. Johnson (R)
William N. Roach (D)	

Ohio

Senators	Representatives
John Sherman (D)	Clifton B. Beach (R)
Clavin S. Brice (D)	Jacob H. Bromwell (R)
	Theodore E. Burton (R)
	Lorenzo Danford (R)
	Francis B. De Witt (R)
	Lucien J. Fenton (R)
	Charles H. Grosvenor (R)
	Stephen R. Harris (R)
	George W. Hulick (R)
	Winfield S. Kerr (R)
	Fernando C. Layton (D)
	Addison S. McClure (R)
	Stephen A. Northway (R)
	Paul J. Sorg (D)
	James H. Southard (R)
	Luther M. Strong (R)
	Charles P. Taft (R)
	Robert W. Tayler (R)
	Henry C. Van Voorhis (R)
	David K. Watson (R)
	George W. Wilson (R)

Oregon

Senators	Representatives
John H. Mitchell (R)	William R. Ellis (R)
George W. McBride (R)	Binger Hermann (R)

Pennsylvania

Senators	Representatives
J. Donald Cameron (R)	Ernest F. Acheson (R)
Matthew S. Quay (R)	Robert Adams, Jr. (R)
	William C. Arnold (R)
	Henry H. Bingham (R)
	Marriott Brosius (R)
	Charles N. Brumm (R)
	James H. Codding (R)
	John Dalzell (R)
	Constantine J. Erdman (D)
	Matthew Griswold (R)
	Galusha A. Grow (R)
	Frederick Halterman (R)
	Alfred C. Harmer (R)
	Joseph J. Hart (D)
	Daniel B. Heiner (R)
	Josiah D. Hicks (R)
	George F. Huff (R)
	Monroe H. Kulp (R)
	John Leisenring (R)
	Fred C. Leonard (R)
	Thaddeus M. Mahon (R)
	Thomas W. Phillips (R)
	John E. Reyburn (R)

Pennsylvania

Senators	Representatives
	John B. Robinson (R)
	Joseph A. Scranton (R)
	James A. Stahle (R)
	Charles W. Stone (R)
	William A. Stone (R)
	Irving P. Wanger (R)
	Ephraim M. Woomer (R)

Rhode Island

Senators	Representatives
Nelson W. Aldrich (R)	Warren O. Arnold (R)
George P. Wetmore (R)	Melville Bull (R)

South Carolina

Senators	Representatives
John L. M. Irby (D)	William Elliott (D)
Benjamin R. Tillman (D)	r. Jun. 1896
	Asbury C. Latimer (D)
	John L. McLaurin (D)
	George W. Murray (R)
	s. 1896
	J. William Stokes (D)
	s. 1896
	Thomas J. Strait (Alliance D)
	W. Jasper Talbert (D)
	Stanyarne Wilson (D)

South Dakota

Senators	Representatives
Richard F. Pettigrew (R)	Robert J. Gamble (R)
James H. Kyle	John A. Pickler (R)

Tennessee

Senators	Representatives
Isham G. Harris (D)	William C. Anderson (R)
William B. Bate (D)	Foster V. Brown (R)
	Nicholas N. Cox (D)
	Henry R. Gibson (R)
	John E. McCall (R)
	James C. McDearmon (D)
	Benton McMillin (D)
	Josiah Patterson (D)
	James D. Richardson (D)
	Joseph E. Washington (D)

Texas

Senators	Representatives
Robert Q. Mills (D)	Jo Abbott (D)
Horace Chilton (D)	Joseph W. Bailey (D)
	Charles K. Bell (D)
	Jeremiah V. Cockrell (D)
	Samuel L. Cooper (D)
	William H. Crain (D)
	d. Feb. 1896
	Miles Crowley (D)
	David B. Culberson (D)
	Joseph C. Hutcheson (D)
	Rudolph Kleberg (D)
	s. 1896
	George H. Noonan (R)
	George C. Pendleton (D)
	Joseph D. Sayers (D)
	Charles H. Yoakum (D)

Utah

Senators	Representative
Frank J. Cannon (R)	Clarence E. Allen (R)
s. 1896	s. 1896
Arthur Brown (R)	
s. 1896	

Vermont

Senators	Representatives
Justin S. Morrill (R)	William W. Grout (R)
Redfield Proctor (R)	H. Henry Powers (R)

Virginia

Senators	Representatives
John W. Daniel (D)	Tazewell Ellett (D)
Thomas S. Martin (D)	William A. Jones (D)
	William R. McKenney (D)
	r. May 1896
	Elisha E. Meredith (D)
	Peter J. Otey (D)
	Claude A. Swanson (D)
	Robert T. Thorp (R)
	s. 1896
	Henry St. George Tucker (D)
	Smith S. Turner (D)
	D. Gardiner Tyler (D)
	James A. Walker (R)

Washington

Senators	Representatives
Watson C. Squire (R)	William H. Doolittle (R)
John L. Wilson (R)	Samuel C. Hyde (R)

West Virginia

Senators	Representatives
Charles J. Faulkner (D)	Alston G. Dayton (R)
Stephen B. Elkins (R)	Blackburn B. Dovener (R)
	James H. Huling (R)
	Warren Miller (R)

Wisconsin

Senators	Representatives
William F. Vilas (D)	Joseph W. Babcock (R)
John L. Mitchell (R)	Samuel S. Barney (R)
	Samuel A. Cook (R)
	Henry A. Cooper (R)
	Michael Griffin (R)
	John J. Jenkins (R)
	Edward S. Minor (R)
	Theobald Otjen (R)
	Edward Sauerhering (R)
	Alexander Stewart (R)

Wyoming

Senators	Representative
Clarence D. Clark (R)	Frank W. Mondell (R)
Francis E. Warren (R)	

Source: Notable Names in American History; A Tabulated Register. Third edition of White's Conspectus of American Biography (1973), 142–144.

TABLE 7.38 FIFTY-FIFTH CONGRESS

Mar. 4, 1897 to Mar. 3, 1899

President of The Senate	President Pro Tempore of The Senate	Speaker of The House of Representatives
Garret A. Hobart	William P. Frye	Thomas B. Reed

Alabama

Senators	Representatives
John T. Morgan (D)	William F. Aldrich (R)
Edmund W. Pettus (D)	s. 1898
	John H. Bankhead (D)
	Willis Brewer (D)
	Henry D. Clayton (D)
	Milford W. Howard (Pop)
	Thomas S. Plowman (D)
	r. Feb. 1898
	Jesse F. Stallings (D)
	George W. Taylor (D)
	Oscar W. Underwood (D)
	Joseph Wheeler (D)

Arkansas

Senators	Representatives
James K. Jones (D)	Stephen Brundidge, Jr. (D)
James H. Berry (D)	Hugh A. Dinsmore (D)
	John S. Little (D)
	Philip D. McCulloch Jr. (D)
	Thomas C. McRae (D)
	William L. Terry (D)

California

Senators	Representatives
Stephen M. White (D)	John A. Barham (R)
George C. Perkins (R)	Charles A. Barlow (D)
	Curtis H. Castle (D)
	Marion De Vries (D)
	Samuel G. Hilborn (R)
	Eugene F. Loud (R)
	James G. Maguire (D)

Colorado

Senators	Representatives
Henry M. Teller (R)	John C. Bell (D)
Edward O. Wolcott (R)	John F. Shafroth (D)

Connecticut

Senators	Representatives
Orville H. Platt (R)	E. Stevens Henry (R)
Joseph R. Hawley (R)	Ebenezer J. Hill (R)
	Charles A. Russell (R)
	Nehemiah D. Sperry (R)

Delaware

Senators	Representative
George Gray (D)	Levin I. Handy (D)
Richard R. Kenney (D)	

Florida

Senators	Representatives
Samuel Pasco (D)	Robert W. Davis (D)
Stephen R. Mallory (D)	Stephen M. Sparkman (D)

Georgia

Senators	Representatives
Augustus O. Bacon (D)	William C. Adamson (D)
Alexander S. Clay (D)	Charles L. Bartlett (D)
	William G. Brantley (D)
	William H. Fleming (D)
	James M. Griggs (D)
	William M. Howard (D)
	Rufus E. Lester (D)
	Elijah B. Lewis (D)
	Leonidas F. Livingston (D)
	John W. Maddox (D)
	Farish C. Tate (D)

Idaho

Senators	Representative
George L. Shoup (R)	James Gunn (P)
Henry Heitfeld (D)	

Illinois

Senators	Representatives
Shelby M. Cullom (R)	Jehu Baker (Fusion)
William E. Mason (R)	Hugh R. Belknap (R)
	Henry S. Boutell (R)
	James R. Campbell (D)
	Joseph G. Cannon (R)
	James A. Connolly (R)
	Edward D. Cooke (R)
	d. Jun. 1897
	George E. Foss (R)
	Joseph V. Graff (R)
	William H. Hinrichsen (D)
	Robert R. Hitt (R)
	Albert J. Hopkins (R)
	Andrew J. Hunter (D)
	Thomas M. Jett (D)
	William Lorimer (R)
	James R. Mann (R)
	Benjamin F. Marsh (R)
	Daniel W. Mills (R)
	George W. Prince (R)
	Walter Reeves (R)
	George W. Smith (R)
	Vespasian Warner (R)
	George E. White (R)

Indiana

Senators	Representatives
David Turpie (D)	Edgar D. Crumpacker (R)
Charles W. Fairbanks (R)	George W. Faris (R)
	Francis M. Griffith (D)
	James A. Hemenway (R)
	Charles L. Henry (R)
	William S. Holman (D)
	d. Apr. 1897
	Henry U. Johnson (R)
	Charles B. Landis (R)
	Robert W. Miers (D)
	Jesse Overstreet (R)
	James M. Robinson (D)
	Lemuel W. Royse (R)
	George W. Steele (R)
	William T. Zenor (D)

Iowa	
Senators	**Representatives**
William B. Allison (R)	Samuel M. Clark (R)
John H. Gear (R)	Robert G. Cousins (R)
	George M. Curtis (R)
	Jonathan P. Dolliver (R)
	Alva L. Hager (R)
	David B. Henderson (R)
	William P. Hepburn (R)
	John A. T. Hull
	John F. Lacey (R)
	George D. Perkins (R)
	Thomas Updegraff (R)

Kansas	
Senators	**Representatives**
Lucien Baker (R)	Jeremiah D. Botkin (Fusion)
William A. Harris (D)	Case Broderick (R)
	Charles Curtis (R)
	Nelson B. McCormick (Pop)
	Mason S. Peters (D)
	Edwin R. Ridgely (People's)
	Jeremiah Simpson (Pop)
	William D. Vincent (Pop)

Kentucky	
Senators	**Representatives**
William Lindsay (D)	Albert S. Berry (D)
William J. DeBoe (R)	John D. Clardy (D)
	David G. Colson (R)
	George M. Davison (R)
	Walter Evans (R)
	Thomas Y. Fitzpatrick (D)
	Samuel J. Pugh (R)
	John S. Rhea (D)
	Evan E. Settle (D)
	David H. Smith (D)
	Charles K. Wheeler (D)

Louisiana	
Senators	**Representatives**
Donelson Caffery (D)	Samuel T. Baird (D)
Samuel D. McEnery (D)	Robert F. Broussard (D)
	Robert C. Davey (D)
	Adolph Meyer (D)
	Henry W. Ogden (D)
	Samuel M. Robertson (D)

Maine	
Senators	**Representatives**
Eugene Hale (R)	Charles A. Boutelle (R)
William P. Frye (R)	Edwin C. Burleigh (R)
	Nelson Dingley, Jr. (R)
	d. Jan. 1899
	Seth L. Milliken (R)
	d. Apr. 1897
	Thomas B. Reed (R)

Maryland	
Senators	**Representatives**
Arthur P. Gorman (D)	William B. Baker (R)
George L. Wellington (D)	Isaac A. Barber (R)
	William S. Booze (R)
	John McDonald (R)
	William W. McIntire (R)
	Sydney E. Mudd (R)

Massachusetts	
Senators	**Representatives**
George F. Hoar (R)	William E. Barrett (R)
Henry Cabot Lodge (R)	Samuel J. Barrows (R)
	John F. Fitzgerald (D)
	Frederick H. Gillett (R)
	William S. Greene (R)
	s. 1898
	William S. Knox (R)
	George P. Lawrence (R)
	William C. Lovering (R)
	Samuel W. McCall (R)
	William H. Moody (R)
	John Simpkins (R)
	d. Mar. 1898
	Charles F. Sprague (R)
	Joseph H. Walker (R)
	George W. Weymouth (R)
	Ashley B. Wright (R)
	d. Aug. 1897

Michigan	
Senators	**Representatives**
James McMillan (R)	Roswell P. Bishop (R)
Julius C. Burrows (R)	Ferdinand Brucker (D)
	John B. Corliss (R)
	Rousseau O. Crump (R)
	Edward L. Hamilton (R)
	William S. Mesick (R)
	Carlos D. Shelden (R)
	Samuel W. Smith (R)
	William Alden Smith (R)
	Horace G. Snover (R)
	George Spalding (R)
	Albert M. Todd

Minnesota	
Senators	**Representatives**
Cushman K. Davis (R)	Frank M. Eddy (R)
Knute Nelson (R)	Loren Fletcher (R)
	Joel P. Heatwole (R)
	James T. McCleary (R)
	R. Page W. Morris (R)
	James A. Tawney (R)
	Frederick C. Stevens (R)

Mississippi	
Senators	**Representatives**
James Z. George (D)	John M. Allen (D)
d. Aug. 1897	Thomas C. Catchings (D)
Hernando D. Money (D)	Andrew F. Fox (D)
s. 1897	Patrick Henry (D)
Edward C. Walthall (D)	William F. Love (D)
d. Apr. 1898	d. Oct. 1898
William V. Sullivan (D)	Frank A. McLain (D)
s. 1898	s. 1898
	Thomas Spight (D)
	s. 1898
	William V. Sullivan (D)
	r. May 1898
	John Sharp Williams (D)

(continued)

TABLE 7.38 (continued)

Mar. 4, 1897 to Mar. 3, 1899

President of The Senate	President Pro Tempore of The Senate	Speaker of The House of Representatives
Garret A. Hobart	William P. Frye	Thomas B. Reed

Missouri

Senators	Representatives
Francis M. Cockrell (D)	Richard Bartholdt (R)
George G. Vest (D)	Maecenas E. Benton (D)
	Richard P. Bland (D)
	Robert N. Bodine (D)
	Champ Clark (D)
	Charles F. Cochran (D)
	James Cooney (D)
	William S. Cowherd (D)
	David A. De Armond (D)
	Alexander M. Dockery (D)
	Charles F. Joy (R)
	James T. Lloyd (D)
	Charles E. Pearce (R)
	Edward Robb (D)
	Willard D. Vandiver (D)

Montana

Senators	Representative
Lee Mantle (R)	Charles S. Hartman (R)
Thomas H. Carter (R)	

Nebraska

Senators	Representatives
William V. Allen (Pop)	William L. Greene (Pop)
John M. Thurston (R)	Samuel Maxwell (Fusion)
	David H. Mercer (R)
	William L. Stark (D)
	Jesse B. Strode (R)
	Roderick D. Sutherland (Pop)

Nevada

Senators	Representative
John P. Jones (R)	Francis G. Newlands (D)
William M. Stewart (R)	

New Hampshire

Senators	Representatives
William E. Chandler (R)	Frank G. Clarke (R)
Jacob H. Gallinger (R)	Cyrus A. Sulloway (R)

New Jersey

Senators	Representatives
James Smith Jr. (D)	Charles N. Fowler (R)
William J. Sewell (R)	John J. Gardner (R)
	Benjamin F. Howell (R)
	Henry C. Loudenslager (R)
	Thomas McEwan Jr. (R)
	Richard W. Parker (R)
	Mahlon Pitney (R)
	r. Jan. 1899
	James F. Stewart (R)

New York

Senators	Representatives
Edward Murphy, Jr. (D)	De Alva S. Alexander (R)
Thomas C. Platt (R)	James J. Belden (R)
	Joseph M. Belford (R)
	Charles G. Bennett (R)
	Thomas J. Bradley (D)
	Henry C. Brewster (R)
	Charles A. Chickering (R)
	Aaron V. S. Cochrane (R)
	Amos Cummings (D)
	Edmund H. Driggs (D)
	Israel F. Fischer (R)
	Wallace T. Foote Jr. (R)
	Charles W. Gillet (R)
	Warren B. Hooker (R)
	r. Nov. 1898
	James R. Howe (R)
	Denis M. Hurley (R)
	d. Feb. 1898
	John H. Ketcham (R)
	Lucius N. Littauer (R)
	Philip B. Low (R)
	George B. McClellan (D)
	Rowland B. Mahany (R)
	John M. Mitchell (R)
	Benjamin B. Odell, Jr. (R)
	Sereno E. Payne (R)
	Lemuel E. Quigg (R)
	George W. Ray (R)
	Richard C. Shannon (R)
	James S. Sherman (R)
	George N. Southwick (R)
	William Sulzer (D)
	John H. G. Vehslage (D)
	James W. Wadsworth (R)
	William L. Ward (R)
	David F. Wilber (R)
	Francis H. Wilson (R)
	r. Sep. 1897

North Carolina

Senators	Representatives
Jeter C. Pritchard (R)	John E. Fowler (Pop)
Marion Butler (Pop)	William W. Kitchin (D)
	Romulus Z. Linney (R)
	Charles H. Martin (Pop)
	Richmond Pearson (R)
	Alonzo C. Shuford (Pop)
	Harry Skinner (Pop)
	William F. Strowd (Pop)
	George H. White (R)

North Dakota

Senators	Representative
Henry C. Hansbrough (R)	Martin N. Johnson (R)
William N. Roach (D)	

Ohio

Senators	Representatives
Marcus A. Hanna (R)	Clifton B. Beach (R)
Joseph B. Foraker (R)	John L. Brenner (D)
	Jacob H. Bromwell (R)
	Seth W. Brown (R)
	Theodore E. Burton (R)
	Lorenzo Danford (R)
	Charles W. F. Dick (R)
	s. 1898
	Lucien J. Fenton (R)

Ohio	
Senators	**Representatives**
	Charles H. Grosvenor (R)
	Winfield S. Kerr (R)
	John J. Lentz (D)
	Archibald Lybrand (R)
	John A. McDowell (D)
	George A. Marshall (D)
	David Meekison (D)
	Stephen A. Northway (R)
	d. Sep. 1898
	James A. Norton (D)
	William B. Shattuc (R)
	James H. Southard (R)
	Robert W. Tayler (R)
	Henry C. Van Voorhis (R)
	Walter L. Weaver (R)

Oregon	
Senators	**Representatives**
George W. McBride (R)	William R. Ellis (R)
Joseph Simon (R)	Thomas H. Tongue (R)
s. 1898	

Pennsylvania	
Senators	**Representatives**
Matthew S. Quay (R)	Ernest F. Acheson (R)
Boies Penrose (R)	Robert Adams, Jr. (R)
	William C. Arnold (R)
	George J. Benner (D)
	Henry H. Bingham (R)
	Marriott Brosius (R)
	Charles N. Brumm (R)
	Thomas S. Butler (R)
	James H. Codding (R)
	William Connell (R)
	John Dalzell (R)
	Samuel A. Davenport (R)
	Daniel Ermentrout (D)
	William H. Graham (R)
	s. 1898
	Galusha A. Grow (R)
	Alfred C. Harmer (R)
	Josiah D. Hicks (R)
	William S. Kirkpatrick (R)
	Monroe H. Kulp (R)
	William McAleer (D)
	Thaddeus M. Mahon (R)
	Marlin E. Olmsted (R)
	Horace B. Packer (R)
	Edward E. Robbins (R)
	Joseph B. Showalter (R)
	Charles W. Stone (R)
	William A. Stone (R)
	r. Nov. 1898
	John C. Sturtevant (R)
	Irving P. Wanger (R)
	Morgan B. Williams (R)
	James R. Young (R)

Rhode Island	
Senators	**Representatives**
Nelson W. Aldrich (R)	Melville Bull (R)
George P. Wetmore (R)	Adin B. Capron (R)

South Carolina	
Senators	**Representatives**
Benjamin R. Tillman (D)	William Elliott (D)
Joseph H. Earle (D)	Asbury C. Latimer (D)
d. May 1897	John L. McLaurin (D)
John L. McLaurin (D)	r. May 1897
s. 1897	James Norton (D)
	J. William Stokes (D)
	Thomas J. Strait (Alliance D)
	W. Jasper Talbert (D)
	Stanyarne Wilson (D)

South Dakota	
Senators	**Representatives**
Richard F. Pettigrew (R)	John E. Kelley (D)
James H. Kyle	Freeman Knowles (Pop)

Tennessee	
Senators	**Representatives**
Isham G. Harris (D)	Walter P. Brownlow (R)
d. Jul. 1897	Edward W. Carmack (D)
Thomas B. Turley (D)	Nicholas N. Cox (D)
s. 1897	John W. Gaines (D)
William B. Bate (D)	Henry R. Gibson (R)
	Benton McMillin (D)
	r. Jan. 1899
	John A. Moon (D)
	Rice A. Pierce (D)
	James D. Richardson (D)
	Thetus W. Sims (D)

Texas	
Senators	**Representatives**
Roger Q. Mills (D)	Joseph W. Bailey (D)
Horace Chilton (D)	Thomas H. Ball (D)
	Robert E. Burke (D)
	Samuel B. Cooper (D)
	John W. Cranford (D)
	d. Mar. 1899
	Reese C. De Graffenreid (D)
	Robert B. Hawley (R)
	Robert L. Henry (D)
	Rudolph Kleberg (D)
	Samuel W. T. Lanham (D)
	Joseph D. Sayers (D)
	r. Jan. 1899
	James L. Slayden (D)
	John H. Stephens (D)

Utah	
Senators	**Representative**
Frank J. Cannon (R)	William H. King (D)
Joseph L. Rawlins (D)	

Vermont	
Senators	**Representatives**
Justin S. Morrill (R)	William W. Grout (R)
d. Dec. 1898	H. Henry Powers (R)
Jonathan Ross (R)	
s. 1899	
Redfield Proctor (R)	

(continued)

TABLE 7.38 (continued)

Mar. 4, 1897 to Mar. 3, 1899

President of The Senate	President Pro Tempore of The Senate	Speaker of The House of Representatives
Garret A. Hobart	William P. Frye	Thomas B. Reed

Virginia

Senators	Representatives

John W. Daniel (D)
Thomas S. Martin (D)
	Sydney P. Epes (D)
	   r. Mar. 1898
	James Hay (D)
	William A. Jones (D)
	John Lamb (D)
	Peter J. Otey (D)
	John F. Rixey (D)
	Claude A. Swanson (D)
	Robert T. Thorp (R)
	   s. 1898
	James A. Walker (D)
	Richard A. Wise (R)
	   s. 1898
	Jacob Yost (R)
	William A. Young (D)
	   r. Apr. 1898

Washington

Senators	Representatives
John L. Wilson (R) George Turner (Fusion)	William C. Jones (R) James Hamilton Lewis (D)

West Virginia

Senators	Representatives
Charles J. Faulkner (D) Stephen B. Elkins (R)	Alston G. Dayton (R) Charles P. Dorr (R) Blackburn B. Dovener (R) Warren Miller (R)

Wisconsin

Senators	Representatives
John L. Mitchell (D) John C. Spooner (R)	Joseph W. Babcock (R) Samuel S. Barney (R) Henry Allen Cooper (R) James H. Davidson (R) Michael Griffin (R) John J. Jenkins (R) Edward S. Minor (R) Theobald Otjen (R) Edward Sauerhering (R) Alexander Stewart (R)

Wyoming

Senators	Representative
Clarence D. Clark (R) Francis E. Warren (R)	John E. Osborne (D)

Source: *Notable Names in American History; A Tabulated Register.* Third edition of *White's Conspectus of American Biography* (1973), 144–147.

TABLE 7.39 FIFTY-SIXTH CONGRESS

Mar. 4, 1899 to Mar. 3, 1901

President of The Senate	President Pro Tempore of The Senate	Speaker of The House of Representatives
Garret A. Hobart	William P. Frye	David B. Henderson

Alabama

Senators	Representatives

John T. Morgan (D)
Edmund W. Pettus (D)
	William F. Aldrich (R)
	John H. Bankhead (D)
	Willis Brewer (D)
	John L. Burnett (D)
	Henry D. Clayton (D)
	William Richardson (D)
	   s. 1900
	Gaston A. Robbins (D)
	   r. Mar. 1900
	Jesse F. Stallings (D)
	George W. Taylor (D)
	Oscar W. Underwood (D)
	Joseph Wheeler (D)
	   r. Apr. 1900

Arkansas

Senators	Representatives
James K. Jones (D) James H. Berry (D)	Stephen Brundidge Jr. (D) Hugh A. Dinsmore (D) John S. Little (D) Philip D. McCulloch, Jr. (D) Thomas C. McRae (D) William L. Terry (D)

California

Senators	Representatives

George C. Perkins (R)
Thomas R. Bard (R)
	John A. Barham (R)
	Marion De Vries (D)
	   r. Aug. 1900
	Julius Kahn (R)
	Eugene F. Loud (R)
	Victor H. Metcalf (R)
	James C. Needham (R)
	Russell J. Waters (R)
	Samuel D. Woods (R)
	   s. 1900

Colorado

Senators	Representatives
Henry M. Teller (R) Edward O. Wolcott (R)	John C. Bell (D) John F. Shafroth (R)

Connecticut

Senators	Representatives
Orville H. Platt (R) Joseph R. Hawley (R)	E. Stevens Henry (R) Ebenezer J. Hill (R) Charles A. Russell (R) Nehemiah D. Sperry (R)

Delaware

Senators	Representatives
Richard R. Kennedy (D) Vacant	John H. Hoffecker (R) d. Jun. 1900 Walter O. Hoffecker (R)

Florida

Senators	Representatives
Stephen R. Mallory (D)	Robert W. Davis (D)
Samuel Pasco (D)	Stephen M. Sparkman (D)
ta. 1899	
James P. Taliaferro (D)	
s. Dec. 1899	

Georgia

Senators	Representatives
Augustus O. Bacon (D)	William C. Adamson (D)
Alexander S. Clay (D)	Charles L. Bartlett (D)
	William G. Brantley (D)
	William H. Fleming (D)
	James M. Griggs (D)
	William M. Howard (D)
	Rufus E. Lester (D)
	Elijah B. Lewis (D)
	Leonidas F. Livingston (D)
	John W. Maddox (D)
	Farish C. Tate (D)

Idaho

Senators	Representative
George L. Shoup (R)	Edgar Wilson (R)
Henry Heitfeld (Pop)	

Illinois

Senators	Representatives
Shelby M. Cullom (R)	Henry S. Boutell (R)
William E. Mason (R)	Ben F. Caldwell (D)
	Joseph G. Cannon (R)
	Joseph B. Crowley (D)
	Thomas Cusack (D)
	George E. Foss (R)
	George P. Foster (D)
	Joseph V. Graff (R)
	Robert R. Hitt (R)
	Albert J. Hopkins (R)
	Thomas M. Jett (D)
	William Lorimer (R)
	James R. Mann (R)
	Benjamin F. Marsh (R)
	Edward T. Noonan (D)
	George W. Prince (R)
	Walter Reeves (R)
	William A. Rodenberg (R)
	George W. Smith (R)
	Vespasian Warner (R)
	James R. Williams (D)
	William E. Williams (D)

Indiana

Senators	Representatives
Charles W. Fairbanks (R)	Abraham L. Brick (R)
Albert J. Beveridge (R)	George W. Cromer (R)
	Edgar D. Crumpacker (R)
	George W. Faris (R)
	Francis M. Griffith (D)
	James A. Hemenway (R)
	Charles B. Landis (R)
	Robert W. Miers (D)
	Jesse Overstreet (R)
	James M. Robinson (D)
	George W. Steele (R)
	James E. Watson (R)
	William T. Zenor (D)

Iowa

Senators	Representatives
William B. Allison (R)	James P. Conner (R)
John H. Gear (R)	s. 1900
d. Jul. 1900	Robert G. Cousins (R)
Jonathan P. Dolliver (R)	Jonathan P. Dolliver (R)
s. 1900	r. Aug. 1900
	Gilbert N. Haugen (R)
	Thomas Hedge (R)
	David B. Henderson (R)
	William P. Hepburn (R)
	John A. T. Hull (R)
	John F. Lacey (R)
	Joseph R. Lane (R)
	Smith McPherson (R)
	r. 1900
	Walter I. Smith (R)
	s. 1900
	Lot Thomas (R)

Kansas

Senators	Representatives
Lucien Baker (R)	Willis J. Bailey (R)
William A. Harris (D)	Justin D. Browersock (R)
	William A. Calderhead (R)
	Charles Curtis (R)
	Chester I. Long (R)
	James M. Miller (R)
	William A. Reeder (R)
	Edwin R. Ridgely (D)

Kentucky

Senators	Representatives
William Lindsay (D)	Henry D. Allen (D)
William J. DeBoe (R)	Albert S. Berry (D)
	Vincent S. Boreing (R)
	Thomas Y. Fitzpatrick (D)
	June W. Gayle (D)
	George G. Gilbert (D)
	Samuel J. Pugh (R)
	John S. Rhea (D-P)
	David H. Smith (D)
	Oscar Turner (D)
	Charles K. Wheeler (D)

Louisiana

Senators	Representatives
Donelson Caffery (D)	Phanor Breazeale (D)
Samuel D. McEnery (D)	Robert F. Broussard (D)
	Robert C. Davey (D)
	Adolph Meyer (D)
	Joseph E. Ransdell (D)
	Samuel M. Robertson (D)

Maine

Senators	Representatives
Eugene Hale (R)	Amos L. Allen (R)
William P. Frye (R)	Charles A. Boutelle (R)
	Edwin C. Burleigh (R)
	Charles E. Littlefield (R)

(continued)

TABLE 7.39 (continued)

Mar. 4, 1899 to Mar. 3, 1901

President of The Senate	President Pro Tempore of The Senate	Speaker of The House of Representatives
Garret A. Hobart	William P. Frye	David B. Henderson

Maryland

Senators	Representatives
George L. Wellington (D)	William B. Baker (R)
Louis E. McComas (R)	James W. Denny (D)
	Josiah L. Kerr (R)
	s. 1900
	Sydney E. Mudd (R)
	George A. Pearre (R)
	John Walter Smith (D)
	r. Jan. 1900
	Frank C. Wachter (R)

Massachusetts

Senators	Representatives
George F. Hoar (R)	John F. Fitzgerald (D)
Henry Cabot Lodge (R)	Frederick H. Gillett (R)
	William S. Greene (R)
	William S. Knox (R)
	George P. Lawrence (R)
	William C. Lovering (R)
	Samuel W. McCall (R)
	William H. Moody (R)
	Henry F. Naphen (D)
	Ernest W. Roberts (R)
	Charles F. Sprague (R)
	John R. Thayer (D)
	George W. Weymouth (R)

Michigan

Senators	Representatives
James McMillan (R)	Roswell P. Bishop (R)
Julius C. Burrows (R)	John B. Corliss (R)
	Rousseau O. Crump (R)
	Joseph W. Fordney (R)
	Washington Gardner (R)
	Edward L. Hamilton (R)
	William S. Mesick (R)
	Carlos D. Shelden (R)
	Henry C. Smith (R)
	Samuel W. Smith (R)
	William Alden Smith (R)
	Edgar Weeks (R)

Minnesota

Senators	Representatives
Cushman K. Davis (R)	Frank M. Eddy (R)
d. Nov. 1900	Loren Fletcher (R)
Charles A. Towne (D)	Joel P. Heatwole (R)
ta. 1900	James T. McCleary (R)
Moses E. Clapp (R)	R. Page W. Morris (R)
s. 1901	Frederick C. Stevens (R)
Knute Nelson (R)	James A. Tawney (R)

Mississippi

Senators	Representatives
Hernando D. Money (D)	John M. Allen (D)
William V. Sullivan (D)	Thomas C. Catchings (D)
	Andrew F. Fox (D)
	Patrick Henry (D)
	Frank A. McLain (D)
	Thomas Spight (D)
	John Sharp Williams (D)

Missouri

Senators	Representatives
Francis M. Cockrell (D)	Richard Bartholdt (R)
George G. Vest (D)	Maecenas E. Benton (D)
	Champ Clark (D)
	Charles F. Cochran (D)
	James Cooney (D)
	William S. Cowherd (D)
	David A. De Armond (D)
	John Dougherty (D)
	Charles F. Joy (R)
	James T. Lloyd (D)
	Charles E. Pearce (R)
	Edward Robb (D)
	William W. Rucker (D)
	Dorsey W. Shackleford (D)
	Willard D. Vandiver (D)

Montana

Senators	Representatives
Thomas H. Carter (R)	Albert J. Campbell (D)
William A. Clark (D)	
r. May 1900	

Nebraska

Senators	Representatives
John M. Thurston (R)	Elmer J. Burkett (R)
William V. Allen (Pop)	David H. Mercer (R)
	William Neville (Pop)
	John S. Robinson (D)
	William L. Stark (D)
	Roderick D. Sutherland (Pop)

Nevada

Senators	Representative
John P. Jones (R)	Francis G. Newlands (D)
William M. Stewart (R)	

New Hampshire

Senators	Representatives
William E. Chandler (R)	Frank G. Clarke (R)
Jacob H. Gallinger (R)	d. Jan. 1901
	Cyrus A. Sulloway (R)

New Jersey	
Senators	**Representatives**
William J. Sewell (R) John Kean (R)	William D. Daly (D) d. Jul. 1900 Charles N. Fowler (R) John J. Gardner (D) Benjamin F. Howell (R) Henry C. Loudenslager (R) Allan L. McDermott (D) s. 1900 Richard W. Parker (R) Joshua S. Salmon (D) James F. Stewart (R)

New York	
Senators	**Representatives**
Thomas C. Platt (R) Chauncey M. Depew (R)	De Alva S. Alexander (R) Thomas J. Bradley (D) William A. Chanler (D) Charles A. Chickering (R) d. Feb. 1900 Bertram T. Clayton (D) Aaron V. S. Cochrane (R) Amos J. Cummings (D) Edmund H. Driggs (D) Michael E. Driscoll (R) Louis W. Emerson (R) John J. Fitzgerald (D) Charles W. Gillet (R) Martin H. Glynn (D) John H. Ketcham (R) Jefferson M. Levy (D) Lucius N. Littauer (R) George B. McClellan (D) Mitchell May (D) Nicholas Muller (D) James M. E. O'Grady (R) Sereno E. Payne (R) George W. Ray (R) Daniel J. Riordan (D) Jacob Ruppert, Jr. (D) William H. Ryan (D) Townsend Scudder (D) Albert D. Shaw (R) s. 1900 James S. Sherman (R) John K. Stewart (R) William Sulzer (D) Arthur Q. Tompkins (R) John Q. Underhill (D) Edward B. Vreeland (R) James W. Wadsworth (R) Frank E. Wilson (D)

North Carolina	
Senators	**Representatives**
Marion Butler (Pop) Jeter C. Pritchard (R)	John W. Atwater (Pop) John D. Bellamy (D) William T. Crawford (D) r. May 1900 William W. Kitchin (D) Theodore F. Kluttz (D) Romulus Z. Linney (R) Richmond Pearson (R) s. 1900 John H. Small (D) Charles R. Thomas (D) George H. White (R)

North Dakota	
Senators	**Representative**
Henry C. Hansbrough (R) Porter J. McCumber (R)	Burleigh F. Spalding (R)

Ohio	
Senators	**Representatives**
Joseph B. Foraker (R) Marcus A. Hanna (R)	John L. Brenner (D) Jacob H. Bromwell (R) Seth W. Brown (R) Theodore E. Burton (R) Charles W. F. Dick (R) Joseph J. Gill (R) Robert B. Gordon (D) Charles H. Grosvenor (R) Winfield S. Kerr (R) John J. Lentz (D) Archibald Lybrand (R) John A. McDowell (D) David Meekison (D) Stephen Morgan (R) James A. Norton (D) Fremont O. Phillips (R) William B. Shattuc (R) James H. Southard (R) Robert W. Tayler (R) Henry C. Van Voorhis (R) Walter L. Weaver (R)

Oregon	
Senators	**Representatives**
George W. McBride (R) Joseph Simon (R)	Malcolm A. Moody (R) Thomas H. Tongue (R)

Pennsylvania	
Senators	**Representatives**
Boies Penrose (R) Matthew S. Quay (R)	Ernest F. Acheson (R) Robert Adams Jr. (R) Laird H. Barber (D) Henry H. Bingham (R) Marriott Brosius (R) Thomas S. Butler (R) William Connell (R) John Dalzell (R) Samuel A. Davenport (R) Stanley W. Davenport (D) Athelston Gaston (D) William H. Graham (R) Henry D. Green (D) Galusha A. Grow (R) James K. P. Hall (D) Alfred C. Harmer (R) d. Mar. 1900 Summers M. Jack (R) William McAleer (D) Thaddeus M. Mahon (R) Edward de V. Morrell (R) s. 1900 Marlin E. Olmsted (R) Horace B. Packer (R) Rufus K. Polk (D) James W. Ryan (D) Joseph B. Showalter (R) Joseph C. Sibley (D) Joseph E. Thropp (R) Irving P. Wanger (R) Charles F. Wright (R) James R. Young (R) Edward Ziegler (D)

(continued)

TABLE 7.39   (continued)

Mar. 4, 1899 to Mar. 3, 1901

President of The Senate	President Pro Tempore of The Senate	Speaker of The House of Representatives
Garret A. Hobart	William P. Frye	David B. Henderson

Rhode Island

Senators	Representatives
Nelson W. Aldrich (R)	Melville Bull (R)
George P. Wetmore (R)	Adin B. Capron (R)

South Carolina

Senators	Representatives
Benjamin R. Tillman (D)	William Elliott (D)
John L. McLaurin (D)	David E. Finley (D)
	Asbury C. Latimer (D)
	James Norton (D)
	J. William Stokes (D)
	W. Jasper Talbert (D)
	Stanyarne Wilson (D)

South Dakota

Senators	Representatives
Richard F. Pettigrew (R)	Charles H. Burke (R)
James H. Kyle	Robert J. Gamble (R)

Tennessee

Senators	Representatives
William B. Bate (D)	Walter P. Brownlow (R)
Thomas B. Turley (D)	Edward W. Carmack (D)
	Nicholas N. Cox (D)
	John W. Gaines (D)
	Henry R. Gibson (R)
	John A. Moon (D)
	Rice A. Pierce (D)
	James D. Richardson (D)
	Thetus W. Sims (D)
	Charles E. Snodgrass (D)

Texas

Senators	Representatives
Horace Chilton (D)	Joseph W. Bailey (D)
Charles A. Culberson (D)	Thomas H. Ball (D)
	Robert E. Burke (D)
	Albert S. Burleson (D)
	Samuel B. Cooper (D)
	Reese C. De Graffenreid (D)
	Robert B. Hawley (R)
	Robert L. Henry (D)
	Rudolph Kleberg (D)
	Samuel W. T. Lanham (D)
	John L. Sheppard (D)
	James L. Slayden (D)
	John H. Stephens (D)

Utah

Senators	Representative
Joseph L. Rawlins (R)	William H. King (D)
Thomas Kearns (R)	s. 1900
s. 1901	

Vermont

Senators	Representatives
Redfield Proctor (R)	William W. Grout (R)
Jonathan Ross (R)	H. Henry Powers (R)
ta. 1899	
William P. Dillingham (R)	
s. 1900	

Virginia

Senators	Representatives
John W. Daniel (D)	Sydney P. Epes (D)
Thomas S. Martin (D)	d. Mar. 1900
	James Hay (D)
	William A. Jones (D)
	John Lamb (D)
	Francis R. Lassiter (D)
	s. 1900
	Peter J. Otey (D)
	Julian M. Quarles (D)
	William F. Rhea (D)
	John F. Rixey (D)
	Claude A. Swanson (D)
	Richard A. Wise (R)
	d. 1900
	William A. Young (D)
	r. Mar. 1900

Washington

Senators	Representatives
George Turner (Fusion)	Francis W. Cushman (R)
Addison G. Foster (R)	Wesley L. Jones (R)

West Virginia

Senators	Representatives
Stephen B. Elkins (R)	Alston G. Dayton (R)
Nathan B. Scott (R)	Blackburn B. Dovener (R)
	Romeo H. Freer (R)
	David E. Johnston (D)

Wisconsin

Senators	Representatives
John C. Spooner (R)	Joseph W. Babcock (R)
Joseph V. Quarles (R)	Samuel S. Barney (R)
	Henry A. Cooper (R)
	Herman B. Dahle (R)
	James H. Davidson (R)
	John J. Esch (R)
	John J. Jenkins (R)
	Edward S. Minor (R)
	Theobald Otjen (R)
	Alexander Stewart (R)

Wyoming

Senators	Representative
Clarence D. Clark (R)	Frank W. Mondell (R)
Francis E. Warren (R)	

Source: Notable Names in American History; A Tabulated Register. Third edition of *White's Conspectus of American Biography* (1973), 147–149.

TABLE 7.40   FIFTY-SEVENTH CONGRESS

Mar. 4, 1901 to Mar. 3, 1903

President of The Senate	President Pro Tempore of The Senate	Speaker of The House of Representatives
Theodore Roosevelt	William P. Frye	David B. Henderson

Alabama

Senators	Representatives
John T. Morgan (D)	John H. Bankhead (D)
Edmund W. Pettus (D)	Sydney J. Bowie (D)
	John L. Burnett (D)
	Henry D. Clayton (D)
	William Richardson (D)
	George W. Taylor (D)
	Charles W. Thompson (D)
	Oscar W. Underwood (D)
	Ariosto A. Wiley (D)

Arkansas

Senators	Representatives
James K. Jones (D)	Stephen Brundidge, Jr. (D)
James H. Berry (D)	Hugh A. Dinsmore (D)
	John S. Little (D)
	Philip D. McCulloch, Jr. (D)
	Thomas C. McRae (D)
	Charles C. Reid (D)

California

Senators	Representatives
George C. Perkins (R)	Frank L. Coombs (R)
Thomas R. Bard (R)	Julius Kahn (R)
	Eugene F. Loud (R)
	James McLachlan (R)
	Victor H. Metcalf (R)
	James C. Needham (R)
	Samuel D. Woods (R)

Colorado

Senators	Representatives
Henry M. Teller (R)	John C. Bell (D)
Thomas M. Patterson (D)	John F. Shafroth (D)

Connecticut

Senators	Representatives
Orville H. Platt (R)	Frank B. Brandegee (R)
Joseph R. Hawley (R)	s. 1902
	E. Stevens Henry (R)
	Ebenezer J. Hill (R)
	Charles A. Russell (R)
	d. Oct. 1902
	Nehemiah D. Sperry (R)

Delaware

Senators	Representative
L. Heisler Ball (R)	L. Heisler Ball (R)
s. 1903	r. Mar. 1903
J. Frank Allee (R)	
s. 1903	

Florida

Senators	Representatives
Stephen R. Mallory (D)	Robert W. Davis (D)
James P. Taliaferro (D)	Stephen M. Sparkman (D)

Georgia

Senators	Representatives
Augustus O. Bacon (D)	William C. Adamson (D)
Alexander S. Clay (D)	Charles L. Bartlett (D)
	William G. Brantley (D)
	William H. Fleming (D)
	James M. Griggs (D)
	William M. Howard (D)
	Rufus E. Lester (D)
	Elijah B. Lewis (D)
	Leonidas F. Livingston (D)
	John W. Maddox (D)
	Farish C. Tate (D)

Idaho

Senators	Representative
Henry Heitfeld (Pop)	Thomas L. Glenn (Pop)
Fred Dubois (R)	

Illinois

Senators	Representatives
Shelby M. Cullom (R)	Henry S. Boutell (R)
William E. Mason (R)	Ben F. Caldwell (D)
	Joseph G. Cannon (R)
	Joseph B. Crowley (D)
	John J. Feely (D)
	George E. Foss (R)
	George P. Foster (D)
	Joseph V. Graff (R)
	Robert R. Hitt (R)
	Albert J. Hopkins (R)
	Thomas M. Jett (D)
	Frederick J. Kern (D)
	James McAndrews (D)
	William F. Mahoney (D)
	James R. Mann (R)
	J. Ross Mickey (D)
	George W. Prince (R)
	Walter Reeves (R)
	Thomas J. Selby (D)
	George W. Smith (R)
	Vespasian Warner (R)
	James R. Williams (D)

Indiana

Senators	Representatives
Charles W. Fairbanks (R)	Abraham L. Brick (R)
Albert J. Beveridge (R)	George W. Cromer (R)
	Edgar D. Crumpacker (R)
	Francis M. Griffith (D)
	James A. Hemenway (R)
	Elias S. Holliday (R)
	Charles B. Landis (R)
	Robert W. Miers (D)
	Jesse Overstreet (R)
	James M. Robinson (D)
	George W. Steele (R)
	James E. Watson (R)
	William T. Zenor (D)

(continued)

TABLE 7.40 (continued)

Mar. 4, 1901 to Mar. 3, 1903

President of The Senate	President Pro Tempore of The Senate	Speaker of The House of Representatives
Theodore Roosevelt	William P. Frye	David B. Henderson

Iowa

Senators	Representatives
William B. Allison (R)	James P. Conner (R)
Jonathan P. Dolliver (R)	Robert G. Cousins (R)
	Gilbert N. Haugen (R)
	Thomas Hedge (R)
	David B. Henderson (R)
	William P. Hepburn (R)
	John A. T. Hull (R)
	John F. Lacey (R)
	John N. W. Rumple (R)
	d. Jan. 1903
	Walter I. Smith (R)
	Lot Thomas (R)

Kansas

Senators	Representatives
William A. Harris (D)	Justin D. Browersock (R)
Joseph R. Burton (R)	William A. Calderhead (R)
	Charles Curtis (R)
	Alfred M. Jackson (D)
	Chester I. Long (R)
	James M. Miller (R)
	William A. Reeder (R)

Kentucky

Senators	Representatives
William J. Deboe (R)	Henry D. Allen (D)
Joseph C. S. Blackburn (D)	Vincent Boreing (R)
	George G. Gilbert (D)
	Daniel L. Gooch (D)
	Harvey S. Irwin (R)
	James N. Kehoe (D)
	J. McKenzie Moss (R)
	s. 1902
	John S. Rhea (D, Pop)
	David H. Smith (D)
	South Trimble (D)
	Charles K. Wheeler (D)
	James B. White (D)

Louisiana

Senators	Representatives
Samuel D. McEnery (D)	Phanor Breazeale (D)
Murphy J. Foster (D)	Robert F. Broussard (D)
	Robert C. Davey (D)
	Adolph Meyer (D)
	Joseph E. Ransdell (D)
	Samuel M. Robertson (D)

Maine

Senators	Representatives
Eugene Hale (R)	Amos L. Allen (R)
William P. Frye (R)	Edwin C. Burleigh (R)
	Charles E. Littlefield (R)
	Llewellyn Powers (R)

Maryland

Senators	Representatives
George L. Wellington (D)	Albert A. Blakeney (R)
Louis E. McComas (R)	William H. Jackson (R)
	Sydney E. Mudd (R)
	George A. Pearre (R)
	Charles R. Schirm (R)
	Frank C. Wachter (R)

Massachusetts

Senators	Representatives
George F. Hoar (R)	Joseph A. Conry (D)
Henry Cabot Lodge (R)	Augustus P. Gardner (R)
	s. 1902
	Frederick H. Gillett (R)
	William S. Greene (R)
	William S. Knox (R)
	George P. Lawrence (R)
	William C. Lovering (R)
	Samuel W. McCall (R)
	William H. Moody (R)
	r. May 1902
	Henry F. Naphen (D)
	Samuel L. Powers (R)
	Ernest W. Roberts (R)
	John R. Thayer (D)
	Charles Q. Tirrell (R)

Michigan

Senators	Representatives
James McMillan (R)	Henry H. Aplin (R)
d. Aug. 1902	Roswell P. Bishop (R)
Russell A. Alger (R)	John B. Corliss (R)
s. 1902	Archibald B. Darragh (R)
Julius C. Burrows (R)	Joseph W. Fordney (R)
	Washington Gardner (R)
	Edward L. Hamilton (R)
	Carlos D. Shelden (R)
	Henry C. Smith (R)
	Samuel W. Smith (R)
	William Alden Smith (R)
	Edgar Weeks (R)

Minnesota

Senators	Representatives
Knute Nelson (R)	Frank M. Eddy (R)
Moses E. Clapp (R)	Loren Fletcher (R)
s. 1903	Joel P. Heatwole (R)
	James T. McCleary (R)
	R. Page W. Morris (R)
	Frederick C. Stevens (R)
	James A. Tawney (R)

Mississippi

Senators	Representatives
Hernando D. Money (D)	Ezekiel S. Candler, Jr. (D)
Anselm J. McLaurin (D)	Andrew F. Fox (D)
	Patrick Henry (D)
	Charles E. Hooker (D)
	Frank A. McLain (D)
	Thomas Spight (D)
	John Sharp Williams (D)

Missouri	
Senators	**Representatives**
Francis M. Cockrell (D)	Richard Bartholdt (R)
George G. Vest (D)	Maecenas E. Benton (D)
	James J. Butler (D)
	s. 1902
	Champ Clark (D)
	Charles F. Cochran (D)
	James Cooney (D)
	William S. Cowherd (D)
	David A. De Armond (D)
	John Dougherty (D)
	Charles F. Joy (R)
	James T. Lloyd (D)
	Edward Robb (D)
	William W. Rucker (D)
	Dorsey W. Shackleford (D)
	Willard D. Vandiver (D)
	George C. R. Wagoner (R)
	s. 1903

Montana	
Senators	**Representative**
William A. Clark (D)	Caldwell Edwards (D, Pop)
Paris Gibson (D)	

Nebraska	
Senators	**Representatives**
William V. Allen (Pop)	Elmer J. Burkett (D)
r. 1901	David H. Mercer (R)
Charles H. Dietrich (R)	William Neville (Pop)
s. 1901	John S. Robinson (D)
Joseph H. Millard (R)	Ashton C. Shallenberger (D)
	William L. Stark (D)

Nevada	
Senators	**Representative**
John P. Jones (R)	Francis G. Newlands (D)
William M. Stewart (R)	

New Hampshire	
Senators	**Representatives**
Jacob H. Gallinger (R)	Frank D. Currier (R)
Henry E. Burnham (R)	Cyrus A. Sulloway (R)

New Jersey	
Senators	**Representatives**
William J. Sewell (R)	De Witt C. Flanagan (D)
d. Dec. 1901	s. 1903
John F. Dryden (R)	Charles N. Fowler (R)
John Kean (R)	John J. Gardner (D)
	Benjamin F. Howell (R)
	Henry C. Loudenslager (R)
	Allan L. McDermott (D)
	Richard W. Parker (R)
	Joshua S. Salmon (D)
	d. May 1902
	James F. Stewart (R)

New York	
Senators	**Representatives**
Thomas C. Platt (R)	De Alva S. Alexander (R)
Chauncey M. Depew (R)	Oliver H. P. Belmont (D)
	Henry Bristow (R)
	Thomas J. Creamer (D)
	Amos J. Cummings (D)
	d. May 1902
	William H. Douglas (R)
	William H. Draper (R)
	Michael E. Driscoll (R)
	John W. Dwight (R)
	s. 1902
	Louis W. Emerson (R)
	John J. Fitzgerald (D)
	Charles W. Gillet (R)
	Henry M. Goldfogle
	Harry A. Hanbury (R)
	John H. Ketcham (R)
	Charles L. Knapp (R)
	Montague Lessler (R)
	s. 1902
	George H. Lindsay (D)
	Lucius N. Littauer (R)
	George B. McClellan (D)
	Nicholas Muller (D)
	r. Dec. 1902
	Sereno E. Payne (R)
	James B. Perkins (R)
	Cornelius A. Pugsley (D)
	George W. Ray (R)
	r. Sep. 1902
	Jacob Ruppert Jr. (D)
	William H. Ryan (D)
	James S. Sherman (R)
	George N. Southwick (R)
	John K. Stewart (R)
	Frederic Storm (R)
	William Sulzer (D)
	Edward Swann (D)
	s. 1902
	Arthur S. Tompkins (R)
	Edward B. Vreeland (R)
	James W. Wadsworth (R)
	Frank E. Wilson (D)

North Carolina	
Senators	**Representatives**
Jeter C. Pritchard (R)	John D. Bellamy (D)
Furnifold McL. Simmons (D)	Edmond S. Blackburn (R)
	Claude Kitchin (D)
	William W. Kitchin (D)
	Theodore F. Kluttz (D)
	James M. Moody (R)
	d. Feb. 1903
	Edward W. Pou (D)
	John H. Small (D)
	Charles R. Thomas (D)

North Dakota	
Senators	**Representative**
Henry C. Hansbrough (R)	Thomas F. Marshall (R)
Porter J. McCumber (R)	

(continued)

TABLE 7.40 (continued)

Mar. 4, 1901 to Mar. 3, 1903

President of The Senate	President Pro Tempore of The Senate	Speaker of The House of Representatives
Theodore Roosevelt	William P. Frye	David B. Henderson

Ohio

Senators	Representatives
Joseph B. Foraker (R) Marcus A. Hanna (R)	Jacob A. Beidler (R) Jacob H. Bromwell (R) Theodore E. Burton (R) John W. Cassingham (D) Charles W. F. Dick (R) Joseph J. Gill (R) Robert B. Gordon (D) Charles H. Grosvenor (R) Charles Q. Hildebrant (R) Thomas B. Kyle (R) Stephen Morgan (R) Robert M. Nevin (R) James A. Norton (D) William B. Shattuc (R) William W. Skiles (R) John S. Snook (R) James H. Southard (R) Robert W. Tayler (R) Emmett Tompkins (R) Henry C. Van Voorhis (R) William R. Warnock (R)

Oregon

Senators	Representatives
Joseph Simon (R) John H. Mitchell (R)	Malcolm A. Moody (R) Thomas H. Tongue (R) d. Jan. 1903

Pennsylvania

Senators	Representatives
Boies Penrose (R) Matthew S. Quay (R)	Ernest F. Acheson (R) Robert Adams, Jr. (R) Arthur L. Bates (R) Alexander Billmeyer (D) s. 1902 Henry H. Bingham (R) Henry Burk (R) Thomas S. Butler (R) Henry B. Cassel (R) William Connell (R) John Dalzell (R) Elias Deemer (R) Alvin Evans (R) Robert H. Foerderer (R) William H. Graham (R) Henry D. Green (D) Galusha A. Grow (R) James K. P. Hall (D) r. Nov. 1902 Summers M. Jack (R) Robert J. Lewis (R) Thaddeus M. Mahon (R) Edward de V. Morrell (R) Howard Mutchler (D) Marlin E. Olmsted (R) Henry W. Palmer (R) George R. Patterson (R) Rufus K. Polk (D) d. Mar. 1902 Joseph B. Showalter (R)

Pennsylvania

Senators	Representatives
	Joseph C. Sibley (R) Irving P. Wanger (R) Charles F. Wright (R) James R. Young (R)

Rhode Island

Senators	Representatives
Nelson W. Aldrich (R) George P. Wetmore (R)	Melville Bull (R) Adin B. Capron (R)

South Carolina

Senators	Representatives
Benjamin R. Tillman (D) John L. McLaurin (D)	William Elliott (D) David E. Finley (D) Joseph T. Johnson (D) Asbury C. Latimer (D) Asbury F. Lever (D) Robert B. Scarborough (D) William J. Talbert (D)

South Dakota

Senators	Representatives
James H. Kyle d. Jul. 1901 Alfred B. Kittredge (R) s. 1901 Robert J. Gamble (R)	Charles H. Burke (R) Eben W. Martin (R)

Tennessee

Senators	Representatives
William B. Bate (D) Edward W. Carmack (D)	Walter P. Brownlow (R) John W. Gaines (D) Henry R. Gibson (R) John A. Moon (D) Lemuel P. Padgett (D) Malcolm R. Patterson (D) Rice A. Pierce (D) James D. Richardson (D) Thetus W. Sims (D) Charles E. Snodgrass (D)

Texas

Senators	Representatives
Charles A. Culberson (D) Joseph W. Bailey (D)	Thomas H. Ball (D) George F. Burgess (D) Albert S. Burleson (D) Samuel B. Cooper (D) Reese C. De Graffenreid (D) d. Aug. 1902 Robert L. Henry (D) Rudolph Kleberg (D) Samuel W. T. Lanham (D) r. Jan. 1903 Choice B. Randell (D) Gordon J. Russell (D) s. 1902 John L. Sheppard (D) d. Oct. 1902 Morris Sheppard (D) s. 1902 James L. Slayden (D) John H. Stephens (D) Dudley G. Wooten (D)

<table>
<tr><td colspan="2" align="center">Utah</td></tr>
<tr><td align="center">Senators</td><td align="center">Representative</td></tr>
<tr><td>Joseph L. Rawlins (D)
Thomas Kearns (R)</td><td>George Sutherland (R)</td></tr>
</table>

Vermont	
Senators	**Representatives**
Redfield Proctor (R) William P. Dillingham (R)	David J. Foster (R) Kittredge Haskins (R)

Virginia	
Senators	**Representatives**

John W. Daniel (D)
Thomas S. Martin (D)
	Henry D. Flood (D)
	Carter Glass (D)
	  s. 1902
	James Hay (D)
	William A. Jones (D)
	John Lamb (D)
	Francis R. Lassiter (D)
	Harry L. Maynard (D)
	Peter J. Otey (D)
	  d. May 1902
	William F. Rhea (D)
	John F. Rixey (D)
	Claude A. Swanson (D)

Washington	
Senators	**Representatives**
George Turner (Fusion) Addison G. Foster (R)	Francis W. Cushman (R) Wesley L. Jones (R)

West Virginia	
Senators	**Representatives**
Stephen B. Elkins (R) Nathan B. Scott (R)	Alston G. Dayton (R) Blackburn B. Dovener (R) Joseph H. Gaines (R) James A. Hughes (R)

Wisconsin	
Senators	**Representatives**
John C. Spooner (R) Joseph V. Quarles (R)	Joseph W. Babcock (R) Samuel S. Barney (R) Webster E. Brown (R) Henry A. Cooper (R) Herman B. Dahle (R) James H. Davidson (R) John J. Esch (R) John J. Jenkins (R) Edward S. Minor (R) Theobald Otjen (R)

Wyoming	
Senators	**Representative**
Clarence D. Clark (R) Francis E. Warren (R)	Frank W. Mondell (R)

Source: Notable Names in American History; A Tabulated Register. Third edition of *White's Conspectus of American Biography* (1973), 150–152.

TABLE 7.41 FIFTY-EIGHTH CONGRESS

Mar. 4, 1903 to Mar. 3, 1905

President of The Senate	President Pro Tempore of The Senate	Speaker of The House of Representatives
Vacant	William P. Frye	Joseph G. Cannon

Alabama	
Senators	**Representatives**

John T. Morgan (D)
Edmund W. Pettus (D)
	John H. Bankhead (D)
	Sydney J. Bowie (D)
	John L. Burnett (D)
	Henry D. Clayton (D)
	J. Thomas Heflin (D)
	  s. 1904
	William Richardson (D)
	George W. Taylor (D)
	Charles W. Thompson (D)
	  d. Mar. 1904
	Oscar W. Underwood (D)
	Ariosto A. Wiley (D)

Arkansas	
Senators	**Representatives**
James H. Berry (D) James P. Clarke (D)	Stephen Brundidge Jr. (D) Hugh A. Dinsmore (D) John S. Little (D) Robert B. Macon (D) Charles C. Reid (D) Joseph T. Robinson (D) Robert M. Wallace (D)

California	
Senators	**Representatives**

George C. Perkins (R)
Thomas R. Bard (R)
	Theodore A. Bell (D)
	Milton J. Daniels (R)
	James N. Gillett (R)
	Joseph R. Knowland (R)
	  s. 1904
	Edward J. Livernash
	  (Union Labor)
	James McLachlan (R)
	Victor H. Metcalf (R)
	  r. Jul. 1904
	James C. Needham (R)
	William J. Wynn (Union Labor)

Colorado	
Senators	**Representatives**

Henry M. Teller (D)
Thomas M. Patterson (D)
	Robert W. Bonynge (R)
	  s. 1904
	Franklin E. Brooks (R)
	Herschel M. Hogg (R)
	John F. Shafroth (D)
	  r. Feb. 1904

Connecticut	
Senators	**Representatives**
Orville H. Platt (R) Joseph R. Hawley (R)	Frank B. Brandegee (R) E. Stevens Henry (R) Ebenezer J. Hill (R) George L. Lilley (R) Nehemiah D. Sperry (R)

(continued)

TABLE 7.41   (continued)

Mar. 4, 1903 to Mar. 3, 1905

President of The Senate	President Pro Tempore of The Senate	Speaker of The House of Representatives
Vacant	William P. Frye	Joseph G. Cannon

Delaware

Senators	Representative
L. Heisler Ball (R) J. Frank Allee (R)	Henry A. Houston (D)

Florida

Senators	Representatives
Stephen R. Mallory (D) James P. Taliaferro (D)	Robert W. Davis (D) William B. Lamar (D) Stephen M. Sparkman (D)

Georgia

Senators	Representatives
Augustus O. Bacon (D) Alexander S. Clay (D)	William C. Adamson (D) Charles L. Bartlett (D) William G. Brantley (D) James M. Griggs (D) Thomas W. Hardwick (D) William M. Howard (D) Rufus E. Lester (D) Elijah B. Lewis (D) Leonidas F. Livingston (D) John W. Maddox (D) Farish C. Tate (D)

Idaho

Senators	Representative
Fred T. Dubois (D) Weldon B. Heyburn (R)	Burton L. French (R)

Illinois

Senators	Representatives
Shelby M. Cullom (R) Albert J. Hopkins (R)	Henry S. Boutell (R) Ben F. Caldwell (D) Joseph G. Cannon (R) Joseph B. Crowley (D) Martin Emerich (D) George E. Foss (R) George P. Foster (D) Charles E. Fuller (R) Joseph V. Graff (R) Robert R. Hitt (R) Philip Knopf (R) William Lorimer (R) James McAndrews (D) William F. Mahoney (D) d. Dec. 1904 James R. Mann (R) Benjamin F. Marsh (R) George W. Prince (R) Henry T. Rainey (D) William A. Rodenberg (R) George W. Smith (R) Howard M. Snapp (R) John A. Sterling (R) Vespasian Warner (R) James R. Williams (D) William W. Wilson (R)

Indiana

Senators	Representatives
Charles W. Fairbanks (R) Albert J. Beveridge (R)	Abraham L. Brick (R) George W. Cromer (R) Edgar D. Crumpacker (R) Francis M. Griffith (R) James A. Hemenway (R) Elias S. Holliday (R) Charles B. Landis (R) Frederick Landis (R) Robert W. Miers (D) Jesse Overstreet (R) James M. Robinson (D) James E. Watson (R) William T. Zenor (D)

Iowa

Senators	Representatives
William B. Allison (R) Jonathan P. Dolliver (R)	Benjamin P. Birdsall (R) James P. Conner (R) Robert G. Cousins (R) Gilbert N. Haugen (R) Thomas Hedge (R) William P. Hepburn (R) John A. T. Hull (R) John F. Lacey (R) Walter I. Smith (R) Lot Thomas (R) Martin J. Wade (D)

Kansas

Senators	Representatives
Joseph R. Burton (R) Chester I. Long (R)	Justin D. Browersock (R) William A. Calderhead (R) Philip P. Campbell (R) Charles Curtis (R) James M. Miller (R) Victor Murdock (R) William A. Reeder (R) Charles F. Scott (R)

Kentucky

Senators	Representatives
Joseph C. S. Blackburn (D) James B. McCreary (D)	George G. Gilbert (D) Daniel L. Gooch (D) Frank A. Hopkins (D) W. Godfrey Hunter (R) Olin M. James (R) James N. Kehoe (D) John S. Rhea (D, Pop) J. Swagar Sherley (D) David H. Smith (D) Augustus O. Stanley (D) South Trimble (D)

Louisiana

Senators	Representatives
Samuel D. McEnery (D) Murphy J. Foster (D)	Phanor Breazeale (D) Robert F. Broussard (D) Robert C. Davey (D) Adolph Meyer (D) Arsene P. Pujo (D) Joseph E. Ransdell (D) Samuel M. Robertson (D)

Maine

Senators	Representatives
Eugene Hale (R) William P. Frye (R)	Amos L. Allen (R) Edwin C. Burleigh (R) Charles E. Littlefield (R) Llewellyn Powers (R)

Maryland

Senators	Representatives
Louis E. McComas (R) Arthur P. Gorman (D)	James W. Denny (D) William H. Jackson (R) Sydney E. Mudd (R) George A. Pearre (R) J. Fred C. Talbott (D) Frank C. Wachter (R)

Massachusetts

Senators	Representatives
George F. Hoar (R) d. Sep. 1904 W. Murray Crane (R) s. 1904 Henry Cabot Lodge (R)	Butler Ames (R) Augustus P. Gardner (R) Frederick H. Gillett (R) William S. Greene (R) John A. Keliher (D) George P. Lawrence (R) William C. Lovering (R) Samuel W. McCall (R) William S. McNary (D) Samuel L. Powers (R) Ernest W. Roberts (R) John A. Sullivan (D) John R. Thayer (D) Charles Q. Tirrell (R)

Michigan

Senators	Representatives
Julius C. Burrows (R) Russell A. Alger (R)	Roswell P. Bishop (R) Archibald B. Darragh (R) Joseph W. Fordney (R) Washington Gardner (R) Edward L. Hamilton (R) George A. Loud (R) Alfred Lucking (D) Henry McMorran (R) Samuel W. Smith (R) William Alden Smith (R) Charles E. Townsend (R) H. Olin Young (R)

Minnesota

Senators	Representatives
Knute Nelson (R) Moses E. Clapp (R)	J. Adam Bede (R) Clarence B. Buckman (R) Charles R. Davis (R) John Lind (D) James T. McCleary (R) Halvor Steenerson (R) Frederick C. Stevens (R) James A. Tawney (R) Andrew J. Volstead (R)

Mississippi

Senators	Representatives
Hernando D. Money (D) Anselm J. McLaurin (D)	Eaton J. Bowers (D) Adam M. Byrd (D) Ezekiel S. Candler, Jr. (D) Wilson S. Hill (D) Benjamin G. Humphreys (D) Frank A. McLain (D) Thomas Spight (D) John Sharp Williams (D)

Missouri

Senators	Representatives
Francis M. Cockrell (D) William J. Stone (D)	Richard Bartholdt (R) Maecenas E. Benton (D) James J. Butler (D) Champ Clark (D) Charles F. Cochran (D) William S. Cowherd (D) David A. De Armond (D) John Dougherty (D) Courtney W. Hamlin (D) John T. Hunt (D) J. Robert Lamar (D) James T. Lloyd (D) Edward Robb (D) William W. Rucker (D) Dorsey W. Shackleford (D) Willard D. Vandiver (D)

Montana

Senators	Representative
William A. Clark (D) Paris Gibson (D)	Joseph M. Dixon (R)

Nebraska

Senators	Representatives
Charles H. Dietrich (R) Joseph H. Millard (R)	Elmer J. Burkett (D) Edmund H. Hinshaw (R) Gilbert M. Hitchcock (D) Moses P. Kinkaid (R) John J. McCarthy (R) George W. Norris (R)

Nevada

Senators	Representative
William M. Stewart (R) Francis G. Newlands (D)	Clarence D. Van Duzer (D)

New Hampshire

Senators	Representatives
Jacob H. Gallinger (R) Henry E. Burnham (R)	Frank D. Currier (R) Cyrus A. Sulloway (R)

(continued)

TABLE 7.41 (continued)

Mar. 4, 1903 to Mar. 3, 1905

President of The Senate	President Pro Tempore of The Senate	Speaker of The House of Representatives
Vacant	William P. Frye	Joseph G. Cannon

New Jersey

Senators	Representatives
John Kean (R)	Allan Benny (D)
John F. Dryden (R)	Charles N. Fowler (R)
	John J. Gardner (D)
	Benjamin F. Howell (R)
	William Hughes (D)
	William M. Lanning (R)
	r. Jun. 1904
	Henry C. Loudenslager (R)
	Allan L. McDermott (D)
	Richard W. Parker (R)
	William H. Wiley (R)
	Ira W. Wood (R)
	s. 1904

New York

Senators	Representatives
Thomas C. Platt (R)	De Alva S. Alexander (R)
Chauncey M. Depew (R)	Robert Baker (D)
	Edward M. Bassett (D)
	Thomas W. Bradley (R)
	W. Bourke Cockran (D)
	s. Mar. 1904
	William H. Douglas (R)
	William H. Draper (R)
	Michael E. Driscoll (R)
	Charles T. Dunwell (R)
	John W. Dwight (R)
	John J. Fitzgerald (D)
	William H. Flack (R)
	Charles W. Gillet (R)
	Henry M. Goldfogle (D)
	Joseph A. Goulden (D)
	Francis B. Harrison (D)
	William Randolph Hearst (D)
	John H. Ketcham (R)
	Charles L. Knapp (R)
	George H. Lindsay (D)
	Lucius N. Littauer (R)
	George B. McClellan (D)
	r. Dec. 1903
	Norton P. Otis (R)
	d. Feb. 1905
	Sereno E. Payne (R)
	James B. Perkins (R)
	Ira E. Rider (D)
	Jacob Ruppert Jr. (D)
	William H. Ryan (D)
	Townsend Scudder (D)
	James S. Sherman (R)
	Francis E. Shober (D)
	George J. Smith (R)
	George N. Southwick (R)
	Timothy D. Sullivan (D)
	William Sulzer (D)
	Edward B. Vreeland (R)
	James W. Wadsworth (R)
	Frank E. Wilson (D)

North Carolina

Senators	Representatives
Furnifold McL. Simmons (D)	James M. Gudger Jr. (D)
Lee S. Overman (D)	Claude Kitchin (D)
	William W. Kitchin (D)
	Theodore F. Kluttz (D)
	Robert N. Page (D)
	Gilbert B. Patterson (D)
	Edward W. Pou (D)
	John H. Small (D)
	Charles R. Thomas (D)
	Edwin Y. Webb (D)

North Dakota

Senators	Representatives
Henry C. Hansbrough (R)	Thomas F. Marshall (R)
Porter J. McCumber (R)	Burleigh F. Spalding (R)

Ohio

Senators	Representatives
Joseph B. Foraker (R)	De Witt C. Badger (D)
Marcus A. Hanna (R)	Jacob A. Beidler (R)
d. Feb. 1904	Theodore E. Burton (R)
Charles W. F. Dick (R)	John W. Cassingham (D)
s. 1904	Charles W. F. Dick (R)
	r. Mar. 1904
	Harvey C. Garber (D)
	Herman P. Goebel (R)
	Charles H. Grosvenor (R)
	Charles Q. Hildebrant (R)
	Amos H. Jackson (D)
	James Kennedy (R)
	Thomas B. Kyle (R)
	Nicholas Longworth (R)
	Stephen Morgan (R)
	Robert M. Nevin (R)
	William W. Skiles (R)
	d. Jan. 1904
	John S. Snook (D)
	James H. Southard (R)
	William A. Thomas (R)
	s. 1904
	Henry C. Van Voorhis (R)
	William R. Warnock (R)
	Amos R. Webber (R)
	s. 1904
	Capell L. Weems (R)

Oregon

Senators	Representatives
John H. Mitchell (R)	Binger Hermann (R)
Charles W. Fulton (R)	John N. Williamson (R)

Pennsylvania

Senators	Representatives
Boies Penrose (R)	Ernest F. Acheson (R)
Matthew S. Quay (R)	Robert Adams, Jr. (R)
d. May 1904	Arthur L. Bates (R)
Philander C. Knox (R)	Henry H. Bingham (R)
s. 1905	James W. Brown (R)
	Henry Burk (R)
	d. Dec. 1903
	Thomas S. Butler (R)
	Henry B. Cassel (R)
	George A. Castor (R)
	s. 1904
	William Connell (R)
	s. 1904

Pennsylvania

Senators	Representatives
	Allen F. Cooper (R)
	John Dalzell (R)
	Elias Deemer (R)
	Charles H. Dickerman (D)
	Solomon R. Dresser (R)
	Alvin Evans (R)
	George Howell (R)
	r. Nov. 1903
	George F. Huff (R)
	Marcus C. L. Kline (D)
	Daniel F. Lafean (R)
	George D. McCreary (R)
	Thaddeus M. Mahon (R)
	Reuben O. Moon (R)
	Edward de V. Morrell (R)
	Marlin E. Olmsted (R)
	Henry W. Palmer (R)
	George R. Patterson (R)
	Henry Kirke Porter
	George Shiras (R)
	Joseph H. Shull (R)
	Joseph C. Sibley (R)
	William O. Smith (R)
	Irving P. Wanger (R)
	Charles F. Wright (R)

Rhode Island

Senators	Representatives
Nelson W. Aldrich (R)	Adin B. Capron (R)
George P. Wetmore (R)	Daniel L. D. Granger (D)

South Carolina

Senators	Representatives
Benjamin R. Tillman (D)	Wyatt Aiken (D)
Asbury C. Latimer (D)	George W. Croft (D)
	d. Mar. 1904
	Theodore G. Croft (D)
	s. 1904
	David E. Finley (D)
	Joseph T. Johnson (D)
	George S. Legare (D)
	Asbury F. Lever (D)
	Robert B. Scarborough (D)

South Dakota

Senators	Representatives
Robert J. Gamble (R)	Charles H. Burke (R)
Alfred B. Kittredge (R)	Eben W. Martin (R)

Tennessee

Senators	Representatives
William B. Bate (D)	Walter P. Brownlow (R)
Edward W. Carmack (D)	Morgan C. Fitzpatrick (D)
	John W. Gaines (D)
	Henry R. Gibson (R)
	John A. Moon (D)
	Lemuel P. Padgett (D)
	Malcolm R. Patterson (D)
	Rice A. Pierce (D)
	James D. Richardson (D)
	Thetus W. Sims (D)

Texas

Senators	Representatives
Charles A. Culberson (D)	Thomas H. Ball (D)
Joseph W. Bailey (D)	r. Nov. 1903
	Jack Beall (D)
	George F. Burgess (D)
	Albert S. Burleson (D)
	Samuel B. Cooper (D)
	Scott Field (D)
	John Nance Garner (D)
	Oscar W. Gillespie (D)
	Alexander W. Gregg (D)
	Robert L. Henry (D)
	John M. Pickney (D)
	Choice B. Randell (D)
	Gordon J. Russell (D)
	Morris Sheppard (D)
	James L. Slayden (D)
	William R. Smith (D)
	John H. Stephens (D)

Utah

Senators	Representative
Thomas Kearns (R)	Joseph Howell (R)
Reed Smoot (R)	

Vermont

Senators	Representatives
Redfield Proctor (R)	David J. Foster (R)
William P. Dillingham (R)	Kittredge Haskins (R)

Virginia

Senators	Representatives
John W. Daniel (D)	Henry D. Flood (D)
Thomas S. Martin (D)	Carter Glass (D)
	James Hay (D)
	William A. Jones (D)
	John Lamb (D)
	Harry L. Maynard (D)
	John F. Rixey (D)
	Campbell Slemp (R)
	Robert G. Southall (D)
	Claude A. Swanson (D)

Washington

Senators	Representatives
Addison G. Foster (R)	Francis W. Cushman (R)
Levi Ankeny (R)	William E. Humphrey (R)
	Wesley L. Jones (R)

West Virginia

Senators	Representatives
Stephen B. Elkins (R)	Alston G. Dayton (R)
Nathan B. Scott (R)	Blackburn B. Dovener (R)
	Joseph H. Gaines (R)
	James A. Hughes (R)
	Harry C. Woodyard (R)

(continued)

TABLE 7.41 (continued)

Mar. 4, 1903 to Mar. 3, 1905

President of The Senate	President Pro Tempore of The Senate	Speaker of The House of Representatives
Vacant	William P. Frye	Joseph G. Cannon

Wisconsin

Senators	Representatives
John C. Spooner (R) Joseph V. Quarles (R)	Henry C. Adams (R) Joseph W. Babcock (R) Webster E. Brown (R) Henry A. Cooper (R) James H. Davidson (R) John J. Esch (R) John J. Jenkins (R) Edward S. Minor (R) Theobald Otjen (R) William H. Stafford (R) Charles H. Weisse (D)

Wyoming

Senators	Representative
Clarence D. Clark (R) Francis E. Warren (R)	Frank W. Mondell (R)

Source: *Notable Names in American History; A Tabulated Register.* Third edition of *White's Conspectus of American Biography* (1973), 152–155.

TABLE 7.42 FIFTY-NINTH CONGRESS

Mar. 4, 1905 to Mar. 3, 1907

President of The Senate	President Pro Tempore of The Senate	Speaker of The House of Representatives
Charles W. Fairbanks	William P. Frye	Joseph G. Cannon

Alabama

Senators	Representatives
John T. Morgan (D) Edmund W. Pettus (D)	John H. Bankhead (D) Sydney J. Bowie (D) John L. Burnett (D) Henry D. Clayton (D) J. Thomas Heflin (D) William Richardson (D) George W. Taylor (D) Oscar W. Underwood (D) Ariosto A. Wiley (D)

Arkansas

Senators	Representatives
James H. Berry (D) James P. Clarke (D)	Stephen Brundidge, Jr. (D) John C. Floyd (D) John S. Little (D) Robert B. Macon (D) Charles C. Reid (D) Joseph T. Robinson (D) Robert M. Wallace (D)

California

Senators	Representatives
George C. Perkins (R) Frank P. Flint (R)	William F. Englebright (R) s. 1907 James N. Gillett r. Nov. 1906 Everis A. Hayes (R) Julius Kahn (R) Joseph R. Knowland (R) Duncan E. McKinlay (R) James McLachlan (R) James C. Needham (R) Sylvester C. Smith (R)

Colorado

Senators	Representatives
Henry M. Teller (R) Thomas M. Patterson (D)	Robert W. Bonynge (R) Franklin E. Brooks (R) Herschel M. Hogg (R)

Connecticut

Senators	Representatives
Orville H. Platt (R) d. Apr. 1905 Frank B. Brandegee (R) s. 1905 Morgan G. Bulkeley (R)	E. Stevens Henry (R) Edwin W. Higgins (R) Ebenezer J. Hill (R) George L. Lilley (R) Nehemiah D. Sperry (R)

Delaware

Senators	Representative
J. Frank Allee (R) Henry A. Du Pont (R) s. 1906	Hiram R. Burton (R)

Florida

Senators	Representatives
Stephen R. Mallory (D) James P. Taliaferro (D)	Frank Clark (R) William B. Lamar (D) Stephen M. Sparkman (D)

Georgia

Senators	Representatives
Augustus O. Bacon (D) Alexander S. Clay (D)	William C. Adamson (D) Charles L. Bartlett (D) Thomas M. Bell (D) William G. Brantley (D) James M. Griggs (D) Thomas W. Hardwick (D) William M. Howard (D) Gordon Lee (D) Rufus E. Lester (D) d. Jun. 1906 Elijah B. Lewis (D) Leonidas F. Livingston (D) James W. Overstreet (D) s. 1906

Idaho

Senators	Representative
Fred T. Dubois (D) Weldon B. Heyburn (R)	Burton L. French (R)

Illinois

Senators	Representatives
Shelby M. Cullom (R)	Henry S. Boutell (R)
Albert J. Hopkins (R)	Joseph G. Cannon (R)
	Pleasant T. Chapman (R)
	Frank S. Dickson (R)
	George E. Foss (R)
	Charles E. Fuller (R)
	Joseph V. Graff (R)
	Robert R. Hitt (R)
	d. Sep. 1906
	Philip Knopf (R)
	William Lorimer (R)
	Frank O. Lowden (R)
	s. 1906
	Charles McGavin (R)
	William B. McKinley (R)
	James McKinney (R)
	Martin B. Madden (R)
	James R. Mann (R)
	Anthony Michalek (R)
	s. 1906
	George W. Prince (R)
	Henry T. Rainey (R)
	Zeno J. Rives (R)
	William A. Rodenberg (R)
	George W. Smith (R)
	Howard M. Snapp (R)
	John A. Sterling (R)
	Charles S. Wharton (R)
	William W. Wilson (R)

Indiana

Senators	Representatives
Albert J. Beveridge (R)	Abraham L. Brick (R)
James A. Hemenway (R)	John C. Chaney (R)
	George W. Cromer (R)
	Edgar D. Crumpacker (R)
	Lincoln Dixon (D)
	John H. Foster (R)
	Newton W. Gilbert (R)
	s. Nov. 1906
	Clarence C. Gilhams (R)
	s. 1906
	Elias S. Holliday (R)
	Charles B. Landis (R)
	Frederick Landis (R)
	Jesse Overstreet (R)
	James E. Watson (R)
	William T. Zenor (D)

Iowa

Senators	Representatives
William B. Allison (R)	Benjamin P. Birdsall (R)
Jonathan P. Dolliver (R)	James P. Conner (R)
	Robert G. Cousins (R)
	Albert F. Dawson (R)
	Gilbert N. Haugen (R)
	Thomas Hedge (R)
	William P. Hepburn (R)
	Elbert H. Hubbard (R)
	John A. T. Hull (R)
	John F. Lacey (R)
	Walter I. Smith (R)

Kansas

Senators	Representatives
Joseph R. Burton (R)	Justin D. Bowersock (R)
r. Jun. 1906	William A. Calderhead (R)
Alfred W. Benson (R)	Philip P. Campbell (R)
ta. 1906	

Kansas

Senators	Representatives
Charles Curtis (R)	Charles Curtis (R)
s. 1907	r. Jan. 1907
Chester I. Long (R)	James M. Miller (R)
	Victor Murdock (R)
	William A. Reeder (R)
	Charles F. Scott (R)

Kentucky

Senators	Representatives
Joseph C. S. Blackburn (D)	Joseph B. Bennett (R)
James B. McCreary (D)	Don C. Edwards (R)
	George G. Gilbert (D)
	Frank A. Hopkins (D)
	Ollie M. James (D)
	James M. Richardson (D)
	Joseph L. Rhinock (D)
	J. Swagar Sherley (D)
	David H. Smith (D)
	Augustus O. Stanley (D)
	South Trimble (D)

Louisiana

Senators	Representatives
Samuel D. McEnery (D)	Robert F. Broussard (D)
Murphy J. Foster (D)	Robert C. Davey (D)
	Adolph Meyer (D)
	Arsene P. Pujo (D)
	Joseph E. Ransdell (D)
	Samuel M. Robertson (D)
	John T. Watkins (D)

Maine

Senators	Representatives
Eugene Hale (R)	Amos L. Allen (R)
William P. Frye (R)	Edwin C. Burleigh (R)
	Charles E. Littlefield (R)
	Llewellyn Powers (R)

Maryland

Senators	Representatives
Arthur P. Gorman (D)	John Gill, Jr. (D)
d. Jun. 1906	Sydney E. Mudd (R)
William P. Whyte (D)	George A. Pearre (R)
s. 1906	Thomas A. Smith (D)
Isidor Rayner (D)	J. Fred C. Talbott (D)
	Frank C. Wachter (R)

Massachusetts

Senators	Representatives
Henry Cabot Lodge (R)	Butler Ames (R)
W. Murray Crane (R)	Augustus P. Gardner (R)
	Frederick H. Gillett (R)
	William S. Greene (R)
	Rockwood Hoar (R)
	d. Nov. 1906
	John A. Keliher (D)
	George P. Lawrence (R)
	William C. Lovering (R)
	Samuel W. McCall (R)
	William S. McNary (D)
	Ernest W. Roberts (R)
	John A. Sullivan (D)
	Charles Q. Tirrell (R)
	Charles G. Washburn (R)
	s. 1907
	John W. Weeks (R)

(continued)

TABLE 7.42 (continued)

Mar. 4, 1905 to Mar. 3, 1907

President of The Senate	President Pro Tempore of The Senate	Speaker of The House of Representatives
Charles W. Fairbanks	William P. Frye	Joseph G. Cannon

Michigan

Senators	Representatives

Julius C. Burrows (R)
Russell A. Alger (R)
  d. Jan. 1907
William Alden Smith (R)
  s. 1907
	Roswell P. Bishop (R)
	Archibald B. Darragh (R)
	Edwin Denby (R)
	Joseph W. Fordney (R)
	Washington Gardner (R)
	Edward L. Hamilton (R)
	George A. Loud (R)
	Henry McMorran (R)
	Samuel W. Smith (R)
	William Alden Smith (R)
	  r. Feb. 1907
	Charles E. Townsend (R)
	H. Olin Young (R)

Minnesota

Senators	Representatives
Knute Nelson (R) Moses E. Clapp (R)	J. Adam Bede (R) Clarence B. Buckman (R) Charles R. Davis (R) Loren Fletcher (R) James T. McCleary (R) Halvor Steenerson (R) Frederick C. Stevens (R) James A. Tawney (R) Andrew J. Volstead (R)

Mississippi

Senators	Representatives
Hernando D. Money (D) Anselm J. McLaurin (D)	Eaton J. Bowers (D) Adam M. Byrd (D) Ezekiel S. Candler, Jr. (D) Wilson S. Hill (D) Benjamin G. Humphreys (D) Frank A. McLain (D) Thomas Spight (D) John Sharp Williams (D)

Missouri

Senators	Representatives

William J. Stone (D)
William Warner (R)
	Richard Bartholdt (R)
	Champ Clark (D)
	Harry M. Coudrey (R)
	  s. 1906
	David A. De Armond (D)
	Edgar C. Ellis (R)
	Frank B. Fulkerson (R)
	John T. Hunt (D)
	Frank B. Klepper (R)
	James T. Lloyd (D)
	Arthur P. Murphy (R)
	Marion E. Rhodes (R)
	William W. Rucker (D)
	Dorsey W. Shackleford (D)
	Cassius M. Shartel (R)
	William T. Tyndall (R)
	John Welborn (R)
	Ernest E. Wood (D)
	  r. Jun. 1906

Montana

Senators	Representative
William A. Clark (D) Thomas H. Carter (R)	Joseph M. Dixon (R)

Nebraska

Senators	Representatives
Joseph H. Millard (R) Elmer J. Burkett (D)	Edmund H. Hinshaw (R) John L. Kennedy (R) Moses P. Kinkaid (R) John J. McCarthy (R) George W. Norris (R) Ernest M. Pollard (R)

Nevada

Senators	Representative
Francis G. Newlands (D) George S. Nixon (R)	Clarence D. Van Duzer (D)

New Hampshire

Senators	Representatives
Jacob H. Gallinger (R) Henry E. Burnham (R)	Frank D. Currier (R) Cyrus A. Sulloway (R)

New Jersey

Senators	Representatives
John Kean (R) John F. Dryden (R)	Henry C. Allen (R) Charles N. Fowler (R) John J. Gardner (D) Benjamin F. Howell (R) Henry C. Loudenslager (R) Allan L. McDermott (D) Richard W. Parker (R) Marshall Van Winkle (R) William H. Wiley (R) Ira W. Wood (R)

New York

Senators	Representatives

Thomas C. Platt (R)
Chauncey M. Depew (R)
	De Alva S. Alexander (R)
	John E. Andrus (R)
	William S. Bennett (R)
	Thomas W. Bradley (R)
	William M. Calder (R)
	W. Bourke Cockran (D)
	William W. Cocks (R)
	William H. Draper (R)
	Michael E. Driscoll (R)
	Charles T. Dunwell (R)
	John W. Dwight (R)
	J. Sloat Fassett (R)
	John J. Fitzgerald (D)
	William H. Flack (R)
	  d. Feb. 1907
	Henry M. Goldfogle (D)
	Joseph A. Goulden (D)
	William Randolph Hearst (D)
	John H. Ketcham (R)
	  d. Nov. 1906
	Charles L. Knapp (R)
	Charles B. Law (R)
	Frank J. Le Fevre (R)
	George H. Lindsay (D)
	Lucius N. Littauer (R)
	J. Van Vechten Olcott (R)
	Herbert Parsons (R)
	Sereno E. Payne (R)

New York	
Senators	**Representatives**
	James B. Perkins (R)
	Daniel B. Perkins (R)
	Daniel J. Riordan (D)
	s. 1906
	Jacob Ruppert, Jr. (D)
	William H. Ryan (D)
	James S. Sherman (R)
	George N. Southwick (R)
	Timothy D. Sullivan (D)
	r. Jul. 1906
	William Sulzer (D)
	Charles A. Towne (D)
	Edward B. Vreeland (R)
	James W. Wadsworth (R)
	George E. Waldo (R)

North Carolina	
Senators	**Representatives**
Furnifold McL. Simmons (D)	Edmond Blackburn (D)
Lee S. Overman (D)	James M. Gudger Jr. (D)
	Claude Kitchin (D)
	William W. Kitchin (D)
	Robert N. Page (D)
	Gilbert B. Patterson (D)
	Edward W. Pou (D)
	John H. Small (D)
	Charles R. Thomas (D)
	Edwin Y. Webb (D)

North Dakota	
Senators	**Representatives**
Henry C. Hansbrough (R)	Asle J. Gronna (R)
Porter J. McCumber (R)	Thomas F. Marshall (R)

Ohio	
Senators	**Representatives**
Joseph B. Foraker (R)	Henry T. Bannon (R)
Charles W. F. Dick (R)	Jacob A. Beidler (R)
	Theodore E. Burton (R)
	William W. Campbell (R)
	Ralph D. Cole (R)
	Beman G. Dawes (R)
	Harvey C. Garber (D)
	Herman P. Goebel (R)
	Charles H. Grosvenor (R)
	J. Warren Keifer (R)
	James Kennedy (R)
	Nicholas Longworth (R)
	Grant E. Mouser (R)
	Robert M. Nevin (R)
	Thomas E. Scroggy (R)
	Martin L. Smyser (R)
	James H. Southard (R)
	Edward L. Taylor, Jr. (R)
	William A. Thomas (R)
	Amos R. Webber (R)
	Capell L. Weems (R)

Oregon	
Senators	**Representative**
John H. Mitchell (R)	Binger Hermann (R)
d. Dec. 1905	
John M. Gearin (D)	
ta. 1906	
Frederick W. Mulkey (R)	
s. 1907	
Charles W. Fulton (R)	

Pennsylvania	
Senators	**Representatives**
Boies Penrose (R)	Ernest F. Acheson (R)
Philander C. Knox (R)	Robert Adams, Jr. (R)
	d. Jun. 1906
	Andrew J. Barchfeld (R)
	Arthur L. Bates (R)
	Henry H. Bingham (R)
	Charles N. Brumm (R)
	s. 1906
	James F. Burke (R)
	Thomas S. Butler (R)
	Henry B. Cassel (R)
	George A. Castor (R)
	d. Feb. 1906
	Allen F. Cooper (R)
	Thomas H. Dale (R)
	John Dalzell (R)
	Elias Deemer (R)
	Solomon R. Dresser (R)
	William H. Graham (R)
	George F. Huff (R)
	Marcus C. L. Kline (D)
	Daniel F. Lafean (R)
	Mial E. Lilley (R)
	George D. McCreary (R)
	Thaddeus M. Mahon (R)
	Reuben O. Moon (R)
	J. Hampton Moore (R)
	s. Dec. 1906
	Edward de V. Morrell (R)
	Marlin E. Olmsted (R)
	Henry W. Palmer (R)
	George R. Patterson (R)
	d. Mar. 1906
	John E. Reyburn (R)
	s. 1906
	John M. Reynolds (R)
	Edmund W. Samuel (R)
	Gustav A. Schneebeli (R)
	Joseph C. Sibley (R)
	William O. Smith (R)
	Irving P. Wanger (R)

Rhode Island	
Senators	**Representatives**
Nelson W. Aldrich (R)	Adin B. Capron (R)
George P. Wetmore (R)	Daniel L. D. Granger (D)

South Carolina	
Senators	**Representatives**
Benjamin R. Tillman (D)	Wyatt Aiken (D)
Asbury C. Latimer (D)	J. Edwin Ellerbe (D)
	David E. Finley (D)
	Joseph T. Johnson (D)
	George S. Legare (D)
	Asbury F. Lever (D)
	James O. Patterson (D)

South Dakota	
Senators	**Representatives**
Robert J. Gamble (R)	Charles H. Burke (R)
Alfred B. Kittredge (R)	Eben W. Martin (R)

(continued)

TABLE 7.42 (continued)

Mar. 4, 1905 to Mar. 3, 1907

President of The Senate	President Pro Tempore of The Senate	Speaker of The House of Representatives
Charles W. Fairbanks	William P. Frye	Joseph G. Cannon

Tennessee

Senators	Representatives
James B. Frazier (D)	Walter P. Brownlow (R)
Edward W. Carmack (D)	Mounce G. Butler (D)
	Finis J. Garrett (D)
	John W. Gaines (D)
	Nathan W. Hale (R)
	William C. Houston (D)
	John A. Moon (D)
	Lemuel P. Padgett (D)
	Malcolm R. Patterson (D)
	r. Nov. 1906
	Thetus W. Sims (D)

Texas

Senators	Representatives
Charles A. Culberson (D)	Jack Beall (D)
Joseph W. Bailey (D)	Moses L. Broocks (D)
	George F. Burgess (D)
	Albert S. Burleson (D)
	Scott Field (D)
	John Nance Garner (D)
	Oscar W. Gillespie (D)
	Alexander W. Gregg (D)
	Robert L. Henry (D)
	John M. Moore (D)
	Choice B. Randell (D)
	Gordon J. Russell (D)
	Morris Sheppard (D)
	James L. Slayden (D)
	William R. Smith (D)
	John H. Stephens (D)

Utah

Senators	Representative
Reed Smoot (R)	Joseph Howell (R)
George Sutherland (R)	

Vermont

Senators	Representatives
Redfield Proctor (R)	David J. Foster (R)
William P. Dillingham (R)	Kittredge Haskins (R)

Virginia

Senators	Representatives
John W. Daniel (D)	Henry D. Flood (D)
Thomas S. Martin (D)	Carter Glass (D)
	James Hay (D)
	William A. Jones (D)
	John Lamb (D)
	Harry L. Maynard (D)
	John F. Rixey (D)
	d. Feb. 1907
	Edward W. Saunders (D)
	s. 1906
	Campbell Slemp (R)
	Robert G. Southall (D)
	Claude A. Swanson (D)
	r. Jan. 1906

Washington

Senators	Representatives
Levi Ankeny (R)	Francis W. Cushman (R)
Samuel H. Piles (R)	William E. Humphrey (R)
	Wesley L. Jones (R)

West Virginia

Senators	Representatives
Stephen B. Elkins (R)	Thomas B. Davis (D)
Nathan B. Scott (R)	Alston G. Dayton (R)
	r. Mar. 1905
	Blackburn B. Dovener (R)
	Joseph H. Gaines (R)
	James A. Hughes (R)
	Harry C. Woodyard (R)

Wisconsin

Senators	Representatives
John C. Spooner (R)	Henry C. Adams (R)
Robert M. La Follette (R)	d. Jul. 1906
	Joseph W. Babcock (R)
	Webster E. Brown (R)
	Henry A. Cooper (R)
	James H. Davidson (R)
	John J. Esch (R)
	John J. Jenkins (R)
	Edward S. Minor (R)
	John M. Nelson (R)
	s. 1906
	Theobald Otjen (R)
	William H. Stafford (R)
	Charles H. Weisse (D)

Wyoming

Senators	Representative
Clarence D. Clark (R)	Frank W. Mondell (R)
Francis E. Warren (R)	

Source: Notable Names in American History; A Tabulated Register. Third edition of *White's Conspectus of American Biography* (1973), 155–158.

TABLE 7.43 SIXTIETH CONGRESS

Mar. 4, 1907 to Mar. 3, 1909

President of The Senate	President Pro Tempore of The Senate	Speaker of The House of Representatives
Charles W. Fairbanks	William P. Frye	Joseph G. Cannon

Alabama

Senators	Representatives
John T. Morgan (D)	John L. Burnett (D)
d. Jun. 1907	Henry D. Clayton (D)
John H. Bankhead (D)	William B. Craig (D)
s. 1907	J. Thomas Heflin (D)
Edmund W. Pettus (D)	Richmond P. Hobson (D)
d. Jul. 1907	William Richardson (D)
Joseph F. Johnston (D)	George W. Taylor (D)
	Oscar W. Underwood (D)
	Ariosto A. Wiley (D)
	d. Jun. 1908
	Oliver C. Wiley (D)
	s. 1908

Arkansas

Senators	Representatives
James P. Clarke (D)	Stephen Brundidge, Jr. (D)
Jeff Davis (D)	William B. Cravens (D)
	John C. Floyd (D)
	Robert B. Macon (D)
	Charles C. Reid (D)
	Joseph T. Robinson (D)
	Robert M. Wallace (D)

California

Senators	Representatives
George C. Perkins (R)	William F. Englebright (R)
Frank P. Flint (R)	Everis A. Hayes (R)
	Julius Kahn (R)
	Joseph R. Knowland (R)
	Duncan E. McKinlay (R)
	James McLachlan (R)
	James C. Needham (R)
	Sylvester C. Smith (R)

Colorado

Senators	Representatives
Henry M. Teller (R)	Robert W. Bonynge (R)
Simon Guggenheim (R)	George W. Cook (R)
	Warren A. Haggott (R)

Connecticut

Senators	Representatives
Morgan G. Bulkeley (R)	E. Stevens Henry (R)
Frank B. Brandegee (R)	Edwin W. Higgins (R)
	Ebenezer J. Hill (R)
	George L. Lilley (R)
	Nehemiah D. Sperry (R)

Delaware

Senators	Representative
Henry A. Du Pont (R)	Hiram R. Burton (R)
Harry A. Richardson (R)	

Florida

Senators	Representatives
Stephen R. Mallory (D)	Frank Clark (R)
d. Dec. 1908	William B. Lamar (D)
William J. Bryan (D)	Stephen M. Sparkman (D)
ta. 1908	
William H. Milton (D)	
s. 1908	
James P. Taliaferro (D)	

Georgia

Senators	Representatives
Augustus O. Bacon (D)	William C. Adamson (D)
Alexander S. Clay (D)	Charles L. Bartlett (D)
	Thomas M. Bell (D)
	William G. Brantley (D)
	Charles G. Edwards (D)
	James M. Griggs (D)
	Thomas W. Hardwick (D)
	William M. Howard (D)
	Gordon Lee (D)
	Elijah B. Lewis (D)
	Leonidas F. Livingston (D)

Idaho

Senators	Representative
Weldon B. Heyburn (R)	Burton L. French (R)
William E. Borah (R)	

Illinois

Senators	Representatives
Shelby M. Cullom (R)	Henry S. Boutell (R)
Albert J. Hopkins (R)	Ben Franklin Caldwell (D)
	Joseph G. Cannon (R)
	Pleasant T. Chapman (R)
	George E. Foss (R)
	Martin D. Foster (D)
	Charles E. Fuller (R)
	Joseph V. Graff (R)
	Philip Knopf (R)
	William Lorimer (R)
	Frank O. Lowden (R)
	James T. McDermott (D)
	Charles McGavin (R)
	William B. McKinley (R)
	James McKinney (R)
	Martin B. Madden (R)
	James R. Mann (R)
	George W. Prince (R)
	Henry T. Rainey (R)
	William A. Rodenberg (R)
	Adolph J. Sabath (D)
	Howard M. Snapp (R)
	John A. Sterling (R)
	Napoleon B. Thistlewood (R)
	s. 1908
	William W. Wilson (R)

Indiana

Senators	Representatives
Albert J. Beveridge (R)	John A. M. Adair (D)
James A. Hemenway (R)	Henry A. Barnhart (D)
	s. 1908
	Abraham L. Brick (R)
	d. Apr. 1908
	John C. Chaney (R)
	William E. Cox (D)
	Edgar D. Crumpacker (R)
	Lincoln Dixon (D)
	John H. Foster (R)
	Clarence C. Gilhams (R)
	Elias S. Holliday (R)
	Charles B. Landis (R)
	Jesse Overstreet (R)
	George W. Rauch (D)
	James E. Watson (R)

Iowa

Senators	Representatives
William B. Allison (R)	Benjamin P. Birdsall (R)
d. Aug. 1908	James P. Conner (R)
Albert B. Cummins (R)	Robert G. Cousins (R)
s. 1908	Albert F. Dawson (R)
Jonathan P. Dolliver (R)	Daniel W. Hamilton (D)
	Gilbert N. Haugen (R)
	William P. Hepburn (R)
	Elbert H. Hubbard (R)
	John A. T. Hull
	Charles A. Kennedy (R)
	Walter I. Smith (R)

(continued)

TABLE 7.43   (continued)

Mar. 4, 1907 to Mar. 3, 1909

President of The Senate	President Pro Tempore of The Senate	Speaker of The House of Representatives
Charles W. Fairbanks	William P. Frye	Joseph G. Cannon

Kansas

Senators	Representatives
Chester I. Long (R)	Daniel R. Anthony, Jr. (R)
Charles Curtis (R)	William A. Calderhead (R)
	Philip P. Campbell (R)
	Edmond H. Madison (R)
	James M. Miller (R)
	Victor Murdock (R)
	William A. Reeder (R)
	Charles F. Scott (R)

Kentucky

Senators	Representatives
James B. McCreary (D)	Joseph B. Bennett (R)
Thomas H. Paynter (D)	Don C. Edwards (R)
	Harvey Helm (D)
	Addison D. James (R)
	Ollie M. James (D)
	Ben Johnson (D)
	William P. Kimball (D)
	John W. Langley (R)
	Joseph L. Rhinock (D)
	J. Swagar Sherley (D)
	Augustus O. Stanley (D)

Louisiana

Senators	Representatives
Samuel D. McEnery (D)	Robert F. Broussard (D)
Murphy J. Foster (D)	Robert C. Davey (D)
	d. Dec. 1908
	Albert Estopinal (D)
	s. 1908
	George K. Favrot (D)
	Adolph Meyer (D)
	d. Mar. 1908
	Arsene P. Pujo (D)
	Joseph E. Ransdell (D)
	John T. Watkins (D)

Maine

Senators	Representatives
Eugene Hale (R)	Amos L. Allen (R)
William P. Frye (R)	Edwin C. Burleigh (R)
	Frank E. Guernsey (R)
	s. 1908
	Charles E. Littlefield (R)
	r. Sep. 1908
	Llewellyn Powers (R)
	d. Jul. 1908
	John P. Swasey (R)
	s. 1908

Maryland

Senators	Representatives
Isidor Rayner (D)	John Gill, Jr. (D)
William P. Whyte (D)	William H. Jackson (R)
d. Mar. 1908	Sydney E. Mudd (R)
John Walter Smith (D)	George A. Pearre (R)
s. 1908	J. Fred C. Talbott (D)
	Harry B. Wolf (D)

Massachusetts

Senators	Representatives
Henry Cabot Lodge (R)	Butler Ames (R)
W. Murray Crane (R)	Augustus P. Gardner (R)
	Frederick H. Gillett (R)
	William S. Greene (R)
	John A. Keliher (D)
	George P. Lawrence (R)
	William C. Lovering (R)
	Samuel W. McCall (R)
	Joseph F. O'Connell (D)
	Andrew J. Peters (D)
	Ernest W. Roberts (R)
	Charles Q. Tirrell (R)
	Charles G. Washburn (R)
	John W. Weeks (R)

Michigan

Senators	Representatives
Julius C. Burrows (R)	Archibald B. Darragh (R)
William Alden Smith (R)	Edwin Denby (R)
	Gerrit J. Diekema (R)
	Joseph W. Fordney (R)
	Washington Gardner (R)
	Edward L. Hamilton (R)
	George A. Loud (R)
	James C. McLaughlin (R)
	Henry McMorran (R)
	Samuel W. Smith (R)
	Charles E. Townsend (R)
	H. Olin Young (R)

Minnesota

Senators	Representatives
Knute Nelson (R)	J. Adam Bede (R)
Moses E. Clapp (R)	Charles R. Davis (R)
	Winfield S. Hammond (D)
	Charles A. Lindbergh (R)
	Frank M. Nye (R)
	Halvor Steenerson (R)
	Frederick C. Stevens (R)
	James A. Tawney (R)
	Andrew J. Volstead (R)

Mississippi

Senators	Representatives
Hernando D. Money (D)	Eaton J. Bowers (D)
Anselm J. McLaurin (D)	Adam M. Byrd (D)
	Ezekiel S. Candler, Jr. (D)
	Wilson S. Hill (D)
	Benjamin G. Humphreys (D)
	Frank A. McLain (D)
	Thomas Spight (D)
	John Sharp Williams (D)

Missouri	
Senators	**Representatives**
William J. Stone (D)	Joshua W. Alexander (D)
William Warner (R)	Richard Bartholdt (R)
	Charles F. Booher (D)
	Henry S. Caulfield (R)
	Champ Clark (D)
	Harry M. Coudrey (R)
	David A. De Armond (D)
	Edgar C. Ellis (R)
	Thomas Hackney (D)
	Courtney W. Hamlin (D)
	J. Robert Lamar (D)
	James T. Lloyd (D)
	William W. Rucker (D)
	Joseph J. Russell (D)
	Dorsey W. Shackleford (D)
	Madison R. Smith (D)

Montana	
Senators	**Representative**
Thomas H. Carter (R)	Charles N. Pray (R)
Joseph M. Dixon (R)	

Nebraska	
Senators	**Representatives**
Elmer J. Burkett (R)	John F. Boyd (R)
Norris Brown (R)	Edmund H. Hinshaw (R)
	Gilbert M. Hitchcock (D)
	Moses P. Kinkaid (R)
	George W. Norris (R)
	Ernest M. Pollard (R)

Nevada	
Senators	**Representative**
Francis G. Newlands (D)	George A. Bartlett (D)
George S. Nixon (R)	

New Hampshire	
Senators	**Representatives**
Jacob H. Gallinger (R)	Frank D. Currier (R)
Henry E. Burnham (R)	Cyrus A. Sulloway (R)

New Jersey	
Senators	**Representatives**
John Kean (R)	Charles N. Fowler (R)
Frank O. Briggs (R)	John J. Gardner (D)
	James A. Hamill (D)
	Benjamin F. Howell (R)
	William Hughes (D)
	Eugene W. Leake (D)
	Henry C. Loudenslager (R)
	Richard W. Parker (R)
	Le Gage Pratt (D)
	Ira W. Wood (R)

New York	
Senators	**Representatives**
Thomas C. Platt (R)	De Alva S. Alexander (R)
Chauncey M. Depew (R)	John E. Andrus (R)
	William S. Bennett (R)
	Thomas W. Bradley (R)
	William M. Calder (R)
	W. Bourke Cockran (D)
	William W. Cocks (R)
	William H. Draper (R)
	Michael E. Driscoll (R)
	Charles T. Dunwell (R)
	d. Jun. 1908
	Cyrus Durey (R)
	John W. Dwight (R)
	George W. Fairchild (R)
	J. Sloat Fassett (R)
	John J. Fitzgerald (D)
	Otto G. Foelker (R)
	s. 1908
	Charles V. Fornes (D)
	Henry M. Goldfogle (D)
	Joseph A. Goulden (D)
	Francis B. Harrison (D)
	Charles L. Knapp (R)
	Charles B. Law (R)
	George H. Lindsay (D)
	Samuel McMillan (R)
	George R. Malby (R)
	J. Van Vechten Olcott (R)
	Herbert Parsons (R)
	Sereno E. Payne (R)
	James B. Perkins (R)
	Peter A. Porter (R,D)
	Daniel J. Riordan (D)
	William H. Ryan (D)
	James S. Sherman (R)
	George N. Southwick (R)
	William Sulzer (D)
	Edward B. Vreeland (R)
	George E. Waldo (R)
	William Willett, Jr. (D)

North Carolina	
Senators	**Representatives**
Furnifold McL. Simmons (D)	William T. Crawford (D)
Lee S. Overman (D)	Hannibal L. Godwin (D)
	Richard N. Hackett (D)
	Claude Kitchin (D)
	William W. Kitchin (D)
	r. Jan. 1909
	Robert N. Page (D)
	Edward W. Pou (D)
	John H. Small (D)
	Charles R. Thomas (D)
	Edwin Y. Webb (D)

North Dakota	
Senators	**Representatives**
Henry C. Hansbrough (R)	Asle J. Gronna (R)
Porter J. McCumber (R)	Thomas F. Marshall (R)

(continued)

TABLE 7.43 (continued)

Mar. 4, 1907 to Mar. 3, 1909

President of The Senate	President Pro Tempore of The Senate	Speaker of The House of Representatives
Charles W. Fairbanks	William P. Frye	Joseph G. Cannon

Ohio

Senators	Representatives
Joseph B. Foraker (R) Charles W. F. Dick (R)	Timothy T. Ansberry (D) William A. Ashbrook (R) Henry T. Bannon (R) Theodore E. Burton (R) Ralph D. Cole (R) Beman G. Dawes (R) Matthew R. Denver (D) Albert Douglas (R) Herman P. Goebel (R) J. Eugene Harding (R) L. Paul Howland (R) J. Warren Keifer (R) James Kennedy (R) J. Ford Laning (R) Nicholas Longworth (R) Grant E. Mouser (R) Isaac R. Sherwood (D) Edward L. Taylor, Jr. (R) William A. Thomas (R) William E. Tou Velle (D) Capell L. Weems (R)

Oklahoma

Senators	Representatives
Thomas P. Gore (D) Robert L. Owen (D)	Charles D. Carter (D) James S. Davenport (D) Scott Ferris (D) Elmer L. Fulton (D) Bird S. McGuire (R)

Oregon

Senators	Representatives
Charles W. Fulton (R) Jonathan Bourne, Jr. (R)	William R. Ellis (R) Willis C. Hawley (R)

Pennsylvania

Senators	Representatives
Boies Penrose (R) Philander C. Knox (R)	Ernest F. Acheson (R) Andrew J. Barchfeld (R) Charles F. Barclay (R) Arthur L. Bates (R) Joseph G. Beale (R) Henry H. Bingham (R) J. Davis Brodhead (D) Charles N. Brumm (R) r. Jan. 1909 James F. Burke (R) Thomas S. Butler (R) Henry B. Cassel (R) Joel Cook (R) Allen F. Cooper (R) John Dalzell (R) Benjamin K. Focht (R) William W. Foulkrod (R) William H. Graham (R) George F. Huff (R) George W. Kipp (D) Daniel F. Lafean (R) John T. Lenahan (D)

Pennsylvania

Senators	Representatives
	George D. McCreary (R) John G. McHenry (D) Reuben O. Moon (R) J. Hampton Moore (R) Thomas D. Nicholls (D) Marlin E. Olmsted (R) John M. Reynolds (R) John H. Rothermel (D) Irving P. Wanger (R) Nelson P. Wheeler (R) William B. Wilson (D)

Rhode Island

Senators	Representatives
Nelson W. Aldrich (R) George P. Wetmore (R)	Adin B. Capron (R) Daniel L. D. Granger (D) d. Feb. 1909

South Carolina

Senators	Representatives

Benjamin R. Tillman (D)
Asbury C. Latimer (D)
  d. Feb. 1908
Frank B. Gary (D)
  s. 1908
	Wyatt Aiken (D)
	J. Edwin Ellerbe (D)
	David E. Finley (D)
	Joseph T. Johnson (D)
	George S. Legare (D)
	Asbury F. Lever (D)
	James O. Patterson (D)

South Dakota

Senators	Representatives
Robert J. Gamble (R) Alfred B. Kittredge (R)	Philo Hall (R) Eben W. Martin (R) William H. Parker (R)

Tennessee

Senators	Representatives
James B. Frazier (D) Robert L. Taylor (D)	Walter P. Brownlow (R) John W. Gaines (D) Finis J. Garrett (D) George W. Gordon (D) Nathan W. Hale (R) William C. Houston (D) Cordell Hull (D) John A. Moon (D) Lemuel P. Padgett (D) Thetus W. Sims (D)

Texas

Senators	Representatives
Charles A. Culberson (D) Joseph W. Bailey (D)	Jack Beall (D) George F. Burgess (D) Albert S. Burleson (D) Samuel B. Cooper (D) John Nance Garner (D) Oscar W. Gillespie (D) Alexander W. Gregg (D) Rufus Hardy (D) Robert L. Henry (D) John M. Moore (D) Choice B. Randell (D) Gordon J. Russell (D) Morris Sheppard (D) James L. Slayden (D) William R. Smith (D) John H. Stephens (D)

Utah

Senators	Representative
Reed Smoot (R) George Sutherland (R)	Joseph Howell (R)

Vermont

Senators	Representatives

Redfield Proctor (R)
  d. Mar. 1908
John W. Stewart (R)
  ta. 1908
Carroll S. Page (R)
  s. 1908
William P. Dillingham (R)
	David J. Foster (R)
	Kittredge Haskins (R)

Virginia

Senators	Representatives
John W. Daniel (D) Thomas S. Martin (D)	Charles C. Carlin (D) Henry D. Flood (D) Carter Glass (D) James Hay (D) William A. Jones (D) John Lamb (D) Francis R. Lassiter (D) Harry L. Maynard (D) Edward W. Saunders (D) C. Bascom Slemp (R) s. 1908

Washington

Senators	Representatives
Levi Ankeny (R) Samuel H. Piles (R)	Francis W. Cushman (R) William E. Humphrey (R) Wesley L. Jones (R)

West Virginia

Senators	Representatives
Stephen B. Elkins (R) Nathan B. Scott (R)	Joseph H. Gaines (R) William P. Hubbard (R) James A. Hughes (R) George C. Sturgiss (R) Harry C. Woodyard (R)

Wisconsin

Senators	Representatives

John C. Spooner (R)
  r. Apr. 1907
Isaac Stephenson (R)
  s. 1907
Robert M. La Follette (R)
	William J. Cary (R)
	Henry A. Cooper (R)
	James H. Davidson (R)
	John J. Esch (R)
	John J. Jenkins (R)
	Gustav Kustermann (R)
	Elmer A. Morse (R)
	James W. Murphy (D)
	John M. Nelson (R)
	William H. Stafford (R)
	Charles H. Weisse (D)

Wyoming

Senators	Representative
Clarence D. Clark (R) Francis E. Warren (R)	Frank W. Mondell (R)

Source: Notable Names in American History; A Tabulated Register. Third edition of *White's Conspectus of American Biography* (1973), 158–161.

TABLE 7.44   SIXTY-FIRST CONGRESS

Mar. 4, 1908 to Mar. 3, 1911

President of The Senate	President Pro Tempore of The Senate	Speaker of The House of Representatives
James S. Sherman	William P. Frye	Joseph G. Cannon

Alabama

Senators	Representatives
John H. Bankhead (D) Joseph F. Johnston (D)	John L. Burnett (D) Henry D. Clayton (D) William B. Craig (D) S. Hubert Dent, Jr. (D) J. Thomas Heflin (D) Richmond P. Hobson (D) William Richardson (D) George W. Taylor (D) Oscar W. Underwood (D)

Arkansas

Senators	Representatives
James P. Clarke (D) Jeff Davis (D)	William B. Cravens (D) John C. Floyd (D) Robert B. Macon (D) William A. Oldfield (D) Joseph T. Robinson (D) Charles C. Reid (D) Robert M. Wallace (D)

California

Senators	Representatives
George C. Perkins (R) Frank P. Flint (R)	William F. Englebright (R) Everis A. Hayes (R) Julius Kahn (R) Joseph R. Knowland (R) Duncan E. McKinlay (R) James McLachlan (R) James C. Needham (R) Sylvester C. Smith (R)

Colorado

Senators	Representatives
Simon Guggenheim (R) Charles J. Hughes, Jr. (D) d. Jan. 1911	John A. Martin (D) Atterson W. Rucker (D) Edward T. Taylor (D)

Connecticut

Senators	Representatives
Morgan G. Bulkeley (R) Frank B. Brandegee (R)	E. Stevens Henry (R) Edwin W. Higgins (R) Ebenezer J. Hill (R) Nehemiah D. Sperry (R) John Q. Tilson (R)

Delaware

Senators	Representative
Henry A. Du Pont (R) Harry A. Richardson (R)	William H. Heald (R)

(continued)

TABLE 7.44 (continued)

Mar. 4, 1908 to Mar. 3, 1911

President of The Senate	President Pro Tempore of The Senate	Speaker of The House of Representatives
James S. Sherman	William P. Frye	Joseph G. Cannon

Florida

Senators	Representatives
James P. Taliaferro (D)	Frank Clark (R)
Duncan U. Fletcher (D)	Dannitte H. Mays (D)
	Stephen M. Sparkman (D)

Georgia

Senators	Representatives
Augustus O. Bacon (D)	William C. Adamson (D)
Alexander S. Clay (D)	Charles L. Bartlett (D)
d. Nov. 1910	Thomas M. Bell (D)
Joseph M. Terrell (D)	William G. Brantley (D)
s. 1910	Charles G. Edwards (D)
	James M. Griggs (D)
	d. Jan. 1910
	Thomas W. Hardwick (D)
	William M. Howard (D)
	Dudley M. Hughes (D)
	Gordon Lee (D)
	Leonidas F. Livingston (D)
	Seaborn A. Roddenbery (D)
	s. 1910

Idaho

Senators	Representative
Weldon B. Heyburn (R)	Thomas R. Hamer (R)
William E. Borah (R)	

Illinois

Senators	Representatives
Shelby M. Cullom (R)	Henry S. Boutell (R)
William Lorimer (R)	Joseph G. Cannon (R)
	Pleasant T. Chapman (R)
	George E. Foss (R)
	Martin D. Foster (D)
	Charles E. Fuller (R)
	Thomas Gallagher (D)
	Joseph V. Graff (R)
	James M. Graham (D)
	William Lorimer (R)
	r. Jun. 1909
	Frank O. Lowden (R)
	Frederick Lundin (R)
	James T. McDermott (D)
	William B. McKinley (R)
	James McKinney (R)
	Martin B. Madden (R)
	James R. Mann (R)
	William J. Moxley (R)
	r. Jun. 1909
	George W. Prince (R)
	Henry T. Rainey (R)
	William A. Rodenberg (R)
	Adolph J. Sabath (D)
	Howard M. Snapp (R)
	John A. Sterling (R)
	Napoleon B. Thistlewood (R)
	William W. Wilson (R)

Indiana

Senators	Representatives
Albert J. Beveridge (R)	John A. M. Adair (D)
Benjamin F. Shively (D)	William O. Barnard (R)
	Henry A. Barnhart (D)
	John W. Boehne (D)
	Cyrus Cline (D)
	William E. Cox (D)
	Edgar D. Crumpacker (R)
	William A. Cullop (D)
	Lincoln Dixon (D)
	Charles A. Korbly (D)
	Martin A. Morrison (D)
	Ralph W. Moss (D)
	George W. Rauch (D)

Iowa

Senators	Representatives
Jonathan P. Dolliver (R)	Albert F. Dawson (R)
d. Oct. 1910	James W. Good (R)
Lafayette Young (R)	Gilbert N. Haugen (R)
ta. 1910	Elbert H. Hubbard (R)
Albert B. Cummins (R)	John A. T. Hull (R)
	William D. Jamieson (D)
	Nathan E. Kendall (R)
	Charles A. Kennedy (R)
	Charles E. Pickett (R)
	Walter I. Smith (R)
	Frank P. Woods (R)

Kansas

Senators	Representatives
Charles Curtis (R)	Daniel R. Anthony, Jr. (R)
Joseph L. Bristow (R)	William A. Calderhead (R)
	Philip P. Campbell (R)
	Edmond H. Madison (R)
	James M. Miller (R)
	Victor Murdock (R)
	William A. Reeder (R)
	Charles F. Scott (R)

Kentucky

Senators	Representatives
Thomas H. Paynter (D)	Joseph B. Bennett (R)
William O. Bradley (R)	James C. Cantrill (D)
	Don C. Edwards (R)
	Harvey Helm (D)
	Ollie M. James (D)
	Ben Johnson (D)
	John W. Langley (R)
	Joseph L. Rhinock (D)
	J. Swagar Sherley (D)
	Augustus O. Stanley (D)
	Robert Y. Thomas, Jr. (D)

Louisiana

Senators	Representatives
Samuel D. McEnery (D)	Robert F. Broussard (D)
d. Jun. 1910	H. Garland Dupre (D)
John R. Thornton (D)	s. 1910
s. 1910	Albert Estopinal (D)
Murphy J. Foster (D)	Samuel L. Gilmore (D)
	d. Jul. 1910
	Arsene P. Pujo (D)
	Joseph E. Ransdell (D)
	John T. Watkins (D)
	Robert C. Wickliffe (D)

Maine	
Senators	**Representatives**
Eugene Hale (R) William P. Frye (R)	Amos L. Allen (R) d. Feb. 1911 Edwin C. Burleigh (R) Frank E. Guernsey (R) John P. Swasey (R)

Maryland	
Senators	**Representatives**
Isidor Rayner (D) John Walter Smith (D)	J. Harry Covington (D) John Gill, Jr. (D) John Kronmiller (R) Sydney E. Mudd (R) George A. Pearre (R) J. Fred C. Talbott (D)

Massachusetts	
Senators	**Representatives**

Henry Cabot Lodge (R)
W. Murray Crane (R)
	Butler Ames (R)
	Eugene N. Foss (D)
	    s. 1910
	Augustus P. Gardner (R)
	Frederick H. Gillett (R)
	William S. Greene (R)
	John A. Keliher (D)
	George P. Lawrence (R)
	William C. Lovering (R)
	    d. Feb. 1910
	Samuel W. McCall (R)
	John J. Mitchell (D)
	    s. 1910
	Joseph F. O'Connell (D)
	Andrew J. Peters (D)
	Ernest W. Roberts (R)
	Charles Q. Tirrell (R)
	    d. Jul. 1910
	Charles G. Washburn (R)
	John W. Weeks (R)

Michigan	
Senators	**Representatives**
Julius C. Burrows (R) William Alden Smith (R)	Edwin Denby (R) Gerrit J. Diekema (R) Francis H. Dodds (R) Joseph W. Fordney (R) Washington Gardner (R) Edward L. Hamilton (R) George A. Loud (R) James C. McLaughlin (R) Henry McMorran (R) Samuel W. Smith (R) Charles E. Townsend (R) H. Olin Young (R)

Minnesota	
Senators	**Representatives**
Knute Nelson (R) Moses E. Clapp (R)	Charles R. Davis (R) Winfield S. Hammond (D) Charles A. Lindbergh (R) Clarence B. Miller (R) Frank M. Nye (R) Halvor Steenerson (R) Frederick C. Stevens (R) James A. Tawney (R) Andrew J. Volstead (R)

Mississippi	
Senators	**Representatives**

Hernando D. Money (D)
Anselm J. McLaurin (D)
    d. Dec. 1909
James Gordon (D)
    ta. 1910
Le Roy Percy (D)
    s. 1910
	Eaton J. Bowers (D)
	Adam M. Byrd (D)
	Ezekiel S. Candler, Jr. (D)
	James W. Collier (D)
	William A. Dickson (D)
	Benjamin G. Humphreys (D)
	Thomas U. Sisson (D)
	Thomas Spight (D)

Missouri	
Senators	**Representatives**

William J. Stone (D)
William Warner (R)
	Joshua W. Alexander (D)
	Richard Bartholdt (R)
	Charles F. Booher (D)
	William P. Borland (D)
	Champ Clark (D)
	Harry M. Coudrey (R)
	Charles A. Crow (R)
	David A. De Armond (D)
	    d. Nov. 1909
	Clement C. Dickinson (D)
	    s. 1910
	Politte Elvins (R)
	Patrick F. Gill (D)
	Courtney W. Hamlin (D)
	James T. Lloyd (D)
	Charles H. Morgan (R)
	Arthur P. Murphy (R)
	William W. Rucker (D)
	Dorsey W. Shackleford (D)

Montana	
Senators	**Representative**
Thomas H. Carter (R) Joseph M. Dixon (R)	Charles N. Pray (R)

Nebraska	
Senators	**Representatives**
Elmer J. Burkett (D) Norris Brown (R)	Edmund H. Hinshaw (RO Gilbert M. Hitchcock (D) Moses P. Kinkaid (R) James P. Latta (D) John A. Maguire (D) George W. Norris (R)

Nevada	
Senators	**Representative**
Francis G. Newlands (D) George S. Nixon (R)	George A. Bartlett (D)

New Hampshire	
Senators	**Representatives**
Jacob H. Gallinger (R) Henry E. Burnham (R)	Frank D. Currier (R) Cyrus A. Sulloway (R)

(continued)

TABLE 7.44 (continued)

Mar. 4, 1908 to Mar. 3, 1911

President of The Senate	President Pro Tempore of The Senate	Speaker of The House of Representatives
James S. Sherman	William P. Frye	Joseph G. Cannon

New Jersey

Senators	Representatives
John Kean (R)	Charles N. Fowler (R)
Frank O. Briggs (R)	John J. Gardner (D)
	James A. Hamill (D)
	Benjamin F. Howell (R)
	William Hughes (D)
	Eugene W. Kinkead (D)
	Henry C. Loudenslager (R)
	Richard W. Parker (R)
	William H. Wiley (R)
	Ira W. Wood (R)

New York

Senators	Representatives
Chauncy M. Depew (R)	De Alva S. Alexander (R)
Elihu Root (R)	John E. Andrus (R)
	William S. Bennett (R)
	Thomas W. Bradley (R)
	William M. Calder (R)
	William W. Cocks (R)
	Micahel F. Conry (D)
	William H. Draper (R)
	Daniel A. Driscoll (D)
	Michael E. Driscoll (R)
	Cyrus Durey (R)
	John W. Dwight (R)
	George W. Fairchild (R)
	J. Sloat Fassett (R)
	Hamilton Fish (R)
	John J. Fitzgerald (D)
	Otto G. Foelker (R)
	Charles V. Fornes (D)
	Henry M. Goldfogle (D)
	Joseph A. Goulden (D)
	Francis B. Harrison (D)
	James S. Havens (D)
	s. 1910
	Charles L. Knapp (R)
	Charles B. Law (R)
	George H. Lindsay (D)
	George R. Malby (R)
	Charles S. Millington (R)
	J. Van Vechten Olcott (R)
	Herbert Parsons (R)
	Sereno E. Payne (R)
	James B. Perkins (R)
	d. Mar. 1910
	Daniel J. Riordan (D)
	James S. Simmons (R)
	George N. Southwick (R)
	William Sulzer (D)
	Edward B. Vreeland (R)
	William Willett, Jr. (D)
	Richard Young (R)

North Carolina

Senators	Representatives
Furnifold McL. Simmons (D)	Charles H. Cowles (R)
Lee S. Overman (D)	Hannibal L. Godwin (D)
	John G. Grant (R)
	Claude Kitchin (D)
	John M. Morehead (R)
	Robert N. Page (D)
	Edward W. Pou (D)
	John H. Small (D)
	Charles R. Thomas (D)
	Edwin Y. Webb (D)

North Dakota

Senators	Representatives
Porter J. McCumber (R)	Asle J. Gronna (R)
Martin N. Johnson (R)	r. 1911
d. Oct. 1909	Louis B. Hanna (R)
Fountain L. Thompson (D)	
r. Jan. 1910	
William E. Purcell (D)	
ta. 1910	
Asle J. Gronna (R)	
s. 1911	

Ohio

Senators	Representatives
Charles W. F. Dick (R)	Carl C. Anderson (D)
Theodore E. Burton (R)	Timothy T. Ansberry (D)
	William A. Ashbrook (D)
	James H. Cassidy (R)
	Ralph D. Cole (R)
	James M. Cox (D)
	Matthew R. Denver (D)
	Albert Douglas (R)
	Herman P. Goebel (R)
	David A. Hollingsworth (R)
	L. Paul Howland (R)
	Adna R. Johnson (R)
	James Joyce (R)
	J. Warren Keifer (R)
	James Kennedy (R)
	Nicholas Longworth (R)
	William G. Sharp (D)
	Isaac R. Sherwood (D)
	Edward L. Taylor, Jr. (R)
	William A. Thomas (R)
	William E. Tou Velle (D)

Oklahoma

Senators	Representatives
Thomas P. Gore (D)	Charles D. Carter (D)
Robert L. Owen (D)	Charles E. Creager (R)
	Scott Ferris (D)
	Bird S. McGuire (R)
	Dick T. Morgan (R)

Oregon

Senators	Representatives
Jonathan Bourne, Jr. (R)	William R. Ellis (R)
George E. Chamberlain (D)	Willis C. Hawley (R)

Pennsylvania	
Senators	**Representatives**

Boies Penrose (R)
George T. Oliver (R)
	Andrew J. Barchfeld (R)
	Charles F. Barclay (R)
	Arthur L. Bates (R)
	Henry H. Bingham (R)
	James F. Burke (R)
	Thomas S. Butler (R)
	Joel Cook (R)
	  d. Dec. 1910
	Allen F. Cooper (R)
	John Dalzell (R)
	Benjamin K. Focht (R)
	William W. Foulkrod (R)
	  d. Nov. 1910
	Alfred B. Garner (R)
	William H. Graham (R)
	William W. Griest (R)
	George F. Huff (R)
	Daniel F. Lafean (R)
	Jonathan N. Langham (R)
	George D. McCreary (R)
	John G. McHenry (D)
	Reuben O. Moon (R)
	J. Hampton Moore (R)
	Thomas D. Nicholls (D)
	Marlin E. Olmsted (R)
	A. Mitchell Palmer (D)
	Henry W. Palmer (R)
	Charles C. Pratt (R)
	John M. Reynolds (R)
	John H. Rothermel (D)
	John K. Tener (R)
	Irving P. Wanger (R)
	Nelson P. Wheeler (R)
	William B. Wilson (D)

Rhode Island	
Senators	**Representatives**
Nelson W. Aldrich (R) George P. Wetmore (R)	Adin B. Capron (R) William P. Sheffield (R)

South Carolina	
Senators	**Representatives**
Benjamin R. Tillman (D) Ellison D. Smith (D)	Wyatt Aiken (D) J. Edwin Ellerbe (D) David E. Finley (D) Joseph T. Johnson (D) George S. Legare (D) Asbury F. Lever (D) James O. Patterson (D)

South Dakota	
Senators	**Representatives**
Robert J. Gamble (R) Coe I. Crawford (R)	Charles H. Burke (R) Eben W. Martin (R)

Tennessee	
Senators	**Representatives**

James B. Frazier (D)
Robert L. Taylor (D)
	Richard W. Austin (R)
	Walter P. Brownlow (R)
	  d. Jul. 1910
	Joseph W. Byrns (D)
	Finis J. Garrett (D)
	George W. Gordon (D)
	William C. Houston (D)
	Cordell Hull (D)
	Zachary D. Massey (R)
	  s. 1910
	John A. Moon (D)
	Lemuel P. Padgett (D)
	Thetus W. Sims (D)

Texas	
Senators	**Representatives**

Charles A. Culberson (D)
Joseph W. Bailey (D)
	Jack Beall (D)
	George F. Burgess (D)
	Albert S. Burleson (D)
	Martin Dies (D)
	John Nance Garner (D)
	Oscar W. Gillespie (D)
	Alexander W. Gregg (D)
	Rufus Hardy (D)
	Robert L. Henry (D)
	Robert M. Lively (D)
	  s. 1910
	John M. Moore (D)
	Choice B. Randell (D)
	Gordon J. Russell (D)
	  r. Jun. 1910
	Morris Sheppard (D)
	James L. Slayden (D)
	William R. Smith (D)
	John H. Stephens (D)

Utah	
Senators	**Representative**
Reed Smoot (R) George Sutherland (R)	Joseph Howell (R)

Vermont	
Senators	**Representatives**
William P. Dillingham (R) Carroll S. Page (R)	David J. Foster (R) Frank Plumley (R)

Virginia	
Senators	**Representatives**

John W. Daniel (D)
  d. Jun. 1910
Claude A. Swanson (D)
  s. 1910
Thomas S. Martin (D)
	Charles C. Carlin (D)
	Henry D. Flood (D)
	Carter Glass (D)
	James Hay (D)
	William A. Jones (D)
	John Lamb (D)
	Francis R. Lassiter (D)
	  d. Oct. 1909
	Harry L. Maynard (D)
	Edward W. Saunders (D)
	C. Bascom Slemp (R)
	Robert Turnbull (D)
	  s. 1910

(continued)

TABLE 7.44 (continued)

Mar. 4, 1908 to Mar. 3, 1911

President of The Senate	President Pro Tempore of The Senate	Speaker of The House of Representatives
James S. Sherman	William P. Frye	Joseph G. Cannon

Washington

Senators	Representatives
Samuel H. Piles (R) Wesley L. Jones (R)	Francis W. Cushman (R) d. Jul. 1909 William E. Humphrey (R) William W. McCredie (R) Miles Poindexter (R)

West Virginia

Senators	Representatives
Stephen B. Elkins (R) d. Jan. 1911 Davis Elkins (R) ta. 1911 Clarence W. Watson (D) s. 1911 Nathan B. Scott (R)	Joseph H. Gaines (R) William P. Hubbard (R) James A. Hughes (R) George C. Sturgiss (R) Harry C. Woodyard (R)

Wisconsin

Senators	Representatives
Robert M. La Follette (R) Isaac Stephenson (R)	William J. Cary (R) Henry A. Cooper (R) James H. Davidson (R) John J. Esch (R) Arthur W. Kopp (R) Gustav Kustermann (R) Irvine L. Lenroot (R) Elmer A. Morse (R) John M. Nelson (R) William H. Stafford (R) Charles H. Weisse (D)

Wyoming

Senators	Representative
Clarence D. Clark (R) Francis E. Warren (R)	Frank W. Mondell (R)

Source: Notable Names in American History; A Tabulated Register. Third edition of *White's Conspectus of American Biography* (1973), 161–163.

TABLE 7.45   SIXTY-SECOND CONGRESS

Mar. 4, 1911 to Mar. 3, 1913

President of The Senate	Presidents Pro Tempore of The Senate	Speaker of The House of Representatives
James S. Sherman	William P. Frye Charles Curtis Augustus O. Bacon Jacob H. Gallinger Henry Cabot Lodge Frank B. Brandegee	Champ Clark

Alabama

Senators	Representatives
John H. Bankhead (D) Joseph F. Johnston (D)	Fred L. Blackmon (D) John L. Burnett (D) Henry D. Clayton (D) S. Hubert Dent, Jr. (D) J. Thomas Heflin (D) Richmond P. Hobson (D) William Richardson (D) George W. Taylor (D) Oscar W. Underwood (D)

Arizona

Senators	Representative
Henry F. Ashurst (D) s. 1912 Marcus A. Smith (D) s. 1912	Carl Hayden (D) s. 1912

Arkansas

Senators	Representatives
James P. Clarke (D) Jeff Davis (D) d. Jan. 1913 John N. Heiskell (D) ta. 1913 William M. Kavanaugh (D) s. 1913	William B. Cravens (D) John C. Floyd (D) William S. Goodwin (D) Henderson M. Jacoway (D) Robert B. Macon (D) William A. Oldfield (D) Joseph T. Robinson (D) r. Jan. 1913 Samuel M. Taylor (D) s. 1913

California

Senators	Representatives
George C. Perkins (R) John D. Works (R)	Everis A. Hayes (R) Julius Kahn (R) William Kent (R) Joseph R. Knowland (R) James C. Needham (R) John E. Raker (D) Sylvester C. Smith (R) d. Jan. 1913 William D. Stephens (R)

Colorado

Senators	Representatives
Simon Guggenheim (R) Charles S. Thomas (D) s. 1913	John A. Martin (D) Atterson W. Rucker (D) Edward T. Taylor (D)

Connecticut

Senators	Representatives
Frank B. Brandegee (R) George P. McLean (R)	E. Stevens Henry (R) Edwin W. Higgins (R) Ebenezer J. Hill (R) Thomas L. Reilly (D) John Q. Tilson (R)

Delaware

Senators	Representative
Henry A. Du Pont (R) Harry A. Richardson (R)	William H. Heald (R)

Florida	
Senators	**Representatives**
Duncan U. Fletcher (D)	Frank Clark (R)
Nathan P. Bryan (D)	Dannitte H. Mays (D)
	Stephen M. Sparkman (D)

Georgia	
Senators	**Representatives**
Augustus O. Bacon (D)	William C. Adamson (D)
Joseph M. Terrell (D)	Charles L. Bartlett (D)
r. Jul. 1911	Thomas M. Bell (D)
Hoke Smith (D)	William G. Brantley (D)
s. 1911	Charles G. Edwards (D)
	Thomas W. Hardwick (D)
	William M. Howard (D)
	Dudley M. Hughes (D)
	Gordon Lee (D)
	Seaborn A. Roddenbery (D)
	Samuel J. Tribble (D)

Idaho	
Senators	**Representative**
Weldon B. Heyburn (R)	Burton L. French (R)
d. Oct. 1911	
Kirtland I. Perky (D)	
ta. 1912	
James H. Brady (R)	
s. 1913	
William E. Borah (R)	

Illinois	
Senators	**Representatives**
Shelby M. Cullom (R)	Frank Buchanan (D)
William Lorimer (R)	Joseph G. Cannon (R)
r. Jul. 1912	Ira C. Copley (R)
	Lynden Evans (D)
	George E. Foss (R)
	Martin D. Foster (D)
	H. Robert Fowler (D)
	Charles E. Fuller (R)
	Thomas Gallagher (D)
	James M. Graham (D)
	James T. McDermott (D)
	John C. McKenzie (R)
	William B. McKinley (R)
	James McKinney (R)
	Martin B. Madden (R)
	James R. Mann (R)
	George W. Prince (R)
	Henry T. Rainey (R)
	William A. Rodenberg (R)
	Adolph J. Sabath (D)
	Edmund J. Stack (D)
	John A. Sterling (R)
	Claudius U. Stone (D)
	Napoleon B. Thistlewood (R)
	William W. Wilson (R)

Indiana	
Senators	**Representatives**
Benjamin F. Shively (D)	John A. M. Adair (D)
John W. Kern (D)	Henry A. Barnhart (D)
	John W. Boehne (D)
	Cyrus Cline (D)
	William E. Cox (D)
	Edgar D. Crumpacker (R)
	William A. Cullop (D)
	Lincoln Dixon (D)
	Finly H. Gray (D)
	Charles A. Korbly (D)
	Martin A. Morrison (D)
	Ralph W. Moss (D)
	George W. Rauch (D)

Iowa	
Senators	**Representatives**
Albert B. Cummins (R)	James W. Good (R)
William S. Kenyon (R)	William R. Green (R)
	Gilbert N. Haugen (R)
	Elbert H. Hubbard (R)
	d. Jun. 1912
	Nathan E. Kendall (R)
	Charles A. Kennedy (R)
	Irvin S. Pepper (D)
	Charles E. Pickett (R)
	Solomon F. Prouty (R)
	George C. Scott (R)
	s. 1912
	Walter I. Smith (R)
	r. Mar. 1911
	Horace M. Towner (R)
	Frank P. Woods (R)

Kansas	
Senators	**Representatives**
Charles Curtis (R)	Daniel R. Anthony, Jr. (R)
Joseph L. Bristow (R)	Philip P. Campbell (R)
	Fred S. Jackson (R)
	Edmond H. Madison (R)
	d. Sep. 1911
	Alexander C. Mitchell (R)
	d. Jul. 1911
	Victor Murdock (R)
	George A. Neeley (D)
	s. 1912
	Rollin R. Rees (R)
	Joseph Taggart (D)
	Isaac D. Young (R)

Kentucky	
Senators	**Representatives**
Thomas H. Paynter (D)	James C. Cantrill (D)
William O. Bradley (R)	William J. Fields (D)
	Harvey Helm (D)
	Ollie M. James (D)
	Ben Johnson (D)
	John W. Langley (R)
	Caleb Powers (R)
	Arthur B. Rouse (D)
	J. Swagar Sherley (D)
	Augustus O. Stanley (D)
	Robert Y. Thomas, Jr. (D)

(continued)

TABLE 7.45   (continued)

Mar. 4, 1911 to Mar. 3, 1913

President of The Senate	Presidents Pro Tempore of The Senate	Speaker of The House of Representatives
James S. Sherman	William P. Frye Charles Curtis Augustus O. Bacon Jacob H. Gallinger Henry Cabot Lodge Frank B. Brandegee	Champ Clark

Louisiana

Senators	Representatives
Murphy J. Foster (D) John R. Thornton (D)	Robert F. Broussard (D) H. Garland Dupre (D) Albert Estopinal (D) Lewis L. Morgan (D) s. 1912 Arsene P. Pujo (D) Joseph E. Ransdell (D) John T. Watkins (D) Robert C. Wickliffe (D) d. Jun. 1912

Maine

Senators	Representatives
William P. Frye (R) d. Aug. 1911 Obadiah Garner (D) s. 1911 Charles F. Johnson (D)	Samuel W. Gould (D) Frank E. Guernsey (R) Asher C. Hinds (R) Daniel J. McGillicuddy (D)

Maryland

Senators	Representatives
Isidor Rayner (D) d. Nov. 1912 William P. Jackson (R) ta. 1912 John Walter Smith (D)	J. Harry Covington (D) George Konig (D) David J. Lewis (D) J. Charles Linthicum (D) Thomas Parran (R) J. Fred C. Talbott (D)

Massachusetts

Senators	Representatives
Henry Cabot Lodge (R) W. Murray Crane (R)	Butler Ames (R) James M. Curley (D) Augustus P. Gardner (R) Frederick H. Gillett (R) William S. Greene (R) Robert O. Harris (R) George P. Lawrence (R) Samuel W. McCall (R) William F. Murray (D) Andrew J. Peters (D) Ernest W. Roberts (R) John A. Thayer (D) John W. Weeks (R) William H. Wilder (R)

Michigan

Senators	Representatives
William Alden Smith (R) Charles E. Townsend (R)	Francis H. Dodds (R) Frank E. Doremus (D) Joseph W. Fordney (R) Edward L. Hamilton (R)

Michigan

Senators	Representatives
	George A. Loud (R) James C. McLaughlin (R) Henry McMorran (R) John M. C. Smith (R) Samuel W. Smith (R) Edwin F. Sweet (D) William W. Wedemeyer (R) d. Jan. 1913 H. Olin Young (R)

Minnesota

Senators	Representatives
Knute Nelson (R) Moses E. Clapp (R)	Sydney Anderson (R) Charles R. Davis (R) Winfield S. Hammond (D) Charles A. Lindbergh (R) Clarence B. Miller (R) Frank M. Nye (R) Halvor Steenerson (R) Frederick C. Stevens (R) Andrew J. Volstead (R)

Mississippi

Senators	Representatives
Le Roy Percy (D) John Sharp Williams (D)	Ezekiel S. Candler, Jr. (D) James W. Collier (D) William A. Dickson (D) Pat Harrison (D) Benjamin G. Humphreys (D) Thomas U. Sisson (D) Hubert D. Stephens (D) Samuel A. Witherspoon (D)

Missouri

Senators	Representatives
William J. Stone (D) James A. Reed (D)	Joshua W. Alexander (D) Richard Bartholdt (R) Charles F. Booher (D) William P. Borland (D) Theron E. Catlin (R) r. Aug. 1912 Champ Clark (D) James A. Daugherty (D) Clement C. Dickinson (D) Leonidas C. Dyer (R) Patrick F. Gill (D) s. 1912 Courtney W. Hamlin (D) Walter L. Hensley (D) James T. Lloyd (D) Thomas L. Rubey (D) William W. Rucker (D) Joseph J. Russell (D) Dorsey W. Shackleford (D)

Montana

Senators	Representative
Joseph M. Dixon (R) Henry L. Myers (D)	Charles N. Pray (R)

Nebraska	
Senators	**Representatives**
Norris Brown (R) Gilbert M. Hitchcock (D)	Moses P. Kinkaid (R) James P. Latta (D) d. Sep. 1911 Charles O. Lobeck (D) John A. Maguire (D) George W. Norris (R) Charles H. Sloan (R) Daniel V. Stephens (D)

Nevada	
Senators	**Representative**
Francis G. Newlands (D) George S. Nixon (R) d. Jun. 1912 William A. Massey (R) ta. 1912 Key Pittman (D) s. 1913	Edwin E. Roberts (R)

New Hampshire	
Senators	**Representatives**
Jacob H. Gallinger (R) Henry E. Burnham (R)	Frank D. Currier (R) Cyrus A. Sulloway (R)

New Jersey	
Senators	**Representatives**
Frank O. Briggs (R) James E. Martine (D)	William J. Browning (R) John J. Gardner (D) James A. Hamill (D) Archibald C. Hart (D) s. 1912 William Hughes (D) r. Sep. 1912 Eugene F. Kinkead (D) Henry C. Loudenslager (R) d. Aug. 1911 Walter I. McCoy (D) Thomas J. Scully (D) Edward W. Townsend (D) William E. Tuttle, Jr. (D) Ira W. Wood (R)

New Mexico	
Senators	**Representatives**
Thomas B. Catron (R) s. 1912 Albert B. Fall (R) s. 1912	George Curry (R) s. 1912 Harvey B. Fergusson (D) s. 1912

New York	
Senators	**Representatives**
Elihu Root (R) James A. O'Gorman (D)	Theron Akin (R) John E. Andrus (R) Steven B. Ayres (D) Thomas W. Bradley (R) William M. Calder (R) Richard E. Connell (D) d. Oct. 1912 Michael F. Conry (D) Henry G. Danforth (R) Henry S. De Forest (R) William H. Draper (R) Daniel A. Driscoll (D) Michael E. Driscoll (R)

New York	
Senators	**Representatives**
	John W. Dwight (R) George W. Fairchild (R) John J. Fitzgerald (D) Charles V. Fornes (D) Henry George Jr. (D) Henry M. Goldfogle (D) Francis B. Harrison (D) John J. Kindred (D) Jefferson M. Levy (D) George H. Lindsay (D) Martin W. Littleton (D) James P. Maher (D) George R. Malby (D) d. Jul. 1912 Edwin A. Merritt, Jr. (R) s. 1912 Luther W. Mott (R) Thomas G. Patten (D) Sereno E. Payne (R) William C. Redfield (D) Daniel J. Riordan (D) James S. Simmons (R) Charles B. Smith (D) William Sulzer (D) r. 1912 Charles A. Talcott (D) Edwin S. Underhill (D) Edward B. Vreeland (R) Frank E. Wilson (D)

North Carolina	
Senators	**Representatives**
Furnifold McL. Simmons (D) Lee S. Overman (D)	Robert L. Doughton (D) John M. Faison (D) Hannibal L. Godwin (D) James M. Gudger, Jr. (D) Claude Kitchin (D) Robert N. Page (D) Edward W. Pou (D) John H. Small (D) Charles M. Stedman (D) Edwin Y. Webb (D)

North Dakota	
Senators	**Representatives**
Porter J. McCumber (R) Asle J. Gronna (R)	Louis B. Hanna (R) r. Jan. 1913 Henry T. Helgesen (R)

Ohio	
Senators	**Representatives**
Theodore E. Burton (R) Atlee Pomerene (D)	Alfred G. Allen (D) Carl C. Anderson (D) d. Oct. 1912 Timothy T. Ansberry (D) William A. Ashbrook (D) Ellsworth R. Bathrick (D) Robert J. Bulkley (D) Horatio C. Claypool (D) James M. Cox (D) r. Jan. 1913 Matthew R. Denver (D) William B. Francis (D) J. Henry Goeke (D) L. Paul Howland (R) Nicholas Longworth (R) James D. Post (D)

(continued)

TABLE 7.45   (continued)

Mar. 4, 1911 to Mar. 3, 1913

President of The Senate	Presidents Pro Tempore of The Senate	Speaker of The House of Representatives
James S. Sherman	William P. Frye Charles Curtis Augustus O. Bacon Jacob H. Gallinger Henry Cabot Lodge Frank B. Brandegee	Champ Clark

Ohio

Senators	Representatives
	William G. Sharp (D) Isaac R. Sherwood (D) Robert M. Switzer (R) Edward L. Taylor, Jr. (R) John J. Whitacre (D) George White (D) Frank B. Willis (R)

Oklahoma

Senators	Representatives
Thomas P. Gore (D) Robert L. Owen (D)	Charles D. Carter (D) James S. Davenport (D) Scott Ferris (D) Bird S. McGuire (R) Dick T. Morgan (R)

Oregon

Senators	Representatives
Jonathan Bourne, Jr. (R) George E. Chamberlain (D)	Willis C. Hawley (R) Abraham W. Lafferty (R)

Pennsylvania

Senators	Representatives

Boies Penrose (R)
George T. Oliver (R)
	William D. B. Ainey (R)
	Andrew J. Barchfeld (R)
	Arthur L. Bates (R)
	Henry H. Bingham (R)
	  d. Mar. 1912
	Charles C. Bowman (R)
	  r. Dec. 1912
	James F. Burke (R)
	Thomas S. Butler (R)
	Thomas S. Crago (R)
	John Dalzell (R)
	Robert E. Diffenderfer (D)
	Michael Donohoe (D)
	John R. Farr (R)
	Benjamin K. Focht (R)
	Curtis H. Gregg (D)
	William W. Griest (R)
	Jesse L. Hartman (R)
	George W. Kipp (D)
	  d. Jul. 1911
	Daniel F. Lafean (R)
	Jonathan N. Langham (R)
	Robert E. Lee (D)
	George D. McCreary (D)
	John G. McHenry (D)
	  d. Dec. 1912
	Charles Matthews (R)
	Reuben O. Moon (R)
	J. Hampton Moore (R)

Pennsylvania

Senators	Representatives
	Marlin E. Olmsted (R) A. Mitchell Palmer (D) Charles E. Patton (R) Stephen G. Porter (R) William S. Reyburn (R) John H. Rothermel (D) Peter M. Speer (R) William S. Vare (R) s. 1912 William B. Wilson (D)

Rhode Island

Senators	Representatives
George P. Wetmore (R) Henry F. Lippitt (R)	George F. O'Shaunessy (D) George H. Utter (R) d. Nov. 1912

South Carolina

Senators	Representatives
Benjamin R. Tillman (D) Ellison D. Smith (D)	Wyatt Aiken (D) James F. Byrnes (D) J. Edwin Ellerbe (D) David E. Finley (D) Joseph T. Johnson (D) George S. Legare (D) d. Jan. 1913 Asbury F. Lever (D)

South Dakota

Senators	Representatives
Robert J. Gamble (R) Coe I. Crawford (R)	Charles H. Burke (R) Eben W. Martin (R)

Tennessee

Senators	Representatives

Robert L. Taylor (D)
  d. Mar. 1912
Newell Sanders (R)
  ta. 1912
William R. Webb (D)
  s. 1913
Luke Lea (D)
	Richard W. Austin (R)
	Joseph W. Byrns (D)
	Finis J. Garrett (D)
	George W. Gordon (D)
	  d. Aug. 1911
	William C. Houston (D)
	Cordell Hull (D)
	Kenneth D. McKellar (D)
	John A. Moon (D)
	Lemuel P. Padgett (D)
	Sam R. Sells (R)
	Thetus W. Sims (D)

Texas

Senators	Representatives

Charles A. Culberson (D)
Joseph W. Bailey (D)
  r. Jan. 1913
Rienzi M. Johnston (D)
  ta. 1913
Morris Sheppard (D)
  s. 1913
	Jack Beall (D)
	George F. Burgess (D)
	Albert S. Burleson (D)
	Oscar Callaway (D)
	Martin Dies (D)
	John Nance Garner (D)
	Alexander W. Gregg (D)
	Rufus Hardy (D)
	Robert L. Henry (D)
	John M. Moore (D)
	Choice B. Randell (D)
	Morris Sheppard (D)
	  r. Feb. 1913
	James L. Slayden (D)

Texas

Senators	Representatives
	William R. Smith (D)
	John H. Stephens (D)
	James Young (D)

Utah

Senators	Representative
Reed Smoot (R)	Joseph Howell (R)
George Sutherland (R)	

Vermont

Senators	Representatives
William P. Dillingham (R)	David J. Foster (R)
Carroll S. Page (R)	d. Mar. 1912
	Frank L. Greene (R)
	s. 1912
	Frank Plumley (R)

Virginia

Senators	Representatives
Thomas S. Martin (D)	Charles C. Carlin (D)
Claude A. Swanson (D)	Henry D. Flood (D)
	Carter Glass (D)
	James Hay (D)
	Edward E. Holland (D)
	William A. Jones (D)
	John Lamb (D)
	Edward W. Saunders (D)
	C. Bascom Slemp (R)
	Robert Turnbull (D)

Washington

Senators	Representatives
Wesley L. Jones (R)	William E. Humphrey (R)
Miles Poindexter (R)	William L. La Follette (R)
	Stanton Warburton (R)

West Virginia

Senators	Representatives
Clarence W. Watson (D)	William G. Brown, Jr. (D)
William E. Chilton (D)	John W. Davis (D)
	John M. Hamilton (D)
	James A. Hughes (R)
	Adam B. Littlepage (D)

Wisconsin

Senators	Representatives
Robert M. La Follette (R)	Victor L. Berger (Socialist)
Isaac Stephenson (R)	Michael E. Burke (D)
	William J. Cary (R)
	Henry A. Cooper (R)
	James H. Davidson (R)
	John J. Esch (R)
	Thomas F. Konop (D)
	Arthur W. Kopp (R)
	Irvine L. Lenroot (R)
	Elmer A. Morse (R)
	John M. Nelson (R)

Wyoming

Senators	Representative
Clarence D. Clark (R)	Frank W. Mondell (R)
Francis E. Warren (R)	

Source: *Notable Names in American History; A Tabulated Register.* Third edition of *White's Conspectus of American Biography* (1973), 163–166.

TABLE 7.46   SIXTY-THIRD CONGRESS

Mar. 4, 1913 to Mar. 3, 1915

President of The Senate	President Pro Tempore of The Senate	Speaker of The House of Representatives
Thomas R. Marshall	James P. Clarke	Champ Clark

Alabama

Senators	Representatives
John H. Bankhead (D)	John W. Abercrombie (D)
Joseph F. Johnston (D)	Fred L. Blackmon (D)
d. Aug. 1913	John L. Burnett (D)
Frank S. White (D)	Henry D. Clayton (D)
s. 1914	r. May 1914
	S. Hubert Dent, Jr. (D)
	Christopher C. Harris (D)
	s. 1914
	J. Thomas Heflin (D)
	Richmond P. Hobson (D)
	William O. Mulkey (D)
	s. 1914
	William Richardson (D)
	d. Mar. 1914
	George W. Taylor (D)
	Oscar W. Underwood (D)

Arizona

Senators	Representative
Henry F. Ashurst (D)	Carl Hayden (D)
Marcus A. Smith (D)	

Arkansas

Senators	Representatives
James P. Clarke (D)	Thaddeus H. Caraway (D)
Joseph T. Robinson (D)	John C. Floyd (D)
	William S. Goodwin (D)
	Henderson M. Jacoway (D)
	William A. Oldfield (D)
	Samuel M. Taylor (D)
	Otis Wingo (D)

California

Senators	Representatives
George C. Perkins (R)	Charles W. Bell (R)
John D. Works (R)	Denver S. Church (D)
	Charles F. Curry (R)
	Everis A. Hayes (R)
	Julius Kahn (R)
	William Kettner (D)
	William Kent
	Joseph R. Knowland (R)
	John I. Nolan (R)
	John E. Raker (D)
	William D. Stephens (R)

(continued)

TABLE 7.46   (continued)

Mar. 4, 1913 to Mar. 3, 1915

President of The Senate	President Pro Tempore of The Senate	Speaker of The House of Representatives
Thomas R. Marshall	James P. Clarke	Champ Clark

Colorado

Senators	Representatives
Charles S. Thomas (D) John F. Shafroth (D)	Edward Keating (D) George J. Kindel (D) Harry H. Seldomridge (D) Edward T. Taylor (D)

Connecticut

Senators	Representatives
Frank B. Brandegee (R) George P. McLean (R)	Jeremiah Donovan (D) William Kennedy (D) Augustine Lonergan (D) Bryan F. Mahan (D) Thomas L. Reilly (D)

Delaware

Senators	Representative
Henry A. Du Pont (R) Willard Saulsbury (D)	Franklin Brockson (D)

Florida

Senators	Representatives
Duncan U. Fletcher (D) Nathan P. Bryan (D)	Frank Clark (R) Claude L'Engle (D) Stephen M. Sparkman (D) Emmett Wilson (D)

Georgia

Senators	Representatives

Augustine O. Bacon (D)
  d. Feb. 1914
William S. West (D)
  ta. 1914
Thomas W. Hardwick (D)
  s. 1914
Hoke Smith (D)
	William C. Adamson (D)
	Charles L. Bartlett (D)
	Thomas M. Bell (D)
	Charles R. Crisp (D)
	Charles G. Edwards (D)
	Thomas W. Hardwick (D)
	  r. Nov. 1914
	William S. Howard (D)
	Dudley M. Hughes (D)
	Gordon Lee (D)
	Frank Park (D)
	Seaborn A. Roddenbery (D)
	  d. Sep. 1913
	Samuel J. Tribble (D)
	Carl Vinson (D)
	  s. 1914
	John R. Walker

Idaho

Senators	Representatives
William E. Borah (R) James H. Brady (R)	Burton L. French (R) Addison T. Smith (R)

Illinois

Senators	Representatives

James H. Lewis (D)
Lawrence Y. Sherman (R)
	William N. Baltz (D)
	Charles M. Borchers (D)
	Fred A. Britten (R)
	Frank Buchanan (D)
	Ira C. Copley (R)
	Louis FitzHenry (D)
	Martin D. Foster (D)
	H. Robert Fowler (D)
	Thomas Gallagher (D)
	George E. Gorman (D)
	James M. Graham (D)
	Robert P. Hill (D)
	William H. Hinebaugh
	  (Progressive)
	Stephen Hoxworth (D)
	James McAndrews (D)
	James T. McDermott (D)
	  s. 1914
	John C. McKenzie (R)
	Martin B. Madden (R)
	James R. Mann (R)
	Frank T. O'Hair (D)
	George W. Prince (R)
	Henry T. Rainey (D)
	Adolph J. Sabath (D)
	Claudius U. Stone (D)
	Lawrence B. Stringer (D)
	Clyde H. Tavenner (D)
	Charles M. Thomson (R)
	William E. Williams (D)

Indiana

Senators	Representatives
Benjamin F. Shively (D) John W. Kern (D)	John A. M. Adair (D) Henry A. Barnhart (D) Cyrus Cline (D) William E. Cox (D) William A. Cullop (D) Lincoln Dixon (D) Finly H. Gray (D) Charles A. Korbly (D) Charles Lieb (D) Martin A. Morrison (D) Ralph W. Moss (D) John B. Peterson (D) George W. Rauch (D)

Iowa

Senators	Representatives

Albert B. Cummins (R)
William S. Kenyon (R)
	Maurice Connolly (D)
	James W. Good (R)
	William R. Green (R)
	Gilbert N. Haugen (R)
	Charles A. Kennedy (R)
	Sanford Kirkpatrick (D)
	Irvin S. Pepper (D)
	  d. Dec. 1913
	Solomon F. Prouty (R)
	George C. Scott (R)
	Horace M. Towner (R)
	Henry Vollmer (D)
	  s. 1914
	Frank P. Woods (R)

Kansas

Senators	Representatives
Joseph L. Bristow (R) William H. Thompson (D)	Daniel R. Anthony, Jr. (R) Philip P. Campbell (R) John R. Connelly (D) Dudley Doolittle (D) Guy T. Helvering (D) Victor Murdock (R) George A. Neeley (D) Joseph Taggart (D)

Kentucky

Senators	Representatives

William O. Bradley (R)
  d. May 1914
Johnson N. Camden (D)
  s. 1914
Ollie M. James (D)
	Alben W. Barkley (D)
	James C. Cantrill (D)
	William J. Fields (D)
	Harvey Helm (D)
	Ben Johnson (D)
	John W. Langley (R)
	Caleb Powers (R)
	Arthur B. Rouse (D)
	J. Swagar Sherley (D)
	Augustus O. Stanley (D)
	Robert Y. Thomas, Jr. (D)

Louisiana

Senators	Representatives
John R. Thornton (D) Joseph E. Ransdell (D)	James B. Aswell (D) Robert F. Broussard (D) H. Garland Dupre (D) J. Walter Elder (D) Albert Estopinal (D) Ladislas Lazaro (D) Lewis L. Morgan (D) John T. Watkins (D)

Maine

Senators	Representatives
Charles F. Johnson (D) Edwin C. Burleigh (R)	Forrest Goodwin (R) d. May 1913 Frank E. Guernsey (R) Asher C. Hinds (R) Daniel J. McGillicuddy (D) John A. Peters (R)

Maryland

Senators	Representatives

John Walter Smith (D)
William P. Jackson (R)
  r. 1914
Blair Lee (D)
  s. 1914
	Charles P. Coady (D)
	J. Harry Covington (D)
	  r. Sep. 1914
	George Konig (D)
	  d. May 1913
	David J. Lewis (D)
	J. Charles Linthicum (D)
	Jesse D. Price (D)
	  s. 1914
	Frank O. Smith (D)
	J. Fred C. Talbott (D)

Massachusetts

Senators	Representatives

Henry Cabot Lodge (R)
John W. Weeks (R)
	James M. Curley (D)
	  r. Feb. 1914
	Frederick S. Deitrick (D)
	James A. Gallivan (D)
	  s. 1914
	Augustus P. Gardner (R)
	Frederick H. Gillett (R)
	Edward Gilmore (D)
	William S. Greene (R)
	John J. Mitchell (D)
	William F. Murray (D)
	  r. Sep. 1914
	Calvin D. Paige (R)
	Andrew J. Peters (D)
	  r. Aug. 1914
	Michael F. Phelan (D)
	Ernest W. Roberts (R)
	John Jacob Rogers (R)
	Thomas C. Thacher (D)
	Allen T. Treadway (R)
	William H. Wilder (R)
	  d. Sep. 1913
	Samuel E. Winslow (R)

Michigan

Senators	Representatives
William Alden Smith (R) Charles E. Townsend (R)	Samuel W. Beakes (D) Louis C. Cramton (R) Frank E. Doremus (D) Joseph W. Fordney (R) Edward L. Hamilton (R) Patrick H. Kelley (R) Francis O. Lindquist (R) William J. MacDonald (Progressive) James C. McLaughlin (R) Carl E. Mapes (R) John M. C. Smith (R) Samuel W. Smith (R) Roy O. Woodruff (R) H. Olin Young (R) r. May 1913

Minnesota

Senators	Representatives
Knute Nelson (R) Moses E. Clapp (R)	Sydney Anderson (R) Charles R. Davis (R) Winfield S. Hammond (D) r. 1915 Charles A. Lindbergh (R) James Manahan (R) Clarence B. Miller (R) George R. Smith (R) Halvor Steenerson (R) Frederick C. Stevens (R) Andrew J. Volstead (R)

Mississippi

Senators	Representatives
John Sharp Williams (D) James K. Vardaman (D)	Ezekiel S. Candler, Jr. (D) James W. Collier (D) Pat Harrison (D) Benjamin G. Humphreys (D) Percy E. Quin (D) Thomas U. Sisson (D) Hubert D. Stephens (D) Samuel A. Witherspoon (D)

(continued)

TABLE 7.46 (continued)

Mar. 4, 1913 to Mar. 3, 1915

President of The Senate	President Pro Tempore of The Senate	Speaker of The House of Representatives
Thomas R. Marshall	James P. Clarke	Champ Clark

Missouri

Senators	Representatives

William J. Stone (D)
James A. Reed (D)
	Joshua W. Alexander (D)
	Richard Bartholdt (R)
	Charles F. Booher (D)
	William P. Borland (D)
	Champ Clark (D)
	Perl D. Decker (D)
	Clement C. Dickinson (D)
	Leonidas C. Dyer (R)
	  r. Jun. 1914
	Michael J. Gill (D)
	  s. 1914
	Courtney W. Hamlin (D)
	Walter L. Hensley (D)
	William L. Igoe (D)
	James T. Lloyd (D)
	Thomas L. Rubey (D)
	William W. Rucker (D)
	Joseph J. Russell (D)
	Dorsey W. Shackleford (D)

Montana

Senators	Representatives
Henry L. Myers (D) Thomas J. Walsh (D)	John M. Evans (D) Tom Stout (D)

Nebraska

Senators	Representatives
Gilbert M. Hitchcock (D) George W. Norris (R)	Silas R. Barton (R) Moses P. Kinkaid (R) Charles O. Lobeck (D) John A. Maguire (D) Charles H. Sloan (R) Daniel V. Stephens (D)

Nevada

Senators	Representative
Francis G. Newlands (D) Key Pittman (D)	Edwin E. Roberts (R)

New Hampshire

Senators	Representatives
Jacob H. Gallinger (R) Henry F. Hollis (D)	Eugene E. Reed (D) Raymond B. Stevens (D)

New Jersey

Senators	Representatives

James E. Martine (D)
William Hughes (D)
	J. Thompson Baker (D)
	Robert G. Bremner (D)
	  d. Feb. 1914
	William J. Browning (R)
	Dow H. Drukker (R)
	  s. 1914
	John J. Eagan (D)
	James A. Hamill (D)
	Archibald C. Hart (D)

New Jersey

Senators	Representatives

	Eugene F. Kinkead (D)
	  r. Feb. 1915
	Walter I. McCoy (D)
	  r. Oct. 1914
	Lewis J. Martin (D)
	  d. May 1913
	Richard W. Parker (R)
	  s. 1914
	Thomas J. Scully (D)
	Edward W. Townsend (D)
	William E. Tuttle, Jr. (D)
	Allan B. Walsh (D)

New Mexico

Senators	Representative
Thomas B. Catron (R) Albert B. Fall (R)	Harvey B. Fergusson (D)

New York

Senators	Representatives

Elihu Root (R)
James A. O'Gorman (D)
	Lathrop Brown (D)
	Henry Bruckner (D)
	William M. Calder (R)
	Jacob A. Cantor (D)
	John F. Carew (D)
	Walter M. Chandler (Progressive)
	John R. Clancy (D)
	Michael F. Conry (D)
	Harry H. Dale (D)
	Henry G. Danforth (R)
	Peter J. Dooling (D)
	Daniel A. Driscoll (D)
	Thomas B. Dunn (R)
	George W. Fairchild (R)
	John J. Fitzgerald (D)
	Henry George, Jr. (D)
	Robert H. Gittins (D)
	Henry M. Goldfogle (D)
	Joseph A. Goulden (D)
	Daniel J. Griffin (D)
	Charles M. Hamilton (R)
	Francis B. Harrison (D)
	  r. Sep. 1913
	Jefferson M. Levy (D)
	George W. Loft (D)
	George McClellan (D)
	James P. Maher (D)
	Edwin A. Merritt, Jr. (R)
	  d. Dec. 1914
	Herman A. Metz (D)
	Luther W. Mott (R)
	James H. O'Brien (D)
	Woodson R. Oglesby (D)
	Denis O'Leary (D)
	  r. Dec. 1914
	James S. Parker (R)
	Thomas G. Patten (D)
	Sereno E. Payne (R)
	  d. Dec. 1914
	Edmund Platt (R)
	Daniel J. Riordan (D)
	Charles B. Smith (D)
	Timothy D. Sullivann (D)
	  d. Aug. 1913
	Charles A. Talcott (D)
	Benjamin I. Taylor (D)
	Peter G. Ten Eyck (D)
	Edwin S. Underhill (D)
	Samuel Wallin (R)
	Frank E. Wilson (D)

North Carolina

Senators	Representatives
Furnifold McL. Simmons (D) Lee S. Overman (D)	Robert L. Doughton (D) John M. Faison (D) Hannibal L. Godwin (D) James M. Gudger, Jr. (D) Claude Kitchin (D) Robert N. Page (D) Edward W. Pou (D) John H. Small (D) Charles M. Stedman (D) Edwin Y. Webb (D)

North Dakota

Senators	Representatives
Porter J. McCumber (R) Asle J. Gronna (R)	Henry T. Helgesen (R) Patrick D. Norton (R) George M. Young (R)

Ohio

Senators	Representatives

Theodore E. Burton (R)
Atlee Pomerene (D)
	Alfred G. Allen (D)
	Timothy T. Ansberry (D)
	    r. Jan. 1915
	William A. Ashbrook (D)
	Ellsworth R. Bathrick (D)
	Stanley E. Bowdle (D)
	Clement L. Brumbaugh (D)
	Robert J. Bulkley (D)
	Horatio C. Claypool (D)
	Robert Crosser (D)
	Simeon D. Fess (R)
	William B. Francis (D)
	Warren Gard (D)
	J. Henry Goeke (D)
	William Gordon (D)
	John A. Key (D)
	James D. Post (D)
	William G. Sharp (D)
	    r. Jul. 1914
	Isaac R. Sherwood (D)
	Robert M. Switzer (R)
	John J. Whitacre (D)
	George White (D)
	Frank B. Willis (R)
	    r. Jan. 1915

Oklahoma

Senators	Representatives
Thomas P. Gore (D) Robert L. Owen (D)	Charles D. Carter (D) James S. Davenport (D) Scott Ferris (D) Bird S. McGuire (R) Dick T. Morgan (R) William H. Murray (D) Joseph B. Thompson (D) Claude Weaver (D)

Oregon

Senators	Representatives
George E. Chamberlain (D) Harry Lane (D)	Willis C. Hawley (R) Abraham W. Lafferty (R) Nicholas J. Sinnott (R)

Pennsylvania

Senators	Representatives
Boies Penrose (R) George T. Oliver (R)	William D. B. Ainey (R) Warren W. Bailey (D) Andrew J. Barchfeld (R) Andrew R. Brodbeck (D) James F. Burke (R) Thomas S. Butler (R) Wooda N. Carr (D) John J. Casey (D) Frank L. Dershem (D) Robert E. Diffenderfer (D) Michael Donohoe (D) George W. Edmonds (R) John R. Farr (R) George S. Graham (R) William W. Griest (R) Willis J. Hulings (Progressive) Abraham L. Keister (R) M. Clyde Kelly (R) Edgar R. Kiess (R) Aaron S. Kreider (R) Jonathan N. Langham (R) Robert E. Lee (D) John V. Lesher (D) Fred E. Lewis (R) J. Washington Logue (D) J. Hampton Moore (R) John M. Morin (R) A. Mitchell Palmer (D) Charles E. Patton (R) Stephen G. Porter (R) John H. Rothermel (D) Arthur R. Rupley (Progressive) Milton W. Shreve (R) Henry W. Temple (R) William S. Vare (R) Anderson H. Walters (R)

Rhode Island

Senators	Representatives
Henry F. Lippitt (R) Le Baron B. Colt (R)	Peter G. Gerry (D) Ambrose Kennedy (R) George F. O'Shaunessy (D)

South Carolina

Senators	Representatives
Benjamin R. Tillman (D) Ellison D. Smith (D)	Wyatt Aiken (D) James F. Byrnes (D) David E. Finley (D) Joseph T. Johnson (D) Asbury F. Lever (D) J. Willard Ragsdale (D) Richard S. Whaley (D)

South Dakota

Senators	Representatives
Coe I. Crawford (R) Thomas Sterling (R)	Charles H. Burke (R) Charles H. Dillon (R) Eben W. Martin (R)

(continued)

TABLE 7.46 (continued)

Mar. 4, 1913 to Mar. 3, 1915

President of The Senate	President Pro Tempore of The Senate	Speaker of The House of Representatives
Thomas R. Marshall	James P. Clarke	Champ Clark

Tennessee

Senators	Representatives
Luke Lea (D) John K. Shields (D)	Richard W. Austin (R) Joseph W. Byrns (D) Finis J. Garrett (D) William C. Houston (D) Cordell Hull (D) Kenneth D. McKellar (D) John A. Moon (D) Lemuel P. Padgett (D) Sam R. Sells (R) Thetus W. Sims (D)

Texas

Senators	Representatives
Charles A. Culberson (D) Morris Sheppard (D)	Jack Beall (D) James P. Buchanan (D) George F. Burgess (D) Albert S. Burleson (D) r. Mar. 1913 Oscar Callaway (D) Martin Dies (D) Joe H. Eagle (D) John Nance Garner (D) Daniel E. Garrett (D) Alexander W. Gregg (D) Rufus Hardy (D) Robert L. Henry (D) Sam Rayburn (D) James L. Slayden (D) William R. Smith (D) John H. Stephens (D) Hatton W. Sumners (D) Horace W. Vaughan (D) James Young (D)

Utah

Senators	Representatives
Reed Smoot (R) George Sutherland (R)	Joseph Howell (R) Jacob Johnson (R)

Vermont

Senators	Representatives
William P. Dillingham (R) Carroll S. Page (R)	Frank L. Greene (R) Frank Plumley (R)

Virginia

Senators	Representatives
Thomas S. Martin (D) Claude A. Swanson (D)	Charles C. Carlin (D) Henry D. Flood (D) Carter Glass (D) James Hay (D) Edward E. Holland (D) William A. Jones (D) Andrew J. Montague (D) Edward W. Saunders (D) C. Bascom Slemp (D) Walter A. Watson (D)

Washington

Senators	Representatives
Wesley L. Jones (R) Miles Poindexter (R)	James W. Bryan (R) Jacob A. Falconer (Progressive) William E. Humphrey (R) Albert Johnson (R) William L. La Follette (R)

West Virginia

Senators	Representatives
William E. Chilton (D) Nathan Goff (R)	Samuel B. Avis (R) William G. Brown, Jr. (D) John W. Davis (D) r. Aug. 1913 James A. Hughes (R) Hunter H. Moss, Jr. (R) Matthew M. Neely (D) Howard Sutherland (R)

Wisconsin

Senators	Representatives
Robert M. La Follette (R) Isaac Stephenson (R)	Edward E. Browne (R) Michael E. Burke (D) William J. Cary (R) Henry A. Cooper (R) John J. Esch (R) James A. Frear (R) Thomas F. Konop (D) Irvine L. Lenroot (R) John M. Nelson (R) Michael K. Reilly (D) William H. Stafford (R)

Wyoming

Senators	Representative
Clarence D. Clark (R) Francis E. Warren (R)	Frank W. Mondell (R)

Source: Notable Names in American History; A Tabulated Register. Third edition of *White's Conspectus of American Biography* (1973), 167–169.

TABLE 7.47 ANNUAL SALARIES OF THE UNITED STATES SENATORS AND REPRESENTATIVES, 1789–1925

Year	Salary
1789[a]	$6 per diem
1816[b]	$1,500 per year
1817	$8 per diem
1856	$3,000 per year
1866	$5,000 per year
1873[c]	$7,500 per year
1874	$5,000 per year
1907	$7,500 per year
1925	$10,000 per year

[a] Salaries of United States senators were raised in 1795 to $7 per diem but in 1796 were returned to $6 per diem.
[b] In 1816 Congress raised its own salary to $1,500 per year. Public outcry forced the repeal of this increase in 1817.
[c] The "Salary Grab" act of 1873 raised congressional salaries to $7,500, but public criticism forced its repeal in 1874.
Source: Austin, Political Facts of the United States Since 1789, Table 1.23.

Leon Czolgosz, an anarchist whose mother came to Alpena, Michigan, from Czechoslovakia a month before Czolgosz was born, killed William McKinley on September 6, 1901. McKinley paid a ceremonial visit to the Pan-American Exposition in Buffalo, New York. Greeting a long line of guests, the president found himself face-to-face with a man who held out a bandaged hand. The gauze concealed a large bore pistol from which Czolgosz fired two shots point blank into the chest and abdomen of McKinley. According to Czolgosz, he shot McKinley because he "didn't believe one man should have so much service and another man should have none." Eight days later, McKinley died, making Theodore Roosevelt president.

TABLE 7.48   PARTISAN COMPOSITION OF THE UNITED STATES SENATE, 1875–1915

Congress	Years	Democratic	Republican	Populist	Other Parties	Total Seats
44th	1875–1877	26	44	. . .	5	75
45th	1877–1879	32	40	. . .	4	76
46th	1879–1881	40	32	. . .	4	76
47th	1881–1883	36	36	. . .	3	75
48th	1883–1885	36	38	. . .	2	76
49th	1885–1887	34	40	. . .	2	76
50th	1887–1889	37	38	. . .	1	76
51st	1889–1891	37	51	. . .	. . .	88
52nd	1891–1893	38	45	1	1	85
53rd	1893–1895	44	41	2	1	88
54th	1895–1897	40	45	3	2	90
55th	1897–1899	35	49	3	3	90
56th	1899–1901	27	57	. . .	5	89
57th	1901–1903	29	55	. . .	6	90
58th	1903–1905	32	57	. . .	1	90
59th	1905–1907	31	58	. . .	1	90
60th	1907–1909	31	61	. . .	. . .	92
61st	1909–1911	32	60	. . .	. . .	92
62nd	1911–1913	44	51	. . .	. . .	95
63rd	1913–1915	51	45	. . .	. . .	96

Source: Austin, *Political Facts of the United States Since 1789,* Table 1.20.

TABLE 7.49   PARTISAN COMPOSITION OF THE UNITED STATES HOUSE OF REPRESENTATIVES, 1875–1915

Congress	Years	Democratic	Republican	Whig	American	Greenback	Populist	Unknown or No Party	Other Parties	Total Seats
44th	1875–1877	174	111	. . .	. . .	. . .	. . .	. . .	8	293
45th	1877–1879	156	137	. . .	. . .	. . .	. . .	. . .	. . .	293
46th	1879–1881	150	137	. . .	. . .	4	. . .	. . .	2	293
47th	1881–1883	129	151	. . .	. . .	4	. . .	. . .	10	293
48th	1883–1885	199	118	. . .	. . .	. . .	. . .	. . .	8	325
49th	1885–1887	183	140	. . .	. . .	1	. . .	. . .	1	325
50th	1887–1889	168	154	. . .	. . .	. . .	. . .	. . .	3	325
51st	1889–1891	152	176	. . .	. . .	. . .	. . .	. . .	3	331
52nd	1891–1893	236	87	. . .	. . .	. . .	4	. . .	5	332
53rd	1893–1895	217	126	. . .	. . .	. . .	7	. . .	6	356
54th	1895–1897	96	253	. . .	. . .	. . .	8	. . .	. . .	357
55th	1897–1899	126	207	. . .	. . .	. . .	12	. . .	12	357
56th	1899–1901	162	189	. . .	. . .	. . .	3	. . .	3	357
57th	1901–1903	153	198	. . .	. . .	. . .	3	. . .	3	357
58th	1903–1905	172	210	. . .	. . .	. . .	. . .	. . .	4	386
59th	1905–1907	135	251	. . .	. . .	. . .	. . .	. . .	. . .	386
60th	1907–1909	167	224	. . .	. . .	. . .	. . .	. . .	. . .	391
61st	1909–1911	172	219	. . .	. . .	. . .	. . .	. . .	. . .	391

Congress	Years	Democratic	Republican	Socialist	Progressive	Farmer Labor	American Labor	Other Parties	Total Seats
62nd	1911–1913	230	162	1	. . .	. . .	. . .	1	394
63rd	1913–1915	291	143	. . .	. . .	. . .	. . .	1	435

Source: Austin, *Political Facts of the United States Since 1789,* Table 1.21.

Unlike other "accidental" presidents, Roosevelt left an indelible mark upon the office, arguably more in foreign policy than anywhere else. In Europe, he insisted that the United States be accepted as an equal power. He accelerated the bonds of friendship, which had been long in the making, between Great Britain and the United States. He treated Latin America like a child over whom he had just won custody and Europe like the loser, informing both parties that the whole Western Hemisphere was an American sphere of influence. In Asia, he made sure the "open door" stayed ajar to American capital and influence.

Major Supreme Court Decisions of the Victorian Age

Munn v. Illinois **(1877)**   In this decision, one of the "Granger cases," the Supreme Court gave states the right to regulate private property in the public interest. The court held that Illinois grain laws setting maximum storage rates did not violate the Fourteenth Amendment's ban on deprivation of property without due process of law and did not restrain interstate commerce. But for the next half-century, the burden of proof was upon the states for their regulatory laws.

Civil Rights Cases **(1883)**   The Supreme Court struck down the Civil Rights Act of 1875, which forbade segregated facilities. Racial equality was delayed for eighty years when the court allowed for private segregation. The guarantee of equal protection under the Fourteenth Amendment applied against state action but not private individuals whose discrimination was beyond federal control. Later *Plessy v. Ferguson* approved segregated public facilities.

United States v. E. C. Knight Co. **(1895)**   In this first ruling on the Sherman Anti-Trust Act of 1890, the court curtailed federal regulation of monopolies by distinguishing between the interstate commerce of monopolies, subject to federal control, and their production activities, which could not be regulated. This distinction between production and commerce impeded federal control of manufacturing until *National Labor Relations Board v. Jones & Laughlin Steel Corp* (1937).

Plessy v. Ferguson **(1896)**   The "separate but equal" doctrine supporting public segregation by law gained the court's approval in this famous ruling, which concerned segregated railroad cars in Louisiana. The court held that so long as equal accommodations were provided, segregation was not discriminatory and did not deprive blacks of equal protection of the laws under the Fourteenth Amendment. This decision stood until *Brown v. Board of Education* (1954).

Lochner v. New York **(1905)**   In this decision, the court struck down a New York law placing limits on maximum working hours for bakers. The law violated the Fourteenth Amendment by restricting individual "freedom of contract" to buy and sell labor and was an excessive use of state police power. This ruling was soon modified in *Muller v. Oregon* (1908), which approved state regulated limits on women's labor on the bases of sociological and economic data that demonstrated the effects on the health and morals of women workers.

Standard Oil Co. of New Jersey v. United States **(1911)**   According to this decision, federal authorities had to apply the "rule of reason" to break up monopolies under the Sherman Anti-Trust Act. Only those combinations in restraint of trade that were contrary to the public interest, and therefore unreasonable, were illegal. The court did allow the breakup of the Standard Oil Company, one of the nation's leading monopolies; this ruling made future breakups of monopolies difficult, which encouraged the merger movement of the 1920s.

TABLE 7.50   SALARIES OF EXECUTIVE BRANCH OFFICERS AND SUPREME COURT JUSTICES, 1871–1912

Year	President	Vice President	Chief Justice	Associate Justice	Cabinet Officers
1871	$25,000	$ 8,000	$ 8,500	$ 8,000	$ 8,000
1873[a]	$50,000	$10,000	$10,500	$10,000	$10,000
1874	$50,000	$ 8,000	$10,500	$10,000	$ 8,000
1903	$50,000	$ 8,000	$13,000	$12,500	$ 8,000
1907	$50,000	$12,000	$13,000	$12,500	$12,000
1909	$75,000	$12,000	$13,000	$12,500	$12,500[b]
1912	$75,000	$12,000	$15,000	$14,500	$12,000

[a]This increase was the result of the famous "Salary Grab" act passed by Congress in 1873. Public outcry against it was strong, and for the most part the raises were rescinded the next year.
[b]The salary of the secretary of state was temporarily reduced to $8,000 so Philander C. Knox, Pennsylvania senator from 1905–1909, could take office in accordance with the constitutional requirement that no senator or representative be appointed to an office which had received a salary increase (see the U.S. Constitution, Article I, Section 6).
Source: Austin, *Political Facts of the United States Since 1789*, Table 1.22.

TABLE 7.51   SUPREME COURT JUSTICES OF THE UNITED STATES APPOINTED BETWEEN 1876 AND 1913

Justice	Tenure	Appointed by
Morrison R. Waite*	1874–1888	Ulysses S. Grant
John Marshall Harlan	1877–1911	Rutherford B. Hayes
William B. Woods	1880–1887	Rutherford B. Hayes
Stanley Matthews	1881–1889	James A. Garfield
Samuel Blatchford	1883–1893	Chester A. Arthur
Horace Gray	1881–1902	Chester A. Arthur
Melville W. Fuller*	1888–1910	Grover Cleveland
Lucius Q. C. Lamar	1888–1893	Grover Cleveland
Rufus W. Peckham	1895–1910	Grover Cleveland
Edward D. White*	1894–1921	Grover Cleveland
David J. Brewer	1889–1910	Benjamin Harrison
Henry B. Brown	1890–1906	Benjamin Harrison
Howell E. Jackson	1893–1895	Benjamin Harrison
George Shiras	1892–1903	Benjamin Harrison
Joseph McKenna	1898–1925	William McKinley
William H. Moody	1906–1910	Theodore Roosevelt
Edward D. White*	1910–1921	William Howard Taft
Mahlon Pitney	1912–1922	William Howard Taft
Willis Van Devanter	1910–1937	William Howard Taft

[a]Denotes a chief justice.
Source: Erik W. Austin, *Political Facts of the United States Since 1789* (1986), 30.

TABLE 7.52   ALABAMA GOVERNORS

Years	Governor and Party
1874–78	George S. Houston (D)
1878–82	Rufus W. Cobb (D)
1882–86	Edward A. O'Neal (D)
1886–90	Thomas Seay (D)
1890–94	Thomas G. Jones (D)
1894–96	William C. Oates (D)
1896–1900	Joseph F. Johnston (D)
1900–01	William J. Samford (D)
1901–04	William D. Jelks (D)
1904–05	Russell McW. Cunningham (D/Acting)
1907–11	Braxton B. Comer (D)
1911–15	Emmett O'Neal (D)

Source: Joseph Nathan Kane, Stephen Anzovin, and Janet Podell, eds. *Facts About the States* (1989), 6.

TABLE 7.53 ALASKA GOVERNORS

Years	District Governor
1884–85	John H. Kinkead
1885–89	A. P. Swineford
1889–93	Lyman E. Knapp
1893–97	James Sheakley
1897–1906	John G. Brady
1906–09	Wilford B. Hoggatt
1909–13	Walter E. Clark

Source: Joseph Nathan Kane, Stephen Anzovin, and Janet Podell, eds. *Facts About the States* (1989), 18.

TABLE 7.54 ARIZONA GOVERNORS

Years	Territorial Governor and Party
1877–78	John P. Joyt (R)
1878–81	John C. Fremont (R)
1881–85	Frederick A. Tritle (R)
1885–89	C. Meyer Zulick (D)
1889–90	Lewis Wolfley (R)
1890–92	John N. Irwin (R)
1892–93	Nathan O. Murphy (R)
1893–96	Lewis C. Hughes (D)
1896–97	Benjamin J. Franklin (R)
1897–98	Myron H. McCord (R)
1898–1902	Nathan O. Murphy (R)
1902–05	Alexander O. Brodie (R)
1905–09	Joseph H. Kibbey (R)
1909–11	Richard E. Sloan (R)

Years	State Governor and Party
1911–19	George W. P. Hunt (D)

Date of Admission
Feb. 14, 1912 (48th)

Source: Joseph Nathan Kane, Stephen Anzovin, and Janet Podell, eds. *Facts About the States* (1989), 27–28.

TABLE 7.55 ARKANSAS GOVERNORS

Years	Governor and Party
1874–77	Augustus H. Garland
1877–81	William R. Miller (D)
1881–83	Thomas J. Churchill (D)
1883–85	James H. Berry (D)
1885–89	Simon P. Hughes
1889–93	James P. Eagle (D)
1893–95	William P. Fishback (D)
1895–97	James P. Clarke (D)
1897–1901	Daniel W. Jones (D)
1901–07	Jeff Davis (D)
1907	John S. Little (D)
1907	John I. Moore (D/Acting)
1907–09	X. O. Pindall (D/Acting)
1909–13	George W. Donaghey (D)
1913	Joseph T. Robinson
1913	J. M. Futrell (D/Acting)

Source: Joseph Nathan Kane, Stephen Anzovin, and Janet Podell, eds. *Facts About the States* (1989), 39.

TABLE 7.56 CALIFORNIA GOVERNORS AND PARTY

Years	Governor and Party
1875–80	William Irwin (D)
1880–83	George C. Perkins (R)
1883–87	George Stoneman (D)
1887	Washington Bartlett (D)
1887–91	Robert W. Waterman (R/Acting)
1891–95	Henry H. Markham (R)
1895–99	James H. Budd (D)
1899–1903	Henry T. Gage (R)
1903–07	George C. Pardee (R)
1907–11	James N. Gillett (R)
1911–17	Hiram A. Johnson (R)

Source: Joseph Nathan Kane, Stephen Anzovin, and Janet Podell, eds. *Facts About the States* (1989), 51.

TABLE 7.57 COLORADO GOVERNORS

Years	Governor and Party
1876–79	John L. Routt (R)
1879–83	Frederick W. Pitkin (R)
1883–85	James B. Grant (D)
1885–87	Benjamin H. Eaton (R)
1887–89	Alva Adams (D)
1889–91	Job A. Cooper (R)
1891–93	John L. Routt (R)
1893–95	Davis H. Waite (Populist)
1895–97	Albert W. McIntire (R)
1897–99	Alva Adams (D)
1899–1901	Charles S. Johnson (D)
1901–03	James B. Orman (D)
1903–05	James H. Peabody (R)
1905	Alva Adams (D)
1905	James H. Peabody (R)
1905–05	Jesse F. McDonald (R)
1907–09	Henry A. Buchtel (R)
1909–13	John F. Shafroth (D)
1913–15	Elias M. Ammons (D)

Date of Admission
Aug. 1, 1876 (38th)

Source: Joseph Nathan Kane, Stephen Anzovin, and Janet Podell, eds. *Facts About The States* (1989), 65–66.

TABLE 7.58 CONNECTICUT GOVERNORS

Years	Governor and Party
1873–77	Charles R. Ingersoll (D)
1877–79	Richard D. Hubbard (D)
1879–81	Charles B. Andrews (R)
1881–83	Hobart B. Bigelow (R)
1883–85	Thomas M. Waller (D)
1885–87	Henry B. Harrison (R)
1887–89	Phineas C. Lounsbury (R)
1889–93	Morgan G. Bulkeley (R)
1893–95	Luzon B. Morris (D)
1895–97	O. Vincent Coffin (R)
1897–99	Lorrin A. Cooke (R)
1899–1901	George E. Lounsbury (R)
1901–03	George P. McLean (R)
1903–05	Abiram Chamberlain (R)
1905–07	Henry Roberts (R)
1907–09	Rollin S. Woodruff (R)
1909	George L. Lilley (R)
1909–11	Frank B. Weeks (R)
1911–15	Simeon E. Baldwin (D)

Source: Joseph Nathan Kane, Stephen Anzovin, and Janet Podell, eds. *Facts About the States* (1989), 77.

TABLE 7.59   DELAWARE GOVERNORS

Years	Governor and Party
1875–79	John P. Cochran (D)
1879–83	John W. Hall (D)
1883–87	Charles C. Stockley (D)
1887–91	Benjamin T. Biggs (D)
1891–95	Robert J. Reynolds (D)
1895	Joshua H. Marvel (R)
1895–97	William T. Watson (D/Acting)
1897–1901	Ebe W. Tunnell (D)
1901–05	John Hunn (R)
1905–09	Preston Lea (R)
1909–13	Simeon S. Pennewill (R)

Source: Joseph Nathan Kane, Stephen Anzovin, and Janet Podell, eds. *Facts About the States* (1989), 87.

TABLE 7.60   FLORIDA GOVERNORS

Years	Governor and Party
1874–77	Marcellus L. Stearns [party not given] (Acting)
1877–81	George F. Drew (D)
1881–85	William D. Bloxham (D)
1885–89	Edward A. Perry (D)
1889–93	Francis P. Fleming (D)
1893–97	Henry L. Mitchell (D)
1897–1901	William D. Bloxham (D)
1901–05	William S. Jennings (D)
1905–09	Napoleon B. Broward (D)
1909–13	Albert W. Gilchrist (D)

Source: Joseph Nathan Kane, Stephen Anzovin, and Janet Podell, eds. *Facts About the States* (1989), 94–95.

TABLE 7.61   GEORGIA GOVERNORS

Years	Governor and Party
1872–77	James M. Smith (D)
1877–82	Alfred H. Colquit (D)
1882–83	Alexander H. Stephens (D)
1883	James S. Boynton (D/Acting)
1883–86	Henry D. McDaniel (D)
1886–90	John B. Gordon (D)
1890–94	William J. Northen (D)
1894–98	William Y. Atkinson (D)
1898–1902	Allen D. Candler (D)
1902–07	Joseph M. Terrell (D)
1907–09	Hoke Smith (D)
1909–11	Joseph M. Brown (D)
1911	Hoke Smith (D)
1911–13	Joseph M. Brown (D)

Source: Joseph Nathan Kane, Stephen Anzovin, and Janet Podell, eds. *Facts About the States* (1989), 107–08.

TABLE 7.62   HAWAII GOVERNORS

Years	Territorial Governor[a]
1900–03	Sanford B. Dole
1903–07	George R. Carter
1907–13	Walter D. Frear

[a] No party given.
Source: Joseph Nathan Kane, Stephen Anzovin, and Janet Podell, eds. *Facts About the States* (1989), 122.

TABLE 7.63   IDAHO GOVERNORS

Years	Territorial Governors
1876–78	Mason Brayman
1878–80	R. A. Sidenbotham (Acting)
1880–83	John B. Neil
1883–84	Edward J. Curtis (Acting)
1884–85	William M. Bunn
1885–89	Edward A. Stevenson
1889–90	George L. Shoup

Years	State Governors
1890	George L. Shoup (R)
1890–93	Norman B. Willey (R)
1893–97	William J. McConnell (R)
1897–1901	Frank Steunenberg (D)
1901–03	Frank W. Hunt (D)
1903–05	John T. Morrison (R)
1905–09	Frank R. Gooding (R)
1909–11	James H. Brady (R)
1911–13	James H. Hawley (D)

Date of Admission
Jul. 3, 1890 (43d)

Source: Joseph Nathan Kane, Stephen Anzovin, and Janet Podell, eds. *Facts About the States* (1989), 133–34.

TABLE 7.64   ILLINOIS GOVERNORS

Years	Governor and Party
1873–77	John L. Beveridge (R)
1877–83	Shelby M. Cullom (R)
1883–85	John M. Hamilton (R)
1885–89	Richard J. Oglesby (R)
1889–93	Joseph W. Fifer (R)
1893–97	John Peter Altgeld (D)
1897–1901	John Riley Tanner (R)
1901–05	Richard Yates (R)
1905–13	Charles S. Deneen

Source: Joseph Nathan Kane, Stephen Anzovin, and Janet Podell, eds. *Facts About the States* (1989), 144.

TABLE 7.65   INDIANA GOVERNORS

Years	Governor and Party
1873–77	Thomas A. Hendricks (D)
1877–80	James D. Williams (D)
1880–81	Isaac P. Gray (D)
1881–85	Albert G. Porter (R)
1885–89	Isaac P. Gray (D)
1889–91	Alvin P. Hovey (R)
1891–93	Ira J. Chase (R)
1893–97	Claude Matthews (D)
1897–1901	James A. Mount (R)
1901–05	Winfield T. Durbin (R)
1905–09	J. Frank Hanly (R)
1909–13	Thomas R. Marshal (D)

Source: Joseph Nathan Kane, Stephen Anzovin, and Janet Podell, eds. *Facts About the States* (1989), 157.

TABLE 7.66   IOWA GOVERNORS

Years	Governor and Party
1876–77	Samuel J. Kirkwood (R)
1877–78	Joshua G. Newbold (R)
1878–82	John H. Gear (R)
1882–86	Buren R. Sherman (R)
1886–90	William Larrabee (R)
1890–94	Horace Boies (D)
1894–96	Frank Dorr Jackson (R)
1896–98	Francis M. Drake (R)
1898–1902	Leslie M. Shaw (R)
1902–08	Albert B. Cummins (R)
1908–09	Warren Garst (R)
1909–13	Beryl F. Carroll (R)

Source: Joseph Nathan Kane, Stephen Anzovin, and Janet Podell, eds. *Facts About the States* (1989), 166.

TABLE 7.69   LOUISIANA GOVERNORS

Years	Governor[a]
1873–77	William Pitt Kellogg
1877–80	Francis Tillou Nicholls
1880–81	Louis Alfred Wiltz
1881–88	Samuel Douglas McEnery
1888–92	Francis Tillou Nicholls
1892–1900	Murphy James Foster
1900–04	William Wright Heard
1904–08	Newton Crain Blanchard
1908–12	Jared Young Sanders
1912–16	Luther Egbert Hall

[a]No party given.
Source: Joseph Nathan Kane, Stephen Anzovin, and Janet Podell, eds. *Facts About the States* (1989), 200.

TABLE 7.67   KANSAS GOVERNORS

Years	Governor and Party
1873–77	Thomas A. Osborn (R)
1877–79	George T. Anthony (R)
1879–83	John P. St. John (R)
1883–85	George W. Glick (D)
1885–89	John A. Martin (R)
1889–93	Lyman U. Humphrey (R)
1893–95	Lorenzo D. Lewelling (Populist-Democrat)
1895–97	Edmund N. Morrill (R)
1897–99	John W. Leedy (D)
1899–1903	William E. Stanley (R)
1903–05	Willis J. Bailey (R)
1905–09	Edward W. Hoch (R)
1909–13	Walter R. Stubbs (R)

Source: Joseph Nathan Kane, Stephen Anzovin, and Janet Podell, eds. *Facts About the States* (1989), 177.

TABLE 7.70   MAINE GOVERNORS

Years	Governor and Party
1876–79	Seldon Connor (R)
1879–80	Alonzo Garcelon (D and Greenback)
1880–81	Daniel F. Davis (R)
1881–83	Harris M. Plaisted (D and Greenback)
1883–87	Frederick Robie (R)
1887	Joseph R. Bodwell (R)
1887–89	Sebastian S. Marble (R/Acting)
1889–93	Edwin C. Burleigh (R)
1893–97	Henry B. Cleaves (R)
1897–1901	Llewellyn Powers (R)
1901–05	John F. Hill (R)
1905–09	William T. Cobb (R)
1909–11	Bert M. Fernald (R)
1911–13	Frederic W. Plaisted (D)

Source: Joseph Nathan Kane, Stephen Anzovin, and Janet Podell, eds. *Facts About the States* (1989), 213.

TABLE 7.68   KENTUCKY GOVERNORS

Years	Governor and Party
1875–79	James B. McCreary (D)
1879–83	Luke P. Blackburn (D)
1883–87	J. Proctor Knott (D)
1887–91	Simon B. Buckner (D)
1891–95	John Young Brown (D)
1895–99	William O. Bradley (R)
1899–1900	William S. Taylor (R)
1900	William Goebel (D)
1900–07	J. C. W. Beckham (D)
1907–11	Augustus E. Willson (R)
1911–15	James B. McCreary (D)

Source: Joseph Nathan Kane, Stephen Anzovin, and Janet Podell, eds. *Facts About the States* (1989), 188.

TABLE 7.71   MARYLAND GOVERNORS

Years	Governor and Party
1876–79	John Lee Carroll (D)
1880–84	William T. Hamilton (D)
1884–85	Robert M. McLane (D)
1885–88	Henry Lloyd (D)
1888–92	Elihu E. Jackson (D)
1892–96	Frank Brown (D)
1896–1900	Lloyd Lowndes (R)
1900–04	John W. Smith (D)
1904–08	Edwin Warfield (D)
1908–12	Austin L. Crothers (D)
1912–16	Phillips L. Goldsborough (R)

Source: Joseph Nathan Kane, Stephen Anzovin, and Janet Podell, eds. *Facts About the States* (1989), 225.

TABLE 7.72 MASSACHUSETTS GOVERNORS

Years	Governor and Party
1876–79	Alex H. Rice (R)
1879–80	Thomas Talbot (R)
1880–83	John D. Long (R)
1883–84	Benjamin F. Butler (D and Independent)
1884–87	George D. Robinson (R)
1887–90	Oliver Ames (R)
1890–91	John Q. A. Brackett (R)
1891–94	William E. Russell (D)
1894–96	Frederick T. Greenhalge (R)
1896–1900	Roger Wolcott (R)
1900–03	W. Murray Crane (R)
1903–05	John L. Bates (R)
1905–06	William L. Douglas (D)
1906–09	Curtis Guild, Jr. (R)
1909–11	Eben S. Draper (R)
1911–14	Eugene N. Foss (Progressive–Democrat)

Source: Joseph Nathan Kane, Stephen Anzovin, and Janet Podell, eds. *Facts About the States* (1989), 237.

TABLE 7.73 MICHIGAN GOVERNORS

Years	Governor and Party
1873–76	John J. Bagley (R)
1877–80	Charles M. Croswell (R)
1881–82	David H. Jerome (R)
1883–84	Josiah W. Begole (D and Greenback)
1885–86	Russell A. Alger (R)
1887–90	Cyrus G. Luce (R)
1891–92	Edwin B. Winans (D)
1893–96	John T. Rich (R)
1897–1900	Hazen S. Pingree (R)
1901–04	Aaron T. Bliss (R)
1905–10	Fred M. Warner (R)
1911–12	Chase S. Osborn (R)
1913–16	Woodbridge N. Ferris (D)

Source: Joseph Nathan Kane, Stephen Anzovin, and Janet Podell, eds. *Facts About the States* (1989), 252.

TABLE 7.74 MINNESOTA GOVERNORS

Years	Governor and Party
1876–82	John S. Pillsbury (R)
1882–87	Lucius F. Hubbard (R)
1887–89	Andrew R. McGill (R)
1889–93	William R. Merriam (R)
1893–95	Knute Nelson (R)
1895–99	David M. Clough (R)
1899–01	John Lind (D)
1901–05	Samuel R. Van Sant (R)
1905–09	John A. Johnson (D)
1909–15	Adolph O. Eberhart (R)

Source: Joseph Nathan Kane, Stephen Anzovin, and Janet Podell, eds. *Facts About the States* (1989), 262–63.

TABLE 7.75 MISSISSIPPI GOVERNORS

Years	Governor and Party
1876–82	John M. Stone (D)
1882–90	Robert Lowry (D)
1890–96	John M. Stone (D)
1896–1900	Anselm J. McLaurin (D)
1900–04	Andrew H. Longino (D)
1904–08	James K. Vardaman (D)
1908–12	Edmund F. Noel (D)
1912–16	Earl L. Brewer (D)

Source: Joseph Nathan Kane, Stephen Anzovin, and Janet Podell, eds. *Facts About the States* (1989), 274.

TABLE 7.76 MISSOURI GOVERNORS

Years	Governor and Party
1875–77	Charles H. Hardin (D)
1877–81	John S. Phelps (D)
1881–85	Thomas T. Crittenden (D)
1885–87	John S. Marmaduke (D)
1887–89	Albert P. Morehouse (D/Acting)
1889–93	David R. Francis (D)
1893–97	William Joel Stone (D)
1897–1901	Lon V. Stephens (D)
1901–05	Alexander M. Dockery (D)
1905–09	Joseph W. Folk (D)
1909–13	Herbert S. Hadley (R)

Source: Joseph Nathan Kane, Stephen Anzovin, and Janet Podell, eds. *Facts About the States* (1989), 285.

TABLE 7.77 MONTANA GOVERNORS

Years	Territorial Governor [a]
1870–83	Benjamin F. Potts
1883–84	J. Schuyler Crosby
1884–85	B. Platt Carpenter
1885–87	Samuel T. Hauser
1887–89	Preston H. Leslie
1889	Benjamin F. White

[a] No party given.

Years	State Governor and Party
1889–93	Joseph K. Toole (D)
1893–97	John E. Rickards (R)
1897–1901	Robert B. Smith (D)
1901–08	Joseph K. Toole (D)
1908–13	Edwin L. Norris (D)
Date of Admission	
Nov. 8, 1889 (41st)	

Source: Joseph Nathan Kane, Stephen Anzovin, and Janet Podell, eds. *Facts About the States* (1989), 296.

TABLE 7.78 NEBRASKA GOVERNORS

Years	Governor and Party
1875–79	Silas Garber (R)
1879–83	Albinus Nance (R)
1883–87	John W. Dawes (R)
1887–91	John Milton Thayer (R/Acting)
1891	James E. Boyd (D)
1891–92	John Milton Thayer (R/Acting)
1892–93	James E. Boyd (D)
1893–95	Lorenzo Crounse (R)
1895–99	Silas Alexander Holcomb (Populist)
1899–1901	William A. Poynter (Populist)
1901	Charles Henry Dietrich (R)
1901–03	Ezra Perin Savage (R)
1903–07	John Hopwood Mickey (R)
1907–09	George Lawson Sheldon (R)
1909–11	Ashton C. Shallenberger (D)
1911–13	Chester Hardy Aldrich (R)

Source: Joseph Nathan Kane, Stephen Anzovin, and Janet Podell, eds. *Facts About the States* (1989), 307.

TABLE 7.79 NEVADA GOVERNORS

Years	Governor and Party
1871–79	L. R. Bradley (D)
1879–83	John H. Kinkead (R)
1883–87	Jewett W. Adams (D)
1887–90	Christopher C. Stephenson (R)
1890–91	Frank Bell (Acting)
1891–95	Roswell K. Colcord (R)
1895–96	John E. Jones (Silver Party)
1896–99	Reinhold Sadler (Silver Party/Acting)
1899–1903	Reinhold Sadler (Silver Party)
1903–08	John Sparks (Silver Democrat)
1908–11	Denver S. Dickerson (Silver Democrat)
1911–15	Tasker L. Oddie (R)

Source: Joseph Nathan Kane, Stephen Anzovin, and Janet Podell, eds. *Facts About the States* (1989), 316–17.

TABLE 7.80 NEW HAMPSHIRE GOVERNORS

Years	Governor and Party
1875–77	Person C. Cheney (R)
1877–79	Benjamin F. Prescott (R)
1879–81	Natt Head (R)
1881–83	Charles H. Bell (R)
1883–85	Samuel W. Hale (R)
1885–87	Moody Currier (R)
1887–89	Charles H. Sawyer (R)
1889–91	David H. Goodell (R)
1891–93	Hiram A. Tuttle (R)
1893–95	John B. Smith (R)
1895–97	Charles A. Busiel (R)
1897–99	George A. Ramsdell (R)
1899–1901	Frank W. Rollins (R)
1901–03	Chester B. Jordan (R)
1903–05	Nahum J. Bachelder (R)
1905–07	John McLane (R)
1907–09	Charles M. Floyd (R)
1909–11	Henry B. Quimby (R)
1911–13	Robert P. Bass (R)

Source: Joseph Nathan Kane, Stephen Anzovin, and Janet Podell, eds. *Facts About the States* (1989), 328.

TABLE 7.81 NEW JERSEY GOVERNORS

Years	Governor and Party
1875–78	Joseph D. Bedle (D)
1878–81	George B. McClellen (D)
1881–84	George C. Ludlow (D)
1884–87	Leon Abbett (D)
1887–90	Robert S. Green (D)
1890–93	Leon Abbett (D)
1893–96	George T. Werts (D)
1896–98	John W. Griggs (R)
1898	Foster M. Voorhees (R/Acting)
1898–99	David O. Watkins (R/Acting)
1899–1902	Foster M. Voorhees (R)
1902–05	Franklin Murphy (R)
1905–08	Edward C. Stokes (R)
1908–11	John Franklin Fort (R)
1911–13	Woodrow Wilson (D)
1913	James F. Fielder (D/Acting)
1913–14	Leon R. Taylor (D/Acting)

Source: Joseph Nathan Kane, Stephen Anzovin, and Janet Podell, eds. *Facts About the States* (1989), 339.

TABLE 7.82 NEW MEXICO GOVERNORS

Years	Territorial Governor[a]
1875–78	Samuel B. Axtell
1878–81	Lewis (Lew) Wallace
1881–85	Lionel A. Sheldon
1885–89	Edmund G. Ross
1889–93	L. Bradford Prince
1893–97	William T. Thornton
1897–1906	Miguel A. Otero
1906–07	Herbert J. Hagerma
1907	J. W. Raynolds (Acting)
1907–10	George Curry
1910–12	William J. Mills

[a] No party given.

Year	State Governor
1912–17	William C. McDonald (D)
Date of Admission	
Jan. 6, 1912 (47th)	

Source: Joseph Nathan Kane, Stephen Anzovin, and Janet Podell, eds. *Facts About the States* (1989), 351.

TABLE 7.83　NEW YORK GOVERNORS

Years	Governor and Party
1875–76	Samuel J. Tilden (D)
1877–79	Lucius Robinson (D)
1880–82	Alonzo B. Cornell (R)
1883–85	Grover Cleveland (D)
1885	David B. Hill (D/Acting)
1886–91	David B. Hill (D)
1892–94	Roswell P. Flower (D)
1895–96	Levi P. Morton (R)
1897–98	Frank S. Black (R)
1899–1900	Theodore Roosevelt (R)
1901–04	Benjamin B. Odell, Jr. (R)
1905–06	Frank W. Higgins (R)
1907–10	Charles Evans Hughes (R)
1910	Horace White (R/Acting)
1911–12	John Alden Dix (D)
1913	William Sulzer (D)
1913–14	Martin Glynn (D/Acting)

Source: Joseph Nathan Kane, Stephen Anzovin, and Janet Podell, eds. *Facts About the States* (1989), 366.

TABLE 7.84　NORTH CAROLINA GOVERNORS

Years	Governor and Party
1874–77	Curtis H. Brogden (R)
1877–79	Zebulon B. Vance (D)
1879–85	Thomas J. Jarvis (D)
1885–89	Alfred M. Scales (D)
1889–91	Daniel G. Fowle (D)
1891–93	Thomas M. Holt (D)
1893–97	Elias Carr (D)
1897–1901	Daniel L. Russell (R)
1901–05	Charles B. Aycock (D)
1905–09	Robert B. Glenn (D)
1901–13	William W. Kitchin (D)

Source: Joseph Nathan Kane, Stephen Anzovin, and Janet Podell, eds. *Facts About the States* (1989), 381.

TABLE 7.85　NORTH DAKOTA GOVERNORS

Years	Territorial Governor[a]
1874–78	John L. Pennington
1878–80	William A. Howard
1880–84	Nehemiah G. Ordway
1884–87	Gilbert A. Pierce
1887–89	Louis K. Church
1889	Arthur C. Melette

[a] No party given.

Years	State Governor and Party
1889–91	John Miller (R)
1891–93	Andrew H. Burke (R)
1893–95	Eli C. D. Shortridge (Democrat–Independent)
1895–97	Roger Allin (R)
1897–98	Frank A. Briggs (R)
1898–99	Joseph M. Devine (R/Acting)
1899–1901	Frederick B. Fancher (R)
1901–05	Frank White (R)
1905–07	Elmore Y. Sarles (R)
1907–13	John Burke (D)

Date of Admission
Nov. 2, 1889 (39th)

Source: Joseph Nathan Kane, Stephen Anzovin, and Janet Podell, eds. *Facts About the States* (1989), 394.

TABLE 7.86　OHIO GOVERNORS

Years	Governor and Party
1876–77	Rutherford B. Hayes (R)
1877–78	Thomas L. Young (R)
1878–80	Richard M. Bishop (D)
1880–84	Charles Foster (R)
1884–86	George Hoadly (D)
1886–90	Joseph B. Foraker (R)
1890–92	James E. Campbell (D)
1892–96	William McKinley (R)
1896–1900	Asa S. Bushnell (R)
1900–04	George K. Nash (R)
1904–06	Myron T. Herrick (R)
1906	John M. Pattison (D)
1906–09	Andrew L. Harris (R)
1909–13	Judson Harmon (D)

Source: Joseph Nathan Kane, Stephen Anzovin, and Janet Podell, eds. *Facts About the States* (1989), 404–405.

TABLE 7.87　OKLAHOMA GOVERNORS

Years	Territorial Governor[a]
1890–91	George W. Steele
1891–92	Robert Martin (Acting)
1892–93	Abraham J. Seay
1893–97	William C. Renfrow
1897–1901	Cassius M. Barnes
1901	William M. Jenkins
1901	William Grimes (Acting)
1901–06	Thompson B. Ferguson
1906–07	Frank Frantz

[a] No party given

Years	State Governor and Party
1907–11	Charles N. Haskell (D)
1911–15	Lee Cruce (D)

Date of Admission
Nov. 16, 1907 (46th)

Source: Joseph Nathan Kane, Stephen Anzovin, and Janet Podell, eds. *Facts About the States* (1989), 415–16.

TABLE 7.88　OREGON GOVERNORS

Years	Governor and Party
1870–77	La Fayette Grover (D)
1877–78	Stephen F. Chadwick (D/Acting)
1878–82	William W. Thayer (D)
1882–87	Zenas F. Moody (R)
1887–95	Sylvester Pennoyer (Democrat–Populist)
1895–99	William P. Lord (R)
1899–1903	T. T. Greer (R)
1903–09	George E. Chamberlain (D)
1909–10	Frank W. Benson (R/Acting)
1910–11	Jay Bowerman (R/Acting)
1911–15	Oswald West (D)

Date of Admission
Nov. 6, 1907 (33rd)

Source: Joseph Nathan Kane, Stephen Anzovin, and Janet Podell, eds. *Facts About the States* (1989), 426.

TABLE 7.89   PENNSYLVANIA GOVERNORS

Years	Governor and Party
1873–79	John Frederick Hartranft (R)
1879–83	Henry Martyn Hoyt (R)
1883–87	Robert Emory Pattison (D)
1887–91	James Addams Beaver (R)
1891–95	Robert Emory Pattison (D)
1895–99	Daniel H. Hastings (R)
1899–1903	William A. Stone (R)
1903–07	Samuel W. Pennypacker (R)
1907–11	Edwin S. Stuart (R)
1911–15	John K. Tener (R)

Source: Joseph Nathan Kane, Stephen Anzovin, and Janet Podell, eds. *Facts About the States* (1989), 439.

TABLE 7.90   RHODE ISLAND GOVERNORS

Years	Governor and Party
1875–77	Henry Lippitt (R)
1877–80	Charles C. Van Zandt (R)
1880–83	Alfred H. Littlefield (R)
1883–85	Augustus O. Bourn (R)
1885–87	George P. Wetmore (R)
1887–88	John W. Davis (D)
1888–89	Royal C. Taft (R)
1889–90	Herbert W. Ladd (R)
1890–91	John W. Davis (D)
1891–92	Herbert W. Ladd (R)
1892–95	D. Russell Brown (R)
1895–97	Charles W. Lippitt (R)
1897–1900	Elisha Dyer (R)
1900–01	William Gregory (R)
1901–03	Charles D. Kimball (R)
1903–05	Lucius F. C. Garvin (D)
1905–07	George H. Utter (R)
1907–09	James H. Higgins (D)
1909–15	Aram J. Pothier (R)

Source: Joseph Nathan Kane, Stephen Anzovin, and Janet Podell, eds. *Facts About the States* (1989), 452.

TABLE 7.91   SOUTH CAROLINA GOVERNORS

Years	Governor and Party
1874–76	Daniel H. Chamberlain (R)
1876–79	Wade Hampton (R)
1879–80	William D. Simpson (D/Acting)
1880	Thomas B. Jeter (D)
1880–82	Johnson Hagood (D)
1882–86	Hugh S. Thompson (D)
1886	John C. Sheppard (D/Acting)
1886–90	John P. Richardson (D)
1890–94	Benjamin R. Tillman (D)
1894–97	John G. Evans (D)
1897–99	William H. Ellerbe (D)
1899–1903	Miles B. McSweeney (D)
1903–07	Duncan C. Heyward (D)
1907–11	Martin F. Ansel (D)
1911–15	Coleman L. Blease (D)

Source: Joseph Nathan Kane, Stephen Anzovin, and Janet Podell, eds. *Facts About the States* (1989), 464.

TABLE 7.92   SOUTH DAKOTA GOVERNORS

Years	Territorial Governor[a]
1874–78	John L. Pennington
1878–80	William A. Howard
1880–84	Nehemiah G. Ordway
1884–89	Gilbert A. Pierce
1889	Arthur C. Mellette

[a] No party given.

Year	State Governor and Party
1889–93	Arthur C. Mellette (R)
1893–97	Charles H. Sheldon (R)
1897–1901	Andrew E. Lee (Populist–Democrat)
1901–05	Charles N. Herreid (R)
1905–07	Samuel H. Elrod (R)
1907–09	Coe I. Crawford (R)
1909–13	Robert S. Vessey (R)

Date of Admission
Nov. 2, 1889 (40th)

Source: Joseph Nathan Kane, Stephen Anzovin, and Janet Podell, eds. *Facts About the States* (1989), 476.

TABLE 7.93   TENNESSEE GOVERNORS

Years	Governor and Party
1875–79	James D. Porter (D)
1879–81	Albert S. Marks (D)
1881–83	Alvin Hawkins (R)
1883–87	William B. Bate (D)
1887–91	Robert L. Taylor (D)
1891–93	John P. Buchanan (D)
1893–97	Peter Turney (D)
1897–99	Robert L. Taylor (D)
1899–1903	Benton McMillin (D)
1903–05	James B. Frazier (D)
1905–07	John I. Cox (D)
1907–11	Malcolm R. Patterson (D)
1911–15	Ben W. Hooper (R)

Source: Joseph Nathan Kane, Stephen Anzovin, and Janet Podell, eds. *Facts About the States* (1989), 486.

TABLE 7.94   TEXAS GOVERNORS

Years	Governor and Party
1876–79	Richard B. Hubbard (D)
1879–83	Oran M. Roberts (D)
1883–87	John Ireland (D)
1887–91	Lawrence S. Ross (R)
1891–95	James S. Hogg (D)
1895–99	Charles A. Culberton (D)
1899–1903	Joseph D. Sayers (D)
1903–07	W. T. Lanham (D)
1907–11	Thomas M. Campbell (D)
1911–15	Oscar B. Colquitt (D)

Source: Joseph Nathan Kane, Stephen Anzovin, and Janet Podell, eds. *Facts About the States* (1989), 499.

TABLE 7.95   UTAH GOVERNORS

Years	Territorial Governor[a]
1875–80	George B. Emery
1880–86	Eli H. Murray
1886–89	Caleb W. West
1889–93	Arthur L. Thomas
1893–96	Caleb W. West

[a] No party given.

Year	State Governor and Party
1896–1905	Heber M. Wells (R)
1905–09	John C. Cutler (R)
1909–17	William Spry (R)
Date of Admission	
Jan. 4, 1896 (45th)	

Source: Joseph Nathan Kane, Stephen Anzovin, and Janet Podell, eds. *Facts About the States* (1989), 514.

TABLE 7.96   VERMONT GOVERNORS

Years	Governor and Party
1874–76	Asahel Peck (R)
1876–78	Horace Fairbanks (R)
1878–80	Redfield Proctor (R)
1880–82	Rosewell Farnham (R)
1882–84	John L. Barstow (R)
1884–86	Samuel E. Pingree (R)
1886–88	Ebenezer J. Ormsbee (R)
1888–90	William P. Dillingham (R)
1890–92	Carroll S. Page (R)
1892–94	Levi K. Fuller (R)
1894–96	Urban A. Woodbury (R)
1896–98	Josiah Grout (R)
1898–1900	Edward C. Smith (R)
1900–02	Wiliam W. Stickney (R)
1902–04	John G. McCullough (R)
1904–06	Charles J. Bell (R)
1906–08	Fletcher D. Proctor (R)
1908–10	George H. Prouty (R)
1910–12	John A. Mead (R)
1912–15	Allen M. Fletcher (R)

Source: Joseph Nathan Kane, Stephen Anzovin, and Janet Podell, eds. *Facts About the States* (1989), 525.

TABLE 7.97   VIRGINIA GOVERNORS

Years	Governor and Party
1874–78	James L. Kemper (D)
1878–82	Frederick Holliday (Conservative)
1882–86	William E. Cameron (Readjuster)
1886–90	Fitzhugh Lee (D)
1890–94	Philip W. McKinney (D)
1894–98	Charles T. O'Ferrall (D)
1898–1902	J. Hoge Tyler (D)
1902–06	Andrew J. Montague (D)
1906–10	Claude A. Swanson (D)
1910–14	William H. Mann (D)

Source: Joseph Nathan Kane, Stephen Anzovin, and Janet Podell, eds. *Facts About the States* (1989), 537.

TABLE 7.98   WASHINGTON GOVERNORS

Years	Territorial Governors[a]
1872–80	Elisha P. Ferry
1880–84	William A. Newell
1884–87	Watson C. Squir
1887–89	Eugene Semple
1889	Miles Conway Moore

[a] No party given.

Year	State Governors
1889–93	Elisha P. Ferry (R)
1893–97	John Harte McGraw (R)
1897–1901	John Rankin Rogers (Democrat/Populist)
1901–05	Henry McBride (R/Acting)
1905–09	Albert Edward Mead (R)
1909	Samuel G. Cosgrove (R)
1909–13	Marion E. Hay (R/Acting)
Date of Admission	
Nov. 11, 1889 (42nd)	

Source: Joseph Nathan Kane, Stephen Anzovin, and Janet Podell, eds. *Facts About the States* (1989), 550.

TABLE 7.99   WEST VIRGINIA GOVERNORS

Years	Governor and Party
1871–77	John J. Jacob (R)
1877–81	Henry M. Mathews (R)
1881–85	Jacob B. Jackson (D)
1885–90	E. Willis Wilson (D)
1890–93	A. Brooks Fleming (D)
1893–97	William A. MacCorkle (D)
1897–1901	George W. Atkinson (R)
1901–05	Albert B. White (R)
1905–09	William M. O. Dawson (R)
1909–13	William E. Glasscock (R)

Source: Joseph Nathan Kane, Stephen Anzovin, and Janet Podell, eds. *Facts About the States* (1989), 563.

TABLE 7.100   WISCONSIN GOVERNORS

Years	Governor and Party
1874–76	William R. Taylor (Democratic/Greenback)
1876–78	Harrison Ludington (R)
1878–82	William E. Smith (R)
1882–89	Jeremiah M. Rusk (R)
1889–91	William D. Hoard (R)
1891–95	George W. Peck (D)
1895–97	William H. Upham (R)
1897–1901	Edward Scofield (R)
1901–06	Robert M. La Follette, Sr. (R)
1906–11	James O. Davidson (R)
1911–15	Francis E. McGovern (R)

Source: Joseph Nathan Kane, Stephen Anzovin, and Janet Podell, eds. *Facts About the States* (1989), 573.

TABLE 7.101 WYOMING GOVERNORS

Years	Territorial Governor [a]
1875–78	John M. Thayer
1878–82	John W. Hoyt
1882–85	William Hale
1885–86	Francis E. Warren
1886	George W. Baxter
1887–89	Thomas Moonlight
1889–90	Francis E. Warren

[a] No party given.

Year	State Governor and Party
1890	Francis E. Warren (R)
1890–91	Amos W. Barber (R/Acting)
1893–95	John E. Osborne (D)
1895–99	William A. Richards (R)
1899–1903	De Forest Richards (R)
1903–05	Fenimore Chatterton (R/Acting)
1905–11	Bryant B. Brooks (R)
1911–15	Joseph M. Carey (D)

Date of Admission
Jul. 10, 1890 (44th)

Source: Joseph Nathan Kane, Stephen Anzovin, and Janet Podell, eds. *Facts About the States* (1989), 583.

TABLE 7.102 DISTRICT OF COLUMBIA AND PUERTO RICO GOVERNORS

District of Columbia	
Governors	Date of Admission
[no governors]	1791, Capital transferred from Philadelphia in 1800

Source: Joseph Nathan Kane, Stephen Anzovin, and Janet Podell, eds. *Facts About the States* (1989), 522.

Puerto Rico	
Governors	Date of Admission
[no governors]	Dec. 10, 1898, Ceded to the United States by Spain after the Spanish-American War

Source: Joseph Nathan Kane, Stephen Anzovin, and Janet Podell, eds. *Facts About the States* (1989), 530–31.

Suffrage Restrictions in the Southern States

While voter participation at the national level was on the increase, southern states were taking deliberate measures to restrict the electorate, especially black voters who had been enfranchised by the Fourteenth and Fifteenth Amendments to the United States Constitution. A variety of techniques was used. Most effective was the poll tax, a per-capita tax on all males twenty-one years of age and over that discouraged the poor, black and white, from voting. Registration procedures with residency requirements disfranchised many who constantly moved to find work. Multiple ballot boxes, secret ballots, and literacy requirements were also devised to prevent thousands of blacks—who, as slaves, were forbidden to learn to read and write—from voting.

Because many of the suffrage restriction provisions also disfranchised poor whites, southern states called conventions—ostensibly to reform voting procedures—to revise their constitutions. These "Jim Crow" constitutions began with Mississippi in 1890 and continued into the twentieth century. Southern states used them to incorporate into state constitutions restrictions on voting, along with clauses such as the "grandfather" clause (voting restricted to those eligible before a specified date, typically before ratification of the Fifteenth Amendment giving blacks the vote) or the "understanding" clause (a literacy restriction typically calling for reading and interpretation of a section of the Constitution) so as to allow poor whites to vote. Constitutional conventions were held in Mississippi in 1890, South Carolina 1895, Louisiana 1896, North Carolina 1900, Alabama 1901, Virginia 1902, Georgia 1908, and Oklahoma 1910.

Financing the Government

Incredible as it may seem today, the federal government had budget surpluses during much of this period. Pres. Chester A. Arthur decided to put the surplus into modernizing the U.S. Navy. Customs duties provided the bulk of the revenue, enabling the nation to keep internal taxes very low. Eventually, the nation would come to rely more heavily on the income tax.

The Military

The GAR

The Grand Army of the Republic, or GAR, was an organization of Union war veterans that grew in the years after the Civil War into a potent political force. Veterans met for encampments ("conventions") to celebrate and relive their Civil War experiences. They became associated as a political force with a political technique known as "waving the bloody shirt" in which the speaker would associate the Democratic Party with disloyalty and rebellion. In the 1880s, they served effectively as a Republican political action committee, with the Civil War veterans' pension system being their most famous achievement. By the 1890s, members numbered over 400,000.

In 1888, the U.S. Congress passed a generous veterans bill to give a lifetime pension to every veteran who had served at least ninety days in the wartime army and was disabled for any reason. If a veteran fell off a porch, he was eligible. Unlike today's government, the U.S. Treasury had a surplus of funds on the order of $100 million per year, which it was anxious to spend.

President Cleveland vetoed this law, and the Republicans ran against him on the slogan "Vote Yourself a Pension" and won the election. The new president, Benjamin Harrison, signed an even more generous Dependent Pensions Act, and the head of the GAR, James "Corporal" Tanner, was appointed to distribute the loot. "God help the surplus" was Tanner's slogan, and he meant it. By the end of Harrison's term, pensions to former Union soldiers reached $160 million. Newspaper gossip columns took wry notice of young women marrying doddering old Yankee soldiers. As late as 1983, forty-one Civil War widows were still receiving a monthly check of about $70 from the federal government.

Southern veterans had to rely on state government appropriations and received none of the federal largesse.

TABLE 7.103 CHRONOLOGY OF PASSAGE OF MAJOR RESTRICTIVE STATUTES IN ALL SOUTHERN STATES, 1870–1918

Year	Poll Tax	Registration	Multiple-Box	Secret Ballot	Literacy Test	Property Test	Understanding Clause	Grandfather Clause
1871	Ga.							
1872								
1873								
1874								
1875	Va.							
1876								
1877	Ga.							
1878								
1879								
1880								
1881	Va. (repealed)							
1882		S.C.	S.C.					
1883								
1884								
1885								
1886								
1887								
1888								
1889	Fla.	Tenn.	Fla.	Tenn.				
1890	Miss. Tenn.			Miss.	Miss.		Miss.	
1891				Ark.				
1892	Ark.							
1893		Ala.		Ala.				
1894		S.C.		Va.				
1895	S.C.				S.C.		S.C.	
1896								
1897		La.		La.				
1898	La.				La.	La.		La.
1899		N.C.	N.C.					
1900	N.C.				N.C.	N.C.		N.C.
1901	Ala.				Ala.	Ala.		Ala.
1902	Va. Tex.				Va.	Va.	Va.	
1903				Tex.				
1904								
1905								
1906								
1907								
1908					Ga.	Ga.	Ga.	Ga.

Source: J. Morgan Kousser, The Shaping of Southern Politics: Suffrage Restriction and the Establishment of the One-Party South, 1880–1910, (1974), 239.

TABLE 7.104 IMPACT OF CHANGES IN CONSTITUTIONAL SUFFRAGE REQUIREMENTS ON VOTER REGISTRATION

Registration figures from the southern states, collected from official and scattered unofficial sources, reveal some of the impact of constitutional changes in suffrage requirements as Jim Crow segregation spread across the South.

State	Year	% Whites Registered	% Blacks Registered
Ala.	1902	74.8	1.3
Ala.	1908[a]	87.7	1.8
Ga.	1904[b]	66.6	28.3
Ga.	1910	73.9	4.3
La.	1898[a,b]	46.6	9.5
La.	1904[a]	52.5	1.1
Miss.	1892[a]	53.8	5.4

State	Year	% Whites Registered	% Blacks Registered
Miss.	1896[a]	76.2	8.5
Miss.	1904	. . .	7.1
Miss.	1908	62.9	7.5
N.C.	1902	. . .	4.6
N.C.	1904	. . .	4.6
S.C.	1896	41.9	3.8
S.C.	1897	73.7	8.2
S.C.	1900	79.8	9.1
S.C.	1904	. . .	13.8
Va.	1900[b]	. . .	. . .
Va.	1904	. . .	15.2
Va.	1905	83.6	13.7

[a]Official registration figures. All others are unofficial estimates.
[b]Denotes registration figure predating constitutional suffrage limitations.
Source: Kousser, The Shaping of Southern Politics: Suffrage Restriction and the Establishment of the One-Party South, 1880–1910, 61.

TABLE 7.105 SOURCES OF FEDERAL REVENUE

1800		1836		1845		1890		1925		1945	
Source	%	Source	%	Source	%	Source	%	Source	%	Source	%
Customs	82.7	Customs	45.9	Customs	91.85	Customs	61.7	Customs	14.4	Individual income	39.9
Int. Rev.	7.5	Public lands	48.9	Public lands	6.9	Liquor & tobacco	38.0	Tobacco	9.1	Corp. income	10.2
All others	10.8	All others	5.2	All others	1.25	All others	3.0	Indiv. income	22.4	Excess profits	23.3
								Corp. income	24.2	Liquor	4.8
								Foreign debt	4.9	Tobacco	1.9
								Estate and gifts	2.9	All others	19.7
								All others	18.4		

Source: From the U.S. Treasury, *Annual Report,* 1945, found in Morris, ed., *Encyclopedia of American History,* 531.

TABLE 7.106 FEDERAL GOVERNMENT FINANCES, 1876–1912

In thousands of dollars

Year	Receipts	Expenditures	Surplus/Deficit
1876	294,096	265,101	28,995
1880	333,527	267,643	65,884
1884	348,520	244,126	104,394
1888	379,266	267,925	111,341
1892	354,938	345,023	9,914
1896	338,142	352,179	−14,037
1900	567,241	520,861	46,380
1904	541,087	583,660	−42,573
1908	601,862	659,196	−57,334
1912	692,609	689,881	2,728

Source: The World Almanac and Encyclopedia 1921, (1920), 421.

Spanish-American War

Secretary of State John Hay called it "a splendid little war." Theodore Roosevelt resigned his post as undersecretary of the navy to fight in it. Crowds gathered in the Midwest to yell, "Remember the *Maine;* to hell with Spain." Americans saw the Spanish-American War as a chance to show their country as a world power. Yet it was a war that exposed the weakness and ineptitude of the U.S. Army. Domestically, it was an opportunity to solidify national unity by having northern and southern boys fight together against Spain. The war set off a chain of events, including a national debate between imperialists and anti-imperialists, that led to the annexation of the Philippines, Hawaii, and Puerto Rico, and almost to the annexation of Cuba.

TABLE 7.107 FEDERAL GOVERNMENT RECEIPTS, BY SOURCE, 1876–1913[a]

Year or Period	Total[b]	Customs	Internal Revenue	Other Receipts Total, Excl. Sales of Public Lands	Sales of Public Lands
1876	294,096	148,072	116,701	29,323	1,129
1877	281,406	130,956	118,620	31,820	976
1878	257,764	130,171	110,581	17,012	1,080
1879	273,827	137,250	113,562	23,016	925
1880	333,522	186,522	124,009	22,995	1,017
1881	360,782	198,160	135,264	27,358	2,202
1882	403,525	220,411	146,498	36,617	4,753
1883	398,288	314,706	144,720	38,861	7,956
1884	348,520	195,067	121,586	31,866	9,811
1885	323,691	181,472	112,499	29,720	5,706
1886	336,440	192,905	116,806	26,729	5,631
1887	371,403	217,287	118,823	35,293	9,254
1888	397,266	219,091	124,297	35,878	11,202
1889	387,050	223,833	130,882	32,336	8,039
1890	403,081	229,669	142,607	30,806	6,358
1891	392,612	219,522	145,686	27,404	4,030
1892	354,938	177,453	153,971	23,514	3,262
1893	385,820	203,355	161,028	21,437	3,182
1894	306,355	131,819	147,111	27,426	1,674
1895	324,729	152,159	143,422	29,149	1,103
1896	338,142	160,022	146,763	31,358	1,006
1897	347,722	176,554	146,689	24,479	865
1898	405,321	149,575	170,901	84,846	1,243
1899	515,961	206,128	273,437	36,395	1,780
1900	567,241	233,165	295,328	38,748	1,837

(continued)

TABLE 7.107 (continued)

Year or Period	Total [b]	Customs	Internal Revenue	Other Receipts	
				Total, Excl. Sales of Public Lands	Sales of Public Lands
1901	587,685	238,585	307,181	41,919	2,965
1902	562,478	254,445	271,880	36,153	4,144
1903	561,881	284,480	230,810	46,591	8,926
1904	541,087	261,275	232,904	46,908	7,453
1905	544,275	261,799	234,096	48,380	4,859
1906	594,984	300,252	249,150	45,582	4,880
1907	665,860	332,233	269,667	63,960	7,879
1908	601,862	286,113	251,711	64,038	9,732
1909	604,320	300,712	246,213	57,396	7,501
1910	675,512	333,683	289,934	51,895	6,356
1911	701,833	314,497	322,529	64,807	5,732
1912	692,609	311,322	321,612	59,657	5,393
1913	714,463	318,891	344,417	60,803	2,910

[a] Figures reported for the period are in thousands of dollars.
[b] Refunds of receipts are excluded starting in 1913; comparable data are not available for prior years.
Source: Austin, Political Facts of the United States Since 1789, Table 6.2.

TABLE 7.108 FEDERAL GOVERNMENT EXPENDITURES, 1876–1912

Numbers given in thousands of dollars.

Year	Total	Dept. of Army	Dept. of Navy	Vets [a]	Interest on Public Debt
1876	265,101	38,071	18,963	28,257	100,243
1880	267,643	38,117	13,537	56,777	95,758
1884	244,126	39,430	17,293	55,429	54,578
1888	267,925	38,522	16,926	80,289	44,715
1892	345,023	46,895	29,174	134,583	23,378
1896	352,179	50,831	27,148	139,434	35,385
1900	520,861	134,775	55,953	140,877	40,160
1904	583,660	165,200	102,956	142,559	24,646
1908	659,196	175,840	118,037	153,892	21,426
1912	689,881	184,123	135,592	153,591	22,616

[a] Compensations and pensions. Includes compensation for service-connected injuries and deaths, as well as pensions for nonservice-connected disabilities and deaths.
Source: Historical Statistics of the United States, Colonial Times to 1957, (1961), 719.

TABLE 7.109 PER CAPITA NATIONAL DEBT

Interest on the debt as a percentage of national income approximated 2.6% at the end of the Civil War, 2.0% after World War I, 2.8% after World War II.

Year	Time Period	Amount
1790	Beginning of National Govt.	$ 19
1816	After War of 1812	15
1866	After Civil War	78
1919	After World War I	240
1948	After World War II	1,720
1958		1,630
1978		3,523

Source: Morris, ed., Encyclopedia of American History, 532; (1982), 737.

TABLE 7.110 MILITARY PERSONNEL ON ACTIVE DUTY, 1876, 1913

Year	Grand Total	Total Army	Total Navy	Total Marine Corps
1876	40,591	28,565	10,046	1,980
1913	154,914	92,756	52,202	9,956

Source: Historical Statistics of the United States, Colonial Times to 1957, 736.

TABLE 7.111 HEADS OF BRANCHES OF THE UNITED STATES ARMED SERVICES, 1869–1914

Name	Years Served	Rank	
Army [a]			
William T. Sherman	1869–1883	General	
Philip H. Sheridan	1883–1888	General	
James McA. Schofield	1888–1895	Lieutenant General	
Nathan A. Miles	1895–1903	Lieutenant General	
Samuel B. M. Young	1903–1904	Lieutenant General	
Adna R. Chaffee	1904–1906	Lieutenant General	
John C. Bates	1906–1906	Lieutenant General	
J. Franklin Bell	1906–1910	Major General	
Leonard Wood	1910–1914	Major General	

Name	Years Served	Initial Rank as Commandant	Final Rank as Commandant
Marine Corps [b]			
Jacob Zeilin	1864–1876	Colonel	Brigadier Gen.
Charles G. McCawley	1876–1891	Colonel	Colonel
Charles Heywood	1891–1903	Colonel	Maj. Gen.
George Elliott	1903–1910	Brigadier Gen.	Maj. Gen.
William P. Biddle	1911–1914	Maj. Gen.	Maj. Gen.

[a] From 1775 to 1903, the head of the army was titled commanding general of the army. In 1903 a General Staff Corps was created and the commander of the army was given the title of "Army Chief of Staff."
[b] The head of the Marine Corps is entitled commandant of the United States Marine Corps.
Source: Austin, Political Facts of the United States Since 1789, Table 5.2.

TABLE 7.112 TOTAL COSTS OF UNITED STATES WARS

In millions of dollars, except percent

War	Estimated Total War Costs	Original War Costs	Veterans' Benefits			Estimated Interest Payments on War Loans	
			Total Costs Under Present Laws	Percent of Original War Costs	Total Costs to 1970	Total	Percent of Original War Costs
Civil War (Union only)	12,952	3,200	8,580	260	8,570	1,172	37
Spanish-American War	6,460	400	6,000	1,505	5,436	60	15

Source: Austin, *Political Facts of the United States Since 1789*, Table 5.4.

Blacks played a large part in both the Cuban and Philippine campaigns. They had been placed in uniform as part of a army plan to prepare for jungle warfare by recruiting "immunes." Racism and medical ignorance led many to believe that blacks possessed a genetic immunity to malaria, yellow fever, and other tropical diseases. Consequently, when the war broke out, four black regiments—two infantry and two cavalry—saw action. Some say that Roosevelt and his Rough Riders would have been overwhelmed when they made their wild charge up San Juan Hill, had it not been for the 10th Negro Cavalry immediately to their left. About 10,000 African Americans served in the war, 4,000 of them in the "immunes."

Another oddity of the war was that most regiments were composed of the urban poor. From largely rural Indiana, for example, of those volunteers who listed their occupations, only 296 were farmers. There were 322 common laborers, 413 artisans, and 118 white-collar clerks. Only forty-seven in the regiment were professionals, and twenty-five were merchants. Another study of a Connecticut regiment found similar figures. In other words, the army of the Spanish-American War was far less representative of the general population than were the armies of the two world wars that followed.

CHAPTER 8 States and Territories

This section contains a compilation of the history and statistics of all the states and territories of the United States, including a short history of each, its official motto, flower and bird, origins of the state name, and demographic and economic facts. (The charters of some states—Kentucky, Maryland, Massachusetts, Pennsylvania, and Virginia—defined them as commonwealths.) Except for a few brief details on early history, the focus is upon the Victorian Age, 1876–1913. In the case of the thirteen original colonies, the ADMISSION DATE is the date of ratification of the Constitution. TOTAL LAND AREA and POPULATION OF MAJOR CITIES are given as of 1910; information on **Business, Famous Natives,** and **Memorable Events** are also confined to the Victorian Age.

Alabama

Alabama was formerly a part of Georgia. During the War of 1812, when the United States established military posts along the Gulf of Mexico, Alabama was made part of the territory of Mississippi. When Mississippi was admitted as a state in 1817, Alabama was designated a territory. ADMISSION DATE: December 14, 1819 (as the 22d state). CAPITAL: Montgomery. NAME: *Alabama* is from the Choctaw and is said to mean "vegetable gatherers." MOTTO: "We Dare Defend our Rights." FLOWER: goldenrod. BIRD: yellowhammer.

Land

TOTAL AREA: 52,250 sq mi. RIVERS: Alabama, Chattahoochee, Mobile, Tennessee, Tennessee-Tombigbee Waterway, Tensaw, Tombigbee. MOUNTAINS: Cumberland, Lookout, Raccoon, and Sand.

Population

1,156,300; (1876) 2,234.884 (1913). MAJOR CITIES: Birmingham (133,000), Mobile (52,000), Montgomery (38,000), Selma (14,000), Anniston (13,000).

Business

In 1900, agricultural production composed 79% of the gross state product. Lumber, timber, turpentine and resin, and cotton were major products. Although primarily an agricultural state, manufacturing industries were increasing. In 1901, 49 cotton mills were in operation and 19 were under construction. More important were the large deposits of iron, coal, limestone, and dolomite especially in the Birmingham district. The state ranked second in U.S. coke production. Manufactures included iron and steel and related foundry and machine-shop products, cast-iron pipe, stoves, car wheels, boilers, and engines. Six railroads headquartered at Birmingham, and large car shops were located there.

Famous Natives

Hugo L. Black, jurist; William Crawford Gorgas, medical doctor; W. C. Handy, blues musician; Helen Keller, author.

Memorable Events

1876	Federal troops withdrew from the state, ending Reconstruction.
1881	Booker T. Washington founded Tuskegee Institute
March 8, 1888	First Alabama steel produced at Birmingham
1898	University of Alabama became coeducational
May 1901	The constitutional convention revised the 1875 constitution and wrote a "Jim Crow" constitution, modeled after North Carolina, with grandfather and literacy clauses.

Alaska

Alaska was purchased from Russia in 1867 for $7.2 million (two cents an acre). It was a district, like the District of Columbia, under congressional control, with three judicial divisions and courts. It had a governor and a surveyor-general who was the secretary and collector of duties. It had no representation in Congress nor a legislature. Congress usually appropriated $30,000 a year for schools. Alaska had an active history during the Victorian Age, most of it associated with gold discoveries. Joe Juneau and Dick Harris made the first major gold strike in 1880 and established the miners' camp named Juneau in 1882; 1896–97 saw 60,000 men pass through Alaska in search of gold in Canada's Yukon along the Klondike River. The following year, gold was found on Anvil Creek near present-day Nome. In 1900, southeastern Alaska gold mines yielded more than $17 million; in 1902, Alaska's most productive gold field was found in the Tanana River Valley, and Fairbanks was founded at the site. ADMISSION DATE: January 3, 1959 (as the 49th state). CAPITAL: Juneau. NAME: From Aleut word *alakshak* meaning "mainland." MOTTO: "North to the future." FLOWER: forget-me-not. BIRD: willow ptarmigan.

Land

TOTAL AREA: 590,884 sq mi. RIVERS: Colville, Porcupine, Noatak, Yukon, Susitna, Copper, Kobuk, Koyukuk, Kuskokwim, Tanana. MOUNTAINS: Alaska Range (Mt. McKinley [Denali] 20,320 ft, highest in North America), Aleutian Range, Brooks Range, Kuskokwim, St. Elias. ISLANDS: Aleutian, Alexander Archipelago, Kodiak, Nunivak, Point Barrow, Pribolof, Seward Peninsula, and St. Lawrence. VOLCANOES: Mount Wrangel, Mount Blackburn, Mount Redoubt, Mount Illiamna, and Mount Augustine.

Population

64,356 (1910), of whom approximately 30,000 were Inuit, Indians, or Aleuts.

Business

Successful attempts were made to grow vegetables and cereals: cabbages raised near Skagway brought $80/ton; potatoes were raised near Dyea with irrigation; barley and oats were sown for hay, which was packed in silos because there was too little sunshine to cure it. Some experiments in growing wild crab apples succeeded. Comparatively few people owned residential land. Mining gold, copper, and iron ore were principal industries. In 1911, a 196-mile railroad joined Cordova and copper mines in the Wrangell Mountains. In 1891, Siberian reindeer were introduced to provide food for Inuit, who were threatened with starvation by the near-extinction of whales and walrus. Salmon canneries turned out a million cases (1899), outstripping those on Puget Sound in Washington.

Famous Natives

Aleksandr Baranov (b. Russia), first governor of Russian America.

Memorable Events

1880s	Gold discoveries at Juneau (1880), Fortymile Creek (1886), Nome (1898), and Fairbanks (1903).
1878	First salmon cannery established.
1884	Civil government was established with the capital at Sitka; the laws of the state of Oregon generally prevailed as administered by federal officials.
May 1902	Mount Redoubt erupted; ashes carried 90 miles; also Mount Blackburn became active and broke up Muir glacier.
1900	Juneau was made the capital.
1902	Conspiracy, led by Alexander McKenzie, president of the East Alaska Gold Company, to get possession of all mining claims at Nome, was exposed and conspirators convicted.
1903	The border between Canada and Alaska was established.
1912	Alaska became a U.S. territory with limited self-rule.
1913	Women were granted the right to vote.

Arizona

Arizona was organized as a territory of the United States on February 24, 1863. It was the last of the 48 conterminous states admitted to the union. In 1900, its population was estimated to be about 122,000: 92,000 whites, 27,000 Native Americans, 1,800 blacks, 1,400 Chinese, and 260 Japanese. A large number of Irish and Cornish miners made up the mining region; farmhands were Swedes, Germans, and Italians; Mexicans numbered one-half the foreign population. The Hopi village of Oraibi was the oldest continuously inhabited town in the United States. ADMISSION DATE: February 14, 1912 (as the 48th state). CAPITAL: Phoenix. MOTTO: "Ditat deus" (God enriches). FLOWER: saguaro cactus blossoms. BIRD: cactus wren.

Land

TOTAL AREA: 113,020 sq mi. RIVERS: Colorado, Gila, Little Colorado, Salt, and Zuni. MOUNTAINS: Black, Gila, Hualpai, Mohawk, San Francisco Peaks.

Population

28,126 (1876); 289,260 (1913). MAJOR CITIES: Tucson (13,000), Phoenix (11,000), Bisbee (9,000), Globe (7,100), Douglas (6,000).

Business

Staple crops were alfalfa, corn, wheat, barley, root crops, vegetables and fruits. Some experimental growing of sugar beets and the date palm was tried. In 1891, cattle in the Arizona territory peaked at 720,940 head; about 5 million pounds of wool were produced from 700,000 sheep. Irrigation made agriculture important. Some evidence suggested Indians also used irrigation. In 1901, 4,210 of the 5,089 farms in the territory and Indian reservation were irrigated. Farms averaged 175 acres. Rainy seasons were in December and July through September. Few reservoirs were built, and the storage capacity of canals was inadequate, but basins were being built to provide a temporary supply of water to last through the droughts and to provide runoff in times of heavy rains. Another technique to get water was the sinking of artesian wells and pumping of water into canals by electricity. Because of the scarcity of water, Arizona was chiefly a mining territory; in 1900, copper smelting and refining was the chief industry, producing $17,286,517, a sum that constituted one-half the industrial produce. In 1907, Arizona led the nation in copper production and has maintained its lead to the present.

Famous Natives

Cochise and Geronimo, Apache leaders.

Memorable Events

1877	A silver strike at Tombstone produced a boom town and population of 15,000 by 1882.
1880	The Southern Pacific Railroad reached Tucson from Yuma and continued eastward to New Mexico in 1881.
October 26, 1881	Wyatt Earp, two of his brothers, and Doc Holliday gunned down three men in Tombstone in the gunfight of the O.K. Corral.
1883	The Atlantic and Pacific Railroad crossed Arizona from east to west.
1886	Apaches were subjugated, and Geronimo surrendered.
1887–1892	The Pleasant Valley War between cattle ranchers and sheep ranchers killed 29.
1889	The territorial capital, previously at Prescott and Tucson, was moved to Phoenix.
1894	Lowell Observatory (later the discoverer of Pluto) was built at Flagstaff.
1906	Congress refused to grant statehood.
1911	Roosevelt Dam and Reservoir was built on Salt River to irrigate 245,940 acres of the Salt River valley.

Arkansas

Arkansas was part of the Louisiana Purchase territory. By the time of the De Soto expedition in 1541, Arkansas was occupied by a variety of peoples: the agrarian Quapaw in the South, the Caddo to the west and south, the Osage in the north, and the Chickasaw and Choctaw in the northeast. ADMISSION DATE: June 15, 1836 (as the 25th state). CAPITAL: Little Rock. NAME: A term for Quapaw tribe given by other Indians. MOTTO: "Regnat Populi" (The people rule). FLOWER: apple blossom. BIRD: mockingbird.

Land

TOTAL AREA: 53,850 sq mi. RIVERS: Arkansas, Mississippi, Ouachita, Red, St. Francis, White. MOUNTAINS: Ozark.

Population

675,300 (1876); 1,656,690 (1913). MAJOR CITIES: Little Rock (46,000), Fort Smith (24,000), Pine Bluff (15,000), Hot Springs (14,000), Argenta (11,000).

Business

Although Arkansas was predominantly agricultural, in the 1890s, manufacturing grew steadily. The chief industry was lumber and timber from pine in the southern portion of the state, cypress swamps in the east, and oak, walnut, hickory, and ash in the north. The value of forest products in 1900 was about $24 million. Flour and grist mills ranked second in industrial importance with a value of $3.7 million. Cotton production was 7.5% of national production, but cotton mills lagged behind those in the rest of the South. In 1900, less than $10 per square mile was invested in cotton mills. Mineral wealth of cannel, anthracite and bituminous coal, iron ore, zinc, galena, manganese, and gypsum was undeveloped.

Memorable Events

1887 Bauxite discovered southwest of Little Rock.
1891 Jim Crow laws segregated railroad coaches and waiting stations.
1892 Adoption of constitutional amendment imposing a poll tax restricted the electorate.
1898 Whites-only primary elections adopted by the Democratic Party.
1901 A number of laws were passed: the law making executions for crime private was changed to require public executions for criminal assault (aimed at deterring "negro crime").
1904 Near Ulm, William H. Fuller grew a 70-acre stand of rice, establishing it as an important crop in the state.
1906 Diamonds discovered near Murfreesboro, which became the site of the only diamond mine in the United States.

California

The history of California may be divided into three periods: The Spanish period (1769–1822), during which ecclesiastical government supported the missions; the Mexican period (1822–46), when Mexican landowners developed a settled agriculture and secularized the missions; and the American period (after 1846), marked by the sudden discovery of gold and the rise of California as a rich and populous state. The state, which was admitted to the union without ever passing through a territorial stage, was known for unique experiments in government. The Constitution of 1879 was adopted under the influence of the workingmen's movement. A precedent was established of bringing legislation to a popular vote in the form of constitutional amendments. A system of home rule was granted to cities of 3,500 or more inhabitants to draw up their own charters and rule themselves without interference by the state legislature. ADMISSION DATE: September 9, 1850 (as the 31st state) CAPITAL: Sacramento. NAME: Spanish, "hot oven." MOTTO: "Eureka" (I have found it). FLOWER: golden poppy. BIRD: California valley quail.

Land

TOTAL AREA: 158,360 sq mi. RIVERS: American, Colorado, Eel, Friant-Kern Canal, Klamath, Russian, Sacramento, Salinas, San Joaquin. MOUNTAINS: Coast Ranges, Klamath, Lassen Peak, Sierra Nevada (Mt. Whitney 14,494 ft).

Population

742,915 (1876); 2,656,750 (1913). MAJOR CITIES: San Francisco (417,000), Los Angeles (319,000), Oakland, (150,000), Sacramento (45,000), Berkeley (40,000).

Business

On January 14, 1848, James W. Marshall discovered gold at Coloma, and within two years, 100,000 people had rushed to California. Gold mining peaked in 1853, and state production shifted to grain and fruit. Fruit growing became the state's most important agricultural industry as California became the leading grower of tropical fruits, such as oranges, lemons, limes, and grapes. Film making emerged late in the Gilded Age but was to achieve its greatest significance later.

Famous Natives

Isadora Duncan, dancer; William Randolph Hearst, publisher; Jack London, author; Lincoln Steffens, reformer; Frederick Jackson Turner, historian.

Memorable Events

1892 Sierra Club founded.
1902 Sinking of the steamship *Walla Walla,* sailing from San Francisco to Puget Sound with 62 passengers and a crew of 79.
April 18, 1906 Earthquake destroyed San Francisco.
1911 The first motion-picture studio moved into Hollywood Hills.

Colorado

Colorado was organized as a territory February 28, 1861. The native peoples of Colorado included the Arapaho and the Cheyenne to the east and the Ute to the west. The state was formed from parts of Kansas, Nebraska, New Mexico, and Utah. ADMISSION DATE: August 1, 1876 (as the 38th state). CAPITAL: Denver. NAME: Spanish for "red." MOTTO: *"Nil sine numine"* (Nothing without Providence). FLOWER: Rocky Mountain columbine. BIRD: lark bunting.

Land

TOTAL AREA: 103,925 sq mi. RIVERS: Arkansas, Colorado, Green, Platte, Rio Grande. MOUNTAINS: Front Range, Laramie, Sangre de Cristo, San Juan, Sawatch Range (Mt. Elbert, 14,443 ft).

Population

132,540 (1876); 880,150 (1913). MAJOR CITIES: Denver (213,000); Pueblo (44,000); Colorado Springs (29,000); Trinidad (10,000); Boulder (9,000).

Business

The chief industries were stock raising, agriculture, and mining. In 1884, the open-range system neared a close with nearly a million cattle in Colorado, many of them driven from Texas. In 1890, more than half the state's improved farmland, a total of about 891,000 acres, was under irrigation, and by 1909, Colorado was first among states in irrigated areage with almost 3 million acres. Due to increased irrigation, flour milling, beet-sugar manufacture, and fruit canning grew. Capital invested in industries in 1900 was $62.8 million; the value of manufactured products amounted to $102.8 million. Denver was a railroad center, a distribution point for the Rocky

Mountain states, and the market for the stock-raising districts. Colorado led in the production of gold and silver ores; the value of lead smelters and refineries accounted for 23% of the total U.S. output. The state ranked ninth in the output of coal.

Famous Natives

Douglas Fairbanks, actor; Zebulon Pike, discoverer of Pike's Peak.

Memorable Events

1877	The University of Colorado opened in Boulder.
1877–80	Heyday of the silver boom at Leadville, which sported an opera house and swelled to a population of 25,000; silver production in the area reached a peak value of $11.5 million.
1879	26 soldiers and Indian agents were killed by the Ute in "Meeker's massacre" in northwestern Colorado.
1880	Ute reservation "reduced" again.
1891	Gold was discovered at Cripple Creek.
1892	The Colorado Fuel & Iron Corporation was founded; its holdings included the only integrated steel plant in the West at Pueblo (it passed under the control of Rockefeller interests in 1903.
1893	The demonetization of silver crippled prices and production of the metal; on November 2, 1893, Colorado gave women the right to vote.
1899	American Smelting and Refining Company, backed by Rockefeller (and later Guggenheim) money, absorbed six of Colorado's largest plants.
August 1, 1901	The quarto-centennial of the admission of Colorado to statehood was celebrated; an address was made by Vice Pres. Theodore Roosevelt, and a statue of Zebulon Pike was unveiled at Colorado Springs.
August 12, 1901	W. B. Helker and C. A. Yont of Denver drove a steam automobile from Colorado Springs to the top of Pike's Peak and back.
1903–04	National Guard troops broke the strikes of the Western Federation of Miners.
1912	Voters approved the adoption of the initiative and referendum.

Connecticut

Connecticut was one of the thirteen original states. Only two states are smaller. The state has been the home of the legendary Yankees, shrewd people of skill, industry, frugality, and inventive genius who took advantage of the region's water power, geographical location, supplies of capital and labor, and joint stock laws to build centers of trade and manufacturing. ADMISSION DATE: January 9, 1788 (as the 5th state). CAPITAL: Hartford. NAME: From Mahican word meaning "beside the long tidal river." MOTTO: *"Qui transtulit sustinet"* (He who transplanted still sustains). FLOWER: mountain laurel. BIRD: American robin.

Land

TOTAL AREA: 4,990 sq mi. RIVERS: Connecticut, Housatonic, Mianus, Naugatuck, Thames. MOUNTAINS: The Berkshires, Mt. Frissell (2,380 ft.).

Population

588,602 (1876); 1,179,306 (1913). MAJOR CITIES: New Haven (134,000), Bridgeport (102,000), Hartford (99,000), Waterbury (73,000), New Britain (44,000).

Business

Forestry and fishing were important industries historically, and Connecticut became an early center of manufacturing. Large insurance and banking interests moved into the state. Hartford has been known as the insurance capital of the world since 1800. Connecticut's quarries provided much of the red sandstone that became known as "brownstone" after it was used to build New York City residences.

Famous Natives

P. T. Barnum, showman; Charles A. Beard, historian; Henry Ward Beecher, reformer; Josiah Willard Gibbs, mathematical physicist; Daniel Coit Gilman, educational administrator; J. P. Morgan, financier; Frederick Law Olmsted, landscape architect; Morrison Remick Waite, jurist.

Memorable Events

1876	U.S. Coast Guard Academy founded and moved to New London in 1910.
January 28, 1878	The first commercial telephone exchange in the world was established in New Haven.
1881	Connecticut University was organized at Storrs.
1882	The national organization of the Knights of Columbus was founded at New Haven.
March 12–14, 1888	A great blizzard devastated much of the state.
August 24, 1893	A harsh storm damaged the Connecticut Valley's tobacco crop.
1901	The legislature passed a bill allowing corporations to obtain charters for a small fee and to be forever free from state taxation and supervision.

Delaware

Delaware was one of the thirteen original colonies and next-to-smallest state in the United States. Under early Dutch control, it was later conquered by the English. The du Pont family achieved a political and economic position unmatched by a single family in any other state. In 1802, E. I. du Pont de Nemours and Co., a gunpowder mill, was founded; it grew into a monopoly before diversifying into banking, media, and real estate. ADMISSION DATE: December 7, 1787 (as the 1st state). CAPITAL: Dover. NAME: From Lord De la Ware, or Delawarr, governor of Virginia, who entered the bay in 1610. MOTTO: "Liberty and independence." FLOWER: peach blossom. BIRD: blue hen chicken.

Land

TOTAL AREA: 2,050 sq mi. RIVERS: Chesapeake and Delaware Canal, Delaware, Nanticoke.

Population

137,971 (1876); 207,824 (1913). MAJOR CITIES: Wilmington (87,000).

Business

The state was famous for its orchards and fruits, which provided the foundation of its industrial base. It lay close to the market cities of Philadelphia and Baltimore. Liberal incorporation laws lured companies to establish their corporate headquarters in Delaware. The principal manufacturing industries were iron and steel products—rolling mills, car shops, machine shops, and shipbuilding plants—and the total value of the products of these industries in 1900 was 30.7% of the gross state product. Between 1890 and 1900, fruit canning and preserving industries advanced by 112%, while the manufacture of fertilizer and of cotton and woolen goods in the same period declined markedly.

Famous Natives

John P. Marquand, writer; Howard Pyle, illustrator.

Memorable Events

1878	First telephones were installed in Wilmington.
1885	Thomas Francis Bayard appointed by Pres. Grover Cleveland as secretary of state.
1889	Law enacted forbidding punishment of women at the whipping-post or pillory.
1897	Delaware adopted its present constitution.
1900	The noted illustrator Howard Pyle opened a school at Wilmington.
1905	Delaware became the last state to abolish the use of the pillory.
1909	The legislature transferred title of the Chesapeake and Delaware Canal to the U.S. government.

District of Columbia

The District of Columbia was formed by a cession of land from the states of Maryland and Virginia of about 1,000 sq. mi. on either side of the Potomac River. Before 1800, Columbia was commonly used to refer to the United States. Washington became the capital on December 1, 1800. In 1878, the administration of the District of Columbia was given to three commissioners, two appointed by the president of the United States from among the residents of the district who have lived there for three years, and a third from the U.S. Army Corps of Engineers. FORMED: March 30, 1791. CAPITAL: Washington. NAME: After Christopher Columbus. MOTTO: *"Justitia omnibus"* (Justice to all). BIRD Wood thrush. FLOWER: American beauty rose.

Land

TOTAL AREA: 70 sq mi. RIVERS: Anacostia, Potomac.

Population

159,254 (1876); 347,446 (1913).

Business

Most of the agricultural land inside the district, about 8,489 acres, was devoted to vegetable, fruit, and dairy farms; African American farmers owned 29 acres. Manufacturing establishments were those having local importance, except the products of government establishments, which formed one-fifth of the manufacturing establishments.

Famous Native

John Philip Sousa, bandleader and composer.

Memorable Events

1894	Coxey's Army marched on Washington in the midst of the nation's worst economic depression to demand relief for the unemployed.
December 1900	A centennial to celebrate the establishment of the seat of government was held in Washington.
1889	The Burnbam Commission suggested plans for beautifying Washington along the lines of the plans of L'Enfant.
1901	The commission's revised plans called for a series of handsome public buildings and the layout of parks, gardens, and avenues in an axial relationship to the Capitol, the White House, and the Washington Monument.

Florida

Florida was first visited by Ponce De León and the Spaniards who landed near St. Augustine in 1513. In 1819, the province was ceded to the United States. Florida is the southernmost state of the Union. Its pleasant climate and proximity to Latin America and the Caribbean have attracted large numbers of the elderly, many immigrants, and millions of tourists. ADMISSION DATE: March 3, 1845 (as the 27th state). CAPITAL: Tallahassee. NAME: By Juan Ponce de León for Pascua Florida (Easter festival of the flowers). MOTTO: "In God we trust." FLOWER: orange blossom. BIRD: Mockingbird.

Land

TOTAL AREA: 58,680 sq mi. RIVERS: Apalachicola, Caloosahatchee, Indian, Kissimmee, Perdido, St. Johns, St. Mary's, Suwanee, Withlacoochee.

Population

236,795 (1876); 822,719 (1913). MAJOR CITIES: Jacksonville (58,000), Tampa (38,000), Pensacola (23,000), Key West (20,000), West Tampa (8,300).

Business

In 1900, agriculture and minerals were the principal industries of the state, but tobacco manufacture ranked first in importance. The immigration of Cuban tobacco makers, the import of Cuban leaf (especially at Tampa), and the success of the "Summatra" wrapper leaf grown in the state made tobacco foremost in agricultural production. Florida ranked second to California in the raising of subtropical fruits: Oranges, lemons, limes, shaddocks, and grapefruit were raised in abundance, and pineapple production doubled in the past five years. Rich veins of phosphate were discovered in 1888; within a year, 440,000 tons were being exported, one half of the total production of the nation. Increasing quantities of phosphate were used inside the state for the production of fertilizer.

Famous Natives

Mary McLeod Bethune, educator and reformer; James Weldon Johnson, lawyer and author; Osceola, Seminole chief; Joseph Warren ("Vinegar Joe") Stillwell, army officer.

Memorable Events

1876	Florida was charged with tampering of its electoral vote in the disputed Tilden-Hayes presidential election.
1878	Statewide yellow-fever epidemic.

1883	First electric lights were installed in a Jacksonville hotel.
1886	Fire destroyed nearly half of Key West; cigar industry moved to Tampa.
1888	Yellow-fever epidemic again ravaged the state.
1898	Thousands of American soldiers embarked from Florida ports for Spanish-American war.
May 3, 1901	A fire that extended for 3 miles destroyed the greater part of the business and residential sections of Jacksonville.
1903	Daytona Beach became the scene of automobile speed tests with an R.E. Olds reaching 68 mph.
1905	Greeks established the sponge industry at Tarpon Springs.
1909	A hurricane destroyed construction work on an railroad to Key West; the railroad was finished in 1912.
1912	Carl Fisher began to develop Miami Beach as a resort.

Georgia

Georgia is one of the thirteen original states, the last of the number to be settled. Georgia has a diverse terrain from the woods of the Blue Ridge Mountains in the north to the alligators of the Okefenokee Swamp in the south. In 1732, George II granted a charter to a corporation for settlement; in 1752, Georgia received a royal patent with the same privileges and regulations as the other colonies. ADMISSION DATE: January 2, 1788 (as the 4th state). CAPITAL: Atlanta. NAME: For King George II of England, 1732. MOTTO: "Wisdom, justice, and moderation." FLOWER: Cherokee rose. BIRD: brown thrasher.

Land

TOTAL AREA: 59,475 sq mi. RIVERS: Altamaha, Apalachicola, Chattahoochee, Flint, Ocmulgee, Oconee, Savannah, Suwanee. MOUNTAINS: Blue Ridge Mountains (Mt. Enotah 4,784 ft).

Population

1,398,952 (1876); 2,732,001 (1913). MAJOR CITIES: Atlanta (155,000), Savannah (65,000), Augusta (41,000), Macon (41,000), Athens (15,000).

Business

Like most other southern states, Georgia's chief industries were agricultural, mainly cotton. Because cotton was the principal crop of the state, naturally Georgia's chief industry would be related manufactures. As manufacturing expanded during the Gilded Age, cottonseed oil and cake ranked among the first of manufactured products; numerous cotton mills grew during the 1880s and 1890s. Turpentine and resin ranked next to cotton in manufacturing importance because of extensive pine forests—especially yellow pine—that covered the state. These forests also supplied large quantities of excellent timber, but destructive methods of harvest threatened them with extinction.

Famous Natives

Tyrus ("Ty") Raymond Cobb, baseball player; John C. Frémont, explorer, politician, and soldier; Joel Chandler Harris, journalist and author; Sidney Lanier, poet.

Memorable Events

1870	Georgia ratified the Fifteenth Amendment and was readmitted to the Union.
1881	International Cotton Exposition held in Atlanta.
1886	John Styth Pemberton, a chemist, invented the formula for Coca-Cola while searching for a cure for hangover.
1893	A cyclone killed 1,000 in Charleston, South Carolina, and Savannah.
1900	In her book, *Georgia Land and People,* Francis Mitchell originated the idea of an annual celebration of the Oglethorpe party's arrival date.
1902	Martha Berry opened a school for poor mountain children.
1907	A statewide prohibition law was passed.
1912	Juliette Gordon Low of Savannah organized the Girl Scouts of America.

Hawaii

Hawaii, or the Sandwich Islands, is a small group of islands in the Pacific Ocean, 2,100 miles west-southwest of San Francisco. The United States acquired the islands by an act of Congress July 7, 1898, and they were organized as the territory of Hawaii by another act of April 30, 1900. First discovered by the Spaniards in 1549 and examined by Captain Hook in 1778, the islands remained independent throughout much of the nineteenth century. In 1893, the reigning Queen Liliuokalani was deposed, and a provisional government was formed. The next year, a republic was proclaimed with a president and a two-house legislature. For military purposes, the islands were attached to the Department of California. ADMISSION DATE: August 21, 1959 (as the 50th state). CAPITAL: Honolulu. NAME: Of unknown origin, maybe from Hawaii Loa, legendary discoverer of the islands or from Hawaiki, the traditional Polynesian homeland. MOTTO: *"Ua mau ke ea o ka aina i de pono"* (The life of the land is perpetuated in righteousness). FLOWER: pua aloalo (yellow hibiscus). BIRD: Hawaiian goose.

Land

TOTAL AREA: 6,640 sq mi. RIVERS: Kaukonahua Stream, Wailuku Stream. VOLCANOES: Hualalai, Kilauea, Mauna Kea (13,796 ft), and Mauna Loa.

Population

In 1900, a population of 154,001 included 61,111 Japanese, 39,656 Hawaiians and part Hawaiians, and 25,767 Chinese. MAJOR CITIES: Honolulu City (52,183), Ewa District (14,627), North Hilo District (12,941), Walluku District (11,742), South Hilo District (9,604).

Business

Sugar manufacture was the major industry of the islands, based upon the continued growing of sugarcane and the labor supply, and the most modern and well-equipped sugar mills were built there. Before 1900, when Hawaii had been made a territory of the United States, Chinese and Japanese labor was brought to the islands to work in the sugar fields. The act of 1900, however, subjected Hawaii to the U.S. immigration laws and restricted alien importations of cheap Asian labor. Sugar production dropped because of insufficient labor. In 1901, Henry E. Cooper, acting governor, asked the federal government to amend immigration laws to allow in a limited number of Chinese, on condition that they engage only in agricultural pursuits.

Famous Natives

Sanford Ballard Dole, jurist, president of the Republic of Hawaii, and governor; Charlotte (b. Ohio) and Luther Halsey Gulick, Camp Fire Girls founders; Victoria Kaiulani, last heiress presumptive to Hawaiian throne; Kamehameha I, king; Kamehameha III, king; Liliuokalani, queen.

Memorable Events

1876	A reciprocity treaty with the United States allowed most goods of the two countries to enter duty-free; this pact greatly stimulated the Hawaiian sugar industry.
1877–1890	More than 55,000 immigrant laborers, half of them Chinese, were brought to the islands as contract workers.
1886	A treaty allowed the introduction of Japanese contract workers and by 1908, 180,000 had arrived.
January 17, 1893	A group of American residents and Hawaiian-born sons of American missionaries deposed Queen Liliuokalani.
July 4, 1894	A new constitution established the Republic of Hawaii and named Sanford B. Dole as president.
August 12, 1898	The United States annexed Hawaii.
1900	An act of Congress established a territorial government; a fire, set by the government to combat the spread of bubonic plague in poorer neighborhoods, got out of control and destroyed Honolulu's Chinatown.
1901	James D. Dole organized the Hawaiian Pineapple Company and by 1919 production reached almost 6 million cases of canned pineapple a year.
1902	Republicans began a domination of legislative elections that lasted until 1954.
1907	A "Gentleman's Agreement" between the U.S. and Japan halted immigration to the U.S. of Japanese laborers; sugar planters began to recruit Filipino workers.
1908	The College of Agriculture and Mechanical Arts opened in Honolulu and became the University of Hawaii in 1920.
1909	The construction of a naval base at Pearl Harbor began.

Idaho

Idaho, part of the original Louisiana Purchase, was created a territory by Congress March 3, 1863. The permanent settlement of the territory began with the discovery of gold in 1860. Mormons here have their greatest influence outside Utah. ADMISSION DATE: July 3, 1890 (as the 43d state). CAPITAL: Boise. NAME: Means "gem of the mountains." MOTTO: *"Salve"* (Welcome or hail). FLOWER: syringa. BIRD: mountain bluebird.

Land

TOTAL AREA: 84,800 sq mi. RIVERS: Bear, Clearwater, Payette, Salmon, Snake. MOUNTAINS: Bitterroot Range, Centennial, Clearwater, Salmon River, Sawtooth Range (Castle Peak, 11,820 ft).

Population

25,566 (1876); 376,843 (1913). MAJOR CITIES: Boise (17,000) Coeur d'Alene (7,300), Pocatello (9,100), Lewiston (6,000), Twin Falls (5,300).

Business

Mining and agriculture were the principal industries of the state. Flour and grist-mill products and car construction and repair were of major importance, but the manufacture of timber and lumber products was the chief industry: approximately 7 million acres of timberland in the state were just beginning to be harvested. In the mountains, gold, lead, silver, and copper are mined; in 1899, Idaho ranked fourth in the production of silver in the nation and produced more than one-fifth of the nation's lead.

Famous Natives

Gutzon Borglum, sculptor; Sacajawea, Native American guide. Ezra Pound, poet.

Memorable Events

1877	Nez Percé, led by Chief Joseph, were pursued through Idaho by federal troops before surrendering in Montana.
1878	40 whites and 78 Indians died in an uprising by the Paiute and the Bannock.
1880	Silver was discovered in the Wood River region.
1882	The Northern Pacific Railroad linked northern Idaho to the east and the Pacific Northwest seaports.
1884	The Oregon Short Line Railroad from Wyoming through southern Idaho to Oregon was completed.
1885	A Test Oath barred Mormons from voting, holding office, or serving on juries; these disabilities were incorporated into the state constitution and remained in force until 1890 when Mormans renounced polygamy; Noah S. Kellogg found silver in Coeur d'Alene.
1890	Agriculture surpassed mining in the total value of production.
1892	Martial law was declared in northern Idaho mining towns, where the dispatch of federal troops helped break a miners' strike; more than 600 union leaders and sympathizers were arrested.
1899	Dynamiting of the Bunker Hill concentrator resulted in the reimposition of martial law and the dispatch of U.S. troops; the Western Federation of Miners was suppressed, and hundreds of miners were imprisoned for six months.
1905	Women received the right to vote.
1907	Clarence Darrow successfully defended "Big Bill" Haywood and two other Western Federation of Miners officials; they were found not guilty of conspiracy in former Idaho governor Frank Steunenberg's murder.
1912	Voters adopted constitutional amendments for the initiative, referendum, and recall.

Illinois

Illinois was first settled by Joliet, Marquette, and the French in 1673; later claimed by the English after a war with the French. Chicago became a major transportation hub with extensive rail networks and a port that served ships from the Atlantic and the Gulf of Mexico. ADMISSION DATE: December 3, 1818 (as the 21st state). CAPITAL: Springfield. NAME: Corruption of *iliniwek* ("tribe of the superior men"), natives at the time of French explorations. MOTTO: "State sovereignty—national union." FLOWER: native violet. BIRD: cardinal.

Land

TOTAL AREA: 56,650 sq mi. RIVERS: Fox, Illinois, Illinois Waterway, Kankakee, Kaskaskia, Mississippi, Ohio, Rock, Vermillion, Wabash.

Population

2,862,679 (1876); 5,894,193 (1913). MAJOR CITIES: Chicago (2,185,283), Peoria (66,950), East St. Louis (58,547), Springfield (51,678), Rockford (45,401).

Business

According to the 1900 census, Illinois ranked as the third manufacturing state in the nation, with industrial wage earners composing 8.2% of the total population. Its rank as a manufacturing state was due to abundant coal and iron supplies and transportation facilities, which make it a natural distribution center for the West and the South. In 1900, Illinois had more railroad mileage than any state in the Union, the total number of miles being 10,997, and Lake Michigan and the Mississippi River offered additional transportation outlets. Slaughtering and meatpacking were the most important industries: Chicago was the great livestock market for the West and Northwest. The manufacture of foundry and machine-shop products ranked second in importance in the state. Mines in the Lake Superior region provided an abundant supply of iron, which increased the iron and steel output. The manufacture of liquor ranked third; the city of Peoria was the largest producer of whiskeys and wines in the United States. The manufacturers of agricultural machines supplied the West with farm machinery.

Famous Natives

Jane Addams, reformer; William Edgar Borah, statesman; William Jennings Bryan, politician; Robert Andrews Millikan, physicist; Carl Sandburg, poet; Lester Frank Ward, sociologist.

Memorable Events

1885	Erection of ten-story Home Insurance Building, prototype of all skyscraper design.
May 4, 1886	Terrorist bombing left nine dead and 130 wounded in Haymarket affair.
1889	Jane Addams established Hull House to help Chicago's poor.
1893	Columbian Exposition, Chicago.
1894	Pres. Grover Cleveland sent federal troops to Chicago to crush the Pullman Car Company railroad strike.
December 30, 1893	A fire in Chicago's Iroquois Theater resulted in 596 deaths.
1912	*Poetry* magazine was founded in Chicago, and Illinois poets Carl Sandburg, Vachel Lindsay, and Edgar Lee Masters were featured in its pages.

Indiana

Indiana was established as a territory in 1800. Originally it constituted a part of New France. In 1763, the territory was ceded to Great Britain. ADMISSION DATE: December 11, 1816 (as the 19th state). CAPITAL: Indianapolis. NAME: For the land of Indians by early settlers. MOTTO: "The crossroads of America." FLOWER: peony. BIRD: cardinal.

Land

TOTAL AREA: 36,350 sq mi. RIVERS: Kankakee, Ohio, Tippecanoe, Wabash, White, Whitewater.

Population

1,859,235 (1876); 2,758,569 (1913). MAJOR CITIES: Indianapolis (233,650), Evansville (69,647), Fort Wayne (63,933), Terre Haute (58,157), South Bend (53,684).

Business

Agriculture formed a large part of Indiana's general wealth, especially swine and corn, and the number of farms in Indiana peaked in 1900 at 221,897. The chief industries were manufacturing—stimulated largely by the extension of railways and the discovery of natural gas—and mechanics. Southern Indiana had large coal deposits and great quarries of limestone. Railways made up for the lack of navigable waterways, and natural gas provided an abundant supply of cheap fuel; in 1899, Indiana ranked first in the nation in the production of natural gas, fourth in petroleum, and sixth in coal. The leading industry of the state, however, was meatpacking; the manufacture of flour and grist-mill products ranked second, followed by liquors. Lumber and timber formed a large part of the state's industries with substantial areas of forest still uncut. Wood products include high-grade wagons, carriages, furniture, and agricultural machines.

Famous Natives

Eugene V. Debs, Socialist and labor organizer; Theodore Dreiser, editor and author; Benjamin Harrison, U.S. president; John N. Hay, statesman; Knute Rockne (b. Norway), football player; Booth Tarkington, author; Wilbur Wright, aviation pioneer.

Memorable Events

1877	James Whitcomb Riley became a regular contributor of verse to the Indianapolis *Journal*.
1889	The Standard Oil Company built one of the world's largest oil refineries in Whiting.
July 4, 1894	Elmer Haines successfully tested his horseless carriage in Kokomo.
1901	The American Socialist Party was founded at Indianapolis with Eugene V. Debs as president.
1906	U.S. Steel established a mill at the company-built town of Gary.
May 30, 1911	The first Indianapolis 500 Memorial Day weekend auto race.

Iowa

Iowa, originally a part of the Louisiana Purchase, was first settled by French Canadians in the 1780s. In 1834, Iowa came under the jurisdiction of Michigan and later Wisconsin before becoming a separate territory in 1838. Iowa lies between two of the great rivers of the central United States, the Mississippi and the Missouri, and has a quarter of the nation's richest and deepest topsoil. ADMISSION DATE: December 28, 1846 (as the 29th state). CAPITAL: Des Moines. NAME: For Iowa tribe. MOTTO: "Our liberties we prize and our rights we will defend." FLOWER: wild rose. BIRD: Eastern gold finch.

Land

TOTAL AREA: 56,025 sq mi. RIVERS: Big Sioux, Des Moines, Mississippi, Missouri.

Population

1,452,377 (1876); 2,278,429 (1913). MAJOR CITIES: Des Moines (86,368); Davenport (43,028); Dubuque (38,494); Cedar Rapids (32,811); Council Bluffs (29,292).

Business

Iowa was primarily an agricultural state. Wholesale slaughtering and meatpacking were the most important industry in the state, amounting to 15.6% of the value of total products. Factory manufacture of butter, cheese, and condensed milk ranked second in importance; flour and grist milling were third. Formerly, the manufacture of lumber and timber were the chief industries, but misuse and exhaustion of timber lands caused a decline, beginning around 1900. Allied to lumber and timber was the manufacture of planing mill products, car construction and repair shops, and the manufacture of agricultural implements.

Famous Natives

William F. ("Buffalo Bill") Cody, showman and scout; Lee De Forest, radio engineer and inventor; John L. Lewis, labor leader; John R. Mott, religious leader; Billy Sunday, baseball player and evangelist.

Memorable Events

1880	Last of the discriminatory laws against blacks is abolished when "white" is removed from the qualifications for legislative office.
July 4, 1884	Statewide prohibition of alcoholic beverages becomes law.
1890	Iowa leads all states in corn production.
1910	With 2,210,050 people, Iowa is the only state to have lost population in the first decade of the twentieth century; mechanization of agriculture and the lure of cheaper lands farther west are believed to be responsible.

Kansas

Kansas was originally a part of the Louisiana Purchase and organized as a territory in 1854 by the Kansas-Nebraska Act. Organized on the basis of popular sovereignty, "Bleeding Kansas" became a rehearsal for the Civil War as pro- and antislavery forces vied for political control over the state. ADMISSION DATE: January 29, 1861 (as the 34th state). CAPITAL: Topeka. NAME: For Kansa or Kaw, "people of the south wind." MOTTO: *"Ad astra per aspera"* (To the stars through adversity). FLOWER: wild native sunflower. BIRD: Western meadow lark.

Land

TOTAL AREA: 82,080 sq mi. RIVERS: Arkansas, Kansas, Missouri, Republican, Saline, Smoky Hill, Solomon.

Population

743,417 (1876); 1,759,915 (1913). MAJOR CITIES: Kansas City (82,331), Wichita (52,450), Topeka (43,684), Leavenworth (19,363), Atchison (16,429).

Business

Agriculture and stock raising were the leading pursuits of the state. The wheat crop of Kansas in 1900 equaled about 3.3% of world production; only about one-fourth of Kansas's wheat was ground there because local mills were too small and freight rates were noncompetitive. Meat products were of chief importance, and Kansas City was the second-largest meatpacking city in the country. Allied to stock raising was the factory manufacture of butter, cheese, and condensed milk, and soap and candles were manufactured from waste products. Flour and grist-mill products ranked second in importance. The smelting and refining of zinc became one of the more important industries; oil and gas fields of southern Kansas produced an unlimited supply of cheap fuel.

Famous Natives

Edgar Lee Masters, author; Carrie Nation (b. Kentucky), prohibitionist; Damon Runyon, author; William Allen White, journalist and writer.

Memorable Events

1877	First telephone installed in Topeka; L. G. A. Copley, a Paola teacher, originated Kansas Day observances.
1878	Black "exodusters" began to arrive from former slave states.
1879	Prohibition amendment was passed by the state's legislature and ratified by voters a year later.
1882	A well near Paola produced a large amount of natural gas.
1886	A great blizzard destroyed cattle herds.
1887	Severe drought caused the end of the agricultural boom.
1889	First county high school in the United States was founded at Chapman.
1890	Menninger Clinic established at Topeka.
1892	Oil was discovered at Neodesha.
October 5, 1892	The Dalton gang raided Coffeyville.
1894	Many companies formed to develop oil and gas fields.
1896	William Allen White wrote the Emporia *Gazette* editorial "What's the Matter with Kansas?"
1900	Carrie Nation began to crusade against saloons.
1901	Dial telephone system first appeared in Kansas.
1903	First helium in United States was discovered in Dexter.
1912	Kansas voted complete suffrage for women.

Commonwealth of Kentucky

The earliest exploration of Kentucky was made in 1767 by John Finley and several companions from North Carolina. In 1769, Daniel Boone, Finley, and others visited the region. In 1775 Daniel Boone concluded a treaty with the Cherokee, and the next year, Kentucky became a part of Virginia. In 1780, it was made a territory. The Commonwealth of Kentucky has traditionally divided between the Blue Grass gentry who supported the Confederacy during the Civil War and the Appalachian settlers who enlisted in the Union. ADMISSION DATE: June 1, 1792 (as the 15th state). CAPITAL: Frankfort. NAME: Corruption of Iroquois *kenta-ke* (meadowland) or Wyandot *kah-ten-tah-teh* (land of tomorrow). MOTTO: "United we stand; divided we fall." FLOWER: trumpet vine. BIRD: cardinal.

Land

TOTAL AREA: 40,400 sq mi. RIVERS: Cumberland, Kentucky, Licking, Ohio, Tennessee. MOUNTAINS: Appalachian (Black Mt. 4,145 ft), Cumberland.

Population

1,517,618 (1876); 2,334,557 (1913). MAJOR CITIES: Louisville (223,928), Covington (53,270), Lexington (35,099), Newport (30,309), Paducah (22,760).

Business

Tobacco was the principal product, totaling 14.2% of the product value of the state in 1900, and Louisville was the largest leaf-tobacco market in the world. Flour and grist-mill products were next in importance. In the manufacture of distilled and malt liquors, Kentucky ranked near the top and was first in the production of corn whiskey. There were two extensive coal mines in the state, and large deposits of iron ore were found, but the lack of transportation facilities prevented their extensive development. Kentucky has long been famous for the breeding of fine horses.

Famous Natives

Louis Dembitz Brandeis, jurist; D. W. Griffith, film maker; John Marshall Harlan, jurist; Samuel Freeman Miller, jurist; Thomas Hunt Morgan, biologist.

Memorable Events

1879	The first telephone exchange in Louisville was opened.
1882	McCoy–Hatfield feud erupted.
1883	The Southern Exposition opened at Louisville.
1888	James William "Honorable Dick" Tate, state treasurer for 20 years, disappeared with one-quarter of a million dollars in state funds.
1890	Tobacco replaced hemp as Kentucky's leading crop.
1897–98	A violent grassroots movement of "tollgate riders" attacked gatekeepers employed by private road companies.
1900	The commonwealth had highest per capita income of the southern states.
1902	Ben Hargis is murdered in "Bloody Breathitt" County, producing a Hargis–Cockrill feud that eventually killed 37 people.
1905–08	The "Black Patch War" witnessed night riders burning tobacco warehouses in organized resistance against prevailing market conditions in the tobacco industry.
1912	The era of family feuds in Kentucky ended with the killing of Ed Callahan of Breathitt County.

Louisiana

The French established the first permanent white settlements in Louisiana. In 1762, France ceded the territory to Spain who in turn re-ceded it to France in 1800, who sold it to the United States in 1803 for the sum of $15 million. African Americans, Cajuns, and Creoles have contributed to the state's distinctive music and cuisine. ADMISSION DATE: April 30, 1812 (as the 18th state). CAPITAL: Baton Rouge. NAME: For King Louis XIV. MOTTO: "Union, justice, and confidence." FLOWER: magnolia. BIRD: Eastern brown pelican.

Land

TOTAL AREA: 48,720 sq mi. RIVERS: Atchafalaya, Mississippi, Ouachita, Pearl, Red, Sabine.

Population

854,734 (1876); 1,742,345 (1913). MAJOR CITIES: New Orleans (339,075), Shreveport (28,015), Baton Rouge (14,897), Lake Charles (11,449), Alexandria (11,213).

Business

Louisiana was another agricultural state whose manufacturing increased rapidly during the Gilded Age. Its industries were largely dependent upon natural resources, such as forests, which cover a large part of the state, and upon the sugarcane, cotton, rice fields, and the excellent transportation facilities afforded by the Gulf of Mexico and the Mississippi River. Facilities at the port of New Orleans stimulated the manufacture of cotton products, such as cottonseed oil and cake. Jute and burlap bags for raw cotton, cottonseed, and fertilizer were also important products. Waterways for the transportation of coal were assured by improvements to the Warrior River (Alabama) and canals from the Mississippi to the Gulf. The discovery of oil promised a cheap fuel for the future. Upper Louisiana was covered with forests of yellow pine, and large stands of them could also be found in the southwestern part of the state. Only a small portion of the pine had been cut, and the state's cypress forests were practically untouched. Except for culling of the choicest white oak, the hardwoods remained in their primal state, but timber interests were attracted to the state in the largest numbers ever.

Famous Natives

Charles "Buddy" Bolden, musician; Ferdinand Joseph La Menthe ("Jelly Roll") Morton, musician; Leonidas K. Polk, clergyman/Confederate general; Henry Hobson Richardson, architect; Edward Douglas White, jurist.

Memorable Events

1877	Home rule was restored under Governor Francis Nicholls.
1879	New Orleans was made an ocean port.
1883	Train service was established between New Orleans and California.
1890	Charles ("Buddy") Bolden, cornetist and pioneer of instrumental jazz, formed his own band in New Orleans.
Nov. 1, 1896	Rural free mail delivery established.
May 12, 1898	The state's new voting qualifications disfranchised most blacks ("Jim Crow" constitution).
June 15, 1910	Evangeline County was founded and named for Evangeline, the heroine of Henry Wadsworth Longfellow's poem.
1901	Petroleum discovered.

Maine

Maine was originally settled by the French in 1603. In 1622, a permanent English settlement was established, and France and England disputed the territory for much of the colony's history. According to the Compromise of 1820, Maine was carved out of the territory of Massachusetts as a free state in order to maintain a balance with the slave states. Maine touches only one other state, New Hampshire. ADMISSION DATE: March 15, 1820 (as the 23d state). CAPITAL: Augusta. NAME: Either from Maine in France or to distinguish mainland from islands in the Gulf of Maine. MOTTO: "Dirigo" (I direct). FLOWER: white pine cone and tassel. BIRD: chickadee

Land

TOTAL AREA: 33,040 sq mi. RIVERS: Alagash, Androscoggin, Aroostock, Kennebec, Machias, Penobscot, Piscataqua, Salmon Falls, St. John. MOUNTAINS: Longfellow (Mt. Katahdin 5,268 ft).

Population

640,128 (1876); 757,358 (1913). MAJOR CITIES: Portland (58,571), Lewiston (26,247), Bangor (24,803), Biddeford (17,079), Auburn (15,064).

Business

In the eighteenth century, canneries, shoe factories, and textiles developed, but Maine's chief industry was the manufacture of cotton goods, due to an excellent water supply and transportation facilities. The increase of mills in the South during the Gilded Age, however, decreased cotton production, and wool products were very important. Because of Maine's extensive forests lumbering and paper making became chief industries: White pine, spruce, and poplar covered the entire northern portion of Maine and were largely untouched. Rough timber and shingles were the most important products of these forests, and nearly all of the wood used to make matches came from Maine. The canning of herring, under the name of sardines, was also significant.

Famous Natives

Neal Dow, temperance reformer; Cyrus Hermann Curtis, publisher; Sarah Orne Jewett, writer; Henry Wadsworth Longfellow, poet; Sir Hiram and Hudson Maxim, inventors; Kenneth Roberts, author; Edwin Arlington Robinson, poet.

Memorable Events

1911   A direct primary, initiative, and referendum were established.

Maryland

The first white settlement in Maryland was made on Kent Island, Chesapeake Bay, in 1631 by Captain William Clayborne with a party of men from Virginia. Later, Cecilius Calvert, Lord Baltimore, received a charter for the first authorized settlement and created a haven for Catholics. ADMISSION DATE: April 28, 1788 (as the 7th state.) CAPITAL: Annapolis. NAME: For Henrietta Maria, queen consort of Charles I. MOTTO: *"Fatti maschii, parole femine"* (Manly deeds, womanly words). FLOWER: black-eyed Susan. BIRD: Baltimore oriole.

Land

TOTAL AREA: 12,210 sq mi. RIVERS: Chester, Choptank, Nanticoke, Patapsco, Patuxent, Pocomoke, Potomac, Susquehanna. MOUNTAINS: Allegheny, Blue Ridge.

Population

873,323 (1876); 1,328,915 (1913). MAJOR CITIES: Baltimore (558,485); Cumberland (21,839); Hagerstown (16,507); Frederick (10,411); Annapolis (8,609).

Business

Canning and fruit preservation, made possible by excellent soil and shipping facilities at railroads and seaports, was the most important industry. Iron and steel manufacturing ranked second; foundry and machine-shop products are third. At the turn of the

twentieth century, the manufacture of cotton products was growing rapidly, and Baltimore was the largest producer of cotton duck in the United States.

Famous Natives

Edwin Thomas Booth, actor; Frederick Douglass, abolitionist; James Gibbons, Roman Catholic prelate; Johns Hopkins, financeer/philanthropist; H. L. Mencken, writer; Upton Sinclair, author; Harriet Tubman, abolitionist.

Memorable Events

1876	Johns Hopkins University opened.
July 20–22, 1877	B&O workers struck and rioted.
1882	Enoch Pratt Free Public Library established.
1889	Steel plant opened at Sparrow's Point and became Maryland's largest manufacturing institution.
May 7, 1889	Johns Hopkins Hospital opened.
1894	Founding of Maryland Women's Suffrage Association.
1904	Downtown Baltimore destroyed by fire.
1905	Noted critic Henry Louis Mencken joined the *Baltimore Sun*.
1910	The nation's first workmen's compensation law requiring compensation for job-related injuries and death passed.

Commonwealth of Massachusetts

The first permanent white settlement in Massachusetts was made in 1620 when 100 English pilgrims seeking religious freedom docked the *Mayflower* at Plymouth. The colony grew with the arrival of new settlers and later played a significant role in the history of the early American republic. ADMISSION DATE: February 6, 1788 (as the 6th state). CAPITAL: Boston. NAME: For Massachuset tribe, whose name means "at or about the great hill." MOTTO: *"Ense petit placidam sub libertate quietem"* (By the sword we seek peace, but peace only under liberty). FLOWER: mayflower. BIRD: chickadee.

Land

TOTAL AREA: 8,315 sq mi. RIVERS: Cape Cod Canal, Charles, Connecticut, Merrimack, Taunton.

Population

1,652,791 (1876); 3,541,940 (1913). MAJOR CITIES: Boston (670,585), Worcester (145,986), Fall River (119,295), Lowell (106,294), Cambridge (104,839).

Business

Abundant water power and good transportation facilities made the state an early leader in industrial development, most noted for its cotton mills. Fishing, trade, textiles, and leather industries were the backbone of the nineteenth-century economy. A large proportion of the machines, which were important in transforming industrial conditions since the introduction of the factory system, were produced in Massachusetts. Worcester, the second largest city of the commonwealth, was the home of the largest wire mills, the American Steel & Wire Company (now the United States Steel Corporation), and the largest plant of the United States Envelope Company. The ample supply of labor facilitated the establishment of factories in the cities.

Famous Natives

Horatio Alger, clergyman/author; Susan B. Anthony, women's rights leader; George Bancroft, historian, diplomat, and Cabinet officer; Clara Barton, nurse; Phillips Brooks, Episcopal bishop; Emily Elizabeth Dickinson, poet; W. E. B. DuBois, educator and reformer; Charles W. Eliot, educator; Ralph Waldo Emerson, philosopher, poet, essayist, and lecturer; William M. Evarts, lawyer and statesman; Marshall Field, merchant; Stephen Johnson Field, jurist; Nathaniel Hawthorne, novelist and writer of tales; Oliver Wendell Holmes, Jr., jurist; Winslow Homer, painter; Gilbert Newton Lewis, physical chemist; James Russell Lowell, author, editor, teacher, and diplomat; Dwight L. Moody, evangelist; Francis Parkman, historian; Charles Sanders Peirce, philosopher, logician, and scientist; Louis Henri Sullivan, architect; Edward Lee Thorndike, educator; James Abbot McNeil Whistler, painter and etcher.

Memorable Events

1876   Alexander Graham Bell invented the telephone in Boston.
1912   A textile workers' strike in Lawrence brought the International Workers of the World to prominence in the East.

Michigan

French missionaries and fur traders were early visitors to Michigan, and the first European settlements were made at Sault Ste. Marie in 1668. Michigan, which became an independent territory in 1805, borders four of the five Great Lakes and has more coastline than any other state except Alaska. ADMISSION DATE: January 26, 1837 (as the 26th state). CAPITAL: Lansing. NAME: From Fox *mesi-kami*, "large lake." MOTTO: *"Si quaeris penisulam amoenam circumspice"* (If you are looking for a beautiful peninsula, look around you). FLOWER: apple blossom. BIRD: robin.

Land

TOTAL AREA: 58,915 sq mi. RIVERS: Brule, Detroit, Kalamazoo, Menominee, Montreal, Muskegon, St. Joseph, St. Mary's.

Population

1,455,786 (1876); 2,931,927 (1913). MAJOR CITIES: Detroit (465,766), Grand Rapids (112,571), Saginaw (50,510), Bay City (45,166), Kalamazoo (39,437).

Business

In the Upper Penisula, lumber and copper were important industries; the northern part of the Lower Penisula was an area of rich farmland. The manufacture of lumber and timber products was the most important industry in the state, other manufacturing being hampered by a lack of coal supply of good quality. In 1888, Michigan produced about one-fourth of the nation's timber, but beginning in the Gilded Age, extravagant and wasteful exploitation of the forests caused a decline in the lumber industry. Public opinion was more supportive of a protective system of forestry. Flour and grist-mill products ranked second, concentrated where shipping facilities and waterpower offered superior advantages. The state also was significant in the furniture industry, especially at Grand Rapids. Wagons, carriages, railroad cars, and agricultural implements were other prime products. Foundry and machine-shop industries were on the rise. In 1890, Michigan led all states in iron-ore production.

Famous Natives

Edna Ferber, writer; Henry Ford, industrialist; Robert Green Ingersoll, orator.

Memorable Events

1900   Olds Motor Works, the first auto factory in Detroit, was completed.
June 12, 1903   Ford Motor Company was organized in Detroit.
1908   Henry Ford introduced the Model T, which sold for $850.

Minnesota

Minnesota was explored by the French in the seventeenth century. In the nineteenth century, it became home to the largest Scandinavian populations in the United States. In 1812, the United States assumed authority within the present limits of the state. In 1819, the military post of Ft. Snelling was established, and in 1837, lumbering operations were begun along the St. Croix River on a small tract of land obtained from the Indians. On March 3, 1849, Minnesota was made a territory of the United States. ADMISSION DATE: May 11, 1858 (as the 32d state). CAPITAL: St. Paul. NAME: From the Siouan language, *minisota* ("sky-tinted waters"). MOTTO: *"L'etoile du nord"* (The star of the north). FLOWER: moccasin flower. BIRD: common loon.

Land

TOTAL AREA: 83,365 sq mi. RIVERS: Minnesota, Mississippi, Red River of the North, St. Croix.

Population

644,346 (1876); 2,177,167 (1913). MAJOR CITIES: Minneapolis (301,408), St. Paul (214,744), Duluth (78,446), Winona (18,583), St. Cloud (10,600).

Business

Immense tracts of white and Norway pine and extensive wheat fields characterized the state and its enterprise. In 1882, nearly 70% of Minnesota land was farmed in wheat, and by 1890, Minnesota led all states in wheat production. Minnesota was also at the forefront of flour and grist-mill products, Minneapolis being the largest center of flour-milling in the nation with the Falls of St. Anthony on the Mississippi River being utilized for power. Lumbering was the second industry of importance, the quality of merchantable pine being greater than that of any other state. Many small lakes and streams in the timber country, many of them connected to the St. Louis and Cloquet rivers, made transportation easy and cheap. Facilities at St. Paul and Minneapolis for the handling of cattle gave slaughtering, meatpacking, and the kindred industries of cheese and butter-making importance. Extensive grain fields made malt liquors a substantial manufacture. The Mesabi Iron range in the north developed the nation's richest source of iron ore.

Famous Natives

Sinclair Lewis, author; William and Charles Mayo, surgeons; Ole Edvart Rölvaag (b. Norway), author; Richard Warren Sears, merchant.

Memorable Events

1883   The Northern Pacific Railroad line from Duluth to the Pacific at Portland, Oregon, was completed.
1889   A hospital opened in Rochester that became world famous as the Mayo Clinic.
November 16, 1890   Discovery of iron-ore potential of the Mesabi Range in northern Minnesota.

1893	James J. Hill's Great Northern Railway stretched to the Pacific, from St. Paul to Seattle.
1894	September forest fires swept over 400 square miles and killed 413, including 197 in Hinckley.
1896	Three-fourths of the Red Lake Chippewa Reservation was opened to whites.
November 5, 1903	The Minneapolis Symphony gave its first concert.
1908	Capital punishment was abolished in Minnesota.

Mississippi

De Soto and La Salle were early explorers of what is now Mississippi. The territory of Mississippi was formed by an act of Congress on April 7, 1798. Civil War losses in property and men (65% of the Southerners who died) and harsh race laws passed in the 1890s have made Mississippi the poorest state in the nation. ADMISSION DATE: December 10, 1817 (as the 20th state). CAPITAL: Jackson. NAME: From Ojibwa *misi sipi*, "great river." MOTTO: *"Virtute et armis"* (By virtue and arms). FLOWER: magnolia. BIRD: mockingbird.

Land

TOTAL AREA: 46,810 sq mi. RIVERS: Big Black, Mississippi, Pearl, Tennessee, Yazoo.

Population

1,010,127 (1876); 1,874,024 (1913). MAJOR CITIES: Meridian (23,285), Jackson (21,262), Vicksburg (20,814), Natchez (11,791), Hattiesburg (11,733).

Business

The alluvial lands along the rivers produced some of the finest cotton in the South. Much of the cotton land along the Yazoo Delta was owned by the state and farmed with the use of convict labor: the use of convicts was a big economic success, the profits for 1901 totaling $150,000. The plan met with popular favor in the state, and several counties adopted a similar system for county convicts. Lumber and timber were the most important industries, constituting about 38.7% of the gross state product in 1900. The rolling pine lands of the interior, containing about 8 million acres, remained largely untouched. Much of the timber was used for building, but also for cheap furniture and boat building and fitting. Cottonseed oil and cake manufacture was second in importance. The production of turpentine and rosin and cotton ginning as well were also important industries.

Memorable Events

1878	A yellow-fever epidemic killed many in the state.
March 11, 1886	A general local-option liquor law was passed.
1904	Separate-but-equal accommodations for whites and blacks on streetcars was mandated.
1908	Statewide prohibition came into effect.

Missouri

In the Louisiana Purchase of 1803, Missouri was included; in 1812, it was made a separate territory. Still one of the nation's most important inland ports, St. Louis, the seat of government, was founded at the confluence of the Mississippi and Missouri rivers and became known as the gateway to the West. The city of Independence got its start provisioning wagons for the Oregon and the Sante Fe trails. The Compromise of 1820 proposed the admission of Missouri as a slave state, the last state to be admitted where slavery was permitted. ADMISSION DATE: August 10, 1821 (as the 24th state). CAPITAL: Jefferson City. NAME: From Missouri Indians. MOTTO: *"Salus populi suprema lex esto"* (The welfare of the people shall be the supreme law). FLOWER: hawthorn. BIRD: bluebird.

Land

TOTAL AREA: 69,415 sq mi. RIVERS: Des Moines, Mississippi, Missouri, Osage, St. Francis. MOUNTAINS: Ozark (Taum Sauk Mt., 1,772 ft).

Population

1,989,546 (1876); 3,351,732 (1913). MAJOR CITIES: St. Louis (687,029), Kansas City (248,381), St. Joseph (77,403), Springfield (35,201), Joplin (32,073).

Business

Slaughtering and meatpacking were the most important industries, and the manufacture of tobacco ranked second. Flour and grist-mill products had an important place because of Missouri's extensive wheat fields. The manufacture of shoes was a comparatively new industry.

Famous Natives

Adophus Busch, brewer; George Washington Carver, botanist; Jesse James, outlaw; Joseph Pulitzer, journalist and newspaper publisher; Mark Twain, writer; John J. ("Black Jack") Pershing, soldier.

Memorable Events

1880	First black newspaper began publication in St. Joseph.
April 1882	Jesse James killed at St. Joseph.
1891	First automobile brought into Missouri.
1904	"Meet Me in St. Louis, Louie" was a popular song at the Louisiana Purchase Exposition (World's Fair).
1908	First school of journalism in the world established at University of Missouri.
February 5, 1911	State capitol burned; first attempt at airmail service was tried, with letter flown from Kinloch Park to Fairgrounds Park, St. Louis, a distance of 10 miles.

Montana

The white settlement of Montana dated from the opening of the gold mines in that region. Montana was established as a territorial government in 1864. An act of February 17, 1873, annexed to Montana a tract of 2,000 square miles previously belonging to Dakota and established the territory's capital at Helena. The state's eastern portion is part of the Great Plains; mountains account for only the western two-fifths of Montana. ADMISSION DATE: November 8, 1889 (as the 41st state). CAPITAL: Helena. NAME: From Spanish *montana*, "mountainous." MOTTO: *"Oro y plata"* (Gold and silver). FLOWER: bitterroot. BIRD: Western meadowlark.

Settlers had to depend on wagon trains for their supplies. Here, a horse train is shown delivering goods in Montana. (Courtesy Milwaukee Public Museum)

Land

TOTAL AREA: 146,080 sq mi. RIVERS: Kootenai, Milk, Missouri, Musselshell, Powder, Yellowstone. MOUNTAINS: Absaroka Range, Beartooth Range (Granite Peak, 12,799 ft), Big Belt Bitterroot Range, Centennial, Crazy, Lewis Range, Little Belt.

Population

31,733 (1876); 417,574 (1913). MAJOR CITIES: Butte (39,165), Great Falls (13,948), Missoula (12,869), Helena (12,515).

Business

Mining, stock raising, and agriculture were the chief enterprises. Hundreds of acres of fine grazing land made the cattle industry important, and the livestock markets of the state ranked among the best in the country. In 1900, Montana's 6 million sheep made the state first in wool growing. However, the smelting and refining of copper and lead became the principal industries, the product of 1900 making up 60% of the entire U.S. output of these ores. Large coal deposits and the abundant supply of nearby timber for use in the mines led to the development of the mining industry. In 1909, homesteaders entered the state (almost 5 million acres in homestead claims were filed in this year), and within a decade, farming supplanted mining as the chief source of income.

Memorable Events

1876	Lakota and Cheyenne defeat U.S. 7th Cavalry under Gen. William Armstrong Custer at Battle of Little Bighorn.
October 5, 1877	Indian fighting virtually ended with the surrender of Chief Joseph and the Nez Percé.
1881–82	Slaughter of buffalo peaked.
1882	Marcus Daly discovered the largest deposit of copper sulphite in the world near Butte.
September 8, 1883	The Northern Pacific Railroad was completed from Lake Superior to the Pacific with the last spike driven at Gold Creek; fewer than 200 buffalo remained in the entire West.
1886	Open grazing peaked with 664,000 cattle and 986,000 sheep.
1886–87	A hard winter killed about half of the cattle.
1887–88	Indians ceded 17.5 million acres north of the Missouri; about 11 million acres remained open to them.
1894	Voters chose Helena as capital.
1910	Glacier National Park was established with 1,013,599 acres.

Nebraska

In 1834, Nebraska was designated as Indian territory and made off-limits to white settlement. Regardless, thousands of whites crossed into the region along the Independence, Mormon, and Oregon trails. Eventually, Congress opened the land to white settlement, which increased rapidly after the Homestead Act of 1862. Newcomers took up ranching and farming under difficult conditions: A severe winter in 1886–87 killed thousands of cattle and forced many large ranchers into bankruptcy. ADMISSION DATE: March 1, 1867 (as the 37th state). CAPITAL: Lincoln. NAME: From Oto *nebrathka*, "flat water." MOTTO: "Equality before the law." FLOWER: goldenrod. BIRD: Western meadowlark.

Land

TOTAL AREA: 77,510 sq mi. RIVERS: Missouri, North Platte, Republican, South Platte.

Population

320,638 (1876); 1,231,605 (1913). MAJOR CITIES: Omaha (124,096), Lincoln (43,973), South Omaha (26,259), Beatrice (9,356).

Business

Slaughtering and meatpacking were the most important industries in the state. Fifteen railroads entered Omaha, and South Omaha was considered one of the great cattle markets of the world. In addition to livestock raised inside the state, sheep and cattle were sent to Nebraska feedlots to be fattened before slaughter. Butter, cheese, condensed milk, flour, grist-mill products, and malt liquors were allied products. A creamery at Lincoln was said to be the largest in the nation. The printing and publishing trade of the Midwest between the Mississippi and the Rocky Mountains was centered in Omaha.

Famous Natives

The Rev. Edward J. Flanagan (b. Ireland), reformer; Willa Sibert Cather (b. Virginia), author; Mahpiua Luta (Red Cloud), Oglala Lakota chief; Roscoe Pound, jurist.

Memorable Events

September 5, 1877	Lakota leader Crazy Horse was killed at Fort Robinson in northwestern Nebraska.
January 9, 1879	Indian resistance ended as most of a small band of Northern Cheyenne was killed at Fort Robinson.
1883	Union Stockyards Company was organized in Omaha.
1885	Homestead filings peaked in Nebraska at 2,141,080 acres.
1890	Populists, exploiting farm distress, won control of both houses of the legislature.
1896	William Jennings Bryan of Lincoln waged the first of his three unsuccessful presidential campaigns as the Democratic Party nominee.
1897	Nebraska was the first state to adopt the initiative and referendum.
1904	The Kincaid Act was signed establishing 640-acre homesteads in northwestern Nebraska, thus ending the reign of cattle barons in the area.

Nevada

Set in the Great Basin Desert, Nevada was part of the Mexican Cession of 1848. The discovery of the Comstock lode brought thousands of miners in 1859, and the boom lasted until the 1870s. Additional strikes of gold and silver in the early 1900s as well as the discovery of copper reinvigorated the economy. In 1910, mainly as a result of renewed mining, the state population doubled over the 1900 population; there were 220 men per 100 women. Nevada receives less rainfall than any other state. ADMISSION DATE: October 31, 1864 (as the 36th state). CAPITAL: Carson City. NAME: From Spanish meaning "snow-covered Sierra." MOTTO: "All for our country." FLOWER: Sagebrush. BIRD: Mountain bluebird.

Land

TOTAL AREA: 110,700 sq mi. RIVERS: Colorado, Humboldt.

Population

54,356 (1876); 94,245 (1913). MAJOR CITY: Reno (10,867).

Business

Gold attracted some miners in 1849, but the real growth of the state dates from the discovery of silver in 1859. Within two years, the population rose from 1,000 to 16,000. Manufacturing industries declined steadily from 1870 to 1890 caused by the decrease in gold and silver mining. In 1900, car construction and repair-shop work were of leading importance, joined by flour and grist milling and the manufacture of butter, cheese, and condensed milk.

Famous Natives

Josiah Royce, philosopher and teacher.

Memorable Events

1877	Mineral production reached a record $47 million, unsurpassed, except for World War II, until 1951.
1879	Several acts were passed by the legislature to prohibit Chinese labor.
1894	Annual mineral production dropped to less than $2 million as the Comstock and other mines petered out.
1894–1902	Heyday of the Silver Party, which sought the remonetization of silver; the party dominated elections to state offices during this period.
March 17, 1897	Bob Fitzsimmons won the world heavyweight championship from Jim Corbett in Carson City and established a tradition of championship fights held in Nevada.
1900	Butch Cassidy's gang robbed the First National Bank in Winnemucca of $32,640; a great silver-gold boom began with the strike at Tonopah in southwestern Nevada.
1905	Las Vegas was founded as a stop in the San Pedro, Los Angeles, and Salt Lake Railroad.
1907	Dispatch of federal troops helped break a strike at Goldfield by the Western Federation of Miners.
1908	Copper production began near Ely, and the area became Nevada's richest mining district.

New Hampshire

New Hampshire was first visited by Europeans in 1614, became a royal province in 1679, and made a public declaration of its independence in 1776 when it established a temporary government. ADMISSION DATE: June 21, 1788 (as the 9th state). CAPITAL: Concord. NAME: For English county of Hampshire. MOTTO: "Live free or die." FLOWER: purple lilac. BIRD: purple finch.

Land

TOTAL AREA: 9,305 sq mi. RIVERS: Connecticut, Merrimack, Piscataqua, Saco, Salmon Falls. MOUNTAINS: White (Mt. Washington, 6,288 ft, highest peak in Northeast).

Population

335,515 (1876); 436,511 (1913). MAJOR CITIES: Manchester (70,063), Nashua (26,005), Concord (21,497), Dover (13,247), Berlin (11,780).

Business

Fishing, trade, and farming were early economic mainstays, but farming in the more fertile valleys of states to the south and west and the prominence of Boston as a trade center eclipsed New Hampshire and caused an economic slump. At the beginning of the Industrial Revolution, the Merrimack River Valley led the way with a tremendous growth in textile-producing mill towns that remained important until World War I. According to the census of 1900, boot and shoe manufacturing formed the leading industry in the state. Woolen goods were second in importance, Manchester being the manufacturing center of this industry. Following, in order of importance, were lumber and timber products, paper and wood pulp, foundry and machine-shop goods, and hosiery and knit goods.

Famous Natives

Salmon P. Chase, statesman and chief justice; Ralph Adams Cram, architect; Mary Baker Eddy, founder, Church of Christ, Scientist; Daniel Chester French, sculptor; Horace Greeley, journalist; Christopher Columbus Langdell, jurist and law teacher; Augustus Saint-Gaudens (b. Ireland), sculptor; Harlan Fiske Stone, 11th chief justice of the United States.

Memorable Events

1877	State constitution amended to abolish the rule that governor, senators, and representatives be of Protestant faith.
May 1, 1903	The state ended 48 years of prohibition by providing liquor licenses.
1909	Adoption of the direct-primary law.

New Jersey

The earliest colony in New Jersey was probably founded at Bergen by the Dutch of New Amsterdam between 1617 and 1620. In 1634, Sir Edmund Polyden obtained a grant of land along the Delaware and named it New Albion. A few years later, a few Swedes and Finns planted several settlements in the same area. In 1664, Charles II of England granted the entire territory between the Connecticut and Delaware Rivers to his brother, the Duke of York, who captured New Amsterdam and controlled the entire region. The first proprietors surrendered their rights to the English crown in 1702. During the American Revolution, more than 100 battles were fought on New Jersey soil. New Jersey lies in a plain between Philadelphia and New York City. ADMISSION DATE: December 18, 1787 (as the 3d state). CAPITAL: Trenton. NAME: After English Channel Island of Jersey. MOTTO: "Liberty and prosperity." FLOWER: purple violet. BIRD: Eastern goldfinch.

Land

TOTAL AREA: 7,815 sq mi. RIVERS: Delaware, Hackensack, Hudson, Passaic. MOUNTAINS: Kittatinny, Ramapo.

Population

1,041,108 (1876); 2,741,607 (1913). MAJOR CITIES: Newark (347,469), Jersey City (267,779), Paterson (125,600), Trenton (96,815), Camden (94,538).

Business

Transportation facilities and proximity to large markets led to New Jersey's rank as the sixth-largest manufacturing state in the nation. According to the 1900 census, the manufacture of textiles was the most important industry in the state, with an investment of $75 million; in the silk industry, the invested capital was about $29 million. The great growth of the silk industry at Paterson began during the 1860s, and in 1900, Paterson ranked first in silk manufacture in the United States. Because the Pennsylvania coal district was only 50 miles from New Jersey's western border, and because a good quantity of iron was also found within New Jersey, the iron and steel industry was also important.

Famous Natives

Nicholas Murray Butler, educator and author; Andrew Dickson White, educator, diplomat, and historian; Frances Willard, reformer.

Memorable Events

1876	The Standard Oil Company built its refinery at Bayonne.
1879	Thomas Alva Edison invented the incandescent electric lamp at Menlo Park.

New Mexico

New Mexico was visited by the Spaniards almost a century before the English landed on the Atlantic coast. Alvar Núñez Cabeza de Vaca reached New Mexico before 1537, an expedition by Marco de Niza followed in 1539, and then another a year later under Coronado. Formal possession was taken in 1595 or 1599 by Juan de Oñate and the missionaries who accompanied his expedition tried to Christianize many of the local Indian tribes. Eventually, the Indians organized a resistance and, in 1680, drove the Spaniards from the area. In 1698, Spain regained possession and held the territory until 1848, when it was ceded to the United States in the Treaty of Guadalupe Hidalgo. A territorial government was formed in 1850. Of all the states, New Mexico has the smallest area covered by water. A higher percentage of Native Americans lives in New Mexico than any other state. ADMISSION DATE: January 6, 1912 (as the 47th state). CAPITAL: Santa Fe. NAME: By Spanish explorers after Mexico. MOTTO: "Crescit eundo" (It grows as it goes). FLOWER: Yucca. BIRD: roadrunner.

Land

TOTAL AREA: 122,580 sq mi. RIVERS: Gila, Pecos, Rio Grande, Zuni. MOUNTAINS: Chuska, Guadalupe, Sacramento, San Andres, Sangre de Cristo.

Population

108,489 (1876); 370,936 (1913). MAJOR CITIES: Albuquerque (11,020), Roswell (6,172), Santa Fe (5,072).

Business

Mining and stock raising were the most important economic activities; agriculture was next. New Mexico had the largest number of sheep of any territory, and several wool-scouring plants were in operation. Some families had sheep herds as large as 250,000 head. By 1880, the wool clip had grown to 4 million pounds a year. In 1890, at the peak of the open ranching system in New Mexico, the state had 1.34 million head of cattle; its population was 94% rural.

Famous Natives

William ("Billy the Kid") Bonney (b. New York), outlaw; Georgia O'Keeffe, painter.

Memorable Events

1876–78	The Lincoln County war pitted cattlemen against merchants in an area comprising one-fifth of the state; Billy the Kid was one of its famous participants.
1879	The Atchison, Topeka, and the Santa Fe Railroad entered New Mexico through the Raton Pass, soon reaching Albuquerque.
July 14, 1881	Sheriff Pat Garrett killed Billy the Kid at a ranch near Fort Summer.
May 1885	Apache chief Geronimo, angered over the eviction of his people to an Arizona reservation, led an uprising against white settlers.
1909–12	Drought forced three-quarters of all homesteaders from New Mexico.
1912	17 were killed in raid by Pancho Villa.

New York

The first white visitors found New York inhabited by various tribes, including the Five Nations of the Iroquois Confederacy. After explorations by Samuel de Champlain and Henry Hudson, the first Dutch settlement was made on Manhattan Island, and the name of New Netherlands was applied to that territory lying between Canada and Virginia. In 1664, New Amsterdam was captured by the English under Colonel Nicolls, and the name New York was given to the whole province. After considerable conflict with the Indians in the French and Indian Wars, the province settled into an uneasy peace, broken by Indian raids on settlements until the Revolutionary War period. Boundaries with Connecticut (1731), Massachusetts (1786), and Vermont and New Hampshire (1790) were finally settled, giving New York its present boundaries. New York's greatest asset has been its location and arteries into the interior. New York Bay is one of the great natural harbors of the world, and the Hudson River is a well-placed asset. After the opening of the Erie Canal in 1825, New York City became a trading center for the Midwest, the Hudson Valley, and the Atlantic coast. Buffalo experienced a boom and became a major industrial port on the Great Lakes. ADMISSION DATE: July 26, 1788 (as the 11th state). CAPITAL: Albany. NAME: For the Duke of York, later James II of England. MOTTO: *Excelsior* (Higher). FLOWER: rose. BIRD: bluebird.

Land

TOTAL AREA: 49,170 sq mi. RIVERS: Allegheny, Delaware, Genesee, Hudson, Mohawk, New York State Barge Canal, Niagara, St. Lawrence, Susquehanna. MOUNTAINS: Adirondack (Mt. Marcy, 5,344 ft), Allegheny, Berkshire Hills, Catskill, Kittatinny, Ramapo.

Population

4,802,826 (1876); 9,690,715 (1913). MAJOR CITIES: New York City (4,766,883), Buffalo (423,715), Rochester (218,149), Syracuse (137,249), Albany (100,253).

Business

Rich soil, excellent climate, extensive forests, and mineral deposits combined with the advantages of location and topography to make New York a rich industrial state. The mild climate around Lakes Ontario and Erie favored horticulture; in the Adirondacks, great forests supported the lumber and paper-making industries—New York ranked first in the production of wood pulp for newspaper stock. Iron was found in several counties. Clay beds along the lower Hudson were the center of one the greatest brick-making districts; near them were also extensive cement beds—New York ranked fourth in the United States (1899) in the production of granite, sandstone, slate, marble, and limestone. After 1893, the state ranked first in the production of salt. The urban population of New York City supported a number of industries in the areas of highly finished articles and luxuries. While the production of confectionary exceeded that of iron and steel in the state, clothing manufacturing was its most important industry, with 4,204 establishments employing 90,017 wage laborers, or 10.6% of the wage earners in the state. The manufacture of foundry and machine-shop products ranked second, and printing and publishing needs held third place. Of the 78,658 manufacturing establishments in the state in 1900, 62,567, or 19.6%, were located in 106 cities and villages.

Famous Natives

George Eastman, camera inventor; Julia Ward Howe, reformer; Washington Irving, author; Henry James, author; Herman Melville, author; John D. Rockefeller, industrialist; Theodore Roosevelt, president; Elizabeth Cady Stanton, suffragette.

Memorable Events

October 28, 1886	The Statue of Liberty was dedicated.
March 11, 1888	The Great Blizzard paralyzed New York City.
1901	Pres. William McKinley was assassinated in Buffalo, and Theodore Roosevelt became president.
October 27, 1904	The first subway in the world began operation in New York City.

North Carolina

The first attempt at settlement of North Carolina was made at Roanoke Island by Ralph Lane. After quarreling with the Indians for a year, the party returned to England. Sir Walter Raleigh, who had dispatched the first group, then sent another group, which mysteriously disappeared, presumably killed by the Indians. Not until the seventeenth century was the first permanent English settlement established when, in 1663, Charles II made land grants to eight noblemen. Later, Albermarle, the name given to the territory, was augumented by settlements from Virginia, New England, and Bermuda. By the eighteenth century, the colony had become known for its tobacco. In 1729, Carolina became a royal province, and North and South Carolina became distinct governments. Last to ratify the Constitution, the state was also the last Southern state to secede from the Union. ADMISSION DATE: Nov 21, 1789 (as the 12th state). CAPITAL: Raleigh. NAME: For King Charles I (*Carolus* is Latin for *Charles*). MOTTO: "*Esse quam videri*" (To be rather than to seem). FLOWER: dogwood. BIRD: cardinal.

Land

TOTAL AREA: 52,250 sq mi. RIVERS: Albermarle, Pee Dee, Roanoke, Yadkin. MOUNTAINS: Black, Blue Ridge, Great Smokey, Unaka.

Population

1,268,394 (1876); 2,304,042 (1913). MAJOR CITIES: Charlotte (34,014), Wilmington (25,748), Raleigh (19,218), Durham (18,241), Winston (17,167).

Business

The manufacture of cotton was the most important industry, having grown by 197% in the 1890s. Lumber and timber ranked next in importance. Tobacco was growing rapidly in importance, and cigarette manufacturing was another significant industry. North Carolina pine was used extensively in buildings as a cheap, hard wood. The state was first in the nation in the production of naval stores, especially turpentine and rosin. Transportation was facilitated by rivers in the east and a long coastline; roads in the west are mountainous and were bad.

Famous Natives

Benjamin Newton and James Buchanan Duke, industrialists/philanthropists; William Sydney Porter (O. Henry), short-story writer.

Memorable Events

1890	James Buchanan Duke's American Tobacco Company was founded.
1903	Wright brothers launched first successful airplane at Kitty Hawk.
1904	Duke's American Tobacco Company controlled three-fourths of the nation's tobacco industry.
1909	Statewide prohibition went into effect under the Turlington Act.

North Dakota

Dakota was originally a part of Minnesota territory, which was organized in 1849 out of the Louisiana Purchase of 1803. Scots-Canadians first settled at Pembina on the Red River near the Canadian border and traded primarily with Winnipeg and St. Paul. In 1859, the first permanent settlements of whites were made in what are now the counties of Clay, Union, and Yankton. On November 2, 1889, the territory was divided into North and South Dakota, which were admitted as states simultaneously. In 1872, the building of the Northern Pacific Railway brought a rapid increase of huge farms, many of which were devastated by drought and severe winters in the 1880s. Thereafter followed a great influx of Norwegians and Germans, whose influence remains today. ADMISSION DATE: November 2, 1889 (as the 39th state). CAPITAL: Bismarck. NAME: For northern section of Dakota territory; *dakota* is Siouan word for "allies." MOTTO: "Liberty and Union, now and forever, one and inseparable." FLOWER: wild prairie rose. BIRD: Western meadowlark.

Land

TOTAL AREA: 70,795 sq mi. RIVERS: Missouri, Red River of the North.

Population

657,740 (1913). MAJOR CITIES: Fargo (14,331), Grand Forks (12,478), Minot (6,188), Bismark (5,443), Devil's Lake 5,157).

Business

North Dakota's economy was primarily agricultural. In 1876, the first of the bonanza farms—giant wheat farms—was established near Casselton. In all, 91 farms of more than 3,000 acres were established, almost all by 1885, after which they were broken up. In 1890, North Dakota ranked second to Minnesota in wheat farming; of the population's 190,183 residents, 43% were foreign-born, including 25,773 from Norway and 23,045 from Canada. Farming was centered in the fertile Red River of the North valley with livestock throughout the remainder of the state. Except in the case of flour and grist mills, most of the manufactures of the state were for home use.

Famous Natives

Vihjalmur Stefansson, explorer.

Memorable Events

May 11, 1876	Federal troops under Gen. George A. Custer left Fort Abraham Lincoln, near Mandan, for their campaign against the Lakota and the Cheyenne, leading to their defeat at the Indians' hands at Little Big Horn.
1881	Sitting Bull's men, who fled to Canada after defeating Custer, surrendered and returned to their reservations; the Northern Pacific reached the Montana border.
1882	Nine million acres of north-central North Dakota were opened to the public despite protests from the Turtle Mountain Chippewa, who did not cede the land until 1892.
1883	Bismark became the capital of Dakota Territory by offering the best bid—$100,000 and 160 acres of land; the University of North Dakota opened at Grand Forks; Theodore Roosevelt came to North Dakota for his health and began to ranch near Medora.
1884	First commercial mining of North Dakota's lignite began.
1885	The first land boom peaked.
1906	The second wave of land fever reached a peak with homestead filings of 2.7 million acres, mostly in arid western North Dakota.
1912	First state to hold presidential primary.

Ohio

In 1680, La Salle and the French explored the Ohio country and soon became involved in quarrels with the English, who claimed most of the area under a grant from their government. By the Treaty of 1763, the French surrendered all the territory west to the Mississippi. The first settlements in Ohio were Marietta in 1788 and Cincinnati in 1789, both on the Ohio River. In 1799, the Northwest Territory was organized, and shortly thereafter, Ohio was given a separate government. Significant migration into the state did not occur until after the War of 1812. ADMISSION DATE: February 19, 1803 (as the 17th state). CAPITAL: Columbus. NAME: From Iroquoian *oheo*, "beautiful." MOTTO: "With God all things are possible." FLOWER: scarlet carnation. BIRD: cardinal.

Land

TOTAL AREA: 41,060 sq mi. RIVERS: Cuyahoga, Maumee, Miami, Muskingum, Ohio, Sandusky, Scioto. MOUNTAINS: Allegheny.

Population

2,984,941; (1876) 4,960,391 (1913). MAJOR CITIES: Cleveland (560,663), Cincinnati (363,591), Columbus (181,511), Toledo (168,497), Dayton (116,577).

Business

Water transportation with the Great Lakes and the Atlantic seaboard and railways into the interior connected the state to important urban and industrial centers. Fertile soil, extensive hardwood forests, and an abundance of coal and natural gas gave Ohio great natural advantages. It led all states west of the Alleghenies in the manufacture of iron and steel; the manufacture of foundry and machine-shop products held second place. The 1870s witnessed the development of a manufacturing base that later became the foundation of the automobile industry. In 1900, Ohio led all other states in the manufacture of metal-working machinery. Flour and grist milling was one of the oldest industries in the state, flour having been sent to New Orleans as early as 1803. Ohio was also a corn-belt state, and much of corn raised there was milled within its borders.

Famous Natives

Sherwood Anderson, writer; George Wesley Bellows, painter and lithographer; Harvey William Cushing, neurological surgeon; George Armstrong Custer, army officer; Clarence Darrow, lawyer and reformer; Paul Laurence Dunbar, poet; Thomas A. Edison, inventor; James A. Garfield, 20th president of the United States; Ulysses S. Grant, 18th president of the United States; Zane Grey, novelist; Marcus A. Hanna, businessman and politician; William Rainey Harper, educator and scholar; Benjamin Harrison, 23rd president of the United States; Rutherford B. Hayes, 19th president of the United States; William Dean Howells, novelist and critic; Charles Franklin Kettering, inventor; William McKinley, 25th president of the United States; George William Norris, statesman; Adolph S. Ochs, newspaper publisher; William Howard Taft, 27th president and 9th chief justice of the United States; Tecumseh, Shawnee chief; Orville Wright, aviation pioneer and inventor.

Memorable Events

1884	The first U.S. electric street railway was placed in operation in Cleveland.
February 23, 1886	In Oberlin, Charles Martin Hall discovered the electrolytic process of making aluminum.
December 10, 1886	The American Federation of Trades and Labor was founded in Columbus, with Samuel Gompers as president.
1892	The state legislature made it unlawful to dismiss a worker for membership in a labor union.
1896	In Akron, B. F. Goodrich Company made the first rubber automobile tire.
1912	Ohio's fourth constitution was adopted.
1913	Spring floods devastated the state and caused 428 deaths and property damage of an estimated $250 million.

Oklahoma

In 1830, what became Oklahoma was created as Indian Territory for the settlement of the "Five Civilized Tribes," the Choctaw, Chickasaw, Cherokee, Creek, and Seminole. Forcibly moved from southeastern United States in a march the Indians labeled "The Trail of Tears," the tribes were promised protection. In March 1889, a rider was attached to an Indian Appropriation bill that opened to homesteaders the center of the territory, an area of about 3 million acres; in April, the land was officially opened and the first Oklahoma "boomers" rushed into the area. The territorial government was formed the following June, and by the same act of Congress, a strip of land known as "No Man's Land," approximately 3.8 million acres, was added as Beaver County. Gradually, other sections were opened. ADMISSION DATE: November 16, 1907 (as the 46th state). CAPITAL: Guthrie until 1910, then Oklahoma City. NAME: From Choctaw *okla humma,* "land of the red people." MOTTO: *"Labor omnia vincit"* (Work overcomes all obstacles). FLOWER: mistletoe. BIRD: scissor-tailed flycatcher.

Land

TOTAL AREA: 70,057 sq mi. RIVERS: Arkansas, Canadian, Cimarron, Red. MOUNTAINS: Ouachita, Ozark Plateau, Wichita.

Population

1,928,312 (1913). MAJOR CITIES: Oklahoma City (64,205), Muskogee (25,278), Tulsa (18,182), Enid (13,799), McAlester (12,954).

Business

Stock raising and agriculture were the primary economic activities of the state, with indications that mining would increase in importance in the future. Cotton growing was important, accompanied by an advance in the manufacturing of cottonseed oil and cake. Lead, zinc, gold, and copper had been found, though not in paying quantities yet, and sandstone and gypsum are widely scattered. In 1900, the most promising mine industry was salt, which was said to be sufficient to supply the nation.

Famous Natives

William Penn Adair Rogers, actor and humorist; James Francis Thorpe, athlete.

Memorable Events

March 2, 1889	A law was passed authorizing the opening of Oklahoma lands; on April 22, the United States opened part of Oklahoma to settlement, and approximately 50,000 settlers rushed in.
May 2, 1890	Congress created a territorial government for the settlers, the last territory in the continental United States.
September 22, 1891	Pres. Benjamin Harrison proclaimed 900,000 acres of Indian land open for general settlement; a second land rush for homesteads occurred.
1893	The Dawes Commission was created to liquidate the affairs of the "Five Civilized Tribes."
1897	A commercial oil well opened at Bartlesville.
1901	Red Fork, a Tulsa oil field, opened.
1910	The state capital was moved from Guthrie to Oklahoma City.

Oregon

Oregon was a name long applied to all the territory claimed by the United States on the Pacific coast, extending from 42°N to 54°N latitude. According to the treaty of 1818, it was jointly occupied by the United States and Great Britain until 1846, when the latter abandoned all claim to territory north of the 49th parallel. The name *Oregon* was then restricted to the region south of that line. In the late 1840s, California gold fever brought many settlers to the area. On August 14, 1848, the Territory of Oregon was organized by an act of Congress. ADMISSION DATE: February 14, 1859 (as the 33d state). CAPITAL: Salem. NAME: Of unknown origin, first applied to Columbia River. MOTTO: "Alis volat propriis" (She flies with her own wings). FLOWER: Oregon grape. BIRD: Western meadowlark.

Land

TOTAL AREA: 96,030 sq mi. RIVERS: Columbia, Snake, Willamette. MOUNTAINS: Cascade Range, Coast Range, Klamath.

Population

141,230 (1876); 753,862 (1913). MAJOR CITIES: Portland (207,214), Salem (14,094), Astoria (9,599), Eugene (9,009), Medford (8,840).

Business

Extensive forests and waterpower made lumber and timber the leading industry. In 1909, Oregon ranked fourth among states in lumber output with 1.9 billion board-feet, compared to 444 million board-feet in 1889. The Columbia River furnished nearly all the canned salmon in the United States, but during the Gilded Age, stringent laws were passed to guard against indiscriminate killing of the salmon. Fish canning was done almost entirely by the Chinese and was centered at Astoria near the mouth of the Columbia. Next to San Francisco, Portland had the largest Chinese community on the West Coast. In 1900, Oregon stood 38th in the United States in population and 30th in manufacturing.

Famous Natives

Hin-mah-too-ya-lat-kekht (Joseph), Nez Percé chief; Edwin Markham, poet; John Reed, journalist/poet/Communist.

Memorable Events

1876   University of Oregon at Eugene opened.
1883   Northern Pacific Railroad completed its link from St. Paul, Minnesota, to Portland.
1887   The Oregon and California Railroad reached San Francisco from Portland; Samuel Gompers, founder of the American Federation of Labor, organized 15 Portland craft unions for skilled workers into a citywide trades assembly.
1902   Voters adopted the initiative and referendum; Crater Lake National Park created.
1905   Lewis and Clark Exposition opened in Portland, commemorating the centennial of the expedition.
1912   Women won the right to vote.

Commonwealth of Pennsylvania

In 1681, the territory west of the Delaware River was granted to William Penn, a Quaker, who colonized it and founded Philadelphia in 1682. Under the Quakers, the colony became known for religious tolerance, peaceful relations with the Indians, and being first among the colonies to abolish slavery. In 1776, a convention presided over by Benjamin Franklin prepared a provisional constitution which was formally adopted in 1790. For 15 years, Philadelphia was the U.S. capital. With access to the Atlantic, the Great Lakes, and the navigable waters of the Ohio-Mississippi Valley, Pennsylvania enjoyed great transportation advantages and took a lead in the opening of the Midwest. ADMISSION DATE: December 12, 1787 (as the 2d state). CAPITAL: Harrisburg. NAME: For Adm. William Penn, father of William Penn. MOTTO: "Virtue, liberty, and independence." FLOWER: mountain laurel. BIRD: ruffed grouse.

Land

TOTAL AREA: 45,215 sq mi. RIVERS: Allegheny, Delaware, Juniata, Monongahela, Ohio, Schuylkill, Susquehanna. MOUNTAINS: Allegheny, Kittatinny, Laurel Hills, Pocono.

Population

3,978,515 (1876); 8,091,510 (1913). MAJOR CITIES: Philadelphia (1,549,008), Pittsburgh (533,905), Scranton (129,867), Reading (96,071), Wilkes-Barre (67,105).

Business

Since 1850, Pennsylvania ranked second in the U.S. in manufactured products and first since 1870 in the amount of power used in manufacturing. Lumber, tanbark, tobacco, cereals, crude petroleum, iron ore, and coal were its resources. Natural gas had been used in manufacturing since 1874, but the gas fields were nearly exhausted. The manufacture of iron and steel was the most important industry with major centers at Pittsburgh, McKeesport, Duquesne, Johnstown, and Newcastle. In 1900, textile manufacturing ranked second among industries of the state—silk being first—having been encouraged by Benjamin Franklin as early as 1750. During the Gilded Age, the carpet industry grew rapidly, as well as worsted goods and knitting production. There were 2,172 establishments engaged in the manufacture of tobacco, chiefly cheap cigars from domestic tobacco.

Famous Natives

Louisa May Alcott, author; James G. Blaine, statesman; Mary Cassatt, painter; Thomas Eakins, artist and teacher; Henry George, economist and reformer; Daniel Coit Gilman, educational administrator; Ross Granville Harrison, biologist; Andrew W. Mellon, financier/philanthropist; Robert E. Peary, naval officer and Arctic explorer; Terence V. Powderly, labor leader and reformer; Henry A. Rowland, physicist.

Memorable Events

1876	Centennial Exposition of Philadelphia where Alexander Graham Bell's new telephone was exhibited.
May 31, 1889	Johnstown flood—the worst in U.S. history—killed 2,200 people.
1892	Pinkerton detectives killed 12 strikers at Homestead steel works near Pittsburgh.
February 2, 1897	The state capitol at Harrisburg burned.
September 11, 1897	Twenty coal miners killed during strike for eight-hour day and other concessions.
August 10, 1898	Cornerstone for new capitol was laid.
1901	Charles M. Schwab became president of United States Steel Corporation, the first billion-dollar corporation.

Commonwealth of Rhode Island

Giovanni da Verrazano in 1524 was the first European to visit the area of Narragansett Bay. The region has also been claimed as the Vinland of the Norse explorers who may have landed on the North American continent four centuries before Columbus. In 1636, Rhode Island was settled at Providence by Roger Williams and dissenters from the Puritan Massachusetts Bay Colony. Providence is also the site of the first Baptist church. At Newport is the first Quaker meetinghouse and the first synagogue. In the nineteenth century, Rhode Island was influenced by immigration and the Industrial Revolution. ADMISSION DATE: May 29, 1790 (as the 13th state). CAPITAL: Providence. NAME: For Rhode Island in Narragansett Bay, named in turn for Mediterranean island of Rhodes. MOTTO: "Hope." FLOWER: violet. BIRD: Rhode Island red.

Land

TOTAL AREA: 1,250 sq mi. RIVERS: Blackstone, Pawcatuck, Providence, Sakonnet.

Population

252,860 (1913); 578,291 (1913). MAJOR CITIES: Providence (224,326), Pawtucket (51,622), Woonsocket (38,125), Newport (27,149), Warwick (26,629).

Business

The manufactures of cotton and woolen goods were the chief industries of the state, second in the United States in the manufacture of cotton goods and third in woolens (1900). Because a method of filling gold with cheaper metals had been perfected, Rhode Island was first in the production of cheap jewelry, which was centered in Providence. Closely allied was the production of silverware. The manufacture of files, rubber and elastic goods, malt liquors, and electrical equipment and supplies were also important industries.

Famous Native

George M. Cohan, actor and producer.

Memorable Events

1885	The Prohibition amendment was added to the state constitution but was repealed in 1889.
1895	The "Rhode Island red" hen was officially recognized as a new breed.
1903	The wireless telegraph was installed in the state.

South Carolina

Jean Ribault, a Frenchman, made the first attempt to colonize the territory now known as South Carolina. In 1663, the province of the Carolinas was created, and English colonists made the first permanent settlement on the banks of the Ashley River. In 1680, a large number of Huguenots and later many Swiss, Scotch, Irish, and German immigrants settled in the territory. Rice plantations worked by slaves were important early, but later, tobacco played a major role. In the back country, settlers eked out a living as tenant farmers. ADMISSION DATE: May 23, 1788 (as the 8th state). CAPITAL: Columbia. NAME: For King Charles II (Carolus is Latin for Charles). MOTTO: "Dum Spiro, Spero" (While I breathe, I hope). FLOWER: yellow jessamine. BIRD: Carolina wren.

Land

TOTAL AREA: 30,570 sq mi. RIVERS: Congaree, Edisto, Pee Dee, Savannah, Tugalos, Wateree. MOUNTAINS: Blue Ridge.

Population

879,589 (1876); 1,570,174 (1913). MAJOR CITIES: Charleston (58,833), Columbia (26,319), Spartanburg (17,517), Greenville (15,741), Anderson (9,654).

Business

By 1910, rice production had mostly ended, and cotton had become the leading crop. While agriculture remained central in the state's economy through the close of the nineteenth century, textile manufacture rapidly advanced to importance in the early twentieth century. With scarcely a cotton mill in the state in 1895, in less than a decade, South Carolina nearly led the nation in the number of spindles and output. The manufacture of lumber and timber ranked second, while phosphate fertilizers ranked third. An experiment in tea growing around Summerville produced successful tea plantations.

Famous Natives

James Francis Byrnes, politician and jurist; DuBose Heyward, author.

Memorable Events

1876	White militants, called Red Shirts, supported the gubernatorial candidate Wade Hampton, a former Confederate general, and intimidated black voters.
August 31, 1886	An earthquake centered in Charleston killed 92 and caused $8 million in damages.
1890	Benjamin R. Tillman, leader of the Farmers Alliance and industrial workers, was elected governor.
August 24, 1893	A hurricane killed 1,000 in Savannah, Georgia, and Charleston.
1895	Blacks were disfranchised by revisions to the constitution.
1896	South Carolina held its first primary.

South Dakota

The U.S. did not organize the Dakota Territory until 1864, and even then little interest was shown in the region until the discovery of gold in 1874. South Dakota was not established as a state until 1889; prior to that year, its history is identical to that of North Dakota. Due to homesteading, the population of the western half of the state increased from 57,575 in 1905 to 137,687 in 1910. ADMISSION DATE: November 2, 1889 (as the 40th state). CAPITAL: Pierre. NAME: For southern section of Dakota Territory; dakota is Siouan word for "allies." MOTTO: "Under God the people rule." FLOWER: pasqueflower. BIRD: ring-necked pheasant.

Land

TOTAL AREA: 77,650 sq mi. RIVERS: Cheyenne, James, Missouri, Moreau, White. MOUNTAINS: Black Hills (Harney Peak, 7,242 ft).

Population

86,779 (1876); 640,924 (1913). MAJOR CITIES: Sioux Falls (14,094), Aberdeen (10,753), Lead (8,392), Watertown (7,010), Mitchell (6,515).

Business

The majority of those who stayed after the gold rush went into cattle ranching, which was a mainstay of the economy through the first half of the twentieth century. In 1883, the land boom peaked in the state; filings in southern Dakota totaled 5,410,687 acres, about 23% of the national total. By 1885, the population of southern South Dakota had risen to 248,569 from 81,781 in 1880. Flour and grist-mill products and the making of butter, cheese, and condensed milk were industries of local importance.

Famous Natives

Martha ("Calamity") Jane Burk (b. Missouri), frontierswoman; Crazy Horse (Tashunka Witco), Oglala-Brulé Lakota chief; Sitting Bull (Tatanka Iyotaka), Hunkpapa Lakota chief.

Memorable Events

August 2, 1876	Wild Bill Hickok was shot in the Black Hills mining town of Deadwood while holding aces over eights (the "dead man's hand"); Calamity Jane was later buried next to him.
1877	The U.S. government wins the Sioux war and take possession of the Black Hills region.
1877	George Hearst bought the Homestake Mine claim for $70,000, and by 1935, it had produced $301 million of gold bullion.
1880	Railroad lines reached the Missouri at Pierre and Chamberlain.
1881	Sitting Bull returned to western South Dakota after five years in Canada, following the Battle of Little Bighorn.
1882	The University of South Dakota was founded at Vermillion.
1889	The Great Sioux Reservation was reduced by about 9 million acres and broken up into five smaller reservations.
1890	Ghost Dance Religion among the Sioux alarmed whites, leading to U.S. troops' massacre of 150 Sioux at Wounded Knee on December 29; 25 soldiers were also killed.
1897	A state referendum repealed the prohibition of liquor.
1904–13	A series of agreements with the Teton Lakota made more than 4 million acres of reservation lands available for purchase by whites.

Tennessee

Tennessee was first claimed by Virginia and then North Carolina. Daniel Boone, the famous frontiersman, traversed the region in the 1760s. In the eighteenth century, cotton and tobacco growers became important in the western part of the state where slavery took root; backwoods settlers in the eastern hills opposed slavery. In 1794, a distinct territorial government was established in Tennessee. ADMISSION DATE: June 1, 1796 (as the 16th state). CAPITAL: Nashville. NAME: From the Indian name of *Tanassee* given the Little Tennessee River. MOTTO: "Agriculture and commerce." FLOWER: iris. BIRD: mockingbird.

Land

TOTAL AREA: 42,050 sq mi. RIVERS: Clinch, Cumberland, Mississippi, Tennessee. MOUNTAINS: Cumberland, Great Smoky, Unaka.

Population

1,428,823 (1876); 2,236,149 (1913). MAJOR CITIES: Memphis (131,105), Nashville (110,364), Chattanooga (44,604), Knoxville (36,346), Jackson (15,779).

Business

The state was famous for the bright tobaccos of Greene County and the fine red shipping tobaccos of the Clarksville district. In order of importance, flour and grist-mill products followed by lumber and timber were the important industries of the state. During the Gilded Age, exploitation of coal, iron, and copper ores made these important growth industries.

Famous Natives

Sequoyah (George Guess), Cherokee scholar.

Memorable Events

1878	The worst yellow-fever epidemic in U.S. history hit Memphis, killing 5,000 out of 19,000.
1890	In the "agrarian revolt," the Farmers' Alliance seized control of the Democratic Party and the governorship.
1905–06	The Black Patch wars.
1907	The local-option law was extended to all include all of Tennessee.
November 9, 1909	Edward Ward Carmack, in a dispute arising out of a bitter context for the gubernatorial nomination, was shot dead by Robin Cooper.
1909	Public opinion, inflamed by Carmack's murder, forced statewide mandatory prohibition through the General Assembly over Governor Malcolm R. Patterson's veto.

Texas

In the 1820s, Mexico won its independence from Spain and gained control of the Spanish borderlands. Land grants were given to impressarios like Stephen F. Austin for the purpose of encouraging settlement in the Texas province. In the 1840s, the United States acquired the entire region after the Mexican-American War. ADMISSION DATE: December 29, 1845 (as the 28th state). CAPITAL: Austin. NAME: From Caddo *tavshas*, "friends." MOTTO: "Friendship." FLOWER: bluebonnet. BIRD: mockingbird.

Land

TOTAL AREA: 265,780 sq mi. RIVERS: Brazos, Colorado Red, Rio Grande. MOUNTAINS: Guadalupe.

Population

1,282,481 (1876); 4,161,777 (1913). MAJOR CITIES: San Antonio (96,614), Dallas (92,104), Houston (78,800), Fort Worth (73,312), Galveston (36,981).

Business

Lumber, cotton, and wheat (sixth in the United States) were produced in abundance. Lumber and timber products were the most important industries. Texas ranked second in the United States in cottonseed oil and cake and cotton ginning. During the Gilded Age, discoveries of great quantities of oil produced a cheap fuel for local use and brought an enormous increase of capital to Texas.

Famous Natives

James Frank Dobie, folklorist; Dwight D. Eisenhower, general and president of the U.S..

Memorable Events

1876	The present state constitution was adopted.
1898	Theodore Roosevelt trained the Rough Riders at San Antonio.
September 8, 1900	A hurricane produced an enormous tidal surge, killing 6,000 at Galveston and leading to the inauguration of the commission form of city government.
1901	Discovery of oil at the great Spindletop oil field.
1910	The first U.S. Army airplane was flown at Fort Sam Houston.

Utah

Utah is located in the middle of the Great Basin between the Rocky Mountains and the Sierra Nevada. After Joseph Smith and his followers were lynched in Illinois, Brigham Young led the members of the Church of Jesus Christ of Latter-Day Saints (Mormons), to the arid Salt Lake Valley in 1847. Polygamy (which the Mormons later renounced) was the chief obstacle to statehood. In 1863, after the discovery of silver, an influx of non-Mormons entered the state, but they still composed less than one-third of the state's population. ADMISSION DATE: January 4, 1896 (as the 45th state). CAPITAL: Salt Lake City. NAME: For Ute Indians. MOTTO: "Industry." FLOWER: sego lily. BIRD: seagull.

Land

TOTAL AREA: 84,970 sq mi. RIVERS: Bear, Colorado, Green, Sevier. MOUNTAINS: La Sal, Uinta (King's Peak, 13,528 ft), Wasatch Range.

Population

121,092 (1876); 405,715 (1913). MAJOR CITIES: Salt Lake City (92,777), Ogden (25,580), Provo (8,925), Logan (7,522).

Business

Utah was primarily a mining and agricultural state but manufacturing increased at the turn of the twentieth century. Smelting and the refining of lead ore was the most important industry; the state produced thirteen percent of U.S. production. Silver was a valuable metal gained in the refining of lead ores. The manufacture of salt from the brine of the Great Salt Lake ranked high in the important industries of 1900. Flour and grist milling, the canning of fruits and vegetables, and the manufacture of beet sugar, malt liquors, and butter and cheese were important agricultural products. During the Victorian period, the state passed labor laws forbidding contractors from coercing labor to work more than an eight-hour day, prohibiting the employment of children under fourteen years of age and women from work in the mines and smelters; proprietors of stores, restaurants, and shops were required to provide seats for their women employees and to permit them to use them when not working. Blacklisting of workers for the purpose of preventing them from joining labor unions was made a misdemeanor.

Famous Native

Maude Adams, actress.

Memorable Events

1885	Because of determined federal efforts to enforce the law against polygamy, 23 persons were convicted and jailed; many polygamous Mormons, including church leaders, went underground; before prosecutions were abandoned in the 1890s, more than 1,000 Utah Mormons were fined or imprisoned.
1887	Seeking statehood, the legislative assembly, with the support of Mormon leaders, enacted a law prohibiting polygamy.
October 6, 1890	A general conference of Mormons unanimously advised church leaders to refrain from the practice of polygamy.
1893	Completion and dedication of the Salt Lake City Temple.
1895	A constitution established for Utah guaranteed no union of church and state and declared polygamous marriage to be "forever prohibited."
1900	200 men died in a mine explosion at Scofield's Winter Quarters Mine.
1905	More than a million acres of Uintah Reservation were opened to white settlement.
1906	Utah Copper Company's Gingham Canyon mine was founded, the largest open-pit copper mine in the world.
1911	The Strawberry Reservoir was completed, diverting the Colorado River water for irrigation and power.

Vermont

Vermont was originally claimed by both New York and New Hampshire. In 1770, Ethan Allen and his Green Mountain Boys stoutly resisted the claims of the New Yorkers, fought well against the British in the Revolution, and declared the area the independent republic of New Connecticut in 1777. ADMISSION DATE: March 4, 1791 (as the 14th state). CAPITAL: Montpelier. NAME: From French *vert mont*, "green mountain." MOTTO: "Freedom and unity." FLOWER: red clover. BIRD: hermit thrush.

Land

TOTAL AREA: 9,565 sq mi. RIVERS: Connecticut, Lamoille, Otter Creek, Poultney, White, Winooski. MOUNTAINS: Green (Mt. Mansfield, 4,393 ft), Taconic.

Population

331,592 (1876); 359,809 (1913). MAJOR CITIES: Burlington (20,468), Rutland (13,546), Barre (10,734), Bennington (8,698), St. Johnsbury (8,098).

Business

An influx of French-Canadians began to develop Vermont's manufacturing base in the nineteenth century. The manufacturing industries were largely dependent upon the natural resources: forests, quarries, and grazing land. Pine and oak were the most important woods, and timber and lumber manufacture ranked first in the state. The lumber industry was centered in Burlington, with important rail connections to Canada and Boston. The making of paper and wood pulp, chiefly at Bellows Falls using the water power of the Connecticut River, were allied industries. A large number of workers were employed in extensive slate, limestone, and granite quarries, making Vermont first in the United States in the tombstone industry. Roofing materials were made from the slate quarries of the southwest, and most of the real sugar maple grown in the United States came from extensive sugar orchards there.

Famous Natives

Chester A. Arthur, U.S. president; John Deere, industrialist; George Dewey, naval officer; John Dewey, philosopher; James Fisk, financier.

Memorable Events

1896   Rudyard Kipling left his Brattleboro home for England after writing two *Jungle Books* and *Captains Courageous* there.

1910   The first airplane flight at St. Johnsbury in northeastern Vermont.

Commonwealth of Virginia

The first known settlers of Virginia were the mound builders of the Mississippi Valley who had outposts in the Appalachian Mountains. The first permanent English settlement in America was made at Jamestown in 1607. The first legislative body to meet on the continent was at James City in 1619 when the first African Americans also landed. In 1624, Virginia became a royal province. In 1744, Virginia purchased from the Indians the rights to make settlements along the Ohio River but in 1781 gave up all claims in the interest of harmony. Roughly one-third of the state broke away during the Civil War and formed the state of West Virginia. ADMISSION DATE: June 25, 1788 (as the 10th state). CAPITAL: Richmond. NAME: For Elizabeth I, called Virgin Queen. MOTTO: *"Sic semper tyrannis"* (Thus always to tyrants). FLOWER: dogwood. BIRD: cardinal.

Land

TOTAL AREA: 42,450 sq mi. RIVERS: James, Potomac, Rappahannock, Roanoke, Shenandoah, York. MOUNTAINS: Allegheny, Blue Ridge, Cumberland, Unaka.

Population

1,397,604 (1876); 2,126,503 (1913).

Business

Until the close of the nineteenth century, Virginia remained very dependent upon labor-intensive tobacco. In 1900, tobacco products were valued at $21 million, first in the United States. Wheat and flour and grist-mill products ranked second in importance. Although most grain was locally consumed, large quantities of flour were transported to the West Indies, South America, Africa, and Europe. The manufacture of lumber and timber products ranked third, but the forests of pine and hardwoods were being depleted rapidly. The shipbuilding yards at Newport News were the largest in the United States, and the U.S. Navy yard at Portsmouth made it first in importance. Iron ore production ranked fifth in the United States, and coal deposits, especially in southwestern Virginia, were substantial.

Famous Natives

Richard E. Byrd, explorer; Willa Cather, novelist; Joseph Eggleston Johnston, soldier and railroad commissioner; Cyrus Hall McCormick, inventor; Matthew Fountaine Maury, oceanographer and naval officer; Walter Reed, doctor; Booker T. Washington, educator; Woodrow Wilson, U.S. president.

Memorable Events

1879   General William Mahone founded the Readjuster Party over the issue of the state debt.

April 24, 1889   The Simpson Dry Dock, the largest in the world, opened at Newport News.

May 12, 1900   The state legislature passed "Jim Crow" laws.

April 26, 1907   The Jamestown Exposition celebrated the 300th anniversary of the landing of English settlers at Cape Henry.

Washington

Washington is in the northwest corner of the contiguous 48 states and was originally the center of a rich Native American culture noted for its ornately carved canoes and totem poles. In 1792, Boston merchant Capt. Robert Gray began to trade in sea otter pelts; in 1810, John Jacob Astor founded a fur company and established a trading post on the Columbia. In 1853, a territorial government was established. ADMISSION DATE: November 11, 1889 (as the 42d state). CAPITAL: Olympia. NAME: For George Washington. MOTTO: *"Alki"* (By and by). FLOWER: rhododendron. BIRD: willow goldfinch.

Land

TOTAL AREA: 69,180 sq mi. RIVERS: Chehalis, Columbia, Pend Oreille, Snake, Yakima. MOUNTAINS: Cascade Range, Olympic.

Population

54,652 (1876); 1,337,166 (1913). MAJOR CITIES: Seattle (237,194), Spokane (104,402), Tacoma (83,743), Everett (24,814), Bellingham (24,298).

Business

The discovery of gold in Alaska and the Yukon stimulated advances in trade and manufacturing in the state. Agriculture and lumbering were the mainstays of the economy. Red fir lumber and cedar shingles were important products. In 1905, with 3,917 million board-feet cut, Washington became the leading lumbering state, doubling its 1900 production. The state was divided into an eastern farming region, rich in dairy products, fruit, and wheat, and a western region that relied largely on the export of lumber products to the Far East. This geographic split is reflected in weather patterns with Pacific-coast Washington getting rain almost daily and the eastern region limited to under 10 inches of rainfall per year. Flour and grist-mill products ranked second to the lumber industry, with canning and preserving of fish third. Salmon and oysters were first shipped to San Francisco in 1850. Puget Sound salmon production peaked in 1913 at 2.5 million cases.

Memorable Events

1885   Anti-Chinese riots resulted in federal troops being sent to Seattle.

June 6, 1887   The first train on the Northern Pacific railroad's transcontinental line reached Tacoma.

1893   Seattle was the terminus of the Great Northern Railroad line.

1901   Alaska-Yukon Exposition at Seattle.

1897   The discovery of gold in the Yukon's Klondike fostered the growth of Seattle as a supply and transportation center.

1899   Mount Rainier National Park established.

1902   Yacolt Burn destroyed 700,000 forested acres south of Puget Sound.

1909   The Alaska-Yukon-Pacific Exposition drew many visitors to the state.

1910   Women received the right to vote.

1912   The initiative, referendum, and recall were enacted.

West Virginia

West Virginia became a state as the consequence of the Civil War. Forty-eight counties in western Virginia, separated from the coast by the mountains, less tied to slavery and better connected to the markets of the Ohio Valley, broke off and reorganized after Virginia seceded. In 1863, the voters chose to become a separate state. ADMISSION DATE: June 20, 1863 (as the 20th state). CAPITAL: Charleston. NAME: For western part of Virginia. MOTTO: *"Montani semper liberi"* (Mountaineers are always free). FLOWER: rhododendron. BIRD: cardinal.

Land

TOTAL AREA: 24,780 sq mi. RIVERS: Big Sandy, Guayandotte, Kanawha, Little Kanawha, Monongahela, Ohio, Potomac. MOUNTAINS: Allegheny, Blue Ridge, Cumberland.

Population

547,880 (1876); 1,303,183 (1913). MAJOR CITIES: Wheeling (41,641), Huntington (31,161), Charleston (22,996), Parkersburg (17,842), Bluefield (11,188).

Business

Farming was the backbone of the economy until the close of the nineteenth century and the opening of the coal fields. Twelve counties in the north along the Ohio River produced more than one-half of the manufactured products of the state. The abundant supplies of coal and natural gas, transportation facilities afforded by the Ohio River, and the proximity to the Pennsylvania's steel districts gave these counties great industrial importance. West Virginia was second only to Pennsylvania in the production of coke. Besides iron and steel, which were centered in Wheeling, lumber and timber products were of secondary importance; they were located mainly in the eastern part of the state, with Charleston as the shipping point.

Famous Natives

Newton Baker, statesman; John W. Davis, politician.

Memorable Events

1882 The 20-year-long Hatfield-McCoy feud erupted in the Tug Valley.
1902 "Mother" Mary Jones campaigned to unionize 7,000 miners in the Kanawha Valley.
1907 The Monogah Mine explosion killed 361 men.
1912 Paint Creek miners struck to gain recognition of the United Mine Workers of America; martial law was imposed until 1913; state prohibition was enacted.

Wisconsin

Native American resistance to white settlement was strong in Wisconsin and not overcome until the Black Hawk wars of 1832. In the early nineteenth century, large numbers of German, Scandinavian, and Dutch farmers immigrated to the state. Wisconsin was founded as a territory in 1836. ADMISSION DATE: May 29, 1848 (as the 30th state). CAPITAL: Madison. NAME: From Ojibwa *wishkonsing,* "place of the bearer." MOTTO: "Forward." FLOWER: wood violet. BIRD: robin.

Land

TOTAL AREA: 56,040 sq mi. RIVERS: Black, Chippewa, Menominee, Mississippi, St. Croix, Wisconsin.

Population

1,211,166 (1876); 2,416,706 (1913). MAJOR CITIES: Milwaukee (373,857), Superior (40,384), Racine (38,002), Oshkosh (33,062), La Crosse (30,417).

Business

Agriculture, especially dairy products, was an extremely important part of Wisconsin's economy. Although the wheat crop was large, nearly one-half of the flour and grist-mill products in 1900 were produced from imported wheat. Lumber and timber products were the most important industry. Foundry and machine shops increased rapidly, producing machinery for motive power and equipment for lumber, flour and paper mills, breweries, and mines. Wisconsin ranked fourth in the United States in the production of malt liquors, an industry centered in Milwaukee.

Famous Natives

King Camp Gillette, inventor and businessman; Harry Houdini, magician; Robert La Follette, politician/reformer; Thorstein Veblen, economist; Frank Lloyd Wright, architect.

Memorable Events

1882 First hydroelectric plant completed at Appleton.
1884 Ringling Brothers circus formed at Baraboo.
1905 The civil service was adopted for state employees.
1910 Milwaukee set precedents by electing the first Socialist congressman (Victor Berger) and the first Socialist mayor of a big city (Emil Seidel).
1911 First state to enact income tax.
1913 First state Workmen's Compensation Law in the United States.

Wyoming

Most of Wyoming was part of the original Louisiana Purchase territory acquired from France in 1803. The western part was acquired by prior settlement, as had Washington, Oregon, and Idaho. Settlement of the territory was slow due to the inhospitable environment and the presence of Indians in the more fertile areas. The building of Fort Laramie in 1834 quickened settlement, and the coming of the Union Pacific railroad in 1869 opened the state to additional settlers. Wyoming was the first state to grant women the vote. Territorial status came in 1869. ADMISSION DATE: July 10, 1890 (as the 44th state). CAPITAL: Cheyenne. NAME: From Delaware *maugh-wau-wa-ma,* "large plains" or "mountains and valleys alternating." MOTTO: "Equal rights." FLOWER: Indian paintbrush. BIRD: meadowlark.

Land

TOTAL AREA: 97,890 sq mi. RIVERS: Bighorn, Green, North Platte, Powder, Snake, Yellowstone. MOUNTAINS: Absaroka, Bighorn, Black Hills, Laramie, Owl Creek, Teton Range, Wind River Range, Wyoming Range.

Population

16,121 (1876); 162,681 (1913). MAJOR CITIES: Cheyenne (11,320), Sheridan (8,408), Laramie (8,237), Rock Springs (5,778).

Business

Stock raising and mining were the chief economic activities. There were no large factories, and the many shops produced mostly for local needs. Iron ore and petroleum were abundant in supply, but transportation difficulties hampered their industrial development. The state was also rich in natural wonders, such as the geysers, forests, and mountains of Yellowstone Park. Wyoming was also called a "geological wonderland." The Meszoic period left rich fossil deposits from little vertebrate ammonites to the giant vertebrate dinosaurs of the Jurassic age. In 1889, a scientific expedition of 80 members spent 40 days exploring and examining fossil exposures and gathering specimens.

Memorable Events

1876	A new treaty opened northeastern Wyoming to white settlement.
1887	The University of Wyoming opened in Laramie with a faculty of seven and a student body of 42.
1892	Big cattlemen hired gunmen to eliminate small ranchers and homesteaders suspected of rustling cattle; the Johnson County War culminated in their unsuccessful attempt to storm Buffalo.
1895	Cody was established, named for William F. Cody (Buffalo Bill), who shot bison to feed railroad workers in Wyoming before organizing his Wild West show.
1897	The first Frontier Days celebration in Cheyenne, featuring what became the world's oldest and biggest rodeo.
1897–1909	Sixteen men and perhaps 10,000 sheep were killed by cattlemen unwilling to share the open range.
1905	The Shoshone and Arapaho relinquished 1,346,320 acres of their reservation, which became available for white settlement.

CHAPTER 9 Cities

Political Machines

The rise of the "boss" and the "political machine" were features of late nineteenth-century urban politics. Escalating demands for sewer, water, housing, police and fire protection, and other services, and burgeoning urban populations of immigrants with votes created the dynamics for ethnic political bosses and their organizations. In exchange for votes, machine politicians fulfilled the needs of neighborhood precincts. The party faithful were also rewarded for their support with political appointments.

The machines acted in very personal ways to serve a hard-pressed population. During the bitter winter of 1870, Boss Tweed of Tammany Hall (the Democratic party organization in New York City) dumped tons of coal on street corners in the slums of New York City. Tim Sullivan gave away thousands of turkeys every Christmas. When block captains reported births and deaths of neighborhood residents or news about people making their first Holy Communion in the Roman Catholic church or celebrating a Jewish bar mitzvah, a ward boss showed up or sent baskets of fruit or flowers. Sometimes, ward politicians threw block parties. In 1871, for example, Mike Norton treated his constituents to 100 kegs of beer, 50 cases of champagne, 20 gallons of brandy, 10 gallons of gin, 200 gallons of turtle soup, 36 hams, 4,000 pounds of corned beef, and 5,000 cigars.

The political machine in power, whether Democrat or Republican, controlled law enforcement. In exchange for cash payments, politicians blinked at illegal businesses: gambling houses, brothels, unlicensed saloons, and opium dens. "Bathhouse" John Coughlan and "Hinkey-Dink" Kenna, of Chicago's "Grey Wolves" (a strong-armed gang), openly collected their tribute at an annual ball for the kings and queens of Chicago vice. Graft and corruption in the awarding of contracts for city services were notorious.

The property-owning middle classes, who shouldered the bills with their taxes, periodically mounted campaigns to eliminate the political machines. The bosses called them "Goo-Goos" (because of their campaigns for *Good Government*). The infamous Tweed Ring, which had bilked New York City of an estimated $200 million, was eventually overthrown in 1872; Chicago's Grey Wolves were thrown out of city hall in 1894; and a major reform campaign swept Abe Ruef, boss of San Francisco, out of office in 1906. But the Goo-Goos did not last because, unlike the ethnic machines, they could not fulfill the needs of downtowners. In fact, immigrants came to regard the Goo-Goos as little more than enemies of their ethnic heritage. In the persons of their ethnic bosses, immigrants could take vicarious pleasure in seeing Poles, Jews, Irishmen, Italians, or blacks succeed in a hostile environment. So the political machine did not disappear from American cities; it merely changed as the old immigrants—Irish, Italians, and Jews—moved up and out of the slums and were replaced with newcomers, such as blacks, Puerto Ricans, and other Hispanics.

Settlement Houses

Settlement houses became one of the most distinctive features of the urban response to the social problems of the Industrial Revolution. Situated in urban districts where the laboring populations lived and worked, the settlement house sought to bring culture, comfort, and uplift to the lives of working men and women. In 1889, Jane Addams and Ellen Gates Starr founded Hull House, the first social settlement, on Chicago's near west side. Addams later defined Hull House as "an experimental effort to aid in the solution of the social

and industrial problems which are engendered by the modern conditions of life in a great city." By 1910 more than 400 settlement houses existed in every major city in the United States.

Settlement houses were typically staffed by young, college-educated (90%) women (60%) who had spurned marriage for social action. Addams and Starr, for example, had graduated from Rockford, Illinois, Female Seminary in 1889. Addams gained a national reputation as a women's rights advocate, Progressive reformer, and peace activist. Religion also motivated many workers; nearly all either came from a ministerial family or contemplated becoming clergy themselves. In 1905, a poll of 339 settlement residents found 88% to be active church members involved in a variety of sectarian youth organizations.

The work of the settlement house included a variety of activities as workers sought to bring art exhibitions, university extension classes, summer schools, Sunday concerts, and special lectures to working-class neighborhoods. Residents also lobbied for changes in child and women's labor laws, public libraries, parks, playgrounds, and better schools. Hull House had a Jane club for working women, a ward club for reformers, sewing and cooking classes, a medical clinic and dispensary, and a labor museum to stir pride in ethnic culture.

City Government by Commission

In 1900, a West Indian hurricane, blowing steadily for 18 hours with winds of 135 miles an hour, swept enormous waves across the city of Galveston, Texas. About 5,000 lives were lost, and property damages were estimated at $17 million. After the storm, the city government, under its mayor, proved unable to deal with the crisis. The Deepwater Commission, composed of commercial experts concerned with developing the harbor, took control of the government and wrote a charter to provide for government by a board to be appointed by the governor of the state.

In 1901, the Galveston charter was modified to provide for a commission form of government, which had a wide influence on municipal government in the United States. The "Galveston plan" came to signify government by commission, rather than by a strong mayor. Typically, cities under this plan elect commissioners who are responsible for major bureaus or commissions, each representing part of the city's services. The commissioners may select a chairman to head the group.

TABLE 9.1   MAYORS OF MAJOR CITIES

The following is a listing of mayors and other chief executives of the top ten cities, selected on the basis of population in 1913.

Baltimore, Maryland	
1877	George P. Kane
1878	F. C. Latrobe
1881	William P. Whyte
1883	F. C. Latrobe
1885	James Hodges

Baltimore, Maryland

1887	F. C. Latrobe
1889	Robert C. Davidson
1891	F. C. Latrobe
1895	Alcaeus Hooper
1897	William T. Malster
1899	Thomas G. Hayes
1903	Robert M. McLane
1904	E. Clay Timanus
1907	J. Barry Mahool
1911	James H. Preston

Boston, Massachusetts

1877	Frederick O. Prince
1878	Henry L. Pierce
1879	Frederick O. Prince
1882	Samuel A. Green
1883	Albert Palmer
1884	Augustus P. Martin
1885	Hugh O'Brien
1889	Thomas N. Hart
1891	Nathan Matthews, Jr.
1895	Edwin U. Curtis
1896	Josiah Quincy
1900	Thomas N. Hart
1902	Patrick A. Collins
1905	Daniel A. Whelton
1906	John F. Fitzgerald
1908	George A. Hibbard
1910	John F. Fitzgerald

Chicago, Illinois

1876	Monroe Heath
1879	Carter H. Harrison, Sr.
1887	John A. Roche
1889	De Witt C. Cregier
1891	Hempstead Washburne
1893	Carter H. Harrison, Sr.
	George B. Swift
	John P. Hopkins
1895	George B. Swift
1897	Carter H. Harrison, Jr.
1905	Edward F. Dunne
1907	Fred A. Busse
1911	Carter H. Harrison, Jr.

Cleveland, Ohio

1877	William G. Rose
1879	P. R. Herrick
1883	John H. Farley
1885	George W. Gardner
1887	Brenton D. Babcock
1889	George W. Gardner
1891	William G. Rose
1893	Robert Blee
1895	Robert E. McKisson
1899	John H. Farley
1901	Tom L. Johnson
1910	Herman Baehr
1912	Newton D. Baker

Detroit, Michigan

1876	Alexander Lewis
1878	George C. Langdon
1880	William G. Thompson
1884	S. B. Grummond
1886	M. H. Chamberlain

Detroit, Michigan

1888	John Pridgeon, Jr.
1897	William Richert
	William C. Maybury
1905	George P. Codd
1907	William B. Thompson
1909	Philip Breitmeyer
1911	William B. Thompson
1913	Oscar B. Marx

Los Angeles, California

1876	Frederick A. MacDougall
1878	James R. Toberman
1882	Cameron E. Thom
1884	Edward F. Spence
1886	William H. Workman
1888	John Bryson
1889	Henry T. Hazard
1892	Thomas E. Rowan
1894	Frank Rader
1896	Meredith P. Snyder
1898	Fred Eaton
1900	Meredith P. Snyder
1904	Owen C. McAleer
1906	Arthur C. Harper
1909	William D. Stephens
	George Alexander
1913	Henry R. Rose

New York, New York

1875	William H. Wickham
1877	Smith Ely
1879	Edward Cooper
1881	William R. Grace
1883	Franklin Edson
1885	William R. Grace
1887	Abram S. Hewitt
1889	Hugh J. Grant
1893	Thomas F. Gilroy
1895	William L. Strong
1898	Robert A. Van Wyck
1902	Seth Low
1904	George B. McClellan
1910	William J. Gaynor
1913	Ardolph L. Kline

Philadelphia, Pennsylvania

1872	William S. Stokley
1881	Samuel G. King
1884	William B. Smith
1887	Edwin H. Fitler
1891	Edwin S. Stuart
1895	Charles F. Warwick
1899	Samuel H. Ashbridge
1903	John Weaver
1907	John E. Reyburn
1911	R. Blankenburg

Pittsburgh, Pennsylvania

1875	William C. McCarthy
1878	Walter Lidwell
1881	Robert W. Lyons
1884	Andrew Fulton
1887	William McCallim
1890	H. J. Gourley
1893	Bernard McKenna
1896	Henry P. Ford
1899	William J. Diehl

(continued)

TABLE 9.1 (continued)

The following is a listing of mayors and other chief executives of the top ten cities, selected on the basis of population in 1913.

Pittsburgh, Pennsylvania	
1901	J. O. Brown
	A. M. Brown
1903	W. G. Hays
1906	George W. Guthrie
1909	William A. Magee

St. Louis, Missouri	
1876	Henry Overstolz
1881	William L. Ewing
1885	David R. Francis
1889	Edward A. Noonan
1893	Cyrus P. Walbridge
1897	Henry Ziegenhein
1901	Rolla Wells
1909	Frederick Kreismann
1913	Henry W. Kiel

Ten Largest Cities in the United States, 1913

Population is the basis of the U.S. rank in 1913. Cities were governed either by a mayor and other city officials or by a commission. Government by commission was first instituted in Galveston, Texas, in 1901 (see page 228). Usually, the commission provided for the election of a certain number of commissioners from the city at large, who, in turn, elected one of their number to act as mayor and divide with each other the administration of the city departments. One might take charge of the fire department, another the police, and a third the health department. A board of five commissioners was common. In some cities, the commission form of government replaced the strong mayor as a reform, sometimes bringing with it the initiative, referendum, and recall.

New York City

Profile

Founded: 1613 (incorporated in present boundaries 1898)
Population (est. 1913): 5,583,871
U.S. Rank, 1913: 1st
Area, 1913: 326.8 square miles
Elevation: sea level to 409 feet above sea level

Ragpickers, handcarts, and advertisements at 23rd Street, west of Third Avenue, New York City, reveal the many faces of the city c. 1896. (Photo by Alice Austen; courtesy, Staten Island Historical Society)

Average Temperatures, 1913: January, 30°F; July, 74°F
Average Annual Precipitation, 1913: 44.6 inches
Type Government, 1913: mayor
Assessed value of all taxable property, 1913: $8,332,066,301

Geography and History

New York City, located on the Atlantic coast at the mouth of the Hudson River, is comprised of five boroughs: Manhattan, the Bronx, Brooklyn, Queens, and Staten Island. Italian explorer Giovanni da Verrazano first explored the region, landing at Staten Island in 1524. Henry Hudson reached Manhattan in 1609 and sailed up the river that later bore his name. The Dutch West India Company in 1624 sent the first permanent white settlers who established Fort Amsterdam, which later became New Amsterdam. In 1626, Mayor Peter Minuit purchased Manhattan from the Canarsie Indians for beads and trinkets supposedly worth $24. The Dutch and the English fought a series of naval wars in the 1660s for control of the region. When Peter Stuyvesant, the Dutch leader, was forced to surrender in 1664, the English renamed the town New York in honor of the Duke of York.

During the nineteenth century, immigrants—first German, Irish, and other Northern European groups and then Italians and East Europeans in the 1890s—transformed New York City into a patchwork of ethnic neighborhoods, each with its own distinct language, religion, and cultural heritage. As Jewish, Catholic, and Protestant traditions clashed, Democratic Party-controlled Tammany Hall (a political machine that dispensed jobs and favors to immigrants in return for their votes) tried to control city politics. Machine politics fed corruption, especially under "Boss" William Marcy Tweed, who led Tammany Hall until he was arrested in 1871 on charges of swindling the city of $200 million. Thereafter, Tammany Hall struggled to govern the city until the reform administration of Fiorello La Guardia during the Great Depression.

While New York City developed as a mosaic of cultures, it also extended its boundaries to include the territory of the city as it is today. This development was hastened by the opening of Brooklyn Bridge in 1883. Brooklyn, the Bronx, Queens, and Staten Island were consolidated with Manhattan in 1898, when an act of the state legislature created "Greater New York." Finally, between 1877 and World War I, New York City emerged as the financial capital of the United States and a world cultural center.

Chicago

Profile

Founded: 1830 (incorporated 1837)
Population (est. 1913): 2,393,325
U.S. Rank, 1913: 2d
Area, 1913: 191.5 square miles
Elevation: 658 feet above sea level
Average Temperatures, 1913: January, 24°F; July, 72°F
Average Annual Precipitation: 33.3 inches
Type Government, 1913: mayor
Assessed value of all taxable property, 1913: $25,784,600

Geography and History

Chicago is located on a plain that extends westward along the southwest shore of Lake Michigan. During this period, frequently changing weather brought temperatures that ranged from very hot in the summer to extremely cold in the winter—on average, temperatures of 96°F or higher occurred during half the summer, and half the winters had temperatures with a minimum low of −15°F. Summer thunderstorms were frequently heavy and sometimes vio-

lent, and strong wind gusts were produced in the downtown central business district because of the tall buildings. The term *windy city,* however, does not refer to the weather but to the alleged propensity of Chicagoans to boast about their city.

In the seventeenth century, Chicago was a fur-trading post. In 1812, angry Potawatomi Indians destroyed Fort Dearborn, built earlier to protect settlers, and killed most of the traders. Completion of the Illinois-Michigan Canal in 1848 turned the city into a marketing center for grain and food products. That same year, the first railroad arrived, and Chicago soon developed into a major livestock and meatpacking center, surpassing Cincinnati as the nation's pork center; Cattle merchants created the Union Stock Yards and Transit Company. Other industries also grew, such as those for farm implements (after Cyrus McCormick opened a factory in 1847), furniture, construction, and fencing. In 1867, George Pullman began to manufacture railroad cars in Chicago. In the following year, merchants Potter Palmer, Marshall Field, and Levi Leter first shipped consumer goods to Midwestern stores. On October 8, 1871, a cataclysmic fire destroyed the entire commercial area, including 8,000 buildings valued at about $200 million; Approximately 90,000 people were left homeless and 300 died.

The city was quickly rebuilt. The meatpacking industry benefited from assembly-line techniques, and technological improvements improved the steel and farm-machinery industries; the United States Steel South Works became one of the world's largest steel producers. In 1893, Chicago became the center of world attention when it held the World's Columbian Exposition to celebrate to 400th anniversary of Christopher Columbus's arrival in America. The exposition attracted 21 million visitors who saw a city at the forefront of architectural innovation and one that became known as the home of the skyscraper; the Chicago Board of Trade building was of special architectural significance. Progressive reform swept the city in the 1890s, bringing a civil service in 1895 and many other reforms.

Philadelphia

Profile

Founded: 1682 (incorporated 1701)
Population (est. 1913): 1,650,000
U.S. Rank, 1913: 3d
Area, 1913: 129.5 square miles
Elevation: 5 to 431 feet above sea level
Average Temperatures, 1913: January, 32°F; July, 76°F
Average Annual Precipitation, 1913: 41.2 inches
Type Government, 1913: mayor and council
Assessed value of all taxable property, 1913: $1,607,916,775

Geography and History

Philadelphia is located on the eastern border of Pennsylvania at the junction of the Delaware and Schuylkill rivers. To the west, the Appalachian Mountains and, to the east, the Atlantic Ocean moderate the climate and prevent extremes of hot or cold temperatures. Occasionally in the summers, the ocean air is trapped in the city, producing humid weather. Precipitation is evenly divided over the year, the summer months producing slightly more rainfall, occasionally enough to flood the Schuylkill River. Snowfall is typically greater in the northern suburbs than in the city, where it often falls as rain. The winter months can produce high winds. Philadelphia is sometimes referred as America's first planned city because it was laid out in a grid pattern with large lots, wide streets, and five city parks, four of which still exist.

The Netherlands claimed the area now known as Philadelphia in 1609 when Henry Hudson, an Englishman in the Dutch service, sailed into Delaware Bay. In about 1647, they began to build trading posts, but in 1664, the English ousted the Dutch.

In 1681, King Charles II of England granted William Penn claim to a territory now known as Pennsylvania in exchange for a debt owed to Penn's father, a wealthy and well-educated member of the Society of Friends, also called Quakers. The Quakers were looked upon with suspicion because of their plain dress, mannerisms, and religious beliefs. Penn himself had been imprisoned on four different occasions for his beliefs, and King Charles was glad to be rid of him and his followers. Penn established a colony known for its religious tolerance and humane treatment of the Indians, from whom Penn chose to purchase the land, despite already having been granted all the land in Pennsylvania.

Economically, Philadelphia was located in a leading agricultural area, and the shipyards thrived on a trade of farm products that were exchanged for sugar and rum in the West Indies; these in turn were traded for English manufactured goods. Nearby supplies of coal and iron enabled Philadelphia to become an early industrial leader. Other significant industries included textiles, printing, publishing, and papermaking. By the time of the American Revolution, Philadelphia was the leading business center of the British Empire. The city's economic success attracted some of the best minds of the day, in-

cluding Benjamin Franklin: his creative genius established the leading newspaper—the *Pennsylvania Gazette*—the first hospital, the first free library, and the first learned society—the American Philosophical Society. Franklin was also instrumental in the founding of the University of Pennsylvania.

During the nineteenth century, the increasing demand for factory workers attracted thousands of migrants—first predominantly Irish and German and then Italian, Jewish, Polish, Slavic immigrants from Europe, and blacks from the South—who helped build the city's industrial base and create distinctive ethnic neighborhoods. The development of the railroad made commuting easier, and the city's economic elite began to move to the suburbs, which became segregated by race, income, and ethnic origin.

St. Louis

Profile
Founded: 1763 (incorporated 1822)
Population (est. 1913): 750,000
U.S. Rank, 1913: 4th

Lunchrooms like this one in St. Louis in 1900 served a growing urban population of clerks, salespeople, and office workers. (Courtesy Prints and Photographs Division, Library of Congress)

Area, 1913: 61.3 square miles
Elevation: 535 feet above sea level
Average Temperatures, 1913: January, 31°F; July, 79°F
Average Annual Precipitation: 37.2 inches
Type Government, 1913: mayor
Assessed value of all taxable property, 1913: $600,794,088

Geography and History

St. Louis, situated just below the confluence of the Mississippi and Missouri rivers, is near the geographic center of the United States. Its climate is characterized by four seasons with no prolonged periods of extreme heat or high humidity; however, warm, moist air from the Gulf of Mexico and polar air masses from Canada produce a variety of weather conditions.

In 1763, Pierre Laclède Liguest, a fur trader, selected the present site; the village was named for the patron saint of King Louis XV of France. After France sold a vast tract of land in 1803—a land deal known as the Louisiana Purchase—St. Louis—part of that tract—developed into a center for fur trappers and traders and a logical point of departure for explorers setting off on westward journeys. Eventually, 50 wagons a day crossed the Mississippi River at St. Louis traveling west.

The arrival of the first steamboat from New Orleans in 1817 was a sign of the city's growing importance as a river trading center. During the Gilded Age, however, railroads replaced steamboats as the primary mode of transportation, and a new route opened to the East: the Eads Bridge, the world's first arched steel-truss bridge, was completed in 1874, and Union Station opened in 1878. The city's new prosperity translated into cultural enrichments, too: the Missouri Botanical Gardens and Tower Grove Park; the St. Louis Symphony, the nation's second oldest symphony orchestra, which formed in 1880, the Mercantile Library Association which opened in 1846 and began to purchase and commission original works of art. Two newspapers reported on the political and social issues of the day: Joseph Pulitzer's *Globe-Democrat* and Carl Schurz's *Westliche Post*. The following year, its city charter separated the city from the county and freed it from state government control, except for general laws.

By 1900, St. Louis had a population of 575,000. The city received worldwide attention in 1904 with the Louisiana Purchase Exposition, a successful year-long round of celebrations and festivities. The ice-cream cone, hot dog, and iced tea were novelties introduced at this world's fair. The first Olympiad to be held in the United States occurred in the city the same year.

Boston

Profile

Founded: 1630 (incorporated 1822)
Population (est. 1913): 733,562
U.S. Rank, 1913: 5th
Area, 1913: 47 square miles
Elevation: Ranges from 0 to 29 feet above sea level
Average Temperatures, 1913: January, 27°F; July, 71°F
Average Annual Precipitation, 1913: 43.4 inches
Type Government, 1913: mayor and council
Assessed value of all taxable property, 1913: $1,520,974,526

Geography and History

Boston is located on Massachusetts's Shawmut Peninsula at the confluence of the Charles and Mystic rivers. Initially, Shawmut was a hilly peninsula separated from the mainland by marshy swamps, mudflats, and inlets. Although the city terrain remains rolling, the leveling of Boston's hills allowed the back-bay marshes to be filled and developed.

Boston's location on the Atlantic Ocean has played an important role in the city's history. Situated on one of the finest natural harbors in the world, Boston quickly became the cultural and mercantile capital of the New England colonies. Variously known as the birthplace of the American Revolution, the port of New England's largest fleet of clipper ships, meeting place of the nation's literati, and the home of many respected cultural and educational institutions, Boston remains the gateway to New England.

Named for the English port in Lincolnshire from which many Puritans emigrated, Boston was settled in 1630 and declared the capital of New England the following year. It very soon reached its preeminence as the cultural and mercantile center of the New England colonies. Always uneasy with British rule, the city emerged as the center of colonial discontent and the seedbed of many revolutionary ideals and leaders. Boston achieved maritime supremacy after the Revolution, trading ocean fish and rum from New England and tobacco from the South for molasses from the West Indies and tea, silks, and spices from India and China. The development of the water-powered loom made Boston an important textile center, and its wool industry grew to rival England's.

In the mid-1800s, waves of Irish immigrants in flight from the potato famine began to arrive; the city experienced a surge in manufacturing, aided by the development of the railroad; and the making of shoes and leather goods emerged as leading industries. During the Civil War, Boston supplied 26,000 soldiers and sailors, became an important military seaport, and gained prominence in the world of finance. The city attracted influential intellectuals who aided in reuniting the nation: poets James Russell Lowell, Henry Wadsworth Longfellow, and John Greenleaf Whittier; novelist Nathaniel Hawthorne; jurist Oliver Wendell Holmes; philosophers Ralph Waldo Emerson and Henry David Thoreau; and historians William H. Prescott and Francis Parkman, who attempted to define the American character.

The urban transportation revolution (which began with the steam-powered railroad in the 1850s and was followed by the cable car in the 1870s and the electric streetcar in the 1890s) and economic change divided the city into distinct districts: working-class neighborhoods, black ghettos, a ring of suburbs, and business districts. The Irish settled in East Boston and Charleston. Boston's black population was already sizable owing to the abolition of slavery in Massachusetts in 1783. By 1900, Boston's population had reached 561,000, swelled by large numbers of Italians who settled in the North End and, along with the French Canadians who arrived next, combined with the Irish to make Boston the nation's second-largest Catholic archdiocese. John F. "Honey-Fitz" Fitzgerald was the city's first Irish mayor, elected to terms in 1906 and 1910. Fishing, food processing, shoemaking, and wool production were major industries until the Great Depression of the 1930s.

Cleveland

Profile

Founded: 1796 (incorporated 1836)
Population (est. 1913): 720,000
U.S. Rank, 1913: 6th
Area, 1913: 51.8 square miles
Elevation: 777 feet above sea level
Average Temperatures, 1913: Unavailable. Temperatures averaged 49.6°, 1970–1980.
Average Annual Precipitation: Unavailable. Annual precipitation averaged 35.4 inches, 1970–1980.
Type Government, 1913: mayor
Assessed value of all taxable property, 1913: $765,754,880

Geography and History

Cleveland extends for 31 miles along the south shore of Lake Erie and is surrounded by mostly level terrain except for an abrupt ridge that rises 500 feet above shore level on the eastern edge of the city. The Cuyahoga River bisects the city from north to south. Westerly to northerly winds off Lake Erie lower summer and raise winter temperatures. Summers are moderately warm and humid, and winters relatively cold and cloudy. Severe thunderstorms often bring damaging winds of 50 miles per hour or more; tornadoes occur frequently.

U.S. General Moses Cleaveland came in 1796 at the behest of the Connecticut Land Company to survey the Western Reserve, a half-million-acre tract of land in northeastern Ohio, which at that time was called "New Connecticut." General Cleaveland plotted a townsite on Lake Erie, copying the New England town-square model. Dysentery and insects, however, drove Cleaveland and his band back to New England. Lorenzo Carter was eventually credited with taming the Western Reserve wilderness, arriving at General Cleaveland's townsite in 1799 and making peace with the Indians in the area. The settlement was named for its original founder; the current spelling of the name can be traced to a newspaper compositor who dropped the first *a* from *Cleaveland* in order to fit the name on the newspaper's masthead.

Cleveland grew as a port and a trade center, especially after the completion of a canal system in 1832 connecting the Ohio River with Lake Erie. In 1847, telegraph lines were installed. The opening of the Soo Canal in 1855 and the arrival of the railroad soon thereafter increased the city's importance as a transportation center. During the Civil War, the ironworks industry grew, aided by the discovery of soft coal in canal beds. After the war, Cleveland advanced as a center of heavy industry. Local fortunes were made in steel and shipping, and captains of industry created a residential district known as "Millionaires Row."

The growth of industry and political reform characterized Cleveland's Gilded Age: in 1870, John D. Rockefeller put Cleveland on the map as the nation's first oil capital; with the growth of industry came also the rise of trade unionism, and Cleveland became the headquarters of the Brotherhood of Locomotive Engineers and national labor meetings. Inventors found a home in the city: Charles Brush, inventor of the carbon arc lamp, founded the Brush Electric Light and Power Company and installed arc lamps throughout the city. He also invented and manufactured the first storage battery. Worcester R. Warner and Ambrose Swasey pioneered automotive gear improvements and designed astronomy instruments.

Heavy industry attracted a large working-class population. In 1870, Cleveland had less than 100,000 people but by 1910 was the sixth largest city in the nation. Accompanying the growth in population was a major change in the ethnic composition, as those of German birth in the city's population were eclipsed in proportion by immigrants, especially those from the Austro-Hungarian empire, mostly from Poland, Czechoslovakia, and Hungary. The number of Cleveland's Slavic and Magyar speakers was above average for American cities; the proportions of Italian and Russian immigrants were below average but still present in large numbers.

Cleveland gained a reputation as a reform city, especially under the leadership of Thomas Loftin Johnson, a captain of the steel and transportation industries who served five terms as mayor (1901–1910). Johnson was influenced by the American social philosopher Henry George, and his administration won high praise from the muckraking journalist Lincoln Steffens, who dubbed Johnson "the nation's best mayor" and Cleveland "the best governed city in the United States." Johnson rode to office on a three-cent-fare campaign and battled his political nemesis, Mark Hanna, who used his en-

trenched power to thwart Johnson's reforms. Johnson improved city life by building new streets and parks, creating a municipal electric company to limit the abuses of private utilities, and introducing city-controlled garbage and refuse collection. He also set high standards for the handling of meat and dairy products and even removed "keep off the grass" signs from the city parks.

Detroit

Profile

Founded: 1701 (incorporated 1815)
Population (est. 1913): 614,486
U.S. Rank, 1913: 7th
Area, 1913: 41.75 square miles
Elevation: 633 feet above sea level
Average Temperatures, 1913: January, 24°F; July 72°F
Average Annual Precipitation: 32.2 inches
Type Government, 1913: mayor
Assessed value of all taxable property, 1913: $491,324,120

Geography and History

Located on the Detroit River, Detroit's climate is influenced by the city's nearness to the Great Lakes and its position in a major storm track. Winter storms can bring a combination of rain, snow, freezing rain, and sleet, possibly with heavy snowfalls. In the summer, storms often pass to the north, permitting periods of warm, humid weather broken by an occasional thunderstorm. Summer nights can be very hot in the central city, which acts as an urban heat island.

In July 1701, Antoine de la Mothe, Sieur de Cadillac, and his party arrived to establish a site to protect French fur-trading interests around the Great Lakes. The river was called *d'Étroit,* meaning "strait" in French. La Mothe and his party built Fort Pontchartrain on the site, naming the fort after Comte de Pontchartrain, King Louis XIV's minister of state. Later, Cadillac named the settlement *ville d'étroit,* or "city of the strait." Eventually, the name was changed to *Detroit.*

During the eighteenth century, Detroit changed hands three times. At the end of the American Revolution, the United States claimed all lands west of the Alleghenies. The British refused to leave, however, until 1796 when General Anthony Wayne defeated the Indians at the Battle of Fallen Timbers. In the War of 1812, General William Hull surrendered the fort to the British, but the United States regained control in 1813 following Oliver H. Perry's victory in the Battle of Lake Erie.

After the June 11, 1805, fire that totally destroyed the city, Augustus B. Woodward, one of the new territory's judges, laid out the city on the basis of Charles L'Énfant's plan for Washington, D.C., with a park in the middle and wide streets radiating outward in a hub-and-spoke pattern. Later, this idea was abandoned, and a grid street pattern was superimposed over the wheel pattern.

The rise of Detroit as an important manufacturing and industrial center in the late nineteenth century was due to a number of factors. Early economic development was spurred in 1826 with the opening of the Erie Canal, the city's access to the Great Lakes, the growing lumber and flour-milling industries, and the availability of a skilled labor force.

After the Civil War, Gilded Age Detroit changed from its earlier role as a country merchant to that of industrial magnate. Iron and steel, foundry, railroad-car, boot-and-shoe, stove, wheel-and-axle, chemical, and pharmaceutical industries all flourished by 1900. In 1896, Charles B. King drove a horseless carriage on Detroit's city streets, and the city's automobile industry was born. Soon, Henry Ford introduced his own version of the conveyance, and Detroit began its ascendancy as the automobile capital of the world.

Detroit Mayor Hazen S. Pingree (1890–1897) gained national attention during his mayoralty with a scheme to aid unemployed workers during the 1893 depression. Pingree wanted to show critics of the relief program that men without jobs were willing to work if given the chance. He located several thousand acres of vacant land in Detroit and appealed to the owners of these sites to let the unemployed plant potatoes. In the first year, the value of the crop exceeded the amount spent in establishing the program. Soon, Pingree's "potato patches" became a model for garden-allotment programs in many major American cities.

Pittsburgh

Profile

Founded: 1758 (incorporated 1816)
Population (est. 1913): 600,000
U.S. Rank, 1913: 8th
Area, 1913: 41 square miles
Elevation: 696 feet above sea level at the river base; 1,369 at the highest point
Average Temperatures, 1913: January, 31°F; July, 75°F
Average Annual Precipitation: 36.4 inches
Type Government, 1913: commission
Assessed value of all taxable property, 1913: $758,366,000

Geography and History

Pittsburgh is located where the Allegheny and Monongahela rivers join to form the Ohio River in the foothills of the Allegheny Mountains. The city's proximity to the Atlantic Ocean and the Great Lakes has a slight affect on its humid climate: About a fourth of Pittsburgh's precipitation falls as snow in the winter months, but from April to October, the sun shines more than 50% of the time.

The Seneca tribe established villages in the 1730s on the site where Pittsburgh now stands. Young Colonel George Washington noted in 1753 that the area was "extremely well suited for a fort." Fort Duquesne was built at the fork of the Allegheny and Monongahela rivers and lasted until 1758 when the British built Fort Pitt in honor of England's prime minister. Fort Pitt was the largest and most elaborate fort in the colonies. Between 1776 and 1790, Pittsburgh was known as the "Gateway to the West."

The city grew as a trading and boat-building center. It also happened to sit atop one of the world's richest coal deposits, and there was an abundance of clay, limestone, natural gas, oil, salt, and sand for glass. Pittsburgh emerged as an industrial leader with the completion in 1834 of the Pennsylvania Canal, connecting the city with Philadelphia, and the arrival in 1852 of the Pennsylvania Railroad. The demand for arms and ammunition in the Civil War gave Pittsburgh's economy a tremendous boost.

After the war, more than one-half of the steel, about a third of the glass, and much of the oil produced in the United States came from Pittsburgh. Industrial giants such as steel manufacturers Andrew Carnegie and Henry Clay Frick invested their money to build bridges, factories, and railroads in the city. It was during this age that Pittsburgh achieved its reputation, now inaccurate, as "the smoky city" and "hell with the lid off" because of its sooty steel mills. Industrial growth attracted immigrants from Europe. In the years from 1870 to 1900, Pittsburgh's population grew from 86,000 to 321,000. Many in the labor force were Poles, Czechs, Hungarians, and other eastern Europeans who composed the largest number of immigrants, beginning in the late 1880s. Labor unions grew in size and strength, and the organization that later became the American Federation of Labor was formed in Pittsburgh in 1881. One of the most highly charged confrontations between management and labor in the nineteenth century happened at Carnegie's Homestead works in 1892 (see pages 60–62).

Baltimore

Profile

Founded: 1696 (incorporated 1797)
Population (est. 1913): 578,000
U.S. Rank, 1913: 9th
Area, 1913: 31.5 square miles
Elevation: 148 feet
Average Temperatures, 1913: January, 33°F; July 77°F
Average Annual Precipitation: 43.2 inches
Type Government, 1913: mayor
Assessed value of all taxable property, 1913: $781,692,000

Geography and History

Baltimore's location on the northern Chesapeake Bay greatly enhanced its social and economic development. Its large natural harbor lies at the mouth of the Patapsco River; streams coursing from the north and west had great velocity, making them ideal sites for water-driven mills. The city is farther inland than other Eastern seaports and more accessible to land-locked areas. Baltimore is protected from harsh weather conditions by the Chesapeake and the Atlantic Ocean to the east and the Appalachian Mountain chain due west. Freezing temperatures rarely occur after mid-April or before the end of October, allowing for approximately 194 frost-free days.

In 1632, King Charles I of England gave George Calvert a vast domain of land in colonial America that became Baltimore County. An area of approximately 550 acres known as "Cole's Harbor" was sold to Baltimore landowners Daniel and Charles Carroll in 1696; they in turn developed it in one-acre lots that became Baltimore Town. By 1750, regular tobacco shipments were leaving Baltimore harbor for Europe, as was locally milled flour and grain, bound for the British slave-and-sugar colonies in the West Indies. When the American Revolution cut off this trade, Congress authorized private citizens to arm and equip their own vessels. Consequently, privateering became a growing industry, and Baltimore became a center for shipbuilding. A slump in maritime trade in 1828 led to the construction of America's first public railroad in Baltimore, linking the city to other parts of the country and expanding commercial opportunities. During the Civil War, Baltimore profited as a military depot.

Baltimore recovered rapidly from the physical and economic damages of the war and began its greatest period of growth and prosperity. In 1904, Baltimore was struck by a fire that started in a cotton warehouse and spread to destroy more than 2,000 buildings. Out of the ruins came improvements to Baltimore's streets and harbor and the construction of a sewer system that was considered one of the most modern of its time.

Los Angeles

Profile

Founded: 1781 (incorporated 1850)
Population (est. 1913): 530,000
U.S. Rank, 1913: 10th
Area, 1913: 107.5 square miles

Elevation: sea level to 5,080 feet above sea level

Average Temperatures, 1913: Not available. Annual temperatures averaged 65.3°, 1970–1980.

Average Annual Precipitation: Not available. Annual precipitation averaged 14.85 inches, 1970–1980.

Type Government, 1913: mayor

Assessed value of all taxable property, 1913: $389,705,515

Geography and History

Los Angeles is located on a hilly coastal plain and is bounded on the south and west by the Pacific Ocean. In the north and west are the foothills of the Santa Monica and San Gabriel mountains. The warm, moist Pacific air keeps temperatures mild throughout the year. Summers are dry and sunny; most of the precipitation occurs in the winters. Unusual weather comes in the form of the Santa Ana winds, hot dusty winds of up to 50 miles per hour from the surrounding mountains, and occasional flash floods in the canyon areas, causing mudslides.

California was first settled by missionaries of the Franciscan Order in the 1770s. The city gets its name from Félipé de Neve, governor of Alta California, who founded a settlement in 1781 called *El Pueblo de Nuestra Señora la Reina de los Angeles,* meaning "the pueblo of our lady the queen of angels."

In the eighteenth century, under Spanish rule, which banned trade with foreign ships, only a few English-speaking inhabitants settled in the area. Whaling and seal hunting were important coastal industries, and a trade in cattle hides and tallow developed at nearby San Pedro. By the 1840s, Los Angeles was the largest town in southern California, and in 1847, after the Mexican-American War, became an American territory. An 1848 gold strike in the Sierra Nevada to the north of Los Angeles produced a gold rush and a market for local beef because many prospectors settled in the area. In 1850, Los Angeles was incorporated and it became known as one of the toughest towns in the West. Murder and lawlessness peaked in 1871 after a mob stormed the Chinatown district, murdering 16 people. Civic leaders and concerned citizens cooperated in bringing law and order to town.

During the Gilded Age, the Southern Pacific Railroad entered the city in 1876, followed by the Santa Fe Railroad in 1885. A rate war between the two companies drove the price of a ticket from the eastern United States down to $5, bringing thousands of settlers to the area and sending real estate prices to unheard-of levels. By 1887, lots were selling for $1,000 per foot around the central plaza area. The boom collapsed within a year, and thousands abandoned the city—sometimes as many as 3,000 a day. The flight led to the creation of a chamber of commerce that launched a campaign to attract new settlers; by 1890, the population had returned to 50,000. Oil discoveries in the city in the 1890s brought another boom, and nearly 1,500 wells opened by 1900. In the early twentieth century, agriculture became important; as a result of its growth, an enormous aqueduct was completed, and the city annexed the San Fernando Valley. A port at San Pedro was added, which enlarged the city's position in the international trade market.

CHAPTER 10 Representative Americans

Jane Addams (1860–1935)

Jane Addams was a humanitarian and social reformer. She graduated from Rockford College (1882) and attended the Woman's Medical College in Philadelphia. During a trip to England (1887), she became interested in social reform. In 1889, with Ellen Gates Starr, she founded Hull House, a settlement house devoted to the improvement of community and civic life in the Chicago slum districts; it was the first of its kind in the United States. Between 1915 and 1934, she crusaded against war and headed the Woman's Peace Party and the International Congress of Women at The Hague. In 1931, Addams was awarded the Nobel Peace Prize. Jane Addams was the author of *Democracy and Social Ethics* (1902), *Twenty Years at Hull House* (1910) and *A New Conscience and an Ancient Evil* (1911).

Susan B. Anthony (1820–1906)

Susan B. Anthony was a social reformer and women's suffrage leader. Reared as a Quaker, she was educated at her father's school and became a schoolteacher (1846–49). She soon abandoned her education career for reform activities. Anthony's first efforts were devoted to temperance; she organized the Woman's State Temperance Society of New York and became involved in the abolitionist movement, advocating black suffrage after the Civil War. Gradually, her main interest centered on the women's suffrage movement. She tried to have a provision inserted into the Fourteenth Amendment to guarantee suffrage to women as well as to black males. In 1869, she became president of the National Woman Suffrage Association and, three years later, became involved in a celebrated case when she registered and voted at the Rochester city elections in a plan to test the legality of women's suffrage. She served as president of the National American Woman Suffrage Association from 1892 to 1900.

Alexander Graham Bell (1847–1922)

Bell, a prominent educator of the deaf and the inventor of the telephone, was born in Edinburgh, Scotland, March 3, 1847. He was educated at McLauren's Academy in Edinburgh and at the Royal High School. In 1867 he became an assistant to his father, Alexander Melville Bell (1819–1905), inventor of a speech system for the deaf. In 1870 Bell accompanied his family to Canada and the following year he began giving special instruction in his father's system to teachers of the deaf in New England cities. In 1872 he opened a normal (teacher's) training school in Boston and served as professor of vocal physiology in the school of oratory of Boston University (1873–77). His work with the deaf and interest in acoustics led him to the research that resulted in the invention of the telephone. At Boston on March 10, 1876, he gave the first practical demonstration of the telephone. The Bell Telephone Company was founded the following year and thereafter commercial development of the telephone proceeded rapidly. Bell gained American citizenship in 1882 and continued his work with the deaf.

The telephone was an immediate success. President Rutherford Hayes put one in the White House in 1878. By 1890 there were 800,000 working telephones in the United States; by 1900, 1.5 million.

Bell's other inventions included the photophone for the transmission of sound by light (1880); the telephone probe for locating metallic traces in the human body (1881); the spectrophone (1881); and the tetrahedral kite (1903). He was also associated with the invention of the wax cyclinder record for the phonograph. He died in Cape Breton Island, Nova Scotia, August 2, 1922.

Edward Bellamy (1850–1898)

In 1888, Edward Bellamy's novel, *Looking Backward, 2000–1887*, was published and within two years had sold 200,000 copies (the equivalent today of a million-copy best-seller). The book led to the formation of about 150 "nationalist clubs," whose members shared Bellamy's vision of the future. It also became the bible of many progressive reformers.

In the book, a young Bostonian of the 1880s falls into a mysterious slumber from which he does not awake until the year 2000. Standing on the threshold of the twenty-first century, he observes the wonders that technology has produced, not a world of sharp class divisions and widespread misery (as in 1887), but a utopia with abundance for all.

In *Looking Backward,* capitalism has been replaced through a democratic revolution (won at the polls); the American people have given up competitive greed and habits of conspicuous consumption because they were un-American. Private ownership of land and industry has given way to state control for the good of all. Everyone contributes to the general welfare of all; none live wastefully or on the backs of others.

Bellamy's ideals were part of an American tradition of socialism, rather than the Marxist version then current in Europe. He called it *Nationalism.* The patriotic face of his ideology made it acceptable to the middle class which, while troubled by the agglomeration of wealth and power in the hands of the few and the wretched poverty of the many, found foreign ideologies abhorrent and frightening.

Martha "Calamity Jane" Canary Burk (1852?–1903)

Martha Jane Canary embodied the rough-and-tumble world of the Wild West in American popular culture. She, along with other legends of the West, personally contributed to the myths surrounding themselves by appearing in Wild West shows that played the cities of America and Europe.

Her nickname "Calamity Jane" derived from her quick outbursts of violent temper and a reputation for meanness that was enhanced by the sudden and mysterious disappearance of several of her string

Women during this period were not only denied the vote, equal pay for the same work as men, and property rights, but they also suffered from cultural restrictions on their personal behavior. Shown here is an unidentified woman in 1896 defying widespread Victorian conventions against women smoking, drinking beer, or revealing their petticoats. (Courtesy Prints and Photographs Division, Library of Congress)

of lovers. She was said to have been "Wild Bill" Hickok's paramour and bore one child.

One historian described her as "big, coarse, strong, vulgar, lewd, and promiscuous." She was usually seen in men's clothing, often chewed tobacco, cursed like a mule driver (one of her occasional occupations), and could drink soldiers under the table. She wrote her own romantic autobiography to support her drinking habit.

Andrew Carnegie (1835–1919)

Andrew Carnegie used corporate consolidation as his means to wealth and power, rising to the top of the steel industry. Born in Scotland, Carnegie emigrated to the United States at the age of 13. He worked as a bobbin boy in a cotton factory, gaining a reputation for hard work, frugality, and ambition before he began his ascent. Investing his earnings wisely and benefiting from a fortuitous discovery of oil on his farm, Carnegie demonstrated his talent for business organization. He foresaw the advantages of having raw materials, the means of transportation and production, and the manufacturing outlets under one ownership. By aggressive manipulation, he forced competitors to sell out to him until he owned iron fields, steamships, railroads, oil—everything necessary to produce steel. By 1880, under the protective umbrella of Congressional legislation and inadequate federal and state regulation, he had gained a monopoly of the steel industry. Near Pittsburgh, he started an immense steel mill on the Monongahela River, later adding the Homestead Steel Works, which became embroiled in labor controversy during the 1890s.

Finally, he sold the Carnegie Steel Works to J. P. Morgan (who created from it what became the U.S. Steel corporation) retired to Scotland, and proceeded to divest himself of an estimated $350 million, endowing schools, libraries, the Carnegie Institute of Technology (now Carnegie-Mellon University), the Carnegie Endowment for Peace, and other institutions.

Carnegie was man of great contrasts, even contradictions. In the name of competition, he crushed his competition. He espoused "individualism" as a virtue and fired his managers when they dared exercise it in ways he did not like. He spoke of the "gospel of wealth" as a sacred duty, without seeming to understand the potential of power to subvert free institutions. His privately owned companies had budgets bigger than some nations, and he had absolute power over his workers; yet he spoke of his business as if it were a hardware store on Main Street, U.S.A.

Carrie (Lane) Chapman Catt (1859–1947)

Carrie Lane Chapman Catt, a prominent national leader of women's suffrage and peace movements, was born in Ripon, Wisconsin, January 9, 1859. In 1880, she graduated from Iowa State College in Ames. In 1890 she joined Susan B. Anthony in South Dakota in her first suffrage campaign.

The women's suffrage movement dated back to the mid-nineteenth century, but the coveted prize of the right to vote remained elusive. Many Americans, women and men—especially of the middle class, from which most of the membership of the movement came—believed that women had no proper place in public life, and that their entry into it would cause them to forfeit what was thought to be their moral influence in the domestic world. Catt began to position the suffrage movement to exploit these prejudices rather than continue to be victimized by them. She quietly downplayed the radical critique of women's status that the early feminists had developed, especially their doubts about marriage. Under her leadership, suffragists also downplayed the traditional argument that women should have the right to vote because they were the equal of men in every way.

In 1902 she founded the International Woman Suffrage Alliance, which held its first conference in Berlin in 1904, and was its president until she retired at the Rome congress in 1923. Catt also organized the National American Woman Suffrage Association (1909–15) and trained women for political action. She marshaled these women on a national scale between 1915 and 1920, to influence Congress to approve the Nineteenth Amendment enfranchising women. After bitter opposition in the U.S. Senate, the amendment was submitted to the states and ratified on August 26, 1920. Catt then reorganized the suffrage association, about two million members, as the National League of Women Voters (1919–20).

In 1925 she gained the cooperation of eleven national women's organizations in the National Committee on the Cause and Cure of

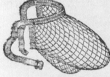

As this ad for corsets from the 1902 Sears Catalog indicates, women were expected to look molded and well proportioned, regardless of the cost to comfort and health. (Author's possession)

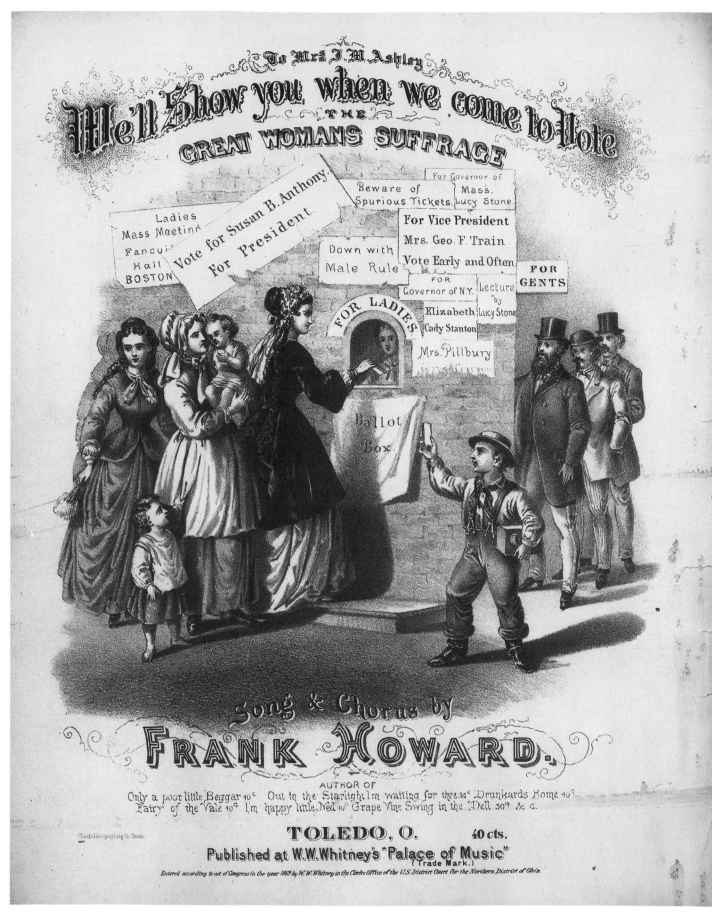

Middle-class women fought for the right of all women to vote throughout the Victorian Age, but their success did not come until after World War I and the passage of the Nineteenth Amendment to the U.S. Constitution. Shown here is a piece of sheet music for "We'll Show You When We Come to Vote," a song used in the campaign. (Courtesy American Antiquarian Society)

War, to launch a campaign of education for U.S. participation in a world organization for peace. After World War II she was vitally interested in the work of the United Nations. She died on March 9, 1947.

Samuel Langhorne Clemens (Mark Twain) (1835–1910)

Samuel Langhorne Clemens, known to his readers as Mark Twain, wrote, with Charles Dudley Warner, *The Gilded Age* (1873), and for many historians the name seemed to suit a period notable for its greed, corruption, and venality. Twain was a local-color writer, but he moved beyond the sentimentality and romance of many of his contemporaries and won the respect of intellectuals and the masses.

Twain was best known for his books about the American West. *The Adventures of Tom Sawyer* (1876) and *Adventures of Huckleberry Finn* (1885) gave him an international reputation; *Life on the Mississippi* (1883) and *Roughing It* (1872) captured the ribald humor and hardships of frontier life. These antisentimental novels were realistic portrayals of life and human weaknesses. Twain's writing embodied both the comic and tragic sides of life and was sensitive to the boiling energy and euphoric materialism of his age.

Twain was a Missourian who deserted a Confederate army unit to go west to Nevada, but he eventually settled in Hartford, Connecticut. He was a brilliant satirist in an age when human vices and follies gave him plenty of material to work with, but his work is not merely humorous. Twain's work embodies a profound understanding of the American character, and illustrates the social stresses of an age undergoing rapid transformation.

Elizabeth Cochran (Nellie Bly) (1864–1922)

At the beginning of the 1890s, Elizabeth Cochran, the orphan daughter of a Pennsylvania miller, became the personification of the "new woman." Cochran shunned the feminists, perhaps because of her humble origins (feminists were overwhelmingly middle class). Born in 1864, forced by her father's death to go to work, and almost entirely self-educated, she turned her talent for self-promotion into international celebrity status.

In 1885, while working at a menial job to support her mother, Cochran responded to the editor of the *Pittsburgh Dispatch* newspaper who had bemoaned the fact that women who did not marry seemed useless to society. In her letter, Cochran eloquently and forcefully argued for opening employment opportunities for girls (who were "just as smart" as boys and were "a great deal quicker to learn"). The editor, who became a lifelong friend, was impressed enough to hire her; as a reporter, she took the name Nellie Bly (from a Stephen Foster song). Bly wrote a series of exposés on working and living conditions in the city ten years in advance of the muckrakers (see Upton Sinclair). She also pioneered the technique of the undercover reporter, actually taking jobs in factories and then reporting on conditions of labor in the first person.

Bly was interested in social reform, but her mastery of self-promotion turned her most famous project into one of journalism's first manufactured stories. As a girl, she had read Jules Verne's *Around the World in Eighty Days*. A number of adventurers had tried to beat the imaginary record and failed. Bly announced that she would make the trip in 75 days. The editors were interested but told Bly they really wanted a man to carry the banner. Bly responded, "Very well. Start the man, and I'll start the same day for some other newspaper and

beat him."

Nellie Bly left New Jersey on November 14, 1889, under the auspices of the *New York World* and returned 72 days later on January 25, 1890.

Suffragists courted Bly, but she spurned them, even expressing oblique disdain for organized feminism. She lectured them to fight for jobs for women, forgo their lecturing and writing, and go to work. After her famous journey she refused to work for the Women's Suffrage Party, saying that she could help more by practicing what they had been preaching.

Nellie Bly marched to her own drum. Shortly after the return from her world trip, she quit journalism and married a 72-year-old manufacturer. She was just 31. He died in 1904, and she ran his factory, designed a steel barrel, provided for the social, medical, and recreational needs of her employees, and paid women the same as men (unheard of at the time). Unfortunately, her Iron Clad Manufacturing Company went bankrupt because of theft by an employee with whom Bly was having an affair. She never regained her celebrity status afterward and died in 1922.

Clarence Darrow (1857–1938)

Clarence Darrow was a lawyer and reformer. He was born in Kinsman, Ohio, April 18, 1857, and spent a year at the University of Michigan Law School. In 1878 he was admitted to the Ohio bar and in 1887 moved to Chicago where he became junior law partner of John Peter Altgeld, later governor of Illinois. He supported many reform movements and opposed capital punishment. He achieved a reputation as a great trial lawyer by winning all but one of more than 50 cases of first degree murder. He gained national prominence in his defense of Eugene V. Debs in the injunction proceedings and conspiracy charges from the rail strike of 1894. In 1907 he successfully defended Haywood, Moyer, and Pettibone, who were charged with being accessories to the murder of Governor Steunenberg of Idaho. Perhaps his most celebrated case was the defense (1924) of Nathan Leopold and Richard Loeb for the kidnapping and murder of Robert Franks. In this case he introduced psychiatric evidence and his masterful summation resulted in the prisoners' receiving life sentences instead of the death penalty. In the 1925 Scopes "monkey" trial he had a celebrated encounter with William Jennings Bryan over the theory of evolution and biblical teaching. He died in Chicago, March 13, 1938.

Eugene V. Debs (1855–1926)

Eugene V. Debs grew up in Terre Haute, Indiana, and became a locomotive fireman after graduation from high school. In 1880, he was elected secretary-treasurer of the Brotherhood of Locomotive Firemen. He also served as city clerk and in 1885 served a term in the Indiana state legislature.

Debs's rise to national prominence began with his organization in 1893 of the militant American Railway Union, which became involved the following year in one of the largest and bitterest strikes in the turbulent history of the railroads: the Pullman strike. In the first two days, about 60,000 railway workers struck in sympathy with the workers of the Pullman Palace Car Company outside Chicago, who had struck after George Pullman slashed their wages 25 to 40 percent in order to maintain profits and pay stockholders. Coming in the midst of a severe economic depression, the strike spread to 20 companies in 27 states. When the federal troops that Pres. Grover Cleveland sent failed to gain control of the situation, Cleveland obtained a court injunction against the railway union on the grounds that it was obstructing delivery of the nation's mail. When Debs defied the injunction, he was jailed for six months (May–November 1895), during which time he became socialist. The legacy of strikebreaking by injunction plagued labor unions for the next three decades.

In 1912, Debs was the most important socialist leader in America. It was the year when 33 cities chose socialist mayors. Debs had run for the presidency on three other occasions: 1900, 1904, and 1908. This time, he polled 6% of the popular vote, the largest vote ever received by a socialist in the United States.

When World War I began, he spoke out against the war. In 1917, Congress passed the Sedition Act, making it a crime to utter "profane, scurrilous, abusive, or disloyal" remarks about the government, and Debs became the most famous case tried under the act. He was convicted, despite never having explicitly advocated violation of the draft laws, and the Supreme Court upheld his conviction in 1919. Seemingly undaunted, Debs ran for the presidency from prison in 1920 and polled a million votes. He was pardoned by President Harding in 1921. Debs died in Elmhurst, Illinois, on October 19, 1926.

W. E. B. Du Bois (1868–1963)

W. E. B. DuBois was born in Great Barrington, Massachusetts, on February 23, 1868. He attended Fisk University before going to Harvard University, where he received his Ph.D. in 1895, the first black American to do so. From 1897 to 1910, he taught history and economics at Atlanta University and in 1903 published *The Souls of Black Folk,* a classic social study of blacks in Philadelphia.

Du Bois's approach to race relations was much more direct and militant than black leader Booker T. Washington, with whose gradualist and accommodationist position Du Bois took issue. In 1910, Du Bois joined the newly formed biracial National Association for the Advancement of Colored People (NAACP). White progressives, including Jane Addams, had joined with the black Niagara Movement to form the NAACP. Du Bois became editor of *Crisis,* the organization's magazine, and made it the impassioned mouthpiece for the black cause in America for 24 years. During his lifetime Du Bois produced a steady stream of articles, books, poems, and novels.

In the NAACP, Du Bois was solidly in the progressive mold: genteel, middle-class, university-educated, and devoted to the idea that the elite should govern. He believed that the "talented tenth" should lead black people to civil equality in the United States. His racial attitudes evolved over the years from biracialism, to a pan-African congress, to favoring an independent black community. The latter attitude caused his break with the NAACP in 1934.

After World War II, Du Bois worked briefly for the NAACP again before finally moving toward the positions represented by the Communist Party, ultimately joining that party and endorsing soviet-style socialism. In 1959, he won the Soviet Union's Lenin Prize. Du Bois emigrated to Ghana, where he died in 1963.

Thomas Alva Edison (1847–1931)

Thomas Alva Edison was born into the great age of invention in American history, and Edison proved to be a man of his time. Most inventors were not scientists; Edison claimed to be more inventor than discoverer because discovery came by accident and invention through deductive reasoning. True to his claim, he made only one scientific discovery (the Edison effect—an electric current produced when a hot wire is near a conductor in a vacuum) but became the greatest single contributor to American technology with hundreds of

inventions. Working long hours with infinite patience, he built up dream laboratories in Menlo Park, New Jersey, and Fort Meyers, Florida, that contained every known material and chemical. He had at his disposal or could obtain any parts or machinery he wanted and could design or have built any imaginable object.

Edison was born on February 11, 1847, in Milan, Ohio. Nothing in his background gave hint to the genius of invention: As a child, he was taught at home by his mother, who was a schoolteacher. But by age 12, he was selling newspapers on a railroad route to finance his experiments.

At age 21, he took a job in a New York brokerage house, where he made some inventive changes in the stock tickers that netted him an astonishing $40,000. He parlayed this sum into a career as a freelance inventor and over the next five years, patented a new invention each month.

Edison fit the stereotype of the absentminded laboratory scientist, forever engrossed in his work. He was partially deaf and, when on the trail of an invention, somewhat testy. Slightly stooped, usually unkempt, typically seen wearing a chemist's white coat, smoking long cigars with fingers stained by the chemicals he used, and his hair dirty and disheveled, he would go for days without food or rest, especially when on the verge of an invention. He even returned to his laboratory on his wedding night to Mary Stilwell, forgetting his young bride.

The Kinetoscope, among his hundreds of important inventions, was developed in the 1880s and was the forerunner of the modern motion-picture projector. The electric light bulb and the phonograph were others of his revolutionary inventions.

Henry Ford (1863–1947)

In the 1890s, Henry Ford worked as an electrical engineer in Detroit's Edison Company and in his spare time experimented upon the gasoline-burning internal combustion engine. By 1896, he had built his first automobile. After manufacturing his first racing car, the "999," he organized the Ford Motor Company, which in 1909 produced the first Model T (popularly known as the "flivver"). The Model T was a standardized vehicle turned out on a mass assembly line because Ford had a dream to "democratize the automobile," to produce thousands of identical vehicles in the same way. On Ford's assembly lines, production was broken down so that each worker performed only one task, constantly repeated, in the production of the finished product. The methods of Ford's engineers made him a worldwide symbol of American industrial technique.

American industry had been moving toward mass production throughout the nineteenth century. Important developments in the firearms industry (interchangeability of parts), tool-and-die companies (precision gauges and jigs), grain milling and iron foundrying (use of conveyor belts to handle materials), in can making (special-purpose machinery), steel production (time and motion studies), meatpacking (slaughterhouse cut-up lines), and bicycle manufacturing (metal stamping and electric resistance welding) all preceded the Ford Motor Company's introduction of the machine-driven assembly line at its Highland Park plant in 1914. The Ford engineers borrowed from past ideas and techniques and applied them to the assembly of 5,000 parts to produce a car.

In 1909, the first year the Model T was built, Ford sold 10,000 cars; in 1914, 248,000 Fords rolled off the production lines.

Most Fords cost $490 each in 1914, about a fourth of what they would have cost ten years earlier. Even this price was beyond the means of many workers, who earned about $2 a day. In 1914, Ford attracted national attention by boosting wages and introducing the eight-hour day into his plant; at the same time, he inaugurated a profit-sharing plan for his employees. These efforts were meant to avert union organizing and gain worker stability. Adapting humans to continually moving machinery exacted its toll in aching backs and other problems, which caused a high turnover of workers. The announcement of the $5 day was made with much ballyhoo in the press, but the effects of the assembly line on workers remained as the following letter from a housewife to Henry Ford in 1914 shows:

> The chain system you have is a slave driver! My God! Mr. Ford. My husband has come home and thrown himself down and won't eat his supper—so done out! Can't it be remedied? . . . That $5 a day is a blessing—a bigger one than you know, but oh they earn it.

In 1915, Ford chartered the *Oscar II* (known as the Ford Peace Ship), which carried a group of pacifists, feminists, and others to Scandinavian nations to try to halt World War I. During the war, he manufactured gun carriages and motors for the U.S. government. In 1918, he ran unsuccessfully for U.S. senator from Michigan. He served as president of Ford Motor Co. until 1919 when he was succeeded by his son Edsel B. Ford. In 1947 when Henry Ford died, Edsel became president and served until his death. The Ford Foundation was established by Henry and Edsel Ford in 1936 and was expanded into a diversified program in educational philanthropy after 1951.

Hamlin Garland (1860–1940)

Hamlin Garland grew up on the farms of Wisconsin and Iowa during the 1860s and 1870s. Unlike the romantic literature of his day, he recalled farm life with little sentimentality. It took him 70 days when he was 11 years old, working "all day, and every day but Sunday," to turn under 150 acres of corn stubble with a horse-drawn plow. He described how men and boys walked the long rows of cornstalks, picking the ears and tossing them into a large wagon being pulled beside them. He described the numb and swollen fingers from cornpicking and the thick dust during wheat harvesting that collected on the face and lips, producing "tears of rage and rebellion." At these times "it seemed hard to be a prairie farmer's son."

Garland was born in Salem, Wisconsin, on September 14, 1860, and moved progressively westward with his family. When he became a young adult, he rebelled against the vicissitudes of pioneering and moved to Boston to begin a literary career. As a realist, he followed in the footsteps of William Dean Howells, his mentor, but he became increasingly bitter as he recorded the frustrations of rural life. His short stories in *Main-Travelled Roads* (1891), *Prairie Folks* (1892), and *Wayside Courtships* (1897), and the novel *Rose of Dutcher's Coolly* (1895) raised storms of protest.

The high country of the American West was his next subject. His Indian stories written during this period (collected in 1923 in *The Book of the American Indian*) proved to be some of the most accurate and sympathetic appraisals of Native Americans. Garland grew increasingly critical of the "excesses" of the naturalists. In 1917, he wrote his most widely acclaimed book, *A Son of the Middle Border*, written in an autobiographical mood and apostrophizing the vanishing frontier. A sequel, *A Daughter of the Middle Border* (1921), won the Pulitzer for biography. During his lifetime, Garland was a force in literary affairs, although later critics sharply divided over his influence upon American letters.

Geronimo (c. 1829–1909)

Between 1881 and 1886, Geronimo led the last major armed resistance to forced settlement on reservations. In 1875 U.S. government officials had ordered all Apache west of the Rio Grande onto the San Carlos reservation on the Gila River in Arizona. For the Apache, reservation life was an ordeal of scarce rations, disease, and boredom. To escape the misery, many fled to the wilderness and led a guerrilla existence, hunting, gathering, raiding, and plundering. Geronimo, who had fought with Cochise, rallied his own band of Chiricahua, and thus his name "became a war cry in the conquering culture."

Among the Chiricahua, Geronimo became respected for his bravery and cunning. Moving back and forth across the U.S.–Mexican border and living among the nomadic and predatory Nednhi band in Mexico's Sierra Madre, Geronimo and his band harassed and evaded U.S. military forces seeking to capture them. He was captured several times by forces under the command of General George Crook, and each time he escaped. Embarrassed, the army replaced Crook with General Nelson Miles, who put 5,000 men in the field to capture 24 renegade Apache.

On September 4, 1886, at Skeleton Canyon, 65 miles south of Apache Pass, where the Apache wars had commenced 25 years earlier, Geronimo and his small band surrendered for the last time. Then he, along with 500 other Apache, was sent by rail in chains to Fort Pickens in Pensacola, Florida. Later, they were moved to Mount Vernon Barracks, Alabama, where at least a fourth of them died from tuberculosis and other diseases. Although other Apache were permitted to return to San Carlos, the citizens of Arizona denied reentry of Geronimo and the Chiricahua to their territory.

Already a legend to many white schoolboys throughout the United States, Geronimo died at Fort Sill, Oklahoma, a prisoner of war, in 1909.

Samuel Gompers (1850–1924)

Samuel Gompers was the most dominant figure in the history of American trade unionism. Born in London on January 27, 1850, Gompers emigrated to New York City in 1863 and became a prominent member of the Cigarmaker's International union. He had followed that trade from an early age and knew firsthand the poverty of New York's tenements, having labored with his father in a tenement sweatshop. He listened to endless discussions among the workers about economics, politics and labor, as they debated whether to follow Karl Marx toward the abolition of private ownership or German socialist Ferdinand Lassalle and his idea of using political means to gain economic emancipation. When Gompers was given his chance to speak, he provided a singularly American response to the growing needs of industrial workers: "Pure and simple unionism," Gompers called it, meaning a strategy of ignoring the growing masses of immigrant and unskilled workers while raising the wages and improving the working conditions of the skilled craftsworkers who were members of the American Federation of Labor (AFL). He represented the cigarmakers at conventions of the AFL until he became president in 1886. He served as AFL president for 40 years until his death, being reelected every year except 1895 when a coalition of socialists engineered his defeat.

His influence within the organization and power to shape trade unionism in America grew with each year. The general adoption of the craft principle of American trade unionism was largely due to Gompers. Where the Knights of Labor had shied away from using the strike, Gompers advocated its use as labor's most formidable weapon. For him, the strike and the boycott were of great value to protect the lives and rights of workers.

Although theoretically a pacifist, when World War I began, he resisted pacifism in the trade unions and threw his support to the Wilson administration, which rewarded him and other moderate labor leaders with high positions in the government. Gompers's partnership with government led to an appointment on the advisory commission of the U.S. Council of National Defense in 1917. The following year, he represented the AFL at the Paris Peace Conference and was appointed chairman of the Peace Conference Commission on Labor Legislation.

He consistently opposed socialist movements among the unions, battled the Industrial Workers of the World, rejected compulsory arbitration in labor disputes, and steered his union clear of political movements that agitated workers. His pragmatic approach gave him a worldwide reputation as a conservative labor leader, and he was the center of controversy all his life. When he died in San Antonio, Texas, on December 13, 1924, he was acknowledged as the labor leader who had most influenced American trade unionism and secured for millions of workers a better life without revolution.

William C. Gorgas (1854–1920)

William C. Gorgas was a sanitarian who received his first degree from the University of the South. Unable to enter West Point, he graduated from Bellevue Hospital Medical College (1879) and after a year's internship was appointed to the U.S. Army Medical Corps. He survived an epidemic of yellow fever at Fort Brown, Texas, and thereafter was assigned to posts where yellow fever was rampant.

In 1898, following the American occupation of Havana, he assumed the post of chief sanitation officer of the city. Once Walter Reed established the cause of yellow fever, Gorgas eliminated the disease by destroying the breeding places of mosquitos. Despite the critics, he did the same thing in the Panama Canal Zone, making Panama City and Colón models of sanitation and winning for himself a worldwide reputation as a top sanitary expert.

Gorgas became surgeon general in 1914 with the rank of brigadier general. In 1916, on behalf of the International Health Board, he went to South America to serve on yellow-fever commissions. During World War I, he was head of the U.S. Army Medical Service and later went on a yellow-fever mission to the west coast of Africa.

Daniel Guggenheim (1856–1930)

Daniel Guggenheim was an industrialist and philanthropist who made his wealth in the copper mining-and-smelting business with his father, Meyer Guggenheim (1828–1905). He soon became the leading figure among seven sons. Largely due to his planning, copper mining, smelting, and refining took place on a large scale.

With his brothers, Daniel Guggenheim assumed control of the American Smelting & Refining Co. (1901), of which he was president or chairman of the board until 1919. Under his guidance, the business became a vast industrial empire that extended to South America and Africa: it developed nitrate fields in Chile, tin mines in Bolivia, and rubber plantations and diamond mines in the Belgian Congo.

He founded the Daniel and Florence Guggenheim Foundation and the Daniel Guggenheim Fund for the promotion of aeronautics. His brother Simon (1867–1941) with his wife established the John Simon Guggenheim Memorial Foundation.

Marcus A. Hanna (1837–1904)

Marcus Alonzo Hanna was a businessman and politician who initially entered the grocery and commission business in Cleveland and in 1867 transferred his earnings to the coal and iron trade in the same city. In 1885, he became head of the firm M.A. Hanna & Co. Hanna also helped launch the Union National Bank, became owner of the Cleveland Opera House and the Cleveland *Herald,* and ran the city's street railway system.

Active in local politics, he was chosen a member of the Republican state committee, and became a power in Ohio politics. William McKinley received Hanna's backing in 1888 for the Ohio governorship (1891, 1893) and later as a presidential aspirant—in 1894 and 1895, in fact, Hanna withdrew from business and devoted himself entirely to launching McKinley as a presidential candidate. A skilled and shrewd political manager, Hanna got McKinley nominated on the first ballot. In recognition of his political acumen, he was selected as chairman of the Republican national committee. By levying business leaders and corporations, he built an unprecedented election coffer of $3.5 million.

In 1897, Hanna was chosen for the U.S. Senate, where he defended corporate interests, supported ship subsidies, and worked for the Panama route for an isthmian canal. He was a close advisor to McKinley and Roosevelt, and although closely identified with big business, he also supported labor's right to organize and chaired the National Civic Federation. Shortly before his death, powerful Republican interests had indicated plans to run him for the presidency in 1904.

John Marshall Harlan (1833–1911)

John Marshall Harlan studied law at Transylvania University and was admitted to the Kentucky Bar (1859). He served as adjutant general of Kentucky (1851), judge of Franklin County (1858), and colonel of the 10th Kentucky Infantry in the Civil War. Harlan was state attorney general (1863–67) and ran twice unsuccessfully for governor (1871, 1875).

President Hayes appointed him to the U.S. Supreme Court (1877–1911). His dissents in 316 cases were notable, especially those in the sugar-trust case (1895) in which he opposed the majority's narrow interpretation of the commerce clause and in *Plessy v. Ferguson* (1896) in which he declares the U.S. Constitution to be "color blind." He wrote the majority opinion sustaining the breakup of the Northern Securities Co. (1904) and the Sherman Anti-Trust Act. Harlan also challenged the majority who held the income tax to be unconstitutional (1895) and dissented in *Lochner v. N.Y.* (1905) on the ground that limiting hours of employment in an unhealthy occupation was a justifiable infringement on liberty of contract. In the *Insular Cases* (1901), he maintained that "the Constitution followed the flag." He declared legislation barring "yellow-dog" contracts (in which workers are required to swear that they will not join or support a union) in railroad employment to infringe the Fifth Amendment (1907).

John Hay (1838–1905)

John Milton Hay, a statesman, was graduated from Brown University (1858) and admitted to the Illinois bar in 1861. He practiced in Springfield and became a part of Abraham Lincoln's circle, accompanying Lincoln to Washington and serving as his private secretary until the president's assassination. After serving in posts at Paris (1865–67), Madrid (1868–70), and Vienna (1867–68), Hay returned to the United States and became an editorial writer on the New York *Tribune* (1870–75). After serving as assistant secretary of state (1879–81), Hay was ambassador to Great Britain (1897–98) and thereafter, until his death, McKinley's and Theodore Roosevelt's secretary of state (1898–1905). He supported the Open Door policy toward China and negotiated the Hay–Pauncefote Treaty with Great Britain (1900–01) and the Hay-Herrán and Hay-Bunau-Varilla treaties with Colombia and Panama respectively. A poet, novelist, and historian, he published *Pike County Ballads* (1871), *Castilian Days* (1871), the antilabor union novel *The Bread-Winners* (1883), and with John G. Nicolay, *Abraham Lincoln, A History* (10 volumes, 1890), and *Abraham Lincoln: Complete Works* (2 volumes, 1894).

James Butler "Wild Bill" Hickok (1837–1876)

Dispensing frontier justice, whether trying horse thieves or dealing with cowboys in western towns on a Saturday night spree or at the end of a long livestock drive, required a certain breed of law enforcer. Actually, it was difficult at times to tell who they were because they were mixed in with the trappers, gamblers, cowboys, miners, and even gunfighters who committed crimes. Some enforcers gained dubious reputations, such as James Butler "Wild Bill" Hickok who drifted west from Illinois in the 1850s. He gained recognition as a rowdy character and notoriety as a "pistoleer." Even the outlaws hesitated to tangle with him. According to legend, as a federal marshal in Hays, Fort Riley, and Abilene, Kansas, he shot to kill but rarely killed anyone who did not deserve it. In his lifetime, he killed at least seven men.

Hickok was the fourth of six children of a Vermont couple who moved to Troy Grove, Illinois where Hickok was born and where his father farmed and operated a general store and established a way station on the Underground Railroad. Young Jim was frequently involved in whisking fugitive slaves away from their pursuers.

By the time he was a teenager, Hickok had gained a reputation as the best shot in northern Illinois; he also proved adept with his fists. In 1855, he brawled with a fellow teamster and thought he had killed him; the 18-year old fled to St. Louis and finally into Kansas, a territory undergoing great strife over the issue of slavery. Hickok joined the Free-State militia.

In 1858, Hickok began a peaceful tenure as the elected constable of Monticello township in Johnson County. Having previously worked as a farmhand, he worked his own homestead claim while in Monticello. He also drove a stagecoach on the Santa Fe Trail. In 1860, as wagonmaster of freight trains for Russell, Majors, & Waddell, Hickok was attacked by a bear, while leading a train through Raton Pass. He killed the bear with his pistols and knife, but he was severely injured. His company sent him to Santa Fe and to Kansas City for treatment and then transferred him to light duties on the Oregon Trail in Nebraska. It was here that Hickok engaged in his notorious fight with Dave McCanles.

During the Civil War, Hickok hired on as a wagonmaster in Sedalia, Missouri; later he worked as a spy and guide under General Samuel P. Curtis. During this time, he had occasion to face down a lynch mob; when a woman shouted "Good for you, Wild Bill!" he was branded with this famous sobriquet. He may have been involved in the Battle of Pea Ridge, Arkansas, in 1862—he was reputedly involved in one dangerous scrape after another.

After the war, Hickok became a gambler in Springfield, Missouri, and there he killed Dave Tutt in a street fight. He ran and lost an election for chief of police of Springfield and then moved to Fort Riley, Kansas, where his older brother was employed as a wagonmaster, scout, and chief herder. Hickok began to scout for Custer's 7th Cavalry and, in 1867, was defeated as a candidate for sheriff of Ellsworth County, Kansas. Nevertheless he found work as a deputy U.S. marshal chasing down army deserters and thieves of government livestock.

The fall of 1868 found Hickok in Colorado with several cattle ranchers when he was surrounded by a hostile band of Cheyenne Indians. Hickok was selected to make a dash for help and safely sped past the Indians. The next year, he was elected sheriff of Ellis County, Kansas, killed two men, lost the next election to his deputy, and moved to Topeka.

Abilene hired him in 1871 as city marshal for $150 a month and a percentage of the fines. When two gamblers at the Bull's Head Saloon refused to remove an obscene symbol of masculinity at the behest of city council, Hickok got into a gunfight with them, killing one of them and his own deputy. A price of $11,000 was placed on his head.

For the next several years, he traveled in the East with Buffalo Bill Cody's Wild West Show and performed rather ineptly in a production billed as "Scouts of the Prairie."

In failing health, the result of gonorrhea, he was arrested in Cheyenne in 1874 for vagrancy. In 1876, he married Agnes Lake but left her after two weeks for the booming gold fields of Dakota Territory. In Deadwood, he spent most of his time gambling at the No. 10 Saloon while writing his wife that he was working hard as a prospector. He was murdered by Jack McCall and was buried owing $50 to the saloon, which raffled his possessions to pay the expenses of his funeral.

William Dean Howells (1837–1920)

Sometimes called "the Dean of American Letters," William Dean Howells presided over the late Gilded Age's literary establishment. An able novelist in his own right, Howells edited the *Atlantic Monthly* (1866–81), in which he published an elegant mix of poetry, stories, and essays that dealt with contemporary issues, usually in a fastidious manner but without the customary sentimentality and romanticism associated with middle- and upper-class reformers.

Howells was a realist. In *The Rise of Silas Lapham* (1885), his best-known novel, a successful manufacturer of paint is put off by the idleness of wealth. But he does not sell his possessions and join the Salvation Army; rather, he finds purpose and happiness only when he loses his fortune and is forced to return to productive work. He treats the desires of the newly rich middle classes for material possessions realistically: Irene, for example, one of Lapham's two daughters, spends her abundant leisure time shopping and on her appearance. Also, like the middle- and upper-class audiences for whom he wrote, Howells found unacceptable graphic depictions of sexual matters or recreations of the degradation of poverty and squalor. Violation of these middle-class taboos he left to the naturalists.

Howells wrote more than 40 volumes of fiction, and his social and economic views tended to become more explicit during the 40 years in which he wrote. Despite the criticism of H. L. Mencken and Sinclair Lewis who in the 1920s damned Howells's realism as "genteel," his treatment of love as namby-pamby, and his optimism as unjustified, later critics reappraised his writing. The bulk of it deals with social problems, not manners, and these are rendered in closely realistic fashion.

Chief Joseph (c. 1840–1904)

When in 1855 Old Chief Joseph (father of this essay's subject) and the Nez Percés were summoned by the Washington Gov. Issac Stevens to a council at Walla Walla, they had been at peace since the Lewis and Clark expedition in 1805. Stevens planned to open up Indian lands to white settlement and limit the various tribes to reservations. The Nez Percé bands under the Christian Chief Joseph agreed to 10,000-square-mile area in the Wallowa Valley—their traditional homeland.

In 1863, white officials called another council and proposed to reduce the Nez Percé reservation to 1,000 square miles, all in western Idaho, which meant the giving up of the entire Wallowa Valley. One faction signed the agreement; Old Joseph and the Lower Nez Percés refused. Returning to the Wallowa Valley, Joseph tore up his Bible in disgust; the Nez Percé pursued a policy of passive resistance until 1871 when Old Chief Joseph died.

Leadership of the band passed to two sons, one with the Christian name Joseph, the other known as Ollokot. Soon after the old chief's death, white settlers moved into the Wallowa Valley and claimed a tract of Indian land. Young Chief Joseph protested, and in 1873 President Grant formally set aside the Wallowa Valley as a Nez Percé reservation.

White homesteaders ignored the designation and threatened to exterminate the tribe if it stayed. Bowing to pressure, in 1875 the president reversed his previous order, and two years later, General O. O. Howard ordered the Lower Nez Percé to a reservation in Idaho. They were given 30 days to relocate their possessions and livestock; failure to comply would be considered an act of war.

The two brothers at first argued for compliance, fearing a major conflict and the loss of Indian life. After a series of confrontations between Indians and settlers, a one-sided battle with the military occurred at White Bird Creek where the Indians as superior marksmen outmaneuvered soldiers on rocky terrain, killing 34 soldiers without losing a man.

After the battle at White Bird Creek, General Howard raised an army of 600 men to pursue the Nez Percé, who now numbered about 700—but at least 550 of these were women, children, and old men unable to fight. Thus began the remarkable and protracted flight of the Nez Percé that ultimately fell just miles short of their goal to reach the Canadian border. General Howard pursued the fleeing Nez Percé back and forth across the territories of Idaho, Wyoming, and Montana territories between June and October, a journey that totaled 1,700 miles. Crossing treacherous rivers, over rolling plains, across the Bitterroot and Bear Paw mountains, and in bitter cold during the final months, the Nez Percé outwitted the U.S. Army, with a superior force and the advantages of telegraph communications, until October.

In the course of their trek to avoid capture, the Nez Percé were joined along the way by remnants of other Indian breakaway bands. Looking Glass, whose people had been driven off their reservation in an unprovoked attack, joined the Nez Percé; other leaders who joined included Tool-hool-hool-zote, Red Echo, Five Wounds, Rainbow, White Bird, and Lean Elk, a mixed-blood Indian known to the whites as Poker Joe.

Over the long journey, a series of skirmishes and the hardships of the long flight gradually reduced the Nez Percé to about 350 women and children and 80 men. Finally, as the exhausted and decimated tribe set up camp in a hollow next to Snake Creek, just 30 miles south of the Canadian border, the army turned howitzers and gatling guns on their position. As winter closed in on their encampment, Chief Joseph, the last remaining leader, decided to surrender. His brother, Looking Glass, and all the other chiefs had been killed.

Joseph mounted a horse and rode slowly toward the rows of bluecoats, several of his warriors following on foot. General Howard gave General Miles the honor of accepting the surrender. It was at this moment that Chief Joseph gave a moving and eloquent speech, (a translator and recording officer was on hand) and carved a special place for himself in history. Joseph had come to symbolize all Indian suffering.

Despite the national sympathy and prominence generated by the speech, he was never granted a return to the Wallowa Valley. Instead, he was sent to Kansas, then to Indian Territory, and finally to the Colville reservation in Washington where he died in 1904 "of a broken heart," according to the reservation doctor.

Robert La Follette (1855–1925)

The career of Wisconsin's Robert "Battlin' Bob" La Follette is almost a history of progressivism in itself. Born in 1855, he studied law and served for three terms as a Republican congressman before 1890. Some have said his itch for reform began with the offer of a bribe to fix the verdict in a trial. La Follette became enraged—for the rest of his life.

In 1900 he became Wisconsin's governor and added his hurricane force to the winds of reform. The system of regulatory laws he installed required every company doing business with the public to follow clear-cut rules and submit to inspections of its operations.

According to La Follette's "Wisconsin Idea," the people needed protection, and it was the government's responsibility to give it to them by using knowledgeable experts to inform itself. For example, insurance premiums could not be kept at reasonable levels unless the government's regulatory body knew what profit was just and what rapacious. The government should rely upon labor experts and economists for an understanding of what was fair in a labor settlement.

Consequently, La Follette formed a close relationship with the University of Wisconsin and used it as a laboratory of experts he could call upon for information. His generous support made it one of the nation's great universities, and in turn, distinguished members of the faculty such as Richard Ely, Selig Perlman, and John Rogers Commons put their expertise at his disposal. The law school helped develop the first legislative reference library in the United States; the School of Agriculture built a close relationship with farmers and their needs and problems.

In politics, he was idealistic but far from naive, building a political organization to protect his reforms that would have been the envy of Boss Tweed, Tammany Hall's notorious machine politician. He used party workers to get out the vote, and he quickly rewarded them with government jobs if they proved themselves honest.

In 1906, La Follette became a U.S. senator and remained so until he died in 1925. He made several tries at the presidency, always presenting himself as the model of incorruptibility. On the stump, with his brown hair, which later turned white, combed straight back, (and waving wildly as he grew older), he looked like an Old Testament prophet, a Jeremiah who had "devoted his life to saving the soul of American society."

Charles Horace Mayo (1865–1939) and William James Mayo (1861–1939)

The two Mayo brothers from Minnesota were sons of a pioneer surgeon of the Northwest. Both took medical degrees, William at the University of Michigan (1883) and Charles at Chicago Medical College (1888) and then gradually assumed their father's practice in

Rochester, Minnesota. Observing the latest clinical and surgical practices in Europe and America, the Mayos became respected surgeons, William in abdominal and Charles in thyroid surgery. Adding general practitioners, surgeons, and labratory scientists, they developed a cooperative group clinic, out of which grew the Mayo Clinic, established in 1912. The brothers also donated about $4 million to establish the Mayo Foundation for Medical Education and Research, later an affiliate of the University of Minnesota. During World War I, they were chief army consultants for the surgical service, each reaching the rank of brigadier general (1921).

Albert A. Michelson (1852–1931)

Virtually all of physicist Albert Abraham Michelson's experiments and research were done in the field of optics. He was brought to the United States as an infant and lived first in Nevada and then California. In 1873, Michelson graduated from the U.S. Naval Academy, where he later served as an instructor in physics and chemistry (1875–77). His postgraduate work took him to Heidelberg, Berlin, and Paris; he taught physics at the Case School of Applied Science in Cleveland, Ohio (1883–89), and Clark University (1889–92). In 1892, he was appointed chief professor in the Ryerson Physical Laboratory and head of the physics department at the newly established University of Chicago, where he stayed until retirement in 1931.

Michelson's improvements of the Foucault apparatus for measuring the speed of light and his work with Edward Williams Morley on the motion of the Earth contributed greatly to Einstein's theory of relativity. He developed the inferometer to measure distance in terms of the wave length of light and was the first to measure the angular diameter of a star. The spectrometer he designed measured the tides in the solid Earth. In 1907, he was awarded the Nobel Prize in Physics.

J. P. Morgan (1837–1913)

John Pierpont Morgan was the father of modern finance capitalism. Born into a prominent family of international bankers in Hartford, Connecticut, Morgan became one of the most formidable of all American financiers, providing the capital for countless enterprises undertaken during the late nineteenth and early twentieth centuries. The piercing eyes, large bulbous nose, and imperious persona became his popular image.

Beginning his career at the top as a lawyer in his father's international banking firm, J. S. Morgan and Company, he founded J. P. Morgan and Company in 1895; it became one of the leading banking houses of the world. Young Morgan proved to be a financial genius, buying, holding, merging, and reorganizing vertically and horizontally entire industries such as railroads, steel, electricity, coal, and steamships. In 1896, the House of Morgan was so powerful that it was able to bail out the U.S. government with a loan (at 4½%) of $62 million in gold to help bring U.S. Treasury gold reserves to $100 million.

With the purchase of Carnegie Steel, capitalized at $1.4 billion, Morgan formed United States Steel, the first billion-dollar industry in America, and pocketed the handsome sum of $62 million in commissions on the deal. By now, he dominated an extraordinarily far-reaching financial empire that included companies such as International Harvester, General Electric, and American Telephone and Telegraph. Morgan and ten associates held 72 directorships in 47 major corporations.

Adolph S. Ochs (1858–1935)

Adolph Simon Ochs made his reputation as a newspaper publisher. He received most of his schooling from his parents and got his early newspaper training in Knoxville, where he served an apprenticeship with the *Chronicle*. In 1878, he gained controlling interest of the *Chattanooga Times,* a newspaper on the brink of failure, and and began a policy of full, accurate, and reliable reporting that marked his subsequent career (1896–1935) as publisher of *The New York Times*. He took over the *Times* when it was also on the verge of bankruptcy, reorganized the newspaper, and made it a model of responsible journalism in a day when sensationalism was at its height in New York City. By 1900, the paper was turning a profit and became known as "the paper of record" because of its extensive coverage of public events and its thoughtful reporting. Ochs's view of a free press was captured in his motto for the *Times:* "All the news that's fit to print," which still occupies a position on the newspaper's front page.

Joseph Pulitzer (1847–1911)

A journalist and newspaper publisher, Joseph Pulitzer arrived in the United States in 1864 and served briefly in the Union army. In 1868, he became a reporter on the *St. Louis Westliche Post* and in 1869 became a member of the Missouri legislature. He rose in politics to become city police commissioner in St. Louis and actively supported the Liberal Republican movement, a reform branch of the party. He was part owner of the *Westliche Post* (1871–73) and was admitted to the bar in the District of Columbia (1876). He purchased the St. Louis *Post* and *Dispatch* and combined them into the *Post-Dispatch,* one of the foremost newspapers of the Midwest. Purchasing the New York *World* from Jay Gould in 1883, he followed a policy of sensational journalism with lurid headlines, comic strips, and crime stories that converted the *World* into a profitable enterprise.

In 1887, he established the *Evening World,* which between 1896 and 1898, competed with Hearst's *Evening Journal* in what was called "yellow journalism." Both aroused public opinion for war against Spain with graphic details of atrocities that Spain was allegedly carrying out against the Cubans. In subsequent years, the *World* became a responsible journal of high standards and independence. Pulitzer announced his intention in 1903 to establish a school of journalism at Columbia University. He made provision in his will of $2 million for its establishment (1912) and for Pulitzer prizes to be awarded annually in many fields of achievement.

Walter Rauschenbusch (1861–1918)

Walter Rauschenbusch was an ordained Baptist minister who took charge of the 2nd German Baptist Church in New York City to work with German immigrants. He had studied economics and theology at the University of Berlin (1891–92), becoming influenced there by the British Fabian movement and the work of the Salvation Army, and at the Rochester Theological Seminary, where he received his A.B. in 1884. Rauschenbusch succeeded his father in 1897 to the chair of New Testament interpretation at Rochester Theological Seminary and gained prominence as an advocate of the "social gospel," the application of Christian principles to social problems. In *Christianity and the Social Crisis* (1907), *Prayers of the Social Awakening* (1910), *Christianizing the Social Order* (1912), and *The Social Principles of Jesus* (1916), he expounded his views of social Darwinism, the doctrine, favored by the unregulated industrialists and financiers, that applied the biological principle of survival of the fittest to economic and social life.

Walter Reed (1851–1902)

Walter Reed was an army surgeon and bacteriologist who had graduated from the University of Virginia (1869) and Bellevue Hospital Medical School, New York City (1870). Entering the Medical Corps of the U.S. Army in 1875, he was assigned to duty as an assistant surgeon. In 1890, Reed was ordered to Baltimore as examiner of recruits and studied at Johns Hopkins Hospital where he was attached to the pathological laboratory, working under Dr. William H. Welch and others in the emerging field of bacteriology. In 1893, he was named professor of bacteriology and clinical microscopy at the newly established Army Medical School.

Just before the outbreak of the Spanish-American War, Reed researched the bacteriology of erysipelas and diptheria, and in 1898 became chairman of a group investigating typhoid fever, a disease affecting the volunteer camps. His report highlighted the importance of transmission by flies, dust, and other agents previously ignored. In 1897–99, Reed and Dr. James Carroll disproved the theory of Dr. Giuseppe Sanarelli of Italy about the cause of yellow fever. Named head of the U.S. Army Yellow Fever Commission in 1900, Reed with his associates (including Carroll) carried out experiments in Cuba that proved conclusively that yellow fever was transmitted by the mosquito. The commission made it possible to control yellow fever and virtually eliminate the disease in the United States and Cuba. The general hospital of the army medical center at Washington, D.C., is named for Reed.

Jacob Riis (1849–1914)

Jacob Riis, born in Ribe, Denmark, arrived in New York City in 1870. Misinformed about America and romantically inclined, upon reaching the port of New York he spent half his money on a large navy revolver, which he wore on the outside of his coat while walking up Broadway, "conscious," he later wrote, "that I was following the fashion of the country." He drifted about in semipoverty for seven years until he became a police reporter, first for the *New York Tribune* and then for the *Evening Sun.*

Beginning in 1877, Riis worked for 22 years in an office on Mulberry Street near police headquarters. The area of the city where he worked—the Lower East Side—became his school and library. Just at "the Bend" where Mulberry Street made a sharp turn he found "the foul core of New York's slums"; he made the area a symbol of his crusade. "For years I walked every morning between two and four o'clock the whole length of Mulberry Street, through the Bend and across the Five Points down to Fulton Ferry." The result was *How the Other Half Lives,* a semi-autobiographical work and descriptive account of what Riis saw and learned on the streets. Not analytical but widely read, the book vacillates between sentimentalism and high-minded reform. Mostly it is a collection of human interest stories.

When Theodore Roosevelt was New York City's police commissioner (1893–95), Riis led him on nighttime excursions into the slums of the city. They became lifelong friends, and Riis later wrote

a biography of Roosevelt. Riis wrote many other books, mostly about slums and tenement living. He was an active reformer, campaigning for slum clearance, parks and playgrounds, and established the Riis Neighborhood House for Social Work (1888–89).

John D. Rockefeller (1839–1937)

John Davison Rockefeller began his public life making money and never stopped for the rest of his life. When the Civil War began, Rockefeller was an accountant. He bought a substitute (someone to take his place in the military draft), and then made a tidy sum selling provisions to the Union Army. He had a consuming passion for riches that influenced his every decision, private and public. For example, he disapproved of drinking and smoking, not because he was a deeply religious Sunday School teacher in the Baptist Church, but because such habits cost money that could be invested. He carefully made record of how he spent every dime. He would remove his stovepipe hat and bend down to pick up a penny.

He made his biggest fortune in crude oil, refining it into kerosene to sell to millions for heat, cooking, and light at a time when the most commonly used substance, whale oil, was exorbitantly priced due to the decimation of the whale population. In 1870, 250 small refineries were engaged in cutthroat competition for the business. Rockefeller shrewdly avoided getting into the business of drilling for oil, which also attracted hundreds of small-time operators; like the robber barons of medieval Europe who located on the narrows of the Rhine and the Danube to plunder the river traffic, Rockefeller controlled the narrows of the oil business—refining.

Controlling an entire business by controlling one stage of the process is known as horizontal integration. Rockefeller used it to establish a monopoly across the business. Within 20 years, his Standard Oil Company controlled 90% of U.S. refining capacity. He persuaded strong competitors to join him and drove weak refiners out of business.

His other practices included cutthroat rate wars. With its superior resources, Standard Oil was able to sell at a loss for a time in order to drive out a competitor who could not withstand the losses. At one point, Rockefeller bought up every barrel stave and hoop in the oil region; competitors could not ship their products. He was also not above using muscle, as he did on one occasion to prevent a refining company from building a pipeline to New York City.

More effective was the "rebate." Because Standard Oil could promise a railroad a fixed and steady volume of business each day, Rockefeller demanded a contract that kicked back to him a portion of his shipping costs—under the table—in return for carrying his kerosene. With competitors paying full price, the rebate gave him a substantial competitive advantage.

Rockefeller used the ancient legal device of the "trust" in order to acquire the vast capital needed to buy out other large producers. According to this arrangement, Standard Oil promised "trust certificates" to refining companies that would turn over their property to be managed and controlled by Standard Oil. Most refiners gave in and became wealthy themselves.

Rockefeller gloated over the consequences of his monopoly, reminding hostile questioners that he had eliminated cutthroat competition and given the consumer a cheaper price for a gallon of kerosene. He made no apologies for what he did and remained a severe critic of competition throughout his life. He had brought order to a chaotic industry. But his concentration of wealth and power caused alarm and resentment in the nation.

Great inequalities of wealth and income characterized the Victorian Age. Fortunes were made in the oil business by men like John D. Rockefeller, whose residence in Cleveland, Ohio, contrasts sharply with the homes of most Americans. Rockefeller and other captains of industry did not hoard their wealth, however. Rather they became benefactors of libraries, art museums, universities, and a variety of philanthropic and charitable organizations. (Courtesy Prints and Photographs Division, Library of Congress)

Elihu Root (1845–1937)

Elihu Root was a statesman, jurist, and diplomat. He graduated from New York University Law School (1867) and began practice in New York. Under presidents McKinley and Roosevelt, he served as secretary of war (1899–1904), where he created a general staff of the army, drew up a constitution for the Philippines, and formulated the Platt Amendment (1901) for governing Cuba. As Roosevelt's secretary of state (1905–09), Root reorganized the consular service and negotiated the Root-Takihara Open Door agreement with Japan (1908). When Republican senator from New York (1909–15), he was chief counsel for the United States in the North Atlantic Fisheries Arbitration (1910).

In 1912, he was awarded the Nobel Prize for peace in recognition of his services as president of the Carnegie Endowment for International Peace (1910–25). He advocated U.S. entry into the League of Nations, was a member of the committee of jurists at the Hague that devised the Permanent Court of International Justice (1920–

21), and was a delegate to the Washington Conference on Limitation of Armaments (1921).

Margaret Sanger (1883–1966)

As a visiting nurse in New York's east side immigrant neighborhoods, Margaret Sanger distributed information about contraception in hopes of preventing unwanted pregnancies among the poor. This activity grew into a lifelong birth-control crusade, encompassing not only the poor but middle-class women who wanted to limit the size of their own families.

Some women used home remedies or assistance from doctors to terminate unwanted pregnancies. Abortions were not uncommon in the late nineteenth century, $10 being the standard fee in New York and Boston. In 1898, the Michigan Board of Health estimated that one third of all pregnancies were voluntarily terminated. Contraceptives were not foolproof but did exist in the form of spermicidal douches, sheaths made from animal intestines, rubber condoms, patent medicines, and early types of diaphragms. Only medical self-help books discussed birth control, childless marriage, and avoiding pregnancy—and not without controversey.

Sanger's crusade raised the hackles of moralists, men and women, who saw birth control as a threat to family and morality. In 1914, Sanger was indicted for mailing "obscene literature" (under New York's Comstock Act of 1873 contraceptive information was classified as obscene). In 1916, the indictment was quashed, but the publicity it stirred up led to the opening of the first birth control clinic in the U.S. (Brooklyn, Oct. 16, 1916). She was forced to flee the country for a year, but she continued her campaign and in 1921 formed the American Birth Control League. The organization enlisted the support of physicians and social workers to convince judges that the distribution of birth-control information was not a threat to the nation's morals. States continued to prohibit the sale of contraceptives, but the issue had been introduced into public discussion.

The Birth Control League became the Planned Parenthood Federation of America in 1946. Today it includes centers in nearly every major city in the U.S. Sanger launched birth control programs in Europe, India, China and Japan. Her numerous publications include *What Every Girl Should Know* (1916); *The Case For Birth Control* (1917); *Woman, Morality, and Birth Control* (1922); *My Fight For Birth Control* (1931); *Margaret Sanger, An Autobiography* (1938).

John Singer Sargent (1856–1925)

John Singer Sargent was an American painter raised in Europe, who studied at the Academy of Fine Arts, Florence. When his parents moved to Paris (1874), he studied at the École des Beaux Arts under Carolus-Duran. He took his first trip to the United States in 1876 and returned to Paris to exhibit at the salons. He generated a storm of criticism in Paris with *Madame X,* his portrait of Madame Gautreau. At age 28, he established a studio in London where his celebrated *Carnation, Lily, Lily, Rose* (1884–86) became the first of a long series of pictures of children and brought him commissions in the United States. Sargent exhibited in Boston (1887), made many visits to that city, and was commissioned to do murals for the Boston Public Library (completed 1916), the Art Museum, and Harvard's Widener Library.

Technically brilliant and stylishly elegant, Sargent was considered primarily a portraitist, but he did original and influential work as a painter of genre *(The Weavers, Neapolitan Children Bathing).* His quickly completed and luminous watercolors *(Melon Boots, White Ships),* painted during his later years, were considered his masterpieces. In 1907, Sargent declined a knighthood on the grounds that he was still a U.S. citizen. During World War I, he was sent by the British government to the front in northern France, where he painted *Gassed* (1919).

Upton Sinclair (1878–1968)

No single force was more influential in spreading the gospel of reform during the Gilded Age than the "muckrakers." Men and women such as Ida Tarbell, who exposed the business practices of John D. Rockefeller and the Standard Oil Company, and Lincoln Steffens, whose telling exposé of corruption in the city government of St. Louis gained national attention, wrote for journals such as *McClure's,* the *Arena, Collier's, Cosmopolitan,* and *Everybody's.* Upton Sin-

clair was probably the most influential muckraker of all.

Sinclair, an obscure young socialist, wrote a serialized novel in 1906 entitled *The Jungle.* The setting was the Chicago stockyards. The story concerned a Lithuanian immigrant who was transformed into a revolutionary anticapitalist by ethnic prejudice and economic exploitation. The mass-circulation magazines would not run the story, so Sinclair turned to a Socialist Party weekly newspaper, the *Appeal to Reason,* which had a large readership; one issue sold more than a million copies. *The Jungle* was a huge success, selling 100,000 copies, one of which reached President Theodore Roosevelt's desk.

The book was less successful as an appeal for socialism. In fact, later chapters where the protagonist turns to the red flag were considered inferior to the rest of the book. But it was immensely successful in popularizing the awful conditions in the Chicago slaughterhouses. *The Jungle* publicized documented cases of rats being ground into sausage, workers with tuberculosis coughing on the meat they packed, and other examples of filth and degradation along the packing line.

Sinclair captured the impact of his work with the comment, "I aimed at the nation's heart and hit it in the stomach." Within months of publication, *The Jungle* led to a federal meat-inspection bill that had been languishing in the Congress, and Roosevelt quickly signed it into law. This law and the Pure Food and Drug Act, which forbade the use of dangerous adulterants in food, brought federal oversight into an area of American life that would have been inconceivable a few years earlier.

In 1940 Sinclair began a popular series of contemporary historical novels covering the period before and during World War II. Lanny Budd, the hero of the series witnesses the rise of nazism in Germany and later becomes a personal representative of President Franklin D. Roosevelt. The series of ten books included *Dragon's Teeth* (1942), winner of the Pulitzer Prize in fiction (1943). In 1953 he published *The Return of Lanny Budd.* His books include *King Coal* (1917) based on his investigation of the Colorado coal strike (1913); *Oil!* (1927), an examination of the Teapot Dome scandal; books about the film industry and evangelism; and *Boston* (1928), an examination of the controversial Sacco-Vanzetti case.

Theobald Smith (1859–1934)

Theobald Smith graduated from the Albany Medical college (1883) and pursued advanced work in biology at Johns Hopkins, Cornell, and the University of Toronto. In 1884, he became director of the newly established pathological laboratory in the Bureau of Animal Industry, Department of Agriculture. Two years later he organized at Columbian (later George Washington University) the first department of bacteriology in any U.S. medical school and was professor there from 1886 to 1895.

Smith studied the diseases of hogs and found their alarming mortality rate to be due to hog cholera and swine plague. In 1898 and 1902, he published studies on the differentiation of the human and bovine types of the tuberculosis bacillus. His published research on Texas cattle fever showed how the parasite was transmitted by the cattle tick, the first demonstration of diseases transmitted by insect carriers.

Smith served as director of the pathological laboratory of the Massachusetts Board of Health (1895–1915), professor of comparative pathology in the Harvard Medical School (1896–1915), and director of the department of animal pathology, Rockefeller Institute for Medicine (1915–29), where he became president (1933). The American livestock industry is greatly indebted to Smith.

Elizabeth Cady Stanton (1815–1902)

Elizabeth Cady Stanton was a social reformer and women's rights leader. In 1832, she graduated from the Troy (N.Y.) Female Seminary and in 1840 married the lawyer and reformer, Henry Brewster Stanton. While attending a London antislavery convention in 1840 with Lucretia C. Mott and other American women, Stanton and the other women were refused official accreditation because of their sex. Afterward, she joined with Mott to plan a women's rights convention that met at the Wesleyan Methodist Church in Seneca Falls, New York, July 19–20, 1848. The Seneca Falls Conference launched the modern women's rights movement. Stanton was active in the abolitionist and temperance movements, but her chief crusade was in behalf of women's rights. After 1851, she worked closely with Susan B. Anthony. She was president of the National Woman Suffrage Association and was coeditor of the *Revolution,* a publication of the feminist movement.

Female Suffrage in the U. S., 1875-1915

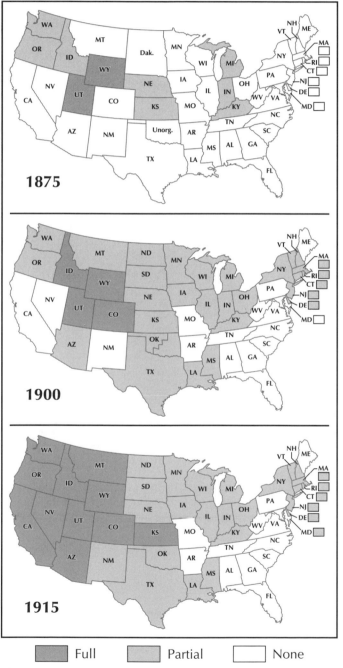

These three maps show the spread of female suffrage in Victorian America. Beginning with Wyoming, only a few states introduced full suffrage for women before 1910, when female suffrage became a major political issue. (Dale Williams)

Lincoln Steffens (1866–1936)

Lincoln Steffens was a journalist and reformer who received a Ph.B. from the University of California then studied abroad at Heidelberg, Munich, Leipzig, and the Sorbonne. In 1892, he returned to New York City to work as a reporter for the *Evening Post,* covering the Lexow Committee's exposé of vice. In 1901, he joined the staff of *McClure's Magazine* and worked with Ida Tarbell and Ray Stannard Baker. Steffens wrote a series of articles, "Tweed Days in St. Louis" (1902), a pioneering "muckraking" article that focused attention on municipal corruption in St. Louis; he followed with a similar article on Minneapolis. His *The Shame of the Cities* (1904) emphasized the link between business and politics. In 1906, with Tarbell and Baker, he took over the *American Magazine* and made it a major reform publication, but he quit the following year to freelance. In 1919, Steffens joined with William C. Bullitt on a mission to Russia, where he met Lenin and exclaimed: "I have seen the future; and it works." Before his death he became disillusioned with reform and advocated a more revolutionary approach.

Louis Henri Sullivan (1856–1924)

Louis Sullivan was one of the leading architects of the age. His idea, "form follows function," established the basis of modern architecture. Sullivan attended Massachusetts Institute of Technology (1872–73) and was admitted to the École des Beaux Arts (1874). As a partner in the architectural firm of Adler and Sullivan (1881–95), he established his reputation as the leading figure in the Chicago school of architecture.

He abandoned the styles of Victorian gothic and romanesque revival in his design of the interior of the Chicago Auditorium (built 1886–90) in favor of the delicate ornamentation that became his trademark. In his designs for the Wainwright Building in St. Louis (1890), the Schiller Building (1892) and the Gage Building (1898) in Chicago, and the Prudential Building in Buffalo, New York (1895), Sullivan evolved the type of designs that would solve the architectural and structural problems of the skyscraper; he was among the first to stress the vertical lines of steel-skeleton construction.

William Graham Sumner (1840–1910)

William Graham Sumner was an economist, political and social scientist, and teacher. Graduated from Yale (1863), he studied for the ministry in Germany and England and was ordained a priest of the Protestant Episcopal Church (1869). He stayed in the ministry until 1872 when he was invited to the newly established chair in political and social science at Yale, a post he retained for the rest of his life.

A noted exponent of laissez-faire economics, he opposed trade unions, social-welfare legislation, and government regulation. As an economist, he favored free trade and opposed free silver. As a sociologist, his work was a path-breaking contribution to the study and interrelationships of all social institutions. His most noted work was *Folkways* (1908). Among his other works are *What Social Classes Owe to Each Other* (1883), *The Financier and Finances of the American Revolution* (2 volumes 1891), and *The Forgotten Man and Other Essays* (1919).

Frederick Winslow Taylor (1856–1915)

The son of a prominent Philadelphia family, Frederick Winslow Taylor became the key figure in industrial management. As a youth, while at a private school, he had a nervous breakdown for which his physicians prescribed work as the cure; therefore, he began to labor at the Midvale Steel Company in Philadelphia. While he worked his way up rapidly, he studied engineering at night and became chief engineer at the factory in the 1880s. Later, he used this experience to rethink the organization of industry.

In *Principles of Scientific Management* (1911), Taylor claimed that time studies of work should form the basis of modern management. Taylor, a pattern maker, machinist, and industrial consultant, sought to eliminate all needless motion in the performance of work for the maximum possible efficiency of labor and the greatest possible profit to employers. At Pennsylvania's Midvale Steel, he first conducted "time and motion studies" in 1898 and went on to test them in bricklaying, arms manufacture, and metal and steel production.

Taylorism, or "scientific" management, caught on in the Victorian Age, a period fascinated with science and with saving time. Taylor's method depended upon four concepts:

1. Analysis (by stopwatch) of tasks in order to reduce performance to the lowest "time rate"
2. Centralized planning and sequencing of each group of tasks, regulated by synchronized factory clocks
3. Detailed monitoring (requiring workers to complete time cards for each task) of each worker's performance
4. Wage payments based upon each worker's adherence to the instructions and "punching" in to the time clock throughout the pay period.

Taylor's method "choreographed the human motions of hands, arms, backs, and legs to perform with clocklike regularity."

Workers responded to efforts to impose the stopwatch as boss in different ways, but most saw the whole "scientific management" process as akin to enslavement. Some decided to go on strike rather than submit to such a regimen, for example at the Massachusetts Watertown Arsenal and in auto plants at Saginaw, Michigan. At Ford Motor Company's Highland Park plant, engineers used time-and-motion studies to manipulate the chain-driven assembly line and the workers who manned it. The result was a high turnover of workers, forcing Ford to institute a wage-and-bonus system to stabilize labor. Others demonstrated, lobbied, and organized campaigns to shorten the workday (eight-hour day) and workweek (40-hour week).

Frederick Jackson Turner (1861–1932)

In 1893 at the Chicago Exposition, Frederick Jackson Turner, a 32-year-old University of Wisconsin history professor, addressed professional historians at the fair and declared the closing of the American frontier. For Turner, the passing of the age of the westward expansion was a momentous event because the frontier had shaped the American character and given definition to American democracy and individualism.

Known in countless textbooks as the "Turner thesis"—the idea that national culture was more a product of mobility and environment and less a derivation from Europe—the thesis is considered by many to have been one of the most original and creative theories ever produced by an American historian. Equally well known is the "safety-valve" theory, a part of the same thesis that argued that the closing of the frontier also meant the loss of an alternative to discontented urban laborers in the East.

From homesteaders on the Plains, sodbusters in Kansas, Mormons trekking to a homeland, or claim jumpers in Oklahoma, whether traveling by covered wagon or automobile, Americans have remained a people on the move. As Turner later noted, of the 1,000 counties in the United States that decreased in population between 1910 and 1920, almost all were rural, and the 2,000 that increased in population were urban and industrial.

Later, historians found a turnover of almost 78% in the five small towns of Grant County, Wisconsin, from 1880 to 1895; another study noted that 20 farmers flocked to the city for every laborer who took up farming. As early as the 1870s, in sections of New England, the Middle Atlantic states, and parts of the Midwest, an urban way of life began to predominate.

Cornelius Vanderbilt, 1794–1877

Cornelius Vanderbilt was one of the first of what Matthew Josephson called robber barons, capitalists of late nineteenth-century America who amassed immense wealth through a combination of shrewdness, ingenuity, and ruthlessness. Vanderbilt was born on Staten Island, New York, and began his business career at the age of 16 when he bought a sailboat and began to ferry freight and passengers between Staten Island and New York City. Eventually, he developed a fleet of oceangoing carriers that sailed the world and gave him the name "commodore," which he proudly proclaimed thereafter.

During the Civil War, he turned his attention to a new and promising carrier, the railroad, and soon became a dominant figure in one of the nation's growth industries of the Industrial Revolution. By 1875, Vanderbilt was worth $100 million and controlled the gigantic New York Central Railroad and 14,000 miles of track, the largest combination of roads under one company.

Vanderbilt heirs carried on the tradition of accumulating wealth through wheeling and dealing in rolling stock: William H. Vanderbilt was noted for his famous comment to a reporter in response to a reminder that he had some responsibility to the public, "The public be damned." The Vanderbilts personified economist Thorstein Veblen's phrase *conspicuous consumption,* a trait for which the growing industrial plutocracy became famous.

Like other families with great fortunes during the Victorian period, the Vanderbilts turned to philanthropy to dispose of some of their vast wealth, most notably giving large gifts to a Methodist seminary in Nashville, Tennessee, renamed Vanderbilt University after the first gift.

Thorstein Veblen (1857–1929)

Thorstein Bunde Veblen was an economist and writer. He graduated from Carleton College, Northfield, Minnesota (1880), and studied at Johns Hopkins, Yale (Ph.D., 1884), and Cornell. His teaching included the University of Chicago (1893–1906), the University of Missouri (1911–18), and the New School for Social Research, New York (1918–20).

The Theory of the Leisure Class (1899) was his first published book; it won him much public acclaim. In it, he analyzed the pecuniary values of the business and middle classes, which he summed up in the famous phrase *conspicuous consumption*. He conceived of the existing economic system as a price system whose cyclical crises gave evidence of its inability to adjust. He proposed as an alternative a system a "Technocracy," with production and distribution to be controlled by engineers.

Among his other works were *The Theory of Business Enterprise* (1904), *Imperial Germany and the Industrial Revolution* (1915), *The Higher Learning in America* (1918), and *The Engineers and the Price System* (1921).

Booker T. Washington (1859–1915)

Booker T. Washington was born into plantation slavery. As a youth, he worked in a salt furnace and a coal mine. In his autobiography *Up from Slavery,* Washington laid out the basic philosophy of hard work and discipline that made him one of the nation's foremost black leaders during the Victorian era. He walked 500 miles to enroll in Hampton (Virginia) Normal and Agricultural Institute, working as a janitor to pay his way. Like his mother, he became a schoolteacher. In 1881, he became the head of Tuskegee Institute and built it from a fledgling school into the nation's foremost institute for vocational training for blacks.

Washington's leadership fit the age in which he lived: he preached the gospel of accommodation to blacks as a strategy for survival, teaching them to be polite, obey the law, and avoid white contact. In a society where blacks were often lynched with impunity (on the average of three a week in the South), during a time when Jim Crow laws forced blacks to eat, shop, play, and live separately from whites, his leadership probably saved lives. He advocated vocational training to make blacks economically independent. He was a stirring public speaker; meanwhile, behind the scenes, he worked in a more aggressive manner to finance some of the earliest cases against segregation and to found the National Negro Business League.

Orville (1871–1948) and Wilbur (1867–1912) Wright

Orville and Wilbur Wright were the pioneers of modern aviation. Wilbur was born on April 16, 1867, in Millville, Indiana, and Orville on August 19, 1871, in Dayton, Ohio. They were sons of a minister with an interest in science and a mother who inspired their mechanical interests. Said to be inveterate tinkerers and builders from early childhood, the Wright brothers were archetypal American inventors—self-taught, curious individuals who accomplished things that were declared impossible by the great and educated.

During the 1890s, the Wrights, familiar with aviation experiments around the world, began to develop their own ideas. By 1900, they had developed their first aviation patent. Experimenting first with kites, they worked with gliders on the sandy dunes at Kitty Hawk, North Carolina, and built the first wind tunnel to test more than 200 wing designs. From these experiments and tests came the science of aerodynamics and a flood of design applications. In 1902 and 1903, they returned to Kitty Hawk to test hundreds of new gliders.

With a knowledge of aerodynamics, they knew what was necessary for powered flight: in 1903, they built a gasoline engine and experimented with a new airscrew. Finally, on December 17, 1903, with five witnesses present and Orville lying on the airplane's wing, they made history with the first flight powered by their own four-cylinder, 12-horsepower, 200-pound gasoline engine.

Soon after, experimenters and innovators built upon the Wright brothers' early efforts. In 1909, Frenchman Louis Blériot flew across the English Channel. International flying meets became commonplace, and country fairs typically included thrilling aerial displays of daring aviators.

Orville and Wilbur continued in the field as designers, promoters, and builders for the rest of their lives. Wilbur died of typhoid in 1912; Orville, in 1948. The Wright brothers launched the air age in America and were part of the spirit of invention that characterized late nineteenth- and early twentieth-century America.

CHAPTER 11 Education

Common Schools and Kindergartens

The primary educational system in the United States expanded during the Victorian Age in size, scope, and substance. In 1876, public schools enrolled 65% of the nation's children between the ages of five and 17; the figure rose to nearly three-fourths (73%) in 1913. Children also spent more time in the common schools (that is, public schools), going from 79 average days attended per enrolled pupil in 1876 to 116 in 1913.

Many rural one-room schools had a single teacher for ages six through 14. During a school day, typically 8 A.M. to 4 P.M., students learned the four Rs: *reading*, *'riting*, *'rithmetic*, and *recitation*. *McGuffey's Eclectic Readers* were commonly used texts; 122 million copies were sold between 1836 and 1922.

McGuffey's readers had a dual mission to teach morality and civics along with reading; chapter titles included "Respect for the Sabbath Rewarded," "The Bible the Best of Classics," and similar uplifting messages. *McGuffey's* taught that the primary purpose of government is the protection of private property; that wealth is an outward sign of inner salvation; that prolonged poverty is a sign of God's disapproval; and that to succeed in life, one needs to be sober, frugal, and energetic. Males were usually the principal characters; when females were introduced, they were represented as models of moral virtue.

School boards also perpetuated the idea of women as naturally virtuous in the preference they showed for women as teachers. Be-

While the U.S. Army fought Indian "insurrections," and gunfighters shot it out in frontier saloons, others on the western plains built schools and educated children. Shown here is Blanche Lamont's school class, Hecla, Montana, 1893. By the turn of the century, Kansas, Iowa, and Nebraska had the highest literacy rates in the nation. (Courtesy Prints and Photographs Division, Library of Congress)

The Tuskegee Institute was founded in 1881 by an act of the Alabama general assembly. The act appropriated only $2,000 a year to support the school. Booker T. Washington headed the school from 1881 until 1915. At his death, he had increased the school's worth to approximately $2 million and established a well-regarded agricultural extension program. The school had about 1,500 students, two-thirds of them below high school level. Pictured here is the history class at Tuskegee Institute in 1902. (Courtesy Prints and Photographs Division, Library of Congress)

tween 1876 and 1913, the number of schoolteachers who were women increased from 58% to 80 percent. They were supervised routinely, however, by male principals and superintendents.

Another major trend in education was the segregation, by law in the South and by custom in the North, of blacks. Native Americans, Hispanic Americans, and Asian Americans were also customarily segregated, making the "common" schools uncommonly white institutions. Roman Catholics and Lutherans often chose to have their children educated in parochial schools. In 1884, the Catholic Church's Third Plenary Council in Baltimore decreed that a parochial school be built near each Catholic church and that parents were obliged to send their children to Catholic schools unless released by the local bishop.

In both parochial and public schools, the kindergarten emerged as a new introductory level of education. Introduced in the United States first in St. Louis in 1873 by followers of the German educator

Friedrich Froebel (1782–1852), the kindergarten spread quickly, to total 225,394 kindergartens in the United States in 1900. Froebel envisioned a child being taught creative play by a model maternal teacher, using games, stories, and songs. William T. Harris, a school superintendent in St. Louis, expanded the meaning of kindergarten to save slum children by teaching them cleanliness, obedience, politeness, and self-control, which they would—presumably—spread to their parents.

High Schools

In the early nineteenth century, high schools were meant to "fit a young man for college." They were private elitist institutions concentrating on classical education. By 1900, the high school had developed into an entirely different kind of institution: mass public

TABLE 11.1   WHAT 14,683 CLEVELAND CHILDREN WERE DOING ON JUNE 23, 1913

		Boys	Girls	Total
Where they were seen	On streets	5,241	2,558	7,799
	In yards	1,583	1,998	3,581
	In vacant lots	686	197	883
	In playgrounds	997	872	1,869
	In alleys	413	138	551
What they were doing	Doing nothing	3,737	2,234	5,961
	Playing	4,601	2,757	7,358
	Working	719	635	1,354
What games they were playing	Baseball	1,448	190	1,638
	Kites	482	49	531
	Sand piles	241	230	471
	Tag	100	53	153
	Jackstones	68	257	325
	Dolls	89	193	282
	Sewing	14	130	144
	Housekeeping	53	191	244
	Horse and wagon	89	24	113
	Bicycle riding	79	13	92
	Minding baby	19	41	60
	Reading	17	35	52
	Roller skating	18	29	47
	Gardening	13	14	27
	Caddy	6	0	6
	Marbles	2	0	2
	Playing in other ways, mostly just fooling	1,863	1,308	3,171

Source: William Graebner and Leonard Richards, eds., *The American Record: Images of the Nation's Past,* Vol. II, *Since 1865* (1988), 141.

TABLE 11.2   PUBLIC SCHOOL ENROLLMENT AND ATTENDANCE, 1876, 1913

Year	Enrollment in Millions	Popul. Ages 5–17	Ave. Length School Term in Days	Ave. Att./ Enrollee in Days
1876	8.9	65%	133	79
1880	9.9	66%	130	31
1890	12.7	69%	135	86
1900	15.5	72%	144	99
1913	18.6	73%	158	116

Source: Historical Statistics of the United States, Colonial Times to 1957, (1961), 207.

TABLE 11.3   PUBLIC SCHOOL TEACHERS, 1876, 1913

Year	Total[a]	Male	Female
1876	259,168	109,780	149,838
1880	286,593	122,795	163,798
1890	363,922	125,525	238,397
1900	423,062	126,588	296,474
1913	565,483	113,213	452,270

[a]Includes classroom teachers and other nonsupervisory staff.
Source: Historical Statistics of the United States, Colonial Times to 1957, 208.

secondary education that was populist, coeducational, and vocational.

Civic-minded Americans in the early twentieth century concerned themselves with the "youth problem." Educators, social scientists, muckrakers, and magazine writers fretted about juvenile

Lacking wood for building, settlers fashioned schools out of sod as they did their homes. Shown here is the sod schoolhouse in Woods County, Oklahoma, 1895. (Courtesy National Archives)

Schoolchildren had to find their own transportation to school. In this picture, a family cow is used to transport children to school in Okanogan, Washington, 1907. (Photo by Frank Matsura. Courtesy National Archives)

misbehavior and delinquency. Popular guidebooks, magazines, "Chautauqua" lecturers and preachers warned anxious middle-class parents about two problems: misconduct and "bad apples." Social problems such as pilfering, drinking, begging, petty larceny, roaming the streets, and fighting characterized the "bad boys." Reformers sought to deal with these problems by having states enact compulsory education statutes (in every state by 1918).

TABLE 11.4 PUBLIC SCHOOL EXPENDITURES, 1876, 1913

Year	Total	Amt. Spent per Pupil in Ave. Daily Att.
1876	83,083	13.63[a]
1880	78,095	. . .
1890	140,507	13.99
1900	214,965	16.67
1913	521,546	32.17

[a] Figure is for 1889, the earliest available.
Source: Historical Statistics of the United States, Colonial Times to 1957, 209.

TABLE 11.6 LITERACY BY RACE AND NATIVITY, 1870–1910, PERCENT FOR POPULATION 10 YEARS OLD AND ABOVE

Nearly 80% of the nonwhite population aged 10 years and above was illiterate in 1870, largely the result of African Americans being forbidden as slaves to read and write. By the end of the Victorian Age, however, as school-enrollment rates increased, less than a third were illiterate.

Year	Total	White			Nonwhite
		Total	Native	Foreign-born	
1870	20.0	11.5	. . .	. . .	79.9
1880	17.0	9.4	8.7	12.0	70.0
1890	13.3	7.7	6.2	13.1	56.8
1900	10.7	6.2	4.6	12.9	44.5
1910	7.7	5.0	3.0	12.7	30.5

Source: Historical Statistics of the United States, Colonial Times to 1957, 214.

TABLE 11.7 TEACHERS AVERAGE ANNUAL SALARY, 1880–1910

Year	Salary
1880	$195
1890	$252
1900	$325
1910	$485

Source: Historical Statistics of the United States, Colonial Times to 1957, 208.

Vocational education also became important. Sons and daughters of working-class parents sought vocational education to help them gain white-collar work. Women students who sought the "commercial course" soon pushed enrollment in such courses to levels that outstripped private business colleges. Increasingly, male students found high school diplomas to be the ticket to jobs as bookkeepers, cashiers, salesmen, and managers.

High schools tended to segregate students into separate courses of study, based upon aptitude tests (pioneered by Hugo Munsterberg in 1910), vocational interests, or the guidance counselors who "tracked" students into career paths. Perhaps to overcome the alienating effects of these essentially undemocratic practices, high schools also adopted programs designed to promote a collective "school spirit." Civics became a required course, a home room period was

TABLE 11.5 SCHOOL ENROLLMENT RATES, BY COLOR AND SEX, 1870–1910, PER 100 POPULATION

Trends in school-enrollment rates show that nonwhites made substantial progress in closing the gap between themselves and whites in the 1870s, lost ground in the 1890s, and made further progress in the 1900s.

Year	Both Sexes			Male			Female		
	Total	White	Nonwhite	Total	White	Nonwhite	Total	White	Nonwhite
1870	48.4	54.4	9.9	49.8	56.0	9.6	46.9	52.7	10.0
1880	57.8	62.0	33.8	59.2	63.5	34.1	56.5	60.5	33.5
1890	54.3	57.9	32.9	54.7	58.5	31.8	53.8	57.2	33.9
1900	50.5	53.6	31.1	50.1	53.4	29.4	50.9	53.9	32.8
1910	59.2	61.3	44.8	59.1	61.4	43.1	59.4	61.3	46.6

Source: Historical Statistics of the United States, Colonial Times to 1957, 2; 213. 1870–90: The population base includes those five to nineteen years old; 1900: The population base includes those five to twenty years old. The classification of the population by race during this period was based upon observation. The nonwhite population consisted of African Americans, Native Americans, Japanese Americans, Chinese Americans, Filipino Americans, and some other groups. Persons of mixed parentage were placed in the category of the nonwhite parent. Persons of Mexican birth or ancestry, who were not definitely Indian or other nonwhite parentage, were classified as white in all censuses during these years.

designed as a time for group activity, and extracurricular activities (student government, clubs, assemblies, publications, and athletics) were adopted by school systems to foster cooperation and introduce an egalitarian atmosphere into an essentially elitist design.

Colleges and Universities

Colleges and universities catered to an even more elitist set than high schools did. In 1870, most offered the traditional concentration in the liberal arts (Latin, philosophy, mathematics, and history) that was designed to prepare boys to become young gentlemen rather than to prepare students for careers or scholarship. A handful of "female seminaries" and colleges before the Civil War also taught the orthodox curriculum, infused with evangelical religion. Between 1880 and 1910, enrollment grew from 116,000 to 355,000 but still included only about 5% of the population ages 18 to 21 by the latter date.

After the Civil War, and especially after 1880, educational facilities multiplied rapidly and changed character. The Morrill Land Grant Act of 1862, the philanthropy of millionaires, the middle-class emphasis upon career preparation, the professionalization of careers, and issues of race and gender all shaped the course of higher education in the late nineteenth century.

The Morrill Act provided federal land to states for the purpose of educating "the industrial classes," especially in "such branches of learning as are related to agriculture and mechanic arts." Thus, it not only fostered technical schools where middle-class youth might learn a profession, but also put the liberal arts within reach of the same students. After Booker T. Washington's Atlanta compromise speech in 1895 and the U.S. Supreme Court decision in *Plessy v. Ferguson* (1896) gave the green light to segregated education, southern state governments established black "agricultural and mechanical" schools patterned after Alabama's Tuskegee Institute (1881). Unlike their white counterparts, black A&Ms trained students not for careers but for manual occupations, usually without access to a liberal-arts curriculum.

Philanthropy figured prominently in the "new education." Gilded Age millionaires competed for honor as patrons of education by constructing buildings, endowing chairs, and funding fellowships at older institutions. Others founded entirely new institutions. For example, Leland Stanford and his wife traveled to Harvard to hear President Charles W. Eliot describe how much it had cost to construct each of Harvard's fine buildings. Mrs. Stanford suddenly exclaimed: "Why, Leland, we can build our own university!" Stanford University in Palo Alto was founded in 1885.

Cornell (1865), Drew (1866), Johns Hopkins (1876), Vanderbilt (1872), and Carnegie Institute of Technology (1905) were all founded through the gifts of moguls and named after them. Russell B. Conwell, the "Acres of Diamonds" preacher, founded Temple University in 1884 for the expressed purpose of training young poor boys to rise in status through education. Duke University was the result of the largesse of a tobacco king; John D. Rockefeller pumped millions into the University of Chicago (1890); and George Eastman, who made his wealth in Kodak cameras, contributed heavily to the University of Rochester.

In the East, separate women's colleges were founded, again with the support of wealthy patrons. Georgia Female College (Wesleyan) and Mount Holyoke dated from before the Civil War. Later in the century, they were joined by Vassar (1861), Wellesley (1870), Smith (1871), Radcliffe (1879), Bryn Mawr (1880), and Barnard (1889). Sometimes, it was necessary to provide "remedial education" to rectify deficiencies in the secondary education of well-to-do young women. Despite the handicaps, the percentage of bachelor's degrees conferred on women rose from 17% in 1876 to 26% in 1913.

In the North and the South, philanthropists and state governments founded institutions for African Americans only. Beginning with Lincoln University in Pennsylvania (founded as the Ashmun Institute in 1854), benefactors supported schools such as Howard University in Washington (1867) and Fisk University (1866) in Nashville. Elsewhere, traditional universities in New England and many of the sectarian colleges of the Ohio Valley admitted small numbers of very well-qualified blacks. W. E. B. Du Bois, founder of the NAACP, earned a Ph.D. at Harvard University. Hamilton S. Smith earned a law degree from Boston University in 1879 (the first African American to do so). In the North and the South, African-American graduates composed a small but dynamic middle class. Suffering the legacy of slavery and the effects of segregated education, about 70% of the African-American population could not read or write in 1910.

Also in small numbers, well-to-do Jews and Catholics took advantage of new opportunities. The Sephardic and German Jews preferred to send their sons to already established institutions such as City College or New York University. Catholics preferred to found their own colleges. Church policy was to prepare middle-class sons and daughters for careers in business and the professions with rigorous training in Catholic church doctrine. Catholic colleges included Notre Dame (1842), Holy Cross (1843), and Boston College (1863).

The transformation of higher education was not simply a matter of more students, universities, and philanthropy. While some institutions such as Yale clung doggedly to the traditional liberal-arts curriculum, the majority adopted the "elective system" pioneered by the College of William and Mary, Washington College in Virginia, and the University of Michigan and most effectively promoted by President Eliot of Harvard. Beginning in 1869, Eliot abandoned the idea of a strict curriculum for all, and allowed individuals to choose their field of study. "Majors" included the traditional subjects but added new disciplines in the social sciences, engineering, and business administration. The new emphasis upon career preparation at the university level reflected the aspirations of upwardly mobile middle-class students.

Graduate education was shaped most influentially by German educators. Before the 1870s, those who wished to learn a profession attached themselves to established practitioners. A would-be lawyer, for example, agreed with an established attorney to sweep floors, do routine office work, help with wills and deeds, and run errands to the courthouse in return for the right to "read law." After a few years, the apprentice could hang out his own shingle. Many physicians learned the same way. Even civil and mechanical engineers learned their professions "on the job" in factories.

German universities, with their emphasis on the scientific methods of research in all fields, including economics, history, and theology, provided the model for graduate training at Johns Hopkins University, which adopted the German strategy from its founding in 1876. Later, Columbia reformed its curricula and administration along the same lines. Teaching methods changed, too, from recitation or explication of texts to lectures based on the results of research.

Specialized academic research led to an explosion in scholarly fields and subfields; for example, a student at the University of Wisconsin in 1876 would have found 35 courses to choose from; in 1915, the student might choose from more than 1,000 courses. The emphasis in 1915 would also have changed, moving away from liberal arts toward the social sciences, such as economics, sociology, and anthropology.

TABLE 11.8   DEGREES CONFERRED, 1876, 1913

Year	All Degrees	Total Bachelors' Degrees	Male	Female	Total M.A.s	Total Ph.Ds
1876	12,871	12,005	9,911	2,094	835	31
1880	13,829	12,896	10,411	2,485	879	54
1890	16,703	15,539	12,857	2,682	1,015	149
1900	29,375	27,410	22,173	5,237	1,583	382
1913	45,959	42,396	31,312	11,084	3,025	538

Source: Historical Statistics of the United States, Colonial Times to 1957, 212.

TABLE 11.9   INSTITUTIONS, FACULTY, AND ENROLLMENT, HIGHER EDUCATION, 1880, 1910

Year	No. Instits.	Total Faculty	Male	Female	Enrollment in Thousands	% Pop. 18–21
1880	811	11,552	7,328	4,194	116	2.7
1910	951	36,480	29,132	7,348	355	5.1

Source: Historical Statistics of the United States, Colonial Times to 1957, 211.

Libraries

The Victorian Era witnessed one of the most active periods of library building in American history. Unlike the years after 1918, philanthropy provided the bulk of the funds for library building. The affluent gave millions to build them. Enoch Pratt donated $1 million to Baltimore for its library. Wealthy lawyer and presidential hopeful Samuel J. Tilden gave New York City $2 million. William Newberry founded Chicago's first public library with a generous bequest of $4 million. Under the direction of the innovative and perspicacious William F. Poole, its first librarian, the Newberry Library became one of the nation's richest collections of books and valuable manuscripts. But the greatest library builder of them all was Andrew Carnegie, who made libraries his principal philanthropy. Before his death in 1919, he had helped to found 2,800 free public libraries. Edward Lippincott Tilton (1861–1933) of the New York firm of McKim, Mead, and White, is the architectual influence behind most of the important library buildings.

TABLE 11.10   MAIN PUBLIC LIBRARY BUILDINGS, 1850–1918

Date	Estimated Number Completed	Estimated Total Cost
1850–1893	500	$15,000,000
1894–1918	1,500	$80,000,000

Source: Donald E. Oehlerts, Books and Blueprints: Building American Public Libraries, (1991), 129.

TABLE 11.11   SOURCE OF FUNDS FOR LARGE PUBLIC LIBRARIES, 1850–1918

Date	Number	Cost	Source of Funds Public	Source of Funds Private
1850–1893	28	$ 7,500,000	25%	75%
1894–1918	60	$36,500,000	40%	60%

Source: Oehlerts, Books and Blueprints: Building American Public Libraries, 130.

TABLE 11.12   PUBLIC LIBRARY BUILDINGS, 1894–1918

Building and Date	Librarian	Architect
Boston, 1894	Theodore Dwight	Charles McKim
Pittsburgh, Carnegie, 1895	Edwin Anderson	Alden and Harlow
Chicago, 1897	Frederick Hild	Charles Coolidge
Milwaukee, 1898	Theresa West	Ferry and Clas
Fall River, Mass, 1899	George Rankin	Bertram Goodhue
Providence, R.I., 1900	William Foster	Alfred Stone
Jersey City, N.J., 1900	Mrs. C. P. Barnes	Henry Bacon
Newark, N.J., 1901	Frank Hill	John Rankin
Atlanta, Carnegie, 1902	Anne Wallace	Albert Ross
Pawtucket, R.I., Sayles, 1902	Minerva Sanders	Bertram Goodhue
Washington, D.C., 1902	Weston Flint	Albert Ross
Nashville, Tenn. Carnegie, 1904		Albert Ross
Grand Rapids, Mich., Ryerson, 1904	Elizabeth Steinmann	Charles Coolidge
Paterson, N.J., Danforth, 1905	George Winchester	Henry Bacon
Syracuse, N.Y. 1905		James Randall
Columbus, Ohio, 1906	John Pugh	Albert Ross
Louisville, Ky., 1908	William Yust	William Tachau
New Orleans, La., 1908	Henry Gill	Diball, Owen and Goldstein
Denver, Colo., 1910	Charles Dudley	Albert Ross
New Haven, Conn., 1911	Willis Stetson	Cass Gilbert
New York, 1911	John Billings	Carrere and Hastings
St. Louis, 1911	Arthur Bostwick	Cass Gilbert
Springfield, Mass., 1911	Hiller Wellman	Edward Tilton
Elizabeth, N.J., 1912	Charles George	Edward Tilton
Portland, Oregon, 1913	Mary Isom	Albert Doyle
Somerville, Mass., 1913	Drew Hall	Edward Tilton
Manchester, N.H., Carpenter, 1914	F. Mabel Winchell	Edward Tilton
San Francisco, 1917	Robert Rea	George Kelham
St. Paul, 1917	Helen McCaine	Electus Litchfield
Indianapolis, 1917	Eliza Browning	Paul Cret

Source: Oehlerts, Books and Blueprints: Building American Public Libraries, 55–56.

CHAPTER 12 Arts and Letters

Literature

Writers of the late nineteenth century explored familiar themes of life in a changing nation. Bret Harte chronicled life in the rough on the western frontier with "The Luck of Roaring Camp" (1870), called "the father of all Western local-color stories." Stephen Crane sought lessons from the past in his masterpiece, *The Red Badge of Courage* (1895), and studied the problems of contemporary urban life in *Maggie: A Girl of the Streets* (1893), an impressionistic novel showing the influence of Zola. Horatio Alger, Jr., published *Ragged Dick* in 1867, the first in a series of 135 books in which he depicted the life of children in the slums and the rise of a fortunate few through a combination of luck and pluck. Immensely popular—more than 16 million copies were sold—Alger's dime novels appealed to the immigrant vision of America's promise. Wholesome goodness was the theme of Louisa May Alcott's *Little Women* (1868), one of the most popular books ever written.

Two writers rose above the rest in critical acclaim for their work, although not necessarily during their lifetimes. Mark Twain, one of the earliest writers to treat race relations, in his masterpiece *Huckleberry Finn* (1885), combined humor with serious social observation. In the genre of local-color writing, he towered over the rest with his wit and mastery of the English language. Henry James, with great and subtle psychological insight, probed the problem of individuality versus social convention, and considered the nature and content of civilized culture. James settled in England because he found American culture stultifying, plain and undeveloped; he set most of his novels in England, France and Italy. Like Twain's, his work is an extended meditation on what it means to be an American. *The American* (1877), *The Europeans* (1878), *Daisy Miller* (1879) and *Portrait of a Lady* (1881) contrast less-cultivated American characters with a sophisticated, perhaps decadent European culture.

Edith Wharton was a novelist whose work is marked by its concern for social form, the moral significance of individual action, and the ironies of social pretension. A devoted admirer of Henry James, she is the author of several classic novels of manners, including *House of Mirth* (1905), *Ethan Frome* (1911), *The Custom of the Country* (1913) and the Pulitzer Prize–winning *The Age of Innocence* (1920).

Realism and naturalism characterized the writing of some authors. William Dean Howells was a realist who disdained the altruistic motives that sentimental writers sometimes imputed to their characters. *The Rise of Silas Lapham* (1885) is his most well-known work. Naturalist writers dealt with subjects that the genteel middle-class saw as taboo; in addition to Crane on prostitution in *Maggie,* Frank Norris, especially in *The Octopus* (1901), depicted characters who were driven by greed to control and manipulate. Theodore Dreiser published his then-scandalous, sexually frank *Sister Carrie* in 1900, the first of his many novels to explore the theme of helpless individuals in the grip of blind, amoral social forces. *Jennie Gerhardt* followed in 1911, and *The Financier,* the first of a trilogy based on the career of the notorious business magnate Charles T. Yerkes, in 1912. His best-known novel is probably *An American Tragedy* of 1925. Jack London was to nature what Mark Twain was to local color, a dominant figure, best seen in his *Call of the Wild* (1903).

Social critique also flourished. Edward Bellamy's *Looking Backward* (1888) was a utopian view of a future America; it sold 200,000 copies in two years. Upton Sinclair's *The Jungle* (1906) exposed corrupt and unsanitary practices in the Chicago stockyards, concluding in an argument for socialism.

Some writers became known for single themes. The socialist Henry George's *Progress and Poverty* (1879) produced a strong following for his single-tax solution to economic inequality. Alfred Thayer Mahan influenced foreign policy for a generation and beyond with *The Influence of Sea Power Upon History, 1600–1783* (1890). He linked strong nations in the past to their dominance of the sea, and his arguments favoring a big U.S. Navy, a strong merchant marine, naval bases, and colonial possessions influenced political thought at home and abroad, especially in Germany.

William James (older brother of Henry James) was a pioneering psychologist and philosopher. His influential works include *Principles of Psychology* (1890), *The Varieties of Religious Experience* (1902), and *Pragmatism* (1907). Henry Adams, grandson of John Quincy Adams, great-grandson of John Adams, was the author of one of the landmark books of American historical writing, the nine-volume *History of the United States During the Administrations of Jefferson and Madison* (1889–1891). He was the anonymous author of two novels of political satire, *Democracy* (1880) and *Esther* (1884), and of the classic, posthumously published autobiography *The Education of Henry Adams* (1918).

TABLE 12.1   BEST-SELLERS, 1895–1913

The following is a list of the best-selling books—one million or more copies—in descending order of sales, published during the Victorian Era. Pamphlets, encyclopedias, hymnals, prayer books, manuals, textbooks, and other "nonbooks" such as picture and game books are excluded. F denotes fiction; J children's books; N nonfiction.

Author	Title	Year	Category
Charles Monroe Sheldon	*In His Steps*	1897	F
L. Frank Baum	*The Wonderful Wizard of Oz*	1900	F
Elbert Hubbard	*A Message to Garcia*	1898	N
Fannie Farmer	*The Boston Cooking School Cook Book*	1896	N
Stephen Crane	*The Red Badge of Courage*	1896	F
Jesse Lyman Hurlburt	*The Story of the Bible*	1904	N
Gene Stratton Porter	*Freckles*	1904	J
Owen Wister	*The Virginian*	1902	F
Kathleen Norris	*Mother*	1911	F
Gene Stratton Porter	*The Harvester*	1911	F
Gene Stratton Porter	*Laddie*	1913	J
Ralph Waldo Trine	*In Tune with the Infinite*	1897	N
John Fox, Jr.	*The Trail of the Lonesome Pine*	1908	F
Winston Churchill	*The Crisis*	1901	F
Mary W. Tileston	*Daily Strength for Daily Needs*	1901	N
Harold Bell Wright	*The Shepherd of the Hills*	1907	F
Arturo Cuyas	*Appleton's English-Spanish, Spanish-English Dictionary*	1903	N
John Fox, Jr.	*The Little Shepherd of Kingdom Come*	1903	F
Florence Barclay	*The Rosary*	1910	F
Eleanor H. Porter	*Pollyanna*	1913	J
Helen Bannerman	*Little Black Sambo*	1899	J
Charles Wagner	*The Simple Life*	1901	N

Source: Alice Payne Hackett, *70 Years of Best Sellers 1895–1965,* (New York & London, 1967), 12–30.

Journalism in the Victorian Era

The American Civil War generated a great interest in newspapers as Americans followed the events of the war and politics. After the war, several influential magazines and newspapers were founded, such as *The Nation* and the San Francisco *Examiner*.

In 1878, Joseph Pulitzer (1847–1911) founded the St. Louis *Post-Dispatch*. The *Post-Dispatch* became one of the nation's great newspapers, appealing to immigrants and advocates of reform. Pulitzer, an immigrant himself, targeted the foreign-born population, and the newspaper served as an agent of acculturation and language acquisition. Pulitzer extended the sensationalism of Civil War journalism with a combination of sex, scandal, and controversy. The flamboyant Pulitzer almost single-handedly developed the people's newspaper and encouraged his mass readership with his special style and panache. Later, he competed with William Randolph Hearst, buying the *New York World* and pushing it to ever greater heights of jingoistic sensationalism in its coverage of the Spanish-American War and the crisis that preceded it.

Large circulation magazines also grew, including some directed toward women such as the *Ladies' Home Journal* (1883) and *Cosmopolitan* (1886). In 1895, Hearst bought the *New York Journal*, and turned it into a crude imitation of Pulitzer's *New York World*, minus the reformer's social conscience. "Yellow journalism" was the name given to sensation-mongering journalism, after a cartoon character in the *New York World* who played irresponsibly on people's emotions. The *New York World*, as well as the Hearst papers, produced lurid and sensationalist accounts of Spanish atrocities in Cuba and the Philippines just before U.S. entry into the Spanish-American War.

Despite its failings, Victorian Age journalism did democratize the medium of communications and produce a more informed and involved public.

TABLE 12.2 NEW BOOKS AND NEW EDITIONS 1892–1913

Year	New Books[a]	New Editions
1892	4,074	788
1900	4,490	1,866
1913	10,607	1,623

[a]From 1880 to 1913, pamphlets were counted but not identified separately from books.
Source: Historical Statistics of the United States, Colonial Times to 1957, 500.

TABLE 12.3 NEWSPAPERS AND PERIODICALS, NUMBER AND CIRCULATION, 1880–1914

Year	Daily Newspapers	
	Number	Circulation in Thousands
1880	971[a]	3,566
1890	1,610[a]	8,387
1900	2,226[a]	15,102
1913	2,580	28,777

[a]Includes a small number of periodicals. In 1914, weekly periodicals numbered 1,379 with a circulation of about 28.5 million readers; weekly newspapers numbered 13,793 with a circulation of 21.9 million; Sunday newspapers numbered 571 with a circulation of 16.5 million.
Source: Historical Statistics of the United States, Colonial Times to 1957, 500.

The Muckrakers

Writers were the most formidable soldiers in the army of the progressive reform movement. Theodore Roosevelt called the new journalists who wrote articles for magazines exposing some particular abuse in American society "muckrakers" after an unattractive character in John Bunyan's classic *Pilgrim's Progress* (1678). The writers were so busy raking muck, Roosevelt said, that they failed to see the good in American society. And it is true that after the success of the early muckrakers, sensation mongers and incompetent hacks produced sloppy research, wild accusations, and ill-founded claims for the sake of sensation. Altogether, in the first decade of the twentieth century, about 2,000 muckraking articles and books were published.

In its finest form, muckraking exposed genuine crimes and abuses and spread the reform impulse. Journals such as *McClure's*, the *Arena*, *Cosmopolitan*, and *Everybody's* hired muckrakers. The discovery of the public appetite for exposure was quite accidental. When *McClure's* editor Samuel S. McClure, who had no special interest in reform, engaged Ida Tarbell and Lincoln Steffens at generous salaries to write articles, he did so not because they were reformers but because they wrote well. Tarbell's serialized *History of the Standard Oil Company* (1904) exposing the dubious business practices of John D. Rockefeller, and Lincoln Steffens's exposure of political corruption in St. Louis caused circulation to soar. Soon they were joined by others who wrote about real and imagined problems. Upton Sinclair, author of *The Jungle* (1906) and many other books, was probably the most influential muckraker of all.

Despite the charlatans, muckraking led to some of the most notable reform achievements of the progressive movement.

Visual Art

Despite the heavy influence of European tradition, painters such as Thomas Eakins and Winslow Homer created a peculiarly American art. Like much of the fiction, visual art of the late nineteenth century was representational and observant of the human condition. Eakins used the camera and new scientific studies of light and anatomy to create a distinctly American style of realism. Homer is best known for his paintings of life near the sea, but his *Snap the Whip* depicts a nostalgic rural scene of boys playing a favorite game.

Frederic Remington re-created—to some extent, created—the Wild West of legend, through 2,739 pictures and the illustrations for 147 books.

James Abbott McNeill Whistler won fame with the subtle painting of his mother entitled *Arrangement in Gray and Black*. In 1884, John Singer Sargent exhibited his famous unflattering portrait of Madame Gautreau, entitled *Madame X*, and was forced to leave Paris.

Mary Cassatt was America's most famous woman artist, accepted in Paris—the only American invited to exhibit—but unrecognized in her own country. Thomas Pollock Anshutz, a student of Eakins, was the nineteenth century's most distinguished African American artist. His *Ironworkers Noontime* characterized his common themes of working-class life. John LaFarge received the first major commission to be awarded an American painter—a mural on the walls of architect Henry Hobson Richardson's Trinity Church in Boston. George Inness emerged as one of America's foremost landscape artists.

In addition, the foundations for modern American painting were laid during this age by a new group of painters known as "The Eight." Among this group, Arthur B. Davies was largely responsible for the Armory show in 1913, which brought to the United States the work of all the leading avant-garde painters of Europe. Davies himself painted idyllic and romantic mood canvases. Other important members of this group included Maurice Prendergast, Robert Henri,

TABLE 12.4 FAMOUS PAINTERS OF THE VICTORIAN ERA

Thomas P. Anshutz	A. B. Frost	Joseph Pennell
John T. Boyle	William J. Glackens	John F. Peto
George Bellows	John Haberle	Maurice Prendergast
Mary Cassatt	William Michael Harnett	Howard Pyle
William Merritt Chase	Childe Hassam	Theodore Robinson
Frederick E. Church	Winslow Homer	Albert P. Ryder
Arthur B. Davies	George Innes	John Singer Sargent
Thomas Wilmer Dewing	Rockwell Kent	John Sloan
Frank Duveneck	John LaFarge	John H. Twachtman
Thomas Eakins	Homer Martin	James A. McNeill Whistler
Louis Eilshemius	Jerome Myers	

Source: E. P. Richardson, *Painting in America.* (New York, 1965), many pages.

John Sloan, George B. Luks, Everett Shinn, Ernest Lawson, and William Glackens, who concerned themselves with the modern urban environment. They were popularly known as "The Ashcan School." Also during this period photography matured and was gradually accepted as a "fine" art, largely through the efforts of Alfred Stieglitz, a photographer who was also an influential editor, writer, and art dealer.

TABLE 12.5 ART MUSEUMS

Listed below are major art museums in the United States that opened during the Victorian period. The list provides name of institution, location, and date of opening.

Gallery	Location	Year
Albright Art Gallery	Buffalo	1905
Art Institute of Chicago	Chicago	1879
Bowdoin College Museum of Fine Arts	Brunswick, Maine	1894
Brooklyn Museum	Brooklyn	1889
Bucks County Historical Society	Doylestown, Pa.	1880
Carnegie Institute	Pittsburgh	1896
Chicago Natural History Museum	Chicago	1893
Cincinnati Art Museum	Cincinnati	1880
City Art Museum	St. Louis	1912
Cleveland Museum of Art	Cleveland	1913
Dallas Museum of Fine Arts	Dallas	1902
Dayton Art Institute	Dayton	1913
Detroit Institute of Arts	Detroit	1884
E. B. Crocker Art Gallery	Sacramento	1885
Ft. Worth Art Museum	Ft. Worth	1910
Hispanic Society of America	New York	1904
Isabella Stewart Gardner Museum	Boston	1900
Isaac Delgado Museum of Art	New Orleans	1910
John Herron Art Museum	Indianapolis	1883
Los Angeles County Museum	Los Angeles	1911
Louisiana State Museum	New Orleans	1906
M.H. de Young Memorial Museum	San Francisco	1895
Memorial Art Gallery	Rochester, N.Y.	1913
Metropolitan Museum of Art	New York	1902
Milwaukee Art Institute	Milwaukee	1888
Minneapolis Institute of Arts	Minneapolis	1883
Museum for the Arts of Decoration	New York	1896
Museum of Fine Arts	Syracuse	1896
Museum of New Mexico	Santa Fe	1909
Museum of the American Numismatic Society	New York	1908
National Collection of Fine Arts	Washington, D.C.	1906

Gallery	Location	Year
New York State Historical Association	Cooperstown	1899
Newark Museum Association	Newark	1909
University Museum of the University of Pennsylvania	Philadelphia	1889
Portland Art Museum	Portland, Oreg.	1892
Rhode Island School of Design, Museum of Art	Providence	1877
Seattle Art Museum	Seattle	1906
Smith College Museum of Art	Northampton, Mass.	1881
Society for the Preservation of New England Antiquities	Boston	1910
Southwest Museum	Los Angeles	1903
Toledo Museum of Art	Toledo	1901
William Hayes Fogg Art Museum	Cambridge	1895
Worcester Art Museum	Worcester, Mass.	1896

Source: Encyclopaedia Britannica, (1960), 15:994.

Architecture

Architectural historians have called this the Age of Elegance, the Age of Indecision, and the Age of Eclecticism. Each description captures trends of the period. Many noted architects built houses for the rich, enriching themselves and enhancing their own reputations. Mimicking European styles was common but selective. Henry Hobson Richardson popularized buildings that were patterned after the Romanesque style, but others began to experiment with a more utilitarian architecture. Louis Sullivan of the Chicago School articulated his guiding principle as "form follows function." His large "skyscraper" buildings, despite their sometimes elaborate ornament, embraced the implications of height and steel-frame construction, and seemed a revolutionary departure from the neo-Gothic, neo-Romanesque and neo-Classic architectural styles that were popular at the time.

TABLE 12.6 FAMOUS ARCHITECTS 1876–1913

Dankmar Adler (1844–1900), with Louis H. Sullivan (1856–1924), of Adler and Sullivan:
 Transportation Building (Chicago, 1893), World's Columbian Exposition
 Stock Exchange Building (Chicago, 1894)
 Wainwright Building (St. Louis, 1891)
 Prudential Building (Buffalo, 1895)   524
Daniel H. Burnham (1846–1912), with John Wellborn Root (1850–91), of Burnham and Root and D. H. Burnham and Company (after 1891):
 Rookery (Chicago, 1886)
 Reliance Building (Chicago, 1895)
 Fisher Building (Chicago, 1896)
 Flatiron Building ([Fuller Building], New York City, 1902)
 Railway Exchange Building (Chicago, 1895)   63–66
John M. Carrère (1858–1911), with Thomas Hastings, of Carrère and Hastings:
 Old Senate Office Building (Washington, D.C., 1909)   71
Thomas Hastings (1860–1929) of Carrère and Hastings:
 Old House Office Building (Washington, D.C., 1908)   71
Ralph Adams Cram (1863–1943), with Bertram Grosvenor Goodhue (1869–1924) and Frank Ferguson (1861–1926), of Cram, Goodhue, and Ferguson:
 All Saints Church (Brookline, Mass., 1895)
 St. Stephen's Church (Cohasset, Mass., 1900)
 First Baptist Church (Pittsburgh, 1909)
 U.S. Military Academy Chapel (West Point, N.Y., 1910)
 Park Avenue Christian Church (New York City, 1911)
 Euclid Avenue Presbyterian Church (Cleveland, 1911)

Landscape Architect

Source: William Dudley Hunt, Jr. *Encyclopedia of American Architecture* (1980), w/pages shown for each entry.

Music

Music of the Victorian period saw a trend away from songs about the Civil War to a focus upon songs of rural nostalgia, urban life, and the hedonistic impulses of the "Gay Nineties." Hymns and sentimental ballads were common in workers' homes during the Victorian years. Blues and ragtime began to dominate popular music at the turn of the century. Broadway musicals and operas entertained elite urban audiences.

TABLE 12.7 FAMOUS SONGS, 1876–1913

The following is a list of the best-known popular or significant songs of the period, cross-referenced by the alternate or multiple titles by which the songs were known.

1876	1877	1878	1879
Dance of the Hours (*La Gioconda*; m. Amilcare Ponchielli) Grandfather's Clock The Hat Father Wore I'll Take You Home Again Kathleen March Slav (m. Tchaikovsky) My Heart Opens at Thy Sweet Voice (*Samson and Dalila*; m. Saint-Saëns) Pizzicati (from the ballet *Sylvia*; m. Délibes) The Rose of Killarney What a Friend We Have in Jesus	Abdulla Bulbul Ameer Chopsticks (original title "The Celebrated Chop Waltz") In the Gloaming The Lost Chord (m. Sir Arthur Sullivan)	Aloha Oe (Farewell to Thee) Carry Me Back to Old Virginny Emmet's Lullaby He Is an Englishmen (*H.M.S. Pinafore*) I Am the Captain of the Pinafore (What Never) (*H.M.S. Pinafore*) I'm Called Little Buttercup (*H.M.S. Pinafore*) In the Evening by the Moonlight The Kerry Dance (an adaptation based on the first eight bars of the melody "The Cuckoo," w.m. Margaret Casson, published in England 1790) Simple Aveu (m. Francis Thomé) Skidmore Fancy Ball When I Was a Lad (*H.M.S. Pinafore*) Where Was Moses When the Lights Went Out?	Alouette (earliest words and music published in Montreal, 1879, but most surely performed before that as a traditional French–Canadian folksong) Atisket, Ataske The Babies on Our Block (Oh Dem) Golden Slippers The Moldau (m. Smetana)
1880	**1881**	**1882**	**1883**
Blow (Knock) the Man Down (sea chantey): first known printed version this year, probably traditional, *c.* 1830 Cradle's Empty Baby's Gone Funiculi—Funicula (m. Luigi Denza) Hear Dem Bells Sailing (,Sailing) (over the Bounding Main) Songs My Mother Taught Me (m. A. Dvořák) Stéphanie-Gavotte (m. Alphons Czibulka) Waves of the Danube (Danube Waves) (m. Ivanovici) *c. 1880* The Old Chisholm Trail	Dar's One More Ribber To Cross Estudiantina (m. P. Lacombe) Loch Lomond (The Bonnie Bonnie Banks, or, Oh! Ye'll Tak' the High Road) (earliest known printing this year, but possibly from 1746 Scotch traditional) My Bonnie Lies Over the Ocean (Bring Back My Bonnie to Me) The Norwegian Dance (m. Grieg) Peek-a-Boo The Spanish Cavalier	Goodbye, My Lover, Goodbye The Skaters (Waltz) (m. Emil Waldteufel) Sweet Violets When the Clock in the Tower Strikes Twelve	The Farmer in the Dell (The Bride Cuts the Cake) La Golondrina (m. Narciso Serradell) A Handful of Earth from Mother's Grave My Nellie's Blue Eyes Only a Pansy Blossom Polly Wolly Doodle Strolling on the Brooklyn Bridge There Is a Tavern in the Town Voices of Spring (m. J. Strauss) When the Robins Nest Again
1884	**1885**	**1886**	**1887**
Always Take Mother's Advice A Boy's Best Friend Is His Mother Clementine Climbing Up the Golden Stairs España (Rhapsody) (m. Chabrier) Listen to My Tale of Woe Love's Old Sweet Song Rock-a-Bye (Hush-a-Bye) Baby (words from *Mother Goose*, 1765) While Strolling Through the Park One Day (The Fountain in the Park) White Wings	American Patrol The Big Rock Candy Mountain Remember Boy, You're Irish	The Gladiator (March) An Irishman's Home Sweet Home Johnny Get Your Gun The Letter That Never Came What the Dickie-Birds Say	Away in the Manger La Cinquantaine (m. Gabriel-Marie) Comrades If You Love Me Darling, Tell Me with Your Eyes Minuet in G (m. Paderewski) A Night on Bald Mountain (m. Mussorgsky) Pictures at an Exhibition (m. Mussorgsky) Slavonic Dances (m. Dvořák) The Swan (m. Saint-Saëns)
1888	**1889**	**1890**	**1891**
Berceuse (*Jocelyn*) (m. B. Godard) Capriccio Espagnol (m. Rimsky-Korsakov) Drill Ye Tarriers Drill L'Internationale Over the Waves (m. Juventino Rosas) Peer Gynt Suite (m. Grieg) Polovtsian Dances (*Prince Igor*; m. Borodin) Scarf Dance (m. Chaminade) Semper Fidelis Where Did You Get That Hat? With All Her Faults I Love Her Still	Down Went McGinty Playmates Slide Kelly Slide The Thunderer (March) The Washington Post (March)	España (Tango) (m. Albéniz) Intermezzo (*Cavalleria Rusticana*: m. Mascagni) Little Annie Roonie Love Will Find a Way (Morse) Maggie Murphy's Home Oh, Promise Me Passing By Scheherazade (m. Rimsky-Korsakov) Sleeping Beauty Waltz (m. Tchaikovsky) Throw Him Down McCloskey	Brown October Ale Death and Transfiguration (m. R. Strauss) (What Shall We Do with) The Drunken Sailor (traditional sea chantey) Hey, Rube! Little Boy Blue March of the Dwarfs (m. Grieg) Molly O! Narcissus The Pardon Came Too Late The Picture That's Turned to the Wall Ta-ra-ra-boom-der-é (de-ay)

1892	1893	1894	1895
After the Ball	The Cat Came Back	Airy, Fairy Lillian	Afternoon of a Faun (m. Debussy)
The Bowery	Do, Do, My Huckleberry Do	And Her Golden Hair Was Hanging	America, the Beautiful
Daddy Wouldn't Buy Me a Bow-Wow	Symphony No. 9 (From the New	Down Her Back	(Casey Would Waltz with the
Daisy Bell (A Bicycle Built for Two)	World) (m. Dvořák)	Dunderbeck, or, Rambling Wreck from	Strawberry Blonde While) The Band
The Man That Broke the Bank at	(Whoopee Ti Yi Yo) Git Along Little	Georgia Tech	Played On
Monte Carlo	Doggies (traditional cowboy song,	Forgotten	The Belle of Avenoo A
My Sweetheart's the Man in the Moon	probably as early as 1880)	His Last Thoughts Were of You	Down in Poverty Row
The Sweetest Story Ever Told (Tell Me	Happy Birthday to You (Good Morning	The Honeymoon March	A Dream
That You Love Me)	to All)	Humoresque (m. Dvořák)	The Hand That Rocks the Cradle
Vesti la Giubba (Pagliacci; m.	Prelude in C# minor	I Don't Want To Play in Your Yard	The Handicap (March)
Leoncavallo)	(m. Rachmaninoff)	I've Been Working on the Railroad, or,	Just Tell Them That You Saw Me
Waltz of the Flowers (The Nutcracker	See, Saw, Margery Daw	The Levee Song, or Someone's in the	King Cotton March
Suite; m. Tchaikovsky)	Two Little Girls in Blue	Kitchen with Dinah, (with new	My Best Girl's a New Yorker (Corker)
	When the Roll Is Called Up Yonder	words in 1903 as "The Eyes of	Paupée Valsante (m. Poldini)
		Texas" (Are Upon You)	Put Me Off at Buffalo
		Kathleen	Rastus on Parade
		The Little Lost Child	Reverie (m. Debussy)
		Mazel Tov	The Streets of Cairo ("Hoochy-Koochy"
		Meditation (Thaïs; m. Massenet)	is the verse)
		My Friend the Major	The Sunshine of Paradise Alley
		My Pearl's a Bowery Girl	Till Eulenspiegel's Merry Prank
		She is More To Be Pitied Than	(m. R. Strauss)
		Censured	
		She May Have Seen Better Days	
		The Sidewalks of New York (East Side,	
		West Side)	
		(Prayer of Thanksgiving) We Gather	
		Together (first published with English	
		words; based on a traditional Dutch	
		tune from 1597)	
		You Can't Play in Our Yard Any More	

1896	1897	1898	1899
All Coons Look Alike to Me	Asleep in the Deep	Because (m. Bowers)	Absent
The Amorous Goldfish	At a Georgia Camp Meeting	Boola Boola (possibly from Hawaii, with	Always (m. Bowers)
El Capitan (March)	Badinage	new words as the "Yale Boola" in	Ben Hur Chariot Race (March)
Chin, Chin, Chinaman	Beautiful Isle of Somewhere	1901)	Come Home, Dewey, We Won't Do a
Eli Green's Cakewalk	Break the News to Mother	The Boy Guessed Right	Thing to You
Elsie from Chelsea	Danny Deever	Ciribiribin (m. Pestalozza)	Doan Ye Cry, Mah Honey
Going for a Pardon	Song of India (M. Rimsky-Korsakov)	The Fortune Teller	The Girl I Loved in Sunny Tennessee
Happy Days in Dixie	The Sorcerer's Apprentice	Gold Will Buy Most Anything But a	Hands Across the Sea (March)
(There'll Be) A Hot Time in the Old	(m. Dukas)	True Girl's Heart	Heart of My Heart (The Story of the
Town (Tonight)	Stars and Stripes Forever	Goodnight, Little Girl, Goodnight	Rose)
I Love You in the Same Old Way—	Take Back Your Gold	Gypsy Love Song (Slumber On)	Hearts and Flowers (melody from
Darling Sue		I Guess I'll Have To Telegraph My Baby	1893.)
In a Persian Garden		It's Always Fair Weather When Good	Hello! Ma Baby
In the Baggage Coach Ahead		Fellows Get Together	I'd Leave My Happy Home for You
I'se Your Nigger If You Want Me, Liza		(A Stein Song)	If You Were Only Mine
Jane		Just One Girl	Mandy Lee
Kentucky Babe		Kiss Me, Honey, Do	Maple Leaf Rag
Laugh and the World Laughs with You		Mister Johnson, Don't Get Gay	My Little Georgia Rose
Love Makes the World Go 'Round		The Moth and the Flame	My Wild Irish Rose
Mister Johnson, Turn Me Loose		Musetta's Waltz (La Bohème; m. Puccini)	O Sole Mio
Mother Was a Lady, or, If Jack Were		My Old New Hampshire Home	On the Banks of the Wabash Far Away
Only Here		Recessional (m. Reginald De Koven)	Pavanne for a Dead Infanta (Princess)
My Gal Is a High Born Lady		The Rosary	(m. Ravel)
The Red River Valley (based on James		Salome	A Picture No Artist Can Paint
Kerrigan's "In the Bright Mohawk		She Is the Belle of New York	She Was Happy Till She Met You
Valley," in its turn based on a		She Was Bred in Old Kentucky	She'll Be Comin' Round the Mountain
traditional Canadian folksong)		When You Were Sweet Sixteen	(based on the traditional Negro
Rustle of Spring (m. Sinding)		Who Dat Say Chicken in Dis Crowd?	melody "When the Chariot Comes")
Sweet Rosie O'Grady		You're Just a Little Nigger, Still You're	Smokey Mokes
To a Wild Rose (Woodland Sketches)		Mine, All Mine	Stay in Your Own Back Yard
When the Saints Go Marching In			There's Where My Heart is Tonight
You're Not the Only Pebble on the			Where the Sweet Magnolias Grow
Beach			Whistling Rufus

1900	1901	1902	1903
Top Hits	*Top Hits*	*Top Hits*	*Top Hits*
A Bird in a Gilded Cage	Finlandia (m. Sibelius)	Because (m. d'Hardelot)	Always Leave Them Laughing When
Down South	Hiawatha	Bill Bailey, Won't You Please Come	You Say Goodbye
The Gladiator's Entry (not "The	I Love You Truly	Home	Bedelia
Gladiator March")	Just A-Wearyin' for You	Down Where the Wurzburger Flows	Dear Old Girl

(continued)

TABLE 12.7 (continued)

The following is a list of the best-known popular or significant songs of the period, cross-referenced by the alternate or multiple titles by which the songs were known.

1900	1901	1902	1903
Goodbye Dolly Gray	Mighty Lak' a Rose	In the Good Old Summertime	Good-bye, Eliza Jane
I Can't Tell Why I Love You, But I Do	Serenade (m. Drigo)	In the Sweet Bye and Bye	I Can't Do the Sum
Just Because She Made Dem Goo-Goo Eyes		Oh, Didn't He Ramble	Ida, Sweet as Apple Cider
Ma Blushin' Rosie	*Notable*	On a Sunday Afternoon	Kashmiri Love Song (Four Indian Love Lyrics)
Strike Up the Band—Here Comes a Sailor	Any Old Place I Can Hang My Hat Is Home Sweet Home to Me	Please Go 'Way and Let Me Sleep	The March of the Toys
Tell Me Pretty Maiden	The Billboard (March)	Pomp and Circumstance (March) (m. Elgar)	(You're the Flower of My Heaart) Sweet Adeline
	Blaze Away (March)	Under the Bamboo Tree	Toyland
Notable	Concerto for Piano, No. 2 (m. Rachmaninoff)		
Absence Makes the Heart Grow Fonder	Davy Jones' Locker	*Notable*	*Adaptations*
The Bridge of Sighs (m. Thornton)	Don't Put Me Off at Buffalo Any More	Come Down Ma Evenin' Star	The Eyes of Texas (Are Upon You), (based on "I've Been Working on the Railroad" (1894))
Creole Belle	Down Where the Cotton Blossoms Grow	Down on the Farm	
Flight of the Bumble Bee (m. Rimsky-Korsakov)	Go Way Back and Sit Down	The Entertainer	
For Old Times' Sake	Hello, Central, Give Me Heaven	If Money Talks, It Ain't on Speaking Terms with Me	*Notable*
Lift Ev'ry Voice and Sing	High Society (March)	Mister Dooley	Congo Love Song
Old Flag Never Touched the Ground	The Honeysuckle and the Bee	The Morris Dance (m. German)	I'm on the Water Wagon Now
Valse Bleue	I've Grown So Used to You	Since Sister Nell Heard Paderewski Play	Lazy Moon
Violets	Josephine, My Jo	When It's All Goin' Out, and Nothin' Comin' In	Melody of Love
	The Maiden with the Dreamy Eyes	Where the Sunset Turns the Ocean's Blue to Gold	Mother o' Mine
	My Castle on the Nile		Navajo
	O Dry Those Tears		Spring, Beautiful Spring (Chimes of Spring) (m. Lincke)
	Panamericana		The Temple Bells (Four Indian Love Lyrics)
	Serenade (m. Toselli)		Under the Anheuser Bush
	The Swan of Tuonela (m. Sibelius)		Waltzing Matilda
	That's Where My Money Goes (possibly earlier)		

1904	1905	1906	1907
Top Hits	*Top Hits*	*Top Hits*	*Top Hits*
Give My Regards to Broadway	Clair de Lune (m. Debussy)	Anchors Aweigh	Bell Bottom Trousers (probably traditional)
Goodbye, Little Girl, Goodbye	Everybody Works But Father	At Dawning	Glow Worm
Goodbye, My Lady Love	Forty-Five Minutes from Broadway	Because You're You	Harrigan
Meet Me in St. Louis, Louis	I Don't Care	The (Little) Bird on Nellie's Hat	I Wish I Had a Girl
Please Come and Play in My Yard	I Want What I Want When I Want It	Chinatown, My Chinatown	It's Delightful To Be Married
Stop Yer Tickling, Jock!	In My Merry Oldsmobile	Every Day Is Ladies' Day to Me	Maxim's (*The Merry Widow*)
Teasing	In the Shade of the Old Apple Tree	I Just Can't Make My Eyes Behave	The Merry Widow Waltz (I Love You So) (*The Merry Widow*) (m. Lehár)
(I Am) The Yankee Doodle Boy	Kiss Me Again	I Love a Lassie (Ma Scotch Bluebell)	On the Road to Mandalay
	Mary's a Grand Old Name	In Old New York (The Streets of New York)	Red Wing
Notable	My Gal Sal (They Call Her Frivolous Sal)	Love Me and the World Is Mine	School Days
Absinthe Frappé	Nobody	National Emblem (March) (parodied as "And the Monkey Wrapped Its Tail Around the Flagpole")	Vilia (*The Merry Widow*) (m. Lehár)
Al Fresco	Rufus Rastus Johnson Brown (What You Goin' To Do When the Rent Comes 'Round)	Sunbonnet Sue	Wal, I Swan!, or, Ebenezer Frye, or, Giddiap Napoleon, It Looks Like Rain
Alexander	So Long Mary	Waiting at the Church (My Wife Won't Let Me)	
Blue Bell	Tammany	Waltz Me Around Again, Willie— 'Round, 'Round, 'Round	*Notable*
Come Back to Sorrento	Wait 'til the Sun Shines, Nellie	Won't You Come Over to My House	Because I'm Married Now
Come Take a Trip in My Airship	The Whistler and His Dog	You're a Grand Old Flag	The Best I Get Is Much Obliged to You
Down on the Brandywine	Will You Love Me in December (as You Do in May)		Budweiser's a Friend of Mine
Fascination (Valse Tzigane)		*Adaptations*	Come Along My Mandy
The Gold and Silver (Waltz) (m. Lehár)	*Notable*	Schnitzelbank (based on "Johnny Schmoker" (1863))	The Farewell (La Partida)
Good-bye, Flo	Daddy's Little Girl		Honey Boy
In Zanzibar—My Little Chimpanzee	Dearie (*Kummer*)	*Revivals*	I Love You So
Life's a Funny Proposition After All	The Leader of the German Band	I Love You Truly (1901)	I'm Afraid To Come Home in the Dark
My Honey Lou	My Irish Molly-O		Take Me Back to New York Town
The Preacher and the Bear	Parade of the Wooden Soldiers	*Notable*	That Lovin' Rag
Souvenir	When the Bell in the Lighthouse Rings Ding Dong	All In Down and Out	There Never Was a Girl Like You
Un Bel Dí (One Fine Day) (*Madama Butterfly*; m. Puccini)	Where the River Shannon Flows	Cheyenne	Tommy, Lad
Valse Triste	A Woman Is Only a Woman, But a Good Cigar Is a Smoke	College Life	Two Blue Eyes
Valse Tzigane (Fascination)		Don't Go in the Lions' Cage Tonight	Two Little Baby Shoes
Way Down in My Heart (I've Got a Feeling for You)		Eli Eli	Waltz Dream
		He Walked Right In, Turned Around and Walked Right Out Again	When a Fellow's on the Level with a Girl That's on the Square
		He's a Cousin of Mine	When We Are M-a-double-r-i-e-d
		I Was Born in Virginia (Ethel Levy's Virginia Song)	You Splash Me and I'll Splash You

1904	1905	1906	1907
		A Lemon in the Garden of Love Moonbeams My Mariuccia Take a Steamboat Nellie Dean Petite Tonkinoise Since Father Went to Work What's the Use of Dreaming Whata's the Use of Loving If You Can't Love All the Time When Love Is Young in the Springtime	

1908	1909	1910	1911
Top Hits Cuddle Up a Little Closer, Lovey Mine Shine On, Harvest Moon Smarty Sweet Violets Take Me Out to the Ball Game *Notable* All for the Love of You Any Old Port in a Storm Daisies Won't Tell Down Among the Sugar Cane Down in Jungle Town Every Little Bit Added to What You've Got Makes Just a Little Bit More Golliwogg's Cake Walk (*Children's Corner*; m. Debussy) La Golondrina Hoo-oo Ain't You Coming Out Tonight If I Had a Thousand Lives To Live In the Garden of My Heart I've Taken Quite a Fancy to You The Longest Way 'Round Is the Sweetest Way Home Love Is Like a Cigarette Roses Bring Dreams of You She Sells Sea-Shells A Vision of Salome The Yama Yama Man You Tell Me Your Dream (I Had a Dream, Dear) You're in the Right Church, But the Wrong Pew	*Top Hits* By the Light of the Silvery Moon Casey Jones From the Land of the Sky Blue Water (Four American Indian Songs) Has Anybody Here Seen Kelly Heaven Will Protect the Working Girl I Love My Wife, But Oh You Kid I Wonder Who's Kissing Her Now I've Got Rings on My Fingers (Mumbo Jumbo Jijjiboo J. O'Shea) Meet Me Tonight in Dreamland My Hero My Pony Boy On Wisconsin Put on Your Old Grey Bonnet That's A Plenty Yip-I-Addy-I-Ay! *Notable* The Cubanola Glide Dollar Princesses I'm Awfully Glad I Met You I've Got a Pain in My Sawdust The Letter Song Moving Day in Jungle Town My Cousin Caruso My Dream of Love Next to Your Mother, Who Do You Love? Nobody Knows, Nobody Cares Rumanian Rhapsody (op. 11, no. 1) (m. Georges Enesco) Waltz (*The Count of Luxenburg*) When I Dream in the Gloaming of You Where My Caravan Has Rested Yiddle on Your Fiddle You Taught Me How To Love You, Now Teach Me To Forget	*Top Hits* Ah! Sweet Mystery of Life (*Naughty Marietta*) Any Little Girl, That's a Nice Little Girl, Is the Right Little Girl for Me Call Me Up Some Rainy Afternoon Caprice Viennois The Chicken Reel Come, Josephine, in My Flying Machine Don't Wake Me Up, I'm Dreaming Down By the Old Mill Stream Every Little Movement (Has a Meaning All Its Own) Gee, But It's Great To Meet a Friend from Your Old Home Town I'd Love To Live in Loveland (with a Girl Like You) I'm Falling in Love with Someone (*Naughty Marietta*) Italian Street Song (*Naughty Marietta*) Let Me Call You Sweetheart Liebesfreud Liebeslied Macushla Mother Machree A Perfect Day Play That Barbershop Chord (Mister Jefferson Lord) Put Your Arms Around Me, Honey Some of These Days Steamboat Bill Stein Song (University of Maine) That's Why They Call Me "Shine" Washington & Lee Swing What's the Matter with Father *Revivals* Passing By (1890) *Notable* All Aboard for Blanket Bay All That I Ask of You Is Love Alma, Where Do You Live The Big Bass Viol By the Saskatchewan Day Dreams (Beautiful) Garden of Roses The Girl with the Flaxen Hair (m. Debussy) Goodbye, Rose Grizzly Bear If He Comes In, I'm Going Out If I Was a Millionaire In All My Dreams I Dream of You In the Shadows I've Got the Time–I've Got the Place, But It's Hard To Find the Girl Life Is Only What You Make It After All Morning Oh, That Beautiful Rag On Mobile Bay	*Top Hits* Alexander's Ragtime Band All Alone (m. Von Tilzer) Billy (For When I Walk) Careless (Kelly's) Love (first printed version this year, but probably traditional c. 1895) Down the Field (March) Everybody's Doing It Now I Want a Girl—Just Like the Girl That Married Dear Old Dad (Look Out For) Jimmy Valentine Little Grey Home in the West My Beautiful Lady (The Kiss Waltz) My Lovin' Honey Man The Oceana Roll Oh You Beautiful Doll Ragtime Violin Roamin' in the Gloamin' Somewhere a Voice Is Calling That Mysterious Rag Too Much Mustard (Très Moutarde) A Wee Deoch-an-Doris The Whiffenpoof Song *Notable* Can't You Take It Back, and Change It for a Boy? Daly's Reel Daphnis et Chloé (m. Ravel) The Firebird (m. Stravinsky; first performed 1910) The Gaby Slide If You Talk in Your Sleep, Don't Mention My Name My Rosary of Dreams A Ring on the Finger Is Worth Two on the Phone The Spaniard That Blighted My Life That Was Before I Met You Till the Sands of the Desert Grow Cold To the Land of My Small Romance When I Was Twenty-one and You Were Sweet Sixteen When You're Away Woodman, Woodman, Spare That Tree

TABLE 12.7 (continued)

The following is a list of the best-known popular or significant songs of the period, cross-referenced by the alternate or multiple titles by which the songs were known.

1908	1909	1910	1911
		Plant a Watermelon on My Grave and Let the Juice Soak Through Silver Bell Tambourin Chinois That Minor Strain That's Yiddishe Love Two Little Love Bees Under the Yum-Yum Tree Waltzes (Der Rosenkavalier) You Are the Ideal of My Dreams	

1912	1913		
Top Hits And the Green Grass Grew All Around Be My Little Baby Bumblebee Down South Everybody Two-Step Giannina Mia (Friml) It's a Long Way to Tipperary (Look Out For) Jimmy Valentine, *see* 1911 Lily of Laguna (Just A Little Love, a Little Kiss Melody (Dawes) The Memphis Blues (On) Moonlight Bay My Melancholy Baby Ragtime Cowboy Joe The Rose of Tralee Row, Row, Row Sweet of Sigma Chi Sympathy That's How I Need You Tipperary, *see* It's a Long Way to Tipperary Waiting for the Robert E. Lee When I Lost You When Irish Eyes Are Smiling When the Midnight Choo-Choo Leaves for Alabam' You Can't Stop Me from Loving You *Notable* After All That I've Been to You Bagdad Daddy Has A Sweetheart, and Mother Is Her Name Funny Bunny Hug Garland of Old Fashioned Roses Hitchy-Koo I'm the Lonesomest Gal in Town Isle o' Dreams Last Night Was the End of the World Love Is Like a Firefly On the Mississippi Roll Dem Roly Boly Eyes Sari Waltz Take a Little Tip from Father They Gotta Quit Kickin' My Dog Around The Wedding Glide When I Get You Alone Tonight When It's Apple Blossom Time in Normandy You're My Baby	*Top Hits* Ballin' the Jack Brighten the Corner Where You Are El Choclo The Curse of an Aching Heart Destiny Waltz (He'd Have To Get Under,) Get Out and Get Under (To Fix Up His Automobile) Goodbye, Boys If I Had My Way My Wife's Gone to the Country (Hurrah! Hurrah!) The Old Rugged Cross Peg o' My Heart Snooky Ookums Sweethearts The Teddy Bear's Picnic That International Rag There's a Long, Long Trail The Trail of the Lonesome Pine Where Did You Get That Girl You Made Me Love You (I Didn't Want To Do It) *Adaptations* Danny Boy (based on a traditional old Irish air ("Londonderry Air") of at least 1855, with added lyrics) (Fifteen Miles [Years] on the) Erie Canal (Low Bridge!—Everybody Down) (based on a traditional folksong.) Marcheta (based on Karl Nicolai's overture to *The Merry Wives of Windsor*) *Notable* All Aboard for Dixieland The Angelus Black and White Rag Don't Blame It All on Broadway I Miss You Most of All Isle d'Amour Nights of Gladness On the Old Fall River Line On the Shores of Italy Panama The Pullman Porters on Parade Rite of Spring (m. Stravinsky) Somebody's Coming to My House Something Seems Tingle-Ingling There's a Girl in the Heart of Maryland What's the Good of Being Good— When No One's Good to Me When You Play in the Game of Love When You're All Dressed Up and No Place To Go You're Here and I'm Here		

Source: Roger Lax and Frederick Smith, *The Great Song Thesaurus* 1984, 20–36.

TABLE 12.8 BOOKS, POEMS, PAINTINGS, MUSIC, ARCHITECTURE, AND SCULPTURE, 1876–1913

The following is an annual listing of the major works of art, literature, music, sculpture, and architecture that appeared during the Victorian Age.

Key: A = Architecture; B = Book; M = Music; P = Painting; Po = Poetry; S = Sculpture; T = Theater

1876	1877	1878	1879
Mark Twain, *The Adventures of Tom Sawyer* (B) Sidney Lanier, "Psalm of the West" (Po) William Cullen Bryant, "A Lifetime" (Po) James Russell Lowell, "An Ode for the Fourth of July, 1876" (Po) Emma Lazarus, "An Ode for the Fourth of July" (Po) Winslow Homer, *Breezing Up* (P) Larkin G. Mead, *Ethan Allen* (S) Henry M. Robert, *Pocket Manual of Rules of Order for Deliberative Assemblies* (B) "Grandfather's Clock" (M)	Thomas Eakins, *William Rush Carving the Allegorical Figure of the Schuykill River* (P) James Abbott McNeill Whistler, *The Falling Rocket* (P) Henry James, *The American* (B) "Walking for Dat Cake" (M)	Henry James, *The Europeans* (B) Henry M. Stanley, *Through the Dark Continent* (B) Moses C. Tyler, *History of American Literature, 1607–1765* (B) Edward Kemeys, *Bison and Wolves* (S) Sidney Lanier, "The Marshes of Glynn" (Po) "Carry Me Back to Old Virginny" (M)	Henry James, *Daisy Miller* (B) George Washington Cable, *Old Creole Days* (B) William Dean Howells, *A Lady of Aroostock* (B) Henry George, *Progress and Poverty* (B) Daniel Chester French, *Ralph Waldo Emerson* (S) Gilbert & Sullivan, *H.M.S. Pinafore* (T) "Oh, Dem Golden Slippers" (M)

1880	1881	1882	1883
Lew Wallace, *Ben-Hur* (B) Henry Adams, *Democracy* (B) Henry Wadsworth Longfellow, *Ultima Thule* (Po) Henry Hobson Richardson, Bellaman House (A) John Knowles Paine, Second Symphony (M) Mark Twain, *A Tramp Abroad* (B)	Helen Hunt Jackson, *A Century of Dishonor* (B) Joel Chandler Harris, *Uncle Remus, His Songs and His Sayings* (B) Henry James, *Portrait of a Lady* (B) John Singer Sargent, *Portrait of a Lady* (P) John Singer Sargent, *Vernon Lee* (P) Stanford White, Newport Casino (A)	Henry Adams, *John Randolph* (B) Mark Twain, *The Prince and the Pauper* (B) John W. Lovell. Produced first of Lovell's Library, 10-cent books	Mark Twain, *Life on the Mississippi* (B) James Whitcomb Riley, *The Old Swimmin' Hole and 'Leven More Poems* (Po) Lester Frank Ward, *Dynamic Sociology* (B) "There is a Tavern in the Town" (M)

1884	1885	1886	1887
Mark Twain, *Adventures of Huckleberry Finn* (B) Helen Hunt Jackson, *Ramona* (B) Sarah Orne Jewett, *A Country Doctor* (B) John Fiske, *Excursions of an Evolutionist* (B) Francis Parkman, *Montcalm and Wolfe* (B) Elihu Vedder, illustrations for *Rubáiyát of Omar Khayyám* John Singer Sargent, *Madame X* (P)	William Dean Howells, *The Rise of Silas Lapham* (B) Josiah Royce, *The Spirit of Modern Philosophy* (B) William Michael Harnett, *After the Hunt* (P) John Donoghue, *Young Sophocles* (S) Josiah Strong, *Our Country* (B) Henry Hobson Richardson, Marshall Field Building (A)	William Gillette, *Held by the Enemy* (T) Francis Hodgson Burnett, *Little Lord Fauntleroy* (B) Henry James, *The Princess Casamassima* (B)	Henry James, *The Aspern Papers* (B) Thomas Nelson Page, *In Old Virginia* (B) Eugene Field, *Culture's Garland* (Po)

1888	1889	1890	1891
Edward Bellamy, *Looking Backward, 2000–1887* (B) James Bryce, *The American Commonwealth* (B) Russell Conwell, *Acres of Diamonds* (B) Walt Whitman, *Leaves of Grass. Augmentation.* (Po) John T. Boyle, *The Stone Age* (P) John La Farge, *Ascension* (P) DeWolf Hopper, first recitation of Ernest Thayer, "Casey at the Bat" (Po)	Mark Twain, *A Connecticut Yankee* (B) Henry Adams, *The History of the United States* (B) William Dean Howells, *Annie Kilburn* (B) Theodore Roosevelt, *The Winning of the West*, vol. 1 (B) Frederick MacMonnies, *Nathan Hale* (S) Edward MacDowell, Second Piano Concerto (M) Bronson Howard, *Shenandoah* (T)	Jacob A. Riis, *How the Other Half Lives* (B) Alfred Thayer Mahan, *The Influence of Sea Power Upon History* (B) John Nicolay & John M. Hay, *Lincoln, A History*. 10 vols. (B) Anna Sewell, *Black Beauty* (B) Rudyard Kipling, *Barrack-Room Ballads* (Po) William Dean Howells, *A Hazard of New Fortunes* (B) Emily Dickinson, *Poems* (Po) Louis H. Sullivan, Wainwright Building, St. Louis (A) Charles "Buddy" Bolden. Formed New Orleans instrumental jazz band (M)	John Fiske, *The American Revolution* (B) Washington Gladden, *Who Wrote the Bible?* (B) Hamlin Garland, *Main-Travelled Roads* (B) Walt Whitman, *Goodbye My Fancy* (Po) Augustus Thomas, *Alabama* (T) Augustus Saint-Gaudens, *Grief* or *Death, or Peace of God* (S)

1892	1893	1894	1895
Walt Whitman, *Leaves of Grass*. Final edition (Po) William Dean Howells, *The Quality of Mercy* (B) Arthur Conan Doyle, *The Adventures of Sherlock Holmes*. First collection (B) Thomas Nelson Page, *The Old South* (B)	Stephen Crane, *Maggie: A Girl of the Streets* (B) Joel Chandler Harris, *Nights with Uncle Remus* (B) William Dean Howells, *The World of Chance* (B) Robert Louis Stevenson, *The Strange Case of Dr. Jekyll and Mr. Hyde* (B)	William Hope Harvey, *Coin's Financial School* (B) William Dean Howells, *A Traveller from Altruria* (B) Rudyard Kipling, *The Jungle Book* (B) Henry Demarest Lloyd, *Wealth Against Commonwealth* (B)	Stephen Crane, *The Red Badge of Courage* (B) George W. Chadwick, *Symphonic Sketches* (M) Katherine Lee Bates, "America the Beautiful" (M) Frederick W. MacMonnies. Bust of Shakespeare (S)

(continued)

TABLE 12.8   (continued)

The following is an annual listing of the major works of art, literature, music, sculpture, and architecture that appeared during the Victorian Age.

Key: A = Architecture; B = Book; M = Music; P = Painting; Po = Poetry; S = Sculpture; T = Theater

1892	1893	1894	1895
James Whitcomb Riley, *Green Fields and Running Brooks* (Po) Winslow Homer, *Coast in Winter* (P) Charles K. Harris, "After the Ball is Over" (M) Frank Lloyd Wright, Charnley House, Chicago (A)	Antonín Dvořák, Symphony No. 9 (From the *New World*) (M) Frederick W. MacMonnies, The Great Fountain of the Court of Honor. Columbian Exposition (S) Daniel Chester French, *The Angel of Death Staying the Sculptor's Hand* (S) ———, *Republic* (S) Frank Lloyd Wright, Winslow Residence, Chicago (A) Louis H. Sullivan, Transportation Building, Columbian Exposition (A)	Mark Twain, *The Tragedy of Pudd'nhead Wilson* (B) Charles Lawler, "The Sidewalks of New York " (M)	Burnham and Root, Reliance Building, Chicago (A)

1896	1897	1898	1899
Henryk Sienkiewicz, *Quo Vadis?* (B) Mark Twain, *Joan of Arc* (B) Sarah Orne Jewett, *The Country of the Pointed Firs* (B) Edwin Arlington Robinson, *The Torrent and the Night Before* (Po) Theodore Roosevelt, *The Winning of the West.* Final volume (B) Charles M. Sheldon, *In His Steps* (B) "There'll Be a Hot Time in the Old Town Tonight." Written by Theodore A. Metz with words by Joseph Hayden (M)	Paul Dresser (Dreiser), "On the Banks of the Wabash, Far Away" (M) Rudyard Kipling, *Captains Courageous* (B) Edwin Arlington Robinson, *The Children of the Night* (Po) Moses Coit Taylor, *The Literary History of the American Revolution* (B)	Ethelbert Nevin, "The Rosary." Lyrics by Robert Cameron Rogers (M) Edward Noyes Westcott, *David Harum* (B) Stephen Crane, *The Open Boat and Other Stories* (B) Peter Finley Dunne, *Mr. Dooley in Peace and War* (B) Henry James, *The Turn of the Screw* (B)	Thorstein Veblen, *The Theory of the Leisure Class* (B) John Dewey, *The School and Society* (B) Frank Norris, *McTeague* (B) Booth Tarkington, *The Gentleman from Indiana* (B) Scott Joplin, "Maple Leaf Rag" (M) Chauncey Olcott, "My Wild Irish Rose" (M) John Philip Sousa, "The Stars and Stripes Forever" (M)

1900	1901	1902	1903
Albert Pinkham Ryder, *Toilers of the Sea* (P) Theodore Dreiser, *Sister Carrie* (B) L. Frank Baum, *The Wonderful Wizard of Oz* (B) Stephen Crane, *Whilomville Stories* (B) William Dean Howells, *Literary Friends and Acquaintances* (B) Jack London, *The Son of the Wolf* (B) *The Galveston Cyclone.* Film *Destruction of the Standard Oil Company Plant at Bayonne.* Film	Frank Norris, *The Octopus* (B) Upton Sinclair, *Springtime and Harvest.* later retitled *King Midas* (B) Porter Steele, "High Society" (M) Booth Tarkington, *Monsieur Beaucaire* (T)	Owen Wister, *The Virginian* (B) Hamlin Garland, *Captain of the Gray-Horse Troop* (B) Henry James, *The Wings of the Dove* (B) Helen Keller, *The Story of My Life* (B) Jack London, *A Daughter of the Snows* (B) Hugh Cannon, "Bill Bailey, Won't You Please Come Home?" (M)	Kate Douglas Wiggin, *Rebecca of Sunnybrook Farm* (B) Henry James, *The Ambassadors* (B) John Fox, Jr., *The Little Shepherd of Kingdom Come* (B) Jack London, *The Call of the Wild* (B) Frank Norris, *The Pit* (B) *The Passion Play.* Film *The Great Train Robbery.* Film Frank Lloyd Wright, Larkin Administration Building, Buffalo (A)

1904	1905	1906	1907
Lincoln Steffens, *Shame of the Cities* (B) Henry James, *The Golden Bowl* (B) Ellen Glasgow, *The Deliverance* (B) O. Henry, *Cabbages and Kings* (B) Jack London, *The Sea Wolf* (B) Ida M. Tarbell, *The History of the Standard Oil Company* (B) Frank Lloyd Wright, Unity Temple, Chicago (A) Gutzon Borglum, *Mares of Diomedes* (S)	Edith Wharton, *The House of Mirth* (B) Thomas Dixon, Jr., *The Clansman* (B) Jack London, *The Game* (B) "Everybody Works But Father." Song (M) David Belasco, *The Girl of the Golden West* (T)	Zane Grey, *The Spirit of the Border* (B) Upton Sinclair, *The Jungle* (B) Ellen Glasgow, *The Wheel of Life* (B) O. Henry, *The Four Million* (B) Jack London, *White Fang* (B) Mark Twain, *What Is Man?* (B) George M. Cohan, *Forty-Five Minutes from Broadway* (T) Ferdinand "Jelly Roll" Morton, "The King Porter Stomp" (M)	Florenz Ziegfeld, *Ziegfeld Follies* (T) Edith Wharton, *The Fruit of the Tree* (B) Frank Lloyd Wright, Robie House, Chicago (A)

1908	1909	1910	1911
John Fox, Jr., *The Trail of the Lonesome Pine* (B) Jack London, *The Iron Heel* (B) Mary Roberts Rinehart, *The Circular Staircase* (B) Upton Sinclair, *The Metropolis* (B)	William Vaughn Moody, *The Faith Healer* (B) *Gertie the Dinosaur.* First animated film	Carrie Jacobs Bond, "A Perfect Day" (M) Ezra Pound, *The Spirit of Romance* (B) O. Henry, *Whirligigs* (B) William Dean Howells, *My Mark Twain: Reminiscences and Criticisms* (B) Henry James, *The Finer Ground* (B)	Harold Bell Wright, *The Winning of Barbara Worth* (B) Theodore Dreiser, *Jennie Gerhardt* (B) Ellen Glasgow, *The Miller of Old Church* (B) O. Henry, *Sixes and Sevens* (B) Henry James, *The Outcry* (B) Jack London, *South Sea Tales* (B)

1908	1909	1910	1911
		Edward Arlington Robinson, *The Town Down the River* (Po) Frederick Converse, *The Pipe of Desire.* Opera	Irving Berlin, "Alexander's Ragtime Band" (M)

1912	1913		
Theodore Dreiser, *The Financier* (B) Willa Cather, *Alexander's Bridge* (B) Zane Grey, *Riders of the Purple Sage* (B) Albert Bigelow Paine, *Mark Twain, A Biography* (B) "Waiting for the *Robert E. Lee*" (M) Rachel Crothers, *He and She* (T) George C. Hazelton and J. Harry Benrimo, *The Yellow Jacket* (T)	Willa Cather, *O Pioneers!* (B) Winston Churchill, *The Inside of the Cup* (B) Ellen Glasgow, *Virginia* (B) O. Henry, *Rolling Stones* (B) Henry James, *A Small Boy and Others* (B) Vachel Lindsay, *General William Booth Enters into Heaven and Other Poems* (Po) Jack London, *The Valley of the Moon* (B) Eleanor Hodgman Porter, *Pollyanna* (B)		

CHAPTER 13 Science and Technology

Science and Invention in the Victorian Era

The period between 1876 and 1913 produced notable achievements in science as well as numerous inventions.

In chemistry, photosalts were discovered (by 1880). Notable work began on colloidal suspensions, especially with silver (from 1889). Josiah Parsons Cooke improved technics in volumetric analysis. Frank Austin Cooke introduced the rotating cathode (before 1903). Josiah Willard Gibbs published work establishing him as the founder of "chemical energetics." Ira Remsen founded U.S. graduate research in chemistry at Johns Hopkins (1876), discovered saccharin (benzoic sulfinide), and elaborated "Remsen's law" on prevention of oxidation in methyl and other groups.

In geology, F. V. Jayden found marine Jurassic fossils in "Red Beds" of the Rocky Mountain area, but it was not until the Jurassic strata were located in California (1885) that the outlines of this formation could be seen. Work of Robert T. Hill (on Texas Cretaceous, 1887) and W. M. Gabb and J. D. Whitney (on California Cretaceous, 1869) contributed to filling out the geological map of the United States. Grove K. Gilbert reported on extinct Lake Bonneville (1879). William H. Dall made major contributions to stratigraphy.

In astronomy, Louis M. Rutherfurd built an astronomical camera, photographed the moon (1864), and then built a micrometer to measure stars. Henry Draper obtained the first successful photograph of the spectrum of a star (1872) and introduced photography of nebulae (1880). Asaph Hall discovered the moon of Mars (1877), and James E. Keeler the composition of Saturn's rings (1886). Samuel P. Langley found a new way to detect temperature differences on the sun. William H. Pickering discovered the ninth satellite of Saturn (1898). Using the work of Percival Lowell, Clyde W. Tombaugh discovered Pluto. George Ellery Hale invented the spectroheliograph (1891) and took the first successful photograph of solar prominence; Hale's efforts also led to the opening of the Mt. Wilson Observatory (1906). Henrietta Leavitt at Harvard announced her "period-luminosity" law that was later applied to measure distances in galaxies.

In paleontology, Othniel Charles Marsh became the first professor of paleontology in the United States (Yale, 1866). He led bone-hunting expeditions for Yale and later (1881) for the U.S. Geological Survey (these discovered 500 new species, 225 new genera, 64 new families, and 19 new orders). Edward D. Cope published his work on herpetology and ichthyology and paved the way for modern classification of North American reptiles, amphibians, and fishes. Henry Fairfield Osborn, professor of zoology at Columbia (1896–1910) and curator of vertebrate paleontology at American Museum of Natural History (1891–1910) popularized knowledge of the field.

In mathematics, James J. Sylvester, the British mathematician, advanced studies in his field at Johns Hopkins and founded the *American Journal of Mathematics*. Josiah Willard Gibbs at Yale published his *Elements of Vector Analysis* (c. 1881–84).

In physics, Albert A. Michelson measured the velocity of light (1878–80) and invented the interferometer to determine, among other things, the length of the standard meter; he also began investigations on the existence of hypothetical ether (1881). Edward W. Morley conducted a famous experiment in 1887 that was the starting point for the development of Einstein's theory of relativity (1905). Robert A. Millikan announced (1911) that he had measured the charge of an electron as a definite constant; he succeeded in proving Einstein's hitherto unproven photoelectric equation and in evaluating Planck's constant.

In biology, Thomas Hunt Morgan used the fruit fly to test Mendel's laws of inheritance; he was the first to use the gene (1909) to describe the parts of chromosomes that control particular characteristics; he discovered sex-linked characteristics (1910) and later (1911, 1913) characteristics of different linkages.

In medicine and public health, cocaine was used as a spinal anesthetic (1884–87). Thomas George Morton performed the first appendectomy. William W. Keen performed the first successful removal of a brain tumor in the United States. William Steward Halstead introduced the use of rubber gloves (c. 1890). At Rochester, Minnesota, the Mayo brothers, William James and Charles Horace, founded the Mayo Clinic (1889) and opened a new era in surgery, stressing diagnosis as well as technique. Hugh H. Young, a urologist, devised a technique of prostatectomy. Theobald Smith conducted basic research in hog cholera, swine plague, and Texas fever in cattle. Walter Reed and his associates carried out experiments in Cuba on soldiers and other volunteers that proved conclusively the theory of mosquito transmission of yellow fever. Daniel D. Palmer founded chiropractics. Radium and X-rays were used against breast (1896) and uterine (1905) cancer, respectively. G. A. Soper documented the role of the healthy carrier, "Typhoid Mary," as a source of the disease (1906). Clifford W. Beers founded the mental hospital movement; lectures by Sigmund Freud and Carl G. Jung at Clark University (1909) advanced psychoanalysis in the United States. Bela Schick devised the "Schick test," a skin test to determine susceptibility to diphtheria.

Bridges

Bridge building evolved with the changes in materials. During the 50 years of railroad development between 1840 and 1890, the iron truss bridge became the standard. In the 1850s, as wrought iron replaced cast iron in bridge construction, many new truss types appeared.

During the 1870s and 1880s, bridges on U.S. railroads began to fail at the rate of 25 per year. The need for more durable spans inaugurated a new age in bridge building—specialization, scientific design, research, specifications, and thorough inspection and testing. The introduction of a new material—steel—marked the beginning of changes in bridge building.

The first extensive use of steel in bridge building came with the construction of the Eads Bridge over the Mississippi River at St. Louis, Missouri (1867–74). In 1878, the first all-steel bridge was built over the Missouri River at Glasgow, South Dakota. The use of steel in the cables and spans of suspension bridges was pioneered by the engineer John A. Roebling in suspension bridges in Pittsburgh, Niagara Falls, Cincinnati and finally the Brooklyn Bridge (1869–83).

With the change from timber and iron to steel, bridge forms could span greater distances and provide more stability. The Metropolis Bridge over the Ohio River, completed in 1917, had the longest truss span to date. In 1909, the Queensboro Bridge over the East River in New York City was completed; unlike any other cantilever bridge, it is a semicontinuous structure with no suspended spans.

TABLE 13.1   BRIDGES

Listed below are the year of opening, name of bridge, location, span, and type of bridge for notable bridges that opened during this period.

Year	Bridge	Location	Span (in feet)	Type
1883	Brooklyn	New York City	1,595½	suspension bridge
1898	Clifton[a]	Niagara Falls	840	steel arch bridge
1903	East Omaha	Missouri River	519	movable bridge
1909	Manhattan	New York City	1,470	suspension bridge
1909	Queensboro	New York City	1,182	cantilever bridge

[a] Railroad bridge.
Source: Encyclopaedia Britannica, (1960), 15:124–28.

TABLE 13.2   DEVELOPMENTS IN TECHNOLOGY, 1876–1913

Year	Inventor	Contribution	Importance
1874	Joseph F. Glidden	barbed wire	Solved problem of fencing range cattle
1876	Melville R. Bissell	carpet sweeper	First practical rug sweeper
1876	Alexander Graham Bell	telephone	revolutionized communication
1877	Thomas Alva Edison	phonograph	Made music available to millions
1879	Thomas Alva Edison	incandescent bulb	Brought electric lighting
1880	W. E. Sawyer	principle of scanning	Made possible the use of only a single wire or channel to transmit a picture, thereby making television possible
1888	George Eastman	hand camera	Revolutionized newspaper journalism
1888	William S. Burroughs	adding machine	Increased business efficiency
1888	Nikola Tesla	first motor to be run by alternating current	Made the transmission of electric power over long distances possible
1892	Thomas A. Edison	electric voting machine	Mechanized vote tallies
1892	John Froelich	motorized tractor	Greatly increased agricultural efficiency
1895	George B. Selden	internal-combustion automobile engine	Began a new mode of transportation
1895	J. Frank Duryea	gasoline-driven motor	Began a new mode of transportation
1896	Guglielmo Marconi	wireless telegraph	Formed the basis for radio transmissions
1903	Orville & Wilbur Wright	first flight of a heavier-than-air craft	Marked the beginning of the air age
1904	Thomas Alva Edison	sound motion picture	Launched a new entertainment/information medium
1913	William M. Burton	crackling oil-refining process	Made production of gasoline from kerosene possible

Source: Richard B. Morris, Encyclopedia of American History, (1965), 558–578.

Soon, the suspension bridge achieved supremacy over the cantilever type.

The Brooklyn Bridge over the East River was the most spectacular suspension bridge of its time, holding for 20 years the record as the world's longest suspension span. It was the work of John A. Roebling, who had designed suspension aqueducts in Pennsylvania and New York in the late 1840s and the world-famous Niagara railway suspension bridge in the 1850s. The latter weakened under the increasing weight of trains and locomotives for 42 years before being replaced by an arch bridge in 1897.

Roebling's crowning achievement and a triumph of engineering was the Brooklyn Bridge, dedicated on May 24, 1883. In 1869, after completing plans and overcoming all obstacles, Roebling died, the result of an accident during final surveys. His son, Washington Roebling, despite suffering from caisson disease, saw the work to its completion.

TABLE 13.3   NUMBER OF PATENTS ISSUED FOR INVENTIONS BY DECADE, 1881–1910

Decade	Patents Issued
1881–1890	207,514
1891–1900	220,608
1901–1910	315,193

Source: Wright, The Universal Almanac, 520–21.

TABLE 13.4   MILESTONES IN MEDICINE, 1876–1913

1876	Robert Koch (German) demonstrates that anthrax is caused by rod-shaped bacterium—the first time a micro-organism is proven to be the cause of a disease.
1881	Louis Pasteur (French) produces vaccine that successfully prevents anthrax.
1890	Emil von Behring (German) and Shibasaburo Kitasato (Japanese) independently discover antitoxins.
1892	Dmitri Ivanovski (Russian) discovers filterable viruses (viruses tiny enough to pass through fine filters that were previously believed to trap all living organisms).
1893	Felix Hoffman (German) develops a process for production of acetylsalicylic acid (aspirin).
1895	Wilhelm Konrad Röentgen (German) discovers X-rays, which soon become a diagnostic tool for medicine and surgery.
1900	Sigmund Freud (Austrian), founder of psychoanalysis, publishes his most important work, The Interpretation of Dreams.
1900	Karl Landsteiner (Austrian), discovers three blood groups, later named A, B, and O; fourth group, to be named AB, discovered in 1902.
1900	Walter Reed (American) established that yellow-fever virus is transmitted by mosquitoes.
1901	Jokichi Takamine (Japanese American) isolates adrenaline, first hormone to be isolated.
1902	Eugene Opie (American) establishes that diabetes results from destruction of specific portions of pancreatic tissue—the islets of Langerhans.
1905	Albert Einhorn (American) synthesized procaine (novocaine), which became the most widely used dental anesthetic.
1906	August von Wassermann (German) develops blood test for syphilis.
1910	Marie Curie (French) isolates pure radium, which came to be used to treat cancer.
1913	Elmer McColuum (American) and Marguerite Davis (American) discovered fat-soluble factor in butterfat, later named vitamin A.
1913	Bela Schick (Hungarian-American) perfects test for determining susceptibility to diphtheria.

Source: The Universal Almanac 1991 (1990), 250–51.

TABLE 13.5 MILESTONES IN EARTH SCIENCES

1880	John Milne (English) invents modern seismograph.
1896	Svante Arrhenius (Swedish) discovers that global temperatures rise with higher levels of carbon dioxide in atmosphere (greenhouse effect).
1902	Léon-Philippe Teisserenc de Bort (French) discovers the stratosphere.
1907	Betram B. Boltwood (American) shows that the age of rocks containing uranium can be determined by measuring the ratio of uranium to lead.
1909	Andrija Mohorovičić (Croatian) discovers boundary between Earth's crust and mantle, now known as Mohorovičić discontinuity or "Moho."
1912	Alfred Wegener (German) proposes theory of continental drift, idea that a single continent—Pangaea—split into present-day continents that have drifted away from each other.

Source: The Universal Almanac 1991, 492.

TABLE 13.6 MAJOR DISCOVERIES IN PHYSICS

1873	James Clerk Maxwell (Scottish) publishes complete theory of electromagnetism, which includes his prediction that radio waves must exist.
1887	Albert Michelson (German-American) and Edward Morley (American) attempt to measure changes in velocity of light produced by motion of Earth through space; inability to find such changes is later interpreted as helping to establish Einstein's special theory of relativity.
1888	Heinrich Hertz (German) produces and detects radio waves.
1895	Wilhelm Konrad Röentgen (German) discovers X-rays.
1896	Antoine-Henri Becquerel (French) discovers natural radioactivity.
1897	Joseph John Thomson (English) discovers the electron.
1900	Max Planck (German) explains behavior of light by proposing that there exists a smallest step that a physical process can take, something he labels *quantum.*
1905	Albert Einstein (German-Swiss-American) shows that photoelectric effect—ejection of electrons from metal by action of light—can be explained if light has particle nature as well as wave nature. Einstein shows that motion of small particles in liquid ("Brownian motion") can be explained by assuming that the liquid is made of molecules. Einstein develops his special theory of relativity and the law $E = MC^2$ (energy equals mass times square of speed of light).
1911	Heike Kamerlingh Onnes (Dutch) discovers superconductivity in metals cooled near to absolute zero.

Source: The Universal Almanac 1991, 504.

TABLE 13.7 MAJOR DISCOVERIES IN LIFE SCIENCES

1894	Marie-Eugène Dubois (Dutch) announces discovery of "Java man," an intermediate between man and simian ancestors, now known to be first discovered specimen of *Homo erectus.*
1898	Mosaic disease of tobacco plants is recognized as being caused by virus, the first identification of a virus (viruses cannot be seen at this time, being known only from their effects).
1900	Three biologists independently rediscover the pioneering work of Gregor Mendel (Austrian, died 1884), who formulated and published in 1866 a theory of the laws of genetics.

Source: The Universal Almanac 1991, 509.

CHAPTER 14 Popular Culture and Sports

The Gay Nineties and the Rise of the Middle Class

The Gay Nineties recalls the nickelodeons, vaudeville shows, days at Coney Island, seaside pavilions, beer gardens, ice cream parlors, bicycling, and the Gibson Girl. The first years of the twentieth century have a reputation as the "good old days." Popular novelists and filmmakers have presented America in this era as less complex, a simpler time of baseball and hot dogs, ragtime music and summer-afternoon bicycle rides.

The genesis of such alluring and seductive images is the rise of the middle class and its values and aspirations that came to dominate American culture. The 1890s and early 1900s marked this period of transition. For millions, these decades were not rosy: to African Americans who were lynched in the South, Native Americans who died at Wounded Knee, infants whose deaths drove mortality to its highest levels in New York City, or the immigrants packed in the slums. That these realities could be eclipsed in favor of the image of the "Gay Nineties" is a measure of growing middle-class cultural influence.

The new middle class, composed of salaried professionals, managers, salespeople, and office workers, mostly living in cities, was not oblivious to social evils. The Progressive reform movement with its characteristic application of expertise to social problems embodied middle-class ideals and habits of thought. Reform embodied the confidence of a people who believed that there could be found a reasonable solution to any problem.

TABLE 14.1 MEMBERSHIP OF FRATERNAL ORGANIZATIONS, C. 1900

Fraternal orders proliferated during the Victorian period. Woodworkers, foresters, and other occupational groups formed organizations that mixed fraternity with preservation of a trade. Jews and Roman Catholics joined organizations that mixed self-help, religion, and ethnic pride. Still other groups created organizations with distinctive dress, secret rituals, and membership devoted to benevolent causes.

Organization	Number of Members in Thousands
Odd Fellows	1,027
Freemasons	903
Modern Woodmen of America	643
Knights of Pythias	517
Ancient Order of United Workmen	420
Improved Order of Red Men	260
Woodmen of the World	252
Knights of Maccabees	228
Royal Arcanum	227
Foresters of America	195
Independent Order of Foresters	187
Ancient Order of Hibernians of America	153
Junior Order of United American Mechanics	104
Benevolent and Protective Order of Elks	100
Ladies' Catholic Benevolent Association	72
Knights of the Golden Eagle	70
Tribe of Ben Hur	67
National Union	60
Knights of Honor	60
Knights and Ladies of Honor	54
Improved Order of Heptasophs	52
Order of United American Mechanics	47
Catholic Benevolent Legion	42
Ancient Order of Foresters	38
Sons of Temperance	33
Independent Order of B'nai B'rith	30
New England Order of Protection	29
Knights of Malta	26
Catholic Knights of America	24
Royal Templars of Temperance	24
United Order of Pilgrim Fathers	23
Brith Abraham Order	19
Star of Bethlehem Order	18
United Ancient Order of Druids	17
Mystic Circle	17
Irish Catholic Benevolent Union	14
American Legion of Honor	8
Smaller Organizations not reported	43
Total	6,103,000

Source: The World Almanac 1902 (1902), 328.

Jell-O, "America's Most Famous Dessert," made its appearance during this period, as shown in a promotional handout of the Genesee Pure Food Company, Leroy, New York, c. 1910. (Courtesy Smithsonian Institution, Warshaw Collection of Business Americana, National Museum of American History)

Marketing advertisements, as shown in this Egg-O-See cold-cereal ad, used modern techniques to connect their product to good health. (Courtesy Smithsonian Institution, Warshaw Collection of Business Americana, National Museum of American History)

TABLE 14.2   LEGAL HOLIDAYS DURING THE VICTORIAN ERA

National (1902)

Jan. 1	in all states except Colo., Mass., and N.H.
Feb. 22	in all states except Colo., Ind. Terr., Miss., and N. Mex.
May 30	Decoration Day (also known as Memorial Day) in all states except Ala., Ark., Colo., Fla., Ga., Idaho, La., Nev., N. Mex., N.C., S.C., and Tex.
Jul. 4	Independence Day in all states except Colo.
Nov. 26	Thanksgiving. Recognized all states.
Dec. 25	Christmas in all states except Colo., which has no statutes regulating holidays, but the majority are observed.

Special Holidays

Jan. 8	Battle of New Orleans in La.
Jan. 19	Gen. Robt. E. Lee's birthday in Ala., Fla., Ga., N.C., S.C., and Va.
Feb. 12	Lincoln's birthday in Conn., Del., Ill., Minn., N.J., N.Y., N. Dak., Pa., Wash., and Wyo.
Jun. 3	Jefferson Davis's birthday in Ala., Fla., Ga., and S.C.
Sep. 7	Labor Day in Ala., Calif., Colo., Conn., Del., D.C., Fla., Ga., Ill., Ind., Iowa, Kans., Maine, Md., Mass., Mich., Minn., Mont., Mo., Nebr., N.H., N.J., N.Y., N. Dak., Ohio, Okla., Oreg., Pa., R.I., S.C., S. Dak., Tenn., Tex., Utah, Va., Wash., and W. Va.
Nov. 3	Election Day in Ariz., Calif., Fla., Idaho, Ind., Kans., Md., Minn., Mo., Mont., Nev., N.H., N.J., N.Y., N. Dak., Okla., Oreg., Pa., R.I., S.C., S. Dak., Tenn., Tex., Wash., W. Va., Wis., Wyo.

Religious Holidays

Good Friday is a holiday in Ala., La., Md., Minn., Pa., and Tenn.; All Saints' Day is a holiday in La.

Anniversaries Sometimes Celebrated

Jan. 19	Lee's birthday
Feb. 14	St. Valentine's Day
Feb. 22	Geo. Washington's birthday
Mar. 17	St. Patrick's day
Jun. 14	Flag Day
Oct. 31	Halloween
Nov. 1	All Saints' Day
Nov. 2	All Souls' Day

Source: The World Almanac 1891 (1891), 25.

Fashions and Role Models

Skirts and shirtwaists (women's blouses tailored to resemble men's shirts) composed the standard informal dress for women of all classes, and the "uniform" of women clerical workers. A shirtwaist could be purchased for anywhere from 50 cents to $7. The Gibson Girl, the "typical American girl" created by the popular magazine illustrator Charles Dana Gibson, was always depicted wearing a shirtwaist and skirt.

The Gibson Girl was by no means a feminist. She took little interest in women's suffrage or other political issues. She was usually presented as coy and flirty, even seductive. She was no shrinking violet either (see profile of Elizabeth Cochran in Chapter 10) but rather robust and athletic. She did not faint after climbing stairs or playing an exhausting game of tennis. She played golf and croquet and rode a bicycle without chaperones. She was quite self-sufficient; indeed, one of Gibson's themes was the insecurity felt by young men in the presence of these self-assured young ladies.

Many women office workers copied the Gibson look because it was both fashionable and practical. Technical training manuals encouraged what a later age called "dressing for success"; for the Victorian Age this meant clothing with the look of efficiency—clean lines, no frills, neither too "feminine" (fluffy or frilly) nor too "masculine" (heavy tweeds and worsteds). A black skirt and a white shirtwaist matched in look the sober, no-nonsense lines of the secretary's typewriter.

Both the lady and mill girl adopted the middle-class ideal. Photographs of young women workers leaving textile factories in Massachusetts and of stenographers in offices in New York City reveal the air of self-assurance that was the hallmark of the Gibson girl. The new independence of women was also indicated in later ages at marriage. In 1890, the average age for a woman on her wedding day was 22, two to three years older than it had been in 1860.

By 1915, the man on the corporate ladder wore one form of dress: the business suit. The "trusty blue serge" introduced in the 1890s descended from several nineteenth-century forms of male wear: the frock coat, the "ditto suit" (coat, vest, and trousers from the same cloth), and the sack coat. The advertisements proclaimed the suit as the symbol of modern masculinity, appropriate to the thinker, expert, and manager. The Prince Albert long coat, the ideal of the 1870s, gave way to the business suit, tie, and white shirt of the 1910s.

The Dime Novel and Wild-West Culture

The most important creator of the legendary Wild West was E. Z. C. Judson, an unsavory character who had been dishonorably discharged from the Union army after the Civil War. Judson, under the pen name Ned Buntline, churned out more than 400 "romantic, blood, guts, and chivalric novels" between 1865 and 1886, mostly

Dime novels, sometimes called pulps after the paper they were printed upon, took the legendary West as their theme and became best-sellers of popular fiction. Shown here is a cover of a dime novel. (Courtesy Denver Public Library, Western History Department)

about western heroes. Judson invented some characters; others were real people he depicted as larger than life. Popular novels of this kind were called *pulps* after the paper they were printed upon or *dime novels* because of their price. Dime novels were popular, especially with young boys.

In the pulps (and later in films), Americans "learned" that bank and train robbers such as Jesse and Frank James along with several cohorts of the Clanton family were really modern-day Robin Hoods, taking from the rich to give to the poor. Billy the Kid (William Bonney), a Brooklyn-born killer, was transformed by the pulps into a tragic hero who was forced into a life of crime because no one cared. The images of "Calamity Jane" Canary, "Wild Bill" Hickok, "Buffalo Bill" Cody, and Hunkpapa Lakota Chief Sitting Bull were likewise created—often bearing little resemblance to their historical models. Wild-West culture thrived long before filmmakers began to make moving pictures.

Gunfights and Gunfighters

During the Victorian Age, the names of many famous gunfighters entered American folklore: Wyatt Earp, Jesse James, James Butler

TABLE 14.3 TOP TWENTY OCCUPATIONS OF GUNFIGHTERS

Rank	Occupation
1.	law officer
2.	cowhand
3.	rancher
4.	farmer
5.	rustler
6.	hired gunfighter
7.	soldier
8.	bandit
9.	gambler
10.	laborer
11.	saloon owner
12.	clerk
13.	train robber
14.	miner
15.	prospector
16.	army scout
17.	stage robber
18.	teamster
19.	bank robber
20.	buffalo hunter

Source: O'Neal, *Encyclopedia of Western Gunfighters* (1979), 8.

TABLE 14.4 YEAR, NUMBER AND PLACE OF GUNFIGHTS

Year	Number of Gunfights	Place
1854	1	Tex.
1856	5	Calif.
1857	1	Calif.
1858	2	Colo., Tex.
1859	4	Tex. (2), Calif., Colo.
1860	2	Idaho, La.
1861	3	Mo. (2), Nebr.
1862	4	Mo., Tenn., Tex., Wyo.
1863	4	Ariz. (2), Mont. (2)
1864	2	Ark., Tex.
1865	6	Calif. (3), Mo., Okla., Tex.
1866	4	Mo. (2), Mex., Tex.
1867	10	Tex. (6), Okla. (2), Wyo. (2)
1868	16	Tex. (10), Nev. (2), Wyo. (2), Kans., Mo.
1869	12	Tex. (5), Kans. (3), Ark., Colo., Mo., Okla.
1870	6	Kans. (4), Tex. (2)
1871	22	Kans. (8), Tex. (5), Calif. (2), N. Mex. (2), Okla. (2), Iowa, Miss., Wyo.
1872	13	Kans. (6), Tex. (2), Calif. (2), Ky., Okla., Utah, Wyo.
1873	27	Kans. (12), Tex. (10), N. Mex. (3), Colo., Okla.
1874	14	Tex. (6), Mo. (2), N. Mex., (2), Okla. (2), Calif., Kans.
1875	13	Tex. (9), N. Mex. (3), Mo.
1876	22	Tex. (11), N. Mex. (5), Dakota (2), Minn. (2), Ariz., Colo.
1877	21	Tex. (12), Kans. (4), N. Mex. (2), Ariz., Fla., Kans.
1878	36	N. Mex. (23), Tex. (10), Kans. (3)
1879	14	N. Mex. (6), Kans. (4), Colo. (2), Tex. (2)

(continued)

TABLE 14.4 (continued)

Year	Number of Gunfights	Place
1880	25	N. Mex. (11), Ariz. (3), Kans. (3), Tex. (3), Calif., Colo., Mexico, Nebr., Nev.
1881	27	N. Mex. (8), Ariz. (7), Tex. (5), Kans. (4), Calif., Colo., Kans.
1882	15	Ariz. (5), Tex. (5), Mo. (2), N. Mex. (2), Colo.
1883	9	Kans. (6), Nebr., N. Mex., Tex.
1884	17	Kans. (5), Tex. (5), N. Mex. (3), Calif., Colo., Mont., Mexico
1885	7	Okla. (3), Tex. (2), Colo., Kans.
1886	7	Tex. (3), Okla. (2), Ariz., N. Mex.
1887	20	Ariz. (9), Tex. (9), Okla. (2)
1888	10	Ariz. (2), Kans. (2), Tex. (2), Ala., Ill., Okla., Tenn.
1889	9	Ariz. (3), Tex. (3), Kans., N. Mex., Okla., Tenn.
1890	9	Okla. (4), Colo., Kans., La., Tex., Utah
1891	10	Kans. (2), Okla. (2), Tex. (2), Ark., Calif., Colo., Wyo.
1892	13	Okla. (7), Calif. (2), Colo., Kans., Wash., Wyo.
1893	11	Okla. (3), Calif. (2), Ark., Kans., La., Mexico, Tex., Wyo.
1894	14	Okla. (5), Tex. (5), Ariz., Mo., Mont., Utah
1895	19	Okla. (10), Tex. (4), Colo., Mo., Mont., N. Mex., Utah
1896	19	Okla. (5), Tex. (4), Ariz. (3), Ark., Calif., Kans., Mexico, Mont., N. Mex., Utah
1897	7	Kans. (2), Mont. (2), Ariz., Tex., Utah
1898	8	Ariz. (5), N. Mex. (2), Colo.
1899	8	Ariz. (3), Wyo. (2), Colo., Tex., Utah
1900	12	Ariz. (5), Colo. (2), Utah (3), Mo., Wyo.
1901	9	Ariz. (5), Okla., Tenn., Tex., Wyo.
1902	8	Ariz. (3), Wash. (3), Oreg., Tex.
1903	2	Tex. (2)
1904	6	Tex. (2), Ariz., Colo., N. Mex., Okla.
1905	5	Okla. (2), Bolivia, N. Mex., Tex.
1906	2	Okla., Mexico
1907	3	Ariz. (2), Colo.
1908	4	N. Mex. (2), Tex., Bolivia
1909	1	Okla.
1911	3	Tex. (2), Ga.
1912	1	Wyo.
1915	2	Okla., Tex.
1917	1	Ariz.
1924	2	Mo., Okla.

Source: O'Neal, *Encyclopedia of Western Gunfighters* (1979), 11–12.

("Wild Bill") Hickok, Johnny Ringo, John Henry ("Doc") Holliday, "Billy the Kid" (aka Henry McCarty or William Bonney), "Butch Cassidy" (Robert Leroy Parker), and the "Sundance Kid" (Harry Longabaugh). The Dalton gang, the Doolin gang, the Powder River gang, and the James gang were also notorious. Gunfighters congregated in saloons, jail offices, bunkhouses, and hideouts.

The men most often involved in terms of occupation were law officers followed by cowboys. A surprising number of farmers, store clerks, schoolteachers, butchers, actors, and others participated in gunfights.

TABLE 14.5 NOTABLE GUN FIGHTS

The following chronology gives the most notable incidents during the period.

Year	Incident	Date/Place
1861	Shootout between the McCanles Gang and "Wild Bill" Hickok	Jul. 12, Rock Creek Station, Nebr.
1864	Hanging of Henry Plummer and many of his Montana outlaws. Hanging of Jack Slade	Mar. 10, Virginia City, Mont.
1865	Duel between Dave Tutt and "Wild Bill" Hickok	Jul. 21, Springfield, Mo.
1870	Fight between "Wild Bill" Hickok and Fort Hays cavalry	Jul. 17, Fort Hays, Kans.
1871	Killing of Bear River Tom Smith	Nov. 2, near Abilene, Kans.
	Mass shootout in Newton saloon	Aug. 20, Newton, Kans.
	Shooting between "Wild Bill" Hickok and Phil Coe	Oct. 5, Abilene, Kans.
1873	Vicious brawl between Arthur McCluskie and Hugh Anderson	Jun., Medicine Lodge, Kans.
	Killing of Sheriff C. B. Whitney by Billy Thompson	Aug. 15, Ellsworth, Kans.
	Horrell War	Lincoln County, N. Mex.
1874	Gunfight between John Younger and detectives	Mar. 16, Monegaw Springs, Mo.
1876	Fight between Bat Masterson and Sgt. Ed King	Jan. 24, Mobeetie, Tex.
	Murder of "Wild Bill" Hickok	Aug. 2, Deadwood, D.T.
	James-Younger raid on Northfield, Minn.	Sep. 7
1877	Horrell-Higgins feud climaxes	around Lampasas, Tex.
1878	Gunfight between Ed Masterson and Texans	Apr. 9, Dodge City, Kans.
	Battle between Texas Rangers and Sam Bass gang	Jul. 19, Round Rock. Tex.
	Hanging of "Wild Bill" Longley	Oct. 11, Giddings, Tex.
	Lincoln County War	Lincoln County, N. Mex.
1880	Pat Garrett's manhunt for "Billy the Kid" and gang	
1881	El Paso gunfight featuring Dallas Stoudenmire and four fatalities	Apr. 14
	"Billy the Kid" shoots his way out of jail	Apr. 28, Lincoln, N. Mex.
	Death of "Billy the Kid"	Jul. 14, Fort Sumner, N. Mex.
	Gunfight at the OK Corral	Oct. 26, Tombstone, Ariz.
1882	Murder of Jesse James	Apr. 3, St. Joseph, Mo.
	Killing of Johnny Ringo	Jul. 14, Turkey Creek Canyon, Ariz.
	Killing of Dallas Stoudenmire by the Manning brothers	Sep. 18, El Paso, Tex.
	Fight between Buckskin Frank Leslie and Billy Claiborne	Nov. 14, Tombstone, Ariz.
1884	Death of Ben Thompson and King Fisher	Mar. 11, San Antonio, Tex.
	Attack on Elfego Baco	Oct., Frisco, N. Mex.
	Medicine Lodge, Kans., bank robbery	Dec. 15
1887	Fight between Luke Short and Long-haired Jim Courtright	Feb. 8, Fort Worth, Tex.
	Peaceful death of "Doc" Holliday	Nov. 8, Glenwood Springs, Colo.
	Arizona's Pleasant Valley War.	
1892	Dalton Gang raid on Coffeyville, Kans.	Oct. 5
	Powder River War	Wyo.
1893	Shootout between the law and the Doolin gang	Sep. 1, Ingalls, Okla.
1895	Killing of John Wesley Hardin by John Selman	Aug. 19, El Paso, Tex.
1896	Death of Bill Doolin by a posse	Aug. 25, Lawson, Okla.

Year	Incident	Date/Place
1898	Heyday of "Butch Cassidy's" Wild Bunch.	
1900	Fight between Jeff Milton and Burt Alvord's gang	Feb. 15, Fairbank, Ariz.
1904	Death of Harvey Logan	May 8, near Glenwood Springs, Colo.
1908	Murder of Pat Garrett	Feb. 29, near Las Cruces, N. Mex.
	Fight between Bolivian soldiers and "Butch Cassidy" and the "Sundance Kid."	
1909	Lynching of Jim ("Killer") Miller	Apr. 19, Ada, Okla.
1924	Killing of Bill Tilghman	Nov. 1, Cromwell, Okla.

Source: O'Neal, *Encyclopedia of Western Gunfighters* (1979), 13–14.

Gunfights were most common during the 1870s and early 1880s. Gunfighting was mostly a post–Civil War phenomenon after important technical improvements had been made in firearms and thousands of men had served in combat. The period ended, except for scattered incidents, after the turn of the century.

Areas of western-styled gunfighting included Texas, the most violent western area. Kansas cattle towns provided favorite spots for gunfighters, followed in importance by New Mexico, Arizona, Oklahoma, California, Colorado, Missouri, and Wyoming, which were each the scenes of more than 70 fights.

Cowboys

Despite the white complexion of cowboys in popular literature and films of the twentieth century, a substantial proportion of them were Mexican or black. In the 1850s, enterprising Texans began to round up half-wild longhorns to drive them to cattle markets in Missouri railroad towns. Although most of the trail bosses were English-speaking, many of the actual workers were Mexicans who called themselves *vaqueros*. *Vaquero*, "cowboy," became *buckaroo* in English. Much of the American folklore and parlance about cowboys was of Mexican derivation.

The cowboy's working outfit was an adaptation of functional Mexican work clothing. The bandana was a washcloth worn around the neck and over the nose and mouth during the dusty cattle drives. The broad-brimmed hat, like the *sombrero*, functioned to keep sun and rain off the face. Made from good-quality beaver felt, the hat also was used as a drinking pot and washbasin.

Real cowboys grew in number with the long cattle drives from deep in the heart of Texas to Abilene, Kansas, which was reached by the transcontinental railroad in 1866. Joseph G. McCoy, a wheeler-dealer from Illinois, saw the possibility of underselling eastern beef with Texas longhorns shipped from Abilene, on whose outskirts he built a series of holding pens. McCoy dispatched agents to Texas to encourage Texans to round up and drive cattle north on a trading route called the Chisholm Trail. In 1867, 35,000 rawboned cattle were sent from Abilene to Chicago. By 1871, 600,000 head were passing through Kansas to other towns along the railroad line as it moved west.

Cow towns along the railroad route gained a reputation as places of wild, rambunctious, and thirsty men looking for a blowout after a long drive. Occasionally, they mixed as equals, but just as often cowboys split along racial lines when they reached their destination towns, where they found segregated restaurants, barber shops, hotels, saloons, and brothels.

Black, white, or Hispanic cowboys were mostly young because the life was so arduous—days in the saddle, cold and damp nights on the bare ground, travel in all kinds of weather—that only the young could take it. Photographs from Abilene and Dodge City and arrest records for drunk and disorderly conduct reveal a population of very young men, mostly under 25 years of age.

Pulp novels glamorized the shootouts that made for exciting reading. But cowboys depended upon skills of horsemanship, roping, and herding, not the Colt revolver that they carried to signal co-workers in the distance. In fact, carrying guns was forbidden in rail towns. Local sheriffs or marshals did not want young men out on a drunken binge packing shooting irons. If buckaroos did not leave their guns in camp outside the towns, they were required to check them at the police station or sheriff's office.

Vaudeville

The French term *vaudeville* first referred to light drama broken by musical interludes, but in the United States vaudeville became a unique entertainment form that had roots in several entertainment traditions. The variety show in saloon music halls, involving an assortment of singers, dancing acts, and comedy skits, was the most immediate progenitor. Usually considered male entertainment because the performers played to raucous saloon audiences who hissed, stamped, jeered, and shouted their approval or disapproval, variety shows had a limited mass appeal until they left the saloon crowd.

In the 1880s, a new generation of promoters began to clean up variety shows and pitch them toward middle-class families. Tony Pastor's New Fourteenth Street theater (1881) was an early attempt to take variety out of the saloon. But it was Benjamin Franklin Keith, a Boston showman who had worked in circuses, tent shows, and dime museums, who transformed the variety show into family entertainment.

Shows borrowed heavily from the circus and Wild-West shows to feature magic, animal acts, juggling, stunts, comedy (often involving "ethnic" humor), and song and dance. Strong men such as Eugene Sandow, "the Modern Hercules," were part of the circus heritage. From the minstrel show, vaudeville borrowed the tradition of the funny- and straight-man dialogue and its blackface performers. The legitimate stage furnished some talent, such as Sarah Bernhardt and Ethel Barrymore, stars of the legitimate theater.

Vaudeville performers, such as singer Lillian Russell, comedienne Fanny Brice, and burlesque queen Eva Tanguay, developed intensely loyal followings. Burt Williams, a highly paid black comedian, achieved his success by playing off stereotypes of African Americans. For some immigrants—Sophie Tucker, Harry Houdini, and Al Jolson—the vaudeville stage became a ladder to success.

Vaudeville encapsulated great chunks of American culture. The tensions and triumphs of an ethnically diverse population rubbing shoulders and striving to get ahead found some release in the exploitation of ethnic humor. The skits and sketches and the rise of stars reinforced and celebrated the ethic of success, so much a part of late nineteenth century American culture. The stage provided larger-than-life figures to admire and emulate, such as Will Rogers, the "Ziegfeld girl" (after Florenz Ziegfeld, the producer of the *Follies,* variety shows featuring a chorus line of pretty showgirls), or Fanny Brice.

From Kinetoscopes and Nickelodeons to Motion Pictures

In 1910, 10,000 movie theaters played to a nationwide audience of more than 10 million weekly, more than all legitimate theaters, variety halls, dime museums, lecture bureaus, concert halls, circuses, and street carnivals combined. Only vaudeville did better, and it would soon be eclipsed by the movies.

The Kinetoscopes and nickelodeons developed as diversions for the middle class. Thomas Edison thought that the same would be true for motion pictures and that they would serve educational purposes. Instead, movies appealed to mass audiences and their popularity rose from the bottom up.

Unlike any other medium, movies spread everyday American life across the national landscape. Kinetoscopes of the 1890s and theater palaces of the late teens showed only silent movies. All across America, people could be simultaneously watching the same movie at the same time. Like the mail-order catalog and the mass-circulation magazines and weeklies, movies made parts of American common culture truly common.

Throughout the nineteenth century, attempts, sometimes comical, were made to put motion on film. For instance, artists created panoramas (long strip paintings that unrolled from giant scrolls before audiences) that fascinated midcentury viewers.

In the 1870s, a famous experiment took place in California at the Palo Alto stud farm of railroad king Leland Stanford. Stanford bet

The city theaters in Victorian America were places where vaudeville shows were staged. Gradually, moving pictures were added as brief features at the end of the show. By 1910, some theaters, like this St. Louis theater, 1910, were places for motion pictures or "nickelodeons" that showed crude moving pictures as a piano played in the background. (Courtesy Prints and Photographs Division, Library of Congress)

$25,000 to prove that a galloping horse sometimes has all four hooves off the ground. To prove his case, Stanford engaged landscape photographer Eadweard Muybridge to record the motions of a running horse. Muybridge, using a series of twenty-four cameras in a row, each shutter being tripped by a string as the horse ran over them, proved that in a canter all four hooves of the horse are periodically off the ground.

In the 1880s, Thomas Edison began to experiment with an instrument to record and reproduce motion. Using celluloid film, he made a Kinetograph to take motion pictures and a Kinetoscope to show them. The Kinetoscope used a 50-foot strip of perforated 35 mm, black-and-white film that moved between a light and a revolving shutter.

After being exhibited at the Chicago World's Fair, the Kinetoscope was installed in parlors, billiard rooms, penny arcades, or storefronts. For a few coins, you could look into a peephole device and see something moving. By today's standards, the "shows" were dull and commonplace: ninety seconds of a man sneezing, a girl dancing, or a child being given a bath. By contrast, vaudeville players juggled Indian clubs, threw custard pies, or built human pyramids. But the wonder and fascination of moving objects captured on film brought in a steady flow of coins. Promoters realized what revenues awaited those who could convert the Kinetoscope into a movie projecting machine with mass audiences.

Moving-picture shows really developed as added attractions following the vaudeville show. In 1895, after the regular show, the vaudeville audience at Koster and Bial's Music Hall in New York was treated to an "added attraction" that included a scene from a prizefight (popular with Kinetoscope fans), a brief dance number, and waves rolling in on the beach at Dover, England. Later, vaudeville motion pictures might include scenes of William McKinley's inauguration, celebrities such as "Buffalo Bill" and Annie Oakley, moving trains and automobiles, Queen Victoria's funeral, Sandow the Strong Man, or Bertholdi the Contortionist. Motion pictures quickly gained in popularity at vaudeville shows; within two decades, the added attraction became the feature as vaudeville houses were converted to movie theaters.

In 1905, the term "nickelodeon" to describe a movies-only, storefront theater appears to have been coined by either John Harris or Harry Davis to name their movie houses in Pittsburgh and McKeesport, Pennsylvania. Regardless of who first used the term, the nickelodeon audiences grew. In 1910, *Scientific American* claimed 20,000 nickelodeons were handling a daily audience of a quarter of a million people.

Mark Sullivan described a typical nickel theater in *Our Times* as a long narrow room with a stage at one end and a white curtain across it. A piano provided background music. The audience of 100 to 450 people was packed closely together into chairs to watch the flashes of light and shadow projected upon the white curtain.

Technically, the projection had a few flaws. The intermittent feed mechanism on the projector caused the screen image to flicker (hence, the *flicks*); hand-cranked cameras produced unevenness in the rate of frames per second. A good projectionist, however, could make these problems seem to disappear by deliberately slowing or speeding up the action to produce comic effects—a prizefighter going down casually or a chase scene at breakneck speed; audiences loved to see action in reverse.

Nickel-theater programs lasted about fifteen to twenty minutes, which made them conveniently accessible to a housewife to visit any time of the day, to factory workers coming home from work, or to children after school. One historian found that families spent an evening or Saturday afternoon together migrating from theater to theater to see the different offerings. In the beginning, most nickel-

TABLE 14.6 MOTION PICTURES

1896	The first motion picture was commercially exhibited at Koster and Bial's Music Hall, New York City.
1900	*Cinderella*, the first film to use "artificially arranged scene," was produced by George Melies, a French producer.
1903	*The Great Train Robbery* earned producer Edwin S. Porter recognition as "the father of story film."
1905	An early nickelodeon movie house was established in Pittsburgh by John P. Harris and Harry Davis; by 1908, between 8,000 and 10,000 were in operation, which expanded the demand for film-production facilities.
1912	Famous Players Films Co. (reorganized as Paramount) was organized and innovated "block booking."
1913	Independent movie makers made Hollywood the center of the industry, supplanting New York.
1913	Serials produced growing interest. The best known were *What Happened to Mary*, *The Perils of Pauline*, and *Ruth of the Rockies*.
1913–16	Mack Sennett's 2-reel comedies (Keystone), with burlesque satire and trick photography, launched "slapstick" comedians, most notably Charlie Chaplain: *The Tramp* (1915), *The Pawnshop* (1916), *Easy Street* (1917), and others.

Source: Morris, Encyclopedia of American History (1965), 628.

odeons located near working-class or immigrant neighborhoods. Four or five storefront theaters crowded together at a busy intersection of trolley lines or along a principal shopping street in a workers' district also proved profitable to promoters.

Soon, more than 4,000 films were being released annually, many imported from France, Germany, and Italy. American studios grew up in warehouses, auditoriums, and lofts in New York City, New Jersey, and Chicago. Films were made from Frank Norris's novel *The Pit* and from *The Perils of Pauline* (1914), a serialized melodrama. Everyday-life themes were played in such films as *The Song of the Shirt* (1910), about the sweatshops; *The Typewriter* (1902), using office humor; and *The Kleptomaniac* (1905), set in a department store.

As the era came to a close, motion pictures began to appeal to a more middle-class clientele. Churches, reformers, and settlement-house workers who had initially condemned movie houses relented when movie producers agreed not to operate on Sunday and not to show "degrading" movies. Producers created a self-regulating body, the National Board of Review of Motion Pictures, that worked with local governments to produce city codes and licensing legislation that averted censorship and brought middle-class Americans to the theaters.

Movies of the 1910s helped to expand the growing middle-class clientele. As movies moved from peephole quickies to full feature presentations, middle-class patrons flocked to the theaters. Finally, D. W. Griffith's *Birth of a Nation* (1915), a three-hour epic about a white southern family rescued from unruly blacks by the Ku Klux Klan, revealed the racist anxieties of the age while also serving as an example of the strides moviemaking had made since the Kinetescope.

Free Silver and *The Wonderful Wizard of Oz*

L. Frank Baum was a restless dreamer who had tried his hand at several careers before he gained fame in children's literature. From 1888 to 1891, he ran a store and newspaper in South Dakota, where he experienced some of the grayness and desolation of agrarian life. An avid supporter of William Jennings Bryan, Baum wrote an enduring allegory on the silver movement, *The Wonderful Wizard of Oz*, published in 1900. It was immediately successful.

Dorothy wore silver slippers (ruby slippers in the movie) symbol of free silver. Silver stood for the common folk; gold was the currency of the idle rich. Dorothy was carried by a cyclone (a victory of the silver forces at the polls) from drought-stricken Kansas to a marvelous land of riches and witches. The Wicked Witch of the East was the eastern money power; the Wicked Witch of the West is said to represent malign nature, mortgage companies, and other obstacles to progress. Other witches included the Good Witch of the North (northern voters) and the Good Witch of the South (support for silver was strong in the South). In order to get back to Kansas, Dorothy had to go through the Emerald City (the greenback-colored national capital).

Characters of the book represented players in the national struggle of farmers to achieve understanding, fair treatment, and equity in the marketplace. The Scarecrow was the farmer who was told that he had no brain but actually possessed abundant common sense. The Tin Woodman was the industrial worker who feared that he had become heartless but instead found a spirit of love and cooperation. The Cowardly Lion depicted the reformer, especially William Jennings Bryan, who turned out to be courageous. The Wizard in the Emerald City represented the money power who was not really powerful at all in the end but a manipulator whose power rested upon illusion and myth. "Oz" was a play on the 16 to 1 (ounces) relationship of silver to gold in the coinage that many debated in the late nineteenth century as the key to financial stability.

The *Oz* stories have remained popular and are still part of most collections of children's literature. In 1939, during the Great Depression, a spectacularly successful movie was made based upon the story.

Chautauqua

In 1874 at Lake Chautauqua in New York's Allegheny Mountains John Vincent, a Methodist clergyman, and Lewis Miller, an Akron, Ohio, businessman, launched a summer program to train Sunday School teachers. Simultaneously, cheap excursion fares on the trains made it feasible to make the trip for the sake of the cool mountain air and relaxation. Chautauqua grew to become one of America's most popular middle-class resorts. Hotels, clubhouses, lecture halls, boardinghouses, parks, classrooms, auditoriums, and permanent summer homes were built on the grounds.

By the turn of the century, a middle-class family could expect to hear lectures by such figures as William Jennings Bryan or watch "magic-lantern" (slide) shows about distant lands by professional world travelers. Distinguished professionals (and quacks) expounded upon their theories about human nature, marital contentment, or childbearing. German oompah bands, Hawaiian dancers, dog and pony shows, Italian acrobats, and Indian fire-eaters provided lighter entertainment.

The success of New York's Chatauqua spawned imitations elsewhere. "Chatauquas" sprang up around lakes and wooded areas with camping facilities; families came to attend lectures, scientific demonstrations, plays, and nondenominational religious exercises. In 1920, there were 21 Chautauqua tent companies operating 93 circuits in the United States and Canada. Programs were presented in 8,580 towns to more than 35 million people.

The Chatauqua movement came to exercise an enormous influence in Protestant America. Theodore Roosevelt called it "the most American thing about America." It has been called a kind of "moral vaudeville" and an early "institution of mass culture" for the rising middle class.

Sports

Auto Racing

In 1909, work began on the first of America's speedways—the Indianapolis Speedway. Road races had originated earlier on Long Island in 1904, but they were discontinued because the cars often went out of control and killed the spectators. The first race on the Indianapolis "oval" was run on August 19, 1909, on an unpaved track. Because of accidents, the track was closed, paved with brick, and reopened in December. Ray Harroun won the first 500-mile race in a Marmon at an average speed of 74.59 miles per hour. Prize money totaled $27,550. Joe Dawson won in 1912 driving a National, and Jules Goux won it in 1913 in a Peugeot, at average speeds of 78.72 and 75.93 miles per hour respectively.

Stock-car racing began somewhat earlier in 1902 with a contest between automobile manufacturers Henry Ford and Alexander Winton in Detroit. Many stock automobiles raced against one another on the sands of Daytona Beach in the early 1900s. The Buick and the Packard achieved recognition for their performance in these races. The sport was short lived, however, because World War I forced U.S. manufacturers to concentrate on mass production instead of racing machines.

Early national champions of auto racing include George Robertson (1909), Ray Harroun (1910), Ralph Mulford (1911), Ralph De Palma (1912), and Earl Cooper (1913).

Barney Oldfield (Berna Eli Oldfield): b. Wauseon, Ohio, January 19, 1878; d. Beverly Hills, California, October 4, 1946.

Barney Oldfield became the most famous of the dusty daredevils, the early race-car drivers whose vehicles were as unpredictable as the dirt roads upon which they ran.

Oldfield began as a bicycle racer and moved to auto racing in October 1902, when he was presented with the chance to drive Henry Ford's 999 in a contest with Alexander Winton's car. Oldfield won, setting a new U.S. speed record, completing the 5-mile course in 5 minutes, 28 seconds. On June 15, 1903, he became the first person to drive an automobile at the pace of a mile a minute, and in 1910, he set a speed record of 81.734 miles per hour at Daytona Beach, Florida.

Oldfield encouraged his reputation as a daredevil driver, often racing with a cigar in his mouth. He had numerous accidents and gave his vehicles such names as Green Dragon, Big Ben, and Golden Submarine. Not noted for his modesty, he once compared himself as a race driver to Henry Ford, the automaker: "I did much the best job of it." He retired in 1918; speed-demon drivers after him sometimes used his name.

Baseball

During the Gilded Age, baseball eclipsed boxing as the nation's leading spectator sport. Fans crowded the grandstands and bleachers on Sunday afternoons to watch professional teams. According to *Harper's Weekly* in 1886, "The fascination of the Game has seized upon the American people, irrespective of age, sex, or other condition." The national pastime entertained Americans at all levels from salesclerks and assembly-line workers to business managers and stenographers. Teams became focal points of civic pride; important

Playing ball in the streets was a favorite pastime for boys in the city. In this scene, boys are playing in San Francisco's streets, c. 1900, in a district where typical housing was five rooms per family that rented for $10 to $12 per month. (Courtesy National Archives)

TABLE 14.7 PENNANT WINNERS

Figures in parentheses after club names indicate in each instance the number of the pennant for that club. The same system is applied to the managers, some of whom won with different clubs.

	National League				
Year	Club	Manager	Won	Lost	Pct.
1876	Chicago (1st)	Albert G. Spalding (1st)	52	14	.788
1877	Boston (1st)	Harry Wright (1st)	31	17	.646
1878	Boston (2d)	Harry Wright (2d)	41	19	.683
1879	Providence (1st)	George Wright (1st)	55	23	.705
1880	Chicago (2d)	Adrian C. Anson (1st)	67	17	.798
1881	Chicago (3d)	Adrian C. Anson (2d)	56	28	.667
1882	Chicago (4th)	Adrian C. Anson (3d)	55	29	.655
1883	Boston (3d)	John F. Morrill (1st)	63	35	.643
1884	Providence (2d)	Frank C. Bancroft (1st)	84	28	.750
1885	Chicago (5th)	Adrian C. Anson (4th)	87	25	.777
1886	Chicago (6th)	Adrian C. Anson (5th)	90	34	.726
1887	Detroit (1st)	William H. Watkins (1st)	79	45	.637
1888	New York (1st)	James Mutrie (1st)	84	47	.641
1889	New York (2d)	James Mutrie (2d)	83	43	.659
1890	Brooklyn (1st)	William McGunnigle (1st)	86	43	.667
1891	Boston (4th)	Frank Selee (1st)	87	51	.630
1892	Boston (5th)	Frank Selee (2d)	102	48	.680
1893	Boston (6th)	Frank Selee (3d)	86	44	.662
1894	Baltimore (1st)	Edward H. Hanlon (1st)	89	39	.695
1895	Baltimore (2d)	Edward H. Hanlon (2d)	87	43	.669
1896	Baltimore (3d)	Edward H. Hanlon (3d)	90	39	.698
1897	Boston (7th)	Frank Selee (4th)	93	39	.705
1898	Boston (8th)	Frank Sele (5th)	102	47	.685
1899	Brooklyn (2d)	Edward H. Hanlon (4th)	88	42	.677
1900	Brooklyn (3d)	Edward H. Hanlon (5th)	82	54	.603
1901	Pittsburgh (1st)	Frederick C. Clarke (1st)	90	49	.647
1902	Pittsburgh (2d)	Frederick C. Clarke (2d)	103	36	.741
1903	Pittsburgh (3d)	Frederick C. Clarke (3d)	91	49	.650
1904	New York (3d)	John J. McGraw (1st)	106	47	.693
1905	New York (4th)	John J. McGraw (2d)	105	48	.686
1906	Chicago (7th)	Frank L. Chance (1st)	116	36	.763
1907	Chicago (8th)	Frank L. Chance (2d)	107	45	.704
1908	Chicago (9th)	Frank L. Chance (3d)	99	55	.643
1909	Pittsburgh (4th)	Frederick C. Clarke (4th)	110	42	.724
1910	Chicago (10th)	Frank L. Chance (4th)	104	50	.675
1911	New York (5th)	John J. McGraw (3d)	99	54	.647
1912	New York (6th)	John J. McGraw (4th)	103	48	.682
1913	New York (7th)	John J. McGraw (5th)	101	51	.664
	American League				
Year	Club	Manager	Won	Lost	Pct.
1901	Chicago (1st)	Clark C. Griffith (1st)	83	53	.610
1902	Philadelphia (1st)	Connie Mack (1st)	83	53	.610
1903	Boston (1st)	James J. Collins (1st)	91	47	.659
1904	Boston (2d)	James J. Collins (2d)	95	59	.617
1905	Philadelphia (2d)	Connie Mack (2d)	92	56	.622
1906	Chicago (2d)	Fielder A. Jones (1st)	93	58	.616
1907	Detroit (1st)	Hugh A. Jennings (1st)	92	58	.613
1908	Detroit (2d)	Hugh A. Jennings (2d)	90	63	.588
1909	Detroit (3d)	Hugh A. Jennings (3d)	98	54	.645
1910	Philadelphia (3d)	Connie Mack (3d)	102	48	.680
1911	Philadelphia (4th)	Connie Mack (4th)	101	50	.669
1912	Boston (3d)	J. Garland Stahl (1st)	105	47	.691
1913	Philadelphia (5th)	Connie Mack (5th)	96	57	.627

Source: Frank G. Menke, *The Encyclopedia of Sports* (1969), 81–82.

TABLE 14.8   WORLD SERIES HIGHLIGHTS

	Highlights	
Year	Teams/Score	Highlights
1903	Boston (A) over Pittsburgh (N), 5–3	The young American League won the first World Series, a best-of-nine affair. The "Pilgrims" (Boston) had to sweep the final four games to win. Bill Dineen and Cy Young each won two games for Boston and held the Pirate immortal Honus Wagner to a single in four games.
1904	No series	Giants owner John T. Brush and manager John McGraw refused to play Boston, calling them an "inferior league."
1905	New York (N) over Philadelphia (A), 4–1	Every game was a shutout with Christy Mathewson of the Giants throwing three. In 27 innings, he allowed 14 hits, struck out 18, and walked one. Game three was pivotal as the Athletics committed five errors.
1906	Chicago (A) over Chicago (N), 4–2	This was the first "subway series" and a stunning upset. The Chicago White Sox had gained a reputation as the "hitless wonders" during the regular season, batting .230 as a club with seven home runs. Meanwhile, the Chicago Cubs had won a record 116 games, still the all-time record. Utilityman George Rohe hit two game-winning triples for the Sox and Ed Walsh pitched for two wins.
1907	Chicago (N) over Detroit (A), 4–0	The Cubs avenged the past year, shutting down Ty Cobb, Sam Crawford, and others with a masterful four-man pitching performance and the hitting of Harry Steinfeldt (.471) and Johnny Evers (.350).
1908	Chicago (N) over Detroit (A), 4–1	Here was the same result, with Johnny Evers repeating his previous year's performance. Player-manager Frank Chance (.421) and outfielder Wildfire Schulte (.389) also had a good series. Ty Cobb led Detroit (.368).
1909	Pittsburgh (N) over Detroit (A), 4–3	The Tigers lost their third straight World Series as Honus Wagner won the "Battle of the Titans" with Ty Cobb. The Pirate shortstop hit .333 with six RBIs and had six stolen bases; Babe Adams pitched three complete games.
1910	Philadelphia (A) over Chicago (N), 4–1	Connie Mack's infielders hit at a .364 pace as the A's rolled over the Cubs. Jack Coombs helped by pitching three winning games and hitting .385. The once-great Cubs pitching staff was aging.
1911	Philadelphia (A) over New York (N), 4–2	The A's, regarded by some as the greatest team over, beat back the strong New York team featuring Mathewson and Rube Marquard. Frank "Home Run" Baker received his nickname by hitting game-winning homers in games two and three.
1912	Boston (A) over New York (N), 4–3	This thrilling series featured an 11-inning tie in game two and an extra-inning final game. Two Giant errors by Freds Merkle and Snodgrass allowed Boston to score two runs in the bottom of the tenth inning of the final game.
1913	Philadelphia (A) over New York (N), 4–1	"Home Run" Baker went on another rampage batting .450 with seven RBIs. Eddie Collins also starred for the As, batting .421 and stealing three bases.

Source: Wright, *The Universal Almanac 1991* (1990), 615–16.

games sometimes received more attention than foreign wars.

Unlike basketball, which originated in the United States, baseball was largely derivative, originating with two children's games—rounders and town ball—and brought to the United States by English immigrants. By the Civil War, a dozen clubs existed in New York City, four in Chicago, and nine in New Orleans, all with distinctly middle-class players and spectators. The Civil War accelerated the diffusion of the game to working-class levels.

By the 1890s, baseball had assumed its modern form: a standardized diamond, formal rules, a published schedule of games, and two major leagues with teams in the most populous cities. The National League was founded in 1876; the American League, the "junior circuit," dates from 1901. Irish-American and German-American owners and players were overrepresented groups, hence heroes like Honus Wagner, "Iron Man" Joe McGinty, John McGraw, and Michael Kelly ("Slide, Kelly, Slide").

Just as in boxing, blacks were denied entry into the white leagues. A first baseman from Iowa, Adrian "Cap" Anson, led the fight to keep black players out of the major leagues. Consequently, black players formed their own leagues.

William Commeyer also left enduring legacies in the game. In 1862, he built an enclosed field in Brooklyn (the first in the country), erected a clubhouse, graded the diamond, and charged admission for the first time. He also began the practice of having "The Star-Span-

gled Banner," which by a presidential order in 1916 became the official anthem of the United States, played before each game. The first World Series between the two league champions, Boston and Pittsburgh, was played in 1903.

Home Run Baker   (John Franklin Baker): b. Trappe, Maryland, March 13, 1886; d. Trappe, Maryland, June 28, 1963.

Frank Baker, if playing today, would not live up to his nickname. In fact, it was given to him not because of his annual or cumulative home-run production but because he hit two home runs in the 1911 World Series, a rare accomplishment at the time.

Baker first played third base for the Philadelphia Athletics and then for New York in the American League. He hit 96 homers in his career during regular season play and three in the six World Series in which he played between 1910–1922. His best year was 1913 when he hit 12 home runs. In three other years, he hit ten home runs.

Baker was more than a slugger. His career batting average was .307. He was elected to the Baseball Hall of Fame in 1955.

The World Series   A championship series between the pennant winners of the National League and the American Association was played at the end of each season between 1882 and 1890, when the American Association folded. Between 1891 and 1901, the top two National League clubs played for the "Temple Cup," but the public

TABLE 14.9   WORLD SERIES, 1903

Boston (A.L.) defeats Pittsburgh (N.L.) 5 games to 3

Team Totals												
	W	AB	H	2B	3B	HR	R	RBI	BA	BB	SO	ERA
BOS A	5	282	71	4	16	2	39	35	.252	13	27	2.03
PIT N	3	271	64	7	9	1	24	23	.236	14	45	3.73

Individual Batting

Boston (A.L.)									Pittsburgh (N.L.)								
Player	AB	H	2B	3B	HR	R	RBI	BA	Player	AB	H	2B	3B	HR	R	RBI	BA
J. Collins, 3b	36	9	1	2	0	5	1	.250	G. Beaumont, of	34	9	0	1	0	6	0	.265
P. Dougherty, of	34	8	0	2	2	3	5	.235	F. Clarke, of	34	9	2	1	0	3	2	.265
C. Stahl, of	33	10	1	3	0	6	3	.303	T. Leach, 3b	33	9	0	4	0	3	7	.273
B. Freeman, of	32	9	0	3	0	6	4	.281	Bransfield, 1b	30	6	0	2	0	3	1	.200
F. Parent, ss	32	9	0	3	0	8	3	.281	J. Sebring, of	30	11	0	1	1	3	5	.367
H. Ferris, 2b	31	9	0	1	0	3	7	.290	C. Ritchey, 2b	27	3	1	0	0	2	2	.111
C. LaChance, 1b	27	6	2	1	0	5	4	.222	H. Wagner, ss	27	6	1	0	0	2	3	.222
L. Criger, c	26	6	0	0	0	1	4	.231	E. Phelps, c	26	6	2	0	0	1	2	.231
C. Young, p	15	2	0	1	0	1	3	.133	D. Phillippe, p	18	4	0	0	0	1	1	.222
B. Dinneen, p.	12	3	0	0	0	1	0	.250	S. Leever, p	4	0	0	0	0	0	0	.000
D. Farrell	2	0	0	0	0	0	1	.000	H. Smith, c	3	0	0	0	0	0	0	.000
J. O'Brien	2	0	0	0	0	0	0	.000	B. Kennedy, p.	2	1	1	0	0	0	0	.500
									B. Veil	2	0	0	0	0	0	0	.000
									G. Thompson, p	1	0	0	0	0	0	0	.000

Errors: L. Criger (3), C. LaChance (3), J. Collins (2), F. Parent (2), H. Ferris (2), P. Dougherty, C. Young

Errors: H. Wagner (6), T. Leach (4), Bransfield (2), E. Phelps (2), F. Clarke, D. Phillippe, B. Veil, H. Smith

Stolen bases: J. Collins (3), C. Stahl (2)

Stolen bases: H. Wagner (3), T. Leach (2), G. Beaumont (2), F. Clarke, Bransfield, C. Ritchey

Individual Pitching

Boston (A.L.)								Pittsburgh (N.L.)							
	W	L	ERA	IP	H	BB	SO	SV		W	L	ERA	IP	H	BB	SO	SV
B. Dineen	3	1	2.06	35	29	8	28	0	D. Phillippe	3	2	3.27	44	38	3	20	0
C. Young	2	1	1.59	34	31	4	17	0	S. Leever	0	2	6.30	10	13	3	2	0
L. Hughes	0	1	9.00	2	4	2	0	0	B. Kennedy	0	1	5.14	7	11	3	3	0
									B. Veil	0	0	1.29	7	6	4	1	0
									G. Thompson	0	0	4.50	2	3	0	1	0

Source: Joseph L. Reichler, ed. *The Baseball Encyclopedia* (1979), 2717.

There was no series in 1904.

TABLE 14.10   WORLD SERIES, 1905

New York (N.L.) defeats Philadelphia (A.L.) 4 games to 1

Team Totals												
	W	AB	H	2B	3B	HR	R	RBI	BA	BB	SO	ERA
NY N	4	153	32	7	0	0	15	13	.209	15	26	0.00
PHI A	1	155	25	5	0	0	3	2	.161	5	25	1.47

Individual Batting

New York (N.L.)									Philadelphia (A.L.)								
Player	AB	H	2B	3B	HR	R	RBI	BA	Player	AB	H	2B	3B	HR	R	RBI	BA
G. Browne, of	22	4	0	0	0	2	1	.182	H. Davis, 1b	20	4	1	0	0	0	0	.200
M. Donlin, of	19	6	1	0	0	4	1	.316	B. Lord, of	20	2	0	0	0	0	2	.100
B. Gilbert, 2b	17	4	0	0	0	1	1	.235	L. Cross, 3b	19	2	0	0	0	0	0	.105
D. McGann, 1b	17	4	2	0	0	1	4	.235	M. Cross, ss	17	3	0	0	0	0	0	.176
S. Mertes, of	17	3	1	0	0	2	3	.176	T. Hartsel, of	17	5	1	0	0	1	0	.294

(continued)

TABLE 14.10   (continued)

New York (N.L.) defeats Philadelphia (A.L.) 4 games to 1

Individual Batting

New York (N.L.) Player	AB	H	2B	3B	HR	R	RBI	BA	Philadelphia (A.L.) Player	AB	H	2B	3B	HR	R	RBI	BA
R. Bresnahan, c	16	5	2	0	0	3	1	.313	D. Murphy, 2b	16	3	1	0	0	0	0	.188
A. Devlin, 3b	16	4	1	0	0	0	1	.250	S. Seybold, of	16	2	0	0	0	0	0	.125
B. Dahlen, ss	15	0	0	0	0	1	1	.000	Schreckengost, c	9	2	1	0	0	2	0	.222
C. Mathewson, p	8	2	0	0	0	1	0	.250	M. Powers, c	7	1	1	0	0	0	0	.143
McGinnity, p.	5	0	0	0	0	0	0	.000	E. Plank, p	6	1	0	0	0	0	0	.167
S. Strang	1	0	0	0	0	0	0	.000	C Bender, p.	5	0	0	0	0	0	0	.000
									A. Coakley, p	2	0	0	0	0	0	0	.000
									D. Hoffman	1	0	0	0	0	0	0	.000

Errors: A. Devlin (2), M. Donlin (2), C. Mathewson, D. McGann

Errors: D. Murphy (4), L. Cross (2), M. Cross (2), T. Hartsel

Stolen bases: A. Devlin (3), B. Dahlen (2), G. Browne (2), M. Donlin (2), R. Bresnahan, B. Gilbert

Stolen bases: T. Hartsel (2)

Individual Pitching

New York (N.L.)	W	L	ERA	IP	H	BB	SO	SV	Philadelphia (A.L.)	W	L	ERA	IP	H	BB	SO	SV
C. Mathewson	3	0	0.00	27	14	1	18	0	C. Bender	1	1	1.06	17	9	6	13	0
McGinnity	1	1	0.00	17	10	3	6	0	E. Plank	0	2	1.59	17	14	4	11	0
R. Ames	0	1	0.00	1	1	1	1	0	A. Coakley	0	1	2.00	9	9	5	2	0

Source: Joseph L. Reichler, ed. *The Baseball Encyclopedia* (1979), 2718.

TABLE 14.11   WORLD SERIES, 1906

Chicago (A.L.) defeats Chicago (N.L.) 4 games to 2

Team Totals

	W	AB	H	2B	3B	HR	R	RBI	BA	BB	SO	ERA
CHI A	4	187	37	10	3	0	22	19	.198	18	35	1.67
CHI N	2	184	36	9	0	0	18	11	.196	18	27	3.40

Individual Batting

Chicago (A.L.) Player	AB	H	2B	3B	HR	R	RBI	BA	Chicago (N.L.) Player	AB	H	2B	3B	HR	R	RBI	BA
F. Isbell, 2b	26	8	4	0	0	4	4	.306	W. Schulte, of	26	7	3	0	0	1	3	.269
E. Hahn, of	22	6	0	0	0	4	0	.273	S. Hofman, of	23	7	1	0	0	3	2	.304
F. Jones, of	21	2	0	0	0	4	0	.095	F. Chance, 1b	21	5	1	0	0	3	0	.238
B. Sullivan, c	21	0	0	0	0	0	0	.000	J. Sheckard, of	21	0	0	0	0	0	1	.000
G. Rohe, 3b	21	7	1	2	0	2	4	.333	J. Evers, 2b	20	3	1	0	0	2	1	.150
P. Dougherty, of	20	2	0	0	0	1	1	.100	Steinfeldt, 3b	20	5	1	0	0	2	2	.250
J. Donahue, 1b	18	6	2	1	0	0	4	.333	J. Tinker, ss	18	3	0	0	0	4	1	.167
G. Davis, ss	13	4	3	0	0	4	6	.308	J. Kling, c	17	3	1	0	0	2	0	.176
L. Tannehill, ss	9	1	0	0	0	1	0	.111	T. Brown, p	6	2	0	0	0	0	0	.333
N. Altrock, p	4	1	0	0	0	0	0	.250	O. Overall, p	4	1	1	0	0	1	0	.250
E. Walsh, p	4	0	0	0	0	1	0	.000	E. Reulbach, p	3	0	0	0	0	0	1	.000
D. White, p	3	0	0	0	0	0	0	.000	P. Moran	2	0	0	0	0	0	0	.000
F. Owen, p	2	0	0	0	0	0	0	.000	J. Pfiester, p	2	0	0	0	0	0	0	.000
McFarland	1	0	0	0	0	0	0	.000	D. Gessler	1	0	0	0	0	0	0	.000
B. O'Neill, of	1	0	0	0	0	1	0	.000									
B. Towne	1	0	0	0	0	0	0	.000									

Errors: F. Isbell (5), G. Rohe (3), G. Davis (2), P. Dougherty, J. Donahue, E. Walsh, B. Sullivan

Errors: J. Tinker (2), J. Pfiester, J. Kling, J. Evers, T. Brown, Steinfeldt

Stolen bases: G. Rohe (2), P. Dougherty (2), F. Isbell, G. Davis

Stolen bases: J. Evers (2), F. Chance (2), J. Tinker (2), J. Sheckard, S. Hofman

Individual Pitching

Chicago (A.L.)	W	L	ERA	IP	H	BB	SO	SV	Chicago (N.L.)	W	L	ERA	IP	H	BB	SO	SV
N. Altrock	1	1	1.00	18	11	2	5	0	T. Brown	1	2	3.66	19.2	14	4	12	0
D. White	1	1	1.80	15	12	7	4	1	O. Overall	0	0	1.50	12	10	3	8	0
E. Walsh	2	0	1.80	15	7	6	17	0	E. Reulbach	1	0	2.45	11	6	8	4	0
F. Owen	0	0	3.00	6	6	3	2	0	J. Pfiester	0	2	6.10	10.1	7	3	11	0

Source: Joseph L. Reichler, ed. *The Baseball Encyclopedia* (1979), 2719.

TABLE 14.12   WORLD SERIES, 1907

Chicago (N.L.) defeats Detroit (A.L.) 4 games to 0

Team Totals

	W	AB	H	2B	3B	HR	R	RBI	BA	BB	SO	ERA
CHI N	4	167	43	6	1	0	19	16	.257	12	25	0.75
DET A	0	172	36	1	2	0	6	6	.209	9	22	1.96

Individual Batting

Chicago (N.L.) Player	AB	H	2B	3B	HR	R	RBI	BA	Detroit (A.L.) Player	AB	H	2B	3B	HR	R	RBI	BA
J. Slagle, of	22	6	0	0	0	3	4	.273	S. Crawford, of	21	5	1	0	0	1	2	.238
J. Sheckard, of	21	5	2	0	0	0	2	.238	G. Schaefer, 2b	21	3	0	0	0	1	0	.143
J. Evers, 2b, ss	20	7	2	0	0	2	1	.350	T. Cobb, of	20	4	0	1	0	1	1	.200
W. Schulte, of	20	5	0	0	0	3	2	.250	B. Coughlin, 3b	20	5	0	0	0	0	0	.250
J. Kling, c	19	4	0	0	0	2	1	.211	C. Rossman, 1b	20	8	0	1	0	1	2	.400
Steinfeldt, 3b	17	8	1	1	0	2	2	.471	D. Jones, of	17	6	0	0	0	1	0	.353
F. Chance, 1b	14	3	1	0	0	3	0	.214	C. O'Leary, ss	17	1	0	0	0	0	0	.059
J. Tinker, ss	13	2	0	0	0	4	1	.154	B. Schmidt, c	12	2	0	0	0	0	0	.167
D. Howard, 1b	5	1	0	0	0	0	0	.200	W. Donovan, p	8	0	0	0	0	0	0	.000
E. Reulbach, p	5	1	0	0	0	0	1	.200	G. Mullin, p	6	0	0	0	0	0	0	.000
O. Overall, p	5	1	0	0	0	0	2	.200	F. Payne, c	4	1	0	0	0	0	1	.250
T. Brown, p	3	0	0	0	0	0	0	.000	J. Archer, c	3	0	0	0	0	0	0	.000
J. Pfiester, p	2	0	0	0	0	0	0	.000	E. Killian, p	2	1	0	0	0	1	0	.500
H. Zimmerman, 2b	1	0	0	0	0	0	0	.000	E. Siever, p	1	0	0	0	0	0	0	.000
P. Moran	0	0	0	0	0	0	0	—									

Errors: J. Evers (3), J. Tinker (3), W. Schulte (2), J. Kling, J. Slagle

Errors: B. Coughlin (2), C. O'Leary (2), B. Schmidt (2), D. Jones, C. Rossman, F. Payne

Stolen bases: J. Slagle (6), J. Evers (3), F. Chance (3), J. Tinker (2), W. Schulte, D. Howard, J. Sheckard, Steinfeldt

Stolen bases: D. Jones (3), C. Rossman (2), B. Coughlin, G. Schaefer

Individual Pitching

Chicago (N.L.)	W	L	ERA	IP	H	BB	SO	SV	Detroit (A.L.)	W	L	ERA	IP	H	BB	SO	SV
O. Overall	1	0	1.00	18	14	4	11	0	W. Donovan	0	1	1.29	21	17	5	16	0
E. Reulbach	1	0	0.75	12	6	3	4	0	G. Mullin	0	2	2.12	17	16	6	7	0
T. Brown	1	0	0.00	9	7	1	4	0	E. Killian	0	0	2.25	4	3	1	1	0
J. Pfiester	1	0	1.00	9	9	1	3	0	E. Siever	0	1	4.50	4	7	0	1	0

Source: Joseph L. Reichler, ed. *The Baseball Encyclopedia* (1979), 2720.

TABLE 14.13 WORLD SERIES, 1908

Chicago (N.L.) defeats Detroit (A.L.) 4 games to 1

Team Totals												
	W	AB	H	2B	3B	HR	R	RBI	BA	BB	SO	ERA
CHI N	4	164	48	4	2	1	24	20	.293	13	26	2.60
DET A	1	158	32	5	0	0	15	14	.203	12	26	3.48

Individual Batting

Chicago (N.L.)									Detroit (A.L.)								
Player	AB	H	2B	3B	HR	R	RBI	BA	Player	AB	H	2B	3B	HR	R	RBI	BA
J. Sheckard, of	21	5	2	0	0	2	1	.238	S. Crawford, of	21	5	1	0	0	2	1	.238
J. Evers, 2b	20	7	1	0	0	5	2	.350	T. Cobb, of	19	7	1	0	0	3	4	.368
F. Chance, 1b	19	8	0	0	0	4	2	.421	C. Rossman, 1b	19	4	0	0	0	3	3	.211
S. Hofman, of	19	6	0	1	0	2	4	.316	C. O'Leary, ss	19	3	0	0	0	2	0	.158
J. Tinker, ss	19	5	0	0	1	2	5	.263	M. McIntyre, of	18	4	1	0	0	2	0	.222
W. Schulte, of	18	7	0	1	0	4	2	.389	G. Schaefer, 3b, 2b	16	2	0	0	0	0	0	.125
J. Kling, c	16	4	1	0	0	2	1	.250	B. Schmidt, c	14	1	0	0	0	0	1	.071
Steinfeldt, 3b	16	4	0	0	0	3	3	.250	B. Coughlin, 3b	8	1	0	0	0	0	1	.125
O. Overall, p	6	2	0	0	0	0	0	.333	R. Downs, 2b	6	1	1	0	0	1	1	.167
T. Brown, p	4	0	0	0	0	0	0	.000	E. Summers, p	5	1	0	0	0	0	1	.200
E. Reulbach, p	3	0	0	0	0	0	0	.000	W. Donovan, p	4	0	0	0	0	0	0	.000
J. Pfiester, p	2	0	0	0	0	0	0	.000	I. Thomas, c	4	2	1	0	0	0	1	.500
D. Howard	1	0	0	0	0	0	0	.000	G. Mullin, p	3	1	0	0	0	1	1	.333
									D Jones	2	0	0	0	0	1	0	.000

Errors: F. Chance (3), J. Evers, Steinfeldt	Errors: T. Cobb (2), C. Rossman (2), M. McIntyre, R. Downs, W. Donovan, B. Coughlin, G. Schaefer, C. O'Leary
Stolen bases: F. Chance (5), J. Evers (2), W. Schulte (2), S. Hofman (2), Steinfeldt, J. Sheckard, J. Tinker	Stolen bases: T. Cobb (2), M. McIntyre, W. Donovan

Individual Pitching

Chicago (N.L.)									Detroit (A.L.)							
	W	L	ERA	IP	H	BB	SO	SV		W	L	ERA	IP	H	BB	SO	SV
O. Overall	2	0	0.98	18.1	7	7	15	0	W. Donovan	0	2	4.24	17	17	4	10	0
T. Brown	2	0	0.00	11	6	1	5	0	E. Summers	0	2	4.30	14.2	18	4	7	0
J. Pfiester	0	1	7.88	8	10	3	1	0	G. Mullin	1	0	1.00	9	7	1	8	0
E. Reulbach	0	0	4.70	7.2	9	1	5	0	E. Killian	0	0	7.71	2.1	5	3	1	0
									G. Winter	0	0	0.00	1	1	1	0	0

Source: Joseph L. Reichler, ed. The Baseball Encyclopedia (1979), 2721.

TABLE 14.14 WORLD SERIES, 1909

Pittsburgh (N.L.) defeats Detroit (A.L.) 4 games to 3

Team Totals												
	W	AB	H	2B	3B	HR	R	RBI	BA	BB	SO	ERA
PIT N	4	223	49	13	1	2	34	25	.220	20	34	3.10
DET A	3	233	55	16	0	2	28	26	.236	20	22	3.10

Individual Batting

Pittsburgh (N.L.)									Detroit (A.L.)								
Player	AB	H	2B	3B	HR	R	RBI	BA	Player	AB	H	2B	3B	HR	R	RBI	BA
D. Miller, 2b	28	7	1	0	0	2	4	.250	D. Jones, of	30	7	0	0	1	6	2	.233
O. Wilson, of	26	4	1	0	0	2	1	.154	S. Crawford, of, 1b	28	7	3	0	1	4	3	.250
B. Abstein, 1b	26	6	2	0	0	3	2	.231	J. Delahanty, 2b	26	9	4	0	0	2	4	.346
T. Leach, of, 3b	25	8	4	0	0	8	2	.320	T. Cobb, of	26	6	3	0	0	3	6	.231
G. Gibson, c	25	6	2	0	0	2	2	.240	T. Jones, 1b	24	6	1	0	0	3	2	.250

Individual Batting

Pittsburgh (N.L.)									Detroit (A.L.)								
Player	AB	H	2B	3B	HR	R	RBI	BA	Player	AB	H	2B	3B	HR	R	RBI	BA
H. Wagner, ss	24	8	2	1	0	4	6	.333	D. Bush, ss	23	6	1	0	0	5	2	.261
B. Byrne, 3b	24	6	1	0	0	5	0	.250	G. Moriarty, 3b	22	6	1	0	0	4	1	.273
F. Clarke, of	19	4	0	0	2	7	7	.211	B. Schmidt, c	18	4	2	0	0	0	4	.222
B. Adams, p	9	0	0	0	0	0	0	.000	G. Mullin, p	16	3	1	0	0	1	0	.188
N. Maddox, p	4	0	0	0	0	0	0	.000	O. Stanage, c	5	1	0	0	0	0	2	.200
V. Willis, p	4	0	0	0	0	0	0	.000	W. Donovan, p	4	0	0	0	0	0	0	.000
H. Hyatt, of	4	0	0	0	0	1	1	.000	M. McIntyre, of	3	0	0	0	0	0	0	.000
P. O'Connor	1	0	0	0	0	0	0	.000	C. O'Leary, 3b	3	0	0	0	0	0	0	.000
L. Leifield, p	1	0	0	0	0	0	0	.000	E. Summers, p	3	0	0	0	0	0	0	.000
D. Phillippe, p	1	0	0	0	0	0	0	.000	E. Willett, p	2	0	0	0	0	0	0	.000
Abbaticchio	1	0	0	0	0	0	0	.000									
H. Camnitz, p	1	0	0	0	0	0	0	.000									

Errors: B. Abstein (5), D. Miller (3), D. Phillippe (2), H. Wagner (2), F. Clarke, B. Byrne, O. Wilson

Errors: D. Bush (5), B. Schmidt (5), J. Delahanty (2), S. Crawford (2), T. Cobb, D. Jones, W. Donovan, E. Willett, T. Jones

Stolen bases: H. Wagner (6), D. Miller (3), F. Clarke (3), G. Gibson (2), B. Byrne, B. Abstein, T. Leach, O. Wilson

Stolen bases: T. Cobb (2), D. Bush, T. Jones, D. Jones, S. Crawford

Individual Pitching

Pittsburgh (N.L.)									Detroit (A.L.)								
	W	L	ERA	IP	H	BB	SO	SV		W	L	ERA	IP	H	BB	SO	SV
B. Adams	3	0	1.33	27	18	6	11	0	G. Mullin	2	1	2.25	32	22	8	20	0
V. Willis	0	1	4.76	11.1	10	8	3	0	W. Donovan	1	1	3.00	12	7	8	7	0
N. Maddox	1	0	1.00	9	10	2	4	0	E. Summers	0	2	8.59	7.1	13	4	4	0
D. Phillippe	0	0	0.00	6	2	1	2	0	E. Willett	0	0	0.00	7.2	3	0	1	0
L. Leifield	0	1	11.25	4	7	1	0	0	R. Works	0	0	9.00	2	4	0	2	0
H. Camnitz	0	1	12.27	3.2	8	2	2	0									

Source: Joseph L. Reichler, ed. *The Baseball Encyclopedia* (1979), 2722.

TABLE 14.15   WORLD SERIES, 1910

Philadelphia (A.L.) defeats Chicago (N.L.) 4 games to 1

Team Totals

	W	AB	H	2B	3B	HR	R	RBI	BA	BB	SO	ERA
PHI A	4	177	56	19	1	1	35	29	.316	17	24	2.76
CHI N	1	158	35	11	1	0	15	13	.222	18	31	4.70

Individual Batting

Philadelphia (A.L.)									Chicago (N.L.)								
Player	AB	H	2B	3B	HR	R	RBI	BA	Player	AB	H	2B	3B	HR	R	RBI	BA
F. Baker, 3b	22	9	3	0	0	6	4	.409	Steinfeldt, 3b	20	2	1	0	0	0	1	.100
B. Lord, of	22	4	2	0	0	3	1	.182	J. Tinker, ss	18	6	2	0	0	2	0	.333
E. Collins, 2b	21	9	4	0	0	5	3	.429	F. Chance, 1b	17	6	1	1	0	1	4	.353
D. Murphy, of	20	7	3	0	1	6	8	.350	W. Schulte, of	17	6	3	0	0	3	2	.353
A. Strunk, of	18	5	1	1	0	2	2	.278	H. Zimmerman, 2b	17	4	1	0	0	0	2	.235
J. Barry, ss	17	4	2	0	0	3	3	.235	S. Hofman, of	15	4	0	0	0	2	2	.267
H. Davis, 1b	17	6	3	0	0	5	2	.353	J. Sheckard, of	14	4	2	0	0	5	1	.286
J. Coombs, p	13	5	1	0	0	0	3	.385	J. King, c	13	1	0	0	0	0	1	.077
L. Thomas, c	12	3	0	0	0	2	1	.250	J. Archer, 1b, c	11	2	1	0	0	1	0	.182
C. Bender, p	6	2	0	0	0	1	1	.333	T. Brown, p	7	0	0	0	0	0	0	.000
T. Hartsel, of	5	1	0	0	0	2	0	.200	G. Beaumont	2	0	0	0	0	1	0	.000
J. Lapp, c	4	1	0	0	0	0	1	.250	K. Cole, p	2	0	0	0	0	0	0	.000
									J. Pfiester, p	2	0	0	0	0	0	0	.000
									H. McIntyre, p	1	0	0	0	0	0	0	.000
									O. Overall, p	1	0	0	0	0	0	0	.000

(continued)

TABLE 14.15 (continued)

Philadelphia (A.L.) defeats Chicago (N.L.) 4 games to 1

Individual Batting																	
Philadelphia (A.L.)									Chicago (N.L.)								
Player	AB	H	2B	3B	HR	R	RBI	BA	Player	AB	H	2B	3B	HR	R	RBI	BA
									T. Needham	1	0	0	0	0	0	0	.000
									J. Kane	0	0	0	0	0	0	0	—

Errors: F. Baker (3), H. Davis (3), J. Coombs (2), A. Strunk, E. Collins, I. Thomas

Errors: Steinfeldt (4), J. Tinker (2), T. Brown, H. McIntyre, S. Hofman, J. Sheckard, W. Schulte, H. Zimmerman

Stolen bases: E. Collins (4), T. Hartsel (2), D. Murphy

Stolen bases: H. Zimmerman, J. Tinker, J. Sheckard

Individual Pitching																	
Philadelphia (A.L.)									Chicago (N.L.)								
	W	L	ERA	IP	H	BB	SO	SV		W	L	ERA	IP	H	BB	SO	SV
J. Coombs	3	0	3.33	27	23	14	17	0	T. Brown	1	2	5.00	18	23	7	14	0
C. Bender	1	1	1.93	18.2	12	4	14	0	K. Cole	0	0	3.38	8	10	3	5	0
									J. Pfiester	0	0	0.00	6.2	9	1	1	0
									H. McIntyre	0	1	6.75	5.1	4	3	3	0
									O. Overall	0	1	9.00	3	6	1	1	0
									E. Reulbach	0	0	13.50	2	3	2	0	0
									I. Richie	0	0	0.00	1	1	0	0	0

Source: Joseph L. Reichler, ed. *The Baseball Encyclopedia* (1979), 2723.

TABLE 14.16   WORLD SERIES, 1911

Pittsburgh (A.L.) defeats New York (N.L.) 4 games to 2

Team Totals												
	W	AB	H	2B	3B	HR	R	RBI	BA	BB	SO	ERA
PHI A	4	205	50	15	0	3	27	20	.244	4	31	1.29
NY N	2	189	33	11	1	0	13	10	.175	14	44	2.83

Individual Batting																	
Philadelphia (A.L.)									New York (N.L.)								
Player	AB	H	2B	3B	HR	R	RBI	BA	Player	AB	H	2B	3B	HR	R	RBI	BA
B. Lord, of	27	5	2	0	0	2	1	.185	J. DeVore, of	24	4	1	0	0	1	3	.167
R. Oldring, of	25	5	2	0	1	2	3	.200	L. Doyle, 2b	23	7	3	1	0	3	1	.304
F. Baker, 3b	24	9	2	0	2	7	5	.375	A. Fletcher, ss	23	3	1	0	0	1	1	.130
H. Davis, 1b	24	5	1	0	0	3	5	.208	B. Herzog, 3b	21	4	2	0	0	3	0	.190
D. Murphy, of	23	7	3	0	0	4	2	.304	R. Murray, of	21	0	0	0	0	0	0	.000
E. Collins, 2b	21	6	1	0	0	4	1	.286	C. Meyers, c	20	6	2	0	0	2	2	.300
J. Barry, ss	19	7	4	0	0	2	2	.368	F. Merkle, 1b	20	3	1	0	0	1	1	.150
L. Thomas, c	12	1	0	0	0	1	1	.083	F. Snodgrass, of	19	2	0	0	0	1	1	.105
C. Bender, p	11	1	0	0	0	0	0	.091	C. Mathewson, p	7	2	0	0	0	0	0	.286
J. Coombs, p	8	2	0	0	0	1	0	.250	B. Becker	3	0	0	0	0	0	0	.000
J. Lapp, c	8	2	0	0	0	1	0	.250	R. Ames, p	2	1	0	0	0	0	0	.500
E. Plank, p	3	0	0	0	0	0	0	.000	D. Crandall, p	2	1	1	0	0	1	1	.500
S. McInnis, 1b	0	0	0	0	0	0	0	—	R. Marquard, p	2	0	0	0	0	0	0	.000
A. Strunk	0	0	0	0	0	0	0	—	H. Wiltse, p	1	0	0	0	0	0	0	.000
									A. Wilson, c	1	0	0	0	0	0	0	.000

Errors: E. Collins (4), J. Barry (3), F. Baker (2), D. Murphy, R. Oldring

Errors: A. Fletcher (4), B. Herzog (3), R. Murray (3), F. Merkel (2), R. Ames, L. Doyle, J. DeVore, C. Mathewson

Stolen bases: E. Collins (2), J. Barry (2)

Stolen bases: B. Herzog (2), L. Doyle (2)

Individual Pitching

	W	L	ERA	IP	H	BB	SO	SV		W	L	ERA	IP	H	BB	SO	SV
			Philadelphia (A.L.)									New York (N.L.)					
C. Bender	2	1	1.04	26	16	8	20	0	C. Mathewson	1	2	2.00	27	25	2	13	0
J. Coombs	1	0	1.35	20	11	6	16	0	R. Marquard	0	1	1.54	11.2	9	1	8	0
E. Plank	1	1	1.86	9.2	6	0	8	0	R. Ames	0	1	2.25	8	6	1	6	0
									D. Crandall	1	0	0.00	4	2	0	2	0
									H. Wiltse	0	0	18.90	3.1	8	0	2	0

Source: Joseph L. Reichler, ed. *The Baseball Encyclopedia* (1979), 2724.

TABLE 14.17   WORLD SERIES, 1912

Boston (A.L.) defeats New York (N.L.) 4 games to 3

Team Totals

	W	AB	H	2B	3B	HR	R	RBI	BA	BB	SO	ERA
BOS A	4	273	60	14	6	1	25	21	.220	19	36	2.92
NY N	3	274	74	14	4	1	31	25	.270	22	39	1.83

Individual Batting

Player	AB	H	2B	3B	HR	R	RBI	BA	Player	AB	H	2B	3B	HR	R	RBI	BA
			Boston (A.L.)									New York (N.L.)					
J. Stahl, 1b	32	9	2	0	0	3	2	.281	L. Doyle, 2b	33	8	1	0	1	5	2	.242
D. Lewis, of	32	5	3	0	0	4	2	.156	F. Merkle, 1b	33	9	2	1	0	5	3	.273
S. Yerkes, 2b	32	8	0	2	0	3	4	.250	F. Snodgrass, of	33	7	2	0	0	2	2	.212
H. Hooper, of	31	9	2	1	0	3	2	.290	R. Murray, of	31	10	4	1	0	5	5	.323
T. Speaker, of	30	9	1	2	0	4	2	.300	B. Herzog, 3b	30	12	4	1	0	6	4	.400
H. Wagner, ss	30	5	1	0	0	1	0	.167	A. Fletcher, ss	28	5	1	0	0	1	3	.179
L. Gardner, 3b	28	5	2	1	1	4	4	.179	C. Meyers, c	28	10	0	1	0	2	3	.357
H. Cady, c	22	3	0	0	0	1	1	.136	J. DeVore, of	24	6	0	0	0	4	0	.250
S. Wood, p	7	2	0	0	0	1	1	.286	C. Mathewson, p	12	2	0	0	0	0	0	.167
B. Carrigan, c	7	0	0	0	0	0	0	.000	J. Tesreau, p	8	3	0	0	0	0	2	.375
H. Bedient, p	6	0	0	0	0	0	0	.000	B. Becker, of	4	0	0	0	0	1	0	.000
R. Collins, p	5	0	0	0	0	0	0	.000	R. Marquard, p	4	0	0	0	0	0	0	.000
C. Hall, p	4	3	1	0	0	0	0	.750	McCormick	4	1	0	0	0	0	1	.250
C. Engle	3	1	1	0	0	1	2	.333	D. Crandall, p	1	0	0	0	0	0	0	.000
B. O'Brien, p	2	0	0	0	0	0	0	.000	A. Wilson, c	1	1	0	0	0	0	0	1.000
N. Ball	1	0	0	0	0	0	0	.000	T. Shafer, ss	0	0	0	0	0	0	0	—
O. Henriksen	1	1	1	0	0	0	1	1.000									

Errors: L. Gardner (4), H. Wagner (3), T. Speaker (2), H. Cady, J. Stahl, D. Lewis, C. Hall, S. Yerkes	**Errors:** L. Doyle (4), A. Fletcher (4), F. Merkle (3), J. DeVore (2), R. Marquard, C. Meyers, A. Wilson, F. Snodgrass
Stolen bases: H. Hooper (2), J. Stahl (2), T. Speaker, H. Wagner	**Stolen bases:** J. DeVore (4), B. Herzog (2), L. Doyle (2), F. Merkle, A. Fletcher, F. Snodgrass, C. Meyers

Individual Pitching

	W	L	ERA	IP	H	BB	SO	SV		W	L	ERA	IP	H	BB	SO	SV
			Boston (A.L.)									New York (N.L.)					
S. Wood	3	1	3.68	22	27	3	21	0	C. Mathewson	0	2	1.57	28.2	23	5	10	0
H. Bedient	1	0	0.50	18	10	7	7	0	J. Tesreau	1	2	3.13	23	19	11	15	0
R. Collins	0	0	1.88	14.1	14	0	6	0	R. Marquard	2	0	0.50	18	14	2	9	0
C. Hall	0	0	3.38	10.2	11	9	1	0	D. Crandall	0	0	0.00	2	1	0	2	0
B. O'Brien	0	2	7.00	9	12	3	4	0	R. Ames	0	0	4.50	2	3	1	0	0

Source: Joseph L. Reichler, ed. *The Baseball Encyclopedia* (1979), 2725.

TABLE 14.18 WORLD SERIES, 1913

Philadelphia (A.L.) defeats New York (N.L.) 4 games to 1

Team Totals												
	W	AB	H	2B	3B	HR	R	RBI	BA	BB	SO	ERA
PHI A	4	174	46	4	4	2	23	21	.264	7	16	2.15
NY N	1	164	33	3	1	1	15	15	.201	8	19	3.60

Individual Batting

Philadelphia (A.L.)									New York (N.L.)								
Player	AB	H	2B	3B	HR	R	RBI	BA	Player	AB	H	2B	3B	HR	R	RBI	BA
E. Murphy, of	22	5	0	0	0	2	0	.227	L. Doyle, 2b	20	3	0	0	0	1	2	.150
R. Oldring, of	22	6	0	1	0	5	0	.273	G. Burns, of	19	3	2	0	0	2	1	.158
J. Barry, ss	20	6	3	0	0	3	2	.300	B. Herzog, 3b	19	1	0	0	0	1	0	.053
F. Baker, 3b	20	9	0	0	1	2	7	.450	T. Shafer, 3b, of	19	3	1	1	0	2	1	.158
E. Collins, 2b	19	8	0	2	0	5	3	.421	A. Fletcher, ss	18	5	0	0	0	1	4	.278
S. McInnis, 1b	17	2	1	0	0	1	2	.118	R. Murray, of	16	4	0	0	0	2	1	.250
A. Strunk of	17	2	0	0	0	3	0	.118	F. Merkle, 1b	13	3	0	0	1	3	3	.231
W. Schang, c	14	5	0	1	1	2	6	.357	L. McLean, c	12	6	0	0	0	0	2	.500
C. Bender, p	8	0	0	0	0	0	1	.000	C. Mathewson, p	5	3	0	0	0	1	1	.600
E. Plank, p	7	1	0	0	0	0	0	.143	D. Crandall, p	4	0	0	0	0	0	0	.000
J. Bush, p	4	1	0	0	0	0	0	.250	C. Meyers, c	4	0	0	0	0	0	0	.000
J. Lapp, c	4	1	0	0	0	0	0	.250	A. Wilson, c	3	0	0	0	0	0	0	.000
									F. Snodgrass, 1b, of	3	1	0	0	0	0	0	.333
									McCormick	2	1	0	0	0	1	0	.500
									H. Wiltse, 1b	2	0	0	0	0	0	0	.000
									J. Tesreau, p	2	0	0	0	0	0	0	.000
									A. Demaree, p	1	0	0	0	0	0	0	.000
									E. Grant	1	0	0	0	0	1	0	.000
									R. Marquard, p	1	0	0	0	0	0	0	.000
									C. Cooper	0	0	0	0	0	0	0	—

Errors: F. Baker, W. Schang, E. Plank, E. Collins, J. Barry

Errors: L. Doyle (3), F. Merkel (2), G. Burns, A. Fletcher

Stolen bases: E. Collins (3), F. Baker, R. Oldring

Stolen bases: R. Murray (2), G. Burns, A. Fletcher, C. Cooper

Individual Pitching

Philadelphia (A.L.)									New York (N.L.)								
	W	L	ERA	IP	H	BB	SO	SV		W	L	ERA	IP	H	BB	SO	SV
E. Plank	1	1	0.95	19	9	3	7	0	C. Mathewson	1	1	0.95	19	14	2	7	0
C. Bender	2	0	4.00	18	19	1	9	0	R. Marquard	0	1	7.00	9	10	3	3	0
J. Bush	1	0	1.00	9	5	4	3	0	J. Tesreau	0	1	5.40	8.1	11	1	4	0
									D. Crandall	0	0	3.86	4.2	4	0	2	0
									A. Demaree	0	1	4.50	4	7	1	0	0

Source: Joseph L. Reichler, ed. *The Baseball Encyclopedia* (1979), 2726.

TABLE 14.19 MOST VALUABLE PLAYER AWARD WINNERS

National League					
Year	Name	Team	HRs	RBIs	Avg.
1911	Frank Schulte	Chicago Cubs	21	121	.300
1912	Larry Doyle	N.Y. Giants	10	90	.330
1913	Jake Daubert	Brooklyn Dodgers	2	52	.350
American League					
Year	Name	Team	HRs	RBIs	Avg.
1911	Ty Cobb	Detroit Tigers	8	144	.420
1912	Tris Speaker	Boston Red Sox	10	98	.383
1913	Walter Johnson (P)	Washington Senators	36W	7L	1.09 ERA

Source: Wright, *The Universal Almanac 1991* (1990), 613.

TABLE 14.20 .400 HITTERS—SINCE 1901

100 or more games

Year	Player	Team/League	Avg.
1901	Nap Lajoie	Philadelphia (AL)	.422
1911	Ty Cobb	Detroit (AL)	.420
1911	Joe Jackson	Cleveland (AL)	.408
1912	Ty Cobb	Detroit (AL)	.410

Source: Joseph L. Reichler, ed., *The Baseball Encyclopedia* (1979), 82.

TABLE 14.21 BATTING CHAMPIONS

National League

Year	Name	Team	Avg.
1876	Roscoe Barnes	Chicago Cubs	.403
1877	James White	Boston Braves	.385
1878	Abner Dalrymple	Milwaukee Brewers	.356
1879	Cap Anson	Chicago Cubs	.407
1880	George Gore	Chicago Cubs	.365
1881	Cap Anson	Chicago Cubs	.399
1882	Dan Brouthers	Buffalo Bisons	.367
1883	Dan Brouthers	Buffalo Bisons	.371
1884	Jim O'Rourke	Buffalo Bisons	.350
1885	Roger Connor	N.Y. Giants	.371
1886	Mike Kelly	Chicago Cubs	.388
1887	Cap Anson	Chicago Cubs	.421
1888	Cap Anson	Chicago Cubs	.343
1889	Dan Brouthers	Boston Braves	.373
1890	Jack Glasscock	N.Y. Giants	.336
1891	Billy Hamilton	Philadelphia Phillies	.338
1892	"Cupid" Childs	Cleveland Spiders	.335
	Dan Brouthers	Brooklyn Dodgers	.335
1893	Hugh Duffy	Boston Braves	.378
1894	Hugh Duffy	Boston Braves	.438
1895	Jesse Burkett	Cleveland Spiders	.423
1896	Jesse Burkett	Cleveland Spiders	.410
1897	Willie Keeler	Baltimore Orioles	.432
1898	Willie Keeler	Baltimore Orioles	.379
1899	Ed Delahanty	Philadelphia Phillies	.408
1900	Honus Wagner	Pittsburgh Pirates	.380
1901	Jesse Burkett	St. Louis Cardinals	.382
1902	C. H. Beaumont	Pittsburgh Pirates	.357
1903	Honus Wagner	Pittsburgh Pirates	.355
1904	Honus Wagner	Pittsburgh Pirates	.349
1905	J. Bentley Seymour	Cincinnati Reds	.377
1906	Honus Wagner	Pittsburgh Pirates	.339
1907	Honus Wagner	Pittsburgh Pirates	.350
1908	Honus Wagner	Pittsburgh Pirates	.354
1909	Honus Wagner	Pittsburgh Pirates	.339
1910	Sherwood Magee	Philadelphia Phillies	.331
1911	Honus Wagner	Pittsburgh Pirates	.334
1912	Heinie Zimmerman	Chicago Cubs	.372
1913	Jake Daubert	Brooklyn Dodgers	.350

American League

Year	Player	Team	Avg.
1901	Nap Lajoie	Philadelphia A's	.422
1902	Ed Delahanty	Washington Senators	.376
1903	Nap Lajoie	Cleveland Indians	.355
1904	Nap Lajoie	Cleveland Indians	.381
1905	Elmer Flick	Cleveland Indians	.306
1906	George Stone	St. Louis Browns	.358
1907	Ty Cobb	Detroit Tigers	.350
1908	Ty Cobb	Detroit Tigers	.324
1909	Ty Cobb	Detroit Tigers	.377
1910	Ty Cobb	Detroit Tigers	.385
1911	Ty Cobb	Detroit Tigers	.420
1912	Ty Cobb	Detroit Tigers	.410
1913	Ty Cobb	Detroit Tigers	.390

Source: Wright, *The Universal Almanac 1991*, 612–13.

TABLE 14.22 PITCHING CHAMPIONS

National League

Year	Player	W.	L.	Pct.
1876	A. G. Spalding, Chi.	47	14	.770
1877	Thomas Bond, Bost.	31	17	.646
1878	Thomas Bond, Bost.	40	19	.678
1879	John M. Ward, Prov.	44	18	.710
1880	Fred Goldsmith, Chi.	22	3	.880
1881	Larry Corcoran, Chi.	31	14	.689
1882	Larry Corcoran, Chi.	27	13	.675
1883	Jim McCormick, Cleve.	27	13	.675
1884	Charles Radbourne, Prov.	60	12	.833
1885	John Clarkson, Chi.	52	16	.765
1886	John Flynn, Chi.	24	6	.800
1887	Charles Getzein, Detroit	29	13	.690
1888	Tim Keefe, N.Y.	35	12	.745
1889	John Clarkson, Bost.	48	19	.716
1890	Tom Lovett, Bklyn.	32	11	.744
1891	John Ewing, N.Y.	22	8	.733
1892	Cy Young, Cleve.	36	10	.783
1893	Henry Gastright, Bost.	15	5	.750
1894	Jouett Meekin, N.Y.	35	11	.761
1895	Willie Hoffer, Balt.	31	7	.816
1896	Willie Hoffer, Balt.	26	7	.788
1897	Amos Rusie, N.Y.	28	8	.778
1898	Ed Lewis, Bost.	25	8	.758
1899	Jay Hughes, Bklyn.	25	5	.833
1900	Joe McGinnity, Bklyn.	20	6	.769
1901	Sam Leever, Pitt.	19	5	.737
1902	Jack Chesbro, Pitt.	28	6	.824
1903	Sam Leever, Pitt.	25	7	.781
1904	Joe McGinnity, N.Y.	35	8	.814
1905	Sam Leever, Pitt.	20	5	.800
1906	Ed Ruelbach, Chi.	19	4	.826
1907	Ed Ruelbach, Chi.	17	4	.810
1908	Ed Reulbach, Chi.	24	7	.774
1909	S. H. Camnitz, Pitt.	25	6	.806
1909	C. Mathewson, N.Y.	25	6	.806
1910	Deacon Phillippe, Pitt.	14	2	.875
1911	Rube Marquard, N.Y.	24	7	.744
1912	C. R. Hendrix, Pitt.	24	9	.774
1913	Grover Alexander, Phila.	22	8	.733

American League

Year	Player	W.	L.	Pct.
1901	Clark Griffith, Chi.	24	7	.774
1902	Rube Waddell, Phila.	23	7	.767
1903	Earl L. Moore, Cleve.	22	7	.759
1904	Jack Chesbro, N.Y.	41	13	.759
1905	Rube Waddell, Phila.	27	10	.730
1906	Eddie Plank, Phila.	19	6	.760
1907	Bill Donovan, Det.	25	4	.862
1908	Ed Walsh, Chi.	40	15	.727
1909	George Mullin, Det.	29	8	.784
1910	Chief Bender, Phila.	23	5	.821
1911	S. A. Gregg. Cleve.	23	7	.767
1912	Joe Wood, Bost.	34	5	.872
1913	Walter Johnson, Wash.	36	7	.837

Source: Frank G. Menke, *The Encyclopedia of Sports* (1969), 77.

TABLE 14.23 WINNERS OF 300 OR MORE GAMES

Player	Years	Won	Lost	Winning %
Charles Radbourne[a]	11	310	191	.619
Mickey Welch[a]	13	316	214	.596
John W. Clarkson[a]	11	328	176	.651
Denton T. "Cy" Young	22	511	313	.620
Charles "Kid" Nichols	15	360	203	.639

Sources: Wright, *The Universal Almanac 1991* (1990), 613; Frank G. Menke, *The Encyclopedia of Sports* (1969).
[a] Pitched in era when distance to plate was 50 feet. Distance changed to 60½ feet in 1893. Nichols' career began 1890, ended 1906. Young's career began in 1890 and ended 1911.

TABLE 14.24 MAJOR LEAGUE BASEBALL ATTENDANCE, 1901–1913

Year	American League	National League	World Series
1901	1,684,000	1,920,000	. . .
1905	3,121,000	2,734,000	92,000
1910	3,271,000	3,495,000	124,000
1913	3,527,000	2,832,000	151,000

Source: *Historical Statistics of the United States, Colonial Times to 1970,* (1975), Part 1, 400.

never really supported the idea. In 1901, the American League began operation, and the two leagues engaged in bidding wars for the top players. In 1903, Pittsburgh in the National League and Boston in the American League, certain winners of the pennant in their leagues, reached a private agreement to hold a "World Series" in October. It was a surprise to many when the newer American League won the title.

Still no agreement existed to play such a series every year, and in 1904, the New York Giants refused to meet the Boston club, likely due to the personal animus of John McGraw against American League president Ban Johnson. The baseball public clamored for a series, however, and in 1905, Giants owner John Brush proposed rules governing a mandatory series to be played each year. With only minor changes, these rules still stand.

TABLE 14.25 NO-HIT GAMES, 1900–1913

The dream of every baseball pitcher is to pitch a game in which he holds the opposition to no hits and no runs and does not permit a man to reach first base—a perfect game. During these years, 1900–13, only two pitchers achieved the feat: Cy Young of the Boston Americans against Philadelphia, May 5, 1904; and Addie Joss, Cleveland Americans against Chicago, October, 1908. Slightly less spectacular but still formidable is the no-hitter, in which the pitcher does not allow a base hit, although a runner or runners may reach base by other means.

Year	Pitcher	Score
1901	Christopher Mathewson, New York, vs. St. Louis NL, Jul. 15	5–0
	Earl L. Moore, Cleveland, vs. Chicago AL, May 9. Moore pitched 9 innings, Chicago not making a hit in that time, but Cleveland lost in the 10th	2–4
1902	James J. Callahan, Chicago, vs. Detroit AL, Sep. 20 (1st game)	3–0
1903	Charles Fraser, Philadelphia, vs. Chicago NL, Sep. 18	10–0

Year	Pitcher	Score
1904	Cy Young, Boston, vs. Philadelphia AL, May 5	3–0
	Jesse N. Tannenhill, Boston, vs. Chicago AL, Aug. 17	6–0
1905	Robert K. Wicker, Chicago, vs. New York NL, Jun. 11, 12 innings; Mertes, NY, made a single in the 10th	1–0
	Christopher Mathewson, New York, vs. Chicago NL, Jun. 13	1–0
	Weldon Henley, Philadelphia, vs. St. Louis AL, Jul. 22 (1st game)	6–0
	William H. Dinneen, Boston, vs. Chicago AL, Sep. 27 (1st game)	2–0
	Frank E. Smith, Chicago, vs. Detroit AL, Sep. 6 (2d game)	15–0
1906	John C. Lush, Philadelphia, vs. Brooklyn NL, May 1	1–0
	Malcolm W. Eason, Brooklyn, vs. St. Louis NL, Jul. 20	2–0
1907	Frank X. Pfeffer, Boston, vs. Cincinnati NL, May 8	6–0
	Nicholas Maddox, Pittsburgh, vs. Brooklyn NL, Sep. 20	2–1
1908	Cy Young, Boston, vs. New York AL, Jun. 30	8–0
	George N. Rucker, Brooklyn, vs. Boston NL, Sep. 5 (2d game)	6–0
	Robert S. Rhoades, Cleveland, vs. Boston AL, Sep. 18	2–0
	Frank E. Smith, Chicago, vs. Philadelphia AL, Sep. 20	1–0
	Adrian C. Joss, Cleveland, vs. Chicago AL, Oct. 2	1–0
1909	Leon K. Ames, New York, vs. Brooklyn NL, Apr. 15. Ames pitched 9 innings, Brooklyn not making a hit in that time, but New York lost in the 13th	0–3
1910	Adrian C. Joss, Cleveland, vs. Chicago AL, Apr. 20	1–0
	Charles A. Bender, Philadelphia, vs. Cleveland AL, May 12	4–0
	Thomas J. Hughes, New York, vs. Cleveland AL, Aug. 30. Highes pitched 9 innings, Cleveland not making a hit in that time. Cleveland made its first hit in the 10th and won in the 11th	0–5
1911	Joseph Wood, Boston, vs. St. Louis AL, Jul. 29, (1st game)	5–0
	Edward A. Walsh, Chicago, vs. Boston AL, Aug. 27	5–0
1912	George E. Mullin, Detroit, vs. St. Louis AL, Jul. 4 (P.M.)	7–0
	Earl Hamilton, St. Louis, vs. Detroit AL, Aug. 30	5–1
	Charles M. Tesreau, New York, vs. Philadelphia NL, Sep. 6 (1st game)	3–0

Source: Frank G. Menke, *The Encyclopedia of Sports* (1969), 79.

Basketball

Basketball is the only major sport devised in the United States with no origins in the sports of other countries. Football evolved from rugby and soccer; hockey was first played by Canadian soldiers; Scottish shepherds sliced the first golf balls; and French clerics first double-faulted in tennis. But basketball is really America's game.

Invented by Dr. James Naismith, the first basketball game was played on December 21, 1891, at the Young Men's Christian Association, Springfield, Massachusetts (now home of the Basketball Hall of Fame). Naismith asked a janitor to find two wooden boxes to use as goals for the new game, and the janitor, Pop Stebbins, brought him two peach baskets, which he hung at a height of 10 feet at each end of the training gymnasium.

TABLE 14.26 BASKETBALL CHAMPIONS

Eastern League (Ivy)				
Year	Team	W.	L.	Pct
1902	Yale	5	3	.675
1903	Yale	7	3	.700
1904	Columbia	10	0	1.000
1905	Columbia	8	0	1.000
1906	Pennsylvania	9	1	.900
1907	Yale	9	1	.900
1908	Pennsylvania	8	0	1.000
1909–10	No competition			
1911	Columbia	7	1	.875
1912	Columbia	8	2	.800
1913	Cornell	7	1	.875

Big Ten				
Year	Team	W.	L.	Pct.
1906	Minnesota	7	1	.875
1907	Chicago, Wisconsin, Minnesota	6	2	.750
1908	Chicago	8	1	.888
1909	Chicago	12	0	1.000
1910	Chicago	9	3	.750
1911	Purdue, Minnesota	8	4	.667
1912	Wisconsin, Purdue	12	0	1.000
1913	Wisconsin	12	0	1.000

Missouri Valley				
Year	Team	W.	L.	Pct.
1908	Kansas	7	2	.778
1909	Kansas	10	2	.833
1910	Kansas	13	1	.929
1911	Kansas	10	2	.833
1912	Kansas, Nebraska	10	2	.833
1913	Nebraska	10	5	.667

Source: Menke, *The Encyclopedia of Sports,* 155–56.

Naismith was a Canadian, orphaned at age nine, a school dropout by 15. As a lumberjack, he began to drink heavily but finally gave up the bottle and graduated from high school at age twenty. He went on to earn doctorates in medicine and divinity and a master's degree in physical education. Family members remember him as a firm Presbyterian minister, a kind and gentle man with a stocky, five-feet eight-inch build, sturdy forearms, and a mustache. Naismith's purpose in inventing the game was to encourage sportsmanship and occupy the winter months. He was not interested in money and once turned down a substantial sum of money for a cigarette endorsement.

Twelve of Naismith's thirteen original rules are still basic, although the game has changed greatly. The peach baskets were replaced quickly by metal ones, and in 1906, the open-hoop basket, like the one used today, was introduced. Another rule change probably saved the game: Originally, rules gave possession to the first team to touch a ball after it went out of bounds. When players trampled spectators trying to touch the ball, some schools erected chicken wire at courtside to protect players and fans from one another before the rule was changed to give the ball to the team who had not knocked it out of play. Backboards were introduced also to keep overzealous spectators from interfering with the game. The rules of basketball did not become standardized until 1934.

As a college sport, basketball's rise to prominence occurred after the Victorian Era. Early college leagues consisted only of the Ivy, Big Ten, and Missouri Valley leagues. Professional basketball on a large scale did not develop until well after World War II.

Bicycling

Different types of bicycles had been in use before the introduction in the 1870s of the "high-wheeler," a vehicle with a six-foot-high front wheel but a small back wheel. Riding the high-wheeler took skill, balance, and daring—the high-wheeler was also called the "bone crusher." Few women could ride it because women's clothes, especially the full skirt, made it almost impossible.

In 1884, John Kemp Stanley designed a "safety" bicycle that made bicycle riding a sport for everyone. It had two wheels of equal size joined by a tubular frame. By 1887, the Victor, a safety bicycle with a dropped frame and no crossbar, appeared for women, increasing the number of women who rode for pleasure. Pneumatic tires, enclosed gears, and coaster brakes completed the changes that relegated the high-wheeler to the museum. On Sundays, the streets were full of bicyclers, many of them women in candy-striped blouses, sporty broad-brimmed hats, and full skirts. By 1888, 50,000 men and women cycled in America. The enthusiasm for this sport/exercise continued. In 1890, 312 U.S. firms were manufacturing 10 million bicycles.

Some moralists condemned the sport for promoting casual relations between members of the opposite sex. Young men and women might leave home in groups for a Sunday ride and then strike up acquaintanceships in parks, away from parents and chaperones. Some worried preachers feared no end to the evils of bicycling.

Despite being far less costly to buy and maintain than a horse, the bicycle was still not inexpensive. In the 1890s, Chicago cyclists could buy a Columbia (Pope Manufacturing Company) or A. G. Spal-

Bicyclemania struck America in the late nineteenth century. More than 10 million enthusiasts learned to ride in the 1880s and 1890s. The League of American Wheelmen formed to exclude professionals hired by bicycle manufacturers from competing in amateur races. Soon 100,000 cyclists were members. Pictured here is a bicycle parade at Hartford, Connecticut, on Main Street looking north from Exchange Corner 1885. Courtesy Prints and Photographs Division, Library of Congress)

ding bicycle for $90. Used bicycles could be found for $35 to $50.

Cycle clubs sprang up with the craze. By 1895, 500 clubs in Chicago, each with its own colors and uniform, organized endurance rides and competitive events. Reading rooms, group outings, and social events were other benefits of membership. The Hermes Club charged a five-dollar initiation fee and dues of fifty cents per month. Most clubs were for cycling and socializing; a few became political lobby groups. The League of American Wheelmen, founded in 1881, lobbied on a national level for better roads and highways.

Boxing

Jack Johnson (John Arthur Johnson): b. Galveston, Texas, March 31, 1878; d. Raleigh, North Carolina, June 10, 1946.

Jack Johnson overcame poverty early in his life and battled racial prejudice throughout his career to become the first black heavyweight boxing champion of the world. He learned to box at a Galveston athletic club. In 1901, he was jailed for participating in an illegal prizefight. Between 1902 and 1908, he fought all over the United States, losing only three bouts.

No white boxer would fight him until the Canadian Tommy Burns agreed to meet him in Sydney, Australia, on December 26, 1908. Police stopped the bout in the fourteenth round to save Burns from further punishment. The win rankled many white Americans, and Johnson exacerbated the hatred of him by gleefully besting every white fighter who fought him. Tragically lacking in discretion, Johnson flaunted his white mistress (later wife) at a time when crossing the color line, especially sexually, was an excuse for lynchings.

In this scene, sailors are shown watching a boxing match on the ship *New York,* July 3, 1899, probably fought by their peers. (Courtesy Prints and Photographs Division, Library of Congress)

TABLE 14.27   BOXING CHAMPIONS

Heavyweights (over 195 lb.)	
Year	Name
1882–92	John L. Sullivan
1892–97	James. J. Corbett
1897–99	Robert Fitzsimmons
1899–1905	James J. Jeffries
1905–06	Marvin Hart
1906–08	Tommy Burns
1908–15	Jack Johnson

Light Heavyweights (175–194 lb.)	
Year	Name
1903	Jack Root, George Gardner
1903–05	Bob Fitzsimmons
1905–12	Philadelphia Jack O'Brien
1912–16	Jack Dillon

Middleweights (160–174 lb.)	
Year	Name
1884–91	Jack "Nonpareil" Dempsey
1891–97	Bob Fitzsimmons
1897–1907	Tommy Ryan
1907–08	Stanley Ketchel, Billy Papke
1908–10	Stanley Ketchel
1911–13	vacant

Welterweights (147–153 lb.)	
Year	Name
1892–94	Billy Smith
1894–96	Tommy Ryan
1896	Kid McCoy
1900	Rube Ferns, Matty Matthews
1901	Rube Ferns
1901–04	Joe Walcott
1904–06	Dude Kid, Joe Walcott, Honey Mellody
1907–11	Mike Sullivan
1911–15	vacant

Lightweights (131–135 lb.)	
Year	Name
1896–99	Kid Lavigne
1899–1902	Frank Erne
1902–08	Joe Gans
1908–10	Battling Nelson
1910–12	Ad Wolgast
1912–14	Willie Ritchie

Featherweights (126–129 lb.)	
Year	Name
1900–01	Terry McGovern, Young Corbett
1901–12	Abe Attell
1912–23	Johnny Kilbane

Source: Wright, *The Universal Almanac 1990,* 629–30.

On July 4, 1910, Jim Jeffries came out of retirement in response to the demand of a prejudiced public as the "great white hope" to dethrone Johnson. The partisan band in Reno, Nevada, played the racist song "All Coons Look Alike to Me" while racial slurs marked Johnson's entry into the ring. When the telegraph announced to the nation that Johnson had knocked Jeffries out in the fifteenth round, racial violence erupted in Houston, Little Rock, and Norfolk. In

Wilmington, Delaware, blacks attacked a white, and whites retaliated with a "lynching bee." Finally in 1912, racism exacted its tribute in the form of a conviction of Johnson under the Mann Act for "transporting women" across state lines "for immoral purposes." (Johnson had taken his common law wife to another state.)

In 1912, after Johnson was convicted of violating the act, he fled to Canada first and then to Europe. He lived lavishly in Europe and continued to fight. His flamboyant ways and a white wife made him unpopular. He remained world champion until April 5, 1915, when at Havana, Cuba, he was knocked out in the sixteenth round by Jess Willard, a white fighter. Over his career, Johnson lost only seven of 114 fights.

In 1920, Johnson returned to the United States and made appearances in vaudeville and at carnivals after serving a year in prison. One result of his career was the banning in New York State in February 1913 of fights between whites and blacks.

Football

Football was a developing sport with no organized professional leagues during the Victorian period. The Ivy League dominated the major college teams with Yale, Harvard, and Princeton being the top teams at the close of the 1902 season. The rivalry between Army and Navy began in 1890, but the Rose Bowl was the only bowl game played during this period. In 1902, Michigan defeated Stanford 49 to 0. The next Rose Bowl game was not played until 1916.

The history of American football is highlighted by several important events. In the fall of 1873, Yale invited Harvard, Princeton, Columbia, and Rutgers to a convention to organize the Intercollegiate Football Association. Harvard declined to attend, and the other members organized their association based upon soccer rules. Harvard then organized its own Foot Ball Club, December 3, 1872, on the basis of rules at the university, where classes of students played what was called the "Boston game." It was different in several ways, but most important, it allowed the ball to be picked up and advanced by running with it. Harvard, in search of teams to play, scheduled intercollegiate competition with McGill University of Montreal, Canada. One game was played at McGill by the English

rugby rules that McGill preferred, the other at Cambridge by the rules of the "Boston game." The games with McGill set the stage for the evolution of football as played in the United States—a game more distinctly American, less British.

Harvard liked the rugby game so much that it scheduled games with Yale and Princeton, who also liked the rugby rules better than the soccer rules that they had been playing under. Consequently, rugby became a popular intercollegiate sport. But rugby served largely as a transitional sport to Americanized football, different from both soccer and rugby.

Gradually, step by step, the rugby rules evolved into something uniquely American. In 1880, the appearance of a quarterback, the substitution of scrimmage for the English scrum, the reduction of players from fifteen to eleven per side, and the naming of team positions altered the game of rugby dramatically. Thereafter came the establishment of downs and the origin and use of signals in 1882. These innovative and far-reaching changes were forerunners of modern football's tactics of blocking, tackling, forward passing, shifts, and formations that were to produce an American-style game built upon speed, skill, and tactical maneuvers. Very early, the size of the players also became a factor.

Another event of great significance in the history of American football took place in 1913 when mighty Army found a gap in its schedule and filled it with lightly regarded Notre Dame. The Army scheduler had heard about little-known Notre Dame and offered the school $1,000 if it would care to play Army. The sum was barely enough to send fifteen players from Indiana to West Point, New York.

Rule changes in the 1880s and 1890s had emphasized brawn. Army had developed the sport with robust players, but Notre Dame had a small-sized squad and stood little chance against the cadets, at least if it played on Army's terms.

After the Notre Dame–Army match was scheduled, Gus Dorais, the Notre Dame quarterback, and Knute Rockne, an end for the team, both of whom had summer jobs at the Cedar Point (Ohio) vacation resort, spent their spare time practicing the forward pass on the beach at Lake Erie. The forward pass had been around for seven years, but had been slighted as a major weapon. Knowing that

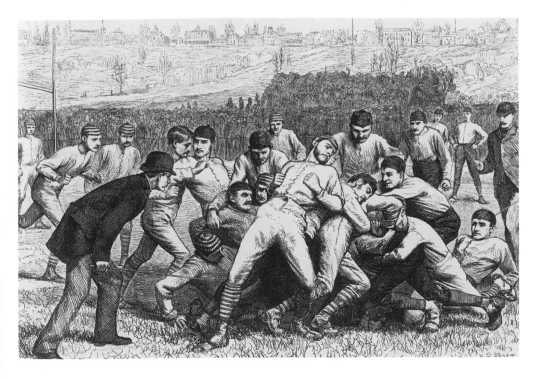

Football developed during this period. The Ivy League pioneered in the sport, and shown here is Yale playing Princeton. (Courtesy Prints and Photographs DIvision, Library of Congress)

the Army matchup was ahead and seeing little hope for winning in a ground game, they worked on the forward pass until they perfected it. Later, the Notre Dame coach decided that it would be a good idea to have another player ready so that Army could not just "key on" Rockne. Thus, Pliska, a back, got private tutoring as a pass-catching end.

When little Notre Dame took the field against the Army giants, few gave them much chance of winning. But Dorais put the forward pass into play, and his tosses baffled the Army defenders, who at first stood around as if paralyzed. When the Army players finally did react to cover Rockne, Dorais would pass to Pliska. The result was a stunning victory in which Notre Dame defeated Army 35 to 13. The unexpected result not only placed the forward pass into the arsenal of college football teams; it also did more to popularize the game with the masses than any single event. In addition, it ended the age when brawn alone would be the determining factor in the outcome of games.

Numbering of players contributed to the development of the game as a spectator sport. Colleges generally took the attitude that numbers were not necessary because students knew the players and it did not matter whether other spectators knew who they were. Consequently, many fans could not identify competing players, a situation made worse on rainy days when players became so smeared with mud that even the rival uniforms became indistinguishable. Without loudspeakers or a scoreboard, spectators often left games not knowing who had scored and sometimes not even knowing who had won.

Washington and Jefferson College first numbered its players in 1908, but then abandoned the practice. Players were not numbered again until 1913 when Amos Alonzo Stagg tried numbering as an experiment at the University of Chicago. It proved a great success but still did not become a common practice until the 1920s.

Football increased in popularity slowly. The Yale Bowl opened in 1914, the most impressive structure of its kind anywhere in the world at the time. Many other stadiums followed thereafter. After World War II, the popularity of football increased greatly, attendance shattering all previous records.

Chronological History of College Football

1869   Princeton and Rutgers pioneered intercollegiate football at New Brunswick, New Jersey, playing games on successive Saturdays—November 6 and November 13. Rutgers won the first, 6 to 4, and Princeton took the second, 8 to 0, both games under soccer rules.

1870   Columbia organized and played both Rutgers and Princeton—soccer rules.

1872   Yale created a football team and played one game, beating Columbia, 3 to 0—soccer rules.

1873   Late in year, Princeton, Rutgers, Columbia and Yale met and drafted a code, with soccer rules prevailing. Harvard declined to join.

May 14, 1874   Harvard defeated McGill under "Boston Game" rules, 3 goals to 0, at Cambridge, Massachusetts.

May 15, 1874   Harvard played McGill University at rugby, introduced by McGill. The game ended in a 0–0 tie.

1875   Yale and Harvard met for the first time, and predominating "Concessionary Rules' were rugby, as advocated by Harvard. Harvard won, 4 goals to 0.

1876   American Intercollegiate Football Association created at Springfield, Massachusetts, membership being Princeton, Rutgers, Columbia, Harvard, and Yale. Yale claimed first championship,

defeating Harvard, Columbia, and Princeton, with E. V. Baker as Yale captain. Rules governing game were those of Rugby Union with changes. A goal was made equal to 4 touchdowns.

1877   Fifteen players constituted a team, arranged as follows: nine men on rush line, one quarterback, two halfbacks, one three-quarter back and two fullbacks. Length of game 90 minutes.

1878   It was decided that players were to discard tights and wear canvas pants and jackets.

1880   Number of players on a side reduced from fifteen to eleven and names of the positions originated. Rugby "scrum" abandoned in favor of a crude scrimmage line, out of which has developed the modern scrimmage line. Position of the quarterback in the scrimmage created, placing him to receive snapback of the ball. He is forbidden to carry the ball. Playing field standardized at 110 × 53 yards, replacing original 140 × 70 yards.

1881   In case of a tie, two additional periods of fifteen minutes each were ordered to be played.

1882   Introduction of the rule on "downs" and "yards" to gain, as follows: "If, on three consecutive downs, a team has not advanced ball 5 yards, or lost 10 yards, it must give up ball to other side at the spot where the final down is made." Signals originated this year. In beginning they consisted of sentences, later of letters beginning sentence. They became numbers in 1885. Teams standardized as follows: seven forwards, one quarterback, two halfbacks, one fullback. Four touchdowns were given precedence over goal from the field; two safeties were made equal to touchdown.

1883   Reorganization of officials provided for two judges, one to be selected by each team, and one impartial referee, the latter's decree to be final.

1883   Numerical scoring introduced with these values: safeties, 1 point; touchdowns, 2 points; goal from touchdown, 4 points; goal from field, 5 points. Referee ordered to take out time for all unnecessary delays. Numerical scoring amended at end of 1884 season to make touchdown 4 points; safety, 2 points; goal after touchdown, 2 points. Origin of interference, then called "guarding."

1885   Harvard faculty prohibited football for the season.

1887   Pennsylvania and Rutgers met in an indoor football game, Madison Square Garden, New York City, the first contest under such conditions.

1888   Rule prohibited blocking with extended arms; tackling extended to point below waist but not below knees.

1889   Walter Camp made first All-America selections.

1890   Yale team appeared wearing extra-long hair—first time this had been featured.

1894   Withdrawal of Harvard and Pennsylvania from association wrecked organization and football was without governing body. University Athletic Club of New York invited Harvard, Pennsylvania, Princeton and Yale to form a rules committee, which was done. It made elaborate revision of code. It was decided that officials should consist of an umpire, referee and linesman; length of game reduced from 90 minutes to 70 minutes, divided into two halves; no player should lay hands upon an opponent unless the opponent had ball, and that no play should be allowed in which more than three men started before ball was in play.

1895   American Intercollegiate Football Association disbanded.

1897   Point scoring changed to following: touchdown, 5 points; goal after touchdown, 1; field goal, 5; safety, 2.

1902   Teams required to change goals following a touchdown or goal from the field.

1904   Value of field goal reduced to 4 points.

1905–1906   Football sank to its lowest depths, owing to great number of deaths and crippling injuries resulting from mass plays where brute strength and great weight were the determining factors. Many college presidents either banned football or threatened to do so unless something was done immediately. Parents of many football players forbade them to play. Pres. Theodore Roosevelt said game must be made safer. With the fate of the game hanging in the balance, football leaders met in the winter of 1905–06, ruled out practically all mass formations, prohibited hurdling, permitted the forward pass and other "safety" rules.

1906 Forward pass introduced. Officials to consist of referee, two umpires and linesman. Length of game reduced to 60 minutes, divided into two halves of 30 minutes each. Distance to gain on downs increased to 10 yards. First forward pass reported thrown by Wesleyan against Yale, with Moore passing and Van Tassel receiving. Yale overwhelmed Wesleyan despite it. In the same season, Yale is reported to have completed a pass against Harvard for a touchdown, Yale winning the game, 6 to 0, the pass constituting the only score.

1907 Office of field judge was created; one of the 2 umpires was eliminated.

1908 Washington and Jefferson occasionally numbered its players, a college innovation that was not continued as a regular thing at W. & J.

1909 Value of field goal reduced to 3 points—the rule today.

1910 Player withdrawn from game for any reason was permitted to return to play in subsequent period. Game divided into quarters of 15 minutes each, instead of old rule of 30-minute halves. Time out between first and second, and third and fourth quarters fixed at 1 minute, with 30 minutes out for rest between halves.

1912 Teams allowed four downs to advance ball 10 yards instead of three. Dimensions of field reduced to 100 yards with extra space of 10 yards behind each goal, the latter being zone in which forward pass might be legally caught by the offensive side. Kick-off, formerly delivered from middle of field, changed to the 40-yard line. Kick-off following a touchback removed from the 25-yard line to the 20-yard line. Value of touchdown increased from 5 to 6 points.

1913 Chicago players numbered in game against Wisconsin.

TABLE 14.28 FOOTBALL PLAYERS, ALL-AMERICA SELECTIONS

Walter Camp's Selections, 1889–1924

A special N.C.A.A. Committee formed in 1954 proved, after exhaustive research, that credit for the selection of the first All-America football team in 1889 should go to Caspar Whitney, a leading sports authority in New York City in the early 1890s, instead of the former Yale star, Walter Camp, as popularly believed. Camp himself gives sole credit to Whitney for the selections from 1889 through 1896 even though the listings were under Camp's name in *Harper's Weekly*. However, Camp skillfully promoted All-America teams, chose them himself beginning in 1897, and his selections appeared in *Collier's Weekly*, a national magazine, until his death on March 14, 1925. Grantland Rice succeeded Camp as the selector for the magazine through 1947.

Rice combined with the Football Writers Association of America in 1948 to make selections for *Look* magazine until his death in 1954.

1889		
Position	Player	School
End	Arthur Cumnock	Harvard
Tackle	Hector W. Cowan	Princeton
Guard	John Cranston	Harvard
Center	William J. George	Princeton
Guard	William W. Heffelfinger	Yale
Tackle	Charles O. Gill	Yale
End	Amos Alonzo Stagg	Yale
Quarterback	Edgar Allen Poe	Princeton
Halfback	James T. Lee	Harvard
Halfback	Roscoe H. Channing Jr.	Princeton
Fullback	Knowlton Ames	Princeton

1890		
Position	Player	School
End	Frank W. Hallowell	Harvard
Tackle	Marshall Newell	Harvard
Guard	Jesse B. Riggs	Princeton
Center	John Cranston	Harvard
Guard	William W. Heffelfinger	Yale
Tackle	William C. Rhodes	Yale
End	Ralph H. Warren	Princeton
Quarterback	Dudley Dean	Harvard
Halfback	John Corbett	Harvard
Halfback	Lee McClung	Yale
Fullback	Sheppard Homans Jr.	Princeton

1891		
Position	Player	School
End	Frank A. Hinkey	Yale
Tackle	Wallace C. Winter	Yale
Guard	William W. Heffelfinger	Yale
Center	John W. Adams	Pennsylvania
Guard	Jesse B. Riggs	Princeton
Tackle	Marshall Newell	Harvard
End	John A. Hartwell	Yale
Quarterback	Phillip King	Princeton
Halfback	Everett J. Lake	Harvard
Halfback	Lee McClung	Yale
Fullback	Sheppard Homans Jr.	Princeton

1892		
Position	Player	School
End	Frank A. Hinkey	Yale
Tackle	A. Hamilton Wallis	Harvard
Guard	Bert Waters	Harvard
Center	William H. Lewis	Harvard
Guard	Arthur L. Wheeler	Princeton
Tackle	Marshall Newell	Harvard
End	Frank W. Hallowell	Harvard
Quarterback	Vance McCormick	Yale
Halfback	Charles Brewer	Harvard
Halfback	Phillip King	Princeton
Fullback	Harry C. Thayer	Pennsylvania

1893		
Position	Player	School
End	Frank A. Hinkey	Yale
Tackle	Langdon Lea	Princeton
Guard	Arthur L. Wheeler	Princeton
Center	William H. Lewis	Harvard
Guard	William O. Hickok	Yale
Tackle	Marshall Newell	Harvard
End	Thomas S. Trenchard	Princeton
Quarterback	Phillip King	Princeton
Halfback	Charles Brewer	Harvard
Halfback	Franklin B. Morse	Princeton
Fullback	Frank S. Butterworth	Yale

(continued)

TABLE 14.28 (continued)

Walter Camp's Selections, 1889–1924

1894

Position	Player	School
End	Frank A. Hinkey	Yale
Tackle	Bert Waters	Harvard
Guard	Arthur L. Wheeler	Princeton
Center	Phillip T. Stillman	Yale
Guard	William O. Hickok	Yale
Tackle	Langdon Lea	Princeton
End	Charles Gelbert	Pennsylvania
Quarterback	George T. Adee	Yale
Halfback	Arthur Knipe	Pennsylvania
Halfback	George H. Brooke	Pennsylvania
Fullback	Frank S. Butterworth	Yale

1895

Position	Player	School
End	Norman Cabot	Harvard
Tackle	Langdon Lea	Princeton
Guard	Charles M. Wharton	Pennsylvania
Center	Al Bull	Pennsylvania
Guard	Dudley Riggs	Princeton
Tackle	Fred T. Murphy	Yale
End	Charles Gelbert	Pennsylvania
Quarterback	Clinton R. Wyckoff	Cornell
Halfback	S. Brinckerhoff Thorne	Yale
Halfback	Charles Brewer	Harvard
Fullback	George H. Brooke	Pennsylvania

1896

Position	Player	School
End	Norman Cabot	Harvard
Tackle	William W. Church	Princeton
Guard	Charles M. Wharton	Pennsylvania
Center	Robert R. Gailey	Princeton
Guard	Wiley Woodruff	Pennsylvania
Tackle	Fred T. Murphy	Yale
End	Charles Gelbert	Pennsylvania
Quarterback	William M. Fincke	Yale
Halfback	Edgar N. Wrightington	Harvard
Halfback	Addison W. Kelly	Princeton
Fullback	John Baird	Princeton

1897

First Team

Position	Player	School
End	Garrett Cochran	Princeton
Tackle	Burr C. Chamberlain	Yale
Guard	T. Truxton Hare	Yale
Center	Alan E. Doucette	Harvard
Guard	Gordon Brown	Yale
Tackle	John Outland	Pennsylvania
End	John A. Hall	Yale
Quarterback	Charles A. H. De Saulles	Yale
Halfback	Benjamin H. Dibblee	Harvard
Halfback	Addison W. Kelly	Princeton
Fullback	John Minds	Pennsylvania

Second Team

Position	Player	School
End	Boyle	Pennsylvania
Tackle	Rodgers	Yale
Guard	Chadwick	Yale
Center	Cadwalader	Yale
Guard	Rinehart	Lafayette

Second Team

Position	Player	School
Tackle	Scales	Army
End	McKeever	Cornell
Quarterback	Young	Cornell
Halfback	Nesbitt	Army
Halfback	Fultz	Brown
Fullback	McBride	Yale

Third Team

Position	Player	School
End	Moulton	Harvard
Tackle	Hillebrand	Princeton
Guard	Bouve	Harvard
Center	Overfield	Pennsylvania
Guard	McCracken	Pennsylvania
Tackle	Donald	Harvard
End	Tracy	Cornell
Quarterback	Baird	Princeton
Halfback	Bannard	Princeton
Halfback	Walbridge	Lafayette
Fullback	Wheeler	Princeton

1898

First Team

Position	Player	School
End	Lew R. Palmer	Princeton
Tackle	A. R. T. Hillebrand	Princeton
Guard	T. Truxton Hare	Pennsylvania
Center	Peter Overfield	Pennsylvania
Guard	Gordon Brown	Yale
Tackle	Burr C. Chamberlain	Yale
End	John W. Hallowell	Harvard
Quarterback	Charles D. Daly	Harvard
Halfback	John Outland	Pennsylvania
Halfback	Benjamin H. Dibblee	Harvard
Fullback	Clarence B. Herschberger	Chicago

Second Team

Position	Player	School
End	Poe	Princeton
Tackle	Steckle	Michigan
Guard	McCracken	Pennsylvania
Center	Cunningham	Michigan
Guard	Boal	Harvard
Tackle	Haughton	Harvard
End	Cochrane	Harvard
Quarterback	Kennedy	Chicago
Halfback	Richardson	Brown
Halfback	Warren	Harvard
Fullback	O'Dea	Wisconsin

Third Team

Position	Player	School
End	Folwell	Pennsylvania
Tackle	Sweetland	Cornell
Guard	Randolph	Penn State
Center	Jaffray	Harvard
Guard	Reed	Cornell
Tackle	Foy	Army
End	Smith	Army
Quarterback	Kromer	Army
Halfback	Raymond	Wesleyan
Halfback	Benedict	Nebraska
Fullback	Romeyn	Army

1899

First Team

Position	Player	School
End	David C. Campbell	Harvard
Tackle	A. R. T. Hillebrand	Princeton
Guard	T. Truxton Hare	Pennsylvania
Center	Peter Overfield	Pennsylvania
Guard	Gordon Brown	Yale
Tackle	George S. Stillmar	Yale
End	Arthur Poe	Princeton
Quarterback	Charles D. Daly	Harvard
Halfback	Isaac Seneca	Carlisle
Halfback	Josiah H. McCracken	Pennsylvania
Fullback	Malcolm L. McBride	Yale

Second Team

Position	Player	School
End	Hallowell	Harvard
Tackle	Wheelock	Carlisle
Guard	Edwards	Princeton
Center	Cunningham	Michigan
Guard	Wright	Columbia
Tackle	Wallace	Pennsylvania
End	Coombs	Pennsylvania
Quarterback	Kennedy	Chicago
Halfback	Richardson	Brown
Halfback	Slaker	Chicago
Fullback	Wheeler	Princeton

Third Team

Position	Player	School
End	Snow	Michigan
Tackle	Alexander	Cornell
Guard	Trout	Lafayette
Center	Burnett	Harvard
Guard	Burden	Harvard
Tackle	Pell	Princeton
End	Hamill	Chicago
Quarterback	Hudson	Carlisle
Halfback	McLean	Michigan
Halfback	Weekes	Columbia
Fullback	O'Dea	Wisconsin

1900

First Team

Position	Player	School
End	David C. Campbell	Harvard
Tackle	James R. Bloomer	Yale
Guard	Gordon Brown	Yale
Center	Herman P. Olcott	Yale
Guard	T. Truxton Hare	Pennsylvania
Tackle	George S. Stillman	Yale
End	John W. Hallowell	Harvard
Quarterback	William M. Fincke	Yale
Halfback	George B. Chadwick	Yale
Halfback	William Morley	Columbia
Fullback	Perry T. W. Hale	Yale

Second Team

Position	Player	School
End	Gould	Yale
Tackle	Wallace	Pennsylvania
Guard	Wright	Columbia
Center	Sargent	Harvard
Guard	Sheldon	Yale
Tackle	Lawrence	Harvard
End	Coy	Yale

Second Team

Position	Player	School
Quarterback	Daly	Harvard
Halfback	Weekes	Columbia
Halfback	Sawin	Harvard
Fullback	Cure	Lafayette

Third Team

Position	Player	School
End	Smith	Army
Tackle	Alexander	Cornell
Guard	Teas	Pennsylvania
Center	Page	Minnesota
Guard	Belknap	Navy
Tackle	Farnsworth	Army
End	Van Hoevenberg	Columbia
Quarterback	Williams	Iowa
Halfback	Reiter	Princeton
Halfback	Sharpe	Yale
Fullback	McCracken	Pennsylvania

1901

First Team

Position	Player	School
End	David C. Campbell	Harvard
Tackle	Oliver F. Cutts	Harvard
Guard	William J. Warner	Cornell
Center	Henry C. Holt	Yale
Guard	William G. Lee	Harvard
Tackle	Paul B. Bunker	Army
End	Ralph T. Davis	Princeton
Quarterback	Charles D. Daly	Army
Halfback	Robert P. Kernan	Harvard
Halfback	Harold Weekes	Columbia
Fullback	Thomas H. Graydon	Harvard

Second Team

Position	Player	School
End	Bowditch	Harvard
Tackle	Blagden	Harvard
Guard	Barnard	Harvard
Center	Rachman	Lafayette
Guard	Hunt	Cornell
Tackle	Wheelock	Carlisle
End	Swan	Yale
Quarterback	De Saulles	Yale
Halfback	Purcell	Cornell
Halfback	Ristine	Harvard
Fullback	Cure	Lafayette

Third Team

Position	Player	School
End	Henry	Princeton
Tackle	Pell	Princeton
Guard	Olcott	Yale
Center	Fisher	Princeton
Guard	Teas	Pennsylvania
Tackle	Goss	Yale
End	Gould	Yale
Quarterback	Johnson	Carlisle
Halfback	Heston	Michigan
Halfback	Morley	Columbia
Fullback	Schoelkopf	Cornell

(continued)

TABLE 14.28   (continued)

Walter Camp's Selections, 1889–1924

1902		
First Team		
Position	Player	School
End	Thomas L. Shevlin	Yale
Tackle	James J. Hogan	Yale
Guard	John R. DeWitt	Princeton
Center	Henry C. Holt	Yale
Guard	Edgar T. Glass	Yale
Tackle	Gilbert Kinney	Yale
End	Edward Bowditch	Harvard
Quarterback	Foster Rockwell	Yale
Halfback	George B. Chadwick	Yale
Halfback	Paul B. Bunker	Army
Fullback	Thomas H. Graydon	Harvard
Second Team		
Position	Player	School
End	Sweeley	Michigan
Tackle	Pierce	Amherst
Guard	Warner	Cornell
Center	Boyers	Army
Guard	Goss	Yale
Tackle	Knowlton	Harvard
End	Davis	Princeton
Quarterback	Weeks	Michigan
Halfback	Barry	Brown
Halfback	Metcalf	Yale
Fullback	Bowman	Yale
Third Team		
Position	Player	School
End	Metzger	Pennsylvania
Tackle	Farr	Chicago
Guard	Lerum	Wisconsin
Center	McCabe	Pennsylvania
Guard	Marshall	Harvard
Tackle	Schact	Minnesota
End	Farmer	Dartmouth
Quarterback	Daly	Army
Halfback	Foulke	Princeton
Halfback	Heston	Michigan
Fullback	Torney	West Point

1903		
First Team		
Position	Player	School
End	Howard H. Henry	Princeton
Tackle	James J. Hogan	Yale
Guard	John R. DeWitt	Princeton
Center	H. J. Hooper	Dartmouth
Guard	Andrew Marshall	Harvard
Tackle	Daniel W. Knowlton	Harvard
End	Charles D. Rafferty	Yale
Quarterback	James E. Johnson	Carlisle
Halfback	William Heston	Michigan
Halfback	J. Dana Kafer	Princeton
Fullback	Richard Smith	Columbia
Second Team		
Position	Player	School
End	Davis	Princeton
Tackle	Thorp	Columbia
Guard	Riley	Army

Second Team		
Position	Player	School
Center	Strathern	Minnesota
Guard	Gilman	Dartmouth
Tackle	Schacht	Minnesota
End	Shevlin	Yale
Quarterback	Whitam	Dartmouth
Halfback	Nichols	Harvard
Halfback	Mitchell	Yale
Fullback	R. Miller	Princeton
Third Team		
Position	Player	School
End	Redden	Michigan
Tackle	Turner	Dartmouth
Guard	Bezdec	Wisconsin
Center	Bruce	Columbia
Guard	Piekarski	Pennsylvania
Tackle	Maddock	Michigan
End	Rogers	Minnesota
Quarterback	Harris	Minnesota
Halfback	Gravar	Michigan
Halfback	Stankard	Holy Cross
Fullback	Salmon	Notre Dame

1904		
First Team		
Position	Player	School
End	Thomas L. Shevlin	Yale
Tackle	James L. Cooney	Princeton
Guard	Frank Piekarski	Pennsylvania
Center	Arthur C. Tipton	Army
Guard	Gilbert Kinney	Yale
Tackle	James J. Hogan	Yale
End	Walter H. Eckersall	Chicago
Quarterback	Vincent Stevenson	Pennsylvania
Halfback	Daniel J. Hurley	Harvard
Halfback	William Heston	Michigan
Fullback	Andrew L. Smith	Pennsylvania
Second Team		
Position	Player	School
End	Weede	Pennsylvania
Tackle	Thorp	Columbia
Guard	Gilman	Dartmouth
Center	Roraback	Yale
Guard	Tripp	Yale
Tackle	Curtiss	Michigan
End	Gillespie	Army
Quarterback	Rockwell	Yale
Halfback	Reynolds	Pennsylvania
Halfback	Hubbard	Amherst
Fullback	Mills	Harvard
Third Team		
Position	Player	School
End	Glaze	Dartmouth
Tackle	Butkiewicz	Pennsylvania
Guard	Short	Princeton
Center	Torrey	Pennsylvania
Guard	Thorpe	Minnesota
Tackle	Doe	Army
End	Rothgeb	Illinois
Quarterback	Harris	Minnesota
Halfback	Hoyt	Yale
Halfback	Vaughan	Dartmouth
Fullback	Bender	Nebraska

1905

First Team

Position	Player	School
End	Thomas L. Shevlin	Yale
Tackle	Otis Lamson	Pennsylvania
Guard	Roswell C. Tripp	Yale
Center	Robert Torrey	Pennsylvania
Guard	Francis H. Burr	Harvard
Tackle	Beaton H. Squires	Harvard
End	Ralph Glaze	Dartmouth
Quarterback	Walter H. Eckersall	Chicago
Halfback	Howard Roome	Yale
Halfback	John H. Hubbard	Amherst
Fullback	James McCormick	Princeton

Second Team

Position	Player	School
End	Catlin	Chicago
Tackle	Forbes	Yale
Guard	Thompson	Cornell
Center	Flanders	Yale
Guard	Schulte	Michigan
Tackle	Curtiss	Michigan
End	Marshall	Minnesota
Quarterback	Hutchinson	Yale
Halfback	Morse	Yale
Halfback	Sheble	Pennsylvania
Fullback	Von Saltza	Columbia

Third Team

Position	Player	School
End	Levene	Pennsylvania
Tackle	Berthke	Wisconsin
Guard	Fletcher	Brown
Center	Gale	Chicago
Guard	Maxwell	Swarthmore
Tackle	Biglow	Yale
End	Tooker	Princeton
Quarterback	Crowell	Swarthmore
Halfback	Hammond	Michigan
Halfback	Findlay	Wisconsin
Fullback	Bezdek	Chicago

1906

First Team

Position	Player	School
End	Robert W. Forbes	Yale
Tackle	Horatio Biglow	Yale
Guard	Francis H. Burr	Harvard
Center	W. T. Dunn	Penn State
Guard	Elmer Ives Thompson	Cornell
Tackle	James L. Cooney	Princeton
End	L. Carpar Wister	Princeton
Quarterback	Walter H. Eckersall	Chicago
Halfback	John W. Hayhew	Brown
Halfback	William F. Knox	Yale
Fullback	Paul L. Veeder	Yale

Second Team

Position	Player	School
End	Dague	Navy
Tackle	Draper	Pennsylvania
Guard	Ziegler	Pennsylvania
Center	Hockenberger	Yale
Guard	Dillon	Princeton
Tackle	Osborn	Harvard
End	Marshall	Minnesota
Quarterback	Jones	Yale

Second Team

Position	Player	School
Halfback	Hollenback	Pennsylvania
Halfback	Wendell	Harvard
Fullback	McCormick	Princeton

Third Team

Position	Player	School
End	Levene	Pennsylvania
Tackle	Weeks	Army
Guard	Kersberg	Harvard
Center	Hunt	Carlisle
Guard	Christy	Army
Tackle	Northcroft	Navy
End	Exendine	Carlisle
Quarterback	E. Dillon	Princeton
Halfback	Morse	Yale
Halfback	Manier	Vanderbilt
Fullback	Garrels	Michigan

1907

First Team

Position	Player	School
End	W. H. Dague Jr.	Navy
Tackle	Dexter Draper	Pennsylvania
Guard	Gus Ziegler	Pennsylvania
Center	Adolph Schulz	Michigan
Guard	William W. Erwin	Army
Tackle	Horatio Biglow	Yale
End	Clarence F. Alcott	Yale
Quarterback	T. A. Dwight Jones	Yale
Halfback	John W. Wendell	Harvard
Halfback	Edwin H. W. Harlan	Princeton
Fullback	James McCormick	Princeton

Second Team

Position	Player	School
End	Exendine	Carlisle
Tackle	Horr	Syracuse
Guard	Rich	Dartmouth
Center	Grant	Harvard
Guard	Thompson	Cornell
Tackle	O'Rourke	Cornell
End	Scarlett	Pennsylvania
Quarterback	Dillon	Princeton
Halfback	Marks	Dartmouth
Halfback	Hollenback	Pennsylvania
Fullback	Coy	Yale

Third Team

Position	Player	School
End	Wister	Princeton
Tackle	Lang	Dartmouth
Guard	Goebel	Yale
Center	Phillips	Princeton
Guard	Krider	Swarthmore
Tackle	Weeks	Army
End	McDonald	Harvard
Quarterback	Steffen	Chicago
Halfback	Capron	Minnesota
Halfback	Hauser	Carlisle
Fullback	Douglas	Annapolis

(continued)

TABLE 14.28 (continued)

Walter Camp's Selections, 1889–1924

1908

First Team

Position	Player	School
End	Hunter Scarlett	Pennsylvania
Tackle	Hamilton Fish	Harvard
Guard	William A. Goebel	Yale
Center	Charles J. Nourse	Harvard
Guard	Clarke W. Tobin	Dartmouth
Tackle	Mark E. Horr	Syracuse
End	George H. Schildmiller	Dartmouth
Quarterback	Walter P. Steffen	Chicago
Halfback	Frederick M. Tibbott	Princeton
Halfback	William A. Hollenback	Pennsylvania
Fullback	Edwin H. Coy	Yale

Second Team

Position	Player	School
End	Dennie	Brown
Tackle	Siegling	Princeton
Guard	Andrus	Yale
Center	Philoon	Army
Guard	Messmer	Wisconsin
Tackle	O'Rourke	Cornell
End	Reifsnider	Navy
Quarterback	Cutler	Harvard
Halfback	Ver Wiebe	Harvard
Halfback	Mayhew	Brown
Fullback	Walder	Cornell

Third Team

Position	Player	School
End	Page	Chicago
Tackle	Draper	Pennsylvania
Guard	Van Hook	Illinois
Center	Brusse	Dartmouth
Guard	Hoar	Harvard
Tackle	Northcroft	Navy
End	Johnson	Army
Quarterback	Miller	Pennsylvania
Halfback	Thorpe	Carlisle
Halfback	Gray	Amherst
Fullback	McCaa	Lafayette

1909

First Team

Position	Player	School
End	Adrien E. Regnier	Brown
Tackle	Hamilton Fish	Harvard
Guard	Albert Benbrook	Michigan
Center	Carroll T. Cooney	Yale
Guard	Hamlin F. Andrus	Yale
Tackle	Henry H. Hobbs	Yale
End	John R. Kilpatrick	Yale
Quarterback	John McGovern	Minnesota
Halfback	Stephen H. Philben	Yale
Halfback	W. M. Minot	Harvard
Fullback	Edward H. Coy	Yale

Second Team

Position	Player	School
End	Bankhart	Dartmouth
Tackle	Lilley	Yale
Guard	Goebel	Yale
Center	P. Withington	Harvard
Guard	Tobin	Dartmouth
Tackle	McKay	Harvard
End	Braddock	Pennsylvania
Quarterback	Howe	Yale
Halfback	Allerdice	Michigan
Halfback	Magidsohn	Michigan
Fullback	Marks	Dartmouth

Third Team

Position	Player	School
End	Page	Chicago
Tackle	Siegling	Princeton
Guard	L. Withington	Harvard
Center	Farnum	Minnesota
Guard	Fisher	Harvard
Tackle	Casey	Michigan
End	McCaffrey	Fordham
Quarterback	Sprackling	Brown
Halfback	Corbett	Harvard
Halfback	Miller	Notre Dame
Fullback	McCaa	Lafayette

1910

First Team

Position	Player	School
End	John R. Kilpatrick	Yale
Tackle	Robert G. McKay	Harvard
Guard	Albert Benbrook	Michigan
Center	Ernest B. Cozens	Pennsylvania
Guard	Robert T. Fisher	Harvard
Tackle	James Walker	Minnesota
End	Stanfield Wells	Michigan
Quarterback	W. Earl Sprackling	Brown
Halfback	Percy Wendell	Harvard
Halfback	Talbot T. Pendleton	Princeton
Fullback	E. LeRoy Mercer	Pennsylvania

Second Team

Position	Player	School
End	L. Smith	Harvard
Tackle	Scully	Yale
Guard	Weir	Army
Center	Morris	Yale
Guard	Brown	Navy
Tackle	Smith	Brown
End	Daley	Dartmouth
Quarterback	Howe	Yale
Halfback	Dalton	Navy
Halfback	Field	Yale
Fullback	McKay	Brown

Third Team

Position	Player	School
End	Eyrich	Cornell
Tackle	Grimm	Washington
Guard	Metzger	Vanderbilt
Center	Sisson	Brown
Guard	Butzer	Illinois
Tackle	Shonka	Nebraska
End	Dean	Wisconsin
Quarterback	McGovern	Minnesota
Halfback	Taylor	Oregon
Halfback	Ramsdell	Pennsylvania
Fullback	H. Corbett	Harvard

1911

First Team

Position	Player	School
End	Sanford B. White	Princeton
Tackle	Edward J. Hart	Princeton
Guard	Robert T. Fisher	Harvard
Center	Henry H. Ketcham	Yale
Guard	Joseph M. Duff Jr.	Princeton
Tackle	Leland S. Devore	Army
End	Douglass M. Bomeisler	Yale
Quarterback	Arthur Howe	Yale
Halfback	Percy Wendell	Harvard
Halfback	Jim Thorpe	Carlisle
Fullback	J. P. Dalton	Navy

Second Team

Position	Player	School
End	Smith	Harvard
Tackle	Munk	Cornell
Guard	Scruby	Chicago
Center	Bluthenthal	Princeton
Guard	McDevitt	Yale
Tackle	Scully	Yale
End	Very	Penn State
Quarterback	Sprackling	Brown
Halfback	Morey	Dartmouth
Halfback	Camp	Yale
Fullback	Rosenwald	Minnesota

Third Team

Position	Player	School
End	Ashbaugh	Brown
Tackle	Buser	Wisconsin
Guard	Francis	Yale
Center	Weems	Navy
Guard	Arnold	Army
Tackle	Brown	Navy
End	Kallett	Syracuse
Quarterback	Capron	Minnesota
Halfback	Mercer	Pennsylvania
Halfback	Wells	Michigan
Fullback	Hudson	Trinity

1912

First Team

Position	Player	School
End	Samuel M. Felton	Harvard
Tackle	Wesley T. Englehorn	Dartmouth
Guard	Stanley B. Pennock	Harvard
Center	Henry H. Ketcham	Yale
Guard	W. John Logan	Princeton
Tackle	Robert P. Butler	Wisconsin
End	Douglass M. Bomeisler	Yale
Quarterback	George M. Crowther	Brown
Halfback	Charles E. Brickley	Harvard
Halfback	Jim Thorpe	Carlisle
Fullback	E. LeRoy Mercer	Pennsylvania

Second Team

Position	Player	School
End	Very	Penn State
Tackle	Probst	Syracuse
Guard	Cooney	Yale
Center	Parmenter	Harvard
Guard	Kulp	Brown
Tackle	Trickey	Iowa
End	Hoeffel	Wisconsin

Second Team

Position	Player	School
Quarterback	Pazzetti	Lehigh
Halfback	Morey	Dartmouth
Halfback	Norgren	Chicago
Fullback	Wendell	Harvard

Third Team

Position	Player	School
End	Ashbaugh	Brown
Tackle	Shaughnessy	Minnesota
Guard	Bennett	Dartmouth
Center	Blumenthal	Princeton
Guard	Brown	Navy
Tackle	Devore	Army
End	Jordan	Bucknell
Quarterback	Bacon	Wesleyan
Halfback	Hardage	Vanderbilt
Halfback	Baker	Princeton
Fullback	Pumpelly	Yale

1913

First Team

Position	Player	School
End	Robert H. Hogsett	Dartmouth
Tackle	Harold R. Ballin	Princeton
Guard	Stanley B. Pennock	Harvard
Center	Paul R. Des Jardien	Chicago
Guard	J. H. Brown Jr.	Navy
Tackle	Nelson S. Talbot	Yale
End	Louis A. Merillat	Army
Quarterback	Ellery C. Huntington Jr.	Colgate
Halfback	James Craig	Michigan
Halfback	Charles E. Brickley	Harvard
Fullback	Edward W. Mahan	Harvard

Second Team

Position	Player	School
End	Fritz	Cornell
Tackle	Butler	Wisconsin
Guard	Busch	Carlisle
Center	Marting	Yale
Guard	Ketcham	Yale
Tackle	Weyand	Army
End	Hardwick	Harvard
Quarterback	Wilson	Yale
Halfback	Spiegel	Washington and Jefferson
Halfback	Guyon	Carlisle
Fullback	Eichenlaub	Notre Dame

Third Team

Position	Player	School
End	Solon	Minnesota
Tackle	Halligan	Nebraska
Guard	Munns	Cornell
Center	Paterson	Michigan
Guard	Talman	Rutgers
Tackle	Storer	Harvard
End	Rockne	Notre Dame
Quarterback	Miller	Penn State
Halfback	Baker	Princeton
Halfback	Nergren	Chicago
Fullback	Whitney	Dartmouth

Source: Menke, *The Encyclopedia of Sports* (1969), 380.

TABLE 14.28 **(continued)**

Walter Camp's Selections, 1889–1924

Scoring Leaders in Points			
Year	Player	School	Total
1912	Jim Thorpe	Carlisle	198
1913	J. (Al) Spiegel	W. and J.	127
Scoring Leaders in Touchdowns			
Year	Player	School	Total
1912	Jim Thorpe	Carlisle	25
1913	J. (Al) Spiegel	W. and J.	21

Source: Menke, *The Encyclopedia of Sports* (1969), 398.

TABLE 14.29 RECORDS OF FAMOUS SERIES[a]

Army-Navy		
Date	Team/Score	Site
Nov. 29, 1890	Navy 24, Army 0	West Point, N.Y.
Nov. 28, 1891	Army 32, Navy 16	Annapolis, Md.
Nov. 26, 1892	Navy 12, Army 4	West Point, N.Y.
Dec. 2, 1893	Navy 6, Army 4	Annapolis, Md.
1894–98	No games	
Dec. 2, 1899	Army 17, Navy 5	Franklin Field, Philadelphia
Dec. 1, 1900	Navy 11, Army 7	Franklin Field, Philadelphia
Nov. 30, 1901	Army 11, Navy 5	Franklin Field, Philadelphia
Nov. 29, 1902	Army 22, Navy 8	Franklin Field, Philadelphia
Nov. 28, 1903	Army 40, Navy 5	Franklin Field, Philadelphia
Nov. 26, 1904	Army 11, Navy 0	Franklin Field, Philadelphia
Dec. 2, 1905	Army 6, Navy 6	Princeton, N.J.
Dec. 1, 1906	Navy 10, Army 0	Franklin Field, Philadelphia
Nov. 30, 1907	Navy 6, Army 0	Franklin Field, Philadelphia
Nov. 28, 1908	Army 6, Navy 4	Franklin Field, Philadelphia
1909	No game	
Nov. 26, 1910	Navy 3, Army 0	Franklin Field, Philadelphia
Nov. 25, 1911	Navy 3, Army 0	Franklin Field, Philadelphia
Nov. 30, 1912	Navy 6, Army 0	Franklin Field, Philadelphia
Nov. 29, 1913	Army 22, Navy 9	Polo Grounds, New York

Yale-Harvard		
Year	Team/Score	Site
1875	Harvard 4g 2t, Yale 0g 0t	New Haven
1876	Yale 1g 0t, Harvard 0g 2t	New Haven
1877	No game	
1878	Yale 1g 0t 2s, Harvard 0g 0t 13s	Boston
1879	Yale 0g 0t 2s, Harvard 0g 0t 4s.	New Haven
1880	Yale 1g 1t 2s, Harvard 0g 0t 9s.	Boston
1881	Yale 0g 0t 0s, Harvard 0g 0t 4s.	New Haven
1882	Yale 1g 3t 0s, Harvard 0g 0t 2s.	Cambridge
1883	Yale 23, Harvard 2	New York
1884	Yale 52, Harvard 0	New Haven
1885	No game	
1886	Yale 29, Harvard 4	Cambridge
1887	Yale 17, Harvard 8	New York
1888	No game	
1889	Yale 6, Harvard 0	Springfield
1890	Harvard 12, Yale 6	Springfield
1891	Yale 10, Harvard 0	Springfield
1892	Yale 6, Harvard 0	Springfield
1893	Yale 6, Harvard 0	Springfield
1894	Yale 12, Harvard 4	Springfield

Yale-Harvard		
Year	Team/Score	Site
1895–96	No games	
1897	Yale 0, Harvard 0	Cambridge
1898	Harvard 17, Yale 0	New Haven
1899	Yale 0, Harvard 0	Cambridge
1900	Yale 28, Harvard 0	New Haven
1901	Harvard 22, Yale 0	Cambridge
1902	Yale 23, Harvard 0	New Haven
1903	Yale 16, Harvard 0	Cambridge
1904	Yale 12, Harvard 0	New Haven
1905	Yale 6, Harvard 0	Cambridge
1906	Yale 6, Harvard 0	New Haven
1907	Yale 12, Harvard 0	Cambridge
1908	Harvard 4, Yale 0	New Haven
1909	Yale 8, Harvard 0	Cambridge
1910	Yale 0, Harvard 0	New Haven
1911	Yale 0, Harvard 0	Cambridge
1912	Harvard 20, Yale 0	New Haven
1913	Harvard 15, Yale 5	Cambridge

Yale-Princeton		
Year	Team/Score	Site
1873	Princeton 3g, Yale 0g	New Haven
1874–75	No games	
1876	Yale 2g, 1t, Princeton 0g, 0t	Hoboken
1877	Yale 0g, 2t, Princeton 0g, 0t	Hoboken
1878	Princeton 1g, Yale 0g	Hoboken
1879	Yale 0g, 0t, Princeton 0g, 0t	Hoboken
1880	Yale 0g, 0t, Princeton 0g, 0t	New York
1881	Yale 0g, 0t, Princeton 0g, 0t	New York
1882	Yale 2g, Princeton 1g	New York
1883	Yale 6, Princeton 0	New York
1884	[b]Yale 6, Princeton 4	New York
1885	Princeton 6, Yale 5	New Haven
1886	[b]Yale 4, Princeton 0	Princeton
1887	Yale 12, Princeton 0	New York
1888	Yale 10, Princeton 0	New York
1889	Princeton 10, Yale 0	New York
1890	Yale 32, Princeton 0	Brooklyn
1891	Yale 19, Princeton 0	New York
1892	Yale 12, Princeton 0	New York
1893	Princeton 6, Yale 0	New York
1894	Yale 24, Princeton 0	New York
1895	Yale 20, Princeton 10	New York
1896	Princeton 24, Yale 6	New York
1897	Yale 6, Princeton 0	New Haven
1898	Princeton 6, Yale 0	Princeton
1899	Princeton 11, Yale 10	New Haven
1900	Yale 29, Princeton 5	Princeton
1901	Yale 12, Princeton 0	New Haven
1902	Yale 12, Princeton 5	Princeton
1903	Princeton 11, Yale 6	New Haven
1904	Yale 12, Princeton 0	Princeton
1905	Yale 23, Princeton 4	New Haven
1906	Yale 0, Princeton 0	Princeton
1907	Yale 12, Princeton 10	New Haven
1908	Yale 11, Princeton 6	Princeton
1909	Yale 17, Princeton 0	New Haven
1910	Yale 5, Princeton 3	Princeton
1911	Princeton 6, Yale 3	New Haven
1912	Yale 6, Princeton 6	Princeton
1913	Yale 3, Princeton 3	New Haven

Princeton-Harvard		
Year	Team/Score	Site
1877 (spring)	Harvard 1g, 2t, Princeton 1t	Cambridge
1877 (fall)	Princeton 1g, 1t, Harvard 1t	Hoboken
1878	Princeton 1t, Harvard 0	Boston
1879	Princeton 1g, Harvard 0	Hoboken
1880	Princeton 2g, 2t, Harvard 1g, 1t	New York
1881	Princeton 0, Harvard 0	New York
1882	Harvard 1g, 1t, Princeton 1g	Cambridge
1883	Princeton 26, Harvard 7	Princeton
1884	Princeton 36, Harvard 6	Cambridge
1885	No game	
1886	Princeton 12, Harvard 0	Princeton
1887	Harvard 12, Princeton 0	Cambridge
1888	Princeton 18, Harvard 6	Princeton
1889	Princeton 41, Harvard 15	Cambridge
1890–94	No games	
1895	Princeton 12, Harvard 4	Princeton
1896	Princeton 12, Harvard 0	Cambridge
1897–1910	No games	
1911	Princeton 8, Harvard 6	Princeton
1912	Harvard 16, Princeton 6	Cambridge
1913	Harvard 3, Princeton 0	Princeton

Source: Menke, *The Encyclopedia of Sports* (1969), 420, 422, 375–81, 423–24.
[a]g—goal; t—touchdown; s—safety.
[b]Games in 1884 and 1886 were stopped by referee because of darkness and were recorded as ties. Yale was leading in both games when play ended. Under the Association rules of the 1880s, two full halves had to be played in order to make a game official.

Golf

The story of golf in the United States began in the 1880s when Joseph Mickle Fox of Philadelphia learned about the sport on a trip to Scotland and introduced the game at his summer house in Foxburg, Pennsylvania, in 1885. The Foxburg Golf Club, founded in 1887, is probably the oldest golf club in the United States.

More telling was the introduction of the game in Yonkers, New York, by John G. Reid on February 22, 1888. Reid asked Robert Lockhart, a friend, to bring back some clubs and balls on his trip to Scotland. Immediately upon Lockhart's return, Reid invited friends to watch him play in a cow pasture in Yonkers. Joining him were John B. Upham, another enthusiast versed in the game, Henry O. Talmadge, Harry Holbrook, Kingman Putnam, and Alexander P. W. Kinnan. The March 1888 blizzard interrupted their demonstration. Afterward, they restarted play on a 30-acre plot at North Broadway and Shonnard Place owned by John C. Shotts, a German butcher. They laid out a six-hole course and played when they liked, apparently with no objection from Shotts.

When summer came, new equipment arrived from Scotland and players seemed addicted to the game. The men played on Sundays, as well as weekdays, bore the brunt of sermons by various preachers and the criticism of passersby who scoffed at the "ridiculous folly" of grown men hitting a little ball from place to place.

On November 14, 1888, Reid gave a dinner party with Upham, Holbrook, Talmadge, and Putnam, who decided to call themselves the St. Andrew's Golf Club after the famous club in Scotland. The next spring, a mixed foursome of Upham teamed with Mrs. Reid and Reid with Carrie Low was staged; Reid and Upham won.

In the spring of 1892, with thirteen active players, the club had to move from the butcher's lot and a new six-hole course was laid out on Palisade Avenue. On warm days, players removed their outer clothing and hung it on an apple tree on the course, gaining them the appellation "the Apple Tree Gang."

Other courses emerged (Middlesboro, Kentucky; Paterson, Lakewood, New Brunswick, and Montclair, New Jersey; Tuxedo, Newburgh, Ardsley, Knollwood, and Rye, New York; Greenwich, Connecticut; Shinnecock and Meadow Brook on Long Island; and Richmond on Staten Island) most of them with nine holes, making the six-hole course of the Apple Tree Gang seem like a "cow-pasture" course. Resentful of being criticized, the St. Andrew's Club took over the General Jacob Odell farm on the Saw Mill River Parkway in Westchester County, New York, had a farewell party for the Apple Tree Gang, and took up new quarters on December 29, 1893.

In 1894, a group of eastern golfers decided to have a tournament to determine a champion and to be "open to the world." Thus began the U.S. Open. Later on December 22, 1894, a general meeting of golf clubs was called to organize championships, adopt rules of play, and regulate amateur status of the players. Only five clubs responded: St. Andrew's (Mount Hope, New York), the Country Club (Brookline, Massachusetts), Newport (Rhode Island) Golf Club, Shinnecock Hills (Long Island), and the Chicago Golf Club, the sole representative from the West. They created the United States Golf Association (U.S.G.A.), the controlling body for the sport in this country ever since.

The U.S.G.A. conducted its first amateur championship in 1895 at Newport with thirty-two players. C. B. Macdonald was declared the winner, being twelve holes up with eleven left to play. The next day, Horace Rollins won the first Open championship on the same course with a 173 for thirty-six holes.

Women took an active interest in the sport from its beginning in Yonkers. When a tournament was planned to decide the men's amateur championship in 1895, the women decided to stage their own tournament. Thirteen contestants played at the New Meadow Brook Club on Long Island, and in medal play, Mrs. C. S. Brown was the winner with 132 strokes for eighteen holes. The following year, the event was changed to match play and has continued since.

Golf had very little public appeal for the first two decades of its existence. Amateur players played in their own clubs; professionals were few in number, mostly teachers of the game. The event that catapulted the game to national prominence was a match in 1913 between Harry Vardon and Ted Ray, English stars who came over to play in the Open (played at Brookline, Massachusetts), one of whom was considered a sure bet to win.

The Vardon–Ray match exploded into national headlines when an unknown twenty-year-old American youth, Francis Ouimet of Boston, previously a caddie, tied Vardon and Ray at 304 and then beat them in a playoff. In the playoff, Ouimet shot a sizzling 72, while Vardon and Ray finished with 77 and 78 respectively.

Ouimet's feat gave great impetus to the game. The story of his win was told and retold. Suddenly, it appeared that everyone wanted to play. Cities laid out public courses. By World War II, millions were playing on 5,700 courses in the United States.

Golf Champions and Statistics

TABLE 14.30 UNITED STATES U.S.G.A. OPEN

Year	Champion	Rounds				Tot.	Site
		1st	2d	3d	4th		
1894	(match play)—Willie Dunn						St. Andrew's
1895	Horace Rawlins	45	46	41	41	173	Newport
1896	James Foulis	78	74	. . .	. . .	152	Shinnecock Hills
1897	Joe Lloyd	83	79	. . .	. . .	162	Chicago
1898	Fred Herd	84	85	75	84	328	Myopia Hunt Club
1899	Willie Smith	77	82	79	77	315	Baltimore
1900	Harry Vardon (England)	79	78	76	80	313	Chicago
1901	Willie Anderson	84	83	83	81	331	Myopia Hunt Club
1902	Lawrence Auchterlonie	78	78	74	77	307	Garden City G.C.
1903	Willie Anderson	73	76	76	82	307	Baltusrol
1904	Willie Anderson	75	78	78	72	303	Glen View
1905	Willie Anderson	81	80	76	77	314	Myopia Hunt Club
1906	Alex Smith	73	74	73	75	295	Onwentsia
1907	Alex Ross	76	74	76	76	302	Philadelphia
1908	Fred McLoed	82	82	81	77	322	Myopia Hunt Club
1909	George Sargent	75	72	72	71	290	Englewood
1910	Alex Smith	73	73	79	73	298	Philadelphia
1911	John J. McDermott	81	72	75	79	307	Chicago
1912	John J. McDermott	74	75	74	71	294	Buffalo
1913	Francis Ouimet	77	74	74	79	304	Brookline

Source: Menke, *The Encyclopedia of Sports* (1969), 458.

TABLE 14.31 U.S.G.A. AMATEUR

Year	Players/Score	Site
1895	Charles B. Macdonald beat C. E. Sands, 12 and 11	Newport (R.I.) G.C.
1896	H. G. Whigham beat J. G. Thorp, 8 and 7	Shinnecock Hills (N.Y.) G.C.
1897	H. G. Whigham beat W. R. Betts, 8 and 6	Chicago G.C., Wheaton, Ill.
1898	Findlay S. Douglas beat W. B. Smith, 5 and 3	Morris County G.C., Morristown, N.J.
1899	H. M. Harriman beat Findlay S. Douglas, 3 and 2	Onwentsia Club, Lake Forest, Ill.
1900	Walter J. Travis beat Findlay S. Douglas, 2 up	Garden City (N.Y.) G.C.
1901	Walter J. Travis beat W. E. Egan, 5 and 4	C.C. of Atlantic City, Atlantic City, N.J.
1902	L. N. James beat E. M. Byers, 4 and 2	Glen View G.C., Golf, Ill.
1903	Walter J. Travis beat E. M. Byers, 5 and 4	Nassau C.C., Glen Cove, N.Y.
1904	H. Chandler Egan beat Fred Herreshoff, 8 and 6	Baltusrol G.C., Short Hills, N.J.
1905	H. Chandler Egan beat D. E. Sawyer, 6 and 5	Chicago G.C., Wheaton, Ill.
1906	E. M. Byers beat G. S. Lyon, 2 up	Englewood (N.J.) G.C.
1907	Jerome D. Travers beat Archibald Graham, 6 and 5	Euclid Club, Cleveland.
1908	Jerome D. Travers beat Max Behr, 8 and 7	Garden City G.C.
1909	R. A. Gardner beat H. Chandler Egan, 4 and 3	Chicago G.C.

Year	Players/Score	Site
1910	W. C. Fownes Jr. beat W. K. Wood, 4 and 3	The Country Club, Brookline, Mass.
1911	Harold H. Hilton beat Fred Herreshoff, 1 up (37 holes)	Apawamis Club, Rye, N.Y.
1912	Jerome D. Travers beat Charles Evans Jr., 7 and 6	Chicago G.C.
1913	Jerome D. Travers beat J. G. Anderson, 5 and 4	Garden City G.C.

Source: Menke, *The Encyclopedia of Sports* (1969), 459.

TABLE 14.32 USGA WOMEN'S AMATEUR

Year	Players/Score	Site
1895	(medal play)—Mrs. C. S. Brown, 132	Meadow Brook G.C., Westbury, N.Y.
1896	Beatrix Hoyt beat Mrs. A. Turnure, 2 and 1	Morris County G.C., Convent, N.J.
1897	Beatrix Hoyt beat Miss N. C. Sargent, 5 and 4	Essex County Club, Manchester, Mass.
1898	Beatrix Hoyt beat Maude K. Wetmore, 5 and 3	Ardsley Club, Ardsley-on-Hudson, N.Y.
1899	Ruth Underhill beat Mrs. Caleb F. Fox, 2 and 1	Philadelphia C.C., Bala, Pa.

Year	Players/Score	Site
1900	Frances C. Griscom beat Margaret Curtis, 6 and 5	Shinnecock Hills (N.Y.) G.C.
1901	Genevieve Hecker beat Lucy Herron, 5 and 3	Baltusrol G.C., Short Hills, N.J.
1902	Genevieve Hecker beat Miss L. A. Wells, 4 and 3	The Country Club, Brookline, Mass.
1903	Bessie Anthony beat Miss J. A. Carpenter, 7 and 6	Chicago G.C., Wheaton, Ill.
1904	Georgiana Bishop beat Mrs. E. F. Sanford, 5 and 3	Merion Cricket Club, Haverford, Pa.
1905	Pauline Mackay beat Margaret Curtis, 1 up	Morris County G.C.
1906	Harriot S. Curtis beat Miss M. B. Adams, 2 and 1	Brae Burn C.C., West Newton, Mass.
1907	Margaret Curtis beat Harriot S. Curtis, 7 and 6	Midlothian C.C., Blue Island, Ill.
1908	Kate C. Harley beat Mrs. T. H. Polhemus, 6 and 5	Chevy Chase (Md.) Club.
1909	Dorothy Campbell beat Mrs. Ronald H. Barlow, 3 and 2	Merion Cricket Club.
1910	Dorothy Campbell beat Mrs. G. M. Martin, 2 and 1	Homewood C.C., Flossmoor, Ill.
1911	Margaret Curtis beat Lillian Hyde, 5 and 3	Baltusrol G.C.
1912	Margaret Curtis beat Mrs. Ronald H. Barlow, 3 and 2	Essex County Club.
1913	Gladys Ravenscroft beat Marion Hollins, 2 up	Wilmington (Del.) C.C.

Source: Menke, The Encyclopedia of Sports, 463.

Horse Racing

Churchill Downs opened in 1875, an event that marked the emergence of horse racing as a "big-time" sport in Kentucky. In the 1870s and 1880s, tracks were built in or near larger cities in all parts of the United States. The importation of thoroughbreds from England increased while owners of horses established their own farms, bringing about the breeding of the American thoroughbred.

Wagering on races is as old as the sport itself. Bookmakers made their first public appearance in 1873. Most of them were English; American bookmakers supplanted them in the late 1870s. Bookmaking was born to provide the number of stakeholders necessary to public wagering. They soon grew into a "profession" making their money by arranging odds against each horse, based upon their ideas of the chances of winning, taking bets, and taking a portion of the total stake before payoff as remuneration. Bookmaking was the only form of wagering on the New York tracks from the 1870s until the 1940s when it was replaced with parimutuel machines. Reform sentiment swept over other racing areas during the Progressive period, causing temporary bans on major racing everywhere, except Maryland and Kentucky where operators used parimutuel machines.

The best-known horse races in this country are three events for three-year-olds: the Kentucky Derby at Churchill Downs in Louisville, the Preakness Stakes at Pimlico in Baltimore, and the Belmont Stakes at Belmont Park in New York. Combined, these races are known as "the triple crown" of thoroughbred racing. Only eight horses (none during this period) have won all three races.

Jumping (steeplechase) races were first held in 1834; many of the courses were abandoned, but some jumping races established during the Victorian Era continue to this day at these major tracks: Belmont, Aqueduct, and Saratoga in New York; Delaware Park near Wilmington; Pimlico and Laurel, Maryland, and Agua Caliente, Tijuana, Mexico.

TABLE 14.33 KENTUCKY DERBY

Year	Winner	Jockey	Wt.	Net. Val.
1875	Aristides	Lewis	100	$2,850
1876	Vagrant	Swim	97	$2,950
1877	Baden Baden	Walker	100	$3,300
1878	Day Star	Carter	100	$4,050
1879	Lord Murphy	Schauer	100	$3,550
1880	Fonso	G. Lewis	105	$3,800
1881	Hindo	J. McLaughlin	105	$4,410
1882	Apollo	Hurd	102	$4,560
1883	Leonatus	W. Donohue	105	$3,750
1884	Buchanan	I. Murphy	110	$3,990
1885	Joe Cotton	Henderson	110	$4,630
1886	Ben Ali	P. Duffy	118	$4,890
1887	Montrose	I. Lewis	118	$4,200
1888	Macbeth II	Covington	115	$4,740
1889	Spokane	Kiley	118	$4,970
1890	Riley	I. Murphy	118	$5,460
1891	Kingman	I. Murphy	122	$4,680
1892	Azra	A. Clayton	122	$4,230
1893	Lookout	Kunze	122	$4,090
1894	Chant	Goodale	122	$4,020
1895	Halma	Perkins	122	$2,970
1896	Ben Brush	Simms	117	$4,850
1897	Typhoon II	F. Garner	117	$4,850
1898	Plaudit	Simms	117	$4,850
1899	Manuel	Taral	117	$4,850
1900	Lieutenant Gibson	Boland	117	$4,850
1901	His Eminence	Winkfield	117	$4,850
1902	Alan-a-Dale	Winkfield	117	$4,850
1903	Judge Himes	H. Booker	117	$4,850
1904	Elwood	Prior	117	$4,850
1905	Agile	J. Martin	122	$4,850
1906	Sir Huron	R. Troxler	117	$4,850
1907	Pink Star	Minder	117	$4,850
1908	Stone Street	A. Pickens	117	$4,850
1909	Wintergreen	V. Powers	117	$4,850
1910	Donau	Herbert	117	$4,850
1911	Meridian	G. Archibald	117	$4,850
1912	Worth	C. H. Shilling	117	$4,850
1913	Donerail	R. Goose	117	$5,475

Source: Menke, The Encyclopedia of Sports, 579.

TABLE 14.34 PREAKNESS STAKES

Year	Winner	Jockey	Wt.	Net. Val.
1873	Survivor	G. Barbee	110	$1,800
1874	Culpepper	M. Donohue	110	$1,900
1875	Tom Ochiltree	L. Hughes	110	$1,900
1876	Shirley	G. Barbee	110	$1,950
1877	Cloverbrook	C. Holloway	110	$1,600
1878	Duke of Magenta	C. Holloway	110	$2,100
1879	Harold	L. Hughes	110	$2,550
1880	Grenada	L. Hughes	110	$2,000
1881	Saunterer	W. Costello	110	$1,950
1882	Vanguard	W. Costello	110	$1,250
1883	Jacobus	G. Barbee	110	$1,635
1884	Knight of Ellerslie	S. H. Fisher	110	$1,905
1885	Tecumseh	J. McLaughlin	118	$2,160
1886	The Bard	S. H. Fisher	118	$2,050
1887	Dunbine	W. Donoghue	118	$1,675
1888	Refund	F. Littlefield	118	$1,185
1889	Buddhist	H. Anderson	118	$1,130
1894	Assignee	F. Taral	122	$1,830
1895	Belmar	F. Taral	115	$1,350
1896	Margrave	H. Griffin	115	$1,350
1897	Paul Kauvar	Thorpe	108	$1,420
1898	Sly Fox	W. Simms	120	$1,500
1899	Half Time	R. Clawson	102	$1,580
1900	Hindus	H. Spencer	110	$1,900
1901	The Parader	Landry	118	$1,605
1902	Old England	L. Jackson	118	$2,240
1903	Flocarline	W. Gannon	113	$1,875
1904	Bryn Mawr	E. Hilderbrand	108	$2,355
1905	Cairngorm	W. Davis	114	$2,200
1906	Whimsical	W. Miller	108	$2,355
1907	Don Enrique	G. Mountain	107	$2,260
1908	Royal Tourist	E. Dugan	112	$2,455
1909	Effendi	W. Doyle	116	$3,225
1910	Layminster	R. Estep	84	$3,300
1911	Watervale	E. Dugan	112	$2,700
1912	Colonel Halloway	C. Turner	107	$1,450
1913	Buskin	J. Butwell	117	$1,670

Source: Menke, *The Encyclopedia of Sports,* 580.

TABLE 14.35 BELMONT STAKES

Year	Winner	Jockey	Wt.	Net. Val.
1876	Algerine	W. Donohue	110	$3,700
1877	Cloverbrook	C. Holloway	110	$5,200
1878	Duke of Magenta	L. Hughes	118	$3,850
1879	Spendthrist	Evans	118	$4,250
1880	Grenada	L. Hughes	118	$2,800
1881	Saunterer	T. Costello	118	$3,000
1882	Forester	J. McLaughlin	118	$2,600
1883	George Kinney	J. McLaughlin	118	$3,070
1884	Panique	J. McLaughlin	118	$3,150
1885	Tyrant	P. Duffy	118	$2,710
1886	Inspector B	J. McLaughlin	118	$2,720
1887	Hanover	J. McLaughlin	118	$2,900
1888	Six Dixon	J. McLaughlin	118	$3,440
1889	Eric	W. Hayward	118	$4,960
1890	Burlington	S. Barnes	125	$8,560
1891	Foxford	E. Garrison	118½	$5,070
1892	Patron	W. Hayward	122	$6,610
1893	Comanche	W. Simms	117	$5,310
1894	Henry of Navarre	W. Simms	117	$6,680
1895	Belmar	F. Taral	119	$2,700
1896	Hastings	H. Griffin	122	$3,025
1897	Scottish Chieftain	J. Scherrer	115	$3,550
1898	Bowling Brook	F. Littlefield	122	$7,810
1899	Jean Bereaud	R. Clawson	122	$9,445
1900	Ildrim	N. Turner	126	$14,790
1901	Commando	H. Spencer	126	$11,595
1902	Masterman	J. Bullman	126	$13,220
1903	Africander	J. Bullman	126	$13,220
1904	Delhi	G. Odom	126	$11,575
1905	Tanya	E. Hilderbrand	121	$17,240
1906	Burgomaster	L. Lyne	126	$22,700
1907	Peter Pan	G. Mountain	126	$22,765
1908	Colin	J. Notter	126	$22,765
1909	Joe Madden	E. Dugan	126	$24,550
1910	Sweep	J. Butwell	126	$9,700
1913	Prince Eugene	R. Troxler	109	$2,825

Source: Menke, *The Encyclopedia of Sports,* 580–81.

Tennis

Tennis has been played since the thirteenth century. Originally, the game was called *court tennis.* The sport caught the fancy of kings and nobility. Lawn tennis developed from court tennis. The game as played today was invented by Major Walter Clopton Wingfield in Wales. It was an adaptation from the ancient game. From the British Isles, the game spread to every country in the world. The Davis Cup, an international competition, is held annually in lawn tennis.

Court Tennis The exact date of introduction of court tennis (played in a rectangular space on a cement floor enclosed by four cement walls with its own special rules) into the United States is unclear. Some date court tennis to a court built by Hollis Hunnewell and Nathaniel Thayer on Buckingham Street, Boston, on the present site of Back Bay Station, in 1876. This is the first court tennis court about which information is available, although other scattered references to courts in eighteenth-century records occur. Jay Gould, Payne Whitney, and Clarence Mackay built lavish courts running into thousands of dollars. Athletic clubs also put in courts, including the racquet clubs of New York City (1891); Boston (1888); Philadelphia; Tuxedo, New York (1900); Chicago (1893); and the Newport, Rhode Island, Casino (1880).

The greatest court tennis players in this country were Thomas Pettitt, a professional who won the world championship in 1885 and 1890. Jay Gould, an amateur and son of the great finance king, was the singles champion (1906) and the only amateur ever to win the world open championship (1914) until 1959.

Lawn Tennis The game of lawn tennis was introduced into the United States via Bermuda by Mary Outerbridge. Just as in England, lawn tennis achieved far greater popularity than the older game from which it derived. Although Major Walter C. Wingfield, a British Army officer, invented lawn tennis, introducing it at a lawn party in Wales in 1873, it was Outerbridge of Staten Island, New York, who brought the game to the United States. Military officers spread Wingfield's game to the island of Bermuda where Outerbridge vacationed in 1874. She watched the play, liked it, and decided that it was a game that would fascinate her friends back home. She learned the game, bought some tennis balls and racquets, and sailed for New York.

In New York, when Outerbridge attempted to clear customs, she encountered problems. Customs agents confiscated the balls and racquets for a week while they determined how much tax to charge on the unusual-looking objects.

The Victorian Era and its conventions of gender behavior posed substantial difficulties for Outerbridge seeking to gain acceptance of her new found pastime. The Outerbridge family had a membership in the Staten Island Cricket and Baseball Club. Outerbridge was given permission to lay out a court on the edge of a cricket field, but she was unable to get her girlfriends to play such an "unladylike" sport that involved chasing after a bouncing ball. Undaunted, Outerbridge coaxed her brothers into playing, and they introduced their male friends to the game. Yet, many men of the Staten Island club remained skittish about participating in a sport because a girl had sponsored it. Moreover, cries of "love" during the scoring seemed to mark it a game for ladies. But the game weathered the storms of opposition and spread to other resorts in Boston, Newport, and Philadelphia, where the wealthy gathered to socialize.

The lack of a set of standardized rules also hampered early development. Outerbridge had brought all the knowledge she could gain, but the game was new at the time that she first came into contact with it in Bermuda, and rules were not standardized. Throughout the 1870s and into the 1880s, increasingly, lawn tennis was played, but different groups used their own rules, and matches were sometimes chaotic and controversial.

To end the confusion, E. H. Outerbridge, Mary's older brother, called a meeting in New York in 1881 of leaders of all the eastern clubs where tennis was played. Together, they formulated a set of rules that standardized the game and specified the size, weight, and so forth of the equipment. These pioneers organized themselves into the United States Lawn Tennis Association, which has continued to be the ruling body of amateur lawn tennis since then.

The first national championship was played in August 1881 at Newport, Rhode Island, with Richard Sears as the winner over W. E. Glyn. Play for the title continued at Newport until it moved to Forest Hills, New York, in 1915. The men's doubles also began in 1881 with F. W. Taylor and Clarence M. Clark winners at Newport. In 1887, the national women's title matches began at the Philadelphia Cricket Club where Ellen F. Hansell won. Women's play continued there before moving to Forest Hills in 1921. Women's doubles started in Philadelphia in 1890, and mixed doubles began in 1892. Grace W. and Ellen C. Roosevelt were winners of the first women's doubles; the first mixed doubles crown went to Mabel E. Cahill and Clarence Hobart.

An important step in the popularization of the sport was taken by Dwight F. Davis of the United States, who in 1900, put up a cup for play between England and the United States. Later, the competition opened to teams of all nations. The Davis Cup directed world attention to the sport.

From its beginnings in the 1870s and for many years thereafter, lawn tennis in the United States was a game for the rich. But in time, public playgrounds were built and equipped with tennis courts, and neighborhoods set aside land for tennis. So the game grew in favor from players in the hundreds in the early decades to the thousands in the early twentieth century. Today the game is played by millions and enjoyed from youth into the middle years.

TABLE 14.36 LEADING STEEPLECHASE JOCKEYS IN U.S., 1905–1913

Year	Jockey	Mts.	Winners
1905	N. Ray	51	19
1906	N. Ray	53	18
1907	H. Boyle	43	15
1908	McKinley	78	27
1909	Donohue	27	13
1910	J. Lynch	37	16
1911	F. Williams	67	25
1912	W. Allen	61	21
1913	W. Allen	61	21
	J. Kermath	74	21

Source: Menke, The Encyclopedia of Sports, 565.

TABLE 14.37 DAVIS CUP CHALLENGE ROUND RECORD

Competition is open to men's teams throughout the world. Except for the first year in 1900, the annual challenge-round matches have been played in the country of the defending champion. The United States did not participate in 1904 and 1912.

Year	Result	Site
1900	United States 5, British Isles 0	Longwood Cricket Club, Boston, Mass.
1901	No competition	
1902	United States 3, British Isles 2	Crescent Athletic Club, Brooklyn, N.Y.
1903	British Isles 4, United States 1	Longwood Cricket Club, Boston, Mass.
1904	British Isles 5, Belgium 0	Wimbledon, England
1905	British Isles 5, United States 0	Wimbledon
1906	British Isles 5, United States 0	Wimbledon
1907	Australia 3, British Isles 2	Wimbledon
1908	Australia 3, United States 2	Melbourne, Australia
1909	Australia 5, United States 0	Sydney, Australia
1910	No competition	
1911	Australia 5, United States 0	Christchurch, New Zealand
1912	British Isles 3, Australia 2	Melbourne
1913	United States 3, British Isles 2	Wimbledon

Source: Menke, The Encyclopedia of Sports (1969), 945.

Wimbledon Champions The United States had no winners in men's singles at Wimbledon, England until 1920 when William Tilden, II, won. Women's singles were won by May G. Sutton in 1905 and 1907.

TABLE 14.38 U.S. OUTDOOR CHAMPIONS

The first national lawn tennis tournament was held in 1881, and until 1911, there were seven championships, including the All-Comers singles and All-Comers doubles for men. The All-Comers events were discontinued after 1911.

Men's Singles

Year	Winner
1881–87	Richard D. Sears
1888–89	Henry W. Slocum Jr.
1890–92	Oliver S. Campbell
1893–94	Robert D. Wrenn
1895	Fred H. Hovey
1896–97	Robert D. Wrenn
1898–1900	Malcolm D. Whitman
1901–02	William A. Larned
1903	Hugh L. Doherty (England)
1904	Holcombe Ward
1905	Beals C. Wright
1906	William J. Clothier
1907–11	William A. Larned
1912–13	Maurice E. McLoughlin

Men's Doubles

Year	Winners
1881	Clarence M. Clark—F. W. Taylor
1882–84	Richard D. Sears—James Dwight
1885	Richard D. Sears—Joseph S. Clark
1886–87	Richard D. Sears—James Dwight
1888	Oliver S. Campbell—Valentine G. Hall
1889	Henry W. Slocum Jr.—Howard A. Taylor
1890	Valentine G. Hall—Clarence Hobart
1891–92	Oliver S. Campbell—Robert P. Huntington Jr.
1893–94	Clarence Hobart—Fred H. Hovey
1895	Malcolm G. Chace—Robert D. Wrenn
1896	Carr B. Neel—Samuel R. Neel
1897–98	Leonard E. Ware—George P. Sheldon Jr.
1899–1901	Holcombe Ward–Dwight F. Davis
1902–03	Reginald F. Doherty—Hugh L. Doherty (England)
1904–06	Holcombe Ward—Beals C. Wright
1907–10	Harold H. Hackett—Frederick B. Alexander
1911	Raymond D. Little—Gustave F. Touchard
1912–14	Maurice E. McLoughlin—Thomas C. Bundy

Women's Singles

Year	Winners
1887	Ellen F. Hansell
1888–89	Bertha L. Townsend
1890	Ellen C. Roosevelt
1891–92	Mabel E. Cahill
1893	Aline M. Terry
1894	Helen R. Helwig
1895	Juliette P. Atkinson
1896	Elisabeth H. Moore
1897–98	Juliette P. Atkinson
1899	Marion Jones
1900	Myrtle McAteer
1901	Elisabeth H. Moore
1902	Marion Jones
1903	Elisabeth H. Moore
1904	May G. Sutton
1905	Elisabeth H. Moore
1906	Helen Homans
1907	Evelyn Sears
1908	Mrs. Maud Bargar-Wallach
1909–11	Hazel V. Hotchkiss

Women's Doubles

Year	Winners
1890	Ellen C. Roosevelt—Grace W. Roosevelt
1891	Mabel E. Cahill—Mrs. W. Fellowes Morgan
1892	Mabel E. Cahill—A. M. McKinley
1893	Aline M. Terry—Hattie Butler
1894–95	Helen R. Helwig—Juliette P. Atkinson
1896	Elisabeth H. Moore—Juliette P. Atkinson
1897–98	Juliette P. Atkinson—Kathleen Atkinson
1899	Jane W. Craven—Myrtle McAteer
1900	Edith Parker—Hallie Champlin
1901	Juliette P. Atkinson—Myrtle McAteer
1902	Juliette P. Atkinson—Marion Jones
1903	Elisabeth H. Moore—Carrie B. Neely
1904	May G. Sutton—Miriam Hall
1905	Helen Homans—Carrie B. Neely
1906	Mrs. L. S. Coe—Mrs. D. S. Platt
1907	Marie Weimer—Carrie B. Neely
1908	Evelyn Sears—Margaret Curtis
1909–10	Hazel V. Hotchkiss—Edith E. Rotch
1911	Hazel V. Hotchkiss—Eleonora Sears
1912	Dorothy Green—Mary K. Browne
1913–14	Mary K. Browne—Mrs. R. H. Williams

Mixed Doubles

Year	Winners
1892	Mabel E. Cahill—Clarence Hobart
1893	Ellen C. Roosevelt—Clarence Hobart
1894–96	Juliette P. Atkinson—Edwin P. Fisher
1897	Laura Hensen—D. L. Magruder
1898	Carrie B. Neely—Edwin P. Fischer
1899	Elizabeth J. Rastall—Albert L. Hoskins
1900	Margaret Hunnewell—Alfred Codman
1901	Marion Jones—Raymond D. Little
1902	Elisabeth H. Moore—Wylie C. Grant
1903	Helen Chapman—Harry F. Allen
1904	Elisabeth H. Moore—Wylie C. Grant
1905	Clarence Hobart—Mrs. Clarence Hobart
1906	Sarah Coffin—Edward B. Dewhurst
1907	May Sayres—Wallace F. Johnson
1908	Edith E. Rotch—Nathaniel W. Niles
1909	Hazel V. Hotchkiss—Wallace F. Johnson
1910	Hazel V. Hotchkiss—Joseph R. Carpenter Jr.
1911	Hazel V. Hotchkiss—Wallace F. Johnson
1912	Mary K. Browne—R. Norris Williams 2d
1913–14	Mary K. Browne—William T. Tilden 2d

Source: Menke, *The Encyclopedia of Sports* (1969), 950.

TABLE 14.39 NATIONAL INTERCOLLEGIATE CHAMPIONS

Tournament was conducted by the United States Lawn Tennis Association prior to 1938.

Singles and Doubles

Year	Winners
1883 (spring)	J. S. Clark, Harvard; J. S. Clark—H. A. Taylor
1883 (fall)	H. A. Taylor, Harvard; H. A. Taylor—P. E. Presby
1884	W. P. Knapp, Yale; W. P. Knapp—W. V. S. Thorne
1885	W. P. Knapp, Yale; W. P. Knapp—A. L. Shipman
1886	G. M. Brinley, Trinity; W. P. Knapp—W. L. Thatcher, Yale
1887	P. S. Sears, Harvard; P. S. Sears—Q. A. Shaw Jr.
1888	P. S. Sears, Harvard; V. G. Hall—O. S. Campbell, Columbia

Singles and Doubles	
Year	Winners
1889	R. P. Huntington Jr., Yale; O. S. Campbell—A. E. Wright, Columbia
1890	F. H. Hovey, Harvard; Q. A. Shaw Jr.—S. T. Chase, Harvard
1891	F. H. Hovey, Harvard; F. H. Hovey—R. D. Wrenn
1892	W. A. Larned, Cornell; R. D. Wrenn—F. D. Winslow, Harvard
1893	M. G. Chace, Brown; M. G. Chace—C. R. Budlong
1894–95	M. G. Chace, Yale; M. G. Chace—A. E. Foote
1896	M. D. Whitman, Harvard; L. E. Ware—W. M. Scudder, Harvard
1897	S. G. Thomson, Princeton; L. E. Ware—M. D. Whitman, Harvard
1898	L. E. Ware, Harvard; L. E. Ware—M. D. Whitman
1899	D. F. Davis, Harvard; D. F. Davis—Holcombe Ward
1900	R. D. Little, Princeton; R. D. Little—F. B. Alexander
1901	F. B. Alexander, Princeton; H. A. Plummer—S. L. Russell, Yale
1902	W. J. Clothier, Harvard; W. J. Clothier—E. W. Leonard
1903	E. B. Dewhurst, Pennsylvania; B. Colston—E. Clapp, Yale
1904	Robert LeRoy, Columbia; K. H. Behr—G. Bodman, Yale
1905	E. B. Dewhurst, Pennsylvania; E. B. Dewhurst—H. B. Register
1906	Robert LeRoy, Columbia; E. B. Wells—A. Spaulding, Yale
1907	G. P. Gardner Jr., Harvard; N. W. Niles—E. S. Dabney, Harvard
1908	N. W. Niles, Harvard; H. M. Tilden—A. Thayer, Pennsylvania
1909	W. F. Johnson, Pennsylvania; W. F. Johnson—A. Thayer
1910	R. A. Holden Jr., Yale; D. Mathey—B. N. Dell, Princeton
1911	E. H. Whitney, Harvard; D. Mathey—C. T. Butler, Princeton
1912	G. M. Church, Princeton; G. M. Church—W. H. Mace
1913	R. N. Williams 2d, Harvard; W. M. Washburn—J. J. Armstrong, Harvard

Source: Menke, The Encyclopedia of Sports (1969), 950–51.

Men's Doubles	
Year	Winner
1900	Calhoun Cragin—J. Parmly Paret
1901	Calhoun Cragin—Oviedo M. Bostwick
1902–04	Wylie C. Grant—Robert LeRoy
1905	Theodore R. Pell—Harry F. Allen
1906–08	Harold H. Hackett—Frederick B. Alexander
1909	Wylie C. Grant—Theodore R. Pell
1910	Gustave F. Touchard—Carlton R. Gardner
1911–12	Frederick B. Alexander—Theodore R. Pell
1913–14	Wylie C. Grant—G. Carleton Shafer

Women's Singles	
Year	Winner
1907	Elisabeth H. Moore
1908–09	Marie Wagner
1910	Mrs. Frederick G. Schmitz
1911	Marie Wagner
1912	No competition
1913–14	Marie Wagner

Women's Doubles	
Year	Winner
1908	Mrs. Helen Helwig Pouch—Elisabeth H. Moore
1909	Elisabeth H. Moore—Erna Marcus
1910	Marie Wagner—Clara Kutroff
1911	Elizabeth C. Bunce—Barbara Fleming
1912	No competition
1913	Marie Wagner—Clara Kutroff

Source: Menke, The Encyclopedia of Sports, 952–953.

TABLE 14.40 UNITED STATES INDOOR CHAMPIONS

Men's Singles	
Year	Winner
1900	J. Appleton Allen
1901	Holcombe Ward
1902	J. Parmly Paret
1903–04	Wylie C. Grant
1905	Edward B. Dewhurst
1906	Wylie C. Grant
1907	Theodore R. Pell
1908	Wylie C. Grant
1909	Theodore R. Pell
1910	Gustave F. Touchard
1911	Theodore R. Pell
1912	Wylie C. Grant
1913–15	Gustave F. Touchard

Swimming

Four standard styles of swimming are recognized internationally: the freestyle, backstroke, butterfly, and breast stroke. Australia achieved early fame as a land of swimmers until the Olympic Club of San Francisco decided in 1903 to hire a tutor for its members. J. Scott Leary was one of the first pupils and broke into the headlines on July 18, 1905, as the first American to swim 100 yards in 60 seconds. He went on to become a swimming sensation in America, attracting others to the sport. Charles M. Daniels observed Leary swimming and adapted the scissors-kick, previously perfected by the Australians, into the "American crawl."

Swimming races for men became part of the modern Olympic games when they were revived in 1896. The United States won its first swimming title when Daniels won the 440-yard (now 400-meter) race in 1904. Within a few Olympiads, the Americans came to dominate men's swimming, until 1932, by which time other countries had developed their own national training programs.

TABLE 14.41   **MEN'S OUTDOOR SWIMMING**

100-Yard Freestyle—100 Meters

Year	Winner	Time
1883	A. F. Camacho	1m 28¼s
1884	H. E. Toussaint	1m 21s
1885	H. Braun	1m 18.4s
1886	H. Braun	1m 29.2s
1887	H. Braun	1m 17.2s
1888	H. Braun	1m 16.2s
1889	W. C. Johnson	1m 22.4s
1800	W. C. Johnson	1m 5.2s
1891	W. C. Johnson	1m 10.6s
1892	A. T. Kenney	1m 18.2s
1893	A. T. Kenney	1m 12.4s
1894	A. T. Kenney	1m 9.6s
1895	No competition	
1896	George R. Whittacker	1m 13.4s
1897	D. B. Renear	1m 7.4s
1898	S. P. Avery	
1899	E. C. Schaeffer	1m 8.6s
1900	E. C. Schaeffer	1m 5.6s
1901	E. C. Schaeffer	1m 10s
1902	E. C. Schaeffer	1m 7s
1903	Fred A. Wenck	1m 9.6s
1904	Zoltan de Holomay	1m 2.8s
1904	Charles M. Daniels	1m 3.8s
1906	Charles M. Daniels	1m
1907	Charles M. Daniels	1m 3.4s
1908	Charles M. Daniels	57.2s
1909–1913	No competition	

220-Yard Freestyle—200 Meters

Year	Winner	Time
1897	D. M. Reeder	2m 57.4s
1898	H. H. Reeder	3m 7.6s
1899	E. C. Schaeffer	2m 53.6s
1900	E. C. Schaeffer	3m 7.2s
1901	E. C. Schaeffer	2m 50.8s
1902	E. C. Schaeffer	2m 58.8s
1903	Charles Ruberl	3m 18.4s
1904	Charles M. Daniels	2m 44.2s
1905	Charles M. Daniels	2m 45s
1906	Charles M. Daniels	2m 42.4s
1907	Charles M. Daniels	3m 13.8s
1908	Charles M. Daniels	2m 36.8s
1909	No competition	
1910	Charles M. Daniels	2m 33s
1911–13	No competition	

440-Yard Freestyle—400 Meters

Year	Winner	Time
1893	A. T. Kenney	6m 24.4s
1894	P. F. Dickey	7m 24.6s
1895–96	No competition	
1897	Howard F. Brewer	7m 8.4s
1898	Dr. Paul Neumann	6m 51.4s
1899	E. C. Schaeffer	6m 48.6s
1900	E. C. Schaeffer	6m 52.8s
1901	E. C. Schaeffer	6m 26s
1902	E. C. Schaeffer	6m 18.2s
1903	T. E. Kitching Jr.	6m 31.6s

440-Yard Freestyle—400 Meters

Year	Winner	Time
1904	Charles M. Daniels	6m 16.2s
1905	L. B. Goodwin	6m 22s
1906	Charles M. Daniels	6m 24s
1907	Charles M. Daniels	6m 26.8s
1908	Charles M. Daniels	5m 54.2s
1909	Charles M. Daniels	5m 57.4s
1910	Charles M. Daniels	5m 59.8s
1911	R. M. Ritter	5m 52.6s
1912	R. E. Frizell	5m 56.8s
1913	J. C. Wheatley	6m 4.6s

880-Yard Freestyle—800 Meters

Year	Winner	Time
1893	W. G. Douglas	13m 39.4s
1894	T. Carey	15m 33s
1895–96	No competition	
1897	Dr. P. Neumann	15m 6.6s
1898	F. A. Wenck	14m 8s
1899	F. A. Wenck	15m 3s
1900	Dr. W. G. Douglas	15m 4.6s
1901	L. B. Goodwin	14m 18.8s
1902	E. C. Schaeffer	13m 27.4s
1903	Charles Ruberl	13m 30.6s
1904	Emil Rausch	13m 11.6s
1905	Charles M. Daniels	12m 58.6s
1906	H. J. Handy	12m 24s
1907	L. B. Goodwin	13m 2.4s
1908	L. B. Goodwin	13m 23s
1909	Charles M. Daniels	12m 18.4s
1910	L. B. Goodwin	13m 12s
1911	L. B. Goodwin	14m 25.8s
1912	L. B. Goodwin	12m 42s
1913	Gilbert E. Tomlinson	12m 49.6s

One-Mile Freestyle—1,500 Meters

Year	Winner	Time
1877	R. Weissenborn	45m 44¼s
1878	H. J. Heath	29m 20s
1879–1882	No competition	
1883	R. P. Magee	29m 42¼s
1884	R. P. Magee (with tide)	25m 41.5s
1885	R. P. Magee (with tide)	22m 38s
1886	R. P. Magee (with tide)	29m 02s
1887	A. Meffert	35m 18.2s
1888	H. Braun	26m 57s
1889	A. Meffert (with tide)	27m 20s
1890	A. Meffert (with tide)	22m 39.4s
1891	J. R. Whitmore (with tide)	24m 11.6s
1892	A. T. Kenney (with tide)	28m 45.4s
1893	G. Whittaker (with tide)	28m 55.4s
1894	A. T. Kenney	33m 34.4s
1895	No competition	
1896	B. A. Hart	30m 27.6s
1897	Dr. P. Neumann	30m 24.4s
1898	F. A. Wenck	29m 51.6s
1899	F. A. Wenck	30m 33.8s
1900	George W. Van Cleaf	34m 45.6s
1901	Otto Wahle	28m 52.6s
1902	E. Carroll Schaeffer	28m 14.6s
1903	Charles Ruberl	28m 05.6s
1904	Emil Rausch	27m 15.2s

One-Mile Freestyle—1,500 Meters

Year	Winner	Time
1905	Charles M. Daniels	26m 41.8s
1906	H. J. Handy	28m 43.4s
1907	H. J. Handy	29m 20.8s
1908	Charles M. Daniels	27m 20.6s
1909	Charles M. Daniels	26m 19.6s
1910	L. B. Goodwin	30m 02.4s
1911	J. H. Reilly	25m 40.4s
1912	L. B. Goodwin	25m 25s
1913	L. B. Goodwin	25m 18.4s

220-Yard Breast Stroke—200 Meters

Year	Winner	Time
1906	A. M. Goersling (200 yards)	3m 01.2s
1907	H. J. Handy (200 yards)	3m 17.6s
1908	A. M. Goersling (200 yards)	2m 46.4s
1909	A. M. Goersling (200 yards)	2m 49s
1910–13	No competition	

Platform Diving

Year	Winner
1909	George W. Gaidzik
1910	George W. Gaidzik
1911	George W. Gaidzik
1912	J. F. Dunn
1913	No competition

Long Distance (4 miles in recent years)

Year	Winner	Time
1909	J. H. Handy	1hr 43m 30s
1910	L. B. Goodwin	1hr 30m 49s
1911	M. McDermott	1hr 41m
1912	Chauncey Heath	1hr 39m 2.2s
1913	M. McDermott	1hr 50m 44.4s

Source: Frank G. Menke, *The Encyclopedia of Sports* (1969), 892, 893, 894, 895.
Source: Wright, ed., *The Universal Almanac* 1990 (1991), 641.

TABLE 14.42   MEN'S INDOOR SWIMMING

100-Yard Freestyle

Year	Winner	Time
1901	E. Carroll Schaeffer	1m 6.8s
1902	H. Lemoyne	1m 4s
1903	L. B. Goodwin	1m 9.2s
1904–05	No competition	
1906	Charles M. Daniels	58s
1907–08	No competition	
1909	Charles M. Daniels	56.8s
1910	Charles M. Daniels	54.8s
1911	Charles M. Daniels	56.8s
1912	Duke Kahanamoku	57.8s
1913	H. J. Hebner	55.4s

220-Yard Freestyle

Year	Winner	Time
1901	E. Carroll Schaeffer (200 yards)	2m 44.8s
1902	H. Lemoyne (200 yards)	2m 30.6s
1903	C. A. Ruberl	2m 54s
1904–05	No competition	
1906	Charles M. Daniels	2m 33.2

220-Yard Freestyle

Year	Winner	Time
1907–08	No competition	
1909	Charles M. Daniels	2m 25.4s
1910	Charles M. Daniels	2m 33s
1911	Charles M. Daniels	2m 26s
1912	Perry McGillivray	2m 34.2s
1913	Perry McGillivray	2m 20s

440-Yard Freestyle

Year	Winner	Time
1901	E. Carroll Schaeffer (400 yards)	5m 26.2s
1902	No competition	
1903	C. A. Ruberl	6m 14s
1904–05	No competition	
1906	Charles M. Daniels	5m 50.4s
1907–09	No competition	

150-Yard Backstroke

Year	Winner	Time
1906	C. A. Ruberl	2m 5.4s
1907–09	No competition	
1910	H. J. Hebner	1m 56.4s
1911	H. J. Hebner	1m 57.2s
1912	H. J. Hebner	1m 55.4s
1913	H. J. Hebner	2m 16.8s

220-Yard Breaststroke—200 Yards

Year	Winner	Time
1906	A. M. Goersling (200 yards)	2m 52.6s
1907–09	No competition	
1910	Michael McDermott (200 yards)	2m 56s
1911	Michael McDermott (200 yards)	2m 43.2s
1912	Michael McDermott (200 yards)	2m 38.8s
1913	Michael McDermott (200 yards)	2m 55.4s

Ten-Foot or Three-Meter Springboard Diving

Year	Winner
1909	F. Bornaman
1910	George Gaidzik
1911	F. Bornaman
1912	G. W. Gaidzik
1913	Arthur McAleenan

Source: Menke, *The Encyclopedia of Sports*, 899, 900, 901, 902, 905.

Track and Field

The first amateur championships in the United States were staged by the New York Athletic Club in 1868; the meet was held indoors. In 1876 colleges, mostly in the east, organized what is now known as the Intercollegiate Association of Amateur Athletes of America (I.C.A.A.A.A.) and staged the nation's pioneer college meet. During the same year, a contest was held to determine the champions of the United States, among collegians and all other amateur athletes. From 1879 through 1888, championships were held under the sponsorship of the National Association of Amateur Athletes of America (N.A.A.A.A.). In 1888, the Amateur Athletic Union of the United States (A.A.U.) came into existence to establish rules for all amateur athletes, collegian or noncollegian, laying the foundation for amateur

Track-and-field events were for men only until the 1920s. In this picture is shown a Central High School track meet, Washington, D.C., 1899. (Courtesy Prints and Photographs Division, Library of Congress)

track-and-field meets, with the I.C.A.A.A.A. handling all strictly collegiate events and the A.A.U. assuming power in amateur athletic programs. Women did not participate in track-and-field events until the 1920s.

Track-and-field meets are divided into two groups: track events and field events. Track events consist of running and hurdling on an oval-shaped running track, usually one-quarter mile long and 18 to 32 feet wide. One side of the track is marked out for short races (dashes). Indoor tracks are much shorter in length (usually 8 to 11 laps to the mile) and use boards, clay, or dirt for the running surface.

Field events—jumping, vaulting, and weight throwing—are usually conducted on the field inside the running track (infield). In some cases, field events are held on a field adjacent to the track.

The shortest races are at distances of 100, 200, and 440 yards (or 100, 200, and 400 meters) outdoors and 50, 60, or 70 yards indoors. The 880-yard (800-meter) run is considered a middle-distance race (more than a quarter but less than a mile in length). Distance races are for 1 mile (1,500 meters) or more. In relay races, four runners make up a team, and each runs a part of the total. In nonmedley relays, each runner covers an equal distance; in medley relays, runners cover varying distances.

Hurdling is a running race in which the runner jumps a series of ten artificial barriers spaced at equal intervals over the entire distance. High-hurdle races are 120 yards; low-hurdle races at the college level are 220 yards.

The broad jump is a horizontal jump for distance; the high jump is a vertical jump over a horizontal bar between two standards. The pole vault is similar in nature except that the jumper uses a 12- to 16-foot pole to clear the bar.

Weight-throwing events utilize the shot put, the discus, and the javelin. The shot put is a 16-pound metal ball that is thrown from a circle 7 feet in diameter. The discus is a wooden disk with a metal rim weighing not less than 4 pounds, 6.4 ounces. The javelin is a pointed spear 8.53 feet long and weighing 1.765 pounds that is hurled from a starting line.

Cross-country running is a special type of long-distance running over a course that is laid out over different surfaces with different obstacles in the countryside. It originated as a sport in England at the time of the revival of modern track and field in the nineteenth century.

U.S. Track-and-Field Champions—Men's Outdoor The first amateur championships in this country were conducted by the New York Athletic Club in 1876, 1877 and 1878. From 1879 through 1888, championships were held under the sponsorship of the National Association of Amateur Athletes of America.

Beginning in 1888 and continuing through the present, the Amateur Athletic Union of the United States has conducted annual championships. Two title meets were held in 1888.

TABLE 14.43 100-YARD DASH

The winners at both meets are listed, the A.A.U. (*) and the N.A.A.A.A. (†)

Year	Champion	Time
1876	F. C. Saportas	10 1/2s
1877	C. C. McIvor	10 1/2s
1878	W. C. Wilmer	10s
1879	B. R. Value	10 3/5s
1880	L. E. Myers	10 2/5s
1881	L. E. Myers	10 1/4s
1882	A. Waldron	. . .
1883	A. Waldron	10 1/4s
1884	M. W. Ford	10 4/5s
1885	M. W. Ford	10 3/5s
1886	M. W. Ford	10 2/5s
1887	C. H. Sherrill	10 2/5s
1888	*F. Westing	10 3/5s
1888	†F. Westing	10s
1889	J. Owen Jr.	10 2/5s
1890	J. Owen Jr.	9 4/5s
1891	L. H. Cary	10 1/5s
1892	H. Jewett	10s
1893	C. W. Stage	10 1/5s
1894	T. I. Lee	10 1/5s
1895	Bernard J. Wefers	10s
1896	Bernard J. Wefers	10 1/5s
1897	Bernard J. Wefers	9 4/5s
1898	F. W. Jarvis	10s
1899	A. C. Kraenzlein	. . .

Year	Champion	Time
1900	M. W. Long	10s
1901	F. M. Sears	9⁴/₅s
1902	P. J. Walsh	10s
1903	Archie Hahn	10¹/₅s
1904	L. Robertson	10²/₅s
1905	Charles L. Parsons	9⁴/₅s
1906	Charles J. Seitz	10¹/₅s
1907	H. J. Huff	10¹/₅s
1908	W. F. Hamilton	10¹/₅s
1909	W. Martin	10¹/₅s
1910	J. M. Rosenberger	10¹/₅s
1911	Gwin Henry	10s
1912	Howard P. Drew	10s
1913	Howard P. Drew	10²/₅s

Source: Frank G. Menke, *The Encyclopedia of Sports* (1969), 965–66.

TABLE 14.44   220-YARD DASH

The winners at both meets are listed, the A.A.U. (*) and the N.A.A.A.A. (†)

Year	Champion	Time
1877	Edward Merritt	24s
1878	W. C. Wilmer	22⁷/₈s
1879	L. E. Myers	23³/₅s
1880	L. E. Myers	23³/₅s
1881	L. E. Myers	23¹/₂s
1882	Henry S. Brooks Jr.	22³/₅s
1883	Henry S. Brooks Jr.	22⁴/₅s
1884	L. E. Myers	24¹/₅s
1885	M. W. Ford	23⁴/₅s
1886	M. W. Ford	23¹/₅s
1887	F. Westing	23¹/₅s
1888	*F. Westing	22¹/₅s
1888	†F. Westing	22²/₅s
1889	J. Owen Jr.	23²/₅s
1890	F. Westing	22¹/₅s
1891	Luther H. Cary	22⁴/₅s
1892	H. Jewett	‡21⁴/₅s
1893	C. W. Stage	22¹/₅s
1894	T. I. Lee	22s
1895	Bernard J. Wefers	21⁴/₅s
1896	Bernard J. Wefers	23s
1897	Bernard J. Wefers	21²/₅s
1898	J. H. Maybury	22²/₅s
1899	M. W. Long	22²/₅s
1900	W. S. Edwards	22s
1901	F. M. Sears	22s
1902	P. J. Walsh	22⁴/₅s
1903	Archie Hahn	23¹/₅s
1904	William Hogenson	22⁴/₅s
1905	Archie Hahn	22¹/₅s
1906	R. L. Young	22²/₅s
1907	H. J. Huff	22¹/₅s
1908	W. F. Keating	22²/₅s
1909	W. F. Dawbarn	22²/₅s
1910	Gwin Henry	22³/₅s
1911	J. Nelson	21⁴/₅s
1912	A. T. Meyer	21⁴/₅s
1913	H. P. Drew	22⁴/₅s

‡With wind.
Source: Frank G. Menke, *The Encyclopedia of Sports* (1969), 966.

TABLE 14.45   440-YARD RUN

The winners at both meets are listed, the A.A.U. (*) and the N.A.A.A.A. (†)

Year	Champion	Time
1876	Edward Merritt	54¹/₂s
1877	Edward Merritt	55¹/₄s
1878	F. W. Brown	54³/₈s
1879	Lawrence E. Myers	52²/₅s
1880	Lawrence E. Myers	52s
1881	Lawrence E. Myers	49²/₅s
1882	Lawrence E. Myers	51³/₅s
1883	Lawrence E. Myers	52¹/₅s
1884	Lawrence E. Myers	55⁴/₅s
1885	H. M. Raborg	54¹/₅s
1886	J. S. Robertson	52s
1887	H. M. Banks	51⁴/₅s
1888	*W. C. Dohm	51s
1888	†T. J. O'Mahoney	53s
1889	W. C. Dohm	51²/₅s
1890	W. C. Downs	50s
1891	W. C. Downs	51s
1892	W. C. Downs	50s
1893	E. W. Allen	50²/₅s
1894	T. F. Keane	51s
1895	T. E. Burke	49³/₅s
1896	T. E. Burke	48⁴/₅s
1897	T. E. Burke	49s
1898	M. W. Long	52s
1899	M. W. Long	50⁴/₅s
1900	M. W. Long	52³/₅s
1901	H. W. Hayes	52²/₅s
1902	F. R. Moulton	50⁴/₅s
1903	H. L. Hillman	52s
1904	D. H. Meyer	51¹/₅s
1905	Frank Waller	49³/₅s
1906	Frank Waller	50¹/₅s
1907	J. B. Taylor	51s
1908	Harry Hillman	49³/₅s
1909	E. F. Lindberg	50²/₅s
1910	W. Hayes	52s
1911	F. J. Lindberg	49s
1912	T. J. Halpin	49²/₅s
1913	C. B. Haff	51¹/₅s

Source: Frank G. Menke, *The Encyclopedia of Sports* (1969), 967.

TABLE 14.46   880-YARD RUN

The winners at both meets are listed, the A.A.U. (*) and the N.A.A.A.A. (†)

Year	Champion	Time
1876	H. Lambe	2m 10s
1877	R. R. Colgate	2m 5³/₄s
1878	Edward Merritt	2m 5¹/₄s
1879	Lawrence E. Myers	2m 1²/₅s
1880	Lawrence E. Myers	2m 4³/₅s
1881	William Smith	2m 4s
1882	W. H. Goodwin Jr.	1m 56⁷/₈s
1883	T. J. Murphy	2m 4²/₅s
1884	Lawrence E. Myers	2m 9⁴/₅s
1885	H. L. Mitchell	2m 2³/₅s
1886	C. M. Smith	2m 4s
1887	G. Tracy	2m 1³/₅s
1888	*G. Tracy	2m 2¹/₅s
1888	†J. W. Moffatt	2m 2¹/₅s
1889	R. A. Ward	2m 6¹/₅s

(continued)

TABLE 14.46 (continued)

Year	Champion	Time
1890	H. L. Dadman	1m 59¹/ss
1891	W. C. Dohm	2m 4¹/ss
1892	T. B. Turner	1m 58³/ss
1893	T. B. Turner	2m 1⁴/ss
1894	Charles H. Kilpatrick	1m 55⁴/ss
1895	Charles H. Kilpatrick	1m 56²/ss
1896	Charles H. Kilpatrick	1m 57³/ss
1897	J. F. Cregan	1m 58³/ss
1898	T. E. Burke	2m ²/ss
1899	H. E. Manvel	1m 58¹/ss
1900	Alex Grant	2m 4¹/ss
1901	H. H. Hayes	2m 2⁴/ss
1902	J. H. Wright	1m 59³/ss
1903	H. V. Valentine	2m 2⁴/ss
1904	H. V. Valentine	2m 4/ss
1905	James D. Lightbody	2m 3³/ss
1906	M. W. Sheppard	1m 55²/ss
1907	M. W. Sheppard	1m 55¹/ss
1908	M. W. Sheppard	1m 55³/ss
1909	C. Edmundson	1m 55¹/ss
1910	Harry Gissing	2m 1⁴/ss
1911	M. W. Sheppard	1m 54¹/ss
1912	M. W. Sheppard	1m 57²/ss
1913	Homer Baker	2m 1/ss

Source: Frank G. Menke, The Encyclopedia of Sports (1969), 968.

TABLE 14.47 1-MILE RUN

The winners at both meets are listed, the A.A.U. (*) and the N.A.A.A.A. (†)

Year	Champion	Time
1876	H. Lambe	4m 51¹/ss
1877	R. Morgan	4m 49³/₄s
1878	T. H. Smith	4m 51¹/₄s
1879	H. M. Pellatt	4m 42²/ss
1880	H. Fredericks	4m 30³/ss
1881	H. Fredericks	4m 32³/ss
1882	H. Fredericks	4m 36²/ss
1883	H. Fredericks	4m 36⁴/ss
1884	P. C. Mederia	4m 36⁴/ss
1885	G. Y. Gilbert	4m 41¹/ss
1886	E. C. Carter	4m 33²/ss
1887	E. C. Carter	4m 30s
1888	*G. M. Gibbs	4m 27¹/ss
1888	†Thomas P. Conneff	4m 32³/ss
1889	A. B. George	4m 36s
1890	A. B. George	4m 24⁴/ss
1891	Thomas P. Conneff	4m 30³/ss
1892	G. W. Orton	4m 27⁴/ss
1893	G. W. Orton	4m 32⁴/ss
1894	G. W. Orton	4m 24²/ss
1895	G. W. Orton	4m 36s
1896	G. W. Orton	4m 27s
1897	J. F. Cregan	4m 27³/ss
1898	J. F. Cregan	4m 47s
1899	Alex Grant	4m 28¹/ss
1900	G. W. Orton	4m 42²/ss
1901	Alex Grant	4m 36²/ss
1902	Alex Grant	4m 35⁴/ss
1903	Alex Grant	4m 52s
1904	D. C. Munson	4m 41¹/ss

Year	Champion	Time
1905	James D. Lightbody	4m 48⁴/ss
1906	F. A. Rodgers	4m 22⁴/ss
1907	J. P. Sullivan	4m 29s
1908	H. L. Trube	4m 25s
1909	Joe Ballard	4m 30¹/ss
1910	J. W. Monument	4m 31s
1911	Abel R. Kiviat	4m 19³/ss
1912	Abel R. Kiviat	4m 18³/ss
1913	Norman S. Taber	4m 26²/ss

Source: Frank G. Menke, The Encyclopedia of Sports (1969), 968.

TABLE 14.48 5-MILE RUN

The winners at both meets are listed, the A.A.U. (*) and the N.A.A.A.A. (†)

Year	Champion	Time
1880	J. H. Gifford	27m 51¹/ss
1881	W. C. Davies	27m 43²/ss
1882	T. F. Delaney	27m 34²/ss
1883	T. F. Delaney	26m 47²/ss
1884	G. Stonebridge	27m 45s
1885	P. D. Skillman	27m 13²/ss
1886	E. C. Carter	27m 4s
1887	E. C. Carter	25m 23³/ss
1888	*Thomas P. Conneff	26m 46²/ss
1889	Thomas P. Conneff	26m 42s
1890	Thomas P. Conneff	25m 37⁴/ss
1891	Thomas P. Conneff	27m 38²/ss
1892	W. D. Day	25m 54²/ss
1893	W. D. Day	26m 8²/ss
1894	C. H. Bean	26m 53²/ss
1895–98	No competition	
1899	{ Alex Grant / R. Grant	28m 30⁴/ss
1900	A. L. Newton	27m 41²/ss
1901	F. M. Kanaly	25m 44⁴/ss
1902	Alex Grant	26m 32s
1903	No competition	
1904	John Joyce	28m 25¹/ss
1905	Frank Verner	28m 57³/ss
1906	William Nelson	26m 22³/ss
1907	J. J. Daly	26m 4s
1908	F. G. Bellars	26m 14⁴/ss
1909	H. McLean	26m 9³/ss
1910	W. J. Kramer	27m 6²/ss
1911	G. V. Bonhag	25m 50²/ss
1912	Hannes Kolehmainen	25m 43²/ss
1913	Hannes Kolehmainen	26m 10³/ss

Source: Frank G. Menke, The Encyclopedia of Sports (1969), 969.

TABLE 14.49 10-MILE RUN

Year	Champion	Time
1889	S. Thomas	53m 58⁴/ss
1890	T. P. Conneff	55m 32³/ss
1891	E. C. Carter	57m 24s
1892	W. O'Keefe	55m 59⁴/ss
1893	E. C. Carter	53m 40¹/ss
1894	E. C. Carter	58m 9¹/ss
1895	No competition	
1896	H. Gray	58m 32²/ss
1897	No competition	
1898	T. G. McGirr	57m 40¹/ss

1899	G. W. Orton	57m 28s
1900–02	No competition	
1903	John Joyce	57m 32s
1904	John Joyce	58m 34¹/₄s
1905	John Joyce	54m 54¹/₅s
1906	No competition	
1907	J. J. Daly	55m 16⁴/₅s
1908	J. L. Eisele	53m 16¹/₅s
1909	G. V. Bonhag	52m 34⁴/₅s
1910	W. C. Bailey	54m 26⁴/₅s
1911	L. Scott	53m 20¹/₅s
1912	H. J. Smith	53m 51²/₅s
1913	Hannes Kolehmainen	51m 3²/₅s

Source: Frank G. Menke, *The Encyclopedia of Sports* (1969), 970.

TABLE 14.50   120-YARD HIGH HURDLES

The winners at both meets are listed, the A.A.U. (*) and the N.A.A.A.A. (†)

Year	Champion	Time
1876	George Hitchock	19s
1877	H. E. Ficken	18¹/₄s
1878	H. E. Ficken	17¹/₄s
1879	J. E. A. Haigh	19s
1880	H. H. Moritz	19¹/₅s
1881	J. T. Tivey	19¹/₈s
1882	J. T. Tivey	16⁴/₅s
1883	S. A. Safford	19²/₅s
1884	S. A. Safford	18¹/₅s
1885	A. A. Jordan	17³/₅s
1886	A. A. Jordan	16¹/₂s
1887	A. A. Jordan	16²/₅s
1888	*A. A. Jordan	161¹/₅s
1889	G. Schwegler	17s
1890	F. T. Ducharme	16s
1891	A. F. Copland	16s
1892	F. C. Puffer	§15²/₅s
1893	F. C. Puffer	16s
1894	S. Chase	15³/₅s
1895	S. Chase	15³/₄s
1896	W. B. Rogers	16¹/₅s
1897	J. H. Thompson Jr.	16s
1898	Alvin C. Kraenzlein	15¹/₅s
1899	Alvin C. Kraenzlein	15⁴/₅s
1900	R. F. Hutchison	16¹/₅s
1901	W. T. Fishleigh	16¹/₅s
1902	R. H. Hatfield	17⁴/₅s
1903	F. W. Schule	16³/₅s
1904	F. Castleman	16¹/₅s
1905	Hugo Friend	16¹/₅s
1906	W. M. Armstrong,	16s
1907	Forrest Smithson	15¹/₅s
1908	A. B. Shaw	15¹/₅s
1909	Forrest Smithson	15⁴/₅s
1910	J. Case	15⁴/₅s
1911	A. B. Shaw	15³/₅s
1912	J. P. Nicholson	15⁴/₅s
1913	F. W. Kelly	16²/₅s

§With wind and five hurdles knocked down.
‡With wind.
Source: Frank G. Menke, *The Encyclopedia of Sports* (1969), 972.

TABLE 14.51   220-YARD LOW HURDLES

The winners at both meets are listed, the A.A.U. (*) and the N.A.A.A.A. (†)

Year	Champion	Time
1887	Alfred F. Copland	27s
1888	*Alfred F. Copland	26⁴/₅s
1888	†Alfred F. Copland	26³/₅s
1889	Alfred F. Copland	27¹/₄s
1890	Fred T. Ducharme	25⁴/₅s
1891	H. H. Morrell	25¹/₅s
1892	F. C. Puffer	25⁴/₅s
1893	F. C. Puffer	25²/₅s
1894	F. C. Puffer	25³/₅s
1895	S. A. Syme	28¹/₅s
1896	J. Buck	25²/₅s
1897	Alvin C. Kraenzlein	25s
1898	Alvin C. Kraenzlein	25²/₅s
1899	Alvin C. Kraenzlein	26¹/₅s
1900	Henry Arnold	27²/₅s
1901	Henry Arnold	26s
1902	H. L. Hillman	27¹/₅s
1903	M. Bockman	26s
1904	J. S. Hill	25¹/₅s
1905	Frank Waller	25⁴/₅s
1906	H. L. Hillman	25¹/₅s
1907	J. J. Eller	25¹/₅s
1908	J. J. Eller	24⁴/₅s
1909	Joe Malcomson	25s
1910	J. J. Eller	25¹/₅s
1911	J. J. Eller	24⁴/₅s
1912	J. J. Eller	25¹/₅s
1913	C. Cory	25³/₅s

Source: Frank G. Menke, *The Encyclopedia of Sports* (1969), 973.

TABLE 14.52   2-MILE STEEPLECHASE

Year	Champion	Time
1889	A. B. George	11m 17²/₅s
1890	W. T. Young	10m 50²/₅s
1891	E. W. Hjertberg	11m 34³/₅s
1892	E. W. Hjertberg	13m 10s
1893	G. W. Orton	12m 2s
1894	G. W. Orton	12m 38⁴/₅s
1895	No competition	
1896	G. W. Orton	10m 58³/₅s
1897	G. W. Orton	12m 8²/₅s
1898	G. W. Orton	11m 41⁴/₅s
1899	G. W. Orton	11m 44³/₅s
1900	A. Grant	12m 19²/₅s
1901	G. W. Orton	11m 58s
1902	A. L. Newton	12m 28⁴/₅s
1903	No competition	
1904	John J. Daly	10m 51⁴/₅s
1905	Harvey Cohn	12m 5¹/₅s
1906–15	No competition	

Source: Frank G. Menke, *The Encyclopedia of Sports* (1969), 974.

TABLE 14.53 7-MILE WALK

This competition was dropped from the program in 1878, resumed in 1879, dropped in 1885, and again resumed in 1912.

Year	Champion	Time
1876	Charles Connor	58m 32.5s
1877	T. H. Armstrong	55m 59.6s
1879	E. E. Merrill	56m 4s
1880	J. B. Clark	54m 47.6s
1881	W. H. Purdy	58m 43s
1882	F. P. Murray	57m 18.5s
1883	W. H. Meek	56m 48.4s
1884	E. F. McDonald	56m 28s
1912	Al Voellmeke	55m 49s
1913	F. Kaiser	55m 9.2s

Source: Frank G. Menke, *The Encyclopedia of Sports* (1969), 975.

TABLE 14.54 HIGH JUMP

The winners at both meets are listed, the A.A.U. (*) and the N.A.A.A.A. (†)

Year	Champion	Height
1876	H. E. Ficken	5ft 5in.
1877	H. E. Ficken	5ft 4in.
1878	H. E. Ficken	5ft 5in.
1879	W. Wunder	5ft 7in.
1880	A. L. Carroll	5ft 5in.
1881	C. W. Durand	5ft 8in.
1882	A. L. Carroll	5ft 7in.
1883	M. W. Ford	5ft 8½in.
1884	J. T. Rindhart	5ft 8in.
1885	W. B. Page	5ft 8⅞in.
1886	W. B. Page	5ft 9in.
1887	W. B. Page	6ft ½in.
1888	*I. D. Wester	5ft 8½in.
1888	†T. M. O'Connor	5ft 9½in.
1889	R. K. Pritchard	5ft 10½in.
1890	H. L. Hallock	5ft 10in.
1891	Alvin Nickerson	5ft 8⅛in.
1892	Michael F. Sweeney	6ft
1893	Michael F. Sweeney	5ft 11in.
1894	Michael F. Sweeney	6ft
1895	Michael F. Sweeney	6ft
1896	C. U. Powell	5ft 9½in.
1897	I. K. Baxter	6ft 2¼in.
1898	I. K. Baxter	6ft
1899	I. K. Baxter	6ft
1900	I. K. Baxter	6ft 1in.
1901	S. S. Jones	6ft 2in.
1902	I. K. Baxter	5ft 7½in.
1903	S. S. Jones	6ft
1904	S. S. Jones	5ft 9in.
1905	H. W. Kerrigan	6ft 1½in.
1906	J. Neil Patterson	5ft 11½in.
1907	Con Leahy	6ft 1in.
1908	H. F. Porter	5ft 11¼in.
1909	Egon Erickson	5ft 11⅗in.
1910	Walter Thomassen	6ft 2in.
1911	Henry Grumpelt H. F. Porter	6ft 3in.
1912	J. O. Johnstone	6ft 3in.
1913	A. W. Richards	6ft 1⅜in.

Source: Frank G. Menke, *The Encyclopedia of Sports* (1969), 980.

TABLE 14.55 BROAD JUMP

The winners at both meets are listed, the A.A.U. (*) and the N.A.A.A.A. (†)

Year	Champion	Distance
1876	I. Frazier	17ft 4in.
1877	W. T. Livingston	18ft 9½in.
1878	W. C. Wilmer	18ft 9in.
1879	F. J. Kilpatrick	19ft 6¾in.
1880	J. S. Voorhees	21ft 4in.
1881	J. S. Voorhees	21ft 4¾in.
1882	J. F. Jenkins Jr.	21ft 5¾in.
1883	M. W. Ford	21ft 7½in.
1884	M. W. Ford	21ft 1½in.
1885	M. W. Ford	21ft 6in.
1886	M. W. Ford	22ft ¾in.
1887	A. A. Jordan	22ft 3½in.
1888	*W. Halpin	23ft
1888	†V. E. Schifferstein	23ft 1¾in.
1889	M. W. Ford	22ft 7½in.
1890	A. F. Copland	23ft 3⅛in.
1891	C. S. Reber	22ft 4½in.
1892	E. W. Goff	22ft 6½in.
1893	C. S. Reber	23ft 4½in.
1894	E. W. Goff	22ft 5in.
1895	E. B. Bloss	22ft 2in.
1896	E. B. Bloss	22ft
1897	E. B. Bloss	21ft 10½in.
1898	Myer Prinstein	23ft 7in.
1899	Alvin C. Kraenzlein	23ft 5in.
1900	H. P. McDonald	22ft
1901	H. P. McDonald	22ft 7in.
1902	Myer Prinstein	21ft 5½in.
1903	P. Molson	22ft 2½in.
1904	Myer Prinstein	22ft 4¾in.
1905	Hugo Friend	22ft 10⅛in.
1906	Myer Prinstein	22ft 4in.
1907	Dan Kelly	23ft 11in.
1908	Platt Adams	21ft 6½in.
1909	Frank Irons	22ft 5in.
1910	Frank Irons	23ft 5⅛in.
1911	Platt Adams	23ft ⅖in.
1912	Platt Adams	22.44ft
1913	P. Stiles	22ft

Source: Frank G. Menke, *The Encyclopedia of Sports* (1969), 981.

TABLE 14.56 POLE VAULT

The winners at both meets are listed, the A.A.U. (*) and the N.A.A.A.A. (†)

Year	Champion	Distance
1877	G. McNichol	9ft 7in.
1878	A. Ing	9ft 4in.
1879	W. J. Van Houten	10ft 4¾in.
1880	W. J. Van Houten	10ft 11in.
1881	W. J. Van Houten	10ft 6in.
1882	B. F. Richardson	10ft
1883	Hugh H. Baxter	11ft ½in.
1884	Hugh H. Baxter	10ft 6in.
1885	Hugh H. Baxter	10ft 3in.
1886	Hugh H. Baxter	10ft 1½in.
1887	T. Ray	11ft ¾in.
1888	*L. D. Godshall	10ft
1888	†G. P. Quin	10ft 1in.
1889	E. L. Stone	10ft
1890	W. S. Rodenbaugh	10ft 6in.

Year	Champion	Distance
1891	T. Luce	10ft 6½in.
1892	T. Luce	11ft
1893	C. T. Buchholz	10ft 6in.
1894	C. T. Buchholz	11ft
1895	H. Thomas	10ft
1896	F. W. Allis	10ft 5in.
1897	J. L. Hurlburt Jr.	11ft 1in.
1898	R. G. Clapp	10ft 9in.
1899	I. K. Baxter	10ft 9in.
1900	Bascom Johnson	11ft 3in.
1901	C. E. Dvorak	11ft 3in.
1902	A. G. Anderson	10ft 9in.
1903	Chas Dvorak	11ft
1904	‡H. L. Gardner / L. G. Williams	10ft 5¼in.
1905	E. C. Glover	11ft 6in.
1906	H. L. Moore / ‡LeRoy Samse	11ft 6in.
1907	E. T. Cooke Jr.	12ft 3in.
1908	W. Happenny	11ft 9in.
1909	R. Paulding	11ft
1910	H. S. Babcock	12ft 1in.
1911	E. T. Cooke Jr / H. Coyle / S. Bellah	12ft 6in.
1912	H. S. Babcock	12ft
1913	S. B. Wagoner	13ft

‡Won jump-off.
Source: Frank G. Menke, *The Encyclopedia of Sports* (1969), 981–82.

TABLE 14.57   SHOT PUT

The winners at both meets are listed, the A.A.U. (*) and the N.A.A.A.A. (†)

Year	Champion	Distance
1876	H. E. Buermeyer	32ft 5in.
1877	H. E. Buermeyer	37ft 2in.
1878	H. E. Buermeyer	37ft 4in.
1879	A. W. Adams	36ft 3⅛in.
1880	A. W. Adams	36ft 4⅞in.
1881	F. L. Lambrecht	37ft 5½in.
1882	F. L. Lambrecht	39ft 9⅞in.
1883	F. L. Lambrecht	43ft
1884	F. L. Lambrecht	39ft 10½in.
1885	F. L. Lambrecht	42ft 2⅜in.
1886	F. L. Lambrecht	42ft 1¼in.
1887	G. R. Gray	42ft 3in.
1888	*G. R. Gray	42ft 10¼in.
1888	†F. L. Lambrecht	42ft 4in.
1889	G. R. Gray	41ft 4in.
1890	G. R. Gray	43ft 9in.
1891	G. R. Gray	§46ft 5¾in.
1892	G. R. Gray	43ft 3¾in.
1893	G. R. Gray	47ft
1894	G. R. Gray	44ft 8in.
1895	W. O. Hickok	43ft
1896	G. R. Gray	44ft 3⅛in.
1897	C. H. Hennemann	42ft 7¾in.
1898	Richard Sheldon	43ft 8⅝in.
1899	Richard Sheldon	40ft ½in.
1900	D. Horgan	46ft 1¼in.
1901	F. G. Beck	42ft 11¼in.
1902	G. R. Gray	46ft 5in.
1903	L. E. J. Feuerbach	42ft 11⅝in.
1904	M. J. Sheridan	40ft 9½in.

Year	Champion	Distance
1905	W. W. Coe	49ft 6in.
1906	W. W. Coe	46ft 10½in.
1907	Ralph Rose	49ft 6½in.
1908	Ralph Rose	49ft ½in.
1909	Ralph Rose	50.26 ft
1910	Ralph Rose	49ft 1in.
1911	P. J. McDonald	47ft 9in.
1912	P. J. McDonald	48.51ft
1913	L. A. Whitney	46ft 2⅝in.

§Shot 8 ounces light.
Source: Frank G. Menke, *The Encyclopedia of Sports* (1969), 982.

TABLE 14.58   DISCUS THROW

Year	Champion	Distance
1897	Charles H. Hennemann	118ft 9in.
1898	Charles H. Hennemann	108ft 8⅝in.
1899	Richard Sheldon	‡
1900	Richard Sheldon	114ft
1901	R. J. Sheridan	111ft 9½in.
1902	R. J. Sheridan	113ft 7in.
1903	J. H. Maddock	113ft
1904	Martin J. Sheridan	119ft 1½in.
1905	Ralph Rose	117ft 5in.
1906	Martin J. Sheridan	129ft 10in.
1907	Martin J. Sheridan	129ft 5¾in.
1908	M. F. Horr	132ft 9in.
1909	Ralph Rose	131.8ft
1910	M. H. Giffin	135ft 9¼in.
1911	Martin J. Sheridan	133ft 9½in.
1912	E. Muller	130.22ft
1913	E. Muller	132ft 7⅛in.

‡Discus short weight.
Source: Frank G. Menke, *The Encyclopedia of Sports* (1969), 983.

TABLE 14.59   JAVELIN THROW

Year	Champion	Distance
1909	Ralph Rose	141.7ft
1910	B. Brodd	163ft 1in.
1911	O. F. Snedigar	165ft 20/100in.
1912	H. Lott	162.65ft
1913	B. Brodd	161ft 3in.

Source: Frank G. Menke, *The Encyclopedia of Sports* (1969), 983.

TABLE 14.60   HAMMER THROW

The winners at both meets are listed, the A.A.U. (*) and the N.A.A.A.A. (†)

Year	Champion	Time
1876	William B. Curtis	76ft 4in.
1877	G. D. Parmly	84ft
1878	William B. Curtis	80ft 2in.
1879	J. G. McDermott	85ft 11½in.
1880	William B. Curtis	87ft 4¼in.
1881	Frank L. Lambrecht	89ft 8in.
1882	Frank L. Lambrecht	93ft ½in.
1883	W. L. Coudon	93ft 11in.
1884	Frank L. Lambrecht	92ft 5in.
1885	Frank L. Lambrecht	96ft 10in.

(continued)

TABLE 14.60 (continued)

Year	Champion	Time
1886	W. L. Coudon	95ft 3in.
1887	C. A. J. Queckberner	102ft 7in.
1888	*W. J. M. Barry	127ft 9in.
1888	†Frank L. Lambrecht	105ft 1in.
1889	J. S. Mitchel	121ft 7½in.
1890	J. S. Mitchel	130ft 8in.
1891	J. S. Mitchel	136ft 1in.
1892	J. S. Mitchel	140ft 11in.
1893	J. S. Mitchel	134ft 8in.
1894	J. S. Mitchel	135ft 9½in.
1895	J. S. Mitchel	139ft 2½in.
1896	J. S. Mitchel	134ft 8¾in.
1897	J. J. Flanagan	148ft 5in.
1898	J. J. Flanagan	151ft 10½in.
1899	J. J. Flanagan	155ft 4½in.
1900	R. J. Sheridan	138ft 2in.
1901	J. J. Flanagan	158ft 10½in.
1902	J. J. Flanagan	151ft 4in.
1903	J. S. Mitchel	140ft 1in.
1904	A. D. Plaw	162ft
1905	A. D. Plaw	163ft 4in.
1906	J. J. Flanagan	166ft 6½in.
1907	J. J. Flanagan	171ft ¾in.
1908	M. J. McGrath	173ft
1909	Lee Talbott	165.8ft
1910	M. J. McGrath	168ft 4½in.
1911	Con Walsh	177ft 6½in.
1912	M. J. McGrath	174.67ft
1913	Patrick J. Ryan	177ft 7¾in.

Source: Frank G. Menke, *The Encyclopedia of Sports* (1969), 984.

TABLE 14.61 56-LB WEIGHT THROW

The winners at both meets are listed, the A.A.U. (*) and the N.A.A.A.A. (†)

Year	Champion	Distance
1878	William B. Curtis	21ft
1879	J. McDermott	22ft 11in.
1880	J. McDermott	24ft 4in.
1881	J. Britton	24ft
1882	H. W. West	24ft 10¼in.
1883	Frank L. Lambrecht	‡25ft 1¼in.
1884	C. A. J. Queckberner	26ft 3¼in.
1885	C. A. J. Queckberner	26ft 3in.
1886	C. A. J. Queckberner	25ft 1in.
1887	C. A. J. Queckberner	25ft
1888	*W. C. Coudon	27ft 9in.
1888	†J. S. Mitchel	26ft 10in.
1889	W. L. Coudon	27ft 9½in.
1890	C. A. J. Queckberner	32ft 10in.
1891	J. S. Mitchel	35ft 3½in.
1892	J. S. Mitchel	34ft 8¼in.
1893	J. S. Mitchel	34ft 5½in.
1894	J. S. Mitchel	33ft 7⅜in.
1895	J. S. Mitchel	32ft 7½in.
1896	J. S. Mitchel	30ft 7in.
1897	J. S. Mitchel	32ft 2in.
1898	Richard Sheldon	30ft 11in.
1899	J. J. Flanagan	33ft 7¼in.
1900	J. S. Mitchel	35ft 5in.
1901	J. J. Flanagan	30ft 6in.
1902	E. Desmarteau	33ft 6in.
1903	J. S. Mitchel	33ft 2¾in.
1904	J. J. Flanagan	35ft 9in.
1905	J. S. Mitchel	33ft 1½in.
1906	J. J. Flanagan	35ft 7in.
1907	J. J. Flanagan	38ft 8in.
1908	J. J. Flanagan	37ft 1½in.
1909	Lee Talbott	33.64ft
1910	Con Walsh	37ft 1½in.
1911	P. J. McDonald	38ft 9⅞in.
1912	Patrick J. Ryan	37.87ft
1912	M. J. McGrath	38ft 5½in.

‡Light weight.
Source: Frank G. Menke, *The Encyclopedia of Sports* (1969), 985.

TABLE 14.62 HOP, STEP, AND JUMP

Year	Champion	Distance
1893	E. B. Bloss	48ft 6in.
1894–1905	No competition	
1906	J. F. O'Connell	45ft 3¾in.
1907	Platt Adams	44ft 9in.
1908	Platt Adams	45ft 4in.
1909	Frank Irons	44.19ft
1910	D. F. Ahearn	48ft ¼in.
1911	D. F. Ahearn	48.16ft
1912	Platt Adams	45.70ft
1913	D. F. Ahearn	50ft

Source: Frank G. Menke, *The Encyclopedia of Sports* (1969), 985.

TABLE 14.63 ALL-AROUND

Year	Champion	Points
1884	W. R. Thompson	5304
1885	M. W. Ford	5045
1886	M. W. Ford	5899
1887	A. A. Jordan	5236
1888	M. W. Ford	5161
1889	A. A. Jordan	5520
1890	A. A. Jordan	5358
1891	A. A. Jordan	6189
1892	E. W. Goff	5232
1893	E. W. Goff	4860
1894	E. W. Goff	5748
1895	J. Cosgrove	4406.50
1896	L. P. Sheldon	5380
1897	E. H. Clark	6244.50
1898	E. C. White	5243
1899	J. Fred Powers	6203
1900	H. Gill	6360.50
1901	A. B. Gunn	5739
1902	A. B. Gunn	6260.50
1903	E. H. Clark	6318.25
1904	Thomas Kiely	6086
1905	M. J. Sheridan	6820.50
1906	Thomas Kiely	6274
1907	M. J. Sheridan	7130.50
1908	J. L. Bredemus	5808
1909	M. J. Sheridan	7385
1910	F. C. Thomson	7009
1911	F. C. Thomson	6709
1912	J. L. Bredemus	6303
1913	F. C. Thomson	7411.50

Source: Frank G. Menke, *The Encyclopedia of Sports* (1969), 987.

TABLE 14.64   CROSS-COUNTRY

Year	Champion	Time
1890	W. D. Day	47m 41s
1891	M. Kennedy	46m 30⁴/₅s
1892	E. C. Carter	43m 54s
1893–96	No competition	
1897	G. W. Orton	35m 58s
1898	G. W. Orton	35m 41²/₅s
1899–1900	No competition	
1901	Jerry Pierce	43m 27¹/₃s
1902	No competition	
1903	John Joyce	32m 23⁴/₅s
1904	No competition	
1905	W. J. Hail	32m 59⁴/₅s
1906	Frank Nebrich	34m 29⁴/₅s
1907	F. G. Bellars	33m 12s
1908	F. G. Bellars	34m 15³/₅s
1909	W. J. Kramer	31m 17¹/₅s
1910	F. G. Bellars	33m 3s
1911	W. J. Kramer	37m 8s
1912	W. J. Kramer	34m 32s
1913	A. R. Kiviat	33m 52s

Source: Frank G. Menke, *The Encyclopedia of Sports* (1969), 987.

TABLE 14.65   CROSS-COUNTRY TEAM

Year	Champion	Points
1907	Irish-American A.C.	29
1908	Trinity A.C. (Maloney, Lees, McCarrick, Taylor, Dietas)	78
1909	No record	
1910	New York A.C. (Bellars, McGinn, Smith, Bailey, Fitzgerald)	27
1911	Irish-American A.C. (McNamara, Collins, Huysman, Donnelly, Nelson)	34
1912	Irish-American A.C. (Johannsen, McNamara, Collins, Huysman, Reynolds)	21
1913	Irish-American A.C. (Kiviat, Barden, Eke, Fogel, Donnelly)	32

Source: Frank G. Menke, *The Encyclopedia of Sports* (1969), 988.

U.S. Track and Field Champions—Men's Indoor

TABLE 14.66   60-YARD DASH

Year	Champion	Time
1906	C. J. Seitz	6.6s
1907	J. F. O'Connell	6.6s
1908	Robert Cloughen	6.6s
1909	R. W. Gill	6.8s
1910	Robert Cloughen	6.8s
1911	A. T. Meyer	6.6s
1912–13	No competition	

Source: Frank G. Menke, *The Encyclopedia of Sports* (1969), 989.

TABLE 14.67   600-YARD RUN

Year	Champion	Time
1906	E. B. Parsons	1m 14.6s
1907	E. B. Parsons	1m 14.4s
1908	Melvin W. Sheppard	1m 14.8s
1909	Melvin W. Sheppard	1m 14.6s
1910	Harry E. Gissing	1m 14s
1911	Abel R. Kiviat	1m 14s
1912	No competition	
1913	Abel R. Kiviat	1m 15.2s

Source: Frank G. Menke, *The Encyclopedia of Sports* (1969), 989.

TABLE 14.68   1,000-YARD RUN

Year	Champion	Time
1906	Melvin W. Sheppard	2m 17.8s
1907	Melvin W. Sheppard	2m 25s
1908	Harry Gissing	2m 20s
1909	Harry Gissing	2m 18.8s
1910	Harry Gissing	2m 20s
1911	Abel R. Kiviat	2m 16.2s
1912	No competition	
1913	Abel R. Kiviat	2m 15.8s

Source: Frank G. Menke, *The Encyclopedia of Sports* (1969), 989–90.

TABLE 14.69   2-MILE RUN

Year	Champion	Time
1899	Alec Grant	10m 4⁴/₅s
1900	Alec Grant	10m 2³/₅s
1901	Alec Grant	9m 40⁴/₅s
1902	No competition	
1903	Alec Grant	9m 55⁴/₅s
1904	George V. Bonhag	9m 44s
1905	George V. Bonhag	9m 54⁴/₅s
1906	George V. Bonhag	9m 47²/₅s
1907	George V. Bonhag	9m 42¹/₅s
1908	M. P. Driscoll	9m 28³/₅s
1909	M. P. Driscoll	9m 39s
1910	J. W. Monument	9m 36¹/₅s
1911	George V. Bonhag	9m 20⁴/₅s
1912	No competition	
1913	W. J. Kramer	9m 19¹/₅s

Source: Frank G. Menke, *The Encyclopedia of Sports* (1969), 990.

TABLE 14.70   60-YARD HIGH HURDLES

Year	Champion	Time
1910	J. L. Hartranft	9.4s
1911	John J. Eller	9.4s
1912	No competition	
1913	J. I. Wendell	9.4s

Source: Frank G. Menke, *The Encyclopedia of Sports* (1969), 991.

TABLE 14.71   1-MILE WALK

(not held, 1898–1906, 1910–1913)

Year	Champion	Time
1897	Harry Ladd	7m 23s
1907	Sam Leibgold	7m 41.2s
1908	Sam Leibgold	7m 19.8s
1909	Sam Leibgold	7m 13.6s

Source: Frank G. Menke, *The Encyclopedia of Sports* (1969), 993.

TABLE 14.72 HIGH JUMP

Year	Champion	Distance
1906	H. A. Gidney	5ft 10½in.
1907	H. F. Porter	6ft 1⅛in.
1908	H. F. Porter	6ft
1909	H. F. Porter	6ft 2¼in.
1910	J. H. Grumpelt	6ft 2in.
1911	S. C. Lawrence	6ft 2⅞in.
1912	No competition	
1913	J. O. Johnstone	6ft 1in.

Source: Frank G. Menke, *The Encyclopedia of Sports* (1969), 994.

TABLE 14.73 POLE VAULT

Year	Champion	Height
1906	A. C. Gilbert	10ft 9in.
1907	Claude A. Allen	11ft 3in.
1908	C. Vezen	11ft 2in.
1909	W. Happeny	11ft 6in.
1910	W. Happeny	11ft 8in.
1911	Gordon B. Dukes	11ft 4in.
1912–13	No competition	

Source: Frank G. Menke, *The Encyclopedia of Sports* (1969), 995.

TABLE 14.74 TEAM

(Points in parentheses.)

Year	Champion
1906	Irish-American AC (89)
1907	New York AC (76)
1908	Irish-American AC (84)
1909	Irish-American AC (69)
1910	New York AC (77)
1911	Irish-American AC (70)
1912	No competition
1913	Irish-American AC (30)

Source: Frank G. Menke, *The Encyclopedia of Sports* (1969), 996.

TABLE 14.75 100-YARD DASH

Year	Champion	Time
1876	H. W. Stevens, Williams	11s
1877	H. H. Lee, Pennsylvania	10.2s
1878	H. H. Lee, Pennsylvania	10¼s
1879	H. H. Lee, Pennsylvania	10.8s
1880	E. J. Wendell, Harvard	10.8s
1881	E. J. Wendell, Harvard	10¼s
1882	H. S. Brooks Jr., Yale	10.2s
1883	S. Derickson Jr., Columbia	10.6s
1884	H. S. Brooks Jr., Yale	10.2s
1885	F. M. Bonine, Michigan	10.6s
1886	E. H. Rogers, Harvard	10.5s
1887	C. H. Sherrill, Yale	10.4s
1888	C. H. Sherrill, Yale	10.6s
1889	C. H. Sherrill, Yale	10.2s
1890	C. H. Sherrill, Yale	10.2s
1891	L. H. Cary, Princeton	10s
1892	W. Swayne Jr., Yale	10.2s
1893	W. M. Richards, Yale	10.2s
1894	E. S. Ramsdell, Pennsylvania	10s
1895	J. V. Crum, Iowa	10s

1896	B. J. Wefers, Georgetown	9.8s
1897	B. J. Wefers, Georgetown	10.4s
1898	J. W. B. Tewksbury, Pennsylvania	10s
1899	J. W. B. Tewksbury, Pennsylvania	10s
1900	A. C. Kraenzlein, Pennsylvania	10.2s
1901	W. T. Lightner, Harvard	*
1902	J. S. Westney, Pennsylvania	*
1903	F. R. Moulton, Yale	*
1904	W. A. Shick Jr., Harvard	10s
1905	W. A. Shick Jr., Harvard	10.2s
1906	N. J. Cartmell, Pennsylvania	10.2s
1907	N. J. Cartmell, Pennsylvania	10s
1908	N. J. Cartmell, Pennsylvania	10.6s
1909	R. C. Foster, Harvard	10.2s
1910	F. L. Ramsdell, Pennsylvania	10s
1911	R. C. Craig, Michigan	9.8s
1912	R. B. Thomas, Princeton	10.2s
1913	J. C. Patterson, Pennsylvania	9.8s

*Finished second; name of winner stricken from records.
†With wind.
Source: Frank G. Menke, *The Encyclopedia of Sports* (1969), 1004.

TABLE 14.76 220-YARD DASH

Year	Champion	Time
1877	H. H. Lee, Pennsylvania	23.5s
1878	H. H. Lee, Pennsylvania	23.6s
1879	E. J. Wendell, Harvard	24.4s
1880	E. J. Wendell Harvard	24.4s
1881	E. J. Wendell, Harvard	23.2s
1882	H. S. Brooks Jr., Yale	22⅝s
1883	H. S. Brooks Jr., Yale	23.2s
1884	Wendell Baker, Harvard	22.4s
1885	Wendell Baker, Harvard	23.6s
1886	Wendell Baker, Harvard	22.8s
1887	E. H. Rogers, Harvard	23s
1888	C. H. Sherrill, Yale	22.6s
1889	C. H. Sherrill, Yale	22.4s
1890	C. H. Sherrill, Yale	22.2s
1891	L. H. Cary, Princeton	21.8s
1892	W. Swayne Jr., Yale	22s
1893	W. M. Richards, Yale	22.6s
1894	E. S. Ramsdell, Pennsylvania	22s
1895	J. V. Crum, Iowa	22s
1896	B. J. Wefers, Georgetown	21.2s
1897	J. H. Colfelt, Princeton	22.6s
1898	J. W. B. Tewksbury, Pennsylvania	21.6s
1899	J. W. B. Tewksbury, Pennsylvania	21.6s
1900	F. J. Jarvis, Princeton	22.2s
1901	F. M. Sears, Cornell	22.6s
1902	W. T. Lightner, Harvard	21.6s
1903	W. T. Lightner, Harvard	22s
1904	W. A. Shick Jr., Harvard	21.4s
1905	W. A. Shick Jr., Harvard	22.2s
1906	N. J. Cartmell, Pennsylvania	23.4s
1907	N. J. Cartmell, Pennsylvania	21.8s
1908	N. J. Cartmell, Pennsylvania	22s
1909	R. C. Foster, Harvard	21.6s
1910	R. C. Craig, Michigan	21.2s
1911	R. C. Craig, Michigan	21.2s
1912	C. D. Reidpath, Syracuse	21.4s
1913	D. F. Lippincott, Pennsylvania	21.2s

Source: Frank G. Menke, *The Encyclopedia of Sports* (1969), 1005.

TABLE 14.77   440-YARD RUN

Year	Champion	Time
1876	H. W. Stevens, Williams	56s
1877	G. M. Hammond, Columbia	54s
1878	A. I. Burton, Columbia	54.2s
1879	C. H. Cogswell, Dartmouth	54.8s
1880	E. J. Wendell, Harvard	55.2s
1881	E. A. Ballard, Pennsylvania	53.8s
1882	W. H. Goodwin Jr., Harvard	53s
1883	W. H. Goodwin Jr., Harvard	51.2s
1884	W. H. Goodwin Jr., Harvard	52.6s
1885	Wendell Baker, Harvard	54.4s
1886	S. G. Wells, Harvard	51.8s
1887	S. G. Wells, Harvard	53.6s
1888	S. G. Wells, Harvard	52.6s
1889	W. C. Dohm, Princeton	50s
1890	W. C. Downs, Harvard	50.6s
1891	G. B. Shattuck, Amherst	49.5s
1892	W. H. Wright, Harvard	50.6s
1893	L. Sayer, Harvard	50.8s
1894	S. M. Merrill, Harvard	50.4s
1895	W. H. Vincent, Harvard	50.8s
1896	T. E. Burke, Boston Univ.	50.4s
1897	T. E. Burke, Boston Univ.	50.4s
1898	F. W. Jarvis, Princeton	50.8s
1899	M. W. Long, Columbia	49.4s
1900	D. Boardman, Yale	49.6s
1901	W. J. Holland, Georgetown	51.6s
1902	W. J. Holland, Georgetown	49.6s
1903	J. E. Haigh, Harvard	50.2s
1904	J. B. Taylor, Pennsylvania	49.2
1905	H. A. Hyman, Pennsylvania	49.4s
1906	H. M. Rogers, Cornell	50.2s
1907	J. B. Taylor, Pennsylvania	48.8s
1908	J. B. Taylor, Pennsylvania	52.2s
1909	T. S. Blumer, Harvard	50.6s
1910	C. D. Reidpath, Syracuse	50s
1911	D. B. Young, Amherst	48.8s
1912	C. D. Reidpath, Syracuse	48s
1913	C. B. Haff, Michigan	48.4s

Source: Frank G. Menke, *The Encyclopedia of Sports* (1969), 1006.

TABLE 14.78   880-YARD RUN

Year	Champion	Time
1876	R. W. Green, Princeton	2m 16.5s
1877	G. M. Hammond, Columbia	2m 20.5s
1878	A. J. Burton, Columbia	2m 8¼s
1879	C. H. Cogswell, Dartmouth	2m 12s
1880	E. A. Ballard, Pennsylvania	2m 9.2s
1881	T. J. Coolidge, Harvard	2m 7⅜s
1882	W. H. Goodwin Jr., Harvard	2m 2.4s
1883	W. H. Goodwin Jr., Harvard	2m 2s
1884	W. H. Goodwin Jr., Harvard	2m 5.5s
1885	H. L. Mitchell, Yale	2m 7.2s
1886	F. R. Smith, Yale	2m 4.2s
1887	R. Faries, Pennsylvania	2m 7s
1888	H. R. Miles, Harvard	2m 2.2s
1889	W. C. Downs, Harvard	2m 2.6s
1890	W. C. Dohm, Princeton	1m 59.2s
1891	W. B. Wright Jr., Yale	1m 59.2s
1892	T. B. Turner, Princeton	1m 59.8s
1893	J. Corbin, Harvard	1m 59.8s
1894	C. H. Kilpatrick, Union	1m 59.2s
1895	E. Hollister, Harvard	2m
1896	E. Hollister, Harvard	1m 56.8s
1897	E. Hollister, Harvard	1m 58.8s
1898	J. F. Cregan, Princeton	1m 58.4s
1899	T. E. Burke, Harvard	1m 58.8s
1900	J. M. Perry, Princeton	2m 3.6s
1901	J. M. Perry, Princeton	2m 3.6s
1902	H. E. Taylor, Amherst	2m ⅗s
1903	L. M. Adsit, Princeton	2m 4.4s
1904	E. B. Parsons, Yale	1m 56.8s
1905	E. B. Parsons, Yale	1m 56s
1906	J. C. Carpenter, Cornell	1m 59.2s
1907	G. Haskins, Pennsylvania	1m 57.8s
1908	L. P. Jones, Pennsylvania	2m 2s
1909	A. F. Beck, Pennsylvania	1m 56.6s
1910	G. Whitely, Princeton	1m 57s
1911	J. P. Jones, Cornell	1m 54.8s
1912	J. P. Jones, Cornell	1m 53.8s
1913	G. E. Brown, Yale	1m 55.2s

Source: Frank G. Menke, *The Encyclopedia of Sports* (1969), 1006–07.

TABLE 14.79   1-MILE RUN

Year	Champion	Time
1876	E. C. Stimson, Dartmouth	4m 58.5s
1877	W. Bearns, Columbia	5m 33s
1878	M. Paton, Princeton	5m 4¾s
1879	'C. H. Trask, Jr., Columbia	5m 24.6s
1880	Theodore Cuyler, Yale	4m 37.6s
1881	Theodore Cuyler, Yale	4m 40⅞s
1882	G. B. Morison, Harvard	4m 40⅞s
1883	G. B. Morison, Harvard	4m 38.6s
1884	R. Faries, Pennsylvania	4m 45.2s
1885	R. Faries, Pennsylvania	4m 46.8s
1886	R. Faries, Pennsylvania	4m 38.8s
1887	W. Harmer, Yale	4m 36.8s
1888	W. Harmer, Yale	4m 37.2s
1889	C. O. Wells, Amherst	4m 29.8s
1890	C. O. Wells, Amherst	4m 35.4s
1891	F. F. Carr, Harvard	4m 34.4s
1892	G. Lowell, Harvard	4m 33.4s
1893	G. O. Jarvis, Wesleyan	4m 34.6s
1894	G. O. Jarvis, Wesleyan	4m 26.8s
1895	G. W. Orton, Pennsylvania	4m 23.4s
1896	G. O. Jarvis, Wesleyan	4m 28.8s
1897	G. W. Orton, Pennsylvania	4m 25s
1898	J. F. Cregan, Princeton	4m 23.6s
1899	J. F. Cregan, Princeton	4m 25.2s.
1900	J. F. Cregan, Princeton	4m 24.4s
1901	H. B. Clark, Harvard	4m 31.2s
1902	R. E. Williams, Princeton	4m 29.2s
1903	W. A. Colwell, Harvard	4m 30.6s
1904	D. C. Munson, Cornell	4m 25.6s
1905	D. C. Munson, Cornell	4m 25.2s

(continued)

TABLE 14.79 (continued)

Year	Champion	Time
1906	G. Haskins, Pennsylvania	4m 29.2s
1907	G. Haskins, Pennsylvania	4m 20.6s
1908	J. P. Halstead, Cornell	4m 30s
1909	W. C. Paull, Pennsylvania	4m 17.8s
1910	P. J. Taylor, Cornell	4m 23.4s
1911	J. P. Jones, Cornell	4m 15.4s
1912	J. P. Jones, Cornell / N. S. Taber, Brown	4m 20.6s
1913	J. P. Jones, Cornell	4m 14.4s

Source: Frank G. Menke, *The Encyclopedia of Sports* (1969), 1007.

TABLE 14.80   2-MILE RUN

Year	Champion	Time
1899	Alex Grant, Pennsylvania	10m 3.4s
1900	Alex Grant, Pennsylvania	9m 51.6s
1901	B. A. Gallagher, Cornell	10m
1902	A. C. Bowen, Pennsylvania	9m 57s
1903	W. E. Schutt, Cornell	9m 40s
1904	W. E. Schutt, Cornell	9m 47.6s
1905	H. J. Hail, Yale	9m 50.6s
1906	C. F. Magoffin, Cornell	9m 56s
1907	Floyd A. Rowe, Michigan	9m 34.8s
1908	H. L. Trube, Cornell	9m 56s
1909	P. J. Taylor, Cornell	9m 27.6s
1910	T. S. Berna, Cornell	9m 40.6s
1911	T. S. Berna, Cornell	9m 25.2s
1912	P. R. Withington, Harvard	9m 24.4s
1913	W. M. McCurdy, Pennsylvania	9m 45.6s

Source: Frank G. Menke, *The Encyclopedia of Sports* (1969), 1008.

TABLE 14.81   120-YARD HIGH HURDLES

Year	Champion	Time
1876	W. J. Wakeman, Yale	18¼s
1877	H. Steven, Princeton	18.5s
1878	J. W. Pryor, Columbia	21.6s
1879	J. E. Cowdin, Harvard	19.2s
1880	H. B. Strong, Lehigh	19.5s
1881	R. T. Morrow, Lehigh	18⅞ss
1882	J. F. Jenkins Jr., Columbia	17.6s
1883	O. Harriman Jr., Princeton	18s
1884	R. Mulford, Columbia	17.5s
1885	W. H. Ludington, Yale	19.2s
1886	W. H. Ludington, Yale	17s
1887	W. H. Ludington, Yale	17.4s
1888	H. Mapes, Columbia	17.2s
1889	H. Mapes, Columbia	16.8s
1890	H. L. Williams, Yale	16.2s
1891	H. L. Williams, Yale	15.8s
1892	H. T. Harding, Columbia	16s
1893	McL. Van Ingen, Yale	16.4s
1894	E. H. Cady, Yale	16s
1895	S. Chase, Dartmouth	15.8s
1896	E. C. Perkins, Yale	16.2s
1897	E. C. Perkins, Yale	16s
1898	A. C. Kraenzlein, Pennsylvania	16.6s
1899	A. C. Kraenzlein, Pennsylvania	15.4s
1900	A. C. Kraenzlein, Pennsylvania	15.4s

Year	Champion	Time
1901	E. J. Clapp, Yale	16.2s
1902	J. H. Converse, Harvard	15.6s
1903	E. J. Clapp, Yale	15.6s
1904	E. J. Clapp, Yale	15.8s
1905	E. S. Amsler, Pennsylvania	15.6s
1906	J. H. Hubbard, Amherst	15.8s
1907	J. C. Garrels, Michigan	15.2s
1908	A. B. Shaw, Dartmouth	15.6s
1909	L. V. Howe, Yale	15.4s
1910	G. A. Chisholm, Yale	16s
1911	G. A. Chisholm, Yale	15.4s
1912	J. I. Wendell, Wesleyan	15.6s
1913	J. I. Wendell, Wesleyan	15.4s

Source: Frank G. Menke, *The Encyclopedia of Sports* (1969), 1008–9.

TABLE 14.82   220-YARD LOW HURDLES

Year	Champion	Time
1888	C. S. Mandel, Harvard	26.8s
1889	Herbert Mapes, Columbia	26.4s
1890	J. P. Lee, Harvard	25.25s
1891	H. L. Williams, Yale	25.2s
1892	G. R. Fearing Jr., Harvard	25.4s
1893	McL. Van Ingen, Yale	26.8s
1894	J. L. Bremer Jr., Harvard	25.2s
1895	J. L. Bremer Jr., Harvard	24.6s
1896	J. L. Bremer Jr., Harvard	25s
1897	E. C. Perkins, Yale	25.8s
1898	A. C. Kraenzlein, Penn	23.6s
1899	A. C. Kraenzlein, Penn	23.8s
1900	A. C. Kraenzlein, Penn	25.2s
1901	E. J. Clapp, Yale	25.4s
1902	J. G. Willis, Harvard	23.8s
1903	E. J. Clapp, Yale	25.2s
1904	E. J. Clapp, Yale	24.6s
1905	F. R. Castleman, Colgate	24.8s
1906	F. R. Castleman, Colgate	25.2s
1907	J. C. Garrels, Michigan	24s
1908	L. V. Howe, Yale	24.6s
1909	L. V. Howe, Yale	24.4s
1910	G. P. Gardner, Harvard	24.4s
1911	G. A. Chisholm, Yale	24.6s
1912	J. B. Craig, Michigan	24.2s
1913	J. I. Wendell, Wesleyan	23.6s

Source: Frank G. Menke, *The Encyclopedia of Sports* (1969), 1009.

TABLE 14.83   HIGH JUMP

Year	Champion	Time
1876	J. W. Pryor, Columbia	5ft 4in.
1877	H. L. Geyelin, Penn	4ft 11in.
1878	J. P. Conover, Columbia	5ft 6½in.
1879	J. P. Conover, Columbia	5ft 8¼in.
1880	A. C. Denniston, Harvard	5ft 1¼in.
1881	W. Soren, Harvard	5ft 2¾in.
1882	W. Soren, Harvard	5ft 6in.
1883	C. H. Atkinson, Harvard	5ft 8½in.
1884	C. H. Atkinson, Harvard	5ft 9¾
1885	W. B. Page Jr., Penn	5ft 11⅝in.
1886	W. B. Page Jr., Penn	5ft 11¾in.
1887	W. B. Page Jr., Penn	5ft 7½in.
1888	I. D. Webster, Penn	5ft 11½in.
1889	I. D. Webster, Penn	5ft 6¾in.
1890	G. R. Fearing Jr., Harvard	5ft 8¼in.

1891	G. R. Fearing Jr., Harvard	6ft
1892	G. R. Fearing Jr., Harvard	6ft ½in.
1893	G. R. Fearing Jr., Harvard	5ft 10¾in.
1894	C. J. Paine, Jr., Harvard	5ft 10½in.
1895	N. T. Leslie, Penn	5ft 11¾in.
1896	J. D. Winsor Jr., Penn	6ft 1in.
1897	J. D. Winsor Jr., Penn	6ft 3in.
1898	W. G. Morse, Harvard C. U. Powell, Cornell A. N. Rice, Harvard J. D. Winsor Jr., Penn	5ft 11⅛in.
1899	I. K. Baxter, Penn	6ft 2in.
1900	S. S. Jones, New York Univ.	5ft 10½in.
1901	S. S. Jones, New York Univ.	5ft 9½in.
1902	W. C. Low, Syracuse	5ft 11in.
1903	R. P. Kernan, Harvard	6ft 1in.
1904	W. C. Lowe, Syracuse	5ft 11in.
1905	J. W. Marshall, Yale	6ft
1906	J. W. Marshall, Yale	5ft 11in.
1907	T. Moffit, Penn	6ft 3¼in.
1908	R. G. Harwood, Harvard E. R. Palmer, Dartmouth	5ft 6½in.
1909	R. G. Harwood, Harvard R. P. Pope, Harvard S. C. Lawrence, Harvard E. R. Palmer, Dartmouth W. Canfield, Yale	5ft 11¼in.
1910	J. W. Burdick, Penn	6ft 1in.
1911	J. W. Burdick, Penn G. C. Farrier, Penn P. W. Dalrymple, M.I.T.	6ft
1912	J. W. Burdick, Penn	6ft ¾in.
1913	E. Beeson, California J. B. Camp, Harvard	6ft ⅛in.

Source: Frank G. Menke, *The Encyclopedia of Sports* (1969), 1011.

TABLE 14.84 BROAD JUMP

Year	Champion	Time
1876	H. L. Willoughby, Penn	18ft 3½in.
1877	H. H. Lee, Penn	19ft 7in.
1878	J. P. Conover, Columbia	19ft 2½in.
1879	J. P. Conover, Columbia	20ft
1880	G. G. Thayer, Penn	20ft 2in.
1881	J. F. Jenkins Jr., Columbia	20ft 9¼in.
1882	J. F. Jenkins Jr., Columbia	20ft 3in.
1883	W. Soren, Harvard	20ft 6in.
1884	O. Bodelsen, Columbia	21ft 3½in.
1885	J. D. Bradley, Harvard	19ft 6in.
1886	C. H. Mapes, Columbia	20ft 11in.
1887	T. G. Shearman Jr., Yale	21ft 11in.
1888	T. G. Shearman Jr., Yale	20ft 8in.
1889	T. G. Shearman Jr., Yale	22ft 6in.
1890	W. C. Dohm, Princeton	22ft 3½in.
1891	V. Mapes, Columbia	22ft 11¼in.
1892	E. B. Bloss, Harvard	22ft 1½in.
1893	E. B. Bloss, Harvard	22ft 9⅝in.
1894	E. S. Ramsdell, Penn	22ft 1in.
1895	L. P. Sheldon, Yale	22ft 8½in.
1896	L. P. Sheldon, Yale	22ft 3¼in.
1897	J. P. Remington, Penn	22ft 4⅞in.
1898	M. Prinstein, Syracuse	23ft 7⅜in.
1899	A. C. Kraenzlein, Penn	24ft 4½in.
1900	M. Prinstein, Syracuse	23ft 8in.
1901	C. W. Kennedy, Columbia	21ft 6⅜in.
1902	A. T. Foster, Amherst	21ft 11in.
1903	W. P. Hubbard, Amherst	22ft 4⅝in.
1904	R. S. Stangland, Columbia	23ft 6½in.
1905	L. W. Simons, Princeton	23ft 2½in.
1906	W. F. Knox, Yale	23ft 4½in.
1907	W. F. Knox, Yale	22ft 10in.
1908	E. T. Cook, Cornell	22ft 8½in.
1909	E. T. Cook, Cornell	22ft 6¼in.
1910	E. M. Roberts, Amherst	22ft 7¼in.
1911	R. Holden, Yale	22ft 3⅝in.
1912	E. L. Mercer, Penn	23ft 10½in.
1913	E. L. Mercer, Penn	23ft 3⅞in.

Source: Frank G. Menke, *The Encyclopedia of Sports* (1969), 1012.

TABLE 14.85 POLE VAULT

Year	Champion	Time
1877	J. W. Pryor, Columbia	7ft 4in.
1878	C. Fabrogou, C.C.N.Y.	9ft
1879	F. H. Lee, Columbia	9ft 3in.
1880	R. B. Tewksbury, Princeton	9ft 4in.
1881	F. W. Dalrymple, Lehigh	8ft 9in.
1882	W. Soren, Harvard	9ft 6in.
1883	H. P. Toler, Princeton	10ft
1884	H. L. Hodge, Princeton	9ft
1885	L. D. Godshall, Lafayette	9ft 7¼in.
1886	A. Stevens, Columbia	10ft 3¼in.
1887	L. D. Godshall, Lafayette	10ft
1888	T. G. Shearman Jr., Yale	9ft 6in.
1889	R. G. Leavitt, Harvard	10ft 5⅛in.
1890	E. D. Ryder, Yale H. F. Welch, Columbia	10ft 7in.
1891	E. D. Ryder, Yale	10ft 9¾in.
1892	O. G. Cartwright, Yale	10ft 5¾in.
1893	C. T. Buchholz, Penn	10ft 10½in.
1894	M. H. Kershow, Yale	10ft 9in.
1895	C. T. Buchholz, Penn	11ft 3¾in.
1896	F. W. Allis, Yale	11ft 1¾in.
1897	B. Johnson, Yale	11ft 3⅝in.
1898	R. G. Clapp, Yale W. W. Hoyt, Harvard	11ft 4¼in.
1899	R. G. Clapp, Yale	11ft 5in.
1900	B. Johnson, Yale	11ft 3¼in.
1901	E. Deakin, Penn A. W. Coleman, Princeton C. Dvorak, Michigan P. A. Moore, Princeton W. Fishleigh, Michigan J. H. Ford, Yale	10ft 9in.
1902	D. S. Horton, Princeton	11ft 7in.
1903	H. L. Gardner, Syracuse	11ft 7in.
1904	W. McLanahan, Yale	11ft 8¾in.
1905	W. R. Dray, Yale	11ft 8in.
1906	A. G. Grant, Harvard T. M. Jackson, Cornell	11ft 10¾in.
1907	W. R. Dray, Yale	11ft 11¾in.
1908	W. R. Dray, Yale A. C. Gilbert, Yale F. T. Nelson, Yale C. S. Campbell, Yale	11ft
1909	C. S. Campbell, Yale	12ft 3¼in.
1910	F. T. Nelson, Yale	12ft 4⅜in.
1911	H. S. Babcock, Columbia	12ft 8⅜in.
1912	R. A. Gardner, Yale	13ft 1in.
1913	T. Fiske, Princeton	12ft 8in.

Source: Frank G. Menke, *The Encyclopedia of Sports* (1969), 1012–13.

TABLE 14.86   SHOT PUT

Year	Champion	Time
1876	J. M. Mann, Princeton	30ft 11½in.
1877	F. Larkin, Princeton	33ft
1878	F. Larkin, Princeton	32ft 11½in.
1879	F. Larkin, Princeton	33ft 8½in.
1880	A. T. Moore, Stevens	35ft 1¼in.
1881	A. T. Moore, Stevens	34ft 11in.
1882	A. T. Moore, Columbia	36ft 3in.
1883	C. H. Kip, Harvard	35ft 8in.
1884	D. W. Reckhart, Columbia	36ft 3¾in.
1885	J. H. Rohrbach, Lafayette*	38ft 1in.
1886	A. B. Coxe, Yale	38ft 9½in.
1887	A. B. Coxe, Yale	40ft 9½in.
1888	H. Pennypacker, Harvard	37ft 3in.
1889	H. H. Janeway, Princeton	36ft 1½in.
1890	H. H. Janeway, Princeton	39ft 6½in.
1891	J. R. Finlay, Harvard	39ft 6¾in.
1892	S. H. Evins, Harvard	39ft 9in.
1893	W. O. Hickok, Yale	41ft ⅛in.
1894	W. O. Hickok, Yale	42ft
1895	W. O. Hickok, Yale	42ft 11½in.
1896	R. Sheldon, Yale	41ft 11½in.
1897	R. Garrett, Princeton	41ft 10¾in.
1898	J. C. McCracken, Penn	43ft 8½in.
1899	J. C. McCracken, Penn	42ft ½in.
1900	F. G. Beck, Yale	44ft 3in.
1901	R. Sheldon, Yale	43ft 9¼in.
1902	F. G. Beck, Yale	44ft 8½in.
1903	F. G. Beck, Yale	46ft
1904	F. H. Schoenfuss, Harvard	44ft 4in
1905	F. J. Porter, Cornell	45ft ½in.
1906	B. T. Stephenson, Harvard	43ft 11⅛in.
1907	W. F. Krueger, Swarthmore	46ft 5½in.
1908	W. F. Krueger, Swarthmore	44ft
1909	C. C. Little, Harvard	46ft 2in.
1910	J. Horner Jr., Michigan	46ft 4½in.
1911	J. Horner Jr., Michigan	46ft 7⅛in.
1912	R. L. Beatty, Columbia	48ft 10¾in.
1913	L. A. Whitney, Dartmouth	47ft 2⅝in.

*Light weight shot.
Source: Frank G. Menke, *The Encyclopedia of Sports* (1969), 1014.

TABLE 14.87   16-LB HAMMER THROW

Year	Champion	Time
1877	G. D. Parmly, Princeton	75ft 10in.
1878	F. Larkin, Princeton	76ft 9in.
1879	F. Larkin, Princeton	87ft 1in.
1880	J. F. Bush, Columbia	84ft 3in.
1881	J. H. Montgomery, Columbia	76ft 9½in.
1882	D. R. Porter, Columbia	87ft 3½in.
1883	C. H. Kip, Harvard	88ft 11in.
1884	A. B. Coxe, Yale	83ft 2in.
1885	A. B. Coxe, Yale	88ft ½in.
1886	A. B. Coxe, Yale	95ft 11in.
1887	A. B. Coxe, Yale	98ft 6in.
1888	A. J. Bowser, Penn	88ft 6½in.
1889	A. J. Bowser, Penn	89ft 10½in.
1890	B. C. Hinman, Columbia	94ft 7in.
1891	J. R. Finlay, Harvard	107ft 7½in.

Year	Champion	Time
1892	S. H. Evins, Harvard	104ft ⅜in.
1893	W. O. Hickok, Yale	110ft 4½in.
1894	W. O. Hickok, Yale	123ft 9in.
1895	W. O. Hickok, Yale	135ft 7½in.
1896	C. Chadwick, Yale	132ft 6½in.
1897	W. G. Woodruff, Penn	136ft 3in.
1898	J. C. McCracken, Penn	149ft 5in.
1899	J. C. McCracken, Penn	144ft 1in.
1900	A. Plaw, California	154ft 4½in.
1901	J. R. DeWitt, Princeton	149ft 4½in.
1902	J. R. DeWitt, Princeton	164ft 10in.
1903	J. R. DeWitt, Princeton	155ft 8in.
1904	J. R. DeWitt, Princeton	161ft 3in.
1905	C. Van Duyne, Syracuse	149ft 11in.
1906	M. F. Horr, Syracuse	147ft 9½in.
1907	M. F. Horr, Syracuse	150ft 1½in.
1908	J. N. Pew, Cornell	155ft 2½in.
1909	L. J. Talcott, Cornell	158ft 9½in.
1910	C. T. Cooney, Yale	152ft 5in.
1911	A. H. Tilley, Dartmouth	145ft 11½in.
1912	T. Cable, Harvard	162ft 4½in.
1913	T. Cable, Harvard	156ft

Source: Frank G. Menke, *The Encyclopedia of Sports* (1969), 1015.

TABLE 14.88   TEAM

From 1876 to 1889, only first places were counted, seconds being counted only in case of a tie. (Points in parentheses.)

Year	Champion
1876	Princeton (4)
1877	Columbia (6)
1878	Columbia (7)
1879	Columbia (6)
1880	Harvard (6)
1881	Harvard (5)
1882	Harvard (6)
1883	Harvard (7)
1884	Harvard (5)
1885	Harvard (4)
1886	Harvard (5)
1887	Yale (6)
1888	Harvard (7)
1889	Yale (4)
1890	Harvard (32)
1891	Harvard (46)
1892	Harvard (48⅔)
1893	Yale (47⅓)
1894	Yale (37)
1895	Yale (30)
1896	Yale (41½)
1897	Penn (34¾)
1898	Penn (50¾)
1899	Penn (57)
1900	Penn (39)
1901	Harvard (46)
1902	Yale (32½)
1903	Yale (43½)
1904	Yale (33½)
1905	Cornell (30½)

Year	School
1906	Cornell (38)
1907	Penn (33)
1908	Cornell (34)
1909	Harvard (39¹/₁₀)
1910	Penn (27½)
1911	Cornell (30½)
1912	Penn (28)
1913	Penn (24)

Source: Frank G. Menke, *The Encyclopedia of Sports* (1969), 1016.

TABLE 14.89   CROSS-COUNTRY

Year	Champion	Time
1908	H. C. Young, Cornell	34m 14s
1909	Tell S. Berna, Cornell	33m 5.5s
1910	John Paul Jones, Cornell	33m 34s
1911	John Paul Jones, Cornell	34m 41.6s
1912	John Paul Jones, Cornell	32m 9.5s
1913	Robert St. B. Boyd, Harvard	34m 37s

Source: Frank G. Menke, *The Encyclopedia of Sports* (1969), 1017.

TABLE 14.90   CROSS-COUNTRY TEAM

Year	School
1908–11	Cornell
1912	Harvard
1913	Cornell

Source: Menke, *The Encyclopedia of Sports* (1969), 1017.

TABLE 14.91   OTHER COLLEGE CONFERENCE CHAMPIONS

Big Ten	
Outdoor	
Year	School
1901–04	Michigan
1905	Chicago
1906	Michigan
1907	Illinois
1908	Chicago
1909	Illinois
1910	Notre Dame
1911	Missouri
1912	California
1913	Illinois
Indoor	
Year	School
1911	Chicago
1912–13	Illinois
Cross Country	
Year	School
1908	Nebraska
1909	Minnesota
1910	Wisconsin
1911	Iowa State
1912–13	Wisconsin

Missouri Valley	
Outdoor	
Year	School
1908	Iowa State
1909	Grinnell
1910	Kansas
1911–13	Missouri

Source: Menke, *The Encyclopedia of Sports* (1969), 1024–26.

TABLE 14.92   BOSTON MARATHON WINNERS

Year	Winner	Time
1897	J. J. McDermott, New York	2h 55m 10s
1898	R. J. MacDonald (Canada)	2h 42m
1899	L. J. Brignoli, Cambridge, Mass.	2h 54m 38s
1900	J. J. Caffrey, Hamilton, Ont.	2h 39m 44.4s
1901	J. J. Caffrey, Hamilton, Ont.	2h 29m 23.6s
1902	Samuel Mellor, Yonkers, N.Y.	2h 43m
1903	J. C. Lorden, Cambridge, Mass.	2h 41m 29.8s
1904	Michael Spring, New York	2h 39m 4.4s
1905	Fred Lorz, Yonkers, N.Y.	2h 38m 25.4s
1906	Timothy Ford, Hampshire A.A.	2h 45m 45s
1907	Thomas Longboat, Toronto	2h 24m 24s
1908	Thomas Morrissey, Yonkers, N.Y.	2h 25m 43.2s
1909	Henri Renaud, Nashua, N.H.	2h 53m 36.8s
1910	Fred L. Cameron, Amherst, Nova Scotia	2h 28m 52.4s
1911	Clarence DeMar, Melrose, Mass.	2h 21m 39.6s
1912	Michael J. Ryan, New York	2h 21m 18.2s
1913	Fritz Carlson, Minneapolis, Minn.	2h 25m 14.8s

Source: Menke, *The Encyclopedia of Sports* (1969), 1027.

Wrestling

Frank Gotch   b. Humboldt, Nebraska, Apr 27, 1878; d. Humboldt, Nebraska, Dec 16, 1917.

Recognized as the greatest American professional wrestler of his time Frank Gotch pursued his career at a time when wrestling was primarily a sport, not the show business exhibition it has become today. Gotch won his first bout on April 2, 1889, and soon attracted enough attention to gain a match with U.S. champion Tom Jenkins on February 2, 1903. He lost but on January 28, 1904, he defeated Jenkins in a rematch for the U.S. title.

Gotch perfected a style of wrestling that Jenkins had devised, known as "catch-as-catch-can." Only the stranglehold was barred; wrestlers were permitted to grip wherever the opportunity presented itself. Gotch used a toehold, which was said to have broken the legs of several opponents. After Jenkins and Gotch, Americans virtually abandoned the older Greco-Roman method.

Gotch retired in 1913 after having defeated such renowned European greats as Yussif Mahmout of Turkey, Emile Maupas of France, and Jim Parr of England. On April 3, 1908, he defeated George Hackenschmidt, the "Russian lion," whom many had regarded as the greatest of all. Hackenschmidt was tremendously powerful. He stood 5 feet 10 inches, weighed between 208 and 225 pounds, and had a reach of 75 inches. He preceded Gotch in his reign and was virtually through when Gotch wrestled him.

In 1906, Gotch met Freddy Beall. In a wild scuffle, Gotch was knocked unconscious against a ring post, and Beall pinned him. Gotch demanded a rematch, during which he toyed with Beall before pinning him in the fall that made him king. Gotch lost only six of 196 matches. He was a man of great strength, daring and bold, but also brainy, a combination that made him superb.

He retired to Humboldt where he became president of a street railway and electric utility. Despite being one of the best-conditioned athletes of his day, he died at age 39 of uremic poisoning.

TABLE 14.93 UNITED STATES AMATEUR WRESTLING CHAMPIONS

105 Pounds

Year	Champion
1889–90	J. B. Reilly
1891	F. Bertsch
1893	C. Monnypenny
1894	R. Bonnett
1896	H. Cotter
1897	G. W. Owen
1899–1900	G. W. Nelson
1901–02	W. Karl
1903–04	R. Curry
1905	J. Heins
1906	W. Lott
1907	G. Taylor
1908	R. Schwartz
1909–10	G. Taylor
1911	H. Donaldson
1912	G. Taylor

108 Pounds

Year	Champion
1913	G. Taylor

115 Pounds

Year	Champion
1889–90	F. Mueller
1891	E. Beck
1893	J. Holt
1894	F. Bertsch
1895	M. Kervin
1896–97	R. Bonnett
1899	R. Bonnett
1900	J. Renzlard
1901	G. Owens
1902–04	G. Mehnert
1905–07	G. Bauer
1908	G. Mehnert
1909	G. Bauer
1910	J. Hein
1911	N. Chapman
1912	W. Strohback
1913	J. Hein

125 Pounds

Year	Champion
1893	W. Troelsch
1894–95	W. Reilly
1896	E. Harris
1897	A. Meanwell
1899	M. Wiley
1900	A. Kurtzman
1901–04	I. Niflot
1905–06	G. Mehnert
1907–08	Louis Dole
1909	L. Ruggiero
1910	M. Himmelhoch
1911–12	G. Bauer
1913	V. Vosen

135 Pounds

Year	Champion
1889	M. Luttbeg
1891	A. Ullman
1893	C. Clark
1894	A. Lippman
1895	J. McGrew
1896	A. Ullman
1897	H. Wolff
1899–1901	M. Wiley
1902	F. Cook
1903–04	B. Bradshaw
1905	I. Niflot
1906	A. Rubin
1907	B. Bradshaw
1908	G. Dole
1909	S. Fleischer
1910	S. Kennedy
1911	P. Franzke
1912	E. Helikman
1913	A. Anderson

145 Pounds

Year	Champion
1897	W. Riggs
1899–1901	M. Wiley
1902	N. Nelson
1903	M. Yokel
1904	O. Roehm
1905	R. Tisney
1906	C. Clapper
1907	Richard Jaeckel
1908	M. Wiley
1909–10	C. Johnson
1911	W. Milchewski
1912	G. Petterson
1913	C. Johnson

158 Pounds

Year	Champion
1888	Dr. Shell
1889	M. Lau
1890	G. Haskin
1891	Z. Von Bockman
1893	W. Osgood
1894	F. Ellis
1895	C. Reinicke
1896	A. Ullman
1897	D. Chesterman
1899	A. Mellinger

1900	M. Wiley
1901–02	J. Schmicker
1903	W. Beckman
1904	C. Erikson
1905	W. Schaefer
1906	J. McAfee
1907	F. Marganes
1908	C. Anderson
1909–10	F. Narganes
1911	C. Gesek
1912–13	J. Smith

175 Pounds

Year	Champion
1913	J. Varga

Heavyweight

Year	Champion
1904–05	B. Hansen
1906	M. McAfee
1907–08	J. Gundersen
1909	E. Payne
1910	F. Motis
1911	H. Grim
1912	A. Kaino
1913	J. Gundersen

Source: Menke, *The Encyclopedia of Sports* (1969), 1070–73.

Despite the limitations on what were considered acceptable women's activities, these women enjoyed sailing on the beach in Ormond, Florida, sometime between 1890 and 1910, even though their attire seems unsuited to such vigorous activity. (Courtesy Prints and Photographs Division, Library of Congress)

Other Leisure Activities

Increasing numbers of Americans took up bowling, visited national monuments, or camped in national parks. Trips on excursion trains were popular, as was wind sailing on the beach. Farm women and their daughters gathered for conversation and quilting.

TABLE 14.94   BOWLING

Year	Number of Bowlers	Number of Teams[a]
1901	1,000	200
1905	3,000	630
1910	7,000	1,400
1913	8,000	1,700

[a]Covers only men's bowling teams in leagues sanctioned by the American Bowling Congress.
Source: *Historical Statistics of the United States, Colonial Times to 1970*, Part 1, 400.

Women in the Midwest, such as these Dakota farm women in the 1890s, found relief from the isolation of rural life in quilting bees, where mothers and daughters came together. (Courtesy State Historical Society of North Dakota)

Although the group of national parks was a later development, camping was enjoyed by a few, such as this camper in Maine in 1888. (Courtesy Prints and Photographs Division, Library of Congress)

In areas where lumbering was prevalent, logging trains were used for Sunday excursions, such as the one here in Harbor Springs, Minnesota, c. 1906. (Courtesy Prints and Photographs Division, Library of Congress)

TABLE 14.95   NATIONAL PARKS AND MONUMENTS: NUMBER AND VISITS, SELECTED YEARS

Year	Total Areas		National Parks		National Monuments	
	Number	Visits	Number	Visits	Number	Visits
1890	3	. . .	3	. . .	0	. . .
1900	12	. . .	7	. . .	5	. . .
1910	44[a]	199,000	13	199,000	26	. . .

[a] The other five areas in 1910 were national historical and military areas.
Source: Historical Statistics of the United States, Colonial Times to 1970, Part 1, 396.

CHAPTER 15 Crime and Punishment

Crime rose precipitously after the Civil War. In cities, gambling dens, saloons, dance halls, and houses of prostitution attracted a growing number of men and women. In rural areas and frontier regions, drifters and desperadoes posed threats to life and property. By 1870, the prison population had nearly doubled from 19,000 in 1860 to 33,000 by 1870. Blacks and immigrants contributed to half of the increase, and native-born whites the other half.

Family feuds, not unknown before the Civil War, became notorious afterward. The mountain feuds of Kentucky, Virginia, and West Virginia, best known for the Hatfield–McCoy feud of 1873–88, became front-page news. Civil War rivalries, population growth and land scarcity, federal and state regulation (in the form of fish and game laws and alcohol taxes) and industrialization that uprooted families and threatened traditional life are explanations historians have stressed for the increases in violence and crime in the mountain South.

Out West, the rapid growth of the postwar cattle industry and the instability produced by the Indian wars were sources of violence and crime. Indians and homesteaders continued to battle one another as Indian lands continued to shrink and homesteaders viewed Indian tribes as obstacles in the pathway of western settlement.

Fierce homesteader–cattle rancher wars plagued the 1880s as farming and ranching clashed in bitter competition for land and water rights. Massive cattle drives trampled over cultivated fields, and farmers threw up fences, stampeded herds, and "rustled" cattle while waving six-shooters. Herders fought back with rumors of Indian uprisings and violence against homesteaders. As sheep grazing shifted to the Plains in the 1870s, cattle ranchers faced another menace leading to range wars. Poisoning water holes (effective against livestock) and spreading grain laced with saltpeter (deadly to sheep but not to cattle) became routine tactics. Dynamiting herds of cattle or driving livestock over cliffs were other methods. More often, guns were used to shoot one another, to kill livestock, or to knock sheep senseless; knives were used to slit the throats of cattle.

Drifters and desperadoes, often Civil War veterans unable to adjust to peaceful pursuits, menaced populations in western towns that

TABLE 15.1 SEX, NATIVITY, RACE, MARITAL STATUS, AGE, HABIT OF LIFE, AND LITERACY OF FEDERAL PRISONERS RECEIVED FROM COURT: SELECTED YEARS 1886–1910

| | | Characteristics of Those Received in Federal and State Facilities | | | | | | | | | | |
| | | | | | | | | Habit of Life | | Literacy | | |
Year	Number Reported	Percent Male	Percent Foreign-Born	Percent White	Percent Other Races	Percent Married	Median Age[a]	Percent Claiming Temperance	Percent Admitting Intemperance	Percent Can Not Read or Write	Percent Can Read Only	Percent Can Read and Write
1886[b]	1,027	(99)	(18)	(74)	(26)	(49)	(31.1)	c	c	c	c	c
1895	1,589	97	16	75	25	39	28.7	70	30	17	3	80
1900	1,536	98	14	66	34	40	28.1	c	c	23	3	74
1905	1,709	98	13	68	32	43	28.9	54	46	18	1	81
1910	1,450	98	20	72	28	45	30.1	54	46	14	1	85

[a] Median age calculated from group data.
[b] Characteristics are for the 1,261 Federal prisoners present on June 30, 1886.
[c] Data not available.
Source: Historical Corrections Statistics in the United States, 1850–1984 (1986), 168.

Judge Roy Bean, the "Law West of the Pecos," is shown here holding court at the old town of Langtry, Texas, in 1900, trying a horse thief. This building served as courthouse and saloon. No other peace officers served in the locality at that time. (Courtesy National Archives)

had scant forces of law and order. Western sheriffs and federal marshals had names and descriptions of thousands of people wanted for murder, arson, robbery, horse stealing, cattle rustling, claim jumping, and other crimes. Some became legends, such as Jesse and Frank James and the Younger brothers, who could not settle down to farming after the war but built careers robbing banks and trains. Martha Jane Canary ("Calamity Jane") achieved fame as a roustabout whose paramours mysteriously disappeared. Even some law officers had questionable reputations: James Butler ("Wild Bill") Hickok became a federal marshal with such a fierce reputation that outlaws feared him. Vigilante courts, made up of local citizens angry over the lack of protection, arose to expedite local justice.

Lynchings

Lynching may be defined as extralegal execution for a real or alleged crime. Between 1882 and 1913, 3,886 individuals in the United States were lynched. Although victims might be male or female, black or white, most were African-American males. The major pretext for lynchings was the assault by black males of white women, although between 1882 and 1903 only about one-third of blacks lynched in the South had committed or were alleged to have committed rape. The other two-thirds were lynched for alleged murder, theft, arson, incendiary language, a bad reputation, testimony on be-

TABLE 15.2   LYNCHINGS BY RACE, 1882–1913

Year	Total	White	Black
1882	113	64	49
1883	130	77	53
1884	211	160	51
1885	184	110	74
1886	138	64	74
1887	120	50	70
1888	137	68	69
1889	170	76	94
1890	96	11	85
1891	184	71	113
1892	230	69	161
1893	152	34	118
1894	192	58	134
1895	179	66	113
1896	123	45	78
1897	158	35	123
1898	120	19	101
1899	106	21	85
1900	115	9	106
1901	130	25	105
1902	92	7	85
1903	99	15	84
1904	83	7	76
1905	62	5	57
1906	65	3	62
1907	60	2	58
1908	97	8	89
1909	82	13	69
1910	76	9	67
1911	67	7	60
1912	63	2	61
1913	52	1	51

Source: Historical Statistics of the United States, Colonial Times to 1957 (1961), 218.

TABLE 15.3   LYNCHINGS BY STATES, 1885 THROUGH 1919, HIGHEST FIVE

State	Number
Georgia	419
Mississippi	393
Texas	294
Louisiana	289
Arkansas	218

Source: The World Almanac and Encyclopedia 1921 (1920), 398.

half of another black, or mistaken identity.

Between 1899 and 1909, two significant changes occurred in lynchings. During this period the proportion of lynchings taking place in the South increased from 82% of total lynchings in the United States to 92%. Simultaneously, the proportion of lynching victims who were white decreased from about one-third to 11.4%. In other words, lynching became increasingly a southern and racial phenomenon.

Lynchings were carried out by a variety of paramilitary-style organizations. Although the Ku Klux Klan had been outlawed by Congressional legislation in 1871 and did not organize again until 1915, other secret groups conducted night rides and lynched their victims by hanging, drowning, shooting, and other means.

The reason why lynching rose so dramatically in the 1890s and swept so powerfully through the South thereafter is not easy to explain, but historians have emphasized the conjunction of sex, race, and economics as fundamental. Crime rates did rise during the economic hard times after the Civil War. The 1890s especially was a decade of recession; black and white males competed with one another to make a living. In the South where interracial tension was already high, blacks readily became scapegoats, victims of false accusations of crime. Any accusation of a sexual crime against a white woman by a black man was almost certain to lead to lynching.

Efforts to end lynching by publicity and legal action were led by the National Association for the Advancement of Colored People (NAACP). In 1919, the Dyer Bill made lynching a federal offense, and although the practice continued, the numbers declined in the 1930s.

Urban Crime

In the cities, street criminals menaced residents. The absence of laws against concealed weapons meant that any drifter or drunk could get hold of a pistol. In 1893, Chicago police arrested one criminal for every eleven residents; the city had eight times more murders than Paris had. The streets of New York City turned young toughs into major outlaws. Gangs members graduated from pilfering to murder. The New York Bowery Boys operated in a territory even the police dared not enter.

America's prison population tripled between 1870 (33,000) and 1920 (93,000). Thirty-one new state and federal penal institutions were built. Reformers, believing that the environment caused crime, crusaded for the removal of criminals from their surroundings and placement in humane reformatories, state prisons, penal farms, and federal penitentiaries where they could be "rehabilitated" through education and vocational training. Despite this, the nation's crime and prison population continued to grow.

Between 1885 and 1904, America averaged 6,597 murders per year. Regionally, in the decade ending in 1913, homicide rates were highest in southern cities (18.2), followed by Pacific-coast cities (10.0), central cities (8.6), and eastern cities (4.9).

The homicide rate among blacks was much higher than whites. During a five-year period when statistics were available, in New Orleans, the black homicide rate was 64.6 per 100,000 compared to 9.5 for whites; in Savannah, Georgia, the comparative rates were 43.8 for blacks and 18.5 for whites; and in Charleston, South Carolina, 60.6 for blacks and 10.7 for whites.

TABLE 15.4   CAUSES FOR WHICH BOYS WERE COMMITTED TO LOUISVILLE, KENTUCKY, INDUSTRIAL SCHOOL, 1906

Offense	White	Black	Total
Incorrigibility	72	27	99
Delinquency	43	13	56
Larceny	4	3	7
Petit larceny	13	9	22
Grand larceny	8	1	9
Burglary	4	3	7
Burglary and larceny	19	3	22
Vagrancy and larceny	1	0	1
Vagrancy	8	2	10
Vagrancy and incorrigibility	3	0	3
Incorrigibility and immorality	1	0	1
Assault	2	1	3
Manslaughter in fourth degree	1	0	1
Felony	1	0	1
Attempted rape	0	1	1
Destruction of property	2	0	2
Obstructing railroad	1	0	1
Disturbing the peace	2	0	2

Source: Graebner and Richard, eds., The American Record: Images of the Past, Vol. II, Since 1865 (1988), 142.

TABLE 15.5   FACTS CONNECTED WITH THE MORAL CONDITION OF THE BOYS WHEN RECEIVED, STATE SCHOOL FOR BOYS, SOUTH PORTLAND, MAINE, 1906

Students were heavily concentrated in the 10–15 age group.

	Number
Whole number received	2,615
Have intemperate parents	881
Lost father	816
Lost mother	654
Relatives in prison	335
Stepparents	491
Idle	1,658
Much neglected	907
Truants	1,140
Sabbath breakers	992
Untruthful	2,053
Profane	1,908

Source: Graebner and Richard, eds., The American Record: Images of the Past, Vol. II, Since 1865 (1988), 142.

TABLE 15.6   COMBINED TOTALS OF PERSONS PRESENT IN LOCAL (JAILS) STATE, AND FEDERAL CORRECTIONAL FACILTITIES BY STATE: 1880, 1890

Region	1880 Census	1890 Census
United States	58,609	82,330
Northest	20,677	28,258
Maine	405	512
N.H.	269	321
Vt.	258	200
Mass.	3,576	5,227
R.I.	317	560
Conn.	718	1,026
N.Y.	8,728	11,468
N.J.	1,573	2,455
Pa.	4,833	6,489
North Central	14,971	19,854
Ohio	2,538	2,909
Ind.	1,613	1,988
Ill.	3,320	3,936
Mich.	1,912	2,155
Wis.	589	1,118
Minn.	426	1,041
Iowa	803	1,016
Mo.	2,041	2,833
N. Dak.	a	97
S. Dak.	a	178
Nebr.	374	655
Kans.	1,295	1,928
South	19,074	27,494
Del.	81	139
Md.	1,259	1,502
D.C.	381	496
Va.	1,543	2,000
W. Va.	389	450
N.C.	1,570	2,033
S.C.	626	1,184
Ga.	1,809	2,938
Fla.	269	667
Ky.	1,398	2,110
Tenn.	2,100	2,451
Ala.	1,353	2,518
Miss.	1,311	1,177
Ark.	756	1,473
La.	1,066	1,609
Okla.	a	a
Tex.	3,163	4,747
West	3,887	6,724
Mont.	76	432
Idaho	32	150
Wyo.	74	74
Colo.	380	902
N. Mex.	40	205
Ariz.	67	250
Utah	58	269
Nev.	199	152
Wash.	81	452
Oreg.	233	440
Calif.	2,647	3,398
Alaska	a	a
Hawaii	a	a

a Not separately enumerated. Total for Dakota Territory was 60 in 1880.
Source: Historical Corrections Statistics in the United States, 1850–1984 (1986), 195

TABLE 15.7 HOMICIDE IN THE UNITED STATES, 1909–1913

rates per 100,000

City	Rate
Memphis	73.3
Charleston	37.2
Atlanta	32.2
Nashville	31.3
Savannah	31.0
New Orleans	24.4
Louisville	16.0
St. Louis	12.7
San Francisco	11.4
Cincinnati	11.1
Chicago	9.5
Indianapolis	9.4
Seattle, Wash.	9.3
Los Angeles	8.9
Washington, D.C.	7.1
Spokane, Wash.	7.5
Cleveland	6.6
Dayton	6.3
New York City	5.6
Pittsburgh	5.5
Providence	5.1
Boston	5.0
Philadelphia	4.7
Buffalo	4.6
Baltimore	4.4
Minneapolis	3.8
Newark, N.J.	3.6
Hartford	3.3
Rochester	3.5
Reading, Pa.	2.9
Total, 31 Cities	8.2

Source: The World Almanac and Encyclopedia 1921, 430.

Despite the prevalence of homicides in American cities, crimes against the person accounted for less than 20% of all crime during the Victorian age. Crimes against property, especially burglary and larceny, were far more typical. In a percentage distribution of offenses reported in 1910 for jail, state, and federal inmates on a given day, nearly 60% of the offenders had committed robbery, embezzlement, larceny, arson, or theft of property. Befitting an age of Victorian values, about as many offenders were incarcerated on morals charges as had committed violent crimes against persons.

TABLE 15.8 PERCENTAGE DISTRIBUTION OF OFFENSES REPORTED FOR JAIL, STATE, AND FEDERAL INMATES PRESENT ON A GIVEN DAY DURING THE YEAR: SELECTED YEARS 1880 AND 1910 [a]

Category and Offense	Offenses of All Inmates 1880 [b]	Principal Offenses of Sentenced Inmates 1910
Person		
Homicide, Manslaughter	8.5	12.8
Assault	9.3	8.6
Rape [d]	1.9	4.0
Other [e]	0.2	k
Total	19.9	25.4
Property		
Robbery	3.4	4.2
Embezzlement, Forgery, Fraud [f]	4.2	4.2
Burglary	17.1	14.6
All Larceny	31.8	19.2
Arson	1.5	k
Stolen Property	0.3	k
Total	58.3	42.2
Morals, Order, Government Charges		
Other Sex-Related Crimes	2.1	0.7
Liquor-Law Violations	0.3	1.9
Drunkenness	6.2	12.3
Disorderly Conduct	3.9	m
Vagrancy	3.6	5.4
Drug-Law Violations	0.1	k
Gambling	0.1	k
Traffic Violations [g]	k	k
Malicious Mischief	0.3	0.4
Carrying and Possessing Weapons	0.3	k
Nonsupport	0.2	k
Revenue-Related Offenses	0.5	k
Military Crimes	0.7	k
Custody Charges [h]	0.2	k
National Security Violations	k	k
Crimes Related to the Admin. of Govt. [i]	0.6	k
Total	19.1	20.7
Other [j]	2.3	11.4
Total Reported	54,005	111,285
Unknown or Unclear	4,602	213

[a] The figures include inmates in all local, State and Federal correctional institutions, except juveniles and offenders in military prisons and mental hospitals.
[b] Eleven percent of the total were classified as awaiting trial.
[d] Includes statutory rape.
[e] Includes kidnapping and sexual assault other than rape.
[f] Extortion and counterfeiting are also included in this category.
[g] Usually driving under the influence of alcohol.
[h] Includes escape, harboring a criminal, and parole violations.
[i] Includes unlawful immigration, perjury, contempt, and related offenses.
[j] Varies in content because of changes in categorization detail, but is largely restricted to those offenses amounting to less than 1 percent of the total. Surveys in 1910 and 1972–73 provided much less detail describing the specific crimes than did those in 1880 or 1923; hence this category is much larger in the former cases.
[k] Not specified.
[m] In 1910, disorderly conduct is combined with the figures under the category entitled "drunkenness."
Source: Historical Corrections Statistics in the United States, 1850–1984, 200.

The Neighborhood Saloon

In turn-of-the-century Chicago, saloons outnumbered groceries, meat markets, and dry-goods stores combined. In 1915, New York City had more than 10,000 licensed saloons, or about one for each 500 persons; Chicago had one for every 335; San Francisco, one every 218, and Houston one for every 198.

City saloons came in various forms. Some served professional and business clientele and were well appointed. At the other extreme were the waterfront dives, gin mills, and barrelhouses for dock workers, sailors, tramps, and the down-and-out. In immigrant enclaves, the German beerhouse did well, as did the German-style beer garden in the suburbs. The beer garden catered to whole families, allowing women and children to be a part of the activities.

Workers' saloons were of three kinds. The occupational saloon drew its customers from nearby docks, mills, or factories. These became meeting halls for union organizations; for example, in Buffalo, at the turn of the century, sixty-three (out of sixty-nine) union organizations met in saloon halls. In the evenings, ethnic saloons drew crowds of immigrants celebrating communal occasions—weddings and holidays—or became meeting places for fraternal orders and clubs. The neighborhood saloon often became a multiethnic gathering place where local ward politicians—themselves members of the ethnic community—combed the crowd for information, issues of concern, and votes. Middle-class men preferred to drink at home, at private clubs, or in hotels.

The everyday routine of a saloon began with an early opening at 5:00 A.M. or 6:00 A.M. to serve workers a morning "bracer" to go with the coffee they carried in their lunch buckets. A free noonday meal drew a large crowd. Then the barkeep had teamsters dropping in throughout the afternoon. About quitting time, the saloon did a brisk business in "growlers," a side- or back-door business with wives and children who came to carry out beer in buckets, cans, or pitchers for the evening meal. In the late evening hours, the saloon returned to a worker's clientele.

Saloons provided a host of services in the city: the only free toilets, watering troughs for teamsters' horses, free newspapers for patrons, check cashing, or money lending. Saloons doubled as convenience stores selling cigars and cigarettes, headache powders, and bonbons (called "wife-pacifiers"). They were also communication centers, places where workers got their mail, left messages, made telephone calls, exchanged political gossip, or heard of work opportunities.

Saloons were also restaurants, serving a varied menu. According to one legend, the practice of Chicago barkeep Joseph C. Mackin of serving a free hot oyster with every drink was the origin of the "free lunch." Regardless of the authenticity of this story, the custom spread across the nation after 1871. Usually set out about 11:00 A.M., the free lunch came with the purchase of a nickel beer. The food, salty and spicy, made patrons thirsty, and included cold meats, sandwiches, hard-boiled eggs, bread, wursts, sliced tomatoes, onions, and radishes. Sometimes, stew or a soup was served. Saloons might hire caterers, or, more often, the bartender's wife would serve.

The saloon ritualized an all-male culture, separate from the world of women and the exigencies of family. Drinking reinforced male solidarity. The custom of "treating," whereby each patron bought a round of drinks and stayed until everyone had done the same, was another rite of hospitality and male camaraderie.

The saloon also constituted a political meeting hall, particularly at the ward or precinct level, a place where politicians could organize their vote. Consequently, at the turn of the century, when mid-

TABLE 15.9 WHAT AMERICANS WERE DRINKING, 1850–1917

Consumption per capita in gallons

Year	Distilled Spirits	Wines	Beers	All Kinds
1850	2.24	0.27	1.58	4.08
1900	1.28	0.39	16.09	17.76
1917	1.60	0.41	17.95	19.95

Source: The Almanac and Encyclopedia 1921. Per-capita figures are misleading because they include children as well as adults, but they do provide a rough estimate of alcohol consumption of the United States.

On the eve of World War I, prohibitionism stalled. In 1914, only one-quarter of the states had prohibition laws, and many of these were loosely enforced, if at all. The war was to provide the reformers with the final weapons they needed to make prohibition a national requirement in 1919 with passage of the Eighteenth Amendment.

dle-class suburban reformers wanted to "reclaim" the city from the ethnic political "machines," temperance and prohibition campaigns could be used as targets of attack. Saloon keepers frequently became involved in politics. According to a common joke, drawn from Lincoln Steffens's *The Shame of the Cities,* the fastest way to empty city-council chambers was to stand and shout, "Your saloon's on fire!" A fictional saloon keeper, Mr. Dooley, created by Finley Peter Dunne and based upon Chicago barkeeper Jim McGarry, became a nationally syndicated commentator on local and national political issues.

Drinking and Temperance

Excessive drinking had first aroused interest in the 1820s. Prohibitionists and temperance advocates for decades battled distillers and ordinary folk who enjoyed a dram or two over the evils of drink. Regardless of whether they supported outright prohibition of alcohol or restrictions on consumption, those against strong drink made it a moral issue.

In the late Victorian age, Frances Willard, head of the Women's Christian Temperance Union, combined the moral crusade against drinking with the battle for women's suffrage. She and her followers entered saloons and invited customers to kneel and pray. Besides shame, the WCTU used politics to advocate the vote for women, both for its own sake and to combat the evils of drink.

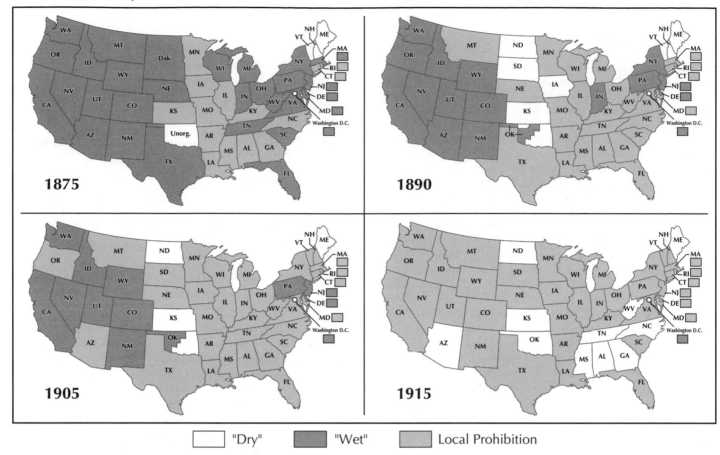

| | "Dry" | | "Wet" | | Local Prohibition |

These four maps show the increasing number of states that chose to outlaw alcoholic beverages, becoming "dry" states, prior to the actual prohibition era, which is usually considered to be the period from 1920 to 1933. (Dale Williams)

The most notable development in the anti-drinking crusade during this period was the stress on its social pathologies. Carry Nation of Kansas was one who had for many years suffered the effects of a drunken husband and poverty. Beginning in 1900, she led a campaign against drinking that gained national attention. Nation led assaults by hatchet-wielding women on saloons, where blurry-eyed customers watched in astonishment as they chopped the place up.

Prostitution and the Mann Act (1910)

Ending prostitution became a goal of the progressives and the women's movement in the early 1900s. Prostitution had long existed in areas of the nation where women were scarce, such as cow towns, mining camps, seaports, migrant farm-worker and logging centers. In large cities, prostitution ranged from lavishly furnished and expensive middle-class brothels to "the cribs," tiny cubicles where whores catered to working men.

Prostitution was clearly a matter for state and local government attention. Progressives, however, demonstrated their belief that government was the key to social reform by joining conservatives in 1910 to use the interstate commerce clause of the Constitution as a weapon against prostitution. Senator James R. Mann of Illinois introduced a measure that attacked the practice, probably exaggerated, of procurers luring girls from the country to become prostitutes elsewhere. The Mann Act forbade transporting women across state lines for "immoral" purposes ("white slavery").

Of course, brothels continued to operate, even if less openly than before and most likely under paid police protection. Streetwalkers, previously the most despised in the trade, became more numerous because they were difficult to catch. Wealthy men continued to find sex for pay, usually in the form of "call girls," women who stayed at home until "called" by a pimp or a hotel employee who worked the streets and lobbies of hotels.

CHAPTER 16 A Documentary Sampler

These documents present readers with the original thoughts, words, and deeds of the people of Victorian America. They represent a blend of social, political, and economic trends. Certain principles guided the selections. Documents are included that caused something to happen or were themselves the result of previous developments. Examples of these are the *Plessy v. Ferguson* decision, Helen Hunt Jackson's *A Century of Dishonor,* and the Sherman Anti Trust Law. Many documents reflect important attitudes of Victorian America, such as Andrew Carnegie's "The Gospel of Wealth," *Mary Antin's America,* or W. E. B. Du Bois's address to the convention of the Niagara Movement. Documents were also chosen to give readers an understanding of social and economic conditions during the age, such as Family Budgets, Xin Jin's prostitution contract, or the poem on the eight-hour day. Finally, some documents were chosen that capture the popular culture or spirit of the age, such as George Washington Plunkitt on "Honest Graft" or Medicine Man Shows. The documents are arranged by topic and chronologically within topics.

African Americans
Ida Wells-Barnett's Antilynching Campaign (1892–95)

Ida Wells-Barnett became editor and part owner of the Memphis Free Speech, *which she used to battle the evil of lynching. Born into slavery in Mississippi in 1862, Wells-Barnett used the brutal lynching of three African-American businessmen in the late 1880s to launch her crusade; she died in 1931 before succeeding in securing a federal antilynching law. The following document is a petition to President William McKinley to protest the lynching of an African-American postmaster in South Carolina.*

Mr. President, the colored citizens of this country in general, and Chicago in particular, desire to respectfully urge that some action be taken by you as chief magistrate of this great nation, first for the apprehension and punishment of the lynchers of Postmaster Baker, of Lake City, S.C.; second, we ask indemnity for the widow and children, both for the murder of the husband and father, and for injuries sustained by themselves; third, we most earnestly desire that national legislation be enacted for the suppression of the national crime of lynching.

For nearly twenty years lynching crimes, which stand side by side with Armenian and Cuban outrages, have been committed and permitted by this Christian nation. Nowhere in the civilized world save the United States of America do men, possessing all civil and political power, go out in bands of 50 and 5,000 to hunt down, shoot, hang or burn to death a single individual, unarmed and absolutely powerless. Statistics show that nearly 10,000 American citizens have been lynched in the past 20 years. To our appeals for justice the stereotyped reply has been that the government could not interfere in a state matter. Postmaster Baker's case was a federal matter, pure and simple. He died at his post of duty in defense of his country's honor, as truly as did ever a soldier on the field of

battle. We refuse to believe this country, so powerful to defend its citizens abroad, is unable to protect its citizens at home. Italy and China have been indemnified by this government for the lynching of their citizens. We ask that the government do as much for its own.

Source: Brier et al., *Who Built America?* (1922), 156.

The Atlanta Compromise, 1895

Booker T. Washington, the most influential African-American leader in the nation during the 1890s, believed the only realistic solution for African Americans living in the "dark night" of Jim Crow segregation was vocational training.

Ignorant and inexperienced, it is not strange that in the first years of our new life we began at the top instead of at the bottom; that a seat in Congress or the state legislature was more sought than real estate or industrial skill; that the political convention or stump speaking had more attractions than starting a dairy farm or a truck garden.

A ship lost at sea for many days suddenly sighted a friendly vessel. From the mast of the unfortunate vessel was seen a signal, "Water, water; we die of thirst!" The answer from the friendly vessel at once came back, "Cast down your bucket where you are." . . . The captain of the distressed vessel, at least heeding the injunction, cast down his bucket, and it came up full of fresh, sparkling water . . . To those of my race who underestimate the importance of cultivating friendly relations with the Southern white man, who is their next-door neighbor, I would say: "Cast down your bucket where you are"—cast it down in making friends in every manly way of the people of all races by whom we are surrounded.

Cast it down in agriculture, mechanics, in commerce, in domestic service, and in the professions. . . . Our greatest danger is that in the great leap from slavery to freedom we may overlook the fact that the masses of us are to live by the productions of our hands, and fail to keep in mind that we shall prosper in proportion as we learn to dignify and glorify common labour, and put brains and skill into the common occupations of life . . . No race can prosper till it learns that there is as much dignity in tilling a field as in writing a poem. It is at the bottom of life we must begin, and not at the top.

To those of the white race who look to the incoming of those of foreign birth and strange tongue and habits for the prosperity of the South, were I permitted I would repeat what I say to my own race, "Cast down your bucket where you are." Cast it down among the eight millions of Negroes whose habits you know, whose fidelity and love you have tested in days when to have proved treacherous meant the ruin of your firesides. Cast down your bucket among these people who have, without strikes and labour wars, tilled your fields, cleared your forests, builded your railroads and cities, and brought forth treasures from the bowels of the earth . . . Casting down your bucket among my people . . . you waste places in your fields, and run your factories. While doing this, you can be sure in the future, as in the past, that you are law-abiding, and unresentful people that the world has seen. . . . In all things that are purely social we can be as separate as the finders, yet one as the hand in all things essential to mutual progress. . . .

The wisest among my race understand that the agitation of questions of social equality is the extremist folly, and that progress in the enjoyment of all the privileges that will come to us must be the result of severe and constant struggle rather than of artificial forcing. No race that has anything to contribute to the markets of the world is long in any degree ostracized. It is important and right that all privileges of the law be ours, but it is vastly more important that we be prepared for the exercise of these privileges. The opportunity to earn a dollar in a factory just now is worth infinitely more than the opportunity to spend a dollar in an opera-house.

Source: Booker T. Washington, *Atlanta Exposition Address*, (1895), in Brown, *America Through the Eyes of Its People*, (1993), 147.

Plessy v. Ferguson (1896)

Plessy v. Ferguson was the landmark case of the U.S. Supreme Court that established "separate but equal" as the basis for segregated facilities. Although the case dealt with separate railway carriages in Louisiana, the Court's ruling was the basis for legal segregation everywhere and gave legal protection to racial apartheid in America for a half-century. Excerpts of the ruling follow.

This case turns upon the constitutionality of an act of the general assembly of the state of Louisiana, passed in 1890, providing for separate railway carriages for the white and colored races. . . .

The constitutionality of this act is attacked upon the ground that it conflicts both with the 13th Amendment of the Constitution, abolishing slavery, and the 14th Amendment, which prohibits certain restrictive legislation on the part of the states.

1. That it does not conflict with the 13th Amendment, which abolished slavery and involuntary servitude, except as a punishment for crime, is too clear for argument. . . . Indeed, we do not understand that the 13th Amendment is strenuously relied upon by the plaintiff. . . .

The object of the [14th] amendment was undoubtedly to enforce the absolute equality of the two races before the law, but in the nature of things it could not have been intended to abolish distinctions based upon color, or to enforce social, as distinguished from political, equality, or a commingling of the two races upon terms unsatisfactory to either. Laws permitting, and even requiring, their separation in places where they are liable to be brought into contact do not necessarily imply the inferiority of either race to the other, and have been generally, if not universally, recognized as within the competency of the state legislatures in the exercise of their police power. . . .

We consider the underlying fallacy of the plaintiff's argument to consist in the assumption that the enforced separation of the two races stamps the colored race with a badge of inferiority. If this be so, it is not by reason of anything found in the act, but solely because the colored race chooses to put that construction upon it. . . .

The argument also assumes that social prejudice may be overcome by legislation, and that equal rights cannot be secured to the Negro except by an enforced commingling of the two races. We cannot accept this proposition. If the two races are to meet on terms of social equality, it must be the result of natural affinities, a mutual appreciation of each other's merits and a voluntary consent of individuals. . . . Legislation is powerless to eradicate racial instincts or abolish distinctions based upon physical differences and the attempt to do so can only result in accentuating the difficulties of the present situation. If the civil and political right of both races be equal, one cannot be inferior to the other civilly or politically. If one race be inferior to the other socially, the Constitution of the United States cannot put them upon the same plane.

Source: Brown, *America Through the Eyes of Its People*, 146.

Literacy Test and Poll Tax, North Carolina, 1899

In the 1890s, legally imposed segregation and disfranchisement were new features of race relations in the South that codified previous customs. Beginning with Mississippi in 1890 and continuing into the twentieth century, southern state legislatures called constitutional conventions, ostensibly for the purpose of reform, and adopted legal instruments to disqualify large numbers of black voters. Excerpts from a North Carolina statute illustrate the use of the literacy test, poll tax, and grandfather clause as tools of disfranchisement.

(Sec. 4.) Every person presenting himself for registration shall be able to read and write any section of the constitution in the English language and before he shall be entitled to vote he shall have paid on or before the first day of March of the year in which he proposes to vote his poll tax as prescribed by law for the previous year. Poll taxes shall be a lien only on assessed property and no process shall issue to enforce the collection of the same except against assessed property.

(Sec. 5.) No male person who was on January one, eighteen hundred and sixty-seven, or at any time prior thereto entitled to vote under the laws of any state in the United States wherein he then resided, and no lineal descendant of any such person, shall be denied the right to register and vote at any election in this state by reason of his failure to possess the educational qualification prescribed in section four of this article: *Provided,* he shall have registered in accordance with the terms of this section prior to December one, nineteen hundred and eight. The general assembly shall provide for a permanent record of all persons who register under this section on or before November first, nineteen hundred and eight: and all such persons shall be entitled to register and vote in all elections by the people in this state unless disqualified under section two of this article: *Provided,* such persons shall have paid their poll tax as requ[i]red by law.

Public Laws of North Carolina, 1899, chapter 218.

Source: Paul D. Escott and David R. Goldfield, *Main Problems in the History of the American South*, Vol. II (1990), 179.

W. E. B. Du Bois, Speech to the Niagara Movement, 1905–1909

The Progressive reform movement included those who fought for racial justice and equality. The Niagara Movement was a loosely organized group of blacks and whites committed to this struggle who organized the National Association for the Advancement of Colored People. The NAACP played a key role, especially in the courts, in overturning the Jim Crow system of legal segregation in the South during the twentieth century. W. E. B. Du Bois, an articulate African-American champion of racial justice, gave the following

The men of the Niagara Movement coming from the toil of the year's hard work and pausing a moment from the earning of their daily bread turn towards the nation and again ask in the name of ten million the privilege of a hearing. In the past year the work of the Negro hater has flourished in the land. Step by step the defenders of the rights of American citizens have retreated. The work of stealing the black man's ballot has progressed and the fifty and more representatives of stolen votes still sit in the nation's capital. Discrimination in travel and public accommodations has so spread that some of our weaker brethren are actually afraid to thunder against color discrimination as such and are simply whispering for ordinary decencies.

Against this the Niagara Movement eternally protests. We will not be satisfied to take one jot or tittle less than our full manhood rights. . . .

In detail our demands are clear and unequivocal. First, we would vote; with the right to vote goes everything: Freedom, manhood, the honor of your wives, the chastity of your daughters, the right to work, and the chance to rise. . . .

Second. We want discrimination in public accommodations to cease. Separation in railway and street cars, based simply on race and color, is un-American, undemocratic, and silly. . . .

Third. We claim the right of freemen to walk, talk, and be with them that wish to be with us. . . .

Fourth. We want the laws enforced against rich as well as poor; against Capitalist as well as Laborer; against white as well as black. . . .

Fifth. We want our children educated. . . . And when we call for education, we mean real education. . . . Education is the development of power and ideal. We want our children trained as intelligent human beings should be, and we will fight for all time against any proposal to educate black boys and girls simply as servants and underlings. . . .

These are some of the chief things which we want. How shall we get them? By voting where we may vote, by persistent, unceasing agitation, by hammering at the truth, by sacrifice and work. . . .

Courage, brothers! The battle for humanity is not lost or losing. All across the skies sit signs of promise. The Slav is rising in his might, the yellow millions are tasting liberty, the black Africans are writhing towards the light, and everywhere the laborer, with ballot in his hand, is voting open the gates of Opportunity and Peace. The morning breaks over the bloodstained hills. We must not falter, we may not shrink. Above are the everlasting stars.

Source: Brier, et al., *Who Built America?*, 202–03.

Cost of Living

Frank H. Streightoff, "The Standard of Living," 1905

The estimated weekly earnings of wage earners in the United States compared to the minimum cost of living is the subject of this document.

Family Budgets, 1904, 1911

"Wages" or "salary" was a critical distinction in workers' pay and status. Wage workers were usually paid by the day or the week.

In some trades—textiles, canning, and the metal-working trades—workers were paid on a piecework basis. Regular or weekly work might depend upon the economy, the foreman, or the season of the year. In 1887, a study by Wisconsin's Departmennt of Labor, Census, and Statistics found that workers in all trades experienced an average 61 days per year of unemployment per person. Although there were considerable variations, depending upon whether one was an unskilled worker or craftsperson, the average annual wage for manufacturing workers in 1900 was $435 or $8.37 per week.

Salaried workers enjoyed regular employment, regular vacation time, time off for holidays, and sickness benefits. They did not live with the fear of sudden layoffs. Salaried workers were paid weekly, bimonthly, or monthly. Middle-class salaries are more difficult to average, but the following budgets of a Boston businessman (the Wells family), a Middle West farmer (the Parnells), and a California teacher (the Allison family) in 1912 demonstrate the higher earnings and expenditures of this group.

U.S. Census Bureau, Bulletin no. 93, Washington, D.C.: Superintendant of Documents (1904), 10; from Lewis M. Hacker and Helene S. Zahler, The Shaping of the American Tradition (1947), 934–36.

MIDDLE-CLASS YEARLY FAMILY BUDGETS

Budget of the Wells Family, 1911

Item	Amount in Dollars	Percentage of Budget
Food	504.00	21.00
Shelter (mortgage, repairs, taxes)	396.00	16.50
Clothes	192.00	8.00
Operating costs		
Help	120.00	
Heat and light	96.00	
Carfare	72.00	
Refurnishing	54.00	
Subtotal	342.00	14.25
Advancement		
Doctor, dentist, medicine	132.00	
Church, charity	168.00	
Vacations, travel, books, amusement	39.00	
Incidentals	89.40	
Insurance (fire and life)	117.60	
Savings	420.00	
Subtotal	966.00	40.25

Budget of the Parnell Family, 1911

Item	Amount in Dollars	Percentage of Budget
Food	600	15.000
Shelter (taxes, repairs, improvements, etc.)	475	11.875
Clothes	450	11.250
Operating	625	15.625
Advancement		
College (son and daughter)	1000	
Insurance (fire and life)	148	
Vacation trips	200	
Gifts, charity, church	60	
Books, etc.	50	
Miscellaneous	182	
Savings	200	
Subtotal	1850	46.250

Advancement expenditures for the Parnell family do not add up to $1850.
Source: Martha B. Bruère, "What Is the Home For," *Outlook* 99 (16 Dec. 1911), 911 (Wells Family); 913 (Parnell Family).

(continued)

Budget of the Allison Family, 1911		
Item	Amount in Dollars	Percentage of Budget
Food	216.00	12.0
Mortgage on home	360.00	20.0
Clothes	225.00	12.5
Operating costs		
Help	59.40	
Gas and electricity	41.40	
Telephone	23.40	
Carfare	70.20	
Laundry	14.40	
Subtotal	208.80	11.6
Advancement		
Insurance	91.80	
Church	10.80	
Books, etc.	64.80	
Amusements	50.40	
Incidentals	50.40	
Savings	522.00	
Subtotal	790.20	43.9

Source: Martha B. Bruère, "Experiments in Spending: The Budgets of a California Schoolteacher and a Massachusetts Clergyman," Woman's Home Companion 38 (Nov. 1911), 14.

TABLE 2 MINIMUM COST OF LIVING FOR ONE YEAR FOR FAMILY OF FIVE, 1908

Rent	$120.
Fuel, 5 tons of coal	35.
1 cord of wood	5.
Food, Groceries	168.
Milk, 1 quart per day at 8 cents	29.20
Vegetables	24.
Meat and fish	96.
Clothing	140.
Church and other organizations	20.
Pleasure	20.
Doctor	12.
Miscellaneous	40.
Total	709.20

This estimate can be summarized thus:

Rent	$120.	16.0%
Food	317.20	44.8
Clothing	140.	19.7
Fuel	40.	5.1

Source: Frank Hatch Streightobb, The Standard of Living Among the Industrial People of America (1911), 161.

TABLE 1 ESTIMATED DISTRIBUTION BY WEEKLY EARNINGS OF AVERAGE NUMBER OF ALL WAGE-EARNERS, AND MEN, WOMEN, AND CHILDREN, 1905

Weekly Earnings	All Wage-earners			Men 16 Years and Over		
	Number	Percentage in Groups	Cumulative Percentage	Number	Percentage in Groups	Cumulative Percentage
Less than $3	225,793	4.1	100.0	92,535	2.2	100.0
$3 to $4	264,426	4.8	95.9	96,569	2.3	97.8
4 to 5	340,113	6.2	91.1	149,531	3.5	95.5
5 to 6	363,693	6.7	84.9	177,550	4.2	92.0
6 to 7	454,285	8.3	78.2	272,288	6.4	87.8
7 to 8	453,203	8.3	69.9	327,726	7.7	81.4
8 to 9	423,689	7.8	61.6	336,669	7.9	73.7
9 to 10	619,465	11.3	53.8	557,046	13.1	65.8
10 to 12	708,858	13.0	42.5	654,435	15.4	52.7
12 to 15	741,036	13.5	29.5	714,816	16.9	37.3
15 to 20	618,314	11.3	16.0	609,797	14.4	20.4
20 to 25	171,844	3.1	4.7	170,571	4.0	6.0
25 and over	85,402	1.6	1.6	85,005	2.0	2.0
Total	5,470,321	100.0		4,244,538	100.0	
	Women 16 Years and Over			Children under 16 Years		
Less than $3	77,826	7.3	100.0	55,432	34.7	100.0
$3 to $4	115,741	10.9	92.7	52,316	32.7	65.3
4 to 5	158,926	14.9	81.8	31,656	19.8	32.6
5 to 6	173,713	16.3	66.9	12,430	7.8	12.8
6 to 7	176,224	16.5	50.6	5,773	3.6	5.0
7 to 8	124,061	11.7	34.1	1,416	0.9	1.4
8 to 9	86,467	8.1	22.4	553	0.3	0.5
9 to 10	62,193	5.8	14.3	226	0.1	0.2
10 to 12	54,340	5.1	8.5	83	0.1	0.1
12 to 15	26,207	2.5	3.4	13	(ª)	(ª)
15 to 20	8,516	0.8	0.9	1	(ª)	(ª)
20 to 25	1,273	0.1	0.1			
25 and over	397	(ª)	(ª)			
Total	1,065,884			159,899		

(ª) Less than one tenth of 1 per cent.
Source: U.S. Census Bureau. Bulletin No. 93 (Washington, D.C.: Supt. of Documents, 1904), 10.

TABLE 3 INCOME AND EXPENDITURES PER FAMILY BY NATIVITY OF HEAD OF FAMILY AND SIZE OF FAMILY, AND PER CENT OF EXPENDITURES FOR VARIOUS PURPOSES

The following table of income and expenditures was based upon a study of 105 native-born U.S. families and 200 foreign-headed families on the Lower West Side of New York City, 1903–05.

Size of Family	Total Families	Total Income	Food	Rent	Clothing	Light and Fuel	Insurance	Sundries	Total Expended	Average Surplus or Deficit	Food	Rent	Clothing	Light and Fuel	Insurance	Sundries	Total Per Cent	Percent of Income Expended
		$	$	$	$	$	$	$	$	$								
United States																		
2	5	851.60	270.18	150.60	83.54	32.17	22.25	214.86	773.60	+78.	34.9	19.5	10.8	4.1	2.9	27.8	100.	90.8
3	11	762.27	203.09	148.45	97.59	36.59	26.42	161.91	764.05	−1.78	38.4	19.4	12.8	4.8	3.4	21.2	100.	100.2
4	23	743.52	294.99	165.64	78.71	40.28	26.89	125.67	732.18	+11.34	40.3	22.6	10.7	5.5	3.7	17.2	100.	98.5
5	22	699.61	326.24	152.14	53.26	40.68	34.34	92.25	698.91	+.70	46.7	21.8	7.6	5.8	4.9	13.2	100.	99.9
6	18	944.89	361.29	171.33	114.09	42.94	29.14	196.15	914.94	+29.95	39.5	18.7	12.5	4.7	3.2	21.4	100.	96.8
7	12	832.75	385.92	167.96	68.37	37.08	45.83	108.34	813.50	+19.25	47.4	20.6	8.4	4.6	5.6	13.3	100.	97.9
8	8	1064.75	498.65	175.	119.37	49.36	41.50	183.87	1067.75	−3.00	46.7	16.4	11.2	4.6	3.9	17.2	100.	100.3
9	5	808.80	374.04	151.80	151.30	34.40	46.80	67.26	825.60	−16.80	45.3	18.4	18.3	4.2	5.6	8.2	100.	102.1
10	1	1046.	520.	180.	140.	40.	52.	114.	1046.	0	49.7	17.2	13.4	3.8	5.	10.9	100.	100.
Total	105	816.61	343.34	161.72	87.61	40.09	33.03	138.36	804.15	+12.46	42.7	20.1	10.9	5.	4.1	17.2	100.	98.5

Average size of family, 5.3.

Size of Family	Total Families	Total Income	Food	Rent	Clothing	Light and Fuel	Insurance	Sundries	Total Expended	Average Surplus or Deficit	Food	Rent	Clothing	Light and Fuel	Insurance	Sundries	Total Per Cent	Percent of Income Expended
Ireland																		
2	0																	
3	0																	
4	6	620.50	280.17	118.83	85.17	37.58	17.58	89.59	628.92	−8.42	44.6	18.9	13.5	6.	2.8	14.2	100.	101.
5	8	712.12	326.40	146.62	62.63	41.81	32.44	100.72	710.62	+1.50	45.9	20.6	8.8	5.9	4.6	14.2	100.	99.8
6	7	790.43	361.91	159.86	53.14	54.31	38.66	130.12	798.	−7.51	45.4	20.	6.7	6.8	4.8	16.3	100.	101.
7	4	1239.75	559.	174.75	164.75	54.33	48.40	291.02	1292.25	−52.50	43.3	13.5	12.8	4.2	3.7	22.5	100.	104.2
8	4	904.25	453.40	131.87	72.98	47.35	31.20	199.20	936.	−31.75	48.4	14.1	7.8	5.1	3.3	21.3	100.	103.5
9	3	1188.33	601.67	249.33	141.67	47.60	39.86	108.20	1188.33	0	50.6	21.	11.9	4.	3.4	9.1	100.	100.
10	3	918.33	485.34	160.67	114.33	51.73	35.01	96.25	943.33	−25.	51.5	17.	12.1	5.5	3.7	10.2	100.	102.7
Total	35	852.83	403.89	156.04	88.66	46.99	33.68	137.95	867.22	−14.39	46.6	18.	10.2	5.4	3.9	15.9	100.	101.7

Average size of family, 6.4.

Size of Family	Total Families	Total Income	Food	Rent	Clothing	Light and Fuel	Insurance	Sundries	Total Expended	Average Surplus or Deficit	Food	Rent	Clothing	Light and Fuel	Insurance	Sundries	Total Per Cent	Percent of Income Expended
England																		
2	0																	
3	1	1000.	338.	144.	125.	85.	0	308.	1000.	0	34.	14.	12.5	8.5	0	31.	100.	100.
4	4	914.25	344.50	187.70	111.25	46.87	16.90	177.03	884.25	+30.	39.	21.2	12.6	5.3	1.9	20.	100.	96.7
5	2	770.	393.	164.	45.	22.70	27.52	143.28	795.50	−25.50	49.4	20.7	5.6	2.8	3.5	18.	100.	103.3
6	3	675.	299.	108.	108.33	41.	37.44	81.23	675.	0	44.3	16.	16.1	6.1	5.5	12.	100.	100.
7	2	951.	468.	180.	72.50	63.20	21.26	136.04	941.	+10.	49.7	19.1	7.7	6.7	2.3	14.5	100.	98.9
8	1	675.	364.	142.50	75.	46.	23.40	24.10	675.	0	53.9	21.1	11.1	6.8	3.5	3.6	100.	100.
9	0																	
10	2	1559.	702.	157.50	130.	50.	31.20	543.30	1614.	−55.	43.5	9.8	8.	3.1	1.9	33.7	100.	103.5
Total	15	927.80	406.87	157.62	97.67	47.55	24.22	195.27	929.20	−1.40	43.8	17.	10.5	5.1	2.6	21.	100.	100.2

Average size of family, 5.9.

Size of Family	Total Families	Total Income	Food	Rent	Clothing	Light and Fuel	Insurance	Sundries	Total Expended	Average Surplus or Deficit	Food	Rent	Clothing	Light and Fuel	Insurance	Sundries	Total Per Cent	Percent of Income Expended
Germany																		
2	1	728.	300.	150.	75.	29.	47.20	51.80	653.	+75.	45.9	23.	11.5	4.4	7.2	8.	100.	89.7
3	0																	
4	3	866.	416.	188.	73.33	43.80	28.60	121.51	871.33	−5.33	47.7	21.6	8.4	5.	3.3	14.	100.	100.6
5	4	966.50	345.50	216.	71.50	38.92	52.12	165.96	890.	+76.50	38.8	24.3	8.	4.4	5.9	18.6	100.	92.1
6	2	1319.50	413.50	286.50	115.	56.10	66.47	294.43	1232.	+87.50	33.6	23.2	9.3	4.6	5.4	23.9	100.	93.4
7	3	974.67	535.60	166.	68.67	45.33	77.29	81.78	974.67	0	55	17	7.	4.7	7.9	8.4	100.	100.
8	3	1113.80	452.67	183.83	108.33	52.34	33.20	210.10	1040.47	+73.33	43.5	17.7	10.4	5.	3.2	20.2	100.	93.4
9	1	1450.	572.	210.	200.	41.	36.40	305.60	1365.	+85.	41.9	15.3	14.7	3.	2.7	22.4	100.	94.1
10	0																	
Total	17	1032.14	429.05	200.62	90.70	44.86	49.54	167.66	982.43	+49.71	43.7	20.4	9.2	4.6	5.	17.1	100.	95.2

Average size of family, 5.9.

(continued)

Federal Legislation
The Sherman Anti Trust Law (1890)

Business consolidation in the form of the trust reduced competition, fostered monopolies, and gave producers unlimited power over consumers. The Sherman Anti Trust Act reflected a growing national concern over monopoly. Already weakened by Congressional compromise, the act depended for its enforcement upon the will of the president and interpretations by the U.S. Supreme Court.

Be it enacted by the Senate and House of Representatives of the United States of America in Congress assembled:

Sec. 1. Every contract, combination in the form of trust, or otherwise, or conspiracy in restraint of trade or commerce

TABLE 3 (continued)

The following table of income and expenditures was based upon a study of 105 native-born U.S. families and 200 foreign-headed families on the Lower West Side of New York City, 1903–05.

Italy

Size of Family	No.	Total Income	Food	Rent	Clothing	Light and Fuel	Insurance	Sundries	Total Expended	Average Surplus or Deficit	Food %	Rent %	Clothing %	Light and Fuel %	Insurance %	Sundries %	Total Per Cent	Per Cent of Income Expended
3	3	478.33	217.33	100.	32.67	31.66	7.80	92.20	481.66	− 3.33	45.1	20.8	6.8	6.6	1.6	19.1	100.	100.7
4	1	797.	271.	216.	30.	38.	31.20	110.80	697.	+100.	38.9	31.	4.3	5.4	4.5	15.9	100.	87.5
5	1	640.	260.	90.	100.	45.	7.80	137.20	640.	0	40.6	14.1	15.6	7.	1.2	21.5	100.	100.
6	3	870.	390.	126.33	108.34	35.80	28.60	168.35	857.42	+ 12.58	45.4	14.7	12.7	4.2	3.4	19.6	100.	98.6
7	1	1162.	416.	216.	166.	24.90	41.60	317.50	1182.	− 20.	35.2	18.3	14.	2.1	3.5	26.9	100.	101.7
8	3	953.67	411.33	189.	106.	51.93	20.80	181.77	960.83	− 7.16	42.8	19.7	11.	5.4	2.2	18.9	100.	100.8
9	0																	
10	2	919.50	384.60	133.50	150.	50.50	22.10	178.80	919.50	0	41.8	14.5	16.3	5.5	2.4	19.5	100.	100.
12	1	1358.	512.20	216.	300.	89.	28.60	212.20	1358.	0	37.7	15.9	22.1	6.6	2.1	15.6	100.	100.
Total	15	846.80	352.29	150.07	109.13	43.74	21.67	164.15	841.05	+ 5.75	41.9	17.8	13.	5.2	2.6	19.5	100.	99.3

Average size of family, 6.6.

France

Size of Family	No.	Total Income	Food	Rent	Clothing	Light and Fuel	Insurance	Sundries	Total Expended	Average Surplus or Deficit	Food %	Rent %	Clothing %	Light and Fuel %	Insurance %	Sundries %	Total Per Cent	Per Cent of Income Expended
2	1	380.	182.	120.	10.	26.	0	42.	380.	0	47.9	31.6	2.6	6.8	0	11.1	100.	100.
3	1	322.	124.	111.	10.50	26.25	21.30	46.95	340.	−18.	36.5	32.6	3.1	7.7	6.3	13.8	100.	105.6
4	0																	
5	1	700.	260.	118.	72.	41.50	0	188.50	680.	+20.	38.2	17.4	10.6	6.1	0	27.7	100.	97.1
6	1	832.	306.80	180.	90.	35.60	30.12	176.48	819.	+13.	37.5	22.	11.	4.3	3.7	21.5	100.	98.4
Total	4	558.50	218.20	132.25	45.63	32.34	12.85	113.48	554.75	+ 3.75	39.3	23.9	8.2	5.8	2.3	20.5	100.	99.3

Average size of family, 4.

Norway and Sweden

Size of Family	No.	Total Income	Food	Rent	Clothing	Light and Fuel	Insurance	Sundries	Total Expended	Average Surplus or Deficit	Food %	Rent %	Clothing %	Light and Fuel %	Insurance %	Sundries %	Total Per Cent	Per Cent of Income Expended
2	1	1000.	260.	186.	83.	33.	0	268.	830.	+170.	31.3	22.4	10.	4.	0	32.3	100.	83.
3	1	1515.	286.	204.	65.	59.	32.30	218.70	865.	+650.	33.1	23.6	7.5	6.8	3.7	25.3	100.	57.1
4	1	1600.	520.	175.30	87.60	40.	7.60	319.50	1150.	+450.	45.2	15.2	7.6	3.5	7.	27.8	100.	71.9
5	1	572.	286.	144.	70.	41.	5.60	25.40	572.	0	50.	25.2	12.2	7.2	1.	4.4	100.	100.
Total	4	1171.75	338.	177.32	176.40	43.25	11.38	207.90	854.25	+317.50	39.6	20.8	8.9	5.1	1.3	24.3	100.	72.9

Average size of family, 3.5.

Switzerland

Size of Family	No.	Total Income	Food	Rent	Clothing	Light and Fuel	Insurance	Sundries	Total Expended	Average Surplus or Deficit	Food %	Rent %	Clothing %	Light and Fuel %	Insurance %	Sundries %	Total Per Cent	Per Cent of Income Expended
4	1	680.	273.	151.	36.	37.35	83.20	99.45	680.	0	40.2	22.2	5.3	5.5	12.2	14.6	100.	100.
6	1	904.	434.20	144.	75.	28.	40.80	147.	869.	+35.	50.	16.6	8.6	3.2	4.7	16.9	100.	96.1
Total	2	792.	353.60	147.50	55.50	32.67	62.	123.23	774.50	+17.50	45.6	19.	7.3	4.2	8.	15.9	100.	97.8

Average size of family, 5.

Nativity of Head of Family	Size of Family	Total Income	Average Expenditure per Family for Food	Rent	Clothing	Light and Fuel	Insurance	Sundries	Total Expended	Average Surplus or Deficit	Per Cent of Expenditure per Family for Food	Rent	Clothing	Light and Fuel	Insurance	Sundries	Total Per Cent	Per Cent of Income Expended
		$	$	$	$	$	$	$	$	$								
*Austria	6	731.	312.	198.	30.	50.	49.20	91.80	731.	0	42.7	27.1	4.1	6.8	6.7	12.6	100.	100.
*Scotland	8	832.	364.	120.	76.	68.20	0	203.80	832.	0	43.8	14.4	9.1	8.2	0	24.5	100.	100.
*Cuba	4	450.	208.	132.	40.	20.	23.40	36.60	460.	−10.	45.2	28.7	8.7	4.3	5.1	8.	100.	102.2

*One family from each of these nationalities.

among the several states or with foreign nations, is hereby declared to be illegal. Every person who shall make any such contract, or engage in any such combination or conspiracy, shall be deemed guilty of a misdemeanor, and on conviction thereof, shall be punished by a fine not exceeding $5,000 or by imprisonment not exceeding one year, or by both said punishments in the discretion of the Court.

Sec. 2. Every person who shall monopolize, or attempt to monopolize, or combine or conspire with any other person or persons to monopolize any part of the trade or commerce among the several states, or with foreign nations, shall be deemed guilty of a misdemeanor, and on conviction thereof, shall be punished by fine not exceeding $5,000, or by imprisonment not exceeding one year, or by both said punishments, in the discretion of the Court.

Sec. 3. Every contract, combination in form or trust or otherwise, or conspiracy, in restraint of trade or commerce in any territory of the United States, or the District of Columbia, or in restraint of trade or commerce between any such Territory and another, or between any such Territory or Territories and State or States or the District of Columbia, or with foreign nations, or between the District of Columbia and any State or States or foreign nations, is hereby declared illegal. Every person who shall make any such contract, or engage in any such combination or conspiracy, shall be deemed guilty of a misdemeanor, and on conviction thereof, shall be punished by fine not exceeding one year, or by both said punishments in the discretion of the Court.

Sec. 4. The several Circuit Courts of the United States are hereby invested with jurisdiction to prevent and restrain violations of this act: and it shall be the duty of the several District-Attorneys of the United States, in their respective districts, under the direction of the Attorney-General to initiate proceedings in equity to prevent and restrain such violations.

Size of Family	Total Families	Total Income	Average Expenditure per Family for						Total Expended	Average Surplus or Deficit	Per Cent of Expenditure per Family for							Per Cent of Income Expended
			Food	Rent	Clothing	Light and Fuel	Insurance	Sundries			Food	Rent	Clothing	Light and Fuel	Insurance	Sundries	Total Per Cent	
		$	$	$	$	$	$	$	$	$								
2	8	795.75	261.61	151.12	73.21	31.10	19.81	179.52	716.37	+79.38	36.5	21.1	10.2	4.3	2.8	25.1	100.	90.
3	17	744.53	272.	140.71	80.71	39.27	21.62	154.78	709.09	+35.44	38.4	19.8	11.4	5.5	3.1	21.8	100.	95.2
4	40	765.15	309.10	162.80	79.50	40.16	25.56	126.67	743.79	+21.36	41.6	21.9	10.7	5.4	3.4	17.	100.	97.2
5	39	728.37	327.24	155.49	58.74	39.95	33.12	106.07	720.61	+ 7.76	45.5	21.6	8.1	5.5	4.6	14.7	100.	98.9
6	36	896.72	360.66	166.69	97.64	44.70	34.62	172.07	875.98	+20.74	41.2	19.1	11.1	5.1	3.9	19.6	100.	97.7
7	22	951.82	446.63	172.20	90.75	43.16	48.16	149.96	950.86	+ .96	47.	18.1	9.5	4.5	5.1	15.8	100.	99.9
8	20	992.22	456.14	165.42	102.05	50.56	32.11	183.56	989.85	+ 2.37	46.1	16.7	10.3	5.1	3.2	18.6	100.	99.8*
9	9	1006.55	471.91	190.78	153.50	39.50	43.33	107.39	1006.44	+ .11	46.9	18.9	15.3	3.9	4.3	10.7	100.	99.99
10	8	1094.75	518.65	155.50	130.37	49.52	32.96	230.87	1117.87	−23.12	46.4	13.9	11.7	4.4	2.9	20.7	100.	102.1
12	1	1358.	512.20	216.	300.	89.	28.60	212.20	1358.	0	37.7	15.9	22.1	6.6	2.1	15.6	100.	100.
Total	200	851.38	363.42	162.26	88.45	42.46	32.35	147.31	836.25	+15.13	43.4	19.4	10.6	5.1	3.9	17.6	100.	98.2

Average size of family, 5.6.

*Due to older German children being boarders—hence more saved.
Source: Louise Bolard More, *Wage-Earners' Budgets* (1907), 75–79.

Such proceedings may be by way of petition setting forth the case and praying that such violation shall be enjoined or otherwise prohibited. When the parties complained of shall have been duly notified of such petition the Court shall proceed, as soon as may be, to the hearing and determination of the case; and pending such petition and before final decree, the court may at any time make such temporary restraining order or prohibition as shall be deemed just in the premises.

Sec. 5. Whenever it shall appear to the Court before which any proceeding under sec. 4 of this act may be pending that the ends of justice require that other parties should be brought before the Court, the Court may cause them to be summoned whether they reside in the district in which the Court is held or not; and subpoenas to that end may be served in any district by the marshal thereof.

Sec. 6. Any property owned under any contract or by any combination, or pursuant to any conspiracy (and being the subject thereof) mentioned in sec. 1 of this act and being in the course of transportation from one state to another, or to a foreign country, shall be forfeited to the United States, and may be seized and condemned by like proceedings as those provided by law for the forfeiture, seizure and condemnation of property imported into the United States contrary to law.

Sec. 7. Any person who shall be injured in his business or property by any other person or corporation by reason of anything forbidden or declared to be unlawful by this act may sue therefore without respect to the amount in controversy, and shall recover threefold the damages by him sustained, and the costs of suit, including a reasonable attorney's fee.

Sec. 8. That the word "person" or "persons" wherever used in this act shall be deemed to include corporations and associations existing under or authorized by the laws of either the United States, the laws of any of the Territories, the laws of any State or the laws of any foreign country.

Approved July 2, 1890.

Source: The World Almanac and Encyclopedia 1918 (1917), 140.

The Sixteenth Amendment to the U.S. Constitution (1913)

The income tax amendment passed during Woodrow Wilson's first administration when the Underwood Tariff drastically reduced tariff rates and reduced revenues. The amendment gave Congress the power it needed to tax incomes:

The Congress shall have power to lay and collect taxes on incomes, from whatever source derived, without apportionment among the several States, and without regard to any census or enumeration.

Source: U.S. Constitution.

Foreign Policy
Josiah Strong, *Our Country*, 1891

Strong was a leading proponent of the theory that it was the "white man's burden" to spread a superior Anglo-Saxon culture to the inferior non-Western cultures. His rationale is contained in this excerpt from his book.

Every race which has deeply impressed itself on the human family has been the representative of some great idea—one or more—which had given direction to the nation's life and form to its civilization. Among the Egyptians this seminal idea was life, among the Persians it was light, among the Hebrews it was purity, among the Greeks it was beauty, among the Romans it was law. The Anglo-Saxon is the representative of two great ideas, which are closely related. One of them is that of civil liberty. Nearly all of the civil liberty in the world is enjoyed by Anglo-Saxons: the English, the British colonists, and the people of the United States. . . . The noblest races have always been lovers of liberty. That love ran strong in early German blood, and has profoundly influenced the institutions of all the branches of the great German family; but it was left for the Anglo-Saxon branch fully to recognize the right of the individual to himself, and formally to declare it the foundation stone of government.

The other great idea of which the Anglo-Saxon is the exponent is that of a pure spiritual Christianity. It was no accident that the great reformation of the sixteenth century originated among a Teutonic, rather than a Latin people. It was the fire of liberty burning in the Saxon heart that flamed up against the absolutism of the Pope. . . .

It is not necessary to argue to those for whom I write that the two great needs of mankind, that all men may be lifted up into the light of the highest Christian civilization, are, first, a pure, spiritual Christianity, and, second, civil liberty. Without controversy, these are the forces which, in the past, have contributed most to the elevation of the human race, and they

TABLE 4   A STUDY OF THE SOURCES OF INCOME

The sources and average amount of income for the 200 families of New York's Lower West Side shows who in the households contributed to the total income of the family.

A. Number of Families with Income from Various Sources by Nativity of Head of Family / B. Percent of Families Having an Income from Various Sources by Nativity of Head of Family

Nativity of Head of Family	Total Families	Average Size of Family	Husband	Wife	Children	Boarders and Lodgers	Other Sources	Husband	Wife	Children	Boarders and Lodgers	Other Sources
			Families with an Income from — Occupation of					Percent of Families with an Income from — Occupation of				
United States	105	5.3	94	55	34	29	68	89.5	52.4	32.4	27.6	64.8
Ireland	35	6.4	25	15	18	11	22	71.4	42.9	51.4	31.4	62.9
England	15	5.9	13	7	7	6	8	86.7	46.7	46.7	40.	53.3
Germany	17	5.9	14	4	5	12	7	82.4	23.5	29.4	70.6	41.2
Italy	15	6.6	13	5	8	3	7	86.7	33.3	53.3	20.	46.7
France	4	4.	3	3	0	0	3	75.	75.	0	0	75.
Norway and Sweden	4	3.5	4	0	0	1	0	100.	0	0	25.	0
Switzerland	2	5.	2	1	0	0	1	100.	50.	0	0	50.
Austria	1	6.	1	1	0	0	0	100.	100.	0	0	100.
Scotland	1	8.	1	1	1	0	0	100.	100.	100.	0	0
Cuba	1	4.	1	1	1	0	1	100.	100.	100.	0	100.
Total foreign	95	6.	77	38	40	33	49	81.1	40.	42.1	34.7	51.6
Total U.S. and foreign	200	5.6	171	93	74	62	117	85.5	46.5	37.	31.	58.5

C. Average Amount of Income from Various Sources by Nativity of Head of Family / D. Percent of Income from Various Sources by Nativity of Head of Family

Nativity of Head of Family	Total Families	Average Size of Family	Husband $	Wife $	Children $	Boarders and Lodgers $	Other Sources $	Total Income of Family $	Husband	Wife	Children	Boarders and Lodgers	Other Sources
			Average Income of all Families from — Occupation of						Per Cent of Income from — Occupation of				
United States	105	5.3	564.51	80.87	57.68	51.70	61.85	816.61	69.1	9.9	7.1	6.3	7.6
Ireland	35	6.4	421.85	87.48	187.69	70.84	84.97	852.83	49.5	10.2	22.	8.3	10.
England	15	5.9	541.50	127.85	88.60	135.	34.85	927.80	58.4	13.8	9.5	14.5	3.8
Germany	17	5.9	580.	59.65	69.18	303.29	20.02	1032.14	56.2	5.8	6.7	29.4	1.9
Italy	15	6.6	487.67	48.87	246.	35.46	28.80	846.80	57.6	5.8	29.	4.2	3.4
France	4	4.	436.69	80.75	0	0	40.06	557.50	78.3	14.5	0	0	7.2
Norway and Sweden	4	3.5	1145.75	0	0	26.	0	1171.75	97.8	0	0	2.2	0
Switzerland	2	5.	754.50	27.50	0	0	10.	792.	95.3	3.5	0	0	1.2
Austria	1	6.	624.	107.	0	0	0	731.	85.4	14.6	0	0	0
Scotland	1	8.	260.	156.	416.	0	0	832.	31.3	18.7	50.	0	0
Cuba	1	4.	72.	75.	275.	0	28.	450.	16.	16.7	61.1	0	6.2
Total foreign	95	6.	514.29	78.34	141.63	108.38	47.17	889.81	57.8	8.8	15.9	12.2	5.3
Total U.S. and foreign	200	5.6	540.65	79.67	97.56	78.62	54.88	851.38	63.5	9.4	11.5	9.2	6.4

E. Average Amount of Income from Various Sources by Nativity of Head of Family

Nativity of Head of Family	Total Families	Average Size of Family	Husband $	Wife $	Children $	Boarders and Lodgers $	Other Sources $	Total Average Income $
			Average Income of Families Having an Income from — Occupation of					
United States	105	5.3	630.57	154.39	178.13	187.19	95.51	816.61
Ireland	35	6.4	590.60	204.11	364.95	225.41	135.18	852.83
England	15	5.9	624.81	273.96	189.86	337.50	65.34	927.80
Germany	17	5.9	704.29	253.50	235.20	429.67	48.63	1032.14
Italy	15	6.6	562.69	146.60	461.25	177.33	61.71	846.80
France	4	4.	582.25	107.67	0	0	54.75	557.50
Norway and Sweden	4	3.5	1145.75	0	0	104.	0	1171.75
Switzerland	2	5.	754.50	55.	0	0	20.	792.

E. Average Amount of Income from Various Sources by Nativity of Head of Family								
			Average Income of Families Having an Income from					
			Occupation of			Boarders and Lodgers	Other Sources	Total Average Income
Nativity of Head of Family	Total Families	Average Size of Family	Husband	Wife	Children			
Austria	1	6.	624.	107.	0	0	0	731.
Scotland	1	8.	260.	156.	416.	0	0	832.
Cuba	1	4.	72.	75.	275.	0	28.	450.
Total foreign	95	6.	634.51	203.75	336.38	312.02	91.45	889.81
Total U.S. and foreign	200	5.6	632.34	171.33	263.67	253.63	93.81	851.38

Source: Louise Bolard More, *Wage-Earners' Budgets* (1907), 84–86.

TABLE 5 WORKING-CLASS YEARLY FAMILY BUDGET

Seamstress

Income

Mrs. M., sewing, 14 weeks, averaged $5.00 a week	$ 70.00
Mrs. M., sewing, 38 weeks, averaged $3.00 a week	114.00
Girl, 13, earned in summer	14.00
Mother, extra work	20.50
St. Vincent de Paul Society, grocery tickets	26.00
St. Vincent de Paul Society, shoes	4.00
Charity Organization Society, for rent	11.50
Total	$260.00

Expenditures

Food	$130.00
Rent	92.75
Clothing	18.00
Fuel	13.00
Medicine	1.00
Moving expenses	3.00
Sundries	2.25
	$260.00

Factory Laborer

Income, Jan. 1, 1904, to Jan. 1, 1905, $489

Expenditures

Food (about $4.00 a week)	$205.00
Rent, $9.00 a month	108.00
Gas and coal	26.00
Clothing	24.00
Clothing for baby	8.00
Furniture	45.00
Books and papers	7.80
Charity	3.00
Recreation in summer	7.00
Gifts	6.00
Loan	27.00
Kitchen needs	8.00
Miscellaneous (stamps, paper, thread, pins, etc.)	14.20
	$489.00

Glassworker

Income

Man, 51½ weeks at $14.00 (3 holidays deducted)	$ 721.00
Woman, for janitor's services, rent-free	132.00
Boy (15), 22 weeks at $3.50, 25 weeks at $4.00	177.00
	$1030.00
Gift from landlord at Christmas	10.00
Total	$1040.00

Expenditures

Food, $10.00 a week, including lunch-money	$ 520.00
Rent	132.00
Clothing	85.00
Light and fuel	48.50
Insurance, .60 a week	31.20
Papers, .11 a week	5.72
Union dues	6.00
Drink for man, $3.00 a week	156.00
Medical attendance	27.00
Church	13.00
Recreation for father and oldest boy	10.00
Sundries	5.58
Total	$1040.00

Source: Louise Bolard More, *Wage-Earners' Budgets* (1907), 152–54 (Seamstress); 159–63 (Factory Laborer); 189–90 (Glassworker).

must continue to be, in the future, the most efficient ministers to its progress. It follows, then, that the Anglo-Saxon, as the great representative of these two ideas, the depositary [sic] of these two greatest blessings, sustains peculiar relations to the world's future, is divinely commissioned to be, in a peculiar sense, his brother's keeper. . . .

There can be no reasonable doubt that North America is to be the great home of the Anglo-Saxon, the principal seat of his power, the center of his life and influence. Not only does it constitute seven-elevenths of his possessions, but this empire is unsevered, while the remaining four-elevenths are fragmentary and scattered over the earth. Australia will have a great population; but its disadvantages, as compared with North America, are too manifest to need mention. Our continent has room and resources and climate, it lies in the pathway of the nations, it belongs to the zone of power, and already, among Anglo-Saxons, do we lead in population and wealth.

Mr. Darwin is not only disposed to see, in the superior vigor of our people, an illustration of his favorite theory of natural selection, but even intimates that the world's history thus far has been simply preparatory for our future, and tributary to it. He says: "There is apparently much truth in the belief that the wonderful progress of the United States, as well as the character of the people, are the results of natural selection; for the more energetic, restless, and courageous men from all parts of Europe have emigrated during the last ten or twelve generations to that great country, and have there succeeded best. . . ."

The time is coming when the pressure of population on the means of subsistence will be felt there as it is now felt in Europe and Asia. Then will the world enter upon a new stage of its history—the final competition of races, for which the Anglo-Saxon is being schooled. Long before the thousands millions are here, the mighty centrifugal tendency, inherent in this stock and strengthened in the United States, will assert itself. Then this race of unequaled energy, with all the majesty of numbers and the might of wealth behind it—the representative, let us hope, of the largest liberty, the purest Christianity, the highest civilization—having developed peculiarly aggressive traits calculated to impress its institutions upon mankind, will spread itself over the earth. If I read not amiss, this powerful race will move down upon Mexico, down upon Central and South America, out upon the islands of the sea, over upon Africa and beyond. And can anyone doubt that the result of this competition of races will be the "survival of the fittest"? . . .

In my own mind, there is no doubt that the Anglo-Saxon is to exercise the commanding influence in the world's future; but the exact nature of that influence is, as yet, undetermined. How far his civilization will be materialistic and atheistic, and how long it will take thoroughly to Christianize and sweeten it, how rapidly he will hasten the coming of the kingdom wherein dwelleth righteousness, or how many ages he may retard it, is still uncertain; but it is now being swiftly determined. . . .

Notwithstanding the great perils which threaten it, I cannot think our civilization will perish; but I believe it is fully in the hand of the Christians of the United States, during the next fifteen or twenty years, to hasten or retard the coming of Christ's kingdom in the world by hundreds, and perhaps thousands, of years. We of this generation and nation occupy the Gibraltar of the ages which command the world's future.

Source: Brown, *America Through the Eyes of Its People*, 133.

McKinley Decides on the Philippines, 1898

In this document, Pres. McKinley sets the path of American foreign policy in the twentieth century with his justification for keeping the Philippines as a spoil of the Spanish-American war.

When next I realized that the Philippines had dropped into our laps, I confess I did not know what to do with them. I sought counsel from all sides—Democrats as well as Republicans—but got little help. I thought first we would take only Manila; then Luzon; then other islands, perhaps, also.

I walked the floor of the White House night after night until midnight; and I am not ashamed to tell you, gentlemen, that I went down on my knees and prayed Almighty God for light and guidance more than one night. And one night late it came to me this way—I don't know how it was, but it came:

(1) That we could not give them back to pain—that would be cowardly and dishonorable;

(2) That we could not turn them over to France or Germany, our commercial rivals in the Orient—that would be bad business and discreditable;

(3) That we could not leave them to themselves—they were unfit for self-government, and they would soon have anarchy and misrule worse then Spain's was; and

(4) That there was nothing left for us to do but to take

them all, and to educate the Filipinos, and uplift and civilize and Christianize them and by God's grace do the very best we could by them, as our fellow men for whom Christ also died

And then I went to bed and went to sleep, and slept soundly, and the next morning I sent for the chief engineer of the War Department (our map-maker), and I told him to put the Philippines on the map of the United States (pointing to a large map on the wall of his office), and there they are and there they will stay while I am President!

Source: C. S. Olcott, *The Life of William McKinley*, Vol. 2 in Brown, *America Through the Eyes of Its People*, 138.

Immigrant Life
Letter of a Swedish Immigrant, 1891

America was a "distant magnet" for thousands of European immigrants. In this letter, a Swedish immigrant, who had emigrated to Minnesota from Norrbottens län in 1891, writes home sixteen years later to tell of his experiences in America. The letter reveals the "push" and "pull" forces of immigration, the hardships of the experience, and the reasons why the author feels he cannot go home.

Born on a medium-sized farm in one of Norrbotten's coastal parishes thirty-odd years ago, with a strong desire to learn, which I early had the chance to satisfy, already as a boy I acquired a strong lust for adventure. I had not, however, thought much about a trip to America, even though I had been in touch with several returned Swedish Americans and though my sister had emigrated to America in my sixteenth year, in the fall of 1889.

But at a book auction at the courthouse in the fall of 1890 I bought a batch of books, and among them I found one with the title *The Truth about America*. I have long since forgotten the author's name, but it was apparently one of your predecessors in the movement to prevent emigration.

This book contained a mass of the most ridiculous lies about America, of the same kind as the stories one reads from time to time in our conservative newspapers back home, with which they think they can frighten the simple Swedes, as when they frighten small children with the boogeyman. They forget that the average Swede knows just as much about American conditions as authors and journalists. The book in question, as I said, painted America in colors as somber as ever any medieval priest could paint the Evil One's abode. This caused me and others who read the book to reflect over what motives could lie behind such a book, and we came to the conclusion that it must be above all to frighten people out of emigrating, and secondly to make the little man satisfied with conditions in Sweden. How successful this was is shown by the fact that all the farm boys in the village to whom I lent the book kept me company over to America the following spring. There were of course many other causes besides, which helped us to decide to leave: the idiotic class differences, lack of the vote, military service, etc. The economic situation was the least important reason, for all of those who went from my home village that spring were from well-to-do farm families.

Although I have now been in this country for sixteen years I still follow the course of events back home and take great interest in the welfare of my homeland. The Swedish American newspapers, of which I read a half dozen, every week include a couple of pages of news from Sweden as well as special correspondence on the events of the day. If the Swedish newspapers would publish half as much about Swedish America, perhaps they would judge us more fairly at home. I have never visited Sweden since I came here, but I feel a deep love for the land where my cradle stood, where my old father lives, and where my mother's remains lie at rest. I have forgotten all that was hard at home and have only the happy memories of childhood left. . . .

Because I do not want my illusions to be crushed, I have never since visited Sweden.

My life here in America has gone through many changes. My "dog years" were especially hard for a youth who was not used to working for others. I worked at sawmills, in the forest, on farms, at a newspaper press, etc., was a census taker and a policeman, until nearly fifteen years ago I got the position in the postal service which I now have. It is not a high position, but under the same circumstances I could never have gotten anything like it in Sweden. My salary is $900—over 3,300 *kronor* a year. When it is considered that when I took the examination for the position I had not gone a single day to an American school and still made a grade of 97 per cent, that is not so bad. My working time is six or seven hours per day.

It could thus never occur to me to leave this position and return to Sweden, where a person who has not acquired academic degrees has no chance to get a position in public service. . . .

The reasons why it would be impossible for Swedish Americans to get along well in Sweden are many: the ridiculous "title sickness" and silly class system, the groveling of the low and the arrogance of the high, the antipathy against Swedish Americans and "self-made men," the bureaucracy and pedantry, the complicated system through which the wealthy seek to keep political power, the forced militarism, and the whole system that makes it impossible to acquire through one's own work as good an income as that mass of good-for-nothings who have managed to obtain certain academic degrees from the state and the commune to do nothing. I consider it fruitless to work against emigration or to try to bring about a remigration of Swedish Americans as long as conditions at home are the way they are. Both Swedes and Swedish Americans have greater demands on life than the ruling class in Sweden is willing to fulfill. Let them therefore go their way. You can surely fill their places with Slavic and other lower kinds of people with smaller requirements and more suitable for your present system, for to expect the ruling class to change the system for the benefit of the little man is expecting too much.

Source: H. Arnold Barton, ed. Letters From The Promised Land: Swedes in America 1840–1914 (1975), 286–89, with permission University of Minnesota Press.

Mary Antin's America, 1912

Mary Antin was a Russian Jew who came with her parents to the United States in 1894. Still just a teenager, she wrote her first book, The Promised Land *(1912). In this excerpt, she provides her version of the immigrant saga.*

On the whole the Russian immigrant in this country is the Jewish immigrant, since we are the most numerous group out of Russia. But to speak for the Jews—the most misunderstood people in the whole of history—ten minutes, in which to clear away 2,000 years of misunderstanding! Your President has probably in this instance, as in other instances, been guided by some inspiration, the source of which none of us may know. I was called by name long before your President notified me that she would call me to this assembly. I was called by name to say what does the Jew bring to America— by a lady from Philadelphia. Miss Repplier, not long ago, in an article in her inimitable fashion, called things by their name, and sometimes miscalled them, spoke of "the Jew in America who has received from us so much and has given us so little." This comment was called down by something that I had said about certain things in American life that did not come up to the American standard. "The Jew who has given so little." Tonight I am the Jew—you are the Americans. Let us look over these things.

What do we bring you besides our poverty and our rags? Men, women, and children—the stuff that nations are built of. What sort of men and women? I shall not seek to tire you with a list of shining names of Jewish notables. If you want to know who's who among the Jews, I refer you to your biographical dictionary. You are as familiar as I am with the name of Jews who shine in the professions, who have done notable service to the state, in politics, in diplomacy, and where you will. . . .

You know as well as I what numbers of Jewish youth are always taking high ranks, high honors in the schools, colleges and universities. You know as well as I do in what numbers our people crowd your lecture halls and your civic centers, in all those places where the spiritual wine of life may be added to our daily bread. These are things that you know. I don't want you to be thinking of any list of Jewish notables.

A very characteristic thing of Jewish life is the democracy of virtue that you find in every Jewish community. We Jews have never depended for our salvation on the supreme constellations of any chosen ones. . . . Our shining ones were to us always examples by means of which the whole community was to be disciplined to what was Jewish virtue.

Take a group of Jews anywhere, and you will have the essence of their Jewishness, though there be not present one single shining luminary. The average Jew presents the average of whatsoever there is of Jewish virtue, talent or capacity.

What is this peculiar Jewish genius? If I must sum it up in a word, I will say that the Jewish genius is a love for living out the things that they believe. What do we believe? We Jews believe that the world is a world of law. Law is another name for our God, and the quest after the law, the formulation of it, has always permeated our schools, and the incorporation of the laws of life, as our scholars noted it down, has been the chief business of the Jewish masses. No wonder that when we come to America, a nation founded as was our ancient nation, a nation founded on law and principle, on an ideal—no wonder that we so quickly find ourselves at home, that presently we fall into the regulation habit of speaking of

America as our own country, until Miss Repplier reproves us, and then we do it no more. I used formerly when speaking of American sins, tribulations, etc., I used to speak of them as "ours"; no more—your sins. I have been corrected.

Why then, now that we have come here, to this nation builded on the same principle as was our nation, no wonder that we so quickly seize on the fundamentals. We make no virtue of the fact—it is the Jewishness in us—that has been our peculiar characteristics, our habit. We need no one from outside of our ranks to remind us of the goodly things we have found and taken from your hands. We have been as eloquent as any that has spoken in appreciation of what we have found here, of liberty, justice, and a square deal. We give thanks. We have rendered thanks, we Jews, some of you are witnesses. We know the value of the gifts that we have found here.

Who shall know the flavor of bread if not they that have gone hungry, and we, who have been for centuries without the bread of justice, we know the full flavor of American justice, liberty, and equality.

To formulate and again formulate, and criticise the law,—what do our Rabbis in the Ghetto besides the study of law? To them used to come our lawyers, to our Rabbis, not to find the way how to get around the law, but to be sure that we were walking straight in the path indicated by the law. So today in America we are busy in the same fashion.

The Jewish virtues, such as they are, are widespread throughout the Jewish masses. Here in New York City is congregated the largest Jewish community in the whole world, and what is true of the Jews of New York, is true of the Jews of America, and the Jews of the world. If I speak of the characteristics of Jewish life on the East side, one of the great characteristics is its restlessness in physical form, due to the oppression of city life, and the greater restlessness, due to the unquenchable, turbulent quest for the truth, and more truth. You know that the East side of New York is a very spawning ground for debate, and debating clubs. There are more boys and girls in debating clubs than in boys' basket ball teams, or baseball teams. I believe in boys playing baseball, but I also believe in that peculiar enthusiasm of our Jewish people for studying the American law, just as they used to study their own law, to see whether any of the American principles find incorporation in American institutions and habits. We are the critics. We are never satisfied with things as they are. Go out and hear the boys and girls. They like to go to school and learn the names of liberty, and equality and justice, and after school they gather in their debating circles and discuss what might be the meaning of these names, and what is their application to life. That is the reason there is so much stirring, rebellion, and protest that comes out of the East side.

In the great labor movement, it is the effort of the people to arrive at a program of economic justice that shall parallel the political justice. Consider for a moment the present condition of the garment-making trade. That is a Jewish trade. Ages ago when the lords of the nations, among whom we lived, were preventing us from engaging in other occupations, they thrust into the hands of our people the needle, and the needle was our tool, why through the needle we have still thought to give expression to the Jewish genius in our life.

This immense clothing industry—a Jewish industry primarily—is today in a better condition as regards unionization, is further on the road to economic justice than any other great industry that you could name. Mind you, the sweatshop we found here when we came here. We took it just as it was,

but the barring of the sweatshop and the organization of the clothing industry in such fashion that it is further in advance, more nearly on a basis that affords just treatment to all concerned—that has been the contribution of our tailor men and tailor women. We have done this thing. . . . The Protocol[1] is a piece of machinery for bringing about justice in this great industry. We have invented that thing, we Jews. We are putting it in operation, we are fighting for its perpetuation. Whatsoever good comes from it, we have done it. . . .

Consider us, if you will, in the most barbarous sense, but I point to this as our great contribution, we are always protesting, and if you want to know the value of that contribution, I remind you that the formulae of the rights of men, which was a criticism of things as they used to be, and a formularizing of things as they ought to be, was at least as efficient as all the armies of the continent put together in the revolutionary war. The Spirit of '76 is the spirit of criticism. We Jews in America are busy at our ancient business of pulling down false gods.

Source: Boller and Story, A More Perfect Union (1992), 99–102.

[1]**The Protocol:** A labor-management agreement recognizing union rights and providing for improved working conditions in the garment industry.

Native Americans
Chief Joseph's Surrender (1877)

The winter of 1877 found Chief Joseph and the remainder of his tribe of Nez Percé Indians on Snake Creek just 30 miles from the Canadian border and freedom. The U.S. Army had pursued them for 1,700 miles to force them onto a reservation. Unable to continue the march or resist any longer, Chief Joseph spoke a moving note of surrender, which was recorded.

Tell General Howard I know his heart. What he told me before, I have in my heart. I am tired of fighting. Our chiefs are killed. Looking Glass is dead. Toohoolhoolzote is dead. The old men are all dead. It is the young men who say yes or no. He who led the young men is dead [Ollikut, his brother]. It is cold and we have no blankets. The little children are freezing to death. My people, some of them, have run away to the hills, and have no blankets, no food. No one knows where they are—perhaps freezing to death. I want to have time to look for my children and see how many I can find. Maybe I shall find them among the dead. Hear me, my chiefs. I am tired. My heart is sick and sad. From where the sun now stands, I will fight no more forever.

Source: Waldman, Atlas of The North American Indian (1985), 135–36.

A Century of Dishonor, 1881

In 1881, Helen Hunt Jackson wrote A Century of Dishonor, *a stinging indictment of America's treatment of Native Americans. This popular book galvanized public opinion by drawing national attention to the plight of Indians. It led to the passage of the Dawes Act, a well-intentioned bill to stabilize Indian life that instead struck a devastating blow to the heart of Native American culture. The following is a letter to the editor of the New York Tribune in which Jackson minces no words in her recital of abuses that Indians have suffered at the hands of the white man.*

There are within the limits of the United States between two hundred and fifty and three hundred thousand Indians, exclusive of those in Alaska. The names of the different tribes and bands, as entered in the statistical table so the Indian Office Reports, number nearly three hundred. One of the most careful estimates which have been made of their numbers and localities gives them as follows: "In Minnesota and States east of the Mississippi, about 32,500; in Nebraska, Kansas, and the Indian Territory, 70,650; in the Territories of Dakota, Montana, Wyoming, and Idaho, 65,000; in Nevada and the Territories of Colorado, New Mexico, Utah, and Arizona, 84,000; and on the Pacific slope, 48,000."

Of these, 130,000 are self-supporting on their own reservations, "receiving nothing from the Government except interest on their own moneys, or annuities granted them in consideration of the cession of their lands to the United States."

Of the remainder, 84,000 are partially supported by the Government—the interest money due them and their annuities, as provided by treaty, being inadequate to their subsistence on the reservations where they are confined. . . .

There are about 55,000 who never visit an agency, over whom the Government does not pretend to have either control or care. These 55,000 "subsist by hunting, fishing, on roots, nuts, berries, etc., and by begging and stealing"; and this also seems to dispose of the accusation that the Indian will not "work for a living." There remains a small portion, about 31,000, that are entirely subsisted by the Government.

There is not among these three hundred bands of Indians one which has not suffered cruelly at the hands either of the Government or of white settlers. The poorer, the more insignificant, the more helpless the band, the more certain the cruelty and outrage to which they have been subjected. This is especially true of the bands on the Pacific slope. These Indians found themselves of a sudden surrounded by and caught up in the great influx of gold-seeking settlers, as helpless creatures on a shore are caught up in a tidal wave. There was not time for the Government to make treaties; not even time for communities to make laws. The tale of the wrongs, the oppressions, the murders of the Pacific-slope Indians in the last thirty years would be a volume by itself, and is too monstrous to be believed.

It makes little difference, however, where one opens the record of the history of the Indians; every page and every year has its dark stain. The story of one tribe is the story of all, varied only differences of time and place; but neither time nor place makes any difference in the main facts. Colorado is as greedy and unjust in 1880 as was Georgia in 1830, and Ohio in 1795; and the United States Government breaks promises now as deftly as then, and with an added ingenuity from long practice.

One of its strongest supports in so doing is the widespread sentiment among the people of dislike to the Indian, of impatience with his presence as a "barrier to civilization" and distrust of it as a possible danger. The old tales of the frontier life, with its horrors of Indian warfare, have gradually, by two or three generations' telling, produced in the average mind something like an hereditary instinct of questioning and unreasoning aversion which it is almost impossible to dislodge or soften. . . .

President after president has appointed commission after commission to inquire into and report upon Indian affairs, and to make suggestions as to the best methods of managing them.

The reports are filled with eloquent statements of wrongs done to the Indians, of perfidies on the part of the Government; they counsel, as earnestly as words can, a trial of the simple and unperplexing expedients of telling truth, keeping promises, making fair bargains, dealing justly in all ways and all things. These reports are bound up with the Government's Annual Reports, and that is the end of them. . . .

"The history of the Government connections with the Indians is a shameful record of broken treaties and unfulfilled promises. The history of the border white man's connection with the Indians is a sickening record of murder, outrage, robbery, and wrongs committed by the former, as the rule, and occasional savage outbreaks and unspeakably barbarous deeds of retaliation by the latter, as the exception.

Taught by the Government that they had rights entitled to respect, when those rights have been assailed by the rapacity of the white man, the arm which should have been raised to protect them has ever been ready to sustain the aggressor.

The testimony of some of the highest military officers of the United States is on record to the effect that, in our Indian wars, almost without exception, the first aggressions have been made by the white man. . . . Every crime committed by a white man against an Indian is concealed and palliated. Every offence committed by an Indian against a white man is borne on the wings of the post or the telegraph to the remotest corner of the land, clothed with all the horrors which the reality or imagination can throw around it. Against such influences as these are the people of the United States need to be warned."

To assume that it would be easy, or by any one sudden stroke of legislative policy possible, to undo the mischief and hurt of the long past, set the Indian policy of the country right for the future, and make the Indians at once safe and happy, is the blunder of a hasty and uninformed judgment. The notion which seems to be growing more prevalent, that simply to make all Indians at once citizens of the United States would be a sovereign and instantaneous panacea for all their ills and all the Government's perplexities, is a very inconsiderate one. To administer complete citizenship of a sudden, all round, to all Indians, barbarous and civilized alike, would be as grotesque a blunder as to dose them all round with any one medicine, irrespective of the symptoms and needs of their diseases. It would kill more than it would cure. Nevertheless, it is true, as was well stated by one of the superintendents of Indian Affairs in 1857, that, "so long as they are not citizens of the United States, their rights of property must remain insecure against invasion. The doors of the federal tribunals being barred against them while wards and dependents, they can only partially exercise the rights of free government, or give to those who make, execute, and construe the few laws they are allowed to enact, dignity sufficient to make them respectable. While they continue individually to gather the crumbs that fall from the table of the United States, idleness, improvidence, and indebtedness will be the rule, and industry, thrift, and freedom from debt the exception. The utter absence of individual title to particular lands deprives every one among them of the chief incentive to labor and exertion—the very mainspring on which the prosperity of a people depends."

All judicious plans and measures for their safety and salvation must embody provisions for their becoming citizens as fast as they are fit, and must protect them till then in every right and particular in which our laws protect other "persons" who are not citizens. . . .

However great perplexity and difficulty there may be in the details of any and every plan possible for doing at this late day anything like justice to the Indian, however, hard it may be for good statesmen and good men to agree upon the things that ought to be done, there certainly is, or ought to be, no perplexity whatever, on difficulty whatever, in agreeing upon certain things that ought not to be done, and which must cease to be done before the first steps can be taken toward righting the wrongs, curing the ills, and wiping out the disgrace to us of the present conditions of our Indians.

Cheating robbing breaking promises-these three are clearly things which must cease to be done. One more thing, also, and that is the refusal of the protection of the law to the Indian's rights of property, "of life, liberty, and the pursuit of happiness."

When these four things have ceased to be done, time, statesmanship, philanthropy, and Christianity can slowly and surely do the rest. Till these four things have ceased to be done, statesmanship and philanthropy alike must work in vain, and even Christianity can reap but small harvest.

Source: Helen Hunt Jackson, Letters to the Editor, *New York Tribune*, 1879, in Brown, *American Through the Eyes of Its People*, 111–12.

Accounts of the Wounded Knee Massacre, 1890

Black Elk gives a detailed account of what happened at Wounded Knee, site of the last "battle" in a long history of Native-European-American conflict: Pres. Harrison also gives his version of the event.

Black Elk

It was about this time that bad news came to us from the north. We heard that some policemen from Standing Rock had gone to arrest Sitting Bull on Grand River, and that he would not let them take him; so there was a fight, and they killed him.

It was now near the end of the Moon of Popping Trees, and I was twenty-seven years old [December, 1890]. We heard that Big Foot was coming down from the Badlands with nearly four hundred people. Some of these were from Sitting Bull's band. They had run away when Sitting Bull was killed, and joined Big Foot on Good River. There were only about a hundred warriors in this band, and all the others were women and children and some old men. They were all starving and freezing, and Big Foot was so sick that they had to bring him along in a pony drag. They had all run away to hide in the Badlands, and they were coming in now because they were starving and freezing. Soldiers were over there looking for them. The soldiers had everything and were not freezing and starving. Near Porcupine Butte the soldiers came up to the Big Foots, and they surrendered and went along with the soldiers to Wounded Knee Creek.

It was in the evening when we heard that the Big Foots were camped over there with the soldiers, about fifteen miles by the old road from where we were. It was the next morning [December 29, 1890] that something terrible happened.

That evening before it happened, I went in to Pine Ridge and heard these things, and while I was there, soldiers started for where the Big Foots were. These made about five hundred soldiers that were there next morning. When I saw them starting I felt that something terrible was going to happen. That night I could hardly sleep at all. I walked around most of the night.

In the morning I went out after my horses, and while I was out I heard shooting off toward the east, and I knew from the sound that it must be wagon-guns [cannon] going off. The sounds went right through my body, and I felt that something terrible would happen. [He donned his ghost shirt, and armed only with a bow, mounted his pony and rode in the direction of the shooting, and was joined on the way by others.]

In a little while we had come to the top of the ridge where, looking to the east, you can see for the first time the monument and the burying ground on the little hill where the church is. That is where the terrible thing started. Just south of the burying ground on the little hill a deep dry gulch runs about east and west, very crooked, and it rises westward to nearly the top of the ridge where we were. It had no name, but the Wasichus [white men] sometimes called Battle Creek now. We stopped on the ridge not far from the head of the dry gulch. Wagon guns were still going off over there on the little hill, and they were going off again where they hit among the gulch. There was much shooting down yonder, and there were many cries, and we could see calvarymen scattered over the hills ahead of us. Calvarymen were riding along the gulch and shooting into it, where the women and children were running away and trying to hide in the gullies and the stunted pines. . . .

We followed down along the dry gulch, and what we saw was terrible. Dead and wounded women and children and little babies were scattered all along there where they had been trying to run away. The soldiers had followed along the gulch, as they ran, and murdered them in there. Sometimes they were in heaps because they had huddled together, and some were scattered all along, sometimes bunches of them had been killed and torn to pieces where the wagon guns hit them. I saw a little baby trying to suck its mother, but she was bloody and dead. There were two little boys at one place in this gulch. They had guns and they had been killing soldiers all by themselves. We could see the soldiers they had killed. The boys were all alone there, and they were not hurt. These were very brave little boys.

When we drove the soldiers back, they dug themselves in, and we were not enough people to drive them out from there. In the evening they marched off up Wounded Knee Creek, and then we saw all that they had done there.

Men and women and children were heaped and scattered all over the flat at the bottom of the little hill where the soldiers had their wagon-guns, and westward up the dry gulch all the way to the high ridge, the dead women and children and babies were scattered.

When I saw this I wished that I had died too, but I was not sorry for the women and children. It was better for them to be happy in the other world, and I wanted to be there too. But before I went there I wanted to have revenge. I thought there might be a day, and we should have revenge.

In the morning the soldiers began to take all the guns away from the Big Foots, who were camped in the flat below the little hill where the monument and burying ground are now. The people had stacked most of their guns, and even their knives, by the teepee where Big Foot was lying sick. Soldiers were on the little hill and all around, and there were soldiers across the dry gulch to the south and over east along Wounded Knee Creek too. The people were nearly surrounded, and the wagon-guns were pointed at them.

It was a good winter day when all this happened. The sun was shining. But after the soldiers marched away from their dirty work, a heavy snow began to fall. The wind came up in the night. There was a big blizzard, and it grew very cold. The snow drifted deep in the crooked gulch, and it was one long grave of butchered women and children and babies, who had never done any harm and were only trying to run away.

Report on Wounded Knee Massacre and the Decrease in Indian Land Acreage, 1891

President Benjamin Harrison, Third Annual Message, December 9, 1891:

The outbreak among the Sioux which occurred in December last is as to its causes and incidents fully reported upon by the War Department and the Department of the Interior. That these Indians had some just complaints, especially in the matter of the reduction of the appropriation for rations and in the delays attending the enactment of laws to enable the Department to perform the engagements entered into with them, is probably true; but the Sioux tribes are naturally warlike and turbulent, and their warriors were excited by their medicine men and chiefs, who preached the coming of an Indian messiah who was to give them power to destroy their enemies. In view of the alarm that prevailed among the white settlers near the reservation and of the fatal consequences that would have resulted from an Indian incursion, I placed at the disposal of General Miles, commanding the Division of the Missouri, all such forces as we thought by him to be required. He is entitled to the credit of having given thorough protection to the settlers and of bringing the hostiles into subjection with the least possible loss of life. . . .

Since March 4, 1889, about 23,000,000 acres have been separated from Indian reservations and added to the public domain for the use of those who desired to secure free homes under our beneficent laws. It is difficult to estimate the increase of wealth which will result from the conversion of these waste lands into farms, but it is more difficult to estimate the betterment which will result to the families that have found renewed hope and courage in the ownership of a home and the assurance of a comfortable subsistence under free and healthful conditions. It is also gratifying to be able to feel, as we may, that this work has proceeded upon lines of justice toward the Indian, and that he may now, if he will, secure to himself the good influences of a settled habitation, the fruits of industry, and the security of citizenship.

Sources: Reprinted from *Black Elk Speaks*, by John G. Neihardt, by permission of The University of Nebraska Press. Copyright 1932, 1959, 1972, by John G. Neihardt. Copyright © 1961 by The John G. Neihardt Trust

Source: Brown, *America Through The Eyes of Its People*, 113.

Nativism

The Secret Oath of the American Protective Association, 1893

A wave of nativism swept America during the period of mass immigration as the new immigrants—large numbers of Roman Catholics and Jews from Eastern Europe—seemed to pose a threat to the American way of life. The American Protective Association gained a following in its anti-Catholic, anti-immigrant stance, and members signed a secret oath pledging themselves to its principles.

I do most solemnly promise and swear that I will always, to the utmost of my ability, labor, plead, and wage a continuous warfare against ignorance and fanaticism; that I will use my utmost power to strike the shackles and chains of blind obedience to the Roman Catholic Church from the hampered and bound consciences of a priest-ridden and church-oppressed people; that I will never allow anyone, a member of the Roman Catholic Church, to become a member of this order, I knowing him to be such; that I will use my influence to promote the interest of all Protestants everywhere in the world that I may be; that I will not employ a Roman Catholic in any capacity, if I can procure the services of a Protestant.

I furthermore promise and swear that I will not aid in building or maintaining, by my resources, any Roman Catholic church or institution of their sect or creed whatsoever, but will do all in my power to retard and break down the power of the Pope, in this country or any other; that I will not enter into any controversy with a Roman Catholic upon the subject of this order, nor will I enter into any agreement with a Roman Catholic to strike or create a disturbance whereby the Catholic employees may undermine and substitute the Protestant co-workers; that in all grievances I will seek only Protestants, and counsel with them to the exclusion of all Roman Catholics, and will not make known to them anything of any nature matured at such conferences.

I furthermore promise and swear that I will not countenance the nomination, in any caucus or convention, of a Roman Catholic for any office in the gift of the American people, and that I will not vote for, or counsel others to vote for, any Roman Catholic, but will vote only for a Protestant, so far as may lie in my power (should there be two Roman Catholics in opposite tickets, I will erase the name on the ticket I vote); that I will at all times endeavor to place the political positions of this government in the hands of Protestants, to the entire exclusion of the Roman Catholic Church, of the members thereof, and the mandate of the Pope.

To all of which I do most solemnly promise and swear, so help me God.

Amen.

Source: Brown, *America Through the Eyes of Its People*, 122.

The United States–China Treaty of 1894

Laws to end mass immigration to the United States were not passed until the 1920s, but restrictive legislation against Asians came much sooner. In 1882, Congress passed the Chinese Exclusion Act to eliminate this group, but smuggling Chinese persons across the lines from Canada and Mexico continued. The following treaty between the United States and China seeks to cut off the flow of Chinese laborers while simultaneously protecting the rights and property of lawful Chinese subjects:

Whereas, On the 17th day of November, A.D. 1880, and of Kwanghali the sixth year, tenth moon, fifteenth day, a treaty was concluded between the United States and China for the purpose of regulating, limiting, or suspending the coming of Chinese laborers to, and their residence in, the United States; and

Whereas, The two Governments desire to cooperate in prohibiting such emigration and to strengthen in other ways the bonds of friendship between the two countries; and,

Whereas, The two Governments are desirous of adopting reciprocal measures for the better protection of the citizens or subjects of each within the jurisdiction of the other. . . .

Article I   The high-contracting parties agree that for a period of ten years beginning with the date of the exchange of the ratifications of this convention, the coming, except under the conditions hereinafter specified, of Chinese laborers to the United States shall be absolutely prohibited.

Article II   The preceding article shall not apply to the return to the United States of any registered Chinese laborer who has a lawful wife, child, or parent in the United States, or property therein of the value of $1,000, or debts of like amount due him and pending settlement. Nevertheless, every such Chinese laborer shall, before leaving the United States, deposit, as a condition of his return, with the Collector of Customs of the district from which he departs, a full description in writing of his family, or property, or debts, as aforesaid, and shall be furnished by said Collector with such certificate of his right to return under this treaty as the laws of the United States may now or hereafter prescribe and not inconsistent with the provisions of this treaty, and should the written description aforesaid be proved to be false, the right of return thereunder, or of continued residence after return, shall in each case be forfeited. And such right of return to the United States shall be exercised within one year from the date of leaving the United States, but such right of return to the United States may be extended for an additional period, not to exceed one year in cases where, by reason of sickness or other cause of disability beyond his control, such Chinese laborer shall be rendered unable sooner to return, which facts

Chinese immigrants clustered in areas such as Chinatown, San Francisco, 1901, for reasons of language, economics, and especially nativist sentiment. (Courtesy Prints and Photographs Division, Library of Congress)

We have no use for them since we got this WONDERFUL WASHER: What a blessing to tired mothers: It costs so little and don't injure the clothes.

The first immigration exclusion act was directed against the Chinese in 1882. During the decade of the 1880s, the Chinese were resented, especially by native-born laborers who disliked competing with them for jobs. In this poster, "The Chinese Must Go," c. 1880s, the intensity of anti-Chinese feeling is obvious. (Courtesy Prints and Photographs Division, Library of Congress)

shall be fully reported to the Chinese Consul at the port of departure, and by him certified, to the satisfaction of the Collector of the port at which such Chinese subjects shall land in the United States. And no such Chinese laborer shall be permitted to enter the United States by land or sea without producing to the proper officer of the customs the return certificate herein required.

Article III The provisions of this convention shall not affect the right at present enjoyed of Chinese subjects, being officials, teachers, students, merchants, or travelers for curiosity or pleasure, but not laborers, of coming to the United States and residing therein. To entitle such Chinese subjects as are above described to admission into the United States, they may produce a certificate from their Government or the Government where they last resided, vizéd [endorsed] by the diplomatic or Consular representative of the United States in the country or port whence they depart. It is also agreed that Chinese laborers shall continue to enjoy the privilege of transit across the territory of the United States in the course of their

journey to or from other countries, subject to such regulations by the Government of the United States as may be necessary to prevent said privilege of transit from being abused.

Article IV In pursuance of Article III, of the immigration treaty between the United States and China, signed at Pekin [Beijing] of the 17th day of November, 1880, (the 15th day of the tenth moon of Kwanghali, sixth year,) it is hereby understood and agreed that Chinese laborers or Chinese of any other class, either permanently or temporarily residing in the United States, shall have for the protection of their persons and property all rights that are given by the laws of the United States to citizens of the most favored nation, excepting the right to become naturalized citizens. And the Government of the United States reaffirms its obligations, as stated in said Article III, to exert all its power to secure protection to the person and property of all Chinese subjects in the United States.

Article V The Government of the United States, having, by an act of Congress, approved May 5, 1892, as amended by an act approved Nov. 3, 1893, required all Chinese laborers lawfully within the limits of the United States before the passage of the first named act to be registered as in said acts provided, with a view of affording them better protection, the Chinese Government will not object to the enforcement of such acts, and reciprocally the Government of the United States recognizes the right of the Government of China to enact and enforce similar laws or regulations for the registration, free of charge, of all laborers, skilled or unskilled, (not merchants as defined by said acts of Congress,) citizens of the United States in China, whether residing within or without the treaty ports. And the Government of the United States agrees that within twelve months from the date of the exchange of the ratifications of this convention, and annually thereafter, it will furnish to the Government of China registers or reports showing the full name, age, occupation, and number or place of residence of all other citizens of the United States, including missionaries, residing both within and without the treaty ports of China, not including, however, diplomatic and other officers of the United States residing or traveling in China upon official business, together with their body and household servants.

Article VI This convention shall remain in force for a period of ten years, beginning with the date of the exchange of ratifications, and if six months before the expiration of the said period of ten years neither Government shall have formally given notice of its final termination to the other, it shall remain in full force for another like period of ten years.

Source: Paul F. Boller, Jr., and Ronald Story, *A More Perfect Union: Documents in U.S. History. Volume II: Since 1865* (1992), 81–83.

Perspectives
The Gilded Age, 1874

Mark Twain (Samuel Clemens), one of the leading novelists of the times, portrayed America as a harsh and materialistic world. In the novel by Mark Twain and Charles Dudley Warner, The Gilded Age: A Tale of Today *(1874) the "Gilded Age" phrase was used to excoriate society's morals and*

He called, with official importance in his mien, at No. —— Wall Street, where a great gilt sign betokened the presence of the headquarters of the "Columbus River Slackwater Navigation Company." He entered and gave a dressy porter his card, and was requested to wait a moment in a sort of anteroom. The porter returned in a minute, and asked whom he would like to see?

"The president of the company, of course."

"He is busy with some gentlemen, sir; says he will be done with them directly."

That a copper-plate card with "Engineer—Chief" on it should be received with such tranquillity as this, annoyed Mr. Brierly not a little.

"Good morning, sir; take a seat—take a seat."

"Thank you, sir," said Harry, throwing as much chill into his manner as his ruffled dignity prompted.

"We perceive by your reports and the reports of the chief superintendent, that you have been making gratifying progress with the work. We are all very much pleased."

"Indeed? We did not discover it from your letters—which we have not received; nor by the treatment our drafts have met with—which were not honored; nor by the reception of any part of the appropriation, no part of it having come to hand."

"Why, my dear Mr. Brierly, there must be some mistake. I am sure we wrote you and also Mr. Sellers, recently—when my clerk comes he will show copies—letters informing you of the ten per cent assessment."

"Oh, certainly, we got those letters. But what we wanted was money to carry on the work—money to pay the men."

"Certainly, certainly—true enough—but we credited you both for a large part of your assessments—I am sure that was in our letters."

"Of course that was in—I remember that."

"Ah, very well, then. Now we begin to understand each other."

"Well, I don't see that we do. There's two months' wages due the men, and—"

"How? Haven't you paid the men?"

"Paid them! How are we going to pay them when you don't honor our drafts?"

"Why, my dear sir, I cannot see how you can find an fault with us. I am sure we have acted in a perfectly straightforward business way. Now let us look at the thing a moment. You subscribed for one hundred shares of the capital stock, at one thousand dollars a share, I believe?"

"Yes, sir, I did."

"And Mr. Sellers took a like amount?"

"Yes, sir."

"Very well. No concern can get along without money. We levied a ten per cent assessment. It was the original understanding that you and Mr. Sellers were to have the positions you now hold, with salaries of six hundred dollars a month each, while in active service. You were duly elected to these places, and you accepted them."

"Certainly."

"Very well. You were given your instructions and put to work. By your reports it appears that you have expended the sum of $9,640 upon the said work. Two months' salary to you two officers amounts altogether to $2,400—about one-eighth of your ten per cent assessment, you see; which leaves you in debt to the company for the other seven-eighths of the assessment—viz., something over $8,000 apiece. Now, instead of requiring you to forward this aggregate of $16,000 or $17,000 to New York, the company voted unanimously to let you pay it over to the contractors, laborers from time to time, and give you credit on the books for it. And they did it without a murmur, too, for they were pleased with the progress you had made, and were glad to pay you that little compliment—and a very neat one it was, too, I am sure. The work you did fell short of $10,000, a trifle. Let me see—$9,640 from $20,000—salary $2,400 added—ah, yes, the balance due the company from yourself and Mr. Sellers is $7,960, which I will take the responsibility of allowing to stand for the present, unless you prefer to draw a check now, and thus—"

"Confound it, do you mean to say that instead of the company owing us $2,400, we owe the company $7,960?"

Source: Warner and Twain, *The Gilded Age,* in Brown, *America Through the Eyes of Its People,* 108.

Andrew Carnegie, "The Gospel of Wealth," 1889

One of the leading industrialists of the age provides a rationale for the accumulation and distribution of wealth amassed by the captains of industry.

The problem of our age is the proper administration of wealth, that the ties of brotherhood may still bind together the rich and poor in harmonious relationship. The conditions of human life have not only been changed, but revolutionized, within the past few hundred years. In former days there was little difference between the dwelling, dress, food, and environment of the chief and those of his retainers. . . . The contrast between the palace of the millionaire and the cottage of the laborer with us to-day measures the change which has come with civilization. This change, however, is not to be deplored, but welcomed as highly beneficial. It is well, say, essential, for the progress of the race that the houses of some should be homes for all that is highest and best in literature and the arts, and for all the refinements of civilization, rather than that none should be so. Much better this great irregularity than universal squalor. Without wealth there can be no Meccenas.

To-day the world obtains commodities of excellent quality at prices which even the preceding generation would have deemed incredible. In the commercial world similar causes have produced similar results, and the race is benefited thereby. The poor enjoy what the rich could not before afford. What were the luxuries have become the necessaries of life. . . .

Objections to the foundations upon which society is based are not in order, because the condition of the race is better with these than it has been with any other which has been tried. . . . No evil, but good, has come to the race from the accumulation of wealth by those who have had the ability and energy to produce it. . . .

We start, then, with a condition of affairs under which the best interests of the race are promoted, but which inevitably gives wealth to the few. . . . What is the proper mode of administering wealth after the laws upon which civilization is founded have thrown it into the hands of the few? . . .

There are but three modes in which surplus wealth can be disposed of. It can be left to the families of the decedents; or it can be bequeathed for public purposes; or, finally, it can be administered by its possessors during their lives. . . .

There remains, then, only one mode of suing great fortunes; but in this we have the true antidote for the temporary unequal distribution of wealth, the reconciliation of the rich and the poor—a reign of harmony, another ideal, differing, indeed, from that of the Communist in requiring only the further evolution of existing conditions, not the total overthrow of our civilization. It is founded upon the most intense Individualism. . . . Under its sway we shall have an ideal State, in which the surplus wealth of the few will become, in the best sense, property of the many, because administering for the common good; and this wealth, passes through the hands of the few, can be made much more potent force for the elevation of our race than if distributed in small sums to the people themselves. Even the poorest can be made to see this, and to agree that great sums gathered by some of their fellow-citizens—spent for public purposes, from which masses reap the principal benefit, are more valuable to them than if scattered among themselves in trifling amounts through the course of many years.

If we consider the results which flow from the Cooper Institute, for instance . . . , and compare these with those who would have ensured for the good of the man form an equal sum distributed by Mr. Cooper in his lifetime in the form of wages, which the highest form of distributing, being work done and not for charity, we can estimate of the possibilities for the improvement of the race which lie embedded in the present law of the accumulation of wealth. . . .

This, then, is held to be the duty of the man of wealth: To set an example of modest, unostentatious living, shunning display or extravagance; to provide moderately for the legitimate wants of those dependent upon him; and, after doing so, to consider all surplus revenues which come to him simply as trust funds, which he is called upon to administer, and strictly bound as a matter of duty to administer in the manner which, in his judgment, is best calculated to produce the most beneficial results for the community—the man of wealth thus becoming the mere trustee and agent for his poorer brethren, bringing to their service his superior wisdom, experience, and ability to administer, doing for them better than they would or could do for them selves. . . .

In bestowing charity, the main consideration should be to help those who will help themselves; to provide part of the means by which those who desire to improve may do so; to give those who desire to rise the aids by which they may rise; to assist, but rarely or never to do all. Neither the individual nor the race is improved by alms giving. Those worthy of assistance, except in rare cases, seldom require assistance. . . .

The rich man is thus almost restricted to following the examples of Peter Cooper, Enoch Pratt of Baltimore, Mr. Pratt of Brooklyn, Senator Stanford, and others, who know that the best means of benefiting the community is to place within its reach the ladders upon which the aspiring can rise—free libraries, parks, and means of recreation, by which men are helped in body and mind; works of art, certain to give pleasure and improve the general condition of the people; in this manner returning their surplus wealth to the mass of their fellows in the forms best calculated to do them lasting good.

Thus is the problem of rich and poor to be solved. The laws of accumulation will be left free, the laws of distribution free. Individualism will continue, but the millionaire will be but a trustee for the poor, intrusted for a season with a great part of the increased wealth of the community, but administering it for the community far better than if could or would have done for itself. The best minds will thus have reached a stage in the development of the race in which it is clearly seen that there is no mode of disposing of surplus wealth creditable to thoughtful and earnest men into whose hands it flows, save by using it year by year for the general good. . . .

Such, in my opinion, is the true gospel concerning wealth, obedience to which is destined some day to solve the problem of the rich and the poor, and to bring "Peace on earth, among men good will."

Source: Andrew Carnegie, "Wealth," *North American Review*, 1889, in Brown, *America Through the Eyes of Its People*, 109.

The Essentials of Scientific Management (1911)

Frederick W. Taylor was an industrial engineer with an intense interest in reducing the time it took workers to accomplish their tasks. He studied time and motion, did analyses of work flows, and made elaborate notes on worker tasks and output. As the chief engineer in a Pennsylvania steel mill, where he first began his work, he concluded from his studies that bosses usually expected too much of workers, and he devised better machinery and a system for the time allotted for every task in the making of steel. When productivity at the mill rose sharply, Taylor's ideas spread throughout industrial America. He resigned his management position to popularize his ideas in books and articles on industrial engineering and administration. He sometimes compared workers insensitively to horses and was known to be an insomniac who required complete silence in order to sleep. The following excerpt of his ideas was taken from remarks he made in 1911 to a special congressional committee on shop management.

Scientific management is not any efficiency device, not a device of any kind for securing efficiency; nor is it any bunch or group of efficiency devices. It is not a new system of figuring costs; it is not a new scheme of paying men; it is not a piecework system; it is not a bonus system; it is not a premium system; it is no scheme for paying men; it is not holding a stop watch on a man and writing things down about him; it is not time study; it is not motion study nor an analysis of the movement of men; it is not the printing and ruling and unloading of a ton or two of blanks on a set of men and saying, "Here's your system; go use it." It is not divided foremanship or functional foremanship; it is not any of the devices which the average man calls to mind when scientific management is spoken of. The average man thinks of one or more of these things when he hears the words "scientific management" mentioned, but scientific management is not any of these devices. I am not sneering at cost-keeping systems, at time study, at functional foremanship, nor at any new and improved scheme of paying men, nor at any efficiency devices, if they are really devices that make for efficiency. I believe in them, but what I am emphasizing is that these devices in whole or in part are not scientific management; they are useful adjuncts to scientific management, so are they also useful adjuncts of other systems of management.

Now, in its essence, scientific management involves a complete mental revolution on the part of the working man engaged in any particular establishment or industry—a complete mental revolution on the part of these men as to their duties toward their work, toward their fellow man, and toward their employers. And it involves the equally complete mental revolution on the part of those on the management's side—the foreman, the superintendent, the owner of the business, the board of directors—a complete mental revolution on their part as to their duties toward their fellow workers in the management, toward their workmen, and toward all of their daily problems. And without this complete mental revolution on both sides scientific management does not exist.

That is the essence of scientific management, this great mental revolution. . . .

I think it is safe to say that in the past a great part of the thought and interest both of the men, on the sides of the management, and of those on the side of the workmen in manufacturing establishments has been centered upon what may be called the proper division of the surplus resulting from their joint efforts, between the management on the one hand, and the workmen on the other hand. The management have been looking for as large a profit as possible for themselves, and the workmen have been looking for as large wages as possible for themselves, and that is what I mean by the division of the surplus. Now, this question of the division of the surplus is a very plain and simple one (for I am announcing no great fact in political economy or anything of that sort). Each article produced in the establishment has its definite selling price. Into the manufacture of this article have gone certain expenses, namely the cost of materials, the expenses connected with selling it, and certain indirect expenses, such as the rent of the building, taxes, insurance, light and power, maintenance of machinery, interest on the plant, etc. Now, if we deduct these several expenses from the selling price, what is left over may be called the surplus. And out of this surplus comes the profit to the manufacturer on the one hand, and the wages of the workmen on the other hand. And it is largely upon the division of this surplus that the attention of the workmen and of the management has been centered in the past. . . .

The great revolution that takes place in the mental attitude of the two parties under scientific management is that both sides take their eyes off the division of the surplus as the all-important matter, and together turn their attention toward increasing the size of the surplus until this surplus becomes so large that it is unnecessary to quarrel over how it shall be divided. They come to see that when they stop pulling against one another, and instead both turn and push shoulder to shoulder in the same direction, the size of the surplus created by their joint efforts is truly astounding. They both realize that when they substitute friendly cooperation and mutual helpfulness for antagonism and strife they are together able to make this surplus so enormously greater than it was in the past that there is ample room for a large increase in wages for the workmen and an equally great increase in profits for the manufacturer. This, gentlemen, is the beginning of the great mental revolution which constitutes the first step toward scientific management. . . .

There is, however, one more change in viewpoint which is absolutely essential to the existence of scientific management. Both sides must recognize as essential the substitution of exact scientific investigation and knowledge for the old individual judgment or opinion, either of the workman or the boss, in all matters relating to the work done in the establishment. And this applies both as to the methods to be employed in doing the work and the time in which each job should be done.

Scientific management cannot be said to exist, then, in any establishment until after this change has taken place in the mental attitude of both the management and the men, both as to their duty to cooperate in producing the largest possible surplus and as to the necessity for substituting exact scientific knowledge for opinions or the old rule of thumb or individual knowledge.

These are the two absolutely essential elements of scientific management.

Source: Boller, Jr., and Story, *A More Perfect Union: Documents in U.S. History,* 61–63.

Popular Culture
Bathing at Coney Island, 1883

Urban Americans found new forms of public leisure and entertainment during this period, including bathing at popular bathhouses and beaches such as those at Coney Island. In the following selection from Richard K. Fox, Bathing at Coney Island, Coney Island Frolics: How New York's Gay Girls and Jolly Boys Enjoy Themselves by the Sea, *the expectations of Victorian America confront changing lifestyles.*

There are various ways of bathing at Coney Island. You can go in at the West End, where they give you a tumbledown closet like a sentry box stuck up in the sand, or at the great hotels where more or less approach to genuine comfort is afforded. The pier, too, is fitted up with extensive bathing houses, and altogether no one who wants a dip in the briny and has a quarter to pay for it need to go without it.

If a man is troubled with illusions concerning the female form divine and wishes to be rid of those illusions he should go to Coney Island and closely watch the thousands of women who bathe there every Sunday.

A woman, or at least most women, in bathing undergoes a transformation that is really wonderful. They waltz into the bathingrooms clad in all the paraphernalia that most gladdens the feminine heart. The hair is gracefully dressed, and appears most abundant; the face is decorated with all that elaborate detail which defies description by one uninitiated in the mysteries of the boudoir; the form is moulded by the milliner to distracting elegance of proportion, and the feet appear aristocratically slender and are arched in French boots.

Thus they appear as they sail past the gaping crowds of men, who make Coney Island a loafing place on Sundays. They seek out their individual dressing-rooms and disappear. Somewhere inside of an hour, they make their appearance ready for the briny surf. If it were not for the men who accompany them it would be impossible to recognize them as the same persons who but a little while ago entered those diminutive rooms. . . .

The broad amphitheatre at Manhattan Beach built at the water's edge is often filled with spectators. Many pay admission fees to witness the feats of swimmers, the clumsiness of beginners and the ludicrous mishaps of the never-absent stout persons. Under the bathinghouse is a sixty horse-power engine. It rinses and washes the suits for the bathers, and its steady puffing is an odd accompaniment to the merry shouts of the bathers and the noise of the shifting crowd ashore. . . .

Going to the beach was popular at Long Beach, California, c. 1900. (Photo by Henry G. Peabody, courtesy National Archives)

A person who intends to bathe at Manhattan or Brighton Beach first buys a ticket and deposits it in a box such as is placed in every elevated railroad station. If he carries valuables he may have them deposited without extra charge in a safe that weighs seven tons and has one thousand compartments.

He encloses them in an envelope and seals it. Then he writes his name partly on the flap of the envelope and partly on the envelope itself. For this envelope he receives a metal check attached to an elastic string, in order that he may wear it about his neck while bathing. This check has been taken from

Large swimming pools, like the Sutro Baths in San Francisco, California, c. 1900, followed Victorian conventions and divided users by sex. (Photo by Henry G. Peabody, courtesy, National Archives)

In Cleveland, Ohio, the Gordon Park Bathing Pavilion (1900–10) was a favorite spot on Sundays in the summertime. (Courtesy Prints and Photographs Division, Library of Congress)

one of the compartments of the safe which bears the same number as the check. Into the same compartment the sealed envelope is put. When the bather returns from the surf he must return the check and must write his name on a piece of paper. This signature is compared with the one on the envelope. Should the bather report that his check has been lost or stolen his signature is deemed a sufficient warrant for the return of the valuables. The safe has double doors in front and behind. Each drawer may be drawn out from either side. When the throng presses six men may be employed at this safe.

Source: Fox, Bathing at Coney Island (1883) in Brown, America Through the Eyes of Its People, 128.

Medicine Men Shows, 1890s

In the backwoods settlements and small-town America, carnivals, circuses, revivals, traveling shows, and even peddlers provided diversion and entertainment. William Naylor describes his experience as part of Doc Porter's Kickapoo Indian Medicine Show.

I was born in New York City on the West Side, but when I was just a baby my people moved up to the Bronx. Our chief diversion on Sundays was to go to Coney Island and ride our bicycles out there. I suppose I always had a flair for the kind of entertainment Coney Island offered. There was a kind of fascination to me in the excitement and glamour of the carnival spirit.

Eventually, when I was about nineteen years old, I joined DOC PORTER'S KICKAPOO INDIAN MEDICINE SHOW. . . .

I stayed with Doc Porter for six years, singing "Poor Mourner, You Shall Be Free," "Kansas," and some of the popular songs like "Two Little Girls in Blue," "Down Went M'Ginty," and "After the Ball." All my work was black-face, and I imagined I was just as good as most vaudeville performers on stages in theaters. We traveled in covered hacks and spring wagons and all our shows were given out of doors. Our lights were gasoline flares on each side of the stage, which was a platform at the back end of the wagon. We traveled all over the small circuits of upper New York, part of Pennsylvania, New Jersey, and as far south as Virginia. In the days of the medicine show there were not so many laws regulating the practice of medicine or the sale of drugs and not so many licenses and restrictions as now. This was especially true in the backwoods towns we'd usually shown in—often towns without railroads and where other shows didn't come.

So Doc Porter didn't have to do anything but drive into a town, pick out a vacant spot somewhere, and set up our pitch there. Everybody would know as soon as we got into a town, but Doc usually hunted up the newspaper office if there was a paper and gave the editor an ad telling where our show was located. That got him on the good side of the editor, and the editor in those backwoods places was an important person. He would call on the marshall, and if there was a mayor he would visit him too. . . .

Once we hit a place back in the hill country of Virginia called Rocky Comfort. It wasn't really a town. There was a water-power grist mill, a store, a blacksmith shop, and about a quarter of a mile up the little valley there was a meeting house, where traveling preachers would sometimes hold revivals, which were called camp meetings.

Doc Porter stopped there to have the horses shod, and it happened there was a camp meeting going on. It looked like a pretty busy place. The natives from miles around had come, brought their families, their hound dogs, and their rifles and were camped out in the grove around the meeting house. Doc got the idea that our Medicine Show would add to the general entertainment and we could give shows between religious services. It worked. Doc was diplomatic and didn't try to compete with the preaching but sort of helped it out and never gave a show while preaching was going on. Instead we'd all attend the services. That put us in solid with the brethren and we sold a lot of medicine.

Doc Porter's medicines were all made up by himself, and he was jealous of the "ancient Kickapoo formulas" he used. They were all made "from roots and barks and the tender succulent foliage of healing, life-giving herbs the Great Manitou of Nature planted in the forests, on the hills, and in the valleys to give his children, the noble tribe of Kickapoos, those priceless secrets of Life and health and Happiness; they were handed down from father to son and from generation to generation—cherished and guarded with the very lives of their possessors? Then when my great-great grandfather saved the life of the Chief Medicine Man of the Kickapoo Tribe, the 'Bounding Cougar,' that great Chief showed his gratitude by giving my noble pioneer ancestor their marvelous formulas and he bade him go forth and give his White Brethren the blessing the Great Manitou had bestowed upon his Red Children."

Doc Porter sure had a great string of palaver, and though I heard it a thousand times I never got tired of listening to his lecture.

One of the tricks Doc Porter used to stimulate sales of his Kickapoo Indian remedies was the psychology of suggestion. Doc had it down fine. He would always wind up his lecture with a detailed description of the symptoms of all the diseases the Kickapoo Indian medicines were supposed to cure. The way he described those diseases—how anybody would feel when they were getting them, or had them or were about to have them—was enough to make anybody shiver. By the time Doc got through describing symptoms, practically everybody in the neighborhood would be imagining they felt at least some of them. Why, I used to sit and listen to Doc's horror stories of diseases till I'd get to feeling the symptoms myself! Doc was a foxy old bird and I guess he wasn't far off base when he'd say, "Most diseases people get are just imagination, anyhow!" . . .

Doc Porter was versatile alright, and nothing ever seemed to stump him. He used to say: "It ain't what anybody knows for certain, but what they think they know for certain that counts, and if people buy Kickapoo Indian Medicine and think it'll cure them, it's darn near sure to cure them. And so they haven't been cheated!"

Which shows that Doc was sincere in believing that the stuff he mixed up out of wild cherry bark, senna leaves, slippery elm bark, sassafras roots, and other "Indian Herbs"—all of which he fortified with about sixty percent of good raw whisky—were genuinely beneficial medicines and that he was a human benefactor. One thing I'm sure of is the tour old Medicine Show gave a lot of people who otherwise didn't have very much entertainment a chance to see and hear something different and be amused.

That's the way a carnival man is. He don't give them anything, yet he gives them something—entertainment, experience, or amusement for the chicken feed he takes away from them at his rack or wheel or ringboard. And if he has a run of "mud-luck," he always finds a way to get out somehow, raise a stake, or climb back into the game. You don't see any genuine old-time carnival birds working the street for a dime, or picking up crumbs from a kitchen back door. They're independent; and even if they're down to the last two bits, you'd never know it by looking at them, or hear it from their own lips. They might do a lot of cussing in private, but never a hardluck story to outsiders. They've always got some kind of idea tucked back in their head that they can pull out and turn into ham-and-egg money somehow. Even if the show goes flat, they'll raise tickets to the next burg someway. And they'll raise it on the square, according to the ethics of the profession: "Give the suckers nothing for their money—but when you give them nothing, you give them something!"

Source: By permission Ann Banks, ed., "Doc Porter's Kickapoo Indian Medicine Show," *First Person America* (1980), 194–98.

Rural Life
A Sharecropping Contract, 1882

Sharecropping arose in the post–Civil War South to become the major form of agricultural labor for most blacks and many whites. The sharecropping and furnishing system prevailed in crops like tobacco and cotton. This 1882 contract lays out the terms and conditions of labor for African-American tenant farmers on small plots in Pitt County, North Carolina. Although not a return to slavery, the contract gives the owner extraordinary control over his tenants, their conditions of work, and the final division of the crop. Note the prohibition against croppers having any of the cotton seed, which would have allowed them to plant their own crop and loosen the grip of the planter.

TO EVERY ONE applying to rent land upon shares, the following conditions must be read and *agreed to.*

To every 30 or 35 acres, I agree to furnish the team, plow, and farming implements, except cotton planters, and I *do not* agree to furnish a cart to every cropper. The croppers are to have half of the cotton, corn and fodder (and peas and pumpkins and potatoes if any are planted) if the following conditions are complied with, but—if not—they are to have only two-fifths. Croppers are to have no part or interest in the cotton seed raised from the crop be planted and worked by them. No vine crops of any description, that is no watermelons . . . squashes or anything of that kind . . . are to be planted in the cotton or corn. All must work under my direction. All plantation work to be done by the croppers. . . .

All croppers must clean out stables and fill them with straw, and haul straw in front of stables whenever I direct. All the cotton must be manured, and enough fertilizer must be brought to manure each crop highly, the croppers to pay for one half of all manure bought, the quantity to be purchased for each crop must be left to me.

No cropper to work off the plantation when there is any work to be done on the land he has rented, or when his work is needed by me or other croppers. . . .

Every cropper must be responsible for all gear and farming implements placed in his hands, and if not returned must be paid for unless it is worn out by use.

Croppers must sow and plow in oats and haul them to the crib, but *must have no part of them.* Nothing to be sold from their crops, nor fodder, nor corn to be carried out of the fields until my rent is all paid, and all amounts they owe me and for which I am responsible are paid in full. . . .

The sale of every cropper's part of the cotton to be made by me when and where I choose to sell, and after deducting all they may owe me and all sums that I may be responsible for on their accounts, to pay them their half of the net proceeds. Work of every description, particularly the work on fences and ditches, to be done to my satisfaction, and must be done over until I am satisfied that it is done as it should be. . . .

Source: Brier, et al., *Who Built America?* 45.

The Omaha Platform, 1892

By 1890, discontented farmers had mounted a third-party movement known as the Populist Party to challenge the regular Democratic and Republican parties. The Omaha Platform was written for the 1892 election and presents their grievances and demands.

Preamble

The conditions which surround us best justify our cooperation; we meet in the midst of a nation brought to the verge of moral, political, and material ruin. Corruption dominates the ballot-box, the Legislatures, the Congress, and touches even the ermine of the bench. The people are demoralized; most of the States have been compelled to isolate the voters at the polling places to prevent universal intimidation and bribery. The newspapers are largely subsidized or muzzled, public opinion silenced, business prostrated, homes covered with mortgages, labor impoverished, and the land concentrating in the hands of capitalists. The urban workmen are denied the right to organize for self-protection, imported pauperized labor beats down their wages, a hireling standing army, unrecognized by our laws, is established to shoot them down, and they are rapidly degenerating into European conditions. The fruits of the toil of millions are boldly stolen to build up colossal fortunes for a few, unprecedented in the history of mankind and the possessors of these, in turn, despise the Republic and endanger liberty. From the same prolific womb of governmental injustice we breed the two great classes—tramps and millionaires. . . .

Assembled on the anniversary of the birthday of the nation, and filled with the spirit of the grand general and chief who established our independence, we seek to restore the government of the Republic to the hands of the "plain people," with which class it originated. We assert our purposes to be identical with the purposes of the National Constitution; to form a more perfect union and establish justice, insure domestic tranquillity, provide for the common defence, promote the general welfare, and secure the blessings of liberty for ourselves and our posterity. . . .

Platform

We declare, therefore—

First.—That the union of the labor forces of the United States this day consummated shall be permanent and perpetual; may its spirit enter into all hearts for the salvation of the Republic and the uplifting of mankind.

Second.—Wealth belongs to him who creates it, and every dollar taken from industry without an equivalent is robbery. "If any will not work, neither shall he eat." The interests of rural and civil labor are the same; their enemies are identical.

Third.—We believe that the time has come when the railroad corporations will either own the people or the people must own the railroads. . . .

FINANCE.—We demand a national currency, safe, sound, and flexible issued by the general government only, a full legal tender for all debts, public and private. . . .

1. We demand free and unlimited coinage of silver and gold at the present legal ration of 16 to 1.
2. We demand that the amount of circulating medium be speedily increased to not less than $50 per capita.
3. We demand a graduated income tax.
4. We believe that the money of the country should be kept as much as possible in the hands of the people, and hence we demand that all State and national revenues shall be limited to the necessary expenses of the government, economically and honestly administered.
5. We demand that postal savings banks be established by the government for the safe deposit of the earnings of the people and to facilitate exchange.

TRANSPORTATION.—Transportation being a means of exchange and a public necessity, the government should own and operate the railroads in the interest of the people. The telegraph and telephone, like the post-office system, being a necessity for the transmission of news, should be owned and operated by the government in the interest of the people.

LAND.—The land, including all the natural sources of wealth, is the heritage of the people, and should not be monopolized for speculative purposes, and alien ownership of land should be prohibited. All land now held by railroads and other corporations in excess of their actual needs, and all lands now owned by aliens should be reclaimed by the government and held for actual settlers only.

Expression of Sentiments

1. **RESOLVED,** That we demand a free ballot, and a fair count of all elections, and pledge ourselves to secure it to every legal voter without Federal intervention, through the adoption by the States of the unperverted Australian or secret ballot system.

2. **RESOLVED,** That the revenue derived from a graduated income tax should be applied to the reduction of the burden of taxation now levied upon the domestic industries of this country.

3. **RESOLVED,** That we pledge our support to fair and liberal pensions to ex-Union soldiers and sailors.

4. **RESOLVED,** That we condemn the fallacy of protecting American labor under the present system, which opens our ports to the pauper and criminal classes of the world and crowds out our wage-earners; and we denounce the present ineffective laws against contract labor, and demand the further restriction of undesirable emigration.

5. **RESOLVED,** That we cordially sympathize with the ef-

forts of organized workingmen to shorten the hours of labor, and demand a rigid enforcement of the existing eight-hour law on Government work, and ask that a penalty clause be added to the said law.

6. **RESOLVED,** That we regard the maintenance of a large standing army of mercenaries, known as the Pinkerton system, as a menace to our liberties, and we demand its abolition. . . .

7. **RESOLVED,** That we commend to the favorable consideration of the people and the reform press the legislative system known as the initiative and referendum.

8. **RESOLVED,** That we favor a constitutional provision limiting the office of President and Vice-president to one term, and providing for the election of Senators of the United States by a direct vote of the people.

9. **RESOLVED,** That we oppose any subsidy or national aid to any private corporation for any purpose.

Source: Brown, *America Through the Eyes of Its People*, 144.

O. E. Rölvaag, *Giants in the Earth,* 1927

Rölvaag provides a picture of the harsh life on the prairie for farm families in the Midwest; farm discontent soon developed into political activism.

In a certain sense, she had to admit to herself, it was lovely up here. The broad expanse stretching away endlessly in every direction, seemed almost like the ocean—especially now, when darkness was falling. It reminded her strongly of the sea, and yet it was very different. . . . This formless prairie had no heart that beat, no waves that sang, no soul that could be touched . . . or cared. . . .

The infinitude surrounding her on every hand had might not have been so oppressive, might even have brought her a measure of peace, if it had not been for the deep silence, which lay heavier here than in a church. Indeed, what was there to break it? She had passed beyond the outposts of civilization; the nearest dwelling places of men were far away. Here no warbling of birds rose on the air, no buzzing of insects sounded; even the wind had died away; the waving blades of grass that trembled to the faintest breath now stood erect and quiet, as if listening, in the great hush of the evening. . . . All along the way, coming out, she had noticed this strange thing; the stillness had grown deeper, the silence more depressing, the farther west they journeyed; it must have been over two weeks now since she had heard a bird sing! Had they travelled into some nameless, abandoned region? Could no living thing exist out here, in the empty, desolate, endless wastes of green and blue? . . . How could existence go on, she thought, desperately? If life is to thrive and endure, it must at least have something to hide behind! . . .

The Children were playing boisterously a little way off. What a terrible noise they made! But she had better let them keep on with their play, as long as they were happy. . . . She sat perfectly quiet, thinking of the long, oh, so interminably long march that they would have to make, back to the place where human beings dwelt. It would be small hardship for her, of course, sitting in the wagon; but she pitied Per Hansa and the boys—and then the poor oxen! . . . He certainly would soon find out for himself that a home for men and women and children could never be established in this wilderness. . . . And how could she bring new life into the world out here! . . .

Slowly her thoughts began to centre on her husband; they grew warm and tender as they dwelt on him. She trembled as they came. . . .

But only for a brief while. As her eyes darted nervously here and there, flitting from object to object and trying to pierce the purple dimness that was steadily closing in, a sense of desolation so profound settled upon her that she seemed unable to think at all. It would not do to gaze any longer at the terror out there, where everything was turning to grim and awful darkness. . . . She threw herself back in the grass and looked up into the heavens. But darkness and infinitude lay there, also—the sense of utter desolation still remained. . . . Suddenly, for the first time, she realized the full extent of her loneliness, the dreadful nature of the fate that had overtaken her. Lying there on her back, and staring up into the quiet sky across which the shadows of night were imperceptibly creeping, she went over in her mind every step of their wanderings, every mile of the distance they had travelled since they had left home. . . .

Winter was ever tightening its grip. The drifting snow flew wildly under a low sky, and stirred up the whole universe into a whirling mass; it swept the plain like the giant broom of a witch, churning up a flurry so thick that people could scarcely open their eyes.

As soon as the weather cleared icy gusts drove through every chink and cranny, leaving white frost behind; people's breaths hung frozen in the air the moment it was out of the mouth; if one touched iron, a piece of skin would be torn away.

At intervals a day of bright sunshine came. Then the whole vast plain flittered with the flashing brilliance of diamonds; the glare was so strong that it burnt the sight; the eyes saw blackness where there was nothing but shining white. . . .

But no sooner had they reached America than the west-fever had smitten the old settlements like a plague. Such a thing had never happened before in the history of mankind; people were intoxicated by bewildering visions; they spoke dazedly, as though under the force of a spell. . . . "Go west! . . . Go west, folks! . . . The farther west, the better the land!" . . . Men beheld in feverish dreams the endless plains, teeming with fruitfulness, glowing, out there where day sank into night—a Beulah Land of corn and wine! . . . She had never dreamed that the good Lord would let such folly loose among men. Were it only the young people who had been caught by the plague, she would not have wondered; but the old had been taken even worse. . . . "Now we're bound west?" said the young. . . . "Wait a minute—we're going along with you!" cried the old, and followed after. . . . Human beings gathered together, in small companies and large—took whatever was movable along, and left the old homestead without as much as a sigh! Ever westward led the course, to where the sun glowed in matchless glory as it sank at night; people drifted about in a sort of delirium, like sea birds in mating time; then they flew toward the sunset, in small flocks, and large—always toward Sunset Land. . . . Now she saw it clearly: here on the trackless plains, the thousand-year-old hunger of the poor after human happiness had been unloosed!

Source: Page 142 from *Giants in The Earth* by O. E. Rölvaag. Copyright 1927 by Harper & Row, Publishers, Inc. Renewed 1955 by Jennie Marie Berdahl Rölvaag. Reprinted by permission of HarperCollins Publishers, Inc.

Urban Life
The Life of the Urban Poor, 1872

In 1872, Charles Loring Brace, founder of the Children's Aid Society, wrote The Dangerous Classes of New York and Twenty Years Among Them. *His hope was to create public awareness of the problems in New York City's slums.*

The intensity of the American temperament is felt in every fibre of these children of poverty and vice. Their crimes have the unrestrained and sanguinary character of a race accustomed to overcome all obstacles. They rifle a bank, where English thieves pick a pocket; they murder, where European proletaires cudgel or fight with fists; in a riot, they begin what seems about to be the sacking of a city, where English rioters would merely batter policemen, or smash lamps. The "dangerous classes" of New York are mainly American-born, but the children of Irish and German immigrants. . . .

There are thousands on thousands in New York who have no assignable home, and "flirt" from attic to attic, and cellar to cellar; there are other thousands more or less connected with criminal enterprises; and still other tens of thousands, poor, hard-pressed, and depending for daily bread on the day's earnings, swarming in tenement-houses, who behold the gilded rewards of toil all about them, but are never permitted to touch them.

All these great masses of destitute, miserable, and criminal persons believe that for ages the rich have had all the good things of life, while to them have been left the evil things. Capital to them is the tyrant.

Let but Law lift its hand from them for a season, or let the civilizing influences of American life fail to reach them, and, if the opportunity offered, we should see an explosion from this class which might leave this city in ashes and blood.

Seventeen year ago, my attention had been called to the extraordinarily degraded condition of the children in a district lying on the west side of the city, between Seventeenth and Nineteenth Streets, and the Seventh and Tenth Avenues. A certain block, called "Misery Row," in Tenth Avenue, was the main seed-bed of crime and poverty in the quarter, and was also invariably a "fever-nest." Here the poor obtained wretched rooms at a comparatively low rent; these they sublet, and thus, in little, crowded, close tenements, were herded men, women and children of all ages. The parents were invariably given to hard drinking, and the children were sent out to beg or to steal. Besides them, other children, who were orphans, or who had run away from drunkards' homes, or had been working on the canal-boats that discharged on the docks near by, drifted into the quarter, as if attracted by the atmosphere of crime and laziness that prevailed in the neighborhood. These slept around the breweries of the ward, or on the hay-barges, or in the old sheds of Eighteenth and Nineteenth Streets. They were mere children, and kept life together by all sorts of street-jobs—helping the brewery laborers, blackening boots, sweeping sidewalks, "smashing baggages" (as they called it), and the like. Herding together, they soon began to form an unconscious society for vagrancy and idleness. Finding that work brought but poor pay, they tried shorter roads to getting money by petty [sic] thefts, in which they were very adroit. Even if they earned a considerable sum by a lucky day's job, they quickly spent it in gambling, or for some folly.

The police soon knew them as "street-rats;" but, like the rats, they were too quick and cunning to be often caught in their petty plunderings, so they gnawed away at the foundations of society undisturbed.

Source: Brown, *America Through the Eyes of Its People,* 125.

How the Other Half Lives (1890)

Jacob Riis, born in Ribe, Denmark, in 1849, emigrated to the United States in 1870. By 1890, he had become a well-known newspaperman in New York City. How the Other Half Lives *made him a household name and included his startling photographs exposing life in slum conditions. Theodore Roosevelt, a budding reformer himself and member of the New York City police board, often accompanied Riis on his journeys into the slums and supported his efforts to reform them. The following is an excerpt from the book.*

When once I asked the agent of a notorious Fourth Ward alley how many people might be living in it I was told: One hundred and forty families, one hundred Irish, thirty-eight Italian, and two that spoke the German tongue. Barring the agent herself there was not a native-born individual in the court. The answer was characteristic of the cosmopolitan character of lower New York, very nearly so of the whole of it, wherever it runs to alleys and courts. One may find for the asking an Italian, a German, a French, African, Spanish, Bohemian, Russian, Scandinavian, Jewish, and Chinese colony. Even the Arab, who peddles "holy earth" from the Battery as a direct importation from Jerusalem, has his exclusive preserves at the lower end of Washington Street. The one thing you shall vainly ask for in the chief city of America is a distinctively American community. . . .

They are not here. In their place has come this queer conglomerate mass of heterogeneous elements, ever striving and working like whiskey and water in one glass, and with the like result: final union and a prevailing taint of whiskey. The once unwelcome Irishman has been followed in his turn by the Italian, the Russian Jew, and the Chinaman, and has himself taken a hand at opposition, quite as bitter and quite as ineffectual, against these later hordes. Wherever these have gone they have crowded him out, possessing the block, the street, the ward with their denser swarms. But the Irishman's revenge is complete. Victorious in defeat over his recent as over his more ancient foe, the one who opposed his coming no less than the one who drove him out, he dictates to both their politics, and, secure in possession of the offices, returns the native his greeting with interest, while collecting the rents of the Italian whose house he has bought with the profits of his saloon. . . .

In justice to the Irish landlord it must be said that like an apt pupil he was merely showing forth the result of the schooling he had received, reenacting, in his own way, the scheme of the tenements. It is only his frankness that shocks. The Irishman does not naturally take kindly to tenement life, though with characteristic versatility he adapts himself to its conditions at once. It does violence, nevertheless, to the best that is in him, and for that very reason of all who come within its sphere soonest corrupts him. The result is a sediment, the product of more than a generation in the city's slums, that, as distinguished from the larger body of his class, justly ranks at the foot of tenement dwellers, the so-called "low Irish" . . .

An impulse toward better things there certainly is. The German ragpicker of thirty years ago, quite as low in the scale as his Italian successor, is the thrifty tradesman or prosperous farmer of today.

The Italian scavenger of our time is fast graduating into exclusive control of the corner fruit-stands, while his black-eyed boy monopolizes the boot-blacking industry in which a few years ago he was an intruder. The Irish hod-carrier in the second generation has become a bricklayer, if not the Alderman of his ward, while the Chinese coolie is in almost exclusive possession of the laundry business. The reason is obvious. The poorest immigrant comes here with the purpose and ambition to better himself and, given half a chance, might be reasonably expected to make the most of it. To the false plea that he prefers the squalid homes in which his kind are housed there could be no better answer. . . .

As emigration from east to west follows the latitude, so does the foreign influx in New York distribute itself along certain well-defined lines that waver and break only under the stronger pressure of a more gregarious race or the encroachments of inexorable business. A feeling of dependence upon mutual effort, natural to strangers in a strange land, unacquainted with its language and customs, sufficiently accounts for this.

The Irishman is the true cosmopolitan immigrant. All-pervading, he shares his lodging with perfect impartiality with the Italian, the Greek, and the "Dutchman," yielding only to sheer force of numbers, and objects equally to them all. A map of the city, colored to designate nationalities, would show more stripes than on the skin of a zebra, and more colors than any rainbow. The city on such a map would fall into two great halves, green for the Irish prevailing in the West Side tenement districts, and blue for the Germans on the East Side. But intermingled with these ground colors would be an odd variety of tints that would give the whole the appearance of an extraordinary crazy-quilt. From down in the Sixth Ward, upon the site of the old Collect Pond that in the days of the fathers drained the hills which are no more, the red of the Italian would be seen forcing its way northward along the line of Mulberry Street to the quarter of the French purple on Bleecker Street and South Fifth Avenue, to lose itself and reappear, after a lapse of miles, in the "Little Italy" of Harlem, east of Second Avenue. Dashes of red, sharply defined, would be seen strung through the Annexed District, northward to the city line. On the West Side the red would be seen overrunning the old Africa of Thompson Street, pushing the black of the negro rapidly uptown, against querulous but unavailing protests, occupying his home, his church, his trade, and all with merciless impartiality.

Hardly less aggressive than the Italian, the Russian and Polish Jew, having overrun the district between Rivington and Division Streets, east of the Bowery, to the point of suffocation, is filling the tenements of the old Seventh Ward to the river front, and disputing with the Italian every foot of available space in the back alleys of Mulberry Street. The two races, differing hopelessly in much, have this in common: they carry their slums with them wherever they go, if allowed to do it. Little Italy already rivals its parent, the "Bend," in foulness. Other nationalities that begin at the bottom make a fresh start when crowded up the ladder. Happily both are manageable, the one by rabbinical, the other by the civil law. Between the dull gray of the Jew, his favorite color, and the Italian red, would be seen squeezed in on the map a sharp streak of yellow, marking the narrow boundaries of Chinatown. Dovetailed in with the German population, the poor but thrifty Bohemian might be picked out by the sombre hue of his life as of his philosophy, struggling against heavy odds in the big human bee-hives of the East Side. Colonies of his people extend northward, with long lapses of space, from below the Cooper Institute more than three miles. The Bohemian is the only foreigner with any considerable representation in the city who counts no wealthy man of his race, none who has not to work hard for a living, or has got beyond the reach of the tenement.

Down near the Battery the West Side emerald would be soiled by a dirty stain, spreading rapidly like a splash of ink on a sheet of blotting paper, headquarters of the Arab tribe, that in a single year has swelled from the original dozen to twelve hundred, intent, every mother's son, on trade and barter. Dots and dashes of color here and there would show where the Finnish sailors worship their djumala (God), the Greek pedlars the ancient name of their race, and the Swiss the goddess of thrift. And so on to the end of the long register, all toiling together in the galling fetters of the tenement. Were the question raised who makes the most of life thus mortgaged, who resists most stubbornly its levelling tendency—knows how to drag even the barracks upward a part of the way at least toward the ideal plane of the home—the palm must be unhesitatingly awarded the Teuton. The Italian and the poor Jew rise only by compulsion. The Chinaman does not rise at all; here, as at home, he simply remains stationary. The Irishman's genius runs to public affairs rather than domestic life; wherever he is mustered in force the saloon is the gorgeous centre of political activity. The German struggles vainly to learn his trick; his Teutonic wit is too heavy, and the political ladder he raises from his saloon usually too short or too clumsy to reach the desired goal. The best part of his life is lived at home, and he makes himself a home independent of the surroundings, giving the lie to the saying, unhappily become a maxim of social truth, that pauperism and drunkenness naturally grow in the tenements. He makes the most of his tenement, and it should be added that whenever and as soon as he can save up money enough, he gets out and never crosses the threshold of one again.

Source: Jacob Riis, *How the Other Half Lives* (1957), 15–21.

George Washington Plunkitt on "Honest Graft," 1890s

Political machines and their bosses were a fixture of urban political life in America's Gilded Age. Immigrants swelled city populations, expanding the needs for social services, housing, jobs, crime protection, utilities, and transportation beyond the capacity of regular political organizations to fill them. In exchange for votes, immigrant bosses organized the ethnic enclaves into precincts and wards and responded to the needs of their constitutents while enriching themselves. Journalist William L. Riordan spent time gathering the reflections of one noted Irish boss of Tammany Hall, the Democratic political machine of New York City. George Washington Plunkitt's humorous definition of what constitutes graft provides an insight into the mind-set of immigrant bosses:

Everybody is talkin' these days about Tammany men growin' rich on graft, but nobody thinks of drawin' the distinction between honest graft and dishonest graft. There's all the difference in the world between the two. Yes, many of our men have grown rich in politics. I have myself. I've made a big fortune out of the game, and I'm gettin' richer every day, but I've not gone in for dishonest graft—blackmailin' gamblers, saloon-keepers, disorderly people, etc.—and neither has any of the men who have made big fortunes in politics.

There's an honest graft, and I'm an example of how it works. I might sum up the whole thing by sayin': 'I seen my opportunities and I took 'em.'

Just let me explain my examples. My party's in power in the city, and it's goin' to undertake a lot of public improvements. Well, I'm tipped off, say, that they're going to lay out a new park at a certain place.

I see my opportunity and I take it. I go to that place and I buy up all the land I can in the neighborhood. Then the board of this or that makes its plan public, and there is a rush to get my land, which nobody cared particular for before.

Ain't it perfectly honest to charge a good price and make a profit on my investment and foresight? Of course it is. Well, that's honest graft. . . .

It's just like lookin' ahead in Wall Street or in the coffee or cotton market.

Now, let me tell you that most politicians who are accused of robbin' the city get rich the same way.

"They didn't steal a dollar from the city treasury. They just seen their opportunities and took them. That is why, when a reform administration comes in and spends a half million dollars in tryin' to find the public robberies they talk about in the campaign, they don't find them.

The books are always all right. The money in the city treasury is all right. Everything is all right. All they can show is that the Tammany heads of departments looked after their friends, within the law, and gave them what opportunities they could to make honest graft. . . .

I've been readin' a book by Lincoln Steffens on *The Shame of the Cities*. Steffens means well but, like all reformers, he don't know how to make distinctions. He can't see no difference between honest graft and dishonest graft and, consequent, he gets things all mixed up. There's the biggest kind of a difference between political looters and politicians who make a fortune out of politics by keepin' their eyes wide open. The looter goes in for himself alone without considerin' his organization or his city. The politician looks after his own interests, the organization's interests, and the city's interests all at the same time. . . .

Source: William L. Riordan, *Plunkitt of Tammany Hall* (1963), 3–6; 29.

"The Preacher and the Slave," 1890s

In the late nineteenth century, union leaders faced formidable obstacles in their efforts to organize workers. Labor unions had no legal standing until the New Deal period. Despite some of the most oppressive conditions men and women ever faced in the workplace, labor organizers waged an uphill battle against antiunion tactics such as firings, evictions from company housing, blacklisting union sympathizers, and "yellow-dog" contracts. The International Workers of the World (IWW), or the "Wobblies," was one of the most militant organizations. Although the IWW never attracted more than 5% of all trade unionists, using giant rallies, massive picket lines, flaming oratory, and revolutionary songs, the Wobblies captured the nation's attention. Joe Hill, songwriter for the IWW, composed the following song, a parody of the popular Salvation Army gospel hymn, sung to the tune "In the Sweet Bye and Bye," to advise the oppressed to seek justice on earth, not in the hereafter.

Long-haired preachers come out every night,
Try to tell you what's wrong and what's right;
But when asked how 'bout something to eat
They will answer with voices so sweet:
Chorus:
You will eat, bye and bye,
In that glorious land above the sky;
Work and Pray, live on hay,
You'll get pie in the sky when you die.

And the starvation army they play,
And they sing and they clap and they pray.
Till they get all your coin on the drum,
Then they'll tell you when you're on the bum:
Holy Rollers and jumpers come out,
And they holler, they jump and they shout.
"Give your money to Jesus," they say,
"He will cure all diseases today."
If you fight hard for children and wife—
Try to get something good in this life—
You're a sinner and bad man, they tell,
When you die you will sure go to hell.
Workingmen of all countries, unite,
Side by side we for freedom will fight:
When the world and its wealth we have gained
To the grafters we'll sing this refrain:
Last Chorus
You will eat, bye and bye,
When you've learned how to cook and to fry.
Chop some wood, 'twill do you good,
And you'll eat in the sweet bye and bye.

Source: Winthrop Jordon and Leon Litwack, *The United States Becoming a World Power* (1991), 463.

Working Conditions and Reform
"Eight Hours for What We Will," 1866

This is a poem writted by I. G. Blanchard in 1866 and set to music in 1872 by the Reverend Jesse H. J. Jones. The song became a rallying cry for labor and its bid for a shorter working day.

We mean to make things over,
    We're tired of toil for naught,
With bare enough to live upon,
    And never an hour for thought;
We want to feel the sunshine,
    And we want to smell the flowers,
We're sure that God has willed it,
    And we mean to have Eight Hours.
We're summoning our forces
    From shipyard, shop and mill;
Eight hours for work, eight hours for rest,
    Eight hours for what we will!

From the factories and workshops,
    In long and weary lines,
From all the sweltering forges,
    From all the sunless mines;
Wherever Toil is wasting
    The force of life to live;
Its bent and battered armies
    Come to claim what God doth give.
And the blazon on its banner
    Doth with hope the nations fill.

Eight hours for work, eight hours for rest,
   Eight hours for what we will!

The voice of God within us
   Is calling us to stand
Erect, as is becoming
   To the work of His right hand.
Should he, to whom the Maker
   His glorious image gave,
The meanest of His creatures crouch,
   A bread-and-butter slave?
Let the shout ring down the valleys
   And echo from ev'ry hill,
Eight hours for work, eight hours for rest,
   Eight hours for what we will!

Source: Brier et al., *Who Built America?* 119.

Xin Jin's Prostitution Contract, 1886

*The Chinese Exclusion Act of 1882 not only banned additional immigra-
tion of Chinese laborers; it also prohibited men from bringing their wives. Of
the 100,000 Chinese immigrants living in the United States between 1880
and 1900, only about 5,000 were women. Most of them worked in laundries
and domestic service; others arrived as indentured prostitutes. The following
contract of Xin Jin, who worked as a prostitute in San Francisco, illustrates
the stringent terms of prostitution in exchange for fare from China.*

THE CONTRACTEE Xin Jin became indebted to her master/
mistress for food and passage from China to San Francisco.
Since she is without funds, she will voluntarily work as a
prostitute at Tan Fu's place for four and one-half years for an
advance of 1,205 yuan (U.S. $524) to pay this debt. There
shall be no interest on the money and Xin Jin shall receive no
wages. At the expiration of the contract, Xin Jin shall be free
to do as she pleases. Until then, she shall first secure the
master/mistress's permission if a customer asks to take her
out. If she has the four loathsome diseases she shall be returned within 100 days; beyond that time the procurer has
no responsibility. Menstruation disorder is limited to one
month's rest only. If Xin Jin becomes sick at any time for
more than 15 days, she shall work one month extra; if she
becomes pregnant, she shall work one year extra. Should Xin
Jin run away before her term is out, she shall pay whatever
expense is incurred in finding and returning her to the
brothel. This is a contract to be retained by the master/mis-
tress as evidence of the agreement. Receipt of 1205 yuan
($524) by Ah Yo. Thumb print of Xin Jin the contractee.
Eighth month 11th day of the 12th year of Guang-zu (1886).

Source: Brier et al., *Who Built America?* 57.

Children in the Coal Mines, 1906

*In 1906, John Spargo described the life of child miners, most of whom
were working because it was necessary to the economic survival of the
household.*

Work in the coal breakers is exceedingly hard and dangerous.
Crouched over the chutes, the boys sit hour after hour, picking out the pieces of slate and other refuse from the coal as
it rushes past to the washers. From the cramped position they
have to assume, most of them become more or less deformed
and bent-backed like old men. When a boy has been working
for some time and begins to get round-shouldered, his fellows
say that "He's got his boy to carry around whenever he goes."

The coal is hard, and accidents to the hands, such as cut,
broken, or crushed fingers, are common among the boys.
Sometimes there is a worse accident: a terrified shriek is
heard, and a boy is mangled and torn in the machinery, or
disappears in the chute to be picked out later smothered and
dead. Clouds of dust fill the breakers and are inhaled by the
boys, laying the foundations for asthma and miners' consumption.

I once stood in a breaker for half an hour and tried to do
the work a twelve-year-old boy was doing day after day, for
ten hours at a stretch, for sixty cents a day. The gloom of the
breaker appalled me. Outside the sun shone brightly, the air
was pellucid, and the birds sang in chorus with the trees and
the rivers. Within the breaker there was blackness, clouds of
deadly dust enfolded everything, the harsh, grinding roar of
the machinery and the ceaseless rushing of coal through the
chutes filled the ears. I tried to pick out the pieces of slate
from the hurrying stream of coal, often missing them; my
hands were bruised and cut in a few minutes; I was covered
from head to foot with coal dust, and for many hours afterwards I was expectorating some of the small particles of anthracite I had swallowed.

I could not do that work and live, but there were boys of
ten and twelve years of age doing it for fifty and sixty cents a
day. Some of them had never been inside of a school; few of
them could read a child's primer. True, some of them attended the night schools, but after working ten hours in the
breaker the educational results from attending school were
practically nil. "We goes fer a good time, an' we keeps de
guys wot's dere hoppin' all de time," said little Owen Jones,
whose work I had been trying to do. . . .

As I stood in that breaker I thought of the reply of the
small boy to Robert Owen [British social reformer]. Visiting
an English coal mine one day, Owen asked a twelve-year-old
if he knew God. The boy stared vacantly at his questioner:
"God?" he said, "God? No, I don't. He must work in some
other mine." It was hard to realize amid the danger and din
and blackness of that Pennsylvania breaker that such a thing
as belief in a great All-good God existed.

From the breakers the boys graduate to the mine depths,
where they become door tenders, switch boys, or mule drivers. Here, far below the surface, work is still more dangerous.
At fourteen and fifteen the boys assume the same risks as the
men, and are surrounded by the same perils. Nor is it in
Pennsylvania only that these conditions exist. In the bituminous mines of West Virginia, boys of nine or ten are frequently employed. I met one little fellow ten years old in Mt.
Carbon, W. Va., last year, who was employed as a "trap boy."
Think of what it means to be a trap boy at ten years of age.
It means to sit alone in a dark mine passage hour after hour,
with no human soul near; to see no living creature except the
mules as they pass with their loads, or a rat or two seeking
to share one's meal; to stand in water or mud that covers the
ankles, chilled to the marrow by the cold draughts that rush
in when you open the trap door for the mules to pass
through; to work for fourteen hours—waiting—opening and
shutting a door—then waiting again—for sixty cents; to reach
the surface when all is wrapped in the mantle of night, and
to fall to the earth exhausted and have to be carried away to
the nearest "shack" to be revived before it is possible to walk
to the farther shack called "home." Boys twelve years of age

may be legally employed in the mines of West Virginia, by day or by night, and for as many hours as the employers care to make them toil or their bodies will stand the strain. Where the disregard of child life is such that this may be done openly and with legal sanction, it is easy to believe what miners have again and again told me—that there are hundreds of little boys of nine and ten years of age employed in the coal mines of this state.

Source: John Spargo, *The Bitter Cry of Children,* (1906), in Brown, *America Through the Eyes of Its People,* 117.

Upton Sinclair, *The Jungle,* 1906

This book on everyday life in Chicago's stockyards had an immediate impact, leading Pres. Theodore Roosevelt to order an investigation of the industry which eventually produced the Meat Inspection Act.

There was another interesting set of statistics that a person might have gathered in Packingtown—those of the various afflictions of the workers. When Jurgis had first inspected the packing plants with Szedvilas, he had marveled while he listened to the tale of all the things that were made out of the carcasses of animals and of all the lesser industries that were maintained there; now he found that each one of these lesser industries was a separate little inferno, in its way as horrible as the killing-beds, the source and fountain of them all. The workers in each of them had their own peculiar diseases. And the wandering visitor might be skeptical about all the swindles, but he could not be skeptical about these, for the worker bore the evidence of them about on his own person—generally he had only to hold out his hand.

There were the men in the pickle rooms, for instance, where old Antanas had gotten his death; scarce a one of these had not some spot of horror on his person. Let a man so much as scrape his finger pushing a truck in the pickle rooms, and he might have a sore that would put him out of the world; all the joints in his fingers might be eaten by the acid, one by one. Of the butchers and floormen, the beef boners and trimmers, and all those who used knives, you could scarcely find a person who had the use of his thumb; time and time again the base of it had been slashed, till it was a mere lump of flesh against which the man pressed the knife to hold it. The hands of these men would be criss-crossed with cuts, until you could no longer pretend to count them or to trace them. They would have no nails—they had worn them off pulling hides; their knuckles were swollen so that their fingers spread out like a fan. There were men who worked in the cooking rooms, in the midst of steam and sickening odors, by artificial light; in these rooms the germs of tuberculosis might live for two years, but the supply was renewed every hour. There were the beef luggers, who carried two-hundred-pound quarters into the refrigerator cars, a fearful kind of work, that began at four o'clock in the morning, and that wore out the most powerful man in a few years. There were those who worked in the chilling rooms, and whose special disease was rheumatism; the time limit that a man could work in the chilling rooms was said to be five years. There were the wool pluckers, whose hands went to pieces even sooner than the hands of the pickle men; for the pelts of the sheep had to be painted with acid to loosen the wool, and then the pluckers had to pull out this wool with their bare hands, till the acid had eaten their fingers off. There

were those who made the tins for the canned meat, and their hands, too, were a maze of cuts, and each cut represented a chance for blood poisoning. Some worked at the stamping machines, and it was very seldom that one could work long there at the pace that was set, and not give out and forget himself, and have a part of his hand chopped off. There were the "hoisters," as they were called, whose task it was to press the lever which lifted the dead cattle off the floor. They ran along upon a rafter, peering down through the damp and the steam, and as old Durham's architects had not built the killing room for the convenience of the hoisters, at every few feet they would have to stoop under a beam, say four feet above the one they ran on, which got them into the habit of stooping, so that in a few years they would be walking like chimpanzees. Worst of any, however, were the fertilizer men, and those who served in the cooking rooms. These people could not be shown to the visitor—for the odor of a fertilizer man would scare any ordinary visitor at a hundred yards, and as for the other men, who worked in tank rooms full of steam and in some of which there were open vats near the level of the floor, their peculiar trouble was that they fell into the vats; and when they were fished out, there was never enough of them left to be worth exhibiting—sometimes they would be overlooked for days, till all but the bones of them had gone out to the world as Durham's Pure Leaf Lard!

* * * * *

Early in the fall Jurgis set out for Chicago again. All the joy went out of tramping as soon as a man could not keep warm in the hay; and, like many thousands of others, he deluded himself with the hope that by coming early he could avoid the rush. He brought fifteen dollars with him, hidden away in one of his shoes, a sum which had been saved from the saloon-keepers, not so much by his conscience, as by the fear which filled him at the thought of being out of work in the city in the wintertime.

He traveled upon the railroad with several other men, hiding in freight cars at night, and liable to be thrown off at any time, regardless of the speed of the train. When he reached the city he left the rest, for he had money and they did not, and he meant to save himself in this fight. He would bring to it all the skill that practice had brought him, and he would stand, whoever fell. On fair nights he would sleep in the park or on a truck or an empty barrel or box, and when it was rainy or cold he would stow himself upon a shelf in a ten-cent lodging-house, or pay three cents for the privileges of a "squatter" in a tenement hallway. He would eat at free lunches, five cents a meal, and never a cent more—so he might keep alive for two months and more, and in that time he would surely find a job. He would have to bid farewell to his summer cleanliness, of course, for he would come out of the first night's lodging with his clothes alive with vermin. There was no place in the city where he could wash even his face, unless he went down to the lake front—and there it would soon be all ice.

First he went to the steel mill and the harvester works, and found that his places there had been filled long ago. He was careful to keep away from the stockyards—he was a single man now, he told himself, and he meant to stay one, to have his wages for his own when he got a job. He began the long, weary round of factories and warehouses, tramping all day, from one end of the city to the other, finding everywhere from ten to a hundred men ahead of him. He watched the newspapers, too—but no longer was he to be taken in by the smooth-spoken agents. He had been told of all those tricks while "on the road."

In the end it was through a newspaper that he got a job, after nearly a month of seeking. It was a call for a hundred laborers, and though he thought it was a "fake," he went because the place was near by. He found a line of men a block long, but as a wagon chanced to come out of an alley and break the line, he saw his chance and sprang to seize a place. Men threatened him and tried to throw him out, but he cursed and made a disturbance to attract a policeman, upon which they subsided, knowing that if the latter interfered it would be to "fire" them all.

An hour or two later he entered a room and confronted a big Irishman behind a desk.

"Ever worked in Chicago before?" the man inquired; and whether it was a good angel that put it into Jurgis's mind, or an intuition of his sharpened wits, he was moved to answer, "No, sir."

"Where do you come from?"

"Kansas City, sir."

"Any references?"

"No sir. I'm just an unskilled man, I've got good arms."

"I want men for hard work—it's all underground, digging tunnels for telephones. Maybe it won't suit you."

"I'm willing, sir—anything for me. What's the pay?"

"Fifteen cents an hour."

"I'm willing, sir."

"All right; go back there and give your name."

So within half an hour he was at work, far underneath the streets of the city. The tunnel was a peculiar one for telephone wires; it was about eight feet high, and with a level floor nearly as wide. It had innumerable branches—a perfect spider-web beneath the city; Jurgis walked over half a mile with his gang to the place where they were to work. Stranger yet, the tunnel was lighted by electricity, and upon it was laid a double-tracked, narrow gauge railroad!

But Jurgis was not there to ask questions, and he did not give the matter a thought. It was nearly a year afterward that he finally learned the meaning of this whole affair. The City Council had passed a quiet and innocent little bill allowing a company to construct telephone conduits under the city streets; and upon the strength of this, a great corporation had proceeded to tunnel all Chicago with a system of railway freight subways. In the city there was a combination of employers, representing hundreds of millions of capital, and formed for the purpose of crushing the labor unions. The chief union which troubled it was the teamsters'; and when these freight tunnels were completed, connecting all the big factories and stores with the railroad depots, they would have the teamsters' union by the throat. Now and then there were rumors and murmurs in the Board of Aldermen, and once there was a committee to investigate—but each time another small fortune was paid over, and the rumors died away; until at last the city woke up with a start to find the work completed. There was a tremendous scandal, of course; it was found that the city records had been falsified and other crimes committed, and some of Chicago's big capitalists got into jail—figuratively speaking. The aldermen declared that they had had no idea of it all, in spite of the fact that the main entrance to the work had been in the rear of the saloon of one of them. . . .

In a work thus carried out, not much thought was given to the welfare of the laborers. On an average, the tunneling cost a life a day and several manglings; it was seldom, however, that more than a dozen or two men heard of any one accident. The work was all done by the new boring-machinery, with as little blasting as possible; but there would be falling rocks and crushed supports and premature explosions—and in addition all the dangers of railroading. So it was that one night, as Jurgis was on his way out with his gang, an engine and a loaded car dashed round one of the innumerable right-angle branches and struck him upon the shoulder, hurling him against the concrete wall and knocking him senseless.

When he opened his eyes again it was to the clanging of the bell of an ambulance. He was lying in it, covered by a blanket, and it was heading its way slowly through the holiday-shopping crowds. They took him to the county hospital, where a young surgeon set his arm, then he was washed and laid upon a bed in a ward with a score or two more of maimed and mangled men.

Source: Sinclair, *The Jungle*, 116–17; 265–69.

The Triangle Factory, 1912

The Triangle Shirtwaist Factory fire (1912) highlighted the plight of workers during the age of Progressive reform. After 146 young women died, the city of New York created a Bureau of Fire Prevention. This document is an account by Pauline Newman of the conditions in the factory.

I'd like to tell you about the kind of world we lived in 75 years ago because all of you probably weren't born then. Seventy-five years is a long time, but I'd like to give you at least a glimpse of that world because it has no resemblance to the world we live in today, in any respect.

That world 75 years ago was a world of incredible exploitation of men, women, and children. I went to work for the Triangle Shirtwaist Company in 1901. The corner of a shop would resemble a kindergarten because we were young, eight, nine, ten years old. It was a world of greed; the human being didn't mean anything. The hours were from 7:30 in the morning to 6:30 at night when it wasn't busy. When the season was on we worked until 9 o'clock. No overtime pay, not even supper money. There was a bakery in the garment center that produced little apple pies the size of this ashtray [holding up ashtray for group to see] and that was what we got for our overtime instead of money.

My wages as a youngster were $1.50 for a seven-day week. I know it sounds exaggerated, but it isn't; it's true. If you worked there long enough and you were satisfactory you got 50 cents a week increase every year. So by the time I left the Triangle Waist Company in 1909, my wages went up to $5.50, and that was quite a wage in those days.

All shops were as bad as the Triangle Waist Company. When you were told Saturday afternoon, through a sign on the elevator, "If you don't come in on Sunday, you needn't come in on Monday," what choice did you have? You had no choice.

I worked on the 9th floor with a lot of youngsters like myself. Our work was not difficult. When the operators were through with sewing shirtwaists, there was a little thread left, and we youngsters would get a little scissors and trim the threads off.

And when the inspectors came around, do you know what happened? The supervisors made all the children climb into one of those crates that they ship material in, and they covered us over with finished shirtwaists until the inspector had left, because of course we were too young to be working in the factory legally.

The Triangle Waist Company was a family affair, all relatives of the owner running the place, watching to see that you did your work, watching when you went to the toilet. And if you were two or three minutes longer than foremen or foreladies thought you should be, it was deducted from your pay. If you came five minutes late in the morning because the freight elevator didn't come down to take you up in time, you were sent home for half a day without pay.

Rubber heels came into use around that time and our employers were the first to use them; you never knew when they would sneak up on you, spying, to be sure you did not talk to each other during working hours.

Most of the women rarely took more than $6.00 a week home, most less. The early sweatshops were usually so dark that gas jets (for light) burned day and night. There was no insulation in the winter, only a pot-bellied stove in the middle of the factory. If you were a finisher and could take your work with you (finishing is a hand operation) you could sit next to the stove in winter. But if you were an operator or a trimmer it was very cold indeed. Of course in the summer you suffocated with practically no ventilation.

There was no drinking water, maybe a tap in the hall, warm, dirty. What were you going to do? Drink this water or none at all. Well, in those days there were vendors who came in with bottles of pop for 2 cents, and much as you disliked to spend the two pennies you got the pop instead of the filthy water in the hall.

The condition was no better and no worse than the tenements where we lived. You got out of the workshop, dark and cold in the winter, hot in summer, dirty unswept floors, no ventilation, and you would go home. What kind of home did you go to? You won't find the tenements we lived in. Some of the rooms didn't have any windows. I lived in a two-room tenement with my mother and two sisters and the bedroom had no windows, the facilities were down in the yard, but that's the way it was in the factories too. In the summer the sidewalk, fire escapes, and the roof of the tenements became bedrooms just to get a breath of air.

We wore cheap clothes, lived in cheap tenements, ate cheap food. There was nothing to look forward to, nothing to expect the next day to be better.

Someone once asked me; "How did you survive?" And I told him, what alternative did we have? You stayed and you survived, that's all.

Source: Brown, *America Through the Eyes of Its People*, 150.

New York World

THEN CAME THE killing of Louis Tikas, the Greek leader of the strikers. We saw the militiamen parley outside the tent city, and a few minutes later, Tikas came out to meet them. We watched them talking. Suddenly an officer raised his rifle, gripping the barrel, and felled Tikas with the butt.

Tikas fell face downward. As he lay there we saw the militiamen fall back. Then they aimed their rifles and deliberately fired them into the unconscious man's body. It was the first murder I had ever seen, for it was a murder and nothing less. Then the miners ran about in the tent colony and women and children scuttled for safety in the [underground] pits which afterwards trapped them.

We watched from our rock shelter while the militia dragged up their machine guns and poured murderous fire into the arroyo from a height by Water Tank Hill above the Ludlow depot. Then came the firing of the tents. . . . The militiamen were thick about the northwest corner of the colony where the fire started and we could see distinctly from our lofty observation place what looked like a blazing torch waved in the midst of militia a few seconds before the general conflagration swept through the place.

Testimony of John D. Rockefeller

CHAIRMAN: And you are willing to go on and let these killings take place . . . rather than go out there and see if you might do something to settle those conditions?

ROCKEFELLER: There is just one thing . . . which can be done, as things are at present, to settle this strike, and that is to unionize the camps; and our interest in labor is so profound . . . that interest demands that the camps shall be open [nonunion] camps that we expect to stand by the [Colorado Fuel and Iron Co.] officers at any cost. . . .

CHAIRMAN: And you will do that if it costs all your property and kills all your employees?

ROCKEFELLER: It is a great principle.

CHAIRMAN: And you would do that rather than recognize the right of men to collective bargaining? Is that what I understand?

ROCKEFELLER: No, sir. Rather than allow outside people to come in and interfere with employees who are thoroughly satisfied with their labor conditions—it was upon a similar principle that the War of the Revolution was carried on. It is a great national issue of the most vital kind.

Source: Brier et al., *Who Built America?* 196–97.

The Ludlow Massacre, Easter Night, 1914

In 1913, John D. Rockefeller's Colorado Fuel and Iron Company led other companies on a drive to break the union which prompted more than 10,000 miners to begin a major strike in September. The battle was protracted and bitter. Finally, on Easter night in 1914, the militia attacked a strikers' tent camp in Ludlow, Colorado, killing fourteen, including eleven children. The following is an excerpt from a New York World *newspaper account; in the second document Rockefeller is questioned by Frank Walsh, a noted reformer and chairman of a Commission on Industrial Relations established by Congress to investigate labor conditions.*

Bibliography

Adams, James Truslow, ed. *Album of American History*. New York: Charles Scribner's Sons, 1946.

———— *Dictionary of American History*. New York: Charles Scribner's Sons, 1940.

Andrews, Wayne. *Architecture, Ambition, and Americans: A Social History of American Architecture*. New York: The Free Press, 1978.

———— *Architecture in America: A Photographic History From the Colonial Period to the Present*. New York: Atheneum Publishers, 1960.

Atlas of American History. Second Revised Edition. New York: Charles Scribner's Sons, 1984.

Austin, Erik W., with the assistance of Jerome M. Clubb. *Political Facts of the United States Since 1789*. New York: Columbia University Press, 1986.

Banks, Ann. *First-Person America*. New York: Alfred Knopf, 1980.

Barnett, Le Roy. *Shipping Literature of the Great Lakes. A Catalog of Company Publications, 1852–1990*. East Lansing: Michigan State University Press, 1992.

Barton, H. Arnold, ed. *Letters From the Promised Land: Swedes in America, 1890–1914*. Minneapolis: University of Minnesota Press, 1975.

Boller, Paul F., Jr., and Ronald Story. *A More Perfect Union: Documents in U.S. History*. Vol. II: Since 1865. Boston: Houghton Mifflin Company, 1992.

Brier, Stephen, et al., eds. *Who Built America? Working People and the Nation's Economy, Politics, Culture, and Society*. Vol II: *From the Gilded Age to the Present*. New York: Pantheon Books, 1992.

Brown, Carol. *America Through the Eyes of Its People: A Collection of Primary Sources*. New York: HarperCollins College Publishers, 1993.

Bureau of the Census. *Historical Statistics of the United States, Colonial Times to 1957*. Washington, D.C.: Government Printing Office, 1961.

Bureau of the Census. *Historical Statistics of the United States, Colonial Times to 1970*. Washington, D.C.: Government Printing Office, 1975.

Cahalan, Margaret Werner. *Historical Correction Statistics in the United States 1850–1984*. Rockville, Md., Westat, Inc., 1986.

Carruth, Gorton. *The Encyclopedia of American Facts and Dates*. 8th Edition. New York: Harper & Row, 1987.

Carruth, Gorton, and Eugene Ehrlich. *Facts and Dates of American Sports*. New York: Harper & Row, 1988.

Cayton, Mary Kupiec, Elliott J. Gorn, and Peter W. Williams, eds. *Encyclopedia of American Social History*. 3 Vols. New York: Scribners, 1993.

Congressional Quarterly Inc. *Members of Congress Since 1789*. Washington, D.C.: Congressional Quarterly Inc., 1977.

Congressional Quarterly Inc. *Presidential Elections Since 1789*. Washington, D.C.: Congressional Quarterly Inc., 1979.

Conlin, Joseph R. *The American Past; A Survey of American History*. San Diego, New York, Chicago, Austin, Washington, D.C., London, Sydney, Tokyo, and Toronto: Harcourt Brace Jovanovich, Publishers, 1990.

Crimmins, Timothy J., and Neil Larry Shumsky. *American Life, American People*. Vol. 2. New York: Harcourt Brace Jovanovich, 1988.

Daniel, Pete, and Raymond Smock. *A Talent for Detail: The Photographs of Miss Frances Benjamin Johnston, 1889–1910*. New York: Harmony Books, 1974.

Department of Commerce. Bureau of the Census. *Religious Bodies 1916*. Part I: Summary and General Tables. Washington, D.C.: Government Printing Office, 1919.

Divine, Robert A., et al. *America Past and Present* (HarperCollins Publishers, 1991).

Encyclopaedia Britannica. 1960 Edition. New York, 1962.

Escott, Paul D., and David R. Goldfield. *Main Problems in the History of the American South*. Vol. II. Lexington, Mass. and Toronto: D. C. Heath and Company, (1990), 179.

Flora, Snowden D. *Tornadoes of the United States*. Norman: University of Oklahoma Press, 1954.

Graebner, William, and Leonard Richards. *The American Record: Images of the Nation's Past*. Vol. Two: *Since 1865*. New York: Alfred A. Knopf, 1988.

Hacker, Louis M., and Helene S. Zahler, *The Shaping of the American Tradition*. New York: Columbia University Press, 1947.

Hackett, Alice Payne. *70 Years of Best-Sellers 1895–1965*. New York & London: R. R. Bowker Co., 1967.

Hickok, Ralph. *New Encyclopedia of Sports*. New York: McGraw-Hill, 1977.

Historical Atlas of the United States. Centennial Edition. Washington, D.C.: National Geographic Society, 1988.

Horowitz, Daniel. *The Morality of Spending: Attitudes Toward the Consumer Society in America, 1875–1940*. Baltimore and London: The Johns Hopkins University Press, 1985.

Hughes, Patrick. *American Weather Stories*. Washington, D.C.: U.S. Department of Commerce, National Oceanic and Atmospheric Administration. Environmental Data Service. U.S. Government Printing Office, 1976.

Hunt, William Dudley, Jr. *Encyclopedia of American Architecture*. Many cities: McGraw Hill, 1980.

Jensen, Oliver. *America's Yesterdays: Images of Our Lost Past Discovered in the Photographic Archives of the Library of Congress*. New York: American Heritage Publishing Co., 1978.

Jensen, Oliver, Joan Paterson Kerr, and Murray Belsky. *American Album*. New York: American Heritage Publishing Co., 1968.

Kane, Joseph Nathan, Steven Anzovin, and Janet Podell, eds. *Facts About the States*. New York: The H. W. Wilson Co., 1989.

Kingston, Mike, and Mary G. Crawford, eds. *Texas Almanac and State Industrial Guide 1990–91*. Dallas: *Dallas Morning News*, 1989.

Kousser, J. Morgan. *The Shaping of Southern Politics: Suffrage Restriction and the Establishment of the One-Party South, 1880–1910*. New Haven and London: Yale University Press, 1974.

Kutler, Stanely I. *Looking for America: The People's History*. II: *Since 1865*. Second Edition. New York: W.W. Norton & Company, 1979.

Lax, Roger, and Frederick Smith, *The Great Song Thesaurus*. New York: Oxford University Press, 1984.

Lewinson, Paul. *Race, Class, & Party: A History of Negro Suffrage and White Politics in the South*. New York: Russell & Russell, Inc., 1963.

Litwack, Leon F., and Winthrop D. Jordan. *The United States Becoming a World Power*. Vol. II. Seventh Edition. Englewood Cliffs, New Jersey: Prentice-Hall, 1991.

Ludlum, David M. *The American Weather Book*. Boston: Houghton Mifflin Company, 1982.

Menke, Frank G. *The Encyclopedia of Sports*. New York: South Brunswick, A.S. Barnes, 1969.

Mitchell, B. R. *International Historical Statistics, the Americas and Australasia*. Detroit: Gale Research Co., 1983.

Moberg, Vilhelm. *Emigrants: A Novel*. New York: Simon and Schuster, 1951.

More, Louise Bolard. *Wage-Earners' Budgets: A Study of Standards and Cost of Living in New York City*. New York: Henry Holt and Company, 1907.

Morris, Richard B., ed. *Encyclopedia of American History*. New York:

Harper & Row, Publishers, 1965, 1982.

Nash, Gary B., et al. *The American People: Creating a Nation and a Society.* New York: Harper & Row Publishers, 1986.

Norton, Mary Beth, et al. *A People and A Nation.* Boston: Houghton Mifflin Company, 1988.

Notable Names in American History; A Tabulated Register. 3rd Edition of White's Conspectus of American Biography. Clifton, N.J.: James T. White and Co., 1973.

Oehlerts, Donald E. *Books and Blueprints: Building America's Public Libraries.* New York and Westport, Conn.: Greenwood Press, 1991.

Peterson, Robert. *Only the Ball was White: A History of Legendary Black Players and All-Black Professional Teams.* New York: Oxford University Press, 1970.

Richardson, E. P. *Painting in America: The Story of 450 Years.* New York: Thomas Y. Crowell Co., 1956.

Riis, Jacob A. *How the Other Half Lives: Studies Among the Tenements of New York.* With introduction by Donald N. Bigelow. New York: Hill and Wang, 1957.

Reichler, Joseph L., ed. *The Baseball Encyclopedia: The Complete and Official Record of Major League Baseball.* 7th Edition. New York: Macmillan Publishing Co., 1988.

Riordan, William, recorder. *Plunkitt of Tammany Hall.* With introduction by Arthur Mann. New York: E.P. Dutton & Co., Inc., 1963.

Roller, David C., and Robert W. Twyman, eds. *The Encyclopedia of Southern History.* Baton Rouge and London: Louisiana State University Press, 1979.

Rölvaag, O. E. *Giants in the Earth.* New York: Harper and Row, 1927.

Salmon, Emily J. And Edward D. C. Campbell, Jr., eds. *The Hornbook of Virginia History: A Ready Reference Guide to the Old Dominion's People, Places, and Past.* Richmond: The Library of Virginia, 1994.

Schlereth, Thomas J. *Victorian America: Transformation in Everyday Life, 1876–1915.* New York: HarperCollins Publishers, 1991.

Schlesinger, Arthur M., Jr., ed. *The Almanac of American History.* New York: G. P. Putnam's Sons, 1983.

Sinclair, Upton. *The Jungle.* New York: Doubleday, Page and Co., 1906.

Spargo, John. *The Bitter Cry of the Children.* London: Macmillan and Co., 1906.

Spofford, Ainsworth R., ed. *An American Almanac and Treasury of Facts, Statistical, Financial, and Political for the Year 1878.* New York and Washington: The American News Co., 1878.

————. *An American Almanac and Treasury of Facts, Statistical, Financial, and Political for the Year 1885.* New York and Washington: The American News Co., 1885.

Straub, Deborah A., and Diane L. Dupuis. *Cities of the United States.* Vol I: *The South.* Vol II: *The West.* Vol III: *The Midwest.* Vol. IV: *The Northeast.* Detroit: Gale Research Inc., 1988.

Streightoff, Frank Hatch. *The Standard of Living Among the Industrial People of America.* Boston and New York: Houghton Mifflin Company, 1911.

Stuart, Paul. *Nations Within a Nation: Historical Statistics of American Indians.* New York and Westport Conn.: Greenwood Press, 1987.

Sutherland, Daniel E. *The Expansion of Everyday Life, 1860–1876.* New York, Cambridge, Philadelphia, San Francisco, London, Mexico City, Sao Paulo, Singapore, Sydney: Harper & Row, Publishers, 1989.

The American Almanac, Year-Book Cyclopedia and Atlas. New York: New York American and Journal Hearst's Chicago American and San Francisco Examiner, 1903.

The National Archives. *The American Image: Photographs from the National Archives, 1860–1960.* New York: Pantheon Books, 1979.

Notable Names in American History. Third edition of White's Conspectus of American Biography. Clifton, New Jersey: James T. White and Co., 1973.

Thornton, Russell. *The American Indian: Holocaust and Survival.* Norman, Okla.: University of Oklahoma Press, 1987.

The Smithsonian Institution. *Images of America.* Smithsonian Books, 1989.

United States Department of Agriculture. *Climate and Man: Yearbook of Agriculture 1941.* Washington, D.C.: U.S. Government Printing, 1941.

United States Department of Commerce. *Climates of the United States.* Washington, D.C., reprint, 1974.

Utley, Robert M. *The Indian Frontier of the American West 1846–1890.* Albuquerque: University of New Mexico Press, 1984.

Ward, David. *Cities and Immigrants: A Geography of Change in Nineteenth-Century America.* New York: Oxford University Press, 1971.

The World Almanac and Encyclopedia 1914. New York: Press Publishing Co., 1913.

The World Almanac 1891. New York: Press Publishing Company, 1891.

The World Almanac and Encyclopedia 1921. New York: Press Publishing Co., 1920.

The World Almanac 1893. New York: Press Publishing Co., 1893.

The World Almanac and Encyclopedia 1920. New York: Press Publishing Co., 1919.

Time-Life Books. *This Fabulous Century, 1870–1900.* New York, 1970.

Waldman, Carl. *Atlas of the North American Indian.* Maps and Illustrations by Molly Braun. New York and Oxford: Facts On File Publications, 1985.

Williams, Michael. *Americans and Their Forests: A Historical Geography.* Cambridge, New York, New Rochelle, Melbourne, and Sydney: Cambridge University Press, 1989.

Wilson, Charles Reagan, William Ferris, Ann J. Abadie, and Mary L. Hart, eds. *Encyclopedia of Southern Culture.* Chapel Hill: University of North Carolina Press, 1989.

World Almanac and Encyclopedia. New York: Press Publishing Co., 1902.

Wolman, Leo. *Ebb and Flow in Trade Unionism.* National Bureau of Economic Research, 1936.

Wright, John W., ed. *The Universal Almanac 1991.* Kansas City and New York: Andrews and McMeel, 1990.

APPENDIX: LIST OF TABLES

Index

This index is arranged alphabetically letter-by-letter. Page numbers in *italic* indicate illustrations or captions. Page numbers followed by *t* indicate tables.

Coxe, A. B. 328t
Coxey, Jacob 28, 56, 62
Coxey's Army 24, 28, 206
Coy, Edward H. 304t
Coy, Edwin H. 304t
Cozens, Ernest B. 304t
"Cradle's Empty Baby's Gone" (song) 264t
Cragin, Aaron H. 101t
Cragin, Calhoun 313t
Crago, Thomas S. 180t
Craig, Alexander K. 133t
Craig, George H. 114t
Craig, J. B. 326t
Craig, James 305t
Craig, R. C. 324t
Craig, Samuel A. 129t
Craig, William B. 166t, 171t
Crain, William H. 122t, 125t, 129t, 134t, 139t, 143t
Cram, Ralph Adams 217, 262t
Cramton, Louis C. 183t
Crandall, D. 290t–292t
Crane, Stephen 260, 260t, 269t, 270t
Crane, W. Murray 159t, 163t, 168t, 173t, 178t, 192t
Cranfill, James B. 27
Cranford, John W. 147t
Cranston, John 299t
Crapo, William W. 101t, 104t, 108t, 112t
Crapsey, Algernon Sidney 32
Crater Lake National Park (Oregon) 221
Craven, Jane W. 312t
Cravens, Jordan E. 103t, 107t, 110t
Cravens, William B. 167t, 171t, 176t
Crawford, Coe I. 175t, 180t, 185t, 195t
Crawford, S. 284t, 287t, 288t
Crawford, William T. 133t, 137t, 151t, 169t
Crazy Horse (Lakota chief) 16, 24, 216, 223
Creager, Charles E. 174t
Creamer, Thomas J. 155t
Cream of Wheat 23
Creeden, Timothy J. 28
Creek Indians 17
Cregan, J. F. 318t, 325t
Cregier, De Witt C. 229t
"Creole Belle" (song) 266t
Cret, Paul 259t
Criger, L. 285t
crime 83, 333–8
Cripple Creek, Colorado 205
Crisis, The (Winston Churchill) 260t
Crisis (magazine) 242
Crisp, Charles F. 115t, 119t, 123t, 126t, 130t–132t, 134t–136t, 138t, 140t
Crisp, Charles R. 140t, 182t
Crittenden, Thomas T. 105t, 192t
Croft, George W. 161t
Croft, Theodore G. 161t
Cromer, George W. 149t, 153t, 158t, 163t
Cromwell, Oklahoma 279t
Crook, George 16, 243
"crop lien" 44
Crosby, J. Schuyler 192t
Crosby, John C. 132t
Cross, L. 285t, 286t
Cross, M. 285t, 286t
cross-country running 323t, 329t
Crosser, Robert 185t
"Cross of Gold" speech (William Jennings Bryan, 1896) 92t
Croswell, Charles M. 192t
Crothers, Austin L. 191t
Crothers, Rachel 271t
Crounse, Lorenzo 101t, 193t
croup 83
Crouse, George W. 125t
Crow, Charles A. 173t
Crow Indian reservation (Montana) 27
Crowley, Joseph B. 149t, 153t, 158t
Crowley, Miles 143t
Crowley, Richard 109t, 112t
Crowther, George C. 141t
Crowther, George M. 305t
Croxton, Thomas 122t

Cruce, Lee 194t
Crude Rubber 71t
Crum, J. V. 324t
Crump, Rousseau O. 141t, 145t, 150t
Crumpacker, Edgar D. 144t, 149t, 153t, 158t, 163t, 167t, 172t, 177t
Cuba 28–33, 78t, 199, 201, 248
"Cubanola Glide, The" (song) 267t
"Cuddle Up a Little Closer, Lovey Mine" (song) 267t
Culberson, Charles A. 152t, 156t, 161t, 166t, 170t, 175t, 180t, 186t
Culberson, David B. 102t, 106t, 110t, 114t, 118t, 122t, 125t, 129t, 134t, 139t, 143t
Culbertson, Charles A. 195t
Culbertson, William C. 129t
Culbertson, William W. 115t
Cullen, William 111t, 115t
Cullom, Shelby M.
   Congress membership 115t, 119t, 123t, 126t, 131t, 135t, 140t, 144t, 149t, 153t, 158t, 163t, 167t, 172t, 177t
   Illinois governor 190t
Cullop, William A. 172t, 177t, 182t
Culpepper (racehorse) 310t
Culture's Garland (Eugene Field poems) 269t
Cumberland, Maryland 212
Cumberland Presbyterian Church 85t
Cummings, Amos J. 124t, 128t, 133t, 137t, 142t, 146t, 151t, 155t
Cummings, Henry J. B. 104t
Cummins, Albert B. 167t, 172t, 177t, 182t, 191t
Cumnock, Arthur 299t
Cunningham, Charles E. 26
Cunningham, Russell McW. 188t
Curie, Marie 273t
Curley, James M. 178t, 183t
currency 71t
Currier, Frank D. 155t, 159t, 164t, 169t, 173t, 179t
Currier, Moody 193t
Curry, Charles F. 181t
Curry, George 179t, 193t
Curry, R. 330t
"Curse of an Aching Heart, The" (song) 268t
Curtin, Andrew G. 113t, 117t, 121t
Curtis, Charles 136t, 140t, 145t, 149t, 154t, 158t, 163t, 168t, 172t, 176t–178t, 180t
Curtis, Cyrus Hermann 212
Curtis, Edward J. 190t
Curtis, Edwin U. 229t
Curtis, George M. 140t, 145t
Curtis, Harriot S. 309t
Curtis, Margaret 309t, 312t
Curtis, Newton M. 133t, 137t, 142t
Curtis, William B. 321t, 322t
Curtis Act (1898) 15, 17
Cusack, Thomas 149t
Cushing, Harvey William 220
Cushman, Francis W. 152t, 157t, 161t, 166t, 171t, 176t
Cushman, Francis W. 152t, 157t
Custer, George Armstrong 24, 215, 219, 220
Custom of the Country, The (Edith Wharton) 260
customs service 199t, 200t
Cutcheon, Byron M. 116t, 120t, 127t
Cutler, Augustus W. 101t, 105t
Cutler, John C. 196t
Cutting, John T. 130t
Cutts, Marsena E. 111t
Cutts, Oliver F. 301t
Cuyahoga City, Ohio 90t
Cuyas, Arturo 260t
Cuyler, Theodore 325t
cyclone 26–8, 207
Czolgosz, Leon 30, 97, 187

D

Dabney, E. S. 313t
"Daddy Has A Sweetheart, and Mother Is Her Name" (song) 268t
"Daddy's Little Girl" (song) 266t
"Daddy Wouldn't Buy Me a Bow-Wow" (song) 265t

Dadman, H. L. 318t
Daggett, Rollin M. 109t
Dague Jr., W. H. 303t
Dahle, Herman B. 152t, 157t
Dahlen, B. 286t
Daily Strength for Daily Needs (Mary W. Tileston) 260t
dairy products 41t
"Daisies Won't Tell" (song) 267t
"Daisy Bell" (song) 265t
Daisy Miller (Henry James) 260, 269t
Dakota Territory 9t, 36t, 277t, 331
Dale, Harry H. 184t
Dale, Thomas H. 165t
Dall, William H. 272
Dallas, Texas 223, 262t
Dalrymple, Abner 293t
Dalrymple, F. W. 327t
Dalrymple, Oliver 37–8
Dalrymple, P. W. 327t
Dalton, J. P. 305t
Dalton Gang 210, 278, 278t
Daly, Charles D. 300t, 301t
Daly, John J. 318t, 319t
Daly, Marcus 215
Daly, William D. 151t
"Daly's Reel" (song) 267t
Dalzell, John
   Congress membership 125t, 129t, 133t, 138t, 142t, 147t, 151t, 156t, 161t, 165t, 170t, 175t, 180t
Danbury Hatters Case (Supreme Court) (1908) 32
"Dance of the Hours" (song) 264t
Danford, Lorenzo 102t, 106t, 142t, 146t
Danforth, Henry G. 179t, 184t
Dangerous Classes of New York and Twenty Years Among Them, The (Charles Loring Brace) 364
Daniel, John W.
   Congress membership 122t, 125t, 130t, 134t, 139t, 143t, 148t, 152t, 157t, 161t, 166t, 171t, 175t
Daniel, William 25
Daniel and Florence Guggenheim Foundation 244
Daniel Guggenheim Fund 244
Daniell, Warren F. 132t
Daniels, Charles 137t, 142t
Daniels, Charles M. 313, 314t, 315t
Daniels, Milton J. 157t
Danish West Indies see Virgin Islands
"Danny Boy" (song) 268t
"Danny Deever" (song) 265t
"Daphnis et Chloé" (song) 267t
Dargan, George W. 117t, 121t, 125t, 129t
Darlington, Smedley 125t, 129t
Darragh, Archibald B. 154t, 159t, 164t, 168t
Darrall, Chester B. 100t, 104t, 111t
Darrow, Clarence 28, 208, 220, 241
"Dar's One More Ribber To Cross" (song) 264t
Daubert, Jake 292t, 293t
Daugherty, James A. 178t
Daughter of the Snows, A (Jack London) 270t
Davenport, Iowa 210
Davenport, Ira 120t
Davenport, James S. 170t, 180t, 185t
Davenport, Samuel A. 147t, 151t
Davenport, Stanley W. 151t
Davey, Robert C. 136t, 145t, 149t, 154t, 158t, 163t, 168t
David Harum (Edward Noyes Westcott) 270t
Davidson, Alexander C. 118t, 122t
Davidson, James H. 148t, 152t, 157t, 162t, 166t, 171t, 176t, 181t
Davidson, James O. 196t
Davidson, Robert C. 229t
Davidson, Robert H. M. 103t, 107t, 111t, 114t, 118t, 122t, 126t
Davies, Arthur B. 261, 262t
Davies, W. C. 318t
Davis, Charles R. 159t, 164t, 168t, 173t, 178t, 183t
Davis, Cushman K. 124t, 128t, 132t, 136t, 141t, 145t, 150t
Davis, D. F. 313t

Davis, Daniel F. 191t
Davis, David 104t, 107t, 110t–112t, 114t
Davis, Dwight F. 311, 312t
Davis, G. 286t
Davis, George R. 107t, 111t, 115t
Davis, H. 285t, 289t, 290t
Davis, Harry 280, 281t
Davis, Henry G. 31, 89t, 103t, 106t, 110t, 114t
Davis, Horace 103t, 107t
Davis, Jeff 167t, 171t, 176t, 189t
Davis, Jefferson 26
Davis, John 131t, 136t
Davis, John W. 181t, 186t, 195t, 226
Davis, Joseph J. 102t, 105t, 109t
Davis, Katherine 23
Davis, Lowndes H. 108t, 112t, 116t
Davis, Marguerite 273t
Davis, Ralph T. 301t
Davis, Robert T. 116t, 120t, 123t
Davis, Robert W. 144t, 149t, 153t, 158t
Davis, Thomas B. 166t
Davis, W. 310t
Davis Cup (tennis) 310, 311, 311t
Davison, George M. 145t
Davy, John M. 101t
"Davy Jones' Locker" (song) 266t
Dawbarn, W. F. 317t
Dawes, Beman G. 165t, 170t
Dawes, Henry L. 101t, 104t, 108t, 112t, 116t, 120t, 123t, 127t, 132t
Dawes, John W. 193t
Dawes, Rufus R. 113t
Dawes Commission 220
Dawes Severalty Act (1887) 14, 17, 26
Daws, Henry G. 93t
Dawson, Albert F. 163t, 167t, 172t
Dawson, Joe 282
Dawson, William 120t
Dawson, William M. O. 196t
Day, W. D. 318t, 323t
Day, William R. 95t
"Day Dreams" (song) 267t
Day Star (racehorse) 309t
Dayton, Alston G. 143t, 148t, 152t, 157t, 161t, 166t
Dayton, Ohio 34, 65, 220, 262t, 336t
Daytona Beach, Florida 207, 282
"dead man's hand" 223
Deadwood, South Dakota 223, 245, 278t
deafness 237
Deakin, E. 327t
Dean, Benjamin 104t
Dean, Dudley 299t
"Dearie" (song) 266t
De Armond, David A. 132t, 137t, 141t, 146t, 150t, 155t, 159t, 164t, 169t, 173t
"Dear Old Girl" (song) 265t
"Death and Transfiguration" (song) 264t
death rate 83
DeBoe, William J. 145t, 149t, 154t
De Bolt, Rezin A. 101t
de Bort, Léon-Philippe Teisserenc 274t
Debs, Eugene V. 241–2
   home state 209
   presidential election, 1900 30, 93t
   presidential election, 1904 31, 93t
   presidential election, 1908 32, 93t
   presidential election, 1912 33, 94t
   Pullman Strike 28
decathlon 17
Decker, Perl D. 184t
Deemer, Elias 156t, 161t, 165t
Deepwater Commission 228
Deere, John 225
Deering, Nathaniel C. 104t, 108t, 111t
De Forest, Henry S. 179t
De Forest, Lee 210
DeForest, Robert E. 130t, 135t
De Graffenreid, Reese C. 147t, 152t, 156t
degrees, university 259t
De Haven, John J. 126t
de Holomay, Zoltan 314t
Deitrick, Frederick S. 183t

Delahanty, Ed 293t
Delahanty, J. 288t
De La Matyr, Gilbert 107t
Delaney, T. F. 318t
De Lano, Milton 124t, 128t
Delaware 205–6 see also specific cities
   African Americans 75t, 88t
   Congressmen
      Forty-fourth 99t
      Forty-fifth 103t
      Forty-sixth 107t
      Forty-seventh 111t
      Forty-eighth 114t
      Forty-ninth 118t
      Fiftieth 122t
      Fifty-first 126t
      Fifty-second 130t
      Fifty-third 135t
      Fifty-fourth 140t
      Fifty-fifth 144t
      Fifty-sixth 148t
      Fifty-seventh 153t
      Fifty-eighth 158t
      Fifty-ninth 162t
      Sixtieth 167t
      Sixty-first 171t
      Sixty-second 176t
      Sixty-third 182t
   farms 36t
   governors 190t
   legal holidays 276t
   Native Americans 17t
   population 17t, 75t
   prisoners 335t
   railroad track 66t
   religion 88t
Delaware, Lackawanna & Western Railroad 48t
Delaware, Ohio 96
Delaware City, Ohio 90t
Delhi (racehorse) 310t
Deliverance, The (Ellen Glasgow) 270t
Dell, B. N. 313t
de Lôme, Enrique 29
DeMar, Clarence 329t
Demaree, A. 292t
Democracy and Social Ethics (Jane Addams) 237
Democracy (Henry Adams) 260, 269t
Democratic Free Silver Convention (1894) 28
Democratic Party
   Compromise of 1877 91, 92
   congressional elections
      1876 24
      1880 24
      1882 25
      1886 26
      1888 26
      1890 27
      1892 27
      1894 28
      1898 30
      1900 30
      1902 31
      1904 31
      1908 32
      1910 33
      1912 34
   House of Representatives composition 187t
   presidential conventions 89t
   presidential elections
      1876 90
      1880 24, 91t
      1884 25, 91t
      1888 26, 92t
      1892 27, 92t
      1896 29, 92t
      1900 30, 93t
      1904 31, 93t
      1908 32, 93t
      1912 33, 94t
   presidential elections 1876 91t
   Senate composition 187t
   whites-only primary elections 204
DeMotte, Mark L. 111t
Dempsey, Jack "Nonpareil" 296t
Denby, Edwin 164t, 168t, 173t
Deneen, Charles S. 190t
Denison, Dudley C. 102t, 106t
Denmark 30

Englebright, William F. 162t, 167t, 171t
Englehorn, Wesley T. 305t
English, James E. 99t
English, Thomas D. 132t, 137t
English, Warren B. 135t
English, William E. 115t
English, William H. 89t, 91t
Enid, Oklahoma 220
Enloe, Benjamin A. 125t, 129t, 134t, 138t
Enoch Pratt Free Public Library (Maryland) 212
Enochs, William H. 133t
"Entertainer, The" (song) 266t
environment 6–8
Epes, James F. 134t, 139t
Epes, Sydney P. 148t, 152t
Episcopalian Church 90t
equal protection guarantee 188
Erdman, Constantine J. 138t, 142t
Erickson, Egon 320t
Eric (racehorse) 310t
"Erie Canal" (song) 268t
Erie Railroad 48t, 56
Erikson, C. 331t
Ermentrout, Daniel 113t, 117t, 121t, 125t, 147t
Erne, Frank 296t
Errett, Russell 106t, 109t, 113t
Erwin, William W. 303t
Esch, John J. 152t, 157t, 162t, 166t, 171t, 176t, 181t, 186t
"España" (song) 264t
Essex City, New Jersey 90t
Estep, R. 310t
Esther (Henry Adams) 260
Estopinal, Albert 168t, 172t, 178t, 183t
"Estudiantina" (song) 264t
Ethan Allen (Larkin G. Mead sculpture) 269t
Ethan Frome (Edith Wharton) 260
ethnic voting 80, 89
Eugene, Oregon 221
Europeans, The (Henry James) 260, 269t
Eustis, James B. 100t, 104t, 119t, 123t, 127t
Evangelical Association 85t
Evans, Alvin 156t, 161t
Evans, H. Clay 129t
Evans, I. Newton 106t, 117t, 121t
Evans, James L. 100t, 104t
Evans, John G. 195t
Evans, John M. 184t
Evans, Lynden 177t
Evans, Walter 140t, 145t
Evans Jr., Charles 308t
Evansville, Indiana 209
Evarts, William B. 94t
Evarts, William M. 120t, 124t, 128t, 213
Evening Journal (Detroit newspaper) 29
Evening Post (New York City newspaper) 251
Evening World (New York City newspaper) 247
Everett, Robert W. 131t
Everett, Washington 225
Everett, William 136t
Everhart, James B. 117t, 121t
Evers, J. 284t, 286t–288t
"Everybody's Doing It Now" (song) 267t
Everybody's (journal) 250, 261
"Everybody Two-Step" (song) 268t
"Everybody Works But Father" (song) 266t, 270t
"Every Day Is Ladies' Day to Me" (song) 266t
"Every Little Bit Added to What You've Got Makes Just a Little Bit More" (song) 267t
"Every Little Movement" (song) 267t
Evins, John H. 106t, 110t, 113t, 117t
Evins, S. H. 328t
Ewart, Hamilton G. 128t
Ewing, John 293t
Ewing, Thomas 106t, 109t
Ewing, William L. 230t
Excursions of an Evolutionist (John Fiske) 269t
executions 26, 204
executive branch of government 188t *see also* president
"Exodusters" 9, 11, *11*, 210
explosions
  Cherry, Illinois 33
  Detroit, Michigan 29
  Hanna, Wyoming 32
  Jacobs Creek, Pennsylvania 32
  Maine (ship) 29
  Monongah, West Virginia 32
  Monongahela, Pennsylvania 32
  Scofield, Utah 30
exports 70, 70t, 71t
Eyck, Peter G. Ten 184t
"Eyes of Texas, The" (song) 266t

F

Fabrogou, C. 327t
Fair, James G. 112t, 116t, 120t
Fairbank, Arizona 279t
Fairbanks, Alaska 202
Fairbanks, Charles W.
  Congress membership 144t, 149t, 153t, 158t, 164t, 166t, 168t, 170t
  presidential election, 1904 31, 89t, 93t
  Theodore Roosevelt Administration 95t
Fairbanks, Douglas 205
Fairbanks, Horace 196t
Fairchild, Benjamin L. 142t
Fairchild, Charles S. 94t
Fairchild, George W. 169t, 174t, 179t, 184t
Fairfield, Vermont 96
Faison, John M. 179t, 185t
Faith Healer, The (William Vaughn Moody) 270t
Falconer, Jacob A. 186t
Fall, Albert B. 179t, 184t
Falling Rocket, The (James Abbott McNeill Whistler painting) 269t
Fall River, Massachusetts 27, 67t, 212, 259t
families 46, 62t, 341
Famous Players Films Co. 281t
Fancher, Frederick B. 194t
"Farewell, The" (song) 266t
Fargo, North Dakota 219
Faries, R. 325t
Faris, George W. 140t, 144t, 149t
Farley, James T. 107t, 110t, 114t
Farley, John H. 229t
Farmer, Fannie 260t
"Farmer in the Dell, The" (song) 264t
Farmer Labor Party 187t
farmers 70, 71, 92 *see also* agriculture; sharecroppers and tenant farmers
Farmers' Alliance 223
Farnham, Rosewell 196t
Farquhar, John M. 120t, 124t, 128t
Farr, Evarts W. 109t
Farr, John R. 180t, 185t
Farrell, D. 285t
Farrier, G. C. 327t
Farwell, Charles B. 100t, 111t, 119t, 123t, 126t
Farwell, Sewall S. 111t
"Fascination" (song) 266t
fashions 276
Fassett, J. Sloat 164t, 169t, 174t
Faulkner, Charles J. 103t, 125t, 130t, 134t, 139t, 143t, 148t
Favrot, George K. 168t
Fearing Jr., G. R. 326t, 327t
Featherstone, Lewis P. 126t
federal government *see also* Congress, U.S.; presidents; Supreme Court
  employees 61t
  expenditures 200t
  finances 199t
  legislation 343–5
  receipts 199t, 200t
  revenue sources 199t
Federal Reserve Act (1913) 71, 72
Federal Reserve System 34, 72
Feely, John J. 153t
Felix Campbell 124t
Fellows, John R. 133t, 137t
Felton, Charles N. 118t, 122t, 130t
Felton, Samuel M. 305t
Felton, William H. 100t, 103t, 107t
Fenton, Lucien J. 142t, 146t
Ferber, Edna 213
Ferdon, John W. 109t
Ferguson, Frank 262t
Ferguson, Thompson B. 194t
Fergusson, Harvey B. 179t, 184t
Fernald, Bert M. 191t
Fernow, Bernhard E. 26
Ferns, Rube 296t
Ferrell, Thomas M. 116t
Ferris, George 23
Ferris, H. 285t
Ferris, Scott 170t, 174t, 180t, 185t
Ferris, Woodbridge N. 192t
Ferry, Elisha P. 196t
Ferry, Orris S. 99t
Ferry, Thomas W. 99t, 101t–106t, 108t, 112t
Ferry and Clas (architectural firm) 259t
Fess, Simeon D. 185t
feuds 211, 278t, 333 *see also* Hatfield-McCoy Feud
Feuerbach, L. E. J. 321t
Ficken, H. E. 319t, 320t
Fiedler, William H. F. 116t
Field, David Dudley 101t
Field, Eugene 269t
Field, James G. 27, 92t
Field, Marshall 213, 231
Field, Scott 161t, 166t
Field, Stephen Johnson 213
Field, Walbridge A. 104t, 108t
Fielder, George B. 137t
Fielder, James F. 193t
Fields, William J. 177t, 183t
Fifer, Joseph W. 190t
Fifth Amendment 244
Filipino-Americans 78, 208
filterable viruses 273t
finance 54t, 70–2
financial panics 32, 56
Financier, The (Theodore Dreiser) 260, 271t
Financier and Finances of the American Revolution (William Graham Sumner) 252
Fincke, William M. 300t, 301t
Findlay, John V. L. 115t
Finer Ground, The (Henry James) 270t
Finerty, John F. 115t
"Finlandia" (song) 265t
Finlay, J. R. 328t
Finley, David E. 152t, 156t, 161t, 165t, 170t, 175t, 180t, 185t
Finley, Ebenezer B. 106t, 109t
Finley, Hugh F. 123t, 127t
Finley, Jesse J. 100t, 103t, 111t
"Firebird, The" (song) 267t
fires *see also* Triangle Fire (1910)
  Baltimore, Maryland 31, 212, 235
  Boston, Massachusetts 28
  Chelsea, Massachusetts 32
  Chicago, Illinois 28, 31, 209
  Cleveland, Ohio 32
  Coney Island, New York 32
  Harrisburg, Pennsylvania 29
  Hinckley, Minnesota 214
  Honolulu, Hawaii 208
  Jacksonville, Florida 30, 207
  Key West, Florida 207
  Milwaukee, Wisconsin 25, 27
  Minneapolis, Minnesota 28
  Mississippi River 26
  New York City 24, 27
  New York Harbor 31
  Pennsylvania 221
  Washington 225
1st Volunteer Cavalry *see* "Rough Riders"
First National Bank (Winnemucca, Nevada) 216
Fischer, Israel F. 142t, 146t
Fish, Hamilton 174t, 304t
Fishback, William P. 189t
Fisher, Carl 207
Fisher, Edwin P. 312t
Fisher, Horatio G. 109t, 113t
Fisher, King 278t
Fisher, Robert T. 304t, 305t
Fisher, S. H. 310t
Fisher, Spencer O. 120t
Fisher, Walter L. 95t
fishing industry 24, 50, *50*, 50t, 51t, 54t
Fishleigh, W. 319t, 327t
Fisk, Clifton B. 26, 92t
Fisk, James 225
Fiske, John 269t
Fiske, T. 327t
Fisk University (Nashville, Tennessee) 258
Fitch, Ashbel P. 124t, 128t, 133t, 137t
Fithian, George W. 126t, 131t, 135t
Fitler, Edwin H. 229t
Fitzgerald, John F. 141t, 145t, 150t, 229t, 233
Fitzgerald, John J. 151t, 155t, 160t, 164t, 169t, 174t, 179t, 184t
FitzHenry, Louis 182t
Fitzpatrick, Morgan C. 161t
Fitzpatrick, Thomas Y. 145t, 149t
Fitzsimmons, Bob 216, 296t
Five Points Gang 83
Five Wounds 246
Flack, William H. 160t, 164t
Flag Day (holiday) 24, 276t
Flagg, Ernest 263t
Flanagan, De Witt C. 155t
Flanagan, Edward J. 216
Flanagan, J. J. 322t
Fleeger, George W. 121t
Fleischer, S. 330t
Fleming, A. Brooks 196t
Fleming, Barbara 313t
Fleming, Francis P. 190t
Fleming, William B. 103t
Fleming, William H. 144t, 149t, 153t
Fletcher, A. 290t–292t
Fletcher, Allen M. 196t
Fletcher, Duncan U. 172t, 177t, 182t
Fletcher, Loren 136t, 141t, 145t, 150t, 154t, 164t
Flick, Elmer 293t
Flick, James P. 127t, 131t
"Flight of the Bumble Bee" (song) 266t
Flint, Frank P. 162t, 167t, 171t
Flint, Weston 259t
Flipper, Henry O. 24
Flocarline (racehorse) 310t
Flood, Henry D. 157t, 161t, 166t, 171t, 175t, 181t, 186t
Flood, Thomas S. 124t, 128t
floods 4–5, 4t *see also* Johnstown, Pennsylvania
  Dayton, Ohio 34
  Kansas, Missouri, and Des Moines rivers 31
  Ohio 220
  Texas 26
Florida 206–7 *see also specific cities*
  African Americans 75t, 88t
  "carpetbag" government ended 24
  Compromise of 1877 92
  Congressmen
    Forty-fourth 100t
    Forty-fifth 103t
    Forty-sixth 107t
    Forty-seventh 111t
    Forty-eighth 114t
    Forty-ninth 118t
    Fiftieth 122t
    Fifty-first 126t
    Fifty-second 130t
    Fifty-third 135t
    Fifty-fourth 140t
    Fifty-fifth 144t
    Fifty-sixth 149t
    Fifty-seventh 153t
    Fifty-eighth 158t
    Fifty-ninth 162t
    Sixtieth 167t
    Sixty-first 172t
    Sixty-second 177t
    Sixty-third 182t
  farms 36t
  governors 190t
  gunfights 277t
  legal holidays 276t
  Native Americans 17t, 26
  population 17t, 75t
  presidential election, 1876 24
  prisoners 335t
  public lands 9t
  railroad track 66t
  religion 88t
Flower, Roswell P. 112t, 128t, 194t
Floyd, Charles M. 193t
Floyd, John C. 162t, 167t, 171t, 176t, 181t
flu *see* influenza
Flye, Edwin 100t
Flynn, John 293t
Focht, Benjamin K. 170t, 175t, 180t
Foelker, Otto G. 169t, 174t
Foerderer, Robert H. 156t
Folger, Charles J. 94t
Folk, Joseph W. 192t
Folkways (William Graham Sumner) 252
Follett, John F. 117t
Folsom, Frances 26
Fonso (racehorse) 309t
food consumption 45t
football *297*, 297–9, 299t–307t
Foot Ball Club (Harvard) 297
Foote, A. E. 313t
Foote Jr., Wallace T. 142t, 146t
Foraker, Joseph B. 146t, 151t, 156t, 160t, 165t, 170t, 194t
Foran, Martin A. 117t, 121t, 125t
Forbes, Robert W. 303t
Ford, George 119t
Ford, Henry 28, 29, 213, 235, 242–3, 282
Ford, Henry P. 229t
Ford, J. H. 327t
Ford, M. W. 316t, 317t, 320t, 322t
Ford, Melbourne H. 124t, 132t
Ford, Nicholas 108t, 112t
Ford, Robert 25
Ford, Timothy 329t
Ford Motor Company 54, *55*, *70*, 213, 242
Fordney, Joseph W. 150t, 154t, 159t, 164t, 168t, 173t, 178t, 183t
foreign-born Americans 80t, 257t, 333t
foreign debt 199t
foreign policy 345–8
forest clearing 52t
Forester (racehorse) 310t
Foresters of America 275t
forest fires 214
Forest Hills, New York 311
forest products 71t
Forest Reserve Act of 1905 7
forestry 54t
Forestry, Division of (Department of Agriculture) 26
"Forgotten" (song) 265t
Forman, William S. 126t, 131t, 135t
Fornes, Charles V. 169t, 174t, 179t
Forney, William H. 99t, 103t, 107t, 110t, 114t, 118t, 122t, 126t, 130t
"For Old Times' Sake" (song) 266t
Forsyth, James 20
Forsythe, Albert P. 107t
Fort, Greenbury L. 100t, 104t, 107t
Fort, John Franklin 193t
Fort Buford, North Dakota 17
Fort Hays, Kansas 278t
Fort Meyers, Florida 242
Fort Pickens (Pensacola, Florida) 243
Fort Riley, Kansas 245
Fort Robinson, Nebraska 216
Fort Sam Houston, Texas 224
Fort Sill, Oklahoma 243
Fort Smith, Arkansas 204
Fort Summer, New Mexico 218
"Fortune Teller, The" (song) 265t
Fort Wayne, Indiana 209
Fort Worth, Texas 223, 262t, 278t
"Forty-five Minutes from Broadway" (song) 266t
Forty-five Minutes from Broadway (theatrical production) 270t
forward pass (football) 297–9
Foss, Eugene N. 173t, 192t

Goldfogle, Henry M. 160t, 164t, 169t, 174t, 179t, 184t
Goldsborough, Phillips L. 191t
Goldsmith, Fred 293t
Goldthwaite, George T. 99t
"Gold Will Buy Most Anything But a True Girl's Heart" (song) 265t
golf 307, 308t, 309t
Goliad, Texas 4t
"Golliwogg's Cake Walk" (song) 267t
"Golondrina, La" (song) 264t, 267t
Golozier, Julius 135t
Gompers, Samuel 23, 26, 55, 220, 221, 243–4
Gooch, Daniel L. 154t, 158t
Good, James W. 172t, 177t, 182t
"Goodbye, Boys" (song) 268t
"Good-bye, Eliza Jane" (song) 266t
"Good-bye, Flo" (song) 266t
"Goodbye, Little Girl, Goodbye" (song) 266t
"Goodbye, My Lady Love" (song) 266t
"Goodbye, My Lover, Goodbye" (song) 264t
"Goodbye, Rose" (song) 267t
"Goodbye Dolly Gray" (song) 266t
Goodbye My Fancy (Walt Whitman poems) 269t
Goode Jr., John 103t, 106t, 110t
Goodell, David H. 193t
Good Friday (holiday) 276t
Goodhue, Bertram 259t, 262t
Goodin, John R. 100t
Gooding, Frank R. 190t
Goodnight, Isaac H. 127t, 131t, 136t
"Goodnight, Little Girl, Goodnight" (song) 265t
Goodwin, Forrest 183t
Goodwin, L. B. 314t, 315t
Goodwin, William S. 176t, 181t
Goodwin Jr., W. H. 317t, 325t
Goodwyn, Albert T. 139t
"Goo-Goos" 228
Goose, R. 309t
Gordon, George W. 170t, 175t, 180t
Gordon, James 173t
Gordon, John B.
  Confederate Veterans organization 26
  Congress membership 100t, 103t, 107t, 131t, 135t, 140t
  Georgia governor 190t
Gordon, Robert B. 151t, 156t
Gordon, William 185t
Gordon Park Bathing Pavilion (Cleveland, Ohio) 360
Gore, George 293t
Gore, Thomas P. 170t, 174t, 180t, 185t
Gorgas, William Crawford 202, 244
Gorman, Arthur P.
  Congress membership 112t, 115t, 119t, 123t, 127t, 132t, 136t, 141t, 145t, 156t, 163t
Gorman, George E. 182t
Gorman, James S. 132t, 136t
"Gospel of Wealth, The" (Andrew Carnegie article) 238, 356–7
Gotch, Frank 329–30
Gould, Jay 25, 27, 55, 310
Gould, Samuel W. 178t
Goulden, Joseph A. 160t, 164t, 169t, 174t, 184t
Gourley, H. J. 229t
Goux, Jules 282
government and politics 89–201
governors see specific state
"Go Way Back and Sit Down" (song) 266t
Grace, William R. 229t
Grady, Benjamin F. 133t, 137t
Graff, Joseph V.
  Congress membership 140t, 144t, 149t, 153t, 158t, 163t, 167t, 172t
graft 365–6
Graham, Archibald 308t
Graham, George S. 185t
Graham, James M. 172t, 177t, 182t
Graham, John H. 137t

Graham, William H. 147t, 151t, 156t, 165t, 170t, 175t
grain 50t
Grand Army of the Republic (GAR) 197
"grandfather" clauses 197, 198t
"Grandfather's Clock" (song) 264t, 269t
Grand Forks, North Dakota 219
Grand Rapids, Michigan 213, 259t
Grand Trunk of Canada Railroad 48t
Grange Movement 46
Granger, Daniel L. D. 161t, 165t, 170t
Granger, Miles T. 122t
Grant, A. G. 327t
Grant, Alex 318t, 319t, 323t, 326t
Grant, E. 292t
Grant, Hugh J. 229t
Grant, James B. 189t
Grant, John G. 174t
Grant, R. 318t
Grant, Ulysses S. 22, 25, 188t, 220, 246
Grant, Wylie C. 312t, 313t
Grant County, Wisconsin 13
Graves, Alexander 116t
Graves, John Temple 32
Gray, Finly H. 177t, 182t
Gray, G. R. 321t
Gray, George 118t, 122t, 126t, 130t, 135t, 140t, 144t
Gray, H. 318t
Gray, Horace 188t
Gray, Isaac P. 190t
Graydon, Thomas H. 301t, 302t
Great Barrington, Massachusetts 242
Great Blizzard (1888) 218
Great Britain 26, 30, 78t, 80t, 311t
Great Falls, Montana 215
Great Lakes 49t, 50t
Great Northern Railroad 48t, 214, 225
Great Sioux Reservation 223
Great Southern Tornado Outbreak (1884) 2, 3, 4t, 25
Great Train Robbery, The (film) 270t, 281t
Great White Fleet 32
Greek-Americans 78
Greek Orthodox Church 78
Greek Orthodox (Hellenic) Church 85t
Greeley, Horace 217
Green, Dorothy 312t
Green, Henry D. 151t, 156t
Green, R. W. 325t
Green, Robert S. 120t, 193t
Green, Samuel A. 229t
Green, Wharton J. 117t, 121t
Green, William R. 177t, 182t
Greenback-Labor Party 24
Greenback Party 24, 25, 91t, 187t
greenbacks 24
Greene, Frank L. 181t, 186t
Greene, William L. 146t
Greene, William S.
  Congress membership 145t, 150t, 154t, 159t, 163t, 168t, 173t, 178t, 183t
Green Fields and Running Brooks (James Whitcomb Riley poems) 270t
Greenhalge, Frederick T. 127t, 192t
greenhouse effect 274t
Greenleaf, Halbert S. 116t, 133t
Greenman, Edward W. 124t
Greenville, South Carolina 222
Greenwich, Connecticut 307
Greenwich Mean Time 69
Greer, T. T. 194t
Gregg, Alexander W. 161t, 166t, 170t, 175t, 180t, 186t
Gregg, Curtis H. 180t
Gregg, S. A. 293t
Gregory, William 195t
Grenada (racehorse) 310t
Gresham, Walter 139t
Gresham, Walter Q. 94t, 95t
Grey, Zane 220, 270t, 271t
Grey Wolves Gang 228

Grief or Death, or Peace of God (Augustus Saint-Gaudens sculpture) 269t
Griest, William W. 175t, 180t, 185t
Griffin, Daniel J. 184t
Griffin, H. 310t
Griffin, Levi T. 136t
Griffin, Michael 139t, 143t, 148t
Griffith, Clark 283t, 293t
Griffith, D. W. 211, 281
Griffith, Francis M. 144t, 149t, 153t, 158t
Griggs, James M. 144t, 149t, 153t, 158t, 162t, 167t, 172t
Griggs, John W. 95t, 193t
Grim, H. 331t
Grimes, Thomas W. 123t, 126t
Grimes, William 194t
Grinnell, Iowa 4t
Griscom, Frances C. 309t
Griswold, Matthew 133t, 142t
"Grizzly Bear" (song) 267t
groceries 63t
Gronna, Asle J. 165t, 169t, 174t, 179t, 185t
Groome, James B. 108t, 112t, 115t
Grosvenor, Charles H.
  Congress membership 121t, 125t, 129t, 138t, 142t, 147t, 151t, 156t, 160t, 165t
Grout, Josiah 196t
Grout, William W.
  Congress membership 114t, 122t, 125t, 129t, 134t, 139t, 143t, 147t, 152t
Grover, La Fayette 106t, 109t, 113t, 194t
Grow, Galusha A. 138t, 142t, 147t, 151t, 156t
Grummond, S. B. 229t
Grumpelt, Henry 320t
Grumpelt, J. H. 324t
Guam 29, 30
Gudger Jr., James M. 160t, 165t, 179t, 185t
Guenther, Richard W. 114t, 118t, 122t, 126t
Guernsey, Frank E. 168t, 173t, 178t, 183t
Guggenheim, Daniel 244
Guggenheim, Simon 167t, 171t, 176t
guidance counselors 257
Guild Jr., Curtis 192t
Guiteau, Charles J. 25, 96, 98, 98
Gulick, Charlotte and Luther Halsey 208
Gundersen, J. 331t
gunfighters and gunfights 277–9, 277t–279t
Gunn, A. B. 322t
Gunn, James 144t
guns 279
Gunter, Thomas M. 99t, 103t, 107t, 110t
Guthrie, George W. 230t
Guthrie, Oklahoma 9, 10, 220
"Gypsy Love Song" (song) 265t

H

Haberle, John 262t
Hackenschmidt, George 330
Hackett, Harold H. 312t, 313t
Hackett, Richard N. 169t
Hackney, Thomas 169t
Hadley, Herbert S. 192t
Hadley, William F. L. 140t
Haff, C. B. 317t, 325t
Hager, Alva L. 136t, 140t, 145t
Hagerma, Herbert J. 193t
Hagerstown, Maryland 212
Haggott, Warren A. 167t
Hagood, Johnson 195t
Hahn, Archie 317t
Hahn, E. 286t
Hahn, Michael 119t
Haigh, J. E. 319t, 325t
Hail, H. J. 323t
Hail, W. J. 323t
Hainer, Eugene J. 137t, 141t
Haines, Charles D. 137t
Haines, Elmer 209
Hale, Eugene

Congress membership 100t, 104t, 111t, 115t, 119t, 123t, 127t, 131t, 136t, 141t, 145t, 149t, 154t, 159t, 163t, 168t, 173t
Hale, George Ellery 272
Hale, John B. 120t
Hale, Nathan W. 166t, 170t
Hale, Perry T. W. 301t
Hale, Samuel W. 193t
Hale, William 197t
Half Time (racehorse) 310t
Hall, Asaph 272
Hall, Benton J. 119t
Hall, C. 291t
Hall, Charles Martin 220
Hall, Darwin S. 128t
Hall, Drew 259t
Hall, G. Stanley 23
Hall, James K. P. 151t, 156t
Hall, John A. 300t
Hall, John W. 190t
Hall, Joshua G. 109t, 112t
Hall, Luther Egbert 191t
Hall, Miriam 312t
Hall, Norman 125t
Hall, Osee M. 132t, 136t
Hall, Philo 170t
Hall, Uriel S. 137t, 141t
Hall, Valentine G. 312t
Halley's Comet 33
Hallock, H. L. 320t
Hall of Fame (New York City) 30
Halloween (holiday) 276t
Hallowell, Edwin 133t
Hallowell, Frank W. 299t
Hallowell, John W. 300t, 301t
Halma (racehorse) 309t
Halpin, T. J. 317t
Halpin, W. 320t
Halsell, John E. 115t, 119t
Halstead, J. P. 326t
Halstead, William Steward 272
Halterman, Frederick 142t
Halvorson, Kittel 132t
Hamer, Thomas R. 172t
Hamill, James A. 169t, 174t, 179t, 184t
Hamilton, Andrew H. 100t, 104t
Hamilton, Billy 293t
Hamilton, Charles M. 184t
Hamilton, Daniel W. 167t
Hamilton, Earl 294t
Hamilton, Edward L.
  Congress membership 145t, 150t, 154t, 159t, 164t, 168t, 173t, 178t, 183t
Hamilton, John M. 181t, 190t
Hamilton, John T. 131t
Hamilton, Morgan C. 102t
Hamilton, Robert 101t
Hamilton, W. F. 317t
Hamilton, William T. 191t
Hamilton City, Ohio 90t
Hamlin, Courtney W. 159t, 169t, 173t, 178t, 184t
Hamlin, Hannibal 100t, 104t, 108t
hammer throw 321t, 322t
Hammond, G. M. 325t
Hammond, John 109t, 112t
Hammond, Nathaniel J. 107t, 111t, 115t, 119t
Hammond, Thomas 135t
Hammond, Winfield S. 168t, 173t, 178t, 183t
Hampton, Wade
  Congress membership 110t, 113t, 117t, 121t, 125t, 129t
  South Carolina governor 195t, 222
Hampton Institute 15, 23
Hampton Roads, Virginia 32
Hanback, Lewis 115t, 119t
Hancock, John 102t, 118t
Hancock, Winfield S. 24, 89t, 91t
"Handful of Earth from Mother's Grave, A" (song) 264t
"Handicap, The" (song) 265t
"Hands Across the Sea" (song) 265t
"Hand That Rocks the Cradle, The" (song) 265t
Handy, H. J. 314t, 315t
Handy, Levin I. 144t

Handy, W. C. 202
Hanford, Benjamin 31, 32
Hanlon, Edward H. 283t
Hanly, J. Frank 140t, 190t
Hanna, John 104t
Hanna, Louis B. 174t, 179t
Hanna, Marcus A. 97, 146t, 151t, 156t, 160t, 220, 244
Hanna, Wyoming 32
Hanover (racehorse) 310t
Hansbrough, Henry C.
  Congress membership 129t, 133t, 137t, 142t, 146t, 151t, 155t, 160t, 165t, 169t
Hansell, Ellen F. 311t, 312t
Hansen, B. 331t
Happeny, W. 321t, 324t
"Happy Birthday to You" (song) 265t
"Happy Days in Dixie" (song) 265t
Haralson, Jeremiah 99t
Harbor Springs, Minnesota 332
Hardeman, Thomas 115t
Hardenbergh, Augustus A. 101t, 105t, 112t
Hardin, Charles H. 192t
Hardin, John Wesley 278t
Harding, H. T. 326t
Harding, J. Eugene 170t
Hardwick, Thomas W. 158t, 162t, 167t, 172t, 177t, 182t
hardwoods 52t
Hardy, Alexander M. 140t
Hardy, John 112t, 116t
Hardy, Rufus 170t, 175t, 180t, 186t
Hare, Darius D. 133t, 138t
Hare, Silas 125t, 129t
Hare, T. Truxton 300t, 301t
Hargis, Ben 211
Hargis-Cockrill Feud 211
Harlan, Edwin H. W. 303t
Harlan, John Marshall 188t, 211, 244
Harley, Kate C. 309t
Harmer, Alfred C.
  Congress membership Forty-fifth 106t, Forty-sixth 109t, Forty-seventh 113t, Forty-eighth 117t, Forty-ninth 121t, Fiftieth 125t, Fifty-first 129t, Fifty-second 133t, Fifty-third 138t, Fifty-fourth 142t, Fifty-fifth 147t, Fifty-sixth 151t
Harmer, W. 325t
Harmon, James 95t
Harmon, Judson 194t
Harnett, William Michael 262t, 269t
Harold (racehorse) 310t
Harper, Arthur C. 229t
Harper, William Rainey 220
Harper's Weekly (magazine) 282
Harries, William H. 132t
"Harrigan" (song) 266t
Harriman, H. M. 308t
Harriman, Job 30
Harriman Jr., O. 326t
Harris, Andrew L. 194t
Harris, Benjamin W. 101t, 104t, 108t, 112t
Harris, Charles K. 27, 270t
Harris, Christopher C. 181t
Harris, Dick 202
Harris, E. 330t
Harris, Henry R. 100t, 103t, 119t
Harris, Henry S. 112t
Harris, Isham G.
  Congress membership Forty-fifth 106t, Forty-sixth 109t, Forty-seventh 113t, Forty-eighth 117t, Forty-ninth 121t, Fiftieth 125t, Fifty-first 129t, Fifty-second 134t, Fifty-third 135t, 136t, 138t, Fifty-fourth 143t, Fifty-fifth 147t
Harris, Joel Chandler 207, 269t
Harris, John 280t, 281t
Harris, John T. 103t, 106t, 110t
Harris, Robert O. 178t
Harris, Stephen R. 142t
Harris, William A. 136t, 145t, 149t, 154t
Harris, William T. 255
Harrisburg, Pennsylvania 29, 221
Harrison, Benjamin 90t, 96–7

Madden, Martin B. 163*t*, 167*t*, 172*t*, 177*t*, 182*t*
Maddock, J. H. 321*t*
Maddox, John W. 135*t*, 140*t*, 144*t*, 149*t*, 153*t*, 158*t*
Maddox, Nicholas 289*t*, 294*t*
Madison, Edmond H. 168*t*, 172*t*, 177*t*
Madison, Wisconsin 226
Madison Square Garden (New York City) 298
Maffett, James T. 125*t*
Magee, R. P. 314*t*
Magee, Sherwood 293*t*
Magee, William A. 230*t*
Maggie: A Girl of the Streets (Stephen Crane) 260, 269*t*
"Maggie Murphy's Home" (song) 264*t*
Magner, Thomas F. 128*t*, 133*t*, 137*t*
Magoffin, C. F. 326*t*
Magoon, Henry S. 103*t*
Magruder, D. L. 312*t*
Maguire, James G. 135*t*, 139*t*, 144*t*
Maguire, John A. 173*t*, 179*t*, 184*t*
Maguire, Matthew 29
Mahan, Alfred Thayer 260, 269*t*
Mahan, Bryan F. 182*t*
Mahan, Edward W. 305*t*
Mahany, Rowland B. 142*t*, 146*t*
Maher, James P. 179*t*, 184*t*
Mahmout, Yussif 329
Mahon, Thaddeus M. 138*t*, 142*t*, 147*t*, 151*t*, 156*t*, 161*t*, 165*t*
Mahone, William 114*t*, 118*t*, 122*t*, 225
Mahoney, Peter P. 121*t*, 124*t*
Mahoney, William F. 153*t*, 158*t*
Mahool, J. Barry 229*t*
"Maiden with the Dreamy Eyes, The" (song) 266*t*
mail-order business 46, *46*
mail service *see* postal service
Maine 211–12 *see also specific cities*
  African Americans 75*t*, 88*t*
  camping *332*
  charcoal pig iron production 53*t*
  Congressmen
    Forty-fourth 100*t*
    Forty-fifth 104*t*
    Forty-sixth 108*t*
    Forty-seventh 111*t*
    Forty-eighth 115*t*
    Forty-ninth 119*t*
    Fiftieth 123*t*
    Fifty-first 127*t*
    Fifty-second 131*t*
    Fifty-third 136*t*
    Fifty-fourth 141*t*
    Fifty-fifth 145*t*
    Fifty-sixth 149*t*
    Fifty-seventh 154*t*
    Fifty-eighth 159*t*
    Fifty-ninth 163*t*
    Sixtieth 168*t*
    Sixty-first 173*t*
    Sixty-second 178*t*
    Sixty-third 183*t*
  farms 36*t*
  governors 191*t*
  legal holidays 276*t*
  Native Americans 17*t*
  population 17*t*, 75*t*
  prisoners 335*t*
  railroad track 66*t*
  religion 88*t*
Maine (ship) 29
Main-Travelled Roads (Hamlin Garland stories) 243, 269*t*
Maish, Levi 102*t*, 106*t*, 125*t*, 129*t*
Majors, Thomas J. 105*t*
malaria 76, 201
Malby, George R. 169*t*, 174*t*, 179*t*
Malcomson, Joe 319*t*
Mallory, Stephen R.
  Congress membership 130*t*, 135*t*, 144*t*, 149*t*, 153*t*, 158*t*, 162*t*, 167*t*
Maloney, Joseph P. 30
Malster, William T. 229*t*
Manahan, James 183*t*
Manchester, New Hampshire 217, 259*t*
Mandel, C. S. 326*t*
Manderson, Charles F.
  Congress membership 116*t*, 120*t*, 124*t*, 126*t*, 128*t*, 130*t*, 132*t*, 134*t*–138*t*
"Mandy Lee" (song) 265*t*
Manhattan Bridge (New York City) 33, 273*t*
Manila, Battle of (Philippines, 1898) 29
Mann, J. M. 328*t*
Mann, James R.
  Congress membership 144*t*, 149*t*, 153*t*, 158*t*, 163*t*, 167*t*, 172*t*, 177*t*, 182*t*
  Mann Act against prostitution 338
  minority leader, House of Representatives, 1899-1919 99*t*
Mann, William H. 196*t*
Mann Act (1910) 33, 34, 338
Manning, Daniel 94*t*
Manning, Vannoy H. 105*t*, 108*t*, 112*t*
Manning brothers 278*t*
Mansur, Charles H. 124*t*, 128*t*, 132*t*
"Man That Broke the Bank at Monte Carlo, The" (song) 265*t*
Mantle, Lee 137*t*, 141*t*, 146*t*
Manuel (racehorse) 309*t*
manufacturing 48*t*, 54*t*, 57*t*, 61*t*
Manvel, H. E. 318*t*
Man Who Looks Around (Mandan Indian) *15*
Mapes, C. H. 327*t*
Mapes, Carl E. 183*t*
Mapes, H. 326*t*
maple 52*t*
"Maple Leaf Rag" (song) 265*t*, 270*t*
Marble, Sebastian S. 191*t*
"Marcheta" (song) 268*t*
"March of the Dwarfs" (song) 264*t*
"March of the Toys, The" (song) 266*t*
March Slav (Tchaikovsky composition) 264*t*
Marconi, Guglielmo 273*t*
Marcus, Erna 313*t*
Mares of Diomedes (Gutzon Borglum sculpture) 270*t*
Marganes, F. 331*t*
Margrave (racehorse) 310*t*
Marianna Mine (Monongahela, Pennsylvania) 32
Marine Corps, U.S. 27–9, 32, 33, 200*t*
Markham, Edwin 221
Markham, Henry H. 118*t*, 189*t*
Marks, Albert S. 195*t*
Mark Twain, A Biography (Albert Bigelow Paine) 271*t*
Marmaduke, John S. 192*t*
Marmon (automobile) 282
Marquand, John P. 206
Marquard, R. 284*t*, 290*t*–292*t*
Marquard, Rube 293*t*
marriage 75*t*
Marsh, Benjamin F.
  Congress membership 104*t*, 107*t*, 111*t*, 135*t*, 140*t*, 144*t*, 149*t*, 158*t*
Marsh, Othniel Charles 272
Marshal, Thomas R. 190*t*
Marshall, Andrew 302*t*
Marshall, George A. 147*t*
Marshall, J. W. 327*t*
Marshall, James W. 139*t*, 204
Marshall, Thomas 94*t*
Marshall, Thomas F. 155*t*, 160*t*, 165*t*, 169*t*
Marshall, Thomas R. 89*t*, 181*t*, 182*t*, 184*t*, 186*t*
"Marshes of Glynn, The" (Sidney Lanier poem) 269*t*
Mars (planet) 272
Martin, Augustus N. 127*t*, 131*t*, 135*t*
Martin, Augustus P. 229*t*
Martin, Benjamin F. 106*t*, 110*t*
Martin, Charles H. 142*t*, 146*t*
Martin, Eben W. 156*t*, 161*t*, 165*t*, 170*t*, 175*t*, 180*t*, 185*t*
Martin, Edward L. 107*t*, 111*t*
Martin, Homer 262*t*
Martin, J. 309*t*
Martin, John 136*t*
Martin, John A. 171*t*, 176*t*, 191*t*
Martin, John M. 118*t*
Martin, Joseph J. 109*t*
Martin, Lewis J. 184*t*
Martin, Mrs. G. M. 309*t*
Martin, Robert 194*t*
Martin, Thomas S.
  Congress membership 143*t*, 148*t*, 152*t*, 157*t*, 161*t*, 166*t*, 171*t*, 175*t*, 181*t*, 186*t*
Martin, W. 317*t*
Martin, William H. 125*t*, 129*t*
Martine, James E. 179*t*, 184*t*
Marvel, Joshua H. 190*t*
Marvin, Francis 137*t*
Marx, Oscar B. 229*t*
Maryland 212 *see also specific cities*
  African Americans 75*t*, 88*t*
  charcoal pig iron production 53*t*
  Congressmen
    Forty-fourth 101*t*
    Forty-fifth 104*t*
    Forty-sixth 108*t*
    Forty-seventh 112*t*
    Forty-eighth 115*t*
    Forty-ninth 119*t*
    Fiftieth 123*t*
    Fifty-first 127*t*
    Fifty-second 132*t*
    Fifty-third 136*t*
    Fifty-fourth 141*t*
    Fifty-fifth 145*t*
    Fifty-sixth 150*t*
    Fifty-seventh 154*t*
    Fifty-eighth 159*t*
    Fifty-ninth 163*t*
    Sixtieth 168*t*
    Sixty-first 173*t*
    Sixty-second 178*t*
    Sixty-third 183*t*
  farms 36*t*
  governors 191*t*
  horse racing 309
  legal holidays 276*t*
  Native Americans 17*t*
  population 17*t*, 75*t*
  prisoners 335*t*
  railroad track 66*t*
  religion 88*t*
Maryland Women's Suffrage Association 212
"Mary's a Grand Old Name" (song) 266*t*
Mason, Joseph 109*t*, 113*t*
Mason, William E. 123*t*, 127*t*, 144*t*, 149*t*, 153*t*
Massachusetts 212–13 *see also specific cities*
  African Americans 75*t*, 88*t*
  charcoal pig iron production 53*t*
  Congressmen
    Forty-fourth 101*t*
    Forty-fifth 104*t*
    Forty-sixth 108*t*
    Forty-seventh 112*t*
    Forty-eighth 116*t*
    Forty-ninth 120*t*
    Fiftieth 123*t*
    Fifty-first 127*t*
    Fifty-second 132*t*
    Fifty-third 136*t*
    Fifty-fourth 141*t*
    Fifty-fifth 145*t*
    Fifty-sixth 150*t*
    Fifty-seventh 154*t*
    Fifty-eighth 159*t*
    Fifty-ninth 163*t*
    Sixtieth 168*t*
    Sixty-first 173*t*
    Sixty-second 178*t*
    Sixty-third 183*t*
  farms 36*t*
  fashions and role models 276
  governors 192*t*
  legal holidays 276*t*
  Native Americans 17*t*
  population 17*t*, 75*t*
  prisoners 335*t*
  railroad track 66*t*
  religion 88*t*
Massey, William A. 179*t*
Massey, Zachary D. 175*t*
Masterman (racehorse) 310*t*
Masters, Edgar Lee 209, 210
Masterson, Bat 278*t*
Matchett, Charles H. 27, 29, 92*t*
mathematics 272
Mathews, Henry M. 196*t*
Mathewson, Christy 284*t*, 286*t*, 290*t*–293*t*
Mathey, D. 313*t*
Matson, Courtland C. 111*t*, 115*t*, 119*t*, 123*t*
Matthews, Charles 180*t*
Matthews, Claude 190*t*
Matthews, Matty 296*t*
Matthews, Stanley 106*t*, 188*t*
Matthews Jr., Nathan 229*t*
Maupas, Emile 329
Maury, Matthew Fountaine 225
Maxey, Samuel B. 102*t*, 106*t*, 110*t*, 114*t*, 118*t*, 122*t*
Maxim, Hiram and Hudson 212
"Maxim's" (song) 266*t*
Maxwell, James Clerk 274*t*
Maxwell, Samuel 146*t*
May, Mitchell 151*t*
Maybury, J. H. 317*t*
Maybury, William C. 116*t*, 120*t*, 229*t*
Mayham, Stephen L. 105*t*
Maynard, Harry L. 157*t*, 161*t*, 166*t*, 171*t*, 175*t*
Maynard, Horace 94*t*
Mayo, Robert M. 118*t*
Mayo, William and Charles 213, 246–7, 272
Mayo Clinic (Rochester, Minnesota) 213, 247, 272
mayors 228*t*–230*t*
Mays, Dannitte H. 172*t*, 177*t*
"Mazel Tov" (song) 265*t*
McAdoo, William 116*t*, 120*t*, 124*t*, 128*t*
McAfee, J. 331*t*
McAfee, M. 331*t*
McAleenan, Arthur 315*t*
McAleer, Owen C. 229*t*
McAleer, William 133*t*, 138*t*, 147*t*, 151*t*
McAlester, Oklahoma 220
McAndrews, James 153*t*, 158*t*, 182*t*
McAteer, Myrtle 312*t*
McBride, George W. 142*t*, 147*t*, 151*t*
McBride, Henry 196*t*
McBride, Malcolm L. 301*t*
McCaine, Helen 259*t*
McCall, Jack 245
McCall, John E. 143*t*
McCall, Samuel W.
  Congress membership 136*t*, 141*t*, 145*t*, 150*t*, 154*t*, 159*t*, 163*t*, 168*t*, 173*t*, 178*t*
McCallim, William 229*t*
McCanles Gang 278*t*
McCarthy, John H. 128*t*
McCarthy, John J. 159*t*, 164*t*
McCarthy, William C. 229*t*
McCawley, Charles G. 200*t*
McClammy, Charles W. 125*t*, 128*t*
McCleary, James T. 136*t*, 141*t*, 145*t*, 150*t*, 154*t*, 159*t*, 164*t*
McClellan, Charles A. O. 127*t*, 131*t*
McClellan, George 184*t*
McClellan, George B. 142*t*, 146*t*, 151*t*, 155*t*, 160*t*, 193*t*, 229*t*
McClung, Lee 299*t*
McClure, Addison S. 113*t*, 142*t*
McClure, Samuel S. 261
McClure's (magazine) 250, 251, 261
McCluskie, Arthur 278*t*
McCoid, Moses A. 108*t*, 111*t*, 115*t*
McColuum, Elmer 273*t*
McComas, Louis E. 115*t*, 119*t*, 123*t*, 127*t*, 150*t*, 154*t*, 159*t*
McConnell, William J. 126*t*, 190*t*
McCook, Anson G. 105*t*, 109*t*, 113*t*
McCord, Myron H. 130*t*, 189*t*
McCormick, Cyrus Hall 225
McCormick, Henry C. 125*t*, 129*t*
McCormick, James 303*t*
McCormick, Jim 291*t*–293*t*
McCormick, John W. 117*t*
McCormick, Nelson B. 145*t*
McCormick, Richard C. 142*t*
McCormick, Vance 299*t*
McCoy, Joseph G. 279
McCoy, Kid 296*t*
McCoy, Walter I. 179*t*, 184*t*
McCoy-Hatfield Feud *see* Hatfield-McCoy Feud
McCracken, J. C. 328*t*
McCracken, Josiah H. 301*t*
McCrary, George W. 94*t*, 100*t*
McCreary, George D. 161*t*, 165*t*, 170*t*, 175*t*, 180*t*
McCreary, James B.
  Congress membership 119*t*, 123*t*, 127*t*, 131*t*, 136*t*, 141*t*, 158*t*, 163*t*, 168*t*
  Kentucky governor 191*t*
McCredie, William W. 176*t*
McCreery, Thomas C. 100*t*, 104*t*
McCulloch, Hugh 94*t*
McCulloch Jr., Philip D. 135*t*, 139*t*, 144*t*, 148*t*, 153*t*
McCullogh, Welty 125*t*
McCullough, John G. 196*t*
McCumber, Porter J.
  Congress membership 151*t*, 155*t*, 160*t*, 165*t*, 169*t*, 174*t*, 179*t*, 185*t*
McCurdy, W. M. 326*t*
McDaniel, Henry D. 190*t*
McDannold, John J. 135*t*
McDearmon, James C. 138*t*, 143*t*
McDermott, Allan L. 151*t*, 155*t*, 160*t*, 164*t*
McDermott, J. G. 321*t*, 322*t*
McDermott, J. J. 329*t*
McDermott, James T. 167*t*, 172*t*, 177*t*, 182*t*
McDermott, John J. 308*t*
McDermott, Michael 315*t*
McDill, James W. 100*t*, 111*t*
McDonald, E. F. 320*t*
McDonald, Edward F. 132*t*
McDonald, H. P. 320*t*
McDonald, Jesse F. 189*t*
McDonald, John 145*t*
McDonald, Joseph E. 100*t*, 104*t*, 107*t*
McDonald, P. J. 321*t*, 322*t*
McDonald, William C. 193*t*
McDowell, Alexander 138*t*
McDowell, John A. 147*t*, 151*t*
McDuffie, John V. 126*t*
McEnery, Samuel D.
  Congress membership 145*t*, 149*t*, 154*t*, 158*t*, 163*t*, 168*t*, 172*t*
  Louisiana governor 191*t*
McEttrick, Michael J. 136*t*
McEwan Jr., Thomas 142*t*, 146*t*
McFarland, William 102*t*
McGann, D. 285*t*, 286*t*
McGann, Lawrence E. 131*t*, 135*t*, 140*t*
McGarry, Jim 337
McGavin, Charles 163*t*, 167*t*
McGill, Andrew R. 192*t*
McGillicuddy, Daniel J. 178*t*, 183*t*
McGillivray, Perry 315*t*
McGinnity, Joe 284, 286*t*, 293*t*
McGirr, T. G. 318*t*
McGovern, Francis E. 196*t*
McGovern, John 304*t*
McGovern, Terry 296*t*
McGowan, Jonas H. 105*t*, 108*t*
McGrath, M. J. 322*t*
McGraw, John 283*t*, 284, 284*t*, 294
McGraw, John Harte 196*t*
McGrew, J. 330*t*
McGuffey's Eclectic Readers 254
McGuire, Bird S. 170*t*, 174*t*, 180*t*, 185*t*
McGunnigle, William 283*t*
McHenry, John G. 170*t*, 175*t*, 180*t*
McInnis, S. 290*t*, 292*t*
McIntire, Albert W. 189*t*
McIntire, William W. 145*t*
McIntyre, H. 289*t*, 290*t*
McIntyre, M. 288*t*, 289*t*
McIvor, C. C. 316*t*
McKaig, William M. 132*t*, 136*t*
McKay, Robert G. 304*t*
McKeesport, Pennsylvania 280
McKeighan, William A. 132*t*
McKellar, Kenneth D. 180*t*, 186*t*
McKenna, Bernard 229*t*
McKenna, Joseph 95*t*, 118*t*, 122*t*, 126*t*, 130*t*, 188*t*